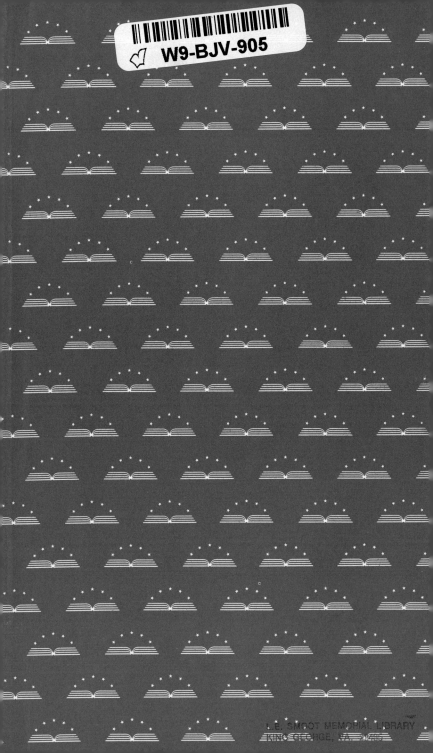

FRANCIS PARKMAN

Francis Parkman

FRANCE AND ENGLAND IN
NORTH AMERICA
VOLUME II

Count Frontenac and New France under Louis XIV
A Half-Century of Conflict
Montcalm and Wolfe

THE LIBRARY OF AMERICA

Distributed to the trade by the Viking Press.

Library of Congress Catalog Card Number: 82-18658
For Cataloging in Publication Data, see end of *Notes* section.
ISBN: 0-940450-11-9

First Printing

Manufactured in the United States of America

DAVID LEVIN
WROTE THE NOTES AND CHRONOLOGY
AND SELECTED THE TEXTS
FOR THIS VOLUME

Grateful acknowledgement is made to the National Endowment for the Humanities and the Ford Foundation for their generous financial support of this series.

Contents

Each section has its own table of contents.

Count Frontenac and New France under Louis XIV. .   1

A Half-Century of Conflict 329

Montcalm and Wolfe 829

Chronology 1505

Note on the Texts 1511

Notes 1514

Index 1517

COUNT FRONTENAC AND NEW FRANCE UNDER LOUIS XIV

Contents

Preface   9

CHAPTER I   1620–1672
COUNT AND COUNTESS FRONTENAC
  Mademoiselle de Montpensier and Madame de Frontenac •
  Orleans • The Maréchale de Camp • Count Frontenac •
  Conjugal Disputes • Early Life of Frontenac • His Courtship
  and Marriage • Estrangement • Scenes at St. Fargeau •
  The Lady of Honor dismissed • Frontenac as a Soldier • He is
  made Governor of New France • Les Divines   13

CHAPTER II   1672–1675
FRONTENAC AT QUEBEC
  Arrival • Bright Prospects • The Three Estates of New France
  • Speech of the Governor • His Innovations • Royal Displea-
  sure • Signs of Storm • Frontenac and the Priests • His
  Attempts to civilize the Indians • Opposition • Complaints
  and Heart-burnings   22

CHAPTER III   1673–1675
FRONTENAC AND PERROT
  La Salle • Fort Frontenac • Perrot • His Speculations • His
  Tyranny • The Bush-rangers • Perrot revolts • Becomes
  alarmed • Dilemma of Frontenac • Mediation of Fénelon •
  Perrot in Prison • Excitement of the Sulpitians • Indignation
  of Fénelon • Passion of Frontenac • Perrot on Trial •
  Strange Scenes • Appeal to the King • Answers of Louis XIV.
  and Colbert • Fénelon rebuked   30

CHAPTER IV   1675–1682
FRONTENAC AND DUCHESNEAU
  Frontenac receives a Colleague • He opposes the Clergy •
  Disputes in the Council • Royal Intervention • Frontenac
  rebuked • Fresh Outbreaks • Charges and Countercharges
  • The Dispute grows hot • Duchesneau condemned and Fron-
  tenac warned • The Quarrel continues • The King loses
  Patience • More Accusations • Factions and Feuds • A Side
  Quarrel • The King threatens • Frontenac denounces the
  Priests • The Governor and the Intendant recalled • Qualities
  of Frontenac   42

CHAPTER V   1682–1684
LE FEBVRE DE LA BARRE

   *His Arrival at Quebec • The Great Fire • A Coming Storm
   • Iroquois Policy • The Danger imminent • Indian Allies of
   France • Frontenac and the Iroquois • Boasts of La Barre •
   His Past Life • His Speculations • He takes Alarm • His
   Dealings with the Iroquois • His Illegal Trade • His Col-
   league denounces him • Fruits of his Schemes • His Anger
   and his Fears*   61

CHAPTER VI   1684
LA BARRE AND THE IROQUOIS

   *Dongan • New York and its Indian Neighbors • The Rival
   Governors • Dongan and the Iroquois • Mission to Onondaga
   • An Iroquois Politician • Warnings of Lamberville • Iro-
   quois Boldness • La Barre takes the Field • His Motives •
   The March • Pestilence • Council at La Famine • The Iro-
   quois defiant • Humiliation of La Barre • The Indian Allies
   • Their Rage and Disappointment • Recall of La Barre*   72

CHAPTER VII   1685–1687
DENONVILLE AND DONGAN

   *Troubles of the New Governor • His Character • English Ri-
   valry • Intrigues of Dongan • English Claims • A Diplomatic Duel • Overt Acts • Anger of Denonville • James II.
   checks Dongan • Denonville emboldened • Strife in the North
   • Hudson's Bay • Attempted Pacification • Artifice of Denonville • He prepares for War*   91

CHAPTER VIII   1687
DENONVILLE AND THE SENECAS

   *Treachery of Denonville • Iroquois Generosity • The Invading
   Army • The Western Allies • Plunder of English Traders •
   Arrival of the Allies • Scene at the French Camp • March of
   Denonville • Ambuscade • Battle • Victory • The Seneca
   Babylon • Imperfect Success*   107

CHAPTER IX   1687–1689
THE IROQUOIS INVASION

   *Altercations • Attitude of Dongan • Martial Preparation •
   Perplexity of Denonville • Angry Correspondence • Recall of
   Dongan • Sir Edmund Andros • Humiliation of Denonville •*

*Distress of Canada • Appeals for Help • Iroquois Diplomacy •
A Huron Macchiavel • The Catastrophe • Ferocity of the Victors • War with England • Recall of Denonville*   120

CHAPTER X   1689, 1690
RETURN OF FRONTENAC
*Versailles • Frontenac and the King • Frontenac sails for
Quebec • Projected Conquest of New York • Designs of the
King • Failure • Energy of Frontenac • Fort Frontenac •
Panic • Negotiations • The Iroquois in Council • Chevalier
d'Aux • Taunts of the Indian Allies • Boldness of Frontenac
• An Iroquois Defeat • Cruel Policy • The Stroke parried*   138

CHAPTER XI   1690
THE THREE WAR-PARTIES
*Measures of Frontenac • Expedition against Schenectady •
The March • The Dutch Village • The Surprise • The Mas-
sacre • Prisoners spared • Retreat • The English and their
Iroquois Friends • The Abenaki War • Revolution at Boston
• Capture of Pemaquid • Capture of Salmon Falls • Capture
of Fort Loyal • Frontenac and his Prisoner • The Canadians
encouraged*   154

CHAPTER XII   1690
MASSACHUSETTS ATTACKS QUEBEC
*English Schemes • Capture of Port Royal • Acadia reduced •
Conduct of Phips • His History and Character • Boston in
Arms • A Puritan Crusade • The March from Albany •
Frontenac and the Council • Frontenac at Montreal • His
War Dance • An Abortive Expedition • An English Raid •
Frontenac at Quebec • Defences of the Town • The Enemy
arrives*   173

CHAPTER XIII   1690
DEFENCE OF QUEBEC
*Phips on the St. Lawrence • Phips at Quebec • A Flag of
Truce • Scene at the Château • The Summons and the An-
swer • Plan of Attack • Landing of the English • The Can-*

nonade • *The Ships repulsed* • *The Land Attack* • *Retreat of Phips* • *Condition of Quebec* • *Rejoicings of the French* • *Distress at Boston*   192

CHAPTER XIV   1690–1694
THE SCOURGE OF CANADA
Iroquois Inroads • *Death of Bienville* • *English Attack* • *A Desperate Fight* • *Miseries of the Colony* • *Alarms* • *A Winter Expedition* • *La Chesnaye burned* • *The Heroine of Verchères* • *Mission Indians* • *The Mohawk Expedition* • *Retreat and Pursuit* • *Relief arrives* • *Frontenac Triumphant*   209

CHAPTER XV   1691–1695
AN INTERLUDE
Appeal of Frontenac • *His Opponents* • *His Services* • *Rivalry and Strife* • *Bishop Saint-Vallier* • *Society at the Château* • *Private Theatricals* • *Alarm of the Clergy* • *Tartuffe* • *A Singular Bargain* • *Mareuil and the Bishop* • *Mareuil on Trial* • *Zeal of Saint-Vallier* • *Scandals at Montreal* • *Appeal to the King* • *The Strife composed* • *Libel against Frontenac*   230

CHAPTER XVI   1690–1694
THE WAR IN ACADIA
State of that Colony • *The Abenakis* • *Acadia and New England* • *Pirates* • *Baron de Saint-Castin* • *Pentegoet* • *The English Frontier* • *The French and the Abenakis* • *Plan of the War* • *Capture of York* • *Villebon* • *Grand War-party* • *Attack of Wells* • *Pemaquid rebuilt* • *John Nelson* • *A Broken Treaty* • *Villieu and Thury* • *Another War-party* • *Massacre at Oyster River*   243

CHAPTER XVII   1690–1697
NEW FRANCE AND NEW ENGLAND
The Frontier of New England • *Border Warfare* • *Motives of the French* • *Needless Barbarity* • *Who were answerable?* • *Father Thury* • *The Abenakis waver* • *Treachery at Pema-*

quid • *Capture of Pemaquid* • *Projected Attack on Boston* •
Disappointment • *Miseries of the Frontier* • *A Captive
Amazon*   267

CHAPTER XVIII   1693–1697
FRENCH AND ENGLISH RIVALRY
Le Moyne d'Iberville • *His Exploits in Newfoundland* • *In
Hudson's Bay* • *The Great Prize* • *The Competitors* • *Fatal
Policy of the King* • *The Iroquois Question* • *Negotiation* •
Firmness of Frontenac • *English Intervention* • *War renewed*
• *State of the West* • *Indian Diplomacy* • *Cruel Measures* •
A Perilous Crisis • *Audacity of Frontenac*   280

CHAPTER XIX   1696–1698
FRONTENAC ATTACKS THE ONONDAGAS
March of Frontenac • *Flight of the Enemy* • *An Iroquois
Stoic* • *Relief for the Onondagas* • *Boasts of Frontenac* • *His
Complaints* • *His Enemies* • *Parties in Canada* • *Views of
Frontenac and the King* • *Frontenac prevails* • *Peace of
Ryswick* • *Frontenac and Bellomont* • *Schuyler at Quebec* •
Festivities • *A Last Defiance*   295

CHAPTER XX   1698
DEATH OF FRONTENAC
His Last Hours • *His Will* • *His Funeral* • *His Eulogist and
his Critic* • *His Disputes with the Clergy* • *His Character*   308

CHAPTER XXI   1699–1701
CONCLUSION
The New Governor • *Attitude of the Iroquois* • *Negotiations* •
Embassy to Onondaga • *Peace* • *The Iroquois and the Allies*
• *Difficulties* • *Death of the Great Huron* • *Funeral Rites* •
The Grand Council • *The Work of Frontenac finished* •
Results   315

Appendix   325

Preface

THE EVENTS recounted in this book group themselves in the main about a single figure, that of Count Frontenac, the most remarkable man who ever represented the crown of France in the New World. From strangely unpromising beginnings, he grew with every emergency, and rose equal to every crisis. His whole career was one of conflict, sometimes petty and personal, sometimes of momentous consequence, involving the question of national ascendency on this continent. Now that this question is put at rest for ever, it is hard to conceive the anxiety which it wakened in our forefathers. But for one rooted error of French policy, the future of the English-speaking races in America would have been more than endangered.

Under the rule of Frontenac occurred the first serious collision of the rival powers, and the opening of the grand scheme of military occupation by which France strove to envelop and hold in check the industrial populations of the English colonies. It was he who made that scheme possible.

In "The Old Régime in Canada," I tried to show from what inherent causes this wilderness empire of the Great Monarch fell at last before a foe, superior indeed in numbers, but lacking all the forces that belong to a system of civil and military centralization. The present volume will show how valiantly, and for a time how successfully, New France battled against a fate which her own organic fault made inevitable. Her history is a great and significant drama, enacted among untamed forests, with a distant gleam of courtly splendors and the regal pomp of Versailles.

The authorities on which the book rests are drawn chiefly from the manuscript collections of the French government in the Archives Nationales, the Bibliothèque Nationale, and, above all, the vast repositories of the Archives of the Marine and Colonies. Others are from Canadian and American sources. I have, besides, availed myself of the collection of French, English, and Dutch documents published by the State of New York, under the excellent editorship of Dr. O'Callaghan, and of the manuscript collections made in

France by the governments of Canada and of Massachusetts. A considerable number of books, contemporary or nearly so with the events described, also help to throw light upon them; and these have all been examined. The citations in the margins represent but a small part of the authorities consulted.

This mass of material has been studied with extreme care, and peculiar pains have been taken to secure accuracy of statement. In the preface of "The Old Régime," I wrote: "Some of the results here reached are of a character which I regret, since they cannot be agreeable to persons for whom I have a very cordial regard. The conclusions drawn from the facts may be matter of opinion: but it will be remembered that the facts themselves can be overthrown only by overthrowing the evidence on which they rest, or bringing forward counter-evidence of equal or greater strength; and neither task will be found an easy one."

The invitation implied in these words has not been accepted. "The Old Régime" was met by vehement protest in some quarters; but, so far as I know, none of the statements of fact contained in it have been attacked by evidence, or even challenged. The lines just quoted are equally applicable to this volume. Should there be occasion, a collection of documentary proofs will be published more than sufficient to make good the positions taken. Meanwhile, it will, I think, be clear to an impartial reader that the story is told, not in the interest of any race or nationality, but simply in that of historical truth.

When, at the age of eighteen, I formed the purpose of writing on French-American history, I meant at first to limit myself to the great contest which brought that history to a close. It was by an afterthought that the plan was extended to cover the whole field, so that the part of the work, or series of works, first conceived, would, following the sequence of events, be the last executed. As soon as the original scheme was formed, I began to prepare for executing it by examining localities, journeying in forests, visiting Indian tribes, and collecting materials. I have continued to collect them ever since, so that the accumulation is now rather formidable; and, if it is to be used at all, it had better be used at once. Therefore,

passing over for the present an intervening period of less decisive importance, I propose to take, as the next subject of
this series, "Montcalm and the Fall of New France."

BOSTON, *1 Jan., 1877.*

Chapter I

COUNT AND COUNTESS FRONTENAC

Mademoiselle de Montpensier and Madame de Frontenac • Orleans • The Maréchale de Camp • Count Frontenac • Conjugal Disputes • Early Life of Frontenac • His Courtship and Marriage • Estrangement • Scenes at St. Fargeau • The Lady of Honor dismissed • Frontenac as a Soldier • He is made Governor of New France • Les Divines

AT VERSAILLES there is the portrait of a lady, beautiful and young. She is painted as Minerva, a plumed helmet on her head, and a shield on her arm. In a corner of the canvas is written *Anne de La Grange-Trianon, Comtesse de Frontenac.* This blooming goddess was the wife of the future governor of Canada.

Madame de Frontenac, at the age of about twenty, was a favorite companion of Mademoiselle de Montpensier, the grand-daughter of Henry IV. and daughter of the weak and dastardly Gaston, Duke of Orleans. Nothing in French annals has found more readers than the story of the exploit of this spirited princess at Orleans during the civil war of the Fronde. Her cousin Condé, chief of the revolt, had found favor in her eyes; and she had espoused his cause against her cousin, the king. The royal army threatened Orleans. The duke, her father, dared not leave Paris; but he consented that his daughter should go in his place to hold the city for Condé and the Fronde.

The princess entered her carriage and set out on her errand, attended by a small escort. With her were three young married ladies, the Marquise de Bréauté, the Comtesse de Fiesque, and the Comtesse de Frontenac. In two days they reached Orleans. The civic authorities were afraid to declare against the king, and hesitated to open the gates to the daughter of their duke, who, standing in the moat with her three companions, tried persuasion and threats in vain. The prospect was not encouraging, when a crowd of boatmen came up from the river and offered the princess their services.

"I accepted them gladly," she writes, "and said a thousand fine things, such as one must say to that sort of people to make them do what one wishes." She gave them money as well as fair words, and begged them to burst open one of the gates. They fell at once to the work; while the guards and officials looked down from the walls, neither aiding nor resisting them. "To animate the boatmen by my presence," she continues, "I mounted a hillock near by. I did not look to see which way I went, but clambered up like a cat, clutching brambles and thorns, and jumping over hedges without hurting myself. Madame de Bréauté, who is the most cowardly creature in the world, began to cry out against me and everybody who followed me; in fact, I do not know if she did not swear in her excitement, which amused me very much." At length, a hole was knocked in the gate; and a gentleman of her train, who had directed the attack, beckoned her to come on. "As it was very muddy, a man took me and carried me forward, and thrust me in at this hole, where my head was no sooner through than the drums beat to salute me. I gave my hand to the captain of the guard. The shouts redoubled. Two men took me and put me in a wooden chair. I do not know whether I was seated in it or on their arms, for I was beside myself with joy. Everybody was kissing my hands, and I almost died with laughing to see myself in such an odd position." There was no resisting the enthusiasm of the people and the soldiers. Orleans was won for the Fronde.[1]

The young Countesses of Frontenac and Fiesque had constantly followed her, and climbed after her through the hole in the gate. Her father wrote to compliment them on their prowess, and addressed his letter *à Mesdames les Comtesses, Maréchales de Camp dans l'armée de ma fille contre le Mazarin.* Officers and soldiers took part in the pleasantry; and, as Madame de Frontenac passed on horseback before the troops, they saluted her with the honors paid to a brigadier.

When the king, or Cardinal Mazarin who controlled him, had triumphed over the revolting princes, Mademoiselle de Montpensier paid the penalty of her exploit by a temporary banishment from the court. She roamed from place to place,

---

[1] *Mémoires de Mademoiselle de Montpensier*, I. 358–363 (ed. 1859).

with a little court of her own, of which Madame de Frontenac was a conspicuous member. During the war, Count Frontenac had been dangerously ill of a fever in Paris; and his wife had been absent for a time, attending him. She soon rejoined the princess, who was at her château of St. Fargeau, three days' journey from Paris, when an incident occurred which placed the married life of her fair companion in an unexpected light. "The Duchesse de Sully came to see me, and brought with her M. d'Herbault and M. de Frontenac. Frontenac had stopped here once before, but it was only for a week, when he still had the fever, and took great care of himself like a man who had been at the door of death. This time he was in high health. His arrival had not been expected, and his wife was so much surprised that everybody observed it, especially as the surprise seemed to be not at all a pleasant one. Instead of going to talk with her husband, she went off and hid herself, crying and screaming because he had said that he would like to have her company that evening. I was very much astonished, especially as I had never before perceived her aversion to him. The elder Comtesse de Fiesque remonstrated with her; but she only cried the more. Madame de Fiesque then brought books to show her her duty as a wife; but it did no good, and at last she got into such a state that we sent for the curé with holy water to exorcise her."[1]

Count Frontenac came of an ancient and noble race, said to have been of Basque origin. His father held a high post in the household of Louis XIII., who became the child's godfather, and gave him his own name. At the age of fifteen, the young Louis showed an incontrollable passion for the life of a soldier. He was sent to the seat of war in Holland, to serve under the Prince of Orange. At the age of nineteen, he was a volunteer at the siege of Hesdin; in the next year, he was at Arras, where he distinguished himself during a sortie of the garrison; in the next, he took part in the siege of Aire; and, in the next, in those of Callioure and Perpignan. At the age of twenty-three, he was made colonel of the regiment of Normandy, which he commanded in repeated battles and sieges of the Italian campaign. He was several times wounded, and

[1] *Mémoires de Mademoiselle de Montpensier*, II. 265. The curé's holy water, or his exhortations, were at last successful.

in 1646 he had an arm broken at the siege of Orbitello. In the same year, when twenty-six years old, he was raised to the rank of *maréchal de camp*, equivalent to that of brigadier-general. A year or two later, we find him at Paris, at the house of his father, on the Quai des Célestins.[1]

In the same neighborhood lived La Grange-Trianon, Sieur de Neuville, a widower of fifty, with one child, a daughter of sixteen, whom he had placed in the charge of his relative, Madame de Bouthillier. Frontenac fell in love with her. Madame de Bouthillier opposed the match, and told La Grange that he might do better for his daughter than to marry her to a man who, say what he might, had but twenty thousand francs a year. La Grange was weak and vacillating: sometimes he listened to his prudent kinswoman, and sometimes to the eager suitor; treated him as a son-in-law, carried love messages from him to his daughter, and ended by refusing him her hand, and ordering her to renounce him on pain of being immured in a convent. Neither Frontenac nor his mistress was of a pliant temper. In the neighborhood was the little church of St. Pierre aux Bœufs, which had the privilege of uniting couples without the consent of their parents; and here, on a Wednesday in October, 1648, the lovers were married in presence of a number of Frontenac's relatives. La Grange was furious at the discovery; but his anger soon cooled, and complete reconciliation followed.[2]

The happiness of the newly wedded pair was short. Love soon changed to aversion, at least on the part of the bride. She was not of a tender nature; her temper was imperious, and she had a restless craving for excitement. Frontenac, on his part, was the most wayward and headstrong of men. She bore him a son; but maternal cares were not to her liking. The infant, François Louis, was placed in the keeping of a nurse at the village of Clion; and his young mother left her husband, to follow the fortunes of Mademoiselle de Montpensier, who for a time pronounced her charming, praised

<hr/>

[1] Pinard, *Chronologie Historique-militaire*, VI.; *Table de la Gazette de France*; Jal, *Dictionnaire Critique, Biographique, et d'Histoire*, art. "Frontenac;" Goyer, *Oraison Funèbre du Comte de Frontenac*.

[2] *Historiettes de Tallemant des Réaux*, IX. 214 (ed. Monmerqué); Jal, *Dictionnaire Critique*, etc.

her wit and beauty, and made her one of her ladies of honor. Very curious and amusing are some of the incidents recounted by the princess, in which Madame de Frontenac bore part; but what is more to our purpose are the sketches traced here and there by the same sharp pen, in which one may discern the traits of the destined saviour of New France. Thus, in the following, we see him at St. Fargeau in the same attitude in which we shall often see him at Quebec.

The princess and the duke her father had a dispute touching her property. Frontenac had lately been at Blois, where the duke had possessed him with his own views of the questions at issue. Accordingly, on arriving at St. Fargeau, he seemed disposed to assume the character of mediator. "He wanted," says the princess, "to discuss my affairs with me: I listened to his preaching, and he also spoke about these matters to Préfontaine (*her man of business*). I returned to the house after our promenade, and we went to dance in the great hall. While we were dancing, I saw Préfontaine walking at the farther end with Frontenac, who was talking and gesticulating. This continued for a long time. Madame de Sully noticed it also, and seemed disturbed by it, as I was myself. I said, 'Have we not danced enough?' Madame de Sully assented, and we went out. I called Préfontaine, and asked him, 'What was Frontenac saying to you?' He answered: 'He was scolding me. I never saw such an impertinent man in my life.' I went to my room, and Madame de Sully and Madame de Fiesque followed. Madame de Sully said to Préfontaine: 'I was very much disturbed to see you talking with so much warmth to Monsieur de Frontenac; for he came here in such ill-humor that I was afraid he would quarrel with you. Yesterday, when we were in the carriage, he was ready to eat us.' The Comtesse de Fiesque said, 'This morning he came to see my mother-in-law, and scolded at her.' Préfontaine answered: 'He wanted to throttle me. I never saw a man so crazy and absurd.' We all four began to pity poor Madame de Frontenac for having such a husband, and to think her right in not wanting to go with him."[1]

Frontenac owned the estate of Isle Savary, on the Indre,

---

[1] *Mémoires de Mademoiselle de Montpensier*, II. 267.

not far from Blois; and here, soon after the above scene, the princess made him a visit. "It is a pretty enough place," she says, "for a man like him. The house is well furnished, and he gave me excellent entertainment. He showed me all the plans he had for improving it, and making gardens, fountains, and ponds. It would need the riches of a superintendent of finance to execute his schemes, and how anybody else should venture to think of them I cannot comprehend."

"While Frontenac was at St. Fargeau," she continues, "he kept open table, and many of my people went to dine with him; for he affected to hold court, and acted as if everybody owed duty to him. The conversation was always about my affair with his Royal Highness (*her father*), whose conduct towards me was always praised, while mine was blamed. Frontenac spoke ill of Préfontaine, and, in fine, said every thing he could to displease me and stir up my own people against me. He praised every thing that belonged to himself, and never came to sup or dine with me without speaking of some *ragoût* or some new sweetmeat which had been served up on his table, ascribing it all to the excellence of the officers of his kitchen. The very meat that he ate, according to him, had a different taste on his board than on any other. As for his silver plate, it was always of good workmanship; and his dress was always of patterns invented by himself. When he had new clothes, he paraded them like a child. One day he brought me some to look at, and left them on my dressing table. We were then at Chambord. His Royal Highness came into the room, and must have thought it odd to see breeches and doublets in such a place. Préfontaine and I laughed about it a great deal. Frontenac took everybody who came to St. Fargeau to see his stables; and all who wished to gain his good graces were obliged to admire his horses, which were very indifferent. In short, this is his way in every thing."[1]

Though not himself of the highest rank, his position at court was, from the courtier point of view, an enviable one. The princess, after her banishment had ended, more than once mentions incidentally that she had met him in the cabinet of the queen. Her dislike of him became intense, and her fondness for his wife changed at last to aversion. She charges

[1] *Mémoires de Mademoiselle de Montpensier*, II. 279; III. 16.

the countess with ingratitude. She discovered, or thought that she discovered, that in her dispute with her father, and in certain dissensions in her own household, Madame de Frontenac had acted secretly in opposition to her interests and wishes. The imprudent lady of honor received permission to leave her service. It was a woful scene. "She saw me get into my carriage," writes the princess, "and her distress was greater than ever. Her tears flowed abundantly: as for me, my fortitude was perfect, and I looked on with composure while she cried. If any thing could disturb my tranquillity, it was the recollection of the time when she laughed while I was crying." Mademoiselle de Montpensier had been deeply offended, and apparently with reason. The countess and her husband received an order never again to appear in her presence; but soon after, when the princess was with the king and queen at a comedy in the garden of the Louvre, Frontenac, who had previously arrived, immediately changed his position, and with his usual audacity took a post so conspicuous that she could not help seeing him. "I confess," she says, "I was so angry that I could find no pleasure in the play; but I said nothing to the king and queen, fearing that they would not take such a view of the matter as I wished."[1]

With the close of her relations with "La Grande Mademoiselle," Madame de Frontenac is lost to sight for a while. In 1669, a Venetian embassy came to France to beg for aid against the Turks, who for more than two years had attacked Candia in overwhelming force. The ambassadors offered to place their own troops under French command, and they asked Turenne to name a general officer equal to the task. Frontenac had the signal honor of being chosen by the first soldier of Europe for this most arduous and difficult position. He went accordingly. The result increased his reputation for ability and courage; but Candia was doomed, and its chief fortress fell into the hands of the infidels, after a protracted struggle, which is said to have cost them a hundred and eighty thousand men.[2]

[1] *Mémoires de Mademoiselle de Montpensier*, III. 270.
[2] *Oraison funèbre du Comte de Frontenac, par le Père Olivier Goyer*. A powerful French contingent, under another command, co-operated with the Venetians under Frontenac.

Three years later, Frontenac received the appointment of Governor and Lieutenant-General for the king in all New France. "He was," says Saint-Simon, "a man of excellent parts, living much in society, and completely ruined. He found it hard to bear the imperious temper of his wife; and he was given the government of Canada to deliver him from her, and afford him some means of living."[1] Certain scandalous songs of the day assign a different motive for his appointment. Louis XIV. was enamoured of Madame de Montespan. She had once smiled upon Frontenac; and it is said that the jealous king gladly embraced the opportunity of removing from his presence, and from hers, a lover who had forestalled him.[2]

Frontenac's wife had no thought of following him across the sea. A more congenial life awaited her at home. She had long had a friend of humbler station than herself, Mademoiselle d'Outrelaise, daughter of an obscure gentleman of Poitou, an amiable and accomplished person, who became through life her constant companion. The extensive building called the Arsenal, formerly the residence of Sully, the minister of Henry IV., contained suites of apartments which were granted to persons who had influence enough to obtain them.

---

[1] *Mémoires du Duc de Saint-Simon*, II. 270; V. 336.

[2] Note of M. Brunet, in *Correspondance de la Duchesse d'Orléans*, I. 200 (ed. 1869).

The following lines, among others, were passed about secretly among the courtiers: —

> "Je suis ravi que le roi, notre sire,
>   Aime la Montespan;
> Moi, Frontenac, je me crève de rire,
>   Sachant ce qui lui pend;
> Et je dirai, sans être des plus bestes,
>   Tu n'as que mon reste,
>   Roi,
>   Tu n'as que mon reste."

Mademoiselle de Montpensier had mentioned in her memoirs, some years before, that Frontenac, in taking out his handkerchief, dropped from his pocket a love-letter to Mademoiselle de Mortemart, afterwards Madame de Montespan, which was picked up by one of the attendants of the princess. The king, on the other hand, was at one time attracted by the charms of Madame de Frontenac, against whom, however, no aspersion is cast.

The Comte de Grignan, son-in-law of Madame de Sévigné, was an unsuccessful competitor with Frontenac for the government of Canada.

The Duc de Lude, grand master of artillery, had them at his disposal, and gave one of them to Madame de Frontenac. Here she made her abode with her friend; and here at last she died, at the age of seventy-five. The annalist Saint-Simon, who knew the court and all belonging to it better than any other man of his time, says of her: "She had been beautiful and gay, and was always in the best society, where she was greatly in request. Like her husband, she had little property and abundant wit. She and Mademoiselle d'Outrelaise, whom she took to live with her, gave the tone to the best company of Paris and the court, though they never went thither. They were called *Les Divines*. In fact, they demanded incense like goddesses; and it was lavished upon them all their lives."

Mademoiselle d'Outrelaise died long before the countess, who retained in old age the rare social gifts which to the last made her apartments a resort of the highest society of that brilliant epoch. It was in her power to be very useful to her absent husband, who often needed her support, and who seems to have often received it.

She was childless. Her son, François Louis, was killed, some say in battle, and others in a duel, at an early age. Her husband died nine years before her; and the old countess left what little she had to her friend Beringhen, the king's master of the horse.[1]

[1] On Frontenac and his family, see Appendix A.

Chapter II

FRONTENAC AT QUEBEC

*Arrival • Bright Prospects • The Three Estates of New France •
Speech of the Governor • His Innovations • Royal Displeasure •
Signs of Storm • Frontenac and the Priests • His Attempts to civi-
lize the Indians • Opposition • Complaints and Heart-burnings*

FRONTENAC was fifty-two years old when he landed at
Quebec. If time had done little to cure his many faults, it
had done nothing to weaken the springs of his unconquerable
vitality. In his ripe middle age, he was as keen, fiery, and per-
versely headstrong as when he quarrelled with Préfontaine in
the hall at St. Fargeau.

Had nature disposed him to melancholy, there was much
in his position to awaken it. A man of courts and camps, born
and bred in the focus of a most gorgeous civilization, he was
banished to the ends of the earth, among savage hordes and
half-reclaimed forests, to exchange the splendors of St. Germain and the dawning glories of Versailles for a stern gray
rock, haunted by sombre priests, rugged merchants and traders, blanketed Indians, and wild bush-rangers. But Frontenac
was a man of action. He wasted no time in vain regrets, and
set himself to his work with the elastic vigor of youth. His
first impressions had been very favorable. When, as he sailed
up the St. Lawrence, the basin of Quebec opened before him,
his imagination kindled with the grandeur of the scene. "I
never," he wrote, "saw any thing more superb than the position of this town. It could not be better situated as the future
capital of a great empire."[1]

That Quebec was to become the capital of a great empire
there seemed in truth good reason to believe. The young king
and his minister Colbert had labored in earnest to build up a
new France in the west. For years past, ship-loads of emigrants had landed every summer on the strand beneath the
rock. All was life and action, and the air was full of promise.

[1] *Frontenac au Ministre, 2 Nov., 1672.*

The royal agent Talon had written to his master: "This part of the French monarchy is destined to a grand future. All that I see around me points to it; and the colonies of foreign nations, so long settled on the sea-board, are trembling with fright in view of what his Majesty has accomplished here within the last seven years. The measures we have taken to confine them within narrow limits, and the prior claim we have established against them by formal acts of possession, do not permit them to extend themselves except at peril of having war declared against them as usurpers; and this, in fact, is what they seem greatly to fear."[1]

Frontenac shared the spirit of the hour. His first step was to survey his government. He talked with traders, colonists, and officials; visited seigniories, farms, fishing-stations, and all the infant industries that Talon had galvanized into life; examined the new ship on the stocks, admired the structure of the new brewery, went to Three Rivers to see the iron mines, and then, having acquired a tolerably exact idea of his charge, returned to Quebec. He was well pleased with what he saw, but not with the ways and means of Canadian travel; for he thought it strangely unbecoming that a lieutenant-general of the king should be forced to crouch on a sheet of bark, at the bottom of a birch canoe, scarcely daring to move his head to the right or left lest he should disturb the balance of the fragile vessel.

At Quebec he convoked the council, made them a speech, and administered the oath of allegiance.[2] This did not satisfy him. He resolved that all Quebec should take the oath together. It was little but a pretext. Like many of his station, Frontenac was not in full sympathy with the centralizing movement of the time, which tended to level ancient rights, privileges, and prescriptions under the ponderous roller of the monarchical administration. He looked back with regret to the day when the three orders of the state, clergy, nobles, and commons, had a place and a power in the direction of national affairs. The three orders still subsisted, in form, if not in substance, in some of the provinces of France; and Frontenac conceived the idea of reproducing them in Canada. Not

[1] *Talon au Ministre, 2 Nov., 1671.*
[2] *Registre du Conseil Souverain.*

only did he cherish the tradition of faded liberties, but he loved pomp and circumstance, above all, when he was himself the central figure in it; and the thought of a royal governor of Languedoc or Brittany, presiding over the estates of his province, appears to have fired him with emulation.

He had no difficulty in forming his order of the clergy. The Jesuits and the seminary priests supplied material even more abundant than he wished. For the order of the nobles, he found three or four *gentilshommes* at Quebec, and these he reinforced with a number of officers. The third estate consisted of the merchants and citizens; and he formed the members of the council and the magistrates into another distinct body, though, properly speaking, they belonged to the third estate, of which by nature and prescription they were the head. The Jesuits, glad no doubt to lay him under some slight obligation, lent him their church for the ceremony that he meditated, and aided in decorating it for the occasion. Here, on the twenty-third of October, 1672, the three estates of Canada were convoked, with as much pomp and splendor as circumstances would permit. Then Frontenac, with the ease of a man of the world and the loftiness of a *grand seigneur*, delivered himself of the harangue he had prepared. He wrote exceedingly well; he is said also to have excelled as an orator; certainly he was never averse to the tones of his own eloquence. His speech was addressed to a double audience: the throng that filled the church, and the king and the minister three thousand miles away. He told his hearers that he had called the assembly, not because he doubted their loyalty, but in order to afford them the delight of making public protestation of devotion to a prince, the terror of whose irresistible arms was matched only by the charms of his person and the benignity of his rule. "The Holy Scriptures," he said, "command us to obey our sovereign, and teach us that no pretext or reason can dispense us from this obedience." And, in a glowing eulogy on Louis XIV., he went on to show that obedience to him was not only a duty, but an inestimable privilege. He dwelt with admiration on the recent victories in Holland, and held forth the hope that a speedy and glorious peace would leave his Majesty free to turn his thoughts to the colony which already owed so much to his fostering care.

"The true means," pursued Frontenac, "of gaining his favor and his support, is for us to unite with one heart in laboring for the progress of Canada." Then he addressed, in turn, the clergy, the nobles, the magistrates, and the citizens. He exhorted the priests to continue with zeal their labors for the conversion of the Indians, and to make them subjects not only of Christ, but also of the king; in short, to tame and civilize them, a portion of their duties in which he plainly gave them to understand that they had not hitherto acquitted themselves to his satisfaction. Next, he appealed to the nobles, commended their gallantry, and called upon them to be as assiduous in the culture and improvement of the colony as they were valiant in its defence. The magistrates, the merchants, and the colonists in general were each addressed in an appropriate exhortation. "I can assure you, messieurs," he concluded, "that if you faithfully discharge your several duties, each in his station, his Majesty will extend to us all the help and all the favor that we can desire. It is needless, then, to urge you to act as I have counselled, since it is for your own interest to do so. As for me, it only remains to protest before you that I shall esteem myself happy in consecrating all my efforts, and, if need be, my life itself, to extending the empire of Jesus Christ throughout all this land, and the supremacy of our king over all the nations that dwell in it."

He administered the oath, and the assembly dissolved. He now applied himself to another work: that of giving a municipal government to Quebec, after the model of some of the cities of France. In place of the syndic, an official supposed to represent the interests of the citizens, he ordered the public election of three aldermen, of whom the senior should act as mayor. One of the number was to go out of office every year, his place being filled by a new election; and the governor, as representing the king, reserved the right of confirmation or rejection. He then, in concert with the chief inhabitants, proceeded to frame a body of regulations for the government of a town destined, as he again and again declares, to become the capital of a mighty empire; and he farther ordained that the people should hold a meeting every six months to discuss questions involving the welfare of the colony. The boldness of these measures will scarcely be appreciated at the present day. The intendant Talon declined, on pretence of a slight illness, to be present at the meeting of the estates. He knew too well the temper of the king, whose constant policy it was to destroy or paralyze every institution or custom that stood in the way of his autocracy. The despatches in which Frontenac announced to his masters what he had done received in due time their answer. The minister Colbert wrote: "Your assembling of the inhabitants to take the oath of fidelity, and your division of them into three estates, may have had a good effect for the moment; but it is well for you to observe that you are always to follow, in the government of Canada, the forms in use here; and since our kings have long regarded it as good for their service not to convoke the states-general of the kingdom, in order, perhaps, to abolish insensibly this ancient usage, you, on your part, should very rarely, or, to speak more correctly, never, give a corporate form to the inhabitants of Canada. You should even, as the colony strengthens, suppress gradually the office of the syndic, who presents petitions in the name of the inhabitants; for it is well that each should speak for himself, and no one for all."[1]

Here, in brief, is the whole spirit of the French colonial rule in Canada; a government, as I have elsewhere shown, of excellent intentions, but of arbitrary methods. Frontenac, filled with the traditions of the past, and sincerely desirous of the good of the colony, rashly set himself against the prevailing current. His municipal government, and his meetings of citizens, were, like his three estates, abolished by a word from the court, which, bold and obstinate as he was, he dared not disobey. Had they been allowed to subsist, there can be little doubt that great good would have resulted to Canada.

Frontenac has been called a mere soldier. He was an excellent soldier, and more besides. He was a man of vigorous and cultivated mind, penetrating observation, and ample travel and experience. His zeal for the colony, however, was often counteracted by the violence of his prejudices, and by two other influences. First, he was a ruined man, who meant to

---

[1] *Frontenac au Roi, 2 Nov., 1672; Ibid., 13 Nov., 1673; Harangue du Comte de Frontenac en l'Assemblée à Quebec; Prestations de Serment, 23 Oct., 1672; Règlement de Police fait par Monsieur le Comte de Frontenac; Colbert à Frontenac, 13 Juin, 1673.*

mend his fortunes; and his wish that Canada should prosper was joined with a determination to reap a goodly part of her prosperity for himself. Again, he could not endure a rival; opposition maddened him, and, when crossed or thwarted, he forgot every thing but his passion. Signs of storm quickly showed themselves between him and the intendant Talon; but the danger was averted by the departure of that official for France. A cloud then rose in the direction of the clergy.

"Another thing displeases me," writes Frontenac, "and this is the complete dependence of the grand vicar and the seminary priests on the Jesuits, for they never do the least thing without their order: so that they (*the Jesuits*) are masters in spiritual matters, which, as you know, is a powerful lever for moving every thing else."[1] And he complains that they have spies in town and country, that they abuse the confessional, intermeddle in families, set husbands against wives, and parents against children, and all, as they say, for the greater glory of God. "I call to mind every day, Monseigneur, what you did me the honor to say to me when I took leave of you, and every day I am satisfied more and more of the great importance to the king's service of opposing the slightest of the attempts which are daily made against his authority." He goes on to denounce a certain sermon, preached by a Jesuit, to the great scandal of loyal subjects, wherein the father declared that the king had exceeded his powers in licensing the trade in brandy when the bishop had decided it to be a sin, together with other remarks of a seditious nature. "I was tempted several times," pursues Frontenac, "to leave the church with my guards and interrupt the sermon; but I contented myself with telling the grand vicar and the superior of the Jesuits, after it was over, that I was very much surprised at what I had heard, and demanded justice at their hands. They greatly blamed the preacher, and disavowed him, attributing his language, after their custom, to an excess of zeal, and making many apologies, with which I pretended to be satisfied; though I told them, nevertheless, that their excuses would not pass current with me another time, and, if the thing happened again, I would put the preacher in a place

---

[1] *Frontenac au Ministre, 2 Nov., 1672.*

where he would learn how to speak. Since then they have been a little more careful, though not enough to prevent one from always seeing their intention to persuade the people that, even in secular matters, their authority ought to be respected above any other. As there are many persons here who have no more brains than they need, and who are attached to them by ties of interest or otherwise, it is necessary to have an eye to these matters in this country more than anywhere else."[1]

The churchmen, on their part, were not idle. The bishop, who was then in France, contrived by some means to acquaint himself with the contents of the private despatches sent by Colbert in reply to the letters of Frontenac. He wrote to another ecclesiastic to communicate what he had learned, at the same time enjoining great caution; "since, while it is well to acquire all necessary information, and to act upon it, it is of the greatest importance to keep secret our possession of such knowledge."[2]

The king and the minister, in their instructions to Frontenac, had dwelt with great emphasis on the expediency of civilizing the Indians, teaching them the French language, and amalgamating them with the colonists. Frontenac, ignorant as yet of Indian nature and unacquainted with the difficulties of the case, entered into these views with great heartiness. He exercised from the first an extraordinary influence over all the Indians with whom he came in contact; and he persuaded the most savage and refractory of them, the Iroquois, to place eight of their children in his hands. Four of these were girls and four were boys. He took two of the boys into his own household, of which they must have proved most objectionable inmates; and he supported the other two, who were younger, out of his own slender resources, placed them in respectable French families, and required them to go daily to school. The girls were given to the charge of the

---

[1] *Frontenac au Ministre, 13 Nov., 1673.*

[2] *Laval à* ——, *1674.* The letter is a complete summary of the contents of Colbert's recent despatch to Frontenac. Then follows the injunction to secrecy, "estant de très-grande conséquence que l'on ne sache pas que l'on aye rien appris de tout cela, sur quoi néanmoins il est bon que l'on agisse et que l'on me donne tous les advis qui seront nécessaires."

Ursulines. Frontenac continually urged the Jesuits to co-operate with him in this work of civilization, but the results of
his urgency disappointed and exasperated him. He complains
that in the village of the Hurons, near Quebec, and under the
control of the Jesuits, the French language was scarcely
known. In fact, the fathers contented themselves with teaching their converts the doctrines and rites of the Roman
Church, while retaining the food, dress, and habits of their
original barbarism.

In defence of the missionaries, it should be said that, when
brought in contact with the French, the Indians usually
caught the vices of civilization without its virtues; but Frontenac made no allowances. "The Jesuits," he writes, "will not
civilize the Indians, because they wish to keep them in perpetual wardship. They think more of beaver skins than of
souls, and their missions are pure mockeries." At the same
time he assures the minister that, when he is obliged to correct them, he does so with the utmost gentleness. In spite of
this somewhat doubtful urbanity, it seems clear that a storm
was brewing; and it was fortunate for the peace of the Canadian Church that the attention of the truculent governor was
drawn to other quarters.

Chapter III

FRONTENAC AND PERROT

*La Salle • Fort Frontenac • Perrot • His Speculations • His Tyr-
anny • The Bush-rangers • Perrot revolts • Becomes alarmed •
Dilemma of Frontenac • Mediation of Fénelon • Perrot in Prison
• Excitement of the Sulpitians • Indignation of Fénelon • Passion
of Frontenac • Perrot on Trial • Strange Scenes • Appeal to the
King • Answers of Louis XIV. and Colbert • Fénelon rebuked*

NOT LONG before Frontenac's arrival, Courcelle, his predecessor, went to Lake Ontario with an armed force, in
order to impose respect on the Iroquois, who had of late become insolent. As a means of keeping them in check, and at
the same time controlling the fur trade of the upper country,
he had recommended, like Talon before him, the building of
a fort near the outlet of the lake. Frontenac at once saw the
advantages of such a measure, and his desire to execute it was
stimulated by the reflection that the proposed fort might be
made not only a safeguard to the colony, but also a source of
profit to himself.

At Quebec, there was a grave, thoughtful, self-contained
young man, who soon found his way into Frontenac's confidence. There was between them the sympathetic attraction of
two bold and energetic spirits; and though Cavelier de la Salle
had neither the irritable vanity of the count, nor his Gallic
vivacity of passion, he had in full measure the same unconquerable pride and hardy resolution. There were but two or
three men in Canada who knew the western wilderness so
well. He was full of schemes of ambition and of gain; and,
from this moment, he and Frontenac seem to have formed an
alliance, which ended only with the governor's recall.

In telling the story of La Salle, I have described the execution of the new plan: the muster of the Canadians, at the call
of Frontenac; the consternation of those of the merchants
whom he and La Salle had not taken into their counsels, and
who saw in the movement the preparation for a gigantic fur
trading monopoly; the intrigues set on foot to bar the enter-

prise; the advance up the St. Lawrence; the assembly of Iroquois at the destined spot; the ascendency exercised over them by the governor; the building of Fort Frontenac on the ground where Kingston now stands, and its final transfer into the hands of La Salle, on condition, there can be no doubt, of sharing the expected profits with his patron.[1]

On the way to the lake, Frontenac stopped for some time at Montreal, where he had full opportunity to become acquainted with a state of things to which his attention had already been directed. This state of things was as follows:—

When the intendant, Talon, came for the second time to Canada, in 1669, an officer named Perrot, who had married his niece, came with him. Perrot, anxious to turn to account the influence of his wife's relative, looked about him for some post of honor and profit, and quickly discovered that the government of Montreal was vacant. The priests of St. Sulpice, feudal owners of the place, had the right of appointing their own governor. Talon advised them to choose Perrot, who thereupon received the desired commission, which, however, was revocable at the will of those who had granted it. The new governor, therefore, begged another commission from the king, and after a little delay he obtained it. Thus he became, in some measure, independent of the priests, who, if they wished to rid themselves of him, must first gain the royal consent.

Perrot, as he had doubtless foreseen, found himself in an excellent position for making money. The tribes of the upper lakes, and all the neighboring regions, brought down their furs every summer to the annual fair at Montreal. Perrot took his measures accordingly. On the island which still bears his name, lying above Montreal and directly in the route of the descending savages, he built a storehouse, and placed it in charge of a retired lieutenant named Brucy, who stopped the Indians on their way, and carried on an active trade with them, to the great profit of himself and his associate, and the great loss of the merchants in the settlements below. This was not all. Perrot connived at the desertion of his own soldiers, who escaped to the woods, became *coureurs de bois*, or bushrangers, traded with the Indians in their villages, and shared their gains with their commander. Many others, too, of these

[1] Discovery of the Great West, chap. vi.

forest rovers, outlawed by royal edicts, found in the governor of Montreal a protector, under similar conditions.

The journey from Quebec to Montreal often consumed a fortnight. Perrot thought himself virtually independent; and relying on his commission from the king, the protection of Talon, and his connection with other persons of influence, he felt safe in his position, and began to play the petty tyrant. The judge of Montreal, and several of the chief inhabitants, came to offer a humble remonstrance against disorders committed by some of the ruffians in his interest. Perrot received them with a storm of vituperation, and presently sent the judge to prison. This proceeding was followed by a series of others, closely akin to it, so that the priests of St. Sulpice, who received their full share of official abuse, began to repent bitterly of the governor they had chosen.

Frontenac had received stringent orders from the king to arrest all the bush-rangers, or *coureurs de bois*; but, since he had scarcely a soldier at his disposal, except his own bodyguard, the order was difficult to execute. As, however, most of these outlaws were in the service of his rival, Perrot, his zeal to capture them rose high against every obstacle. He had, moreover, a plan of his own in regard to them, and had already petitioned the minister for a galley, to the benches of which the captive bush-rangers were to be chained as rowers, thus supplying the representative of the king with a means of transportation befitting his dignity, and at the same time giving wholesome warning against the infraction of royal edicts.[1] Accordingly, he sent orders to the judge, at Montreal, to seize every *coureur de bois* on whom he could lay hands.

The judge, hearing that two of the most notorious were lodged in the house of a lieutenant named Carion, sent a constable to arrest them; whereupon Carion threatened and maltreated the officer of justice, and helped the men to escape. Perrot took the part of his lieutenant, and told the judge that he would put him in prison, in spite of Frontenac, if he ever dared to attempt such an arrest again.[2]

When Frontenac heard what had happened, his ire was doubly kindled. On the one hand, Perrot had violated the

---

[1] *Frontenac au Ministre, 2 Nov., 1672.*

[2] *Mémoire des Motifs qui ont obligé M. le Comte de Frontenac de faire arrêter le Sieur Perrot.*

authority lodged by the king in the person of his representative; and, on the other, the mutinous official was a rival in trade, who had made great and illicit profits, while his superior had, thus far, made none. As a governor and as a man, Frontenac was deeply moved; yet, helpless as he was, he could do no more than send three of his guardsmen, under a lieutenant named Bizard, with orders to arrest Carion and bring him to Quebec.

The commission was delicate. The arrest was to be made in the dominions of Perrot, who had the means to prevent it, and the audacity to use them. Bizard acted accordingly. He went to Carion's house, and took him prisoner; then proceeded to the house of the merchant Le Ber, where he left a letter, in which Frontenac, as was the usage on such occasions, gave notice to the local governor of the arrest he had ordered. It was the object of Bizard to escape with his prisoner before Perrot could receive the letter; but, meanwhile, the wife of Carion ran to him with the news, and the governor suddenly arrived, in a frenzy of rage, followed by a sergeant and three or four soldiers. The sergeant held the point of his halberd against the breast of Bizard, while Perrot, choking with passion, demanded, "How dare you arrest an officer in my government without my leave?" The lieutenant replied that he acted under orders of the governor-general, and gave Frontenac's letter to Perrot, who immediately threw it into his face, exclaiming: "Take it back to your master, and tell him to teach you your business better another time. Meanwhile you are my prisoner." Bizard protested in vain. He was led to jail, whither he was followed a few days after by Le Ber, who had mortally offended Perrot by signing an attestation of the scene he had witnessed. As he was the chief merchant of the place, his arrest produced a great sensation, while his wife presently took to her bed with a nervous fever.

As Perrot's anger cooled, he became somewhat alarmed. He had resisted the royal authority, and insulted its representative. The consequences might be serious; yet he could not bring himself to retrace his steps. He merely released Bizard, and sullenly permitted him to depart, with a letter to the governor-general, more impertinent than apologetic.[1]

[1] *Mémoire des Motifs*, etc.

Frontenac, as his enemies declare, was accustomed, when enraged, to foam at the mouth. Perhaps he did so when he learned the behavior of Perrot. If he had had at command a few companies of soldiers, there can be little doubt that he would have gone at once to Montreal, seized the offender, and brought him back in irons; but his body-guard of twenty men was not equal to such an enterprise. Nor would a muster of the militia have served his purpose; for the settlers about Quebec were chiefly peaceful peasants, while the denizens of Montreal were disbanded soldiers, fur traders, and forest adventurers, the best fighters in Canada. They were nearly all in the interest of Perrot, who, if attacked, had the temper as well as the ability to make a passionate resistance. Thus civil war would have ensued, and the anger of the king would have fallen on both parties. On the other hand, if Perrot were left unpunished, the *coureurs de bois*, of whom he was the patron, would set no bounds to their audacity, and Frontenac, who had been ordered to suppress them, would be condemned as negligent or incapable.

Among the priests of St. Sulpice at Montreal was the Abbé Salignac de Fénelon, half-brother of the celebrated author of *Télémaque*. He was a zealous missionary, enthusiastic and impulsive, still young, and more ardent than discreet. One of his uncles had been the companion of Frontenac during the Candian war, and hence the count's relations with the missionary had been very friendly. Frontenac now wrote to Perrot, directing him to come to Quebec and give account of his conduct; and he coupled this letter with another to Fénelon, urging him to represent to the offending governor the danger of his position, and advise him to seek an interview with his superior, by which the difficulty might be amicably adjusted. Perrot, dreading the displeasure of the king, soothed by the moderate tone of Frontenac's letter, and moved by the assurances of the enthusiastic abbé, who was delighted to play the part of peace-maker, at length resolved to follow his counsel. It was mid-winter. Perrot and Fénelon set out together, walked on snow-shoes a hundred and eighty miles down the frozen St. Lawrence, and made their appearance before the offended count.

Frontenac, there can be little doubt, had never intended

that Perrot, once in his power, should return to Montreal as its governor; but that, beyond this, he meant harm to him, there is not the least proof. Perrot, however, was as choleric and stubborn as the count himself; and his natural disposition had not been improved by several years of petty autocracy at Montreal. Their interview was brief, but stormy. When it ended, Perrot was a prisoner in the château, with guards placed over him by day and night. Frontenac made choice of one La Nouguère, a retired officer, whom he knew that he could trust, and sent him to Montreal to command in place of its captive governor. With him he sent also a judge of his own selection. La Nouguère set himself to his work with vigor. Perrot's agent or partner, Brucy, was seized, tried, and imprisoned; and an active hunt was begun for his *coureurs de bois*. Among others, the two who had been the occasion of the dispute were captured and sent to Quebec, where one of them was solemnly hanged before the window of Perrot's prison; with the view, no doubt, of producing a chastening effect on the mind of the prisoner. The execution was fully authorized, a royal edict having ordained that bush-ranging was an offence punishable with death.[1] As the result of these proceedings, Frontenac reported to the minister that only five *coureurs de bois* remained at large; all the rest having returned to the settlements and made their submission, so that farther hanging was needless.

Thus the central power was vindicated, and Montreal brought down from her attitude of partial independence. Other results also followed, if we may believe the enemies of Frontenac, who declare that, by means of the new commandant and other persons in his interest, the governor-general possessed himself of a great part of the trade from which he had ejected Perrot, and that the *coureurs de bois*, whom he hanged when breaking laws for his rival, found complete impunity when breaking laws for him.

Meanwhile, there was a deep though subdued excitement among the priests of St. Sulpice. The right of naming their own governor, which they claimed as seigniors of Montreal, had been violated by the action of Frontenac in placing La Nouguère in command without consulting them. Perrot was

[1] *Édits et Ordonnances*, I. 73.

a bad governor; but it was they who had chosen him, and the recollection of his misdeeds did not reconcile them to a successor arbitrarily imposed upon them. Both they and the colonists, their vassals, were intensely jealous of Quebec; and, in their indignation against Frontenac, they more than half forgave Perrot. None among them all was so angry as the Abbé Fénelon. He believed that he had been used to lure Perrot into a trap; and his past attachment to the governor-general was turned into wrath. High words had passed between them; and, when Fénelon returned to Montreal, he vented his feelings in a sermon plainly levelled at Frontenac.[1] So sharp and bitter was it, that his brethren of St. Sulpice hastened to disclaim it; and Dollier de Casson, their Superior, strongly reproved the preacher, who protested in return that his words were not meant to apply to Frontenac in particular, but only to bad rulers in general. His offences, however, did not cease with the sermon; for he espoused the cause of Perrot with more than zeal, and went about among the colonists to collect attestations in his favor. When these things were reported to Frontenac, his ire was kindled, and he summoned Fénelon before the council at Quebec to answer the charge of instigating sedition.

Fénelon had a relative and friend in the person of the Abbé d'Urfé, his copartner in the work of the missions. D'Urfé, anxious to conjure down the rising storm, went to Quebec to seek an interview with Frontenac; but, according to his own account, he was very ill received, and threatened with a prison. On another occasion, the count showed him a letter in which D'Urfé was charged with having used abusive language concerning him. Warm words ensued, till Frontenac, grasping his cane, led the abbé to the door and dismissed him, berating him from the top of the stairs in tones so angry that the sentinel below spread the report that he had turned his visitor out of doors.[2]

Two offenders were now arraigned before the council of Quebec: the first was Perrot, charged with disobeying the royal edicts and resisting the royal authority; the other was

---

[1] *Information faite par nous, Charles le Tardieu, Sieur de Tilly.* Tilly was a commissioner sent by the council to inquire into the affair.

[2] *Mémoire de M. d'Urfé à Colbert*, extracts in Faillon.

the Abbé Fénelon. The councillors were at this time united in the interest of Frontenac, who had the power of appointing and removing them. Perrot, in no way softened by a long captivity, challenged the governor-general, who presided at the council board, as a party to the suit and his personal enemy, and took exception to several of the members as being connections of La Nouguère. Frontenac withdrew, and other councillors or judges were appointed provisionally; but these were challenged in turn by the prisoner, on one pretext or another. The exceptions were overruled, and the trial proceeded, though not without signs of doubt and hesitation on the part of some of the councillors.[1]

Meanwhile, other sessions were held for the trial of Fénelon; and a curious scene ensued. Five councillors and the deputy attorney-general were seated at the board, with Frontenac as presiding judge, his hat on his head and his sword at his side, after the established custom. Fénelon, being led in, approached a vacant chair, and was about to seat himself with the rest, when Frontenac interposed, telling him that it was his duty to remain standing while answering the questions of the council. Fénelon at once placed himself in the chair, and replied that priests had the right to speak seated and with heads covered.

"Yes," returned Frontenac, "when they are summoned as witnesses, but not when they are cited to answer charges of crime."

"My crimes exist nowhere but in your head," replied the abbé. And, putting on his hat, he drew it down over his brows, rose, gathered his cassock about him, and walked in a defiant manner to and fro. Frontenac told him that his conduct was wanting in respect to the council, and to the governor as its head. Fénelon several times took off his hat, and pushed it on again more angrily than ever, saying at the same time that Frontenac was wanting in respect to his character of priest, in citing him before a civil tribunal. As he persisted in his refusal to take the required attitude, he was at length told that he might leave the room. After being kept for a time

[1] All the proceedings in the affair of Perrot will be found in full in the *Registre des Jugements et Délibérations du Conseil Supérieur*. They extend from the end of January to the beginning of November, 1674.

in the ante-room in charge of a constable, he was again brought before the council, when he still refused obedience, and was ordered into a sort of honorable imprisonment.[1]

This behavior of the effervescent abbé, which Frontenac justly enough characterizes as unworthy of his birth and his sacred office, was, nevertheless, founded on a claim sustained by many precedents. As an ecclesiastic, Fénelon insisted that the bishop alone, and not the council, had the right to judge him. Like Perrot, too, he challenged his judges as parties to the suit, or otherwise interested against him. On the question of jurisdiction, he had all the priests on his side. Bishop Laval was in France; and Bernières, his grand vicar, was far from filling the place of the strenuous and determined prelate. Yet the ecclesiastical storm rose so high that the councillors, discouraged and daunted, were no longer amenable to the will of Frontenac; and it was resolved at last to refer the whole matter to the king. Perrot was taken from the prison, which he had occupied from January to November, and shipped for France, along with Fénelon. An immense mass of papers was sent with them for the instruction of the king; and Frontenac wrote a long despatch, in which he sets forth the offences of Perrot and Fénelon, the pretensions of the ecclesiastics, the calumnies he had incurred in his efforts to serve his Majesty, and the insults heaped upon him, "which no man but me would have endured so patiently." Indeed, while the suits were pending before the council, he had displayed a calmness and moderation which surprised his opponents. "Knowing as I do," he puruses, "the cabals and intrigues that are rife here, I must expect that every thing will be said against me that the most artful slander can devise. A governor in this country would greatly deserve pity, if he were left without support; and, even should he make mistakes, it would surely be very pardonable, seeing that there is no snare that is not spread for him, and that, after avoiding a hundred of them, he will hardly escape being caught at last."[2]

[1] *Conteste entre le Gouverneur et l'Abbé de Fénelon; Jugements et Déliberations du Conseil Supérieur, 21 Août, 1674.*

[2] *Frontenac au Ministre, 14 Nov., 1674.* In a preceding letter, sent by way of Boston, and dated 16 February, he says that he could not suffer Perrot to go unpunished without injury to the regal authority, which he is resolved to defend to the last drop of his blood.

In his charges of cabal and intrigue, Frontenac had chiefly in view the clergy, whom he profoundly distrusted, excepting always the Récollet friars, whom he befriended because the bishop and the Jesuits opposed them. The priests on their part declare that he persecuted them, compelled them to take passports like laymen when travelling about the colony, and even intercepted their letters. These accusations and many others were carried to the king and the minister by the Abbé d'Urfé, who sailed in the same ship with Fénelon. The moment was singularly auspicious to him. His cousin, the Marquise d'Allègre, was on the point of marrying Seignelay, the son of the minister Colbert, who, therefore, was naturally inclined to listen with favor to him and to Fénelon, his relative. Again, Talon, uncle of Perrot's wife, held a post at court, which brought him into close personal relations with the king. Nor were these the only influences adverse to Frontenac and propitious to his enemies. Yet his enemies were disappointed. The letters written to him both by Colbert and by the king are admirable for calmness and dignity. The following is from that of the king:—

"Though I do not credit all that has been told me concerning various little annoyances which you cause to the ecclesiastics, I nevertheless think it necessary to inform you of it, in order that, if true, you may correct yourself in this particular, giving to all the clergy entire liberty to go and come throughout all Canada without compelling them to take out passports, and at the same time leaving them perfect freedom as regards their letters. I have seen and carefully examined all that you have sent touching M. Perrot; and, after having also seen all the papers given by him in his defence, I have condemned his action in imprisoning an officer of your guard. To punish him, I have had him placed for a short time in the Bastile, that he may learn to be more circumspect in the discharge of his duty, and that his example may serve as a warning to others. But after having thus vindicated my authority, which has been violated in your person, I will say, in order that you may fully understand my views, that you should not without absolute necessity cause your commands to be executed within the limits of a local government, like that of Montreal, without first informing its governor, and also that the ten months of imprisonment which you have made him undergo seems to me sufficient for his fault. I therefore sent him to the Bastile merely as a public reparation for having violated my authority. After keeping him there a few days, I shall send him back to his government, ordering him first to see you and make apology to you for all that has passed; after which I desire that you retain no resentment against him, and that you treat him in accordance with the powers that I have given him."[1]

Colbert writes in terms equally measured, and adds: "After having spoken in the name of his Majesty, pray let me add a word in my own. By the marriage which the king has been pleased to make between the heiress of the house of Allègre and my son, the Abbé d'Urfé has become very closely connected with me, since he is cousin german of my daughter-in-law; and this induces me to request you to show him especial consideration, though, in the exercise of his profession, he will rarely have occasion to see you."

As D'Urfé had lately addressed a memorial to Colbert, in which the conduct of Frontenac is painted in the darkest colors, the almost imperceptible rebuke couched in the above lines does no little credit to the tact and moderation of the stern minister.

Colbert next begs Frontenac to treat with kindness the priests of Montreal, observing that Bretonvilliers, their Superior at Paris, is his particular friend. "As to M. Perrot," he continues, "since ten months of imprisonment at Quebec and three weeks in the Bastile may suffice to atone for his fault, and since also he is related or connected with persons for whom I have a great regard, I pray you to accept kindly the apologies which he will make you, and, as it is not at all likely that he will fall again into any offence approaching that which he has committed, you will give me especial pleasure in granting him the honor of your favor and friendship."[2]

Fénelon, though the recent marriage had allied him also to Colbert, fared worse than either of the other parties to the dispute. He was indeed sustained in his claim to be judged by an ecclesiastical tribunal; but his Superior, Bretonvilliers, for-

[1] *Le Roi à Frontenac, 22 Avril, 1675.*
[2] *Colbert à Frontenac, 13 Mai, 1675.*

bade him to return to Canada, and the king approved the prohibition. Bretonvilliers wrote to the Sulpitian priests of Montreal: "I exhort you to profit by the example of M. de Fénelon. By having busied himself too much in worldly matters, and meddled with what did not concern him, he has ruined his own prospects and injured the friends whom he wished to serve. In matters of this sort, it is well always to stand neutral."[1]

[1] *Lettre de Bretonvilliers, 7 Mai, 1675*; extract in Faillon. Fénelon, though wanting in prudence and dignity, had been an ardent and devoted missionary. In relation to these disputes, I have received much aid from the research of Abbé Faillon, and from the valuable paper of Abbé Verreau, *Les deux Abbés de Fénelon*, printed in the Canadian *Journal de l'Instruction Publique*, Vol. VIII.

Chapter IV

1675–1682

FRONTENAC AND DUCHESNEAU

Frontenac receives a Colleague • He opposes the Clergy • Disputes in the Council • Royal Intervention • Frontenac rebuked • Fresh Outbreaks • Charges and Countercharges • The Dispute grows hot • Duchesneau condemned and Frontenac warned • The Quarrel continues • The King loses Patience • More Accusations • Factions and Feuds • A Side Quarrel • The King threatens • Frontenac denounces the Priests • The Governor and the Intendant recalled • Qualities of Frontenac

---

WHILE WRITING to Frontenac in terms of studied mildness, the king and Colbert took measures to curb his power. In the absence of the bishop, the appointment and removal of councillors had rested wholly with the governor; and hence the council had been docile under his will. It was now ordained that the councillors should be appointed by the king himself.[1] This was not the only change. Since the departure of the intendant Talon, his office had been vacant; and Frontenac was left to rule alone. This seems to have been an experiment on the part of his masters at Versailles, who, knowing the peculiarities of his temper, were perhaps willing to try the effect of leaving him without a colleague. The experiment had not succeeded. An intendant was now, therefore, sent to Quebec, not only to manage the details of administration, but also to watch the governor, keep him, if possible, within prescribed bounds, and report his proceedings to the minister. The change was far from welcome to Frontenac, whose delight it was to hold all the reins of power in his own hands; nor was he better pleased with the return of Bishop Laval, which presently took place. Three preceding governors had quarrelled with that uncompromising prelate; and there was little hope that Frontenac and he would keep the peace. All the signs of the sky foreboded storm.

The storm soon came. The occasion of it was that old

[1] *Édits et Ordonnances*, I. 84.

vexed question of the sale of brandy, which has been fully treated in another volume,[1] and on which it is needless to dwell here. Another dispute quickly followed; and here, too, the governor's chief adversaries were the bishop and the ecclesiastics. Duchesneau, the new intendant, took part with them. The bishop and his clergy were, on their side, very glad of a secular ally; for their power had greatly fallen since the days of Mézy, and the rank and imperious character of Frontenac appear to have held them in some awe. They avoided as far as they could a direct collision with him, and waged vicarious war in the person of their friend the intendant. Duchesneau was not of a conciliating spirit, and he felt strong in the support of the clergy; while Frontenac, when his temper was roused, would fight with haughty and impracticable obstinacy for any position which he had once assumed, however trivial or however mistaken. There was incessant friction between the two colleagues in the exercise of their respective functions, and occasions of difference were rarely wanting.

The question now at issue was that of honors and precedence at church and in religious ceremonies, matters of substantial importance under the Bourbon rule. Colbert interposed, ordered Duchesneau to treat Frontenac with becoming deference, and warned him not to make himself the partisan of the bishop;[2] while, at the same time, he exhorted Frontenac to live in harmony with the intendant.[3] The dispute continued till the king lost patience.

"Through all my kingdom," he wrote to the governor, "I do not hear of so many difficulties on this matter (*of ecclesiastical honors*) as I see in the church of Quebec."[4] And he directs him to conform to the practice established in the city of Amiens, and to exact no more; "since you ought to be satisfied with being the representative of my person in the country where I have placed you in command."

At the same time, Colbert corrects the intendant. "A memorial," he wrote, "has been placed in my hands, touching various ecclesiastical honors, wherein there continually ap-

---

[1] The Old Régime in Canada.
[2] *Colbert à Duchesneau, 1 Mai, 1677.*
[3] *Ibid., 18 Mai, 1677.*
[4] *Le Roy à Frontenac, 25 Avril, 1679.*

pears a great pretension on your part, and on that of the bishop of Quebec in your favor, to establish an equality between the governor and you. I think I have already said enough to lead you to know yourself, and to understand the difference between a governor and an intendant; so that it is no longer necessary for me to enter into particulars, which could only serve to show you that you are completely in the wrong."[1]

Scarcely was this quarrel suppressed, when another sprang up. Since the arrival of the intendant and the return of the bishop, the council had ceased to be in the interest of Frontenac. Several of its members were very obnoxious to him; and chief among these was Villeray, a former councillor whom the king had lately reinstated. Frontenac admitted him to his seat with reluctance. "I obey your orders," he wrote mournfully to Colbert; "but Villeray is the principal and most dangerous instrument of the bishop and the Jesuits."[2] He says, farther, that many people think him to be a Jesuit in disguise, and that he is an intriguing busybody, who makes trouble everywhere. He also denounces the attorney-general, Auteuil, as an ally of the Jesuits. Another of the reconstructed council, Tilly, meets his cordial approval; but he soon found reason to change his mind concerning him.

The king had recently ordered that the intendant, though holding only the third rank in the council, should act as its president.[3] The commission of Duchesneau, however, empowered him to preside only in the absence of the governor;[4] while Frontenac is styled "chief and president of the council" in several of the despatches addressed to him. Here was an inconsistency. Both parties claimed the right of presiding, and both could rest their claim on a clear expression of the royal will.

Frontenac rarely began a new quarrel till the autumn vessels had sailed for France; because a full year must then elapse before his adversaries could send their complaints to the king, and six months more before the king could send back his an-

[1] *Colbert à Duchesneau, 8 Mai, 1679.*

[2] *Frontenac au Ministre, 14 Nov., 1674.*

[3] *Declaration du Roy, 23 Sept., 1675.*

[4] "Presider au Conseil Souverain *en l'absence du dit Sieur de Frontenac.*"
— *Commission de Duchesneau, 5 Juin, 1675.*

swer. The governor had been heard to say, on one of these occasions, that he should now be master for eighteen months, subject only to answering with his head for what he might do. It was when the last vessel was gone in the autumn of 1678 that he demanded to be styled *chief and president* on the records of the council; and he showed a letter from the king in which he was so entitled.[1] In spite of this, Duchesneau resisted, and appealed to precedent to sustain his position. A long series of stormy sessions followed. The councillors in the clerical interest supported the intendant. Frontenac, chafed and angry, refused all compromise. Business was stopped for weeks. Duchesneau lost temper, and became abusive. Auteuil tried to interpose in behalf of the intendant. Frontenac struck the table with his fist, and told him fiercely that he would teach him his duty. Every day embittered the strife. The governor made the declaration usual with him on such occasions, that he would not permit the royal authority to suffer in his person. At length he banished from Quebec his three most strenuous opponents, Villeray, Tilly, and Auteuil, and commanded them to remain in their country houses till they received his farther orders. All attempts at compromise proved fruitless; and Auteuil, in behalf of the exiles, appealed piteously to the king.

The answer came in the following summer: "Monsieur le Comte de Frontenac," wrote Louis XIV., "I am surprised to learn all the new troubles and dissensions that have occurred in my country of New France, more especially since I have clearly and strongly given you to understand that your sole care should be to maintain harmony and peace among all my subjects dwelling therein; but what surprises me still more is that in nearly all the disputes which you have caused you have advanced claims which have very little foundation. My edicts, declarations, and ordinances had so plainly made known to you my will, that I have great cause of astonishment that you, whose duty it is to see them faithfully executed, have yourself set up pretensions entirely opposed to them. You have wished to be styled chief and president on the records of the Supreme Council, which is contrary to my edict concerning that coun-

[1] This letter, still preserved in the *Archives de la Marine*, is dated *12 Mai, 1678*. Several other letters of Louis XIV. give Frontenac the same designation.

cil; and I am the more surprised at this demand, since I am very sure that you are the only man in my kingdom who, being honored with the title of governor and lieutenant-general, would care to be styled chief and president of such a council as that of Quebec."

He then declares that neither Frontenac nor the intendant is to have the title of president, but that the intendant is to perform the functions of presiding officer, as determined by the edict. He continues:—

"Moreover, your abuse of the authority which I have confided to you in exiling two councillors and the attorney-general for so trivial a cause cannot meet my approval; and, were it not for the distinct assurances given me by your friends that you will act with more moderation in future, and never again fall into offences of this nature, I should have resolved on recalling you."[1]

Colbert wrote to him with equal severity: "I have communicated to the king the contents of all the despatches which you have written to me during the past year; and as the matters of which they treat are sufficiently ample, including dissensions almost universal among those whose duty it is to preserve harmony in the country under your command, his Majesty has been pleased to examine all the papers sent by all the parties interested, and more particularly those appended to your letters. He has thereupon ordered me distinctly to make known to you his intentions." The minister then proceeds to reprove him sharply in the name of the king, and concludes: "It is difficult for me to add any thing to what I have just said. Consider well that, if it is any advantage or any satisfaction to you that his Majesty should be satisfied with your services, it is necessary that you change entirely the conduct which you have hitherto pursued."[2]

---

[1] *Le Roy à Frontenac, 29 Avril, 1680.* A decree of the council of state soon after determined the question of presidency in accord with this letter. *Édits et Ordonnances*, I. 238.

[2] *Colbert à Frontenac, 4 Dec., 1679.* This letter seems to have been sent by a special messenger by way of New England. It was too late in the season to send directly to Canada. On the quarrel about the presidency, *Duchesneau au Ministre, 10 Nov., 1679; Auteuil au Ministre, 10 Aug., 1679; Contestations entre le Sieur Comte de Frontenac et M. Duchesneau, Chevalier.* This last paper consists of voluminous extracts from the records of the council.

This, one would think, might have sufficed to bring the governor to reason, but the violence of his resentments and antipathies overcame the very slender share of prudence with which nature had endowed him. One morning, as he sat at the head of the council board, the bishop on his right hand, and the intendant on his left, a woman made her appearance with a sealed packet of papers. She was the wife of the councillor Amours, whose chair was vacant at the table. Important business was in hand, the registration of a royal edict of amnesty to the *coureurs de bois*. The intendant, who well knew what the packet contained, demanded that it should be opened. Frontenac insisted that the business before the council should proceed. The intendant renewed his demand, the council sustained him, and the packet was opened accordingly. It contained a petition from Amours, stating that Frontenac had put him in prison, because, having obtained in due form a passport to send a canoe to his fishing station of Matane, he had afterwards sent a sail-boat thither without applying for another passport. Frontenac had sent for him, and demanded by what right he did so. Amours replied that he believed that he had acted in accordance with the intentions of the king; whereupon, to borrow the words of the petition, "Monsieur the governor fell into a rage, and said to your petitioner, 'I will teach you the intentions of the king, and you shall stay in prison till you learn them;' and your petitioner was shut up in a chamber of the château, wherein he still remains." He proceeds to pray that a trial may be granted him according to law.[1]

Discussions now ensued which lasted for days, and now and then became tempestuous. The governor, who had declared that the council had nothing to do with the matter, and that he could not waste time in talking about it, was not always present at the meetings, and it sometimes became necessary to depute one or more of the members to visit him. Auteuil, the attorney-general, having been employed on this unenviable errand, begged the council to dispense him from such duty in future, "by reason," as he says, "of the abuse, ill treatment, and threats which he received from Monsieur the governor, when he last had the honor of being deputed to

[1] *Registre du Conseil Supérieur, 16 Août, 1681.*

confer with him, the particulars whereof he begs to be excused from reporting, lest the anger of Monsieur the governor should be kindled against him still more."[1] Frontenac, hearing of this charge, angrily denied it, saying that the attorney-general had slandered and insulted him, and that it was his custom to do so. Auteuil rejoined that the governor had accused him of habitual lying, and told him that he would have his hand cut off. All these charges and countercharges may still be found entered in due form on the old records of the council at Quebec.

It was as usual upon the intendant that the wrath of Frontenac fell most fiercely. He accuses him of creating cabals and intrigues, and causing not only the council, but all the country, to forget the respect due to the representative of his Majesty. Once, when Frontenac was present at the session, a dispute arose about an entry on the record. A draft of it had been made in terms agreeable to the governor, who insisted that the intendant should sign it. Duchesneau replied that he and the clerk would go into the adjoining room, where they could examine it in peace, and put it into a proper form. Frontenac rejoined that he would then have no security that what he had said in the council would be accurately reported. Duchesneau persisted, and was going out with the draft in his hand, when Frontenac planted himself before the door, and told him that he should not leave the council chamber till he had signed the paper. "Then I will get out of the window, or else stay here all day," returned Duchesneau. A lively debate ensued, and the governor at length yielded the point.[2]

The imprisonment of Amours was short, but strife did not cease. The disputes in the council were accompanied throughout with other quarrels which were complicated with them, and which were worse than all the rest, since they involved more important matters and covered a wider field. They related to the fur trade, on which hung the very life of the colony. Merchants, traders, and even *habitants*, were ranged in two contending factions. Of one of these Frontenac was the chief. With him were La Salle and his lieutenant, La Forêt; Du Lhut, the famous leader of *coureurs de bois*; Bois-

[1] *Registre du Conseil Supérieur, 4 Nov., 1681.*
[2] *Registre du Conseil Supérieur, 1681.*

seau, agent of the farmers of the revenue; Barrois, the governor's secretary; Bizard, lieutenant of his guard; and various
others of greater or less influence. On the other side were the
members of the council, with Aubert de la Chesnaye, Le
Moyne and all his sons, Louis Joliet, Jacques Le Ber, Sorel,
Boucher, Varennes, and many more, all supported by the intendant Duchesneau, and also by his fast allies, the ecclesiastics. The faction under the lead of the governor had every
advantage, for it was sustained by all the power of his office.
Duchesneau was beside himself with rage. He wrote to the
court letters full of bitterness, accused Frontenac of illicit
trade, denounced his followers, and sent huge bundles of
procès-verbaux and attestations to prove his charges.

But if Duchesneau wrote letters, so too did Frontenac; and
if the intendant sent proofs, so too did the governor. Upon
the unfortunate king and the still more unfortunate minister
fell the difficult task of composing the quarrels of their servants, three thousand miles away. They treated Duchesneau
without ceremony. Colbert wrote to him: "I have examined
all the letters, papers, and memorials that you sent me by the
return of the vessels last November, and, though it appears
by the letters of M. de Frontenac that his conduct leaves
something to be desired, there is assuredly far more to blame
in yours than in his. As to what you say concerning his violence, his trade with the Indians, and in general all that you
allege against him, the king has written to him his intentions;
but since, in the midst of all your complaints, you say many
things which are without foundation, or which are no concern of yours, it is difficult to believe that you act in the spirit
which the service of the king demands; that is to say, without
interest and without passion. If a change does not appear in
your conduct before next year, his Majesty will not keep you
in your office."[1]

At the same time, the king wrote to Frontenac, alluding to
the complaints of Duchesneau, and exhorting the governor to
live on good terms with him. The general tone of the letter is
moderate, but the following significant warning occurs in it:
"Although no gentleman in the position in which I have

[1] *Colbert à Duchesneau, 15 Mai, 1678.*

placed you ought to take part in any trade, directly or indirectly, either by himself or any of his servants, I nevertheless now prohibit you absolutely from doing so. Not only abstain from trade, but act in such a manner that nobody can even suspect you of it; and this will be easy, since the truth will readily come to light."[1]

Exhortation and warning were vain alike. The first ships which returned that year from Canada brought a series of despatches from the intendant, renewing all his charges more bitterly than before. The minister, out of patience, replied by berating him without mercy. "You may rest assured," he concludes, "that, did it not appear by your later despatches that the letters you have received have begun to make you understand that you have forgotten yourself, it would not have been possible to prevent the king from recalling you."[2]

Duchesneau, in return, protests all manner of deference to the governor, but still insists that he sets the royal edicts at naught; protects a host of *coureurs de bois* who are in league with him; corresponds with Du Lhut, their chief; shares his illegal profits, and causes all the disorders which afflict the colony. "As for me, Monseigneur, I have done every thing within the scope of my office to prevent these evils; but all the pains I have taken have only served to increase the aversion of Monsieur the governor against me, and to bring my ordinances into contempt. This, Monseigneur, is a true account of the disobedience of the *coureurs de bois*, of which I twice had the honor to speak to Monsieur the governor; and I could not help telling him, with all possible deference, that it was shameful to the colony and to us that the king, our master, of whom the whole world stands in awe, who has just given law to all Europe, and whom all his subjects adore, should have the pain of knowing that, in a country which has received so many marks of his paternal tenderness, his orders are violated and scorned; and a governor and an intendant stand by, with folded arms, content with saying that the evil is past remedy. For having made these representations to him, I drew on myself words so full of contempt and insult that I was forced to leave his room to appease his anger. The next

[1] *Le Roy à Frontenac, 12 Mai, 1678.*
[2] *Colbert à Duchesneau, 25 Avril, 1679.*

morning I went to him again, and did all I could to have my ordinances executed; but, as Monsieur the governor is interested with many of the *coureurs de bois*, it is useless to attempt to do any thing. He has gradually made himself master of the trade of Montreal; and, as soon as the Indians arrive, he sets guards in their camp, which would be very well, if these soldiers did their duty and protected the savages from being annoyed and plundered by the French, instead of being employed to discover how many furs they have brought, with a view to future operations. Monsieur the governor then compels the Indians to pay his guards for protecting them; and he has never allowed them to trade with the inhabitants till they had first given him a certain number of packs of beaver skins, which he calls his presents. His guards trade with them openly at the fair, with their bandoleers on their shoulders."

He says, farther, that Frontenac sends up goods to Montreal, and employs persons to trade in his behalf; and that, what with the beaver skins exacted by him and his guards under the name of presents, and those which he and his favorites obtain in trade, only the smaller part of what the Indians bring to market ever reaches the people of the colony.[1]

This despatch, and the proofs accompanying it, drew from the king a sharp reproof to Frontenac.

"What has passed in regard to the *coureurs de bois* is entirely contrary to my orders; and I cannot receive in excuse for it your allegation that it is the intendant who countenances them by the trade he carries on, for I perceive clearly that the fault is your own. As I see that you often turn the orders that I give you against the very object for which they are given, beware not to do so on this occasion. I shall hold you answerable for bringing the disorder of the *coureurs de bois* to an end throughout Canada; and this you will easily succeed in doing, if you make a proper use of my authority. Take care not to persuade yourself that what I write to you comes from the ill offices of the intendant. It results from what I fully know from every thing which reaches me from Canada, proving but too well what you are doing there. The bishop, the

[1] *Duchesneau au Ministre, 10 Nov., 1679.*

ecclesiastics, the Jesuit fathers, the Supreme Council, and, in a word, everybody, complain of you; but I am willing to believe that you will change your conduct, and act with the moderation necessary for the good of the colony."[1]

Colbert wrote in a similar strain; and Frontenac saw that his position was becoming critical. He showed, it is true, no sign of that change of conduct which the king had demanded; but he appealed to his allies at court to use fresh efforts to sustain him. Among the rest, he had a strong friend in the Maréchal de Bellefonds, to whom he wrote, in the character of an abused and much-suffering man: "You exhort me to have patience, and I agree with you that those placed in a position of command cannot have too much. For this reason, I have given examples of it here such as perhaps no governor ever gave before; and I have found no great difficulty in doing so, because I felt myself to be the master. Had I been in a private station, I could not have endured such outrageous insults without dishonor. I have always passed over in silence those directed against me personally; and have never given way to anger, except when attacks were made on the authority of which I have the honor to be the guardian. You could not believe all the annoyances which the intendant tries to put upon me every day, and which, as you advise me, I scorn or disregard. It would require a virtue like yours to turn them to all the good use of which they are capable; yet, great as the virtue is which has enabled you to possess your soul in tranquillity amid all the troubles of the court, I doubt if you could preserve such complete equanimity among the miserable tumults of Canada."[2]

Having given the principal charges of Duchesneau against Frontenac, it is time to give those of Frontenac against Duchesneau. The governor says that all the *coureurs de bois* would be brought to submission but for the intendant and his allies, who protect them, and carry on trade by their means; that the seigniorial house of Duchesneau's partner, La Chesnaye, is the constant resort of these outlaws; and that he and his associates have large storehouses at Montreal, Isle St. Paul, and Rivière du Loup, whence they send goods into the In-

[1] *Le Roy à Frontenac, 29 Avril, 1680.*
[2] *Frontenac au Maréchal de Bellefonds, 14 Nov., 1680.*

dian country, in contempt of the king's orders.[1] Frontenac also complains of numberless provocations from the intendant. "It is no fault of mine that I am not on good terms with M. Duchesneau; for I have done every thing I could to that end, being too submissive to your Majesty's commands not to suppress my sharpest indignation the moment your will is known to me. But, Sire, it is not so with him; and his desire to excite new disputes, in the hope of making me appear their principal author, has been so great that the last ships were hardly gone, when, forgetting what your Majesty had enjoined upon us both, he began these dissensions afresh, in spite of all my precautions. If I depart from my usual reserve in regard to him, and make bold to ask justice at the hands of your Majesty for the wrongs and insults I have undergone, it is because nothing but your authority can keep them within bounds. I have never suffered more in my life than when I have been made to appear as a man of violence and a disturber of the officers of justice: for I have always confined myself to what your Majesty has prescribed; that is, to exhorting them to do their duty when I saw that they failed in it. This has drawn upon me, both from them and from M. Duchesneau, such cutting affronts that your Majesty would hardly credit them."[2]

In 1681, Seignelay, the son of Colbert, entered upon the charge of the colonies; and both Frontenac and Duchesneau hastened to congratulate him, protest their devotion, and overwhelm him with mutual accusations. The intendant declares that, out of pure zeal for the king's service, he shall tell him every thing. "Disorder," he says, "reigns everywhere; universal confusion prevails throughout every department of business; the pleasure of the king, the orders of the Supreme Council, and my ordinances remain unexecuted; justice is openly violated, and trade is destroyed; violence, upheld by authority, decides every thing; and nothing consoles the people, who groan without daring to complain, but the hope, Monseigneur, that you will have the goodness to condescend to be moved by their misfortunes. No position could be more distressing than mine, since, if I conceal the truth from you,

[1] *Mémoire et Preuves du Désordre des Coureurs de Bois.*
[2] *Frontenac au Roy, 2 Nov., 1681.*

I fail in the obedience I owe the king, and in the fidelity that I vowed so long since to Monseigneur, your father, and which I swear anew at your hands; and if I obey, as I must, his Majesty's orders and yours, I cannot avoid giving offence, since I cannot render you an account of these disorders without informing you that M. de Frontenac's conduct is the sole cause of them."[1]

Frontenac had written to Seignelay a few days before: "I have no doubt whatever that M. Duchesneau will, as usual, overwhelm me with fabrications and falsehoods, to cover his own ill conduct. I send proofs to justify myself, so strong and convincing that I do not see that they can leave any doubt; but, since I fear that their great number might fatigue you, I have thought it better to send them to my wife, with a full and exact journal of all that has passed here day by day, in order that she may extract and lay before you the principal portions.

"I send you in person merely the proofs of the conduct of M. Duchesneau, in barricading his house and arming all his servants, and in coming three weeks ago to insult me in my room. You will see thereby to what a pitch of temerity and lawlessness he has transported himself, in order to compel me to use violence against him, with the hope of justifying what he has asserted about my pretended outbreaks of anger."[2]

The mutual charges of the two functionaries were much the same; and, so far at least as concerns trade, there can be little doubt that they were well founded on both sides. The strife of the rival factions grew more and more bitter: canes and sticks played an active part in it, and now and then we hear of drawn swords. One is reminded at times of the intestine feuds of some mediæval city, as, for example, in the following incident, which will explain the charge of Frontenac against the intendant of barricading his house and arming his servants: —

On the afternoon of the twentieth of March, a son of Duchesneau, sixteen years old, followed by a servant named Vautier, was strolling along the picket fence which bordered the descent from the Upper to the Lower Town of Quebec. The boy was amusing himself by singing a song, when Frontenac's

---

[1] *Duchesneau au Ministre, 13 Nov., 1681.*
[2] *Frontenac au Ministre, 2 Nov., 1681.*

partisan, Boisseau, with one of the guardsmen, approached, and, as young Duchesneau declares, called him foul names, and said that he would give him and his father a thrashing. The boy replied that he would have nothing to say to a fellow like him, and would beat him if he did not keep quiet; while the servant, Vautier, retorted Boisseau's abuse, and taunted him with low birth and disreputable employments. Boisseau made report to Frontenac, and Frontenac complained to Duchesneau, who sent his son, with Vautier, to give the governor his version of the affair. The bishop, an ally of the intendant, thus relates what followed. On arriving with a party of friends at the château, young Duchesneau was shown into a room in which were the governor and his two secretaries, Barrois and Chasseur. He had no sooner entered than Frontenac seized him by the arm, shook him, struck him, called him abusive names, and tore the sleeve of his jacket. The secretaries interposed, and, failing to quiet the governor, opened the door and let the boy escape. Vautier, meanwhile, had remained in the guard-room, where Boisseau struck at him with his cane; and one of the guardsmen went for a halberd to run him through the body. After this warm reception, young Duchesneau and his servant took refuge in the house of his father. Frontenac demanded their surrender. The intendant, fearing that he would take them by force, for which he is said to have made preparation, barricaded himself and armed his household. The bishop tried to mediate, and after protracted negotiations young Duchesneau was given up, whereupon Frontenac locked him in a chamber of the château, and kept him there a month.[1]

The story of Frontenac's violence to the boy is flatly denied by his friends, who charge Duchesneau and his partisans with circulating libels against him, and who say, like Frontenac himself, that the intendant used every means to exasperate him, in order to make material for accusations.[2]

The disputes of the rival factions spread through all Can-

---

[1] *Mémoire de l'Evesque de Québec, Mars, 1681* (printed in *Revue Canadienne*, 1873). The bishop is silent about the barricades of which Frontenac and his friends complain in several letters.

[2] See, among other instances, the *Défense de M. de Frontenac par un de ses Amis*, published by Abbé Verreau in the *Revue Canadienne*, 1873.

ada. The most heinous offence in the eyes of the court with which each charged the other was the carrying of furs to the English settlements; thus defrauding the revenue, and, as the king believed, preparing the ruin of the colony. The intendant farther declared that the governor's party spread among the Indians the report of a pestilence at Montreal, in order to deter them from their yearly visit to the fair, and thus by means of *coureurs de bois* obtain all their beaver skins at a low price. The report, according to Duchesneau, had no other foundation than the fate of eighteen or twenty Indians, who had lately drunk themselves to death at La Chine.[1]

Montreal, in the mean time, was the scene of a sort of by-play, in which the chief actor was the local governor, Perrot. He and Frontenac appear to have found it for their common interest to come to a mutual understanding; and this was perhaps easier on the part of the count, since his quarrel with Duchesneau gave sufficient employment to his natural pugnacity. Perrot was now left to make a reasonable profit from the illicit trade which had once kindled the wrath of his superior; and, the danger of Frontenac's anger being removed, he completely forgot the lessons of his imprisonment.

The intendant ordered Migeon, bailiff of Montreal, to arrest some of Perrot's *coureurs de bois*. Perrot at once arrested the bailiff, and sent a sergeant and two soldiers to occupy his house, with orders to annoy the family as much as possible. One of them, accordingly, walked to and fro all night in the bed-chamber of Migeon's wife. On another occasion, the bailiff invited two friends to supper: Le Moyne d'Iberville and one Bouthier, agent of a commercial house at Rochelle. The conversation turned on the trade carried on by Perrot. It was overheard and reported to him, upon which he suddenly appeared at the window, struck Bouthier over the head with his cane, then drew his sword, and chased him while he fled for his life. The seminary was near at hand, and the fugitive clambered over the wall. Dollier de Casson dressed him in the hat and cassock of a priest, and in this disguise he escaped.[2] Per-

[1] *Plumitif du Conseil Souverain, 1681.*

[2] *Conduite du Sieur Perrot, Gouverneur de Montréal en la Nouvelle France, 1681; Plainte du Sieur Bouthier, 10 Oct., 1680; Procès-verbal des huissiers de Montréal.*

rot's avidity sometimes carried him to singular extremities. "He has been seen," says one of his accusers, "filling barrels of brandy with his own hands, and mixing it with water to sell to the Indians. He bartered with one of them his hat, sword, coat, ribbons, shoes, and stockings, and boasted that he had made thirty pistoles by the bargain, while the Indian walked about town equipped as governor."[1]

Every ship from Canada brought to the king fresh complaints of Duchesneau against Frontenac, and of Frontenac against Duchesneau; and the king replied with rebukes, exhortations, and threats to both. At first he had shown a disposition to extenuate and excuse the faults of Frontenac, but every year his letters grew sharper. In 1681 he wrote: "Again I urge you to banish from your mind the difficulties which you have yourself devised against the execution of my orders; to act with mildness and moderation towards all the colonists, and divest yourself entirely of the personal animosities which have thus far been almost your sole motive of action. In conclusion, I exhort you once more to profit well by the directions which this letter contains; since, unless you succeed better herein than formerly, I cannot help recalling you from the command which I have intrusted to you."[2]

The dispute still went on. The autumn ships from Quebec brought back the usual complaints, and the long-suffering king at length made good his threat. Both Frontenac and Duchesneau received their recall, and they both deserved it.[3]

The last official act of the governor, recorded in the register of the council of Quebec, is the formal declaration that his rank in that body is superior to that of the intendant.[4]

The key to nearly all these disputes lies in the relations between Frontenac and the Church. The fundamental quarrel

[1] *Conduite du Sieur Perrot.* La Barre, Frontenac's successor, declares that the charges against Perrot were false, including the attestations of Migeon and his friends; that Dollier de Casson had been imposed upon, and that various persons had been induced to sign unfounded statements without reading them. *La Barre au Ministre, 4 Nov., 1683.*

[2] *Le Roy à Frontenac, 30 Avril, 1681.*

[3] La Barre says that Duchesneau was far more to blame than Frontenac. *La Barre au Ministre, 1683.* This testimony has weight, since Frontenac's friends were La Barre's enemies.

[4] *Registre du Conseil Supérieur, 16 Fév., 1682.*

was generally covered by superficial issues, and it was rarely that the governor fell out with anybody who was not in league with the bishop and the Jesuits. "Nearly all the disorders in New France," he writes, "spring from the ambition of the ecclesiastics, who want to join to their spiritual authority an absolute power over things temporal, and who persecute all who do not submit entirely to them." He says that the intendant and the councillors are completely under their control, and dare not decide any question against them; that they have spies everywhere, even in his house; that the bishop told him that he could excommunicate even a governor, if he chose; that the missionaries in Indian villages say that they are equals of Onontio, and tell their converts that all will go wrong till the priests have the government of Canada; that directly or indirectly they meddle in all civil affairs; that they trade even with the English of New York; that, what with Jesuits, Sulpitians, the bishop, and the seminary of Quebec, they hold two-thirds of the good lands of Canada; that, in view of the poverty of the country, their revenues are enormous; that, in short, their object is mastery, and that they use all means to compass it.[1] The recall of the governor was a triumph to the ecclesiastics, offset but slightly by the recall of their instrument, the intendant, who had done his work, and whom they needed no longer.

Thus far, we have seen Frontenac on his worst side. We shall see him again under an aspect very different. Nor must it be supposed that the years which had passed since his government began, tempestuous as they appear on the record, were wholly given over to quarrelling. They had their periods of uneventful calm, when the wheels of administration ran as smoothly as could be expected in view of the condition of the colony. In one respect at least, Frontenac had shown a remarkable fitness for his office. Few white men have ever equalled or approached him in the art of dealing with Indians. There seems to have been a sympathetic relation between

---

[1] Frontenac, *Mémoire adressé à Colbert, 1677.* This remarkable paper will be found in the *Découvertes et Établissements des Français dans l'Amérique Septentrionale; Mémoires et Documents Originaux,* edited by M. Margry. The paper is very long, and contains references to attestations and other proofs which accompanied it, especially in regard to the trade of the Jesuits.

him and them. He conformed to their ways, borrowed their rhetoric, flattered them on occasion with great address, and yet constantly maintained towards them an attitude of paternal superiority. When they were concerned, his native haughtiness always took a form which commanded respect without exciting anger. He would not address them as *brothers*, but only as *children*; and even the Iroquois, arrogant as they were, accepted the new relation. In their eyes Frontenac was by far the greatest of all the "Onontios," or governors of Canada. They admired the prompt and fiery soldier who played with their children, and gave beads and trinkets to their wives; who read their secret thoughts and never feared them, but smiled on them when their hearts were true, or frowned and threatened them when they did amiss. The other tribes, allies of the French, were of the same mind; and their respect for their Great Father seems not to have been permanently impaired by his occasional practice of bullying them for purposes of extortion.

Frontenac appears to have had a liking not only for Indians, but also for that roving and lawless class of the Canadian population, the *coureurs de bois*, provided always that they were not in the service of his rivals. Indeed, as regards the Canadians generally, he refrained from the strictures with which succeeding governors and intendants freely interlarded their despatches. It was not his instinct to clash with the humbler classes, and he generally reserved his anger for those who could retort it.

He had the air of distinction natural to a man familiar all his life with the society of courts, and he was as gracious and winning on some occasions as he was unbearable on others. When in good humor, his ready wit and a certain sympathetic vivacity made him very agreeable. At times he was all sunshine, and his outrageous temper slumbered peacefully till some new offence wakened it again; nor is there much doubt that many of his worst outbreaks were the work of his enemies, who knew his foible, and studied to exasperate him. He was full of contradictions; and, intolerant and implacable as he often was, there were intervals, even in his bitterest quarrels, in which he displayed a surprising moderation and patience. By fits he could be magnanimous. A woman once brought him a petition in burlesque verse. Frontenac wrote a jocose answer. The woman, to ridicule him, contrived to have both petition and answer slipped among the papers of a suit pending before the council. Frontenac had her fined a few francs, and then caused the money to be given to her children.[1]

When he sailed for France, it was a day of rejoicing to more than half the merchants of Canada, and, excepting the Récollets, to all the priests; but he left behind him an impression, very general among the people, that, if danger threatened the colony, Count Frontenac was the man for the hour.

[1] Note by Abbé Verreau, in *Journal de l'Instruction Publique* (Canada), VIII. 127.

Chapter V

1682–1684

LE FEBVRE DE LA BARRE

*His Arrival at Quebec • The Great Fire • A Coming Storm •
Iroquois Policy • The Danger imminent • Indian Allies of France
• Frontenac and the Iroquois • Boasts of La Barre • His Past Life
• His Speculations • He takes Alarm • His Dealings with the Iro-
quois • His Illegal Trade • His Colleague denounces him • Fruits
of his Schemes • His Anger and his Fears*

WHEN the new governor, La Barre, and the new intendant, Meules, arrived at Quebec, a dismal greeting
waited them. All the Lower Town was in ashes, except the
house of the merchant Aubert de la Chesnaye, standing alone
amid the wreck. On a Tuesday, the fourth of August, at ten
o'clock in the evening, the nuns of the Hôtel-Dieu were
roused from their early slumbers by shouts, outcries, and the
ringing of bells; "and," writes one of them, "what was our
terror to find it as light as noonday, the flames burned so
fiercely and rose so high." Half an hour before, Chartier de
Lotbinière, judge of the king's court, heard the first alarm,
ran down the descent now called Mountain Street, and found
every thing in confusion in the town below. The house of
Etienne Planchon was in a blaze; the fire was spreading to
those of his neighbors, and had just leaped the narrow street
to the storehouse of the Jesuits. The season was excessively
dry; there were no means of throwing water except kettles
and buckets, and the crowd was bewildered with excitement
and fright. Men were ordered to tear off roofs and pull down
houses; but the flames drove them from their work, and at
four o'clock in the morning fifty-five buildings were burnt to
the ground. They were all of wood, but many of them were
storehouses filled with goods; and the property consumed
was more in value than all that remained in Canada.[1]

Under these gloomy auspices, Le Febvre de la Barre began

[1] Chartier de Lotbinière, *Procès-verbal sur l'Incendie de la Basse Ville*; *Meules
au Ministre, 6 Oct., 1682*; Juchereau, *Histoire de l'Hôtel-Dieu de Québec*, 256.

his reign. He was an old officer who had achieved notable exploits against the English in the West Indies, but who was now to be put to a test far more severe. He made his lodging in the château; while his colleague, Meules, could hardly find a shelter. The buildings of the Upper Town were filled with those whom the fire had made roofless, and the intendant was obliged to content himself with a house in the neighboring woods. Here he was ill at ease, for he dreaded an Indian war and the scalping-knives of the Iroquois.[1]

So far as his own safety was concerned, his alarm was needless; but not so as regarded the colony with whose affairs he was charged. For those who had eyes to see it, a terror and a woe lowered in the future of Canada. In an evil hour for her, the Iroquois had conquered their southern neighbors, the Andastes, who had long held their ground against them, and at one time threatened them with ruin. The hands of the confederates were now free; their arrogance was redoubled by victory, and, having long before destroyed all the adjacent tribes on the north and west,[2] they looked for fresh victims in the wilderness beyond. Their most easterly tribe, the Mohawks, had not forgotten the chastisement they had received from Tracy and Courcelle. They had learned to fear the French, and were cautious in offending them; but it was not so with the remoter Iroquois. Of these, the Senecas at the western end of the "Long House," as they called their fivefold league, were by far the most powerful, for they could muster as many warriors as all the four remaining tribes together; and they now sought to draw the confederacy into a series of wars, which, though not directed against the French, threatened soon to involve them. Their first movement westward was against the tribes of the Illinois. I have already described their bloody inroad in the summer of 1680.[3] They made the valley of the Illinois a desert, and returned with several hundred prisoners, of whom they burned those that were useless, and incorporated the young and strong into their own tribe.

This movement of the western Iroquois had a double incentive, their love of fighting and their love of gain. It was a

[1] *Meules au Ministre, 6 Oct., 1682.*
[2] Jesuits in North America.
[3] Discovery of the Great West.

war of conquest and of trade. All the five tribes of the league had become dependent on the English and Dutch of Albany for guns, powder, lead, brandy, and many other things that they had learned to regard as necessities. Beaver skins alone could buy them, but to the Iroquois the supply of beaver skins was limited. The regions of the west and north-west, the upper Mississippi with its tributaries, and, above all, the forests of the upper lakes, were occupied by tribes in the interest of the French, whose missionaries and explorers had been the first to visit them, and whose traders controlled their immense annual product of furs. La Salle, by his newly built fort of St. Louis, engrossed the trade of the Illinois and Miami tribes; while the Hurons and Ottawas, gathered about the old mission of Michillimackinac, acted as factors for the Sioux, the Winnebagoes, and many other remote hordes. Every summer they brought down their accumulated beaver skins to the fair at Montreal; while French bush-rangers roving through the wilderness, with or without licenses, collected many more.[1]

It was the purpose of the Iroquois to master all this traffic, conquer the tribes who had possession of it, and divert the entire supply of furs to themselves, and through themselves to the English and Dutch. That English and Dutch traders urged them on is affirmed by the French, and is very likely. The accomplishment of the scheme would have ruined Canada. Moreover, the Illinois, the Hurons, the Ottawas, and all the other tribes threatened by the Iroquois, were the allies and "children" of the French, who in honor as in interest were bound to protect them. Hence, when the Seneca invasion of the Illinois became known, there was deep anxiety in the colony, except only among those in whom hatred of the monopolist La Salle had overborne every consideration of the public good. La Salle's new establishment of St. Louis was in the path of the invaders; and, if he could be crushed, there was wherewith to console his enemies for all else that might ensue.

Bad as was the posture of affairs, it was made far worse by an incident that took place soon after the invasion of the Illinois. A Seneca chief engaged in it, who had left the main

[1] Duchesneau, *Memoir on Western Indians in N. Y. Colonial Docs.*, IX. 160.

body of his countrymen, was captured by a party of Winne-bagoes to serve as a hostage for some of their tribe whom the Senecas had lately seized. They carried him to Michillimacki-nac, where there chanced to be a number of Illinois, married to Indian women of that neighborhood. A quarrel ensued be-tween them and the Seneca, whom they stabbed to death in a lodge of the Kiskakons, one of the tribes of the Ottawas. Here was a *casus belli* likely to precipitate a war fatal to all the tribes about Michillimackinac, and equally fatal to the trade of Canada. Frontenac set himself to conjure the rising storm, and sent a messenger to the Iroquois to invite them to a con-ference.

He found them unusually arrogant. Instead of coming to him, they demanded that he should come to them, and many of the French wished him to comply; but Frontenac refused, on the ground that such a concession would add to their in-solence, and he declined to go farther than Montreal, or at the utmost Fort Frontenac, the usual place of meeting with them. Early in August he was at Montreal, expecting the ar-rival of the Ottawas and Hurons on their yearly descent from the lakes. They soon appeared, and he called them to a sol-emn council. Terror had seized them all. "Father, take pity on us," said the Ottawa orator, "for we are like dead men." A Huron chief, named the Rat, declared that the world was turned upside down, and implored the protection of Onon-tio, "who is master of the whole earth." These tribes were far from harmony among themselves. Each was jealous of the other, and the Ottawas charged the Hurons with trying to make favor with the common enemy at their expense. Fron-tenac told them that they were all his children alike, and ad-vised them to live together as brothers, and make treaties of alliance with all the tribes of the lakes. At the same time, he urged them to make full atonement for the death of the Sen-eca murdered in their country, and carefully to refrain from any new offence.

Soon after there was another arrival. La Forêt, the officer in command at Fort Frontenac, appeared, bringing with him a famous Iroquois chief called Decanisora or Tegannisorens, attended by a number of warriors. They came to invite Fron-tenac to meet the deputies of the five tribes at Oswego, within their own limits. Frontenac's reply was characteristic. "It is for the father to tell the children where to hold council, not for the children to tell the father. Fort Frontenac is the proper place, and you should thank me for going so far every summer to meet you." The Iroquois had expressed pacific intentions towards the Hurons and Ottawas. For this Frontenac commended him, but added: "The Illinois also are children of Onontio, and hence brethren of the Iroquois. Therefore they, too, should be left in peace; for Onontio wishes that all his family should live together in union." He confirmed his words with a huge belt of wampum. Then, addressing the flattered deputy as a great chief, he desired him to use his influence in behalf of peace, and gave him a jacket and a silk cravat, both trimmed with gold, a hat, a scarlet ribbon, and a gun, with beads for his wife, and red cloth for his daughter. The Iroquois went home delighted.[1]

Perhaps on this occasion Frontenac was too confident of his influence over the savage confederates. Such at least was the opinion of Lamberville, Jesuit missionary at Onondaga, the Iroquois capital. From what he daily saw around him, he thought the peril so imminent that concession on the part of the French was absolutely necessary, since not only the Illinois, but some of the tribes of the lakes, were in danger of speedy and complete destruction. "Tegannisorens loves the French," he wrote to Frontenac, "but neither he nor any other of the upper Iroquois fear them in the least. They annihilate our allies, whom by adoption of prisoners they convert into Iroquois; and they do not hesitate to avow that after enriching themselves by our plunder, and strengthening themselves by those who might have aided us, they will pounce all at once upon Canada, and overwhelm it in a single campaign." He adds that within the past two years they have reinforced themselves by more than nine hundred warriors, adopted into their tribes.[2]

Such was the crisis when Frontenac left Canada at the moment when he was needed most, and Le Febvre de la Barre came to supplant him. The new governor introduces himself with a burst of rhodomontade. "The Iroquois," he writes to

[1] For the papers on this affair, see *N. Y. Colonial Docs.*, IX.
[2] *P. Jean de Lamberville à Frontenac, 20 Sept., 1682.*

the king, "have twenty-six hundred warriors. I will attack them with twelve hundred men. They know me before seeing me, for they have been told by the English how roughly I handled them in the West Indies." This bold note closes rather tamely; for the governor adds, "I think that if the Iroquois believe that your Majesty would have the goodness to give me some help, they will make peace, and let our allies alone, which would save the trouble and expense of an arduous war."[1] He then begs hard for troops, and in fact there was great need of them, for there were none in Canada; and even Frontenac had been compelled in the last year of his government to leave unpunished various acts of violence and plunder committed by the Iroquois. La Barre painted the situation in its blackest colors, declared that war was imminent, and wrote to the minister, "We shall lose half our trade and all our reputation, if we do not oppose these haughty conquerors."[2]

A vein of gasconade appears in most of his letters, not however accompanied with any conclusive evidence of a real wish to fight. His best fighting days were past, for he was sixty years old; nor had he always been a man of the sword. His early life was spent in the law; he had held a judicial post, and had been intendant of several French provinces. Even the military and naval employments, in which he afterwards acquitted himself with credit, were due to the part he took in forming a joint-stock company for colonizing Cayenne.[3] In fact, he was but half a soldier; and it was perhaps for this reason that he insisted on being called, not *Monsieur le Gouverneur*, but *Monsieur le Général*. He was equal to Frontenac neither in vigor nor in rank, but he far surpassed him in avidity. Soon after his arrival, he wrote to the minister that he should not follow the example of his predecessors in making money out of his government by trade; and in consideration

[1] *La Barre au Roy*, (4 Oct. ?) *1682.*

[2] *La Barre à Seignelay, 1682.*

[3] He was made governor of Cayenne, and went thither with Tracy in 1664. Two years later, he gained several victories over the English, and recaptured Cayenne, which they had taken in his absence. He wrote a book concerning this colony, called *Description de la France Équinoctiale*. Another volume, called *Journal du Voyage du Sieur de la Barre en la Terre Ferme et Isle de Cayenne*, was printed at Paris in 1671.

of these good intentions he asked for an addition to his pay.[1]
He then immediately made alliances with certain merchants
of Quebec for carrying on an extensive illicit trade, backed by
all the power of his office. Now ensued a strange and miserable complication. Questions of war mingled with questions
of personal gain. There was a commercial revolution in the
colony. The merchants whom Frontenac excluded from his
ring now had their turn. It was they who, jointly with the
intendant and the ecclesiastics, had procured the removal of
the old governor; and it was they who gained the ear of the
new one. Aubert de la Chesnaye, Jacques Le Ber, and the rest
of their faction, now basked in official favor; and La Salle, La
Forêt, and the other friends of Frontenac, were cast out.
There was one exception. Greysolon Du Lhut, leader of *coureurs de bois*, was too important to be thus set aside. He was
now as usual in the wilderness of the north, the roving chief
of a half savage crew, trading, exploring, fighting, and laboring with persistent hardihood to foil the rival English traders
of Hudson's Bay. Inducements to gain his adhesion were
probably held out to him by La Barre and his allies: be this
as it may, it is certain that he acted in harmony with the faction of the new governor. With La Forêt it was widely different. He commanded Fort Frontenac, which belonged to La
Salle, when La Barre's associates, La Chesnaye and Le Ber,
armed with an order from the governor, came up from Montreal, and seized upon the place with all that it contained. The
pretext for this outrage was the false one that La Salle had not
fulfilled the conditions under which the fort had been granted to
him. La Forêt was told that he might retain his command, if he
would join the faction of La Barre; but he refused, stood true
to his chief, and soon after sailed for France.

La Barre summoned the most able and experienced persons
in the colony to discuss the state of affairs. Their conclusion
was that the Iroquois would attack and destroy the Illinois,
and, this accomplished, turn upon the tribes of the lakes, conquer or destroy them also, and ruin the trade of Canada.[2]
Dark as was the prospect, La Barre and his fellow-speculators

---

[1] *La Barre à Seignelay, 1682.*

[2] *Conference on the State of Affairs with the Iroquois, Oct., 1682,* in *N. Y.
Colonial Docs.*, IX. 194.

flattered themselves that the war could be averted for a year at least. The Iroquois owed their triumphs as much to their sagacity and craft as to their extraordinary boldness and ferocity. It had always been their policy to attack their enemies in detail, and while destroying one to cajole the rest. There seemed little doubt that they would leave the tribes of the lakes in peace till they had finished the ruin of the Illinois; so that if these, the allies of the colony, were abandoned to their fate, there would be time for a profitable trade in the direction of Michillimackinac.

But hopes seemed vain and prognostics illusory, when, early in spring, a report came that the Seneca Iroquois were preparing to attack, in force, not only the Illinois, but the Hurons and Ottawas of the lakes. La Barre and his confederates were in dismay. They already had large quantities of goods at Michillimackinac, the point immediately threatened; and an officer was hastily despatched, with men and munitions, to strengthen the defences of the place.[1] A small vessel was sent to France with letters begging for troops. "I will perish at their head," wrote La Barre to the king, "or destroy your enemies;"[2] and he assures the minister that the Senecas must be attacked or the country abandoned.[3] The intendant, Meules, shared something of his alarm, and informed the king that "the Iroquois are the only people on earth who do not know the grandeur of your Majesty."[4]

While thus appealing to the king, La Barre sent Charles le Moyne as envoy to Onondaga. Through his influence, a deputation of forty-three Iroquois chiefs was sent to meet the governor at Montreal. Here a grand council was held in the newly built church. Presents were given the deputies to the value of more than two thousand crowns. Soothing speeches were made them; and they were urged not to attack the tribes of the lakes, nor to plunder French traders, *without permission*.[5] They assented; and La Barre then asked, timidly,

---

[1] *La Barre au Ministre, 4 Nov., 1683.*

[2] *La Barre au Roy, 30 Mai, 1683.*

[3] *La Barre au Ministre, 30 Mai, 1683.*

[4] *Meules au Roy, 2 Juin, 1683.*

[5] Soon after La Barre's arrival, La Chesnaye is said to have induced him to urge the Iroquois to plunder all traders who were not provided with passports from the governor. The Iroquois complied so promptly, that they

why they made war on the Illinois. "Because they deserve to die," haughtily returned the Iroquois orator. La Barre dared not answer. They complained that La Salle had given guns, powder, and lead to the Illinois; or, in other words, that he had helped the allies of the colony to defend themselves. La Barre, who hated La Salle and his monopolies, assured them that he should be punished.[1] It is affirmed, on good authority, that he said more than this, and told them they were welcome to plunder and kill him.[2] The rapacious old man was playing with a two-edged sword.

Thus the Illinois, with the few Frenchmen who had tried to defend them, were left to perish; and, in return, a brief and doubtful respite was gained for the tribes of the lakes. La Barre and his confederates took heart again. Merchandise, in abundance, was sent to Michillimackinac, and thence to the remoter tribes of the north and west. The governor and his partner, La Chesnaye, sent up a fleet of thirty canoes;[3] and, a little later, they are reported to have sent more than a hundred. This forest trade robbed the colonists, by forestalling the annual market of Montreal; while a considerable part of the furs acquired by it were secretly sent to the English and Dutch of New York. Thus the heavy duties of the custom-house at Quebec were evaded; and silver coin was received in payment, instead of questionable bills of exchange.[4] Frontenac had not been faithful to his trust; but, compared to his successor, he was a model of official virtue.

La Barre busied himself with ostentatious preparation for

---

stopped and pillaged, at Niagara, two canoes belonging to La Chesnaye himself, which had gone up the lakes in Frontenac's time, and therefore were without passports. *Recueil de ce qui s'est passé en Canada au Sujet de la Guerre, etc., depuis l'année 1682.* (Published by the Historical Society of Quebec.) This was not the only case in which the weapons of La Barre and his partisans recoiled against themselves.

[1] Belmont, *Histoire du Canada* (a contemporary chronicle).

[2] See Discovery of the Great West. La Barre denies the assertion, and says that he merely told the Iroquois that La Salle should be sent home.

[3] *Mémoire adressé à MM. les Intéressés en la Société de la Ferme et Commerce du Canada, 1683.*

[4] These statements are made in a memorial of the agents of the custom-house, in letters of Meules, and in several other quarters. La Barre is accused of sending furs to Albany under pretext of official communication with the governor of New York.

war; built vessels at Fort Frontenac, and sent up fleets of canoes, laden or partly laden with munitions. But his accusers say that the king's canoes were used to transport the governor's goods, and that the men sent to garrison Fort Frontenac were destined, not to fight the Iroquois, but to sell them brandy. "Last year," writes the intendant, "Monsieur de la Barre had a vessel built, for which he made his Majesty pay heavily;" and he proceeds to say that it was built for trade, and was used for no other purpose. "If," he continues, "the two (king's) vessels now at Fort Frontenac had not been used for trading, they would have saved us half the expense we have been forced to incur in transporting munitions and supplies. The pretended necessity of having vessels at this fort, and the consequent employing of carpenters, and sending up of iron, cordage, sails, and many other things, at his Majesty's charge, was simply in the view of carrying on trade." He says, farther, that in May last, the vessels, canoes, and men being nearly all absent on this errand, the fort was left in so defenceless a state that a party of Senecas, returning from their winter hunt, took from it a quantity of goods, and drank as much brandy as they wanted. "In short," he concludes, "it is plain that Monsieur de la Barre uses this fort only as a depot for the trade of Lake Ontario."[1]

In the spring of 1683, La Barre had taken a step as rash as it was lawless and unjust. He sent the Chevalier de Baugis, lieutenant of his guard, with a considerable number of canoes and men, to seize La Salle's fort of St. Louis on the river Illinois; a measure which, while gratifying the passions and the greed of himself and his allies, would greatly increase the danger of rupture with the Iroquois. Late in the season, he despatched seven canoes and fourteen men, with goods to the value of fifteen or sixteen thousand livres, to trade with the tribes of the Mississippi. As he had sown, so he reaped. The seven canoes passed through the country of the Illinois. A large war party of Senecas and Cayugas invaded it in February. La Barre had told their chiefs that they were welcome to plunder the canoes of La Salle. The Iroquois were not discriminating. They fell upon the governor's canoes, seized all

[1] *Meules à Seignelay, 8 July, 1684.* This accords perfectly with statements made in several memorials of La Salle and his friends.

the goods, and captured the men.[1] Then they attacked Baugis at Fort St. Louis. The place, perched on a rock, was strong, and they were beaten off; but the act was one of open war.

When La Barre heard the news, he was furious.[2] He trembled for the vast amount of goods which he and his fellow-speculators had sent to Michillimackinac and the lakes. There was but one resource: to call out the militia, muster the Indian allies, advance to Lake Ontario, and dictate peace to the Senecas, at the head of an imposing force; or, failing in this, to attack and crush them. A small vessel lying at Quebec was despatched to France, with urgent appeals for immediate aid, though there was little hope that it could arrive in time. She bore a long letter, half piteous, half bombastic, from La Barre to the king. He declared that extreme necessity and the despair of the people had forced him into war, and protested that he should always think it a privilege to lay down life for his Majesty. "I cannot refuse to your country of Canada, and your faithful subjects, to throw myself, with unequal forces, against the foe, while at the same time begging your aid for a poor, unhappy people on the point of falling victims to a nation of barbarians." He says that the total number of men in Canada capable of bearing arms is about two thousand; that he received last year a hundred and fifty raw recruits; and that he wants, in addition, seven or eight hundred good soldiers. "Recall me," he concludes, "if you will not help me, for I cannot bear to see the country perish in my hands." At the same time, he declares his intention to attack the Senecas, with or without help, about the middle of August.[3]

Here we leave him, for a while, scared, excited, and blustering.

[1] There appears no doubt that La Barre brought this upon himself. His successor, Denonville, writes that the Iroquois declared that, in plundering the canoes, they thought they were executing the orders they had received to plunder La Salle's people. Denonville, *Mémoire adressé au Ministre sur les Affaires de la Nouvelle France, 10 Août, 1688.* The Iroquois told Dongan, in 1684, "that they had not don any thing to the French but what Monsr. delaBarr Ordered them, which was that if they mett with any French hunting without his passe to take what they had from them." *Dongan to Denonville, 9 Sept., 1687.*

[2] "Ce qui mit M. de la Barre en fureur." Belmont, *Histoire du Canada.*

[3] *La Barre au Roy, 5 Juin, 1684.*

Chapter VI

1684

LA BARRE AND THE IROQUOIS

Dongan • New York and its Indian Neighbors • The Rival Governors • Dongan and the Iroquois • Mission to Onondaga • An Iroquois Politician • Warnings of Lamberville • Iroquois Boldness • La Barre takes the Field • His Motives • The March • Pestilence • Council at La Famine • The Iroquois defiant • Humiliation of La Barre • The Indian Allies • Their Rage and Disappointment • Recall of La Barre

---

THE DUTCH COLONY of New Netherland had now become the English colony of New York. Its proprietor, the Duke of York, afterwards James II. of England, had appointed Colonel Thomas Dongan its governor. He was a Catholic Irish gentleman of high rank, nephew of the famous Earl of Tyrconnel, and presumptive heir to the earldom of Limerick. He had served in France, was familiar with its language, and partial to its king and its nobility; but he nevertheless gave himself with vigor to the duties of his new trust.

The Dutch and English colonists aimed at a share in the western fur trade, hitherto a monopoly of Canada; and it is said that Dutch traders had already ventured among the tribes of the Great Lakes, boldly poaching on the French preserves. Dongan did his utmost to promote their interests, so far at least as was consistent with his instructions from the Duke of York, enjoining him to give the French governor no just cause of offence.[1]

[1] *Sir John Werden to Dongan, 4 Dec., 1684; N. Y. Col. Docs.*, III. 353. Werden was the duke's secretary.

Dongan has been charged with instigating the Iroquois to attack the French. The Jesuit Lamberville, writing from Onondaga, says, on the contrary, that he hears that the "governor of New England (*New York*), when the Mohawk chiefs asked him to continue the sale of powder to them, replied that it should be continued so long as they would not make war on Christians." *Lamberville à La Barre, 10 Fév., 1684.*

The French ambassador at London complained that Dongan excited the Iroquois to war, and Dongan denied the charge. *N. Y. Col. Docs.*, III. 506, 509.

For several years past, the Iroquois had made forays against the borders of Maryland and Virginia, plundering and killing the settlers; and a declared rupture between those colonies and the savage confederates had more than once been imminent. The English believed that these hostilities were instigated by the Jesuits in the Iroquois villages. There is no proof whatever of the accusation; but it is certain that it was the interest of Canada to provoke a war which might, sooner or later, involve New York. In consequence of a renewal of such attacks, Lord Howard of Effingham, governor of Virginia, came to Albany in the summer of 1684, to hold a council with the Iroquois.

The Oneidas, Onondagas, and Cayugas were the offending tribes. They all promised friendship for the future. A hole was dug in the court-yard of the council house, each of the three threw a hatchet into it, and Lord Howard and the representative of Maryland added two others; then the hole was filled, the song of peace was sung, and the high contracting parties stood pledged to mutual accord.[1] The Mohawks were also at the council, and the Senecas soon after arrived; so that all the confederacy was present by its deputies. Not long before, La Barre, then in the heat of his martial preparations, had sent a messenger to Dongan with a letter, informing him that, as the Senecas and Cayugas had plundered French canoes and assaulted a French fort, he was compelled to attack them, and begging that the Dutch and English colonists should be forbidden to supply them with arms.[2] This letter produced two results, neither of them agreeable to the writer: first, the Iroquois were fully warned of the designs of the French; and, secondly, Dongan gained the opportunity he wanted of asserting the claim of his king to sovereignty over the confederacy, and possession of the whole country south of the Great Lakes. He added that, if the Iroquois had done wrong, he would require them, as British subjects, to make reparation; and he urged La Barre, for the sake of peace between the two colonies, to refrain from his intended invasion of British territory.[3]

[1] Report of Conferences at Albany, in Colden, *History of the Five Nations*, 50 (ed. 1727, Shea's reprint).

[2] *La Barre à Dongan, 15 Juin, 1684.*

[3] *Dongan à La Barre, 24 Juin, 1684.*

Dongan next laid before the assembled sachems the complaints made against them in the letter of La Barre. They replied by accusing the French of carrying arms to their enemies, the Illinois and the Miamis. "Onontio," said their orator, "calls us his children, and then helps our enemies to knock us in the head." They were somewhat disturbed at the prospect of La Barre's threatened attack; and Dongan seized the occasion to draw from them an acknowledgment of subjection to the Duke of York, promising in return that they should be protected from the French. They did not hesitate. "We put ourselves," said the Iroquois speaker, "under the great sachem Charles, who lives over the Great Lake, and under the protection of the great Duke of York, brother of your great sachem." But he added a moment after, "Let your friend (*King Charles*) who lives over the Great Lake know that we are a free people, though united to the English."[1] They consented that the arms of the Duke of York should be planted in their villages, being told that this would prevent the French from destroying them. Dongan now insisted that they should make no treaty with Onontio without his consent; and he promised that, if their country should be invaded, he would send four hundred horsemen and as many foot soldiers to their aid.

As for the acknowledgment of subjection to the king and the Duke of York, the Iroquois neither understood its full meaning nor meant to abide by it. What they did clearly understand was that, while they recognized Onontio, the governor of Canada, as their father, they recognized Corlaer, the governor of New York, only as their brother.[2] Dongan, it seems, could not, or dared not, change this mark of equality. He did his best, however, to make good his claims, and sent Arnold Viele, a Dutch interpreter, as his envoy to Onondaga. Viele set out for the Iroquois capital, and thither we will follow him.

---

[1] Speech of the Onondagas and Cayugas, in Colden, *Five Nations*, 68 (1727).

[2] Except the small tribe of the Oneidas, who addressed Corlaer as *Father*. *Corlaer* was the official Iroquois name of the governor of New York; *Onas* (the Feather, or Pen), that of the governor of Pennsylvania; and *Assarigoa* (the Big Knife, or Sword), that of the governor of Virginia. Corlaer, or Cuyler, was the name of a Dutchman whom the Iroquois held in great respect.

He mounted his horse, and in the heats of August rode westward along the valley of the Mohawk. On a hill a bow-shot from the river, he saw the first Mohawk town, Kaghnawaga, encircled by a strong palisade. Next he stopped for a time at Gandagaro, on a meadow near the bank; and next, at Canajora, on a plain two miles away. Tionondogué, the last and strongest of these fortified villages, stood like the first on a hill that overlooked the river, and all the rich meadows around were covered with Indian corn. The largest of the four contained but thirty houses, and all together could furnish scarcely more than three hundred warriors.[1]

When the last Mohawk town was passed, a ride of four or five days still lay before the envoy. He held his way along the old Indian trail, now traced through the grass of sunny meadows, and now tunnelled through the dense green of shady forests, till it led him to the town of the Oneidas, containing about a hundred bark houses, with twice as many fighting men, the entire force of the tribe. Here, as in the four Mohawk villages, he planted the scutcheon of the Duke of York, and, still advancing, came at length to a vast open space where the rugged fields, patched with growing corn, sloped upwards into a broad, low hill, crowned with the clustered lodges of Onondaga. There were from one to two hundred of these large bark dwellings, most of them holding several families. The capital of the confederacy was not fortified at this time, and its only defence was the valor of some four hundred warriors.[2]

In this focus of trained and organized savagery, where ferocity was cultivated as a virtue, and every emotion of pity stifled as unworthy of a man; where ancient rites, customs, and traditions were held with the tenacity of a people who joined the extreme of wildness with the extreme of conservatism,—here burned the council fire of the five confederate tribes; and here, in time of need, were gathered their

---

[1] *Journal of Wentworth Greenhalgh, 1677*, in *N. Y. Col. Docs.*, III. 250.

[2] *Journal of Greenhalgh.* The site of Onondaga, like that of all the Iroquois towns, was changed from time to time, as the soil of the neighborhood became impoverished, and the supply of wood exhausted. Greenhalgh, in 1677, estimated the warriors at three hundred and fifty; but the number had increased of late by the adoption of prisoners.

bravest and their wisest to debate high questions of policy and war.

The object of Viele was to confirm the Iroquois in their very questionable attitude of subjection to the British crown, and persuade them to make no treaty or agreement with the French, except through the intervention of Dongan, or at least with his consent. The envoy found two Frenchmen in the town, whose presence boded ill to his errand. The first was the veteran colonist of Montreal, Charles le Moyne, sent by La Barre to invite the Onondagas to a conference. They had known him, in peace or war, for a quarter of a century; and they greatly respected him. The other was the Jesuit Jean de Lamberville, who had long lived among them, and knew them better than they knew themselves. Here, too, was another personage who cannot pass unnoticed. He was a famous Onondaga orator named Otréouati, and called also Big Mouth, whether by reason of the dimensions of that feature or the greatness of the wisdom that issued from it. His contemporary, Baron La Hontan, thinking perhaps that his French name of La Grande Gueule was wanting in dignity, Latinized it into Grangula; and the Scotchman, Colden, afterwards improved it into Garangula, under which high-sounding appellation Big Mouth has descended to posterity. He was an astute old savage, well trained in the arts of Iroquois rhetoric, and gifted with the power of strong and caustic sarcasm, which has marked more than one of the chief orators of the confederacy. He shared with most of his countrymen the conviction that the earth had nothing so great as the league of the Iroquois; but, if he could be proud and patriotic, so too he could be selfish and mean. He valued gifts, attentions, and a good meal, and would pay for them abundantly in promises, which he kept or not, as his own interests or those of his people might require. He could use bold and loud words in public, and then secretly make his peace with those he had denounced. He was so given to rough jokes that the intendant, Meules, calls him a buffoon; but his buffoonery seems to have been often a cover to his craft. He had taken a prominent part in the council of the preceding summer at Montreal; and, doubtless, as he stood in full dress before the governor and the officers, his head plumed, his face painted, his figure draped in a colored blanket, and his feet decked with embroidered moccasins, he was a picturesque and striking object. He was less so as he squatted almost naked by his lodge fire, with a piece of board laid across his lap, chopping rank tobacco with a scalping-knife to fill his pipe, and entertaining the grinning circle with grotesque stories and obscene jests. Though not one of the hereditary chiefs, his influence was great. "He has the strongest head and the loudest voice among the Iroquois," wrote Lamberville to La Barre. "He calls himself your best friend. . . . He is a venal creature, whom you do well to keep in pay. I assured him I would send him the jerkin you promised."[1] Well as the Jesuit knew the Iroquois, he was deceived if he thought that Big Mouth was securely won.

Lamberville's constant effort was to prevent a rupture. He wrote with every opportunity to the governor, painting the calamities that war would bring, and warning him that it was vain to hope that the league could be divided, and its three eastern tribes kept neutral, while the Senecas were attacked. He assured him, on the contrary, that they would all unite to fall upon Canada, ravaging, burning, and butchering along the whole range of defenceless settlements. "You cannot believe, Monsieur, with what joy the Senecas learned that you might possibly resolve on war. When they heard of the preparations at Fort Frontenac, they said that the French had a great mind to be stripped, roasted, and eaten; and that they will see if their flesh, which they suppose to have a salt taste, by reason of the salt which we use with our food, be as good as that of their other enemies."[2] Lamberville also informs the governor that the Senecas have made ready for any emergency, buried their last year's corn, prepared a hiding place in the depth of the forest for their old men, women, and children, and stripped their towns of every thing that they value; and that their fifteen hundred warriors will not shut themselves up in forts, but fight under cover, among trees and in the tall grass, with little risk to themselves and extreme danger to the invader. "There is no profit," he says, "in fighting with

[1] *Letters of Lamberville* in *N. Y. Col. Docs.*, IX. For specimens of Big Mouth's skill in drawing, see *ibid.*, IX. 386.

[2] *Lamberville to La Barre, 11 July, 1684*, in *N. Y. Col. Docs.*, IX. 253.

this sort of banditti, whom you cannot catch, but who will catch many of your people. The Onondagas wish to bring about an agreement. Must the father and the children, they ask, cut each other's throats?"

The Onondagas, moved by the influence of the Jesuit and the gifts of La Barre, did in fact wish to act as mediators between their Seneca confederates and the French; and to this end they invited the Seneca elders to a council. The meeting took place before the arrival of Viele, and lasted two days. The Senecas were at first refractory, and hot for war, but at length consented that the Onondagas might make peace for them, if they could; a conclusion which was largely due to the eloquence of Big Mouth.

The first act of Viele was a blunder. He told the Onondagas that the English governor was master of their country; and that, as they were subjects of the king of England, they must hold no council with the French without permission. The pride of Big Mouth was touched. "You say," he exclaimed to the envoy, "that we are subjects of the king of England and the Duke of York; but we say that we are brothers. We must take care of ourselves. The coat of arms which you have fastened to that post cannot defend us against Onontio. We tell you that we shall bind a covenant chain to our arm and to his. We shall take the Senecas by one hand and Onontio by the other, and their hatchet and his sword shall be thrown into deep water."[1]

Thus well and manfully did Big Mouth assert the independence of his tribe, and proclaim it the arbiter of peace. He told the warriors, moreover, to close their ears to the words of the Dutchman, who spoke as if he were drunk;[2] and it was resolved at last that he, Big Mouth, with an embassy of chiefs and elders, should go with Le Moyne to meet the French governor.

While these things were passing at Onondaga, La Barre had finished his preparations, and was now in full campaign. Before setting out, he had written to the minister that he was about to advance on the enemy, with seven hundred Canadians, a hundred and thirty regulars, and two hundred mission

---

[1] Colden, *Five Nations*, 80 (1727).

[2] *Lamberville to La Barre, 28 Aug., 1684*, in N. Y. Col. Docs., IX. 257.

Indians; that more Indians were to join him on the way; that Du Lhut and La Durantaye were to meet him at Niagara with a body of *coureurs de bois* and Indians from the interior; and that, "when we are all united, we will perish or destroy the enemy."[1] On the same day, he wrote to the king: "My purpose is to exterminate the Senecas; for otherwise your Majesty need take no farther account of this country, since there is no hope of peace with them, except when they are driven to it by force. I pray you do not abandon me; and be assured that I shall do my duty at the head of your faithful colonists."[2]

A few days after writing these curiously incoherent epistles, La Barre received a letter from his colleague, Meules, who had no belief that he meant to fight, and was determined to compel him to do so, if possible. "There is a report," wrote the intendant, "that you mean to make peace. It is doing great harm. Our Indian allies will despise us. I trust the story is untrue, and that you will listen to no overtures. The expense has been enormous. The whole population is roused."[3] Not satisfied with this, Meules sent the general a second letter, meant, like the first, as a tonic and a stimulant. "If we come to terms with the Iroquois, without first making them feel the strength of our arms, we may expect that, in future, they will do every thing they can to humiliate us, because we drew the sword against them, and showed them our teeth. I do not think that any course is now left for us but to carry the war to their very doors, and do our utmost to reduce them to such a point that they shall never again be heard of as a nation, but only as our subjects and slaves. If, after having gone so far, we do not fight them, we shall lose all our trade, and bring this country to the brink of ruin. The Iroquois, and especially the Senecas, pass for great cowards. The Reverend Father Jesuit, who is at Prairie de la Madeleine, told me as much yesterday; and, though he has never been among them, he assured me that he has heard everybody say so. But, even if they were brave, we ought to be very glad of it; since then we could hope that they would wait our attack, and give us a chance to beat them. If we do not destroy them, they will

[1] *La Barre au Ministre, 9 July, 1684.*

[2] *La Barre au Roy, même date.*

[3] *Meules à La Barre, 15 July, 1684.*

destroy us. I think you see but too well that your honor and the safety of the country are involved in the results of this war."[1]

While Meules thus wrote to the governor, he wrote also to the minister, Seignelay, and expressed his views with great distinctness. "I feel bound in conscience to tell you that nothing was ever heard of so extraordinary as what we see done in this country every day. One would think that there was a divided empire here between the king and the governor; and, if things should go on long in this way, the governor would have a far greater share than his Majesty. The persons whom Monsieur la Barre has sent this year to trade at Fort Frontenac have already shared with him from ten to twelve thousand crowns." He then recounts numerous abuses and malversations on the part of the governor. "In a word, Monseigneur, this war has been decided upon in the cabinet of Monsieur the general, along with six of the chief merchants of the country. If it had not served their plans, he would have found means to settle every thing; but the merchants made him understand that they were in danger of being plundered, and that, having an immense amount of merchandise in the woods in nearly two hundred canoes fitted out last year, it was better to make use of the people of the country to carry on war against the Senecas. This being done, he hopes to make extraordinary profits without any risk, because one of two things will happen: either we shall gain some considerable advantage over the savages, as there is reason to hope, if Monsieur the general will but attack them in their villages; or else we shall make a peace which will keep every thing safe for a time. These are assuredly the sole motives of this war, which has for principle and end nothing but mere interest. He says himself that there is good fishing in troubled waters.[2]

"With all our preparations for war, and all the expense in which Monsieur the general is involving his Majesty, I will

---

[1] *Meules à La Barre, 14 Août, 1684.* This and the preceding letter stand, by a copyist's error, in the name of La Barre. They are certainly written by Meules.

[2] The famous *voyageur*, Nicolas Perrot, agrees with the intendant. "Ils (*La Barre et ses associés*) s'imaginèrent que sitost que le François viendroit à paroistre, l'Irroquois luy demanderoit miséricorde, qu'il seroit facile d'establir

take the liberty to tell you, Monseigneur, though I am no prophet, that I discover no disposition on the part of Monsieur the general to make war against the aforesaid savages. In my belief, he will content himself with going in a canoe as far as Fort Frontenac, and then send for the Senecas to treat of peace with them, and deceive the people, the intendant, and, if I may be allowed with all possible respect to say so, his Majesty himself.

"P.S.—I will finish this letter, Monseigneur, by telling you that he set out yesterday, July 10th, with a detachment of two hundred men. All Quebec was filled with grief to see him embark on an expedition of war *tête-à-tête* with the man named La Chesnaye. Everybody says that the war is a sham, that these two will arrange every thing between them, and, in a word, do whatever will help their trade. The whole country is in despair to see how matters are managed."[1]

After a long stay at Montreal, La Barre embarked his little army at La Chine, crossed Lake St. Louis, and began the ascent of the upper St. Lawrence. In one of the three companies of regulars which formed a part of the force was a young subaltern, the Baron la Hontan, who has left a lively account of the expedition. Some of the men were in flat boats, and some were in birch canoes. Of the latter was La Hontan, whose craft was paddled by three Canadians. Several times they shouldered it through the forest to escape the turmoil of the rapids. The flat boats could not be so handled, and were dragged or pushed up in the shallow water close to the bank, by gangs of militia men, toiling and struggling among the rocks and foam. The regulars, unskilled in such matters, were spared these fatigues, though tormented night and day by

---

des magasins, construire des barques dans le lac Ontario, et que c'estoit un moyen de trouver des richesses." *Mémoire sur les Mœurs, Coustumes, et Relligion des Sauvages*, chap. xxi.

The Sulpitian, Abbé Belmont, says that the avarice of the merchants was the cause of the war; that they and La Barre wished to prevent the Iroquois from interrupting trade; and that La Barre aimed at an indemnity for the sixteen hundred livres in merchandise which the Senecas had taken from his canoes early in the year. Belmont adds that he wanted to bring them to terms without fighting.

[1] *Meules au Ministre, 8–11 Juillet, 1684.*

swarms of gnats and mosquitoes, objects of La Hontan's bitterest invective. At length the last rapid was passed, and they
moved serenely on their way, threaded the mazes of the
Thousand Islands, entered what is now the harbor of Kingston, and landed under the palisades of Fort Frontenac.

Here the whole force was soon assembled, the regulars in
their tents, the Canadian militia and the Indians in huts and
under sheds of bark. Of these red allies there were several
hundred: Abenakis and Algonquins from Sillery, Hurons
from Lorette, and converted Iroquois from the Jesuit mission
of Saut St. Louis, near Montreal. The camp of the French
was on a low, damp plain near the fort; and here a malarious
fever presently attacked them, killing many and disabling
many more. La Hontan says that La Barre himself was
brought by it to the brink of the grave. If he had ever entertained any other purpose than that of inducing the Senecas to
agree to a temporary peace, he now completely abandoned it.
He dared not even insist that the offending tribe should meet
him in council, but hastened to ask the mediation of the
Onondagas, which the letters of Lamberville had assured him
that they were disposed to offer. He sent Le Moyne to persuade them to meet him on their own side of the lake, and,
with such of his men as were able to move, crossed to the
mouth of Salmon River, then called La Famine.

The name proved prophetic. Provisions fell short from bad
management in transportation, and the men grew hungry and
discontented. September had begun; the place was unwholesome, and the malarious fever of Fort Frontenac infected the
new encampment. The soldiers sickened rapidly. La Barre,
racked with suspense, waited impatiently the return of Le
Moyne. We have seen already the result of his mission, and
how he and Lamberville, in spite of the envoy of the English
governor, gained from the Onondaga chiefs the promise to
meet Onontio in council. Le Moyne appeared at La Famine
on the third of the month, bringing with him Big Mouth and
thirteen other deputies. La Barre gave them a feast of bread,
wine, and salmon trout, and on the morning of the fourth the
council began.

Before the deputies arrived, the governor had sent the sick
men homeward in order to conceal his helpless condition;

and he now told the Iroquois that he had left his army at Fort Frontenac, and had come to meet them attended only by an escort. The Onondaga politician was not to be so deceived. He, or one of his party, spoke a little French; and during the night, roaming noiselessly among the tents, he contrived to learn the true state of the case from the soldiers.

The council was held on an open spot near the French encampment. La Barre was seated in an arm-chair. The Jesuit Bruyas stood by him as interpreter, and the officers were ranged on his right and left. The Indians sat on the ground in a row opposite the governor; and two lines of soldiers, forming two sides of a square, closed the intervening space. Among the officers was La Hontan, a spectator of the whole proceeding. He may be called a man in advance of his time; for he had the caustic, sceptical, and mocking spirit which a century later marked the approach of the great revolution, but which was not a characteristic of the reign of Louis XIV. He usually told the truth when he had no motive to do otherwise, and yet was capable at times of prodigious mendacity.[1] There is no reason to believe that he indulged in it on the present occasion, and his account of what he now saw and heard may probably be taken as substantially correct. According to him, La Barre opened the council as follows:—

"The king my master, being informed that the Five Nations of the Iroquois have long acted in a manner adverse to peace, has ordered me to come with an escort to this place, and to send Akouessan (*Le Moyne*) to Onondaga to invite the principal chiefs to meet me. It is the wish of this great king that you and I should smoke the calumet of peace together, provided that you promise, in the name of the Mohawks, Oneidas, Onondagas, Cayugas, and Senecas, to give entire satisfaction and indemnity to his subjects, and do nothing in future which may occasion rupture."

Then he recounted the offences of the Iroquois. First, they had maltreated and robbed French traders in the country of

---

[1] La Hontan attempted to impose on his readers a marvellous story of pretended discoveries beyond the Mississippi; and his ill repute in the matter of veracity is due chiefly to this fabrication. On the other hand, his account of what he saw in the colony is commonly in accord with the best contemporary evidence.

the Illinois; "wherefore," said the governor, "I am ordered to demand reparation, and in case of refusal to declare war against you."

Next, "the warriors of the Five Nations have introduced the English into the lakes which belong to the king my master, and among the tribes who are his children, in order to destroy the trade of his subjects, and seduce these people from the obedience they owe him. I am willing to forget this; but, should it happen again, I am expressly ordered to declare war against you."

Thirdly, "the warriors of the Five Nations have made sundry barbarous inroads into the country of the Illinois and Miamis, seizing, binding, and leading into captivity an infinite number of these savages in time of peace. They are the children of my king, and are not to remain your slaves. They must at once be set free and sent home. If you refuse to do this, I am expressly ordered to declare war against you."

La Barre concluded by assuring Big Mouth, as representing the Five Nations of the Iroquois, that the French would leave them in peace if they made atonement for the past, and promised good conduct for the future; but that, if they did not heed his words, their villages should be burned, and they themselves destroyed. He added, though he knew the contrary, that the governor of New York would join him in war against them.

During the delivery of this martial harangue, Big Mouth sat silent and attentive, his eyes fixed on the bowl of his pipe. When the interpreter had ceased, he rose, walked gravely two or three times around the lines of the assembly, then stopped before the governor, looked steadily at him, stretched his tawny arm, opened his capacious jaws, and uttered himself as follows:—

"Onontio, I honor you, and all the warriors who are with me honor you. Your interpreter has ended his speech, and now I begin mine. Listen to my words.

"Onontio, when you left Quebec, you must have thought that the heat of the sun had burned the forests that make our country inaccessible to the French, or that the lake had overflowed them so that we could not escape from our villages. You must have thought so, Onontio; and curiosity to see such a fire or such a flood must have brought you to this place. Now your eyes are opened; for I and my warriors have come to tell you that the Senecas, Cayugas, Onondagas, Oneidas, and Mohawks are all alive. I thank you in their name for bringing back the calumet of peace which they gave to your predecessors; and I give you joy that you have not dug up the hatchet which has been so often red with the blood of your countrymen.

"Listen, Onontio. I am not asleep. My eyes are open; and by the sun that gives me light I see a great captain at the head of a band of soldiers, who talks like a man in a dream. He says that he has come to smoke the pipe of peace with the Onondagas; but I see that he came to knock them in the head, if so many of his Frenchmen were not too weak to fight. I see Onontio raving in a camp of sick men, whose lives the Great Spirit has saved by smiting them with disease. Our women had snatched war-clubs, and our children and old men seized bows and arrows to attack your camp, if our warriors had not restrained them, when your messenger, Akouessan, appeared in our village."

He next justified the pillage of French traders on the ground, very doubtful in this case, that they were carrying arms to the Illinois, enemies of the confederacy; and he flatly refused to make reparation, telling La Barre that even the old men of his tribe had no fear of the French. He also avowed boldly that the Iroquois had conducted English traders to the lakes. "We are born free," he exclaimed, "we depend neither on Onontio nor on Corlaer. We have the right to go whithersoever we please, to take with us whomever we please, and buy and sell of whomever we please. If your allies are your slaves or your children, treat them like slaves or children, and forbid them to deal with anybody but your Frenchmen.

"We have knocked the Illinois in the head, because they cut down the tree of peace and hunted the beaver on our lands. We have done less than the English and the French, who have seized upon the lands of many tribes, driven them away, and built towns, villages, and forts in their country.

"Listen, Onontio. My voice is the voice of the Five Tribes of the Iroquois. When they buried the hatchet at Cataraqui (*Fort Frontenac*) in presence of your predecessor, they planted the tree of peace in the middle of the fort, that it might be a post of traders and not of soldiers. Take care that all the soldiers you have brought with you, shut up in so small a fort, do not choke this tree of peace. I assure you in the name of the Five Tribes that our warriors will dance the dance of the calumet under its branches; and that they will sit quiet on their mats and never dig up the hatchet, till their brothers, Onontio and Corlaer, separately or together, make ready to attack the country that the Great Spirit has given to our ancestors."

The session presently closed; and La Barre withdrew to his tent, where, according to La Hontan, he vented his feelings in invective, till reminded that good manners were not to be expected from an Iroquois. Big Mouth, on his part, entertained some of the French at a feast which he opened in person by a dance. There was another session in the afternoon, and the terms of peace were settled in the evening. The tree of peace was planted anew; La Barre promised not to attack the Senecas; and Big Mouth, in spite of his former declaration, consented that they should make amends for the pillage of the traders. On the other hand, he declared that the Iroquois would fight the Illinois to the death; and La Barre dared not utter a word in behalf of his allies. The Onondaga next demanded that the council fire should be removed from Fort Frontenac to La Famine, in the Iroquois country. This point was yielded without resistance; and La Barre promised to decamp and set out for home on the following morning.[1]

Such was the futile and miserable end of the grand expedition. Even the promise to pay for the plundered goods was contemptuously broken.[2] The honor rested with the Iroquois. They had spurned the French, repelled the claims of the English, and by act and word asserted their independence of both.

La Barre embarked and hastened home in advance of his men. His camp was again full of the sick. Their comrades

---

[1] The articles of peace will be found in *N. Y. Col. Docs.*, IX. 286. Compare *Memoir of M. de la Barre regarding the War against the Senecas, ibid.*, 239. These two documents do not agree as to date, one placing the council on the 4th and the other on the 5th.

[2] This appears from the letters of Denonville, La Barre's successor.

placed them, shivering with ague fits, on board the flat-boats and canoes; and the whole force, scattered and disordered, floated down the current to Montreal. Nothing had been gained but a thin and flimsy truce, with new troubles and dangers plainly visible behind it. The better to understand their nature, let us look for a moment at an episode of the campaign.

When La Barre sent messengers with gifts and wampum belts to summon the Indians of the Upper Lakes to join in the war, his appeal found a cold response. La Durantaye and Du Lhut, French commanders in that region, vainly urged the surrounding tribes to lift the hatchet. None but the Hurons would consent, when, fortunately, Nicolas Perrot arrived at Michillimackinac on an errand of trade. This famous *coureur de bois*—a very different person from Perrot, governor of Montreal—was well skilled in dealing with Indians. Through his influence, their scruples were overcome; and some five hundred warriors, Hurons, Ottawas, Ojibwas, Pottawatamies, and Foxes, were persuaded to embark for the rendezvous at Niagara, along with a hundred or more Frenchmen. The fleet of canoes, numerous as a flock of blackbirds in autumn, began the long and weary voyage. The two commanders had a heavy task. Discipline was impossible. The French were scarcely less wild than the savages. Many of them were painted and feathered like their red companions, whose ways they imitated with perfect success. The Indians, on their part, were but half-hearted for the work in hand, for they had already discovered that the English would pay twice as much for a beaver skin as the French; and they asked nothing better than the appearance of English traders on the lakes, and a safe peace with the Iroquois, which should open to them the market of New York. But they were like children with the passions of men, inconsequent, fickle, and wayward. They stopped to hunt on the shore of Michigan, where a Frenchman accidentally shot himself with his own gun. Here was an evil omen. But for the efforts of Perrot, half the party would have given up the enterprise, and paddled home. In the Strait of Detroit there was another hunt, and another accident. In firing at a deer, an Indian wounded his own brother. On this the tribesmen of the wounded man proposed to kill the

French, as being the occasion of the mischance. Once more the skill of Perrot prevailed; but when they reached the Long Point of Lake Erie, the Foxes, about a hundred in number, were on the point of deserting in a body. As persuasion failed, Perrot tried the effect of taunts. "You are cowards," he said to the naked crew, as they crowded about him with their wild eyes and long lank hair. "You do not know what war is: you never killed a man and you never ate one, except those that were given you tied hand and foot." They broke out against him in a storm of abuse. "You shall see whether we are men. We are going to fight the Iroquois; and, unless you do your part, we will knock you in the head." "You will never have to give yourselves the trouble," retorted Perrot, "for at the first war-whoop you will all run off." He gained his point. Their pride was roused, and for the moment they were full of fight.[1]

Immediately after, there was trouble with the Ottawas, who became turbulent and threatening, and refused to proceed. With much ado, they were persuaded to go as far as Niagara, being lured by the rash assurance of La Durantaye that three vessels were there, loaded with a present of guns for them. They carried their canoes by the cataract, launched them again, paddled to the mouth of the river, and looked for the vessels in vain. At length a solitary sail appeared on the lake. She brought no guns, but instead a letter from La Barre, telling them that peace was made, and that they might all go home. Some of them had paddled already a thousand miles, in the hope of seeing the Senecas humbled. They turned back in disgust, filled with wrath and scorn against the governor and all the French. Canada had incurred the contempt, not only of enemies, but of allies. There was danger that these tribes would repudiate the French alliance, welcome the English traders, make peace at any price with the Iroquois, and carry their beaver skins to Albany instead of Montreal.

The treaty made at La Famine was greeted with contumely through all the colony. The governor found, however, a comforter in the Jesuit Lamberville, who stood fast in the position

[1] *La Potherie*, II. 159 (ed. 1722). Perrot himself, in his *Mœurs des Sauvages*, briefly mentions the incident.

which he had held from the beginning. He wrote to La Barre: "You deserve the title of saviour of the country for making peace at so critical a time. In the condition in which your army was, you could not have advanced into the Seneca country without utter defeat. The Senecas had double palisades, which could not have been forced without great loss. Their plan was to keep three hundred men inside, and to perpetually harass you with twelve hundred others. All the Iroquois were to collect together, and fire only at the legs of your people, so as to master them, and burn them at their leisure, and then, after having thinned their numbers by a hundred ambuscades in the woods and grass, to pursue you in your retreat even to Montreal, and spread desolation around it."[1]

La Barre was greatly pleased with this letter, and made use of it to justify himself to the king. His colleague, Meules, on the other hand, declared that Lamberville, anxious to make favor with the governor, had written only what La Barre wished to hear. The intendant also informs the minister that La Barre's excuses are a mere pretence; that everybody is astonished and disgusted with him; that the sickness of the troops was his own fault, because he kept them encamped on wet ground for an unconscionable length of time; that Big Mouth shamefully befooled and bullied him; that, after the council at La Famine, he lost his wits, and went off in a fright; that, since the return of the troops, the officers have openly expressed their contempt for him; and that the people would have risen against him, if he, Meules, had not taken measures to quiet them.[2] These, with many other charges, flew across the sea from the pen of the intendant.

The next ship from France brought the following letter from the king:—

MONSIEUR DE LA BARRE,—Having been informed that your years do not permit you to support the fatigues inseparable from your office of governor and lieutenant-general in Canada, I send you this letter to acquaint you that I have selected Monsieur de Denonville to serve in your place; and

[1] *Lamberville to La Barre, 9 Oct., 1684,* in *N. Y. Col. Docs.,* IX. 260.
[2] *Meules au Ministre, 10 Oct., 1684.*

my intention is that, on his arrival, after resigning to him the command, with all instructions concerning it, you embark for your return to France.

LOUIS.

La Barre sailed for home; and the Marquis de Denonville, a pious colonel of dragoons, assumed the vacant office.

Chapter VII

DENONVILLE AND DONGAN

Troubles of the New Governor • His Character • English Rivalry
• Intrigues of Dongan • English Claims • A Diplomatic Duel •
Overt Acts • Anger of Denonville • James II. checks Dongan •
Denonville emboldened • Strife in the North • Hudson's Bay •
Attempted Pacification • Artifice of Denonville • He
prepares for War

D ENONVILLE embarked at Rochelle in June, with his wife and a part of his family. Saint-Vallier, the destined bishop, was in the same vessel; and the squadron carried five hundred soldiers, of whom a hundred and fifty died of fever and scurvy on the way. Saint-Vallier speaks in glowing terms of the new governor. "He spent nearly all his time in prayer and the reading of good books. The Psalms of David were always in his hands. In all the voyage, I never saw him do any thing wrong; and there was nothing in his words or acts which did not show a solid virtue and a consummate prudence, as well in the duties of the Christian life as in the wisdom of this world."[1]

When they landed, the nuns of the Hôtel-Dieu were overwhelmed with the sick. "Not only our halls, but our church, our granary, our hen-yard, and every corner of the hospital where we could make room, were filled with them."[2]

Much was expected of Denonville. He was to repair the mischief wrought by his predecessor, and restore the colony to peace, strength, and security. The king had stigmatized La Barre's treaty with the Iroquois as disgraceful, and expressed indignation at his abandonment of the Illinois allies. All this was now to be changed; but it was easier to give the order at Versailles than to execute it in Canada. Denonville's difficulties were great; and his means of overcoming them were small. What he most needed was more troops and more

---

[1] Saint-Vallier, *État Présent de l'Église*, 4 (Quebec, 1856).
[2] Juchereau, *Hôtel-Dieu*, 283.

money. The Senecas, insolent and defiant, were still attacking the Illinois; the tribes of the north-west were angry, contemptuous, and disaffected; the English of New York were urging claims to the whole country south of the Great Lakes, and to a controlling share in all the western fur trade; while the English of Hudson's Bay were competing for the traffic of the northern tribes, and the English of New England were seizing upon the fisheries of Acadia, and now and then making piratical descents upon its coast. The great question lay between New York and Canada. Which of these two should gain mastery in the west?

Denonville, like Frontenac, was a man of the army and the court. As a soldier, he had the experience of thirty years of service; and he was in high repute, not only for piety, but for probity and honor. He was devoted to the Jesuits, an ardent servant of the king, a lover of authority, filled with the instinct of subordination and order, and, in short, a type of the ideas, religious, political, and social, then dominant in France. He was greatly distressed at the disturbed condition of the colony; while the state of the settlements, scattered in broken lines for two or three hundred miles along the St. Lawrence, seemed to him an invitation to destruction. "If we have a war," he wrote, "nothing can save the country but a miracle of God."

Nothing was more likely than war. Intrigues were on foot between the Senecas and the tribes of the lakes, which threatened to render the appeal to arms a necessity to the French. Some of the Hurons of Michillimackinac were bent on allying themselves with the English. "They like the manners of the French," wrote Denonville; "but they like the cheap goods of the English better." The Senecas, in collusion with several Huron chiefs, had captured a considerable number of that tribe and of the Ottawas. The scheme was that these prisoners should be released, on condition that the lake tribes should join the Senecas and repudiate their alliance with the French.[1] The governor of New York favored this intrigue to the utmost.

Denonville was quick to see that the peril of the colony rose, not from the Iroquois alone, but from the English of

[1] *Denonville au Ministre, 12 Juin, 1686.*

New York, who prompted them. Dongan understood the situation. He saw that the French aimed at mastering the whole interior of the continent. They had established themselves in the valley of the Illinois, had built a fort on the lower Mississippi, and were striving to entrench themselves at its mouth. They occupied the Great Lakes; and it was already evident that, as soon as their resources should permit, they would seize the avenues of communication throughout the west. In short, the grand scheme of French colonization had begun to declare itself. Dongan entered the lists against them. If his policy should prevail, New France would dwindle to a feeble province on the St. Lawrence: if the French policy should prevail, the English colonies would remain a narrow strip along the sea. Dongan's cause was that of all these colonies; but they all stood aloof, and left him to wage the strife alone. Canada was matched against New York, or rather against the governor of New York. The population of the English colony was larger than that of its rival; but, except the fur traders, few of the settlers cared much for the questions at issue.[1] Dongan's chief difficulty, however, rose from the relations of the French and English kings. Louis XIV. gave Denonville an unhesitating support. James II., on the other hand, was for a time cautious to timidity. The two monarchs were closely united. Both hated constitutional liberty, and both held the same principles of supremacy in church and state; but Louis was triumphant and powerful, while James, in conflict with his subjects, was in constant need of his great ally, and dared not offend him.

The royal instructions to Denonville enjoined him to humble the Iroquois, sustain the allies of the colony, oppose the schemes of Dongan, and treat him as an enemy, if he encroached on French territory. At the same time, the French ambassador at the English court was directed to demand from James II. precise orders to the governor of New York for a complete change of conduct in regard to Canada and the Iroquois.[2] But Dongan, like the French governors, was not easily

[1] New York had about 18,000 inhabitants (Brodhead, *Hist. N. Y.*, II. 458). Canada, by the census of 1685, had 12,263.

[2] *Seignelay to Barillon, French Ambassador at London*, in *N. Y. Col. Docs.*, IX. 269.

controlled. In the absence of money and troops, he intrigued busily with his Indian neighbors. "The artifices of the English," wrote Denonville, "have reached such a point that it would be better if they attacked us openly and burned our settlements, instead of instigating the Iroquois against us for our destruction. I know beyond a particle of doubt that M. Dongan caused all the five Iroquois nations to be assembled last spring at Orange (*Albany*), in order to excite them against us, by telling them publicly that I meant to declare war against them." He says, further, that Dongan supplies them with arms and ammunition, incites them to attack the colony, and urges them to deliver Lamberville, the priest at Onondaga, into his hands. "He has sent people, at the same time, to our Montreal Indians to entice them over to him, promising them missionaries to instruct them, and assuring them that he would prevent the introduction of brandy into their villages. All these intrigues have given me not a little trouble throughout the summer. M. Dongan has written to me, and I have answered him as a man may do who wishes to dissimulate and does not feel strong enough to get angry."[1]

Denonville, accordingly, while biding his time, made use of counter intrigues, and, by means of the useful Lamberville, freely distributed secret or "underground" presents among the Iroquois chiefs; while the Jesuit Engelran was busy at Michillimackinac in adroit and vigorous efforts to prevent the alienation of the Hurons, Ottawas, and other lake tribes. The task was difficult; and, filled with anxiety, the father came down to Montreal to see the governor, "and communicate to me," writes Denonville, "the deplorable state of affairs with our allies, whom we can no longer trust, owing to the discredit into which we have fallen among them, and from which we cannot recover, except by gaining some considerable advantage over the Iroquois; who, as I have had the honor to inform you, have labored incessantly since last autumn to rob us of all our allies, by using every means to make treaties with them independently of us. You may be assured, Monseigneur, that the English are the chief cause of the arrogance and insolence of the Iroquois, adroitly using them to

[1] *Denonville à Seignelay, 8 Nov., 1686.*

extend the limits of their dominion, and uniting with them as one nation, insomuch that the English claims include no less than the Lakes Ontario and Erie, the region of Saginaw (*Michigan*), the country of the Hurons, and all the country in the direction of the Mississippi."[1]

The most pressing danger was the defection of the lake tribes. "In spite of the king's edicts," pursues Denonville, "the *coureurs de bois* have carried a hundred barrels of brandy to Michillimackinac in a single year; and their libertinism and debauchery have gone to such an extremity that it is a wonder the Indians have not massacred them all to save themselves from their violence and recover their wives and daughters from them. This, Monseigneur, joined to our failure in the last war, has drawn upon us such contempt among all the tribes that there is but one way to regain our credit, which is to humble the Iroquois by our unaided strength, without asking the help of our Indian allies."[2] And he begs hard for a strong reinforcement of troops.

Without doubt, Denonville was right in thinking that the chastising of the Iroquois, or at least the Senecas, the head and front of mischief, was a matter of the last necessity. A crushing blow dealt against them would restore French prestige, paralyze English intrigue, save the Illinois from destruction, and confirm the wavering allies of Canada. Meanwhile, matters grew from bad to worse. In the north and in the west, there was scarcely a tribe in the French interest which was not either attacked by the Senecas or cajoled by them into alliances hostile to the colony. "We may set down Canada as lost," again writes Denonville, "if we do not make war next year; and yet, in our present disordered state, war is the most dangerous thing in the world. Nothing can save us but the sending out of troops and the building of forts and block-houses. Yet I dare not begin to build them; for, if I do, it will bring down all the Iroquois upon us before we are in a condition to fight them."

Nevertheless, he made what preparations he could, begging all the while for more soldiers, and carrying on at the same time a correspondence with his rival, Dongan. At first, it was

[1] *Denonville à Seignelay, 12 Juin, 1686.*
[2] *Ibid.*

courteous on both sides; but it soon grew pungent, and at last acrid. Denonville wrote to announce his arrival, and Dongan replied in French: "Sir, I have had the honor of receiving your letter, and greatly rejoice at having so good a neighbor, whose reputation is so widely spread that it has anticipated your arrival. I have a very high respect for the king of France, of whose bread I have eaten so much that I feel under an obligation to prevent whatever can give the least umbrage to our masters. M. de la Barre is a very worthy gentleman, but he has not written to me in a civil and befitting style."[1]

Denonville replied with many compliments: "I know not what reason you may have had to be dissatisfied with M. de la Barre; but I know very well that I should reproach myself all my life if I could fail to render to you all the civility and attention due to a person of so great rank and merit. In regard to the affair in which M. de la Barre interfered, as you write me, I presume you refer to his quarrel with the Senecas. As to that, Monsieur, I believe you understand the character of that nation well enough to perceive that it is not easy to live in friendship with a people who have neither religion, nor honor, nor subordination. The king, my master, entertains affection and friendship for this country solely through zeal for the establishment of religion here, and the support and protection of the missionaries whose ardor in preaching the faith leads them to expose themselves to the brutalities and persecutions of the most ferocious of tribes. You know better than I what fatigues and torments they have suffered for the sake of Jesus Christ. I know your heart is penetrated with the glory of that name which makes Hell tremble, and at the mention of which all the powers of Heaven fall prostrate. Shall we be so unhappy as to refuse them our master's protection? You are a man of rank and abounding in merit. You love our holy religion. Can we not then come to an understanding to sustain our missionaries by keeping those fierce tribes in respect and fear?"[2]

This specious appeal for maintaining French Jesuits on English territory, or what was claimed as such, was lost on Don-

[1] *Dongan to Denonville, 13 Oct., 1685*, in N. Y. Col. Docs., IX. 292.
[2] *Denonville to Dongan, 5 Juin, 1686*, N. Y. Col. Docs., III. 456.

gan, Catholic as he was. He regarded them as dangerous political enemies, and did his best to expel them, and put English priests in their place. Another of his plans was to build a fort at Niagara, to exclude the French from Lake Erie. Denonville entertained the same purpose, in order to exclude the English; and he watched eagerly the moment to execute it. A rumor of the scheme was brought to Dongan by one of the French *coureurs de bois*, who often deserted to Albany, where they were welcomed and encouraged. The English governor was exceedingly wroth. He had written before in French out of complaisance. He now dispensed with ceremony, and wrote in his own peculiar English: "I am informed that you intend to build a fort at Ohniagero (*Niagara*) on this side of the lake, within my Master's territoryes without question. I cannot beleev that a person that has your reputation in the world would follow the steps of Monsr. Labarr, and be ill advized by some interested persons in your Governt. to make disturbance between our Masters subjects in those parts of the world for a little pelttree (*peltry*). I hear one of the Fathers (*the Jesuit Jean de Lamberville*) is gone to you, and th'other that stayed (*Jacques de Lamberville*) I have sent for him here lest the Indians should insult over him, tho' it's a thousand pittys that those that have made such progress in the service of God should be disturbed, and that by the fault of those that laid the foundation of Christianity amongst these barbarous people; setting apart the station I am in, I am as much Monsr. Des Novilles (*Denonville's*) humble servant as any friend he has, and will ommit no opportunity of manifesting the same. Sir, your humble servant, Thomas Dongan."[1]

Denonville in reply denied that he meant to build a fort at Niagara, and warned Dongan not to believe the stories told him by French deserters. "In order," he wrote, "that we may live on a good understanding, it would be well that a gentleman of your character should not give protection to all the rogues, vagabonds, and thieves who desert us and seek refuge with you, and who, to gain your favor, think they cannot do better than tell nonsensical stories about us, which they will continue to do so long as you listen to them."[2]

[1] *Dongan to Denonville, 22 May, 1686*, in N. Y. Col. Docs., III. 455.

[2] *Denonville à Dongan, 20 Juin, 1686.*

The rest of the letter was in terms of civility, to which Dongan returned: "Beleive me it is much joy to have soe good a neighbour of soe excellent qualifications and temper, and of a humour altogether differing from Monsieur de la Barre, your predecessor, who was so furious and hasty and very much addicted to great words, as if I had bin to have bin frighted by them. For my part, I shall take all immaginable care that the Fathers who preach the Holy Gospell to those Indians over whom I have power bee not in the least ill treated, and upon that very accompt have sent for one of each nation to come to me, and then those beastly crimes you reproove shall be checked severely, and all my endevours used to surpress their filthy drunkennesse, disorders, debauches, warring, and quarrels, and whatsoever doth obstruct the growth and enlargement of the Christian faith amongst those people." He then, in reply to an application of Denonville, promised to give up "runawayes."[1]

Promise was not followed by performance; and he still favored to the utmost the truant Frenchmen who made Albany their resort, and often brought with them most valuable information. This drew an angry letter from Denonville. "You were so good, Monsieur, as to tell me that you would give up all the deserters who have fled to you to escape chastisement for their knavery. As most of them are bankrupts and thieves, I hope that they will give you reason to repent having harbored them, and that your merchants who employ them will be punished for trusting such rascals."[2] To the great wrath of the French governor, Dongan persisted in warning the Iroquois that he meant to attack them. "You proposed, Monsieur," writes Denonville, "to submit every thing to the decision of our masters. Nevertheless, your emissary to the Onondagas told all the Five Nations in your name to pillage and make war on us." Next, he berates his rival for furnishing the Indians with rum. "Think you that religion will make any progress, while your traders supply the savages in abundance with the liquor which, as you ought to know, converts them into demons and their lodges into counterparts of Hell?"

"Certainly," retorts Dongan, "our Rum doth as little hurt

[1] *Dongan to Denonville, 26 July, 1686*, in *N. Y. Col. Docs.*, III. 460.
[2] *Denonville à Dongan, 1 Oct., 1686.*

as your Brandy, and, in the opinion of Christians, is much more wholesome."[1]

Each tried incessantly to out-general the other. Denonville, steadfast in his plan of controlling the passes of the western country, had projected forts, not only at Niagara, but also at Toronto, on Lake Erie, and on the Strait of Detroit. He thought that a time had come when he could, without rashness, secure this last important passage; and he sent an order to Du Lhut, who was then at Michillimackinac, to occupy it with fifty *coureurs de bois*.[2] That enterprising chief accordingly repaired to Detroit, and built a stockade at the outlet of Lake Huron on the western side of the strait. It was not a moment too soon. The year before, Dongan had sent a party of armed traders in eleven canoes, commanded by Johannes Rooseboom, a Dutchman of Albany, to carry English goods to the upper lakes. They traded successfully, winning golden opinions from the Indians, who begged them to come every year; and, though Denonville sent an officer to stop them at Niagara, they returned in triumph, after an absence of three months.[3] A larger expedition was organized in the autumn of 1686. Rooseboom again set out for the lakes with twenty or more canoes. He was to winter among the Senecas, and wait the arrival of Major McGregory, a Scotch officer, who was to leave Albany in the spring with fifty men, take command of the united parties, and advance to Lake Huron, accompanied by a band of Iroquois, to form a general treaty of trade and alliance with the tribes claimed by France as her subjects.[4]

Denonville was beside himself at the news. He had already urged upon Louis XIV. the policy of buying the colony of New York, which he thought might easily be done, and which, as he said, "would make us masters of the Iroquois without a war." This time he wrote in a less pacific mood: "I have a mind to go straight to Albany, storm their fort, and burn every thing."[5] And he begged for soldiers more earnestly

---

[1] *Dongan to Denonville, 1 Dec., 1686*, in N. Y. Col. Docs., III. 462.

[2] *Denonville à Du Lhut, 6 Juin, 1686.*

[3] Brodhead, *Hist. of New York*, II. 429; *Denonville au Ministre, 8 Mai, 1686.*

[4] Brodhead, *Hist. of New York*, II. 443; *Commission of McGregory*, in N. Y. Col. Docs., IX. 318.

[5] *Denonville au Ministre, 16 Nov., 1686.*

than ever. "Things grow worse and worse. The English stir up the Iroquois against us, and send parties to Michillimack-inac to rob us of our trade. It would be better to declare war against them than to perish by their intrigues."[1]

He complained bitterly to Dongan, and Dongan replied: "I beleeve it is as lawfull for the English as the French to trade amongst the remotest Indians. I desire you to send me word who it was that pretended to have my orders for the Indians to plunder and fight you. That is as false as 'tis true that God is in heaven. I have desired you to send for the deserters. I know not who they are but had rather such Rascalls and Bankrouts, as you call them, were amongst their own coun-trymen."[2]

He had, nevertheless, turned them to good account; for, as the English knew nothing of western geography, they em-ployed these French bush-rangers to guide their trading par-ties. Denonville sent orders to Du Lhut to shoot as many of them as he could catch.

Dongan presently received despatches from the English court, which showed him the necessity of caution; and, when next he wrote to his rival, it was with a chastened pen: "I hope your Excellency will be so kinde as not desire or seeke any correspondence with our Indians of this side of the Great lake (*Ontario*): if they doe amisse to any of your Governmt. and you make it known to me, you shall have all justice done." He complained mildly that the Jesuits were luring their Iroquois converts to Canada; "and you must pardon me if I tell you that is not the right way to keepe fair correspon-dence. I am daily expecting Religious men from England, which I intend to put amongst those five nations. I desire you would order Monsr. de Lamberville that soe long as he stayes amongst those people he would meddle only with the affairs belonging to his function. Sir, I send you some Oranges, hearing that they are a rarity in your partes."[3]

"Monsieur," replies Denonville, "I thank you for your or-anges. It is a great pity that they were all rotten."

[1] *Ibid.*, 15 Oct., 1686.

[2] *Dongan to Denonville, 1 Dec., 1686; Ibid., 20 June, 1687*, in N. Y. Col. Docs., III. 462, 465.

[3] *Ibid., 20 Juin, 1687*, in N. Y. Col. Docs., III. 465.

The French governor, unlike his rival, felt strong in the support of his king, who had responded amply to his appeals for aid; and the temper of his letters answered to his improved position. "I was led, Monsieur, to believe, by your civil language in the letter you took the trouble to write me on my arrival, that we should live in the greatest harmony in the world; but the result has plainly shown that your intentions did not at all answer to your fine words." And he upbraids him without measure for his various misdeeds: "Take my word for it. Let us devote ourselves to the accomplishment of our masters' will; let us seek, as they do, to serve and promote religion; let us live together in harmony, as they desire. I repeat and protest, Monsieur, that it rests with you alone; but do not imagine that I am a man to suffer others to play tricks on me. I willingly believe that you have not ordered the Iroquois to plunder our Frenchmen; but, whilst I have the honor to write to you, you know that Salvaye, Gédeon Petit, and many other rogues and bankrupts like them, are with you, and boast of sharing your table. I should not be surprised that you tolerate them in your country; but I am astonished that you should promise me not to tolerate them, that you so promise me again, and that you perform nothing of what you promise. Trust me, Monsieur, make no promise that you are not willing to keep."[1]

Denonville, vexed and perturbed by his long strife with Dongan and the Iroquois, presently found a moment of comfort in tidings that reached him from the north. Here, as in the west, there was violent rivalry between the subjects of the two crowns. With the help of two French renegades, named Radisson and Groseilliers, the English Company of Hudson's Bay, then in its infancy, had established a post near the mouth of Nelson River, on the western shore of that dreary inland sea. The company had also three other posts, called Fort Albany, Fort Hayes, and Fort Rupert, at the southern end of the bay. A rival French company had been formed in Canada, under the name of the Company of the North; and it resolved on an effort to expel its English competitors. Though it was a time of profound peace between the two kings, Denonville

[1] *Denonville à Dongan, 21 Aug., 1687; Ibid., no date (1687).*

warmly espoused the plan; and, in the early spring of 1686, he sent the Chevalier de Troyes from Montreal, with eighty or more Canadians, to execute it.[1] With Troyes went Iberville, Sainte-Hélène, and Maricourt, three of the sons of Charles Le Moyne; and the Jesuit Silvy joined the party as chaplain.

They ascended the Ottawa, and thence, from stream to stream and lake to lake, toiled painfully towards their goal. At length, they neared Fort Hayes. It was a stockade with four bastions, mounted with cannon. There was a strong blockhouse within, in which the sixteen occupants of the place were lodged, unsuspicious of danger. Troyes approached at night. Iberville and Sainte-Hélène with a few followers climbed the palisade on one side, while the rest of the party burst the main gate with a sort of battering ram, and rushed in, yelling the war-whoop. In a moment, the door of the blockhouse was dashed open, and its astonished inmates captured in their shirts.

The victors now embarked for Fort Rupert, distant forty leagues along the shore. In construction, it resembled Fort Hayes. The fifteen traders who held the place were all asleep at night in their blockhouse, when the Canadians burst the gate of the stockade and swarmed into the area. One of them mounted by a ladder to the roof of the building, and dropped lighted hand-grenades down the chimney, which, exploding among the occupants, told them unmistakably that something was wrong. At the same time, the assailants fired briskly on them through the loopholes, and, placing a petard under the walls, threatened to blow them into the air. Five, including a woman, were killed or wounded; and the rest cried for quarter. Meanwhile, Iberville with another party attacked a vessel anchored near the fort, and, climbing silently over her side, found the man on the watch asleep in his blanket. He sprang up and made fight, but they killed him, then stamped on the deck to rouse those below, sabred two of them as they

---

[1] The Compagnie du Nord had a grant of the trade of Hudson's Bay from Louis XIV. The bay was discovered by the English, under Hudson; but the French had carried on some trade there before the establishment of Fort Nelson. Denonville's commission to Troyes merely directs him to build forts, and "se saisir des voleurs coureurs de bois et autres que nous savons avoir pris et arrêté plusieurs de nos François commerçants avec les sauvages."

came up the hatchway, and captured the rest. Among them was Bridger, governor for the company of all its stations on the bay.

They next turned their attention to Fort Albany, thirty leagues from Fort Hayes, in a direction opposite to that of Fort Rupert. Here there were about thirty men, under Henry Sargent, an agent of the company. Surprise was this time impossible; for news of their proceedings had gone before them, and Sargent, though no soldier, stood on his defence. The Canadians arrived, some in canoes, some in the captured vessel, bringing ten captured pieces of cannon, which they planted in battery on a neighboring hill, well covered by intrenchments from the English shot. Here they presently opened fire; and, in an hour, the stockade with the houses that it enclosed was completely riddled. The English took shelter in a cellar, nor was it till the fire slackened that they ventured out to show a white flag and ask for a parley. Troyes and Sargent had an interview. The Englishman regaled his conqueror with a bottle of Spanish wine; and, after drinking the health of King Louis and King James, they settled the terms of capitulation. The prisoners were sent home in an English vessel which soon after arrived; and Maricourt remained to command at the bay, while Troyes returned to report his success to Denonville.[1]

This buccaneer exploit exasperated the English public, and it became doubly apparent that the state of affairs in America could not be allowed to continue. A conference had been arranged between the two powers, even before the news came from Hudson's Bay; and Count d'Avaux appeared at London as special envoy of Louis XIV. to settle the questions at issue. A treaty of neutrality was signed at Whitehall, and commissioners were appointed on both

---

[1]On the capture of the forts at Hudson's Bay, see La Potherie, I. 147–163; the letter of Father Silvy, chaplain of the expedition, in Saint-Vallier, État Présent, 43; and Oldmixon, British Empire in America, I. 561–564 (ed. 1741). An account of the preceding events will be found in La Potherie and Oldmixon; in Jerémie, Relation de la Baie de Hudson; and in N. Y. Col. Docs., IX. 796–802. Various embellishments have been added to the original narratives by recent writers, such as an imaginary hand-to-hand fight of Iberville and several Englishmen in the blockhouse of Fort Hayes.

sides.[1] Pending the discussion, each party was to refrain from acts of hostility or encroachment; and, said the declaration of the commissioners, "to the end the said agreement may have the better effect, we do likewise agree that the said serene kings shall immediately send necessary orders in that behalf to their respective governors in America."[2] Dongan accordingly was directed to keep a friendly correspondence with his rival, and take good care to give him no cause of complaint.[3]

It was this missive which had dashed the ardor of the English governor, and softened his epistolary style. More than four months after, Louis XIV. sent corresponding instructions to Denonville;[4] but, meantime, he had sent him troops, money, and munitions in abundance, and ordered him to attack the Iroquois towns. Whether such a step was consistent with the recent treaty of neutrality may well be doubted; for, though James II. had not yet formally claimed the Iroquois as British subjects, his representative had done so for years with his tacit approval, and out of this claim had risen the principal differences which it was the object of the treaty to settle.

Eight hundred regulars were already in the colony, and eight hundred more were sent in the spring, with a hundred and sixty-eight thousand livres in money and supplies.[5] Denonville was prepared to strike. He had pushed his preparations actively, yet with extreme secrecy; for he meant to fall on the Senecas unawares, and shatter at a blow the mainspring of English intrigue. Harmony reigned among the chiefs of the colony, military, civil, and religious. The intendant Meules had been recalled on the complaints of the gov-

---

[1] *Traité de Neutralité pour l'Amérique, conclu à Londres le 16 Nov., 1686*, in *Mémoires des Commissaires*, II. 86.

[2] *Instrument for preventing Acts of Hostility in America* in N. Y. Col. Docs., III. 505.

[3] *Order to Gov. Dongan, 22 Jan., 1687*, in N. Y. Col. Docs., III. 504.

[4] *Louis XIV. à Denonville, 17 Juin, 1687*. At the end of March, the king had written that "he did not think it expedient to make any attack on the English."

[5] *Abstract of Letters*, in N. Y. Col. Docs., IX. 314. This answers exactly to the statement of the *Mémoire adressé au Régent*, which places the number of troops in Canada at this time at thirty-two companies of fifty men each.

ernor, who had quarrelled with him; and a new intendant, Champigny, had been sent in his place. He was as pious as Denonville himself, and, like him, was in perfect accord with the bishop and the Jesuits. All wrought together to promote the new crusade.

It was not yet time to preach it, or at least Denonville thought so. He dissembled his purpose to the last moment, even with his best friends. Of all the Jesuits among the Iroquois, the two brothers Lamberville had alone held their post. Denonville, in order to deceive the enemy, had directed these priests to urge the Iroquois chiefs to meet him in council at Fort Frontenac, whither, as he pretended, he was about to go with an escort of troops, for the purpose of conferring with them. The two brothers received no hint whatever of his real intention, and tried in good faith to accomplish his wishes; but the Iroquois were distrustful, and hesitated to comply. On this, the elder Lamberville sent the younger with letters to Denonville to explain the position of affairs, saying at the same time that he himself would not leave Onondaga except to accompany the chiefs to the proposed council. "The poor father," wrote the governor, "knows nothing of our designs. I am sorry to see him exposed to danger; but, should I recall him, his withdrawal would certainly betray our plans to the Iroquois." This unpardonable reticence placed the Jesuit in extreme peril; for the moment the Iroquois discovered the intended treachery they would probably burn him as its instrument. No man in Canada had done so much as the elder Lamberville to counteract the influence of England and serve the interests of France, and in return the governor exposed him recklessly to the most terrible of deaths.[1]

In spite of all his pains, it was whispered abroad that there was to be war; and the rumor was brought to the ears of Dongan by some of the Canadian deserters. He lost no time

[1] *Denonville au Ministre, 9 Nov., 1686; Ibid., 8 Juin, 1687.* Denonville at last seems to have been seized with some compunction, and writes: "Tout cela me fait craindre que le pauvre père n'ayt de la peine à se retirer d'entre les mains de ces barbares ce qui m'inquiète fort." Dongan, though regarding the Jesuit as an insidious enemy, had treated him much better, and protected him on several occasions, for which he received the emphatic thanks of Dablon, superior of the missions. *Dablon to Dongan* (1685?), in *N. Y. Col. Docs.*, III. 454.

in warning the Iroquois, and their deputies came to beg his help. Danger humbled them for the moment; and they not only recognized King James as their sovereign, but consented at last to call his representative *Father* Corlaer instead of *Brother*. Their father, however, dared not promise them soldiers; though, in spite of the recent treaty, he caused gunpowder and lead to be given them, and urged them to recall the powerful war-parties which they had lately sent against the Illinois.[1]

Denonville at length broke silence, and ordered the militia to muster. They grumbled and hesitated, for they remembered the failures of La Barre. The governor issued a proclamation, and the bishop a pastoral mandate. There were sermons, prayers, and exhortations in all the churches. A revulsion of popular feeling followed; and the people, says Denonville, "made ready for the march with extraordinary animation." The church showered blessings on them as they went, and daily masses were ordained for the downfall of the foes of Heaven and of France.[2]

[1] Colden, 97 (1727), *Denonville au Ministre, 8 Juin, 1687*.

[2] Saint-Vallier, *État Présent*. Even to the moment of marching, Denonville pretended that he meant only to hold a peace council at Fort Frontenac. "J'ai toujours publié que je n'allois qu'à l'assemblée générale projetée à Cataracouy (*Fort Frontenac*). J'ai toujours tenu ce discours jusqu'au temps de la marche." *Denonville au Ministre, 8 Juin, 1687*.

Chapter VIII

1687

DENONVILLE AND THE SENECAS

Treachery of Denonville • Iroquois Generosity • The Invading Army • The Western Allies • Plunder of English Traders • Arrival of the Allies • Scene at the French Camp • March of Denonville • Ambuscade • Battle • Victory • The Seneca Babylon • Imperfect Success

---

A HOST of flat-boats filled with soldiers, and a host of Indian canoes, struggled against the rapids of the St. Lawrence, and slowly made their way to Fort Frontenac. Among the troops was La Hontan. When on his arrival he entered the gate of the fort, he saw a strange sight. A row of posts was planted across the area within, and to each post an Iroquois was tied by the neck, hands, and feet, "in such a way," says the indignant witness, "that he could neither sleep nor drive off the mosquitoes." A number of Indians attached to the expedition, all of whom were Christian converts from the mission villages, were amusing themselves by burning the fingers of these unfortunates in the bowls of their pipes, while the sufferers sang their death songs. La Hontan recognized one of them who, during his campaign with La Barre, had often feasted him in his wigwam; and the sight so exasperated the young officer that he could scarcely refrain from thrashing the tormentors with his walking stick.[1]

Though the prisoners were Iroquois, they were not those against whom the expedition was directed; nor had they, so far as appears, ever given the French any cause of complaint. They belonged to two neutral villages, called Kenté and Ganneious, on the north shore of Lake Ontario, forming a sort of colony, where the Sulpitians of Montreal had established a mission.[2] They hunted and fished for the garrison of the fort, and had been on excellent terms with it. Denonville, however, feared that they would report his movements to their rela-

[1] *La Hontan*, I. 93–95 (1709).
[2] Ganneious or Ganéyout was on an arm of the lake a little west of the present town of Fredericksburg. Kenté or Quinte was on Quinte Bay.

tions across the lake; but this was not his chief motive for seizing them. Like La Barre before him, he had received orders from the court that, as the Iroquois were robust and strong, he should capture as many of them as possible, and send them to France as galley slaves.[1] The order, without doubt, referred to prisoners taken in war; but Denonville, aware that the hostile Iroquois were not easily caught, resolved to entrap their unsuspecting relatives.

The intendant Champigny accordingly proceeded to the fort in advance of the troops, and invited the neighboring Iroquois to a feast. They came to the number of thirty men and about ninety women and children, whereupon they were surrounded and captured by the intendant's escort and the two hundred men of the garrison. The inhabitants of the village of Ganneious were not present; and one Perré, with a strong party of Canadians and Christian Indians, went to secure them. He acquitted himself of his errand with great address, and returned with eighteen warriors and about sixty women and children. Champigny's exertions did not end here. Learning that a party of Iroquois were peaceably fishing on an island in the St. Lawrence, he offered them also the hospitalities of Fort Frontenac; but they were too wary to be entrapped. Four or five Iroquois were however caught by the troops on their way up the river. They were in two or more parties, and they all had with them their women and children, which was never the case with Iroquois on the war-path. Hence the assertion of Denonville, that they came with hostile designs, is very improbable. As for the last six months he had constantly urged them, by the lips of Lamberville, to visit him and smoke the pipe of peace, it is not unreasonable to suppose that these Indian families were on their way to the colony in consequence of his invitations. Among them were the son and brother of Big Mouth, who of late had been an advocate of peace; and, in order not to alienate him, these two were eventually set free. The other warriors were tied like the rest to stakes at the fort.

The whole number of prisoners thus secured was fifty-one, sustained by such food as their wives were able to get for

[1] *Le Roy à La Barre, 21 Juillet, 1684; Le Roy à Denonville et Champigny, 30 Mars, 1687.*

them. Of more than a hundred and fifty women and children captured with them, many died at the fort, partly from excitement and distress, and partly from a pestilential disease. The survivors were all baptized, and then distributed among the mission villages in the colony. The men were sent to Quebec, where some of them were given up to their Christian relatives in the missions who had claimed them, and whom it was not expedient to offend; and the rest, after being baptized, were sent to France, to share with convicts and Huguenots the horrible slavery of the royal galleys.[1]

Before reaching Fort Frontenac, Denonville, to his great relief, was joined by Lamberville, delivered from the peril to which the governor had exposed him. He owed his life to an act of magnanimity on the part of the Iroquois, which does them signal honor. One of the prisoners at Fort Frontenac had contrived to escape, and, leaping sixteen feet to the ground from the window of a blockhouse, crossed the lake, and gave the alarm to his countrymen. Apparently, it was from him that the Onondagas learned that the invitations of Onontio were a snare; that he had entrapped their relatives, and was about to fall on their Seneca brethren with all the force of Canada. The Jesuit, whom they trusted and esteemed, but who had been used as an instrument to beguile

---

[1] The authorities for the above are Denonville, Champigny, Abbé Belmont, Bishop Saint-Vallier, and the author of *Recueil de ce qui s'est passé en Canada au Sujet de la Guerre, etc., depuis l'année 1682.*

Belmont, who accompanied the expedition, speaks of the affair with indignation, which was shared by many French officers. The bishop, on the other hand, mentions the success of the stratagem as a reward accorded by Heaven to the piety of Denonville. *État Présent de l'Église*, 91, 92 (reprint, 1856).

Denonville's account, which is sufficiently explicit, is contained in the long journal of the expedition which he sent to the court, and in several letters to the minister. Both Belmont and the author of the *Recueil* speak of the prisoners as having been "pris par l'appât d'un festin."

Mr. Shea, usually so exact, has been led into some error by confounding the different acts of this affair. By Denonville's official journal, it appears that, on the 19th June, Perré, by his order, captured several Indians on the St. Lawrence; that, on the 25th June, the governor, then at Rapide Plat on his way up the river, received a letter from Champigny, informing him that he had seized all the Iroquois near Fort Frontenac; and that, on the 3d July, Perré, whom Denonville had sent several days before to attack Ganneious, arrived with his prisoners.

them, was summoned before a council of the chiefs. They were in a fury at the news; and Lamberville, as much astonished by it as they, expected instant death, when one of them is said to have addressed him to the following effect: "We know you too well to believe that you meant to betray us. We think that you have been deceived as well as we; and we are not unjust enough to punish you for the crime of others. But you are not safe here. When once our young men have sung the war-song, they will listen to nothing but their fury; and we shall not be able to save you." They gave him guides, and sent him by secret paths to meet the advancing army.[1]

Again the fields about Fort Frontenac were covered with tents, camp-sheds, and wigwams. Regulars, militia, and Indians, there were about two thousand men; and, besides these, eight hundred regulars just arrived from France had been left at Montreal to protect the settlers.[2] Fortune thus far had smiled on the enterprise, and she now gave Denonville a fresh proof of her favor. On the very day of his arrival, a canoe came from Niagara with news that a large body of allies from the west had reached that place three days before, and were waiting his commands. It was more than he had dared to hope. In the preceding autumn, he had ordered Tonty, commanding at the Illinois, and La Durantaye, commanding at Michillimackinac, to muster as many *coureurs de bois* and Indians as possible, and join him early in July at Niagara. The distances were vast, and the difficulties incalculable. In the

[1] I have ventured to give this story on the sole authority of Charlevoix, for the contemporary writers are silent concerning it. Mr. Shea thinks that it involves a contradiction of date; but this is entirely due to confounding the capture of prisoners by Perré at Ganneious on July 8d with the capture by Champigny at Fort Frontenac about June 20th. Lamberville reached Denonville's camp, one day's journey from the fort, on the evening of the 29th. (*Journal of Denonville.*) This would give four and a half days for news of the treachery to reach Onondaga, and four and a half days for the Jesuit to rejoin his countrymen.

Charlevoix, with his usual carelessness, says that the Jesuit Milet had also been used to lure the Iroquois into the snare, and that he was soon after captured by the Oneidas, and delivered by an Indian matron. Milet's captivity did not take place till 1689–90.

[2] Denonville. Champigny says 832 regulars, 930 militia, and 300 Indians. This was when the army left Montreal. More Indians afterwards joined it. Belmont says 1,800 French and Canadians and about 300 Indians.

eyes of the pious governor, their timely arrival was a manifest sign of the favor of Heaven. At Fort St. Louis, of the Illinois, Tonty had mustered sixteen Frenchmen and about two hundred Indians, whom he led across the country to Detroit; and here he found Du Lhut, La Forêt, and La Durantaye, with a large body of French and Indians from the upper lakes.[1] It had been the work of the whole winter to induce these savages to move. Presents, persuasion, and promises had not been spared; and while La Durantaye, aided by the Jesuit Engelran, labored to gain over the tribes of Michillimackinac, the indefatigable Nicolas Perrot was at work among those of the Mississippi and Lake Michigan. They were of a race unsteady as aspens and fierce as wild-cats, full of mutual jealousies, without rulers, and without laws; for each was a law to himself. It was difficult to persuade them, and, when persuaded, scarcely possible to keep them so. Perrot, however, induced some of them to follow him to Michillimackinac, where many hundreds of Algonquin savages were presently gathered: a perilous crew, who changed their minds every day, and whose dancing, singing, and yelping might turn at any moment into war-whoops against each other or against their hosts, the French. The Hurons showed more stability; and La Durantaye was reasonably sure that some of them would follow him to the war, though it was clear that others were bent on allying themselves with the Senecas and the English. As for the Pottawatamies, Sacs, Ojibwas, Ottawas, and other Algonquin hordes, no man could foresee what they would do.[2]

Suddenly a canoe arrived with news that a party of English traders was approaching. It will be remembered that two bands of Dutch and English, under Rooseboom and McGregory, had prepared to set out together for Michillimackinac, armed with commissions from Dongan. They had rashly changed their plan, and parted company. Rooseboom took the lead, and McGregory followed some time after. Their hope was that, on reaching Michillimackinac, the Indians of the place, attracted by their cheap goods and their abundant

[1] Tonty, *Mémoire* in Margry, *Relations Inédites*.
[2] The name of Ottawas, here used specifically, was often employed by the French as a generic term for the Algonquin tribes of the Great Lakes.

supplies of rum, would declare for them and drive off the French; and this would probably have happened, but for the prompt action of La Durantaye. The canoes of Rooseboom, bearing twenty-nine whites and five Mohawks and Mohicans, were not far distant, when, amid a prodigious hubbub, the French commander embarked to meet him with a hundred and twenty *coureurs de bois*.[1] Behind them followed a swarm of Indian canoes, whose occupants scarcely knew which side to take, but for the most part inclined to the English. Rooseboom and his men, however, naturally thought that they came to support the French; and, when La Durantaye bore down upon them with threats of instant death if they made the least resistance, they surrendered at once. The captors carried them in triumph to Michillimackinac, and gave their goods to the delighted Indians.

"It is certain," wrote Denonville, "that, if the English had not been stopped and pillaged, the Hurons and Ottawas would have revolted and cut the throats of all our Frenchmen."[2] As it was, La Durantaye's exploit produced a revulsion of feeling, and many of the Indians consented to follow him. He lost no time in leading them down the lake to join Du Lhut at Detroit; and, when Tonty arrived, they all paddled for Niagara. On the way, they met McGregory with a party about equal to that of Rooseboom. He had with him a considerable number of Ottawa and Huron prisoners whom the Iroquois had captured, and whom he meant to return to their countrymen as a means of concluding the long projected triple alliance between the English, the Iroquois, and the tribes of the lakes. This bold scheme was now completely crushed. All the English were captured and carried to Niagara, whence they and their luckless precursors were sent prisoners to Quebec.

La Durantaye and his companions, with a hundred and eighty *coureurs de bois* and four hundred Indians, waited impatiently at Niagara for orders from the governor. A canoe despatched in haste from Fort Frontenac soon appeared; and

[1] Attestation of N. Harmentse and others of Rooseboom's party, *N. Y. Col. Docs.*, III. 436. La Potherie says, three hundred.

[2] *Denonville au Ministre, 25 Août, 1687.*

they were directed to repair at once to the rendezvous at Iron-dequoit Bay, on the borders of the Seneca country.[1]

Denonville was already on his way thither: On the fourth of July, he had embarked at Fort Frontenac with four hundred bateaux and canoes, crossed the foot of Lake Ontario, and moved westward along the southern shore. The weather was rough, and six days passed before he descried the low headlands of Irondequoit Bay. Far off on the glimmering water, he saw a multitude of canoes advancing to meet him. It was the flotilla of La Durantaye. Good management and good luck had so disposed it that the allied bands, concentring from points more than a thousand miles distant, reached the rendezvous on the same day. This was not all. The Ottawas of Michillimackinac, who refused to follow La Durantaye, had changed their minds the next morning, embarked in a body, paddled up the Georgian Bay of Lake Huron, crossed to Toronto, and joined the allies at Niagara. White and red, Denonville now had nearly three thousand men under his command.[2]

All were gathered on the low point of land that separates Irondequoit Bay from Lake Ontario. "Never," says an eyewitness, "had Canada seen such a sight; and never, perhaps, will she see such a sight again. Here was the camp of the regulars from France, with the general's head-quarters; the camp of the four battalions of Canadian militia, commanded by the *noblesse* of the country; the camp of the Christian Indians; and, farther on, a swarm of savages of every nation. Their features were different, and so were their manners, their weapons, their decorations, and their dances. They sang and whooped and harangued in every accent and tongue. Most of them wore nothing but horns on their heads, and the tails of beasts behind their backs. Their faces were painted red or green, with black or white spots; their ears and noses were

---

[1] The above is drawn from papers in *N. Y. Col. Docs.*, III. 436, IX. 324, 336, 346, 405; Saint-Vallier, *État Présent*, 92; Denonville, *Journal*; Belmont, *Histoire du Canada*; La Potherie, II. chap. xvi.; La Hontan, I. 96. Colden's account is confused and incorrect.

[2] *Recueil de ce qui s'est passé en Canada depuis 1682*; *Captain Duplessis's Plan for the Defence of Canada*, in *N. Y. Col. Docs.*, IX. 447.

hung with ornaments of iron; and their naked bodies were daubed with figures of various sorts of animals."[1]

These were the allies from the upper lakes. The enemy, meanwhile, had taken alarm. Just after the army arrived, three Seneca scouts called from the edge of the woods, and demanded what they meant to do. "To fight you, you blockheads," answered a Mohawk Christian attached to the French. A volley of bullets was fired at the scouts; but they escaped, and carried the news to their villages.[2] Many of the best warriors were absent. Those that remained, four hundred or four hundred and fifty by their own accounts, and eight hundred by that of the French, mustered in haste; and, though many of them were mere boys, they sent off the women and children, hid their most valued possessions, burned their chief town, and prepared to meet the invaders.

On the twelfth, at three o'clock in the afternoon, Denonville began his march, leaving four hundred men in a hastily built fort to guard the bateaux and canoes. Troops, officers, and Indians, all carried their provisions at their backs. Some of the Christian Mohawks guided them; but guides were scarcely needed, for a broad Indian trail led from the bay to the great Seneca town, twenty-two miles southward. They marched three leagues through the open forests of oak, and encamped for the night. In the morning, the heat was intense. The men gasped in the dead and sultry air of the woods, or grew faint in the pitiless sun, as they waded waist-deep through the rank grass of the narrow intervales. They passed safely through two dangerous defiles, and, about two in the afternoon, began to enter a third. Dense forests covered the hills on either hand. La Durantaye with Tonty and his cousin Du Lhut led the advance, nor could all Canada have supplied three men better for the work. Each led his band of *coureurs de bois*, white Indians, without discipline, and scarcely capable of it, but brave and accustomed to the woods. On their left were the Iroquois converts from the missions of Saut St. Louis and the Mountain of Montreal, fighting under the influence of their ghostly prompters against their own country-

---

[1] The first part of the extract is from Belmont; the second, from Saint-Vallier.

[2] *Information received from several Indians*, in N. Y. Col. Docs., III. 444.

men. On the right were the pagan Indians from the west. The woods were full of these painted spectres, grotesquely horrible in horns and tail; and among them flitted the black robe of Father Engelran, the Jesuit of Michillimackinac. Nicolas Perrot and two other bush-ranging Frenchmen were assigned to command them, but in fact they obeyed no man. These formed the vanguard, eight or nine hundred in all, under an excellent officer, Callières, governor of Montreal. Behind came the main body under Denonville, each of the four battalions of regulars alternating with a battalion of Canadians. Some of the regulars wore light armor, while the Canadians were in plain attire of coarse cloth or buckskin. Denonville, oppressed by the heat, marched in his shirt. "It is a rough life," wrote the marquis, "to tramp afoot through the woods, carrying one's own provisions in a haversack, devoured by mosquitoes, and faring no better than a mere soldier."[1] With him was the Chevalier de Vaudreuil, who had just arrived from France in command of the eight hundred men left to guard the colony, and who, eager to take part in the campaign, had pushed forward alone to join the army. Here, too, were the Canadian seigniors at the head of their vassals, Berthier, La Valterie, Granville, Longueuil, and many more. A guard of rangers and Indians brought up the rear.

Scouts thrown out in front ran back with the report that they had reached the Seneca clearings, and had seen no more dangerous enemy than three or four women in the cornfields. This was a device of the Senecas to cheat the French into the belief that the inhabitants were still in the town. It had the desired effect. The vanguard pushed rapidly forward, hoping to surprise the place, and ignorant that, behind the ridge of thick forests on their right, among a tangled growth of beech-trees in the gorge of a brook, three hundred ambushed warriors lay biding their time.

Hurrying forward through the forest, they left the main body behind, and soon reached the end of the defile. The woods were still dense on their left and front; but on their right lay a great marsh, covered with alder thickets and rank grass. Suddenly the air was filled with yells, and a rapid though distant fire was opened from the thickets and the for-

[1] *Denonville au Ministre, 8 Juin, 1687.*

est. Scores of painted savages, stark naked, some armed with swords and some with hatchets, leaped screeching from their ambuscade, and rushed against the van. Almost at the same moment a burst of whoops and firing sounded in the defile behind. It was the ambushed three hundred supporting the onset of their countrymen in front; but they had made a fatal mistake. Deceived by the numbers of the vanguard, they supposed it to be the whole army, never suspecting that Denonville was close behind with sixteen hundred men. It was a surprise on both sides. So dense was the forest that the advancing battalions could see neither the enemy nor each other. Appalled by the din of whoops and firing, redoubled by the echoes of the narrow valley, the whole army was seized with something like a panic. Some of the officers, it is said, threw themselves on the ground in their fright. There were a few moments of intense bewilderment. The various corps became broken and confused, and moved hither and thither without knowing why. Denonville behaved with great courage. He ran, sword in hand, to where the uproar was greatest, ordered the drums to beat the charge, turned back the militia of Berthier who were trying to escape, and commanded them and all others whom he met to fire on whatever looked like an enemy. He was bravely seconded by Callières, La Valterie, and several other officers. The Christian Iroquois fought well from the first, leaping from tree to tree, and exchanging shots and defiance with their heathen countrymen; till the Senecas, seeing themselves confronted by numbers that seemed endless, abandoned the field, after heavy loss, carrying with them many of their dead and all of their wounded.[1]

Denonville made no attempt to pursue. He had learned the dangers of this blind warfare of the woods; and he feared that the Senecas would waylay him again in the labyrinth of bushes that lay between him and the town. "Our troops," he says, "were all so overcome by the extreme heat and the long march that we were forced to remain where we were till morning. We had the pain of witnessing the usual cruelties of the Indians, who cut the dead bodies into quarters, like butchers meat, to put into their kettles, and opened most of

[1] For authorities, see note at the end of the chapter. The account of Charlevoix is contradicted at several points by the contemporary writers.

them while still warm to drink the blood. Our rascally Otta-was particularly distinguished themselves by these barbarities, as well as by cowardice; for they made off in the fight. We had five or six men killed on the spot, and about twenty wounded, among whom was Father Engelran, who was badly hurt by a gun-shot. Some prisoners who escaped from the Senecas tell us that they lost forty men killed outright, twenty-five of whom we saw butchered. One of the escaped prisoners saw the rest buried, and he saw also more than sixty very dangerously wounded."[1]

In the morning, the troops advanced in order of battle through a marsh covered with alders and tall grass, whence they had no sooner emerged than, says Abbé Belmont, "we began to see the famous Babylon of the Senecas, where so many crimes have been committed, so much blood spilled, and so many men burned. It was a village or town of bark, on the top of a hill. They had burned it a week before. We found nothing in it but the graveyard and the graves, full of snakes and other creatures; a great mask, with teeth and eyes of brass, and a bearskin drawn over it, with which they per-formed their conjurations."[2] The fire had also spared a num-ber of huge receptacles of bark, still filled with the last season's corn; while the fields around were covered with the growing crop, ripening in the July sun. There were hogs, too, in great number; for the Iroquois did not share the antipathy with which Indians are apt to regard that unsavory animal, and from which certain philosophers have argued their de-scent from the Jews.

The soldiers killed the hogs, burned the old corn, and hacked down the new with their swords. Next they advanced to an abandoned Seneca fort on a hill half a league distant, and burned it, with all that it contained. Ten days were passed in the work of havoc. Three neighboring villages were levelled, and all their fields laid waste. The amount of corn destroyed was prodigious. Denonville reckons it at the ab-surdly exaggerated amount of twelve hundred thousand bushels.

---

[1] *Denonville au Ministre, 25 Août, 1687.* In his journal, written afterwards, he says that the Senecas left twenty-seven dead on the field, and carried off twenty more, besides upwards of sixty mortally wounded.

[2] Belmont. A few words are added from Saint-Vallier.

The Senecas, laden with such of their possessions as they could carry off, had fled to their confederates in the east; and Denonville did not venture to pursue them. His men, feasting without stint on green corn and fresh pork, were sickening rapidly, and his Indian allies were deserting him. "It is a miserable business," he wrote, "to command savages, who, as soon as they have knocked an enemy in the head, ask for nothing but to go home and carry with them the scalp, which they take off like a skull-cap. You cannot believe what trouble I had to keep them till the corn was cut."

On the twenty-fourth, he withdrew, with all his army, to the fortified post at Irondequoit Bay, whence he proceeded to Niagara, in order to accomplish his favorite purpose of building a fort there. The troops were set at work, and a stockade was planted on the point of land at the eastern angle between the River Niagara and Lake Ontario, the site of the ruined fort built by La Salle nine years before.[1] Here he left a hundred men, under the Chevalier de Troyes, and, embarking with the rest of the army, descended to Montreal.

The campaign was but half a success. Joined to the capture of the English traders on the lakes, it had, indeed, prevented the defection of the western Indians, and in some slight measure restored their respect for the French, of whom, nevertheless, one of them was heard to say that they were good for nothing but to make war on hogs and corn. As for the Senecas, they were more enraged than hurt. They could rebuild their bark villages in a few weeks; and, though they had lost their harvest, their confederates would not let them starve.[2] A converted Iroquois had told the governor before his departure that, if he overset a wasps' nest, he must crush the wasps, or they would sting him. Denonville left the wasps alive.

---

[1] *Procès-verbal de la Prise de Possession de Niagara, 31 Julliet, 1687.* There are curious errors of date in this document regarding the proceedings of La Salle.

[2] The statement of some later writers, that many of the Senecas died during the following winter in consequence of the loss of their corn, is extremely doubtful. Captain Duplessis, in his *Plan for the Defence of Canada*, 1690, declares that not one of them perished of hunger.

DENONVILLE'S CAMPAIGN AGAINST THE SENECAS.—The chief authorities on this matter are the journal of Denonville, of which there is a translation in the *Colonial Documents of New York*, IX.; the letters of Denonville to the Minister; the *État Présent de l'Église de la Colonie Française*, by Bishop Saint-Vallier; the *Recueil de ce qui s'est passé en Canada au Sujet de la Guerre, tant des Anglais que des Iroquois, depuis l'année 1682*; and the excellent account by Abbé Belmont in his chronicle called *Histoire du Canada*. To these may be added La Hontan, Tonty, Nicolas Perrot, La Potherie, and the Senecas examined before the authorities of Albany, whose statements are printed in the *Colonial Documents*, III. These are the original sources. Charlevoix drew his account from a portion of them. It is inexact, and needs the correction of his learned annotator, Mr. Shea. Colden, Smith, and other English writers follow La Hontan.

The researches of Mr. O. H. Marshall, of Buffalo, have left no reasonable doubt as to the scene of the battle, and the site of the neighboring town. The Seneca ambuscade was on the marsh and the hills immediately north and west of the present village of Victor; and their chief town, called Gannagaro by Denonville, was on the top of Boughton's Hill, about a mile and a quarter distant. Immense quantities of Indian remains were formerly found here, and many are found to this day. Charred corn has been turned up in abundance by the plough, showing that the place was destroyed by fire. The remains of the fort burned by the French are still plainly visible on a hill a mile and a quarter from the ancient town. A plan of it will be found in Squier's *Aboriginal Monuments of New York*. The site of the three other Seneca towns destroyed by Denonville, and called Totiakton, Gannondata, and Gannongarae, can also be identified. See Marshall, in *Collections N. Y. Hist. Soc., 2d Series*, II. Indian traditions of historical events are usually almost worthless; but the old Seneca chief Dyunehogawah, or "John Blacksmith," who was living a few years ago at the Tonawanda reservation, recounted to Mr. Marshall with remarkable accuracy the story of the battle as handed down from his ancestors who lived at Gannagaro, close to the scene of action. Gannagaro was the Canagorah of Wentworth Greenhalgh's Journal. The old Seneca, on being shown a map of the locality, placed his finger on the spot where the fight took place, and which was long known to the Senecas by the name of Dyagodiyu, or "The Place of a Battle." It answers in the most perfect manner to the French contemporary descriptions.

Chapter IX

1687–1689

THE IROQUOIS INVASION

Altercations • Attitude of Dongan • Martial Preparation • Perplexity of Denonville • Angry Correspondence • Recall of Dongan • Sir Edmund Andros • Humiliation of Denonville • Distress of Canada • Appeals for Help • Iroquois Diplomacy • A Huron Macchiavel • The Catastrophe • Ferocity of the Victors • War with England • Recall of Denonville

WHEN Dongan heard that the French had invaded the Senecas, seized English traders on the lakes, and built a fort at Niagara, his wrath was kindled anew. He sent to the Iroquois, and summoned them to meet him at Albany; told the assembled chiefs that the late calamity had fallen upon them because they had held councils with the French without asking his leave; forbade them to do so again, and informed them that, as subjects of King James, they must make no treaty, except by the consent of his representative, the governor of New York. He declared that the Ottawas and other remote tribes were also British subjects; that the Iroquois should unite with them, to expel the French from the west; and that all alike should bring down their beaver skins to the English at Albany. Moreover, he enjoined them to receive no more French Jesuits into their towns, and to call home their countrymen whom these fathers had converted and enticed to Canada. "Obey my commands," added the governor, "for that is the only way to eat well and sleep well, without fear or disturbance." The Iroquois, who wanted his help, seemed to assent to all he said. "We will fight the French," exclaimed their orator, "as long as we have a man left."[1]

At the same time, Dongan wrote to Denonville demanding the immediate surrender of the Dutch and English captured on the lakes. Denonville angrily replied that he would keep the prisoners, since Dongan had broken the treaty of neutral-

---

[1] *Dongan's Propositions to the Five Nations; Answer of the Five Nations, N. Y. Col. Docs.,* III. 438, 441.

ity by "giving aid and comfort to the savages." The English
governor, in return, upbraided his correspondent for invading
British territory. "I will endevour to protect his Majesty's
subjects here from your unjust invasions, till I hear from the
King, my Master, who is the greatest and most glorious Monarch that ever set on a Throne, and would do as much to
propagate the Christian faith as any prince that lives. He did
not send me here to suffer you to give laws to his subjects. I
hope, notwithstanding all your trained souldiers and greate
Officers come from Europe, that our masters at home will
suffer us to do ourselves justice on you for the injuries and
spoyle you have committed on us; and I assure you, Sir, if
my Master gives leave, I will be as soon at Quebeck as you
shall be att Albany. What you alleage concerning my assisting
the Sinnakees (*Senecas*) with arms and ammunition to warr
against you was never given by mee untill the sixt of August
last, when understanding of your unjust proceedings in invading the King my Master's territorys in a hostill manner, I
then gave them powder, lead, and armes, and united the five
nations together to defend that part of our King's dominions
from your jnjurious invasion. And as for offering them men,
in that you doe me wrong, our men being all buisy then at
their harvest, and I leave itt to your judgment whether there
was any occasion when only foure hundred of them engaged
with your whole army. I advise you to send home all the
Christian and Indian prisoners the King of England's subjects
you unjustly do deteine. This is what I have thought fitt to
answer to your reflecting and provoking letter."[1]

As for the French claims to the Iroquois country and the
upper lakes, he turned them to ridicule. They were founded,
in part, on the missions established there by the Jesuits. "The
King of China," observes Dongan, "never goes anywhere
without two Jessuits with him. I wonder you make not the
like pretence to that Kingdome." He speaks with equal irony
of the claim based on discovery: "Pardon me if I say itt is a
mistake, except you will affirme that a few loose fellowes ram-
bling amongst Indians to keep themselves from starving gives
the French a right to the Countrey." And of the claim based
on geographical divisions: "Your reason is that some rivers or

[1] *Dongan to Denonville, 9 Sept., 1687,* in *N. Y. Col. Docs.,* III. 472.

rivoletts of this country run out into the great river of Canada. O just God! what new, farr-fetched, and unheard-of pretence is this for a title to a country. The French King may
have as good a pretence to all those Countrys that drink clarett and Brandy."[1] In spite of his sarcasms, it is clear that the
claim of prior discovery and occupation was on the side of
the French.

The dispute now assumed a new phase. James II. at length
consented to own the Iroquois as his subjects, ordering Dongan to protect them, and repel the French by force of arms,
should they attack them again.[2] At the same time, conferences
were opened at London between the French ambassador and
the English commissioners appointed to settle the questions
at issue. Both disputants claimed the Iroquois as subjects, and
the contest wore an aspect more serious than before.

The royal declaration was a great relief to Dongan. Thus
far he had acted at his own risk; now he was sustained by the
orders of his king. He instantly assumed a warlike attitude;
and, in the next spring, wrote to the Earl of Sunderland that
he had been at Albany all winter, with four hundred infantry,
fifty horsemen, and eight hundred Indians. This was not
without cause, for a report had come from Canada that the
French were about to march on Albany to destroy it. "And
now, my Lord," continues Dongan, "we must build forts in
ye countrey upon ye great Lakes, as ye French doe, otherwise
we lose ye Countrey, ye Bever trade, and our Indians."[3] Denonville, meanwhile, had begun to yield, and promised to
send back McGregory and the men captured with him.[4] Dongan, not satisfied, insisted on payment for all the captured
merchandise, and on the immediate demolition of Fort Niagara. He added another demand, which must have been singularly galling to his rival. It was to the effect that the
Iroquois prisoners seized at Fort Frontenac, and sent to the
galleys in France, should be surrendered as British subjects to

[1] *Dongan's Fourth Paper to the French Agents, N. Y. Col. Docs.*, III. 528.

[2] *Warrant authorizing Governor Dongan to protect the Five Nations, 10 Nov.,
1687, N. Y. Col. Docs.*, III. 503.

[3] *Dongan to Sunderland, Feb., 1688, N. Y. Col. Docs.*, III. 510.

[4] *Denonville à Dongan, 2 Oct., 1687.* McGregory soon arrived, and Dongan
sent him back to Canada as an emissary with a civil message to Denonville.
Dongan to Denonville, 10 Nov., 1687.

the English ambassador at Paris or the secretary of state in London.[1]

Denonville was sorely perplexed. He was hard pressed, and eager for peace with the Iroquois at any price; but Dongan was using every means to prevent their treating of peace with the French governor until he had complied with all the English demands. In this extremity, Denonville sent Father Vaillant to Albany, in the hope of bringing his intractable rival to conditions less humiliating. The Jesuit played his part with ability, and proved more than a match for his adversary in dialectics; but Dongan held fast to all his demands. Vaillant tried to temporize, and asked for a truce, with a view to a final settlement by reference to the two kings.[2] Dongan referred the question to a meeting of Iroquois chiefs, who declared in reply that they would make neither peace nor truce till Fort Niagara was demolished and all the prisoners restored. Dongan, well pleased, commended their spirit, and assured them that King James, "who is the greatest man the sunn shines uppon, and never told a ly in his life, has given you his Royall word to protect you."[3] Vaillant returned from his bootless errand; and a stormy correspondence followed between the two governors. Dongan renewed his demands, then protested his wish for peace, extolled King James for his pious zeal, and declared that he was sending over missionaries of his own to convert the Iroquois.[4] What Denonville wanted was not their conversion by Englishmen, but their conversion by Frenchmen, and the presence in their towns of those most useful political agents, the Jesuits.[5] He replied angrily, charging Dongan with preventing the conversion of the Iroquois

[1] *Dongan to Denonville, 31 Oct., 1687; Dongan's First Demand of the French Agents, N. Y. Col. Docs.*, III. 515, 520.

[2] The papers of this discussion will be found in *N. Y. Col. Docs.*, III.

[3] *Dongan's Reply to the Five Nations, Ibid.*, III. 535.

[4] *Dongan to Denonville, 17 Feb., 1688, Ibid.*, III. 519.

[5] "Il y a une nécessité indispensable pour les intérais de la Religion et de la Colonie de restablir les missionaries Jésuites dans tous les villages Iroquois: si vous ne trouvés moyen de faire retourner ces Pères dans leurs anciennes missions, vous devés en attendre beaucoup de malheur pour cette Colonie; car je dois vous dire que jusqu'icy c'est leur habilité qui a soutenu les affaires du pays par leur sçavoir-faire à gouverner les esprits de ces barbares, qui ne sont Sauvages que de nom." Denonville, *Mémoire adressé au Ministre, 9 Nov., 1688*.

by driving off the French missionaries, and accusing him, farther, of instigating the tribes of New York to attack Canada.[1] Suddenly there was a change in the temper of his letters. He wrote to his rival in terms of studied civility; declared that he wished he could meet him, and consult with him on the best means of advancing the cause of true religion; begged that he would not refuse him his friendship; and thanked him in warm terms for befriending some French prisoners whom he had saved from the Iroquois, and treated with great kindness.[2]

This change was due to despatches from Versailles, in which Denonville was informed that the matters in dispute would soon be amicably settled by the commissioners; that he was to keep on good terms with the English commanders, and, what pleased him still more, that the king of England was about to recall Dongan.[3] In fact, James II. had resolved on remodelling his American colonies. New York, New Jersey, and New England had been formed into one government under Sir Edmund Andros; and Dongan was summoned home, where a regiment was given him, with the rank of major-general of artillery. Denonville says that, in his efforts to extend English trade to the Great Lakes and the Mississippi, his late rival had been influenced by motives of personal gain. Be this as it may, he was a bold and vigorous defender of the claims of the British crown.

Sir Edmund Andros now reigned over New York; and, by the terms of his commission, his rule stretched westward to the Pacific. The usual official courtesies passed between him and Denonville; but Andros renewed all the demands of his predecessor, claimed the Iroquois as subjects, and forbade the

---

[1] *Denonville à Dongan, 24 Avril, 1688; Ibid., 12 Mai, 1688.* Whether the charge is true is questionable. Dongan had just written that, if the Iroquois did harm to the French, he was ordered to offer satisfaction, and had already done so.

[2] *Denonville à Dongan, 18 Juin, 1688; Ibid., 5 Juillet, 1688; Ibid., 20 Aug., 1688.* "Je n'ai donc qu'à vous asseurer que toute la Colonie a une très-parfaite reconnoissance des bons offices que ces pauvres malheureux ont reçu de vous et de vos peuples."

[3] *Mémoire pour servir d'Instruction au Sr. Marquis de Denonville, 8 Mars, 1688; Le Roy à Denonville, même date; Seignelay à Denonville, même date.* Louis XIV. had demanded Dongan's recall. How far this had influenced the action of James II. it is difficult to say.

French to attack them.[1] The new governor was worse than the old. Denonville wrote to the minister: "I send you copies of his letters, by which you will see that the spirit of Dongan has entered into the heart of his successor, who may be less passionate and less interested, but who is, to say the least, quite as much opposed to us, and perhaps more dangerous by his suppleness and smoothness than the other was by his violence. What he has just done among the Iroquois, whom he pretends to be under his government, and whom he prevents from coming to meet me, is a certain proof that neither he nor the other English governors, nor their people, will refrain from doing this colony all the harm they can."[2]

While these things were passing, the state of Canada was deplorable, and the position of its governor as mortifying as it was painful. He thought with good reason that the maintenance of the new fort at Niagara was of great importance to the colony, and he had repeatedly refused the demands of Dongan and the Iroquois for its demolition. But a power greater than sachems and governors presently intervened. The provisions left at Niagara, though abundant, were atrociously bad. Scurvy and other malignant diseases soon broke out among the soldiers. The Senecas prowled about the place, and no man dared venture out for hunting, fishing, or firewood.[3] The fort was first a prison, then a hospital, then a charnel-house, till before spring the garrison of a hundred men was reduced to ten or twelve. In this condition, they were found towards the end of April by a large war-party of friendly Miamis, who entered the place and held it till a French detachment at length arrived for its relief.[4] The garrison of Fort Frontenac had suffered from the same causes, though not to the same degree. Denonville feared that he should be forced to abandon them both. The way was so long and so danger-

[1] *Andros to Denonville, 21 Aug., 1688; Ibid., 29 Sept., 1688.*

[2] *Mémoire de l'Estat Présent des Affaires de ce Pays depuis le 10me Aoust, 1688, jusqu'au dernier Octobre de la mesme année.* He declares that the English are always "itching for the western trade," that their favorite plan is to establish a post on the Ohio, and that they have made the attempt three times already.

[3] Denonville, *Mémoire du 10 Aoust, 1688.*

[4] *Recueil de ce qui s'est passé en Canada depuis l'année 1682.* The writer was an officer of the detachment, and describes what he saw. Compare La Potherie, II. 210; and La Hontan, I. 131 (1709).

ous, and the governor had grown of late so cautious, that he dreaded the risk of maintaining such remote communications. On second thought, he resolved to keep Frontenac and sacrifice Niagara. He promised Dongan that he would demolish it, and he kept his word.[1]

He was forced to another and a deeper humiliation. At the imperious demand of Dongan and the Iroquois, he begged the king to send back the prisoners entrapped at Fort Frontenac, and he wrote to the minister: "Be pleased, Monseigneur, to remember that I had the honor to tell you that, in order to attain the peace necessary to the country, I was obliged to promise that I would beg you to send back to us the prisoners I sent you last year. I know you gave orders that they should be well treated, but I am informed that, though they were well enough treated at first, your orders were not afterwards executed with the same fidelity. If ill treatment has caused them all to die,—for they are people who easily fall into dejection, and who die of it,—and if none of them come back, I do not know at all whether we can persuade these barbarians not to attack us again."[2]

What had brought the marquis to this pass? Famine, destitution, disease, and the Iroquois were making Canada their prey. The fur trade had been stopped for two years; and the people, bereft of their only means of subsistence, could contribute nothing to their own defence. Above Three Rivers, the whole population was imprisoned in stockade forts hastily built in every seigniory.[3] Here they were safe, provided that they never ventured out; but their fields were left untilled, and the governor was already compelled to feed many of them at the expense of the king. The Iroquois roamed among the deserted settlements or prowled like lynxes about the forts, waylaying convoys and killing or capturing stragglers.

[1] *Denonville à Dongan, 20 Aoust, 1688; Procès-verbal of the Condition of Fort Niagara, 1688*; N. Y. Col. Docs., IX. 386. The palisades were torn down by Denonville's order on the 15th of September. The rude dwellings and storehouses which they enclosed, together with a large wooden cross, were left standing. The commandant De Troyes had died, and Captain Desbergères had been sent to succeed him.

[2] Denonville, *Mémoire du 10 Aoust, 1688.*

[3] In the Dêpot des Cartes de la Marine, there is a contemporary manuscript map, on which all these forts are laid down.

Their war-parties were usually small; but their movements were so mysterious and their attacks so sudden, that they spread a universal panic through the upper half of the colony. They were the wasps which Denonville had failed to kill.

"We should succumb," wrote the distressed governor, "if our cause were not the cause of God. Your Majesty's zeal for religion, and the great things you have done for the destruction of heresy, encourage me to hope that you will be the bulwark of the Faith in the new world as you are in the old. I cannot give you a truer idea of the war we have to wage with the Iroquois than by comparing them to a great number of wolves or other ferocious beasts, issuing out of a vast forest to ravage the neighboring settlements. The people gather to hunt them down; but nobody can find their lair, for they are always in motion. An abler man than I would be greatly at a loss to manage the affairs of this country. It is for the interest of the colony to have peace at any cost whatever. For the glory of the king and the good of religion, we should be glad to have it an advantageous one; and so it would have been, but for the malice of the English and the protection they have given our enemies."[1]

And yet he had, one would think, a reasonable force at his disposal. His thirty-two companies of regulars were reduced by this time to about fourteen hundred men, but he had also three or four hundred Indian converts, besides the militia of the colony, of whom he had stationed a large body under Vaudreuil at the head of the Island of Montreal. All told, they were several times more numerous than the agile warriors who held the colony in terror. He asked for eight hundred more regulars. The king sent him three hundred. Affairs grew worse, and he grew desperate. Rightly judging that the best means of defence was to take the offensive, he conceived the plan of a double attack on the Iroquois, one army to assail the Onondagas and Cayugas, another the Mohawks and Oneidas.[2] Since to reach the Mohawks as he proposed, by the way of Lake Champlain, he must pass through territory indisputably British, the attempt would be a flagrant violation of

[1] *Denonville au Roy, 1688; Ibid., Mémoire du 10 Aoust, 1688; Ibid., Mémoire du 9 Nov., 1688.*

[2] *Plan for the Termination of the Iroquois War, N. Y. Col. Docs., IX. 375.*

the treaty of neutrality. Nevertheless, he implored the king to send him four thousand soldiers to accomplish it.[1] His fast friend, the bishop, warmly seconded his appeal. "The glory of God is involved," wrote the head of the church, "for the Iroquois are the only tribe who oppose the progress of the gospel. The glory of the king is involved, for they are the only tribe who refuse to recognize his grandeur and his might. They hold the French in the deepest contempt; and, unless they are completely humbled within two years, his Majesty will have no colony left in Canada."[2] And the prelate proceeds to tell the minister how, in his opinion, the war ought to be conducted. The appeal was vain. "His Majesty agrees with you," wrote Seignelay, "that three or four thousand men would be the best means of making peace, but he cannot spare them now. If the enemy breaks out again, raise the inhabitants, and fight as well as you can till his Majesty is prepared to send you troops."[3]

A hope had dawned on the governor. He had been more active of late in negotiating than in fighting, and his diplomacy had prospered more than his arms. It may be remembered that some of the Iroquois entrapped at Fort Frontenac had been given to their Christian relatives in the mission villages. Here they had since remained. Denonville thought that he might use them as messengers to their heathen countrymen, and he sent one or more of them to Onondaga with gifts and overtures of peace. That shrewd old politician, Big Mouth, was still strong in influence at the Iroquois capital, and his name was great to the farthest bounds of the confederacy. He knew by personal experience the advantages of a neutral position between the rival European powers, from both of whom he received gifts and attentions; and he saw that what was good for him was good for the confederacy, since, if it gave itself to neither party, both would court its alliance. In his opinion, it had now leaned long enough towards the English; and a change of attitude had become expedient. Therefore, as Denonville promised the return of the

---

[1] Denonville, *Mémoire du 8 Aoust, 1688.*

[2] Saint-Vallier, *Mémoire sur les Affaires du Canada pour Monseigneur le Marquis de Seignelay.*

[3] *Mémoire du Ministre adressé à Denonville, 1 Mai, 1689.*

prisoners, and was plainly ready to make other concessions, Big Mouth, setting at naught the prohibitions of Andros, consented to a conference with the French. He set out at his leisure for Montreal, with six Onondaga, Cayuga, and Oneida chiefs; and, as no diplomatist ever understood better the advantage of negotiating at the head of an imposing force, a body of Iroquois warriors, to the number, it is said, of twelve hundred, set out before him, and silently took path to Canada.

The ambassadors paddled across the lake and presented themselves before the commandant of Fort Frontenac, who received them with distinction, and ordered Lieutenant Perelle to escort them to Montreal. Scarcely had the officer conducted his august charge five leagues on their way, when, to his amazement, he found himself in the midst of six hundred Iroquois warriors, who amused themselves for a time with his terror, and then accompanied him as far as Lake St. Francis, where he found another body of savages nearly equal in number. Here the warriors halted, and the ambassadors with their escort gravely pursued their way to meet Denonville at Montreal.[1]

Big Mouth spoke haughtily, like a man who knew his power. He told the governor that he and his people were subjects neither of the French nor of the English; that they wished to be friends of both; that they held their country of the Great Spirit; and that they had never been conquered in war. He declared that the Iroquois knew the weakness of the French, and could easily exterminate them; that they had formed a plan of burning all the houses and barns of Canada, killing the cattle, setting fire to the ripe grain, and then, when the people were starving, attacking the forts; but that he, Big Mouth, had prevented its execution. He concluded by saying that he was allowed but four days to bring back the governor's reply; and that, if he were kept waiting longer, he would not answer for what might happen.[2] Though it appeared by some expressions in his speech that he was ready

---

[1] *Relation des Événements de la Guerre, 30 Oct., 1688.*

[2] *Declaration of the Iroquois in presence of M. de Denonville, N. Y. Col. Docs.,* IX. 384; *Relation des Événements de la Guerre, 30 Oct., 1688;* Belmont, *Histoire du Canada.*

to make peace only with the French, leaving the Iroquois free to attack the Indian allies of the colony, and though, while the ambassadors were at Montreal, their warriors on the river above actually killed several of the Indian converts, Denonville felt himself compelled to pretend ignorance of the outrage.[1] A declaration of neutrality was drawn up, and Big Mouth affixed to it the figures of sundry birds and beasts as the signatures of himself and his fellow-chiefs.[2] He promised, too, that within a certain time deputies from the whole confederacy should come to Montreal and conclude a general peace.

The time arrived, and they did not appear. It became known, however, that a number of chiefs were coming from Onondaga to explain the delay, and to promise that the deputies should soon follow. The chiefs in fact were on their way. They reached La Famine, the scene of La Barre's meeting with Big Mouth; but here an unexpected incident arrested them, and completely changed the aspect of affairs.

Among the Hurons of Michillimackinac there was a chief of high renown named Kondiaronk, or the Rat. He was in the prime of life, a redoubted warrior, and a sage counsellor. The French seem to have admired him greatly. "He is a gallant man," says La Hontan, "if ever there was one;" while Charlevoix declares that he was the ablest Indian the French ever knew in America, and that he had nothing of the savage but the name and the dress. In spite of the father's eulogy, the moral condition of the Rat savored strongly of the wigwam. He had given Denonville great trouble by his constant intrigues with the Iroquois, with whom he had once made a plot for the massacre of his neighbors, the Ottawas, under cover of a pretended treaty.[3] The French had spared no pains to gain him; and he had at length been induced to declare for them, under a pledge from the governor that the war should never cease till the Iroquois were destroyed. During the summer, he raised a party of forty warriors, and came down the

---

[1] *Callières à Seignelay, Jan., 1689.*
[2] See the signatures in *N. Y. Col. Docs.*, IX. 385, 386.
[3] Nicolas Perrot, 143.

lakes in quest of Iroquois scalps.[1] On the way, he stopped at Fort Frontenac to hear the news, when, to his amazement, the commandant told him that deputies from Onondaga were coming in a few days to conclude peace, and that he had better go home at once.

"It is well," replied the Rat.

He knew that for the Hurons it was not well. He and his tribe stood fully committed to the war, and for them peace between the French and the Iroquois would be a signal of destruction, since Denonville could not or would not protect his allies. The Rat paddled off with his warriors. He had secretly learned the route of the expected deputies; and he shaped his course, not, as he had pretended, for Michillimackinac, but for La Famine, where he knew that they would land. Having reached his destination, he watched and waited four or five days, till canoes at length appeared, approaching from the direction of Onondaga. On this, the Rat and his friends hid themselves in the bushes.

The new comers were the messengers sent as precursors of the embassy. At their head was a famous personage named Decanisora, or Tegannisorens, with whom were three other chiefs, and, it seems, a number of warriors. They had scarcely landed when the ambushed Hurons gave them a volley of bullets, killed one of the chiefs, wounded all the rest, and then, rushing upon them, seized the whole party except a warrior who escaped with a broken arm. Having secured his prisoners, the Rat told them that he had acted on the suggestion of Denonville, who had informed him that an Iroquois war-party was to pass that way. The astonished captives protested that they were envoys of peace. The Rat put on a look of amazement, then of horror and fury, and presently burst into invectives against Denonville for having made him the instrument of such atrocious perfidy. "Go, my brothers," he exclaimed, "go home to your people. Though there is war between us, I give you your liberty. Onontio has made me do so black a deed that I shall never be happy again till your five tribes take a just vengeance upon him." After giving them

[1] *Denonville à Seignelay, 9 Nov., 1688.* La Hontan saw the party set out, and says that there were about a hundred of them.

guns, powder, and ball, he sent them on their way, well pleased with him and filled with rage against the governor.

In accordance with Indian usage, he, however, kept one of them to be adopted, as he declared, in place of one of his followers whom he had lost in the skirmish; then, recrossing the lake, he went alone to Fort Frontenac, and, as he left the gate to rejoin his party, he said coolly, "I have killed the peace: we shall see how the governor will get out of this business."[1] Then, without loss of time, he repaired to Michillimackinac, and gave his Iroquois prisoner to the officer in command. No news of the intended peace had yet reached that distant outpost; and, though the unfortunate Iroquois told the story of his mission and his capture, the Rat declared that it was a crazy invention inspired by the fear of death, and the prisoner was immediately shot by a file of soldiers. The Rat now sent for an old Iroquois who had long been a prisoner at the Huron village, telling him with a mournful air that he was free to return to his people, and recount the cruelty of the French, who, had put their countryman to death. The liberated Iroquois faithfully acquitted himself of his mission.[2]

One incident seemed for a moment likely to rob the intriguer of the fruits of his ingenuity. The Iroquois who had escaped in the skirmish contrived to reach Fort Frontenac some time after the last visit of the Rat. He told what had happened; and, after being treated with the utmost attention, he was sent to Onondaga, charged with explanations and regrets. The Iroquois dignitaries seemed satisfied, and Denon-

[1]"Il dit, J'ai tué la paix." Belmont, *Histoire du Canada*. "Le Rat passa ensuite seul à Catarakouy (*Fort Frontenac*) sans vouloir dire le tour qu'il avoit fait, dit seulement estant hors de la porte, en s'en allant, Nous verrons comme le gouverneur se tirera d'affaire." Denonville.

[2]La Hontan, I. 189 (1709). Most of the details of the story are drawn from this writer, whose statement I have compared with that of Denonville, in his letter dated Nov. 9, 1688; of Callières, Jan., 1689; of the *Abstract of Letters from Canada*, in *N. Y. Col. Docs.*, IX. 393; and of the writer of *Relation des Événements de la Guerre, 30 Oct., 1688*. Belmont notices the affair with his usual conciseness. La Hontan's account is sustained by the others in most, though not in all of its essential points. He calls the Huron chief *Adario, ou le Rat*. He is elsewhere mentioned as Kondiaronk, Kondiaront, Soüoïas, and Soüaïti. La Hontan says that the scene of the treachery was one of the rapids of the St. Lawrence, but more authentic accounts place it at La Famine.

ville wrote to the minister that there was still good hope of peace. He little knew his enemy. They could dissemble and wait; but they neither believed the governor nor forgave him. His supposed treachery at La Famine, and his real treachery at Fort Frontenac, filled them with a patient but unextinguishable rage. They sent him word that they were ready to renew the negotiation; then they sent again, to say that Andros forbade them. Without doubt they used his prohibition as a pretext. Months passed, and Denonville remained in suspense. He did not trust his Indian allies, nor did they trust him. Like the Rat and his Hurons, they dreaded the conclusion of peace, and wished the war to continue, that the French might bear the brunt of it, and stand between them and the wrath of the Iroquois.[1]

In the direction of the Iroquois, there was a long and ominous silence. It was broken at last by the crash of a thunderbolt. On the night between the fourth and fifth of August, a violent hail-storm burst over Lake St. Louis, an expansion of the St. Lawrence a little above Montreal. Concealed by the tempest and the darkness, fifteen hundred warriors landed at La Chine, and silently posted themselves about the houses of the sleeping settlers, then screeched the war-whoop, and began the most frightful massacre in Canadian history. The houses were burned, and men, women, and children indiscriminately butchered. In the neighborhood were three stockade forts, called Rémy, Roland, and La Présentation; and they all had garrisons. There was also an encampment of two hundred regulars about three miles distant, under an officer named Subercase, then absent at Montreal on a visit to Denonville, who had lately arrived with his wife and family. At four o'clock in the morning, the troops in this encampment heard a cannon-shot from one of the forts. They were at once ordered under arms. Soon after, they saw a man running towards them, just escaped from the butchery. He told his story, and passed on with the news to Montreal, six miles distant. Then several fugitives appeared, chased by a band of Iroquois, who gave over the pursuit at sight of the soldiers, but pillaged several houses before their eyes. The day was well advanced before Subercase arrived. He ordered the troops to

[1] *Denonville au Ministre, 9 Nov., 1688.*

march. About a hundred armed inhabitants had joined them, and they moved together towards La Chine. Here they found the houses still burning, and the bodies of their inmates strewn among them or hanging from the stakes where they had been tortured. They learned from a French surgeon, escaped from the enemy, that the Iroquois were all encamped a mile and a half farther on, behind a tract of forest. Subercase, whose force had been strengthened by troops from the forts, resolved to attack them; and, had he been allowed to do so, he would probably have punished them severely, for most of them were helplessly drunk with brandy taken from the houses of the traders. Sword in hand, at the head of his men, the daring officer entered the forest; but, at that moment, a voice from the rear commanded a halt. It was that of the Chevalier de Vaudreuil, just come from Montreal, with positive orders from Denonville to run no risks and stand solely on the defensive. Subercase was furious. High words passed between him and Vaudreuil, but he was forced to obey.

The troops were led back to Fort Roland, where about five hundred regulars and militia were now collected under command of Vaudreuil. On the next day, eighty men from Fort Rémy attempted to join them; but the Iroquois had slept off the effect of their orgies, and were again on the alert. The unfortunate detachment was set upon by a host of savages, and cut to pieces in full sight of Fort Roland. All were killed or captured, except Le Moyne de Longueuil, and a few others, who escaped within the gate of Fort Rémy.[1]

Montreal was wild with terror. It had been fortified with palisades since the war began; but, though there were troops in the town under the governor himself, the people were in mortal dread. No attack was made either on the town or on any of the forts, and such of the inhabitants as could reach them were safe; while the Iroquois held undisputed possession of the open country, burned all the houses and barns over an extent of nine miles, and roamed in small parties,

---

[1] *Recueil de ce qui s'est passé en Canada depuis l'année 1682; Observations on the State of Affairs in Canada, 1689,* N. Y. Col. Docs., IX. 431; Belmont. *Histoire du Canada; Frontenac au Ministre, 15 Nov., 1689.* This detachment was commanded by Lieutenant de la Rabeyre, and consisted of fifty French and thirty Indian converts.

pillaging and scalping, over more than twenty miles. There is no mention of their having encountered opposition; nor do they seem to have met with any loss but that of some warriors killed in the attack on the detachment from Fort Rémy, and that of three drunken stragglers who were caught and thrown into a cellar in Fort La Présentation. When they came to their senses, they defied their captors, and fought with such ferocity that it was necessary to shoot them. Charlevoix says that the invaders remained in the neighborhood of Montreal till the middle of October, or more than two months; but this seems incredible, since troops and militia enough to drive them all into the St. Lawrence might easily have been collected in less than a week. It is certain, however, that their stay was strangely long. Troops and inhabitants seem to have been paralyzed with fear.

At length, most of them took to their canoes, and recrossed Lake St. Louis in a body, giving ninety yells to show that they had ninety prisoners in their clutches. This was not all; for the whole number carried off was more than a hundred and twenty, besides about two hundred who had the good fortune to be killed on the spot. As the Iroquois passed the forts, they shouted, "Onontio, you deceived us, and now we have deceived you." Towards evening, they encamped on the farther side of the lake, and began to torture and devour their prisoners. On that miserable night, stupefied and speechless groups stood gazing from the strand of La Chine at the lights that gleamed along the distant shore of Châteaugay, where their friends, wives, parents, or children agonized in the fires of the Iroquois, and scenes were enacted of indescribable and nameless horror. The greater part of the prisoners were, however, reserved to be distributed among the towns of the confederacy, and there tortured for the diversion of the inhabitants. While some of the invaders went home to celebrate their triumph, others roamed in small parties through all the upper parts of the colony, spreading universal terror.[1]

---

[1] The best account of the descent of the Iroquois at La Chine is that of the *Recueil de ce qui s'est passé en Canada, 1682–1712.* The writer was an officer under Subercase, and was on the spot. Belmont, superior of the mission of Montreal, also gives a trustworthy account in his *Histoire du Canada.* Compare La Hontan, I. 193 (1709), and La Potherie, II. 229. Farther particulars

Canada lay bewildered and benumbed under the shock of this calamity; but the cup of her misery was not full. There was revolution in England. James II., the friend and ally of France, had been driven from his kingdom, and William of Orange had seized his vacant throne. Soon there came news of war between the two crowns. The Iroquois alone had brought the colony to the brink of ruin; and now they would be supported by the neighboring British colonies, rich, strong, and populous, compared to impoverished and depleted Canada.

A letter of recall for Denonville was already on its way.[1] His successor arrived in October, and the marquis sailed for France. He was a good soldier in a regular war, and a subordinate command; and he had some of the qualities of a good governor, while lacking others quite as essential. He had more activity than vigor, more personal bravery than firmness, and more clearness of perception than executive power. He filled his despatches with excellent recommendations, but was not the man to carry them into effect. He was sensitive, fastidious, critical, and conventional, and plumed himself on his honor, which was not always able to bear a strain; though

---

are given in the letters of Callières, 8 Nov.; Champigny, 16 Nov.; and Frontenac, 15 Nov. Frontenac, after visiting the scene of the catastrophe a few weeks after it occurred, writes: "Ils (*les Iroquois*) avoient bruslé plus de trois lieues de pays, saccagé toutes les maisons jusqu'aux portes de la ville, enlevé plus de six vingt personnes, tant hommes, femmes, qu'enfants, après avoir massacré plus de deux cents dont ils avoient cassé la teste aux uns, bruslé, rosty, et mangé les autres, ouvert le ventre des femmes grosses pour en arracher les enfants, et fait des cruautez inouïes et sans exemple." The details given by Belmont, and by the author of *Histoire de l'Eau de Vie en Canada*, are no less revolting. The last-mentioned writer thinks that the massacre was a judgment of God upon the sale of brandy at La Chine.

Some Canadian writers have charged the English with instigating the massacre. I find nothing in contemporary documents to support the accusation. Denonville wrote to the minister, after the Rat's treachery came to light, that Andros had forbidden the Iroquois to attack the colony. Immediately after the attack at La Chine, the Iroquois sachems, in a conference with the agents of New England, declared that "we did not make war on the French at the persuasion of our brethren at Albany; for we did not so much as acquaint them of our intention till fourteen days after our army had begun their march." *Report of Conference* in Colden, 103.

[1] *Le Roy à Denonville, 31 Mai, 1689.*

as regards illegal trade, the besetting sin of Canadian governors, his hands were undoubtedly clean.[1] It is said that he had an instinctive antipathy for Indians, such as some persons have for certain animals; and the *coureurs de bois*, and other lawless classes of the Canadian population, appeared to please him no better. Their license and insubordination distressed him, and he constantly complained of them to the king. For the Church and its hierarchy his devotion was unbounded; and his government was a season of unwonted sunshine for the ecclesiastics, like the balmy days of the Indian summer amid the gusts of November. They exhausted themselves in eulogies of his piety; and, in proof of its depth and solidity, Mother Juchereau tells us that he did not regard station and rank as very useful aids to salvation. While other governors complained of too many priests, Denonville begged for more. All was harmony between him and Bishop Saint-Vallier; and the prelate was constantly his friend, even to the point of justifying his worst act, the treacherous seizure of the Iroquois neutrals.[2] When he left Canada, the only mourner besides the churchmen was his colleague, the intendant Champigny; for the two chiefs of the colony, joined in a common union with the Jesuits, lived together in unexampled concord. On his arrival at court, the good offices of his clerical allies gained for him the highly honorable post of governor of the royal children, the young Dukes of Burgundy, Anjou, and Berri.

[1] "I shall only add one article, on which possibly you will find it strange that I have said nothing; namely, whether the governor carries on any trade. I shall answer, no; but my Lady the Governess (*Madame la Gouvernante*), who is disposed not to neglect any opportunity for making a profit, had a room, not to say a shop, full of goods, till the close of last winter, in the château of Quebec, and found means afterwards to make a lottery to get rid of the rubbish that remained, which produced her more than her good merchandise." *Relation of the State of Affairs in Canada, 1688,* in *N. Y. Col. Docs.,* IX. 388. This paper was written at Quebec.

[2] Saint-Vallier, *État Présent,* 91, 92 (Quebec, 1856).

Chapter X

RETURN OF FRONTENAC

Versailles • Frontenac and the King • Frontenac sails for Quebec • Projected Conquest of New York • Designs of the King • Failure • Energy of Frontenac • Fort Frontenac • Panic • Negotiations • The Iroquois in Council • Chevalier d'Aux • Taunts of the Indian Allies • Boldness of Frontenac • An Iroquois Defeat • Cruel Policy • The Stroke parried

THE SUN of Louis XIV. had reached its zenith. From a morning of unexampled brilliancy it had mounted to the glare of a cloudless noon; but the hour of its decline was near. The mortal enemy of France was on the throne of England, turning against her from that new point of vantage all the energies of his unconquerable genius. An invalid built the Bourbon monarchy, and another invalid battered and defaced the imposing structure: two potent and daring spirits in two frail bodies, Richelieu and William of Orange.

Versailles gave no sign of waning glories. On three evenings of the week, it was the pleasure of the king that the whole court should assemble in the vast suite of apartments now known as the Halls of Abundance, of Venus, of Diana, of Mars, of Mercury, and of Apollo. The magnificence of their decorations, pictures of the great Italian masters, sculptures, frescoes, mosaics, tapestries, vases and statues of silver and gold; the vista of light and splendor that opened through the wide portals; the courtly throngs, feasting, dancing, gaming, promenading, conversing, formed a scene which no palace of Europe could rival or approach. Here were all the great historic names of France, princes, warriors, statesmen, and all that was highest in rank and place; the flower, in short, of that brilliant society, so dazzling, captivating, and illusory. In former years, the king was usually present, affable and gracious, mingling with his courtiers and sharing their amusements; but he had grown graver of late, and was more often in his cabinet, laboring with his ministers on the task of administration, which his extravagance and ambition made every day more burdensome.[1]

There was one corner of the world where his emblem, the sun, would not shine on him. He had done his best for Canada, and had got nothing for his pains but news of mishaps and troubles. He was growing tired of the colony which he had nursed with paternal fondness, and he was more than half angry with it because it did not prosper. Denonville's letters had grown worse and worse; and, though he had not heard as yet of the last great calamity, he was sated with ill tidings already.

Count Frontenac stood before him. Since his recall, he had lived at court, needy and no longer in favor; but he had influential friends, and an intriguing wife, always ready to serve him. The king knew his merits as well as his faults; and, in the desperate state of his Canadian affairs, he had been led to the resolution of restoring him to the command from which, for excellent reasons, he had removed him seven years before. He now told him that, in his belief, the charges brought against him were without foundation.[2] "I send you back to Canada," he is reported to have said, "where I am sure that you will serve me as well as you did before; and I ask nothing more of you."[3] The post was not a tempting one to a man in his seventieth year. Alone and unsupported,—for the king, with Europe rising against him, would give him no more troops,—he was to restore the prostrate colony to hope and courage, and fight two enemies with a force that had proved no match for one of them alone. The audacious count trusted himself, and undertook the task; received the royal instructions, and took his last leave of the master whom even he after a fashion honored and admired.

[1] Saint-Simon speaks of these assemblies. The halls in question were finished in 1682; and a minute account of them, and of the particular use to which each was destined, was printed in the *Mercure Français* of that year. See also Soulié, *Notice du Musée impérial de Versailles*, where copious extracts from the *Mercure* are given. The *grands appartements* are now entirely changed in appearance, and turned into an historic picture gallery.

[2] *Journal de Dangeau*, II. 390. Frontenac, since his recall, had not been wholly without marks of royal favor. In 1685, the king gave him a "gratification" of 3,500 francs. *Ibid.*, I. 205.

[3] Goyer, *Oraison Funèbre du Comte de Frontenac*.

He repaired to Rochelle, where two ships of the royal navy were waiting his arrival, embarked in one of them, and sailed for the New World. An heroic remedy had been prepared for the sickness of Canada, and Frontenac was to be the surgeon. The cure, however, was not of his contriving. Denonville had sent Callières, his second in command, to represent the state of the colony to the court, and beg for help. Callières saw that there was little hope of more troops or any considerable supply of money; and he laid before the king a plan, which had at least the recommendations of boldness and cheapness. This was to conquer New York with the forces already in Canada, aided only by two ships of war. The blow, he argued, should be struck at once, and the English taken by surprise. A thousand regulars and six hundred Canadian militia should pass Lake Champlain and Lake George in canoes and bateaux, cross to the Hudson and capture Albany, where they would seize all the river craft and descend the Hudson to the town of New York, which, as Callières stated, had then about two hundred houses and four hundred fighting men. The two ships were to cruise at the mouth of the harbor, and wait the arrival of the troops, which was to be made known to them by concerted signals, whereupon they were to enter and aid in the attack. The whole expedition, he thought, might be accomplished in a month; so that by the end of October the king would be master of all the country. The advantages were manifold. The Iroquois, deprived of English arms and ammunition, would be at the mercy of the French; the question of English rivalry in the west would be settled for ever; the king would acquire a means of access to his colony incomparably better than the St. Lawrence, and one that remained open all the year; and, finally, New England would be isolated, and prepared for a possible conquest in the future.

The king accepted the plan with modifications, which complicated and did not improve it. Extreme precautions were taken to insure secrecy; but the vast distances, the difficult navigation, and the accidents of weather appear to have been forgotten in this amended scheme of operation. There was, moreover, a long delay in fitting the two ships for sea. The wind was ahead, and they were fifty-two days in reaching Chedabucto, at the eastern end of Nova Scotia. Thence Frontenac and Callières had orders to proceed in a merchant ship to Quebec, which might require a month more; and, on arriving, they were to prepare for the expedition, while at the same time Frontenac was to send back a letter to the naval commander at Chedabucto, revealing the plan to him, and ordering him to sail to New York to co-operate in it. It was the twelfth of September when Chedabucto was reached, and the enterprise was ruined by the delay. Frontenac's first step in his new government was a failure, though one for which he was in no way answerable.[1]

It will be well to observe what were the intentions of the king towards the colony which he proposed to conquer. They were as follows: If any Catholics were found in New York, they might be left undisturbed, provided that they took an oath of allegiance to the king. Officers, and other persons who had the means of paying ransoms, were to be thrown into prison. All lands in the colony, except those of Catholics swearing allegiance, were to be taken from their owners, and granted under a feudal tenure to the French officers and soldiers. All property, public or private, was to be seized, a portion of it given to the grantees of the land, and the rest sold on account of the king. Mechanics and other workmen might, at the discretion of the commanding officer, be kept as prisoners to work at fortifications and do other labor. The rest of the English and Dutch inhabitants, men, women, and children, were to be carried out of the colony and dispersed in New England, Pennsylvania, or other places, in such a manner that they could not combine in any attempt to recover their property and their country. And, that the conquest might be perfectly secure, the nearest settlements of New En-

[1] *Projet du Chevalier de Callières de former une Expédition pour aller attaquer Orange, Manatte, etc.; Résumé du Ministre sur la Proposition de M. de Callières; Autre Mémoire de M. de Callières sur son Projet d'attaquer la Nouvelle York; Mémoire des Armes, Munitions, et Ustensiles nécessaires pour l'Entreprise proposée par M. de Callières; Observations du Ministre sur le Projet et le Mémoire ci-dessus; Observations du Ministre sur le Projet d'Attaque de la Nouvelle York; Autre Mémoire de M. de Callières au Sujet de l'Entreprise proposée; Autre Mémoire de M. de Callières sur le même Sujet.*

gland were to be destroyed, and those more remote laid under contribution.[1]

In the next century, some of the people of Acadia were torn from their homes by order of a British commander. The act was harsh and violent, and the innocent were involved with the guilty; but many of the sufferers had provoked their fate, and deserved it.

Louis XIV. commanded that eighteen thousand unoffending persons should be stripped of all that they possessed, and cast out to the mercy of the wilderness. The atrocity of the plan is matched by its folly. The king gave explicit orders, but he gave neither ships nor men enough to accomplish them; and the Dutch farmers, goaded to desperation, would have cut his sixteen hundred soldiers to pieces. It was the scheme of a man blinded by a long course of success. Though perverted by flattery and hardened by unbridled power, he was not cruel by nature; and here, as in the burning of the Palatinate and the persecution of the Huguenots, he would have stood aghast, if his dull imagination could have pictured to him the miseries he was preparing to inflict.[2]

With little hope left that the grand enterprise against New

---

[1] *Mémoire pour servir d'Instruction à Monsieur le Comte de Frontenac sur l'Entreprise de la Nouvelle York, 7 Juin, 1689.* "Si parmy les habitans de la Nouvelle York il se trouve des Catholiques de la fidelité desquels il croye se pouvoir asseurer, il pourra les laisser dans leurs habitations après leur avoir fait prester serment de fidelité à sa Majesté. . . . Il pourra aussi garder, s'il le juge à propos, des artisans et autres gens de service nécessaires pour la culture des terres ou pour travailler aux fortifications en qualité de prisonniers . . . . Il faut retenir en prison les officiers et les principaux habitans desquels on pourra retirer des rançons. A l'esgard de tous les autres estrangers (*ceux qui ne sont pas Français*) hommes, femmes, et enfans, sa Majesté trouve à propos qu'ils soient mis hors de la Colonie et envoyez à la Nouvelle Angleterre, à la Pennsylvanie, ou en d'autres endroits qu'il jugera à propos, par mer ou par terre, ensemble ou séparément, le tout suivant qu'il trouvera plus seur pour les dissiper et empescher qu'en se réunissant ils ne puissent donner occasion à des entreprises de la part des ennemis contre cette Colonie. Il envoyera en France les Français fugitifs qu'il y pourra trouver, et particulièrement ceux de la Religion Prétendue-Reformée (*Huguenots*)." A translation of the entire document will be found in *N. Y. Col. Docs.*, IX. 422.

[2] On the details of the projected attack of New York, *Le Roy à Denonville, 7 Juin, 1689; Le Ministre à Denonville, même date; Le Ministre à Frontenac, même date; Ordre du Roy à Vaudreuil, même date; Le Roy au Sieur de la Caffinière, même date; Champigny au Ministre, 16 Nov., 1689.*

York could succeed, Frontenac made sail for Quebec, and, stopping by the way at Isle Percée, learned from Récollet missionaries the irruption of the Iroquois at Montreal. He hastened on; but the wind was still against him, and the autumn woods were turning brown before he reached his destination. It was evening when he landed, amid fireworks, illuminations, and the firing of cannon. All Quebec came to meet him by torchlight; the members of the council offered their respects, and the Jesuits made him an harangue of welcome.[1] It was but a welcome of words. They and the councillors had done their best to have him recalled, and hoped that they were rid of him for ever; but now he was among them again, rasped by the memory of real or fancied wrongs. The count, however, had no time for quarrelling. The king had told him to bury old animosities and forget the past, and for the present he was too busy to break the royal injunction.[2] He caused boats to be made ready, and in spite of incessant rains pushed up the river to Montreal. Here he found Denonville and his frightened wife. Every thing was in confusion. The Iroquois were gone, leaving dejection and terror behind them. Frontenac reviewed the troops. There were seven or eight hundred of them in the town, the rest being in garrison at the various forts. Then he repaired to what was once La Chine, and surveyed the miserable waste of ashes and desolation that spread for miles around.

To his extreme disgust, he learned that Denonville had sent a Canadian officer by secret paths to Fort Frontenac, with orders to Valrenne, the commandant, to blow it up, and return with his garrison to Montreal. Frontenac had built the fort, had given it his own name, and had cherished it with a paternal fondness, reinforced by strong hopes of making money out of it. For its sake he had become the butt of scandal and opprobrium; but not the less had he always stood its strenuous and passionate champion. An Iroquois envoy had lately with great insolence demanded its destruction of Denonville; and this alone, in the eyes of Frontenac, was ample reason for maintaining it at any cost.[3] He still had hope that

[1] La Hontan, I. 199.
[2] *Instruction pour le Sieur Comte de Frontenac, 7 Juin, 1689.*
[3] *Frontenac au Ministre, 15 Nov., 1689.*

it might be saved, and with all the energy of youth he proceeded to collect canoes, men, provisions, and arms; battled against dejection, insubordination, and fear, and in a few days despatched a convoy of three hundred men to relieve the place, and stop the execution of Denonville's orders. His orders had been but too promptly obeyed. The convoy was scarcely gone an hour, when, to Frontenac's unutterable wrath, Valrenne appeared with his garrison. He reported that he had set fire to every thing in the fort that would burn, sunk the three vessels belonging to it, thrown the cannon into the lake, mined the walls and bastions, and left matches burning in the powder magazine; and, further, that when he and his men were five leagues on their way to Montreal a dull and distant explosion told them that the mines had sprung. It proved afterwards that the destruction was not complete; and the Iroquois took possession of the abandoned fort, with a large quantity of stores and munitions left by the garrison in their too hasty retreat.[1]

There was one ray of light through the clouds. The unwonted news of a victory came to Montreal. It was small, but decisive, and might be an earnest of greater things to come. Before Frontenac's arrival, Denonville had sent a reconnoitring party up the Ottawa. They had gone no farther than the Lake of Two Mountains, when they met twenty-two Iroquois in two large canoes, who immediately bore down upon them, yelling furiously. The French party consisted of twenty-eight *coureurs de bois* under Du Lhut and Mantet, excellent partisan chiefs, who manœuvred so well that the rising sun blazed full in the eyes of the advancing enemy, and spoiled their aim. The French received their fire, which wounded one man; then, closing with them while their guns were empty, gave them a volley, which killed and wounded eighteen of their number. One swam ashore. The remaining three were captured, and given to the Indian allies to be burned.[2]

This gleam of sunshine passed, and all grew black again.

---

[1] *Frontenac au Ministre, 15 Nov., 1689; Recueil de ce qui s'est passé en Canada depuis l'année 1682.*

[2] *Frontenac au Ministre, 15 Nov., 1689; Champigny au Ministre, 16 Nov., 1689.* Compare Belmont, whose account is a little different; also *N. Y. Col. Docs.*, IX. 435.

On a snowy November day, a troop of Iroquois fell on the settlement of La Chesnaye, burned the houses, and vanished with a troop of prisoners, leaving twenty mangled corpses on the snow.[1] "The terror," wrote the bishop, "is indescribable." The appearance of a few savages would put a whole neighborhood to flight.[2] So desperate, wrote Frontenac, were the needs of the colony, and so great the contempt with which the Iroquois regarded it, that it almost needed a miracle either to carry on war or make peace. What he most earnestly wished was to keep the Iroquois quiet, and so leave his hands free to deal with the English. This was not easy, to such a pitch of audacity had late events raised them. Neither his temper nor his convictions would allow him to beg peace of them, like his predecessor; but he had inordinate trust in the influence of his name, and he now took a course which he hoped might answer his purpose without increasing their insolence. The perfidious folly of Denonville in seizing their countrymen at Fort Frontenac had been a prime cause of their hostility; and, at the request of the late governor, the surviving captives, thirteen in all, had been taken from the galleys, gorgeously clad in French attire, and sent back to Canada in the ship which carried Frontenac. Among them was a famous Cayuga war-chief called Ourehaoué, whose loss had infuriated the Iroquois.[3] Frontenac gained his good-will on the voyage; and, when they reached Quebec, he lodged him in the château, and treated him with such kindness that the chief became his devoted admirer and friend. As his influence was great among his people, Frontenac hoped that he might use him with success to bring about an accommodation. He placed three of the captives at the disposal of the Cayuga, who forthwith sent them to Onondaga with a message which the governor had dictated, and which was to the following effect: "The great Onontio, whom you all know, has come back again. He does not blame you for what you

[1] Belmont, *Histoire du Canada; Frontenac à* ———, *17 Nov., 1689; Champigny au Ministre, 16 Nov., 1689.* This letter is not the one just cited. Champigny wrote twice on the same day.

[2] *N. Y. Col. Docs.*, IX. 435.

[3] Ourehaoué was not one of the neutrals entrapped at Fort Frontenac, but was seized about the same time by the troops on their way up the St. Lawrence.

have done; for he looks upon you as foolish children, and blames only the English, who are the cause of your folly, and have made you forget your obedience to a father who has always loved and never deceived you. He will permit me, Ourehaoué, to return to you as soon as you will come to ask for me, not as you have spoken of late, but like children speaking to a father."[1] Frontenac hoped that they would send an embassy to reclaim their chief, and thus give him an opportunity to use his personal influence over them. With the three released captives, he sent an Iroquois convert named Cut Nose with a wampum belt to announce his return.

When the deputation arrived at Onondaga and made known their errand, the Iroquois magnates, with their usual deliberation, deferred answering till a general council of the confederacy should have time to assemble; and, meanwhile, they sent messengers to ask the mayor of Albany, and others of their Dutch and English friends, to come to the meeting. They did not comply, merely sending the government interpreter, with a few Mohawk Indians, to represent their interests. On the other hand, the Jesuit Milet, who had been captured a few months before, adopted, and made an Oneida chief, used every effort to second the designs of Frontenac. The authorities of Albany tried in vain to induce the Iroquois to place him in their hands. They understood their interests too well, and held fast to the Jesuit.[2]

The grand council took place at Onondaga on the twenty-second of January. Eighty chiefs and sachems, seated gravely on mats around the council fire, smoked their pipes in silence for a while; till at length an Onondaga orator rose, and announced that Frontenac, the old Onontio, had returned with Ourehaoué and twelve more of their captive friends, that he meant to rekindle the council fire at Fort Frontenac, and that he invited them to meet him there.[3]

[1] *Frontenac au Ministre, 30 Avril, 1690.*

[2] Milet was taken in 1689, not, as has been supposed, in 1690. *Lettre du Père Milet, 1691*, printed by Shea.

[3] Frontenac declares that he sent no such message, and intimates that Cut Nose had been tampered with by persons over-anxious to conciliate the Iroquois, and who had even gone so far as to send them messages on their own account. These persons were Lamberville, François Hertel, and one of the Le Moynes. Frontenac was very angry at this interference, to which he ascribes

"Ho, ho, ho," returned the eighty senators, from the bottom of their throats. It was the unfailing Iroquois response to a speech. Then Cut Nose, the governor's messenger, addressed the council: "I advise you to meet Onontio as he desires. Do so, if you wish to live." He presented a wampum belt to confirm his words, and the conclave again returned the same guttural ejaculation.

"Ourehaoué sends you this," continued Cut Nose, presenting another belt of wampum: "by it he advises you to listen to Onontio, if you wish to live."

When the messenger from Canada had ceased, the messenger from Albany, a Mohawk Indian, rose and repeated word for word a speech confided to him by the mayor of that town, urging the Iroquois to close their ears against the invitations of Onontio.

Next rose one Cannehoot, a sachem of the Senecas, charged with matters of grave import; for they involved no less than the revival of that scheme, so perilous to the French, of the union of the tribes of the Great Lakes in a triple alliance with the Iroquois and the English. These lake tribes, disgusted with the French, who, under Denonville, had left them to the mercy of the Iroquois, had been impelled, both by their fears and their interests, to make new advances to the confederacy, and had first addressed themselves to the Senecas, whom they had most cause to dread. They had given up some of the Iroquois prisoners in their hands, and promised soon to give up the rest. A treaty had been made; and it was this event which the Seneca sachem now announced to the council. Having told the story to his assembled colleagues, he exhibited and explained the wampum belts and other tokens brought by the envoys from the lakes, who represented nine distinct tribes or bands from the region of Michillimackinac. By these tokens, the nine tribes declared that they came to learn wisdom of the Iroquois and the English; to wash off the war-paint, throw down the tomahawk, smoke the pipe of peace, and unite with them as one body. "Onontio is drunk," such was the interpretation of the fourth wampum belt; "but

---

the most mischievous consequences. Cut Nose, or Nez Coupé, is called Adarahta by Colden, and Gagniegaton, or Red Bird, by some French writers.

we, the tribes of Michillimackinac, wash our hands of all his actions. Neither we nor you must defile ourselves by listening to him." When the Seneca sachem had ended, and when the ejaculations that echoed his words had ceased, the belts were hung up before all the assembly, then taken down again, and distributed among the sachems of the five Iroquois tribes, excepting one, which was given to the messengers from Albany. Thus was concluded the triple alliance, which to Canada meant no less than ruin.

"Brethren," said an Onondaga sachem, "we must hold fast to our brother Quider (*Peter Schuyler, mayor of Albany*), and look on Onontio as our enemy, for he is a cheat."

Then they invited the interpreter from Albany to address the council, which he did, advising them not to listen to the envoys from Canada. When he had ended, they spent some time in consultation among themselves, and at length agreed on the following message, addressed to Corlaer, or New York, and to Kinshon, the Fish, by which they meant New England, the authorities of which had sent them the image of a fish as a token of alliance:[1] —

"Brethren, our council fire burns at Albany. We will not go to meet Onontio at Fort Frontenac. We will hold fast to the old chain of peace with Corlaer, and we will fight with Onontio. Brethren, we are glad to hear from you that you are preparing to make war on Canada, but tell us no lies.

"Brother Kinshon, we hear that you mean to send soldiers against the Indians to the eastward; but we advise you, now that we are all united against the French, to fall upon them at once. Strike at the root: when the trunk is cut down, all the branches fall with it.

"Courage, Corlaer! courage, Kinshon! Go to Quebec in the spring; take it, and you will have your feet on the necks of the French and all their friends."

Then they consulted together again, and agreed on the following answer to Ourehaoué and Frontenac: —

"Ourehaoué, the whole council is glad to hear that you have come back.

"Onontio, you have told us that you have come back again,

---

[1] The wooden image of a codfish still hangs in the State House at Boston, the emblem of a colony which lived chiefly by the fisheries.

and brought with you thirteen of our people who were carried prisoners to France. We are glad of it. You wish to speak with us at Cataraqui (*Fort Frontenac*). Don't you know that your council fire there is put out? It is quenched in blood. You must first send home the prisoners. When our brother Ourehaoué is returned to us, then we will talk with you of peace. You must send him and the others home this very winter. We now let you know that we have made peace with the tribes of Michillimackinac. You are not to think, because we return you an answer, that we have laid down the tomahawk. Our warriors will continue the war till you send our countrymen back to us."[1]

The messengers from Canada returned with this reply. Unsatisfactory as it was, such a quantity of wampum was sent with it as showed plainly the importance attached by the Iroquois to the matters in question. Encouraged by a recent success against the English, and still possessed with an overweening confidence in his own influence over the confederates, Frontenac resolved that Ourehaoué should send them another message. The chief, whose devotion to the count never wavered, accordingly despatched four envoys, with a load of wampum belts, expressing his astonishment that his countrymen had not seen fit to send a deputation of chiefs to receive him from the hands of Onontio, and calling upon them to do so without delay, lest he should think that they had forgotten him. Along with the messengers, Frontenac ventured to send the Chevalier d'Aux, a half-pay officer, with orders to observe the disposition of the Iroquois, and impress them in private talk with a sense of the count's power, of his good-will to them, and of the wisdom of coming to terms with him, lest, like an angry father, he should be forced at last to use the rod. The chevalier's reception was a warm one.

[1] The account of this council is given, with condensation and the omission of parts not essential, from Colden (105–112, ed. 1747). It will serve as an example of the Iroquois method of conducting political business, the habitual regularity and decorum of which has drawn from several contemporary French writers the remark that in such matters the five tribes were savages only in name. The reply to Frontenac is also given by Monseignat (*N. Y. Col. Docs.*, IX. 465), and, after him, by La Potherie. Compare Le Clercq, *Établissement de la Foy*, II. 403. Ourehaoué is the Tawerahet of Colden.

They burned two of his attendants, forced him to run the gauntlet, and, after a vigorous thrashing, sent him prisoner to Albany. The last failure was worse than the first. The count's name was great among the Iroquois, but he had trusted its power too far.[1]

The worst of news had come from Michillimackinac. La Durantaye, the commander of the post, and Carheil, the Jesuit, had sent a messenger to Montreal in the depth of winter to say that the tribes around them were on the point of revolt. Carheil wrote that they threatened openly to throw themselves into the arms of the Iroquois and the English; that they declared that the protection of Onontio was an illusion and a snare; that they once mistook the French for warriors, but saw now that they were no match for the Iroquois, whom they had tamely allowed to butcher them at Montreal, without even daring to defend themselves; that when the French invaded the Senecas they did nothing but cut down corn and break canoes, and since that time they had done nothing but beg peace for themselves, forgetful of their allies, whom they expected to bear the brunt of the war, and then left to their fate; that they had surrendered through cowardice the prisoners they had caught by treachery, and this, too, at a time when the Iroquois were burning French captives in all their towns; and, finally, that, as the French would not or could not make peace for them, they would make peace for themselves. "These," pursued Carheil, "are the reasons they give us to prove the necessity of their late embassy to the Senecas; and by this one can see that our Indians are a great deal more clear-sighted than they are thought to be, and that it is hard to conceal from their penetration any thing that can help or harm their interests. What is certain is that, if the Iroquois are not stopped, they will not fail to come and make themselves masters here."[2]

Charlevoix thinks that Frontenac was not displeased at this bitter arraignment of his predecessor's administration. At the

[1] *Message of Ourehaoué*, in *N. Y. Col. Docs.*, III. 735; *Instructions to Chevalier d'Eau*, *Ibid.*, 733; *Chevalier d'Aux au Ministre, 15 Mai, 1693.* The chevalier's name is also written *d'O*. He himself wrote it as in the text.

[2] *Carheil à Frontenac, 1690.* Frontenac did not receive this letter till September, and acted on the information previously sent him. Charlevoix's version of the letter does not conform with the original.

same time, his position was very embarrassing. He had no men to spare; but such was the necessity of saving Michilli-mackinac, and breaking off the treaty with the Senecas, that when spring opened he sent Captain Louvigny with a hundred and forty-three Canadians and six Indians to rein-force the post and replace its commander, La Durantaye. Two other officers with an additional force were ordered to accom-pany him through the most dangerous part of the journey. With them went Nicolas Perrot, bearing a message from the count to his rebellious children of Michillimackinac. The fol-lowing was the pith of this characteristic document: —

"I am astonished to learn that you have forgotten the pro-tection that I always gave you. Do you think that I am no longer alive; or that I have a mind to stand idle, like those who have been here in my place? Or do you think that, if eight or ten hairs have been torn from my children's heads when I was absent, I cannot put ten handfuls of hair in the place of every one that was pulled out? You know that before I protected you the ravenous Iroquois dog was biting every-body. I tamed him and tied him up; but, when he no longer saw me, he behaved worse than ever. If he persists, he shall feel my power. The English have tried to win him by flatter-ies, but I will kill all who encourage him. The English have deceived and devoured their children, but I am a good father who loves you. I loved the Iroquois once, because they obeyed me. When I knew that they had been treacherously captured and carried to France, I set them free; and, when I restore them to their country, it will not be through fear, but through pity, for I hate treachery. I am strong enough to kill the English, destroy the Iroquois, and whip you, if you fail in your duty to me. The Iroquois have killed and captured you in time of peace. Do to them as they have done to you, do to the English as they would like to do to you, but hold fast to your true father, who will never abandon you. Will you let the English brandy that has killed you in your wigwams lure you into the kettles of the Iroquois? Is not mine better, which has never killed you, but always made you strong?"[1]

[1] *Parole (de M. de Frontenac) qui doit être dite à l'Outaouais pour le dissuader de l'Alliance qu'il veut faire avec l'Iroquois et l'Anglois.* The message is long. Only the principal points are given above.

Charged with this haughty missive, Perrot set out for Michillimackinac along with Louvigny and his men. On their way up the Ottawa, they met a large band of Iroquois hunters, whom they routed with heavy loss. Nothing could have been more auspicious for Perrot's errand. When towards mid-summer they reached their destination, they ranged their canoes in a triumphal procession, placed in the foremost an Iroquois captured in the fight, forced him to dance and sing, hung out the *fleur-de-lis*, shouted *Vive le Roi*, whooped, yelled, and fired their guns. As they neared the village of the Ottawas, all the naked population ran down to the shore, leaping, yelping, and firing, in return. Louvigny and his men passed on, and landed at the neighboring village of the French settlers, who, drawn up in battle array on the shore, added more yells and firing to the general uproar; though, amid this joyous fusillade of harmless gunpowder, they all kept their bullets ready for instant use, for they distrusted the savage multitude. The story of the late victory, however, confirmed as it was by an imposing display of scalps, produced an effect which averted the danger of an immediate outbreak.

The fate of the Iroquois prisoner now became the point at issue. The French hoped that the Indians in their excitement could be induced to put him to death, and thus break their late treaty with his countrymen. Besides the Ottawas, there was at Michillimackinac a village of Hurons under their crafty chief, the Rat. They had pretended to stand fast for the French, who nevertheless believed them to be at the bottom of all the mischief. They now begged for the prisoner, promising to burn him. On the faith of this pledge, he was given to them; but they broke their word, and kept him alive, in order to curry favor with the Iroquois. The Ottawas, intensely jealous of the preference shown to the Hurons, declared in their anger that the prisoner ought to be killed and eaten. This was precisely what the interests of the French demanded; but the Hurons still persisted in protecting him. Their Jesuit missionary now interposed, and told them that, unless they "put the Iroquois into the kettle," the French would take him from them. After much discussion, this argument prevailed. They planted a stake, tied him to it, and

began to torture him; but, as he did not show the usual fortitude of his countrymen, they declared him unworthy to die
the death of a warrior, and accordingly shot him.[1]

Here was a point gained for the French, but the danger
was not passed. The Ottawas could disavow the killing of the
Iroquois; and, in fact, though there was a great division of
opinion among them, they were preparing at this very time
to send a secret embassy to the Seneca country to ratify the
fatal treaty. The French commanders called a council of all
the tribes. It met at the house of the Jesuits. Presents in abundance were distributed. The message of Frontenac was reinforced by persuasion and threats; and the assembly was told
that the five tribes of the Iroquois were like five nests of
muskrats in a marsh, which the French would drain dry, and
then burn with all its inhabitants. Perrot took the disaffected
chiefs aside, and with his usual bold adroitness diverted them
for the moment from their purpose. The projected embassy
was stopped, but any day might revive it. There was no safety
for the French, and the ground of Michillimackinac was hollow under their feet. Every thing depended on the success of
their arms. A few victories would confirm their wavering allies; but the breath of another defeat would blow the fickle
crew over to the enemy like a drift of dry leaves.

[1] "Le Père Missionnaire des Hurons, prévoyant que cette affaire auroit
peut-être une suite qui pourrait être préjudiciable aux soins qu'il prenoit de
leur instruction, demanda qu'il lui fut permis d'aller à leur village pour les
obliger de trouver quelque moyen qui fut capable d'appaiser le ressentiment
des François. Il leur dit que ceux-ci vouloient absolument que l'on mit *l'Iroquois à la chaudière*, et que si on ne le faisoit, on devoit venir le leur enlever."
La Potherie, II. 237 (1722). By the "result prejudicial to his cares for their
instruction" he seems to mean their possible transfer from French to English
influences. The expression *mettre à la chaudière*, though derived from canni-
bal practices, is often used figuratively for torturing and killing. The missionary in question was either Carheil or another Jesuit, who must have acted
with his sanction.

Chapter XI

1690

THE THREE WAR-PARTIES

Measures of Frontenac • Expedition against Schenectady • The March • The Dutch Village • The Surprise • The Massacre • Prisoners spared • Retreat • The English and their Iroquois Friends • The Abenaki War • Revolution at Boston • Capture of Pemaquid • Capture of Salmon Falls • Capture of Fort Loyal • Frontenac and his Prisoner • The Canadians encouraged

WHILE STRIVING to reclaim his allies, Frontenac had not forgotten his enemies. It was of the last necessity to revive the dashed spirits of the Canadians and the troops; and action, prompt and bold, was the only means of doing so. He resolved, therefore, to take the offensive, not against the Iroquois, who seemed invulnerable as ghosts, but against the English; and by striking a few sharp and rapid blows to teach both friends and foes that Onontio was still alive. The effect of his return had already begun to appear, and the energy and fire of the undaunted veteran had shot new life into the dejected population. He formed three war-parties of picked men, one at Montreal, one at Three Rivers, and one at Quebec; the first to strike at Albany, the second at the border settlements of New Hampshire, and the third at those of Maine. That of Montreal was ready first. It consisted of two hundred and ten men, of whom ninety-six were Indian converts, chiefly from the two mission villages of Saut St. Louis and the Mountain of Montreal. They were Christian Iroquois whom the priests had persuaded to leave their homes and settle in Canada, to the great indignation of their heathen countrymen, and the great annoyance of the English colonists, to whom they were a constant menace. When Denonville attacked the Senecas, they had joined him; but of late they had shown reluctance to fight their heathen kinsmen, with whom the French even suspected them of collusion. Against the English, however, they willingly took up the hatchet. The French of the party were for the most part *coureurs de bois*. As the sea is the sailor's element, so the forest was theirs. Their merits were hardihood and skill in woodcraft; their chief faults were insubordination and lawlessness. They had shared the general demoralization that followed the inroad of the Iroquois, and under Denonville had proved mutinous and unmanageable. In the best times, it was a hard task to command them, and one that needed, not bravery alone, but tact, address, and experience. Under a chief of such a stamp, they were admirable bush-fighters, and such were those now chosen to lead them. D'Aillebout de Mantet and Le Moyne de Sainte-Hélène, the brave son of Charles Le Moyne, had the chief command, supported by the brothers Le Moyne d'Iberville and Le Moyne de Bienville, with Repentigny de Montesson, Le Ber du Chesne, and others of the sturdy Canadian *noblesse*, nerved by adventure and trained in Indian warfare.[1]

It was the depth of winter when they began their march, striding on snow-shoes over the vast white field of the frozen St. Lawrence, each with the hood of his blanket coat drawn over his head, a gun in his mittened hand, a knife, a hatchet, a tobacco pouch, and a bullet pouch at his belt, a pack on his shoulders, and his inseparable pipe hung at his neck in a leather case. They dragged their blankets and provisions over the snow on Indian sledges. Crossing the forest to Chambly, they advanced four or five days up the frozen Richelieu and the frozen Lake Champlain, and then stopped to hold a council. Frontenac had left the precise point of attack at the discretion of the leaders, and thus far the men had been ignorant of their destination. The Indians demanded to know it. Mantet and Sainte-Hélène replied that they were going to Albany. The Indians demurred. "How long is it," asked one of them, "since the French grew so bold?" The commanders answered that, to regain the honor of which their late misfortunes had robbed them, the French would take Albany or die in the attempt. The Indians listened sullenly; the decision was postponed, and the party moved forward again. When after eight

[1] *Relation de Monseignat, 1689-90.* There is a translation of this valuable paper in *N. Y. Col. Docs.*, IX. 462. The party, according to three of their number, consisted at first of 160 French and 140 Christian Indians, but was reduced by sickness and desertion to 250 in all. *Examination of three French prisoners taken by y^e. Maquas (Mohawks), and brought to Skinnectady, who were examined by Peter Schuyler, Mayor of Albany, Domine Godevridus Dellius, and some of y^e. Gentle^n. that went from Albany a purpose.*

days they reached the Hudson, and found the place where two paths diverged, the one for Albany and the other for Schenectady, they all without farther words took the latter. Indeed, to attempt Albany would have been an act of desperation. The march was horrible. There was a partial thaw, and they waded knee-deep through the half melted snow, and the mingled ice, mud, and water of the gloomy swamps. So painful and so slow was their progress, that it was nine days more before they reached a point two leagues from Schenectady. The weather had changed again, and a cold, gusty snowstorm pelted them. It was one of those days when the trees stand white as spectres in the sheltered hollows of the forest, and bare and gray on the wind-swept ridges. The men were half dead with cold, fatigue, and hunger. It was four in the afternoon of the eighth of February. The scouts found an Indian hut, and in it were four Iroquois squaws, whom they captured. There was a fire in the wigwam; and the shivering Canadians crowded about it, stamping their chilled feet and warming their benumbed hands over the blaze. The Christian chief of the Saut St. Louis, known as Le Grand Agnié, or the Great Mohawk, by the French, and by the Dutch called Kryn, harangued his followers, and exhorted them to wash out their wrongs in blood. Then they all advanced again, and about dark reached the river Mohawk, a little above the village. A Canadian named Gignières, who had gone with nine Indians to reconnoitre, now returned to say that he had been within sight of Schenectady, and had seen nobody. Their purpose had been to postpone the attack till two o'clock in the morning; but the situation was intolerable, and the limit of human endurance was reached. They could not make fires, and they must move on or perish. Guided by the frightened squaws, they crossed the Mohawk on the ice, toiling through the drifts amid the whirling snow that swept down the valley of the darkened stream, till about eleven o'clock they descried through the storm the snow-beplastered palisades of the devoted village. Such was their plight that some of them afterwards declared that they would all have surrendered if an enemy had appeared to summon them.[1]

Schenectady was the farthest outpost of the colony of New

[1] Colden, 114 (ed. 1747).

York. Westward lay the Mohawk forests; and Orange, or Albany, was fifteen miles or more towards the south-east. The village was oblong in form, and enclosed by a palisade which had two gates, one towards Albany and the other towards the Mohawks. There was a blockhouse near the eastern gate, occupied by eight or nine Connecticut militia men under Lieutenant Talmage. There were also about thirty friendly Mohawks in the place, on a visit. The inhabitants, who were all Dutch, were in a state of discord and confusion. The revolution in England had produced a revolution in New York. The demagogue Jacob Leisler had got possession of Fort William, and was endeavoring to master the whole colony. Albany was in the hands of the anti-Leisler or conservative party, represented by a convention of which Peter Schuyler was the chief. The Dutch of Schenectady for the most part favored Leisler, whose emissaries had been busily at work among them; but their chief magistrate, John Sander Glen, a man of courage and worth, stood fast for the Albany convention, and in consequence the villagers had threatened to kill him. Talmage and his Connecticut militia were under orders from Albany; and therefore, like Glen, they were under the popular ban. In vain the magistrate and the officer entreated the people to stand on their guard. They turned the advice to ridicule, laughed at the idea of danger, left both their gates wide open, and placed there, it is said, two snow images as mock sentinels. A French account declares that the village contained eighty houses, which is certainly an exaggeration. There had been some festivity during the evening, but it was now over; and the primitive villagers, fathers, mothers, children, and infants, lay buried in unconscious sleep. They were simple peasants and rude woodsmen, but with human affections and capable of human woe.

The French and Indians stood before the open gate, with its blind and dumb warder, the mock sentinel of snow. Iberville went with a detachment to find the Albany gate, and bar it against the escape of fugitives; but he missed it in the gloom, and hastened back. The assailants were now formed into two bands, Sainte-Hélène leading the one and Mantet the other. They passed through the gate together in dead silence: one turned to the right and the other to the left, and they filed around the village between the palisades and the houses till the two leaders met at the farther end. Thus the place was completely surrounded. The signal was then given: they all screeched the war-whoop together, burst in the doors with hatchets, and fell to their work. Roused by the infernal din, the villagers leaped from their beds. For some it was but a momentary nightmare of fright and horror, ended by the blow of the tomahawk. Others were less fortunate. Neither women nor children were spared. "No pen can write, and no tongue express," wrote Schuyler, "the cruelties that were committed."[1] There was little resistance, except at the block-house, where Talmage and his men made a stubborn fight; but the doors were at length forced open, the defenders killed or taken, and the building set on fire. Adam Vrooman, one of the villagers, saw his wife shot and his child brained against the door-post; but he fought so desperately that the assailants promised him his life. Orders had been given to spare Peter Tassemaker, the domine or minister, from whom it was thought that valuable information might be obtained; but he was hacked to pieces, and his house burned. Some, more agile or more fortunate than the rest, escaped at the eastern gate, and fled through the storm to seek shelter at Albany or at houses along the way. Sixty persons were killed outright, of whom thirty-eight were men and boys, ten were women, and twelve were children.[2] The number captured appears to have been between eighty and ninety. The thirty Mohawks in the town were treated with studied kindness by the victors, who declared that they had no quarrel with them, but only with the Dutch and English.

The massacre and pillage continued two hours; then the prisoners were secured, sentinels posted, and the men told to rest and refresh themselves. In the morning, a small party crossed the river to the house of Glen, which stood on a rising ground half a mile distant. It was loopholed and pali-

---

[1] "The women bigg with Childe rip'd up, and the Children alive throwne into the flames, and their heads dashed to pieces against the Doors and windows." *Schuyler to the Council of Connecticut, 15 Feb., 1690.* Similar statements are made by Leisler. See *Doc. Hist. N. Y.*, I. 307, 310.

[2] *List of y*. *People kild and destroyed by y*. *French of Canida and there Indians at Skinnechtady*, in *Doc. Hist. N. Y.*, I. 304.

saded; and Glen had mustered his servants and tenants, closed his gates, and prepared to defend himself. The French told him to fear nothing, for they had orders not to hurt a chicken of his; whereupon, after requiring them to lay down their arms, he allowed them to enter. They urged him to go with them to the village, and he complied; they on their part leaving one of their number as a hostage in the hands of his followers. Iberville appeared at the gate with the Great Mohawk, and, drawing his commission from the breast of his coat, told Glen that he was specially charged to pay a debt which the French owed him. On several occasions, he had saved the lives of French prisoners in the hands of the Mohawks; and he, with his family, and, above all, his wife, had shown them the greatest kindness. He was now led before the crowd of wretched prisoners, and told that not only were his own life and property safe, but that all his kindred should be spared. Glen stretched his privilege to the utmost, till the French Indians, disgusted at his multiplied demands for clemency, observed that everybody seemed to be his relation.

Some of the houses had already been burned. Fire was now set to the rest, excepting one, in which a French officer lay wounded, another belonging to Glen, and three or four more which he begged the victors to spare. At noon Schenectady was in ashes. Then the French and Indians withdrew, laden with booty. Thirty or forty captured horses dragged their sledges; and a troop of twenty-seven men and boys were driven prisoners into the forest. About sixty old men, women, and children were left behind, without farther injury, in order, it is said, to conciliate the Mohawks in the place, who had joined with Glen in begging that they might be spared. Of the victors, only two had been killed.[1]

[1] Many of the authorities on the burning of Schenectady will be found in the *Documentary History of New York*, I. 297–312. One of the most important is a portion of the long letter of M. de Monseignat, comptroller-general of the marine in Canada, to a lady of rank, said to be Madame de Maintenon. Others are contemporary documents preserved at Albany, including, among others, the lists of killed and captured, letters of Leisler to the governor of Maryland, the governor of Massachusetts, the governor of Barbadoes, and the Bishop of Salisbury; of Robert Livingston to Sir Edmund Andros and to Captain Nicholson; and of Mr. Van Cortlandt to Sir Edmund Andros. One of the best contemporary authorities is a letter of Schuyler and his colleagues

At the outset of the attack, Simon Schermerhorn threw himself on a horse, and galloped through the eastern gate. The French shot at and wounded him; but he escaped, reached Albany at daybreak, and gave the alarm. The soldiers and inhabitants were called to arms, cannon were fired to rouse the country, and a party of horsemen, followed by some friendly Mohawks, set out for Schenectady. The Mohawks had promised to carry the news to their three towns on the river above; but, when they reached the ruined village, they were so frightened at the scene of havoc that they would not go farther. Two days passed before the alarm reached the Mohawk towns. Then troops of warriors came down on snowshoes, equipped with tomahawk and gun, to chase the retiring French. Fifty young men from Albany joined them; and they followed the trail of the enemy, who, with the help of their horses, made such speed over the ice of Lake Champlain that it seemed impossible to overtake them. They thought the pursuit abandoned; and, having killed and eaten most of their horses, and being spent with fatigue, they moved more slowly as they neared home, when a band of Mohawks, who had followed stanchly on their track, fell upon a party of stragglers, and killed or captured fifteen or more, almost within sight of Montreal.

Three of these prisoners, examined by Schuyler, declared

---

to the governor and council of Massachusetts, 15 February, 1690, preserved in the Massachusetts archives, and printed in the third volume of Mr. Whitmore's *Andros Tracts*. La Potherie, Charlevoix, Colden, Smith, and many others, give accounts at second-hand.

Johannes Sander, or Alexander, Glen, was the son of a Scotchman of good family. He was usually known as Captain Sander. The French wrote the name *Cendre*, which became transformed into *Condre*, and then into *Coudre*. In the old family Bible of the Glens, still preserved at the placed named by them Scotia, near Schenectady, is an entry in Dutch recording the "murders" committed by the French, and the exemption accorded to Alexander Glen on account of services rendered by him and his family to French prisoners. See *Proceedings of N. Y. Hist. Soc.*, 1846, 118.

The French called Schenectady Corlaer or Corlar, from Van Curler, its founder. Its treatment at their hands was ill deserved, as its inhabitants, and notably Van Curler himself, had from the earliest times been the protectors of French captives among the Mohawks. Leisler says that only one-sixth of the inhabitants escaped unhurt.

that Frontenac was preparing for a grand attack on Albany in the spring. In the political confusion of the time, the place was not in fighting condition; and Schuyler appealed for help to the authorities of Massachusetts. "Dear neighbours and friends, we must acquaint you that nevir poor People in the world was in a worse Condition than we are at Present, no Governour nor Command, no money to forward any expedition, and scarce Men enough to maintain the Citty. We have here plainly laid the case before you, and doubt not but you will so much take it to heart, and make all Readinesse in the Spring to invade Canida by water."[1] The Mohawks were of the same mind. Their elders came down to Albany to condole with their Dutch and English friends on the late disaster. "We are come," said their orator, "with tears in our eyes, to lament the murders committed at Schenectady by the perfidious French. Onontio comes to our country to speak of peace, but war is at his heart. He has broken into our house at both ends, once among the Senecas and once here; but we hope to be revenged. Brethren, our covenant with you is a silver chain that cannot rust or break. We are of the race of the bear; and the bear does not yield, so long as there is a drop of blood in his body. Let us all be bears. We will go together with an army to ruin the country of the French. Therefore, send in all haste to New England. Let them be ready with ships and great guns to attack by water, while we attack by land."[2] Schuyler did not trust his red allies, who, however, seem on this occasion to have meant what they said. He lost no time in sending commissioners to urge the several governments of New England to a combined attack on the French.

New England needed no prompting to take up arms; for she presently learned to her cost that, though feeble and prostrate, Canada could sting. The war-party which attacked Schenectady was, as we have seen, but one of three which Frontenac had sent against the English borders. The second, aimed at New Hampshire, left Three Rivers on the twenty-

[1] *Schuyler, Wessell, and Van Rensselaer to the Governor and Council of Massachusetts, 15 Feb., 1690, in Andros Tracts, III. 114.*
[2] *Propositions made by the Sachems of y[e]. Maquase (Mohawk) Castles to y[e]. Mayor, Aldermen, and Commonality of y[e]. Citty of Albany, y[e]. 25 day of february, 1690, in Doc. Hist. N. Y., II. 164–169.*

eighth of January, commanded by François Hertel. It consisted of twenty-four Frenchmen, twenty Abenakis of the Sokoki band, and five Algonquins. After three months of excessive hardship in the vast and rugged wilderness that intervened, they approached the little settlement of Salmon Falls on the stream which separates New Hampshire from Maine; and here for a moment we leave them, to observe the state of this unhappy frontier.

It was twelve years and more since the great Indian outbreak, called King Philip's War, had carried havoc through all the borders of New England. After months of stubborn fighting, the fire was quenched in Massachusetts, Plymouth, and Connecticut; but in New Hampshire and Maine it continued to burn fiercely till the treaty of Casco, in 1678. The principal Indians of this region were the tribes known collectively as the Abenakis. The French had established relations with them through the missionaries; and now, seizing the opportunity, they persuaded many of these distressed and exasperated savages to leave the neighborhood of the English, migrate to Canada, and settle first at Sillery near Quebec and then at the falls of the Chaudière. Here the two Jesuits, Jacques and Vincent Bigot, prime agents in their removal, took them in charge; and the missions of St. Francis became villages of Abenaki Christians, like the village of Iroquois Christians at Saut St. Louis. In both cases, the emigrants were sheltered under the wing of Canada; and they and their tomahawks were always at her service. The two Bigots spared no pains to induce more of the Abenakis to join these mission colonies. They were in good measure successful, though the great body of the tribe still clung to their ancient homes on the Saco, the Kennebec, and the Penobscot.[1]

There were ten years of critical and dubious peace along the English border, and then the war broke out again. The occasion of this new uprising is not very clear, and it is hardly worth while to look for it. Between the harsh and reckless borderer on the one side, and the fierce savage on the other,

---

[1] The Abenaki migration to Canada began as early as the autumn of 1675 (*Relation, 1676–77*). On the mission of St. Francis on the Chaudière, see Bigot, *Relation, 1684; Ibid., 1685.* It was afterwards removed to the river St. Francis.

a single spark might at any moment set the frontier in a blaze. The English, however, believed firmly that their French rivals had a hand in the new outbreak; and, in fact, the Abenakis told some of their English captives that Saint-Castin, a French adventurer on the Penobscot, gave every Indian who would go to the war a pound of gunpowder, two pounds of lead, and a supply of tobacco.[1] The trading house of Saint-Castin, which stood on ground claimed by England, had lately been plundered by Sir Edmund Andros, and some of the English had foretold that an Indian war would be the consequence; but none of them seem at this time to have suspected that the governor of Canada and his Jesuit friends had any part in their woes. Yet there is proof that this was the case; for Denonville himself wrote to the minister at Versailles that the successes of the Abenakis on this occasion were due to the "good understanding which he had with them," by means of the two brothers Bigot and other Jesuits.[2]

Whatever were the influences that kindled and maintained the war, it spread dismay and havoc through the English settlements. Andros at first made light of it, and complained of

[1] Hutchinson, *Hist. Mass.*, I. 326. Compare *N. Y. Col. Docs.*, IV. 282, 476.

[2] "En partant de Canada, j'ay laissé une très grande disposition à attirer au Christianisme la plus grande partie des sauvages Abenakis qui abitent les bois du voisinage de Baston. Pour cela il faut les attirer à la mission nouvellement établie près Québec sous le nom de S. François de Sale. Je l'ai vue en peu de temps au nombre de six cents âmes venues du voisinage de Baston. Je l'ay laissée en estat d'augmenter beaucoup si elle est protegée; j'y ai fait quelque dépense qui n'est pas inutile. *La bonne intelligence que j'ai eue avec ces sauvages par les soins des Jésuites, et surtout des deux pères Bigot frères a fait le succès de toutes les attaques qu'ils ont faites sur les Anglois cet esté*, aux quels ils ont enlevé 16 forts, outre celuy de Pemcuit (*Pemaquid*) ou il y avoit 20 pièces de canon, et leur ont tué plus de 200 hommes." *Denonville au Ministre, Jan., 1690.*

It is to be observed that this Indian outbreak began in the summer of 1688, when there was peace between France and England. News of the declaration of war did not reach Canada till July, 1689. (Belmont.) Dover and other places were attacked in June of the same year.

The intendant Champigny says that most of the Indians who attacked the English were from the mission villages near Quebec. *Champigny au Ministre, 16 Nov., 1689.* He says also that he supplied them with gunpowder for the war.

The "forts" taken by the Indians on the Kennebec at this time were nothing but houses protected by palisades. They were taken by treachery and surprise. *Lettre du Père Thury, 1689.* Thury says that 142 men, women, and children were killed.

the authorities of Boston, because in his absence they had sent troops to protect the settlers; but he soon changed his mind, and in the winter went himself to the scene of action with seven hundred men. Not an Indian did he find. They had all withdrawn into the depths of the frozen forest. Andros did what he could, and left more than five hundred men in garrison on the Kennebec and the Saco, at Casco Bay, Pemaquid, and various other exposed points. He then returned to Boston, where surprising events awaited him. Early in April, news came that the Prince of Orange had landed in England. There was great excitement. The people of the town rose against Andros, whom they detested as the agent of the despotic policy of James II. They captured his two forts with their garrisons of regulars, seized his frigate in the harbor, placed him and his chief adherents in custody, elected a council of safety, and set at its head their former governor, Bradstreet, an old man of eighty-seven. The change was disastrous to the eastern frontier. Of the garrisons left for its protection the winter before, some were partially withdrawn by the new council; while others, at the first news of the revolution, mutinied, seized their officers, and returned home.[1] These garrisons were withdrawn or reduced, partly perhaps because the hated governor had established them, partly through distrust of his officers, some of whom were taken from the regulars, and partly because the men were wanted at Boston. The order of withdrawal cannot be too strongly condemned. It was a part of the bungling inefficiency which marked the military

[1] Andros, *Account of Forces in Maine*, in *3 Mass. Hist. Coll.*, I. 85. Compare *Andros Tracts*, I. 177; *Ibid.*, II. 181, 193, 207, 213, 217; *Ibid.*, III. 232; *Report of Andros* in *N. Y. Col. Docs.*, III. 722. The order for the reduction of the garrisons and the return of the suspected officers was passed at the first session of the council of safety, 20 April. The agents of Massachusetts at London endeavored to justify it. See *Andros Tracts*, III. 34. The only regular troops in New England were two companies brought by Andros. Most of them were kept at Boston, though a few men and officers were sent to the eastern garrison. These regulars were regarded with great jealousy, and denounced as "a crew that began to teach New England to Drab, Drink, Blaspheme, Curse, and Damm." *Ibid.*, II. 50.

In their hatred of Andros, many of the people of New England held the groundless and foolish belief that he was in secret collusion with the French and Indians. Their most dangerous domestic enemies were some of their own traders, who covertly sold arms and ammunition to the Indians.

management of the New England governments from the close of Philip's war to the peace of Utrecht.

When spring opened, the Indians turned with redoubled fury against the defenceless frontier, seized the abandoned stockades, and butchered the helpless settlers. Now occurred the memorable catastrophe at Cocheco, or Dover. Two squaws came at evening and begged lodging in the palisaded house of Major Waldron. At night, when all was still, they opened the gates and let in their savage countrymen. Waldron was eighty years old. He leaped from his bed, seized his sword, and drove back the assailants through two rooms; but, as he turned to snatch his pistols, they stunned him by the blow of a hatchet, bound him in an arm-chair, and placed him on a table, where after torturing him they killed him with his own sword.

The crowning event of the war was the capture of Pemaquid, a stockade work, mounted with seven or eight cannon. Andros had placed in it a garrison of a hundred and fifty-six men, under an officer devoted to him. Most of them had been withdrawn by the council of safety; and the entire force of the defenders consisted of Lieutenant James Weems and thirty soldiers, nearly half of whom appear to have been absent at the time of the attack.[1] The Indian assailants were about a hundred in number, all Christian converts from mission villages. By a sudden rush, they got possession of a number of houses behind the fort, occupied only by women and children, the men being at their work.[2] Some ensconced themselves in the cellars, and others behind a rock on the seashore, whence they kept up a close and galling fire. On the next day, Weems surrendered, under a promise of life, and, as the English say, of liberty to himself and all his followers.

[1] Andros in *3 Mass. Hist. Coll.*, I. 85. The original commanding officer, Brockholes, was reputed a "papist." Hence his removal. *Andros Tracts*, III. 35. Andros says that but eighteen men were left in the fort. A list of them in the archives of Massachusetts, certified by Weems himself, shows that there were thirty. Doubt is thrown on this certificate by the fact that the object of it was to obtain a grant of money in return for advances of pay made by Weems to his soldiers. Weems was a regular officer. A number of letters from him, showing his condition before the attack, will be found in Johnston, *History of Bristol, Bremen, and Pemaquid*.

[2] *Captivity of John Gyles*. Gyles was one of the inhabitants.

The fourteen men who had survived the fire, along with a number of women and children, issued from the gate, upon which some were butchered on the spot, and the rest, excepting Weems and a few others, were made prisoners. In other respects, the behavior of the victors is said to have been creditable. They tortured nobody, and their chiefs broke the rum barrels in the fort, to prevent disorder. Father Thury, a priest of the seminary of Quebec, was present at the attack; and the assailants were a part of his Abenaki flock. Religion was one of the impelling forces of the war. In the eyes of the Indian converts, it was a crusade against the enemies of God. They made their vows to the Virgin before the fight; and the squaws, in their distant villages on the Penobscot, told unceasing beads, and offered unceasing prayers for victory.[1]

The war now ran like wildfire through the settlements of Maine and New Hampshire. Sixteen fortified houses, with or without defenders, are said to have fallen into the hands of the enemy; and the extensive district then called the county of Cornwall was turned to desolation. Massachusetts and Plymouth sent hasty levies of raw men, ill-armed and ill-officered, to the scene of action. At Casco Bay, they met a large body of Indians, whom they routed after a desultory fight of six hours; and then, as the approaching winter seemed to promise a respite from attack, most of them were withdrawn and disbanded.

---

[1]Thury, *Relation du Combat des Canibas*. Compare Hutchinson, *Hist. Mass.*, I. 352, and Mather, *Magnalia*, II. 590 (ed. 1853). The murder of prisoners after the capitulation has been denied. Thury incidentally confirms the statement, when, after saying that he exhorted the Indians to refrain from drunkenness and cruelty, he adds that, in consequence, they did not take a single scalp, and "*tuèrent sur le champ ceux qu'ils voulurent tuer.*"

English accounts place the number of Indians at from two to three hundred. Besides the persons taken in the fort, a considerable number were previously killed, or captured in the houses and fields. Those who were spared were carried to the Indian towns on the Penobscot, the seat of Thury's mission. La Motte-Cadillac, in his *Mémoire sur l'Acadie, 1692*, says that 80 persons in all were killed; an evident exaggeration. He adds that Weems and six men were spared at the request of the chief, Madockawando. The taking of Pemaquid is remarkable as one of the very rare instances in which Indians have captured a fortified place otherwise than by treachery or surprise. The exploit was undoubtedly due to French prompting. We shall see hereafter with what energy and success Thury incited his flock to war.

It was a false and fatal security. Through snow and ice and storm, Hertel and his band were moving on their prey. On the night of the twenty-seventh of March, they lay hidden in the forest that bordered the farms and clearings of Salmon Falls. Their scouts reconnoitred the place, and found a fortified house with two stockade forts, built as a refuge for the settlers in case of alarm. Towards daybreak, Hertel, dividing his followers into three parties, made a sudden and simultaneous attack. The settlers, unconscious of danger, were in their beds. No watch was kept even in the so-called forts; and, when the French and Indians burst in, there was no time for their few tenants to gather for defence. The surprise was complete; and, after a short struggle, the assailants were successful at every point. They next turned upon the scattered farms of the neighborhood, burned houses, barns, and cattle, and laid the entire settlement in ashes. About thirty persons of both sexes and all ages were tomahawked or shot; and fifty-four, chiefly women and children, were made prisoners. Two Indian scouts now brought word that a party of English was advancing to the scene of havoc from Piscataqua, or Portsmouth, not many miles distant. Hertel called his men together, and began his retreat. The pursuers, a hundred and forty in number, overtook him about sunset at Wooster River, where the swollen stream was crossed by a narrow bridge. Hertel and his followers made a stand on the farther bank, killed and wounded a number of the English as they attempted to cross, kept up a brisk fire on the rest, held them in check till night, and then continued their retreat. The prisoners, or some of them, were given to the Indians, who tortured one or more of the men, and killed and tormented children and infants with a cruelty not always equalled by their heathen countrymen.[1]

[1] The archives of Massachusetts contain various papers on the disaster at Salmon Falls. Among them is the report of the authorities of Portsmouth to the governor and council at Boston, giving many particulars, and asking aid. They estimate the killed and captured at upwards of eighty, of whom about one fourth were men. They say that about twenty houses were burnt, and mention but one fort. The other, mentioned in the French accounts, was probably a palisaded house. Speaking of the combat at the bridge, they say, "We fought as long as we could distinguish friend from foe. We lost two killed and six or seven wounded, one mortally." The French accounts say

Hertel continued his retreat to one of the Abenaki villages on the Kennebec. Here he learned that a band of French and Indians had lately passed southward on their way to attack the English fort at Casco Bay, on the site of Portland. Leaving at the village his eldest son, who had been badly wounded at Wooster River, he set out to join them with thirty-six of his followers. The band in question was Frontenac's third war-party. It consisted of fifty French and sixty Abenakis from the mission of St. Francis; and it had left Quebec in January, under a Canadian officer named Portneuf and his lieutenant, Courtemanche. They advanced at their leisure, often stopping to hunt, till in May they were joined on the Kennebec by a large body of Indian warriors. On the twenty-fifth, Portneuf encamped in the forest near the English forts, with a force which, including Hertel's party, the Indians of the Kennebec, and another band led by Saint-Castin from the Penobscot, amounted to between four and five hundred men.[1]

Fort Loyal was a palisade work with eight cannon, standing on rising ground by the shore of the bay, at what is now the foot of India Street in the city of Portland. Not far distant were four blockhouses and a village which they were designed to protect. These with the fort were occupied by about a hundred men, chiefly settlers of the neighborhood, under Captain Sylvanus Davis, a prominent trader. Around lay rough and broken fields stretching to the skirts of the forest half a mile distant. Some of Portneuf's scouts met a straggling Scotchman, and could not resist the temptation of killing him. Their scalp-yells alarmed the garrison, and thus the advantage of surprise was lost. Davis resolved to keep his men within their defences, and to stand on his guard; but there

---

fourteen. This letter is accompanied by the examination of a French prisoner, taken the same day. Compare Mather, *Magnalia*, II. 595; Belknap, *Hist. New Hampshire*, I. 207; *Journal of Rev. John Pike* (*Proceedings of Mass. Hist. Soc.* 1875); and the French accounts of Monseignat and La Potherie. Charlevoix adds various embellishments, not to be found in the original sources. Later writers copy and improve upon him, until Hertel is pictured as charging the pursuers sword in hand, while the English fly in disorder before him.

[1] *Declaration of Sylvanus Davis*; Mather, *Magnalia*, II. 603.

was little or no discipline in the yeoman garrison, and thirty young volunteers under Lieutenant Thaddeus Clark sallied out to find the enemy. They were too successful; for, as they approached the top of a hill near the woods, they observed a number of cattle staring with a scared look at some object on the farther side of a fence; and, rightly judging that those they sought were hidden there, they raised a cheer, and ran to the spot. They were met by a fire so close and deadly that half their number were shot down. A crowd of Indians leaped the fence and rushed upon the survivors, who ran for the fort; but only four, all of whom were wounded, succeeded in reaching it.[1]

The men in the blockhouses withdrew under cover of night to Fort Loyal, where the whole force of the English was now gathered along with their frightened families. Portneuf determined to besiege the place in form; and, after burning the village, and collecting tools from the abandoned blockhouses, he opened his trenches in a deep gully within fifty yards of the fort, where his men were completely protected. They worked so well that in three days they had wormed their way close to the palisade; and, covered as they were in their burrows, they lost scarcely a man, while their enemies suffered severely. They now summoned the fort to surrender. Davis asked for a delay of six days, which was refused; and in the morning the fight began again. For a time the fire was sharp and heavy. The English wasted much powder in vain efforts to dislodge the besiegers from their trenches; till at length, seeing a machine loaded with a tar-barrel and other combustibles shoved against their palisades, they asked for a parley. Up to this time, Davis had supposed that his assailants were all Indians, the French being probably dressed and painted like their red allies. "We demanded," he says, "if there were any French among them, and if they would give us quarter. They answered that they were Frenchmen, and that they would give us good quarter. Upon this, we sent out to them again to know from whence they came, and if they would give us good quarter for our men, women, and children, both wounded and sound, and (to demand) that we should have

[1] *Relation de Monseignat*; La Potherie, III. 79.

liberty to march to the next English town, and have a guard for our defence and safety; then we would surrender; and also that the governour of the French should hold up his hand and swear by the great and ever living God that the several articles should be performed: all which he did solemnly swear."

The survivors of the garrison now filed through the gate, and laid down their arms. They with their women and children were thereupon abandoned to the Indians, who murdered many of them, and carried off the rest. When Davis protested against this breach of faith, he was told that he and his countrymen were rebels against their lawful king, James II. After spiking the cannon, burning the fort, and destroying all the neighboring settlements, the triumphant allies departed for their respective homes, leaving the slain unburied where they had fallen.[1]

Davis with three or four others, more fortunate than their companions, was kept by the French, and carried to Canada. "They were kind to me," he says, "on my travels through the country. I arrived at Quebeck the 14th of June, where I was civilly treated by the gentry, and soon carried to the fort before the governour, the Earl of Frontenack." Frontenac told him that the governor and people of New York were the cause of the war, since they had stirred up the Iroquois against Canada, and prompted them to torture French pris-

---

[1] Their remains were buried by Captain Church, three years later.

On the capture of Fort Loyal, compare Monseignat and La Potherie with Mather, *Magnalia*, II. 603, and the *Declaration of Sylvanus Davis*, in *3 Mass. Hist. Coll.*, I. 101. Davis makes curious mistakes in regard to French names, his rustic ear not being accustomed to the accents of the Gallic tongue. He calls Courtemanche, Monsieur Corte de March, and Portneuf, Monsieur Burniffe or Burneffe. To these contemporary authorities may be added the account given by Le Clercq, *Établissement de la Foy*, II. 393, and a letter from Governor Bradstreet of Massachusetts to Jacob Leisler in *Doc. Hist. N. Y.*, II. 259. The French writers of course say nothing of any violation of faith on the part of the victors, but they admit that the Indians kept most of the prisoners. Scarcely was the fort taken, when four English vessels appeared in the harbor, too late to save it. Willis, in his *History of Portland* (ed. 1865), gives a map of Fort Loyal and the neighboring country. In the Massachusetts archives is a letter from Davis, written a few days before the attack, complaining that his fort is in wretched condition.

oners.[1] Davis replied that New York and New England were distinct and separate governments, each of which must answer for its own deeds; and that New England would gladly have remained at peace with the French, if they had not set on the Indians to attack her peaceful settlers. Frontenac admitted that the people of New England were not to be regarded in the same light with those who had stirred up the Indians against Canada; but he added that they were all rebels to their king, and that if they had been good subjects there would have been no war. "I do believe," observes the captive Puritan, "that there was a popish design against the Protestant interest in New England as in other parts of the world." He told Frontenac of the pledge given by his conqueror, and the violation of it. "We were promised good quarter," he reports himself to have said, "and a guard to conduct us to our English; but now we are made captives and slaves in the hands of the heathen. I thought I had to do with Christians that would have been careful of their engagements, and not to violate and break their oaths. Whereupon the governour shaked his head, and, as I was told, was very angry with Burniffe (*Portneuf*)."

Frontenac was pleased with his prisoner, whom he calls a *bonhomme*. He told him in broken English to take courage, and promised him good treatment; to which Davis replied that his chief concern was not for himself, but for the captives in the hands of the Indians. Some of these were afterwards ransomed by the French, and treated with much kindness, as was also Davis himself, to whom the count gave lodging in the château.

The triumphant success of his three war-parties produced on the Canadian people all the effect that Frontenac had expected. This effect was very apparent, even before the last two victories had become known. "You cannot believe, Monseigneur," wrote the governor, speaking of the capture of Schenectady, "the joy that this slight success has caused, and how much it contributes to raise the people from their dejection and terror."

One untoward accident damped the general joy for a mo-

[1] I am unable to discover the foundation of this last charge.

ment. A party of Iroquois Christians from the Saut St. Louis had made a raid against the English borders, and were returning with prisoners. One evening, as they were praying at their camp near Lake Champlain, they were discovered by a band of Algonquins and Abenakis who were out on a similar errand, and who, mistaking them for enemies, set upon them and killed several of their number, among whom was Kryn, the great Mohawk, chief of the mission of the Saut. This mishap was near causing a rupture between the best Indian allies of the colony; but the difference was at length happily adjusted, and the relatives of the slain propitiated by gifts.[1]

[1] The attacking party consisted of some of the Abenakis and Algonquins who had been with Hertel, and who had left the main body after the destruction of Salmon Falls. Several of them were killed in the skirmish, and among the rest their chief, Hopehood, or Wohawa, "that memorable tygre," as Cotton Mather calls him.

Chapter XII

MASSACHUSETTS ATTACKS QUEBEC

English Schemes • Capture of Port Royal • Acadia reduced • Conduct of Phips • His History and Character • Boston in Arms • A Puritan Crusade • The March from Albany • Frontenac and the Council • Frontenac at Montreal • His War Dance • An Abortive Expedition • An English Raid • Frontenac at Quebec • Defences of the Town • The Enemy arrives

WHEN Frontenac sent his war-parties against New York and New England, it was in the hope not only of reanimating the Canadians, but also of teaching the Iroquois that they could not safely rely on English aid, and of inciting the Abenakis to renew their attacks on the border settlements. He imagined, too, that the British colonies could be chastised into prudence and taught a policy of conciliation towards their Canadian neighbors; but he mistook the character of these bold and vigorous though not martial communities. The plan of a combined attack on Canada seems to have been first proposed by the Iroquois; and New York and the several governments of New England, smarting under French and Indian attacks, hastened to embrace it. Early in May, a congress of their delegates was held in the city of New York. It was agreed that the colony of that name should furnish four hundred men, and Massachusetts, Plymouth, and Connecticut three hundred and fifty-five jointly; while the Iroquois afterwards added their worthless pledge to join the expedition with nearly all their warriors. The colonial militia were to rendezvous at Albany, and thence advance upon Montreal by way of Lake Champlain. Mutual jealousies made it difficult to agree upon a commander; but Fitz-John Winthrop of Connecticut was at length placed at the head of the feeble and discordant band.

While Montreal was thus assailed by land, Massachusetts and the other New England colonies were invited to attack Quebec by sea; a task formidable in difficulty and in cost, and one that imposed on them an inordinate share in the burden of the war. Massachusetts hesitated. She had no money, and she was already engaged in a less remote and less critical enterprise. During the winter, her commerce had suffered from French cruisers, which found convenient harborage at Port Royal, whence also the hostile Indians were believed to draw supplies. Seven vessels, with two hundred and eighty-eight sailors, were impressed, and from four to five hundred militiamen were drafted for the service.[1] That rugged son of New England, Sir William Phips, was appointed to the command. He sailed from Nantasket at the end of April, reached Port Royal on the eleventh of May, landed his militia, and summoned Meneval, the governor, to surrender. The fort, though garrisoned by about seventy soldiers, was scarcely in condition to repel an assault; and Meneval yielded without resistance, first stipulating, according to French accounts, that private property should be respected, the church left untouched, and the troops sent to Quebec or to France.[2] It was found, however, that during the parley a quantity of goods, belonging partly to the king and partly to merchants of the place, had been carried off and hidden in the woods.[3] Phips thought this a sufficient pretext for plundering the merchants, imprisoning the troops, and desecrating the church. "We cut down the cross," writes one of his followers, "rifled their church, pulled down their high altar, and broke their images."[4] The houses of the two priests were also pillaged. The people were promised security to life, liberty, and property, on condition of swearing allegiance to King William and Queen Mary; "which," says the journalist, "they did with great acclamation," and thereupon they were left unmolested.[5] The lawful portion of the booty included twenty-one

[1] *Summary of Muster Roll*, appended to *A Journal of the Expedition from Boston against Port Royal*, among the papers of George Chalmers in the Library of Harvard College.

[2] *Relation de la Prise du Port Royal par les Anglois de Baston, pièce anonyme, 27 Mai, 1690*.

[3] *Journal of the Expedition from Boston against Port Royal*.

[4] *Ibid.*

[5] *Relation de Monseignat*. Nevertheless, a considerable number seem to have refused the oath, and to have been pillaged. The *Relation de la Prise du Port Royal par les Anglois de Baston*, written on the spot immediately after the event, says that, except that nobody was killed, the place was treated as if

pieces of cannon, with a considerable sum of money belonging to the king. The smaller articles, many of which were taken from the merchants and from such of the settlers as refused the oath, were packed in hogsheads and sent on board the ships. Phips took no measures to secure his conquest, though he commissioned a president and six councillors, chosen from the inhabitants, to govern the settlement till farther orders from the crown or from the authorities of Massachusetts. The president was directed to constrain nobody in the matter of religion; and he was assured of protection and support so long as he remained "faithful to our government," that is, the government of Massachusetts.[1] The little Puritan commonwealth already gave itself airs of sovereignty.

Phips now sent Captain Alden, who had already taken possession of Saint-Castin's post at Penobscot, to seize upon La Hêve, Chedabucto, and other stations on the southern coast. Then, after providing for the reduction of the settlements at the head of the Bay of Fundy, he sailed, with the rest of the fleet, for Boston, where he arrived triumphant on the thirtieth of May, bringing with him, as prisoners, the French governor, fifty-nine soldiers, and the two priests, Petit and Trouvé. Massachusetts had made an easy conquest of all Acadia; a conquest, however, which she had neither the men nor the money to secure by sufficient garrisons.

The conduct of the New England commander in this affair does him no credit. It is true that no blood was split, and no revenge taken for the repeated butcheries of unoffending and defenceless settlers. It is true, also, that the French appear to have acted in bad faith. But Phips, on the other hand, displayed a scandalous rapacity. Charlevoix says that he robbed Meneval of all his money; but Meneval himself affirms that he gave it to the English commander for safe keeping, and that Phips and his wife would return neither the money nor various other articles belonging to the captive governor,

---

taken by assault. Meneval also says that the inhabitants were pillaged. *Meneval au Ministre, 29 Mai, 1690*; also *Rapport de Champigny, Oct., 1690.* Meneval describes the New England men as excessively irritated at the late slaughter of settlers at Salmon Falls and elsewhere.

[1] *Journal of the Expedition, etc.*

whereof the following are specified: "Six silver spoons, six silver forks, one silver cup in the shape of a gondola, a pair of pistols, three new wigs, a gray vest, four pair of silk garters, two dozen of shirts, six vests of dimity, four nightcaps with lace edgings, all my table service of fine tin, all my kitchen linen," and many other items which give an amusing insight into Meneval's housekeeping.[1]

Meneval, with the two priests, was confined in a house at Boston, under guard. He says that he petitioned the governor and council for redress; "but, as they have little authority and stand in fear of Phips, who is supported by the rabble, to which he himself once belonged, and of which he is now the chief, they would do nothing for me."[2] This statement of Meneval is not quite correct: for an order of the council is on record, requiring Phips to restore his chest and clothes; and, as the order received no attention, Governor Bradstreet wrote to the refractory commander a note, enjoining him to obey it at once.[3] Phips thereupon gave up some of the money and the worst part of the clothing, still keeping the rest.[4] After long delay, the council released Meneval: upon which, Phips and the populace whom he controlled demanded that he should be again imprisoned; but the "honest people" of the

[1] *An Account of the Silver and Effects which Mr. Phips keeps back from Mr. Meneval*, in *3 Mass. Hist. Coll.*, I. 115.

Monseignat and La Potherie describe briefly this expedition against Port Royal. In the archives of Massachusetts are various papers concerning it, among which are Governor Bradstreet's instructions to Phips, and a complete invoice of the plunder. Extracts will be found in Professor Bowen's *Life of Phips*, in Sparks's *American Biography*, VII. There is also an order of council, "Whereas the French soldiers lately brought to this place from Port Royal *did surrender on capitulation*," they shall be set at liberty. Meneval, *Lettre au Ministre, 29 Mai, 1690*, says that there was a capitulation, and that Phips broke it. Perrot, former governor of Acadia, accuses both Meneval and the priest Petit of being in collusion with the English. *Perrot à de Chevry, 2 Juin, 1690*. The same charge is made as regards Petit in *Mémoire sur l'Acadie, 1691*.

Charlevoix's account of this affair is inaccurate. He ascribes to Phips acts which took place weeks after his return, such as the capture of Chedabucto.

[2] *Mémoire présenté à M. de Ponchartrain par M. de Meneval, 6 Avril, 1691.*

[3] This note, dated 7 Jan., 1691, is cited by Bowen in his *Life of Phips*, Sparks's *American Biography*, VII.

[4] *Mémoire de Meneval.*

town took his part, his persecutor was forced to desist, and he set sail covertly for France.[1] This, at least, is his own account of the affair.

As Phips was to play a conspicuous part in the events that immediately followed, some notice of him will not be amiss. He is said to have been one of twenty-six children, all of the same mother, and was born in 1650 at a rude border settlement, since called Woolwich, on the Kennebec. His parents were ignorant and poor; and till eighteen years of age he was employed in keeping sheep. Such a life ill suited his active and ambitious nature. To better his condition, he learned the trade of ship-carpenter, and, in the exercise of it, came to Boston, where he married a widow with some property, beyond him in years, and much above him in station. About this time, he learned to read and write, though not too well, for his signature is like that of a peasant. Still aspiring to greater things, he promised his wife that he would one day command a king's ship and own a "fair brick house in the Green Lane of North Boston," a quarter then occupied by citizens of the better class. He kept his word at both points. Fortune was inauspicious to him for several years; till at length, under the pressure of reverses, he conceived the idea of conquering fame and wealth at one stroke, by fishing up the treasure said to be stored in a Spanish galleon wrecked fifty years before somewhere in the West Indian seas. Full of this project, he went to England, where, through influences which do not plainly appear, he gained a hearing from persons in high places, and induced the admiralty to adopt his scheme. A frigate was given him, and he sailed for the West Indies; whence, after a long search, he returned unsuccessful, though not without adventures which proved his mettle. It was the epoch of the buccaneers; and his crew, tired of a vain and toilsome search, came to the quarterdeck, armed with cutlasses, and demanded of their captain that he should turn pirate with them. Phips, a tall and powerful man, instantly fell upon them with his fists, knocked down the ringleaders, and awed them all into submission. No long after, there was a more formidable mu-

[1] *Ibid.*

tiny; but, with great courage and address, he quelled it for a time, and held his crew to their duty till he had brought the ship into Jamaica, and exchanged them for better men.

Though the leaky condition of the frigate compelled him to abandon the search, it was not till he had gained information which he thought would lead to success; and, on his return, he inspired such confidence that the Duke of Albemarle, with other noblemen and gentlemen, gave him a fresh outfit, and despatched him again on his Quixotic errand. This time he succeeded, found the wreck, and took from it gold, silver, and jewels to the value of three hundred thousand pounds sterling. The crew now leagued together to seize the ship and divide the prize; and Phips, pushed to extremity, was compelled to promise that every man of them should have a share in the treasure, even if he paid it himself. On reaching England, he kept his pledge so well that, after redeeming it, only sixteen thousand pounds was left as his portion, which, however, was an ample fortune in the New England of that day. He gained, too, what he valued almost as much, the honor of knighthood. Tempting offers were made him of employment in the royal service; but he had an ardent love for his own country, and thither he presently returned.

Phips was a rude sailor, bluff, prompt, and choleric. He never gave proof of intellectual capacity; and such of his success in life as he did not owe to good luck was due probably to an energetic and adventurous spirit, aided by a blunt frankness of address that pleased the great, and commended him to their favor. Two years after the expedition to Port Royal, the king, under the new charter, made him governor of Massachusetts, a post for which, though totally unfit, he had been recommended by the elder Mather, who, like his son Cotton, expected to make use of him. He carried his old habits into his new office, cudgelled Brinton, the collector of the port, and belabored Captain Short of the royal navy with his cane. Far from trying to hide the obscurity of his origin, he leaned to the opposite foible, and was apt to boast of it, delighting to exhibit himself as a self-made man. New England writers describe him as honest in private dealings; but, in accordance with his coarse nature, he seems to have thought that any thing is fair in war. On the other hand, he was warmly patriotic, and was almost as ready to serve New England as to serve himself.[1]

When he returned from Port Royal, he found Boston alive with martial preparation. A bold enterprise was afoot. Massachusetts of her own motion had resolved to attempt the conquest of Quebec. She and her sister colonies had not yet recovered from the exhaustion of Philip's war, and still less from the disorders that attended the expulsion of the royal governor and his adherents. The public treasury was empty, and the recent expeditions against the eastern Indians had been supported by private subscription. Worse yet, New England had no competent military commander. The Puritan gentlemen of the original emigration, some of whom were as well fitted for military as for civil leadership, had passed from the stage; and, by a tendency which circumstances made inevitable, they had left none behind them equally qualified. The great Indian conflict of fifteen years before had, it is true, formed good partisan chiefs, and proved that the New England yeoman, defending his family and his hearth, was not to be surpassed in stubborn fighting; but, since Andros and his soldiers had been driven out, there was scarcely a single man in the colony of the slightest training or experience in regular war. Up to this moment, New England had never asked help of the mother country. When thousands of savages burst on her defenceless settlements, she had conquered safety and peace with her own blood and her own slender resources; but now, as the proposed capture of Quebec would inure to the profit of the British crown, Bradstreet and his council thought it not unfitting to ask for a supply of arms and ammunition, of which they were in great need.[2] The request was refused, and no aid of any kind came from the English government, whose resources were engrossed by the Irish war.

While waiting for the reply, the colonial authorities urged on their preparations, in the hope that the plunder of Quebec

---

[1] An excellent account of Phips will be found in Professor Bowen's biographical notice, already cited. His Life by Cotton Mather is excessively eulogistic.

[2] *Bradstreet and Council to the Earl of Shrewsbury, 29 Mar., 1690; Danforth to Sir H. Ashurst, 1 April, 1690.*

would pay the expenses of its conquest. Humility was not among the New England virtues, and it was thought a sin to doubt that God would give his chosen people the victory over papists and idolaters; yet no pains were spared to ensure the divine favor. A proclamation was issued, calling the people to repentance; a day of fasting was ordained; and, as Mather expresses it, "the wheel of prayer was kept in continual motion."[1] The chief difficulty was to provide funds. An attempt was made to collect a part of the money by private subscription;[2] but, as this plan failed, the provisional government, already in debt, strained its credit yet farther, and borrowed the needful sums. Thirty-two trading and fishing vessels, great and small, were impressed for the service. The largest was a ship called the "Six Friends," engaged in the dangerous West India trade, and carrying forty-four guns. A call was made for volunteers, and many enrolled themselves; but, as more were wanted, a press was ordered to complete the number. So rigorously was it applied that, what with voluntary and enforced enlistment, one town, that of Gloucester, was deprived of two-thirds of its fencible men.[3] There was not a moment of doubt as to the choice of a commander, for Phips was imagined to be the very man for the work. One John Walley, a respectable citizen of Barnstable, was made second in command with the modest rank of major; and a sufficient number of ship-masters, merchants, master mechanics, and substantial farmers, were commissioned as subordinate officers. About the middle of July, the committee charged with the preparations reported that all was ready. Still there was a long delay. The vessel sent early in spring to ask aid from England had not returned. Phips waited for her as long as he dared, and the best of the season was over when he resolved to put to sea. The rustic warriors, duly formed into companies, were sent on board; and the fleet sailed from Nantasket on the ninth of August. Including sailors, it carried twenty-two hundred men, with provi-

---

[1] *Mass. Colonial Records, 12 Mar., 1690*; Mather, *Life of Phips.*

[2] *Proposals for an Expedition against Canada*, in *3 Mass. Hist. Coll.*, X. 119.

[3] *Rev. John Emerson to Wait Winthrop, 26 July, 1690.* Emerson was the minister of Gloucester. He begs for the release of the impressed men.

sions for four months, but insufficient ammunition and no pilot for the St. Lawrence.[1]

While Massachusetts was making ready to conquer Quebec by sea, the militia of the land expedition against Montreal had mustered at Albany. Their strength was even less than was at first proposed; for, after the disaster at Casco, Massachusetts and Plymouth had recalled their contingents to defend their frontiers. The rest, decimated by dysentery and small-pox, began their match to Lake Champlain, with bands of Mohawk, Oneida, and Mohegan allies. The western Iroquois were to join them at the lake, and the combined force was then to attack the head of the colony, while Phips struck at its heart.

Frontenac was at Quebec during most of the winter and the early spring. When he had despatched the three war-parties, whose hardy but murderous exploits were to bring this double storm upon him, he had an interval of leisure, of which he made a characteristic use. The English and the Iroquois were not his only enemies. He had opponents within as well as without, and he counted as among them most of the members of the supreme council. Here was the bishop, representing that clerical power which had clashed so often with the civil rule; here was that ally of the Jesuits, the intendant Champigny, who, when Frontenac arrived, had written mournfully to Versailles that he would do his best to live at peace with him; here were Villeray and Auteuil, whom the governor had once banished, Damours, whom he had imprisoned, and others scarcely more agreeable to him. They and their clerical friends had conspired for his recall seven or eight years before; they had clung to Denonville, that faithful son of the Church, in spite of all his failures; and they had seen with troubled minds the return of King Stork in the person of the haughty and irascible count. He on his part felt his power. The country was in deadly need of him, and looked to him for salvation; while the king had shown him such

---

[1] Mather, *Life of Phips*, gives an account of the outfit. Compare the *Humble Address of Divers of the Gentry, Merchants and others inhabiting in Boston, to the King's Most Excellent Majesty*. Two officers of the expedition, Walley and Savage, have left accounts of it, as Phips would probably have done, had his literary acquirements been equal to the task.

marks of favor, that, for the moment at least, his enemies must hold their peace. Now, therefore, was the time to teach them that he was their master. Whether trivial or important the occasion mattered little. What he wanted was a conflict and a victory, or submission without a conflict.

The supreme council had held its usual weekly meetings since Frontenac's arrival; but as yet he had not taken his place at the board, though his presence was needed. Auteuil, the attorney-general, was thereupon deputed to invite him. He visited the count at his apartment in the château, but could get from him no answer, except that the council was able to manage its own business, and that he would come when the king's service should require it. The councillors divined that he was waiting for some assurance that they would receive him with befitting ceremony; and, after debating the question, they voted to send four of their number to repeat the invitation, and beg the governor to say what form of reception would be agreeable to him. Frontenac answered that it was for them to propose the form, and that, when they did so, he would take the subject into consideration. The deputies returned, and there was another debate. A ceremony was devised, which it was thought must needs be acceptable to the count; and the first councillor, Villeray, repaired to the château to submit it to him. After making him an harangue of compliment, and protesting the anxiety of himself and his colleagues to receive him with all possible honor, he explained the plan, and assured Frontenac that, if not wholly satisfactory, it should be changed to suit his pleasure. "To which," says the record, "Monsieur the governor only answered that the council could consult the bishop and other persons acquainted with such matters." The bishop was consulted, but pleaded ignorance. Another debate followed; and the first councillor was again despatched to the château, with proposals still more deferential than the last, and full power to yield, in addition, whatever the governor might desire. Frontenac replied that, though they had made proposals for his reception when he should present himself at the council for the first time, they had not informed him what ceremony they meant to observe when he should come to the subsequent sessions. This point also having been thoroughly debated,

Villeray went again to the count, and with great deference laid before him the following plan: That, whenever it should be his pleasure to make his first visit to the council, four of its number should repair to the château, and accompany him, with every mark of honor, to the palace of the intendant, where the sessions were held; and that, on his subsequent visits, two councillors should meet him at the head of the stairs, and conduct him to his seat. The envoy farther protested that, if this failed to meet his approval, the council would conform itself to all his wishes on the subject. Frontenac now demanded to see the register in which the proceedings on the question at issue were recorded. Villeray was directed to carry it to him. The records had been cautiously made; and, after studying them carefully, he could find nothing at which to cavil.

He received the next deputation with great affability, told them that he was glad to find that the council had not forgotten the consideration due to his office and his person, and assured them, with urbane irony, that, had they offered to accord him marks of distinction greater than they felt were due, he would not have permitted them thus to compromise their dignity, having too much regard for the honor of a body of which he himself was the head. Then, after thanking them collectively and severally, he graciously dismissed them, saying that he would come to the council after Easter, or in about two months.[1] During four successive Mondays, he had forced the chief dignitaries of the colony to march in deputations up and down the rugged road from the intendant's palace to the chamber of the château where he sat in solitary state. A disinterested spectator might see the humor of the

[1] "M. le Gouverneur luy a répondu qu'il avoit reconnu avec plaisir que la Compagnie (*le Conseil*) conservoit la considération qu'elle avoit pour son caractère et pour sa personne, et qu'elle pouvoit bien s'assurer qu'encore qu'elle luy eust fait des propositions au delà de ce qu'elle auroit cru devoir faire pour sa reception au Conseil, il ne les auroit pas acceptées, l'honneur de la Compagnie luy estant d'autant plus considérable, qu'en estant le chef, il n'auroit rien voulu souffrir qui peust estre contraire à sa dignité." *Registre du Conseil Souverain, séance du 13 Mars, 1690.* The affair had occupied the preceding sessions of 20 and 27 February and 6 March. The submission of the councillors did not prevent them from complaining to the minister. *Champigny au Ministre, 10 Mai, 1691; Mémoire instructif sur le Canada, 1691.*

situation; but the council felt only its vexations. Frontenac had gained his point: the enemy had surrendered unconditionally.

Having settled this important matter to his satisfaction, he again addressed himself to saving the country. During the winter, he had employed gangs of men in cutting timber in the forests, hewing it into palisades, and dragging it to Quebec. Nature had fortified the Upper Town on two sides by cliffs almost inaccessible, but it was open to attack in the rear; and Frontenac, with a happy prevision of approaching danger, gave his first thoughts to strengthening this, its only weak side. The work began as soon as the frost was out of the ground, and before midsummer it was well advanced. At the same time, he took every precaution for the safety of the settlements in the upper parts of the colony, stationed detachments of regulars at the stockade forts, which Denonville had built in all the parishes above Three Rivers, and kept strong scouting parties in continual movement in all the quarters most exposed to attack. Troops were detailed to guard the settlers at their work in the fields, and officers and men were enjoined to use the utmost vigilance. Nevertheless, the Iroquois war-parties broke in at various points, burning and butchering, and spreading such terror that in some districts the fields were left untilled and the prospects of the harvest ruined.

Towards the end of July, Frontenac left Major Prévost to finish the fortifications, and, with the intendant Champigny, went up to Montreal, the chief point of danger. Here he arrived on the thirty-first; and, a few days after, the officer commanding the fort at La Chine sent him a messenger in hot haste with the startling news that Lake St. Louis was "all covered with canoes."[1] Nobody doubted that the Iroquois were upon them again. Cannon were fired to call in the troops from the detached posts; when alarm was suddenly turned to joy by the arrival of other messengers to announce that the new comers were not enemies, but friends. They were the Indians of the upper lakes descending from Michillimackinac to trade at Montreal. Nothing so auspicious had happened

---

[1] "Que le lac estoit tout couvert de canots." *Frontenac au Ministre, 9 et 12 Nov., 1690.*

since Frontenac's return. The messages he had sent them in the spring by Louvigny and Perrot, reinforced by the news of the victory on the Ottawa and the capture of Schenectady, had had the desired effect; and the Iroquois prisoner whom their missionary had persuaded them to torture had not been sacrificed in vain. Despairing of an English market for their beaver skins, they had come as of old to seek one from the French.

On the next day, they all came down the rapids, and landed near the town. There were fully five hundred of them, Hurons, Ottawas, Ojibwas, Pottawatamies, Crees, and Nipissings, with a hundred and ten canoes laden with beaver skins to the value of nearly a hundred thousand crowns. Nor was this all; for, a few days after, La Durantaye, late commander at Michillimackinac, arrived with fifty-five more canoes, manned by French traders, and filled with valuable furs. The stream of wealth dammed back so long was flowing upon the colony at the moment when it was most needed. Never had Canada known a more prosperous trade than now in the midst of her danger and tribulation. It was a triumph for Frontenac. If his policy had failed with the Iroquois, it had found a crowning success among the tribes of the lakes.

Having painted, greased, and befeathered themselves, the Indians mustered for the grand council which always preceded the opening of the market. The Ottawa orator spoke of nothing but trade, and, with a regretful memory of the cheapness of English goods, begged that the French would sell them at the same rate. The Huron touched upon politics and war, declaring that he and his people had come to visit their old father and listen to his voice, being well assured that he would never abandon them, as others had done, nor fool away his time, like Denonville, in shameful negotiations for peace; and he exhorted Frontenac to fight, not the English only, but the Iroquois also, till they were brought to reason. "If this is not done," he said, "my father and I shall both perish; but, come what may, we will perish together."[1] "I answered," writes Frontenac, "that I would fight the Iroquois

---

[1] La Potherie, III. 94; Monseignat, *Relation*; *Frontenac au Ministre, 9 et 12 Nov., 1690*.

till they came to beg for peace, and that I would grant them
no peace that did not include all my children, both white and
red, for I was the father of both alike."

Now ensued a curious scene. Frontenac took a hatchet,
brandished it in the air and sang the war-song. The principal
Frenchmen present followed his example. The Christian Iroquois of the two neighboring missions rose and joined them,
and so also did the Hurons and the Algonquins of Lake Nipissing, stamping and screeching like a troop of madmen;
while the governor led the dance, whooping like the rest. His
predecessor would have perished rather than play such a part
in such company; but the punctilious old courtier was himself
half Indian at heart, as much at home in a wigwam as in the
halls of princes. Another man would have lost respect in Indian eyes by such a performance. In Frontenac, it roused his
audience to enthusiasm. They snatched the proffered hatchet
and promised war to the death.[1]

Then came a solemn war-feast. Two oxen and six large
dogs had been chopped to pieces for the occasion, and boiled
with a quantity of prunes. Two barrels of wine with abundant
tobacco were also served out to the guests, who devoured the
meal in a species of frenzy.[2] All seemed eager for war except
the Ottawas, who had not forgotten their late dalliance with
the Iroquois. A Christian Mohawk of the Saut St. Louis
called them to another council, and demanded that they
should explain clearly their position. Thus pushed to the wall,
they no longer hesitated, but promised like the rest to do all
that their father should ask.

Their sincerity was soon put to the test. An Iroquois convert called La Plaque, a notorious reprobate though a good

[1] "Je leur mis moy-mesme la hache à la main en chantant la chanson de
guerre pour m'accommoder à leurs façons de faire." *Frontenac au Ministre, 9
et 12 Nov., 1690.*

"Monsieur de Frontenac commença la Chanson de guerre, la Hache a la
main, les principaux Chefs des François se joignant a luy avec de pareilles
armes, la chanterent ensemble. Les Iroquois du Saut et de la Montagne, les
Hurons et les Nipisiriniens donnerent encore le branle: l'on eut dit, Monsieur, que ces Acteurs étoient des possedez par les gestes et les contorsions
qu'ils faisoient. Les *Sassakouez*, où les cris et les hurlemens que M.ʳ de Frontenac étoit obligé de faire pour se conformer à leur manière, augmentoit
encore la fureur bachique." La Potherie, III. 97.

[2] La Potherie, III. 96, 98.

warrior, had gone out as a scout in the direction of Albany. On the day when the market opened and trade was in full activity, the buyers and sellers were suddenly startled by the sound of the death-yell. They snatched their weapons, and for a moment all was confusion; when La Plaque, who had probably meant to amuse himself at their expense, made his appearance, and explained that the yells proceeded from him. The news that he brought was, however, sufficiently alarming. He declared that he had been at Lake St. Sacrement, or Lake George, and had seen there a great number of men making canoes as if about to advance on Montreal. Frontenac, thereupon, sent the Chevalier de Clermont to scout as far as Lake Champlain. Clermont soon sent back one of his followers to announce that he had discovered a party of the enemy, and that they were already on their way down the Richelieu. Frontenac ordered cannon to be fired to call in the troops, crossed the St. Lawrence followed by all the Indians, and encamped with twelve hundred men at La Prairie to meet the expected attack. He waited in vain. All was quiet, and the Ottawa scouts reported that they could find no enemy. Three days passed. The Indians grew impatient, and wished to go home. Neither English nor Iroquois had shown themselves; and Frontenac, satisfied that their strength had been exaggerated, left a small force at La Prairie, recrossed the river, and distributed the troops again among the neighboring parishes to protect the harvesters. He now gave ample presents to his departing allies, whose chiefs he had entertained at his own table, and to whom, says Charlevoix, he bade farewell "with those engaging manners which he knew so well how to assume when he wanted to gain anybody to his interest." Scarcely were they gone, when the distant cannon of La Prairie boomed a sudden alarm.

The men whom La Plaque had seen near Lake George were a part of the combined force of Connecticut and New York, destined to attack Montreal. They had made their way along Wood Creek to the point where it widens into Lake Champlain, and here they had stopped. Disputes between the men of the two colonies, intestine quarrels in the New York militia, who were divided between the two factions engendered by the late revolution, the want of provisions, the want of canoes, and the ravages of small-pox, had ruined an enterprise which had been mismanaged from the first. There was no birch bark to make more canoes, and owing to the lateness of the season the bark of the elms would not peel. Such of the Iroquois as had joined them were cold and sullen; and news came that the three western tribes of the confederacy, terrified by the small-pox, had refused to move. It was impossible to advance; and Winthrop, the commander, gave orders to return to Albany, leaving Phips to conquer Canada alone.[1] But first, that the campaign might not seem wholly futile, he permitted Captain John Schuyler to make a raid into Canada with a band of volunteers. Schuyler left the camp at Wood Creek with twenty-nine whites and a hundred and twenty Indians, passed Lake Champlain, descended the Richelieu to Chambly, and fell suddenly on the settlement of La Prairie, whence Frontenac had just withdrawn with his forces. Soldiers and inhabitants were reaping in the wheat-fields. Schuyler and his followers killed or captured twenty-five, including several women. He wished to attack the neighboring fort, but his Indians refused; and after burning houses, barns, and hay-ricks, and killing a great number of cattle, he seated himself with his party at dinner in the adjacent woods, while cannon answered cannon from Chambly, La Prairie, and Montreal, and the whole country was astir. "We thanked the Governor of Canada," writes Schuyler, "for his salute of heavy artillery during our meal."[2]

[1] On this expedition see the *Journal of Major General Winthrop*, in *N. Y. Col. Docs.*, IV. 193; *Publick Occurrences, 1690,* in *Historical Magazine*, I. 228; and various documents in *N. Y. Col. Docs.*, III. 727, 752, and in *Doc. Hist. N. Y.*, II. 266, 288. Compare La Potherie, III. 126, and *N. Y. Col. Docs.*, IX. 513. These last are French statements. A Sokoki Indian brought to Canada a greatly exaggerated account of the English forces, and said that disease had been spread among them by boxes of infected clothing, which they themselves had provided in order to poison the Canadians. Bishop Laval, *Lettre du 20 Nov., 1690,* says that there was a quarrel between the English and their Iroquois allies, who, having plundered a magazine of spoiled provisions, fell ill, and thought that they were poisoned. Colden and other English writers seem to have been strangely ignorant of this expedition. The Jesuit Michel Germain declares that the force of the English alone amounted to four thousand men (*Relation de la Défaite des Anglois, 1690*). About one tenth of this number seem actually to have taken the field.

[2] *Journal of Captain John Schuyler*, in *Doc. Hist. N. Y.*, II. 285. Compare La Potherie, III. 101, and *Relation de Monseignat.*

The English had little to boast in this affair, the paltry termination of an enterprise from which great things had been expected. Nor was it for their honor to adopt the savage and cowardly mode of warfare in which their enemies had led the way. The blow that had been struck was less an injury to the French than an insult; but, as such, it galled Frontenac excessively, and he made no mention of it in his despatches to the court. A few more Iroquois attacks and a few more murders kept Montreal in alarm till the tenth of October, when matters of deeper import engaged the governor's thoughts.

A messenger arrived in haste at three o'clock in the afternoon, and gave him a letter from Prévost, town major of Quebec. It was to the effect that an Abenaki Indian had just come over land from Acadia, with news that some of his tribe had captured an English woman near Portsmouth, who told them that a great fleet had sailed from Boston to attack Quebec. Frontenac, not easily alarmed, doubted the report. Nevertheless, he embarked at once with the intendant in a small vessel, which proved to be leaky, and was near foundering with all on board. He then took a canoe, and towards evening set out again for Quebec, ordering some two hundred men to follow him. On the next day, he met another canoe, bearing a fresh message from Prévost, who announced that the English fleet had been seen in the river, and that it was already above Tadoussac. Frontenac now sent back Captain de Ramsay with orders to Callières, governor of Montreal, to descend immediately to Quebec with all the force at his disposal, and to muster the inhabitants on the way. Then he pushed on with the utmost speed. The autumnal storms had begun, and the rain pelted him without ceasing; but on the morning of the fourteenth he neared the town. The rocks of Cape Diamond towered before him; the St. Lawrence lay beneath them, lonely and still; and the Basin of Quebec outspread its broad bosom, a solitude without a sail. Frontenac had arrived in time.

He landed at the Lower Town, and the troops and the armed inhabitants came crowding to meet him. He was delighted at their ardor.[1] Shouts, cheers, and the waving of hats greeted the old man as he climbed the steep ascent of Moun-

[1] *Frontenac au Ministre, 9 et 12 Nov., 1690.*

tain Street. Fear and doubt seemed banished by his presence.
Even those who hated him rejoiced at his coming, and hailed
him as a deliverer. He went at once to inspect the fortifications. Since the alarm a week before, Prévost had accomplished wonders, and not only completed the works begun in
the spring, but added others to secure a place which was a
natural fortress in itself. On two sides, the Upper Town
scarcely needed defence. The cliffs along the St. Lawrence and
those along the tributary river St. Charles had three accessible
points, guarded at the present day by the Prescott Gate, the
Hope Gate, and the Palace Gate. Prévost had secured them
by barricades of heavy beams and casks filled with earth. A
continuous line of palisades ran along the strand of the St.
Charles, from the great cliff called the Saut au Matelot to the
palace of the intendant. At this latter point began the line of
works constructed by Frontenac to protect the rear of the
town. They consisted of palisades, strengthened by a ditch
and an embankment, and flanked at frequent intervals by
square towers of stone. Passing behind the garden of the Ursulines, they extended to a windmill on a hillock called Mt.
Carmel, and thence to the brink of the cliffs in front. Here
there was a battery of eight guns near the present Public Garden; two more, each of three guns, were planted at the top
of the Saut au Matelot; another at the barricade of the Palace
Gate; and another near the windmill of Mt. Carmel; while a
number of light pieces were held in reserve for such use as
occasion might require. The Lower Town had no defensive
works; but two batteries, each of three guns, eighteen and
twenty-four pounders, were placed here at the edge of the
river.[1]

Two days passed in completing these defences under the
eye of the governor. Men were flocking in from the parishes
far and near; and on the evening of the fifteenth about
twenty-seven hundred, regulars and militia, were gathered
within the fortifications, besides the armed peasantry of Beauport and Beaupré, who were ordered to watch the river below

[1] *Relation de Monseignat; Plan de Québec, par Villeneuve, 1690; Relation du
Mercure Galant, 1691*. The summit of Cape Diamond, which commanded the
town, was not fortified till three years later, nor were any guns placed here
during the English attack.

the town, and resist the English, should they attempt to land.[1] At length, before dawn on the morning of the sixteenth, the sentinels on the Saut au Matelot could descry the slowly moving lights of distant vessels. At daybreak the fleet was in sight. Sail after sail passed the Point of Orleans and glided into the Basin of Quebec. The excited spectators on the rock counted thirty-four of them. Four were large ships, several others were of considerable size, and the rest were brigs, schooners, and fishing craft, all thronged with men.

[1] *Diary of Sylvanus Davis*, prisoner in Quebec, in *Mass. Hist. Coll.* 3, I. 101. There is a difference of ten days in the French and English dates, the *New Style* having been adopted by the former and not by the latter.

Chapter XIII

1690

DEFENCE OF QUEBEC

Phips on the St. Lawrence • Phips at Quebec • A Flag of Truce • Scene at the Château • The Summons and the Answer • Plan of Attack • Landing of the English • The Cannonade • The Ships repulsed • The Land Attack • Retreat of Phips • Condition of Quebec • Rejoicings of the French • Distress at Boston

---

THE DELAY at Boston, waiting aid from England that never came, was not propitious to Phips; nor were the wind and the waves. The voyage to the St. Lawrence was a long one; and when he began, without a pilot, to grope his way up the unknown river, the weather seemed in league with his enemies. He appears, moreover, to have wasted time. What was most vital to his success was rapidity of movement; yet, whether by his fault or his misfortune, he remained three weeks within three days' sail of Quebec.[1] While anchored off Tadoussac, with the wind ahead, he passed the idle hours in holding councils of war and framing rules for the government of his men; and, when at length the wind veered to the east, it is doubtful if he made the best use of his opportunity.[2]

He presently captured a small vessel, commanded by Granville, an officer whom Prévost had sent to watch his movements. He had already captured, near Tadoussac, another vessel, having on board Madame Lalande and Madame Joliet, the wife and the mother-in-law of the discoverer of the Mississippi.[3] When questioned as to the condition of Quebec, they told him that it was imperfectly fortified, that its cannon were dismounted, and that it had not two hundred men to defend it. Phips was greatly elated, thinking that, like Port Royal, the capital of Canada would fall without a blow. The

[1] *Journal of Major Walley*, in Hutchinson, *Hist. Mass.*, I. 470.
[2] "Ils ne profitèrent pas du vent favorable pour nous surprendre comme ils auroient pu faire." Juchereau, 320.
[3] "Les Demoiselles Lalande et Joliet." The title of *madame* was at this time restricted to married women of rank. The wives of the *bourgeois*, and even of the lesser nobles, were called *demoiselles*.

statement of the two prisoners was true, for the most part, when it was made; but the energy of Prévost soon wrought a change.

Phips imagined that the Canadians would offer little resistance to the Puritan invasion; for some of the Acadians had felt the influence of their New England neighbors, and shown an inclination to them. It was far otherwise in Canada, where the English heretics were regarded with abhorrence. Whenever the invaders tried to land at the settlements along the shore, they were met by a rebuff. At the river Ouelle, Francheville, the curé put on a cap and capote, took a musket, led his parishioners to the river, and hid with them in the bushes. As the English boats approached their ambuscade, they gave the foremost a volley, which killed nearly every man on board; upon which the rest sheared off. It was the same when the fleet neared Quebec. Bands of militia, vigilant, agile, and well commanded, followed it along the shore, and repelled with showers of bullets every attempt of the enemy to touch Canadian soil.

When, after his protracted voyage, Phips sailed into the Basin of Quebec, one of the grandest scenes on the western continent opened upon his sight: the wide expanse of waters, the lofty promontory beyond, and the opposing heights of Levi; the cataract of Montmorenci, the distant range of the Laurentian Mountains, the warlike rock with its diadem of walls and towers, the roofs of the Lower Town clustering on the strand beneath, the Château St. Louis perched at the brink of the cliff, and over it the white banner, spangled with *fleurs-de-lis*, flaunting defiance in the clear autumnal air. Perhaps, as he gazed, a suspicion seized him that the task he had undertaken was less easy than he had thought; but he had conquered once by a simple summons to surrender, and he resolved to try its virtue again.

The fleet anchored a little below Quebec; and towards ten o'clock the French saw a boat put out from the admiral's ship, bearing a flag of truce. Four canoes went from the Lower Town, and met it midway. It brought a subaltern officer, who announced himself as the bearer of a letter from Sir William Phips to the French commander. He was taken into one of the canoes and paddled to the quay, after being completely blindfolded by a bandage which covered half his face. Prévost received him as he landed, and ordered two sergeants to take him by the arms and lead him to the governor. His progress was neither rapid nor direct. They drew him hither and thither, delighting to make him clamber in the dark over every possible obstruction; while a noisy crowd hustled him, and laughing women called him Colin Maillard, the name of the chief player in blindman's buff.[1] Amid a prodigious hubbub, intended to bewilder him and impress him with a sense of immense warlike preparation, they dragged him over the three barricades of Mountain Street, and brought him at last into a large room of the château. Here they took the bandage from his eyes. He stood for a moment with an air of astonishment and some confusion. The governor stood before him, haughty and stern, surrounded by French and Canadian officers, Maricourt, Sainte-Hélène, Longueuil, Villebon, Valrenne, Bienville, and many more, bedecked with gold lace and silver lace, perukes and powder, plumes and ribbons, and all the martial foppery in which they took delight, and regarding the envoy with keen, defiant eyes.[2] After a moment, he recovered his breath and his composure, saluted Frontenac, and, expressing a wish that the duty assigned him had been of a more agreeable nature, handed him the letter of Phips. Frontenac gave it to an interpreter, who read it aloud in French that all might hear. It ran thus:—

"*Sir William Phips, Knight, General and Commander-in-chief in and over their Majesties' Forces of New England, by Sea and Land, to Count Frontenac, Lieutenant-General and Governour for the French King at Canada; or, in his absence, to his Deputy, or him or them in chief command at Quebeck:*

"The war between the crowns of England and France doth not only sufficiently warrant, but the destruction made by the French and Indians, under your command and

---

[1] Juchereau, 323.

[2] "Tous ces Officiers s'étoient habillés le plus proprement qu'ils pûrent, les galons d'or et d'argent, les rubans, les plumets, la poudre, et la frisure, rien ne manquoit," etc. *Ibid.*

encouragement, upon the persons and estates of their Majesties' subjects of New England, without provocation on
their part, hath put them under the necessity of this expedition for their own security and satisfaction. And although
the cruelties and barbarities used against them by the
French and Indians might, upon the present opportunity,
prompt unto a severe revenge, yet, being desirous to avoid
all inhumane and unchristian-like actions, and to prevent
shedding of blood as much as may be,

"I, the aforesaid William Phips, Knight, do hereby, in
the name and in the behalf of their most excellent Majesties, William and Mary, King and Queen of England, Scotland, France, and Ireland, Defenders of the Faith, and by
order of their said Majesties' government of the Massachu-
set-colony in New England, demand a present surrender of
your forts and castles, undemolished, and the King's and
other stores, unimbezzled, with a seasonable delivery of all
captives; together with a surrender of all your persons and
estates to my dispose: upon the doing whereof, you may
expect mercy from me, as a Christian, according to what
shall be found for their Majesties' service and the subjects'
security. Which, if you refuse forthwith to do, I am come
provided, and am resolved, by the help of God, in whom I
trust, by force of arms to revenge all wrongs and injuries
offered, and bring you under subjection to the Crown of
England, and, when too late, make you wish you had accepted of the favour tendered.

"Your answer positive in an hour, returned by your own
trumpet, with the return of mine, is required upon the peril
that will ensue."[1]

When the reading was finished, the Englishman pulled his
watch from his pocket, and handed it to the governor. Frontenac could not, or pretended that he could not, see the hour.
The messenger thereupon told him that it was ten o'clock,
and that he must have his answer before eleven. A general cry
of indignation arose; and Valrenne called out that Phips was

---

[1] See the Letter in Mather, *Magnalia*, I. 186. The French kept a copy of it,
which, with an accurate translation, in parallel columns, was sent to Versailles, and is still preserved in the Archives de la Marine. The text answers
perfectly to that given by Mather.

nothing but a pirate, and that his man ought to be hanged. Frontenac contained himself for a moment, and then said to the envoy:—

"I will not keep you waiting so long. Tell your general that I do not recognize King William; and that the Prince of Orange, who so styles himself, is a usurper, who has violated the most sacred laws of blood in attempting to dethrone his father-in-law. I know no king of England but King James. Your general ought not to be surprised at the hostilities which he says that the French have carried on in the colony of Massachusetts; for, as the king my master has taken the king of England under his protection, and is about to replace him on his throne by force of arms, he might have expected that his Majesty would order me to make war on a people who have rebelled against their lawful prince." Then, turning with a smile to the officers about him: "Even if your general offered me conditions a little more gracious, and if I had a mind to accept them, does he suppose that these brave gentlemen would give their consent, and advise me to trust a man who broke his agreement with the governor of Port Royal, or a rebel who has failed in his duty to his king, and forgotten all the favors he had received from him, to follow a prince who pretends to be the liberator of England and the defender of the faith, and yet destroys the laws and privileges of the kingdom and overthrows its religion? The divine justice which your general invokes in his letter will not fail to punish such acts severely."

The messenger seemed astonished and startled; but he presently asked if the governor would give him his answer in writing.

"No," returned Frontenac, "I will answer your general only by the mouths of my cannon, that he may learn that a man like me is not to be summoned after this fashion. Let him do his best, and I will do mine;" and he dismissed the Englishman abruptly. He was again blindfolded, led over the barricades, and sent back to the fleet by the boat that brought him.[1]

---

[1] *Lettre de Sir William Phips à M. de Frontenac, avec sa Réponse verbale; Relation de ce qui s'est passé à la Descente des Anglois à Québec au mois d'Octobre, 1690.* Compare Monseignat, *Relation.* The English accounts, though more brief, confirm those of the French.

Phips had often given proof of personal courage, but for the past three weeks his conduct seems that of a man conscious that he is charged with a work too large for his capacity. He had spent a good part of his time in holding councils of war; and now, when he heard the answer of Frontenac, he called another to consider what should be done. A plan of attack was at length arranged. The militia were to be landed on the shore of Beauport, which was just below Quebec, though separated from it by the St. Charles. They were then to cross this river by a ford practicable at low water, climb the heights of St. Geneviève, and gain the rear of the town. The small vessels of the fleet were to aid the movement by ascending the St. Charles as far as the ford, holding the enemy in check by their fire, and carrying provisions, ammunition, and intrenching tools, for the use of the land troops. When these had crossed and were ready to attack Quebec in the rear, Phips was to cannonade it in front, and land two hundred men under cover of his guns to effect a diversion by storming the barricades. Some of the French prisoners, from whom their captors appear to have received a great deal of correct information, told the admiral that there was a place a mile or two above the town where the heights might be scaled and the rear of the fortifications reached from a direction opposite to that proposed. This was precisely the movement by which Wolfe afterwards gained his memorable victory; but Phips chose to abide by the original plan.[1]

While the plan was debated, the opportunity for accomplishing it ebbed away. It was still early when the messenger returned from Quebec; but, before Phips was ready to act, the day was on the wane and the tide was against him. He lay quietly at his moorings when, in the evening, a great shouting, mingled with the roll of drums and the sound of fifes, was heard from the Upper Town. The English officers asked their prisoner, Granville, what it meant. "Ma foi, Messieurs," he replied, "you have lost the game. It is the governor of Montreal with the people from the country above. There is nothing for you now but to pack and go home." In fact, Callières had arrived with seven or eight hundred men, many

---

[1] *Journal of Major Walley*; Savage, *Account of the Late Action of the New Englanders* (Lond. 1691).

of them regulars. With these were bands of *coureurs de bois* and other young Canadians, all full of fight, singing and whooping with martial glee as they passed the western gate and trooped down St. Louis Street.[1]

The next day was gusty and blustering; and still Phips lay quiet, waiting on the winds and the waves. A small vessel, with sixty men on board, under Captain Ephraim Savage, ran in towards the shore of Beauport to examine the landing, and stuck fast in the mud. The Canadians plied her with bullets, and brought a cannon to bear on her. They might have waded out and boarded her, but Savage and his men kept up so hot a fire that they forbore the attempt; and, when the tide rose, she floated again.

There was another night of tranquillity; but at about eleven on Wednesday morning the French heard the English fifes and drums in full action, while repeated shouts of "God save King William!" rose from all the vessels. This lasted an hour or more; after which a great number of boats, loaded with men, put out from the fleet and rowed rapidly towards the shore of Beauport. The tide was low, and the boats grounded before reaching the landing-place. The French on the rock could see the troops through telescopes, looking in the distance like a swarm of black ants, as they waded through mud and water, and formed in companies along the strand. They were some thirteen hundred in number, and were commanded by Major Walley.[2] Frontenac had sent three hundred sharpshooters, under Sainte-Hélène, to meet them and hold them in check. A battalion of troops followed; but, long before they could reach the spot, Sainte-Hélène's men, with a few militia from the neighboring parishes, and a band of Huron warriors from Lorette, threw themselves into the thickets along the front of the English, and opened a distant but galling fire upon the compact bodies of the enemy. Walley ordered a charge. The New England men rushed, in a disorderly manner, but with great impetuosity, up the rising

[1] Juchereau, 325, 326.

[2] "Between 12 and 1,300 men." Walley, *Journal*. "About 1,200 men." Savage, *Account of the Late Action*. Savage was second in command of the militia. Mather says, 1,400. Most of the French accounts say, 1,500. Some say, 2,000; and La Hontan raises the number to 3,000.

ground; received two volleys, which failed to check them; and drove back the assailants in some confusion. They turned, however, and fought in Indian fashion with courage and address, leaping and dodging among trees, rocks, and bushes, firing as they retreated, and inflicting more harm than they received. Towards evening they disappeared; and Walley, whose men had been much scattered in the desultory fight, drew them together as well as he could, and advanced towards the St. Charles, in order to meet the vessels which were to aid him in passing the ford. Here he posted sentinels, and encamped for the night. He had lost four killed and about sixty wounded, and imagined that he had killed twenty or thirty of the enemy. In fact, however, their loss was much less, though among the killed was a valuable officer, the Chevalier de Clermont, and among the wounded the veteran captain of Beauport, Juchereau de Saint-Denis, more than sixty-four years of age. In the evening, a deserter came to the English camp, and brought the unwelcome intelligence that there were three thousand armed men in Quebec.[1]

Meanwhile, Phips, whose fault hitherto had not been an excess of promptitude, grew impatient, and made a premature movement inconsistent with the preconcerted plan. He left his moorings, anchored his largest ships before the town, and prepared to cannonade it; but the fiery veteran, who watched him from the Château St. Louis, anticipated him, and gave him the first shot. Phips replied furiously, opening fire with every gun that he could bring to bear; while the rock paid him back in kind, and belched flame and smoke from all its

[1] On this affair, Walley, *Journal*; Savage, *Account of the Late Action* (in a letter to his brother); Monseignat, *Relation*; *Relation de la Descente des Anglois*; *Relation de 1682–1712*; La Hontan, I. 213. "M. le comte de Frontenac se trouva avec 3,000 hommes." Belmont, *Histoire du Canada*, A.D. 1690. The prisoner Captain Sylvanus Davis, in his diary, says, as already mentioned, that on the day before Phips's arrival so many regulars and militia arrived that, with those who came with Frontenac, there were about 2,700. This was before the arrival of Callières, who, according to Davis, brought but 300. Thus the three accounts of the deserter, Belmont, and Davis, tally exactly as to the sum total.

An enemy of Frontenac writes, "Ce n'est pas sa présence qui fit prendre la fuite aux Anglois, mais le grand nombre de François auxquels ils virent bien que celuy de leurs guerriers n'étoit pas capable de faire tête." *Remarques sur l'Oraison Funèbre de feu M. de Frontenac.*

batteries. So fierce and rapid was the firing, that La Hontan compares it to volleys of musketry; and old officers, who had seen many sieges, declared that they had never known the like.[1] The din was prodigious, reverberated from the surrounding heights, and rolled back from the distant mountains in one continuous roar. On the part of the English, however, surprisingly little was accomplished beside noise and smoke. The practice of their gunners was so bad that many of their shot struck harmlessly against the face of the cliff. Their guns, too, were very light, and appear to have been charged with a view to the most rigid economy of gunpowder; for the balls failed to pierce the stone walls of the buildings, and did so little damage that, as the French boasted, twenty crowns would have repaired it all.[2] Night came at length, and the turmoil ceased.

Phips lay quiet till daybreak, when Frontenac sent a shot to waken him, and the cannonade began again. Sainte-Hélène had returned from Beauport; and he, with his brother Maricourt, took charge of the two batteries of the Lower Town, aiming the guns in person, and throwing balls of eighteen and twenty-four pounds with excellent precision against the four largest ships of the fleet. One of their shots cut the flag-staff of the admiral, and the cross of St. George fell into the river. It drifted with the tide towards the north shore; whereupon several Canadians paddled out in a birch canoe, secured it, and brought it back in triumph. On the spire of the cathedral in the Upper Town had been hung a picture of the Holy Family, as an invocation of divine aid. The Puritan gunners wasted their ammunition in vain attempts to knock it down. That it escaped their malice was ascribed to miracle, but the miracle would have been greater if they had hit it.

At length, one of the ships, which had suffered most, hauled off and abandoned the fight. That of the admiral had fared little better, and now her condition grew desperate. With her rigging torn, her mainmast half cut through, her mizzen-mast splintered, her cabin pierced, and her hull riddled with shot, another volley seemed likely to sink her, when Phips ordered her to be cut loose from her moorings, and she drifted out of fire, leaving cable and anchor behind. The re-

[1] La Hontan, I. 216; Juchereau, 326.
[2] Père Germain, *Relation de la Défaite des Anglois.*

maining ships soon gave over the conflict, and withdrew to stations where they could neither do harm nor suffer it.[1]

Phips had thrown away nearly all his ammunition in this futile and disastrous attack, which should have been deferred till the moment when Walley, with his land force, had gained the rear of the town. Walley lay in his camp, his men wet, shivering with cold, famished, and sickening with the small-pox. Food, and all other supplies, were to have been brought him by the small vessels, which should have entered the mouth of the St. Charles and aided him to cross it. But he waited for them in vain. Every vessel that carried a gun had busied itself in cannonading, and the rest did not move. There appears to have been insubordination among the masters of these small craft, some of whom, being owners or part-owners of the vessels they commanded, were probably unwilling to run them into danger. Walley was no soldier; but he saw that to attempt the passage of the river without aid, under the batteries of the town and in the face of forces twice as numerous as his own, was not an easy task. Frontenac, on his part, says that he wished him to do so, knowing that the attempt would ruin him.[2] The New England men were eager to push on; but the night of Thursday, the day of Phips's repulse, was so cold that ice formed more than an inch in thickness, and the half-starved militia suffered intensely. Six field-pieces, with their ammunition, had been sent ashore; but they were nearly useless, as there were no means of moving them. Half a barrel of musket powder, and one biscuit for each man, were also landed; and with this meagre aid Walley was left to capture Quebec. He might, had he dared, have made a dash across the ford on the morning of Thursday, and assaulted the town in the rear while Phips was cannonading it in front; but his courage was not equal to so desperate a venture. The firing ceased, and the possible opportunity was lost. The citizen soldier despaired of success; and, on the morning of Friday, he went on board the admiral's ship to explain his situation. While he was gone, his men put them-

[1] Besides authorities before cited, Le Clercq, *Établissement de la Foy*, II. 434; La Potherie, III. 118; *Rapport de Champigny*, *Oct.*, *1690*; Laval, *Lettre à* ——, *20 Nov.*, *1690*.

[2] *Frontenac au Ministre*, *12 et 19 Nov.*, *1690*.

selves in motion, and advanced along the borders of the St. Charles towards the ford. Frontenac, with three battalions of regular troops, went to receive them at the crossing; while Sainte-Hélène, with his brother Longueuil, passed the ford with a body of Canadians, and opened fire on them from the neighboring thickets. Their advance parties were driven in, and there was a hot skirmish, the chief loss falling on the New England men, who were fully exposed. On the side of the French, Sainte-Hélène was mortally wounded, and his brother was hurt by a spent ball. Towards evening, the Canadians withdrew, and the English encamped for the night. Their commander presently rejoined them. The admiral had given him leave to withdraw them to the fleet, and boats were accordingly sent to bring them off; but, as these did not arrive till about daybreak, it was necessary to defer the embarkation till the next night.

At dawn, Quebec was all astir with the beating of drums and the ringing of bells. The New England drums replied; and Walley drew up his men under arms, expecting an attack, for the town was so near that the hubbub of voices from within could plainly be heard. The noise gradually died away; and, except a few shots from the ramparts, the invaders were left undisturbed. Walley sent two or three companies to beat up the neighboring thickets, where he suspected that the enemy was lurking. On the way, they had the good luck to find and kill a number of cattle, which they cooked and ate on the spot; whereupon, being greatly refreshed and invigorated, they dashed forward in complete disorder, and were soon met by the fire of the ambushed Canadians. Several more companies were sent to their support, and the skirmishing became lively. Three detachments from Quebec had crossed the river; and the militia of Beauport and Beaupré had hastened to join them. They fought like Indians, hiding behind trees or throwing themselves flat among the bushes, and laying repeated ambuscades as they slowly fell back. At length, they all made a stand on a hill behind the buildings and fences of a farm; and here they held their ground till night, while the New England men taunted them as cowards who would never fight except under cover.[1]

[1] *Relation de la Descente des Anglois.*

Walley, who with his main body had stood in arms all day, now called in the skirmishers, and fell back to the landing-place, where, as soon as it grew dark, the boats arrived from the fleet. The sick men, of whom there were many, were sent on board, and then, amid floods of rain, the whole force embarked in noisy confusion, leaving behind them in the mud five of their cannon. Hasty as was their parting, their conduct on the whole had been creditable; and La Hontan, who was in Quebec at the time, says of them, "They fought vigorously, though as ill-disciplined as men gathered together at random could be; for they did not lack courage, and, if they failed, it was by reason of their entire ignorance of discipline, and because they were exhausted by the fatigues of the voyage." Of Phips he speaks with contempt, and says that he could not have served the French better if they had bribed him to stand all the while with his arms folded. Some allowance should, nevertheless, be made him for the unmanageable character of the force under his command, the constitution of which was fatal to military subordination.

On Sunday, the morning after the re-embarkation, Phips called a council of officers, and it was resolved that the men should rest for a day or two, that there should be a meeting for prayer, and that, if ammunition enough could be found, another landing should be attempted; but the rough weather prevented the prayer-meeting, and the plan of a new attack was fortunately abandoned.

Quebec remained in agitation and alarm till Tuesday, when Phips weighed anchor and disappeared, with all his fleet, behind the Island of Orleans. He did not go far, as indeed he could not, but stopped four leagues below to mend rigging, fortify wounded masts, and stop shot-holes. Subercase had gone with a detachment to watch the retiring enemy; and Phips was repeatedly seen among his men, on a scaffold at the side of his ship, exercising his old trade of carpenter. This delay was turned to good use by an exchange of prisoners. Chief among those in the hands of the French was Captain Davis, late commander at Casco Bay; and there were also two young daughters of Lieutenant Clark, who had been killed at the same place. Frontenac himself had humanely ransomed these children from the Indians; and Madame de Champigny, wife of the intendant, had, with equal kindness, bought from them a little girl named Sarah Gerrish, and placed her in charge of the nuns at the Hôtel-Dieu, who had become greatly attached to her, while she, on her part, left them with reluctance. The French had the better in these exchanges, receiving able-bodied men, and returning, with the exception of Davis, only women and children.

The heretics were gone, and Quebec breathed freely again. Her escape had been a narrow one; not that three thousand men, in part regular troops, defending one of the strongest positions on the continent, and commanded by Frontenac, could not defy the attacks of two thousand raw fishermen and farmers, led by an ignorant civilian, but the numbers which were a source of strength were at the same time a source of weakness.[1] Nearly all the adult males of Canada were gathered at Quebec, and there was imminent danger of starvation. Cattle from the neighboring parishes had been hastily driven into the town; but there was little other provision, and before Phips retreated the pinch of famine had begun. Had he come a week earlier or stayed a week later, the French themselves believed that Quebec would have fallen, in the one case for want of men, and in the other for want of food.

The Lower Town had been abandoned by its inhabitants, who bestowed their families and their furniture within the solid walls of the seminary. The cellars of the Ursuline convent were filled with women and children, and many more took refuge at the Hôtel-Dieu. The beans and cabbages in the garden of the nuns were all stolen by the soldiers; and their wood-pile was turned into bivouac fires. "We were more dead than alive when we heard the cannon," writes Mother Juchereau; but the Jesuit Fremin came to console them, and their prayers and their labors never ceased. On the day when the firing was heaviest, twenty-six balls fell into their yard and garden, and were sent to the gunners at the batteries, who returned them to their English owners. At the convent of the

---

[1] The small-pox had left probably less than 2,000 effective men in the fleet when it arrived before Quebec. The number of regular troops in Canada by the roll of 1689 was 1,418. Nothing had since occurred to greatly diminish the number. Callières left about fifty in Montreal, and perhaps also a few in the neighboring forts. The rest were in Quebec.

Ursulines, the corner of a nun's apron was carried off by a cannon-shot as she passed through her chamber. The sister-hood began a *novena*, or nine days' devotion, to St. Joseph, St. Ann, the angels, and the souls in purgatory; and one of their number remained day and night in prayer before the images of the Holy Family. The bishop came to encourage them; and his prayers and his chants were so fervent that they thought their last hour was come.[1]

The superior of the Jesuits, with some of the elder mem-bers of the Order, remained at their college during the attack, ready, should the heretics prevail, to repair to their chapel, and die before the altar. Rumor exaggerated the numbers of the enemy, and a general alarm pervaded the town. It was still greater at Lorette, nine miles distant. The warriors of that mission were in the first skirmish at Beauport; and two of them, running off in a fright, reported at the village that the enemy were carrying every thing before them. On this, the villagers fled to the woods, followed by Father Germain, their missionary, to whom this hasty exodus suggested the flight of the Holy Family into Egypt.[2] The Jesuits were thought to have special reason to fear the Puritan soldiery, who, it was reported, meant to kill them all, after cutting off their ears to make necklaces.[3]

When news first came of the approach of Phips, the bishop was absent on a pastoral tour. Hastening back, he entered Quebec at night, by torchlight, to the great joy of its inmates, who felt that his presence brought a benediction. He issued a pastoral address, exhorting his flock to frequent and full confession and constant attendance at mass, as the means of insuring the success of their arms.[4] Laval, the former bishop, aided his efforts. "We appealed," he writes, "to God, his Holy Mother, to all the Angels, and to all the Saints."[5] Nor was the appeal in vain: for each day seemed to bring some new token of celestial favor; and it is not surprising that the head-

[1] *Récit d'une Réligieuse Ursuline*, in *Les Ursulines de Québec*, I. 470.

[2] "Il nous ressouvint alors de la fuite de Nostre Seigneur en Égypte." Père Germain, *Relation*.

[3] *Ibid.*

[4] *Lettre pastorale pour disposer les Peuples de ce Diocèse à se bien deffendre contre les Anglois* (Reg. de l'Évêché de Québec).

[5] *Laval à ——, Nov. 20, 1690.*

winds which delayed the approach of the enemy, the cold and the storms which hastened his departure, and, above all, his singularly innocent cannonade, which killed but two or three persons, should have been accepted as proof of divine intervention. It was to the Holy Virgin that Quebec had been most lavish of its vows, and to her the victory was ascribed.

One great anxiety still troubled the minds of the victors. Three ships, bringing large sums of money and the yearly supplies for the colony, were on their way to Quebec; and nothing was more likely than that the retiring fleet would meet and capture them. Messengers had been sent down the river, who passed the English in the dark, found the ships at St. Paul's Bay, and warned them of the danger. They turned back, and hid themselves within the mouth of the Saguenay; but not soon enough to prevent Phips from discovering their retreat. He tried to follow them; but thick fogs arose, with a persistent tempest of snow, which completely baffled him, and, after waiting five days, he gave over the attempt. When he was gone, the three ships emerged from their hiding-place, and sailed again for Quebec, where they were greeted with a universal jubilee. Their deliverance was ascribed to Saint Ann, the mother of the Virgin, and also to St. Francis Xavier, whose name one of them bore.

Quebec was divided between thanksgiving and rejoicing. The captured flag of Phips's ship was borne to the cathedral in triumph; the bishop sang *Te Deum*; and, amid the firing of cannon, the image of the Virgin was carried to each church and chapel in the place by a procession, in which priests, people, and troops all took part. The day closed with a grand bonfire in honor of Frontenac.

One of the three ships carried back the news of the victory, which was hailed with joy at Versailles; and a medal was struck to commemorate it. The ship carried also a despatch from Frontenac. "Now that the king has triumphed by land and sea," wrote the old soldier, "will he think that a few squadrons of his navy would be ill employed in punishing the insolence of these genuine old parliamentarians of Boston, and crushing them in their den and the English of New York as well? By mastering these two towns, we shall secure the whole sea-coast, besides the fisheries of the Grand Bank, which is no slight matter: and this would be the true, and perhaps the only, way of bringing the wars of Canada to an end; for, when the English are conquered, we can easily reduce the Iroquois to complete submission."[1]

Phips returned crestfallen to Boston late in November; and one by one the rest of the fleet came straggling after him, battered and weather-beaten. Some did not appear till February, and three or four never came at all. The autumn and early winter were unusually stormy. Captain Rainsford, with sixty men, was wrecked on the Island of Anticosti, where more than half their number died of cold and misery.[2] In the other vessels, some were drowned, some frost-bitten, and above two hundred killed by small-pox and fever.

At Boston, all was dismay and gloom. The Puritan bowed before "this awful frown of God," and searched his conscience for the sin that had brought upon him so stern a chastisement.[3] Massachusetts, already impoverished, found herself in extremity. The war, instead of paying for itself, had burdened her with an additional debt of fifty thousand pounds.[4] The sailors and soldiers were clamorous for their pay; and, to satisfy them, the colony was forced for the first time in its history to issue a paper currency. It was made receivable at a premium for all public debts, and was also fortified by a provision for its early redemption by taxation; a provision which was carried into effect in spite of poverty and distress.[5]

[1] *Frontenac au Ministre, 9 et 12 Nov., 1690.*

[2] Mather, *Magnalia*, I. 192.

[3] *The Governor and Council to the Agents of Massachusetts*, in *Andros Tracts*, III. 53.

[4] *Address of the Gentry, Merchants, and others, Ibid.*, II. 236.

[5] The following is a literal copy of a specimen of this paper money, which varied in value from two shillings to ten pounds:—

No. (2161) 10[s]

This Indented Bill of Ten Shillings, due from the Massachusetts Colony to the Possessor, shall be in value equal to Money, and shall be accordingly accepted by the Treasurer and Receivers subordinate to him in all Publick Payments, and for any Stock at any time in the Treasury Boston in New England, December the 10th 1690. By Order of the General Court.

| Seal of Massachusetts. | PETER TOWNSEND ADAM WINTHROP TIM. THORNTON | } *Com[tee]* |

Massachusetts had made her usual mistake. She had confidently believed that ignorance and inexperience could match the skill of a tried veteran, and that the rude courage of her fishermen and farmers could triumph without discipline or leadership. The conditions of her material prosperity were adverse to efficiency in war. A trading republic, without trained officers, may win victories; but it wins them either by accident or by an extravagant outlay in money and life.

When this paper came into the hands of the treasurer, it was burned. Nevertheless, owing to the temporary character of the provisional government, it fell for a time to the value of from fourteen to sixteen shillings in the pound.

In the Bibliothèque Nationale is the original draft of a remarkable map, by the engineer Villeneuve, of which a *fac-simile* is before me. It represents in detail the town and fortifications of Quebec, the surrounding country, and the positions of the English fleet and land forces, and is entitled *PLAN DE QUÉBEC, et de ses Enuirons, EN LA NOUVELLE FRANCE, ASSIÉGÉ PAR LES ANGLOIS, le 16 d'Octobre 1690 jusqu'au 22 dud. mois qu'ils s'en allerent, apprès auoir esté bien battus PAR M.* LE COMTE DE FRONTENAC, gouuerneur general du Pays.*

Chapter XIV

THE SCOURGE OF CANADA

Iroquois Inroads • Death of Bienville • English Attack • A Desperate Fight • Miseries of the Colony • Alarms • A Winter Expedition • La Chesnaye burned • The Heroine of Verchères • Mission Indians • The Mohawk Expedition • Retreat and Pursuit • Relief arrives • Frontenac Triumphant

---

O NE of Phips's officers, charged with the exchange of prisoners at Quebec, said as he took his leave, "We shall make you another visit in the spring;" and a French officer returned, with martial courtesy, "We shall have the honor of meeting you before that time." Neither side made good its threat, for both were too weak and too poor. No more war-parties were sent that winter to ravage the English border; for neither blankets, clothing, ammunition, nor food could be spared. The fields had lain untilled over half Canada; and, though four ships had arrived with supplies, twice as many had been captured or driven back by English cruisers in the Gulf. The troops could not be kept together; and they were quartered for subsistence upon the settlers, themselves half famished.

Spring came at length, and brought with it the swallows, the bluebirds, and the Iroquois. They rarely came in winter, when the trees and bushes had no leaves to hide them, and their movements were betrayed by the track of their snow-shoes; but they were always to be expected at the time of sowing and of harvest, when they could do most mischief. During April, about eight hundred of them, gathering from their winter hunting-grounds, encamped at the mouth of the Ottawa, whence they detached parties to ravage the settlements. A large band fell upon Point aux Trembles, below Montreal, burned some thirty houses, and killed such of the inmates as could not escape. Another band attacked the Mission of the Mountain, just behind the town, and captured thirty-five of the Indian converts in broad daylight. Others prowled among the deserted farms on both shores of the St.

Lawrence; while the inhabitants remained pent in their stockade forts, with misery in the present and starvation in the future.

Troops and militia were not wanting. The difficulty was to find provisions enough to enable them to keep the field. By begging from house to house, getting here a biscuit and there a morsel of bacon, enough was collected to supply a considerable party for a number of days; and a hundred and twenty soldiers and Canadians went out under Vaudreuil to hunt the hunters of men. Long impunity had made the Iroquois so careless that they were easily found. A band of about forty had made their quarters at a house near the fort at Repentigny, and here the French scouts discovered them early in the night. Vaudreuil and his men were in canoes. They lay quiet till one o'clock, then landed, and noiselessly approached the spot. Some of the Iroquois were in the house, the rest lay asleep on the ground before it. The French crept towards them, and by one close volley killed them all. Their comrades within sprang up in dismay. Three rushed out, and were shot: the others stood on their defence, fired from windows and loopholes, and killed six or seven of the French, who presently succeeded in setting fire to the house, which was thatched with straw. Young François de Bienville, one of the sons of Charles Le Moyne, rushed up to a window, shouted his name like an Indian warrior, fired on the savages within, and was instantly shot dead. The flames rose till surrounding objects were bright as day. The Iroquois, driven to desperation, burst out like tigers, and tried to break through their assailants. Only one succeeded. Of his companions, some were shot, five were knocked down and captured, and the rest driven back into the house, where they perished in the fire. Three of the prisoners were given to the inhabitants of Repentigny, Point aux Trembles, and Boucherville, who, in their fury, burned them alive.[1]

For weeks, the upper parts of the colony were infested by wolfish bands howling around the forts, which they rarely

[1] *Relation de Bénac, 1691; Relation de ce qui s'est passé de plus considérable en Canada, 1690, 1691*; La Potherie, III. 134; *Relation de 1682–1712; Champigny au Ministre, 12 May, 1691*. The name of Bienville was taken, after his death, by one of his brothers, the founder of New Orleans.

ventured to attack. At length, help came. A squadron from France, strong enough to beat off the New England privateers which blockaded the St. Lawrence, arrived at Quebec with men and supplies; and a strong force was despatched to break up the Iroquois camp at the Ottawa. The enemy vanished at its approach; and the suffering farmers had a brief respite, which enabled them to sow their crops, when suddenly a fresh alarm was sounded from Sorel to Montreal, and again the settlers ran to their forts for refuge.

Since the futile effort of the year before, the English of New York, still distracted by the political disorders that followed the usurpation of Leisler, had fought only by deputy, and contented themselves with hounding on the Iroquois against the common enemy. These savage allies at length lost patience, and charged their white neighbors with laziness and fear. "You say to us, 'Keep the French in perpetual alarm.' Why don't you say, 'We will keep the French in perpetual alarm'?"[1] It was clear that something must be done, or New York would be left to fight her battles alone. A war-party was therefore formed at Albany, and the Indians were invited to join it. Major Peter Schuyler took command; and his force consisted of two hundred and sixty-six men, of whom a hundred and twenty were English and Dutch, and the rest Mohawks and Wolves, or Mohegans.[2] He advanced to a point on the Richelieu ten miles above Fort Chambly, and, leaving his canoes under a strong guard, marched towards La Prairie de la Madeleine, opposite Montreal.

Scouts had brought warning of his approach; and Callières, the local governor, crossed the St. Lawrence, and encamped at La Prairie with seven or eight hundred men.[3] Here he remained for a week, attacked by fever and helpless in bed. The fort stood a few rods from the river. Two battalions of regulars lay on a field at the right; and the Canadians and Indians were bivouacked on the left, between the fort and a small stream, near which was a windmill. On the evening of the tenth of August, a drizzling rain began to fall; and the Canadians thought more of seeking shelter than of keeping watch.

[1] Colden, 125, 140.
[2] *Official Journal of Schuyler*, in *N. Y. Col. Docs.*, III. 800.
[3] *Relation de Bénac*; *Relation de 1682–1712.*

They were, moreover, well supplied with brandy, and used it freely.[1] At an hour before dawn, the sentry at the mill descried objects like the shadows of men silently advancing along the borders of the stream. They were Schuyler's vanguard. The soldier cried, "Qui vive?" There was no answer. He fired his musket, and ran into the mill. Schuyler's men rushed in a body upon the Canadian camp, drove its occupants into the fort, and killed some of the Indian allies, who lay under their canoes on the adjacent strand.

The regulars on the other side of the fort, roused by the noise, sprang to arms and hastened to the spot. They were met by a volley, which laid some fifty of them on the ground, and drove back the rest in disorder. They rallied and attacked again; on which, Schuyler, greatly outnumbered, withdrew his men to a neighboring ravine, where he once more repulsed his assailants, and, as he declares, drove them into the fort with great loss. By this time it was daylight. The English, having struck their blow, slowly fell back, hacking down the corn in the fields, as it was still too green for burning, and pausing at the edge of the woods, where their Indians were heard for some time uttering frightful howls, and shouting to the French that they were not men, but dogs. Why the invaders were left to retreat unmolested, before a force more than double their own, does not appear. The helpless condition of Callières and the death of Saint-Cirque, his second in command, scarcely suffice to explain it. Schuyler retreated towards his canoes, moving, at his leisure, along the forest path that led to Chambly. Tried by the standard of partisan war, his raid had been a success. He had inflicted great harm and suffered little; but the affair was not yet ended.

A day or two before, Valrenne, an officer of birth and ability, had been sent to Chambly, with about a hundred and sixty troops and Canadians, a body of Huron and Iroquois converts, and a band of Algonquins from the Ottawa. His orders were to let the English pass, and then place himself in their rear to cut them off from their canoes. His scouts had discovered their advance; and, on the morning of the attack, he set his force in motion, and advanced six or seven miles towards La Prairie, on the path by which Schuyler was re-

[1] "La débauche fut extrême en toute manière." Belmont.

treating. The country was buried in forests. At about nine o'clock, the scouts of the hostile parties met each other, and their war-whoops gave the alarm. Valrenne instantly took possession of a ridge of ground that crossed the way of the approaching English. Two large trees had fallen along the crest of the acclivity; and behind these the French crouched, in a triple row, well hidden by bushes and thick standing trunks. The English, underrating the strength of their enemy, and ignorant of his exact position, charged impetuously, and were sent reeling back by a close and deadly volley. They repeated the attack with still greater fury, and dislodged the French from their ambuscade. Then ensued a fight, which Frontenac declares to have been the most hot and stubborn ever known in Canada. The object of Schuyler was to break through the French and reach his canoes: the object of Valrenne was to drive him back upon the superior force at La Prairie. The cautious tactics of the bush were forgotten. Three times the combatants became mingled together, firing breast to breast, and scorching each other's shirts by the flash of their guns. The Algonquins did themselves no credit; and at first some of the Canadians gave way, but they were rallied by Le Ber Duchesne, their commander, and afterwards showed great bravery. On the side of the English, many of the Mohegan allies ran off; but the whites and the Mohawks fought with equal desperation. In the midst of the tumult, Valrenne was perfectly cool, directing his men with admirable vigor and address, and barring Schuyler's retreat for more than an hour. At length, the French were driven from the path. "We broke through the middle of their body," says Schuyler, "until we got into their rear, trampling upon their dead; then faced about upon them, and fought them until we made them give way; then drove them, by strength of arm, four hundred paces before us; and, to say the truth, we were all glad to see them retreat."[1] He and his followers continued their march unmolested, carrying their wounded men, and leaving about forty dead behind them, along with one of their flags, and all their knapsacks, which they had thrown off when the fray began. They reached the banks of the Riche-

[1] *Major Peter Schuyler's Journal of his Expedition to Canada*, in N. Y. Col. Docs., III. 800. "Les ennemis enfoncèrent notre embuscade." Belmont.

lieu, found their canoes safe, and, after waiting several hours for stragglers, embarked for Albany.

Nothing saved them from destruction but the failure of the French at La Prairie to follow their retreat, and thus enclose them between two fires. They did so, it is true, at the eleventh hour, but not till the fight was over and the English were gone. The Christian Mohawks of the Saut also appeared in the afternoon, and set out to pursue the enemy, but seem to have taken care not to overtake them; for the English Mohawks were their relatives, and they had no wish for their scalps. Frontenac was angry at their conduct; and, as he rarely lost an opportunity to find fault with the Jesuits, he laid the blame on the fathers in charge of the mission, whom he sharply upbraided for the shortcomings of their flock.[1]

He was at Three Rivers at a ball when news of the disaster at La Prairie damped the spirits of the company, which, however, were soon revived by tidings of the fight under Valrenne and the retreat of the English, who were reported to have left two hundred dead on the field. Frontenac wrote an account of the affair to the minister, with high praise of Valrenne and his band, followed by an appeal for help. "What with fighting and hardship, our troops and militia are wasting away." "The enemy is upon us by sea and land." "Send us a thousand men next spring, if you want the colony to be saved." "We are perishing by inches; the people are in the depths of poverty;

---

[1] As this fight under Valrenne has been represented as a French victory against overwhelming odds, it may be well to observe the evidence as to the numbers engaged. The French party consisted, according to Bénac, of 160 regulars and Canadians, besides Indians. La Potherie places it at 180 men, and Frontenac at 200 men. These two estimates do not include Indians; for the author of the *Relation* of 1682–1712, who was an officer on the spot at the time, puts the number at 300 soldiers, Canadians, and savages.

Schuyler's official return shows that his party consisted of 120 whites, 80 Mohawks, and 66 River Indians (Mohegans): 266 in all. The French writer Bénac places the whole at 280, and the intendant Champigny at 300. The other French estimates of the English force are greatly exaggerated. Schuyler's strength was reduced by 27 men left to guard the canoes, and by a number killed or disabled at La Prairie. The force under Valrenne was additional to the 700 or 800 men at La Prairie (*Relation, 1682–1712*). Schuyler reported his loss in killed at 21 whites, 16 Mohawks, and 6 Mohegans, besides many wounded. The French statements of it are enormously in excess of this, and are irreconcilable with each other.

the war has doubled prices so that nobody can live." "Many families are without bread. The inhabitants desert the country, and crowd into the towns."[1] A new enemy appeared in the following summer, almost as destructive as the Iroquois. This was an army of caterpillars, which set at naught the maledictions of the clergy, and made great havoc among the crops. It is recorded that along with the caterpillars came an unprecedented multitude of squirrels, which, being industriously trapped or shot, proved a great help to many families.

Alarm followed alarm. It was reported that Phips was bent on revenge for his late discomfiture, that great armaments were afoot, and that a mighty host of "Bostonnais" was preparing another descent. Again and again Frontenac begged that one bold blow should be struck to end these perils and make King Louis master of the continent, by despatching a fleet to seize New York. If this were done, he said, it would be easy to take Boston and the "rebels and old republican leaven of Cromwell" who harbored there; then burn the place, and utterly destroy it.[2] Villebon, governor of Acadia, was of the same mind. "No town," he told the minister, "could be burned more easily. Most of the houses are covered with shingles, and the streets are very narrow."[3] But the king could not spare a squadron equal to the attempt; and Frontenac was told that he must wait. The troops sent him did not supply his losses.[4] Money came every summer in sums which now seem small, but were far from being so in the eyes of the king, who joined to each remittance a lecture on economy and a warning against extravagance.[5]

The intendant received his share of blame on these occasions, and he usually defended himself vigorously. He tells his

---

[1] *Lettres de Frontenac et de Champigny, 1691, 1692.*

[2] Frontenac in *N. Y. Col. Docs.*, IX. 496, 506.

[3] Villebon in *N. Y. Col. Docs.*, IX. 507.

[4] The returns show 1,313 regulars in 1691, and 1,120 in 1692.

[5] *Lettres du Roy et du Ministre, 1690–1694.* In 1691, the amount allowed for *extraordinaires de guerre* was 99,000 livres (*francs*). In 1692, it was 193,000 livres, a part of which was for fortifications. In the following year, no less than 750,000 livres were drawn for Canada, "ce qui ne se pourroit pas supporter, si cela continuoit de la mesme force," writes the minister. (*Le Ministre à Frontenac, 13 Mars, 1694.*) This last sum probably included the pay of the troops.

master that "war-parties are necessary, but very expensive. We rarely pay money; but we must give presents to our Indians, and fit out the Canadians with provisions, arms, ammunition, moccasons, snow-shoes, sledges, canoes, capotes, breeches, stockings, and blankets. This costs a great deal, but without it we should have to abandon Canada." The king complained that, while the great sums he was spending in the colony turned to the profit of the inhabitants, they contributed nothing to their own defence. The complaint was scarcely just; for, if they gave no money, they gave their blood with sufficient readiness. Excepting a few merchants, they had nothing else to give; and, in the years when the fur trade was cut off, they lived chiefly on the pay they received for supplying the troops and other public services. Far from being able to support the war, they looked to the war to support them.[1]

The work of fortifying the vital points of the colony, Quebec, Three Rivers, and Montreal, received constant stimulus from the alarms of attack, and, above all, from a groundless report that ten thousand "Bostonnais" had sailed for Quebec. The sessions of the council were suspended, and the councillors seized pick and spade. The old defences of the place were reconstructed on a new plan, made by the great engineer Vauban. The settlers were mustered together from a distance of twenty leagues, and compelled to labor, with little or no pay, till a line of solid earthworks enclosed Quebec from Cape Diamond to the St. Charles. Three Rivers and Montreal were also strengthened. The cost exceeded the estimates, and drew upon Frontenac and Champigny fresh admonitions from Versailles.[2]

---

[1] "Sa Majesté fait depuis plusieurs années des sacrifices immenses en Canada. L'avantage en demeure presque tout entier au profit des habitans et des marchands qui y resident. Ces dépenses se font pour leur seureté et pour leur conservation. Il est juste que ceux qui sont en estat secourent le public." *Mémoire du Roy, 1693.* "Les habitans de la colonie ne contribuent en rien à tout ce que Sa Majesté fait pour leur conservation, pendant que ses sujets du Royaume donnent tout ce qu'ils ont pour son service." *Le Ministre à Frontenac, 13 Mars, 1694.*

[2] *Lettres du Roy et du Ministre, 1693, 1694.* Cape Diamond was now for the first time included within the line of circumvallation at Quebec. A strong stone redoubt, with sixteen cannon, was built upon its summit.

In 1854, in demolishing a part of the old wall between the fort of Quebec

The bounties on scalps and prisoners were another occasion of royal complaint. Twenty crowns had been offered for each male white prisoner, ten crowns for each female, and ten crowns for each scalp, whether Indian or English.[1] The bounty on prisoners produced an excellent result, since instead of killing them the Indian allies learned to bring them to Quebec. If children, they were placed in the convents; and, if adults, they were distributed to labor among the settlers. Thus, though the royal letters show that the measure was one of policy, it acted in the interest of humanity. It was not so with the bounty on scalps. The Abenaki, Huron, and Iroquois converts brought in many of them; but grave doubts arose whether they all came from the heads of enemies.[2] The scalp of a Frenchman was not distinguishable from the scalp of an Englishman, and could be had with less trouble. Partly for this reason, and partly out of economy, the king gave it as his belief that a bounty of one crown was enough; though the governor and the intendant united in declaring that the scalps of the whole Iroquois confederacy would be a good bargain for his Majesty at ten crowns apiece.[3]

The river Ottawa was the main artery of Canada, and to stop it was to stop the flow of her life blood. The Iroquois

---

and the adjacent "Governor's Garden," a plate of copper was found with a Latin inscription, of which the following is a translation: —

"In the year of Grace, 1693, under the reign of the Most August, Most Invincible, and Most Christian King, Louis the Great, Fourteenth of that name, the Most Excellent and Most Illustrious Lord, Louis de Buade, Count of Frontenac, twice Viceroy of all New France, after having three years before repulsed, routed, and completely conquered the rebellious inhabitants of New England, who besieged this town of Quebec, and who threatened to renew their attack this year, constructed, at the charge of the king, this citadel, with the fortifications therewith connected, for the defence of the country and the safety of the people, and for confounding yet again a people perfidious towards God and towards its lawful king. And he has laid this first stone."

[1] *Champigny au Ministre, 21 Sept., 1692*.

[2] *Relation de 1682–1712.*

[3] *Mémoire du Roy aux Sieurs Frontenac et Champigny, 1693; Frontenac et Champigny au Ministre, 4 Nov., 1693.* The bounty on prisoners was reduced in the same proportion, showing that economy was the chief object of the change.

knew this; and their constant effort was to close it so completely that the annual supply of beaver skins would be prevented from passing, and the colony be compelled to live on credit. It was their habit to spend the latter part of the winter in hunting among the forests between the Ottawa and the upper St. Lawrence, and then, when the ice broke up, to move in large bands to the banks of the former stream, and lie in ambush at the Chaudière, the Long Saut, or other favorable points, to waylay the passing canoes. On the other hand, it was the constant effort of Frontenac to drive them off and keep the river open; an almost impossible task. Many conflicts, great and small, took place with various results; but, in spite of every effort, the Iroquois blockade was maintained more than two years. The story of one of the expeditions made by the French in this quarter will show the hardship of the service, and the moral and physical vigor which it demanded.

Early in February, three hundred men under Dorvilliers were sent by Frontenac to surprise the Iroquois in their hunting-grounds. When they were a few days out, their leader scalded his foot by the upsetting of a kettle at their encampment near Lake St. Francis; and the command fell on a youth named Beaucour, an officer of regulars, accomplished as an engineer, and known for his polished wit. The march through the snow-clogged forest was so terrible that the men lost heart. Hands and feet were frozen; some of the Indians refused to proceed, and many of the Canadians lagged behind. Shots were heard, showing that the enemy were not far off; but cold, hunger, and fatigue had overcome the courage of the pursuers, and the young commander saw his followers on the point of deserting him. He called them together, and harangued them in terms so animating that they caught his spirit, and again pushed on. For four hours more they followed the tracks of the Iroquois snow-shoes, till they found the savages in their bivouac, set upon them, and killed or captured nearly all. There was a French slave among them, scarcely distinguishable from his owners. It was an officer named La Plante, taken at La Chine three years before. "He would have been killed like his masters," says La Hontan, "if he had not cried out with all his might, '*Miséricorde, sauvez-*

moi, je suis Français.'"[1] Beaucour brought his prisoners to Quebec, where Frontenac ordered that two of them should be burned. One stabbed himself in prison; the other was tortured by the Christian Hurons on Cape Diamond, defying them to the last. Nor was this the only instance of such fearful reprisal. In the same year, a number of Iroquois captured by Vaudreuil were burned at Montreal at the demand of the Canadians and the mission Indians, who insisted that their cruelties should be paid back in kind. It is said that the purpose was answered, and the Iroquois deterred for a while from torturing their captives.[2]

The brunt of the war fell on the upper half of the colony. The country about Montreal, and for nearly a hundred miles below it, was easily accessible to the Iroquois by the routes of Lake Champlain and the upper St. Lawrence; while below Three Rivers the settlements were tolerably safe from their incursions, and were exposed to attack solely from the English of New England, who could molest them only by sailing up from the Gulf in force. Hence the settlers remained on their farms, and followed their usual occupations, except when Frontenac drafted them for war parties. Above Three Rivers, their condition was wholly different. A traveller passing through this part of Canada would have found the houses empty. Here and there he would have seen all the inhabitants of a parish laboring in a field together, watched by sentinels, and generally guarded by a squad of regulars. When one field was tilled, they passed to the next; and this communal process was repeated when the harvest was ripe. At night, they took refuge in the fort; that is to say, in a cluster of log cabins, surrounded by a palisade. Sometimes, when long exemption from attack had emboldened them, they ventured back to their farm-houses, an experiment always critical and sometimes fatal. Thus the people of La Chesnaye, forgetting a sharp lesson they had received a year or two before, returned to their homes in fancied security. One evening a bachelor of the parish made a visit to a neighboring widow, bringing with him his gun and a small dog. As he was taking his leave,

---

[1] La Potherie, III. 156; *Relation de ce qui s'est passé de plus considérable en Canada, 1691, 1692*; La Hontan, I. 233.

[2] *Relation, 1682–1712.*

his hostess, whose husband had been killed the year before, told him that she was afraid to be left alone, and begged him to remain with her, an invitation which he accepted. Towards morning, the barking of his dog roused him; when, going out, he saw the night lighted up by the blaze of burning houses, and heard the usual firing and screeching of an Iroquois attack. He went back to his frightened companion, who also had a gun. Placing himself at a corner of the house, he told her to stand behind him. A number of Iroquois soon appeared, on which he fired at them, and, taking her gun, repeated the shot, giving her his own to load. The warriors returned his fire from a safe distance, and in the morning withdrew altogether, on which the pair emerged from their shelter, and succeeded in reaching the fort. The other inhabitants were all killed or captured.[1]

Many incidents of this troubled time are preserved, but none of them are so well worth the record as the defence of the fort at Verchères by the young daughter of the seignior. Many years later, the Marquis de Beauharnais, governor of Canada, caused the story to be written down from the recital of the heroine herself. Verchères was on the south shore of the St. Lawrence, about twenty miles below Montreal. A strong blockhouse stood outside the fort, and was connected with it by a covered way. On the morning of the twenty-second of October, the inhabitants were at work in the fields, and nobody was left in the place but two soldiers, two boys, an old man of eighty, and a number of women and children. The seignior, formerly an officer of the regiment of Carignan, was on duty at Quebec; his wife was at Montreal; and their daughter Madeleine, fourteen years of age, was at the landing-place not far from the gate of the fort, with a hired man named Laviolette. Suddenly she heard firing from the direction where the settlers were at work, and an instant after Laviolette cried out, "Run, Mademoiselle, run! here come the Iroquois!" She turned and saw forty or fifty of them at the distance of a pistol-shot. "I ran for the fort, commending myself to the Holy Virgin. The Iroquois who chased after me, seeing that they could not catch me alive before I reached the

[1] *Relation, 1682–1712.*

gate, stopped and fired at me. The bullets whistled about my ears, and made the time seem very long. As soon as I was near enough to be heard, I cried out, *To arms! to arms!* hoping that somebody would come out and help me; but it was of no use. The two soldiers in the fort were so scared that they had hidden in the blockhouse. At the gate, I found two women crying for their husbands, who had just been killed. I made them go in, and then shut the gate. I next thought what I could do to save myself and the few people with me. I went to inspect the fort, and found that several palisades had fallen down, and left openings by which the enemy could easily get in. I ordered them to be set up again, and helped to carry them myself. When the breaches were stopped, I went to the blockhouse where the ammunition is kept, and here I found the two soldiers, one hiding in a corner, and the other with a lighted match in his hand. 'What are you going to do with that match?' I asked. He answered, 'Light the powder, and blow us all up.' 'You are a miserable coward,' said I, 'go out of this place.' I spoke so resolutely that he obeyed. I then threw off my bonnet; and, after putting on a hat and taking a gun, I said to my two brothers: 'Let us fight to the death. We are fighting for our country and our religion. Remember that our father has taught you that gentlemen are born to shed their blood for the service of God and the king.' "

The boys, who were twelve and ten years old, aided by the soldiers, whom her words had inspired with some little courage, began to fire from the loopholes upon the Iroquois, who, ignorant of the weakness of the garrison, showed their usual reluctance to attack a fortified place, and occupied themselves with chasing and butchering the people in the neighboring fields. Madeleine ordered a cannon to be fired, partly to deter the enemy from an assault, and partly to warn some of the soldiers, who were hunting at a distance. The women and children in the fort cried and screamed without ceasing. She ordered them to stop, lest their terror should encourage the Indians. A canoe was presently seen approaching the landing-place. It was a settler named Fontaine, trying to reach the fort with his family. The Iroquois were still near; and Madeleine feared that the new comers would be killed, if something were not done to aid them. She appealed to the soldiers, but their courage was not equal to the attempt; on which, as she declares, after leaving Laviolette to keep watch at the gate, she herself went alone to the landing-place. "I thought that the savages would suppose it to be a ruse to draw them towards the fort, in order to make a sortie upon them. They did suppose so, and thus I was able to save the Fontaine family. When they were all landed, I made them march before me in full sight of the enemy. We put so bold a face on it, that they thought they had more to fear than we. Strengthened by this reinforcement, I ordered that the enemy should be fired on whenever they showed themselves. After sunset, a violent north-east wind began to blow, accompanied with snow and hail, which told us that we should have a terrible night. The Iroquois were all this time lurking about us; and I judged by their movements that, instead of being deterred by the storm, they would climb into the fort under cover of the darkness. I assembled all my troops, that is to say, six persons, and spoke to them thus: 'God has saved us to-day from the hands of our enemies, but we must take care not to fall into their snares to-night. As for me, I want you to see that I am not afraid. I will take charge of the fort with an old man of eighty and another who never fired a gun; and you, Pierre Fontaine, with La Bonté and Gachet (our two soldiers), will go to the blockhouse with the women and children, because that is the strongest place; and, if I am taken, don't surrender, even if I am cut to pieces and burned before your eyes. The enemy cannot hurt you in the blockhouse, if you make the least show of fight.' I placed my young brothers on two of the bastions, the old man on the third, and I took the fourth; and all night, in spite of wind, snow, and hail, the cries of 'All's well' were kept up from the blockhouse to the fort, and from the fort to the blockhouse. One would have thought that the place was full of soldiers. The Iroquois thought so, and were completely deceived, as they confessed afterwards to Monsieur de Callières, whom they told that they had held a council to make a plan for capturing the fort in the night but had done nothing because such a constant watch was kept.

"About one in the morning, the sentinel on the bastion by the gate called out, 'Mademoiselle, I hear something.' I went to him to find what it was; and by the help of the snow, which covered the ground, I could see through the darkness a number of cattle, the miserable remnant that the Iroquois had left us. The others wanted to open the gate and let them in, but I answered: 'God forbid. You don't know all the tricks of the savages. They are no doubt following the cattle, covered with skins of beasts, so as to get into the fort, if we are simple enough to open the gate for them.' Nevertheless, after taking every precaution, I thought that we might open it without risk. I made my two brothers stand ready with their guns cocked in case of surprise, and so we let in the cattle.

"At last, the daylight came again; and, as the darkness disappeared, our anxieties seemed to disappear with it. Everybody took courage except Mademoiselle Marguérite, wife of the Sieur Fontaine, who being extremely timid, as all Parisian women are, asked her husband to carry her to another fort. . . He said, 'I will never abandon this fort while Mademoiselle Madelon (*Madeleine*) is here.' I answered him that I would never abandon it; that I would rather die than give it up to the enemy; and that it was of the greatest importance that they should never get possession of any French fort, because, if they got one, they would think they could get others, and would grow more bold and presumptuous than ever. I may say with truth that I did not eat or sleep for twice twenty-four hours. I did not go once into my father's house, but kept always on the bastion, or went to the blockhouse to see how the people there were behaving. I always kept a cheerful and smiling face, and encouraged my little company with the hope of speedy succor.

"We were a week in constant alarm, with the enemy always about us. At last Monsieur de la Monnerie, a lieutenant sent by Monsieur de Callières, arrived in the night with forty men. As he did not know whether the fort was taken or not, he approached as silently as possible. One of our sentinels, hearing a slight sound, cried, 'Qui vive?' I was at the time dozing, with my head on a table and my gun lying across my arms. The sentinel told me that he heard a voice from the river. I went up at once to the bastion to see whether it was Indians or Frenchmen. I asked, 'Who are you?' One of them answered, 'We are Frenchmen: it is La Monnerie, who comes to bring you help.' I caused the gate to be opened, placed a sentinel there, and went down to the river to meet them. As soon as I saw Monsieur de la Monnerie, I saluted him, and said, 'Monsieur, I surrender my arms to you.' He answered gallantly, 'Mademoiselle, they are in good hands.' 'Better than you think,' I returned. He inspected the fort, and found every thing in order, and a sentinel on each bastion. 'It is time to relieve them, Monsieur,' said I: 'we have not been off our bastions for a week.' "[1]

A band of converts from the Saut St. Louis arrived soon after, followed the trail of their heathen countrymen, overtook them on Lake Champlain, and recovered twenty or more French prisoners. Madeleine de Verchères was not the only heroine of her family. Her father's fort was the Castle Dangerous of Canada; and it was but two years before that her mother, left with three or four armed men, and beset by the Iroquois, threw herself with her followers into the blockhouse, and held the assailants two days at bay, till the Marquis de Crisasi came with troops to her relief.[2]

From the moment when the Canadians found a chief whom they could trust, and the firm old hand of Frontenac grasped the reins of their destiny, a spirit of hardihood and energy grew up in all this rugged population; and they faced their stern fortunes with a stubborn daring and endurance that merit respect and admiration.

Now, as in all their former wars, a great part of their suffering was due to the Mohawks. The Jesuits had spared no pains to convert them, thus changing them from enemies to friends; and their efforts had so far succeeded that the mission

---

[1] *Récit de Mlle. Magdelaine de Verchères, âgée de 14 ans* (Collection de l'Abbé Ferland). It appears from Tanguay, *Dictionnaire Généalogique*, that Marie-Madeleine Jarret de Verchères was born in April, 1678, which corresponds to the age given in the *Récit*. She married Thomas Tarieu de la Naudière in 1706, and M. de la Perrade, or Prade, in 1722. Her brother Louis was born in 1680, and was therefore, as stated in the *Récit*, twelve years old in 1692. The birthday of the other, Alexander, is not given. His baptism was registered in 1682. One of the brothers was killed at the attack of Haverhill, in 1708.

Madame de Ponchartrain, wife of the minister, procured a pension for life to Madeleine de Verchères. Two versions of her narrative are before me. There are slight variations between them, but in all essential points they are the same. The following note is appended to one of them: "Ce récit fut fait par ordre de M. de Beauharnois, gouverneur du Canada."

[2] La Potherie, I. 326.

colony of Saut St. Louis contained a numerous population of Mohawk Christians.[1] The place was well fortified; and troops were usually stationed here, partly to defend the converts and partly to ensure their fidelity. They had sometimes done excellent service for the French; but many of them still remembered their old homes on the Mohawk, and their old ties of fellowship and kindred. Their heathen countrymen were jealous of their secession, and spared no pains to reclaim them. Sometimes they tried intrigue, and sometimes force. On one occasion, joined by the Oneidas and Onondagas, they appeared before the palisades of St. Louis, to the number of more than four hundred warriors; but, finding the bastions manned and the gates shut, they withdrew discomfited. It was of great importance to the French to sunder them from their heathen relatives so completely that reconciliation would be impossible, and it was largely to this end that a grand expedition was prepared against the Mohawk towns.

All the mission Indians in the colony were invited to join it, the Iroquois of the Saut and Mountain, Abenakis from the Chaudière, Hurons from Lorette, and Algonquins from Three Rivers. A hundred picked soldiers were added, and a large band of Canadians. All told, they mustered six hundred and twenty-five men, under three tried leaders, Mantet, Courtemanche, and La Noue. They left Chambly at the end of January, and pushed southward on snow-shoes. Their way was over the ice of Lake Champlain, for more than a century the great thoroughfare of war-parties. They bivouacked in the forest by squads of twelve or more; dug away the snow in a circle, covered the bared earth with a bed of spruce boughs, made a fire in the middle, and smoked their pipes around it. Here crouched the Christian savage, muffled in his blanket, his unwashed face still smirched with soot and vermilion, relics of the war-paint he had worn a week before when he danced the war-dance in the square of the mission village; and here sat the Canadians, hooded like Capuchin monks, but irrepressible in loquacity, as the blaze of the camp-fire glowed on their hardy visages and fell in fainter radiance on the rocks and pines behind them.

[1] This mission was also called Caghnawaga. The village still exists, at the head of the rapid of St. Louis, or La Chine.

Sixteen days brought them to the two lower Mohawk towns. A young Dutchman who had been captured three years before at Schenectady, and whom the Indians of the Saut had imprudently brought with them, ran off in the night, and carried the alarm to the English. The invaders had no time to lose. The two towns were a quarter of a league apart. They surrounded them both on the night of the sixteenth of February, waited in silence till the voices within were hushed, and then captured them without resistance, as most of the inmates were absent. After burning one of them, and leaving the prisoners well guarded in the other, they marched eight leagues to the third town, reached it at evening, and hid in the neighboring woods. Through all the early night, they heard the whoops and songs of the warriors within, who were dancing the war-dance for an intended expedition. About midnight, all was still. The Mohawks had posted no sentinels; and one of the French Indians, scaling the palisade, opened the gate to his comrades. There was a short but bloody fight. Twenty or thirty Mohawks were killed, and nearly three hundred captured, chiefly women and children. The French commanders now required their allies, the mission Indians, to make good a promise which, at the instance of Frontenac, had been exacted from them by the governor of Montreal. It was that they should kill all their male captives, a proceeding which would have averted every danger of future reconciliation between the Christian and heathen Mohawks. The converts of the Saut and the Mountain had readily given the pledge, but apparently with no intention to keep it; at least, they now refused to do so. Remonstrance was useless; and, after burning the town, the French and their allies began their retreat, encumbered by a long train of prisoners. They marched two days, when they were hailed from a distance by Mohawk scouts, who told them that the English were on their track, but that peace had been declared in Europe, and that the pursuers did not mean to fight, but to parley. Hereupon the mission Indians insisted on waiting for them, and no exertion of the French commanders could persuade them to move. Trees were hewn down, and a fort made after the Iroquois fashion, by encircling the camp with a high and dense abatis of trunks and

branches. Here they lay two days more, the French disgusted
and uneasy, and their savage allies obstinate and impracticable.

Meanwhile, Major Peter Schuyler was following their trail,
with a body of armed settlers hastily mustered. A troop of
Oneidas joined him; and the united parties, between five and
six hundred in all, at length appeared before the fortified
camp of the French. It was at once evident that there was to
be no parley. The forest rang with war-whoops; and the English Indians, unmanageable as those of the French, set at
work to entrench themselves with felled trees. The French
and their allies sallied to dislodge them. The attack was fierce,
and the resistance equally so. Both sides lost ground by turns.
A priest of the mission of the Mountain, named Gay, was in
the thick of the fight; and, when he saw his neophytes run,
he threw himself before them, crying, "What are you afraid
of? We are fighting with infidels, who have nothing human
but the shape. Have you forgotten that the Holy Virgin is
our leader and our protector, and that you are subjects of the
King of France, whose name makes all Europe tremble?"[1]
Three times the French renewed the attack in vain; then gave
over the attempt, and lay quiet behind their barricade of trees.
So also did their opponents. The morning was dark and
stormy, and the driving snow that filled the air made the position doubly dreary. The English were starving. Their slender
stock of provisions had been consumed or shared with the
Indians, who, on their part, did not want food, having resources unknown to their white friends. A group of them
squatted about a fire invited Schuyler to share their broth; but
his appetite was spoiled when he saw a human hand ladled
out of the kettle. His hosts were breakfasting on a dead
Frenchman.

All night the hostile bands, ensconced behind their sylvan
ramparts, watched each other in silence. In the morning, an
Indian deserter told the English commander that the French
were packing their baggage. Schuyler sent to reconnoitre, and
found them gone. They had retreated unseen through the
snow-storm. He ordered his men to follow; but, as most of
them had fasted for two days, they refused to do so till an

[1] *Journal de Jacques Le Ber*, extract in Faillon, *Vie de Mlle. Le Ber, Appendix.*

expected convoy of provisions should arrive. They waited till the next morning, when the convoy appeared: five biscuits were served out to each man, and the pursuit began. By great efforts, they nearly overtook the fugitives, who now sent them word that, if they made an attack, all the prisoners should be put to death. On this, Schuyler's Indians refused to continue the chase. The French, by this time, had reached the Hudson, where to their dismay they found the ice breaking up and drifting down the stream. Happily for them, a large sheet of it had become wedged at a turn of the river, and formed a temporary bridge, by which they crossed, and then pushed on to Lake George. Here the soft and melting ice would not bear them; and they were forced to make their way along the shore, over rocks and mountains, through sodden snow and matted thickets. The provisions, of which they had made a dépôt on Lake Champlain, were all spoiled. They boiled moccasons for food, and scraped away the snow to find hickory and beech nuts. Several died of famine, and many more, unable to move, lay helpless by the lake; while a few of the strongest toiled on to Montreal to tell Callières of their plight. Men and food were sent them; and from time to time, as they were able, they journeyed on again, straggling towards their homes, singly or in small parties, feeble, emaciated, and in many instances with health irreparably broken.[1]

"The expedition," says Frontenac, "was a glorious success." However glorious, it was dearly bought; and a few more such victories would be ruin. The governor presently achieved a success more solid and less costly. The wavering mood of the north-western tribes, always oscillating between the French and the English, had caused him incessant anxiety; and he had lost no time in using the defeat of Phips to confirm them in alliance with Canada. Courtemanche was sent up the Ottawa to carry news of the French triumph, and stimulate the

---

[1] On this expedition, *Narrative of Military Operations in Canada*, in *N. Y. Col. Docs.*, IX. 550; *Relation de ce qui s'est passé de plus remarquable en Canada, 1692, 1693; Callières au Ministre, 7 Sept., 1693*; La Potherie, III. 169; *Relation de 1682–1712*; Faillon, *Vie de Mlle. Le Ber*, 313; Belmont, *Hist. du Canada*; Beyard and Lodowick, *Journal of the Late Actions of the French at Canada; Report of Major Peter Schuyler*, in *N. Y. Col. Docs.*, IV. 16; Colden, 142.

The minister wrote to Callières, finding great fault with the conduct of the mission Indians. *Ponchartrain à Callières, 8 Mai, 1694.*

savages of Michillimackinac to lift the hatchet. It was a desperate venture; for the river was beset, as usual, by the Iroquois. With ten followers, the daring partisan ran the gauntlet of a thousand dangers, and safely reached his destination; where his gifts and his harangues, joined with the tidings of victory, kindled great excitement among the Ottawas and Hurons. The indispensable but most difficult task remained: that of opening the Ottawa for the descent of the great accumulation of beaver skins, which had been gathering at Michillimackinac for three years, and for the want of which Canada was bankrupt. More than two hundred Frenchmen were known to be at that remote post, or roaming in the wilderness around it; and Frontenac resolved on an attempt to muster them together, and employ their united force to protect the Indians and the traders in bringing down this mass of furs to Montreal. A messenger, strongly escorted, was sent with orders to this effect, and succeeded in reaching Michillimackinac, though there was a battle on the way, in which the officer commanding the escort was killed. Frontenac anxiously waited the issue, when after a long delay the tidings reached him of complete success. He hastened to Montreal, and found it swarming with Indians and *coureurs de bois*. Two hundred canoes had arrived, filled with the coveted beaver skins. "It is impossible," says the chronicle, "to conceive the joy of the people, when they beheld these riches. Canada had awaited them for years. The merchants and the farmers were dying of hunger. Credit was gone, and everybody was afraid that the enemy would waylay and seize this last resource of the country. Therefore it was, that none could find words strong enough to praise and bless him by whose care all this wealth had arrived. *Father of the People*, *Preserver of the Country*, seemed terms too weak to express their gratitude."[1]

While three years of arrested sustenance came down together from the lakes, a fleet sailed up the St. Lawrence, freighted with soldiers and supplies. The horizon of Canada was brightening.

[1] *Relation de ce qui s'est passé de plus remarquable en Canada, 1692, 1693.* Compare La Potherie, III. 185.

Chapter XV

AN INTERLUDE

*Appeal of Frontenac • His Opponents • His Services • Rivalry and
Strife • Bishop Saint-Vallier • Society at the Château • Private
Theatricals • Alarm of the Clergy • Tartuffe • A Singular Bar-
gain • Mareuil and the Bishop • Mareuil on Trial • Zeal of Saint-
Vallier • Scandals at Montreal • Appeal to the King • The Strife
composed • Libel against Frontenac*

WHILE the Canadians hailed Frontenac as a father, he
found also some recognition of his services from his
masters at the court. The king wrote him a letter with his
own hand, to express satisfaction at the defence of Quebec,
and sent him a gift of two thousand crowns. He greatly
needed the money, but prized the letter still more, and wrote
to his relative, the minister Ponchartrain: "The gift you procured for me, this year, has helped me very much towards
paying the great expenses which the crisis of our affairs and
the excessive cost of living here have caused me; but, though
I receive this mark of his Majesty's goodness with the utmost
respect and gratitude, I confess that I feel far more deeply the
satisfaction that he has been pleased to express with my services. The raising of the siege of Quebec did not deserve all
the attention that I hear he has given it in the midst of so
many important events, and therefore I must needs ascribe it
to your kindness in commending it to his notice. This leads
me to hope that whenever some office, or permanent employment, or some mark of dignity or distinction, may offer itself,
you will put me on the list as well as others who have the
honor to be as closely connected with you as I am; for it
would be very hard to find myself forgotten because I am in
a remote country, where it is more difficult and dangerous to
serve the king than elsewhere. I have consumed all my property. Nothing is left but what the king gives me; and I have
reached an age where, though neither strength nor good-will
fail me as yet, and though the latter will last as long as I live,
I see myself on the eve of losing the former: so that a post a

little more secure and tranquil than the government of Canada will soon suit my time of life; and, if I can be assured of your support, I shall not despair of getting such a one. Please then to permit my wife and my friends to refresh your memory now and then on this point."[1] Again, in the following year: "I have been encouraged to believe that the gift of two thousand crowns, which his Majesty made me last year, would be continued; but apparently you have not been able to obtain it, for I think that you know the difficulty I have in living here on my salary. I hope that, when you find a better opportunity, you will try to procure me this favor. My only trust is in your support; and I am persuaded that, having the honor to be so closely connected with you, you would reproach yourself, if you saw me sink into decrepitude, without resources and without honors."[2] And still again he appeals to the minister for "some permanent and honorable place attended with the marks of distinction, which are more grateful than all the rest to a heart shaped after the right pattern."[3] In return for these sturdy applications, he got nothing for the present but a continuance of the king's gift of two thousand crowns.

Not every voice in the colony sounded the governor's praise. Now, as always, he had enemies in state and Church. It is true that the quarrels and the bursts of passion that marked his first term of government now rarely occurred, but this was not so much due to a change in Frontenac himself as to a change in the conditions around him. The war made him indispensable. He had gained what he wanted, the consciousness of mastery; and under its soothing influence he was less irritable and exacting. He lived with the bishop on terms of mutual courtesy, while his relations with his colleague, the intendant, were commonly smooth enough on the surface; for Champigny, warned by the court not to offend him, treated him with studied deference, and was usually treated in return with urbane condescension. During all this time, the intendant was complaining of him to the minister. "He is spending a great deal of money; but he is master, and does

[1] *Frontenac au Ministre, 20 Oct., 1691.*

[2] *Ibid., 15 Sept., 1692.*

[3] *Ibid., 25 Oct., 1693.*

what he pleases. I can only keep the peace by yielding every thing."[1] "He wants to reduce me to a nobody." And, among other similar charges, he says that the governor receives pay for garrisons that do not exist, and keeps it for himself. "Do not tell that I said so," adds the prudent Champigny, "for it would make great trouble, if he knew it."[2] Frontenac, perfectly aware of these covert attacks, desires the minister not to heed "the falsehoods and impostures uttered against me by persons who meddle with what does not concern them."[3] He alludes to Champigny's allies, the Jesuits, who, as he thought, had also maligned him. "Since I have been here, I have spared no pains to gain the good-will of Monsieur the intendant, and may God grant that the counsels which he is too ready to receive from certain persons who have never been friends of peace and harmony do not some time make division between us. But I close my eyes to all that, and shall still persevere."[4] In another letter to Ponchartrain, he says: "I write you this in private, because I have been informed by my wife that charges have been made to you against my conduct since my return to this country. I promise you, Monseigneur, that, whatever my accusers do, they will not make me change conduct towards them, and that I shall still treat them with consideration. I merely ask your leave most humbly to represent that, having maintained this colony in full prosperity during the ten years when I formerly held the government of it, I nevertheless fell a sacrifice to the artifice and fury of those whose encroachments, and whose excessive and unauthorized power, my duty and my passionate affection for the service of the king obliged me in conscience to repress. My recall, which made them masters in the conduct of the government, was followed by all the disasters which overwhelmed this unhappy colony. The millions that the king spent here, the troops that he sent out, and the Canadians that he took into pay, all went for nothing. Most of the soldiers, and no small number of brave Canadians, perished in enterprises ill devised and ruinous to the country, which I found on my arrival ravaged with

[1] *Champigny au Ministre, 12 Oct., 1691.*

[2] *Ibid., 4 Nov., 1693.*

[3] *Frontenac au Ministre, 15 Sept., 1692.*

[4] *Ibid., 20 Oct., 1691.*

unheard-of cruelty by the Iroquois, without resistance, and in sight of the troops and of the forts. The inhabitants were discouraged, and unnerved by want of confidence in their chiefs; while the friendly Indians, seeing our weakness, were ready to join our enemies. I was fortunate enough and diligent enough to change this deplorable state of things, and drive away the English, whom my predecessors did not have on their hands, and this too with only half as many troops as they had. I am far from wishing to blame their conduct. I leave you to judge it. But I cannot have the tranquillity and freedom of mind which I need for the work I have to do here, without feeling entire confidence that the cabal which is again forming against me cannot produce impressions which may prevent you from doing me justice. For the rest, if it is thought fit that I should leave the priests to do as they like, I shall be delivered from an infinity of troubles and cares, in which I can have no other interest than the good of the colony, the trade of the kingdom, and the peace of the king's subjects, and of which I alone bear the burden, as well as the jealousy of sundry persons, and the iniquity of the ecclesiastics, who begin to call impious those who are obliged to oppose their passions and their interests."[1]

As Champigny always sided with the Jesuits, his relations with Frontenac grew daily more critical. Open rupture at length seemed imminent, and the king interposed to keep the peace. "There has been discord between you under a show of harmony," he wrote to the disputants.[2] Frontenac was exhorted to forbearance and calmness; while the intendant was told that he allowed himself to be made an instrument of others, and that his charges against the governor proved nothing but his own ill-temper.[3] The minister wrote in vain. The bickerings that he reproved were but premonitions of a greater strife.

Bishop Saint-Vallier was a rigid, austere, and contentious prelate, who loved power as much as Frontenac himself, and

---

[1] "L'iniquité des ecclésiastiques qui commencent à traiter d'impies ceux qui sont obligés de resister à leurs passions et à leurs interêts." *Frontenac au Ministre, 20 Oct., 1691.*

[2] *Mémoire du Roy pour Frontenac et Champigny, 1694.*

[3] *Le Ministre à Frontenac, 8 May, 1694; Le Ministre à Champigny, même date.*

thought that, as the deputy of Christ, it was his duty to exercise it to the utmost. The governor watched him with a jealous eye, well aware that, though the pretensions of the Church to supremacy over the civil power had suffered a check, Saint-Vallier would revive them the moment he thought he could do so with success. I have shown elsewhere the severity of the ecclesiastical rule at Quebec, where the zealous pastors watched their flock with unrelenting vigilance, and associations of pious women helped them in the work.[1] This naturally produced revolt, and tended to divide the town into two parties, the worldly and the devout. The love of pleasure was not extinguished, and various influences helped to keep it alive. Perhaps none of these was so potent as the presence in winter of a considerable number of officers from France, whose piety was often less conspicuous than their love of enjoyment. At the Château St. Louis a circle of young men, more or less brilliant and accomplished, surrounded the governor, and formed a centre of social attraction. Frontenac was not without religion, and he held it becoming a man of his station not to fail in its observances; but he would not have a Jesuit confessor, and placed his conscience in the keeping of the Récollet friars, who were not politically aggressive, and who had been sent to Canada expressly as a foil to the rival order. They found no favor in the eyes of the bishop and his adherents, and the governor found none for the support he lent them.

The winter that followed the arrival of the furs from the upper lakes was a season of gayety without precedent since the war began. All was harmony at Quebec till the carnival approached, when Frontenac, whose youthful instincts survived his seventy-four years, introduced a startling novelty which proved the signal of discord. One of his military circle, the sharp-witted La Motte-Cadillac, thus relates this untoward event in a letter to a friend: "The winter passed very pleasantly, especially to the officers, who lived together like comrades; and, to contribute to their honest enjoyment, the count caused two plays to be acted, 'Nicomede' and 'Mithridate.'" It was an amateur performance, in which the officers took part along with some of the ladies of Quebec. The suc-

[1] Old Régime, chap. xxii.

cess was prodigious, and so was the storm that followed. Half a century before, the Jesuits had grieved over the first ball in Canada. Private theatricals were still more baneful. "The clergy," continues La Motte, "beat their alarm drums, armed cap-a-pie, and snatched their bows and arrows. The Sieur Glandelet was first to begin, and preached two sermons, in which he tried to prove that nobody could go to a play without mortal sin. The bishop issued a mandate, and had it read from the pulpits, in which he speaks of certain impious, impure, and noxious comedies, insinuating that those which had been acted were such. The credulous and infatuated people, seduced by the sermons and the mandate, began already to regard the count as a corrupter of morals and a destroyer of religion. The numerous party of the pretended devotees mustered in the streets and public places, and presently made their way into the houses, to confirm the weak-minded in their illusion, and tried to make the stronger share it; but, as they failed in this almost completely, they resolved at last to conquer or die, and persuaded the bishop to use a strange device, which was to publish a mandate in the church, whereby the Sieur de Mareuil, a half-pay lieutenant, was interdicted the use of the sacraments."[1]

This story needs explanation. Not only had the amateur actors at the château played two pieces inoffensive enough in themselves, but a report had been spread that they meant next to perform the famous "Tartuffe" of Molière, a satire which, while purporting to be levelled against falsehood, lust, greed, and ambition, covered with a mask of religion, was rightly thought by a portion of the clergy to be levelled against themselves. The friends of Frontenac say that the report was a hoax. Be this as it may, the bishop believed it. "This worthy prelate," continues the irreverent La Motte, "was afraid of 'Tartuffe,' and had got it into his head that the count meant to have it played, though he had never thought of such a thing. Monsieur de Saint-Vallier sweated blood and water to stop a torrent which existed only in his imagination." It was now that he launched his two mandates, both on the same day; one denouncing comedies in general and "Tartuffe" in particular, and the other smiting Mareuil, who, he says, "uses

[1] *La Motte-Cadillac à* ———, *28 Sept., 1694.*

language capable of making Heaven blush," and whom he elsewhere stigmatizes as "worse than a Protestant."[1] It was Mareuil who, as reported, was to play the part of Tartuffe; and on him, therefore, the brunt of episcopal indignation fell. He was not a wholly exemplary person. "I mean," says La Motte, "to show you the truth in all its nakedness. The fact is that, about two years ago, when the Sieur de Mareuil first came to Canada, and was carousing with his friends, he sang some indecent song or other. The count was told of it, and gave him a severe reprimand. This is the charge against him. After a two years' silence, the pastoral zeal has wakened, because a play is to be acted which the clergy mean to stop at any cost."

The bishop found another way of stopping it. He met Frontenac, with the intendant, near the Jesuit chapel, accosted him on the subject which filled his thoughts, and offered him a hundred pistoles if he would prevent the playing of "Tartuffe." Frontenac laughed, and closed the bargain. Saint-Vallier wrote his note on the spot; and the governor took it, apparently well pleased to have made the bishop disburse. "I thought," writes the intendant, "that Monsieur de Frontenac would have given him back the paper." He did no such thing, but drew the money on the next day and gave it to the hospitals.[2]

Mareuil, deprived of the sacraments, and held up to reprobation, went to see the bishop, who refused to receive him; and it is said that he was taken by the shoulders and put out of doors. He now resolved to bring his case before the council; but the bishop was informed of his purpose, and anticipated it. La Motte says "he went before the council on the first of February, and denounced the Sieur de Mareuil, whom he declared guilty of impiety towards God, the Virgin, and the Saints, and made a fine speech in the absence of the count, interrupted by the effusions of a heart which seemed

[1] *Mandement au Sujet des Comédies, 16 Jan., 1694; Mandement au Sujet de certaines Personnes qui tenoient des Discours impies, même date; Registre du Conseil Souverain.*

[2] This incident is mentioned by La Motte-Cadillac; by the intendant, who reports it to the minister; by the minister Ponchartrain, who asks Frontenac for an explanation; by Frontenac, who passes it off as a jest; and by several other contemporary writers.

filled with a profound and infinite charity, but which, as he said, was pushed to extremity by the rebellion of an indocile child, who had neglected all his warnings. This was, nevertheless, assumed; I will not say entirely false."

The bishop did, in fact, make a vehement speech against Mareuil before the council on the day in question; Mareuil stoutly defending himself, and entering his appeal against the episcopal mandate.[1] The battle was now fairly joined. Frontenac stood alone for the accused. The intendant tacitly favored his opponents. Auteuil, the attorney-general, and Villeray, the first councillor, owed the governor an old grudge; and they and their colleagues sided with the bishop, with the outside support of all the clergy, except the Récollets, who, as usual, ranged themselves with their patron. At first, Frontenac showed great moderation, but grew vehement, and then violent, as the dispute proceeded; as did also the attorney-general, who seems to have done his best to exasperate him. Frontenac affirmed that, in depriving Mareuil and others of the sacraments, with no proof of guilt and no previous warning, and on allegations which, even if true, could not justify the act, the bishop exceeded his powers, and trenched on those of the king. The point was delicate. The attorney-general avoided the issue, tried to raise others, and revived the old quarrel about Frontenac's place in the council, which had been settled fourteen years before. Other questions were brought up, and angrily debated. The governor demanded that the debates, along with the papers which introduced them, should be entered on the record, that the king might be informed of every thing; but the demand was refused. The discords of the council chamber spread into the town. Quebec was divided against itself. Mareuil insulted the bishop; and some of his scapegrace sympathizers broke the prelate's windows at night, and smashed his chamber-door.[2] Mareuil was at last ordered to prison, and the whole affair was referred to the king.[3]

These proceedings consumed the spring, the summer, and a part of the autumn. Meanwhile, an access of zeal appeared

[1] *Registre du Conseil Souverain, 1 et 8 Fév., 1694.*

[2] *Champigny au Ministre, 27 Oct., 1694.*

[3] *Registre du Conseil Souverain; Requeste du Sieur de Mareuil, Nov., 1694.*

to seize the bishop; and he launched interdictions to the right and left. Even Champigny was startled when he refused the sacraments to all but four or five of the military officers for alleged tampering with the pay of their soldiers, a matter wholly within the province of the temporal authorities.[1] During a recess of the council, he set out on a pastoral tour, and, arriving at Three Rivers, excommunicated an officer named Desjordis for a reputed intrigue with the wife of another officer. He next repaired to Sorel, and, being there on a Sunday, was told that two officers had neglected to go to mass. He wrote to Frontenac, complaining of the offence. Frontenac sent for the culprits, and rebuked them; but retracted his words when they proved by several witnesses that they had been duly present at the rite.[2] The bishop then went up to Montreal, and discord went with him.

Except Frontenac alone, Callières, the local governor, was the man in all Canada to whom the country owed most; but, like his chief, he was a friend of the Récollets, and this did not commend him to the bishop. The friars were about to receive two novices into their order, and they invited the bishop to officiate at the ceremony. Callières was also present, kneeling at a *prie-dieu*, or prayer-desk, near the middle of the church. Saint-Vallier, having just said mass, was seating himself in his arm-chair, close to the altar, when he saw Callières at the *prie-dieu*, with the position of which he had already found fault as being too honorable for a subordinate governor. He now rose, approached the object of his disapproval, and said, "Monsieur, you are taking a place which belongs only to Monsieur de Frontenac." Callières replied that the place was that which properly belonged to him. The bishop rejoined that, if he did not leave it, he himself would leave the church. "You can do as you please," said Callières; and the prelate withdrew abruptly through the sacristy, refusing any farther part in the ceremony.[3] When the services were

---

[1] *Champigny au Ministre, 24 Oct., 1694.* Trouble on this matter had begun some time before. *Mémoire du Roy pour Frontenac et Champigny, 1694; Le Ministre à l'Évêque, 8 Mai, 1694.*

[2] *La Motte-Cadillac à ———, 28 Sept., 1694; Champigny au Ministre, 27 Oct., 1694.*

[3] *Procès-verbal du Père Hyacinthe Perrault, Commissaire Provincial des Récollets* (*Archives Nationales*); *Mémoire touchant le Démeslé entre M. l'Évesque de Québec et le Chevalier de Callières* (*Ibid.*).

over, he ordered the friars to remove the obnoxious *prie-dieu*. They obeyed; but an officer of Callières replaced it, and, unwilling to offend him, they allowed it to remain. On this, the bishop laid their church under an interdict; that is, he closed it against the celebration of all the rites of religion.[1] He then issued a pastoral mandate, in which he charged Father Joseph Denys, their superior, with offences which he "dared not name for fear of making the paper blush."[2] His tongue was less bashful than his pen; and he gave out publicly that the father superior had acted as go-between in an intrigue of his sister with the Chevalier de Callières.[3] It is said that the accusation was groundless, and the character of the woman wholly irreproachable. The Récollets submitted for two months to the bishop's interdict, then refused to obey longer, and opened their church again.

Quebec, Three Rivers, Sorel, and Montreal had all been ruffled by the breeze of these dissensions, and the farthest outposts of the wilderness were not too remote to feel it. La Motte-Cadillac had been sent to replace Louvigny in the command of Michillimackinac, where he had scarcely arrived, when trouble fell upon him. "Poor Monsieur de la Motte-Cadillac," says Frontenac, "would have sent you a journal to show you the persecutions he has suffered at the post where I placed him, and where he does wonders, having great influence over the Indians, who both love and fear him, but he has had no time to copy it. Means have been found to excite against him three or four officers of the posts dependent on

[1] *Mandement ordonnant de fermer l'Église des Récollets, 13 Mai, 1694.*

[2] "Le Supérieur du dit Couvent estant lié avec le Gouverneur de la dite ville par des interests que tout le monde scait et qu'on n'oseroit exprimer de peur de faire rougir le papier." *Extrait du Mandement de l'Évesque de Québec* (*Archives Nationales*). He had before charged Mareuil with language "capable de faire rougir le ciel."

[3] "M.ʳ l'Évesque accuse publiquement le Rev. Père Joseph, supérieur des Récollets de Montréal, d'être l'entremetteur d'une galanterie entre sa sœur et le Gouverneur. Cependant M.ʳ l'Évesque sait certainement que le Père Joseph est l'un des meilleurs et des plus saints religieux de son ordre. Ce qu'il allègue du prétendu commerce entre le Gouverneur et la Dame de la Naudière (*sœur du Père Joseph*) est entièrement faux, et il l'a publié avec scandale, sans preuve et contre toute apparence, la ditte Dame ayant toujours eu une conduite irréprochable." *Mémoire touchant le Démeslé, etc.* Champigny also says that the bishop has brought this charge, and that Callières declares that he has told a falsehood. *Champigny au Ministre, 27 Oct., 1694.*

his, who have put upon him such strange and unheard of affronts, that I was obliged to send them to prison when they came down to the colony. A certain Father Carheil, the Jesuit who wrote me such insolent letters a few years ago, has played an amazing part in this affair. I shall write about it to Father La Chaise, that he may set it right. Some remedy must be found; for, if it continues, none of the officers who were sent to Michillimackinac, the Miamis, the Illinois, and other places, can stay there on account of the persecutions to which they are subjected, and the refusal of absolution as soon as they fail to do what is wanted of them. Joined to all this is a shameful traffic in influence and money. Monsieur de Tonty could have written to you about it, if he had not been obliged to go off to the Assinneboins, to rid himself of all these torments."[1] In fact, there was a chronic dispute at the forest outposts between the officers and the Jesuits, concerning which matter much might be said on both sides.

The bishop sailed for France. "He has gone," writes Callières, "after quarrelling with everybody." The various points in dispute were set before the king. An avalanche of memorials, letters, and *procès-verbaux*, descended upon the unfortunate monarch; some concerning Mareuil and the quarrels in the council, others on the excommunication of Desjordis, and others on the troubles at Montreal. They were all referred to the king's privy council.[2] An adjustment was effected: order, if not harmony, was restored; and the usual distribution of advice, exhortation, reproof, and menace, was made to the parties in the strife. Frontenac was commended for defending the royal prerogative, censured for violence, and admonished to avoid future quarrels.[3] Champigny was reproved for not supporting the governor, and told that "his Majesty sees with great pain that, while he is making extraordinary efforts to sustain Canada at a time so critical, all his cares and all his outlays are made useless by your misunderstanding with

---

[1] *Frontenac à M. de Lagny, 2 Nov., 1695.*

[2] *Arrest qui ordonne que les Procédures faites entre le Sieur Évesque de Québec et les Sieurs Mareuil, Desjordis, etc., seront évoquez au Conseil Privé de Sa Majesté, 3 Juillet, 1695.*

[3] *Le Ministre à Frontenac, 4 Juin, 1695; Ibid., 8 Juin, 1695.*

Monsieur de Frontenac."[1] The attorney-general was sharply reprimanded, told that he must mend his ways or lose his place, and ordered to make an apology to the governor.[2] Villeray was not honored by a letter, but the intendant was directed to tell him that his behavior had greatly displeased the king. Callières was mildly advised not to take part in the disputes of the bishop and the Récollets.[3] Thus was conjured down one of the most bitter as well as the most needless, trivial, and untimely, of the quarrels that enliven the annals of New France.

A generation later, when its incidents had faded from memory, a passionate and reckless partisan, Abbé La Tour, published, and probably invented, a story which later writers have copied, till it now forms an accepted episode of Canadian history. According to him, Frontenac, in order to ridicule the clergy, formed an amateur company of comedians expressly to play "Tartuffe;" and, after rehearsing at the château during three or four months, they acted the piece before a large audience. "He was not satisfied with having it played at the château, but wanted the actors and actresses and the dancers, male and female, to go in full costume, with violins, to play it in all the religious communities, except the Récollets. He took them first to the house of the Jesuits, where the crowd entered with him; then to the Hospital, to the hall of the paupers, whither the nuns were ordered to repair; then he went to the Ursuline Convent, assembled the sisterhood, and had the piece played before them. To crown the insult, he wanted next to go to the seminary, and repeat the spectacle there; but, warning having been given, he was met on the way, and begged to refrain. He dared not persist, and withdrew in very ill-humor."[4]

Not one of numerous contemporary papers, both official and private, and written in great part by enemies of Frontenac, contains the slightest allusion to any such story, and many of them are wholly inconsistent with it. It may safely

---

[1] *Le Ministre à Champigny, 4 Juin, 1695; Ibid., 8 Juin, 1695.*

[2] *Le Ministre à d'Auteuil, 8 Juin, 1695.*

[3] *Le Ministre à Callières, 8 Juin, 1695.*

[4] La Tour, *Vie de Laval, liv.* xii.

be set down as a fabrication to blacken the memory of the governor, and exhibit the bishop and his adherents as victims of persecution.[1]

[1] Had an outrage, like that with which Frontenac is here charged, actually taken place, the registers of the council, the letters of the intendant and the attorney-general, and the records of the bishopric of Quebec would not have failed to show it. They show nothing beyond a report that "Tartuffe" was to be played, and a payment of money by the bishop in order to prevent it. We are left to infer that it was prevented accordingly. I have the best authority— that of the superior of the convent (1871), herself a diligent investigator into the history of her community—for stating that neither record nor tradition of the occurrence exists among the Ursulines of Quebec; and I have been unable to learn that any such exists among the nuns of the Hospital (Hôtel-Dieu). The contemporary *Récit d'une Religieuse Ursuline* speaks of Frontenac with gratitude, as a friend and benefactor, as does also Mother Juchereau, superior of the Hôtel-Dieu.

Chapter XVI

1690–1694

THE WAR IN ACADIA

State of that Colony • The Abenakis • Acadia and New England • Pirates • Baron de Saint-Castin • Pentegoet • The English Frontier • The French and the Abenakis • Plan of the War • Capture of York • Villebon • Grand War-party • Attack of Wells • Pemaquid rebuilt • John Nelson • A Broken Treaty • Villieu and Thury • Another War-party • Massacre at Oyster River

---

AMID domestic strife, the war with England and the Iroquois still went on. The contest for territorial mastery was fourfold: first, for the control of the west; secondly, for that of Hudson's Bay; thirdly, for that of Newfoundland; and, lastly, for that of Acadia. All these vast and widely sundered regions were included in the government of Frontenac. Each division of the war was distinct from the rest, and each had a character of its own. As the contest for the west was wholly with New York and her Iroquois allies, so the contest for Acadia was wholly with the "Bostonnais," or people of New England.

Acadia, as the French at this time understood the name, included Nova Scotia, New Brunswick, and the greater part of Maine. Sometimes they placed its western boundary at the little River St. George, and sometimes at the Kennebec. Since the wars of D'Aulnay and La Tour, this wilderness had been a scene of unceasing strife; for the English drew their eastern boundary at the St. Croix, and the claims of the rival nationalities overlapped each other. In the time of Cromwell, Sedgwick, a New England officer, had seized the whole country. The peace of Breda restored it to France: the Chevalier de Grandfontaine was ordered to reoccupy it, and the king sent out a few soldiers, a few settlers, and a few women as their wives.[1] Grandfontaine held the nominal command for a time, followed by a succession of military chiefs, Chambly, Marson,

---

[1] In 1671, 30 *garçons* and 30 *filles* were sent by the king to Acadia, at the cost of 6,000 livres. *État de Dépenses, 1671.*

and La Vallière. Then Perrot, whose malpractices had cost him the government of Montreal, was made governor of Acadia; and, as he did not mend his ways, he was replaced by Meneval.[1]

One might have sailed for days along these lonely coasts, and seen no human form. At Canseau, or Chedabucto, at the eastern end of Nova Scotia, there was a fishing station and a fort; Chibuctou, now Halifax, was a solitude; at La Hêve there were a few fishermen; and thence, as you doubled the rocks of Cape Sable, the ancient haunt of La Tour, you would have seen four French settlers, and an unlimited number of seals and sea-fowl. Ranging the shore by St. Mary's Bay, and entering the Strait of Annapolis Basin, you would have found the fort of Port Royal, the chief place of all Acadia. It stood at the head of the basin, where De Monts had planted his settlement nearly a century before. Around the fort and along the neighboring river were about ninety-five small houses; and at the head of the Bay of Fundy were two other settlements, Beaubassin and Les Mines, comparatively stable and populous. At the mouth of the St. John were the abandoned ruins of La Tour's old fort; and on a spot less exposed, at some distance up the river, stood the small wooden fort of Jemsec, with a few intervening clearings. Still sailing westward, passing Mount Desert, another scene of ancient settlement, and entering Penobscot Bay, you would have found the Baron de Saint-Castin with his Indian harem at Pentegoet, where the town of Castine now stands. All Acadia was comprised in these various stations, more or less permanent, together with one or two small posts on the Gulf of St. Lawrence, and the huts of an errant population of fishermen and fur traders. In the time of Denonville, the colonists numbered less than a thousand souls. The king, busied with nursing Canada, had neglected its less important dependency.[2]

Rude as it was, Acadia had charms, and it has them still: in

[1] Grandfontaine, 1670; Chambly, 1673; Marson, 1678; La Vallière, the same year, Marson having died; Perrot, 1684; Meneval, 1687. The last three were commissioned as local governors, in subordination to the governor-general. The others were merely military commandants.

[2] The census taken by order of Meules in 1686 gives a total of 885 persons, of whom 592 were at Port Royal, and 127 at Beaubassin. By the census of 1693, the number had reached 1,009.

its wilderness of woods and its wilderness of waves; the rocky ramparts that guard its coasts; its deep, still bays and foaming headlands; the towering cliffs of the Grand Menan; the innumerable islands that cluster about Penobscot Bay; and the romantic highlands of Mount Desert, down whose gorges the sea-fog rolls like an invading host, while the spires of fir-trees pierce the surging vapors like lances in the smoke of battle.

Leaving Pentegoet, and sailing westward all day along a solitude of woods, one might reach the English outpost of Pemaquid, and thence, still sailing on, might anchor at evening off Casco Bay, and see in the glowing west the distant peaks of the White Mountains, spectral and dim amid the weird and fiery sunset.

Inland Acadia was all forest, and vast tracts of it are a primeval forest still. Here roamed the Abenakis with their kindred tribes, a race wild as their haunts. In habits they were all much alike. Their villages were on the waters of the Androscoggin, the Saco, the Kennebec, the Penobscot, the St. Croix, and the St. John; here in spring they planted their corn, beans, and pumpkins, and then, leaving them to grow, went down to the sea in their birch canoes. They returned towards the end of summer, gathered their harvest, and went again to the sea, where they lived in abundance on ducks, geese, and other water-fowl. During winter, most of the women, children, and old men remained in the villages; while the hunters ranged the forest in chase of moose, deer, caribou, beavers, and bears.

Their summer stay at the seashore was perhaps the most pleasant, and certainly the most picturesque, part of their lives. Bivouacked by some of the innumerable coves and inlets that indent these coasts, they passed their days in that alternation of indolence and action which is a second nature to the Indian. Here in wet weather, while the torpid water was dimpled with rain-drops, and the upturned canoes lay idle on the pebbles, the listless warrior smoked his pipe under his roof of bark, or launched his slender craft at the dawn of the July day, when shores and islands were painted in shadow against the rosy east, and forests, dusky and cool, lay waiting for the sunrise.

The women gathered raspberries or whortleberries in the

open places of the woods, or clams and oysters in the sands and shallows, adding their shells as a contribution to the shell-heaps that have accumulated for ages along these shores. The men fished, speared porpoises, or shot seals. A priest was often in the camp watching over his flock, and saying mass every day in a chapel of bark. There was no lack of altar candles, made by mixing tallow with the wax of the bayberry, which abounded among the rocky hills, and was gathered in profusion by the squaws and children.

The Abenaki missions were a complete success. Not only those of the tribe who had been induced to migrate to the mission villages of Canada, but also those who remained in their native woods, were, or were soon to become, converts to Romanism, and therefore allies of France. Though less ferocious than the Iroquois, they were brave, after the Indian manner, and they rarely or never practised cannibalism.

Some of the French were as lawless as their Indian friends. Nothing is more strange than the incongruous mixture of the forms of feudalism with the independence of the Acadian woods. Vast grants of land were made to various persons, some of whom are charged with using them for no other purpose than roaming over their domains with Indian women. The only settled agricultural population was at Port Royal, Beaubassin, and the Basin of Minas. The rest were fishermen, fur traders, or rovers of the forest. Repeated orders came from the court to open a communication with Quebec, and even to establish a line of military posts through the intervening wilderness, but the distance and the natural difficulties of the country proved insurmountable obstacles. If communication with Quebec was difficult, that with Boston was easy; and thus Acadia became largely dependent on its New England neighbors, who, says an Acadian officer, "are mostly fugitives from England, guilty of the death of their late king, and accused of conspiracy against their present sovereign; others of them are pirates, and they are all united in a sort of independent republic."[1] Their relations with the Acadians were of a mixed sort. They continually encroached on Acadian fishing grounds, and we hear at one time of a hundred of their vessels thus engaged. This was not all. The interlopers

[1] *Mémoire du Sieur Bergier, 1685.*

often landed and traded with the Indians along the coast. Meneval, the governor, complained bitterly of their arrogance. Sometimes, it is said, they pretended to be foreign pirates, and plundered vessels and settlements, while the aggrieved parties could get no redress at Boston. They also carried on a regular trade at Port Royal and Les Mines or Grand Pré, where many of the inhabitants regarded them with a degree of favor which gave great umbrage to the military authorities, who, nevertheless, are themselves accused of seeking their own profit by dealings with the heretics; and even French priests, including Petit, the curé of Port Royal, are charged with carrying on this illicit trade in their own behalf, and in that of the seminary of Quebec. The settlers caught from the "Bostonnais" what their governor stigmatizes as English and parliamentary ideas, the chief effect of which was to make them restive under his rule. The Church, moreover, was less successful in excluding heresy from Acadia than from Canada. A number of Huguenots established themselves at Port Royal, and formed sympathetic relations with the Boston Puritans. The bishop at Quebec was much alarmed. "This is dangerous," he writes. "I pray your Majesty to put an end to these disorders."[1]

A sort of chronic warfare of aggression and reprisal, closely akin to piracy, was carried on at intervals in Acadian waters by French private armed vessels on one hand, and New England private armed vessels on the other. Genuine pirates also frequently appeared. They were of various nationality, though usually buccaneers from the West Indies. They preyed on New England trading and fishing craft, and sometimes attacked French settlements. One of their most notorious exploits was the capture of two French vessels and a French fort at Chedabucto by a pirate, manned in part, it is said, from Massachusetts.[2] A similar proceeding of earlier date was the

[1] *L'Évêque au Roy, 10 Nov., 1683.* For the preceding pages, the authorities are chiefly the correspondence of Grandfontaine, Marson, La Vallière, Meneval, Bergier, Goutins, Perrot, Talon, Frontenac, and other officials. A large collection of Acadian documents, from the archives of Paris, is in my possession. I have also examined the Acadian collections made for the government of Canada and for that of Massachusetts.

[2] Meneval, *Mémoire, 1688*; Denonville, *Mémoire, 18 Oct., 1688*; *Procès-verbal du Pillage de Chedabucto*; *Relation de la Boullaye, 1688*.

act of Dutchmen from St. Domingo. They made a descent on
the French fort of Pentegoet, on Penobscot Bay. Chambly,
then commanding for the king in Acadia, was in the place.
They assaulted his works, wounded him, took him prisoner,
and carried him to Boston, where they held him at ransom.
His young ensign escaped into the woods, and carried the
news to Canada; but many months elapsed before Chambly
was released.[1]

This young ensign was Jean Vincent de l'Abadie, Baron de
Saint-Castin, a native of Béarn, on the slopes of the Pyrenees,
the same rough, strong soil that gave to France her Henri IV.
When fifteen years of age, he came to Canada with the regiment of Carignan-Salières, ensign in the company of Chambly; and, when the regiment was disbanded, he followed his
natural bent, and betook himself to the Acadian woods. At
this time there was a square bastioned fort at Pentegoet,
mounted with twelve small cannon; but after the Dutch attack it fell into decay.[2] Saint-Castin, meanwhile, roamed the
woods with the Indians, lived like them, formed connections
more or less permanent with their women, became himself a
chief, and gained such ascendency over his red associates that,
according to La Hontan, they looked upon him as their tutelary god. He was bold, hardy, adroit, tenacious; and, in
spite of his erratic habits, had such capacity for business, that,
if we may believe the same somewhat doubtful authority, he
made a fortune of three or four hundred thousand crowns.
His gains came chiefly through his neighbors of New England, whom he hated, but to whom he sold his beaver skins
at an ample profit. His trading house was at Pentegoet, now

[1] *Frontenac au Ministre, 14 Nov., 1674; Frontenac à Leverett, gouverneur de
Baston, 24 Sept., 1674; Frontenac to the Governor and Council of Massachusetts, 25
May, 1675* (see *3 Mass. Hist. Coll.,* I. 64); *Colbert à Frontenac, 15 May, 1675.*
Frontenac supposed the assailants to be buccaneers. They had, however, a
commission from William of Orange. Hutchinson says that the Dutch again
took Pentegoet in 1676, but were driven off by ships from Boston, as the
English claimed the place for themselves.

[2] On its condition in 1670, *Estat du Fort et Place de Pentegoet fait en l'année
1670, lorsque les Anglois l'ont rendu.* In 1671, fourteen soldiers and eight laborers
were settled near the fort. *Talon au Ministre, 2 Nov., 1671.* In the next year,
Talon recommends an *envoi de filles* for the benefit of Pentegoet. *Mémoire sur
le Canada, 1672.* As late as 1698, we find Acadian officials advising the reconstruction of the fort.

called Castine, in or near the old fort; a perilous spot, which he occupied or abandoned by turns, according to the needs of the time. Being a devout Catholic he wished to add a resident priest to his establishment for the conversion of his Indian friends; but, observes Father Petit of Port Royal, who knew him well, "he himself has need of spiritual aid to sustain him in the paths of virtue."[1] He usually made two visits a year to Port Royal, where he gave liberal gifts to the church of which he was the chief patron, attended mass with exemplary devotion, and then, shriven of his sins, returned to his squaws at Pentegoet. Perrot, the governor, maligned him; the motive, as Saint-Castin says, being jealousy of his success in trade, for Perrot himself traded largely with the English and the Indians. This, indeed, seems to have been his chief occupation; and, as Saint-Castin was his principal rival, they were never on good terms. Saint-Castin complained to Denonville. "Monsieur Petit," he writes, "will tell you every thing. I will only say that he (*Perrot*) kept me under arrest from the twenty-first of April to the ninth of June, on pretence of a little weakness I had for some women, and even told me that he had your orders to do it: but that is not what troubles him; and as I do not believe there is another man under heaven who will do meaner things through love of gain, even to selling brandy by the pint and half-pint before strangers in his own house, because he does not trust a single one of his servants,—I see plainly what is the matter with him. He wants to be the only merchant in Acadia."[2]

Perrot was recalled this very year; and his successor, Meneval, received instructions in regard to Saint-Castin, which show that the king or his minister had a clear idea both of the baron's merits and of his failings. The new governor was ordered to require him to abandon "his vagabond life among the Indians," cease all trade with the English, and establish a permanent settlement. Meneval was farther directed to assure him that, if he conformed to the royal will, and led a life "more becoming a gentleman," he might expect to receive proofs of his Majesty's approval.[3]

[1] Petit in Saint-Vallier, *Estat de l'Église*, 39 (1856).
[2] *Saint-Castin à Denonville, 2 Juillet, 1687.*
[3] *Instruction du Roy au Sieur de Meneval, 5 Avril, 1687.*

In the next year, Meneval reported that he had represented to Saint-Castin the necessity of reform, and that in consequence he had abandoned his trade with the English, given up his squaws, married, and promised to try to make a solid settlement.[1] True he had reformed before, and might need to reform again; but his faults were not of the baser sort: he held his honor high, and was free-handed as he was bold. His wife was what the early chroniclers would call an Indian princess; for she was the daughter of Madockawando, chief of the Penobscots.

So critical was the position of his post at Pentegoet that a strong fort and a sufficient garrison could alone hope to maintain it against the pirates and the "Bostonnais." Its vicissitudes had been many. Standing on ground claimed by the English, within territory which had been granted to the Duke of York, and which, on his accession to the throne, became a part of the royal domain, it was never safe from attack. In 1686, it was plundered by an agent of Dongan. In 1687, it was plundered again; and in the next year Andros, then royal governor, anchored before it in his frigate, the "Rose," landed with his attendants, and stripped the building of all it contained, except a small altar with pictures and ornaments, which they found in the principal room. Saint-Castin escaped to the woods; and Andros sent him word by an Indian that his property would be carried to Pemaquid, and that he could have it again by becoming a British subject. He refused the offer.[2]

The rival English post of Pemaquid was destroyed, as we have seen, by the Abenakis in 1689; and, in the following year, they and their French allies had made such havoc among the border settlements that nothing was left east of the Piscataqua except the villages of Wells, York, and Kittery. But a change had taken place in the temper of the savages, mainly due to the easy conquest of Port Royal by Phips, and to an expedition of the noted partisan Church by which they had suffered considerable losses. Fear of the English on one hand, and the attraction of their trade on the other, disposed many of them

[1] *Mémoire du Sieur de Meneval sur l'Acadie, 10 Sept., 1688.*

[2] *Mémoire présenté au Roy d'Angleterre, 1687*; *Saint-Castin à Denonville, 7 Juillet, 1687*; *Hutchinson Collection, 562, 563*; *Andros Tracts, I. 118.*

to peace. Six chiefs signed a truce with the commissioners of Massachusetts, and promised to meet them in council to bury the hatchet for ever.

The French were filled with alarm. Peace between the Abenakis and the "Bostonnais" would be disastrous both to Acadia and to Canada, because these tribes held the passes through the northern wilderness, and, so long as they were in the interest of France, covered the settlements on the St. Lawrence from attack. Moreover, the government relied on them to fight its battles. Therefore, no pains were spared to break off their incipient treaty with the English, and spur them again to war. Villebon, a Canadian of good birth, one of the brothers of Portneuf, was sent by the king to govern Acadia. Presents for the Abenakis were given him in abundance; and he was ordered to assure them of support, so long as they fought for France.[1] He and his officers were told to join their war-parties; while the Canadians, who followed him to Acadia, were required to leave all other employments and wage incessant war against the English borders. "You yourself," says the minister, "will herein set them so good an example, that they will be animated by no other desire than that of making profit out of the enemy: there is nothing which I more strongly urge upon you than to put forth all your ability and prudence to prevent the Abenakis from occupying themselves in any thing but war, and by good management of the supplies which you have received for their use to enable them to live by it more to their advantage than by hunting."[2]

Armed with these instructions, Villebon repaired to his post, where he was joined by a body of Canadians under

---

[1] *Mémoire pour servir d'Instruction au Sieur de Villebon, 1691.*

[2] "Comme vostre principal objet doit estre de faire la guerre sans relâche aux Anglois, il faut que vostre plus particulière application soit de detourner de tout autre employ les François qui sont avec vous, en leur donnant de vostre part un si bon exemple en cela qu'ils ne soient animez que du désir de chercher à faire du proffit sur les ennemis. Je n'ay aussy rien à vous recommander plus fortement que de mettre en usage tout ce que vous pouvez avoir de capacité et de prudence afin que les Canibas (*Abenakis*) ne s'employent qu'à la guerre, et que par l'economie de ce que vous avez à leur fournir ils y puissent trouver leur subsistance et plus d'avantage qu'à la chasse." *Le Ministre à Villebon, Avril, 1692.* Two years before, the king had ordered that the Abenakis should be made to attack the English settlements.

Portneuf. His first step was to reoccupy Port Royal; and, as there was nobody there to oppose him, he easily succeeded. The settlers renounced allegiance to Massachusetts and King William, and swore fidelity to their natural sovereign.[1] The capital of Acadia dropped back quietly into the lap of France; but, as the "Bostonnais" might recapture it at any time, Villebon crossed to the St. John, and built a fort high up the stream at Naxouat, opposite the present city of Fredericton. Here no "Bostonnais" could reach him, and he could muster war-parties at his leisure.

One thing was indispensable. A blow must be struck that would encourage and excite the Abenakis. Some of them had had no part in the truce, and were still so keen for English blood that a deputation of their chiefs told Frontenac at Quebec that they would fight, even if they must head their arrows with the bones of beasts.[2] They were under no such necessity. Guns, powder, and lead were given them in abundance; and Thury, the priest on the Penobscot, urged them to strike the English. A hundred and fifty of his converts took the war-path, and were joined by a band from the Kennebec. It was January; and they made their way on snow-shoes along the frozen streams, and through the deathly solitudes of the winter forest, till, after marching a month, they neared their destination, the frontier settlement of York. In the afternoon of the fourth of February, they encamped at the foot of a high hill, evidently Mount Agamenticus, from the top of which the English village lay in sight. It was a collection of scattered houses along the banks of the river Agamenticus and the shore of the adjacent sea. Five or more of them were built for defence, though owned and occupied by families like the other houses. Near the sea stood the unprotected house of the chief man of the place, Dummer, the minister. York appears to have contained from three to four hundred persons of all ages, for the most part rude and ignorant borderers.

The warriors lay shivering all night in the forest, not daring to make fires. In the morning, a heavy fall of snow began. They moved forward, and soon heard the sound of an axe. It

[1] *Procès-verbal de la Prise de Possession du Port Royal, 27 Sept., 1691.*
[2] *Paroles des Sauvages de la Mission de Pentegoet.*

was an English boy chopping wood. They caught him, extorted such information as they needed, then tomahawked
him, and moved on, till, hidden by the forest and the thick
snow, they reached the outskirts of the village. Here they divided into two parties, and each took its station. A gun was
fired as a signal, upon which they all yelled the war-whoop,
and dashed upon their prey. One party mastered the nearest
fortified house, which had scarcely a defender but women.
The rest burst into the unprotected houses, killing or capturing the astonished inmates. The minister was at his door, in
the act of mounting his horse to visit some distant parishioners, when a bullet struck him dead. He was a graduate of
Harvard College, a man advanced in life, of some learning,
and greatly respected. The French accounts say that about a
hundred persons, including women and children, were killed,
and about eighty captured. Those who could, ran for the fortified houses of Preble, Harmon, Alcock, and Norton, which
were soon filled with the refugees. The Indians did not attack
them, but kept well out of gun-shot, and busied themselves
in pillaging, killing horses and cattle, and burning the unprotected houses. They then divided themselves into small bands,
and destroyed all the outlying farms for four or five miles
around.

The wish of King Louis was fulfilled. A good profit had
been made out of the enemy. The victors withdrew into the
forest with their plunder and their prisoners, among whom
were several old women and a number of children from three
to seven years old. These, with a forbearance which does
them credit, they permitted to return uninjured to the nearest
fortified house, in requital, it is said, for the lives of a number
of Indian children spared by the English in a recent attack on
the Androscoggin. The wife of the minister was allowed to
go with them; but her son remained a prisoner, and the agonized mother went back to the Indian camp to beg for his
release. They again permitted her to return; but, when she
came a second time, they told her that, as she wanted to be a
prisoner, she should have her wish. She was carried with the
rest to their village, where she soon died of exhaustion and
distress. One of the warriors arrayed himself in the gown of

the slain minister, and preached a mock sermon to the captive parishioners.[1]

Leaving York in ashes, the victors began their march homeward; while a body of men from Portsmouth followed on their trail, but soon lost it, and failed to overtake them. There was a season of feasting and scalp-dancing at the Abenaki towns; and then, as spring opened, a hundred of the warriors set out to visit Villebon, tell him of their triumph, and receive the promised gifts from their great father the king. Villebon and his brothers, Portneuf, Neuvillette, and Desîles, with their Canadian followers, had spent the winter chiefly on the St. John, finishing their fort at Naxouat, and preparing for future operations. The Abenaki visitors arrived towards the end of April, and were received with all possible distinction. There were speeches, gifts, and feasting; for they had done much, and were expected to do more. Portneuf sang a war-song in their language; then he opened a barrel of wine: the guests emptied it in less than fifteen minutes, sang, whooped, danced, and promised to repair to the rendezvous at Saint-Castin's station of Pentegoet.[2] A grand war-party was afoot; and a new and withering blow was to be struck against the English border. The guests set out for Pentegoet, followed by Portneuf, Desîles, La Brognerie, several other officers, and twenty Canadians. A few days after, a large band of Micmacs arrived; then came the Malicite warriors from their village of Medoctec; and at last Father Baudoin appeared, leading another band of Micmacs from his mission of Beaubassin. Speeches, feasts, and gifts were made to them all; and they all followed the rest to the appointed rendezvous.

[1] The best French account of the capture of York is that of Champigny in a letter to the minister, 5 Oct., 1692. His information came from an Abenaki chief, who was present. The journal of Villebon contains an exaggerated account of the affair, also derived from Indians. Compare the English accounts in Mather, Williamson, and Niles. These writers make the number of slain and captives much less than that given by the French. In the contemporary journal of Rev. John Pike, it is placed at 48 killed and 73 taken.

Two fortified houses of this period are still (1875) standing at York. They are substantial buildings of squared timber, with the upper story projecting over the lower, so as to allow a vertical fire on the heads of assailants. In one of them some of the loopholes for musketry are still left open. They may or may not have been originally enclosed by palisades.

[2] Villebon, *Journal de ce qui s'est passé à l'Acadie, 1691, 1692.*

At the beginning of June, the site of the town of Castine was covered with wigwams and the beach lined with canoes. Malicites and Micmacs, Abenakis from the Penobscot and Abenakis from the Kennebec, were here, some four hundred warriors in all.[1] Here, too, were Portneuf and his Canadians, the Baron de Saint-Castin and his Indian father-in-law, Madockawando, with Moxus, Egeremet, and other noted chiefs, the terror of the English borders. They crossed Penobscot Bay, and marched upon the frontier village of Wells.

Wells, like York, was a small settlement of scattered houses along the sea-shore. The year before, Moxus had vainly attacked it with two hundred warriors. All the neighboring country had been laid waste by a murderous war of detail, the lonely farm-houses pillaged and burned, and the survivors driven back for refuge to the older settlements.[2] Wells had been crowded with these refugees; but famine and misery had driven most of them beyond the Piscataqua, and the place was now occupied by a remnant of its own destitute inhabitants, who, warned by the fate of York, had taken refuge in five fortified houses. The largest of these, belonging to Joseph Storer, was surrounded by a palisade, and occupied by fifteen armed men, under Captain Convers, an officer of militia. On the ninth of June, two sloops and a sail-boat ran up the neighboring creek, bringing supplies and fourteen more men. The succor came in the nick of time. The sloops had scarcely anchored, when a number of cattle were seen running frightened and wounded from the woods. It was plain that an enemy was lurking there. All the families of the place now gathered within the palisades of Storer's house, thus increasing his force to about thirty men; and a close watch was kept throughout the night.

In the morning, no room was left for doubt. One John Diamond, on his way from the house to the sloops, was seized by Indians and dragged off by the hair. Then the whole

---

[1] *Frontenac au Ministre, 15 Sept., 1692.*

[2] The ravages committed by the Abenakis in the preceding year among the scattered farms of Maine and New Hampshire are said by Frontenac to have been "impossible to describe." Another French writer says that they burned more than 200 houses.

body of savages appeared swarming over the fields, so confident of success that they neglected their usual tactics of surprise. A French officer, who, as an old English account says, was "habited like a gentleman," made them an harangue: they answered with a burst of yells, and then attacked the house, firing, screeching, and calling on Convers and his men to surrender. Others gave their attention to the two sloops, which lay together in the narrow creek, stranded by the ebbing tide. They fired at them for a while from behind a pile of planks on the shore, and threw many fire-arrows without success, the men on board fighting with such cool and dexterous obstinacy that they held them all at bay, and lost but one of their own number. Next, the Canadians made a huge shield of planks, which they fastened vertically to the back of a cart. La Brognerie with twenty-six men, French and Indians, got behind it, and shoved the cart towards the stranded sloops. It was within fifty feet of them, when a wheel sunk in the mud, and the machine stuck fast. La Brognerie tried to lift the wheel, and was shot dead. The tide began to rise. A Canadian tried to escape, and was also shot. The rest then broke away together, some of them, as they ran, dropping under the bullets of the sailors.

The whole force now gathered for a final attack on the garrison house. Their appearance was so frightful, and their clamor so appalling, that one of the English muttered something about surrender. Convers returned, "If you say that again, you are a dead man." Had the allies made a bold assault, he and his followers must have been overpowered; but this mode of attack was contrary to Indian maxims. They merely leaped, yelled, fired, and called on the English to yield. They were answered with derision. The women in the house took part in the defence, passed ammunition to the men, and sometimes fired themselves on the enemy. The Indians at length became discouraged, and offered Convers favorable terms. He answered, "I want nothing but men to fight with." An Abenaki who spoke English cried out: "If you are so bold, why do you stay in a garrison house like a squaw? Come out and fight like a man!" Convers retorted, "Do you think I am fool enough to come out with thirty men to fight five hundred?" Another Indian shouted, "Damn you, we'll cut you small as tobacco before morning." Convers returned a contemptuous defiance.

After a while, they ceased firing, and dispersed about the neighborhood, butchering cattle and burning the church and a few empty houses. As the tide began to ebb, they sent a fire-raft in full blaze down the creek to destroy the sloops; but it stranded, and the attempt failed. They now wreaked their fury on the prisoner Diamond, whom they tortured to death, after which they all disappeared. A few resolute men had foiled one of the most formidable bands that ever took the war-path in Acadia.[1]

The warriors dispersed to their respective haunts; and, when a band of them reached the St. John, Villebon coolly declares that he gave them a prisoner to burn. They put him to death with all their ingenuity of torture. The act, on the part of the governor, was more atrocious, as it had no motive of reprisal, and as the burning of prisoners was not the common practice of these tribes.[2]

The warlike ardor of the Abenakis cooled after the failure at Wells, and events that soon followed nearly extinguished it. Phips had just received his preposterous appointment to the government of Massachusetts. To the disgust of its inhab-

[1] Villebon, *Journal de ce qui s'est passé à l'Acadie, 1691, 1692*; Mather, *Magnalia*, II. 613; Hutchinson, *Hist. Mass.*, II. 67; Williamson, *History of Maine*, I. 631; Bourne, *History of Wells*, 213; Niles, *Indian and French Wars*, 229. Williamson, like Sylvanus Davis, calls Portneuf *Burneffe* or *Burniffe*. He, and other English writers, call La Brognerie *Labocree*. The French could not recover his body, on which, according to Niles and others, was found a pouch "stuffed full of relics, pardons, and indulgences." The prisoner Diamond told the captors that there were thirty men in the sloops. They believed him, and were cautious accordingly. There were, in fact, but fourteen. Most of the fighting was on the tenth. On the evening of that day, Convers received a reinforcement of six men. They were a scouting party, whom he had sent a few days before in the direction of Salmon River. Returning, they were attacked, when near the garrison house, by a party of Portneuf's Indians. The sergeant in command instantly shouted, "Captain Convers, send your men round the hill, and we shall catch these dogs." Thinking that Convers had made a sortie, the Indians ran off, and the scouts joined the garrison without loss.

[2] "Le 18me (*Août*) un sauvage anglois fut pris au bas de la rivière de St. Jean. Je le donnai à nos sauvages pour estre brulé, ce qu'ils firent le lendemain. On ne peut rien adjouter aux tourmens qu'ils luy firent souffrir." Villebon, *Journal, 1691, 1692*.

itants, the stubborn colony was no longer a republic. The new governor, unfit as he was for his office, understood the needs of the eastern frontier, where he had spent his youth; and he brought a royal order to rebuild the ruined fort at Pemaquid. The king gave the order, but neither men, money, nor munitions to execute it; and Massachusetts bore all the burden. Phips went to Pemaquid, laid out the work, and left a hundred men to finish it. A strong fort of stone was built, the abandoned cannon of Casco mounted on its walls, and sixty men placed in garrison.

The keen military eye of Frontenac saw the danger involved in the re-establishment of Pemaquid. Lying far in advance of the other English stations, it barred the passage of war-parties along the coast, and was a standing menace to the Abenakis. It was resolved to capture it. Two ships of war, lately arrived at Quebec, the "Poli" and the "Envieux," were ordered to sail for Acadia with above four hundred men, take on board two or three hundred Indians at Pentegoet, reduce Pemaquid, and attack Wells, Portsmouth, and the Isles of Shoals; after which, they were to scour the Acadian seas of "Bostonnais" fishermen.

At this time, a gentleman of Boston, John Nelson, captured by Villebon the year before, was a prisoner at Quebec. Nelson was nephew and heir of Sir Thomas Temple, in whose right he claimed the proprietorship of Acadia, under an old grant of Oliver Cromwell. He was familiar both with that country and with Canada, which he had visited several times before the war. As he was a man of birth and breeding, and a declared enemy of Phips, and as he had befriended French prisoners, and shown especial kindness to Meneval, the captive governor of Acadia, he was treated with distinction by Frontenac, who, though he knew him to be a determined enemy of the French, lodged him at the château, and entertained him at his own table.[1] Madockawando, the father-in-law of Saint-Castin, made a visit to Frontenac; and Nelson, who spoke both French and Indian, contrived to gain from him and from other sources a partial knowledge of the intended expedition. He was not in favor at Boston; for, though one of the foremost in the overthrow of Andros, his creed and his char-

[1] *Champigny au Ministre, 4 Nov., 1693.*

acter savored more of the Cavalier than of the Puritan. This
did not prevent him from risking his life for the colony. He
wrote a letter to the authorities of Massachusetts, and then
bribed two soldiers to desert and carry it to them. The deserters were hotly pursued, but reached their destination, and
delivered their letter. The two ships sailed from Quebec; but
when, after a long delay at Mount Desert, they took on board
the Indian allies and sailed onward to Pemaquid, they found
an armed ship from Boston anchored in the harbor. Why they
did not attack it, is a mystery. The defences of Pemaquid were
still unfinished, the French force was far superior to the English, and Iberville, who commanded it, was a leader of un-
questionable enterprise and daring. Nevertheless, the French
did nothing, and soon after bore away for France. Frontenac
was indignant, and severely blamed Iberville, whose sister was
on board his ship, and was possibly the occasion of his inaction.[1]

Thus far successful, the authorities of Boston undertook an
enterprise little to their credit. They employed the two deserters, joined with two Acadian prisoners, to kidnap Saint-
Castin, whom, next to the priest Thury, they regarded as their
most insidious enemy. The Acadians revealed the plot, and
the two soldiers were shot at Mount Desert. Nelson was sent
to France, imprisoned two years in a dungeon of the Château
of Angoulême, and then placed in the Bastile. Ten years
passed before he was allowed to return to his family at
Boston.[2]

[1] *Frontenac au Ministre, 25 Oct., 1693.*

[2] Lagny, *Mémoire sur l'Acadie, 1692; Mémoire sur l'Enlèvement de Saint-Castin; Frontenac au Ministre, 25 Oct., 1693; Relation de ce qui s'est passé de plus
remarquable, 1690, 1691* (capture of Nelson); *Frontenac au Ministre, 15 Sept.,
1692; Champigny au Ministre, 15 Oct., 1692.* Champigny here speaks of Nelson
as the most audacious of the English, and the most determined on the destruction of the French. Nelson's letter to the authorities of Boston is printed
in Hutchinson, I. 338. It does not warn them of an attempt against Pemaquid, of the rebuilding of which he seems not to have heard, but only of a
design against the seaboard towns. Compare *N. Y. Col. Docs.,* IX. 555. In the
same collection is a *Memorial on the Northern Colonies,* by Nelson, a paper
showing much good sense and penetration. After an imprisonment of four
and a half years, he was allowed to go to England on parole; a friend in
France giving security of 15,000 livres for his return, in case of his failure to
procure from the king an order for the fulfilment of the terms of the capitu-

The French failure at Pemaquid completed the discontent of the Abenakis; and despondency and terror seized them when, in the spring of 1693, Convers, the defender of Wells, ranged the frontier with a strong party of militia, and built another stone fort at the falls of the Saco. In July, they opened a conference at Pemaquid; and, in August, thirteen of their chiefs, representing, or pretending to represent, all the tribes from the Merrimac to the St. Croix, came again to the same place to conclude a final treaty of peace with the commissioners of Massachusetts. They renounced the French alliance, buried the hatchet, declared themselves British subjects, promised to give up all prisoners, and left five of their chief men as hostages.[1] The frontier breathed again. Security and hope returned to secluded dwellings buried in a treacherous forest, where life had been a nightmare of horror and fear; and the settler could go to his work without dreading to find at evening his cabin burned and his wife and children murdered. He was fatally deceived, for the danger was not past.

It is true that some of the Abenakis were sincere in their pledges of peace. A party among them, headed by Madockawando, were dissatisfied with the French, anxious to recover their captive countrymen, and eager to reopen trade with the English. But there was an opposing party, led by the chief Taxous, who still breathed war; while between the two was an unstable mob of warriors, guided by the impulse of the hour.[2] The French spared no efforts to break off the peace. The two missionaries, Bigot on the Kennebec and Thury on the Penobscot, labored with unwearied energy to urge the savages to war. The governor, Villebon, flattered them, feasted them, adopted Taxous as his brother, and, to honor

---

lation of Port Royal. (*Le Ministre à Bégon, 13 Jan., 1694.*) He did not succeed, and the king forbade him to return. It is characteristic of him that he preferred to disobey the royal order, and thus incur the high displeasure of his sovereign, rather than break his parole and involve his friend in loss. La Hontan calls him a "fort galant homme." There is a portrait of him at Boston, where his descendants are represented by the prominent families of Winthrop, Derby, and Borland.

[1] For the treaty in full, Mather, *Magnalia*, II. 625.

[2] The state of feeling among the Abenakis is shown in a letter of Thury to Frontenac, 11 Sept., 1694, and in the journal of Villebon for 1693.

the occasion, gave him his own best coat. Twenty-five hundred pounds of gunpowder, six thousand pounds of lead, and a multitude of other presents, were given this year to the Indians of Acadia.[1] Two of their chiefs had been sent to Versailles. They now returned, in gay attire, their necks hung with medals, and their minds filled with admiration, wonder, and bewilderment.

The special duty of commanding Indians had fallen to the lot of an officer named Villieu, who had been ordered by the court to raise a war-party and attack the English. He had lately been sent to replace Portneuf, who had been charged with debauchery and peculation. Villebon, angry at his brother's removal, was on ill terms with his successor; and, though he declares that he did his best to aid in raising the war-party, Villieu says, on the contrary, that he was worse than indifferent. The new lieutenant spent the winter at Naxouat, and on the first of May went up in a canoe to the Malicite village of Medoctec, assembled the chiefs, and invited them to war. They accepted the invitation with alacrity. Villieu next made his way through the wilderness to the Indian towns of the Penobscot. On the ninth, he reached the mouth of the Mattawamkeag, where he found the chief Taxous, paddled with him down the Penobscot, and, at midnight on the tenth, landed at a large Indian village, at or near the place now called Passadumkeag. Here he found a powerful ally in the Jesuit Vincent Bigot, who had come from the Kennebec, with three Abenakis, to urge their brethren of the Penobscot to break off the peace. The chief envoy denounced the treaty of Pemaquid as a snare; and Villieu exhorted the assembled warriors to follow him to the English border, where honor and profit awaited them. But first he invited them to go back with him to Naxouat to receive their presents of arms, ammunition, and every thing else that they needed.

They set out with alacrity. Villieu went with them, and they all arrived within a week. They were feasted and gifted to their hearts' content; and then the indefatigable officer led them back by the same long and weary routes which he had passed and repassed before, rocky and shallow streams, chains of wilderness lakes, threads of water writhing through

[1] *Estat de Munitions, etc., pour les Sauvages de l'Acadie, 1693.*

swamps where the canoes could scarcely glide among the water-weeds and alders. Villieu was the only white man. The governor, as he says, would give him but two soldiers, and these had run off. Early in June, the whole flotilla paddled down the Penobscot to Pentegoet. Here the Indians divided their presents, which they found somewhat less ample than they had imagined. In the midst of their discontent, Madockawando came from Pemaquid with news that the governor of Massachusetts was about to deliver up the Indian prisoners in his hands, as stipulated by the treaty. This completely changed the temper of the warriors. Madockawando declared loudly for peace, and Villieu saw all his hopes wrecked. He tried to persuade his disaffected allies that the English only meant to lure them to destruction, and the missionary Thury supported him with his utmost eloquence. The Indians would not be convinced; and their trust in English good faith was confirmed, when they heard that a minister had just come to Pemaquid to teach their children to read and write. The news grew worse and worse. Villieu was secretly informed that Phips had been off the coast in a frigate, invited Madockawando and other chiefs on board, and feasted them in his cabin, after which they had all thrown their hatchets into the sea, in token of everlasting peace. Villieu now despaired of his enterprise, and prepared to return to the St. John; when Thury, wise as the serpent, set himself to work on the jealousy of Taxous, took him aside, and persuaded him that his rival, Madockawando, had put a slight upon him in presuming to make peace without his consent. "The effect was marvellous," says Villieu. Taxous, exasperated, declared that he would have nothing to do with Madockawando's treaty. The fickle multitude caught the contagion, and asked for nothing but English scalps; but, before setting out, they must needs go back to Passadumkeag to finish their preparations.

Villieu again went with them, and on the way his enterprise and he nearly perished together. His canoe overset in a rapid at some distance above the site of Bangor: he was swept down the current, his head was dashed against a rock, and his body bruised from head to foot. For five days he lay helpless with fever. He had no sooner recovered than he gave the Indians a war-feast, at which they all sang the war-song, except

Madockawando and some thirty of his clansmen, whom the others made the butt of their taunts and ridicule. The chief began to waver. The officer and the missionary beset him with presents and persuasion, till at last he promised to join the rest.

It was the end of June when Villieu and Thury, with one Frenchman and a hundred and five Indians, began their long canoe voyage to the English border. The savages were directed to give no quarter, and told that the prisoners already in their hands would insure the safety of their hostages in the hands of the English.[1] More warriors were to join them from Bigot's mission on the Kennebec. On the ninth of July, they neared Pemaquid; but it was no part of their plan to attack a garrisoned post. The main body passed on at a safe distance; while Villieu approached the fort, dressed and painted like an Indian, and accompanied by two or three genuine savages, carrying a packet of furs, as if on a peaceful errand of trade. Such visits from Indians had been common since the treaty; and, while his companions bartered their beaver skins with the unsuspecting soldiers, he strolled about the neighborhood and made a plan of the works. The party was soon after joined by Bigot's Indians, and the united force now amounted to two hundred and thirty. They held a council to determine where they should make their attack, but opinions differed. Some were for the places west of Boston, and others for those nearer at hand. Necessity decided them. Their provisions were gone, and Villieu says that he himself was dying of hunger. They therefore resolved to strike at the nearest settlement, that of Oyster River, now Durham, about twelve miles from Portsmouth. They cautiously moved forward, and sent scouts in advance, who reported that the inhabitants kept no watch. In fact, a messenger from Phips had assured them that the war was over, and that they could follow their usual vocations without fear.

Villieu and his band waited till night, and then made their approach. There was a small village; a church; a mill; twelve fortified houses, occupied in most cases only by families; and many unprotected farm-houses, extending several miles along

[1]Villebon, *Mémoire, Juillet, 1694*; *Instruction du S. de Villebon au S. de Villieu*.

the stream. The Indians separated into bands, and, stationing themselves for a simultaneous attack at numerous points, lay patiently waiting till towards day. The moon was still bright when the first shot gave the signal, and the slaughter began. The two palisaded houses of Adams and Drew, without garrisons, were taken immediately, and the families butchered. Those of Edgerly, Beard, and Medar were abandoned, and most of the inmates escaped. The remaining seven were successfully defended, though several of them were occupied only by the families which owned them. One of these, belonging to Thomas Bickford, stood by the river near the lower end of the settlement. Roused by the firing, he placed his wife and children in a boat, sent them down the stream, and then went back alone to defend his dwelling. When the Indians appeared, he fired on them, sometimes from one loophole and sometimes from another, shouting the word of command to an imaginary garrison, and showing himself with a different hat, cap, or coat, at different parts of the building. The Indians were afraid to approach, and he saved both family and home. One Jones, the owner of another of these fortified houses, was wakened by the barking of his dogs, and went out, thinking that his hog-pen was visited by wolves. The flash of a gun in the twilight of the morning showed the true nature of the attack. The shot missed him narrowly; and, entering the house again, he stood on his defence, when the Indians, after firing for some time from behind a neighboring rock, withdrew and left him in peace. Woodman's garrison house, though occupied by a number of men, was attacked more seriously, the Indians keeping up a long and brisk fire from behind a ridge where they lay sheltered; but they hit nobody, and at length disappeared.[1]

Among the unprotected houses, the carnage was horrible. A hundred and four persons, chiefly women and children half naked from their beds, were tomahawked, shot, or killed by slower and more painful methods. Some escaped to the fortified houses, and others hid in the woods. Twenty-seven were kept alive as prisoners. Twenty or more houses were burned; but, what is remarkable, the church was spared. Fa-

[1] Woodman's garrison house is still standing, having been carefully preserved by his descendants.

ther Thury entered it during the massacre, and wrote with chalk on the pulpit some sentences, of which the purport is not preserved, as they were no doubt in French or Latin.

Thury said mass, and then the victors retreated in a body to the place where they had hidden their canoes. Here Taxous, dissatisfied with the scalps that he and his band had taken, resolved to have more; and with fifty of his own warriors, joined by others from the Kennebec, set out on a new enterprise. "They mean," writes Villieu in his diary, "to divide into bands of four or five, and knock people in the head by surprise, which cannot fail to produce a good effect."[1] They did in fact fall a few days after on the settlements near Groton, and killed some forty persons.

Having heard from one of the prisoners a rumor of ships on the way from England to attack Quebec, Villieu thought it necessary to inform Frontenac at once. Attended by a few Indians, he travelled four days and nights, till he found Bigot at an Abenaki fort on the Kennebec. His Indians were completely exhausted. He took others in their place, pushed forward again, reached Quebec on the twenty-second of August, found that Frontenac had gone to Montreal, followed him thither, told his story, and presented him with thirteen English scalps.[2] He had displayed in the achievement of his detestable exploit an energy, perseverance, and hardihood rarely equalled; but all would have been vain but for the help of his clerical colleague Father Pierre Thury.[3]

[1] "Casser des testes à la surprise après s'estre divisés en plusieurs bandes de quatre au cinq, ce qui ne peut manquer de faire un bon effect." Villieu, *Relation*.

[2] "Dans cette assemblée M. de Villieu avec 4 sauvages qu'il avoit amenés de l'Accadie présenta à Monsieur le Comte de Frontenac 13 chevelures angloises." *Callières au Ministre, 19 Oct., 1694.*

[3] The principal authority for the above is the very curious *Relation du Voyage fait par le Sieur de Villieu . . . pour faire la Guerre aux Anglois au printemps de l'an 1694.* It is the narrative of Villieu himself, written in the form of a journal, with great detail. He also gives a brief summary in a letter to the minister, 7 Sept. The best English account is that of Belknap, in his *History of New Hampshire.* Cotton Mather tells the story in his usual unsatisfactory and ridiculous manner. Pike, in his journal, says that ninety-four persons in all were killed or taken. Mather says, "ninety four or a hundred." The *Provincial Record of New Hampshire* estimates it at eighty. Charlevoix claims two hundred and thirty, and Villieu himself but a hundred and thirty-one. Cham-

THE INDIAN TRIBES OF ACADIA.—The name *Abenaki* is generic, and of very loose application. As employed by the best French writers at the end of the seventeenth century, it may be taken to include the tribes from the Kennebec eastward to the St. John. These again may be sub-divided as follows. First, the Canibas (Kenibas), or tribes of the Kennebec and adjacent waters. These with kindred neighboring tribes on the Saco, the Androscoggin, and the Sheepscot, have been held by some writers to be the Abenakis proper, though some of them, such as the Sokokis or Pequawkets of the Saco, spoke a dialect distinct from the rest. Secondly, the tribes of the Penobscot, called Tarratines by early New England writers, who sometimes, however, give this name a more extended application. Thirdly, the Malicites (Marechites) of the St. Croix and the St. John. These, with the Penobscots or Tarratines, are the Etchemins of early French writers. All these tribes speak dialects of Algonquin, so nearly related that they understand each other with little difficulty. That eminent Indian philologist, Mr. J. Hammond Trumbull, writes to me: "The Malicite, the Penobscot, and the Kennebec, or Caniba, are dialects of the same language, which may as well be called *Abenaki*. The first named differs more considerably from the other two than do these from each other. In fact the Caniba and the Penobscot are merely provincial dialects, with no greater difference than is found in two English counties." The case is widely different with the Micmacs, the Souriquois of the French, who occupy portions of Nova Scotia and New Brunswick, and who speak a language which, though of Algonquin origin, differs as much from the Abenaki dialects as Italian differs from French, and was once described to me by a Malicite (Passamaquoddy) Indian as an unintelligible jargon.

---

pigny, Frontenac, and Callières, in their reports to the court, adopt Villieu's statements. Frontenac says that the success was due to the assurances of safety which Phips had given the settlers.

In the Massachusetts archives is a letter to Phips, written just after the attack. The devastation extended six or seven miles. There are also a number of depositions from persons present, giving a horrible picture of the cruelties practised.

Chapter XVII

NEW FRANCE AND NEW ENGLAND

The Frontier of New England • Border Warfare • Motives of the French • Needless Barbarity • Who were answerable? • Father Thury • The Abenakis waver • Treachery at Pemaquid • Capture of Pemaquid • Projected Attack on Boston • Disappointment • Miseries of the Frontier • A Captive Amazon

---

THIS STROKE," says Villebon, speaking of the success at Oyster River, "is of great advantage, because it breaks off all the talk of peace between our Indians and the English. The English are in despair, for not even infants in the cradle were spared."[1]

I have given the story in detail, as showing the origin and character of the destructive raids, of which New England annalists show only the results. The borders of New England were peculiarly vulnerable. In Canada, the settlers built their houses in lines, within supporting distance of each other, along the margin of a river which supplied easy transportation for troops; and, in time of danger, they all took refuge in forts under command of the local seigniors, or of officers with detachments of soldiers. The exposed part of the French colony extended along the St. Lawrence about ninety miles. The exposed frontier of New England was between two and three hundred miles long, and consisted of farms and hamlets, loosely scattered through an almost impervious forest. Mutual support was difficult or impossible. A body of Indians and Canadians, approaching secretly and swiftly, dividing into small bands, and falling at once upon the isolated houses of an extensive district, could commit prodigious havoc in a short time, and with little danger. Even in so-called villages, the houses were far apart, because, except on the sea-shore, the people lived by farming. Such as were able to do so

[1] "Ce coup est très-avantageux, parcequ'il rompte tous les pourparlers de paix entre nos sauvages et les Anglois. Les Anglois sont au désespoir de ce qu'ils ont tué jusqu'aux enfants au berceau." *Villebon au Ministre, 19 Sept., 1694.*

fenced their dwellings with palisades, or built them of solid timber, with loopholes, a projecting upper story like a block-house, and sometimes a flanker at one or more of the corners. In the more considerable settlements, the largest of these for-tified houses was occupied, in time of danger, by armed men, and served as a place of refuge for the neighbors. The pali-saded house defended by Convers at Wells was of this sort, and so also was the Woodman house at Oyster River. These were "garrison houses," properly so called, though the name was often given to fortified dwellings occupied only by the family. The French and Indian war-parties commonly avoided the true garrison houses, and very rarely captured them, ex-cept unawares; for their tactics were essentially Iroquois, and consisted, for the most part, in pouncing upon peaceful set-tlers by surprise, and generally in the night. Combatants and non-combatants were slaughtered together. By parading the number of slain, without mentioning that most of them were women and children, and by counting as forts mere private houses surrounded with palisades, Charlevoix and later writ-ers have given the air of gallant exploits to acts which deserve a very different name. To attack military posts, like Casco and Pemaquid, was a legitimate act of war; but systematically to butcher helpless farmers and their families can hardly pass as such, except from the Iroquois point of view.

The chief alleged motive for this ruthless warfare was to prevent the people of New England from invading Canada, by giving them employment at home; though, in fact, they had never thought of invading Canada till after these attacks began. But for the intrigues of Denonville, the Bigots, Thury, and Saint-Castin, before war was declared, and the destruc-tion of Salmon Falls after it, Phips's expedition would never have taken place. By successful raids against the borders of New England, Frontenac roused the Canadians from their de-jection, and prevented his red allies from deserting him; but, in so doing, he brought upon himself an enemy who, as Charlevoix himself says, asked only to be let alone. If there was a political necessity for butchering women and children on the frontier of New England, it was a necessity created by the French themselves.

There was no such necessity. Massachusetts was the only

one of the New England colonies which took an aggressive part in the contest. Connecticut did little or nothing. Rhode Island was non-combatant through Quaker influence; and New Hampshire was too weak for offensive war. Massachusetts was in no condition to fight, nor was she impelled to do so by the home government. Canada was organized for war, and must fight at the bidding of the king, who made the war and paid for it. Massachusetts was organized for peace; and, if she chose an aggressive part, it was at her own risk and her own cost. She had had fighting enough already against infuriated savages far more numerous than the Iroquois, and poverty and political revolution made peace a necessity to her. If there was danger of another attack on Quebec, it was not from New England, but from Old; and no amount of frontier butchery could avert it.

Nor, except their inveterate habit of poaching on Acadian fisheries, had the people of New England provoked these barbarous attacks. They never even attempted to retaliate them, though the settlements of Acadia offered a safe and easy revenge. Once, it is true, they pillaged Beaubassin; but they killed nobody, though countless butcheries in settlements yet more defenceless were fresh in their memory.[1]

With New York, a colony separate in government and widely sundered in local position, the case was different. Its rulers had instigated the Iroquois to attack Canada, possibly before the declaration of war, and certainly after it; and they had no right to complain of reprisal. Yet the frontier of New York was less frequently assailed, because it was less exposed; while that of New England was drenched in blood, because it was open to attack, because the Abenakis were convenient instruments for attacking it, because the adhesion of these tribes was necessary to the maintenance of French power in Acadia, and because this adhesion could best be secured by

[1] The people of Beaubassin had taken an oath of allegiance to England in 1690, and pleaded it as a reason for exemption from plunder; but it appears by French authorities that they had violated it (*Observations sur les Depêches touchant l'Acadie, 1695*), and their priest Baudoin had led a band of Micmacs to the attack of Wells (Villebon, *Journal*). When the "Bostonnais" captured Port Royal, they are described by the French as excessively irritated by the recent slaughter at Salmon Falls, yet the only revenge they took was plundering some of the inhabitants.

inciting them to constant hostility against the English. They were not only needed as the barrier of Canada against New England, but the French commanders hoped, by means of their tomahawks, to drive the English beyond the Piscataqua, and secure the whole of Maine to the French crown.

Who were answerable for these offences against Christianity and civilization? First, the king; and, next, the governors and military officers who were charged with executing his orders, and who often executed them with needless barbarity. But a far different responsibility rests on the missionary priests, who hounded their converts on the track of innocent blood. The Acadian priests are not all open to this charge. Some of them are even accused of being too favorable to the English; while others gave themselves to their proper work, and neither abused their influence, nor perverted their teaching to political ends. The most prominent among the apostles of carnage, at this time, are the Jesuit Bigot on the Kennebec, and the seminary priest Thury on the Penobscot. There is little doubt that the latter instigated attacks on the English frontier before the war, and there is conclusive evidence that he had a hand in repeated forays after it began. Whether acting from fanaticism, policy, or an odious compound of both, he was found so useful, that the minister Ponchartrain twice wrote him letters of commendation, praising him in the same breath for his care of the souls of the Indians and his zeal in exciting them to war. "There is no better man," says an Acadian official, "to prompt the savages to any enterprise."[1] The king was begged to reward him with money; and Ponchartrain wrote to the bishop of Quebec to increase his pay out of the allowance furnished by the government to the Acadian clergy, because he, Thury, had persuaded the Abenakis to begin the war anew.[2]

The French missionaries are said to have made use of sin-

---

[1] Tibièrge, *Mémoire sur l'Acadie, 1695.*

[2] "Les témoignages qu'on a rendu à Sa Majesté de l'affection et du zêle du S.‏ de Thury, missionaire chez les Canibas (*Abenakis*), pour son service, et particulièrement dans l'engagement où il a mis les Sauvages de recommencer la guerre contre les Anglois, m'oblige de vous prier de luy faire une plus forte part sur les 1,500 livres de gratification que Sa Majesté accorde pour les ecclésiastiques de l'Acadie." *Le Ministre à l'Évesque de Québec, 16 Avril, 1695.*

"Je suis bien aise de me servir de cette occasion pour vous dire que j'ay

gular methods to excite their flocks against the heretics. The Abenaki chief Bomaseen, when a prisoner at Boston in 1696, declared that they told the Indians that Jesus Christ was a Frenchman, and his mother, the Virgin, a French lady; that the English had murdered him, and that the best way to gain his favor was to revenge his death.[1]

Whether or not these articles of faith formed a part of the teachings of Thury and his fellow apostles, there is no doubt that it was a recognized part of their functions to keep their converts in hostility to the English, and that their credit with the civil powers depended on their success in doing so. The same holds true of the priests of the mission villages in Canada. They avoided all that might impair the warlike spirit of the neophyte, and they were well aware that in savages the warlike spirit is mainly dependent on native ferocity. They taught temperance, conjugal fidelity, devotion to the rites of their religion, and submission to the priest; but they left the savage a savage still. In spite of the remonstrances of the civil authorities, the mission Indian was separated as far as possible from intercourse with the French, and discouraged from learning the French tongue. He wore a crucifix, hung wampum on the shrine of the Virgin, told his beads, prayed three times a day, knelt for hours before the Host, invoked the saints, and confessed to the priest; but, with rare exceptions, he murdered, scalped, and tortured like his heathen countrymen.[2]

----

esté informé, non seulement de vostre zêle et de vostre application pour vostre mission, et du progrès qu'elle fait pour l'avancement de la religion avec les sauvages, mais encore de vos soins pour les maintenir dans le service de Sa Majesté et pour les encourager aux expeditions de guerre." *Le Ministre à Thury, 23 Avril, 1697.* The other letter to Thury, written two years before, is of the same tenor.

[1] Mather, *Magnalia*, II. 629. Compare Dummer, *Memorial, 1709,* in *Mass. Hist. Coll., 3 Ser.,* I., and the same writer's *Letter to a Noble Lord concerning the Late Expedition to Canada, 1712.* Dr. Charles T. Jackson, the geologist, when engaged in the survey of Maine in 1836, mentions, as an example of the simplicity of the Acadians of Madawaska, that one of them asked him "if Bethlehem, where Christ was born, was not a town in France." *First Report on the Geology of Maine,* 72. Here, perhaps, is a tradition from early missionary teaching.

[2] The famous Ouréhaoué, who had been for years under the influence of the priests, and who, as Charlevoix says, died "un vrai Chrétien," being told on his death-bed how Christ was crucified by the Jews, exclaimed with fervor: "Ah! why was not I there? I would have revenged him: I would have

The picture has another side, which must not pass unnoticed. Early in the war, the French of Canada began the merciful practice of buying English prisoners, and especially children, from their Indian allies. After the first fury of attack, many lives were spared for the sake of this ransom. Sometimes, but not always, the redeemed captives were made to work for their benefactors. They were uniformly treated well, and often with such kindness that they would not be exchanged, and became Canadians by adoption.

Villebon was still full of anxiety as to the adhesion of the Abenakis. Thury saw the danger still more clearly, and told Frontenac that their late attack at Oyster River was due more to levity than to any other cause; that they were greatly alarmed, wavering, half stupefied, afraid of the English, and distrustful of the French, whom they accused of using them as tools.[1] It was clear that something must be done; and nothing could answer the purpose so well as the capture of Pemaquid, that English stronghold which held them in constant menace, and at the same time tempted them by offers of

---

had their scalps." La Potherie, IV. 91. Charlevoix, after his fashion on such occasions, suppresses the revenge and the scalping, and instead makes the dying Christian say, "I would have prevented them from so treating my God."

The savage custom of forcing prisoners to run the gauntlet, and sometimes beating them to death as they did so, was continued at two, if not all, of the mission villages down to the end of the French domination. General Stark of the Revolution, when a young man, was subjected to this kind of torture at St. Francis, but saved himself by snatching a club from one of the savages, and knocking the rest to the right and left as he ran. The practice was common, and must have had the consent of the priests of the mission.

At the Sulpitian mission of the Mountain of Montreal, unlike the rest, the converts were taught to speak French and practise mechanical arts. The absence of such teaching in other missions was the subject of frequent complaint, not only from Frontenac, but from other officers. La Motte-Cadillac writes bitterly on the subject, and contrasts the conduct of the French priests with that of the English ministers, who have taught many Indians to read and write, and reward them for teaching others in turn, which they do, he says, with great success. *Mémoire contenant une Description détaillée de l'Acadie, etc., 1693*. In fact, Eliot and his co-workers took great pains in this respect. There were at this time thirty Indian churches in New England, according to the *Diary of President Stiles*, cited by Holmes.

[1] *Thury à Frontenac, 11 Sept., 1694.*

goods at a low rate. To the capture of Pemaquid, therefore, the French government turned its thoughts.

One Pascho Chubb, of Andover, commanded the post, with a garrison of ninety-five militia-men. Stoughton, governor of Massachusetts, had written to the Abenakis, upbraiding them for breaking the peace, and ordering them to bring in their prisoners without delay. The Indians of Bigot's mission, that is to say, Bigot in their name, retorted by a letter to the last degree haughty and abusive. Those of Thury's mission, however, were so anxious to recover their friends held in prison at Boston that they came to Pemaquid, and opened a conference with Chubb. The French say that they meant only to deceive him.[1] This does not justify the Massachusetts officer, who, by an act of odious treachery, killed several of them, and captured the chief, Egeremet. Nor was this the only occasion on which the English had acted in bad faith. It was but playing into the hands of the French, who saw with delight that the folly of their enemies had aided their own intrigues.[2]

Early in 1696, two ships of war, the "Envieux" and the "Profond," one commanded by Iberville and the other by Bonaventure, sailed from Rochefort to Quebec, where they took on board eighty troops and Canadians; then proceeded to Cape Breton, embarked thirty Micmac Indians, and steered for the St. John. Here they met two British frigates and a provincial tender belonging to Massachusetts. A fight ensued. The forces were very unequal. The "Newport," of twenty-four guns, was dismasted and taken; but her companion frigate along with the tender escaped in the fog. The French then anchored at the mouth of the St. John, where Villebon and the priest Simon were waiting for them, with fifty more Micmacs. Simon and the Indians went on board; and they all sailed for Pentegoet, where Villieu, with twenty-five soldiers, and Thury and Saint-Castin, with some three hundred Abenakis, were ready to join them. After the usual feasting, these

[1] Villebon, *Journal, 1694–1696.*
[2] N. Y. Col. Docs., IX. 613, 616, 642, 643; La Potherie, III. 258; *Callières au Ministre, 25 Oct., 1695; Rev. John Pike to Governor and Council, 7 Jan., 1694* (1695), in Johnston, *Hist. of Bristol and Bremen*; Hutchinson, *Hist. Mass.*, II. 81, 90.

new allies paddled for Pemaquid; the ships followed; and on the next day, the fourteenth of August, they all reached their destination.

The fort of Pemaquid stood at the west side of the promontory of the same name, on a rocky point at the mouth of Pemaquid River. It was a quadrangle, with ramparts of rough stone, built at great pains and cost, but exposed to artillery, and incapable of resisting heavy shot. The government of Massachusetts, with its usual military fatuity, had placed it in the keeping of an unfit commander, and permitted some of the yeoman garrison to bring their wives and children to this dangerous and important post.

Saint-Castin and his Indians landed at New Harbor, half a league from the fort. Troops and cannon were sent ashore; and, at five o'clock in the afternoon, Chubb was summoned to surrender. He replied that he would fight, "even if the sea were covered with French ships and the land with Indians." The firing then began; and the Indian marksmen, favored by the nature of the ground, ensconced themselves near the fort, well covered from its cannon. During the night, mortars and heavy ships' guns were landed, and by great exertion were got into position, the two priests working lustily with the rest. They opened fire at three o'clock on the next day. Saint-Castin had just before sent Chubb a letter, telling him that, if the garrison were obstinate, they would get no quarter, and would be butchered by the Indians. Close upon this message followed four or five bomb-shells. Chubb succumbed immediately, sounded a parley, and gave up the fort, on condition that he and his men should be protected from the Indians, sent to Boston, and exchanged for French and Abenaki prisoners. They all marched out without arms; and Iberville, true to his pledge, sent them to an island in the bay, beyond the reach of his red allies. Villieu took possession of the fort, where an Indian prisoner was found in irons, half dead from long confinement. This so enraged his countrymen that a massacre would infallibly have taken place but for the precaution of Iberville.

The cannon of Pemaquid were carried on board the ships, and the small arms and ammunition given to the Indians. Two days were spent in destroying the works, and then the victors withdrew in triumph. Disgraceful as was the prompt surrender of the fort, it may be doubted if, even with the best defence, it could have held out many days; for it had no casemates, and its occupants were defenceless against the explosion of shells. Chubb was arrested for cowardice on his return, and remained some months in prison. After his release, he returned to his family at Andover, twenty miles from Boston; and here, in the year following, he and his wife were killed by Indians, who seem to have pursued him to this apparently safe asylum to take revenge for his treachery toward their countrymen.[1]

The people of Massachusetts, compelled by a royal order to build and maintain Pemaquid, had no love for it, and underrated its importance. Having been accustomed to spend their money as they themselves saw fit, they revolted at compulsion, though exercised for their good. Pemaquid was nevertheless of the utmost value for the preservation of their hold on Maine, and its conquest was a crowning triumph to the French.

The conquerors now projected a greater exploit. The Marquis de Nesmond, with a powerful squadron of fifteen ships, including some of the best in the royal navy, sailed for Newfoundland, with orders to defeat an English squadron supposed to be there, and then to proceed to the mouth of the Penobscot, where he was to be joined by the Abenaki warriors and fifteen hundred troops from Canada. The whole united force was then to fall upon Boston. The French had an exact knowledge of the place. Meneval, when a prisoner there, lodged in the house of John Nelson, had carefully examined it; and so also had the Chevalier d'Aux; while La Motte-Cadillac had reconnoitred the town and harbor before the war began. An accurate map of them was made for the use of the expedition, and the plan of operations was arranged with great care. Twelve hundred troops and Canadi-

[1] Baudoin, *Journal d'un Voyage fait avec M. d'Iberville*. Baudoin was an Acadian priest, who accompanied the expedition, which he describes in detail. *Relation de ce qui s'est passé, etc., 1695, 1696*; *Des Goutins au Ministre, 23 Sept., 1696*; Hutchinson, *Hist. Mass.*, II. 89; Mather, *Magnalia*, II. 633. A letter from Chubb, asking to be released from prison, is preserved in the archives of Massachusetts. I have examined the site of the fort, the remains of which are still distinct.

ans were to land with artillery at Dorchester, and march at once to force the barricade across the neck of the peninsula on which the town stood. At the same time, Saint-Castin was to land at Noddle's Island, with a troop of Canadians and all the Indians; pass over in canoes to Charlestown; and, after mastering it, cross to the north point of Boston, which would thus be attacked at both ends. During these movements, two hundred soldiers were to seize the battery on Castle Island, and then land in front of the town near Long Wharf, under the guns of the fleet.

Boston had about seven thousand inhabitants, but, owing to the seafaring habits of the people, many of its best men were generally absent; and, in the belief of the French, its available force did not much exceed eight hundred. "There are no soldiers in the place," say the directions for attack, "at least there were none last September, except the garrison from Pemaquid, who do not deserve the name." An easy victory was expected. After Boston was taken, the land forces, French and Indian, were to march on Salem, and thence northward to Portsmouth, conquering as they went; while the ships followed along the coast to lend aid, when necessary. All captured places were to be completely destroyed after removing all valuable property. A portion of this plunder was to be abandoned to the officers and men, in order to encourage them, and the rest stowed in the ships for transportation to France.[1]

[1] *Mémoire sur l'Entreprise de Baston, pour M. le Marquis de Nesmond, Versailles, 21 Avril, 1697; Instruction à M. le Marquis de Nesmond, même date; Le Roy à Frontenac, même date; Le Roy à Frontenac et Champigny, 27 Avril, 1697; Le Ministre à Nesmond, 28 Avril, 1697; Ibid., 15 Juin, 1697; Frontenac au Ministre, 15 Oct., 1697; Carte de Baston, par le S. Franquelin, 1697.* This is the map made for the use of the expedition. A *fac-simile* of it is before me. The conquest of New York had originally formed part of the plan. *Lagny au Ministre, 20 Jan., 1695.* Even as it was, too much was attempted, and the scheme was fatally complicated by the operations at Newfoundland. Four years before, a projected attack on Quebec by a British fleet, under Admiral Wheeler, had come to nought from analogous causes.

The French spared no pains to gain accurate information as to the strength of the English settlements. Among other reports on this subject there is a curious *Mémoire sur les Établissements anglois au delà de Pemaquid, jusqu'à Baston.* It was made just after the capture of Pemaquid, with a view to farther operations. Saco is described as a small fort a league above the mouth of the river Saco, with four cannon, but fit only to resist Indians. At Wells, it says,

Notice of the proposed expedition had reached Frontenac in the spring; and he began at once to collect men, canoes, and supplies for the long and arduous march to the rendezvous. He saw clearly the uncertainties of the attempt; but, in spite of his seventy-seven years, he resolved to command the land force in person. He was ready in June, and waited only to hear from Nesmond. The summer passed; and it was not till September that a ship reached Quebec with a letter from the marquis, telling him that head winds had detained the fleet till only fifty days' provision remained, and it was too late for action. The enterprise had completely failed, and even at Newfoundland nothing was accomplished. It proved a positive advantage to New England, since a host of Indians, who would otherwise have been turned loose upon the borders, were gathered by Saint-Castin at the Penobscot to wait for the fleet, and kept there idle all summer.

It is needless to dwell farther on the war in Acadia. There were petty combats by land and sea; Villieu was captured and carried to Boston; a band of New England rustics made a futile attempt to dislodge Villebon from his fort at Naxouat; while, throughout the contest, rivalry and jealousy rankled among the French officials, who continually maligned each other in tell-tale letters to the court. Their hope that the Abenakis would force back the English boundary to the Piscataqua was never fulfilled. At Kittery, at Wells, and even among the ashes of York, the stubborn settlers held their ground, while war-parties prowled along the whole frontier, from the Kennebec to the Connecticut. A single incident will show the nature of the situation, and the qualities which it sometimes called forth.

Early in the spring that followed the capture of Pemaquid, a band of Indians fell, after daybreak, on a number of farm-

---

all the settlers have sought refuge in four *petits forts*, of which the largest holds perhaps 20 men, besides women and children. At York, all the people have gathered into one fort, where there are about 40 men. At Portsmouth there is a fort, of slight account, and about a hundred houses. This neighborhood, no doubt including Kittery, can furnish at most about 300 men. At the Isles of Shoals there are some 280 fishermen, who are absent, except on Sundays. In the same manner, estimates are made for every village and district as far as Boston.

houses near the village of Haverhill. One of them belonged to a settler named Dustan, whose wife Hannah had borne a child a week before, and lay in the house, nursed by Mary Neff, one of her neighbors. Dustan had gone to his work in a neighboring field, taking with him his seven children, of whom the youngest was two years old. Hearing the noise of the attack, he told them to run to the nearest fortified house, a mile or more distant, and, snatching up his gun, threw himself on one of his horses and galloped towards his own house to save his wife. It was too late: the Indians were already there. He now thought only of saving his children; and, keeping behind them as they ran, he fired on the pursuing savages, and held them at bay till he and his flock reached a place of safety. Meanwhile, the house was set on fire, and his wife and the nurse carried off. Her husband, no doubt, had given her up as lost, when, weeks after, she reappeared, accompanied by Mary Neff and a boy, and bringing ten Indian scalps. Her story was to the following effect.

The Indians had killed the new-born child by dashing it against a tree, after which the mother and the nurse were dragged into the forest, where they found a number of friends and neighbors, their fellows in misery. Some of these were presently tomahawked, and the rest divided among their captors. Hannah Dustan and the nurse fell to the share of a family consisting of two warriors, three squaws, and seven children, who separated from the rest, and, hunting as they went, moved northward towards an Abenaki village, two hundred and fifty miles distant, probably that of the mission on the Chaudière. Every morning, noon, and evening, they told their beads, and repeated their prayers. An English boy, captured at Worcester, was also of the party. After a while, the Indians began to amuse themselves by telling the women that, when they reached the village, they would be stripped, made to run the gauntlet, and severely beaten, according to custom.

Hannah Dustan now resolved on a desperate effort to escape, and Mary Neff and the boy agreed to join in it. They were in the depths of the forest, half way on their journey, and the Indians, who had no distrust of them, were all asleep about their camp fire, when, late in the night, the two women and the boy took each a hatchet, and crouched silently by the bare heads of the unconscious savages. Then they all struck at once, with blows so rapid and true that ten of the twelve were killed before they were well awake. One old squaw sprang up wounded, and ran screeching into the forest, followed by a small boy whom they had purposely left unharmed. Hannah Dustan and her companions watched by the corpses till daylight; then the Amazon scalped them all, and the three made their way back to the settlements, with the trophies of their exploit.[1]

[1] This story is told by Mather, who had it from the women themselves, and by Niles, Hutchinson, and others. An entry in the contemporary journal of Rev. John Pike fully confirms it. The facts were notorious at the time. Hannah Dustan and her companions received a bounty of £50 for their ten scalps; and the governor of Maryland, hearing of what they had done, sent them a present.

Chapter XVIII

1693–1697

FRENCH AND ENGLISH RIVALRY

Le Moyne d'Iberville • His Exploits in Newfoundland • In Hudson's Bay • The Great Prize • The Competitors • Fatal Policy of the King • The Iroquois Question • Negotiation • Firmness of Frontenac • English Intervention • War renewed • State of the West • Indian Diplomacy • Cruel Measures • A Perilous Crisis • Audacity of Frontenac

N O CANADIAN, under the French rule, stands in a more conspicuous or more deserved eminence than Pierre Le Moyne d'Iberville. In the seventeenth century, most of those who acted a prominent part in the colony were born in Old France; but Iberville was a true son of the soil. He and his brothers, Longueuil, Serigny, Assigny, Maricourt, Sainte-Hélène, the two Châteauguays, and the two Bienvilles, were, one and all, children worthy of their father, Charles Le Moyne of Montreal, and favorable types of that Canadian *noblesse*, to whose adventurous hardihood half the continent bears witness. Iberville was trained in the French navy, and was already among its most able commanders. The capture of Pemaquid was, for him, but the beginning of greater things; and, though the exploits that followed were outside the main theatre of action, they were too remarkable to be passed in silence.

The French had but one post of any consequence on the Island of Newfoundland, the fort and village at Placentia Bay; while the English fishermen had formed a line of settlements two or three hundred miles along the eastern coast. Iberville had represented to the court the necessity of checking their growth, and to that end a plan was settled, in connection with the expedition against Pemaquid. The ships of the king were to transport the men; while Iberville and others associated with him were to pay them, and divide the plunder as their compensation. The chronicles of the time show various similar bargains between the great king and his subjects.

Pemaquid was no sooner destroyed, than Iberville sailed for

Newfoundland, with the eighty men he had taken at Quebec; and, on arriving, he was joined by as many more, sent him from the same place. He found Brouillan, governor of Placentia, with a squadron formed largely of privateers from St. Malo, engaged in a vain attempt to seize St. John, the chief post of the English. Brouillan was a man of harsh, jealous, and impracticable temper; and it was with the utmost difficulty that he and Iberville could act in concert. They came at last to an agreement, made a combined attack on St. John, took it, and burned it to the ground. Then followed a new dispute about the division of the spoils. At length it was settled. Brouillan went back to Placentia, and Iberville and his men were left to pursue their conquests alone.

There were no British soldiers on the island. The settlers were rude fishermen without commanders, and, according to the French accounts, without religion or morals. In fact, they are described as "worse than Indians." Iberville now had with him a hundred and twenty-five soldiers and Canadians, besides a few Abenakis from Acadia.[1] It was mid-winter when he began his march. For two months he led his hardy band through frost and snow, from hamlet to hamlet, along those forlorn and desolate coasts, attacking each in turn and carrying havoc everywhere. Nothing could exceed the hardships of the way, or the vigor with which they were met and conquered. The chaplain Baudoin gives an example of them in his diary. "January 18th. The roads are so bad that we can find only twelve men strong enough to beat the path. Our snowshoes break on the crust, and against the rocks and fallen trees hidden under the snow, which catch and trip us; but, for all that, we cannot help laughing to see now one, and now another, fall headlong. The Sieur de Martigny fell into a river, and left his gun and his sword there to save his life."

A panic seized the settlers, many of whom were without arms as well as without leaders. They imagined the Canadians to be savages, who scalped and butchered like the Iroquois. Their resistance was feeble and incoherent, and Iberville carried all before him. Every hamlet was pillaged and burned; and, according to the incredible report of the French writers,

---

[1] The reinforcement sent him from Quebec consisted of fifty soldiers, thirty Canadians, and three officers. *Frontenac au Ministre, 28 Oct., 1696.*

two hundred persons were killed and seven hundred captured, though it is admitted that most of the prisoners escaped. When spring opened, all the English settlements were destroyed, except the post of Bonavista and the Island of Carbonnière, a natural fortress in the sea. Iberville returned to Placentia, to prepare for completing his conquest, when his plans were broken by the arrival of his brother Serigny, with orders to proceed at once against the English at Hudson's Bay.[1]

It was the nineteenth of May, when Serigny appeared with five ships of war, the "Pelican," the "Palmier," the "Wesp," the "Profond," and the "Violent." The important trading-post of Fort Nelson, called Fort Bourbon by the French, was the destined object of attack. Iberville and Serigny had captured it three years before, but the English had retaken it during the past summer, and, as it commanded the fur-trade of a vast interior region, a strong effort was now to be made for its recovery. Iberville took command of the "Pelican," and his brother of the "Palmier." They sailed from Placentia early in July, followed by two other ships of the squadron, and a vessel carrying stores. Before the end of the month they entered the bay, where they were soon caught among masses of floating ice. The store-ship was crushed and lost, and the rest were in extreme danger. The "Pelican" at last extricated herself, and sailed into the open sea; but her three consorts were nowhere to be seen. Iberville steered for Fort Nelson, which was several hundred miles distant, on the western shore of this dismal

[1] On the Newfoundland expedition, the best authority is the long diary of the chaplain Baudoin, *Journal du Voyage que j'ai fait avec M. d'Iberville*; also, *Mémoire sur l'Entreprise de Terreneuve, 1696.* Compare La Potherie, I. 24–52. A deposition of one Phillips, one Roberts, and several others, preserved in the Public Record Office of London, and quoted by Brown in his *History of Cape Breton*, makes the French force much greater than the statements of the French writers. The deposition also says that at the attack of St. John's "the French took one William Brew, an inhabitant, a prisoner, and cut all round his scalp, and then, by strength of hands, stript his skin from the forehead to the crown, and so sent him into the fortifications, assuring the inhabitants that they would serve them all in like manner if they did not surrender."

St. John's was soon after reoccupied by the English.

Baudoin was one of those Acadian priests who are praised for services "en empeschant les sauvages de faire la paix avec les Anglois, ayant mesme esté en guerre avec eux." *Champigny au Ministre, 24 Oct., 1694.*

inland sea. He had nearly reached it, when three sail hove in sight; and he did not doubt that they were his missing ships. They proved, however, to be English armed merchantmen: the "Hampshire" of fifty-two guns, and the "Daring" and the "Hudson's Bay" of thirty-six and thirty-two. The "Pelican" carried but forty-four, and she was alone. A desperate battle followed, and from half past nine to one o'clock the cannonade was incessant. Iberville kept the advantage of the wind, and, coming at length to close quarters with the "Hampshire," gave her repeated broadsides between wind and water, with such effect that she sank with all on board. He next closed with the "Hudson's Bay," which soon struck her flag; while the "Daring" made sail, and escaped. The "Pelican" was badly damaged in hull, masts, and rigging; and the increasing fury of a gale from the east made her position more critical every hour. She anchored, to escape being driven ashore; but the cables parted, and she was stranded about two leagues from the fort. Here, racked by the waves and the tide, she split amidships; but most of the crew reached land with their weapons and ammunition. The northern winter had already begun, and the snow lay a foot deep in the forest. Some of them died from cold and exhaustion, and the rest built huts and kindled fires to warm and dry themselves. Food was so scarce that their only hope of escape from famishing seemed to lie in a desperate effort to carry the fort by storm, but now fortune interposed. The three ships they had left behind in the ice arrived with all the needed succors. Men, cannon, and mortars were sent ashore, and the attack began.

Fort Nelson was a palisade work, garrisoned by traders and other civilians in the employ of the English fur company, and commanded by one of its agents, named Bailey. Though it had a considerable number of small cannon, it was incapable of defence against any thing but musketry; and the French bombs soon made it untenable. After being three times summoned, Bailey lowered his flag, though not till he had obtained honorable terms; and he and his men marched out with arms and baggage, drums beating and colors flying.

Iberville had triumphed over the storms, the icebergs, and the English. The north had seen his prowess, and another fame awaited him in the regions of the sun; for he became the father of Louisiana, and his brother Bienville founded New Orleans.[1]

These northern conflicts were but episodes. In Hudson's Bay, Newfoundland, and Acadia, the issues of the war were unimportant, compared with the momentous question whether France or England should be mistress of the west; that is to say, of the whole interior of the continent. There was a strange contrast in the attitude of the rival colonies towards this supreme prize: the one was inert, and seemingly indifferent; the other, intensely active. The reason is obvious enough. The English colonies were separate, jealous of the crown and of each other, and incapable as yet of acting in concert. Living by agriculture and trade, they could prosper within limited areas, and had no present need of spreading beyond the Alleghanies. Each of them was an aggregate of persons, busied with their own affairs, and giving little heed to matters which did not immediately concern them. Their rulers, whether chosen by themselves or appointed in England, could not compel them to become the instruments of enterprises in which the sacrifice was present, and the advantage remote. The neglect in which the English court left them, though wholesome in most respects, made them unfit for aggressive action; for they had neither troops, commanders, political union, military organization, nor military habits. In communities so busy, and governments so popular, much could not be done, in war, till the people were roused to the necessity of doing it; and that awakening was still far distant. Even New York, the only exposed colony, except Massachusetts and New Hampshire, regarded the war merely as a nuisance to be held at arm's length.[2]

In Canada, all was different. Living by the fur trade, she needed free range and indefinite space. Her geographical position determined the nature of her pursuits; and her pursuits developed the roving and adventurous character of her people, who, living under a military rule, could be directed at will to such ends as their rulers saw fit. The grand French scheme

[1] On the capture of Fort Nelson, *Iberville au Ministre, 8 Nov., 1697*; Jérémie, *Relation de la Baye de Hudson*; La Potherie, I. 85–109. All these writers were present at the attack.

[2] See note at the end of the chapter.

of territorial extension was not born at court, but sprang from Canadian soil, and was developed by the chiefs of the colony, who, being on the ground, saw the possibilities and requirements of the situation, and generally had a personal interest in realizing them. The rival colonies had two different laws of growth. The one increased by slow extension, rooting firmly as it spread; the other shot offshoots, with few or no roots, far out into the wilderness. It was the nature of French colonization to seize upon detached strategic points, and hold them by the bayonet, forming no agricultural basis, but attracting the Indians by trade, and holding them by conversion. A musket, a rosary, and a pack of beaver skins may serve to represent it, and in fact it consisted of little else.

Whence came the numerical weakness of New France, and the real though latent strength of her rivals? Because, it is answered, the French were not an emigrating people; but, at the end of the seventeenth century, this was only half true. The French people were divided into two parts, one eager to emigrate, and the other reluctant. The one consisted of the persecuted Huguenots, the other of the favored Catholics. The government chose to construct its colonies, not of those who wished to go, but of those who wished to stay at home. From the hour when the edict of Nantes was revoked, hundreds of thousands of Frenchmen would have hailed as a boon the permission to transport themselves, their families, and their property to the New World. The permission was fiercely refused, and the persecuted sect was denied even a refuge in the wilderness. Had it been granted them, the valleys of the west would have swarmed with a laborious and virtuous population, trained in adversity, and possessing the essential qualities of self-government. Another France would have grown beyond the Alleghanies, strong with the same kind of strength that made the future greatness of the British colonies. British America was an asylum for the oppressed and the suffering of all creeds and nations, and population poured into her by the force of a natural tendency. France, like England, might have been great in two hemispheres, if she had placed herself in accord with this tendency, instead of opposing it; but despotism was consistent with itself, and a mighty opportunity was for ever lost.

As soon could the Ethiopian change his skin as the priest-ridden king change his fatal policy of exclusion. Canada must be bound to the papacy, even if it blasted her. The contest for the west must be waged by the means which Bourbon policy ordained, and which, it must be admitted, had some great advantages of their own, when controlled by a man like Frontenac. The result hung, for the present, on the relations of the French with the Iroquois and the tribes of the lakes, the Illinois, and the valley of the Ohio, but, above all, on their relations with the Iroquois; for, could they be conquered or won over, it would be easy to deal with the rest.

Frontenac was meditating a grand effort to inflict such castigation as would bring them to reason, when one of their chiefs, named Tareha, came to Quebec with overtures of peace. The Iroquois had lost many of their best warriors. The arrival of troops from France had discouraged them; the war had interrupted their hunting; and, having no furs to barter with the English, they were in want of arms, ammunition, and all the necessaries of life. Moreover, Father Milet, nominally a prisoner among them, but really an adopted chief, had used all his influence to bring about a peace; and the mission of Tareha was the result. Frontenac received him kindly. "My Iroquois children have been drunk; but I will give them an opportunity to repent. Let each of your five nations send me two deputies, and I will listen to what they have to say." They would not come, but sent him instead an invitation to meet them and their friends, the English, in a general council at Albany; a proposal which he rejected with contempt. Then they sent another deputation, partly to him and partly to their Christian countrymen of the Saut and the Mountain, inviting all alike to come and treat with them at Onondaga. Frontenac, adopting the Indian fashion, kicked away their wampum belts, rebuked them for tampering with the mission Indians, and told them that they were rebels, bribed by the English; adding that, if a suitable deputation should be sent to Quebec to treat squarely of peace, he still would listen, but that, if they came back with any more such proposals as they had just made, they should be roasted alive.

A few weeks later, the deputation appeared. It consisted of two chiefs of each nation, headed by the renowned orator

Decanisora, or, as the French wrote the name, Tegannisorens. The council was held in the hall of the supreme council at Quebec. The dignitaries of the colony were present, with priests, Jesuits, Récollets, officers, and the Christian chiefs of the Saut and the Mountain. The appearance of the ambassadors bespoke their destitute plight; for they were all dressed in shabby deer-skins and old blankets, except Decanisora, who was attired in a scarlet coat laced with gold, given him by the governor of New York. Colden, who knew him in his old age, describes him as a tall, well-formed man, with a face not unlike the busts of Cicero. "He spoke," says the French reporter, "with as perfect a grace as is vouchsafed to an uncivilized people;" buried the hatchet, covered the blood that had been spilled, opened the roads, and cleared the clouds from the sun. In other words, he offered peace; but he demanded at the same time that it should include the English. Frontenac replied, in substance: "My children are right to come submissive and repentant. I am ready to forgive the past, and hang up the hatchet; but the peace must include all my other children, far and near. Shut your ears to English poison. The war with the English has nothing to do with you, and only the great kings across the sea have power to stop it. You must give up all your prisoners, both French and Indian, without one exception. I will then return mine, and make peace with you, but not before." He then entertained them at his own table, gave them a feast described as "magnificent," and bestowed gifts so liberally, that the tattered ambassadors went home in embroidered coats, laced shirts, and plumed hats. They were pledged to return with the prisoners before the end of the season, and they left two hostages as security.[1]

Meanwhile, the authorities of New York tried to prevent the threatened peace. First, Major Peter Schuyler convoked the chiefs at Albany, and told them that, if they went to ask peace in Canada, they would be slaves for ever. The Iroquois

[1] On these negotiations, and their antecedents, Callières, *Relation de ce qui s'est passé de plus remarquable en Canada depuis Sept., 1692, jusqu'au Départ des Vaisseaux en 1693*; La Motte-Cadillac, *Mémoire des Negociations avec les Iroquois, 1694*; *Callières au Ministre, 19 Oct., 1694*; La Potherie, III. 200–220; Colden, *Five Nations*, chap. x.; *N. Y. Col. Docs.*, IV. 85.

declared that they loved the English, but they repelled every attempt to control their action. Then Fletcher, the governor, called a general council at the same place, and told them that they should not hold councils with the French, or that, if they did so, they should hold them at Albany in presence of the English. Again they asserted their rights as an independent people. "Corlaer," said their speaker, "has held councils with our enemies, and why should not we hold councils with his?" Yet they were strong in assurances of friendship, and declared themselves "one head, one heart, one blood, and one soul, with the English." Their speaker continued: "Our only reason for sending deputies to the French is that we are brought so low, and none of our neighbors help us, but leave us to bear all the burden of the war. Our brothers of New England, Pennsylvania, Maryland, and Virginia, all of their own accord took hold of the covenant chain, and called themselves our allies; but they have done nothing to help us, and we cannot fight the French alone, because they are always receiving soldiers from beyond the Great Lake. Speak from your heart, brother: will you and your neighbors join with us, and make strong war against the French? If you will, we will break off all treaties, and fight them as hotly as ever; but, if you will not help us, we must make peace."

Nothing could be more just than these reproaches; and, if the English governor had answered by a vigorous attack on the French forts south of the St. Lawrence, the Iroquois warriors would have raised the hatchet again with one accord. But Fletcher was busy with other matters; and he had besides no force at his disposal but four companies, the only British regulars on the continent, defective in numbers, ill-appointed, and mutinous.[1] Therefore he answered not with acts, but with words. The negotiation with the French went on, and Fletcher called another council. It left him in a worse position than before. The Iroquois again asked for help: he could not promise it, but was forced to yield the point, and tell them that he consented to their making peace with Onontio.

It is certain that they wanted peace, but equally certain that

[1] Fletcher is, however, charged with gross misconduct in regard to the four companies, which he is said to have kept at about half their complement, in order to keep the balance of their pay for himself.

they did not want it to be lasting, and sought nothing more than a breathing time to regain their strength. Even now some of them were for continuing the war; and at the great council at Onondaga, where the matter was debated, the Onondagas, Oneidas, and Mohawks spurned the French proposals, and refused to give up their prisoners. The Cayugas and some of the Senecas were of another mind, and agreed to a partial compliance with Frontenac's demands. The rest seem to have stood passive in the hope of gaining time.

They were disappointed. In vain the Seneca and Cayuga deputies buried the hatchet at Montreal, and promised that the other nations would soon do likewise. Frontenac was not to be deceived. He would accept nothing but the frank fulfilment of his conditions, refused the proffered peace, and told his Indian allies to wage war to the knife. There was a dog-feast and a war-dance, and the strife began anew.

In all these conferences, the Iroquois had stood by their English allies, with a fidelity not too well merited. But, though they were loyal towards the English, they had acted with duplicity towards the French, and, while treating of peace with them, had attacked some of their Indian allies, and intrigued with others. They pursued with more persistency than ever the policy they had adopted in the time of La Barre, that is, to persuade or frighten the tribes of the west to abandon the French, join hands with them and the English, and send their furs to Albany instead of Montreal; for the sagacious confederates knew well that, if the trade were turned into this new channel, their local position would enable them to control it. The scheme was good; but, with whatever consistency their chiefs and elders might pursue it, the wayward ferocity of their young warriors crossed it incessantly, and murders alternated with intrigues. On the other hand, the western tribes, who since the war had been but ill supplied with French goods and French brandy, knew that they could have English goods and English rum in great abundance, and at far less cost; and thus, in spite of hate and fear, the intrigue went on. Michillimackinac was the focus of it, but it pervaded all the west. The position of Frontenac was one of great difficulty, and the more so that the intestine quarrels of his allies excessively complicated the mazes of forest diplomacy. This heterogeneous multitude, scattered in tribes and groups of tribes over two thousand miles of wilderness, was like a vast menagerie of wild animals; and the lynx bristled at the wolf, and the panther grinned fury at the bear, in spite of all his efforts to form them into a happy family under his paternal rule.

La Motte-Cadillac commanded at Michillimackinac, Courtemanche was stationed at Fort Miamis, and Tonty and La Forêt at the fortified rock of St. Louis on the Illinois; while Nicolas Perrot roamed among the tribes of the Mississippi, striving at the risk of his life to keep them at peace with each other, and in alliance with the French. Yet a plot presently came to light, by which the Foxes, Mascontins, and Kickapoos were to join hands, renounce the French, and cast their fortunes with the Iroquois and the English. There was still more anxiety for the tribes of Michillimackinac, because the results of their defection would be more immediate. This important post had at the time an Indian population of six or seven thousand souls, a Jesuit mission, a fort with two hundred soldiers, and a village of about sixty houses, occupied by traders and *coureurs de bois*. The Indians of the place were in relations more or less close with all the tribes of the lakes. The Huron village was divided between two rival chiefs: the Baron, who was deep in Iroquois and English intrigue; and the Rat, who, though once the worst enemy of the French, now stood their friend. The Ottawas and other Algonquins of the adjacent villages were savages of a lower grade, tossed continually between hatred of the Iroquois, distrust of the French, and love of English goods and English rum.[1]

La Motte-Cadillac found that the Hurons of the Baron's band were receiving messengers and peace belts from New York and her red allies, that the English had promised to build a trading house on Lake Erie, and that the Iroquois had invited the lake tribes to a grand convention at Detroit. These

---

[1] "Si les Outaouacs (*Ottawas*) et Hurons concluent la paix avec l'Iroquois sans nostre participation, et donnent chez eux l'entrée à l'Anglois pour le commerce, la Colonie est entièrement ruinée, puisque c'est le seul (*moyen*) par lequel ce pays-cy puisse subsister, et l'on peut asseurer que si les sauvages goustent une fois du commerce de l'Anglois, ils rompront pour toujours avec les François, parcequ'ils ne peuvent donner les marchandises qu'à un prix beaucoup plus hault." *Frontenac au Ministre, 25 Oct., 1696.*

belts and messages were sent, in the Indian expression, "underground," that is, secretly; and the envoys who brought them came in the disguise of prisoners taken by the Hurons. On one occasion, seven Iroquois were brought in; and some of the French, suspecting them to be agents of the negotiation, stabbed two of them as they landed. There was a great tumult. The Hurons took arms to defend the remaining five; but at length suffered themselves to be appeased, and even gave one of the Iroquois, a chief, into the hands of the French, who, says La Potherie, determined to "make an example of him." They invited the Ottawas to "drink the broth of an Iroquois." The wretch was made fast to a stake, and a Frenchman began the torture by burning him with a red-hot gun-barrel. The mob of savages was soon wrought up to the required pitch of ferocity; and, after atrociously tormenting him, they cut him to pieces, and ate him.[1] It was clear that the more Iroquois the allies of France could be persuaded to burn, the less would be the danger that they would make peace with the confederacy. On another occasion, four were tortured at once; and La Motte-Cadillac writes, "If any more prisoners are brought me, I promise you that their fate will be no sweeter."[2]

The same cruel measures were practised when the Ottawas came to trade at Montreal. Frontenac once invited a band of them to "roast an Iroquois," newly caught by the soldiers; but as they had hamstrung him, to prevent his escape, he bled to death before the torture began.[3] In the next spring, the revolting tragedy of Michillimackinac was repeated at Montreal, where four more Iroquois were burned by the soldiers, inhabitants, and Indian allies. "It was the mission of Canada," says a Canadian writer, "to propagate Christianity and civilization."[4]

[1] La Potherie, II. 298.

[2] *La Motte-Cadillac à* ———, *3 Aug., 1695.* A translation of this letter will be found in Sheldon, *Early History of Michigan.*

[3] *Relation de ce qui s'est passé de plus remarquable entre les François et les Iroquois durant la présente année, 1695.* There is a translation in N. Y. Col. Docs., IX. Compare La Potherie, who misplaces the incident as to date.

[4] This last execution was an act of reprisal: "J'abandonnay les 4 prisonniers aux soldats, habitants, et sauvages, qui les bruslerent par représailles de deux du Sault que cette nation avoit traitté de la mesme manière." *Callières au Ministre, 20 Oct., 1696.*

Every effort was vain. La Motte-Cadillac wrote that matters grew worse and worse, and that the Ottawas had been made to believe that the French neither would nor could protect them, but meant to leave them to their fate. They thought that they had no hope except in peace with the Iroquois, and had actually gone to meet them at an appointed rendezvous. One course alone was now left to Frontenac, and this was to strike the Iroquois with a blow heavy enough to humble them, and teach the wavering hordes of the west that he was, in truth, their father and their defender. Nobody knew so well as he the difficulties of the attempt; and, deceived perhaps by his own energy, he feared that, in his absence on a distant expedition, the governor of New York would attack Montreal. Therefore, he had begged for more troops. About three hundred were sent him, and with these he was forced to content himself.

He had waited, also, for another reason. In his belief, the re-establishment of Fort Frontenac, abandoned in a panic by Denonville, was necessary to the success of a campaign against the Iroquois. A party in the colony vehemently opposed the measure, on the ground that the fort would be used by the friends of Frontenac for purposes of trade. It was, nevertheless, very important, if not essential, for holding the Iroquois in check. They themselves felt it to be so; and, when they heard that the French intended to occupy it again, they appealed to the governor of New York, who told them that, if the plan were carried into effect, he would march to their aid with all the power of his government. He did not, and perhaps could not, keep his word.[1]

In the question of Fort Frontenac, as in every thing else, the opposition to the governor, always busy and vehement, found its chief representative in the intendant, who told the minister that the policy of Frontenac was all wrong; that the public good was not its object; that he disobeyed or evaded the orders of the king; and that he had suffered the Iroquois to delude him by false overtures of peace. The representations of the intendant and his faction had such effect, that Ponchartrain wrote to the governor that the plan of re-establish-

[1] Colden, 178. Fletcher could get no men from his own or neighboring governments. See *note*, at the end of the chapter.

ing Fort Frontenac "must absolutely be abandoned." Frontenac, bent on accomplishing his purpose, and doubly so because his enemies opposed it, had anticipated the orders of the minister, and sent seven hundred men to Lake Ontario to repair the fort. The day after they left Montreal, the letter of Ponchartrain arrived. The intendant demanded their recall. Frontenac refused. The fort was repaired, garrisoned, and victualled for a year.

A successful campaign was now doubly necessary to the governor, for by this alone could he hope to avert the consequences of his audacity. He waited no longer, but mustered troops, militia, and Indians, and marched to attack the Iroquois.[1]

MILITARY INEFFICIENCY OF THE BRITISH COLONIES. — "His Majesty has subjects enough in those parts of America to drive out the French from Canada; but they are so *crumbled into little governments*, and so disunited, that they have hitherto afforded little assistance to each other, and now seem in a much worse disposition to do it for the future." This is the complaint of the Lords of Trade. Governor Fletcher writes bitterly: "Here every little government sets up for despotic power, and allows no appeal to the Crown, but, by a little juggling, defeats all commands and injunctions from the King." Fletcher's complaint was not unprovoked. The Queen had named him commander-in-chief, during the war, of the militia of several of the colonies, and empowered him to call on them for contingents of men, not above 350 from Massachusetts, 250 from Virginia, 160 from Maryland, 120 from Connecticut, 48 from Rhode Island, and 80 from Pennsylvania. This measure excited the jealousy of the colonies, and several of them remonstrated on constitutional grounds; but the attorney-general, to whom the question was referred, reported that the crown had power, under certain limitations, to appoint a commander-in-chief. Fletcher, therefore, in his character as such, called for a portion of the men; but scarcely one could he get. He was met by excuses and evasions, which, especially in the case of Connecticut, were of a most vexatious character. At last, that colony, tired by his importunities, condescended to furnish him with twenty-five men. With the others, he was less fortunate, though Virginia and Maryland compounded with a sum of money. Each colony claimed the control of its own militia, and was anxious to avoid the establishment of any precedent which might deprive it of the right. Even in the military management of each separate colony, there was scarcely less

[1] The above is drawn from the correspondence of Frontenac, Champigny, La Motte-Cadillac, and Callières, on one hand, and the king and the minister on the other. The letters are too numerous to specify. Also, from the official *Relation de ce qui s'est passé de plus remarquable en Canada, 1694, 1695,* and *Ibid., 1695, 1696; Mémoire soumis au Ministre de ce qui résulte des Avis reçus du Canada en 1695;* Champigny, *Mémoire concernant le Fort de Cataracouy;* La Potherie, II. 284–302, IV. 1–80; Colden, chaps. x., xi.

difficulty. A requisition for troops from a royal governor was always regarded with jealousy, and the provincial assemblies were slow to grant money for their support. In 1692, when Fletcher came to New York, the assembly gave him 300 men, for a year; in 1693, they gave him an equal number; in 1694, they allowed him but 170, he being accused, apparently with truth, of not having made good use of the former levies. He afterwards asked that the force at his disposal should be increased to 500 men, to guard the frontier; and the request was not granted. In 1697 he was recalled; and the Earl of Bellomont was commissioned governor of New York, Massachusetts, and New Hampshire, and captain-general, during the war, of all the forces of those colonies, as well as of Connecticut, Rhode Island, and New Jersey. The close of the war quickly ended this military authority; but there is no reason to believe that, had it continued, the earl's requisitions for men, in his character of captain-general, would have had more success than those of Fletcher. The whole affair is a striking illustration of the original isolation of communities, which afterwards became welded into a nation. It involved a military paralysis almost complete. Sixty years later, under the sense of a great danger, the British colonies were ready enough to receive a commander-in-chief, and answer his requisitions.

A great number of documents bearing upon the above subject will be found in the *New York Colonial Documents*, IV.

Chapter XIX

1696−1698

FRONTENAC ATTACKS THE ONONDAGAS

March of Frontenac • Flight of the Enemy • An Iroquois Stoic • Relief for the Onondagas • Boasts of Frontenac • His Complaints • His Enemies • Parties in Canada • Views of Frontenac and the King • Frontenac prevails • Peace of Ryswick • Frontenac and Bellomont • Schuyler at Quebec • Festivities • A Last Defiance

---

O N THE FOURTH of July, Frontenac left Montreal, at the head of about twenty-two hundred men. On the nineteenth he reached Fort Frontenac, and on the twenty-sixth he crossed to the southern shore of Lake Ontario. A swarm of Indian canoes led the way; next followed two battalions of regulars, in bateaux, commanded by Callières; then more bateaux, laden with cannon, mortars, and rockets; then Frontenac himself, surrounded by the canoes of his staff and his guard; then eight hundred Canadians, under Ramesay; while more regulars and more Indians, all commanded by Vaudreuil, brought up the rear. In two days they reached the mouth of the Oswego; strong scouting-parties were sent out to scour the forests in front; while the expedition slowly and painfully worked its way up the stream. Most of the troops and Canadians marched through the matted woods along the banks; while the bateaux and canoes were pushed, rowed, paddled, or dragged forward against the current. On the evening of the thirtieth, they reached the falls, where the river plunged over ledges of rock which completely stopped the way. The work of "carrying" was begun at once. The Indians and Canadians carried the canoes to the navigable water above, and gangs of men dragged the bateaux up the portage-path on rollers. Night soon came, and the work was continued till ten o'clock by torchlight. Frontenac would have passed on foot like the rest, but the Indians would not have it so. They lifted him in his canoe upon their shoulders, and bore him in triumph, singing and yelling, through the forest and along the margin of the rapids, the blaze of the torches lighting the strange procession, where plumes of officers and uniforms of the governor's guard mingled with the feathers and scalp-locks of naked savages.

When the falls were passed, the troops pushed on as before along the narrow stream, and through the tangled labyrinths on either side; till, on the first of August, they reached Lake Onondaga, and, with sails set, the whole flotilla glided before the wind, and landed the motley army on a rising ground half a league from the salt springs of Salina. The next day was spent in building a fort to protect the canoes, bateaux, and stores; and, as evening closed, a ruddy glow above the southern forest told them that the town of Onondaga was on fire.

The Marquis de Crisasy was left, with a detachment, to hold the fort; and, at sunrise on the fourth, the army moved forward in order of battle. It was formed in two lines, regulars on the right and left, and Canadians in the centre. Callières commanded the first line, and Vaudreuil the second. Frontenac was between them, surrounded by his staff officers and his guard, and followed by the artillery, which relays of Canadians dragged and lifted forward with inconceivable labor. The governor, enfeebled by age, was carried in an armchair; while Callières, disabled by gout, was mounted on a horse, brought for the purpose in one of the bateaux. To Subercase fell the hard task of directing the march among the dense columns of the primeval forest, by hill and hollow, over rocks and fallen trees, through swamps, brooks, and gullies, among thickets, brambles, and vines. It was but eight or nine miles to Onondaga; but they were all day in reaching it, and evening was near when they emerged from the shadows of the forest into the broad light of the Indian clearing. The maize-fields stretched before them for miles, and in the midst lay the charred and smoking ruins of the Iroquois capital. Not an enemy was to be seen, but they found the dead bodies of two murdered French prisoners. Scouts were sent out, guards were set, and the disappointed troops encamped on the maize-fields.

Onondaga, formerly an open town, had been fortified by the English, who had enclosed it with a double range of strong palisades, forming a rectangle, flanked by bastions at the four corners, and surrounded by an outer fence of tall poles. The place was not defensible against cannon and mortars; and the four hundred warriors belonging to it had been but slightly reinforced from the other tribes of the confederacy, each of which feared that the French attack might be directed against itself. On the approach of an enemy of five times their number, they had burned their town, and retreated southward into distant forests.

The troops were busied for two days in hacking down the maize, digging up the *caches*, or hidden stores of food, and destroying their contents. The neighboring tribe of the Oneidas sent a messenger to beg peace. Frontenac replied that he would grant it, on condition that they all should migrate to Canada, and settle there; and Vaudreuil, with seven hundred men, was sent to enforce the demand. Meanwhile, a few Onondaga stragglers had been found; and among them, hidden in a hollow tree, a withered warrior, eighty years old, and nearly blind. Frontenac would have spared him; but the Indian allies, Christians from the mission villages, were so eager to burn him that it was thought inexpedient to refuse them. They tied him to the stake, and tried to shake his constancy by every torture that fire could inflict; but not a cry nor a murmur escaped him. He defied them to do their worst, till, enraged at his taunts, one of them gave him a mortal stab. "I thank you," said the old Stoic, with his last breath; "but you ought to have finished as you began, and killed me by fire. Learn from me, you dogs of Frenchmen, how to endure pain; and you, dogs of dogs, their Indian allies, think what you will do when you are burned like me."[1]

Vaudreuil and his detachment returned within three days, after destroying Oneida, with all the growing corn, and seiz-

[1] *Relation de ce qui s'est passé, etc., 1695, 1696*; La Potherie, III. 279. Callières and the author of the Relation of 1682–1712 also speak of the extraordinary fortitude of the victim. The Jesuits say that it was not the Christian Indians who insisted on burning him, but the French themselves, "qui voulurent absolument qu'il fût brulé à petit feu, ce qu'ils executèrent eux-mêmes. Un Jesuite le confessa et l'assista à la mort, l'encourageant à souffrir courageusement et *chrétiennement* les tourmens." *Relation de 1696* (Shea), 10. This writer adds that, when Frontenac heard of it, he ordered him to be spared; but it was too late. Charlevoix misquotes the old Stoic's last words, which were, according to the official Relation of 1695–6: "Je te remercie mais tu aurais bien dû achever de me faire mourir par le feu. Apprenez, chiens de François, à souffrir, et vous sauvages leurs allies, qui êtes les chiens des chiens, souvenez vous de ce que vous devez faire quand vous serez en pareil état que moi."

ing a number of chiefs as hostages for the fulfilment of the demands of Frontenac. There was some thought of marching on Cayuga, but the governor judged it to be inexpedient; and, as it would be useless to chase the fugitive Onondagas, nothing remained but to return home.[1]

While Frontenac was on his march, Governor Fletcher had heard of his approach, and called the council at New York to consider what should be done. They resolved that "it will be very grievous to take the people from their labour; and there is likewise no money to answer the charge thereof." Money was, however, advanced by Colonel Cortlandt and others; and the governor wrote to Connecticut and New Jersey for their contingents of men; but they thought the matter no concern of theirs, and did not respond. Fletcher went to Albany with the few men he could gather at the moment, and heard on his arrival that the French were gone. Then he convoked the chiefs, condoled with them, and made them presents. Corn was sent to the Onondagas and Oneidas to support them through the winter, and prevent the famine which the French hoped would prove their destruction.

What Frontenac feared had come to pass. The enemy had saved themselves by flight; and his expedition, like that of Denonville, was but half successful. He took care, however, to announce it to the king as a triumph.

"Sire, the benedictions which Heaven has ever showered upon your Majesty's arms have extended even to this New World; whereof we have had visible proof in the expedition I have just made against the Onondagas, the principal nation of the Iroquois. I had long projected this enterprise, but the difficulties and risks which attended it made me regard it as

---

[1] On the expedition against the Onondagas, *Callières au Ministre, 20 Oct., 1696*; *Frontenac au Ministre, 25 Oct., 1696*; *Frontenac et Champigny au Ministre (lettre commune) 26 Oct., 1696*; *Relation de ce qui s'est passé, etc., 1695, 1696*; *Relation, 1682–1712*; *Relation des Jesuites, 1696* (Shea); *Doc. Hist. N. Y.,* I. 323–355; La Potherie, III. 270–282; *N. Y. Col. Docs.,* IV. 242.

Charlevoix charges Frontenac on this occasion with failing to pursue his advantage, lest others, and especially Callières, should get more honor than he. The accusation seems absolutely groundless. His many enemies were silent about it at the time; for the king warmly commends his conduct on the expedition, and Callières himself, writing immediately after, gives him nothing but praise.

imprudent; and I should never have resolved to undertake it, if I had not last year established an *entrepôt* (*Fort Frontenac*), which made my communications more easy, and if I had not known, beyond all doubt, that this was absolutely the only means to prevent our allies from making peace with the Iroquois, and introducing the English into their country, by which the colony would infallibly be ruined. Nevertheless, by unexpected good fortune, the Onondagas, who pass for masters of the other Iroquois, and the terror of all the Indians of this country, fell into a sort of bewilderment, which could only have come from on High; and were so terrified to see me march against them in person, and cover their lakes and rivers with nearly four hundred sail, that, without availing themselves of passes where a hundred men might easily hold four thousand in check, they did not dare to lay a single ambuscade, but, after waiting till I was five leagues from their fort, they set it on fire with all their dwellings, and fled, with their families, twenty leagues into the depths of the forest. It could have been wished, to make the affair more brilliant, that they had tried to hold their fort against us, for we were prepared to force it and kill a great many of them; but their ruin is not the less sure, because the famine, to which they are reduced, will destroy more than we could have killed by sword and gun.

"All the officers and men have done their duty admirably; and especially M. de Callières, who has been a great help to me. I know not if your Majesty will think that I have tried to do mine, and will hold me worthy of some mark of honor that may enable me to pass the short remainder of my life in some little distinction; but, whether this be so or not, I most humbly pray your Majesty to believe that I will sacrifice the rest of my days to your Majesty's service with the same ardor I have always felt."[1]

The king highly commended him, and sent him the cross of the Military Order of St. Louis. Callières, who had deserved it less, had received it several years before; but he had not found or provoked so many defamers. Frontenac complained to the minister that his services had been slightly and tardily requited. This was true, and it was due largely to the

[1] *Frontenac au Roy, 25 Oct., 1696.*

complaints excited by his own perversity and violence. These complaints still continued; but the fault was not all on one side, and Frontenac himself had often just reason to retort them. He wrote to Ponchartrain: "If you will not be so good as to look closely into the true state of things here, I shall always be exposed to detraction, and forced to make new apologies, which is very hard for a person so full of zeal and uprightness as I am. My secretary, who is going to France, will tell you all the ugly intrigues used to defeat my plans for the service of the king, and the growth of the colony. I have long tried to combat these artifices, but I confess that I no longer feel strength to resist them, and must succumb at last, if you will not have the goodness to give me strong support."[1]

He still continued to provoke the detraction which he deprecated, till he drew, at last, a sharp remonstrance from the minister. "The dispute you have had with M. de Champigny is without cause, and I confess I cannot comprehend how you could have acted as you have done. If you do things of this sort, you must expect disagreeable consequences, which all the desire I have to oblige you cannot prevent. It is deplorable, both for you and for me, that, instead of using my goodwill to gain favors from his Majesty, you compel me to make excuses for a violence which answers no purpose, and in which you indulge wantonly, nobody can tell why."[2]

Most of these quarrels, however trivial in themselves, had a solid foundation, and were closely connected with the great question of the control of the west. As to the measures to be taken, two parties divided the colony; one consisting of the governor and his friends, and the other of the intendant, the Jesuits, and such of the merchants as were not in favor with Frontenac. His policy was to protect the Indian allies at all risks, to repel by force, if necessary, every attempt of the English to encroach on the territory in dispute, and to occupy it by forts which should be at once posts of war and commerce and places of rendezvous for traders and *voyageurs*. Champigny and his party denounced this system; urged that the forest posts should be abandoned, that both garrisons and traders should be recalled, that the French should not go to

[1] *Frontenac au Ministre, 25 Oct., 1696.*
[2] *Le Ministre à Frontenac, 21 Mai, 1698.*

the Indians, but that the Indians should come to the French, that the fur trade of the interior should be carried on at Montreal, and that no Frenchman should be allowed to leave the settled limits of the colony, except the Jesuits and persons in their service, who, as Champigny insisted, would be able to keep the Indians in the French interest without the help of soldiers.

Strong personal interests were active on both sides, and gave bitterness to the strife. Frontenac, who always stood by his friends, had placed Tonty, La Forêt, La Motte-Cadillac, and others of their number, in charge of the forest posts, where they made good profit by trade. Moreover, the licenses for trading expeditions into the interior were now, as before, used largely for the benefit of his favorites. The Jesuits also declared, and with some truth, that the forest posts were centres of debauchery, and that the licenses for the western trade were the ruin of innumerable young men. All these reasons were laid before the king. In vain Frontenac represented that to abandon the forest posts would be to resign to the English the trade of the interior country, and at last the country itself. The royal ear was open to his opponents, and the royal instincts reinforced their arguments. The king, enamoured of subordination and order, wished to govern Canada as he governed a province of France; and this could be done only by keeping the population within prescribed bounds. Therefore, he commanded that licenses for the forest trade should cease, that the forest posts should be abandoned and destroyed, that all Frenchmen should be ordered back to the settlements, and that none should return under pain of the galleys. An exception was made in favor of the Jesuits, who were allowed to continue their western missions, subject to restrictions designed to prevent them from becoming a cover to illicit fur trade. Frontenac was also directed to make peace with the Iroquois, even, if necessary, without including the western allies of France; that is, he was authorized by Louis XIV. to pursue the course which had discredited and imperilled the colony under the rule of Denonville.[1]

[1] *Mémoire du Roy pour Frontenac et Champigny, 26 Mai, 1696*; *Ibid., 27 Avril, 1697*; *Registres du Conseil Supérieur, Édit du 21 Mai, 1696*.

"Ce qui vous avez mandé de l'accommodement des Sauvages alliés avec les

The intentions of the king did not take effect. The policy of Frontenac was the true one, whatever motives may have entered into his advocacy of it. In view of the geographical, social, political, and commercial conditions of Canada, the policy of his opponents was impracticable, and nothing less than a perpetual cordon of troops could have prevented the Canadians from escaping to the backwoods. In spite of all the evils that attended the forest posts, it would have been a blunder to abandon them. This quickly became apparent. Champigny himself saw the necessity of compromise. The instructions of the king were scarcely given before they were partially withdrawn, and they soon became a dead letter. Even Fort Frontenac was retained after repeated directions to abandon it. The policy of the governor prevailed; the colony returned to its normal methods of growth, and so continued to the end.

Now came the question of peace with the Iroquois, to whose mercy Frontenac was authorized to leave his western allies. He was the last man to accept such permission. Since the burning of Onondaga, the Iroquois negotiations with the western tribes had been broken off, and several fights had occurred, in which the confederates had suffered loss and been roused to vengeance. This was what Frontenac wanted, but at the same time it promised him fresh trouble; for, while he was determined to prevent the Iroquois from making peace with the allies without his authority, he was equally determined to compel them to do so with it. There must be peace, though not till he could control its conditions.

The Onondaga campaign, unsatisfactory as it was, had had its effect. Several Iroquois chiefs came to Quebec with overtures of peace. They brought no prisoners, but promised to bring them in the spring; and one of them remained as a hostage that the promise should be kept. It was nevertheless

---

Irocois n'a pas permis à Sa Majesté d'entrer dans la discution de la manière de faire l'abandonnement des postes des François dans la profondeur des terres, particulièrement à Missilimackinac. . . En tout cas vous ne devez pas manquer de donner ordre pour ruiner les forts et tous les édifices qui pourront y avoir esté faits." *Le Ministre à Frontenac, 26 Mai, 1696.*

Besides the above, many other letters and despatches on both sides have been examined in relation to these questions.

broken under English influence; and, instead of a solemn embassy, the council of Onondaga sent a messenger with a wampum belt to tell Frontenac that they were all so engrossed in bewailing the recent death of Black Kettle, a famous war chief, that they had no strength to travel; and they begged that Onontio would return the hostage, and send to them for the French prisoners. The messenger farther declared that, though they would make peace with Onontio, they would not make it with his allies. Frontenac threw back the peacebelt into his face. "Tell the chiefs that, if they must needs stay at home to cry about a trifle, I will give them something to cry for. Let them bring me every prisoner, French and Indian, and make a treaty that shall include all my children, or they shall feel my tomahawk again." Then, turning to a number of Ottawas who were present: "You see that I can make peace for myself when I please. If I continue the war, it is only for your sake. I will never make a treaty without including you, and recovering your prisoners like my own."

Thus the matter stood, when a great event took place. Early in February, a party of Dutch and Indians came to Montreal with news that peace had been signed in Europe; and, at the end of May, Major Peter Schuyler, accompanied by Dellius, the minister of Albany, arrived with copies of the treaty in French and Latin. The scratch of a pen at Ryswick had ended the conflict in America, so far at least as concerned the civilized combatants. It was not till July that Frontenac received the official announcement from Versailles, coupled with an address from the king to the people of Canada.

OUR FAITHFUL AND BELOVED, — The moment has arrived ordained by Heaven to reconcile the nations. The ratification of the treaty concluded some time ago by our ambassadors with those of the Emperor and the Empire, after having made peace with Spain, England, and Holland, has everywhere restored the tranquillity so much desired. Strasbourg, one of the chief ramparts of the empire of heresy, united for ever to the Church and to our Crown; the Rhine established as the barrier between France and Germany; and, what touches us even more, the worship of the True Faith authorized by a solemn engagement with sovereigns of another religion, are the advantages secured by this last treaty. The Author of so many blessings manifests Himself so clearly that we cannot but recognize His goodness; and the visible impress of His all-powerful hand is as it were the seal He has affixed to justify our intent to cause all our realm to serve and obey Him, and to make our people happy. We have begun by the fulfilment of our duty in offering Him the thanks which are His due; and we have ordered the archbishops and bishops of our kingdom to cause *Te Deum* to be sung in the cathedrals of their dioceses. It is our will and our command that you be present at that which will be sung in the cathedral of our city of Quebec, on the day appointed by the Count of Frontenac, our governor and lieutenant-general in New France. Herein fail not, for such is our pleasure.

Louis.[1]

There was peace between the two crowns; but a serious question still remained between Frontenac and the new governor of New York, the Earl of Bellomont. When Schuyler and Dellius came to Quebec, they brought with them all the French prisoners in the hands of the English of New York, together with a promise from Bellomont that he would order the Iroquois, subjects of the British crown, to deliver to him all those in their possession, and that he would then send them to Canada under a safe escort. The two envoys demanded of Frontenac, at the same time, that he should deliver to them all the Iroquois in his hands. To give up Iroquois prisoners to Bellomont, or to receive through him French prisoners whom the Iroquois had captured, would have been an acknowledgment of British sovereignty over the five confederate tribes. Frontenac replied that the earl need give himself no trouble in the matter, as the Iroquois were rebellious subjects of King Louis; that they had already repented and begged peace; and that, if they did not soon come to conclude it, he should use force to compel them.

Bellomont wrote, in return, that he had sent arms to the Iroquois, with orders to defend themselves if attacked by the French, and to give no quarter to them or their allies; and he

[1] *Lettre du Roy pour faire chanter le Te Deum, 12 Mars, 1698.*

added that, if necessary, he would send soldiers to their aid. A few days after, he received fresh news of Frontenac's warlike intentions, and wrote in wrath as follows:—

SIR.—Two of our Indians, of the Nation called Onondages, came yesterday to advise me that you had sent two renegades of their Nation to them, to tell them and the other tribes, except the Mohawks, that, in case they did not come to Canada within forty days to solicit peace from you, they may expect your marching into their country at the head of an army to constrain them thereunto by force. I, on my side, do this very day send my lieutenant-governor with the king's troops to join the Indians, and to oppose any hostilities you will attempt; and, if needs be, I will arm every man in the Provinces under my government to repel you, and to make reprisals for the damage which you will commit on our Indians. This, in a few words, is the part I will take, and the resolution I have adopted, whereof I have thought it proper by these presents to give you notice.

I am, Sir, yours, &c.,

EARL OF BELLOMONT.

NEW YORK, 22d August, 1698.

To arm every man in his government would have been difficult. He did, however, what he could, and ordered Captain Nanfan, the lieutenant-governor, to repair to Albany; whence, on the first news that the French were approaching, he was to march to the relief of the Iroquois with the four shattered companies of regulars and as many of the militia of Albany and Ulster as he could muster. Then the earl sent Wessels, mayor of Albany, to persuade the Iroquois to deliver their prisoners to him, and make no treaty with Frontenac. On the same day, he despatched Captain John Schuyler to carry his letters to the French governor. When Schuyler reached Quebec, and delivered the letters, Frontenac read them with marks of great displeasure. "My Lord Bellomont threatens me," he said. "Does he think that I am afraid of him? He claims the Iroquois, but they are none of his. They call me father, and they call him brother; and shall not a father chastise his children when he sees fit?" A conversation followed, in which Frontenac asked the envoy what was the strength of Bellomont's government. Schuyler parried the question by a grotesque exaggeration, and answered that the earl could bring about a hundred thousand men into the field. Frontenac pretended to believe him, and returned with careless gravity that he had always heard so.

The following Sunday was the day appointed for the *Te Deum* ordered by the king; and all the dignitaries of the colony, with a crowd of lesser note, filled the cathedral. There was a dinner of ceremony at the château, to which Schuyler was invited; and he found the table of the governor thronged with officers. Frontenac called on his guests to drink the health of King William. Schuyler replied by a toast in honor of King Louis; and the governor next gave the health of the Earl of Bellomont. The peace was then solemnly proclaimed, amid the firing of cannon from the batteries and ships; and the day closed with a bonfire and a general illumination. On the next evening, Frontenac gave Schuyler a letter in answer to the threats of the earl. He had written with trembling hand, but unshaken will and unbending pride:—

"I am determined to pursue my course without flinching; and I request you not to try to thwart me by efforts which will prove useless. All the protection and aid you tell me that you have given, and will continue to give, the Iroquois, against the terms of the treaty, will not cause me much alarm, nor make me change my plans, but rather, on the contrary, engage me to pursue them still more."[1]

As the old soldier traced these lines, the shadow of death was upon him. Toils and years, passions and cares, had

[1] On the questions between Bellomont and Frontenac, *Relation de ce qui s'est passé, etc., 1697, 1698*; *Champigny au Ministre, 12 Juillet, 1698*; *Frontenac au Ministre, 18 Oct., 1698*; *Frontenac et Champigny au Ministre (lettre commune), 15 Oct., 1698*; *Callières au Ministre, même date, etc.* The correspondence of Frontenac and Bellomont, the report of Peter Schuyler and Dellius, the journal of John Schuyler, and other papers on the same subjects, will be found in *N. Y. Col. Docs.*, IV. John Schuyler was grandfather of General Schuyler of the American Revolution. Peter Schuyler and his colleague Dellius brought to Canada all the French prisoners in the hands of the English of New York, and asked for English prisoners in return; but nearly all of these preferred to remain, a remarkable proof of the kindness with which the Canadians treated their civilized captives.

wasted his strength at last, and his fiery soul could bear him up no longer. A few weeks later he was lying calmly on his death-bed.

Chapter XX

DEATH OF FRONTENAC

*His Last Hours • His Will • His Funeral • His Eulogist and his
Critic • His Disputes with the Clergy • His Character*

IN NOVEMBER, when the last ship had gone, and Canada
was sealed from the world for half a year, a mortal illness
fell upon the governor. On the twenty-second, he had
strength enough to dictate his will, seated in an easy-chair in
his chamber at the château. His colleague and adversary,
Champigny, often came to visit him, and did all in his power
to soothe his last moments. The reconciliation between them
was complete. One of his Récollet friends, Father Olivier
Goyer, administered extreme unction; and, on the afternoon
of the twenty-eighth, he died, in perfect composure and full
possession of his faculties. He was in his seventy-eighth year.

He was greatly beloved by the humbler classes, who, days
before his death, beset the château, praising and lamenting
him. Many of higher station shared the popular grief. "He
was the love and delight of New France," says one of them:
"churchmen honored him for his piety, nobles esteemed him
for his valor, merchants respected him for his equity, and the
people loved him for his kindness."[1] "He was the father of
the poor," says another, "the protector of the oppressed, and
a perfect model of virtue and piety."[2] An Ursuline nun regrets
him as the friend and patron of her sisterhood, and so also
does the superior of the Hôtel-Dieu.[3] His most conspicuous
though not his bitterest opponent, the intendant Champigny,
thus announced his death to the court: "I venture to send this
letter by way of New England to tell you that Monsieur le
Comte de Frontenac died on the twenty-eighth of last month,
with the sentiments of a true Christian. After all the disputes
we have had together, you will hardly believe, Monseigneur,

[1] La Potherie, I. 244, 246.
[2] Hennepin, 41 (1704). Le Clerc speaks to the same effect.
[3] *Histoire des Ursulines de Québec*, I. 508; Juchereau, 378.

how truly and deeply I am touched by his death. He treated me during his illness in a manner so obliging, that I should be utterly void of gratitude if I did not feel thankful to him."[1]

As a mark of kind feeling, Frontenac had bequeathed to the intendant a valuable crucifix, and to Madame de Champigny a reliquary which he had long been accustomed to wear. For the rest, he gave fifteen hundred livres to the Récollets, to be expended in masses for his soul, and that of his wife after her death. To her he bequeathed all the remainder of his small property, and he also directed that his heart should be sent her in a case of lead or silver.[2] His enemies reported that she refused to accept it, saying that she had never had it when he was living, and did not want it when he was dead.

On the Friday after his death, he was buried as he had directed, not in the cathedral, but in the church of the Récollets, a preference deeply offensive to many of the clergy. The bishop officiated; and then the Récollet, Father Goyer, who had attended his death-bed, and seems to have been his confessor, mounted the pulpit, and delivered his funeral oration. "This funeral pageantry," exclaimed the orator, "this temple draped in mourning, these dim lights, this sad and solemn music, this great assembly bowed in sorrow, and all this pomp and circumstance of death, may well penetrate your hearts. I will not seek to dry your tears, for I cannot contain my own. After all, this is a time to weep, and never did people weep for a better governor."

A copy of this eulogy fell into the hands of an enemy of Frontenac, who wrote a running commentary upon it. The copy thus annotated is still preserved at Quebec. A few passages from the orator and his critic will show the violent conflict of opinion concerning the governor, and illustrate in some sort, though with more force than fairness, the contradictions of his character: —

THE ORATOR. "This wise man, to whom the Senate of Venice listened with respectful attention, because he spoke

[1] *Champigny au Ministre, 22 Dec., 1698.*

[2] *Testament du Comte de Frontenac.* I am indebted to Abbé Bois of Maskinongé for a copy of this will. Frontenac expresses a wish that the heart should be placed in the family tomb at the Church of St. Nicolas des Champs.

before them with all the force of that eloquence which you, Messieurs, have so often admired,—[1]

THE CRITIC. *"It was not his eloquence that they admired, but his extravagant pretensions, his bursts of rage, and his unworthy treatment of those who did not agree with him."*

THE ORATOR. "This disinterested man, more busied with duty than with gain,—

THE CRITIC. *"The less said about that the better."*

THE ORATOR. "Who made the fortune of others, but did not increase his own,—

THE CRITIC. *"Not for want of trying, and that very often in spite of his conscience and the king's orders."*

THE ORATOR. "Devoted to the service of his king, whose majesty he represented, and whose person he loved,—

THE CRITIC. *"Not at all. How often has he opposed his orders, even with force and violence, to the great scandal of everybody!"*

THE ORATOR. "Great in the midst of difficulties, by that consummate prudence, that solid judgment, that presence of mind, that breadth and elevation of thought, which he retained to the last moment of his life,—

THE CRITIC. *"He had in fact a great capacity for political manœuvres and tricks; but as for the solid judgment ascribed to him, his conduct gives it the lie, or else, if he had it, the vehemence of his passions often unsettled it. It is much to be feared that his presence of mind was the effect of an obstinate and hardened self-confidence by which he put himself above everybody and every thing, since he never used it to repair, so far as in him lay, the public and private wrongs he caused. What ought he not to have done here, in this temple, to ask pardon for the obstinate and furious heat with which he so long persecuted the Church; upheld and even instigated rebellion against her; protected libertines, scandal-mongers, and creatures of evil life against the ministers of Heaven; molested, persecuted, vexed persons most eminent in vir-*

---

[1] Alluding to an incident that occurred when Frontenac commanded a Venetian force for the defence of Candia against the Turks.

tue, nay, even the priests and magistrates, who defended the cause of God; sustained in all sorts of ways the wrongful and scandalous traffic in brandy with the Indians; permitted, approved, and supported the license and abuse of taverns; authorized and even introduced, in spite of the remonstrances of the servants of God, criminal and dangerous diversions; tried to decry the bishop and the clergy, the missionaries, and other persons of virtue, and to injure them, both here and in France, by libels and calumnies; caused, in fine, either by himself or through others, a multitude of disorders, under which this infant church has groaned for many years! What, I say, ought he not to have done before dying to atone for these scandals, and give proof of sincere penitence and compunction? God gave him full time to recognize his errors, and yet to the last he showed a great indifference in all these matters. When, in presence of the Holy Sacrament, he was asked according to the ritual, 'Do you not beg pardon for all the ill examples you may have given?' he answered, 'Yes,' but did not confess that he had ever given any. In a word, he behaved during the few days before his death like one who had led an irreproachable life, and had nothing to fear. And this is the presence of mind that he retained to his last moment!"

THE ORATOR. "Great in dangers by his courage, he always came off with honor, and never was reproached with rashness,—

THE CRITIC. *"True; he was not rash, as was seen when the Bostonnais besieged Quebec."*

THE ORATOR. "Great in religion by his piety, he practised its good works in spirit and in truth,—

THE CRITIC. *"Say rather that he practised its forms with parade and ostentation: witness the inordinate ambition with which he always claimed honors in the Church, to which he had no right; outrageously affronted intendants, who opposed his pretensions; required priests to address him when preaching, and in their intercourse with him demanded from them humiliations which he did not exact from the meanest military officer. This was his way of making himself great in* religion and piety, *or, more truly, in vanity and hypocrisy. How can a man be called* great in religion, *when he openly holds opinions entirely opposed to the True Faith,* such as, that all men are predestined, *that* Hell will not last for ever, *and the like?*"

THE ORATOR. "His very look inspired esteem and confidence,—

THE CRITIC. *"Then one must have taken him at exactly the right moment, and not when he was foaming at the mouth with rage."*

THE ORATOR. "A mingled air of nobility and gentleness; a countenance that bespoke the probity that appeared in all his acts, and a sincerity that could not dissimulate,—

THE CRITIC. *"The eulogist did not know the old fox."*

THE ORATOR. "An inviolable fidelity to friends,—

THE CRITIC. *"What friends? Was it persons of the other sex? Of these he was always fond, and too much for the honor of some of them."*

THE ORATOR. "Disinterested for himself, ardent for others, he used his credit at court only to recommend their services, excuse their faults, and obtain favors for them,—

THE CRITIC. *"True; but it was for his creatures and for nobody else."*

THE ORATOR. "I pass in silence that reading of spiritual books which he practised as an indispensable duty more than forty years; that holy avidity with which he listened to the word of God,—

THE CRITIC. *"Only if the preacher addressed the sermon to him, and called him* Monseigneur. *As for his reading, it was often Jansenist books, of which he had a great many, and which he greatly praised and lent freely to others."*

THE ORATOR. "He prepared for the sacraments by meditation and retreat,—

THE CRITIC. *"And generally came out of his retreat more excited than ever against the Church."*

THE ORATOR. "Let us not recall his ancient and noble descent, his family connected with all that is greatest in the army, the magistracy, and the government; Knights, Marshals of France, Governors of Provinces, Judges, Councillors, and Ministers of State: let us not, I say, recall all these without remembering that their examples roused this generous heart to noble emulation; and, as an expiring flame grows brighter as it dies, so did all the virtues of his race unite at last in him to end with glory a long line of great men, that shall be no more except in history."

THE CRITIC. *"Well laid on, and too well for his hearers to believe him. Far from agreeing that all these virtues were collected in the person of his pretended* hero, *they would find it very hard to admit that he had even one of them."*[1]

It is clear enough from what quiver these arrows came. From the first, Frontenac had set himself in opposition to the most influential of the Canadian clergy. When he came to the colony, their power in the government was still enormous, and even the most devout of his predecessors had been forced into conflict with them to defend the civil authority; but, when Frontenac entered the strife, he brought into it an irritability, a jealous and exacting vanity, a love of rule, and a passion for having his own way, even in trifles, which made him the most exasperating of adversaries. Hence it was that many of the clerical party felt towards him a bitterness that was far from ending with his life.

The sentiment of a religion often survives its convictions. However heterodox in doctrine, he was still wedded to the observances of the Church, and practised them, under the ministration of the Récollets, with an assiduity that made full amends to his conscience for the vivacity with which he opposed the rest of the clergy. To the Récollets their patron was the most devout of men; to his ultramontane adversaries, he was an impious persecutor.

---

[1] *Oraison Funèbre du très-haut et très-puissant Seigneur Louis de Buade, Comte de Frontenac et de Palluau, etc., avec des remarques critiques, 1698.* That indefatigable investigator of Canadian history, the late M. Jacques Viger, to whom I am indebted for a copy of this eulogy, suggested that the anonymous critic may have been Abbé la Tour, author of the *Vie de Laval*. If so, his statements need the support of more trustworthy evidence. The above extracts are not consecutive, but are taken from various parts of the manuscript.

His own acts and words best paint his character, and it is needless to enlarge upon it. What perhaps may be least forgiven him is the barbarity of the warfare that he waged, and the cruelties that he permitted. He had seen too many towns sacked to be much subject to the scruples of modern humanitarianism; yet he was no whit more ruthless than his times and his surroundings, and some of his contemporaries find fault with him for not allowing more Indian captives to be tortured. Many surpassed him in cruelty, none equalled him in capacity and vigor. When civilized enemies were once within his power, he treated them, according to their degree, with a chivalrous courtesy, or a generous kindness. If he was a hot and pertinacious foe, he was also a fast friend; and he excited love and hatred in about equal measure. His attitude towards public enemies was always proud and peremptory, yet his courage was guided by so clear a sagacity that he never was forced to recede from the position he had taken. Towards Indians, he was an admirable compound of sternness and conciliation. Of the immensity of his services to the colony there can be no doubt. He found it, under Denonville, in humiliation and terror; and he left it in honor, and almost in triumph.

In spite of Father Goyer, greatness must be denied him; but a more remarkable figure, in its bold and salient individuality and sharply marked light and shadow, is nowhere seen in American history.[1]

[1] There is no need to exaggerate the services of Frontenac. Nothing could be more fallacious than the assertion, often repeated, that in his time Canada withstood the united force of all the British colonies. Most of these colonies took no part whatever in the war. Only two of them took an aggressive part, New York and Massachusetts. New York attacked Canada twice, with the two inconsiderable war-parties of John Schuyler in 1690 and of Peter Schuyler in the next year. The feeble expedition under Winthrop did not get beyond Lake George. Massachusetts, or rather her seaboard towns, attacked Canada once. Quebec, it is true, was kept in alarm during several years by rumors of another attack from the same quarter; but no such danger existed, as Massachusetts was exhausted by her first effort. The real scourge of Canada was the Iroquois, supplied with arms and ammunition from Albany.

Chapter XXI

CONCLUSION

The New Governor • Attitude of the Iroquois • Negotiations • Embassy to Onondaga • Peace • The Iroquois and the Allies • Difficulties • Death of the Great Huron • Funeral Rites • The Grand Council • The Work of Frontenac finished • Results

---

IT DID NOT need the presence of Frontenac to cause snappings and sparks in the highly electrical atmosphere of New France. Callières took his place as governor *ad interim*, and in due time received a formal appointment to the office. Apart from the wretched state of his health, undermined by gout and dropsy, he was in most respects well fitted for it; but his deportment at once gave umbrage to the excitable Champigny, who declared that he had never seen such *hauteur* since he came to the colony. Another official was still more offended. "Monsieur de Frontenac," he says, "was no sooner dead than trouble began. Monsieur de Callières, puffed up by his new authority, claims honors due only to a marshal of France. It would be a different matter if he, like his predecessor, were regarded as the father of the country, and the love and delight of the Indian allies. At the review at Montreal, he sat in his carriage, and received the incense offered him with as much composure and coolness as if he had been some divinity of this New World." In spite of these complaints, the court sustained Callières, and authorized him to enjoy the honors that he had assumed.[1]

His first and chief task was to finish the work that Frontenac had shaped out, and bring the Iroquois to such submission as the interests of the colony and its allies demanded. The fierce confederates admired the late governor, and, if they themselves are to be believed, could not help lamenting him; but they were emboldened by his death, and the difficulty of dealing with them was increased by it. Had they been sure of

[1] *Champigny au Ministre, 26 Mai, 1699; La Potherie au Ministre, 2 Juin, 1699; Vaudreuil et La Potherie au Ministre, même date.*

effectual support from the English, there can be little doubt that they would have refused to treat with the French, of whom their distrust was extreme. The treachery of Denonville at Fort Frontenac still rankled in their hearts, and the English had made them believe that some of their best men had lately been poisoned by agents from Montreal. The French assured them, on the other hand, that the English meant to poison them, refuse to sell them powder and lead, and then, when they were helpless, fall upon and destroy them. At Montreal, they were told that the English called them their negroes; and, at Albany, that if they made peace with Onontio, they would sink into "perpetual infamy and slavery." Still, in spite of their perplexity, they persisted in asserting their independence of each of the rival powers, and played the one against the other, in order to strengthen their position with both. When Bellomont required them to surrender their French prisoners to him, they answered: "We are the masters; our prisoners are our own. We will keep them or give them to the French, if we choose." At the same time, they told Callières that they would bring them to the English at Albany, and invited him to send thither his agents to receive them. They were much disconcerted, however, when letters were read to them which showed that, pending the action of commissioners to settle the dispute, the two kings had ordered their respective governors to refrain from all acts of hostility, and join forces, if necessary, to compel the Iroquois to keep quiet.[1] This, with their enormous losses, and their desire to recover their people held captive in Canada, led them at last to serious thoughts of peace. Resolving at the same time to try the temper of the new Onontio, and yield no more than was absolutely necessary, they sent him but six ambassadors, and no prisoners. The ambassadors marched in single file to the place of council; while their chief, who led the way, sang a dismal song of lamentation for the French slain in the war, calling on them to thrust their heads above ground, behold the good work of peace, and banish every thought of vengeance. Callières proved, as they had hoped, less inexorable

[1] *Le Roy à Frontenac, 25 Mars, 1699.* Frontenac's death was not known at Versailles till April. *Le Roy d'Angleterre à Bellomont, 2 Avril, 1699*; La Potherie, IV. 128; *Callières à Bellomont, 7 Août, 1699.*

than Frontenac. He accepted their promises, and consented to send for the prisoners in their hands, on condition that within thirty-six days a full deputation of their principal men should come to Montreal. The Jesuit Bruyas, the Canadian Maricourt, and a French officer named Joncaire went back with them to receive the prisoners.

The history of Joncaire was a noteworthy one. The Senecas had captured him some time before, tortured his companions to death, and doomed him to the same fate. As a preliminary torment, an old chief tried to burn a finger of the captive in the bowl of his pipe, on which Joncaire knocked him down. If he had begged for mercy, their hearts would have been flint; but the warrior crowd were so pleased with this proof of courage that they adopted him as one of their tribe, and gave him an Iroquois wife. He lived among them for many years, and gained a commanding influence, which proved very useful to the French. When he, with Bruyas and Maricourt, approached Onondaga, which had long before risen from its ashes, they were greeted with a fusillade of joy, and regaled with the sweet stalks of young maize, followed by the more substantial refreshment of venison and corn beaten together into a pulp and boiled. The chiefs and elders seemed well inclined to peace; and, though an envoy came from Albany to prevent it, he behaved with such arrogance that, far from dissuading his auditors, he confirmed them in their resolve to meet Onontio at Montreal. They seemed willing enough to give up their French prisoners, but an unexpected difficulty arose from the prisoners themselves. They had been adopted into Iroquois families; and, having become attached to the Indian life, they would not leave it. Some of them hid in the woods to escape their deliverers, who, with their best efforts, could collect but thirteen, all women, children, and boys. With these, they returned to Montreal, accompanied by a peace embassy of nineteen Iroquois.

Peace, then, was made. "I bury the hatchet," said Callières, "in a deep hole, and over the hole I place a great rock, and over the rock I turn a river, that the hatchet may never be dug up again." The famous Huron, Kondiaronk, or the Rat, was present, as were also a few Ottawas, Abenakis, and converts of the Saut and the Mountain. Sharp words passed between them and the ambassadors; but at last they all laid down their hatchets at the feet of Onontio, and signed the treaty together. It was but a truce, and a doubtful one. More was needed to confirm it, and the following August was named for a solemn act of ratification.[1]

Father Engelran was sent to Michillimackinac, while Courtemanche spent the winter and spring in toilsome journeyings among the tribes of the west. Such was his influence over them that he persuaded them all to give up their Iroquois prisoners, and send deputies to the grand council. Engelran had had scarcely less success among the northern tribes; and early in July a great fleet of canoes, conducted by Courtemanche, and filled with chiefs, warriors, and Iroquois prisoners, paddled down the lakes for Montreal. Meanwhile Bruyas, Maricourt, and Joncaire had returned on the same errand to the Iroquois towns; but, so far as concerned prisoners, their success was no greater than before. Whether French or Indian, the chiefs were slow to give them up, saying that they had all been adopted into families who would not part with them unless consoled for the loss by gifts. This was true; but it was equally true of the other tribes, whose chiefs had made the necessary gifts, and recovered the captive Iroquois. Joncaire and his colleagues succeeded, however, in leading a large deputation of chiefs and elders to Montreal.

Courtemanche with his canoe fleet from the lakes was not far behind; and when their approach was announced, the chronicler, La Potherie, full of curiosity, went to meet them at the mission village of the Saut. First appeared the Iroquois, two hundred in all, firing their guns as their canoes drew near, while the mission Indians, ranged along the shore, returned the salute. The ambassadors were conducted to a capacious lodge, where for a quarter of an hour they sat smoking with immovable composure. Then a chief of the mission made a speech, and then followed a feast of boiled dogs. In the morning they descended the rapids to Montreal, and

[1]On these negotiations, La Potherie, IV. lettre xi.; *N. Y. Col. Docs.*, IX. 708, 711, 715; Colden, 200; *Callières au Ministre, 16 Oct., 1700*; *Champigny au Ministre, 22 Juillet, 1700*; *La Potherie au Ministre, 11 Août, 1700*; *Ibid., 16 Oct., 1700*; *Callières et Champigny au Ministre, 18 Oct., 1700*. See also *N. Y. Col. Docs.*, IV., for a great number of English documents bearing on the subject.

in due time the distant roar of the saluting cannon told of their arrival.

They had scarcely left the village, when the river was covered with the canoes of the western and northern allies. There was another fusillade of welcome as the heterogeneous company landed, and marched to the great council-house. The calumet was produced, and twelve of the assembled chiefs sang a song, each rattling at the same time a dried gourd half full of peas. Six large kettles were next brought in, containing several dogs and a bear suitably chopped to pieces, which being ladled out to the guests were despatched in an instant, and a solemn dance and a supper of boiled corn closed the festivity.

The strangers embarked again on the next day, and the cannon of Montreal greeted them as they landed before the town. A great quantity of evergreen boughs had been gathered for their use, and of these they made their wigwams outside the palisades. Before the opening of the grand council, a multitude of questions must be settled, jealousies soothed, and complaints answered. Callières had no peace. He was busied for a week in giving audience to the deputies. There was one question which agitated them all, and threatened to rekindle the war. Kondiaronk, the Rat, the foremost man among all the allied tribes, gave utterance to the general feeling: "My father, you told us last autumn to bring you all the Iroquois prisoners in our hands. We have obeyed, and brought them. Now let us see if the Iroquois have also obeyed, and brought you our people whom they captured during the war. If they have done so, they are sincere; if not, they are false. But I know that they have not brought them. I told you last year that it was better that they should bring their prisoners first. You see now how it is, and how they have deceived us."

The complaint was just, and the situation became critical. The Iroquois deputies were invited to explain themselves. They stalked into the council-room with their usual haughty composure, and readily promised to surrender the prisoners in future, but offered no hostages for their good faith. The Rat, who had counselled his own and other tribes to bring their Iroquois captives to Montreal, was excessively mortified at finding himself duped. He came to a later meeting, when this and other matters were to be discussed; but he was so weakened by fever that he could not stand. An arm-chair was brought him; and, seated in it, he harangued the assembly for two hours, amid a deep silence, broken only by ejaculations of approval from his Indian hearers. When the meeting ended, he was completely exhausted; and, being carried in his chair to the hospital, he died about midnight. He was a great loss to the French; for, though he had caused the massacre of La Chine, his services of late years had been invaluable. In spite of his unlucky name, he was one of the ablest North American Indians on record, as appears by his remarkable influence over many tribes, and by the respect, not to say admiration, of his French contemporaries.

The French charged themselves with the funeral rites, carried the dead chief to his wigwam, stretched him on a robe of beaver skin, and left him there lying in state, swathed in a scarlet blanket, with a kettle, a gun, and a sword at his side, for his use in the world of spirits. This was a concession to the superstition of his countrymen; for the Rat was a convert, and went regularly to mass.[1] Even the Iroquois, his deadliest foes, paid tribute to his memory. Sixty of them came in solemn procession, and ranged themselves around the bier; while one of their principal chiefs pronounced an harangue, in which he declared that the sun had covered his face that day in grief for the loss of the great Huron.[2] He was buried on the next morning. Saint-Ours, senior captain, led the funeral train with an escort of troops, followed by sixteen Huron warriors in robes of beaver skin, marching four and four, with faces painted black and guns reversed. Then came the clergy, and then six war-chiefs carrying the coffin. It was decorated with flowers, and on it lay a plumed hat, a sword, and a gorget. Behind it were the brother and sons of the dead

[1] La Potherie, IV. 229. Charlevoix suppresses the kettle and gun, and says that the dead chief wore a sword and a uniform, like a French officer. In fact, he wore Indian leggins and a capote under his scarlet blanket.

[2] Charlevoix says that these were Christian Iroquois of the missions. Potherie, his only authority, proves them to have been heathen, as their chief mourner was a noted Seneca, and their spokesman, Avenano, was the accredited orator of the Oneidas, Onondagas, Cayugas, and Senecas, in whose name he made the funeral harangue.

chief, and files of Huron and Ottawa warriors; while Madame de Champigny, attended by Vaudreuil and all the military officers, closed the procession. After the service, the soldiers fired three volleys over the grave; and a tablet was placed upon it, carved with the words,—

CY GIT LE RAT, CHEF DES HURONS.

All this ceremony pleased the allied tribes, and helped to calm their irritation. Every obstacle being at length removed or smoothed over, the fourth of August was named for the grand council. A vast, oblong space was marked out on a plain near the town, and enclosed with a fence of branches. At one end was a canopy of boughs and leaves, under which were seats for the spectators. Troops were drawn up in line along the sides; the seats under the canopy were filled by ladies, officials, and the chief inhabitants of Montreal; Callières sat in front, surrounded by interpreters; and the Indians were seated on the grass around the open space. There were more than thirteen hundred of them, gathered from a distance of full two thousand miles, Hurons and Ottawas from Michillimackinac, Ojibwas from Lake Superior, Crees from the remote north, Pottawatamies from Lake Michigan, Mascoutins, Sacs, Foxes, Winnebagoes, and Menominies from Wisconsin, Miamis from the St. Joseph, Illinois from the river Illinois, Abenakis from Acadia, and many allied hordes of less account; each savage painted with diverse hues and patterns, and each in his dress of ceremony, leathern shirts fringed with scalp-locks, colored blankets or robes of bison hide and beaver skin, bristling crests of hair or long lank tresses, eagle feathers or horns of beasts. Pre-eminent among them all sat their valiant and terrible foes, the warriors of the confederacy. "Strange," exclaims La Potherie, "that four or five thousand should make a whole new world tremble. New England is but too happy to gain their good graces; New France is often wasted by their wars, and our allies dread them over an extent of more than fifteen hundred leagues." It was more a marvel than he knew, for he greatly overrates their number.

Callières opened the council with a speech, in which he told the assembly that, since but few tribes were represented at the treaty of the year before, he had sent for them all to ratify it; that he now threw their hatchets and his own into a pit so deep that nobody could find them; that henceforth they must live like brethren; and, if by chance one should strike another, the injured brother must not revenge the blow, but come for redress to him, Onontio, their common father. Nicolas Perrot and the Jesuits who acted as interpreters repeated the speech in five different languages; and, to confirm it, thirty-one wampum belts were given to the thirty-one tribes present. Then each tribe answered in turn. First came Hassaki, chief of an Ottawa band known as Cut Tails. He approached with a majestic air, his long robe of beaver skin trailing on the grass behind him. Four Iroquois captives followed, with eyes bent on the ground; and, when he stopped before the governor, they seated themselves at his feet. "You asked us for our prisoners," he said, "and here they are. I set them free because you wish it, and I regard them as my brothers." Then turning to the Iroquois deputies: "Know that if I pleased I might have eaten them; but I have not done as you would have done. Remember this when we meet, and let us be friends." The Iroquois ejaculated their approval.

Next came a Huron chief, followed by eight Iroquois prisoners, who, as he declared, had been bought at great cost, in kettles, guns, and blankets, from the families who had adopted them. "We thought that the Iroquois would have done by us as we have done by them; and we were astonished to see that they had not brought us our prisoners. Listen to me, my father, and you, Iroquois, listen. I am not sorry to make peace, since my father wishes it, and I will live in peace with him and with you." Thus, in turn, came the spokesmen of all the tribes, delivering their prisoners and making their speeches. The Miami orator said: "I am very angry with the Iroquois, who burned my son some years ago; but to-day I forget all that. My father's will is mine. I will not be like the Iroquois, who have disobeyed his voice." The orator of the Mississagas came forward, crowned with the head and horns of a young bison bull, and, presenting his prisoners, said: "I place them in your hands. Do with them as you like. I am only too proud that you count me among your allies."

The chief of the Foxes now rose from his seat at the farther end of the enclosure, and walked sedately across the whole open space towards the stand of spectators. His face was painted red, and he wore an old French wig, with its abundant curls in a state of complete entanglement. When he reached the chair of the governor, he bowed, and lifted the wig like a hat, to show that he was perfect in French politeness. There was a burst of laughter from the spectators; but Callières, with ceremonious gravity, begged him to put it on again, which he did, and proceeded with his speech, the pith of which was briefly as follows: "The darkness is gone, the sun shines bright again, and now the Iroquois is my brother."

Then came a young Algonquin war-chief, dressed like a Canadian, but adorned with a drooping red feather and a tall ridge of hair like the crest of a cock. It was he who slew Black Kettle, that redoubted Iroquois whose loss filled the confederacy with mourning, and who exclaimed as he fell, "Must I, who have made the whole earth tremble, now die by the hand of a child!" The young chief spoke concisely and to the purpose: "I am not a man of counsel: it is for me to listen to your words. Peace has come, and now let us forget the past."

When he and all the rest had ended, the orator of the Iroquois strode to the front, and in brief words gave in their adhesion to the treaty. "Onontio, we are pleased with all you have done, and we have listened to all you have said. We assure you by these four belts of wampum that we will stand fast in our obedience. As for the prisoners whom we have not brought you, we place them at your disposal, and you will send and fetch them."

The calumet was lighted. Callières, Champigny, and Vaudreuil drew the first smoke, then the Iroquois deputies, and then all the tribes in turn. The treaty was duly signed, the representative of each tribe affixing his mark, in the shape of some bird, beast, fish, reptile, insect, plant, or nondescript object.

"Thus," says La Potherie, "the labors of the late Count Frontenac were brought to a happy consummation." The work of Frontenac was indeed finished, though not as he would have finished it. Callières had told the Iroquois that till they surrendered their Indian prisoners he would keep in his own hands the Iroquois prisoners surrendered by the allied tribes. To this the spokesman of the confederacy coolly replied: "Such a proposal was never made since the world began. Keep them, if you like. We will go home, and think no more about them; but, if you gave them to us without making trouble, and gave us our son Joncaire at the same time, we should have no reason to distrust your sincerity, and should all be glad to send you back the prisoners we took from your allies." Callières yielded, persuaded the allies to agree to the conditions, gave up the prisoners, and took an empty promise in return. It was a triumph for the Iroquois, who meant to keep their Indian captives, and did in fact keep nearly all of them.[1]

The chief objects of the late governor were gained. The power of the Iroquois was so far broken that they were never again very formidable to the French. Canada had confirmed her Indian alliances, and rebutted the English claim to sovereignty over the five tribes, with all the consequences that hung upon it. By the treaty of Ryswick, the great questions at issue in America were left to the arbitrament of future wars; and meanwhile, as time went on, the policy of Frontenac developed and ripened. Detroit was occupied by the French, the passes of the west were guarded by forts, another New France grew up at the mouth of the Mississippi, and lines of military communication joined the Gulf of Mexico with the Gulf of St. Lawrence; while the colonies of England lay passive between the Alleghanies and the sea till roused by the trumpet that sounded with wavering notes on many a bloody field to peal at last in triumph from the Heights of Abraham.

[1] The council at Montreal is described at great length by La Potherie, a spectator. There is a short official report of the various speeches, of which a translation will be found in N. Y. Col. Docs., IX. 722. Callières himself gives interesting details. (Callières au Ministre, 4 Oct., 1701.) A great number of papers on Indian affairs at this time will be found in N. Y. Col. Docs., IV.

Joncaire went for the prisoners whom the Iroquois had promised to give up, and could get but six of them. Callières au Ministre, 31 Oct., 1701. The rest were made Iroquois by adoption.

According to an English official estimate made at the end of the war, the Iroquois numbered 2,550 warriors in 1689, and only 1,230 in 1698. N. Y. Col. Docs., IV. 420. In 1701, a French writer estimates them at only 1,200 warriors. In other words, their strength was reduced at least one half. They afterwards partially recovered it by the adoption of prisoners, and still more by the adoption of an entire kindred tribe, the Tuscaroras. In 1720, the English reckon them at 2,000 warriors. N. Y. Col. Docs., V. 557.

APPENDIX

THE FAMILY OF FRONTENAC

COUNT FRONTENAC's grandfather was

ANTOINE DE BUADE, Seigneur de Frontenac, Baron de Palluau, Conseiller d'État, Chevalier des Ordres du Roy, son premier maitre d'hôtel, et gouverneur de St. Germain-en-Laye. By Jeanne Secontat, his wife, he had, among other children,

HENRI DE BUADE, Chevalier, Baron de Palluau et mestre de camp (*colonel*) du régiment de Navarre, who, by his wife Anne Phélippeaux, daughter of Raymond Phélippeaux, Secretary of State, had, among other children,

LOUIS DE BUADE, Comte de Palluau et Frontenac, Seigneur de l'Isle-Savary, mestre de camp du régiment de Normandie, maréchal de camp dans les armées du Roy, et gouverneur et lieutenant général en Canada, Acadie, Isle de Terreneuve, et autres pays de la France septentrionale. Louis de Buade had by his wife, Anne de La Grange-Trianon, one son, François Louis, killed in Germany, while in the service of the king, and leaving no issue.

The foregoing is drawn from a comparison of the following authorities, all of which will be found in the Bibliothèque Nationale of Paris, where the examination was made: *Mémoires de Marolles, abbé de Villeloin*, II. 201; L'Hermite-Souliers, *Histoire Généalogique de la Noblesse de Touraine*; Du Chesne, *Recherches Historiques de l' Ordre du Saint-Esprit*; Morin, *Statuts de l' Ordre du Saint-Esprit*; Marolles de Villeloin, *Histoire des Anciens Comtes d' Anjou*; Père Anselme, *Grands Officiers de la Couronne*; Pinard, *Chronologie Historique-militaire*; *Table de la Gazette de France*. In this matter of the Frontenac genealogy, I am much indebted to the kind offices of my friend, James Gordon Clarke, Esq.

When, in 1600, Henry IV. was betrothed to Marie de Medicis, Frontenac, grandfather of the governor of Canada, described as "ung des plus antiens serviteurs du roy," was sent to Florence by the king to carry his portrait to his affianced bride. *Mémoires de Philippe Hurault*, 448 (Petitot).

The appointment of Frontenac to the post, esteemed as highly honorable, of *maître d'hôtel* in the royal household, immediately followed. There is a very curious book, the journal of Jean Héroard, a physician charged with the care of the infant Dauphin, afterwards Louis XIII., born in 1601. It records every act of the future monarch: his screaming and kicking in the arms of his nurses, his refusals to be washed and dressed, his resistance when his hair was combed; how he scratched his governess, and called her names; how he quarrelled with the children of his father's mistresses, and at the age of four declined to accept them as brothers and sisters; how his mother slighted him; and how his father sometimes caressed, sometimes teased, and sometimes corrected him with his own hand. The details of the royal nursery are, we may add, astounding for their grossness; and the language and the manners amid which the infant monarch grew up were worthy of the days of Rabelais.

Frontenac and his children appear frequently, and not unfavorably, on the pages of this singular diary. Thus, when the Dauphin was three years old, the king, being in bed, took him and a young Frontenac of about the same age, set them before him, and amused himself by making them rally each other in their infantile language. The infant Frontenac had a trick of stuttering, which the Dauphin caught from him, and retained for a long time. Again, at the age of five, the Dauphin, armed with a little gun, played at soldier with two of the Frontenac children in the hall at St. Germain. They assaulted a town, the rampart being represented by a balustrade before the fireplace. "The Dauphin," writes the journalist, "said that he would be a musketeer, and yet he spoke sharply to the others who would not do as he wished. The king said to him, 'My boy, you are a musketeer, but you speak like a general.'" Long after, when the Dauphin was in his fourteenth year, the following entry occurs in the physician's diary:—

St. Germain, Sunday, 22d (*July, 1614*). "He (*the Dauphin*) goes to the chapel of the terrace, then mounts his horse and goes to find M. de Souvré and M. de Frontenac, whom he surprises as they were at breakfast at the small house near the quarries. At half past one, he mounts again, in hunting boots; goes to the park with M. de Frontenac as a guide, chases a stag, and catches him. It was his first stag-hunt."

Of Henri de Buade, father of the governor of Canada, but little is recorded. When in Paris, he lived, like his son after him, on the Quai des Célestins, in the parish of St. Paul. His son, Count Frontenac, was born in 1620, seven years after his father's marriage. Apparently his birth took place elsewhere than in Paris, for it is not recorded with those of Henri de Buade's other children, on the register of St. Paul (Jal, *Dictionnaire Critique, Biographique, et d'Histoire*). The story told by Tallemant des Réaux concerning his marriage (see page 16) seems to be mainly true. Colonel Jal says: "On conçoit que j'ai pu être tenté de connaître ce qu'il y a de vrai dans les récits de Saint-Simon et de Tallemant des Réaux; voici ce qu'après bien des recherches, j'ai pu apprendre. Mlle La Grange fit, en effet, un mariage à demi secret. Ce ne fut point à sa paroisse que fut bénie son union avec M. de Frontenac, mais dans une des petites églises de la Cité qui avaient le privilège de recevoir les amants qui s'unissaient malgré leurs parents, et ceux qui regularisaient leur position et s'épousaient un peu avant— quelquefois après—la naissance d'un enfant. Ce fut à St. Pierreaux-Bœufs que, le mercredy, 28 Octobre, 1648, 'Messire Louis de Buade, Chevalier, comte de Frontenac, conseiller du Roy en ses conseils, mareschal des camps et armées de S. M., et maistre de camp du régiment du Normandie,' épousa 'demoiselle Anne de La Grange, fille de Messire Charles de La Grange, conseiller du Roy et maistre des comptes' de la paroisse de St. Paul comme M. de Frontenac, 'en vertu de la dispense . . . obtenue de M. l'official de Paris par laquelle il est permis au Sr de Buade et demoiselle de La Grange de célébrer leur marriage suyvant et conformément à la permission qu'ils en ont obtenue du Sr Coquerel, vicaire de St. Paul, devant le premier curé ou vicaire sur ce requis, en gardant les solennités en ce cas requises et accoutumées.' " Jal then gives the signatures to the act of marriage, which, except that of the bride, are all of the Frontenac family.

A HALF-CENTURY OF CONFLICT

Contents

PREFACE   337

CHAPTER I   1700–1713
EVE OF WAR

*The Spanish Succession • Influence of Louis XIV. on History •
French Schemes of Conquest in America • New York • Unfit-
ness of the Colonies for War • The Five Nations • Doubt and
Vacillation • The Western Indians • Trade and Politics*   339

CHAPTER II   1694–1704
DETROIT

*Michillimackinac • La Mothe-Cadillac • His Disputes with
the Jesuits • Opposing Views • Plans of Cadillac • His Memorial to the Court • His Opponents • Detroit founded •
The New Company • Detroit changes Hands • Strange Act
of the Five Nations*   348

CHAPTER III   1703–1713
QUEEN ANNE'S WAR

*The Forest of Maine • A Treacherous Peace • A Frontier
Village • Wells and its People • Attack upon it • Border
Ravages • Beaubassin's War-Party • The "Woful Decade" •
A Wedding Feast • A Captive Bridegroom*   359

CHAPTER IV   1704–1740
DEERFIELD

*Hertel de Rouville • A Frontier Village • Rev. John Williams
• The Surprise • Defence of the Stebbins House • Attempted
Rescue • The Meadow Fight • The Captives • The Northward
March • Mrs. Williams killed • The Minister's Journey •
Kindness of Canadians • A Stubborn Heretic • Eunice
Williams • Converted Captives • John Sheldon's Mission •
Exchange of Prisoners • An English Squaw • The Gill Family*   373

CHAPTER V   1704–1713
THE TORMENTED FRONTIER

*Border Raids • Haverhill • Attack and Defence • War to
the Knife • Motives of the French • Proposed Neutrality •
Joseph Dudley • Town and Country*   399

CHAPTER VI 1700–1710
THE OLD RÉGIME IN ACADIA

*The Fishery Question • Privateers and Pirates • Port Royal •
Official Gossip • Abuse of Brouillan • Complaints of De Goutin • Subercase and his Officers • Church and State • Paternal Government* 410

CHAPTER VII 1704–1710
ACADIA CHANGES HANDS

*Reprisal for Deerfield • Major Benjamin Church • His
Ravages at Grand-Pré • Port Royal Expedition • Futile Pro-
ceedings • A Discreditable Affair • French Successes in New-
foundland • Schemes of Samuel Vetch • A Grand Enterprise
• Nicholson's Advance • An Infected Camp • Ministerial
Promises broken • A New Scheme • Port Royal attacked •
Acadia conquered* 417

CHAPTER VIII 1710, 1711
WALKER'S EXPEDITION

*Scheme of La Ronde Denys • Boston warned against British
Designs • Boston to be ruined • Plans of the Ministry •
Canada doomed • British Troops at Boston • The Colonists
denounced • The Fleet sails for Quebec • Forebodings of
the Admiral • Storm and Wreck • Timid Commanders •
Retreat • Joyful News for Canada • Pious Exultation
• Fanciful Stories • Walker disgraced* 440

CHAPTER IX 1712–1749
LOUISBOURG AND ACADIA

*Peace of Utrecht • Perilous Questions • Louisbourg founded •
Annapolis attacked • Position of the Acadians • Weakness of
the British Garrison • Apathy of the Ministry • French Intrigue • Clerical Politicans • The Oath of Allegiance •
Acadians refuse it • Their Expulsion proposed • They take
the Oath* 458

CHAPTER X 1713–1724
SEBASTIEN RALE

*Boundary Disputes • Outposts of Canada • The Earlier and
Later Jesuits • Religion and Politics • The Norridgewocks and
their Missionary • A Hollow Peace • Disputed Land Claims •*

Council at Georgetown • Attitude of Rale • Minister and
Jesuit • The Indians waver • An Outbreak • Covert War
• Indignation against Rale • War declared • Governor
and Assembly • Speech of Samuel Sewall • Penobscots
attack Fort St. George • Reprisal • Attack on Norridgewock •
Death of Rale   477

CHAPTER XI   1724, 1725
LOVEWELL'S FIGHT
Vaudreuil and Dummer • Embassy to Canada • Indians
intractable • Treaty of Peace • The Pequawkets • John
Lovewell • A Hunting Party • Another Expedition • The
Ambuscade • The Fight • Chaplain Frye • His Fate • The
Survivors • Susanna Rogers   502

CHAPTER XII   1712
THE OUTAGAMIES AT DETROIT
The West and the Fur-Trade • New York and Canada •
Indian Population • The Firebrands of the West • Detroit in
1712 • Dangerous Visitors • Suspense • Timely Succors • The
Outagamies attacked • Their Desperate Position • Overtures
• Wavering Allies • Conduct of Dubuisson • Escape of the
Outagamies • Pursuit and Attack • Victory and Carnage   517

CHAPTER XIII   1697–1750
LOUISIANA
The Mississippi to be occupied • English Rivalry • Iberville •
Bienville • Huguenots • Views of Louis XIV. • Wives for the
Colony • Slaves • La Mothe-Cadillac • Paternal Government
• Crozat's Monopoly • Factions • The Mississippi Company •
New Orleans • The Bubble bursts • Indian Wars • The
Colony firmly established • The two Heads of New France   534

CHAPTER XIV   1700–1732
THE OUTAGAMIE WAR
The Western Posts • Detroit • The Illinois • Perils of the
West • The Outagamies • Their Turbulence • English Insti-
gation • Louvigny's Expedition • Defeat of Outagamies •
Hostilities renewed • Lignery's Expedition • Outagamies at-
tacked by Villiers • By Hurons and Iroquois • La Butte des
Morts • The Sacs and Foxes   552

CHAPTER XV   1697–1741
FRANCE IN THE FAR WEST
   *French Explorers • Le Sueur on the St. Peter's • Canadians
   on the Missouri • Juchereau de Saint-Denis • Bénard de la
   Harpe on Red River • Adventures of Du Tisné • Bourgmont
   visits the Comanches • The Brothers Mallet in Colorado and
   New Mexico • Fabry de la Bruyère*   565

CHAPTER XVI   1716–1761
SEARCH FOR THE PACIFIC
   *The Western Sea • Schemes for reaching it • Journey of
   Charlevoix • The Sioux Mission • Varennes de la Vérendrye
   • His Enterprise • His Disasters • Visits the Mandans • His
   Sons • Their Search for the Western Sea • Their Adventures
   • The Snake Indians • A Great War-Party • The Rocky
   Mountains • A Panic • Return of the Brothers • Their
   Wrongs and their Fate*   580

CHAPTER XVII   1700–1750
THE CHAIN OF POSTS
   *Opposing Claims • Attitude of the Rival Nations • America
   a French Continent • England a Usurper • French Demands
   • Magnanimous Proposals • Warlike Preparation • Niagara
   • Oswego • Crown Point • The Passes of the West secured*   606

CHAPTER XVIII   1744, 1745
A MAD SCHEME
   *War of the Austrian Succession • The French seize Canseau
   and attack Annapolis • Plan of Reprisal • William Vaughan
   • Governor Shirley • He advises an Attack on Louisbourg •
   The Assembly refuses, but at last consents • Preparation •
   William Pepperrell • George Whitefield • Parson Moody
   • The Soldiers • The Provincial Navy • Commodore
   Warren • Shirley as an Amateur Soldier • The Fleet sails*   616

CHAPTER XIX   1745
LOUISBOURG BESIEGED
   *Seth Pomeroy • The Voyage • Canseau • Unexpected Succors
   • Delays • Louisbourg • The Landing • The Grand Battery
   taken • French Cannon turned on the Town • Weakness of
   Duchambon • Sufferings of the Besiegers • Their Hardihood •*

*Their Irregular Proceedings • Joseph Sherburn • Amateur
Gunnery • Camp Frolics • Sectarian Zeal • Perplexities of
Pepperrell*   636

CHAPTER XX   1745
LOUISBOURG TAKEN
  *A Rash Resolution • The Island Battery • The Volunteers •
  The Attack • The Repulse • Capture of the "Vigilant" • A
  Sortie • Skirmishes • Despondency of the French • English
  Camp threatened • Pepperrell and Warren • Warren's Plan
  • Preparation for a General Attack • Flag of Truce
  • Capitulation • State of the Fortress • Parson Moody •
  Soldiers dissatisfied • Disorders • Army and Navy • Rejoicings
  • England repays Provincial Outlays*   654

CHAPTER XXI   1745–1747
DUC D'ANVILLE
  *Louisbourg after the Conquest • Mutiny • Pestilence • Ste-
  phen Williams • His Diary • Scheme of conquering Canada
  • Newcastle's Promises • Alarm in Canada • Promises broken
  • Plan against Crown Point • Startling News • D'Anville's
  Fleet • Louisbourg to be avenged • Disasters of D'Anville •
  Storm • Pestilence • Famine • Death of D'Anville • Suicide
  of the Vice-Admiral • Ruinous Failure • Return Voyage •
  Defeat of La Jonquière*   672

CHAPTER XXII   1745–1747
ACADIAN CONFLICTS
  *Efforts of France • Apathy of Newcastle • Dilemma of Aca-
  dians • Their Character • Danger of the Province • Plans
  of Shirley • Acadian Priests • Political Agitators • Noble's
  Expedition • Ramesay at Beaubassin • Noble at Grand-Pré •
  A Winter March • Defeat and Death of Noble • Grand-Pré
  re-occupied by the English • Threats of Ramesay against the
  Acadians • The British Ministry will not protect them*   688

CHAPTER XXIII   1740–1747
WAR AND POLITICS
  *Governor and Assembly • Saratoga destroyed • William John-
  son • Border Ravages • Upper Ashuelot • French "Military
  Movements" • Number Four • Niverville's Attack • Phineas
  Stevens • The French repulsed*   712

CHAPTER XXIV   1745–1748
FORT MASSACHUSETTS
  *Frontier Defence • Northfield and its Minister • Military
  Criticisms of Rev. Benjamin Doolittle • Rigaud de Vaudreuil
  • His Great War-Party • He attacks Fort Massachusetts •
  Sergeant Hawks and his Garrison • A Gallant Defence
  • Capitulation • Humanity of the French • Ravages •
  Return to Crown Point • Peace of Aix-la-Chapelle* 728

APPENDIX
A. *France claims All North America except the Spanish
    Colonies* 747
B. *French Views of the Siege of Louisbourg* 761
C. *Shirley's Relations with the Acadians* 791

Preface

THIS BOOK, forming Part VI. of the series called France and England in North America, fills the gap between Part V., "Count Frontenac," and Part VII., "Montcalm and Wolfe;" so that the series now forms a continuous history of the efforts of France to occupy and control this continent.

In the present volumes the nature of the subject does not permit an unbroken thread of narrative, and the unity of the book lies in its being throughout, in one form or another, an illustration of the singularly contrasted characters and methods of the rival claimants to North America.

Like the rest of the series, this work is founded on original documents. The statements of secondary writers have been accepted only when found to conform to the evidence of contemporaries, whose writings have been sifted and collated with the greatest care. As extremists on each side have charged me with favoring the other, I hope I have been unfair to neither.

The manuscript material collected for the preparation of the series now complete forms about seventy volumes, most of them folios. These have been given by me from time to time to the Massachusetts Historical Society, in whose library they now are, open to the examination of those interested in the subjects of which they treat. The collection was begun forty-five years ago, and its formation has been exceedingly slow, having been retarded by difficulties which seemed insurmountable, and for years were so in fact. Hence the completion of the series has required twice the time that would have sufficed under less unfavorable conditions.

BOSTON, *March 26, 1892*.

Chapter I

1700—1713

EVE OF WAR

The Spanish Succession • Influence of Louis XIV. on History •
French Schemes of Conquest in America • New York • Unfitness
of the Colonies for War • The Five Nations • Doubt and Vacilla-
tion • The Western Indians • Trade and Politics

THE WAR which in the British colonies was called Queen Anne's War, and in England the War of the Spanish Succession, was the second of a series of four conflicts which ended in giving to Great Britain a maritime and colonial preponderance over France and Spain. So far as concerns the colonies and the sea, these several wars may be regarded as a single protracted one, broken by intervals of truce. The three earlier of them, it is true, were European contests, begun and waged on European disputes. Their American part was incidental and apparently subordinate, yet it involved questions of prime importance in the history of the world.

The War of the Spanish Succession sprang from the ambition of Louis XIV. We are apt to regard the story of that gorgeous monarch as a tale that is told; but his influence shapes the life of nations to this day. At the beginning of his reign two roads lay before him, and it was a momentous question for posterity, as for his own age, which one of them he would choose: whether he would follow the wholesome policy of his great minister Colbert, or obey his own vanity and arrogance, and plunge France into exhausting wars; whether he would hold to the principle of tolerance embodied in the Edict of Nantes, or do the work of fanaticism and priestly ambition. The one course meant prosperity, progress, and the rise of a middle class: the other meant bankruptcy and the Dragonades; and this was the King's choice. Crushing taxation, misery, and ruin followed, till France burst out at last in a frenzy, drunk with the wild dreams of Rousseau. Then came the Terror and the Napoleonic wars, and reaction on reaction, revolution on revolution, down to our own day.

Louis placed his grandson on the throne of Spain, and in-

339

sulted England by acknowledging as her rightful king the son of James II., whom she had deposed. Then England declared war. Canada and the northern British colonies had had but a short breathing time since the Peace of Ryswick; both were tired of slaughtering each other, and both needed rest. Yet before the declaration of war, the Canadian officers of the Crown prepared, with their usual energy, to meet the expected crisis. One of them wrote: "If war be declared, it is certain that the King can very easily conquer and ruin New England." The French of Canada often use the name "New England" as applying to the British colonies in general. They are twice as populous as Canada, he goes on to say; but the people are great cowards, totally undisciplined, and ignorant of war, while the Canadians are brave, hardy, and well trained. We have, besides, twenty-eight companies of regulars, and could raise six thousand warriors from our Indian allies. Four thousand men could easily lay waste all the northern English colonies, to which end we must have five ships of war, with one thousand troops on board, who must land at Penobscot, where they must be joined by two thousand regulars, militia, and Indians, sent from Canada by way of the Chaudière and the Kennebec. Then the whole force must go to Portsmouth, take it by assault, leave a garrison there, and march to Boston, laying waste all the towns and villages by the way; after destroying Boston, the army must march for New York, while the fleet follows along the coast. "Nothing could be easier," says the writer, "for the road is good, and there is plenty of horses and carriages. The troops would ruin everything as they advanced, and New York would quickly be destroyed and burned."[1]

Another plan, scarcely less absurd, was proposed about the same time by the celebrated Le Moyne d'Iberville. The essential point, he says, is to get possession of Boston; but there are difficulties and risks in the way. Nothing, he adds, referring to the other plan, seems difficult to persons without experience; but unless we are prepared to raise a great and costly armament, our only hope is in surprise. We should make it in winter, when the seafaring population, which is

[1] *Premier Projet pour L'Expédition contre la Nouvelle Angleterre, 1701. Second Projet*, etc. Compare *N. Y. Col. Docs.*, IX. 725.

the chief strength of the place, is absent on long voyages. A thousand Canadians, four hundred regulars, and as many Indians should leave Quebec in November, ascend the Chaudière, then descend the Kennebec, approach Boston under cover of the forest, and carry it by a night attack. Apparently he did not know that but for its lean neck—then but a few yards wide—Boston was an island, and that all around for many leagues the forest that was to have covered his approach had already been devoured by numerous busy settlements. He offers to lead the expedition, and declares that if he is honored with the command, he will warrant that the New England capital will be forced to submit to King Louis, after which New York can be seized in its turn.[1]

In contrast to those incisive proposals, another French officer breathed nothing but peace. Brouillan, governor of Acadia, wrote to the governor of Massachusetts to suggest that, with the consent of their masters, they should make a treaty of neutrality. The English governor being dead, the letter came before the council, who received it coldly. Canada, and not Acadia, was the enemy they had to fear. Moreover, Boston merchants made good profit by supplying the Acadians with necessaries which they could get in no other way; and in time of war these profits, though lawless, were greater than in time of peace. But what chiefly influenced the council against the overtures of Brouillan was a passage in his letter reminding them that, by the Treaty of Ryswick, the New England people had no right to fish within sight of the Acadian coast. This they flatly denied, saying that the New England people had fished there time out of mind, and that if Brouillan should molest them, they would treat it as an act of war.[2]

While the New England colonies, and especially Massachusetts and New Hampshire, had most cause to deprecate a war,

[1] *Mémoire du Sieur d'Iberville sur Boston et ses Dépendances, 1700* (1701?). Baron de Saint-Castin also drew up a plan for attacking Boston in 1702, with lists of necessary munitions and other supplies.

[2] *Brouillan à Bellomont, 10 Août, 1701. Conseil de Baston à Brouillan, 22 Août, 1701.* Brouillan acted under royal orders, having been told, in case of war being declared, to propose a treaty with New England, unless he should find that he can "se garantir des insultes des Anglais" and do considerable harm to their trade, in which case he is to make no treaty. *Mémoire du Roy au Sieur de Brouillan, 23 Mars, 1700.*

the prospect of one was also extremely unwelcome to the people of New York. The conflict lately closed had borne hard upon them through the attacks of the enemy, and still more through the derangement of their industries. They were distracted, too, with the factions rising out of the recent revolution under Jacob Leisler. New York had been the bulwark of the colonies farther south, who, feeling themselves safe, had given their protector little help, and that little grudgingly, seeming to regard the war as no concern of theirs. Three thousand and fifty-one pounds, provincial currency, was the joint contribution of Virginia, Maryland, East Jersey, and Connecticut to the aid of New York during five years of the late war.[1] Massachusetts could give nothing, even if she would, her hands being full with the defence of her own borders. Colonel Quary wrote to the Board of Trade that New York could not bear alone the cost of defending herself; that the other colonies were "stuffed with commonwealth notions," and were "of a sour temper in opposition to government," so that Parliament ought to take them in hand and compel each to do its part in the common cause.[2] To this Lord Cornbury adds that Rhode Island and Connecticut are even more stubborn than the rest, hate all true subjects of the Queen, and will not give a farthing to the war so long as they can help it.[3] Each province lived in selfish isolation, recking little of its neighbor's woes.

New York, left to fight her own battles, was in a wretched condition for defence. It is true that, unlike the other colonies, the King had sent her a few soldiers, counting at this time about one hundred and eighty, all told;[4] but they had been left so long without pay that they were in a state of scandalous destitution. They would have been left without rations had not three private gentlemen—Schuyler, Livingston, and Cortlandt—advanced money for their supplies, which seems never to have been repaid.[5] They are reported to have been "without shirts, breeches, shoes, or stockings," and "in

[1] Schuyler, *Colonial New York*, I. 431, 432.
[2] *Col. Quary to the Lords of Trade, 16 June, 1703.*
[3] *Cornbury to the Lords of Trade, 9 Sept. 1703.*
[4] *Bellomont to the Lords of Trade, 28 Feb. 1700.*
[5] *Ibid.*

such a shameful condition that the women when passing them are obliged to cover their eyes." "The Indians ask," says the Governor, " 'Do you think us such fools as to believe that a King who cannot clothe his soldiers can protect us from the French, with their fourteen hundred men all well equipped?' "[1]

The forts were no better than their garrisons. The Governor complains that those of Albany and Schenectady "are so weak and ridiculous that they look more like pounds for cattle than forts." At Albany the rotten stockades were falling from their own weight.

If New York had cause to complain of those whom she sheltered, she herself gave cause of complaint to those who sheltered her. The Five Nations of the Iroquois had always been her allies against the French, had guarded her borders and fought her battles. What they wanted in return was gifts, attentions, just dealings, and active aid in war; but they got them in scant measure. Their treatment by the province was short-sighted, if not ungrateful. New York was a mixture of races and religions not yet fused into a harmonious body politic, divided in interests and torn with intestine disputes. Its Assembly was made up in large part of men unfitted to pursue a consistent scheme of policy, or spend the little money at their disposal on any objects but those of present and visible interest. The royal governors, even when personally competent, were hampered by want of means and by factious opposition. The Five Nations were robbed by land-speculators, cheated by traders, and feebly supported in their constant wars with the French. Spasmodically, as it were, on occasions of crisis, they were summoned to Albany, soothed with such presents as could be got from unwilling legislators, or now and then from the Crown, and exhorted to fight vigorously in the common cause. The case would have been far worse but for a few patriotic men, with Peter Schuyler at their head, who understood the character of these Indians, and labored strenuously to keep them in what was called their allegiance.

The proud and fierce confederates had suffered greatly in the late war. Their numbers had been reduced about one half,

[1] Schuyler, *Colonial New York*, I. 488.

and they now counted little more than twelve hundred warriors. They had learned a bitter and humiliating lesson, and their arrogance had changed to distrust and alarm. Though hating the French, they had learned to respect their military activity and prowess, and to look askance on the Dutch and English, who rarely struck a blow in their defence, and suffered their hereditary enemy to waste their fields and burn their towns. The English called the Five Nations British subjects, on which the French taunted them with being British slaves, and told them that the King of England had ordered the Governor of New York to poison them. This invention had great effect. The Iroquois capital, Onondaga, was filled with wild rumors. The credulous savages were tossed among doubts, suspicions, and fears. Some were in terror of poison, and some of witchcraft. They believed that the rival European nations had leagued to destroy them and divide their lands, and that they were bewitched by sorcerers, both French and English.[1]

After the Peace of Ryswick, and even before it, the French Governor kept agents among them. Some of these were soldiers, like Joncaire, Maricourt, or Longueuil, and some were Jesuits, like Bruyas, Lamberville, or Vaillant. The Jesuits showed their usual ability and skill in their difficult and perilous task. The Indians derived various advantages from their presence, which they regarded also as a flattering attention; while the English, jealous of their influence, made feeble attempts to counteract it by sending Protestant clergymen to Onondaga. "But," writes Lord Bellomont, "it is next to impossible to prevail with the ministers to live among the Indians. They (the Indians) are so nasty as never to wash their hands, or the utensils they dress their victuals with."[2] Even had their zeal been proof to these afflictions, the ministers would have been no match for their astute opponents. In vain Bellomont assured the Indians that the Jesuits were "the greatest lyars and impostors in the world."[3] In vain he offered a hundred dollars for every one of them whom they should deliver into his hands. They would promise to expel them;

---

[1] *N. Y. Col. Docs.*, IV. 658.

[2] *Bellomont to the Lords of Trade, 17 Oct. 1700.*

[3] *Conference of Bellomont with the Indians, 26 Aug. 1700.*

but their minds were divided, and they stood in fear of each other. While one party distrusted and disliked the priests, another was begging the Governor of Canada to send more. Others took a practical view of the question. "If the English sell goods cheaper than the French, we will have ministers; if the French sell them cheaper than the English, we will have priests." Others, again, wanted neither Jesuits nor ministers, "because both of you (English and French) have made us drunk with the noise of your praying."[1]

The aims of the propagandists on both sides were secular. The French wished to keep the Five Nations neutral in the event of another war: the English wished to spur them to active hostility; but while the former pursued their purpose with energy and skill, the efforts of the latter were intermittent and generally feeble.

"The Nations," writes Schuyler, "are full of factions." There was a French party and an English party in every town, especially in Onondaga, the centre of intrigue. French influence was strongest at the western end of the confederacy, among the Senecas, where the French officer, Joncaire, an Iroquois by adoption, had won many to France; and it was weakest at the eastern end, among the Mohawks, who were nearest to the English settlements. Here the Jesuits had labored long and strenuously in the work of conversion, and from time to time they had led their numerous proselytes to remove to Canada, where they settled at St. Louis, or Caughnawaga, on the right bank of the St. Lawrence, a little above Montreal, where their descendants still remain. It is said that at the beginning of the eighteenth century two thirds of the Mohawks had thus been persuaded to cast their lot with the French, and from enemies to become friends and allies. Some of the Oneidas and a few of the other Iroquois nations joined them and strengthened the new mission settlement; and the Caughnawagas afterwards played an important part between the rival European colonies.

The "Far Indians," or "Upper Nations," as the French called them, consisted of the tribes of the Great Lakes and adjacent regions, Ottawas, Pottawattamies, Sacs, Foxes, Sioux, and many more. It was from these that Canada drew

[1] *Journal of Bleeker and Schuyler on their visit to Onondaga, Aug., Sept. 1701.*

the furs by which she lived. Most of them were nominal friends and allies of the French, who in the interest of trade strove to keep these wild-cats from tearing each other's throats, and who were in constant alarm lest they should again come to blows with their old enemies, the Five Nations, in which case they would call on Canada for help, thus imperilling those pacific relations with the Iroquois confederacy which the French were laboring constantly to secure.

In regard to the "Far Indians," the French, the English, and the Five Iroquois Nations all had distinct and opposing interests. The French wished to engross their furs, either by inducing the Indians to bring them down to Montreal, or by sending traders into their country to buy them. The English, with a similar object, wished to divert the "Far Indians" from Montreal and draw them to Albany; but this did not suit the purpose of the Five Nations, who, being sharp politicians and keen traders, as well as bold and enterprising warriors, wished to act as middle-men between the beaver-hunting tribes and the Albany merchants, well knowing that good profit might thus accrue. In this state of affairs the converted Iroquois settled at Caughnawaga played a peculiar part. In the province of New York, goods for the Indian trade were of excellent quality and comparatively abundant and cheap; while among the French, especially in time of war, they were often scarce and dear. The Caughnawagas accordingly, whom neither the English nor the French dared offend, used their position to carry on a contraband trade between New York and Canada. By way of Lake Champlain and the Hudson they brought to Albany furs from the country of the "Far Indians," and exchanged them for guns, blankets, cloths, knives, beads, and the like. These they carried to Canada and sold to the French traders, who in this way, and often in this alone, supplied themselves with the goods necessary for bartering furs from the "Far Indians." This lawless trade of the Caughnawagas went on even in time of war; and opposed as it was to every principle of Canadian policy, it was generally connived at by the French authorities as the only means of obtaining the goods necessary for keeping their Indian allies in good humor.

It was injurious to English interests; but the fur-traders of Albany and also the commissioners charged with Indian affairs, being Dutchmen converted by force into British subjects, were, with a few eminent exceptions, cool in their devotion to the British Crown; while the merchants of the port of New York, from whom the fur-traders drew their supplies, thought more of their own profits than of the public good. The trade with Canada through the Caughnawagas not only gave aid and comfort to the enemy, but continually admitted spies into the colony, from whom the Governor of Canada gained information touching English movements and designs.

The Dutch traders of Albany and the importing merchants who supplied them with Indian goods had a strong interest in preventing active hostilities with Canada, which would have spoiled their trade. So, too, and for similar reasons, had influential persons in Canada. The French authorities, moreover, thought it impolitic to harass the frontiers of New York by war parties, since the Five Nations might come to the aid of their Dutch and English allies, and so break the peaceful relations which the French were anxious to maintain with them. Thus it happened that, during the first six or seven years of the eighteenth century, there was a virtual truce between Canada and New York, and the whole burden of the war fell upon New England, or rather upon Massachusetts, with its outlying district of Maine and its small and weak neighbor, New Hampshire.[1]

[1] The foregoing chapter rests on numerous documents in the Public Record Office, Archives de la Marine, Archives Nationales, *N. Y. Colonial Documents*, Vols. IV., V., IX., and the *Second and Third Series of the Correspondance Officielle* at Ottawa.

Chapter II

DETROIT

Michillimackinac • La Mothe-Cadillac • His Disputes with the Je-
suits • Opposing Views • Plans of Cadillac • His Memorial to the
Court • His Opponents • Detroit founded • The New Company •
Detroit changes Hands • Strange Act of the Five Nations

IN THE FEW years of doubtful peace that preceded Queen
Anne's War, an enterprise was begun, which, nowise in
accord with the wishes and expectations of those engaged in
it, was destined to produce as its last result an American city.

Antoine de La Mothe-Cadillac commanded at Michillimackinac, whither Frontenac had sent him in 1694. This old
mission of the Jesuits, where they had gathered the remnants
of the lake tribes dispersed by the Iroquois at the middle of
the seventeenth century, now savored little of its apostolic beginnings. It was the centre of the Western fur-trade and the
favorite haunt of the *coureurs de bois*. Brandy and squaws
abounded, and according to the Jesuit Carheil, the spot where
Marquette had labored was now a witness of scenes the most
unedifying.[1]

At Michillimackinac was seen a curious survival of Huron-
Iroquois customs. The villages of the Hurons and Ottawas,
which were side by side, separated only by a fence, were surrounded by a common enclosure of triple palisades, which,
with the addition of loopholes for musketry, were precisely
like those seen by Cartier at Hochelaga, and by Champlain in
the Onondaga country. The dwellings which these defences
enclosed were also after the old Huron-Iroquois pattern, —
those long arched structures covered with bark which Brebeuf
found by the shores of Matchedash Bay, and Jogues on the
banks of the Mohawk. Besides the Indians, there was a
French colony at the place, chiefly of fur-traders, lodged in
log cabins, roofed with cedar bark, and forming a street along
the shore close to the palisaded villages of the Hurons and

[1] See *Old Régime in Canada*, p. 1364.

Ottawas. The fort, known as Fort Buade, stood at the head of the little bay.[1]

The Hurons and Ottawas were thorough savages, though the Hurons retained the forms of Roman Catholic Christianity. This tribe, writes Cadillac, "are reduced to a very small number; and it is well for us that they are, for they are ill-disposed and mischievous, with a turn for intrigue and a capacity for large undertakings. Luckily, their power is not great; but as they cannot play the lion, they play the fox, and do their best to make trouble between us and our allies."

La Mothe-Cadillac[2] was a captain in the colony troops, and an admirer of the late governor, Frontenac, to whose policy he adhered, and whose prejudices he shared. He was amply gifted with the kind of intelligence that consists in quick observation, sharpened by an inveterate spirit of sarcasm, was energetic, enterprising, well instructed, and a bold and sometimes a visionary schemer, with a restless spirit, a nimble and biting wit, a Gascon impetuosity of temperament, and as much devotion as an officer of the King was forced to profess, coupled with small love of priests and an aversion to Jesuits.[3] Carheil and Marest, missionaries of that order at Michillimackinac, were objects of his especial antipathy, which they fully returned. The two priests were impatient of a military commandant to whose authority they were in some small measure subjected; and they imputed to him the disorders which he did not, and perhaps could not, prevent. They were opposed also to the traffic in brandy, which was favored by

[1] *Relation de la Mothe-Cadillac*, in Margry, V. 75.

[2] He wrote his name as above. It is often written La Motte, which has the advantage of conveying the pronunciation unequivocally to an unaccustomed English ear. La Mothe-Cadillac came of a good family of Languedoc. His father, Jean de La Mothe, seigneur de Cadillac et de Launay, or Laumet, was a counsellor in the Parliament of Toulouse. The date of young Cadillac's birth is uncertain. The register of his marriage places it in 1661, and that of his death in 1657. Another record, cited by Farmer in his *History of Detroit*, makes it 1658. In 1703 he himself declared that he was forty-seven years old. After serving as lieutenant in the regiment of Clairembault, he went to Canada about the year 1683. He became skilled in managing Indians, made himself well acquainted with the coasts of New England, and strongly urged an attack by sea on New York and Boston, as the only sure means of securing French ascendency. He was always in opposition to the clerical party.

[3] See *La Mothe-Cadillac à ——, 3 Août, 1695.*

Cadillac on the usual ground that it attracted the Indians, and so prevented the English from getting control of the fur-trade,—an argument which he reinforced by sanitary considerations based on the supposed unwholesomeness of the fish and smoked meat which formed the chief diet of Michilli-mackinac. "A little brandy after the meal," he says, with the solemnity of the learned Purgon, "seems necessary to cook the bilious meats and the crudities they leave in the stomach."[1]

Cadillac calls Carheil, superior of the mission, the most passionate and domineering man he ever knew, and further declares that the Jesuit tried to provoke him to acts of violence, in order to make matter of accusation against him. If this was Carheil's aim, he was near succeeding. Once, in a dispute with the commandant on the brandy trade, he upbraided him sharply for permitting it; to which Cadillac replied that he only obeyed the orders of the court. The Jesuit rejoined that he ought to obey God, and not man,—"on which," says the commandant, "I told him that his talk smelt of sedition a hundred yards off, and begged that he would amend it. He told me that I gave myself airs that did not belong to me, holding his fist before my nose at the same time. I confess I almost forgot that he was a priest, and felt for a moment like knocking his jaw out of joint; but, thank God, I contented myself with taking him by the arm, pushing him out, and ordering him not to come back."[2]

Such being the relations of the commandant and the Father Superior, it is not surprising to find the one complaining that he cannot get absolved from his sins, and the other painting the morals and manners of Michillimackinac in the blackest colors.

I have spoken elsewhere of the two opposing policies that

---

[1] *La Mothe-Cadillac à* ——, *3 Août, 1695.*

[2] "Il me dit que je me donnois des airs qui ne m'appartenoient pas, en me portant le poing au nez. Je vous avoue, Monsieur, que je pensai oublier qu'il étoit prêtre, et que je vis le moment où j'allois luy démonter la mâchoire; mais, Dieu merci, je me contentai de le prendre par le bras et de le pousser dehors, avec ordre de n'y plus rentrer." Margry, V. (author's edition), Introduction, CIV. This introduction, with other editorial matter, is omitted in the edition of M. Margry's valuable collection, printed under a vote of the American Congress.

divided Canada,—the policies of concentration and of expansion, on the one hand leaving the West to the keeping of the Jesuits, and confining the population to the borders of the St. Lawrence; on the other, the occupation of the interior of the continent by posts of war and trade.[1] Through the force of events the latter view had prevailed; yet while the military chiefs of Canada could not but favor it, the Jesuits were unwilling to accept it, and various interests in the colony still opposed it openly or secretly. Frontenac had been its strongest champion, and Cadillac followed in his steps. It seemed to him that the time had come for securing the West for France.

The strait—*détroit*—which connects Lake Huron with Lake Erie was the most important of all the Western passes. It was the key of the three upper lakes, with the vast countries watered by their tributaries, and it gave Canada her readiest access to the valley of the Mississippi. If the French held it, the English would be shut out from the Northwest; if, as seemed likely, the English should seize it, the Canadian fur-trade would be ruined.[2] The possession of it by the French would be a constant curb and menace to the Five Nations, as well as a barrier between those still formidable tribes and the Western Indians, allies of Canada; and when the intended French establishment at the mouth of the Mississippi should be made, Detroit would be an indispensable link of communication between Canada and Louisiana.

Denonville had recognized the importance of the position, and it was by his orders that Greysolon Dulhut, in 1686, had occupied it for a time, and built a picket fort near the site of Fort Gratiot.[3]

It would be idle to imagine that the motives of Cadillac were wholly patriotic. Fur-trading interests were deeply involved in his plans, and bitter opposition was certain. The fur-trade, in its nature, was a constant breeder of discord. The people of Montreal would have the tribes come down every summer from the West and Northwest and hold a fair under the palisades of their town. It is said that more than four

---

[1] See *Count Frontenac*, 300.

[2] Robert Livingston urged the occupation of Detroit as early as 1700. *N. Y. Col. Docs.*, IV. 650.

[3] *Denonville à Dulhut, 6 Juin, 1686. Count Frontenac*, 99.

hundred French families lived wholly or in part by this home trade, and therefore regarded with deep jealousy the establishment of interior posts, which would forestall it. Again, every new Western post would draw away trade from those already established, and every trading license granted to a company or an individual would rouse the animosity of those who had been licensed before. The prosperity of Detroit would be the ruin of Michillimackinac, and those whose interests centred at the latter post angrily opposed the scheme of Cadillac.

He laid his plans before Count de Maurepas by a characteristic memorial, apparently written in 1699. In this he proposed to gather all the tribes of the lakes at Detroit, civilize them and teach them French, "insomuch that from pagans they would become children of the Church, and therefore good subjects of the King." They will form, he continues, a considerable settlement, "strong enough to bring the English and the Iroquois to reason, or, with help from Montreal, to destroy both of them." Detroit, he adds, should be the seat of trade, which should not be permitted in the countries beyond it. By this regulation the intolerable glut of beaver-skins, which spoils the market, may be prevented. This proposed restriction of the beaver trade to Detroit was enough in itself to raise a tempest against the whole scheme. "Cadillac well knows that he has enemies," pursues the memorial, "but he keeps on his way without turning or stopping for the noise of the puppies who bark after him."[1]

Among the essential features of his plan was a well-garrisoned fort, and a church, served not by Jesuits alone, but also by Recollet friars and priests of the Missions Etrangères. The idea of this ecclesiastical partnership was odious to the Jesuits, who felt that the West was their proper field, and that only they had a right there. Another part of Cadillac's proposal pleased them no better. This was his plan of civilizing the Indians and teaching them to speak French; for it was the reproach of the Jesuit missions that they left the savage a savage still, and asked little of him but the practice of certain rites and the passive acceptance of dogmas to him incomprehensible.

[1] "Sans se destourner et sans s'arrester au bruit des jappereaux qui crient après luy." *Mémoire de La Mothe-Cadillac adressé au Comte de Maurepas.*

"It is essential," says the memorial, "that in this matter of teaching the Indians our language the missionaries should act in good faith, and that his Majesty should have the goodness to impose his strictest orders upon them; for which there are several good reasons. The first and most stringent is that when members of religious orders or other ecclesiastics undertake anything, they never let it go. The second is that by not teaching French to the Indians they make themselves necessary [as interpreters] to the King and the Governor. The third is that if all Indians spoke French, all kinds of ecclesiastics would be able to instruct them. This might cause them [the Jesuits] to lose some of the presents they get; for though these Reverend Fathers come here only for the glory of God, yet the one thing does not prevent the other,"—meaning that God and Mammon may be served at once. "Nobody can deny that the priests own three quarters of Canada. From St. Paul's Bay to Quebec, there is nothing but the seigniory of Beauport that belongs to a private person. All the rest, which is the best part, belongs to the Jesuits or other ecclesiastics. The Upper Town of Quebec is composed of six or seven superb palaces belonging to Hospital Nuns, Ursulines, Jesuits, Recollets, Seminary priests, and the Bishop. There may be some forty private houses, and even these pay rent to the ecclesiastics, which shows that *the one thing does not prevent the other*." From this it will be seen that, in the words of one of his enemies, Cadillac "was not quite in the odor of sanctity."

"One may as well knock one's head against a wall," concludes the memorial, "as hope to convert the Indians in any other way [than that of civilizing them]; for thus far all the fruits of the missions consist in the baptism of infants who die before reaching the age of reason."[1] This was not literally true, though the results of the Jesuit missions in the West had been meagre and transient to a surprising degree.

Cadillac's plan of a settlement at Detroit was not at first received with favor by Callières, the governor; while the intendant, Champigny, a fast friend of the Jesuits, strongly opposed it. By their order the chief inhabitants of Quebec met at the Château St. Louis, Callières, Champigny, and Cadillac

[1] *Mémoire adressé au Comte de Maurepas*, in Margry, V. 138.

himself being present. There was a heated debate on the beaver-trade, after which the Intendant commanded silence, explained the projects of Cadillac, and proceeded to oppose them. His first point was that the natives should not be taught French, because the Indian girls brought up at the Ursuline Convent led looser lives than the young squaws who had received no instruction, while it was much the same with the boys brought up at the Seminary.

"M. de Champigny," returned the sarcastic Cadillac, "does great honor to the Ursulines and the Seminary. It is true that some Indian women who have learned our language have lived viciously; but that is because their teachers were too stiff with them, and tried to make them nuns."[1]

Champigny's position, as stated by his adversary, was that "all intimacy of the Indians with the French is dangerous and corrupting to their morals," and that their only safety lies in keeping them at a distance from the settlements. This was the view of the Jesuits, and there is much to be said in its favor; but it remains not the less true that conversion must go hand in hand with civilization, or it is a failure and a fraud.

Cadillac was not satisfied with the results of the meeting at the Château St. Louis, and he wrote to the minister: "You can never hope that this business will succeed if it is discussed here on the spot. Canada is a country of cabals and intrigues, and it is impossible to reconcile so many different interests."[2] He sailed for France, apparently in the autumn of 1699, to urge his scheme at court. Here he had an interview with the colonial minister, Ponchartrain, to whom he represented the military and political expediency of his proposed establishment;[3] and in a letter which seems to be addressed to La Touche, chief clerk in the Department of Marine and Colonies, he promised that the execution of his plan would insure the safety of Canada and the ruin of the British colonies.[4] He asked for fifty soldiers and fifty Canadians to begin the work, to be followed in the next year by twenty or thirty families

---

[1] La Mothe-Cadillac, *Rapport au Ministre, 1700*, in Margry, V. 157.

[2] *Rapport au Ministre, 1700*.

[3] Cadillac's report of this interview is given in Sheldon, *Early History of Michigan*, 85–91.

[4] *La Mothe-Cadillac à un premier commis, 18 Oct. 1700*, in Margry, V. 166.

and by two hundred picked men of various trades, sent out at the King's charge, along with priests of several communities, and nuns to attend the sick and teach the Indian girls. "I cannot tell you," continues Cadillac, "the efforts my enemies have made to deprive me of the honor of executing my project; but so soon as M. de Ponchartrain decides in its favor, the whole country will applaud it."

Ponchartrain accepted the plan, and Cadillac returned to Canada commissioned to execute it. Early in June, 1701, he left La Chine with a hundred men in twenty-five canoes loaded with provisions, goods, munitions, and tools. He was accompanied by Alphonse de Tonty, brother of Henri de Tonty, the companion of La Salle, and by two half-pay lieutenants, Dugué and Chacornacle, together with a Jesuit and a Recollet.[1] Following the difficult route of the Ottawa and Lake Huron, they reached their destination on the 24th of July, and built a picket fort sixty yards square, which by order of the Governor they named Fort Ponchartrain.[2] It stood near the west bank of the strait, about forty paces from the water.[3] Thus was planted the germ of the city of Detroit.

Cadillac sent back Chacornacle with the report of what he had done, and a description of the country written in a strain of swelling and gushing rhetoric in singular contrast with his usual sarcastic utterances. "None but enemies of the truth," his letter concludes, "are enemies of this establishment, so necessary to the glory of the King, the progress of religion, and the destruction of the throne of Baal."[4]

What he had, perhaps, still more at heart was making money out of it by the fur-trade. By command of the King a radical change had lately been made in this chief commerce of Canada, and the entire control of it had been placed in the hands of a company in which all Canadians might take shares. But as the risks were great and the conditions ill-defined, the number of subscribers was not much above one hundred and

---

[1] *Callières au Ministre, 4 Oct. 1701. Autre lettre du même, sans date,* in Margry, V. 187, 190.

[2] *Callières et Champigny au Ministre, sans date.*

[3] *Relation du Destroit* (by the Jesuit who accompanied the expedition).

[4] *Description de la Rivière du Détroit, jointe à la lettre de MM. de Callières et de Champigny, 8 Oct. 1701.*

fifty; and the rest of the colony found themselves shut out from the trade,—to the ruin of some, and the injury of all.[1]

All trade in furs was restricted to Detroit and Fort Frontenac, both of which were granted to the company, subject to be resumed by the King at his pleasure.[2] The company was to repay the eighty thousand francs which the expedition to Detroit had cost; and to this was added various other burdens. The King, however, was to maintain the garrison.

All the affairs of the company were placed in the hands of seven directors, who began immediately to complain that their burdens were too heavy, and to beg for more privileges; while an outcry against the privileges already granted rose from those who had not taken shares in the enterprise. Both in the company and out of it there was nothing but discontent. None were worse pleased than the two Jesuits, Carheil and Marest, who saw their flocks at Michillimackinac, both Hurons and Ottawas, lured away to a new home at Detroit. Cadillac took a peculiar satisfaction in depriving Carheil of his converts, and in 1703 we find him writing to the minister, Ponchartrain, that only twenty-five Hurons are left at Michillimackinac; and "I hope," he adds, "that in the autumn I shall pluck this last feather from his wing; and I am convinced that this obstinate priest will die in his parish without one parishioner to bury him."[3]

If the Indians came to Detroit, the French would not come. Cadillac had asked for five or six families as the modest beginning of a settlement; but not one had appeared. The Indians, too, were angry because the company asked too much for its goods; while the company complained that a forbidden trade, fatal to its interests, went on through all the region of the Upper Lakes. It was easy to ordain a monopoly, but impossible to enforce it. The prospects of the new establishment

[1] *Callières au Ministre, 9 Nov. 1700.*

[2] *Traité fait avec la Compagnie de la Colonie de Canada, 31 Oct. 1701.*

[3] *Lamothe-Cadillac à Ponchartrain, 31 Aoust, 1703* (Margry, V. 301). On Cadillac's relations with the Jesuits, see *Conseils tenus par Lamothe-Cadillac avec les Sauvages* (Margry, V. 253–300); also a curious collection of Jesuit letters sent by Cadillac to the minister, with copious annotations of his own. He excepts from his strictures Father Engelran, who, he says, incurred the ill-will of the other Jesuits by favoring the establishment of Detroit, and he also has a word of commendation for Father Germain.

were deplorable; and Cadillac lost no time in presenting his views of the situation to the court. "Detroit is good, or it is bad," he writes to Ponchartrain. "If it is good, it ought to be sustained, without allowing the people of Canada to deliberate any more about it. If it is bad, the court ought to make up its mind concerning it as soon as may be. I have said what I think. I have explained the situation. You have felt the need of Detroit, and its utility for the glory of God, the progress of religion, and the good of the colony. Nothing is left me to do but to imitate the governor of the Holy City,—take water, and wash my hands of it." His aim now appears. He says that if Detroit were made a separate government, and he were put at the head of it, its prospects would improve. "You may well believe that the company cares for nothing but to make a profit out of it. It only wants to have a storehouse and clerks; no officers, no troops, no inhabitants. Take this business in hand, Monseigneur, and I promise that in two years your Detroit shall be established of itself." He then informs the minister that as the company complain of losing money, he has told them that if they will make over their rights to him, he will pay them back all their past outlays. "I promise you," he informs Ponchartrain, "that if they accept my proposal and you approve it, I will make our Detroit flourish. Judge if it is agreeable to me to have to answer for my actions to five or six merchants [the directors of the company], who not long ago were blacking their masters' boots." He is scarcely more reserved as to the Jesuits. "I do what I can to make them my friends, but, impiety apart, one had better sin against God than against them; for in that case one gets one's pardon, whereas in the other the offence is never forgiven in this world, and perhaps never would be in the other, if their credit were as great there as it is here."[1]

The letters of Cadillac to the court are unique. No governor of New France, not even the audacious Frontenac, ever wrote to a minister of Louis XIV. with such off-hand free-

[1] *La Mothe-Cadillac à Ponchartrain 31 Août, 1703.* "Toute impiété à part, il vaudroit mieux pescher contre Dieu que contre eux, parce que d'un costé on en reçoit son pardon, et de l'autre, l'offense, mesme prétendue, n'est jamais remise dans ce monde, et ne le seroit peut-estre jamais dans l'autre, si leur crédit y estoit aussi grand qu'il est dans ce pays."

dom of language as this singular personage,—a mere captain in the colony troops; and to a more stable and balanced character it would have been impossible.

Cadillac's proposal was accepted. The company was required to abandon Detroit to him on his paying them the expenses they had incurred. Their monopoly was transferred to him; but as far as concerned beaver-skins, his trade was limited to twenty thousand francs a year. The Governor was ordered to give him as many soldiers as he might want, permit as many persons to settle at Detroit as might choose to do so, and provide missionaries.[1] The minister exhorted him to quarrel no more with the Jesuits, or anybody else, to banish blasphemy and bad morals from the post, and not to offend the Five Nations.

The promised era of prosperity did not come. Detroit lingered on in a weak and troubled infancy, disturbed, as we shall see, by startling incidents. Its occupation by the French produced a noteworthy result. The Five Nations, filled with jealousy and alarm, appealed to the King of England for protection, and, the better to insure it, conveyed the whole country from Lake Ontario northward to Lake Superior, and westward as far as Chicago, "unto our souveraigne Lord King William the Third" and his heirs and successors forever. This territory is described in the deed as being about eight hundred miles long and four hundred wide, and was claimed by the Five Nations as theirs by right of conquest.[2] It of course included Detroit itself. The conveyance was drawn by the English authorities at Albany in a form to suit their purposes, and included terms of subjection and sovereignty which the signers could understand but imperfectly, if at all. The Five Nations gave away their land to no purpose. The French remained in undisturbed possession of Detroit. The English made no attempt to enforce their title, but they put the deed on file, and used it long after as the base of their claim to the region of the Lakes.

[1] *Ponchartrain à La Mothe-Cadillac, 14 Juin, 1704.*

[2] *Deed from the Five Nations to the King of their Beaver Hunting Ground,* in *N. Y. Col. Docs.,* IV. 908. It is signed by the totems of sachems of all the Nations.

Chapter III

QUEEN ANNE'S WAR

The Forest of Maine • A Treacherous Peace • A Frontier Village • Wells and its People • Attack upon it • Border Ravages • Beaubassin's War Party • The "Woful Decade" • A Wedding Feast • A Captive Bridegroom

---

F OR UNTOLD ages Maine had been one unbroken forest, and it was so still. Only along the rocky seaboard or on the lower waters of one or two great rivers a few rough settlements had gnawed slight indentations into this wilderness of woods, and a little farther inland some dismal clearing around a blockhouse or stockade let in the sunlight to a soil that had lain in shadow time out of mind. This waste of savage vegetation survives, in some part, to this day, with the same prodigality of vital force, the same struggle for existence and mutual havoc that mark all organized beings, from men to mushrooms. Young seedlings in millions spring every summer from the black mould, rich with the decay of those that had preceded them, crowding, choking, and killing each other, perishing by their very abundance; all but a scattered few, stronger than the rest, or more fortunate in position, which survive by blighting those about them. They in turn, as they grow, interlock their boughs, and repeat in a season or two the same process of mutual suffocation. The forest is full of lean saplings dead or dying with vainly stretching towards the light. Not one infant tree in a thousand lives to maturity; yet these survivors form an innumerable host, pressed together in struggling confusion, squeezed out of symmetry and robbed of normal development, as men are said to be in the level sameness of democratic society. Seen from above, their mingled tops spread in a sea of verdure basking in light; seen from below, all is shadow, through which spots of timid sunshine steal down among legions of lank, mossy trunks, toadstools and rank ferns, protruding roots, matted bushes, and rotting carcases of fallen trees. A generation ago one might find here and there the rugged trunk of some great pine lifting its verdant spire above the undistinguished myriads of the forest. The woods of Maine had their aristocracy; but the axe of the woodman has laid them low, and these lords of the wilderness are seen no more.

The life and light of this grim solitude were in its countless streams and lakes, from little brooks stealing clear and cold under the alders, full of the small fry of trout, to the mighty arteries of the Penobscot and the Kennebec; from the great reservoir of Moosehead to a thousand nameless ponds shining in the hollow places of the forest.

It had and still has its beast of prey,—wolves, savage, cowardly, and mean; bears, gentle and mild compared to their grisly relatives of the Far West, vegetarians when they can do no better, and not without something grotesque and quaint in manners and behavior; sometimes, though rarely, the strong and sullen wolverine; frequently the lynx; and now and then the fierce and agile cougar.

The human denizens of this wilderness were no less fierce, and far more dangerous. These were the various tribes and sub-tribes of the Abenakis, whose villages were on the Saco, the Kennebec, the Penobscot, and the other great watercourses. Most of them had been converted by the Jesuits, and, as we have seen already, some had been persuaded to remove to Canada, like the converted Iroquois of Caughnawaga.[1] The rest remained in their native haunts, where, under the direction of their missionaries, they could be used to keep the English settlements in check.

We know how busily they plied their tomahawks in William and Mary's War, and what havoc they made among the scattered settlements of the border.[2] Another war with France was declared on the 4th of May, 1702, on which the Abenakis again assumed a threatening attitude. In June of the next year Dudley, Governor of Massachusetts, called the chiefs of the various bands to a council at Casco. Here presently appeared the Norridgewocks from the Kennebec, the Penobscots and Androscoggins from the rivers that bear their names, the Penacooks from the Merrimac, and the Pequawkets from the Saco, all well armed, and daubed with ceremonial paint. The

[1] *Count Frontenac,* 162.
[2] *Ibid.,* Chaps. XI., XVI., XVII.

principal among them, gathered under a large tent, were addressed by Dudley in a conciliatory speech. Their orator replied that they wanted nothing but peace, and that their thoughts were as far from war as the sun was from the earth,—words which they duly confirmed by a belt of wampum.[1] Presents were distributed among them and received with apparent satisfaction, while two of their principal chiefs, known as Captain Samuel and Captain Bomazeen, declared that several French missionaries had lately come among them to excite them against the English, but that they were "firm as mountains," and would remain so "as long as the sun and moon endured." They ended the meeting with dancing, singing, and whoops of joy, followed by a volley of musketry, answered by another from the English. It was discovered, however, that the Indians had loaded their guns with ball, intending, as the English believed, to murder Dudley and his attendants if they could have done so without danger to their chiefs, whom the Governor had prudently kept about him. It was afterwards found, if we may believe a highly respectable member of the party, that two hundred French and Indians were on their way, "resolved to seize the Governor, Council, and gentlemen, and then to sacrifice the inhabitants at pleasure;" but when they arrived, the English officials had been gone three days.[2]

The French Governor, Vaudreuil, says that about this time some of the Abenakis were killed or maltreated by English-

[1] Penhallow, *History of the Wars of New England with the Eastern Indians*, 16 (ed. 1859). Penhallow was present at the council. In Judge Sewall's clumsy abstract of the proceedings (*Diary of Sewall*, II. 85) the Indians are represented as professing neutrality. The Governor and Intendant of Canada write that the Abenakis had begun a treaty of neutrality with the English, but that as "les Jésuites observoient les sauvages, le traité ne fut pas conclu." They add that Rale, Jesuit missionary at Norridgewock, informs them that his Indians were ready to lift the hatchet against the English. *Vaudreuil et Beauharnois au Ministre, 1703.*

[2] Penhallow, 17, 18 (ed. 1859). There was a previous meeting of conciliation between the English and the Abenakis in 1702. The Jesuit Bigot says that the Indians assured him that they had scornfully repelled the overtures of the English, and told them that they would always stand fast by the French. *Relation des Abenakis, 1702.* This is not likely. The Indians probably lied both to the Jesuit and to the English, telling to each what they knew would be most acceptable.

men. It may have been so; desperadoes, drunk or sober, were not rare along the frontier: but Vaudreuil gives no particulars, and the only English outrage that appears on record at the time was the act of a gang of vagabonds who plundered the house of the younger Saint-Castin, where the town of Castine now stands. He was Abenaki by his mother; but he was absent when the attack took place, and the marauders seem to have shed no blood. Nevertheless, within six weeks after the Treaty of Casco, every unprotected farm-house in Maine was in a blaze.

The settlements of Maine, confined to the southwestern corner of what is now the State of Maine, extended along the coast in a feeble and broken line from Kittery to Casco. Ten years of murderous warfare had almost ruined them. East of the village of Wells little was left except one or two forts and the so-called "garrisons," which were private houses pierced with loopholes and having an upper story projecting over the lower, so that the defenders could fire down on assailants battering the door or piling fagots against the walls. A few were fenced with palisades, as was the case with the house of Joseph Storer, at the east end of Wells, where an overwhelming force of French and Indians had been gallantly repulsed in the summer of 1692.[1] These fortified houses were, however, very rarely attacked, except by surprise and treachery. In case of alarm such of the inhabitants as found time took refuge in them with their families, and left their dwellings to the flames; for the first thought of the settler was to put his women and children beyond reach of the scalping-knife. There were several of these asylums in different parts of Wells; and without them the place must have been abandoned. In the little settlement of York, farther westward, there were five of them, which had saved a part of the inhabitants when the rest were surprised and massacred.

Wells was a long, straggling settlement, consisting at the beginning of William and Mary's War of about eighty houses and log-cabins,[2] strung at intervals along the north side of the rough track, known as the King's Road, which ran parallel to the sea. Behind the houses were rude, half-cleared pas-

[1] See *Count Frontenac*, 255.
[2] Bourne, *History of Wells and Kennebunk*.

tures, and behind these again, the primeval forest. The cultivated land was on the south side of the road, in front of the houses, and beyond it spread great salt-marshes, bordering the sea and haunted by innumerable game-birds.

The settlements of Maine were a dependency of Massachusetts,—a position that did not please their inhabitants, but which they accepted because they needed the help of their Puritan neighbors, from whom they differed widely both in their qualities and in their faults. The Indian wars that checked their growth had kept them in a condition more than half barbarous. They were a hard-working and hard-drinking race; for though tea and coffee were scarcely known, the land flowed with New England rum, which was ranked among the necessaries of life. The better sort could read and write in a bungling way; but many were wholly illiterate, and it was not till long after Queen Anne's War that the remoter settlements established schools, taught by poor students from Harvard or less competent instructors, and held at first in private houses or under sheds. The church at Wells had been burned by the Indians; and though the settlers were beggared by the war, they voted in town meeting to build another. The new temple, begun in 1699, was a plain wooden structure thirty feet square. For want of money the windows long remained unglazed, the walls without plaster, and the floor without seats; yet services were duly held here under direction of the minister, Samuel Emery, to whom they paid £45 a year, half in provincial currency, and half in farm produce and firewood.

In spite of these efforts to maintain public worship, they were far from being a religious community; nor were they a peaceful one. Gossip and scandal ran riot; social jealousies abounded; and under what seemed entire democratic equality, the lazy, drunken, and shiftless envied the industrious and thrifty. Wells was infested, moreover, by several "frightfully turbulent women," as the chronicle styles them, from whose rabid tongues the minister himself did not always escape; and once, in its earlier days, the town had been indicted for not providing a ducking-stool to correct these breeders of discord.

Judicial officers were sometimes informally chosen by popular vote, and sometimes appointed by the Governor of Massachusetts from among the inhabitants. As they knew no law, they gave judgment according to their own ideas of justice, and their sentences were oftener wanting in wisdom than in severity. Until after 1700 the county courts met by beat of drum at some of the primitive inns or taverns with which the frontier abounded.

At Wells and other outlying and endangered hamlets life was still exceedingly rude. The log-cabins of the least thrifty were no better furnished than Indian wigwams. The house of Edmond Littlefield, reputed the richest man in Wells, consisted of two bedrooms and a kitchen, which last served a great variety of uses, and was supplied with a table, a pewter pot, a frying-pan, and a skillet; but no chairs, cups, saucers, knives, forks, or spoons. In each of the two bedrooms there was a bed, a blanket, and a chest. Another village notable— Ensign John Barrett—was better provided, being the possessor of two beds, two chests and a box, four pewter dishes, four earthen pots, two iron pots, seven trays, two buckets, some pieces of wooden-ware, a skillet, and a frying-pan. In the inventory of the patriarchal Francis Littlefield, who died in 1712, we find the exceptional items of one looking-glass, two old chairs, and two old books. Such of the family as had no bed slept on hay or straw, and no provision for the toilet is recorded.[1]

On the 10th of August, 1703, these rugged borderers were about their usual callings, unconscious of danger,—the women at their household work, the men in the fields or on the more distant salt-marshes. The wife of Thomas Wells had reached the time of her confinement, and her husband had gone for a nurse. Some miles east of Wells's cabin lived Stephen Harding,—hunter, blacksmith, and tavern-keeper, a sturdy, good-natured man, who loved the woods, and whose frequent hunting trips sometimes led him nearly to the White Mountains. Distant gunshots were heard from the westward, and his quick eye presently discovered Indians approaching, on which he told his frightened wife to go with their infant to a certain oak-tree beyond the creek while he waited to learn whether the strangers were friends or foes.

[1] The above particulars are drawn from the *History of Wells and Kennebunk*, by the late Edward E. Bourne, of Wells,—a work of admirable thoroughness, fidelity, and candor.

That morning several parties of Indians had stolen out of the dismal woods behind the houses and farms of Wells, and approached different dwellings of the far-extended settlement at about the same time. They entered the cabin of Thomas Wells, where his wife lay in the pains of childbirth, and murdered her and her two small children. At the same time they killed Joseph Sayer, a neighbor of Wells, with all his family.

Meanwhile Stephen Harding, having sent his wife and child to a safe distance, returned to his blacksmith's shop, and, seeing nobody, gave a defiant whoop; on which four Indians sprang at him from the bushes. He escaped through a back-door of the shop, eluded his pursuers, and found his wife and child in a cornfield, where the woman had fainted with fright. They spent the night in the woods, and on the next day, after a circuit of nine miles, reached the palisaded house of Joseph Storer.

They found the inmates in distress and agitation. Storer's daughter Mary, a girl of eighteen, was missing. The Indians had caught her, and afterwards carried her prisoner to Canada. Samuel Hill and his family were captured, and the younger children butchered. But it is useless to record the names and fate of the sufferers. Thirty-nine in all, chiefly women and children, were killed or carried off, and then the Indians disappeared as quickly and silently as they had come, leaving many of the houses in flames.

This raid upon Wells was only part of a combined attack on all the settlements from that place to Casco. Those eastward of Wells had been, as we have seen, abandoned in the last war, excepting the forts and fortified houses; but the inhabitants, reassured, no doubt, by the Treaty of Casco, had begun to return. On this same day, the 10th of August, they were startled from their security. A band of Indians mixed with Frenchmen fell upon the settlements about the stone fort near the Falls of the Saco, killed eleven persons, captured twenty-four, and vainly attacked the fort itself. Others surprised the settlers at a place called Spurwink, and killed or captured twenty-two. Others, again, destroyed the huts of the fishermen at Cape Porpoise, and attacked the fortified house at Winter Harbor, the inmates of which, after a brave resistance, were forced to capitulate. The settlers at Scarborough were also in a fortified house, where they made a long and obstinate defence till help at last arrived. Nine families were settled at Purpooduck Point, near the present city of Portland. They had no place of refuge, and the men, being, no doubt, fishermen, were all absent, when the Indians burst into the hamlet, butchered twenty-five women and children, and carried off eight.

The fort at Casco, or Falmouth, was held by Major March, with thirty-six men. He had no thought of danger, when three well-known chiefs from Norridgewock appeared with a white flag, and asked for an interview. As they seemed to be alone and unarmed, he went to meet them, followed by two or three soldiers and accompanied by two old men named Phippeny and Kent, inhabitants of the place. They had hardly reached the spot when the three chiefs drew hatchets from under a kind of mantle which they wore and sprang upon them, while other Indians, ambushed near by, leaped up and joined in the attack. The two old men were killed at once; but March, who was noted for strength and agility, wrenched a hatchet from one of his assailants, and kept them all at bay till Sergeant Hook came to his aid with a file of men and drove them off.

They soon reappeared, burned the deserted cabins in the neighborhood, and beset the garrison in numbers that continually increased, till in a few days the entire force that had been busied in ravaging the scattered settlements was gathered around the place. It consisted of about five hundred Indians of several tribes, and a few Frenchmen under an officer named Beaubassin. Being elated with past successes, they laid siege to the fort, sheltering themselves under a steep bank by the water-side and burrowing their way towards the rampart. March could not dislodge them, and they continued their approaches till the third day, when Captain Southack, with the Massachusetts armed vessel known as the "Province Galley," sailed into the harbor, recaptured three small vessels that the Indians had taken along the coast, and destroyed a great number of their canoes, on which they gave up their enterprise and disappeared.[1]

[1] On these attacks on the frontier of Maine, Penhallow, who well knew the country and the people, is the best authority. Niles, in his *Indian and French*

Such was the beginning of Queen Anne's War. These attacks were due less to the Abenakis than to the French who set them on. "Monsieur de Vaudreuil," writes the Jesuit historian Charlevoix, "formed a party of these savages, to whom he joined some Frenchmen under the direction of the Sieur de Beaubassin, when they effected some ravages of no great consequence; they killed, however, about three hundred men." This last statement is doubly incorrect. The whole number of persons killed and carried off during the August attacks did not much exceed one hundred and sixty;[1] and these were of both sexes and all ages, from octogenarians to new-born infants. The able-bodied men among them were few, as most of the attacks were made upon unprotected houses in the absence of the head of the family; and the only fortified place captured was the garrison-house at Winter Harbor, which surrendered on terms of capitulation. The instruments of this ignoble warfare and the revolting atrocities that accompanied it, were all, or nearly all, converted Indians of the missions. Charlevoix has no word of disapproval for it, and seems to regard its partial success as a gratifying one so far as it went.

One of the objects was, no doubt, to check the progress of the English settlements; but, pursues Charlevoix, "the essential point was to commit the Abenakis in such a manner that they could not draw back."[2] This object was constantly kept in view. The French claimed at this time that the territory of Acadia reached as far westward as the Kennebec, which therefore formed, in their view, the boundary between the rival nations, and they trusted in the Abenakis to defend this assumed line of demarcation. But the Abenakis sorely needed English guns, knives, hatchets, and kettles, and nothing but

---

Wars, copies him without acknowledgment, but not without blunders. As regards the attack on Wells, what particulars we have are mainly due to the research of the indefatigable Bourne. Compare Belknap, I. 330; Folsom, *History of Saco and Biddeford*, 198; *Coll. Maine Hist. Soc.*, III. 140, 348; Williamson, *History of Maine*, II. 42. Beaubassin is called "Bobasser" in most of the English accounts.

[1] The careful and well-informed Belknap puts it at only 130. *History of New Hampshire*, I. 331.

[2] Charlevoix, II. 289–290 (quarto edition).

the utmost vigilance could prevent them from coming to terms with those who could supply their necessities. Hence the policy of the French authorities on the frontier of New England was the opposite of their policy on the frontier of New York. They left the latter undisturbed, lest by attacking the Dutch and English settlers they should stir up the Five Nations to attack Canada; while, on the other hand, they constantly spurred the Abenakis against New England, in order to avert the dreaded event of their making peace with her.

The attack on Wells, Casco, and the intervening settlements was followed by murders and depredations that lasted through the autumn and extended along two hundred miles of frontier. Thirty Indians attacked the village of Hampton, killed the widow Mussey, a famous Quakeress, and then fled to escape pursuit. At Black Point nineteen men going to their work in the meadows were ambushed by two hundred Indians, and all but one were shot or captured. The fort was next attacked. It was garrisoned by eight men under Lieutenant Wyatt, who stood their ground for some time, and then escaped by means of a sloop in the harbor. At York the wife and children of Arthur Brandon were killed, and the Widow Parsons and her daughter carried off. At Berwick the Indians attacked the fortified house of Andrew Neal, but were repulsed with the loss of nine killed and many wounded, for which they revenged themselves by burning alive Joseph Ring, a prisoner whom they had taken. Early in February a small party of them hovered about the fortified house of Joseph Bradley at Haverhill, till, seeing the gate open and nobody on the watch, they rushed in. The woman of the house was boiling soap, and in her desperation she snatched up the kettle and threw the contents over them with such effect that one of them, it is said, was scalded to death. The man who should have been on the watch was killed, and several persons were captured, including the woman. It was the second time that she had been a prisoner in Indian hands. Half starved and bearing a heavy load, she followed her captors in their hasty retreat towards Canada. After a time she was safely delivered of an infant in the midst of the winter forest; but the child pined for want of sustenance, and the Indians hastened its death by throwing hot coals into its mouth when it cried.

The astonishing vitality of the woman carried her to the end of the frightful journey. A Frenchman bought her from the Indians, and she was finally ransomed by her husband.

By far the most dangerous and harassing attacks were those of small parties skulking under the edge of the forest, or lying hidden for days together, watching their opportunity to murder unawares, and vanishing when they had done so. Against such an enemy there was no defence. The Massachusetts Government sent a troop of horse to Portsmouth, and another to Wells. These had the advantage of rapid movement in case of alarm along the roads and forest-paths from settlement to settlement; but once in the woods, their horses were worse than useless, and they could only fight on foot. Fighting, however, was rarely possible; for on reaching the scene of action they found nothing but mangled corpses and burning houses.

The best defence was to take the offensive. In September Governor Dudley sent three hundred and sixty men to the upper Saco, the haunt of the Pequawket tribe; but the place was deserted. Major, now Colonel, March soon after repeated the attempt, killing six Indians and capturing as many more. The General Court offered £40 for every Indian scalp, and one Captain Tyng, in consequence, surprised an Indian village in midwinter and brought back five of these disgusting trophies. In the spring of 1704 word came from Albany that a band of French Indians had built a fort and planted corn at Co-os meadows, high up the river Connecticut. On this, one Caleb Lyman with five friendly Indians, probably Mohegans, set out from Northampton, and after a long march through the forest, surprised, under cover of a thunderstorm, a wigwam containing nine warriors,—bound, no doubt, against the frontier. They killed seven of them; and this was all that was done at present in the way of reprisal or prevention.[1]

The murders and burnings along the borders were destined to continue with little variety and little interruption during ten years. It was a repetition of what the pedantic Cotton Mather calls *Decennium luctuosum*, or the "woful decade" of William and Mary's War. The wonder is that the outlying settlements were not abandoned. These ghastly, insidious,

---

[1] Penhallow, *Wars of New England with the Eastern Indians*.

and ever-present dangers demanded a more obstinate courage than the hottest battle in the open field.

One curious frontier incident may be mentioned here, though it did not happen till towards the end of the war. In spite of poverty, danger, and tribulation, marrying and giving in marriage did not cease among the sturdy borderers; and on a day in September there was a notable wedding feast at the palisaded house of John Wheelwright, one of the chief men of Wells. Elisha Plaisted was to espouse Wheelwright's daughter Hannah, and many guests were assembled, some from Portsmouth, and even beyond it. Probably most of them came in sail-boats; for the way by land was full of peril, especially on the road from York, which ran through dense woods, where Indians often waylaid the traveller. The bridegroom's father was present with the rest. It was a concourse of men in homespun, and women and girls in such improvised finery as their poor resources could supply; possibly, in default of better, some wore nightgowns, more or less disguised, over their daily dress, as happened on similar occasions half a century later among the frontiersmen of west Virginia.[1] After an evening of rough merriment and gymnastic dancing, the guests lay down to sleep under the roof of their host or in adjacent barns and sheds. When morning came, and they were preparing to depart, it was found that two horses were missing; and not doubting that they had strayed away, three young men, Sergeant Tucker, Joshua Downing, and Isaac Cole, went to find them. In a few minutes several gunshots were heard. The three young men did not return. Downing and Cole were killed, and Tucker was wounded and made prisoner.

Believing that, as usual, the attack came from some small scalping party, Elisha Plaisted and eight or ten more threw themselves on the horses that stood saddled before the house, and galloped across the fields in the direction of the firing; while others ran to cut off the enemy's retreat. A volley was presently heard, and several of the party were seen running back towards the house. Elisha Plaisted and his companions had fallen into an ambuscade of two hundred Indians. One or more of them were shot, and the unfortunate bridegroom

[1] Doddridge, *Notes on Western Virginia and Pennsylvania.*

was captured. The distress of his young wife, who was but eighteen, may be imagined.

Two companies of armed men in the pay of Massachusetts were then in Wells, and some of them had come to the wedding. Seventy marksmen went to meet the Indians, who ensconced themselves in the edge of the forest, whence they could not be dislodged. There was some desultory firing, and one of the combatants was killed on each side, after which the whites gave up the attack, and Lieutenant Banks went forward with a flag of truce, in the hope of ransoming the prisoners. He was met by six chiefs, among whom were two noted Indians of his acquaintance, Bomazeen and Captain Nathaniel. They well knew that the living Plaisted was worth more than his scalp; and though they would not come to terms at once, they promised to meet the English at Richmond's Island in a few days and give up both him and Tucker on payment of a sufficient ransom. The flag of truce was respected, and Banks came back safe, bringing a hasty note to the elder Plaisted from his captive son. This note now lies before me, and it runs thus, in the dutiful formality of the olden time:

SIR,—I am in the hands of a great many Indians, with which there is six captains. They say that what they will have for me is 50 pounds, and thirty pounds for Tucker, my fellow prisoner, in good goods, as broadcloth, some provisions, some tobacco pipes, Pomisstone [pumicestone], stockings, and a little of all things. If you will, come to Richmond's Island in 5 days at farthest, for here is 200 Indians, and they belong to Canada.

If you do not come in 5 days, you will not see me, for Captain Nathaniel the Indian will not stay no longer, for the Canada Indians is not willing for to sell me. Pray, Sir, don't fail, for they have given me one day, for the days were but 4 at first. Give my kind love to my dear wife. This from your dutiful son till death,

ELISHA PLAISTED

The alarm being spread and a sufficient number of men mustered, they set out to attack the enemy and recover the prisoners by force; but not an Indian could be found.

Bomazeen and Captain Nathaniel were true to the rendez-vous; in due time Elisha Plaisted was ransomed and restored to his bride.[1]

[1] On this affair, the note of Elisha Plaisted in Massachusetts Archives; *Richard Waldron to Governor Dudley, Portsmouth, 19 Sept. 1712*; Bourne, *Wells and Kennebunk*, 278.

Chapter IV

1704—1740

DEERFIELD

*Hertel de Rouville • A Frontier Village • Rev. John Williams •
The Surprise • Defence of the Stebbins House • Attempted Rescue
• The Meadow Fight • The Captives • The Northward March •
Mrs. Williams killed • The Minister's Journey • Kindness of
Canadians • A Stubborn Heretic • Eunice Williams • Con-
verted Captives • John Sheldon's Mission • Exchange of Prisoners
• An English Squaw • The Gill Family*

ABOUT midwinter the Governor of Canada sent another
large war-party against the New England border. The
object of attack was an unoffending hamlet, that from its position could never be a menace to the French, and the destruction of which could profit them nothing. The aim of the
enterprise was not military, but political. "I have sent no war-
party towards Albany," writes Vaudreuil, "because we must
do nothing that might cause a rupture between us and the
Iroquois; but we must keep things astir in the direction of
Boston, or else the Abenakis will declare for the English." In
short, the object was fully to commit these savages to hostility
against New England, and convince them at the same time
that the French would back their quarrel.[1]

The party consisted, according to French accounts, of fifty
Canadians and two hundred Abenakis and Caughnawagas,—
the latter of whom, while trading constantly with Albany,
were rarely averse to a raid against Massachusetts or New
Hampshire.[2] The command was given to the younger Hertel
de Rouville, who was accompanied by four of his brothers.
They began their march in the depth of winter, journeyed

---

[1] *Vaudreuil au Ministre, 14 Nov. 1703; Ibid., 3 Avril, 1704; Vaudreuil et Beauharnois au Ministre, 17 Nov. 1704.* French writers say that the English surprised
and killed some of the Abenakis, who thereupon asked help from Canada.
This perhaps refers to the expeditions of Colonel March and Captain Tyng,
who, after the bloody attacks upon the settlements of Maine, made reprisal
upon Abenaki camps.

[2] English accounts make the whole number 342.

nearly three hundred miles on snow-shoes through the forest, and approached their destination on the afternoon of the 28th of February, 1704. It was the village of Deerfield,—which then formed the extreme northwestern frontier of Massachusetts, its feeble neighbor, the infant settlement of Northfield, a little higher up the Connecticut, having been abandoned during the last war. Rouville halted his followers at a place now called Petty's Plain, two miles from the village; and here, under the shelter of a pine forest, they all lay hidden, shivering with cold,—for they dared not make fires,—and hungry as wolves, for their provisions were spent. Though their numbers, by the lowest account, were nearly equal to the whole population of Deerfield,—men, women, and children,—they had no thought of an open attack, but trusted to darkness and surprise for an easy victory.

Deerfield stood on a plateau above the river meadows, and the houses—forty-one in all—were chiefly along the road towards the villages of Hadley and Hatfield, a few miles distant. In the middle of the place, on a rising ground called Meeting-house Hill, was a small square wooden meeting-house. This, with about fifteen private houses, besides barns and sheds, was enclosed by a fence of palisades eight feet high, flanked by "mounts," or block-houses, at two or more of the corners. The four sides of this palisaded enclosure, which was called the fort, measured in all no less than two hundred and two rods, and within it lived some of the principal inhabitants of the village, of which it formed the centre or citadel. Chief among its inmates was John Williams, the minister, a man of character and education, who, after graduating at Harvard, had come to Deerfield when it was still suffering under the ruinous effects of King Philip's War, and entered on his ministry with a salary of sixty pounds in depreciated New England currency, payable, not in money, but in wheat, Indian-corn, and pork.[1] His parishioners built him a house, he married, and had now eight children, one of whom was absent with friends at Hadley.[2] His next neighbor was Benoni Stebbins, sergeant in the county militia, who lived a few rods from the meeting-house. About fifty yards distant, and near

[1] Stephen W. Williams, *Biographical Memoir of Rev. John Williams.*
[2] *Account of y* destruction of Deref*d, Feb. 29, 1703/4.*

the northwest angle of the enclosure, stood the house of Ensign John Sheldon, a framed building, one of the largest in
the village, and, like that of Stebbins, made bullet-proof by a
layer of bricks between the outer and inner sheathing, while
its small windows and its projecting upper story also helped
to make it defensible.

The space enclosed by the palisade, though much too large
for effective defence, served in time of alarm as an asylum for
the inhabitants outside, whose houses were scattered,—some
on the north towards the hidden enemy, and some on the
south towards Hadley and Hatfield. Among those on the
south side was that of the militia captain, Jonathan Wells,
which had a palisade of its own, and, like the so-called fort,
served as an asylum for the neighbors.

These private fortified houses were sometimes built by the
owners alone, though more often they were the joint work of
the owners and of the inhabitants, to whose safety they contributed. The palisade fence that enclosed the central part of
the village was made under a vote of the town, each inhabitant being required to do his share; and as they were greatly
impoverished by the last war, the General Court of the province remitted for a time a part of their taxes in consideration
of a work which aided the general defence.[1]

Down to the Peace of Ryswick the neighborhood had been
constantly infested by scalping-parties, and once the village
had been attacked by a considerable force of French and Indians, who were beaten off. Of late there had been warnings
of fresh disturbance. Lord Cornbury, Governor of New York,
wrote that he had heard through spies that Deerfield was
again to be attacked, and a message to the same effect came
from Peter Schuyler, who had received intimations of the
danger from Mohawks lately on a visit to their Caughnawaga
relatives. During the autumn the alarm was so great that the
people took refuge within the palisades, and the houses of the
enclosure were crowded with them; but the panic had now
subsided, and many, though not all, had returned to their
homes. They were reassured by the presence of twenty vol-

---

[1] Papers in the Archives of Massachusetts. Among these, a letter of Rev.
John Williams to the Governor, 21 Oct. 1703, states that the palisade is rotten,
and must be rebuilt.

unteers from the villages below, who, on application from the minister, Williams, the General Court had sent as a garrison to Deerfield, where they were lodged in the houses of the villagers. On the night when Hertel de Rouville and his band lay hidden among the pines there were in all the settlement a little less than three hundred souls, of whom two hundred and sixty-eight were inhabitants, twenty were yeomen soldiers of the garrison, two were visitors from Hatfield, and three were negro slaves. They were of all ages, — from the Widow Allison, in her eighty-fifth year, to the infant son of Deacon French, aged four weeks.[1]

Heavy snows had lately fallen and buried the clearings, the meadow, and the frozen river to the depth of full three feet. On the northwestern side the drifts were piled nearly to the top of the palisade fence, so that it was no longer an obstruction to an active enemy.

As the afternoon waned, the sights and sounds of the little border hamlet were, no doubt, like those of any other rustic New England village at the end of a winter day, — an ox-sledge creaking on the frosty snow as it brought in the last load of firewood, boys in homespun snowballing each other in the village street, farmers feeding their horses and cattle in the barns, a matron drawing a pail of water with the help of one of those long well-sweeps still used in some remote districts, or a girl bringing a pail of milk from the cow-shed. In the houses, where one room served as kitchen, dining-room, and parlor, the housewife cooked the evening meal, children sat at their bowls of mush and milk, and the men of the family, their day's work over, gathered about the fire, while perhaps some village coquette sat in the corner with fingers busy at the spinning-wheel, and ears intent on the stammered wooings of her rustic lover. Deerfield kept early hours, and it is likely that by nine o'clock all were in their beds. There was a patrol inside the palisade, but there was little discipline among these extemporized soldiers; the watchers grew care-

[1] The names of nearly all the inhabitants are preserved, and even the ages of most of them have been ascertained, through the indefatigable research of Mr. George Sheldon, of Deerfield, among contemporary records. The house of Thomas French, the town clerk, was not destroyed, and his papers were saved.

less as the frosty night went on; and it is said that towards morning they, like the villagers, betook themselves to their beds.

Rouville and his men, savage with hunger, lay shivering under the pines till about two hours before dawn; then, leaving their packs and their snow-shoes behind, they moved cautiously towards their prey. There was a crust on the snow strong enough to bear their weight, though not to prevent a rustling noise as it crunched under the feet of so many men. It is said that from time to time Rouville commanded a halt, in order that the sentinels, if such there were, might mistake the distant sound for rising and falling gusts of wind. In any case, no alarm was given till they had mounted the palisade and dropped silently into the unconscious village. Then with one accord they screeched the war-whoop, and assailed the doors of the houses with axes and hatchets. The hideous din startled the minister, Williams, from his sleep. Half-wakened, he sprang out of bed, and saw dimly a crowd of savages bursting through the shattered door. He shouted to two soldiers who were lodged in the house; and then, with more valor than discretion, snatched a pistol that hung at the head of the bed, cocked it, and snapped it at the breast of the foremost Indian, who proved to be a Caughnawaga chief. It missed fire, or Williams would, no doubt, have been killed on the spot. Amid the screams of his terrified children, three of the party seized him and bound him fast; for they came well provided with cords, since prisoners had a market value. Nevertheless in the first fury of their attack they dragged to the door and murdered two of the children and a negro woman called Parthena, who was probably their nurse. In an upper room lodged a young man named Stoddard, who had time to snatch a cloak, throw himself out of the window, climb the palisade, and escape in the darkness. Half-naked as he was, he made his way over the snow to Hatfield, binding his bare feet with strips torn from the cloak.

They kept Williams shivering in his shirt for an hour while a frightful uproar of yells, shrieks, and gunshots sounded from without. At length they permitted him, his wife, and five remaining children to dress themselves. Meanwhile the Indians and their allies burst into most of the houses, killed such of the men as resisted, butchered some of the women and children, and seized and bound the rest. Some of the villagers escaped in the confusion, like Stoddard, and either fled half dead with cold towards Hatfield, or sought refuge in the fortified house of Jonathan Wells.

The house of Stebbins, the minister's next neighbor, had not been attacked so soon as the rest, and the inmates had a little time for preparation. They consisted of Stebbins himself, with his wife and five children, David Hoyt, Joseph Catlin, Benjamin Church, a namesake of the old Indian fighter of Philip's War, and three other men,—probably refugees who had brought their wives and families within the palisaded enclosure for safety. Thus the house contained seven men, four or five women, and a considerable number of children. Though the walls were bullet-proof, it was not built for defence. The men, however, were well supplied with guns, powder, and lead, and they seem to have found some means of barricading the windows. When the enemy tried to break in, they drove them back with loss. On this, the French and Indians gathered in great numbers before the house, showered bullets upon it, and tried to set it on fire. They were again repulsed, with the loss of several killed and wounded; among the former a Caughnawaga chief, and among the latter a French officer. Still the firing continued. If the assailants had made a resolute assault, the defenders must have been overpowered; but to risk lives in open attack was contrary to every maxim of forest warfare. The women in the house behaved with great courage, and moulded bullets, which the men shot at the enemy. Stebbins was killed outright, and Church was wounded, as was also the wife of David Hoyt. At length most of the French and Indians, disgusted with the obstinacy of the defence, turned their attention to other quarters; though some kept up their fire under cover of the meeting-house and another building within easy range of gunshot.

This building was the house of Ensign John Sheldon, already mentioned. The Indians had had some difficulty in mastering it; for the door being of thick oak plank, studded with nails of wrought iron and well barred, they could not break it open. After a time, however, they hacked a hole in it, through which they fired and killed Mrs. Sheldon as she sat on the edge of a bed in a lower room. Her husband, a man of great resolution, seems to have been absent. Their son John, with Hannah his wife, jumped from an upper chamber window. The young woman sprained her ankle in the fall, and lay helpless, but begged her husband to run to Hatfield for aid, which he did, while she remained a prisoner. The Indians soon got in at a back door, seized Mercy Sheldon, a little girl of two years, and dashed out her brains on the door-stone. Her two brothers and her sister Mary, a girl of sixteen, were captured. The house was used for a short time as a de-pot for prisoners, and here also was brought the French offi-cer wounded in the attack on the Stebbins house. A family tradition relates that as he lay in great torment he begged for water, and that it was brought him by one of the prisoners, Mrs. John Catlin, whose husband, son, and infant grandson had been killed, and who, nevertheless, did all in her power to relieve the sufferings of the wounded man. Probably it was in recognition of this charity that when the other prisoners were led away, Mrs. Catlin was left behind. She died of grief a few weeks later.

The sun was scarcely an hour high when the miserable drove of captives was conducted across the river to the foot of a mountain or high hill. Williams and his family were soon compelled to follow, and his house was set on fire. As they led him off he saw that other houses within the palisade were burning, and that all were in the power of the enemy except that of his neighbor Stebbins, where the gallant defenders still kept their assailants at bay. Having collected all their prison-ers, the main body of the French and Indians began to with-draw towards the pine forest, where they had left their packs and snow-shoes, and to prepare for a retreat before the coun-try should be roused, first murdering in cold blood Marah Carter, a little girl of five years, whom they probably thought unequal to the march. Several parties, however, still lingered in the village, firing on the Stebbins house, killing cattle, hogs, and sheep, and gathering such plunder as the place afforded.

Early in the attack, and while it was yet dark, the light of burning houses, reflected from the fields of snow, had been seen at Hatfield, Hadley, and Northampton. The alarm was sounded through the slumbering hamlets, and parties of men mounted on farm-horses, with saddles or without, hastened to the rescue, not doubting that the fires were kindled by Indians. When the sun was about two hours high, between thirty and forty of them were gathered at the fortified house of Jonathan Wells, at the southern end of the village. The houses of this neighborhood were still standing, and seem not to have been attacked; the stubborn defence of the Stebbins house having apparently prevented the enemy from pushing much beyond the palisaded enclosure. The house of Wells was full of refugee families. A few Deerfield men here joined the horsemen from the lower towns, as also did four or five of the yeoman soldiers who had escaped the fate of most of their comrades. The horsemen left their horses within Wells's fence; he himself took the lead, and the whole party rushed in together at the southern gate of the palisaded enclosure, drove out the plunderers, and retook a part of their plunder. The assailants of the Stebbins house, after firing at it for three hours, were put to flight, and those of its male occupants who were still alive joined their countrymen, while the women and children ran back for harborage to the house of Wells.

Wells and his men, now upwards of fifty, drove the flying enemy more than a mile across the river meadows, and ran in headlong pursuit over the crusted snow, killing a considerable number. In the eagerness of the chase many threw off their overcoats, and even their jackets. Wells saw the danger, and vainly called on them to stop. Their blood was up, and most of them were young and inexperienced.

Meanwhile the firing at the village had been heard by Rouville's main body, who had already begun their retreat northward. They turned back to support their comrades, and hid themselves under the bank of the river till the pursuers drew near, when they gave them a close volley and rushed upon them with the war-whoop. Some of the English were shot down, and the rest driven back. There was no panic. "We retreated," says Wells, "facing about and firing." When they reached the palisade they made a final stand, covering by their fire such of their comrades as had fallen within range of musket-shot, and thus saving them from the scalping-knife.

The French did not try to dislodge them. Nine of them had been killed, several were wounded, and one was captured.[1]

The number of English carried off prisoners was one hundred and eleven, and the number killed was according to one list forty-seven, and according to another fifty-three, the latter including some who were smothered in the cellars of their burning houses. The names, and in most cases the ages, of both captives and slain are preserved. Those who escaped with life and freedom were, by the best account, one hundred and thirty-seven. An official tabular statement, drawn up on the spot, sets the number of houses burned at seventeen. The house of the town clerk, Thomas French, escaped, as before mentioned, and the town records, with other papers in his charge, were saved. The meeting-house also was left standing. The house of Sheldon was hastily set on fire by the French and Indians when their rear was driven out of the village by Wells and his men; but the fire was extinguished, and "the Old Indian House," as it was called, stood till the year 1849. Its door, deeply scarred with hatchets, and with a hole cut near the middle, is still preserved in the Memorial Hall at Deerfield.[2]

Vaudreuil wrote to the minister, Ponchartrain, that the French lost two or three killed, and twenty or twenty-one wounded, Rouville himself being among the latter. This cannot include the Indians, since there is proof that the enemy

[1] On the 31st of May, 1704, Jonathan Wells and Ebenezer Wright petitioned the General Court for compensation for the losses of those who drove the enemy out of Deerfield and chased them into the meadow. The petition, which was granted, gives an account of the affair, followed by a list of all the men engaged. They number fifty-seven, including the nine who were killed. A list of the plunder re-taken from the enemy, consisting of guns, blankets, hatchets, etc., is also added. Several other petitions for the relief of men wounded at the same time are preserved in the archives of Massachusetts. In 1736 the survivors of the party, with the representatives of those who had died, petitioned the General Court for allotments of land, in recognition of their services. This petition also was granted. It is accompanied by a narrative written by Wells. These and other papers on the same subject have been recently printed by Mr. George Sheldon, of Deerfield.

[2] After the old house was demolished, this door was purchased by my friend Dr. Daniel Denison Slade, and given by him to the town of Deerfield, on condition that it should be carefully preserved. For an engraving of "the Old Indian House," see Hoyt, *Indian Wars* (ed. 1824).

left behind a considerable number of their dead. Wherever resistance was possible, it had been of the most prompt and determined character.[1]

Long before noon the French and Indians were on their northward march with their train of captives. More armed men came up from the settlements below, and by midnight about eighty were gathered at the ruined village. Couriers had been sent to rouse the country, and before evening of the next day (the 1st of March) the force at Deerfield was increased to two hundred and fifty; but a thaw and a warm rain had set in, and as few of the men had snow-shoes, pursuit was out of the question. Even could the agile savages and their allies have been overtaken, the probable consequence would have been the murdering of the captives to prevent their escape.

In spite of the foul blow dealt upon it, Deerfield was not abandoned. Such of its men as were left were taken as soldiers into the pay of the province, while the women and children were sent to the villages below. A small garrison was also stationed at the spot, under command of Captain Jonathan Wells, and thus the village held its ground till the storm of war should pass over.[2]

[1] Governor Dudley, writing to Lord ——— on 21 April, 1704, says that thirty dead bodies of the enemy were found in the village and on the meadow. Williams, the minister, says that they did not seem inclined to rejoice over their success, and continued for several days to bury members of their party who died of wounds on the return march. He adds that he learned in Canada that they lost more than forty, though Vaudreuil assured him that they lost but eleven.

[2] On the attack of Deerfield, Williams, *The Redeemed Captive Returning to Zion*. This is the narrative of the minister, John Williams. *Account of the Captivity of Stephen Williams, written by himself*. This is the narrative of one of the minister's sons, eleven years old when captured. It is printed in the Appendix to the *Biographical Memoir of Rev. John Williams* (Hartford, 1837); *An account of ye destruction at Derefd. febr. 29, 1703/4*, in *Proceedings of the Mass. Hist. Soc.*, 1867, p. 478. This valuable document was found among the papers of Fitz-John Winthrop, Governor of Connecticut. The authorities of that province, on hearing of the catastrophe at Deerfield, promptly sent an armed force to its relief, which, however, could not arrive till long after the enemy were gone. The paper in question seems to be the official report of one of the Connecticut officers. After recounting what had taken place, he gives a tabular list of the captives, the slain, and those who escaped, with the estimated losses in property of each inhabitant. The list of captives is not quite complete. Compare the lists given by Stephen Williams at the end of his narra-

We have seen that the minister, Williams, with his wife and family were led from their burning house across the river to the foot of the mountain, where the crowd of terrified and disconsolate captives—friends, neighbors, and relatives—were already gathered. Here they presently saw the fight in the meadow, and were told that if their countrymen attempted a rescue, they should all be put to death. "After this," writes Williams, "we went up the mountain, and saw the smoke of the fires in town, and beheld the awful desolation of Deerfield; and before we marched any farther they killed a sucking child of the English."

The French and Indians marched that afternoon only four or five miles,—to Greenfield meadows,—where they stopped to encamp, dug away the snow, laid spruce-boughs on the ground for beds, and bound fast such of the prisoners as seemed able to escape. The Indians then held a carousal on some liquor they had found in the village, and in their drunken rage murdered a negro man belonging to Williams. In spite of their precautions, Joseph Alexander, one of the prisoners, escaped during the night, at which they were greatly incensed; and Rouville ordered Williams to tell his com-

---

tive. The town records of Hatfield give various particulars concerning the attack on its unfortunate neighbor, as do the letters of Col. Samuel Partridge, commanding the militia of the county. Hoyt, *Antiquarian Researches*, gives a valuable account of it. The careful and unwearied research of Mr. George Sheldon, the lineal descendant of Ensign John Sheldon, among all sources, public or private, manuscript or in print, that could throw light on the subject cannot be too strongly commended, and I am indebted to him for much valued information.

Penhallow's short account is inexact, and many of the more recent narratives are not only exaggerated, but sometimes absurdly incorrect.

The French notices of the affair are short, and give few particulars. Vaudreuil in one letter sets the number of prisoners at one hundred and fifty, and increases it in another to two hundred and fifty. Ramesay, Governor of Montreal, who hated Hertel de Rouville, and bore no love to Vaudreuil, says that fifty-six women and children were murdered on the way to Canada,—which is a gross exaggeration. *Ramesay au Ministre, 14 Nov. 1704.* The account by Dr. Ethier in the *Revue Canadienne* of 1874 is drawn entirely from the *Redeemed Captive* of Williams, with running comments by the Canadian writer, but no new information. The comments chiefly consist in praise of Williams for truth when he speaks favorably of the Canadians, and charges of lying when he speaks otherwise.

panions in misfortune that if any more of them ran off, the rest should be burned alive.[1]

The prisoners were the property of those who had taken them. Williams had two masters; one of the three who had seized him having been shot in the attack on the house of Stebbins. His principal owner was a surly fellow who would not let him speak to the other prisoners; but as he was presently chosen to guard the rear, the minister was left in the hands of his other master, who allowed him to walk beside his wife and help her on the way. Having borne a child a few weeks before, she was in no condition for such a march, and felt that her hour was near. Williams speaks of her in the strongest terms of affection. She made no complaint, and accepted her fate with resignation. "We discoursed," he says, "of the happiness of those who had God for a father and friend, as also that it was our reasonable duty quietly to submit to his will." Her thoughts were for her remaining children, whom she commended to her husband's care. Their intercourse was short. The Indian who had gone to the rear of the train soon returned, separated them, ordered Williams to the front, "and so made me take a last farewell of my dear wife, the desire of my eyes and companion in many mercies and afflictions." They came soon after to Green River, a stream then about knee-deep, and so swift that the water had not frozen. After wading it with difficulty, they climbed a snow-covered hill beyond. The minister, with strength almost spent, was permitted to rest a few moments at the top; and as the other prisoners passed by in turn, he questioned each for news of his wife. He was not left long in suspense. She had fallen from weakness in fording the stream, but gained her feet again, and, drenched in the icy current, struggled to the farther bank, when the savage who owned her, finding that she could not climb the hill, killed her with one stroke of his hatchet. Her body was left on the snow till a few of her townsmen, who had followed the trail, found it a day or two after, carried it back to Deerfield, and buried it in the churchyard.

On the next day the Indians killed an infant and a little girl

[1] John Williams, *The Redeemed Captive*. Compare Stephen Williams, *Account of the Captivity*, etc.

of eleven years; on the day following, Friday, they toma-hawked a woman, and on Saturday four others. This apparent cruelty was in fact a kind of mercy. The victims could not keep up with the party, and the death-blow saved them from a lonely and lingering death from cold and starvation. Some of the children, when spent with the march, were carried on the backs of their owners,—partly, perhaps, through kind-ness, and partly because every child had its price.

On the fourth day of the march they came to the mouth of West River, which enters the Connecticut a little above the present town of Brattleboro'. Some of the Indians were dis-contented with the distribution of the captives, alleging that others had got more than their share; on which the whole troop were mustered together, and some changes of owner-ship were agreed upon. At this place, dog-trains and sledges had been left, and these served to carry their wounded, as well as some of the captive children. Williams was stripped of the better part of his clothes, and others given him instead, so full of vermin that they were a torment to him through all the journey. The march now continued with pitiless speed up the frozen Connecticut, where the recent thaw had cov-ered the ice with slush and water ankle-deep.

On Sunday they made a halt, and the minister was permit-ted to preach a sermon from the text, "Hear, all people, and behold my sorrow: my virgins and my young men are gone into captivity." Then amid the ice, the snow, the forest, and the savages, his forlorn flock joined their voices in a psalm.[1] On Monday, guns were heard from the rear, and the Indians and their allies, in great alarm, bound their prisoners fast, and prepared for battle. It proved, however, that the guns had been fired at wild geese by some of their own number; on which they recovered their spirits, fired a volley for joy, and boasted that the English could not overtake them.[2] More women fainted by the way and died under the hatchet,— some with pious resignation, some with despairing apathy, some with a desperate joy.

[1] The small stream at the mouth of which Williams is supposed to have preached is still called Williams River.

[2] Stephen Williams, *Account of the Captivity*, etc. His father also notices the incident.

Two hundred miles of wilderness still lay between them and the Canadian settlements. It was a waste without a house or even a wigwam; except here and there the bark shed of some savage hunter. At the mouth of White River, the party divided into small bands,—no doubt in order to subsist by hunting, for provisions were fast failing. The Williams family were separated. Stephen was carried up the Connecticut; Samuel and Eunice, with two younger children, were carried off in various directions; while the wretched father, along with two small children of one of his parishioners, was compelled to follow his Indian masters up the valley of White River. One of the children—a little girl—was killed on the next morning by her Caughnawaga owner, who was unable to carry her.[1] On the next Sunday, the minister was left in camp with one Indian and the surviving child,—a boy of nine,—while the rest of the party were hunting. "My spirit," he says, "was almost overwhelmed within me." But he found comfort in the text, "Leave thy fatherless children, I will preserve them alive." Nor was his hope deceived. His youngest surviving child,—a boy of four,— though harshly treated by his owners, was carried on their shoulders or dragged on a sledge to the end of the journey. His youngest daughter—seven years old—was treated with great kindness throughout. Samuel and Eunice suffered much from hunger, but were dragged on sledges when too faint to walk. Stephen nearly starved to death; but after eight months in the forest, he safely reached Chambly with his Indian masters.

Of the whole band of captives, only about half ever again saw friends and home. Seventeen broke down on the way and were killed; while David Hoyt and Jacob Hix died of starvation at Coos meadows, on the upper Connecticut. During the entire march, no woman seems to have been subjected to violence; and this holds true, with rare exceptions, in all the Indian wars of New England. This remarkable forbearance towards female prisoners, so different from the practice of many Western tribes, was probably due to a form of superstition, aided perhaps by the influence of the mission-

---

[1] The name Macquas (Mohawks) is always given to the Caughnawagas by the elder Williams.

aries.[1] It is to be observed, however, that the heathen savages of King Philip's War, who had never seen a Jesuit, were no less forbearing in this respect.

The hunters of Williams's party killed five moose, the flesh of which, smoked and dried, was carried on their backs and that of the prisoner, whom they had provided with snow-shoes. Thus burdened, the minister toiled on, following his masters along the frozen current of White River till, crossing the snowy backs of the Green Mountains, they struck the headwaters of the stream then called French River, now the Winooski, or Onion. Being in great fear of a thaw, they pushed on with double speed. Williams was not used to snow-shoes, and they gave him those painful cramps of the legs and ankles called in Canada *mal à la raquette*. One morning at dawn, he was waked by his chief master and ordered to get up, say his prayers, and eat his breakfast, for they must make a long march that day. The minister was in despair. "After prayer," he says, "I arose from my knees; but my feet were so tender, swollen, bruised, and full of pain that I could scarce stand upon them without holding on the wigwam. And when the Indians said, 'You must run to-day,' I answered I could not run. My master, pointing to his hatchet, said to me, 'Then I must dash out your brains and take your scalp.'" The Indian proved better than his word, and Williams was suffered to struggle on as he could. "God wonderfully supported me," he writes, "and my strength was restored and renewed to admiration." He thinks that he walked that day forty miles on the snow. Following the Winooski to its mouth, the party reached Lake Champlain a little north of the present city of Burlington. Here the swollen feet of the prisoner were tortured by the rough ice, till snow began to fall and cover it with a soft carpet. Bending under his load, and powdered by the falling flakes, he toiled on till, at noon of a Saturday, lean, tired, and ragged, he and his masters reached the French outpost of Chambly, twelve or fifteen miles from Montreal.

Here the unhappy wayfarer was treated with great kindness both by the officers of the fort and by the inhabitants, one of

[1] The Iroquois are well known to have had superstitions in connection with sexual abstinence.

the chief among whom lodged him in his house and welcomed him to his table. After a short stay at Chambly, Williams and his masters set out in a canoe for Sorel. On the way a Frenchwoman came down to the bank of the river and invited the party to her house, telling the minister that she herself had once been a prisoner among the Indians, and knew how to feel for him. She seated him at a table, spread a tablecloth, and placed food before him, while the Indians, to their great indignation, were supplied with a meal in the chimney-corner. Similar kindness was shown by the inhabitants along the way till the party reached their destination, the Abenaki village of St. Francis, to which his masters belonged. Here there was a fort, in which lived two Jesuits, directors of the mission, and here Williams found several English children, captured the summer before during the raid on the settlements of Maine, and already transformed into little Indians both in dress and behavior. At the gate of the fort one of the Jesuits met him, and asked him to go into the church and give thanks to God for sparing his life, to which he replied that he would give thanks in some other place. The priest then commanded him to go, which he refused to do. When on the next day the bell rang for mass, one of his Indian masters seized him and dragged him into the church, where he got behind the door, and watched the service from his retreat with extreme disapprobation. One of the Jesuits telling him that he would go to hell for not accepting the apostolic traditions, and trusting only in the Bible, he replied that he was glad to know that Christ was to be his judge, and not they. His chief master, who was a zealot in his way, and as much bound to the rites and forms of the Church as he had been before his conversion, to his "medicines," or practices of heathen superstition, one day ordered him to make the sign of the cross, and on his refusal, tried to force him. But as the minister was tough and muscular, the Indian could not guide his hand. Then, pulling out a crucifix that hung at his neck, he told Williams in broken English to kiss it; and being again refused, brandished his hatchet over him and threatened to knock out his brains. This failing of the desired effect, he threw down the hatchet and said he would first bite out the minister's finger-nails,—a form of torture then in vogue among the northern Indians, both converts and heathen. Williams offered him a hand and invited him to begin; on which he gave the thumb-nail a gripe with his teeth, and then let it go, saying, "No good minister, bad as the devil." The failure seems to have discouraged him, for he made no further attempt to convert the intractable heretic.

The direct and simple narrative of Williams is plainly the work of an honest and courageous man. He was the most important capture of the year; and the Governor, hearing that he was at St. Francis, despatched a canoe to request the Jesuits of the mission to send him to Montreal. Thither, therefore, his masters carried him, expecting, no doubt, a good price for their prisoner. Vaudreuil, in fact, bought him, exchanged his tattered clothes for good ones, lodged him in his house, and, in the words of Williams, "was in all respects relating to my outward man courteous and charitable to admiration." He sent for two of the minister's children who were in the town, bought his eldest daughter from the Indians, and promised to do what he could to get the others out of their hands. His youngest son was bought by a lady of the place, and his eldest by a merchant. His youngest daughter, Eunice, then seven or eight years old, was at the mission of St. Louis, or Caughnawaga. Vaudreuil sent a priest to conduct Williams thither and try to ransom the child. But the Jesuits of the mission flatly refused to let him speak to or see her. Williams says that Vaudreuil was very angry at hearing of this; and a few days after, he went himself to Caughnawaga with the minister. This time the Jesuits, whose authority within their mission seemed almost to override that of the Governor himself, yielded so far as to permit the father to see his child, on condition that he spoke to no other English prisoner. He talked with her for an hour, exhorting her never to forget her catechism, which she had learned by rote. Vaudreuil and his wife afterwards did all in their power to procure her ransom; but the Indians, or the missionaries in their name, would not let her go. "She is there still," writes Williams two years later, "and has forgotten to speak English." What grieved him still more, Eunice had forgotten her catechism.

While he was at Montreal, his movements were continually

watched, lest he should speak to other prisoners and prevent their conversion. He thinks these precautions were due to the priests, whose constant endeavor it was to turn the captives, or at least the younger and more manageable among them, into Catholics and Canadians. The Governor's kindness towards him never failed, though he told him that he should not be set free till the English gave up one Captain Baptiste, a noted sea-rover whom they had captured some time before.

He was soon after sent down the river to Quebec along with the superior of the Jesuits. Here he lodged seven weeks with a member of the council, who treated him kindly, but told him that if he did not avoid intercourse with the other English prisoners he would be sent farther away. He saw much of the Jesuits, who courteously asked him to dine; though he says that one of them afterwards made some Latin verses about him, in which he was likened to a captive wolf. Another Jesuit told him that when the mission Indians set out on their raid against Deerfield, he charged them to baptize all children before killing them,—such, he said, was his desire for the salvation even of his enemies. To murdering the children after they were baptized, he appears to have made no objection. Williams says that in their dread lest he should prevent the conversion of the other prisoners, the missionaries promised him a pension from the King and free intercourse with his children and neighbors if he would embrace the Catholic faith and remain in Canada; to which he answered that he would do so without reward if he thought their religion was true, but as he believed the contrary, "the offer of the whole world would tempt him no more than a blackberry."

To prevent him more effectually from perverting the minds of his captive countrymen, and fortifying them in their heresy, he was sent to Château Richer, a little below Quebec, and lodged with the parish priest, who was very kind to him. "I am persuaded," he writes, "that he abhorred their sending down the heathen to commit outrages against the English, saying it is more like committing murders than carrying on war."

He was sorely tried by the incessant efforts to convert the prisoners. "Sometimes they would tell me my children, sometimes my neighbors, were turned to be of their religion. Some made it their work to allure poor souls by flatteries and great promises; some threatened, some offered abuse to such as refused to go to church and be present at mass; and some they industriously contrived to get married among them. I understood they would tell the English that I was turned, that they might gain them to change their religion. These their endeavors to seduce to popery were very exercising to me."

After a time he was permitted to return to Quebec, where he met an English Franciscan, who, he says, had been sent from France to aid in converting the prisoners. Lest the minister should counteract the efforts of the friar, the priests had him sent back to Château Richer; "but," he observes, "God showed his dislike of such a persecuting spirit; for the very next day the Seminary, a very famous building, was most of it burnt down, by a joiner letting a coal of fire drop among the shavings."[1]

The heaviest of all his tribulations now fell upon him. His son Samuel, about sixteen years old, had been kept at Montreal under the tutelage of Father Meriel, a priest of St.-Sulpice. The boy afterwards declared that he was promised great rewards if he would make the sign of the cross, and severe punishment if he would not. Proving obstinate, he was whipped till at last he made the sign; after which he was told to go to mass, and on his refusal, four stout boys of the school were ordered to drag him in. Williams presently received a letter in Samuel's handwriting, though dictated, as the father believed, by his priestly tutors. In this was recounted, with many edifying particulars, the deathbed conversion of two New England women; and to the minister's unspeakable grief and horror, the messenger who brought the letter told him that the boy himself had turned Catholic. "I have heard the news," he wrote to his recreant son, "with the most distressing, afflicting, sorrowful spirit. Oh, I pity you, I mourn over you day and night. Oh, I pity your weakness that, through the craftiness of man, you are turned from the simplicity of the gospel." Though his correspondence was strictly watched, he managed to convey to the boy a long

[1]Williams remarks that the Seminary had also been burned three years before. This was the fire of November, 1701. See *Old Régime in Canada*, 1370.

exposition, from his own pen, of the infallible truth of Calvinistic orthodoxy, and the damnable errors of Rome. This, or something else, had its effect. Samuel returned to the creed of his fathers; and being at last exchanged, went home to Deerfield, where he was chosen town-clerk in 1713, and where he soon after died.[1]

Williams gives many particulars of the efforts of the priests to convert the prisoners, and his account, like the rest of his story, bears the marks of truth. There was a treble motive for conversion: it recruited the Church, weakened the enemy, and strengthened Canada, since few of the converts would peril their souls by returning to their heretic relatives. The means of conversion varied. They were gentle when gentleness seemed likely to answer the purpose. Little girls and young women were placed in convents, where it is safe to assume that they were treated with the most tender kindness by the sisterhood, who fully believed that to gain them to the faith was to snatch them from perdition. But when they or their brothers proved obdurate, different means were used. Threats of hell were varied by threats of a whipping, which, according to Williams, were often put into execution. Parents were rigorously severed from their families; though one Lalande, who had been set to watch the elder prisoners, reported that they would persist in trying to see their children, till some of them were killed in the attempt. "Here," writes Williams, "might be a history in itself of the trials and sufferings of many of our children, who, after separation from grown persons, have been made to do as they would have them. I mourned when I thought with myself that I had one child with the Maquas [Caughnawagas], a second turned papist, and a little child of six years of age in danger to be instructed in popery, and knew full well that all endeavors would be used to prevent my seeing or speaking with them." He also says that he and others were told that if they would turn Catholic their children should be restored to them; and among other devices, some of his parishioners were assured that their pastor himself had seen the error of his ways and bowed in submission to Holy Church.

In midwinter, not quite a year after their capture, the pris-

[1] Note of Mr. George Sheldon.

oners were visited by a gleam of hope. John Sheldon, accompanied by young John Wells, of Deerfield, and Captain Livingston, of Albany, came to Montreal with letters from Governor Dudley, proposing an exchange. Sheldon's wife and infant child, his brother-in-law, and his son-in-law had been killed. Four of his children, with his daughter-in-law, Hannah,—the same who had sprained her ankle in leaping from her chamber window,—besides others of his near relatives and connections, were prisoners in Canada; and so also was the mother of young Wells. In the last December, Sheldon and Wells had gone to Boston and begged to be sent as envoys to the French Governor. The petition was readily granted, and Livingston, who chanced to be in the town, was engaged to accompany them. After a snow-shoe journey of extreme hardship they reached their destination and were received with courtesy by Vaudreuil. But difficulties arose. The French, and above all the clergy, were unwilling to part with captives, many of whom they hoped to transform into Canadians by conversion and adoption. Many also were in the hands of the Indians, who demanded payment for them,— which Dudley had always refused, declaring that he would not "set up an Algiers trade" by buying them from their pretended owners; and he wrote to Vaudreuil that for his own part he "would never permit a savage to tell him that any Christian prisoner was at his disposal." Vaudreuil had insisted that his Indians could not be compelled to give up their captives, since they were not subjects of France, but only allies,— which, so far as concerned the mission Indians within the colony, was but a pretext. It is true, however, that the French authorities were in such fear of offending even these that they rarely ventured to cross their interests or their passions. Other difficulties were raised, and though the envoys remained in Canada till late in spring, they accomplished little. At last, probably to get rid of their importunities, five prisoners were given up to them,—Sheldon's daughter-in-law, Hannah; Esther Williams, eldest daughter of the minister; a certain Ebenezer Carter; and two others unknown. With these, Sheldon and his companions set out in May on their return; and soon after they were gone, four young men, Baker, Nims, Kellogg, and Petty, desperate at being left in captivity, made their escape from Montreal, and reached Deerfield before the end of June, half dead with hunger.

Sheldon and his party were escorted homeward by eight soldiers under Courtemanche, an officer of distinction, whose orders were to "make himself acquainted with the country." He fell ill at Boston, where he was treated with much kindness, and on his recovery was sent home by sea, along with Captain Vetch and Samuel Hill, charged to open a fresh negotiation. With these, at the request of Courtemanche, went young William Dudley, son of the Governor.[1]

They were received at Quebec with a courtesy qualified by extreme caution, lest they should spy out the secrets of the land. The mission was not very successful, though the elder Dudley had now a good number of French prisoners in his hands, captured in Acadia or on the adjacent seas. A few only of the English were released, including the boy, Stephen Williams, whom Vaudreuil had bought for forty crowns from his Indian master.

In the following winter John Sheldon made another journey on foot to Canada, with larger powers than before. He arrived in March, 1706, and returned with forty-four of his released countrymen, who, says Williams, were chiefly adults permitted to go because there was no hope of converting them. The English Governor had by this time seen the necessity of greater concessions, and had even consented to release the noted Captain Baptiste, whom the Boston merchants regarded as a pirate. In the same summer Samuel Appleton and John Bonner, in the brigantine "Hope," brought a considerable number of French prisoners to Quebec, and returned to Boston at the end of October with fifty-seven English, of all ages. For three, at least, of this number money was paid by the English, probably on account of prisoners bought by Frenchmen from the Indians. The minister, Williams, was exchanged for Baptiste, the so-called pirate, and two of his children were also redeemed, though the Caughnawagas, or their

---

[1] The elder Dudley speaks with great warmth of Courtemanche, who, on his part, seems equally pleased with his entertainers. Young Dudley was a boy of eighteen. "Il a du mérite," says Vaudreuil. *Dudley to Vaudreuil, 4 July, 1705; Vaudreuil au Ministre, 19 Oct. 1705.*

missionaries, refused to part with his daughter Eunice. Williams says that the priests made great efforts to induce the prisoners to remain in Canada, tempting some with the prospect of pensions from the King, and frightening others with promises of damnation, joined with predictions of shipwreck on the way home. He thinks that about one hundred were left in Canada, many of whom were children in the hands of the Indians, who could easily hide them in the woods, and who were known in some cases to have done so. Seven more were redeemed in the following year by the indefatigable Sheldon, on a third visit to Canada.[1]

The exchanged prisoners had been captured at various times and places. Those from Deerfield amounted in all to about sixty, or a little more than half the whole number carried off. Most of the others were dead or converted. Some married Canadians, and others their fellow captives. The history of some of them can be traced with certainty. Thus, Thomas French, blacksmith and town clerk of Deerfield, and deacon of the church, was captured, with his wife and six children. His wife and infant child were killed on the way to Canada. He and his two eldest children were exchanged and brought home. His daughter Freedom was converted, baptized under the name of Marie Françoise, and married to Jean Daulnay, a Canadian. His daughter Martha was baptized as Marguerite and married to Jacques Roy, on whose death she married Jean Louis Ménard, by whom she became ancestress of Joseph Plessis, eleventh bishop of Quebec. Elizabeth Corse, eight years old when captured, was baptized under her own name, and married to Jean Dumontel. Abigail Stebbins, baptized as Marguerite, lived many years at Boucherville, wife of Jacques de Noyon, a sergeant in the colony troops. The widow Sarah Hurst, whose youngest child, Benjamin, had

---

[1] In 1878 Miss C. Alice Baker, of Cambridge, Mass., a descendant of Abigail Stebbins, read a paper on John Sheldon before the Memorial Association at Deerfield. It is the result of great research, and contains much original matter, including correspondence between Sheldon and the captives when in Canada, as well as a full and authentic account of his several missions. Mr. George Sheldon has also traced out with great minuteness the history of his ancestor's negotiations.

been murdered on the Deerfield meadows, was baptized as Marie Jeanne.[1] Joanna Kellogg, eleven years old when taken, married a Caughnawaga chief, and became, at all points, an Indian squaw.

She was not alone in this strange transformation. Eunice Williams, the namesake of her slaughtered mother, remained in the wigwams of the Caughnawagas, forgot, as we have seen, her English and her catechism, was baptized, and in due time married to an Indian of the tribe, who thenceforward called himself Williams. Thus her hybrid children bore her family name. Her father, who returned to his parish at Deerfield, and her brother Stephen, who became a minister like his parent, never ceased to pray for her return to her country and her faith. Many years after, in 1740, she came with her husband to visit her relatives in Deerfield, dressed as a squaw and wrapped in an Indian blanket. Nothing would induce her to stay, though she was persuaded on one occasion to put on a civilized dress and go to church; after which she impatiently discarded her gown and resumed her blanket. As she was kindly treated by her relatives, and as no attempt was made to detain her against her will, she came again in the next year, bringing two of her half-breed children; and twice afterwards repeated the visit. She and her husband were offered a tract of land if they would settle in New England; but she positively refused, saying that it would endanger her soul. She lived to a great age, a squaw to the last.[2]

One of her grandsons, Eleazer Williams, turned Protestant, was educated at Dartmouth College at the charge of friends

[1] The above is drawn mainly from extracts made by Miss Baker from the registers of the Church of Notre Dame at Montreal. Many of the acts of baptism bear the signature of Father Meriel, so often mentioned in the narrative of Williams. Apparently, Meriel spoke English. At least there is a letter in English from him, relating to Eunice Williams, in the Massachusetts Archives, Vol. 51. Some of the correspondence between Dudley and Vaudreuil concerning exchange of prisoners will be found among the Paris documents in the State House at Boston. Copies of these papers were printed at Quebec in 1883–1885, though with many inaccuracies.

[2] Stephen W. Williams, *Memoir of the Rev. John Williams*, 53. *Sermon preached at Mansfield, Aug. 4, 1741, on behalf of Mrs. Eunice, the daughter of Rev. John Williams; by Solomon Williams, A.M. Letter of Mrs. Colton, great granddaughter of John Williams* (in appendix to the *Memoir of Rev. John Williams*).

in New England, and was for a time missionary to the Indians of Green Bay, in Wisconsin. His character for veracity was not of the best. He deceived the excellent antiquarian, Hoyt, by various inventions touching the attack on Deerfield, and in the latter part of his life tried to pass himself off as the lost Dauphin, son of Louis XVI.[1]

Here it may be observed that the descendants of young captives brought into Canada by the mission Indians during the various wars with the English colonies became a considerable element in the Canadian population. Perhaps the most prominent example is that of the Gill family. A few years after the capture of Deerfield, Samuel Gill, a boy of fourteen, was taken by the Abenakis on the Connecticut, near the present town of Greenfield. They carried him to St. Francis, where he was converted, and in 1715 married to a young girl whose family name was James, and who had been captured at the same time and place. In 1866 the late Abbé Maurault, missionary at St. Francis, computed their descendants at nine hundred and fifty-two, in whose veins French, English, and Abenaki blood were mixed in every conceivable proportion. He gives the tables of genealogy in full, and says that two hundred and thirteen of this prolific race still bear the surname of Gill. "If," concludes the worthy priest, "one should trace out all the English families brought into Canada by the Abenakis, one would be astonished at the number of persons who to-day are indebted to these savages for the blessing of being Catholics

[1] I remember to have seen Eleazer Williams at my father's house in Boston, when a boy. My impression of him is that of a good-looking and somewhat portly man, showing little trace of Indian blood, and whose features, I was told, resembled those of the Bourbons. Probably this likeness, real or imagined, suggested the imposition he was practising at the time. The story of the "Bell of St. Regis" is probably another of his inventions. It is to the effect that the bell of the church at Deerfield was carried by the Indians to the mission of St. Regis, and that it is there still. But there is reason to believe that there was no church bell at Deerfield, and it is certain that St. Regis did not exist till more than a half century after Deerfield was attacked. It has been said that the story is true, except that the name of Caughnawaga should be substituted for that of St. Regis, but the evidence for this conjecture is weak. On the legend of the bell, see Le Moine, *Maple Leaves, New Series* (1873) 29; *Proceedings of the Mass. Hist. Soc.*, 1869, 1870, 311; *Hist. Mag. 2d Series*, IX. 401. Hough, *Hist. St. Lawrence and Franklin Counties*, 116, gives the story without criticism.

and the advantage of being Canadians,"[1] — an advantage for which French-Canadians are so ungrateful that they migrate to the United States by myriads.

[1] Maurault, *Hist. des Abenakis*, 377. I am indebted to R. A. Ramsay, Esq., of Montreal, for a paper on the Gill family, by Mr. Charles Gill, who confirms the statements of Maurault so far as relates to the genealogies.

John and Zechariah Tarbell, captured when boys at Groton, became Caughnawaga chiefs, and one of them, about 1760, founded the mission of St. Regis. Green, *Groton during the Indian Wars*, 116, 117–120.

Chapter V

THE TORMENTED FRONTIER

Border Raids • Haverhill • Attack and Defence • War to the Knife • Motives of the French • Proposed Neutrality • Joseph Dudley • Town and Country

I HAVE told the fate of Deerfield in full, as an example of the desolating raids which for years swept the borders of Massachusetts and New Hampshire. The rest of the miserable story may be passed more briefly. It is in the main a weary detail of the murder of one, two, three, or more men, women, or children waylaid in fields, woods, and lonely roads, or surprised in solitary cabins. Sometimes the attacks were on a larger scale. Thus, not long after the capture of Deerfield, a band of fifty or more Indians fell at dawn of day on a hamlet of five houses near Northampton. The alarm was sounded, and they were pursued. Eight of the prisoners were rescued, and three escaped; most of the others being knocked in the head by their captors. At Oyster River the Indians attacked a loopholed house, in which the women of the neighboring farms had taken refuge while the men were at work in the fields. The women disguised themselves in hats and jackets, fired from the loopholes, and drove off the assailants. In 1709, a hundred and eighty French and Indians again attacked Deerfield, but failed to surprise it, and were put to flight. At Dover, on a Sunday, while the people were at church, a scalping party approached a fortified house, the garrison of which consisted of one woman,—Esther Jones, who, on seeing them, called out to an imaginary force within, "Here they are! come on! come on!"—on which the Indians disappeared.

Soon after the capture of Deerfield, the French authorities, being, according to the prisoner Williams, "wonderfully lifted up with pride," formed a grand war-party, and assured the minister that they would catch so many prisoners that they should not know what to do with them. Beaucour, an officer of great repute, had chief command, and his force consisted of between seven and eight hundred men, of whom about a hundred and twenty were French, and the rest mission Indians.[1] They declared that they would lay waste all the settlements on the Connecticut,—meaning, it seems, to begin with Hatfield. "This army," says Williams, "went away in such a boasting, triumphant manner that I had great hopes God would discover and disappoint their designs." In fact, their plans came to nought, owing, according to French accounts, to the fright of the Indians; for a soldier having deserted within a day's march of the English settlements, most of them turned back, despairing of a surprise, and the rest broke up into small parties to gather scalps on the outlying farms.[2]

In the summer of 1708 there was a more successful attempt. The converts of all the Canadian missions were mustered at Montreal, where Vaudreuil, by exercising, as he says, "the patience of an angel," soothed their mutual jealousies and persuaded them to go upon a war-party against Newbury, Portsmouth, and other New England villages. Fortunately for the English, the Caughnawagas were only half-hearted towards the enterprise; and through them the watchful Peter Schuyler got hints of it which enabled him, at the eleventh hour, to set the intended victims on their guard. The party consisted of about four hundred, of whom one hundred were French, under twelve young officers and cadets; the whole commanded by Saint-Ours des Chaillons and Hertel de Rouville. For the sake of speed and secrecy, they set out in three bodies, by different routes. The rendezvous was at Lake Winnepesaukee, where they were to be joined by the Norridgewocks, Penobscots, and other eastern Abenakis. The Caughnawagas and Hurons turned back by reason of evil omens and a disease which broke out among them. The rest met on the shores of the lake,—probably at Alton Bay,—where, after waiting in vain for their Eastern allies, they resolved to make no attempt on Portsmouth or Newbury, but to turn all their strength upon the smaller village of Haverhill, on the Merrimac. Advancing quickly under cover of night, they made their onslaught at half an hour before dawn, on Sunday, the 29th of August.

[1] *Vaudreuil et Beauharnois au Ministre, 17 Nov. 1704.*
[2] *Ibid.; Vaudreuil au Ministre, 16 Nov. 1704; Ramesay au Ministre, 14 Nov. 1704.* Compare Penhallow.

Haverhill consisted of between twenty and thirty dwelling-houses, a meeting-house, and a small picket fort. A body of militia from the lower Massachusetts towns had been hastily distributed along the frontier, on the vague reports of danger sent by Schuyler from Albany; and as the intended point of attack was unknown, the men were of necessity widely scattered. French accounts say that there were thirty of them in the fort at Haverhill, and more in the houses of the villagers; while others still were posted among the distant farms and hamlets.

In spite of darkness and surprise, the assailants met a stiff resistance and a hot and persistent fusillade. Vaudreuil says that they could dislodge the defenders only by setting fire to both houses and fort. In this they were not very successful, as but few of the dwellings were burned. A fire was kindled against the meeting-house, which was saved by one Davis and a few others, who made a dash from behind the adjacent parsonage, drove the Indians off, and put out the flames. Rolfe, the minister, had already been killed while defending his house. His wife and one of his children were butchered; but two others—little girls of six and eight years—were saved by the self-devotion of his maid-servant, Hagar, apparently a negress, who dragged them into the cellar and hid them under two inverted tubs, where they crouched, dumb with terror, while the Indians ransacked the place without finding them. English accounts say that the number of persons killed—men, women, and children—was forty-eight; which the French increase to a hundred.

The distant roll of drums was presently heard, warning the people on the scattered farms; on which the assailants made a hasty retreat. Posted near Haverhill were three militia officers,—Turner, Price, and Gardner,—lately arrived from Salem. With such men as they had with them, or could hastily get together, they ambushed themselves at the edge of a piece of woods, in the path of the retiring enemy, to the number, as the French say, of sixty or seventy, which it is safe to diminish by a half. The French and Indians, approaching rapidly, were met by a volley which stopped them for the moment; then, throwing down their packs, they rushed on, and after a sharp skirmish broke through the ambuscade and continued their retreat. Vaudreuil sets their total loss at eight killed and eighteen wounded,—the former including two officers, Verchères and Chambly. He further declares that in the skirmish all the English, except ten or twelve, were killed outright; while the English accounts say that the French and Indians took to the woods, leaving nine of their number dead on the spot, along with their medicine chest and all their packs.[1]

Scarcely a hamlet of the Massachusetts and New Hampshire borders escaped a visit from the nimble enemy. Groton, Lancaster, Exeter, Dover, Kittery, Casco, Kingston, York, Berwick, Wells, Winter Harbor, Brookfield, Amesbury, Marlborough, were all more or less infested, usually by small scalping parties, hiding in the outskirts, waylaying stragglers, or shooting men at work in the fields, and disappearing as soon as their blow was struck. These swift and intangible persecutors were found a far surer and more effectual means of annoyance than larger bodies. As all the warriors were converts of the Canadian missions, and as prisoners were an article of value, cases of torture were not very common; though now and then, as at Exeter, they would roast some poor wretch alive, or bite off his fingers and sear the stumps with red-hot tobacco pipes.

This system of petty, secret, and transient attack put the impoverished colonies to an immense charge in maintaining a cordon of militia along their northern frontier,—a precaution often as vain as it was costly; for the wily savages, covered by the forest, found little difficulty in dodging the scouting-parties, pouncing on their victims, and escaping. Rewards were offered for scalps; but one writer calculates that, all things considered, it cost Massachusetts a thousand pounds of her currency to kill an Indian.[2]

In 1703–1704, six hundred men were kept ranging the woods all winter without finding a single Indian, the enemy

---

[1] *Vaudreuil au Ministre, 5 Nov. 1708*; *Vaudreuil et Raudot au Ministre, 14 Nov. 1708*; Hutchinson, II. 156; *Mass. Hist. Coll.*, 2d Series, IV. 129; Sewall, *Diary*, II. 234. Penhallow.

[2] The rewards for scalps were confined to male Indians thought old enough to bear arms,—that is to say, above twelve years. *Act of General Court, 19 Aug. 1706.*

having deserted their usual haunts and sought refuge with the French, to emerge in February for the destruction of Deerfield. In the next summer, nineteen hundred men were posted along two hundred miles of frontier.[1] This attitude of passive defence exasperated the young men of Massachusetts, and it is said that five hundred of them begged Dudley for leave to make a raid into Canada, on the characteristic condition of choosing their own officers. The Governor consented; but on a message from Peter Schuyler that he had at last got a promise from the Caughnawagas and other mission Indians to attack the New England borders no more, the raid was countermanded, lest it should waken the tempest anew.[2]

What was the object of these murderous attacks, which stung the enemy without disabling him, confirmed the Indians in their native savagery, and taught the French to emulate it? In the time of Frontenac there was a palliating motive for such barbarous warfare. Canada was then prostrate and stunned under the blows of the Iroquois war. Successful war-parties were needed as a tonic and a stimulant to rouse the dashed spirits of French and Indians alike; but the remedy was a dangerous one, and it drew upon the colony the attack under Sir William Phips, which was near proving its ruin. At present there was no such pressing call for butchering women, children, and peaceful farmers. The motive, such as it was, lay in the fear that the Indian allies of France might pass over to the English, or at least stand neutral. These allies were the Christian savages of the missions, who, all told, from the Caughnawagas to the Micmacs, could hardly have mustered a thousand warriors. The danger was that the Caughnawagas, always open to influence from Albany, might be induced to lay down the hatchet and persuade the rest to follow their example. Therefore, as there was for the time a vir-

---

[1] *Dudley to Lord* ———, *21 April, 1704. Address of Council and Assembly to the Queen, 12 July, 1704.* The burden on the people was so severe that one writer—not remarkable, however, for exactness of statement—declares that he "is credibly informed that some have been forced to cut open their beds and sell the feathers to pay their taxes." The general poverty did not prevent a contribution in New England for the suffering inhabitants of the island of St. Christopher.

[2] *Vaudreuil au Ministre, 12 Nov. 1708.* Vaudreuil says that he got his information from prisoners.

tual truce with New York, no pains were spared to commit them irrevocably to war against New England. With the Abenaki tribes of Maine and New Hampshire the need was still more urgent, for they were continually drawn to New England by the cheapness and excellence of English goods; and the only sure means to prevent their trading with the enemy was to incite them to kill him. Some of these savages had been settled in Canada, to keep them under influence and out of temptation; but the rest were still in their native haunts, where it was thought best to keep them well watched by their missionaries, as sentinels and outposts to the colony.

There were those among the French to whom this barbarous warfare was repugnant. The minister, Ponchartrain, by no means a person of tender scruples, also condemned it for a time. After the attack on Wells and other places under Beaubassin in 1703, he wrote: "It would have been well if this expedition had not taken place. I have certain knowledge that the English want only peace, knowing that war is contrary to the interests of all the colonies. Hostilities in Canada have always been begun by the French."[1] Afterwards, when these bloody raids had produced their natural effect and spurred the sufferers to attempt the ending of their woes once for all by the conquest of Canada, Ponchartrain changed his mind and encouraged the sending out of war-parties, to keep the English busy at home.

The schemes of a radical cure date from the attack on Deerfield and the murders of the following summer. In the autumn we find Governor Dudley urging the capture of Quebec. "In the last two years," he says, "the Assembly of Massachusetts has spent about £50,000 in defending the

---

[1] *Resumé d'une Lettre de MM. de Vaudreuil et de Beauharnois du 15 Nov. 1703, avec les Observations du Ministre.* Subercase, governor of Acadia, writes on 25 Dec. 1708, that he hears that a party of Canadians and Indians have attacked a place on the *Maramet* (Merrimac), "et qu'ils y ont égorgé 4 à 500 personnes sans faire quartier aux femmes ni aux enfans." This is an exaggerated report of the affair of Haverhill. M. de Chevry writes in the margin of the letter: "Ces actions de cruauté devroient être modérées;" to which Ponchartrain adds: "Bon; les défendre." His attitude, however, was uncertain; for as early as 1707 we find him approving Vaudreuil for directing the missionaries to prompt the Abenakis to war. *N. Y. Col. Docs.*, IX. 805.

Province, whereas three or four of the Queen's ships and fifteen hundred New England men would rid us of the French and make further outlay needless,"—a view, it must be admitted, sufficiently sanguine.[1]

But before seeking peace with the sword, Dudley tried less strenuous methods. It may be remembered that in 1705 Captain Vetch and Samuel Hill, together with the Governor's young son William, went to Quebec to procure an exchange of prisoners. Their mission had also another object. Vetch carried a letter from Dudley to Vaudreuil, proposing a treaty of neutrality between their respective colonies, and Vaudreuil seems to have welcomed the proposal. Notwithstanding the pacific relations between Canada and New York, he was in constant fear that Dutch and English influence might turn the Five Nations into open enemies of the French; and he therefore declared himself ready to accept the proposals of Dudley, on condition that New York and the other English colonies should be included in the treaty, and that the English should be excluded from fishing in the Gulf of St. Lawrence and the Acadian seas. The first condition was difficult, and the second impracticable; for nothing could have induced the people of New England to accept it. Vaudreuil, moreover, would not promise to give up prisoners in the hands of the Indians, but only to do what he could to persuade their owners to give them up. The negotiations dragged on for several years. For the first three or four months Vaudreuil stopped his warparties; but he let them loose again in the spring, and the New England borders were tormented as before.

The French Governor thought that the New England country people, who had to bear the brunt of the war, were ready to accept his terms. The French court approved the plan, though not without distrust; for some enemy of the Governor told Ponchartrain that under pretence of negotiations he and Dudley were carrying on trading speculations,— which is certainly a baseless slander.[2] Vaudreuil on his part had strongly suspected Dudley's emissary, Vetch, of illicit trade during his visit to Quebec; and perhaps there was

[1] *Dudley to ———, 26 Nov. 1704.*
[2] *Abrégé d'une lettre de M. de Vaudreuil, avec les notes du Ministre, 19 Oct. 1705.*

ground for the suspicion. It is certain that Vetch, who had visited the St. Lawrence before, lost no opportunity of studying the river, and looked forward to a time when he could turn his knowledge to practical account.[1]

Joseph Dudley, governor of Massachusetts and New Hampshire, was the son of a former Governor of Massachusetts, that upright, sturdy, narrow, bigoted old Puritan, Thomas Dudley, in whose pocket was found after his death the notable couplet:

> "Let men of God in courts and churches watch
> O'er such as do a toleration hatch."

Such a son of such a father was the marvel of New England. Those who clung to the old traditions and mourned for the old theocracy under the old charter, hated Joseph Dudley as a renegade; and the worshippers of the Puritans have not forgiven him to this day. He had been president of the council under the detested Andros, and when that representative of the Stuarts was overthrown by a popular revolution, both he and Dudley were sent prisoners to England. Here they found a reception different from the expectations and wishes of those who sent them. Dudley became a member of Parliament and lieutenant-governor of the Isle of Wight, and was at length, in the beginning of the reign of Queen Anne, sent back to govern those who had cast him out. Any governor imposed on them by England would have been an offence; but Joseph Dudley was more than they could bear.

He found bitter opposition from the old Puritan party. The two Mathers, father and son, who through policy had at first favored him, soon denounced him with insolent malignity, and the honest and conscientious Samuel Sewall regarded him with as much asperity as his kindly nature would permit. To the party of religious and political independency he was an abomination, and great efforts were made to get him recalled. Two pamphlets of the time, one printed in 1707 and the other

[1] On the negotiations for neutrality, see the correspondence and other papers in the *Paris Documents* in the Boston State House; also *N. Y. Col. Docs.*, IX. 770, 776, 779, 809; Hutchinson, II. 141.

in the next year, reflect the bitter animosity he excited.[1] Both seem to be the work of several persons, one of whom, there can be little doubt, was Cotton Mather; for it is not easy to mistake the mingled flippancy and pedantry of his style. He bore the Governor a grudge, for Dudley had chafed him in his inordinate vanity and love of power.

If Dudley loved himself first, he loved his native New England next, and was glad to serve her if he could do so in his own way and without too much sacrifice of his own interests. He was possessed by a restless ambition, apparently of the cheap kind that prefers the first place in a small community to the second in a large one. He was skilled in the arts of the politician, and knew how, by attentions, dinners, or commissions in the militia, to influence his Council and Assembly to do his will. His abilities were beyond question, and his manners easy and graceful; but his instincts were arbitrary. He stood fast for prerogative, and even his hereditary Calvinism had strong Episcopal leanings. He was a man of the world in the better as well as the worse sense of the term; was loved and admired by some as much as he was hated by others; and in the words of one of his successors, "had as many virtues as can consist with so great a thirst for honor and power."[2]

His enemies, however, set no bounds to their denunciation. "All the people here are bought and sold betwixt the Governour and his son Paul," says one. "It is my belief," says another, probably Cotton Mather, "that he means to help the French and Indians to destroy all they can." And again, "He is a criminal governour. . . . His God is Mammon, his aim is the ruin of his country." The meagreness and uncertainty of his salary, which was granted by yearly votes of the Assembly, gave color to the charge that he abused his official position to improve his income. The worst accusation against him was that of conniving in trade with the French and Indians under pretence of exchanging prisoners. Six prominent men

---

[1] *A Memorial of the Present Deplorable State of New England, Boston, 1707. The Deplorable State of New England, by Reason of a Covetous and Treacherous Governour and Pusillanimous Counsellors, London, 1708.* The first of the above is answered by a pamphlet called a *Modest Inquiry.* All three are reprinted in *Mass. Hist. Coll., 5th Series,* VI.

[2] Hutchinson, II. 194.

of the colony, Borland, Vetch, Lawson, Rous, Phillips, and Coffin, only three of whom were of New England origin, were brought to trial before the Assembly for trading at Port Royal, and it was said that Dudley, though he had no direct share in the business, found means to make profit from it. All the accused were convicted and fined. The more strenuous of their judges were for sending them to jail, and Rous was to have been sentenced to "sit an hour upon the gallows with a rope about his neck;" but the Governor and Council objected to these severities, and the Assembly forbore to impose them. The popular indignation against the accused was extreme, and probably not without cause.[1] There was no doubt an illicit trade between Boston and the French of Acadia, who during the war often depended on their enemies for the necessaries of life, since supplies from France, precarious at the best, were made doubly so by New England cruisers. Thus the Acadians and their Indian allies were but too happy to exchange their furs for very modest supplies of tools, utensils, and perhaps, at times, of arms, powder, and lead.[2] What with privateering and illicit trade, it was clear that the war was a source of profit to some of the chief persons in Boston. That place, moreover, felt itself tolerably safe from attack, while the borders were stung from end to end as by a swarm of wasps; and thus the country conceived the idea that the town was fattening at its expense. Vaudreuil reports to the minister that the people of New England want to avenge themselves by an attack on Canada, but that their chief men are for a policy of defence. This was far from being wholly true; but the notion that the rural population bore a grudge against Boston had taken strong hold of the French, who even believed that if the town

[1] The agent of Massachusetts at London, speaking of the three chief offenders, says that they were neither "of English extraction, nor natives of the place, and two of them were very new comers." Jeremiah Dummer, *Letter to a Noble Lord concerning the late Expedition to Canada*.

[2] The French naval captain Bonaventure says that the Acadians were forced to depend on Boston traders, who sometimes plundered them, and sometimes sold them supplies. *Bonaventure au Ministre, 30 Nov. 1705.* Colonel Quary, Judge of Admiralty at New York, writes: "There hath been and still is, as I am informed, a Trade carried on with Port Royal by some of the topping men of that government [Boston], under colour of sending and receiving Flaggs of truce." *Quary to the Lords of Trade, 10 Jan. 1708.*

were attacked, the country would not move hand or foot to help it. Perhaps it was well for them that they did not act on the belief, which, as afterwards appeared, was one of their many mistakes touching the character and disposition of their English neighbors.

The sentences on Borland and his five companions were annulled by the Queen and Council, on the ground that the Assembly was not competent to try the case.[1] The passionate charges against Dudley and a petition to the Queen for his removal were equally unavailing. The Assemblies of Massachusetts and New Hampshire, the chief merchants, the officers of militia, and many of the ministers sent addresses to the Queen in praise of the Governor's administration;[2] and though his enemies declared that the votes and signatures were obtained by the arts familiar to him, his recall was prevented, and he held his office seven years longer.

[1] *Council Record*, in Hutchinson, II. 144.

[2] These addresses are appended to *A Modest Inquiry into the Grounds and Occasions of a late Pamphlet intituled a Memorial of the present Deplorable State of New England. London, 1707.*

Chapter VI

THE OLD RÉGIME

IN ACADIA

The Fishery Question • Privateers and Pirates • Port Royal • Official Gossip • Abuse of Brouillan • Complaints of De Goutin • Subercase and his Officers • Church and State • Paternal Government

---

THE FRENCH province of Acadia, answering to the present Nova Scotia and New Brunswick, was a government separate from Canada and subordinate to it. Jacques François de Brouillan, appointed to command it, landed at Chibucto, the site of Halifax, in 1702, and crossed by hills and forests to the Basin of Mines, where he found a small but prosperous settlement. "It seems to me," he wrote to the minister, "that these people live like true republicans, acknowledging neither royal authority nor courts of law."[1] It was merely that their remoteness and isolation made them independent, of necessity, so far as concerned temporal government. When Brouillan reached Port Royal he found a different state of things. The fort and garrison were in bad condition; but the adjacent settlement, primitive as it was, appeared on the whole duly submissive.

Possibly it would have been less so if it had been more prosperous; but the inhabitants had lately been deprived of fishing, their best resource, by a New England privateer which had driven their craft from the neighboring seas; and when the Governor sent Lieutenant Neuvillette in an armed vessel to seize the interloping stranger, a fight ensued, in which the lieutenant was killed, and his vessel captured. New England is said to have had no less than three hundred vessels every year in these waters.[2] Before the war a French officer proposed that New England sailors should be hired to teach the Acadians how to fish, and the King seems to have ap-

---

[1] *Brouillan au Ministre, 6 Oct. 1702.*

[2] *Mémoire de Subercase.*

proved the plan.[1] Whether it was adopted or not, New England in peace or war had a lion's share of the Acadian fisheries. "It grieves me to the heart," writes Subercase, Brouillan's successor, "to see Messieurs les Bastonnais enrich themselves in our domain; for the base of their commerce is the fish which they catch off our coasts, and send to all parts of the world."

When the war broke out, Brouillan's fighting resources were so small that he was forced to depend largely for help on sea-rovers of more than doubtful character. They came chiefly from the West Indies,—the old haunt of buccaneers,—and were sometimes mere pirates, and sometimes semi-piratical privateers commissioned by French West Indian governors. Brouillan's successor writes that their opportunities are good, since at least a thousand vessels enter Boston every year.[2] Besides these irregular allies, the Governor usually had at his disposal two French frigates of thirty and sixty guns, to which was opposed the Massachusetts navy, consisting of a ship of fifty-six guns, and the "province galley," of twenty-two. In 1710 one of these Massachusetts vessels appeared off the coast escorting a fishing fleet of no less than two hundred and fifty sail, some of which were afterwards captured by French corsairs. A good number of these last, however, were taken from time to time by Boston sea-rovers, who, like their enemies, sometimes bore a close likeness to pirates. They seized French fishing and trading vessels, attacked French corsairs, sometimes traded with the Acadians, and sometimes plundered them. What with West India rum brought by the French freebooters, and New England rum brought by the English, it is reported that one could get drunk in Acadia for two sous.

Port Royal, now Annapolis, was the seat of government, and the only place of any strength in the colony. The fort, a sodded earthwork, lately put into tolerable repair by the joint labor of the soldiers and inhabitants, stood on the point of land between the mouth of the River Annapolis and that of the small stream now called Allen's River, whence it looked

[1] *Mémoire du Roy au Sieur de Brouillan, 23 Mars, 1700; Le Ministre à Villebon, 9 Avril, 1700.*

[2] *Subercase au Ministre, 3 Jan. 1710.*

down the long basin, or land-locked bay, which, framed in hills and forests, had so won the heart of the Baron de Poutrincourt a century before.[1] The garrison was small, counting in 1704 only a hundred and eighty-five soldiers and eight commissioned officers. At the right of the fort, between it and the mouth of the Annapolis, was the Acadian village, consisting of seventy or eighty small houses of one story and an attic, built of planks, boards, or logs, simple and rude, but tolerably comfortable. It had also a small, new wooden church, to the building of which the inhabitants had contributed eight hundred francs, while the King paid the rest. The inhabitants had no voice whatever in public affairs, though the colonial minister had granted them the privilege of travelling in time of peace without passports. The ruling class, civil and military, formed a group apart, living in or near the fort, in complete independence of public opinion, supposing such to have existed. They looked only to their masters at Versailles; and hence a state of things as curious as it was lamentable. The little settlement was a hotbed of gossip, backbiting, and slander. Officials of every degree were continually trying to undermine and supplant each other, besieging the minister with mutual charges. Brouillan, the governor, was a frequent object of attack. He seems to have been of an irritable temper, aggravated perhaps by an old unhealed wound in the cheek, which gave him constant annoyance. One writer declares that Acadia languishes under selfish greed and petty tyranny; that everything was hoped from Brouillan when he first came, but that hope has changed to despair; that he abuses the King's authority to make money, sells wine and brandy at retail, quarrels with officers who are not punctilious enough in saluting him, forces the inhabitants to catch seal and cod for the King, and then cheats them of their pay, and countenances an obnoxious churchwarden whose daughter is his mistress. "The country groans, but dares not utter a word," concludes the accuser, as he closes his indictment.[2]

Brouillan died in the autumn of 1705, on which M. de Goutin, a magistrate who acted as intendant, and was therefore at

[1] *Pioneers of France in the New World*, 187, 188.
[2] La Touche, *Mémoire sur l'Acadie, 1702* (adressé à Ponchartrain).

once the colleague of the late Governor and a spy upon him, writes to the minister that "the divine justice has at last taken pity on the good people of this country," but that as it is base to accuse a dead man, he will not say that the public could not help showing their joy at the late Governor's departure; and he adds that the deceased was charged with a scandalous connection with the Widow de Freneuse. Nor will he reply, he says, to the Governor's complaint to the court about a pretended cabal, of which he, De Goutin, was the head, and which was in reality only three or four honest men, incapable of any kind of deviation, who used to meet in a friendly way, and had given offence by not bowing down before the beast.[1]

Then he changes the subject, and goes on to say that on a certain festal occasion he was invited by Bonaventure, who acted as governor after the death of Brouillan, to share with him the honor of touching off a bonfire before the fort gate; and that this excited such envy, jealousy, and discord that he begs the minister, once for all, to settle the question whether a first magistrate has not the right to the honor of touching off a bonfire jointly with a governor.

De Goutin sometimes discourses of more serious matters. He tells the minister that the inhabitants have plenty of cattle, and more hemp than they can use, but neither pots, scythes, sickles, knives, hatchets, kettles for the Indians, nor salt for themselves. "We should be fortunate if our enemies would continue to supply our necessities and take the beaver-skins with which the colony is gorged;" adding, however, that the Acadians hate the English, and will not trade with them if they can help it.[2]

In the next year the "Bastonnais" were again bringing supplies, and the Acadians again receiving them. The new Governor, Subercase, far from being pleased at this, was much annoyed, or professed to be so, and wrote to Ponchartrain, "Nobody could suffer more than I do at seeing the English

---

[1] "Que trois ou quatre amis, honnêtes gens, incapables de gauchir en quoique ce soit, pour n'avoir pas fléché devant la bête, aient été qualifiés de cabalistes." *De Goutin au Ministre, 4 Déc. 1705.*

[2] *De Goutin au Ministre, 22 Déc. 1707.* In 1705 Bonaventure, in a time of scarcity, sent a vessel to Boston to buy provisions, on pretence of exchanging prisoners. *Bonaventure au Ministre, 30 Nov. 1705.*

so coolly carry on their trade under our very noses." Then he proceeds to the inevitable personalities. "You wish me to write without reserve of the officers here; I have little good to tell you;" and he names two who to the best of his belief have lost their wits, a third who is incorrigibly lazy, and a fourth who is eccentric; adding that he is tolerably well satisfied with the rest, except M. de la Ronde. "You see, Monseigneur, that I am as much in need of a madhouse as of barracks; and what is worse, I am afraid that the *mauvais esprit* of this country will drive me crazy too."[1] "You write to me," he continues, "that you are informed that M. Labat has killed some cattle belonging to the inhabitants. If so, he has expiated his fault by blowing off his thumb by the bursting of his gun while he was firing at a sheep. I am sure that the moon has a good deal to do with his behavior; he always acts very strangely when she is on the wane."

The charge brought against Brouillan in regard to Madame de Freneuse was brought also against Bonaventure in connection with the same lady. "The story," says Subercase, "was pushed as far as hell could desire;"[2] and he partially defends the accused, declaring that at least his fidelity to the King is beyond question.

De Goutin had a quarrel with Subercase, and writes: "I do all that is possible to live on good terms with him, and to that end I walk as if in the chamber of a sick prince whose sleep is of the lightest." As Subercase defends Bonaventure, De Goutin attacks him, and gives particulars concerning him and Madame de Freneuse which need not be recounted here. Then comes a story about a quarrel caused by some cows belonging to Madame de Freneuse which got into the garden of Madame de Saint-Vincent, and were driven out by a soldier who presumed to strike one of them with a long stick. "The facts," gravely adds De Goutin, "have been certified to me as I have the honor to relate them to your Grandeur."[3] Then the minister is treated to a story of one Allein. "He

[1] "Ne me fasse à mon tour tourner la cervelle." *Subercase au Ministre, 20 Déc. 1708.*

[2] "On a poussé la chose aussi loin que l'enfer le pouvait désirer." *Subercase au Ministre, 20 Déc. 1708.*

[3] *De Goutin au Ministre, 29 Déc. 1708.*

insulted Madame de Belleisle at the church door after high mass, and when her son, a boy of fourteen, interposed, Allein gave him such a box on the ear that it drew blood; and I am assured that M. Petit, the priest, ran to the rescue in his sacerdotal robes." Subercase, on his side, after complaining that the price of a certain canoe had been unjustly deducted from his pay, though he never had the said canoe at all, protests to Ponchartrain, "there is no country on earth where I would not rather live than in this, by reason of the ill-disposed persons who inhabit it."[1]

There was the usual friction between the temporal and the spiritual powers. "The Church," writes Subercase, "has long claimed the right of commanding here, or at least of sharing authority with the civil rulers."[2] The Church had formerly been represented by the Capuchin friars, and afterwards by the Recollets. Every complaint was of course carried to the minister. In 1700 we find M. de Villieu, who then held a provisional command in the colony, accusing the ecclesiastics of illicit trade with the English.[3] Bonaventure reports to Ponchartrain that Père Félix, chaplain of the fort, asked that the gate might be opened, in order that he might carry the sacraments to a sick man, his real object being to marry Captain Duvivier to a young woman named Marie Muis de Pouboncoup,—contrary, as the Governor thought, to the good of the service. He therefore forbade the match; on which the priests told him that when they had made up their minds to do anything, nobody had power to turn them from it; and the chaplain presently added that he cared no more for the Governor than for the mud on his shoes.[4] He carried his point and married Duvivier, in spite of the commander.

Every King's ship from Acadia brought to Ponchartrain letters full of matters like these. In one year, 1703, he got at least fourteen such. If half of what Saint-Simon tells us of him is true, it is not to be supposed that he gave himself much trouble concerning them. This does not make it the less astonish-

---

[1] *Subercase au Ministre, 20 Déc. 1708.*

[2] *Ibid.*

[3] *Villieu au Ministre, 20 Oct. 1700.*

[4] "Il répondit qu'il se soucioit de moi comme de la boue de ses souliers." *Bonaventure au Ministre, 30 Nov. 1705.*

ing that in the midst of a great and disastrous war a minister of state should be expected to waste time on matters worthy of a knot of old gossips babbling round a tea-table. That pompous spectre which calls itself the Dignity of History would scorn to take note of them; yet they are highly instructive, for the morbid anatomy of this little colony has a scientific value as exhibiting, all the more vividly for the narrowness of the field, the workings of an unmitigated paternalism acting from across the Atlantic. The King's servants in Acadia pestered his minister at Versailles with their pettiest squabbles, while Marlborough and Eugene were threatening his throne with destruction.[1] The same system prevailed in Canada; but as there the field was broader and the men often larger, the effects are less whimsically vivid than they appear under the Acadian microscope. The two provinces, however, were ruled alike; and about this time the Canadian Intendant Raudot was writing to Ponchartrain in a strain worthy of De Goutin, Subercase, or Bonaventure.[2]

[1] These letters of Acadian officials are in the Archives du Ministère de la Marine et des Colonies at Paris. Copies of some of them will be found in the 3d series of the *Correspondance Officielle* at Ottawa.

[2] *Raudot au Ministre, 20 Sept. 1709*. The copy before me covers 108 folio pages, filled with gossiping personalities.

Chapter VII

ACADIA CHANGES HANDS

Reprisal for Deerfield • Major Benjamin Church • His Ravages at Grand-Pré • Port Royal Expedition • Futile Proceedings • A Discreditable Affair • French Successes in Newfoundland • Schemes of Samuel Vetch • A Grand Enterprise • Nicholson's Advance • An Infected Camp • Ministerial Promises broken • A New Scheme • Port Royal attacked • Acadia conquered

WHEN war-parties from Canada struck the English borders, reprisal was difficult against those who had provoked it. Canada was made almost inaccessible by a hundred leagues of pathless forest, prowled by her Indian allies, who were sure to give the alarm of an approaching foe; while, on the other hand, the New Englanders could easily reach Acadia by their familiar element, the sea; and hence that unfortunate colony often made vicarious atonement for the sins of her Northern sister. It was from French privateers and fishing-vessels on the Acadian seas that Massachusetts drew most of the prisoners whom she exchanged for her own people held captive in Canada.

Major Benjamin Church, the noted Indian fighter of King Philip's War, was at Tiverton in Rhode Island when he heard of Hertel de Rouville's attack on Deerfield. Boiling with rage, he mounted his horse and rode to Boston to propose a stroke of retaliation. Church was energetic, impetuous, and bull-headed, sixty-five years old, and grown so fat that when pushing through the woods on the trail of Indians, he kept a stout sergeant by him to hoist him over fallen trees. Governor Dudley approved his scheme, and appointed him to command the expedition, with the rank of colonel. Church repaired to his native Duxbury; and here, as well as in Plymouth and other neighboring settlements, the militia were called out, and the veteran readily persuaded a sufficient number to volunteer under him. With the Indians of Cape Cod he found more difficulty; they being, as his son observes, "a people that need much treating, especially with drink." At last, however, some of them were induced to join him. Church now returned to Boston, and begged that an attack on Port Royal might be included in his instructions, which was refused, on the ground that a plan to that effect had been laid before the Queen, and that nothing could be done till her answer was received. The Governor's enemies seized the occasion to say that he wished Port Royal to remain French, in order to make money by trading with it.

The whole force, including Indians and sailors, amounted to about seven hundred men; they sailed to Matinicus in brigs and sloops, the province galley, and two British frigates. From Matinicus most of the sailing-vessels were sent to Mount Desert to wait orders, while the main body rowed eastward in whale-boats. Touching at St. Castin's fort, where the town of Castine now stands, they killed or captured everybody they found there. Receiving false information that there was a large war-party on the west side of Passamaquoddy Bay, they hastened to the place, reached it in the night, and pushed into the woods in hope of surprising the enemy. The movement was difficult; and Church's men, being little better than a mob, disregarded his commands, and fell into disorder. He raged and stormed; and presently, in the darkness and confusion, descrying a hut or cabin on the farther side of a small brook, with a crowd gathered about it, he demanded what was the matter, and was told that there were Frenchmen inside who would not come out. "Then knock them in the head," shouted the choleric old man; and he was obeyed. It was said that the victims belonged to a party of Canadians captured just before, under a promise of life. Afterwards, when Church returned to Boston, there was an outcry of indignation against him for this butchery. In any case, however, he could have known nothing of the alleged promise of quarter.

To hunt Indians with an endless forest behind them was like chasing shadows. The Acadians were surer game. Church sailed with a part of his force up the Bay of Fundy, and landed at Grand-Pré,—a place destined to a dismal notoriety half a century later. The inhabitants of this and the neighboring settlements made some slight resistance, and killed a lieutenant named Baker, and one soldier, after which they fled;

when Church, first causing the houses to be examined, to make sure that nobody was left in them, ordered them to be set on fire. The dikes were then broken, and the tide let in upon the growing crops.[1] In spite of these harsh proceedings, he fell far short in his retaliation for the barbarities at Deerfield; since he restrained his Indians and permitted no woman or child to be hurt, at the same time telling his prisoners that if any other New England village were treated as Deerfield had been, he would come back with a thousand Indians and leave them free to do what they pleased. With this bluster, he left the unfortunate peasants in the extremity of terror, after carrying off as many of them as were needed for purposes of exchange. A small detachment was sent to Beaubassin, where it committed similar havoc.

Church now steered for Port Royal, which he had been forbidden to attack. The two frigates and the transports had by this time rejoined him, and in spite of Dudley's orders to make no attempt on the French fort, the British and provincial officers met in council to consider whether to do so. With one voice they decided in the negative, since they had only four hundred men available for landing, while the French garrison was no doubt much stronger, having had ample time to call the inhabitants to its aid. Church, therefore, after trying the virtue of a bombastic summons to surrender, and destroying a few houses, sailed back to Boston. It was a miserable retaliation for a barbarous outrage; as the guilty were out of reach, the invaders turned their ire on the innocent.[2]

If Port Royal in French hands was a source of illicit gain to some persons in Boston, it was also an occasion of loss by the privateers and corsairs it sent out to prey on trading and fishing-vessels, while at the same time it was a standing men-

---

[1] Church, *Entertaining Passages*. "Un habitant des Mines a dit que les ennemis avaient été dans toutes les rivières, qu'il n'y restait plus que quatre habitations en entier, le restant ayant été brulé." *Expéditions faites par les Anglois, 1704.* "Qu'ils avaient . . . brulé toutes les maisons à la reserve du haut des rivières." Labat, *Invasion des Anglois, 1704.*

[2] On this affair, Thomas Church, *Entertaining Passages* (1716). The writer was the son of Benjamin Church. Penhallow; Belknap, I. 266; *Dudley to ——, 21 April, 1704*; Hutchinson, II. 132; *Deplorable State of New England*; *Entreprise des Anglais sur l'Acadie, 1704*; *Expéditions faites par les Anglais de la Nouvelle Angleterre, 1704*; Labat, *Invasion des Anglois de Baston, 1704.*

ace as the possible naval base for one of those armaments against the New England capital which were often threatened, though never carried into effect. Hence, in 1707 the New England colonists made, in their bungling way, a serious attempt to get possession of it.

Dudley's enemies raised the old cry that at heart he wished Port Royal to remain French, and was only forced by popular clamor to countenance an attack upon it. The charge seems a malicious slander. Early in March he proposed the enterprise to the General Court; and the question being referred to a committee, they reported that a thousand soldiers should be raised, vessels impressed, and her Majesty's frigate "Deptford," with the province galley, employed to convoy them. An Act was passed accordingly.[1] Two regiments were soon afoot, one uniformed in red, and the other in blue; one commanded by Colonel Francis Wainwright, and the other by Colonel Winthrop Hilton. Rhode Island sent eighty more men, and New Hampshire sixty, while Connecticut would do nothing. The expedition sailed on the 13th of May, and included one thousand and seventy-six soldiers, with about four hundred and fifty sailors.

The soldiers were nearly all volunteers from the rural militia, and their training and discipline were such as they had acquired in the uncouth frolics and plentiful New England rum of the periodical "muster days." There chanced to be one officer who knew more or less of the work in hand. This was the English engineer Rednap, sent out to look after the fortifications of New York and New England. The commander-in-chief was Colonel John March, of Newbury, who had popular qualities, had seen frontier service, and was personally brave, but totally unfit for his present position. Most of the officers were civilians from country towns,—Ipswich, Topsfield, Lynn, Salem, Dorchester, Taunton, or Weymouth.[2] In the province galley went, as secretary of the expedition, that intelligent youth, William Dudley, son of the Governor.

New England has been blamed for not employing trained

---

[1] *Report of a Committee to consider his Excellency's Speech, 12 March, 1707. Resolve for an Expedition against Port Royal* (Massachusetts Archives).

[2] *Autobiography of Rev. John Barnard*, one of the five chaplains of the expedition.

officers to command her levies; but with the exception of Rednap, and possibly of Captain Samuel Vetch, there were none in the country, nor were they wanted. In their stubborn and jealous independence, the sons of the Puritans would have resented their presence. The provincial officers were, without exception, civilians. British regular officers, good, bad, or indifferent, were apt to put on airs of superiority which galled the democratic susceptibilities of the natives, who, rather than endure a standing military force imposed by the mother-country, preferred to suffer if they must, and fight their own battles in their own crude way. Even for irregular warfare they were at a disadvantage; Canadian feudalism developed good partisan leaders, which was rarely the case with New England democracy. Colonel John March was a tyro set over a crowd of ploughboys, fishermen, and mechanics, officered by tradesmen, farmers, blacksmiths, village magnates, and deacons of the church; for the characters of deacon and militia officer were often joined in one. These improvised soldiers commonly did well in small numbers, and very ill in large ones.

Early in June the expedition sailed into Port Royal Basin, and Lieutenant-Colonel Appleton, with three hundred and fifty men, landed on the north shore, four or five miles below the fort, marched up to the mouth of the Annapolis, and was there met by an ambushed body of French, who, being outnumbered, presently took to their boats and retreated to the fort. Meanwhile, March, with seven hundred and fifty men, landed on the south shore and pushed on to the meadows of Allen's River, which they were crossing in battle array when a fire blazed out upon them from a bushy hill on the farther bank, where about two hundred French lay in ambush under Subercase, the governor. March and his men crossed the stream, and after a skirmish that did little harm to either side, the French gave way. The English then advanced to a hill known as the Lion Rampant, within cannon-shot of the fort, and here began to intrench themselves, stretching their lines right and left towards the Annapolis on the one hand, and Allen's River on the other, so as to form a semicircle before the fort, where all the inhabitants had by this time taken refuge.

Soon all was confusion in the New England camp,—the consequence of March's incapacity for a large command, and the greenness and ignorance of both himself and his subordinates. There were conflicting opinions, wranglings, and disputes. The men, losing all confidence in their officers, became unmanageable. "The devil was at work among us," writes one of those present. The engineer, Rednap, the only one of them who knew anything of the work in hand, began to mark out the batteries; but soon lost temper, and declared that "it was not for him to venture his reputation with such ungovernable and undisciplined men and inconstant officers."[1] He refused to bring up the cannon, saying that it could not be done under the fire of the fort; and the naval captains were of the same opinion.

One of the chaplains, Rev. John Barnard, being of a martial turn and full of zeal, took it upon him to make a plan of the fort; and to that end, after providing himself with pen, ink, paper, and a horse-pistol, took his seat at a convenient spot; but his task was scarcely begun when it was ended by a cannon-ball that struck the ground beside him, peppered him with gravel, and caused his prompt retreat.[2]

French deserters reported that there were five hundred men in the fort, with forty-two heavy cannon, and that four or five hundred more were expected every day. This increased the general bewilderment of the besiegers. There was a council of war. Rednap declared that it would be useless to persist; and after hot debate and contradiction, it was resolved to decamp. Three days after, there was another council, which voted to bring up the cannon and open fire, in spite of Rednap and the naval captains; but in the next evening a third council resolved again to raise the siege as hopeless. This disgusted the rank and file, who were a little soothed by an order to destroy the storehouse and other buildings outside the fort; and, ill led as they were, they did the work thoroughly. "Never did men act more boldly," says the witness before quoted; "they threatened the enemy to his nose, and would have taken the fort if the officers had shown any spirit. They found it hard to bring them off. At the end we broke up with

[1] *A Boston Gentleman to his Friend, 13 June, 1707* (Mass. Archives).
[2] *Autobiography of Rev. John Barnard.*

the confusion of Babel, and went about our business like fools."[1]

The baffled invaders sailed crestfallen to Casco Bay, and a vessel was sent to carry news of the miscarriage to Dudley, who, vexed and incensed, ordered another attempt. March was in a state of helpless indecision, increased by a bad cold; but the Governor would not recall him, and chose instead the lamentable expedient of sending three members of the provincial council to advise and direct him. Two of them had commissions in the militia; the third, John Leverett, was a learned bachelor of divinity, formerly a tutor in Harvard College, and soon after its president,—capable, no doubt, of preaching Calvinistic sermons to the students, but totally unfit to command men or conduct a siege.

Young William Dudley was writing meanwhile to his father how jealousies and quarrels were rife among the officers, how their conduct bred disorder and desertion among the soldiers, and how Colonel March and others behaved as if they had nothing to do but make themselves popular.[2] Many of the officers seem, in fact, to have been small politicians in search of notoriety, with an eye to votes or appointments. Captain Stuckley, of the British frigate, wrote to the Governor in great discontent about the "nonsensical malice" of Lieutenant-Colonel Appleton, and adds, "I don't see what good I can do by lying here, where I am almost murdered by mosquitoes."[3]

The three commissioners came at last, with a reinforcement of another frigate and a hundred recruits, which did not supply losses, as the soldiers had deserted by scores. In great ill-humor, the expedition sailed back to Port Royal, where it was found that reinforcements had also reached the French, including a strongly manned privateer from Martinique. The New England men landed, and there was some sharp skirmishing in an orchard. Chaplain Barnard took part in the fray. "A shot brushed my wig," he says, "but I was mercifully preserved. We soon drove them out of the orchard, killed a few of them, desperately wounded the privateer captain, and after that we all embarked and returned to Boston as fast as

---

[1] *A Boston Gentleman to his Friend, 13 June* (old style), *1707*. The final attack here alluded to took place on the night of the 16th of June (new style).

[2] *William Dudley to Governor Dudley, 24 June, 1707.*

[3] *Stuckley to Dudley, 28 June, 1707.*

we could." This summary statement is imperfect, for there was a good deal of skirmishing from the 13th August to the 20th, when the invaders sailed for home. March was hooted as he walked Boston streets, and children ran after him crying "Wooden sword!" There was an attempt at a court-martial; but so many officers were accused, on one ground or another, that hardly enough were left to try them, and the matter was dropped. With one remarkable exception, the New England militia reaped scant laurels on their various expeditions eastward; but of all their shortcomings, this was the most discreditable.[1]

Meanwhile events worthy of note were passing in Newfoundland. That island was divided between the two conflicting powers; the chief station of the French being at Placentia, and that of the English at St. John. In January, 1705, Subercase, who soon after became governor of Acadia, marched with four hundred and fifty soldiers, Canadians, and buccaneers, aided by a band of Indians, against St. John, a fishing-village defended by two forts, the smaller, known as the castle, held by twelve men, and the larger, called Fort William, by forty men under Captain Moody. The latter was attacked by the French, who were beaten off; on which they burned the unprotected houses and fishing-huts with a brutality equal to that of Church in Acadia, and followed up the exploit by destroying the hamlet at Ferryland and all the defenceless hovels and fish-stages along the shore towards Trinity Bay and Bonavista.[2]

Four years later, the Sieur de Saint-Ovide, a nephew of

[1] A considerable number of letters and official papers on this expedition will be found in the 51st and 71st volumes of the Massachusetts Archives. See also Hutchinson, II. 151, and Belknap, I. 273. The curious narrative of the chaplain, Barnard, is in *Mass. Hist. Coll., 3d Series*, V. 189–196. The account in the *Deplorable State of New England* is meant solely to injure Dudley. The chief French accounts are *Entreprise des Anglois contre l'Acadie, 26 Juin, 1707; Subercase au Ministre, même date; Labat au Ministre, 6 Juillet, 1707; Relation* appended to Dièreville, *Voyage de l'Acadie*. The last is extremely loose and fanciful. Subercase puts the English force at three thousand men, whereas the official returns show it to have been, soldiers and sailors, about half this number.

[2] Penhallow puts the French force at five hundred and fifty. Jeremiah Dummer, *Letter to a Noble Lord concerning the late Expedition to Canada*, says that the havoc committed occasioned a total loss of £80,000.

Brouillan, late governor at Port Royal, struck a more creditable blow. He set out from Placentia on the 13th of December, 1708, with one hundred and sixty-four men, and on the 1st of January approached Fort William two hours before day, found the gate leading to the covered way open, entered with a band of volunteers, rapidly crossed the ditch, planted ladders against the wall, and leaped into the fort, then, as he declares, garrisoned by a hundred men. His main body followed close. The English were taken unawares; their commander, who showed great courage, was struck down by three shots, and after some sharp fighting the place was in the hands of the assailants. The small fort at the mouth of the harbor capitulated on the second day, and the palisaded village of the inhabitants, which, if we are to believe Saint-Ovide, contained nearly six hundred men, made little resistance. St. John became for the moment a French possession; but Costebelle, governor at Placentia, despaired of holding it, and it was abandoned in the following summer.[1]

About this time a scheme was formed for the permanent riddance of New England from war-parties by the conquest of Canada.[2] The prime mover in it was Samuel Vetch, whom we have seen as an emissary to Quebec for the exchange of prisoners, and also as one of the notables fined for illicit trade with the French. He came of a respectable Scotch family. His grandfather, his father, three of his uncles, and one of his brothers were Covenanting ministers, who had suffered some persecution under Charles II. He himself was destined for the ministry; but his inclinations being in no way clerical, he and his brother William got commissions in the army and took an active part in the war that ended with the Peace of Ryswick.

In the next year the two brothers sailed for the Isthmus of Panama as captains in the band of adventurers embarked in the disastrous enterprise known as the Darien Scheme. Wil-

[1] *Saint-Ovide au Ministre, 20 Jan. 1709; Ibid., 6 Sept. 1709; Rapport de Costebelle, 26 Fév. 1709.* Costebelle makes the French force one hundred and seventy-five.

[2] Some of the French officials in Acadia foresaw aggressive action on the part of the English in consequence of the massacre at Haverhill. "Le coup que les Canadiens viennent de faire, où Mars, plus féroce qu'en Europe, a donné carrière à sa rage, me fait appréhender une représaille." *De Goutin au Ministre, 29 Déc. 1708.*

liam Vetch died at sea, and Samuel repaired to New York, where he married a daughter of Robert Livingston, one of the chief men of the colony, and engaged largely in the Canadian trade. From New York he went to Boston, where we find him when the War of the Spanish Succession began. During his several visits to Canada he had carefully studied the St. Lawrence and its shores, and boasted that he knew them better than the Canadians themselves.[1] He was impetuous, sanguine, energetic, and headstrong, astute withal, and full of ambition. A more vigorous agent for the execution of the proposed plan of conquest could not have been desired. The General Court of Massachusetts, contrary to its instinct and its past practice, resolved, in view of the greatness of the stake, to ask this time for help from the mother-country, and Vetch sailed for England, bearing an address to the Queen, begging for an armament to aid in the reduction of Canada and Acadia. The scheme waxed broader yet in the ardent brain of the agent; he proposed to add Newfoundland to the other conquests, and when all was done in the North, to sail to the Gulf of Mexico and wrest Pensacola from the Spaniards; by which means, he writes, "Her Majesty shall be sole empress of the vast North American continent." The idea was less visionary than it seems. Energy, helped by reasonable good luck, might easily have made it a reality, so far as concerned the possessions of France.

The court granted all that Vetch asked. On the 11th of March he sailed for America, fully empowered to carry his plans into execution, and with the assurance that when Canada was conquered, he should be its governor. A squadron bearing five regiments of regular troops was promised. The colonies were to muster their forces in all haste. New York was directed to furnish eight hundred men; New Jersey, two hundred; Pennsylvania, one hundred and fifty; and Connecticut, three hundred and fifty; the whole to be at Albany by the middle of May, and to advance on Montreal by way of Wood Creek and Lake Champlain, as soon as they should hear that the squadron had reached Boston. Massachusetts,

[1] Patterson, *Memoir of Hon. Samuel Vetch*, in *Collections of the Nova Scotia Historical Society*, IV. Compare a paper by Gen. James Grant Wilson in *International Review*, November, 1881.

New Hampshire, and Rhode Island were to furnish twelve hundred men, to join the regulars in attacking Quebec by way of the St. Lawrence.[1]

Vetch sailed from Portsmouth in the ship "Dragon," accompanied by Colonel Francis Nicholson, late Lieutenant-Governor of New York, who was to take an important part in the enterprise. The squadron with the five regiments was to follow without delay. The weather was bad, and the "Dragon," beating for five weeks against head-winds, did not enter Boston harbor till the evening of the 28th of April. Vetch, chafing with impatience, for every moment was precious, sent off expresses that same night to carry the Queen's letters to the Governors of Rhode Island, Connecticut, New Jersey, and Pennsylvania. Dudley and his council met the next morning, and to them Vetch delivered the royal message, which was received, he says, "with the dutiful obedience becoming good subjects, and all the marks of joy and thankfulness."[2] Vetch, Nicholson, and the Massachusetts authorities quickly arranged their plans. An embargo was laid on the shipping; provision was made for raising men and supplies and providing transportation. When all was in train, the two emissaries hired a sloop for New York, and touching by the way at Rhode Island, found it in the throes of the annual election of governor. Yet every warlike preparation was already made, and Vetch and his companion sailed at once for New Haven to meet Saltonstall, the newly elected governor of Connecticut. Here, too, all was ready, and the envoys, well pleased, continued their voyage to New York, which they reached on the 18th of May. The governor, Lord Lovelace, had lately died, and Colonel Ingoldsby, the lieutenant-governor, acted in his place. The Assembly was in session, and being summoned to the council chamber, the members were addressed by Vetch and Nicholson with excellent effect.

In accepting the plan of conquest, New York completely changed front. She had thus far stood neutral, leaving her

---

[1] *Instructions to Colonel Vetch, 1 March, 1709; The Earl of Sunderland to Dudley, 28 April, 1709; The Queen to Lord Lovelace, 1 March, 1709; The Earl of Sunderland to Lord Lovelace, 28 April, 1709.*

[2] *Journal of Vetch and Nicholson* (Public Record Office). This is in the form of a letter, signed by both, and dated at New York, 29 June, 1709.

neighbors to defend themselves, and carrying on an active trade with the French and their red allies. Still, it was her interest that Canada should become English; thus throwing open to her the trade of the Western tribes; and the promises of aid from England made the prospects of the campaign so flattering that she threw herself into the enterprise, though not without voices of protest; for while the frontier farmers and some prominent citizens like Peter Schuyler thought that the time for action had come, the Albany traders and their allies, who fattened on Canadian beaver, were still for peace at any price.[1]

With Pennsylvania and New Jersey the case was different. The one, controlled by non-combatant Quakers and safe from French war-parties, refused all aid; while the other, in less degree under the same military blight, would give no men, though granting a slow and reluctant contribution of £3,000, taking care to suppress on the record every indication that the money was meant for military uses. New York, on the other hand, raised her full contingent, and Massachusetts and New Hampshire something more, being warm in the faith that their borders would be plagued with war-parties no longer.

It remained for New York to gain the help of the Five Nations of the Iroquois, to which end Abraham Schuyler went to Onondaga, well supplied with presents. The Iroquois capital was now, as it had been for years, divided between France and England. French interests were represented by the two Jesuits, Mareuil and Jacques Lamberville. The skilful management of Schuyler, joined to his gifts and his rum, presently won over so many to the English party, and raised such excitement in the town, that Lamberville thought it best to set out for Montreal with news of what was going on. The intrepid Joncaire, agent of France among the Senecas, was scandalized at what he calls the Jesuit's flight, and wrote to the commandant of Fort Frontenac that its effect on the Indians was such that he, Joncaire, was in peril of his life.[2] Yet he stood his ground, and managed so well that he held the Senecas firm in their neutrality. Lamberville's colleague, Mareuil, whose position was still more critical, was persuaded by Schuyler that his only safety was in going with him to Al-

---

[1] *Thomas Cockerill to Mr. Popple, 2 July, 1709.*
[2] Joncaire in *N. Y. Col. Docs.*, IX. 838.

bany, which he did; and on this the Onondagas, excited by rum, plundered and burned the Jesuit mission-house and chapel.[1] Clearly, the two priests at Onondaga were less hungry for martyrdom than their murdered brethren, Jogues, Brebeuf, Lallemant, and Charles Garnier; but it is to be remembered that the Canadian Jesuit of the first half of the seventeenth century was before all things an apostle, and his successor of a century later was before all things a political agent.

As for the Five Nations, that once haughty confederacy, in spite of divisions and waverings, had conceived the idea that its true policy lay, not in siding with either of the European rivals, but in making itself important to both, and courted and caressed by both. While some of the warriors sang the war-song at the prompting of Schuyler, they had been but half-hearted in doing so; and even the Mohawks, nearest neighbors and best friends of the English, sent word to their Canadian kindred, the Caughnawagas, that they took up the hatchet only because they could not help it.

The attack on Canada by way of the Hudson and Lake Champlain was to have been commanded by Lord Lovelace or some officer of his choice; but as he was dead, Ingoldsby, his successor in the government of the province, jointly with the governors of several adjacent colonies who had met at New York, appointed Colonel Nicholson in his stead.[2] Nicholson went to Albany, whence, with about fifteen hundred men, he moved up the Hudson, built a stockade fort opposite Saratoga, and another at the spot known as the Great Carrying Place. This latter he called Fort Nicholson,—a name which it afterwards exchanged for that of Fort Lydius, and later still for that of Fort Edward, which the town that occupies the site owns to this day.[3] Thence he cut a rough roadway through the woods to where Wood Creek, choked with beaver dams, writhed through flat green meadows, walled in by rock and forest. Here he built another fort, which was

[1] Mareuil in *N. Y. Col. Docs.*, IX. 836, text and note. *Vaudreuil au Ministre, 14 Nov. 1709.*

[2] "If I had not accepted the command, there would have been insuperable difficulties" (arising from provincial jealousies). *Nicholson to Sunderland, 8 July, 1709.*

[3] Forts Nicholson, Lydius, and Edward were not the same, but succeeded each other on the same ground.

afterwards rebuilt and named Fort Anne. Wood Creek led to Lake Champlain, and Lake Champlain to Chambly and Montreal,—the objective points of the expedition. All was astir at the camp. Flat-boats and canoes were made, and stores brought up from Albany, till everything was ready for an advance the moment word should come that the British fleet had reached Boston. Vetch, all impatience, went thither to meet it, as if his presence could hasten its arrival.

Reports of Nicholson's march to Wood Creek had reached Canada, and Vaudreuil sent Ramesay, governor of Montreal, with fifteen hundred troops, Canadians, and Indians, to surprise his camp. Ramesay's fleet of canoes had reached Lake Champlain, and was half way to the mouth of Wood Creek, when his advance party was discovered by English scouts, and the French commander began to fear that he should be surprised in his turn; in fact, some of his Indians were fired upon from an ambuscade. All was now doubt, perplexity, and confusion. Ramesay landed at the narrows of the lake, a little south of the place now called Crown Point. Here, in the dense woods, his Indians fired on some Canadians whom they took for English. This was near producing a panic. "Every tree seemed an enemy," writes an officer present. Ramesay lost himself in the woods, and could not find his army. One Deruisseau, who had gone out as a scout, came back with the report that nine hundred Englishmen were close at hand. Seven English canoes did in fact appear, supported, as the French in their excitement imagined, by a numerous though invisible army in the forest; but being fired upon, and seeing that they were entering a hornet's nest, the English sheered off. Ramesay having at last found his army, and order being gradually restored, a council of war was held, after which the whole force fell back to Chambly, having accomplished nothing.[1]

Great was the alarm in Canada when it became known that the enemy aimed at nothing less than the conquest of the

---

[1] *Mémoire sur le Canada, Année 1709*. This paper, which has been ascribed to the engineer De Léry, is printed in *Collection de Manuscrits relatifs à la Nouvelle France*, I. 615, (Quebec, 1883,) printed from the MS. *Paris Documents* in the Boston State House. The writer of the *Mémoire* was with Ramesay's expedition. Also *Ramesay à Vaudreuil, 19 Oct. 1709*, and *Vaudreuil au Minis-*

colony. One La Plaine spread a panic at Quebec by reporting
that, forty-five leagues below, he had seen eight or ten ships
under sail and heard the sound of cannon. It was afterwards
surmised that the supposed ships were points of rocks seen
through the mist at low tide, and the cannon the floundering
of whales at play.[1] Quebec, however, was all excitement, in
expectation of attack. The people of the Lower Town took
refuge on the rock above; the men of the neighboring parishes were ordered within the walls; and the women and children, with the cattle and horses, were sent to hiding-places in
the forest. There had been no less consternation at Montreal,
caused by exaggerated reports of Iroquois hostility and the
movements of Nicholson. It was even proposed to abandon
Chambly and Fort Frontenac, and concentrate all available
force to defend the heart of the colony. "A most bloody war
is imminent," wrote Vaudreuil to the minister, Ponchartrain.

Meanwhile, for weeks and months Nicholson's little army
lay in the sultry valley of Wood Creek, waiting those tidings
of the arrival of the British squadron at Boston which were
to be its signal of advance. At length a pestilence broke out.
It is said to have been the work of the Iroquois allies, who
thought that the French were menaced with ruin, and who,
true to their policy of balancing one European power against
the other, poisoned the waters of the Creek by throwing into
it, above the camp, the skins and offal of the animals they had
killed in their hunting. The story may have some foundation,
though it rests only on the authority of Charlevoix. No contemporary writer mentions it; and Vaudreuil says that the
malady was caused by the long confinement of the English in
their fort. Indeed, a crowd of men, penned up through the
heats of midsummer in a palisaded camp, ill-ordered and un-
clean as the camps of the raw provincials usually were, and

---

tre, 14 Nov. 1709. Charlevoix says that Ramesay turned back because he believed that there were five thousand English at Wood Creek; but Ramesay
himself makes their number only one thousand whites and two hundred Indians. He got his information from two Dutchmen caught just after the
alarm near Pointe à la Chevelure (Crown Point). He turned back because he
had failed to surprise the English, and also, it seems, because there were
disagreements among his officers.

[1] *Monseigneur de Saint-Vallier et l'Hôpital Général de Québec,* 203.

infested with pestiferous swarms of flies and mosquitoes, could hardly have remained in health. Whatever its cause, the disease, which seems to have been a malignant dysentery, made more havoc than the musket and the sword. A party of French who came to the spot late in the autumn, found it filled with innumerable graves.

The British squadron, with the five regiments on board, was to have reached Boston at the middle of May. On the 20th of that month the whole contingent of Massachusetts, New Hampshire, and Rhode Island was encamped by Boston harbor, with transports and stores, ready to embark for Quebec at ten hours' notice.[1] When Vetch, after seeing everything in readiness at New York, returned to Boston on the 3d of July, he found the New England levies encamped there still, drilled diligently every day by officers whom he had brought from England for the purpose. "The bodies of the men," he writes to Lord Sunderland, "are in general better than in Europe, and I hope their courage will prove so too; so that nothing in human probability can prevent the success of this glorious enterprise but the too late arrival of the fleet."[2] But of the fleet there was no sign. "The government here is put to vast expense," pursues Vetch, "but they cheerfully pay it, in hopes of being freed from it forever hereafter. All that they can do now is to fast and pray for the safe and speedy arrival of the fleet, for which they have already had two public fast-days kept."

If it should not come in time, he continues, "it would be the last disappointment to her Majesty's colonies, who have so heartily complied with her royal order, and would render them much more miserable than if such a thing had never been undertaken." Time passed, and no ships appeared. Vetch wrote again: "I shall only presume to acquaint your Lordship how vastly uneasy all her Majesty's loyall subjects here on this continent are. Pray God hasten the fleet."[3] Dudley, scarcely less impatient, wrote to the same

---

[1] *Dudley to Sunderland, 14 Aug. 1709.*

[2] *Vetch to Sunderland, 2 Aug. 1709.* The pay of the men was nine shillings a week, with eightpence a day for provisions; and most of them had received an enlistment bounty of £12.

[3] *Vetch to Sunderland, 12 Aug. 1709.* Dudley writes with equal urgency two days later.

effect. It was all in vain, and the soldiers remained in their camp, monotonously drilling day after day through all the summer and half the autumn. At length, on the 11th of October, Dudley received a letter from Lord Sunderland, informing him that the promised forces had been sent to Portugal to meet an exigency of the European war. They were to have reached Boston, as we have seen, by the middle of May. Sunderland's notice of the change of destination was not written till the 27th of July, and was eleven weeks on its way, thus imposing on the colonists a heavy and needless tax in time, money, temper, and, in the case of the expedition against Montreal, health and life.[1] What was left of Nicholson's force had fallen back before Sunderland's letter came, making a scapegoat of the innocent Vetch, cursing him, and wishing him hanged.

In New England the disappointment and vexation were extreme; but, not to lose all the fruits of their efforts, the governors of Massachusetts, Connecticut, New Hampshire, and Rhode Island met and resolved to attack Port Royal if the captains of several British frigates then at New York and Boston would take part in the enterprise. To the disgust of the provincials, the captains, with one exception, refused, on the score of the late season and the want of orders.

A tenacious energy has always been a characteristic of New England, and the hopes of the colonists had been raised too high to be readily abandoned. Port Royal was in their eyes a pestilent nest of privateers and pirates that preyed on the New England fisheries; and on the refusal of the naval commanders to join in an immediate attack, they offered to the court to besiege the place themselves next year, if they could count on the help of four frigates and five hundred soldiers, to be at Boston by the end of March.[2] The Assembly of Massachusetts requested Nicholson, who was on the point of sailing for Eu-

[1] *Letters of Nicholson, Dudley, and Vetch, 20 June to 24 Oct. 1709.*

[2] *Joint Letter of Nicholson, Dudley, Vetch, and Moody to Sunderland, 24 Oct. 1709*; also *Joint Letter of Dudley, Vetch, and Moody to Sunderland, 25 Oct. 1709*; *Abstracts of Letters and Papers relating to the Attack of Port Royal, 1709* (Public Record Office); *Address of ye Inhabitants of Boston and Parts adjacent, 1709.* Moody, named above, was the British naval captain who had consented to attack Port Royal.

rope, to beg her Majesty to help them in an enterprise which would be so advantageous to the Crown, "and which, by the long and expensive war, we are so impoverished and enfeebled as not to be in a capacity to effect."[1]

Nicholson sailed in December, and Peter Schuyler soon followed. New York, having once entered on the path of war, saw that she must continue in it; and to impress the Five Nations with the might and majesty of the Queen, and so dispose them to hold fast to the British cause, Schuyler took five Mohawk chiefs with him to England. One died on the voyage; the rest arrived safe, and their appearance was the sensation of the hour. They were clad, at the Queen's expense, in strange and gay attire, invented by the costumer of one of the theatres; were lodged and feasted as the guests of the nation, driven about London in coaches with liveried servants, conducted to dockyards, arsenals, and reviews, and saluted with cannon by ships of war. The Duke of Shrewsbury presented them to Queen Anne,—one as emperor of the Mohawks, and the other three as kings,—and the Archbishop of Canterbury solemnly gave each of them a Bible. Steele and Addison wrote essays about them, and the Dutch artist Verelst painted their portraits, which were engraved in mezzotint.[2] Their presence and the speech made in their name before the court seem to have had no small effect in drawing attention to the war in America and inclining the ministry towards the proposals of Nicholson. These were accepted, and he sailed for America commissioned to command the enterprise against Port Royal, with Vetch as adjutant-general.[3]

[1] *Order of Assembly, 27 Oct. 1709.* Massachusetts had spent about £22,000 on her futile expedition of 1707, and, with New Hampshire and Rhode Island, a little more than £46,000 on that of 1709, besides continual outlay in guarding her two hundred miles of frontier,—a heavy expense for the place and time.

[2] See J. R. Bartlett, in *Magazine of American History*, March, 1878, and Schuyler, *Colonial New York*, II. 34–39. The chiefs returned to America in May on board the "Dragon." An elaborate pamphlet appeared in London, giving an account of them and their people. A set of the mezzotint portraits, which are large and well executed, is in the John Carter Brown collection at Providence. For photographic reproductions, see Winsor, *Nar. and Crit. Hist.*, V. 107. Compare Smith, *Hist. N. Y.*, I. 204 (1830).

[3] *Commission of Colonel Francis Nicholson, 18 May, 1710. Instructions to Colonel Nicholson, same date.*

Colonel Francis Nicholson had held some modest military positions, but never, it is said, seen active service. In colonial affairs he had played an important part, and in the course of his life governed at different times, Virginia, New York, Maryland, and Carolina. He had a robust, practical brain, capable of broad views and large schemes. One of his plans was a confederacy of the provinces to resist the French, which, to his great indignation, Virginia rejected. He had Jacobite leanings, and had been an adherent of James II.; but being no idealist, and little apt to let his political principles block the path of his interests, he turned his back on the fallen cause and offered his services to the Revolution. Though no pattern of domestic morals, he seems to have been officially upright, and he wished well to the colonies, saving always the dominant interests of England. He was bold, ambitious, vehement, and sometimes headstrong and perverse.

Though the English ministry had promised aid, it was long in coming. The Massachusetts Assembly had asked that the ships should be at Boston before the end of March; but it was past the middle of May before they sailed from Plymouth. Then, towards midsummer, a strange spasm of martial energy seems to have seized the ministry, for Viscount Shannon was ordered to Boston with an additional force, commissioned to take the chief command and attack, not Port Royal, but Quebec.[1] This ill-advised change of plan seems to have been reconsidered; at least, it came to nothing.[2]

Meanwhile, the New England people waited impatiently for the retarded ships. No order had come from England for raising men, and the colonists resolved this time to risk nothing till assured that their labor and money would not be wasted. At last, not in March, but in July, the ships appeared. Then all was astir with preparation. First, the House of Representatives voted thanks to the Queen for her "royal aid."

[1] *Instructions to Richard Viscount Shannon, July, 1710.* A report of the scheme reached Boston. Hutchinson, II. 164.

[2] The troops, however, were actually embarked. *True State of the Forces commanded by the Right Honᵇˡᵉ The Lord Viscount Shannon, as they were Embark'ᵈ the 14ᵗʰ of October, 1710.* The total was three thousand two hundred and sixty-five officers and men. Also, *Shannon to Sunderland, 16 Oct. 1710.* The absurdity of the attempt at so late a season is obvious. Yet the fleet lay some weeks more at Portsmouth, waiting for a fair wind.

Next, it was proclaimed that no vessel should be permitted to leave the harbor "till the service is provided;" and a committee of the House proceeded to impress fourteen vessels to serve as transports. Then a vote was passed that nine hundred men be raised as the quota of Massachusetts, and a month's pay in advance, together with a coat worth thirty shillings, was promised to volunteers; a committee of three being at the same time appointed to provide the coats. On the next day appeared a proclamation from the Governor announcing the aforesaid "encouragements," calling on last year's soldiers to enlist again, promising that all should return home as soon as Port Royal was taken, and that each might keep as his own forever the Queen's musket that would be furnished him. Now came an order to colonels of militia to muster their regiments on a day named, read the proclamation at the head of each company, and if volunteers did not come forward in sufficient number, to draft as many men as might be wanted, appointing, at the same time, officers to conduct them to the rendezvous at Dorchester or Cambridge; and, by a stringent and unusual enactment, the House ordered that they should be quartered in private houses, with or without the consent of the owners, "any law or usage to the contrary notwithstanding." Sailors were impressed without ceremony to man the transports; and, finally, it was voted that a pipe of wine, twenty sheep, five pigs, and one hundred fowls be presented to the Honorable General Nicholson for his table during the expedition.[1] The above, with slight variation, may serve as an example of the manner in which, for several generations, men were raised in Massachusetts to serve against the French.

Autumn had begun before all was ready. Connecticut, New Hampshire, and Rhode Island sent their contingents; there was a dinner at the Green Dragon Tavern in honor of Nicholson, Vetch, and Sir Charles Hobby, the chief officers of the expedition; and on the 18th of September the whole put to sea.

On the 24th the squadron sailed into the narrow entrance of Port Royal, where the tide runs like a mill-stream. One vessel was driven upon the rocks, and twenty-six men were drowned. The others got in safely, and anchored above Goat

[1] *Archives of Massachusetts*, Vol. LXXI., where the original papers are preserved.

Island, in sight of the French fort. They consisted of three fourth-rates,—the "Dragon," the "Chester," and the "Falmouth;" two fifth-rates,—the "Lowestoffe" and the "Feversham;" the province galley, one bomb-ketch, twenty-four small transports, two or three hospital ships, a tender, and several sloops carrying timber to make beds for cannon and mortars. The landing force consisted of four hundred British marines, and about fifteen hundred provincials, divided into four battalions.[1] Its unnecessary numbers were due to the belief of Nicholson that the fort had been reinforced and strengthened.

In the afternoon of the 25th they were all on shore; Vetch with his two battalions on the north side, and Nicholson with the other two on the south. Vetch marched to his camping-ground, on which, in the words of Nicholson's journal, "the French began to fire pretty thick." On the next morning Nicholson's men moved towards the fort, hacking their way through the woods and crossing the marshes of Allen's River, while the French fired briskly with cannon from the ramparts, and small-arms from the woods, houses, and fences. They were driven back, and the English advance guard intrenched itself within four hundred yards of the works. Several days passed in landing artillery and stores, cannonading from the fort and shelling from the English bomb-ketch, when on the 29th, Ensign Perelle, with a drummer and a flag of truce, came to Nicholson's tent, bringing a letter from Subercase, who begged him to receive into his camp and under his protection certain ladies of the fort who were distressed by the bursting of the English shells. The conduct of Perelle was irregular, as he had not given notice of his approach by beat of drum and got himself and attendants blindfolded before entering the camp. Therefore Nicholson detained him, sending back an officer of his own with a letter to the effect that he would receive the ladies and lodge them in the same house with the French ensign, "for the Queen, my royal mistress,

[1] *Nicholson and Vetch to the Secretary of State, 16 Sept. 1710*; Hutchinson, II. 164; Penhallow. Massachusetts sent two battalions of four hundred and fifty men each, and Connecticut one battalion of three hundred men, while New Hampshire and Rhode Island united their contingents to form a fourth battalion.

hath not sent me hither to make war against women." Subercase on his part detained the English officer, and wrote to Nicholson:

> SIR,—You have one of my officers, and I have one of yours; so that now we are equal. However, that hinders me not from believing that once you have given me your word, you will keep it very exactly. On that ground I now write to tell you, sir, that to prevent the spilling of both English and French blood, I am ready to hold up both hands for a capitulation that will be honorable to both of us.[1]

In view of which agreement he adds that he defers sending the ladies to the English camp.

Another day passed, during which the captive officers on both sides were treated with much courtesy. On the next morning, Sunday, October 1st, the siege-guns, mortars, and coehorns were in position; and after some firing on both sides, Nicholson sent Colonel Tailor and Captain Abercrombie with a summons to surrender the fort. Subercase replied that he was ready to listen to proposals; the firing stopped, and within twenty-four hours the terms were settled. The garrison were to march out with the honors of war, and to be carried in English ships to Rochelle or Rochefort. The inhabitants within three miles of the fort were to be permitted to remain, if they chose to do so, unmolested, in their homes during two years, on taking an oath of allegiance and fidelity to the Queen.

Two hundred provincials marched to the fort gate and formed in two lines on the right and left. Nicholson advanced between the ranks, with Vetch on one hand and Hobby on the other, followed by all the field-officers. Subercase came to meet them, and gave up the keys, with a few words of compliment. The French officers and men marched out with shouldered arms, drums beating, and colors flying, saluting the English commander as they passed; then the English troops marched in, raised the union flag, and drank the Queen's health amid a general firing of cannon from the fort

---

[1] The contemporary English translation of this letter is printed among the papers appended to *Nicholson's Journal* in *Collections of the Nova Scotia Historical Society*, I.

and ships. Nicholson changed the name of Port Royal to Annapolis Royal; and Vetch, already commissioned as governor,
took command of the new garrison, which consisted of two
hundred British marines, and two hundred and fifty provincials who had offered themselves for the service.

The English officers gave a breakfast to the French ladies
in the fort. Sir Charles Hobby took in Madame de Bonaventure, and the rest followed in due order of precedence; but as
few of the hosts could speak French, and few of the guests
could speak English, the entertainment could hardly have
been a lively one.

The French officers and men in the fort when it was taken
were but two hundred and fifty-eight. Some of the soldiers
and many of the armed inhabitants deserted during the siege,
which, no doubt, hastened the surrender; for Subercase, a
veteran of more than thirty years' service, had borne fair repute as a soldier.

Port Royal had twice before been taken by New England
men,—once under Major Sedgwick in 1654, and again under
Sir William Phipps in the last war; and in each case it had
been restored to France by treaty. This time England kept
what she had got; and as there was no other place of strength
in the province, the capture of Port Royal meant the conquest
of Acadia.[1]

[1] In a letter to Ponchartrain, *1 Oct. 1710* (new style), Subercase declares that
he has not a sou left, nor any credit. "I have managed to borrow enough to
maintain the garrison for the last two years, and have paid what I could by
selling all my furniture." Charlevoix's account of the siege has been followed
by most writers, both French and English; but it is extremely incorrect. It
was answered by one De Gannes, apparently an officer under Subercase, in a
paper called *Observations sur les Erreurs de la Relation du Siège du Port Royal
. . . faittes sur de faux mémoires par le révérend Père Charlevoix*, whom De
Gannes often contradicts flatly. Thus Charlevoix puts the besieging force at
thirty-four hundred men, besides officers and sailors, while De Gannes puts
it at fourteen hundred; and while Charlevoix says that the garrison were famishing, his critic says that they were provisioned for three months. See the
valuable notes to Shea's *Charlevoix*, V. 227–232.

The journal of Nicholson was published "by authority" in the *Boston News
Letter, Nov. 1710*, and has been reprinted, with numerous accompanying documents, including the French and English correspondence during the siege,
in the *Collections of the Nova Scotia Historical Society*, I.

Vaudreuil, before the siege, sent a reinforcement to Subercase, who, by a
strange infatuation, refused it. *N. Y. Col. Docs.*, IX. 853.

Chapter VIII

1710–1711

WALKER'S EXPEDITION

Scheme of La Ronde Denys • Boston warned against British Designs • Boston to be ruined • Plans of the Ministry • Canada doomed • British Troops at Boston • The Colonists denounced • The Fleet sails for Quebec • Forebodings of the Admiral • Storm and Wreck • Timid Commanders • Retreat • Joyful News for Canada • Pious Exultation • Fanciful Stories • Walker disgraced

MILITARY aid from Old England to New, promised in one year and actually given in the next, was a fact too novel and surprising to escape the notice either of friends or of foes.

The latter drew strange conclusions from it. Two Irish deserters from an English station in Newfoundland appeared at the French post of Placentia full of stories of British and provincial armaments against Canada. On this, an idea seized the French commandant, Costebelle, and he hastened to make it known to the colonial minister. It was to the effect that the aim of England was not so much to conquer the French colonies as to reduce her own to submission, especially Massachusetts,—a kind of republic which has never willingly accepted a governor from its king.[1] In sending ships and soldiers to the "Bastonnais" under pretence of helping them to conquer their French neighbors, Costebelle is sure that England only means to bring them to a dutiful subjection. "I do not think," he writes on another occasion, "that they are so blind as not to see that they will insensibly be brought under the yoke of the Parliament of Old England; but by the cruelties that the Canadians and Indians exercise in continual incursions upon their lands, I judge that they would rather be delivered from the inhumanity of such neighbors than preserve all the former powers of their little repub-

[1] *Rapport de Costebelle, 14 Oct. 1709. Ibid., 3 Déc. 1709.*

lic."[1] He thinks, however, that the design of England ought to be strongly represented to the Council at Boston, and that M. de la Ronde Denys will be a good man to do it, as he speaks English, has lived in Boston, and has many acquaintances there.[2]

The minister, Ponchartrain, was struck by Costebelle's suggestion, and wrote both to him and to Vaudreuil in high approval of it. To Vaudreuil he says: "Monsieur de Costebelle has informed me that the chief object of the armament made by the English last year was to establish their sovereignty at Boston and New York, the people of these provinces having always maintained a sort of republic, governed by their council, and having been unwilling to receive absolute governors from the kings of England. This destination of the armament seems to me probable, and it is much to be wished that the Council at Boston could be informed of the designs of the English court, and shown how important it is for that province to remain in the state of a republic. The King would even approve our helping it to do so. If you see any prospect of success, no means should be spared to secure it. The matter is of the greatest importance, but care is essential to employ persons who have the talents necessary for conducting it, besides great secrecy and prudence, as well as tried probity and fidelity. This affair demands your best attention, and must be conducted with great care and precaution, in order that no false step may be taken."[3]

Ponchartrain could not be supposed to know that while,

[1] "Je ne les crois pas assez aveugles pour ne point s'apercevoir qu'insensiblement ils vont subir le joug du parlement de la vieille Angleterre, mais par les cruautés que les Canadiens et sauvages exercent sur leurs terres par des courses continuelles je juge qu'ils aiment encore mieux se délivrer de l'inhumanité de semblables voisins que de conserver toute l'ancienne autorité de leur petite république." *Costebelle au Ministre, 3 Déc. 1710.* He clung tenaciously to this idea, and wrote again in 1712 that "les cruautés de nos sauvages, qui font horreur à rapporter," would always incline the New England people to peace. They had, however, an opposite effect.

[2] It is more than probable that La Ronde Denys, who had studied the "Bastonnais" with care, first gave the idea to Costebelle.

[3] *Ponchartrain à Vaudreuil, 10 Août, 1710. Ponchartrain à Costebelle, même date.* These letters are in answer to the reports of Costebelle, before cited.

under her old charter, Massachusetts, called by him and other Frenchmen, the government of Boston, had chosen her own governor, New York had always received hers from the court. What is most curious in this affair is the attitude of Louis XIV., who abhorred republics, and yet was prepared to bolster up one or more of them beyond the Atlantic,—thinking, no doubt, that they would be too small and remote to be dangerous.

Costebelle, who had suggested the plan of warning the Council at Boston, proceeded to unfold his scheme for executing it. This was to send La Ronde Denys to Boston in the spring, under the pretext of treating for an exchange of prisoners, which would give him an opportunity of insinuating to the colonists that "the forces which the Queen of England sends to join their own for the conquest of Acadia and Canada have no object whatever but that of ravishing from them the liberties they have kept so firmly and so long, but which would be near ruin if the Queen should become mistress of New France by the fortune of war; and that either they must have sadly fallen from their ancient spirit, or their chiefs have been corrupted by the Court of London, if they do not see that they are using their own weapons for the destruction of their republic."[1]

La Ronde Denys accordingly received his instructions, which authorized him to negotiate with the "Bastonnais" as with an independent people, and offer them complete exemption from French hostility if they would promise to give no more aid to Old England either in ships or men. He was told at the same time to approach the subject with great caution, and unless he found willing listeners, to pass off the whole as a pleasantry.[2] He went to Boston, where he was detained in consequence of preparations then on foot for attacking Canada. He tried to escape; but his vessel was seized and moored

---

[1] *Costebelle à Ponchartrain, 3 Déc. 1710.*

[2] *Instructions pour Monsieur de la Ronde, Capitaine d'Infanterie des Détachements de la Marine, 1711.* "Le dit sieur de la Ronde pourroit entrer en négociation et se promettre de faire cesser toutes sortes d'hostilités du côté du Canada, supposé que les Bastonnais promissent d'en faire de même de leur côté, et qu'ils ne donnassent aucun secours à l'avenir, d'hommes ni de vaisseaux, aux puissances de la vieille Angleterre et d'Ecosse."

under the guns of the town, and it is needless to say that his mission was a failure.

The idea of Costebelle, or rather of La Ronde,—for it probably originated with him,—was not without foundation; for though there is no reason to believe that in sending ships and soldiers against the French, England meant to use them against the liberties of her own colonies, there can be no doubt that she thought those liberties excessive and troublesome; and, on the other side, while the people of Massachusetts were still fondly attached to the land of their fathers, and still called it "Home," they were at the same time enamoured of their autonomy, and jealously watchful against any abridgment of it.

While La Ronde Denys was warning Massachusetts of the danger of helping England to conquer Canada, another Frenchman, in a more prophetic spirit, declared that England would make a grave mistake if she helped her colonies to the same end. "There is an antipathy," this writer affirms, "between the English of Europe and those of America, who will not endure troops from England even to guard their forts;" and he goes on to say that if the French colonies should fall, those of England would control the continent from Newfoundland to Florida. "Old England"—such are his words— "will not imagine that these various provinces will then unite, shake off the yoke of the English monarchy, and erect themselves into a democracy."[1] Forty or fifty years later, several Frenchmen made the same prediction; but at this early day, when the British provinces were so feeble and divided, it is truly a remarkable one.

The anonymous prophet regards the colonies of England, Massachusetts above all, as a standing menace to those of France; and he proposes a drastic remedy against the danger. This is a powerful attack on Boston by land and sea, for which he hopes that God will prepare the way. "When Boston is reduced, we would call together all the chief men of the other towns of New England, who would pay heavy sums

[1] "La vieille Angleterre ne s'imaginera pas que ces diverses Provinces se réuniront, et, secouant le joug de la monarchie Anglaise, s'érigeront en démocratie." *Mémoire sur la Nouvelle Angleterre, 1710, 1711.* (Archives de la Marine.)

to be spared from the flames. As for Boston, it should be pillaged, its workshops, manufactures, shipyards, all its fine establishments ruined, and its ships sunk." If these gentle means are used thoroughly, he thinks that New England will cease to be a dangerous rival for some time, especially if "Rhodelene" (Rhode Island) is treated like Boston.[1]

While the correspondent of the French court was thus consigning New England to destruction, an attack was preparing against Canada less truculent but quite as formidable as that which he urged against Boston. The French colony was threatened by an armament stronger in proportion to her present means of defence than that which brought her under British rule half a century later. But here all comparison ceases; for there was no Pitt to direct and inspire, and no Wolfe to lead.

The letters of Dudley, the proposals of Vetch, the representations of Nicholson, the promptings of Jeremiah Dummer, agent of Massachusetts in England, and the speech made to the Queen by the four Indians who had been the London sensation of the last year, had all helped to draw the attention of the ministry to the New World, and the expediency of driving the French out of it. Other influences conspired to the same end, or in all likelihood little or nothing would have been done. England was tiring of the Continental war, the costs of which threatened ruin. Marlborough was rancorously attacked, and his most stanch supporters, the Whigs, had given place to the Tories, led by the Lord Treasurer, Harley, and the Secretary of State, St. John, soon afterwards Lord Bolingbroke. Never was party spirit more bitter; and the new ministry found a congenial ally in the coarse and savage but powerful genius of Swift, who, incensed by real or imagined slights from the late minister, Godolphin, gave all his strength to the winning side.

---

[1]"Pour Baston, il faudrait la piller, ruiner ses ateliers, ses manufactures, tous ses beaux établissements, couler bas ses navires, . . . ruiner les ateliers de construction de navires." *Mémoire sur la Nouvelle Angleterre, 1710, 1711.* The writer was familiar with Boston and its neighborhood, and had certainly spent some time there. Possibly he was no other than La Ronde Denys himself, after the failure of his mission to excite the "Bastonnais" to refuse co-operation with British armaments. He enlarges with bitterness on the extent of the fisheries, foreign trade, and ship-building of New England.

The prestige of Marlborough's victories was still immense. Harley and St. John dreaded it as their chief danger, and looked eagerly for some means of counteracting it. Such means would be supplied by the conquest of New France. To make America a British continent would be an achievement almost worth Blenheim or Ramillies, and one, too, in which Britain alone would be the gainer; whereas the enemies of Marlborough, with Swift at their head, contended that his greatest triumphs turned more to the profit of Holland or Germany than of England.[1] Moreover, to send a part of his army across the Atlantic would tend to cripple his movements and diminish his fame.

St. John entered with ardor into the scheme. Seven veteran regiments, five of which were from the army in Flanders, were ordered to embark. But in the choice of commanders the judgment of the ministers was not left free; there were influences that they could not disregard. The famous Sarah, Duchess of Marlborough, lately the favorite of the feeble but wilful Queen, had lost her good graces and given place to Mrs. Masham, one of the women of her bedchamber. The new favorite had a brother, John Hill, known about the court as Jack Hill, whom Marlborough had pronounced good for nothing, but who had been advanced to the rank of colonel, and then of brigadier, through the influence of Mrs. Masham; and though his agreeable social qualities were his best recommendation, he was now appointed to command the troops on the Canada expedition. It is not so clear why the naval command was given to Admiral Sir Hovenden Walker, a man whose incompetence was soon to become notorious.

Extreme care was taken to hide the destination of the fleet. Even the Lords of the Admiralty were kept ignorant of it. Some thought the ships bound for the West Indies; some for the South Sea. Nicholson was sent to America with orders to the several colonies to make ready men and supplies. He landed at Boston on the 8th of June. The people of the town, who were nearly all Whigs, were taken by surprise, expecting no such enterprise on the part of the Tory ministry; and their perplexity was not diminished when they were told that the fleet was at hand, and that they were to supply it forthwith

[1] See Swift, *Conduct of the Allies*.

with provisions for ten weeks.[1] There was no time to lose. The governors of New York, Connecticut, and Rhode Island were summoned to meet at New London, and Dudley and Nicholson went thither to join them. Here plans were made for the double attack; for while Walker and Hill sailed up the St. Lawrence against Quebec, Nicholson, as in the former attempt, was to move against Montreal by way of Lake Champlain. In a few days the arrangements were made, and the governors hastened back to their respective posts.[2]

When Dudley reached Boston, he saw Nantasket Roads crowded with transports and ships of war, and the pastures of Noddle's Island studded with tents. The fleet had come on the 24th, having had what the Admiral calls "by the blessing of God a favorable and extraordinary passage, being but seven weeks and two days between Plymouth and Nantasket."[3]

The Admiral and the General had been welcomed with all honor. The provincial Secretary, with two members of the Council, conducted them to town amid salutes from the batteries of Copp's Hill and Fort Hill, and the Boston militia regiment received them under arms; after which they were feasted at the principal tavern and accompanied in ceremony to the lodgings provided for them.[4] When the troops were disembarked and the tents pitched, curious townspeople and staring rustics crossed to Noddle's Island, now East Boston, to gaze with wonder on a military pageant the like of which New England had never seen before. Yet their joy at this unlooked-for succor was dashed with deep distrust and jealousy. They dreaded these new and formidable friends, with their imperious demeanor and exacting demands. The British officers, on their part, were no better pleased with the colonists, and one of them, Colonel King, of the artillery, thus gives

[1] Boston, devoted to fishing, shipbuilding, and foreign trade, drew most of its provisions from neighboring colonies. Dummer, *Letter to a Noble Lord.* The people only half believed that the Tory ministry were sincere in attacking Canada, and suspected that the sudden demand for provisions, so difficult to meet at once, was meant to furnish a pretext for throwing the blame of failure upon Massachusetts. Hutchinson, II. 173.

[2] *Minutes of Proceedings of the Congress of Governors, June, 1711.*

[3] *Walker to Burchett, Secretary of the Admiralty, 14 Aug. 1711.*

[4] *Abstract of the Journal of the Governor, Council, and Assembly of the Province of the Massachusetts Bay.*

vent to his feelings: "You'll find in my Journal what Difficul-
tyes we mett with through the Misfortune that the Coloneys
were not inform'd of our Coming two Months sooner, and
through the Interestedness, ill Nature, and Sowerness of these
People, whose Government, Doctrine, and Manners, whose
Hypocracy and canting, are insupportable; and no man living
but one of Gen'l Hill's good Sense and good Nature could
have managed them. But if such a Man mett with nothing he
could depend on, altho' vested with the Queen's Royal Power
and Authority, and Supported by a Number of Troops sufficient to reduce by force all the Coloneys, 't is easy to determine the Respect and Obedience her Majesty may reasonably
expect from them." And he gives it as his conviction that till
all the colonies are deprived of their charters and brought under one government, "they will grow more stiff and disobedient every Day."[1]

It will be seen that some coolness on the part of the Bostonians was not unnatural. But whatever may have been the
popular feeling, the provincial authorities did their full part
towards supplying the needs of the new-comers; for Dudley,
with his strong Tory leanings, did not share the prevailing
jealousy, and the country members of the Assembly were anxious before all things to be delivered from war-parties. The
problem was how to raise the men and furnish the supplies
in the least possible time. The action of the Assembly, far
from betraying any slackness, was worthy of a military dicta-
torship. All ordinary business was set aside. Bills of credit for
£40,000 were issued to meet the needs of the expedition. It
was ordered that the prices of provisions and other necessaries
of the service should stand fixed at the point where they stood
before the approach of the fleet was known. Sheriffs and con-
stables, jointly with the Queen's officers, were ordered to
search all the town for provisions and liquors, and if the owners refused to part with them at the prescribed prices, to break
open doors and seize them. Stringent and much-needed Acts
were passed against harboring deserters. Provincial troops, in
greater number than the ministry had demanded, were ordered to be raised at once, and quartered upon the citizens,
with or without their consent, at the rate of eightpence a day

[1] *King to Secretary St. John, 25 July, 1711.*

for each man.[1] Warrants were issued for impressing pilots, and also mechanics and laborers, who, in spite of Puritan scruples, were required to work on Sundays.

Such measures, if imposed by England, would have roused the most bitter resentment. Even when ordered by their own representatives, they caused a sullen discontent among the colonists, and greatly increased the popular dislike of their military visitors. It was certain that when the expedition sailed and the operation of the new enactments ceased, prices would rise; and hence the compulsion to part with goods at low fixed rates was singularly trying to the commercial temper. It was a busy season, too, with the farmers, and they showed no haste to bring their produce to the camp. Though many of the principal inhabitants bound themselves by mutual agreement to live on their family stores of salt provisions, in order that the troops might be better supplied with fresh, this failed to soothe the irritation of the British officers, aggravated by frequent desertions, which the colonists favored, and by the impossibility of finding pilots familiar with the St. Lawrence. Some when forced into the service made their escape, to the great indignation of Walker, who wrote to the Governor: "Her Majesty will resent such actions in a very signal manner; and when it shall be represented that the people live here as if there were no king in Israel, but every one does what seems right in his own eyes, measures will be taken to put things upon a better foot for the future."[2] At length, however, every preparation was made, the supplies were all on board, and after a grand review of the troops on the fields of Noddle's Island, the whole force set sail on the 30th of July, the provincials wishing them success, and heartily rejoicing that they were gone.

The fleet consisted of nine ships of war and two bomb-ketches, with about sixty transports, store-ships, hospital-ships, and other vessels, British and provincial. They carried

[1] The number demanded from Massachusetts was one thousand, and that raised by her was eleven hundred and sixty. *Dudley to Walker, 27 July, 1711.*

[2] Walker prints this letter in his Journal. Colonel King writes in his own Journal: "The conquest of Canada will naturally lead the Queen into changing their present disorderly government;" and he thinks that the conviction of this made the New Englanders indifferent to the success of the expedition.

the seven British regiments, numbering, with the artillery train, about fifty-five hundred men, besides six hundred marines and fifteen hundred provincials; counting, with the sailors, nearly twelve thousand in all.[1]

Vetch commanded the provincials, having been brought from Annapolis for that purpose. The great need was of pilots. Every sailor in New England who had seen the St. Lawrence had been pressed into the service, though each and all declared themselves incapable of conducting the fleet to Quebec. Several had no better knowledge of the river than they had picked up when serving as soldiers under Phips twenty-one years before. The best among them was the veteran Captain Bonner, who afterwards amused his old age by making a plan of Boston, greatly prized by connoisseurs in such matters. Vetch had studied the St. Lawrence in his several visits to Quebec, but, like Bonner, he had gone up the river only in sloops or other small craft, and was, moreover, no sailor. One of Walker's ships, the "Chester," sent in advance to cruise in the Gulf, had captured a French vessel commanded by one Paradis, an experienced old voyager, who knew the river well. He took a bribe of five hundred pistoles to act as pilot; but the fleet would perhaps have fared better if he had refused the money. He gave such dismal accounts of the Canadian winter that the Admiral could see nothing but ruin ahead, even if he should safely reach his destination. His tribulation is recorded in his Journal. "That which now chiefly took up my thoughts, was contriving how to secure the ships if we got up to Quebec; for *the ice in the river freezing to the bottom* would have utterly destroyed and bilged them as much as if they had been squeezed between rocks."[2] These misgivings may serve to give the measure of his professional judgment. Afterwards, reflecting on the situation, he sees cause for gratitude in his own mishaps; "because, had we arrived safe at Quebec, our provisions would have been reduced to a very small proportion, not exceeding eight or nine weeks at short

[1] The above is drawn from the various lists and tables in Walker, *Journal of the Canada Expedition.* The armed ships that entered Boston in June were fifteen in all; but several had been detached for cruising. The number of British transports, store-ships, etc., was forty, the rest being provincial.

[2] Walker, *Journal: Introduction.*

allowance, so that between ten and twelve thousand men must have been left to perish with the extremity of cold and hunger. I must confess the melancholy contemplation of this (had it happened) strikes me with horror; for how dismal must it have been to have beheld the seas and earth locked up by adamantine frosts, and swoln with high mountains of snow, in a barren and uncultivated region; great numbers of brave men famishing with hunger, and drawing lots who should die first to feed the rest."[1]

All went well till the 18th of August, when there was a strong head-wind, and the ships ran into the Bay of Gaspé. Two days after, the wind shifted to the southeast, and they set sail again, Walker in his flagship, the "Edgar," being at or near the head of the fleet. On the evening of the 22d they were at some distance above the great island of Anticosti. The river is here about seventy miles wide, and no land had been seen since noon of the day before. There was a strong east wind, with fog. Walker thought that he was not far from the south shore, when in fact he was at least fifty miles from it, and more than half that distance north of his true course. At eight in the evening the Admiral signalled the fleet to bring to, under mizzen and maintopsails, with heads turned southward. At half-past ten, Paddon, the captain of the "Edgar," came to tell him that he saw land which he supposed must be the south shore; on which Walker, in a fatal moment, signalled for the ships to wear and bring to, with heads northward. He then turned into his berth, and was falling asleep, when a military officer, Captain Goddard, of Seymour's regiment, hastily entered, and begged him to come on deck, saying that there were breakers on all sides. Walker, scornful of a landsman, and annoyed at being disturbed, answered impatiently and would not stir. Soon after, Goddard appeared again, and implored him for Heaven's sake to come up and see for himself, or all would be lost. At the same time the Admiral heard a great noise and trampling, on which he turned out of his berth, put on his dressing-gown and slippers, and going in this attire on deck, found a scene of fright and confusion. At first he could see nothing, and shouted to

---

[1] Walker *Journal: Introduction*, 25.

the men to reassure them; but just then the fog opened, the moon shone out, and the breaking surf was plainly visible to leeward. The French pilot, who at first could not be found, now appeared on deck, and declared, to the astonishment of both the Admiral and Captain Paddon, that they were off the north shore. Paddon, in his perplexity, had ordered an anchor to be let go; Walker directed the cable to be cut, and, making all sail, succeeded in beating to windward and gaining an offing.[1]

The ship that carried Colonel King, of the artillery, had a narrow escape. King says that she anchored in a driving rain, "with a shoal of rocks on each quarter within a cable's length of us, which we plainly perceived by the waves breaking over them in a very violent manner." They were saved by a lull in the gale; for if it had continued with the same violence, he pursues, "our anchors could not have held, and the wind and the vast seas which ran, would have broke our ship into ten thousand pieces against the rocks. All night we heard nothing but ships firing and showing lights, as in the utmost distress."[2]

Vetch, who was on board the little frigate "Despatch," says that he was extremely uneasy at the course taken by Walker on the night of the storm. "I told Colonel Dudley and Captain Perkins, commander of the 'Despatch,' that I wondered what the Flag meant by that course, and why he did not steer west and west-by-south."[3] The "Despatch" kept well astern, and so escaped the danger. Vetch heard through the fog guns firing signals of distress; but three days passed before he knew how serious the disaster was. The ships of war had all escaped; but eight British transports, one storeship, and one sutler's sloop were dashed to pieces.[4] "It was lamentable to hear the shrieks of the sinking, drowning, departing souls," writes the New England commissary, Sheaf, who was very near sharing their fate.

The disaster took place at and near a rocky island, with adjacent reefs, lying off the north shore and called Isle aux

[1] Walker, *Journal*, 124, 125.
[2] King, *Journal*.
[3] Vetch, *Journal*.
[4] King, *Journal*.

Œufs. On the second day after it happened, Walker was told by the master of one of the wrecked transports that 884 soldiers had been lost, and he gives this hasty estimate in his published Journal; though he says in his Introduction to it that the total loss of officers, soldiers, and sailors was scarcely nine hundred.[1] According to a later and more trustworthy statement, the loss of the troops was 29 officers, 676 sergeants, corporals, drummers, and private soldiers, and 35 women attached to the regiments; that is, a total of 740 lives.[2] The loss of the sailors is not given; but it could scarcely have exceeded two hundred.

The fleet spent the next two days in standing to and fro between the northern and southern shores, with the exception of some of the smaller vessels employed in bringing off the survivors from the rocks of Isle aux Œufs. The number thus saved was, according to Walker, 499. On the 25th he went on board the General's ship, the "Windsor," and Hill and he resolved to call a council of war. In fact, Hill had already got his colonels together. Signals were made for the captains of the men-of-war to join them, and the council began.

"Jack Hill," the man about town, placed in high command by the influence of his sister, the Queen's tire-woman, had now an opportunity to justify his appointment and prove his mettle. Many a man of pleasure and fashion, when put to the proof, has revealed the latent hero within him; but Hill was not one of them. Both he and Walker seemed to look for nothing but a pretext for retreat; and when manhood is conspicuously wanting in the leaders, a council of war is rarely disposed to supply it. The pilots were called in and examined, and they all declared themselves imperfectly acquainted with the St. Lawrence, which, as some of the captains observed, they had done from the first. Sir William Phips, with pilots still more ignorant, had safely carried his fleet to Quebec in 1690, as Walker must have known, for he had with him

[1] Compare Walker, *Journal*, 45, and *Ibid.*, 127, 128. He elsewhere intimates that his first statement needed correction.

[2] *Report of ye Soldiers, etc., Lost*. (Public Record Office.) This is a tabular statement, giving the names of the commissioned officers and the positions of their subordinates, regiment by regiment. All the French accounts of the losses are exaggerations.

Phips's Journal of the voyage. The expedition had lost about a twelfth part of its soldiers and sailors, besides the transports that carried them; with this exception there was no reason for retreat which might not as well have been put forward when the fleet left Boston. All the war-ships were safe, and the loss of men was not greater than might have happened in a single battle. Hill says that Vetch, when asked if he would pilot the fleet to Quebec, refused to undertake it;[1] but Vetch himself gives his answer as follows: "I told him [the Admiral] I never was bred to sea, nor was it any part of my province; but I would do my best by going ahead and showing them where the difficulty of the river was, which I knew pretty well."[2] The naval captains, however, resolved that by reason of the ignorance of the pilots and the dangerous currents it was impossible to go up to Quebec.[3] So discreditable a backing out from a great enterprise will hardly be found elsewhere in English annals. On the next day Vetch, disappointed and indignant, gave his mind freely to the Admiral. "The late disaster cannot, in my humble opinion, be anyways imputed to the difficulty of the navigation, but to the wrong course we steered, which most unavoidably carried us upon the north shore. Who directed that course you best know; and as our return without any further attempt would be a vast reflection upon the conduct of this affair, so it would be of very fatal consequence to the interest of the Crown and all the British colonies upon this continent."[4] His protest was fruitless. The fleet retraced its course to the gulf, and then steered for Spanish River,—now the harbor of Sydney,—in the island of Cape Breton; the Admiral consoling himself with the reflection that the wreck was a blessing in disguise and a merciful intervention of Providence to save the expedition from the freezing, starvation, and cannibalism which his imagination had conjured up.[5]

The frigate "Sapphire" was sent to Boston with news of the

[1] *Hill to Dudley, 25 Aug. 1711.*

[2] Vetch, *Journal*. His statement is confirmed by the report of the council.

[3] *Report of a Consultation of Sea Officers belonging to the Squadron under Command of Sir Hovenden Walker, Kt., 25 Aug. 1711.* Signed by Walker and eight others.

[4] *Vetch to Walker, 26 Aug. 1711.*

[5] Walker, *Journal, Introduction,* 25.

wreck and the retreat, which was at once despatched to Nicholson, who, if he continued his movement on Montreal, would now be left to conquer Canada alone. His force consisted of about twenty-three hundred men, white and red, and when the fatal news reached him he was encamped on Wood Creek, ready to pass Lake Champlain. Captain Butler, a New York officer at the camp, afterwards told Kalm, the Swedish naturalist, that when Nicholson heard what had happened, he was beside himself with rage, tore off his wig, threw it on the ground and stamped upon it, crying out "Roguery! Treachery!"[1] When his fit was over, he did all that was now left for him to do,—burned the wooden forts he had built, marched back to Albany, and disbanded his army, after leaving one hundred and fifty men to protect the frontier against scalping-parties.[2]

Canada had been warned of the storm gathering against her. Early in August, Vaudreuil received letters from Costebelle, at Placentia, telling him that English prisoners had reported mighty preparations at Boston against Quebec, and that Montreal was also to be attacked.[3] The colony was ill prepared for the emergency, but no effort was spared to give the enemy a warm reception. The militia were mustered, Indians called together, troops held in readiness, and defences strengthened. The saints were invoked, and the aid of Heaven was implored by masses, processions, and penances, as in New England by a dismal succession of fasts. Mother Juchereau de Saint-Denis tells us how devout Canadians prayed for help from God and the most holy Virgin; "since their glory was involved, seeing that the true religion would quickly perish if the English should prevail." The general alarm produced effects which, though transient, were thought highly commendable while they lasted. The ladies, according to Mother Juchereau, gave up their ornaments, and became more modest and more pious. "Those of Montreal," pursues the worthy nun, "even outdid those of Quebec; for they bound themselves by oath to wear neither ribbons nor lace, to keep their throats covered, and to observe various holy practices for the

[1] Kalm, *Travels*, II. 135.
[2] Schuyler, *Colonial New York*, II. 48.
[3] *Vaudreuil au Ministre, 25 Oct. 1711*.

space of a year." The recluse of Montreal, Mademoiselle Le Ber, who, by reason of her morbid seclusion and ascetic life, was accounted almost a saint, made a flag embroidered with a prayer to the Virgin, to be borne against the heretical bands of Nicholson.

When that commander withdrew, his retreat, though not the cause of it, was quickly known at Montreal, and the forces gathered there went down to Quebec to aid in repelling the more formidable attack by sea. Here all was suspense and expectancy till the middle of October, when the report came that two large ships had been seen in the river below. There was great excitement, for they were supposed to be the van of the British fleet; but alarm was soon turned to joy by the arrival of the ships, which proved to be French. On the 19th, the Sieur de la Valterie, who had come from Labrador in September, and had been sent down the river again by Vaudreuil to watch for the English fleet, appeared at Quebec with tidings of joy. He had descended the St. Lawrence in a canoe, with two Frenchmen and an Indian, till, landing at Isle aux Œufs on the 1st of October, they met two French sailors or fishermen loaded with plunder, and presently discovered the wrecks of seven English ships, with, as they declared, fifteen or sixteen hundred dead bodies on the strand hard by, besides dead horses, sheep, dogs, and hens, three or four hundred large iron-hooped casks, a barrel of wine and a barrel and a keg of brandy, cables, anchors, chains, planks, boards, shovels, picks, mattocks, and piles of old iron three feet high.[1]

"The least devout," writes Mother Juchereau, "were touched by the grandeur of the miracle wrought in our behalf,—a marvellous effect of God's love for Canada, which, of all these countries, is the only one that professes the true religion."

Quebec was not ungrateful. A solemn mass was ordered every month during a year, to be followed by the song of Moses after the destruction of Pharaoh and his host.[2] Amazing reports were spread concerning the losses of the English.

[1] *Déposition de François de Marganne, Sieur de la Valterie; par devant Nous, Paul Dupuy, Ecuyer, Conseiller du Roy, etc., 19 Oct. 1711.*

[2] *Monseigneur de Saint-Vallier et l'Histoire de l'Hôpital Général de Québec,* 209.

About three thousand of "these wretches"—so the story ran—died after reaching land, without counting the multitudes drowned in the attempt; and even this did not satisfy divine justice, for God blew up one of the ships by lightning during the storm. Vessels were sent to gather up the spoils of the wreck, and they came back, it was reported, laden with marvellous treasures, including rich clothing, magnificent saddles, plate, silver-hilted swords, and the like; bringing also the gratifying announcement that though the autumn tides had swept away many corpses, more than two thousand still lay on the rocks, naked and in attitudes of despair.[1] These stories, repeated by later writers, find believers to this day.[2]

When Walker and his ships reached Spanish River, he called another council of war. The question was whether, having failed to take Quebec, they should try to take Placentia; and it was resolved that the short supply of provisions, the impossibility of getting more from Boston before the 1st of November, and the risks of the autumnal storms, made the attempt impracticable. Accordingly, the New England transports sailed homeward, and the British fleet steered for the Thames.

Swift writes on the 6th of October in his Journal to Stella: "The news of Mr. Hill's miscarriage in his expedition came to-day, and I went to visit Mrs. Masham and Mrs. Hill, his two sisters, to condole with them." A week after, he mentions the arrival of the General himself; and again on the 16th writes thus: "I was to see Jack Hill this morning, who made that unfortunate expedition; and there is still more misfortune, for that ship which was admiral of his fleet [the "Edgar"] is blown up in the Thames by an accident and carelessness of some rogue, who was going, as they think, to steal some gunpowder: five hundred men are lost."

A report of this crowning disaster reached Quebec, and Mother Juchereau does not fail to improve it. According to

[1] Juchereau, *Histoire de l'Hôtel-Dieu de Québec*, 473–491. La Ronde Denys says that nearly one thousand men were drowned, and that about two thousand died of injuries received. *La Ronde au Ministre, 30 Déc. 1711.*

[2] Some exaggeration was natural enough. Colonel Lee, of the Rhode Island contingent, says that a day or two after the wreck he saw "the bodies of twelve or thirteen hundred brave men, with women and children, lying in heaps." *Lee to Governor Cranston, 12 Sept. 1711.*

her, the Admiral, stricken with divine justice, and wrought to desperation, blew up the ship himself, and perished with all on board, except only two men.

There was talk of an examination into the causes of the failure, but nothing was done. Hill, strong in the influence of Mrs. Masham, reaped new honors and offices. Walker, more answerable for the result, and less fortunate in court influence, was removed from command, and his name was stricken from the half-pay list. He did not, however, blow himself up, but left England and emigrated to South Carolina, whence, thinking himself ill-treated by the authorities, he removed to Barbadoes, and died some years later.[1]

[1] Walker's Journal was published in 1720, with an Introduction of forty-eight pages, written in bad temper and bad taste. The Journal contains many documents, printed in full. In the Public Record Office are preserved the Journals of Hill, Vetch, and King. Copies of these, with many other papers on the same subject, from the same source, are before me. Vetch's Journal and his letter to Walker after the wreck are printed in the *Collections of the Nova Scotia Historical Society*, Vol. IV.

It appears by the muster-rolls of Massachusetts that what with manning the coast-guard vessels, defending the frontier against Indians, and furnishing her contingent to the Canada expedition, more than one in five of her able-bodied men were in active service in the summer of 1711. Years passed before she recovered from the effects of her financial exhaustion.

Chapter IX

LOUISBOURG AND ACADIA

Peace of Utrecht • Perilous Questions • Louisbourg founded • Annapolis attacked • Position of the Acadians • Weakness of the British Garrison • Apathy of the Ministry • French Intrigue • Clerical Politicians • The Oath of Allegiance • Acadians refuse it • Their Expulsion proposed • They take the Oath

---

THE GREAT European war was drawing to an end, and with it the American war, which was but its echo. An avalanche of defeat and disaster had fallen upon the old age of Louis XIV., and France was burdened with an insupportable load of debt. The political changes in England came to her relief. Fifty years later, when the elder Pitt went out of office and Bute came in, France had cause to be grateful; for the peace of 1763 was far more favorable to her than it would have been under the imperious war minister. It was the same in 1712. The Whigs who had fallen from power would have wrung every advantage from France; the triumphant Tories were eager to close with her on any terms not so easy as to excite popular indignation. The result was the Treaty of Utrecht, which satisfied none of the allies of England, and gave to France conditions more favorable than she had herself proposed two years before. The fall of Godolphin and the disgrace of Marlborough were a godsend to her.

Yet in America Louis XIV. made important concessions. The Five Nations of the Iroquois were acknowledged to be British subjects; and this became in future the preposterous foundation for vast territorial claims of England. Hudson Bay, Newfoundland, and Acadia, "according to its ancient limits," were also given over by France to her successful rival; though the King parted from Acadia with a reluctance shown by the great offers he made for permission to retain it.[1]

But while the Treaty of Utrecht seemed to yield so much,

---

[1] *Offres de la France; Demandes de l'Angleterre et Réponses de la France*, in *Memorials of the English and French Commissaries concerning the Limits of Acadia*.

and yielded so much in fact, it staved off the settlement of questions absolutely necessary for future peace. The limits of Acadia, the boundary line between Canada and the British colonies, and the boundary between those colonies and the great western wilderness claimed by France, were all left unsettled, since the attempt to settle them would have rekindled the war. The peace left the embers of war still smouldering, sure, when the time should come, to burst into flame. The next thirty years were years of chronic, smothered war, disguised, but never quite at rest. The standing subjects of dispute were three, very different in importance. First, the question of Acadia: whether the treaty gave England a vast country, or only a strip of sea-coast. Next, that of northern New England and the Abenaki Indians, many of whom French policy still left within the borders of Maine, and whom both powers claimed as subjects or allies. Last and greatest was the question whether France or England should hold the valleys of the Mississippi and the Great Lakes, and with them the virtual control of the continent. This was the triple problem that tormented the northern English colonies for more than a generation, till it found a solution at last in the Seven Years' War.

Louis XIV. had deeply at heart the recovery of Acadia. Yet the old and infirm King, whose sun was setting in clouds after half a century of unrivalled splendor, felt that peace was a controlling necessity, and he wrote as follows to his plenipotentiaries at Utrecht: "It is so important to prevent the breaking off of the negotiations that the King will give up both Acadia and Cape Breton, if necessary for peace; but the plenipotentiaries will yield this point only in the last extremity, for by this double cession Canada will become useless, the access to it will be closed, the fisheries will come to an end, and the French marine be utterly destroyed."[1] And he adds that if the English will restore Acadia, he, the King, will give them, not only St. Christopher, but also the islands of St. Martin and St. Bartholomew.

The plenipotentiaries replied that the offer was refused, and that the best they could do without endangering the peace

---

[1] *Mémoire du Roy à ses Plénipotentiaires, 20 Mars, 1712.*

was to bargain that Cape Breton should belong to France.[1] On this, the King bid higher still for the coveted province, and promised that if Acadia were returned to him, the fortifications of Placentia should be given up untouched, the cannon in the forts of Hudson Bay abandoned to the English, and the Newfoundland fisheries debarred to Frenchmen,[2] — a remarkable concession; for France had fished on the banks of Newfoundland for two centuries, and they were invaluable to her as a nursery of sailors. Even these offers were rejected, and England would not resign Acadia.

Cape Breton was left to the French. This large island, henceforth called by its owners Isle Royale, lies east of Acadia, and is separated from it only by the narrow Strait of Canso. From its position, it commands the chief entrance of the gulf and river of St. Lawrence. Some years before, the Intendant Raudot had sent to the court an able paper, in which he urged its occupation and settlement, chiefly on commercial and industrial grounds. The war was then at its height; the plan was not carried into effect, and Isle Royale was still a wilderness. It was now proposed to occupy it for military and political reasons. One of its many harbors, well fortified and garrisoned, would guard the approaches of Canada, and in the next war furnish a base for attacking New England and recovering Acadia.

After some hesitation the harbor called Port à l'Anglois was chosen for the proposed establishment, to which the name of Louisbourg was given, in honor of the King. It lies near the southeastern point of the island, where an opening in the iron-bound coast, at once easily accessible and easily defended, gives entrance to a deep and sheltered basin, where a fleet of war-ships may find good anchorage. The proposed fortress was to be placed on the tongue of land that lies between this basin and the sea. The place, well chosen from the point of view of the soldier or the fisherman, was unfit for an agricultural colony, its surroundings being barren hills studded with spruce and fir, and broad marshes buried in moss.

In spite of the losses and humiliations of the war, great

[1] *Précis de ce qui s'est passé pendant la Négotiation de la Paix d'Utrecht au Sujet de l'Acadie; Juillet, 1711 –Mai, 1712.*
[2] *Mémoire du Roy, 20 Avril, 1712.*

expectations were formed from the new scheme. Several years earlier, when the proposals of Raudot were before the Marine Council, it was confidently declared that a strong fortress on Cape Breton would make the King master of North America. The details of the establishment were settled in advance. The King was to build the fortifications, supply them with cannon, send out eight companies of soldiers, besides all the usual officers of government, establish a well-endowed hospital, conducted by nuns, as at Quebec, provide Jesuits and Récollets as chaplains, besides Filles de la Congrégation to teach girls, send families to the spot, support them for two years, and furnish a good number of young women to marry the soldiers.[1]

This plan, or something much like it, was carried into effect. Louisbourg was purely and solely the offspring of the Crown and its ally, the Church. In time it grew into a compact fishing town of about four thousand inhabitants, with a strong garrison and a circuit of formidable ramparts and batteries. It became by far the strongest fortress on the Atlantic coast, and so famous as a resort of privateers that it was known as the Dunquerque of America.

What concerns us now is its weak and troubled infancy. It was to be peopled in good part from the two lost provinces of Acadia and Newfoundland, whose inhabitants were to be transported to Louisbourg or other parts of Isle Royale, which would thus be made at once and at the least possible cost a dangerous neighbor to the newly acquired possessions of England. The Micmacs of Acadia, and even some of the Abenakis, were to be included in this scheme of immigration.

In the autumn, the commandant of Plaisance, or Placentia,—the French stronghold in Newfoundland,—received the following mandate from the King:—

MONSIEUR DE COSTEBELLE,—I have caused my orders to be given you to evacuate the town and forts of Plaisance and the other places of your government of Newfoundland, ceded to my dear sister the Queen of Great Britain. I have given my orders for the equipment of the vessels necessary to make the evacuation and transport you, with the officers,

[1] *Mémoire sur l'Isle du Cap Breton, 1709.*

garrison, and inhabitants of Plaisance and other places of Newfoundland, to my Isle Royale, vulgarly called Cape Breton; but as the season is so far advanced that this cannot be done without exposing my troops and my subjects to perishing from cold and misery, and placing my vessels in evident peril of wreck, I have judged it proper to defer the transportation till the next spring.[1]

The inhabitants of Placentia consisted only of twenty-five or thirty poor fishermen, with their families,[2] and some of them would gladly have become English subjects and stayed where they were; but no choice was given them. "Nothing," writes Costebelle, "can cure them of the error, to which they obstinately cling, that they are free to stay or go, as best suits their interest."[3] They and their fishing-boats were in due time transported to Isle Royale, where for a while their sufferings were extreme.

Attempts were made to induce the Indians of Acadia to move to the new colony; but they refused, and to compel them was out of the question. But by far the most desirable accession to the establishment of Isle Royale would be that of the Acadian French, who were too numerous to be transported in the summary manner practised in the case of the fishermen of Placentia. It was necessary to persuade rather than compel them to migrate, and to this end great reliance was placed on their priests, especially Fathers Pain and Dominique. Ponchartrain himself wrote to the former on the subject. The priest declares that he read the letter to his flock, who answered that they wished to stay in Acadia; and he adds that the other Acadians were of the same mind, being unwilling to leave their rich farms and risk starvation on a wild and barren island.[4] "Nevertheless," he concludes, "we shall fulfil the intentions of his Majesty by often holding before their eyes that religion for which they ought to make every sacrifice." He and his brother priests kept their word. Freedom of worship was pledged on certain conditions to the Acadians

[1] *Le Roy à Costebelle, 29 Sept. 1713.*

[2] *Recensement des Habitans de Plaisance et Iles de St. Pierre, rendus à Louisbourg avec leurs Femmes et Enfans, 5 Nov. 1714.*

[3] *Costebelle au Ministre, 19 Juillet, 1713.*

[4] *Félix Pain à Costebelle, 23 Sept. 1713.*

by the Treaty of Utrecht, and no attempt was ever made to deprive them of it; yet the continual declaration of their missionaries that their souls were in danger under English rule was the strongest spur to impel them to migrate.

The condition of the English in Acadia since it fell into their hands had been a critical one. Port Royal, thenceforth called Annapolis Royal, or simply Annapolis, had been left, as before mentioned, in charge of Colonel Vetch, with a heterogeneous garrison of four hundred and fifty men.[1] The Acadians of the *banlieue*—a term defined as covering a space of three miles round the fort—had been included in the capitulation, and had taken an oath of allegiance to Queen Anne, binding so long as they remained in the province. Some of them worked for the garrison and helped to repair the fort, which was in a ruinous condition. Meanwhile the Micmac Indians remained fiercely hostile to the English; and in June, 1711, aided by a band of Penobscots, they ambuscaded and killed or captured nearly seventy of them. This completely changed the attitude of the Acadians. They broke their oath, rose against their new masters, and with their Indian friends, invested the fort to the number of five or six hundred. Disease, desertion, and the ambuscade had reduced the garrison to about two hundred effective men, and the defences of the place were still in bad condition.[2] The assailants, on the other hand, had no better leader than the priest, Gaulin, missionary of the Micmacs and prime mover in the rising. He presently sailed for Placentia to beg for munitions and a commander; but his errand failed, the siege came to nought, and the besiegers dispersed. Vaudreuil, from whom the Acadians had begged help, was about to send it when news of the approach of Walker's fleet forced him to keep all his strength for his own defence.

[1] Vetch was styled "General and Commander-in-chief of all his Majesty's troops in these parts, and Governor of the fort of Annapolis Royal, country of l'Accady and Nova Scotia." Hence he was the first English governor of Nova Scotia after its conquest in 1710. He was appointed a second time in 1715, Nicholson having served in the interim.

[2] *Narrative of Paul Mascarene*, addressed to Nicholson. According to French accounts, a pestilence at Annapolis had carried off three fourths of the garrison. *Gaulin à —— 5 Sept. 1711; Cahouet au Ministre, 20 Juillet, 1711.* In reality a little more than one hundred had died.

From this time to the end of the war, the chief difficulties of the Governor of Acadia rose, not from the enemy, but from the British authorities at home. For more than two years he, with his starved and tattered garrison, were treated with absolute neglect. He received no orders, instructions, or money.[1] Acadia seemed forgotten by the ministry, till Vetch heard at last that Nicholson was appointed to succeed him.

Now followed the Treaty of Utrecht, the cession of Acadia to England, and the attempt on the part of France to induce the Acadians to remove to Isle Royale. Some of the English officials had once been of opinion that this French Catholic population should be transported to Martinique or some other distant French colony, and its place supplied by Protestant families sent from England or Ireland.[2] Since the English Revolution, Protestantism was bound up with the new political order, and Catholicism with the old. No Catholic could favor the Protestant succession, and hence politics were inseparable from creed. Vetch, who came of a race of hot and stubborn Covenanters, had been one of the most earnest for replacing the Catholic Acadians by Protestants; but after the peace he and others changed their minds. No Protestant colonists appeared, nor was there the smallest sign that the government would give itself the trouble to attract any. It was certain that if the Acadians removed at all, they would go, not to Martinique or any other distant colony, but to the new military establishment of Isle Royale, which would thus become a strong and dangerous neighbor to the feeble British post of Annapolis. Moreover, the labor of the French inhabitants was useful and sometimes necessary to the English garrison, which depended mainly on them for provisions; and if they left the province, they would leave it a desert, with the prospect of long remaining so.

Hence it happened that the English were for a time almost as anxious to keep the Acadians in Acadia as they were forty years later to get them out of it; nor had the Acadians themselves any inclination to leave their homes. But the French authorities needed them at Isle Royale, and made every effort

[1] Passages from Vetch's letters, in Patterson, *Memoir of Vetch.*
[2] *Vetch to the Earl of Dartmouth, 22 Jan. 1711; Memorial of Council of War at Annapolis, 14 Oct. 1710.*

to draw them thither. By the fourteenth article of the Treaty of Utrecht such of them as might choose to leave Acadia were free to do so within the space of a year, carrying with them their personal effects; while a letter of Queen Anne, addressed to Nicholson, then governor of Acadia, permitted the emigrants to sell their lands and houses.

The missionary Félix Pain had reported, as we have seen, that they were, in general, disposed to remain where they were; on which Costebelle, who now commanded at Louisbourg, sent two officers, La Ronde Denys and Pensens, with instructions to set the priests at work to persuade their flocks to move.[1] La Ronde Denys and his colleague repaired to Annapolis, where they promised the inhabitants vessels for their removal, provisions for a year, and freedom from all taxation for ten years. Then, having been well prepared in advance, the heads of families were formed in a circle, and in presence of the English Governor, the two French officers, and the priests Justinien, Bonaventure, and Gaulin, they all signed, chiefly with crosses, a paper to the effect that they would live and die subjects of the King of France.[2] A few embarked at once for Isle Royale in the vessel "Marie-Joseph," and the rest were to follow within the year.

This result was due partly to the promises of La Ronde Denys, and still more to a pastoral letter from the Bishop of Quebec, supporting the assurances of the missionaries that the heretics would rob them of the ministrations of the Church. This was not all. The Acadians about Annapolis had been alienated by the conduct of the English authorities, which was not conciliating, and on the part of the Governor was sometimes outrageous.[3] Yet those of the *banlieue* had no right to complain, since they had made themselves liable to the penalties of treason by first taking an oath of allegiance to Queen Anne, and then breaking it by trying to seize her fort.[4]

Governor Nicholson, like his predecessor, was resolved to

[1] Costebelle, *Instruction au Capitaine de la Ronde, 1714.*

[2] *Ecrit des Habitants d'Annapolis Royale, 25 Aoust, 1714; Mémoire de La Ronde Denys, 30 Aoust, 1714.*

[3] In 1711, however, the missionary Félix Pain says, "The English have treated the Acadians with much humanity." *Père Félix à —— 8 Sept. 1711.*

[4] This was the oath taken after the capitulation, which bound those who took it to allegiance so long as they remained in the province.

keep the Acadians in the province if he could. This personage, able, energetic, perverse, headstrong, and unscrupulous, conducted himself, even towards the English officers and soldiers, in a manner that seems unaccountable, and that kindled their utmost indignation.[1] Towards the Acadians his behavior was still worse. As Costebelle did not keep his promise to send vessels to bring them to Isle Royale, they built small ones for themselves, and the French authorities at Louisbourg sent them the necessary rigging. Nicholson ordered it back, forbade the sale of their lands and houses,—a needless stretch of power, as there was nobody to buy,—and would not let them sell even their personal effects, coolly setting at nought both the Treaty of Utrecht and the letter of the Queen.[2]

Nicholson was but a short time at Annapolis, leaving the government, during most of his term, to his deputies, Caulfield and afterwards Doucette, both of whom roundly denounce their principal for his general conduct, while both, in one degree or another, followed his example in preventing so far as they could the emigration of the Acadians. Some of them, however, got away, and twelve or fifteen families who settled at Port Toulouse, on Isle Royale, were near perishing from cold and hunger.[3]

From Annapolis the French agents, La Ronde Denys and Pensens, proceeded to the settlements about Chignecto and the Basin of Mines,—the most populous and prosperous parts of Acadia. Here they were less successful than before. The people were doubtful and vacillating; ready enough to promise, but slow to perform. While declaring with perfect sincerity their devotion to "our invincible monarch," as they called King Louis, who had just been compelled to surrender their country, they clung tenaciously to the abodes of their fathers. If they had wished to emigrate, the English Governor had no power to stop them. From Baye Verte, on the isthmus, they had frequent and easy communication with the

---

[1] "As he used to curse and Damm Governor Vetch and all his friends, he is now served himself in the same manner." *Adams to Steele, 24 Jan. 1715.*

[2] For a great number of extracts from documents on this subject see a paper by Abbé Casgrain in *Canada Français*, I. 411–414; also the documentary supplement of the same publication.

[3] *La Ronde Denys au Ministre, 3 Déc. 1715.*

French at Louisbourg, which the English did not and could not interrupt. They were armed, and they far outnumbered the English garrison; while at a word they could bring to their aid the Micmac warriors, who had been taught to detest the English heretics as foes of God and man. To say that they wished to leave Acadia, but were prevented from doing so by a petty garrison at the other end of the province, so feeble that it could hardly hold Annapolis itself, is an unjust reproach upon a people who, though ignorant and weak of purpose, were not wanting in physical courage. The truth is that from this time to their forced expatriation in 1755, all the Acadians except those of Annapolis and its immediate neighborhood were free to go or stay at will. Those of the eastern parts of the province especially, who formed the greater part of the population, were completely their own masters. This was well known to the French authorities. The Governor of Louisbourg complains of the apathy of the Acadians.[1] Saint-Ovide declares that they do not want to fulfil the intentions of the King and remove to Isle Royale. Costebelle makes the same complaint; and again, after three years of vain attempts to overcome their reluctance, he writes that every effort has failed to induce them to migrate.

From this time forward the state of affairs in Acadia was a peculiar one. By the Treaty of Utrecht it was a British province, and the nominal sovereignty resided at Annapolis, in the keeping of the miserable little fort and the puny garrison, which as late as 1743 consisted of but five companies, counting, when the ranks were full, thirty-one men each.[2] More troops were often asked for, and once or twice were promised; but they were never sent. "This has been hitherto no more than a mock government, its authority never yet having extended beyond cannon-shot of the fort," wrote Governor Philipps in 1720. "It would be more for the honour of the Crown, and profit also, to give back the country to the

[1] *Costebelle au Ministre, 15 Jan. 1715.*

[2] *Governor Mascarene to the Secretary of State, 1 Dec. 1743.* At this time there was also a blockhouse at Canso, where a few soldiers were stationed. These were then the only British posts in the province. In May, 1727, Philipps wrote to the Lords of Trade: "Everything there [at Annapolis] is wearing the face of ruin and decay," and the ramparts are "lying level with the ground in breaches sufficiently wide for fifty men to enter abreast."

French, than to be contented with the name only of government."[1] Philipps repaired the fort, which, as the engineer Mascarene says, "had lain tumbling down" before his arrival; but Annapolis and the whole province remained totally neglected and almost forgotten by England till the middle of the century. At one time the soldiers were in so ragged a plight that Lieutenant-Colonel Armstrong was forced to clothe them at his own expense.[2]

While this seat of British sovereignty remained in unchanging feebleness for more than forty years, the French Acadians were multiplying apace. Before 1749 they were the only white inhabitants of the province, except ten or twelve English families who, about the year 1720, lived under the guns of Annapolis. At the time of the cession the French population seems not to have exceeded two thousand souls, about five hundred of whom lived within the *banlieue* of Annapolis, and were therefore more or less under English control. They were all alike a simple and ignorant peasantry, prosperous in their humble way, and happy when rival masters ceased from troubling, though vexed with incessant quarrels among themselves, rising from the unsettled boundaries of their lands, which had never been properly surveyed. Their mental horizon was of the narrowest, their wants were few, no military service was asked of them by the English authorities, and they paid no taxes to the government. They could even indulge their strong appetite for litigation free of cost; for when, as often happened, they brought their land disputes before the Council at Annapolis, the cases were settled and the litigants paid no fees. Their communication with the English officials was carried on through deputies chosen by themselves, and often as ignorant as their constituents, for a remarkable equality prevailed through this primitive little society.

Except the standing garrison at Annapolis, Acadia was as completely let alone by the British government as Rhode Island or Connecticut. Unfortunately, the traditional British policy of inaction towards her colonies was not applicable in the case of a newly conquered province with a disaffected population and active, enterprising, and martial neighbors

[1] *Philipps to Secretary Craggs, 26 Sept. 1720.*
[2] *Selections from the Public Documents of Nova Scotia, 18, note.*

bent on recovering what they had lost. Yet it might be supposed that a neglect so invigorating in other cases, might have developed among the Acadians habits of self-reliance and faculties of self-care. The reverse took place; for if England neglected Acadia, France did not; and though she had renounced her title to it, she still did her best to master it and make it hers again. The chief instrument of her aggressive policy was the Governor of Isle Royale, whose station was the fortress of Louisbourg, and who was charged with the management of Acadian affairs. At all the Acadian settlements he had zealous and efficient agents in the missionary priests, who were sent into the province by the Bishop of Quebec, or in a few cases by their immediate ecclesiastical superiors in Isle Royale.

The Treaty of Utrecht secured freedom of worship to the Acadians under certain conditions. These were that they should accept the sovereignty of the British Crown, and that they and their pastors should keep within the limits of British law.[1] Even supposing that by swearing allegiance to Queen Anne the Acadians had acquired the freedom of worship which the treaty gave them on condition of their becoming British subjects, it would have been an abuse of this freedom to use it for subverting the power that had granted it. Yet this is what the missionaries did. They were not only priests of the Roman Church, they were also agents of the King of France; and from first to last they labored against the British government in the country that France had ceded to the British Crown. So confident were they, and with so much reason, of the weakness of their opponents that they openly avowed that their object was to keep the Acadians faithful to King Louis. When two of their number, Saint-Poncy and Chevereaux, were summoned before the Council at Annapolis, they answered, with great contempt, "We are here on the business of the King of France." They were ordered to leave Acadia. One of them stopped among the Indians at Cape Sable; the other, in defiance of the Council, was sent back to Annapolis

---

[1] "Those who are willing to remain there [in Acadia] and to be subject to the kingdom of Great Britain, are to enjoy the free exercise of their religion according to the usage of the Church of Rome, as far as the laws of Great Britain do allow the same." *Treaty of Utrecht, 14th article.*

by the Governor of Isle Royale.[1] Apparently he was again ordered away; for four years later the French Governor, in expectation of speedy war, sent him to Chignecto with orders secretly to prepare the Acadians for an attack on Annapolis.[2]

The political work of the missionaries began with the cession of the colony, and continued with increasing activity till 1755, kindling the impotent wrath of the British officials, and drawing forth the bitter complaints of every successive Governor. For this world and the next, the priests were fathers of their flocks, generally commanding their attachment, and always their obedience. Except in questions of disputed boundaries, where the Council alone could settle the title, the ecclesiastics took the place of judges and courts of justice, enforcing their decisions by refusal of the sacraments.[3] They often treated the British officials with open scorn. Governor Armstrong writes to the Lords of Trade: "Without some particular directions as to the insolent behavior of those priests, the people will never be brought to obedience, being by them incited to daily acts of rebellion." Another Governor complains that they tell the Acadians of the destitution of the soldiers and the ruinous state of the fort, and assure them that the Pretender will soon be king of England, and that Acadia will then return to France.[4] "The bearer, Captain Bennett," writes Armstrong, "can further tell your Grace of the disposition of the French inhabitants of this province, and of the conduct of their missionary priests, who instil hatred into both Indians and French against the English."[5] As to the Indians, Governor Philipps declares that their priests hear a general confession from them twice a year, and give them absolution on condition of always being enemies of the English.[6] The condition was easy, thanks to the neglect of the British government, which took no pains to conciliate the Micmacs, while the French Governor of Isle Royale corresponded secretly with them and made them yearly presents.

[1] *Minutes of Council, 18 May, 1736. Governor Armstrong to the Secretary of State, 22 Nov. 1736.*

[2] *Minutes of Council, 18 Sept. 1740*, in *Nova Scotia Archives.*

[3] *Governor Mascarene to Père des Enclaves, 29 Juin, 1741.*

[4] *Deputy-Governor Doucette to the Secretary of State, 5 Nov. 1717.*

[5] *Governor Armstrong to the Secretary of State, 30 April, 1727.*

[6] *Governor Philipps to Secretary Craggs, 26 Sept. 1720.*

In 1720 Philipps advised the recall of the French priests, and the sending of others in their place, as the only means of making British subjects of the Acadians,[1] who at that time, having constantly refused the oath of allegiance, were not entitled, under the treaty, to the exercise of their religion. Governor Armstrong wrote sixteen years after: "By some of the above papers your Grace will be informed how high the French government carries its pretensions over its priests' obedience; and how to prevent the evil consequences I know not, unless we could have missionaries from places independent of that Crown."[2] He expresses a well-grounded doubt whether the home government will be at the trouble and expense of such a change, though he adds that there is not a missionary among either Acadians or Indians who is not in the pay of France.[3] Gaulin, missionary of the Micmacs, received a "gratification" of fifteen hundred livres, besides an annual allowance of five hundred, and is described in the order granting it as a "brave man, capable even of leading these savages on an expedition."[4] In 1726 he was brought before the Council at Annapolis charged with incendiary conduct among both Indians and Acadians; but on asking pardon and promising never more to busy himself with affairs of government, he was allowed to remain in the province, and even to act as curé of the Mines.[5] No evidence appears that the British authorities ever molested a priest, except when detected in practices alien to his proper functions and injurious to the government. On one occasion when two cures were vacant, one through sedition and the other apparently through illness or death,

[1] *Governor Philipps to Secretary Craggs, 26 May, 1720.*

[2] *Armstrong to the Secretary of State, 22 Nov. 1736.* The dismissal of French priests and the substitution of others was again recommended some time after.

[3] The motives for paying priests for instructing the people of a province ceded to England are given in a report of the French Marine Council. The Acadians "ne pourront jamais conserver un véritable attachement à la religion et *à leur légitime souverain* sans le secours d'un missionnaire" (*Délibérations du Conseil de Marine, 23 Mai, 1719,* in *Le Canada-Français*). The Intendant Bégon highly commends the efforts of the missionaries to keep the Acadians in the French interest (*Bégon au Ministre, 25 Sept. 1715*), and Vaudreuil praises their zeal in the same cause (*Vaudreuil au Ministre, 31 Oct. 1717*).

[4] *Délibérations du Conseil de Marine, 3 Mai, 1718.*

[5] *Record of Council at Annapolis, 11 and 24 Oct. 1726.*

Lieutenant-Governor Armstrong requested the Governor of Isle Royale to send two priests "of known probity" to fill them.[1]

Who were answerable for the anomalous state of affairs in the province,—the *imperium in imperio* where the inner power waxed and strengthened every day, and the outer relatively pined and dwindled? It was not mainly the Crown of France nor its agents, secular or clerical. Their action under the circumstances, though sometimes inexcusable, was natural, and might have been foreseen. Nor was it the Council at Annapolis, who had little power either for good or evil. It was mainly the neglect and apathy of the British ministers, who seemed careless as to whether they kept Acadia or lost it, apparently thinking it not worth their notice.

About the middle of the century they wakened from their lethargy, and warned by the signs of the times, sent troops and settlers into the province at the eleventh hour. France and her agents took alarm, and redoubled their efforts to keep their hold on a country which they had begun to regard as theirs already. The settlement of the English at Halifax startled the French into those courses of intrigue and violence which were the immediate cause of the removal of the Acadians in 1755.

At the earlier period which we are now considering, the storm was still remote. The English made no attempt either to settle the province or to secure it by sufficient garrisons; they merely tried to bind the inhabitants by an oath of allegiance which the weakness of the government would constantly tempt them to break. When George I. came to the throne, Deputy-Governor Caulfield tried to induce the inhabitants to swear allegiance to the new monarch. The Acadians asked advice of Saint-Ovide, governor at Louisbourg, who sent them elaborate directions how to answer the English demand and remain at the same time faithful children of France. Neither Caulfield nor his successor could carry their point. The Treaty of Utrecht, as we have seen, gave the Acadians a year in which to choose between remaining in the province and becoming British subjects, or leaving it as subjects of the King of France. The year had long ago expired, and most of

[1] *Armstrong to Saint-Ovide, 17 June, 1732.*

them were still in Acadia, unwilling to leave it, yet refusing to own King George. In 1720 General Richard Philipps, the governor of the province, set himself to the task of getting the oath taken, while the missionaries and the French officers at Isle Royale strenuously opposed his efforts. He issued a proclamation ordering the Acadians to swear allegiance to the King of England or leave the country, without their property, within four months. In great alarm, they appealed to their priests, and begged the Récollet, Père Justinien, curé of Mines, to ask advice and help from Saint-Ovide, successor of Costebelle at Louisbourg, protesting that they would abandon all rather than renounce their religion and their King.[1] At the same time they prepared for a general emigration by way of the isthmus and Baye Verte, where it would have been impossible to stop them.[2]

Without the influence of their spiritual and temporal advisers, to whom they turned in all their troubles, it is clear that the Acadians would have taken the oath and remained in tranquil enjoyment of their homes; but it was then thought important to French interests that they should remove either to Isle Royale or to Isle St. Jean, now Prince Edward's Island. Hence no means were spared to prevent them from becoming British subjects, if only in name; even the Micmacs were enlisted in the good work, and induced to threaten them with their enmity if they should fail in allegiance to King Louis. Philipps feared that the Acadians would rise in arms if he insisted on the harsh requirements of his proclamation; in which case his position would have been difficult, as they now outnumbered his garrison about five to one. Therefore he extended indefinitely the term of four months, that he had fixed for their final choice, and continued to urge and persuade, without gaining a step towards the desired result. In vain he begged for aid from the British authorities. They would do nothing for him, but merely observed that while the French

[1] *The Acadians to Saint-Ovide, 6 May, 1720*, in *Public Documents of Nova Scotia*, 25. This letter was evidently written for them,—no doubt by a missionary.

[2] "They can march off at their leisure, by way of the Baye Verte, with their effects, without danger of being molested by this garrison, which scarce suffices to secure the Fort." *Philipps to Secretary Craggs, 26 May, 1720*.

officers and priests had such influence over the Acadians, they would never be good subjects, and so had better be put out of the country.[1] This was easier said than done; for at this very time there were signs that the Acadians and the Micmacs would unite to put out the English garrison.[2]

Philipps was succeeded by a deputy-governor, Lieutenant-Colonel Armstrong,—a person of ardent impulses and unstable disposition. He applied himself with great zeal and apparent confidence to accomplishing the task in which his principal had failed. In fact, he succeeded in 1726 in persuading the inhabitants about Annapolis to take the oath, with a proviso that they should not be called upon for military service; but the main body of the Acadians stiffly refused. In the next year he sent Ensign Wroth to Mines, Chignecto, and neighboring settlements to renew the attempt on occasion of the accession of George II. The envoy's instructions left much to his discretion or his indiscretion, and he came back with the signatures, or crosses, of the inhabitants attached to an oath so clogged with conditions that it left them free to return to their French allegiance whenever they chose.

Philipps now came back to Acadia to resume his difficult task. And here a surprise meets us. He reported a complete success. The Acadians, as he declared, swore allegiance without reserve to King George; but he does not tell us how they were brought to do so. Compulsion was out of the question. They could have cut to pieces any part of the paltry English garrison that might venture outside the ditches of Annapolis, or they might have left Acadia, with all their goods and chattels, with no possibility of stopping them. The taking of the oath was therefore a voluntary act.

But what was the oath? The words reported by Philipps were as follows: "I promise and swear sincerely, on the faith of a Christian, that I will be entirely faithful, and will truly obey his Majesty King George the Second, whom I recognize as sovereign lord of Acadia or Nova Scotia. So help me God."

---

[1] *The Board of Trade to Philipps, 28 Dec. 1720.*

[2] *Délibérations du Conseil de Marine, Aoust, 1720.* The attempt against the garrison was probably opposed by the priests, who must have seen the danger that it would rouse the ministry into sending troops to the province, which would have been disastrous to their plans.

To this the Acadians affixed their crosses, or, in exceptional cases, their names. Recently, however, evidence has appeared that, so far at least as regards the Acadians on and near Mines Basin, the effect of the oath was qualified by a promise on the part of Philipps that they should not be required to take up arms against either French or Indians; they on their part promising never to take up arms against the English. This statement is made by Gaudalie, curé of the parish of Mines, and Noiville, priest at Pigiquid, or Pisiquid, now Windsor.[1] In fact, the English never had the folly to call on the Acadians to fight for them; and the greater part of this peace-loving people were true to their promise not to take arms against the English, though a considerable number of them did so, especially at the beginning of the Seven Years' War. It was to this promise, whether kept or broken, that they owed their name of Neutral French.

From first to last, the Acadians remained in a child-like dependence on their spiritual and temporal guides. Not one of their number stands out prominently from among the rest. They seem to have been totally devoid of natural leaders, and, unhappily for themselves, left their fate in the hands of others. Yet they were fully aware of their numerical strength, and had repeatedly declared, in a manner that the English officers called insolent, that they would neither leave the country nor swear allegiance to King George. The truth probably is that those who governed them had become convinced that this simple population, which increased rapidly, and could always be kept French at heart, might be made more useful to France in Acadia than out of it, and that it was needless farther to oppose the taking of an oath which would leave them in quiet possession of their farms without making any change in their feelings, and probably none in their actions. By force of natural increase Acadia would in time become the seat of a large population ardently French and ardently Catholic; and while officials in France sometimes complained of the reluctance of the Acadians to move to Isle Royale, those who directed

---

[1] *Certificat de Charles de la Gaudalie, prêtre, curé missionnaire de la paroisse des Mines, et Noël-Alexandre Noiville, . . . curé de l'Assomption et de la Sainte Famille de Pigiguit*; printed in Rameau, *Une Colonie Féodale en Amérique* (ed. 1889) II. 53.

them in their own country seem to have become willing that they should stay where they were and place themselves in such relations with the English as should leave them free to increase and multiply undisturbed. Deceived by the long apathy of the British government, French officials did not foresee that a time would come when it would bestir itself to make Acadia English in fact as well as in name.[1]

[1]The preceding chapter is based largely on two collections of documents relating to Acadia,—the *Nova Scotia Archives*, or *Selections from the Public Documents of Nova Scotia*, printed in 1869 by the government of that province, and the mass of papers collected by Rev. H. R. Casgrain and printed in the documentary department of *Le Canada-Français*, a review published under direction of Laval University at Quebec. Abbé Casgrain, with passionate industry, has labored to gather everything in Europe or America that could tell in favor of the French and against the English. Mr. Akins, the editor of the *Nova Scotia Archives*, leans to the other side, so that the two collections supplement each other. Both are copious and valuable. Besides these, I have made use of various documents from the archives of Paris not to be found in either of the above-named collections.

Chapter X

1713 – 1724

SEBASTIEN RALE

Boundary Disputes • Outposts of Canada • The Earlier and Later Jesuits • Religion and Politics • The Norridgewocks and their Missionary • A Hollow Peace • Disputed Land Claims • Council at Georgetown • Attitude of Rale • Minister and Jesuit • The Indians waver • An Outbreak • Covert War • Indignation against Rale • War declared • Governor and Assembly • Speech of Samuel Sewall • Penobscots attack Fort St. George • Reprisal • Attack on Norridgewock • Death of Rale

B EFORE the Treaty of Utrecht, the present Nova Scotia, New Brunswick, and a part of Maine were collectively called Acadia by the French; but after the treaty gave Acadia to England, they insisted that the name meant only Nova Scotia. The English on their part claimed that the cession of Acadia made them owners, not only of the Nova Scotian peninsula, but of all the country north of it to the St. Lawrence, or at least to the dividing ridge or height of land.

This and other disputed questions of boundary were to be settled by commissioners of the two powers; but their meeting was put off for forty years, and then their discussions ended in the Seven Years' War. The claims of the rival nations were in fact so discordant that any attempt to reconcile them must needs produce a fresh quarrel. The treaty had left a choice of evils. To discuss the boundary question meant to renew the war; to leave it unsettled was a source of constant irritation; and while delay staved off a great war, it quickly produced a small one.

The river Kennebec, which was generally admitted by the French to be the dividing line between their possessions and New England,[1] was regarded by them with the most watchful jealousy. Its headwaters approached those of the Canadian river Chaudière, the mouth of which is near Quebec; and by

---

[1] In 1700, however, there was an agreement, under the Treaty of Ryswick, which extended the English limits as far as the River St. George, a little west of the Penobscot.

ascending the former stream and crossing to the headwaters of the latter, through an intricacy of forests, hills, ponds, and marshes, it was possible for a small band of hardy men, unencumbered by cannon, to reach the Canadian capital, as was done long after by the followers of Benedict Arnold. Hence it was thought a matter of the last importance to close the Kennebec against such an attempt. The Norridgewock band of the Abenakis, who lived on the banks of that river, were used to serve this purpose and to form a sort of advance-guard to the French colony, while other kindred bands on the Penobscot, the St. Croix, and the St. John, were expected to aid in opposing a living barrier to English intrusion. Missionaries were stationed among all these Indians to keep them true to Church and King. The most important station, that of the Norridgewocks, was in charge of Father Sebastien Rale, the most conspicuous and interesting figure among the later French-American Jesuits.

Since the middle of the seventeenth century a change had come over the Jesuit missions of New France. Nothing is more striking or more admirable than the self-devoted apostleship of the earlier period.[1] The movement in Western Europe known as the Renaissance was far more than a revival of arts and letters,—it was an awakening of intellectual, moral, and religious life; the offspring of causes long in action, and the parent of other movements in action to this day. The Protestant Reformation was a part of it. That revolt against Rome produced a counter Renaissance in the bosom of the ancient Church herself. In presence of that peril she woke from sloth and corruption, and girded herself to beat back the invading heresies, by force or by craft, by inquisitorial fires, by the arms of princely and imperial allies, and by the self-sacrificing enthusiasm of her saints and martyrs. That time of danger produced the exalted zeal of Xavier and the intense, thoughtful, organizing zeal of Loyola. After a century had passed, the flame still burned, and it never shone with a purer or brighter radiance than in the early missions of New France.

Such ardors cannot be permanent; they must subside, from the law of their nature. If the great Western mission had been a success, the enthusiasm of its founders might have main-

[1] See *Jesuits in North America in the Seventeenth Century.*

tained itself for some time longer; but that mission was extinguished in blood. Its martyrs died in vain, and the burning faith that had created it was rudely tried. Canada ceased to be a mission. The civil and military powers grew strong, and the Church no longer ruled with undivided sway. The times changed, and the men changed with them. It is a characteristic of the Jesuit Order, and one of the sources of its strength, that it chooses the workman for his work, studies the qualities of its members, and gives to each the task for which he is fitted best. When its aim was to convert savage hordes and build up another Paraguay in the Northern wilderness, it sent a Jogues, a Brébeuf, a Charles Garnier, and a Gabriel Lalemant, like a forlorn hope, to storm the stronghold of heathendom. In later times it sent other men to meet other needs and accomplish other purposes.

Before the end of the seventeenth century the functions of the Canadian Jesuit had become as much political as religious; but if the fires of his apostolic zeal burned less high, his devotion to the Order in which he had merged his personality was as intense as before. While in constant friction with the civil and military powers, he tried to make himself necessary to them, and in good measure he succeeded. Nobody was so able to manage the Indian tribes and keep them in the interest of France. "Religion," says Charlevoix, "is the chief bond by which the savages are attached to us;" and it was the Jesuit above all others who was charged to keep this bond firm.

The Christianity that was made to serve this useful end did not strike a deep root. While humanity is in the savage state, it can only be Christianized on the surface; and the convert of the Jesuits remained a savage still. They did not even try to civilize him. They taught him to repeat a catechism which he could not understand, and practise rites of which the spiritual significance was incomprehensible to him. He saw the symbols of his new faith in much the same light as the superstitions that had once enchained him. To his eyes the crucifix was a fetich of surpassing power, and the Mass a beneficent "medicine," or occult influence, of supreme efficacy. Yet he would not forget his old rooted beliefs, and it needed the constant presence of the missionary to prevent him from returning to them.

Since the Iroquois had ceased to be a danger to Canada, the active alliance of the Western Indians had become less important to the colony. Hence the missions among them had received less attention, and most of these tribes had relapsed into heathenism. The chief danger had shifted eastward, and was, or was supposed to be, in the direction of New England. Therefore the Eastern missions were cultivated with diligence, whether those within or adjoining the settled limits of Canada, like the Iroquois mission of Caughnawaga, the Abenaki missions of St. Francis and Becancour, and the Huron mission of Lorette, or those that served as outposts and advance-guards of the colony, like the Norridgewock Abenakis of the Kennebec, or the Penobscot Abenakis of the Penobscot. The priests at all these stations were in close correspondence with the government, to which their influence over their converts was invaluable. In the wilderness dens of the Hurons or the Iroquois, the early Jesuit was a marvel of self-sacrificing zeal; his successor, half missionary and half agent of the King, had thought for this world as well as the next.

Sebastien Rale,[1] born in Franche-Comté in 1657, was sent to the American missions in 1689 at the age of thirty-two. After spending two years among the Abenakis of Canada, then settled near the mouth of the Chaudière, he was sent for two years more to the Illinois, and thence to the Abenakis of the Kennebec, where he was to end his days.

Near where the town of Norridgewock now stands, the Kennebec curved round a broad tongue of meadow land, in the midst of a picturesque wilderness of hills and forests. On this tongue of land, on ground a few feet above the general level, stood the village of the Norridgewocks, fenced with a stockade of round logs nine feet high. The enclosure was square; each of its four sides measured one hundred and sixty feet, and each had its gate. From the four gates ran two streets, or lanes, which crossed each other in the middle of the village. There were twenty-six Indian houses, or cabins, within the stockade, described as "built much after the English manner," though probably of logs. The church was out-

[1] So written by himself in an autograph letter of 18 Nov. 1712. It is also spelled Rasle, Rasles, Ralle, and, very incorrectly, Rallé, or Rallee.

side the enclosure, about twenty paces from the east gate.[1] Such was the mission village of Norridgewock in 1716. It had risen from its ashes since Colonel Hilton destroyed it in 1705, and the church had been rebuilt by New England workmen hired for the purpose.[2] A small bell, which is still preserved at Brunswick, rang for Mass at early morning, and for vespers at sunset. Rale's leisure hours were few. He preached, exhorted, catechised the young converts, counselled their seniors for this world and the next, nursed them in sickness, composed their quarrels, tilled his own garden, cut his own firewood, cooked his own food, which was of Indian corn, or, at a pinch, of roots and acorns, worked at his Abenaki vocabulary, and, being expert at handicraft, made ornaments for the church, or moulded candles from the fruit of the bayberry, or wax-myrtle.[3] Twice a year, summer and winter, he followed his flock to the sea-shore and the islands, where they lived at their ease on fish and seals, clams, oysters, and seafowl.

This Kennebec mission had been begun more than half a century before; yet the conjurors, or "medicine men,"—natural enemies of the missionary,—still remained obdurate and looked on the father askance, though the body of the tribe were constant at Mass and confession, and regarded him with loving reverence. He always attended their councils, and, as he tells us, his advice always prevailed; but he was less fortunate when he told them to practise no needless cruelty in their wars, on which point they were often disobedient children.[4]

---

[1] The above particulars are taken from an inscription on a manuscript map in the library of the Maine Historical Society, made in 1716 by Joseph Heath, one of the principal English settlers on the Kennebec, and for a time commandant of the fort at Brunswick.

[2] When Colonel Westbrook and his men came to Norridgewock in 1722, they found a paper pinned to the church door, containing, among others, the following words, in the handwriting of Rale, meant as a fling at the English invaders: "It [the church] is ill built, because the English don't work well. It is not finished, although five or six Englishmen have wrought here during four years, and the Undertaker [contractor], who is a great Cheat, hath been paid in advance for to finish it." The money came from the Canadian government.

[3] *Myrica cerifera.*

[4] The site of the Indian village is still called Indian Old Point. Norridgewock is the Naurantsouak, or Narantsouak, of the French. For Rale's mission

Rale was of a strong, enduring frame, and a keen, vehement, caustic spirit. He had the gift of tongues, and was as familiar with the Abenaki and several other Indian languages as he was with Latin.[1] Of the genuineness of his zeal there is no doubt, nor of his earnest and lively interest in the fortunes of the wilderness flock of which he was the shepherd for half his life. The situation was critical for them and for him. The English settlements were but a short distance below, while those of the French could be reached only by a hard journey of twelve or fourteen days.

With two intervals of uneasy peace, the borders of Maine had been harried by war-parties for thirty-eight years; and since 1689 these raids had been prompted and aided by the French. Thus it happened that extensive tracts, which before Philip's War were dotted with farm-houses and fishing hamlets, had been abandoned, and cultivated fields were turning again to forests. The village of Wells had become the eastern frontier. But now the Treaty of Utrecht gave promise of lasting tranquillity. The Abenakis, hearing that they were to be backed no longer by the French, became alarmed, sent messengers to Casco, and asked for peace. In July there was a convention at Portsmouth, when delegates of the Norridgewocks, Penobscots, Malecites, and other Abenaki bands met Governor Dudley and the councillors of Massachusetts and New Hampshire. A paper was read to them by sworn interpreters, in which they confessed that they had broken former treaties, begged pardon for "past rebellions, hostilities, and violations of promises," declared themselves subjects of Queen Anne, pledged firm friendship with the English, and promised them that they might re-enter without molestation on all their former possessions. Eight of the principal Abenaki

---

life, see two letters of his, 15 Oct. 1722, and 12 Oct. 1722, and a letter of Père La Chasse, Superior of the Missions, 29 Oct. 1724. These are printed in the *Lettres Edifiantes*, XVII., XXIII.

[1] Père La Chasse, in his eulogy of Rale, says that there was not a language on the continent with which he had not some acquaintance. This is of course absurd. Besides a full knowledge of the Norridgewock Abenaki, he had more or less acquaintance with two other Algonkin languages,—the Ottawa and the Illinois,—and also with the Huron; which is enough for one man.

chiefs signed this document with their totemic marks, and the rest did so, after similar interpretation, at another convention in the next year.[1] Indians when in trouble can waive their pride and lavish professions and promises; but when they called themselves subjects of Queen Anne, it is safe to say that they did not know what the words meant.

Peace with the Indians was no sooner concluded than a stream of settlers began to move eastward to reoccupy the lands that they owned or claimed in the region of the lower Kennebec. Much of this country was held in extensive tracts, under old grants of the last century, and the proprietors offered great inducements to attract emigrants. The government of Massachusetts, though impoverished by three wars, of which it had borne the chief burden, added what encouragements it could. The hamlets of Saco, Scarborough, Falmouth, and Georgetown rose from their ashes, mills were built on the streams, old farms were retilled, and new ones cleared. A certain Dr. Noyes, who had established a sturgeon fishery on the Kennebec, built at his own charge a stone fort at Cushnoc, or Augusta; and it is said that as early as 1714 a blockhouse was built many miles above, near the mouth of the Sebasticook.[2] In the next year, Fort George was built at the lower falls of the Androscoggin; and, some years later, Fort Richmond, on the Kennebec, at the site of the present town of Richmond.[3]

Some of the claims to these Kennebec lands were based on old Crown patents, some on mere prescription, some on Indian titles, good or bad. Rale says that an Englishman would give an Indian a bottle of rum, and get from him in return a

[1] This treaty is given in full by Penhallow. It is also printed from the original draft by Mr. Frederic Kidder, in his *Abenaki Indians: their Treaties of 1713 and 1717.* The two impressions are substantially the same, but with verbal variations. The version of Kidder is the more complete, in giving not only the Indian totemic marks, but also the autographs in fac-simile of all the English officials. Rale gives a dramatic account of the treaty, which he may have got from the Indians, and which omits their submission and their promises.

[2] It was standing in 1852, and a sketch of it is given by Winsor, *Narrative and Critical History,* V. 185. I have some doubts as to the date of erection.

[3] Williamson, *History of Maine,* II. 88, 97. Compare Penhallow.

large tract of land.[1] Something like this may have happened; though in other cases the titles were as good as Indian titles usually are, the deeds being in regular form and signed by the principal chiefs for a consideration which they thought sufficient. The lands of Indians, however, are owned, so far as owned at all, by the whole community; and in the case of the Algonquin tribes the chiefs had no real authority to alienate them without the consent of the tribesmen. Even supposing this consent to have been given, the Norridgewocks would not have been satisfied; for Rale taught them that they could not part with their lands, because they held them in trust for their children, to whom their country belonged as much as to themselves.

Long years of war and mutual wrong had embittered the Norridgewocks against their English neighbors, with whom, nevertheless, they wished to be at peace, because they feared them, and because their trade was necessary to them.

The English borderers, on their part, regarded the Indians less as men than as vicious and dangerous wild animals. In fact, the benevolent and philanthropic view of the American savage is for those who are beyond his reach. It has never yet been held by any whose wives and children have lived in danger of his scalping-knife. In Boston and other of the older and safer settlements, the Indians had found devoted friends before Philip's War; and even now they had apologists and defenders, prominent among whom was that relic of antique Puritanism, old Samuel Sewall, who was as conscientious and humane as he was prosy, narrow, and sometimes absurd, and whose benevolence towards the former owners of the soil was trebly reinforced by his notion that they were descendants of the ten lost tribes of Israel.[2]

The intrusion of settlers, and the building of forts and blockhouses on lands which they still called their own, irritated and alarmed the Norridgewocks, and their growing resentment was fomented by Rale, both because he shared it himself, and because he was prompted by Vaudreuil. Yet,

---

[1] *Remarks out of the Fryar Sebastian Rale's Letter from Norridgewock, Feb. 7, 1720,* in the *Common Place Book* of Rev. Henry Flynt.

[2] Sewall's *Memorial relating to the Kennebec Indians* is an argument against war with them.

dreading another war with the English, the Indians kept quiet for a year or two, till at length the more reckless among them began to threaten and pilfer the settlers.

In 1716, Colonel Samuel Shute came out to succeed Dudley as governor, and in the next summer he called the Indians to a council at Georgetown, a settlement on Arrowsick Island, at the mouth of the Kennebec. Thither he went in the frigate "Squirrel," with the councillors of Massachusetts and New Hampshire; while the deputies of the Norridgewocks, Penobscots, Pequawkets, or Abenakis of the Saco, and Assagunticooks, or Abenakis of the Androscoggin, came in canoes to meet him, and set up their wigwams on a neighboring island. The council opened on the 9th of August, under a large tent, over which waved the British flag. The oath was administered to the interpreters by the aged Judge Sewall, and Shute then made the Indians a speech in which he told them that the English and they were subjects of the great, good, and wise King George; that as both peoples were under the same king, he would gladly see them also of the same religion, since it was the only true one; and to this end he gave them a Bible and a minister to teach them,—pointing to Rev. Joseph Baxter, who stood near by. And he further assured them that if any wrong should be done them, he would set it right. He then condescended to give his hand to the chiefs, telling them, through the interpreter, that it was to show his affection.

The Indians, after their usual custom, deferred their answer to the next day, when the council again met, and the Norridgewock chief, Wiwurna, addressed the Governor as spokesman for his people. In defiance of every Indian idea of propriety, Shute soon began to interrupt him with questions and remarks. Wiwurna remonstrated civilly; but Shute continued his interruptions, and the speech turned to a dialogue, which may be abridged thus, Shute always addressing himself, not to the Indian orator, but to the interpreter.

The orator expressed satisfaction at the arrival of the Governor, and hoped that peace and friendship would now prevail.

GOVERNOR (*to the interpreter*). Tell them that if they behave themselves, I shall use them kindly.

ORATOR (*as rendered by the interpreter*).   Your Excellency was pleased to say that we must obey King George. We will if we like his way of treating us.

GOVERNOR.   They must obey him.

ORATOR.   We will if we are not disturbed on our lands.

GOVERNOR.   Nor must they disturb the English on theirs.

ORATOR.   We are pleased that your Excellency is ready to hear our complaints when wrong is done us.

GOVERNOR.   They must not pretend to lands that belong to the English.

ORATOR.   We beg leave to go on in order with our answer.

GOVERNOR.   Tell him to go on.

ORATOR.   If there should be any quarrel and bloodshed, we will not avenge ourselves, but apply to your Excellency. We will embrace in our bosoms the English that have come to settle on our land.

GOVERNOR.   They must not call it their land, for the English have bought it of them and their ancestors.

ORATOR.   We pray leave to proceed with our answer, and talk about the land afterwards.

Wiwurna, then, with much civility, begged to be excused from receiving the Bible and the minister, and ended by wishing the Governor good wind and weather for his homeward voyage.

There was another meeting in the afternoon, in which the orator declared that his people were willing that the English should settle on the west side of the Kennebec as far up the river as a certain mill; on which the Governor said to the interpreter: "Tell them we want nothing but our own, and that that we will have;" and he ordered an old deed of sale, signed by six of their chiefs, to be shown and explained to them. Wiwurna returned that though his tribe were uneasy about their lands, they were willing that the English should keep what they had got, excepting the forts. On this point there was a sharp dialogue, and Shute said bluntly that if he saw fit, he should build a fort at every new settlement. At this all the Indians rose abruptly and went back to their camp, leaving behind an English flag that had been given them.

Rale was at the Indian camp, and some of them came back in the evening with a letter from him, in which he told Shute that the Governor of Canada had asked the King of France whether he had ever given the Indians' land to the English, to which the King replied that he had not, and would help the Indians to repel any encroachment upon them. This cool assumption on the part of France of paramount right to the Abenaki country incensed Shute, who rejected the letter with contempt.

As between the Governor and the Indian orator, the savage had shown himself by far the more mannerly; yet so unwilling were the Indians to break with the English that on the next morning, seeing Shute about to re-embark, they sent messengers to him to apologize for what they called their rudeness, beg that the English flag might be returned to them, and ask for another interview, saying that they would appoint another spokesman instead of Wiwurna, who had given so much offence. Shute consented, and the meeting was held. The new orator presented a wampum belt, expressed a wish for peace, and said that his people wished the English to extend their settlements as far as they had formerly done. Shute, on his part, promised that trading-houses should be established for supplying their needs, and that they should have a smith to mend their guns, and an interpreter of their own choice. Twenty chiefs and elders then affixed their totemic marks to a paper, renewing the pledges made four years before at Portsmouth, and the meeting closed with a dance in honor of the Governor.[1]

The Indians, as we have seen, had shown no eagerness to accept the ministrations of Rev. Joseph Baxter. The Massachusetts Assembly had absurdly tried to counteract the influence of Rale by offering £150 a year in their depreciated currency to any one of their ministers who would teach Calvinism to the Indians. Baxter, whom Rale, with characteristic exaggeration, calls the ablest of the Boston ministers, but who

[1] A full report of this conference was printed at the time in Boston. It is reprinted in *N. H. Historical Collections*, II. 242, and *N. H. Provincial Papers*, III. 693. Penhallow was present at the meeting, but his account of it is short. The accounts of Williamson and Hutchinson are drawn from the above-mentioned report.

was far from being so, as he was the pastor of the small country village of Medfield, took up the task, and, with no experience of Indian life or knowledge of any Indian language,
entered the lists against an adversary who had spent half his
days among savages, had gained the love and admiration of
the Norridgewocks, and spoke their language fluently. Baxter,
with the confidence of a novice, got an interpreter and began
to preach, exhort, and launch sarcasms against the doctrines
and practices of the Roman Church. Rale excommunicated
such of his flock as listened to him;[1] yet some persisted in
doing so, and three of these petitioned the English Governor
to order "a small praying-house" to be built for their use.[2]

Rale, greatly exasperated, opened a correspondence with
Baxter, and wrote a treatise for his benefit, in which, through
a hundred pages of polemical Latin, he proved that the
Church of Rome was founded on a rock. This he sent to
Baxter, and challenged him to overthrow his reasons. Baxter
sent an answer for which Rale expresses great scorn as to both
manner and matter. He made a rejoinder, directed not only
against his opponent's arguments, but against his Latin, in
which he picked flaws with great apparent satisfaction. He
says that he heard no more from Baxter for a long time, but
at last got another letter, in which there was nothing to the
purpose, the minister merely charging him with an irascible
and censorious spirit. This letter is still preserved, and it does
not answer to Rale's account of it. Baxter replies to his correspondent vigorously, defends his own Latin, attacks that of
Rale, and charges him with losing temper.[3]

Rale's correspondence with the New England ministers
seems not to have been confined to Baxter. A paper is preserved, translated apparently from a Latin original, and entitled, "Remarks out of the Fryar Sebastian Rale's Letter from
Norridgewock, Feb. 7, 1720." This letter appears to have been
addressed to some Boston minister, and is of a scornful and

[1] *Shute to Rale, 21 Feb. 1718.*

[2] This petition is still in the Massachusetts Archives, and is printed by Dr.
Francis in *Sparks's American Biography*, New Series, XVII. 259.

[3] This letter was given by Mr. Adams, of Medfield, a connection of the
Baxter family, to the Massachusetts Historical Society, in whose possession it
now is, in a worn condition. It was either captured with the rest of Rale's
papers and returned to the writer, or else is a duplicate kept by Baxter.

defiant character, using language ill-fitted to conciliate, as thus: "You must know that a missionary is not a cipher, like a minister;" or thus: "A Jesuit is not a Baxter or a Boston minister." The tone is one of exasperation dashed with contempt, and the chief theme is English encroachment and the inalienability of Indian lands.[1] Rale says that Baxter gave up his mission after receiving the treatise on the infallible supremacy of the true Church; but this is a mistake, as the minister made three successive visits to the Eastern country before he tired of his hopeless mission.

In the letter just quoted, Rale seems to have done his best to rasp the temper of his New England correspondent. He boasts of his power over the Indians, who, as he declares, always do as he advises them. "Any treaty with the Governor," he goes on to say, "and especially that of Arrowsick, is null and void if I do not approve it, for I give them so many reasons against it that they absolutely condemn what they have done." He says further that if they do not drive the English from the Kennebec, he will leave them, and that they will then lose both their lands and their souls; and he adds that, if necessary, he will tell them that they may make war.[2] Rale wrote also to Shute; and though the letter is lost, the Governor's answer shows that it was sufficiently aggressive.

The wild Indian is unstable as water. At Arrowsick, the Norridgewocks were all for peace; but when they returned to their village their mood changed, and, on the representations of Rale, they began to kill the cattle of the English settlers on the river below, burn their haystacks, and otherwise annoy them.[3] The English suspected that the Jesuit was the source of their trouble; and as they had always regarded the lands in

[1] This curious paper is in the *Common Place Book* of Rev. Henry Flynt, of which the original is in the library of the Massachusetts Historical Society.

[2] See Francis, *Life of Rale*, where the entire passage is given.

[3] Rale wrote to the Governor of Canada that it was "sur Les Représentations qu'Il Avoit fait aux Sauvages de Sa Mission" that they had killed "un grand nombre de Bestiaux apartenant aux Anglois," and threatened them with attack if they did not retire. *Réponse fait par MM. Vaudreuil et Bégon au Mémoire du Roy du 8 Juin, 1721.* Rale told the Governor of Massachusetts, on another occasion, that his character as a priest permitted him to give the Indians nothing but counsels of peace. Yet as early as 1703 he wrote to Vaudreuil that the Abenakis were ready, at a word from him, to lift the hatchet against the English. *Beauharnois et Vaudreuil au Ministre, 15 Nov. 1703.*

question as theirs, by virtue of the charter of the Plymouth Company in 1620, and the various grants under it, as well as by purchase from the Indians, their ire against him burned high. Yet afraid as the Indians were of another war, even Rale could scarcely have stirred them to violence, but for the indignities put upon them by Indian-hating ruffians of the border, vicious rum-selling traders, and hungry land-thieves. They had still another cause of complaint. Shute had promised to build trading-houses where their wants should be supplied without fraud and extortion; but he had not kept his word, and could not keep it, for reasons that will soon appear.

In spite of such provocations, Norridgewock was divided in opinion. Not only were the Indians in great dread of war, but they had received English presents to a considerable amount, chiefly from private persons interested in keeping them quiet. Hence, to Rale's great chagrin, there was an English party in the village so strong that when the English authorities demanded reparation for the mischief done to the settlers, the Norridgewocks promised two hundred beaver-skins as damages, and gave four hostages as security that they would pay for misdeeds in the past, and commit no more in the future.[1]

Rale now feared that his Indians would all go over to the English and tamely do their bidding; for though most of them, when he was present, would denounce the heretics and boast of the brave deeds they would do against them, yet after a meeting with English officials, they would change their minds and accuse their spiritual father of lying. It was clear that something must be done to end these waverings, lest the lands in dispute should be lost to France forever.

The Norridgewocks had been invited to another interview with the English at Georgetown; and Rale resolved, in modern American phrase, to "capture the meeting." Vaudreuil and the Jesuit La Chasse, superior of the mission, lent their aid. Messengers were sent to the converted Indians of Can-

---

[1] *Joseph Heath and John Minot to Shute, 1 May, 1719.* Rale says that these hostages were seized by surprise and violence; but Vaudreuil complains bitterly of the faintness of heart which caused the Indians to give them (*Vaudreuil à Rale, 15 Juin, 1721*), and both he and the Intendant lay the blame on the English party at Norridgewock, who "with the consent of all the Indians of that mission, had the weakness to give four hostages." *Réponse de Vaudreuil et Bégon au Mémoire du Roy du 8 Juin, 1721.*

ada, whose attachment to France and the Church was past all doubt, and who had been taught to abhor the English as children of the devil. The object of the message was to induce them to go to the meeting at Georgetown armed and equipped for any contingency.

They went accordingly,—Abenakis from Becancour and St. Francis, Hurons from Lorette, and Iroquois from Caughnawaga, besides others, all stanch foes of heresy and England. Rale and La Chasse directed their movements and led them first to Norridgewock, where their arrival made a revolution. The peace party changed color like a chameleon, and was all for war. The united bands, two hundred and fifty warriors in all, paddled down the Kennebec along with the two Jesuits and two French officers, Saint-Castin and Croisil. In a few days the English at Georgetown saw them parading before the fort, well armed, displaying French flags,—feathers dangling from their scalp-locks, and faces fantastically patterned in vermilion, ochre, white clay, soot, and such other pigments as they could find or buy.

They were met by Captain Penhallow and other militia officers of the fort, to whom they gave the promised two hundred beaver-skins, and demanded the four hostages in return; but the hostages had been given as security, not only for the beaver-skins, but also for the future good behavior of the Indians, and Penhallow replied that he had no authority to surrender them. On this they gave him a letter to the Governor, written for them by Père de la Chasse, and signed by their totems. It summoned the English to leave the country at once, and threatened to rob and burn their houses in case of refusal.[1] The threat was not executed, and they presently disappeared, but returned in September in increased numbers,

[1] *Eastern Indians' Letter to the Governour, 27 July, 1721*, in *Mass. Hist. Coll., Second Series*, VIII. 259. This is the original French. It is signed with totems of all the Abenaki bands, and also of the Caughnawagas, Iroquois of the Mountain, Hurons, Micmacs, Montagnais, and several other tribes. On this interview, Penhallow; Belknap II. 51; *Shute to Vaudreuil, 21 July, 1721* (O. S.); *Ibid., 23 April, 1722*; Rale in *Lettres Edifiantes*, XVII. 285. Rale blames Shute for not being present at the meeting, but a letter of the Governor shows that he had never undertaken to be there. He could not have come in any case, from the effects of a fall, which disabled him for some months even from going to Portsmouth to meet the Legislature. *Provincial Papers of New Hampshire*, III. 822.

burned twenty-six houses and attacked the fort, in which the inhabitants had sought refuge. The garrison consisted of forty men, who, being reinforced by the timely arrival of several whale-boats bringing thirty more, made a sortie. A skirmish followed; but being outnumbered and outflanked, the English fell back behind their defences.[1]

The French authorities were in a difficult position. They thought it necessary to stop the progress of English settlement along the Kennebec; and yet, as there was peace between the two Crowns, they could not use open force. There was nothing for it but to set on the Abenakis to fight for them. "I am well pleased," wrote Vaudreuil to Rale, "that you and Père de la Chasse have prompted the Indians to treat the English as they have done. My orders are to let them want for nothing, and I send them plenty of ammunition." Rale says that the King allowed him a pension of six thousand livres a year, and that he spent it all "in good works." As his statements are not remarkable for precision, this may mean that he was charged with distributing the six thousand livres which the King gave every year in equal shares to the three Abenaki missions of Medoctec, Norridgewock, and Panawamské, or Penobscot, and which generally took the form of presents of arms, gunpowder, bullets, and other munitions of war, or of food and clothing to support the squaws and children while the warriors were making raids on the English.[2]

Vaudreuil had long felt the delicacy of his position, and even before the crisis seemed near he tried to provide against it, and wrote to the minister that he had never called the Abenakis subjects of France, but only allies, in order to avoid responsibility for anything they might do.[3] "The English," he

---

[1] Williamson, *Hist. of Maine*, II. 119; Penhallow. Rale's account of the affair, found among his papers at Norridgewock, is curiously exaggerated. He says that he himself was with the Indians, and "to pleasure the English" showed himself to them several times,—a point which the English writers do not mention, though it is one which they would be most likely to seize upon. He says that fifty houses were burned, and that there were five forts, two of which were of stone, and that in one of these six hundred armed men, besides women and children, had sought refuge, though there was not such a number of men in the whole region of the Kennebec.

[2] Vaudreuil, *Mémoire adressé au Roy, 5 Juin, 1723.*

[3] *Vaudreuil au Ministre, 6 Sept. 1716.*

says elsewhere, "must be prevented from settling on Abenaki lands; and to this end we must let the Indians act for us (*laisser agir les sauvages*)."[1]

Yet while urging the need of precaution, he was too zealous to be always prudent; and once, at least, he went so far as to suggest that French soldiers should be sent to help the Abenakis,—which, he thought, would frighten the English into retreating from their settlements; whereas if such help were refused, the Indians would go over to the enemy.[2] The court was too anxious to avoid a rupture to permit the use of open force, and would only promise plenty of ammunition to Indians who would fight the English, directing at the same time that neither favors nor attentions should be given to those who would not.[3]

The half-breed officer, Saint-Castin, son of Baron Vincent de Saint-Castin by his wife, a Penobscot squaw, bore the double character of a French lieutenant and an Abenaki chief, and had joined with the Indians in their hostile demonstration at Arrowsick Island. Therefore, as chief of a tribe styled subjects of King George, the English seized him, charged him with rebellion, and brought him to Boston, where he was examined by a legislative committee. He showed both tact and temper, parried the charges against him, and was at last set at liberty. His arrest, however, exasperated his tribesmen, who soon began to burn houses, kill settlers, and commit various acts of violence, for all of which Rale was believed to be mainly answerable. There was great indignation against him. He himself says that a reward of a thousand pounds sterling was offered for his head, but that the English should not get it for all their sterling money. It does not appear that such a reward was offered, though it is true that the Massachusetts House of Representatives once voted five hundred pounds in their currency—then equal to about a hundred and eighty pounds sterling—for the same purpose; but as the Governor and Council refused their concurrence, the Act was of no effect.

---

[1] *Extrait d'une Liasse de Papiers concernant le Canada, 1720.* (Archives du Ministère des Affaires Etrangères.)

[2] *Réponse de Vaudreuil et Bégon au Mémoire du Roy, 8 Juin, 1721.*

[3] *Bégon à Rale, 14 Juin, 1721.*

All the branches of the government, however, presently joined in sending three hundred men to Norridgewock, with a demand that the Indians should give up Rale "and the other heads and fomentors of their rebellion." In case of refusal they were to seize the Jesuit and the principal chiefs and bring them prisoners to Boston. Colonel Westbrook was put in command of the party. Rale, being warned of their approach by some of his Indians, swallowed the consecrated wafers, hid the sacred vessels, and made for the woods, where, as he thinks, he was saved from discovery by a special intervention of Providence. His papers fell into the hands of Westbrook, including letters that proved beyond all doubt that he had acted as agent of the Canadian authorities in exciting his flock against the English.[1]

Incensed by Westbrook's invasion, the Indians came down the Kennebec in large numbers, burned the village of Brunswick, and captured nine families at Merry-meeting Bay; though they soon set them free, except five men whom they kept to exchange for the four hostages still detained at Boston.[2] At the same time they seized several small vessels in the harbors along the coast. On this the Governor and Council declared war against the Eastern Indians, meaning the Abenakis and their allies, whom they styled traitors and robbers.

In Massachusetts many persons thought that war could not be justified, and were little disposed to push it with vigor. The direction of it belonged to the Governor in his capacity of Captain-General of the Province. Shute was an old soldier who had served with credit as lieutenant-colonel under Marlborough; but he was hampered by one of those disputes which in times of crisis were sure to occur in every British province whose governor was appointed by the Crown. The Assembly, jealous of the representative of royalty, and looking back mournfully to their virtual independence under the lamented old charter, had from the first let slip no opportunity

[1] Some of the papers found in Rale's "strong box" are still preserved in the Archives of Massachusetts, including a letter to him from Vaudreuil, dated at Quebec, 25 Sept. 1721, in which the French Governor expresses great satisfaction at the missionary's success in uniting the Indians against the English, and promises military aid, if necessary.

[2] Wheeler, *History of Brunswick, Topsham, and Harpswell*, 54.

to increase its own powers and abridge those of the Governor, refused him the means of establishing the promised trading-houses in the Indian country, and would grant no money for presents to conciliate the Norridgewocks. The House now wanted, not only to control supplies for the war, but to direct the war itself and conduct operations by committees of its own. Shute made his plans of campaign, and proceeded to appoint officers from among the frontier inhabitants, who had at least the qualification of being accustomed to the woods. One of them, Colonel Walton, was obnoxious to some of the representatives, who brought charges against him, and the House demanded that he should be recalled from the field to answer to them for his conduct. The Governor objected to this as an encroachment on his province as commander-in-chief. Walton was now accused of obeying orders of the Governor in contravention of those of the representatives, who thereupon passed a vote requiring him to lay his journal before them. This was more than Shute could bear. He had the character of a good-natured man; but the difficulties and mortifications of his position had long galled him, and he had got leave to return to England and lay his case before the King and Council. The crisis had now come. The Assembly were for usurping all authority, civil and military. Accordingly, on the 1st of January, 1723, the Governor sailed in a merchant ship for London, without giving notice of his intention to anybody except two or three servants.[1]

The burden of his difficult and vexatious office fell upon the Lieutenant-Governor, William Dummer. When he first met the Council in his new capacity, a whimsical scene took place. Here, among the rest, was the aged, matronly countenance of the worthy Samuel Sewall, deeply impressed with the dignity and importance of his position as senior member of the Board. At his best he never had the faintest sense of humor or perception of the ludicrous, and being now perhaps touched with dotage, he thought it incumbent upon him to address a few words of exhortation and encouragement to the incoming chief magistrate. He rose from his seat with long locks, limp and white, drooping from under his black skull-

[1] Hutchinson, II. 261. On these dissensions compare Palfrey, *Hist. of New England*, IV., 406–428.

cap,—for he abhorred a wig as a sign of backsliding,—and in a voice of quavering solemnity spoke thus:—

"If your Honour and this Honourable Board please to give me leave, I would speak a Word or two upon this solemn Occasion. Altho the unerring Providence of God has brought you to the Chair of Government in a cloudy and tempestuous season, yet you have this for your Encouragement, that the people you Have to do with are a part of the Israel of God, and you may expect to have of the Prudence and Patience of Moses communicated to you for your Conduct. It is evident that our Almighty Saviour counselled the first planters to remove hither and Settle here, and they dutifully followed his Advice, and therefore He will never leave nor forsake them nor Theirs; so that your Honour must needs be happy in sincerely seeking their Interest and Welfare, which your Birth and Education will incline you to do. *Difficilia quæ pulchra.* I promise myself that they who sit at this Board will yield their Faithful Advice to your Honour according to the Duty of their Place."

Having thus delivered himself to an audience not much more susceptible of the ludicrous than he was, the old man went home well pleased, and recorded in his diary that the Lieutenant-Governor and Councillors rose and remained standing while he was speaking, "and they expressed a handsom Acceptance of what I had said; *Laus Deo.*"[1]

Dummer was born in New England, and might, therefore, expect to find more favor than had fallen to his predecessor; but he was the representative of royalty, and could not escape the consequences of being so. In earnest of what was in store for him, the Assembly would not pay his salary, because he had sided with the Governor in the late quarrel. The House voted to dismiss Colonel Walton and Major Moody, the chief officers appointed by Shute; and when Dummer reminded it that this was a matter belonging to him as commander-in-chief, it withheld the pay of the obnoxious officers and refused all supplies for the war till they should be removed.

[1] *Sewall Papers*, III. 317, 318.

Dummer was forced to yield.[1] The House would probably have pushed him still farther, if the members had not dreaded the effect of Shute's representations at court, and feared lest persistent encroachment on the functions of the Governor might cost them their charter, to which, insufficient as they thought it, and far inferior to the one they had lost, they clung tenaciously as the palladium of their liberties. Yet Dummer needed the patience of Job; for his Assembly seemed more bent on victories over him than over the Indians.

There was another election, which did not improve the situation. The new House was worse than the old, being made up largely of narrow-minded rustics, who tried to relieve the Governor of all conduct of the war by assigning it to a committee chosen from among themselves; but the Council would not concur with them.

Meanwhile the usual ravages went on. Farm-houses were burned, and the inmates waylaid and killed, while the Indians generally avoided encounters with armed bodies of whites. Near the village of Oxford four of them climbed upon the roof of a house, cut a hole in it with their hatchets, and tried to enter. A woman who was alone in the building, and who had two loaded guns and two pistols, seeing the first savage struggling to shove himself through the hole, ran to him in desperation and shot him; on which the others dragged the body back and disappeared.[2]

There were several attempts of a more serious kind. The small wooden fort at the river St. George, the most easterly English outpost, was attacked, but the assailants were driven off. A few weeks later it was attacked again by the Penobscots under their missionary, Father Lauverjat. Other means failing, they tried to undermine the stockade; but their sap caved in from the effect of rains, and they retreated, with severe loss. The warlike contagion spread to the Indians of Nova Scotia. In July the Micmacs seized sixteen or seventeen fishing-smacks at Canso; on which John Eliot, of Boston, and John Robinson, of Cape Ann, chased the marauders in two sloops, retook most of the vessels, and killed a good number of the Indians. In the autumn a war-party, under the noted chief

[1] Palfrey, IV. 432, 433.
[2] Penhallow. Hutchinson II. 279.

Grey Lock, prowled about the village of Rutland, met the minister, Joseph Willard, and attacked him. He killed one savage and wounded another, but was at last shot and scalped.[1]

The representatives had long been bent on destroying the mission village of the Penobscots on the river of that name; and one cause of their grudge against Colonel Walton was that, by order of the Governor, he had deferred a projected attack upon it. His successor, Colonel Westbrook, now took the work in hand, went up the Penobscot in February with two hundred and thirty men in sloops and whaleboats, left these at the head of navigation, and pushed through the forest to the Indian town called Panawamské by the French. It stood apparently above Bangor, at or near Passadumkeag. Here the party found a stockade enclosure fourteen feet high, seventy yards long, and fifty yards wide, containing twenty-three houses, which Westbrook, a better woodsman than grammarian, reports to have been "built regular." Outside the stockade stood the chapel, "well and handsomely furnished within and without, and on the south side of that the Fryer's dwelling-house."[2] This "Fryer" was Father Lauverjat, who had led his flock to the attack of the fort at the St. George. Both Indians and missionary were gone. Westbrook's men burned the village and chapel, and sailed back to the St. George. In the next year, 1724, there was a more noteworthy stroke; for Dummer, more pliant than Shute, had so far soothed his Assembly that it no longer refused money for the war. It was resolved to strike at the root of the evil, seize Rale, and destroy Norridgewock. Two hundred and eight men in four companies, under Captains Harmon, Moulton, and Brown, and Lieutenant Bean, set out from Fort Richmond in seventeen whaleboats on the 8th of August. They left the boats at Taconic Falls in charge of a lieutenant and forty men, and on the morning of the 10th the main body, accompanied by three Mohawk Indians, marched through the forest for Norridgewock. Towards evening they saw two squaws, one of whom they brutally shot, and captured the other, who proved to be the wife of the noted chief Boma-

---

[1] Penhallow. Temple and Sheldon, *History of Northfield*, 195.

[2] *Westbrook to Dummer, 23 March, 1723*, in *Collections Mass. Hist. Soc., 2d Series*, VIII. 264.

zeen. She gave them a full account of the state of the village, which they approached early in the afternoon of the 12th. In the belief that some of the Indians would be in their corn-fields on the river above, Harmon, who was in command, divided the force, and moved up the river with about eighty men, while Moulton, with as many more, made for the village, advancing through the forest with all possible silence. About three o'clock he and his men emerged from a tangle of trees and bushes, and saw the Norridgewock cabins before them, no longer enclosed with a stockade, but open and un-protected. Not an Indian was stirring, till at length a warrior came out from one of the huts, saw the English, gave a star-tled war-whoop, and ran back for his gun. Then all was dis-may and confusion. Squaws and children ran screaming for the river, while the warriors, fifty or sixty in number, came to meet the enemy. Moulton ordered his men to reserve their fire till the Indians had emptied their guns. As he had fore-seen, the excited savages fired wildly, and did little or no harm. The English, still keeping their ranks, returned a volley with deadly effect. The Indians gave one more fire, and then ran for the river. Some tried to wade to the farther side, the water being low; others swam across, while many jumped into their canoes, but could not use them, having left the pad-dles in their houses. Moulton's men followed close, shooting the fugitives in the water or as they climbed the farther bank.

When they returned to the village they found Rale in one of the houses, firing upon some of their comrades who had not joined in the pursuit. He presently wounded one of them, on which a lieutenant named Benjamin Jaques burst open the door of the house, and, as he declared, found the priest load-ing his gun for another shot. The lieutenant said further that he called on him to surrender, and that Rale replied that he would neither give quarter nor take it; on which Jaques shot him through the head.[1] Moulton, who had given orders that Rale should not be killed, doubted this report of his subor-dinate so far as concerned the language used by Rale, though believing that he had exasperated the lieutenant by provoking

---

[1] Hutchinson, II. 283 (ed. 1795). Hutchinson had the story from Moulton. Compare the tradition in the family of Jaques, as told by his great-grandson, in *Historical Magazine*, VIII. 177.

expressions of some kind. The old chief Mogg had shut himself up in another house from which he fired and killed one of Moulton's three Mohawks, whose brother then beat in the door and shot the chief dead. Several of the English followed, and brutally murdered Mogg's squaw and his two children. Such plunder as the village afforded, consisting of three barrels of gunpowder, with a few guns, blankets, and kettles, was then seized; and the Puritan militia thought it a meritorious act to break what they called the "idols" in the church, and carry off the sacred vessels.

Harmon and his party returned towards night from their useless excursion to the cornfields, where they found nobody. In the morning a search was made for the dead, and twenty-six Indians were found and scalped, including the principal chiefs and warriors of the place. Then, being anxious for the safety of their boats, the party marched for Taconic Falls. They had scarcely left the village when one of the two surviving Mohawks, named Christian, secretly turned back, set fire to the church and the houses, and then rejoined the party. The boats were found safe, and embarking, they rowed down to Richmond with their trophies.[1]

The news of the fate of the Jesuit and his mission spread joy among the border settlers, who saw in it the end of their troubles. In their eyes, Rale was an incendiary, setting on a horde of bloody savages to pillage and murder. While they thought him a devil, he passed in Canada for a martyred saint. He was neither the one nor the other, but a man with the qualities and faults of a man,—fearless, resolute, endur-

[1] The above rests on the account of Hutchinson, which was taken from the official Journal of Harmon, the commander of the expedition, and from the oral statements of Moulton, whom Hutchinson examined on the subject. Charlevoix, following a letter of La Chasse in the Jesuit *Lettres Edifiantes*, gives a widely different story. According to him, Norridgewock was surprised by eleven hundred men, who first announced their presence by a general volley, riddling all the houses with bullets. Rale, says La Chasse, ran out to save his flock by drawing the rage of the enemy on himself; on which they raised a great shout and shot him dead at the foot of the cross in the middle of the village. La Chasse does not tell us where he got the story; but as there were no French witnesses, the story must have come from the Indians, who are notorious liars where their interest and self-love are concerned. Nobody competent to judge of evidence can doubt which of the two statements is the more trustworthy.

ing; boastful, sarcastic, often bitter and irritating; a vehement partisan; apt to see things, not as they were, but as he wished them to be; given to inaccuracy and exaggeration, yet no doubt sincere in opinions and genuine in zeal; hating the English more than he loved the Indians; calling himself their friend, yet using them as instruments of worldly policy, to their danger and final ruin. In considering the ascription of martyrdom, it is to be remembered that he did not die because he was an apostle of the faith, but because he was the active agent of the Canadian government.

There is reason to believe that he sometimes exercised a humanizing influence over his flock. The war which he helped to kindle was marked by fewer barbarities—fewer tortures, mutilations of the dead, and butcheries of women and infants—than either of the preceding wars. It is fair to assume that this was due in part to him, though it was chiefly the result of an order given, at the outset, by Shute that noncombatants in exposed positions should be sent to places of safety in the older settlements.[1]

[1] It is also said that Rale taught some of his Indians to read and write,—which was unusual in the Jesuit missions. On his character, compare the judicial and candid *Life of Rale*, by Dr. Convers Francis, in Sparks's *American Biography, New Series*, VII.

Chapter XI

1724, 1725

LOVEWELL'S FIGHT

*Vaudreuil and Dummer • Embassy to Canada • Indians intrac-
table • Treaty of Peace • The Pequawkets • John Lovewell • A
Hunting Party • Another Expedition • The Ambuscade • The
Fight • Chaplain Frye • His Fate • The Survivors •
Susanna Rogers*

THE DEATH of Rale and the destruction of Norridgewock
did not at once end the war. Vaudreuil turned all the
savages of the Canadian missions against the borders, not
only of Maine, but of western Massachusetts, whose peaceful
settlers had given no offence. Soon after the Norridgewock
expedition, Dummer wrote to the French Governor, who had
lately proclaimed the Abenakis his allies: "As they are subjects
of his Britannic Majesty, they cannot be your allies, except
through me, his representative. You have instigated them to
fall on our people in the most outrageous manner. I have seen
your commission to Sebastien Rale. But for your protection
and incitements they would have made peace long ago."[1]

In reply, Vaudreuil admitted that he had given a safe-con-
duct and a commission to Rale, which he could not deny, as
the Jesuit's papers were in the hands of the English Governor. "You will have to answer to your King for his murder,"
he tells Dummer. "It would have been strange if I had abandoned our Indians to please you. I cannot help taking the part
of our allies. You have brought your troubles upon yourself.
I advise you to pull down all the forts you have built on the
Abenaki lands since the Peace of Utrecht. If you do so, I will
be your mediator with the Norridgewocks. As to the murder
of Rale, I leave that to be settled between the two Crowns."[2]

Apparently the French court thought it wise to let the
question rest, and make no complaint. Dummer, however,
gave his views on the subject to Vaudreuil. "Instead of

[1] *Dummer to Vaudreuil, 15 Sept. 1724.*
[2] *Vaudreuil à Dummer, 29 Oct. 1724.*

preaching peace, love, and friendship, agreeably to the Christian religion, Rale was an incendiary, as appears by many letters I have by me. He has once and again appeared at the head of a great many Indians, threatening and insulting us. If such a disturber of the peace has been killed in the heat of action, nobody is to blame but himself. I have much more cause to complain that Mr. Willard, minister of Rutland, who is innocent of all that is charged against Rale, and always confined himself to preaching the Gospel, was slain and scalped by your Indians, and his scalp carried in triumph to Quebec."

Dummer then denies that France has any claim to the Abenakis, and declares that the war between them and the English is due to the instigations of Rale and the encouragements given them by Vaudreuil. But he adds that in his wish to promote peace he sends two prominent gentlemen, Colonel Samuel Thaxter and Colonel William Dudley, as bearers of his letter.[1]

Mr. Atkinson, envoy on the part of New Hampshire, joined Thaxter and Dudley, and the three set out for Montreal, over the ice of Lake Champlain. Vaudreuil received them with courtesy. As required by their instructions, they demanded the release of the English prisoners in Canada, and protested against the action of the French Governor in setting on the Indians to attack English settlements when there was peace between the two Crowns. Vaudreuil denied that he had done so, till they showed him his own letters to Rale, captured at Norridgewock. These were unanswerable; but Vaudreuil insisted that the supplies sent to the Indians were only the presents which they received every year from the King. As to the English prisoners, he said that those in the hands of the Indians were beyond his power; but that the envoys could have those whom the French had bought from their captors, on paying back the price they had cost. The demands were exorbitant, but sixteen prisoners were ransomed, and bargains were made for ten more. Vaudreuil proposed to Thaxter and his colleagues to have an interview with the Indians, which they at first declined, saying that they had no powers to treat with them, though, if the Indians wished to

---

[1] *Dummer to Vaudreuil, 19 Jan. 1725.* This, with many other papers relating to these matters, is in the Massachusetts Archives.

ask for peace, they were ready to hear them. At length a meeting was arranged. The French Governor writes: "Being satisfied that nothing was more opposed to our interests than a peace between the Abenakis and the English, I thought that I would sound the chiefs before they spoke to the English envoys, and insinuate to them everything that I had to say."[1] This he did with such success that, instead of asking for peace, the Indians demanded the demolition of the English forts, and heavy damages for burning their church and killing their missionary. In short, to Vaudreuil's great satisfaction, they talked nothing but war. The French despatch reporting this interview has the following marginal note: "Nothing better can be done than to foment this war, which at least retards the settlements of the English;" and against this is written, in the hand of the colonial minister, the word "*Approved.*"[2] This was, in fact, the policy pursued from the first, and Rale had been an instrument of it. The Jesuit La Chasse, who spoke both English and Abenaki, had acted as interpreter, and so had had the meeting in his power, as he could make both parties say what he pleased. The envoys thought him more anti-English than Vaudreuil himself, and ascribed the intractable mood of the Indians to his devices. Under the circumstances, they made a mistake in consenting to the interview at all. The Governor, who had treated them with civility throughout, gave them an escort of soldiers for the homeward journey, and they and the redeemed prisoners returned safely to Albany.

The war went on as before, but the Indians were fast growing tired of it. The Penobscots had made themselves obnoxious by their attacks on Fort St. George, and Captain Heath marched across country from the Kennebec to punish them. He found their village empty. It was built, since Westbrook's attack, at or near the site of Bangor, a little below Indian Old

[1] *Dépêche de Vaudreuil, 7 Août, 1725.* "Comme j'ai toujours été persuadé que rien n'est plus opposé à nos intérêts que la paix des Abenakis avec les Anglais (la sureté de cette colonie du côté de l'est ayant été l'unique objet de cette guerre), je songeai à pressentir ces sauvages avant qu'ils parlassent aux Anglais et à leur insinuer tout ce que j'avais à leur dire." *Vaudreuil au Ministre, 22 Mai, 1725.*

[2] *N. Y. Col. Docs.*, IX. 949.

Town,—the present abode of the tribe,—and consisted of fifty wigwams, which Heath's men burned to the ground.

One of the four hostages still detained at Boston, together with another Indian captured in the war, was allowed to visit his people, under a promise to return. Strange to say, the promise was kept. They came back bringing a request for peace from their tribesmen. On this, commissioners were sent to the St. George, where a conference was held with some of the Penobscot chiefs, and it was arranged that deputies of that people should be sent to Boston to conclude a solid peace. After long delay, four chiefs appeared, fully empowered, as they said, to make peace, not for the Penobscots only, but for the other Abenaki tribes, their allies. The speeches and ceremonies being at last ended, the four deputies affixed their marks to a paper in which, for themselves and those they represented, they made submission "unto his most excellent Majesty George, by the grace of God king of Great Britain, France, and Ireland, defender of the Faith," etc., promising to "cease and forbear all acts of hostility, injuries, and discord towards all his subjects, and never confederate or combine with any other nation to their prejudice." Here was a curious anomaly. The English claimed the Abenakis as subjects of the British Crown, and at the same time treated with them as a foreign power. Each of the four deputies signed the above-mentioned paper, one with the likeness of a turtle, the next with that of a bird, the third with the untutored portrait of a beaver, and the fourth with an extraordinary scrawl, meant, it seems, for a lobster,—such being their respective totems. To these the Lieutenant-Governor added the seal of the province of Massachusetts, coupled with his own autograph.

In the next summer, and again a year later, other meetings were held at Casco Bay with the chiefs of the various Abenaki tribes, in which, after prodigious circumlocution, the Boston treaty was ratified, and the war ended.[1] This time the Massachusetts Assembly, taught wisdom by experience, furnished a guarantee of peace by providing for government trading houses in the Indian country, where goods were supplied, through responsible hands, at honest prices.

[1] Penhallow gives the Boston treaty. For the ratifications, see *Collections of the Maine Hist. Soc.*, III. 377, 407.

The Norridgewocks, with whom the quarrel began, were completely broken. Some of the survivors joined their kindred in Canada, and others were merged in the Abenaki bands of the Penobscot, Saco, or Androscoggin. Peace reigned at last along the borders of New England; but it had cost her dear. In the year after the death of Rale, there was an incident of the conflict too noted in its day, and too strongly rooted in popular tradition, to be passed unnoticed.

Out of the heart of the White Mountains springs the river Saco, fed by the bright cascades that leap from the crags of Mount Webster, brawling among rocks and bowlders down the great defile of the Crawford Notch, winding through the forests and intervales of Conway, then circling northward by the village of Fryeburg in devious wanderings by meadows, woods, and mountains, and at last turning eastward and southward to join the sea.

On the banks of this erratic stream lived an Abenaki tribe called the Sokokis. When the first white man visited the country, these Indians lived at the Falls, a few miles from the mouth of the river. They retired before the English settlers, and either joined their kindred in Maine, or migrated to St. Francis and other Abenaki settlements in Canada; but a Sokoki band called Pigwackets, or Pequawkets, still kept its place far in the interior, on the upper waters of the Saco, near Pine Hill, in the present town of Fryeburg. Except a small band of their near kindred on Lake Ossipee, they were the only human tenants of a wilderness many thousand square miles in extent. In their wild and remote abode they were difficult of access, and the forest and the river were well stocked with moose, deer, bear, beaver, otter, lynx, fisher, mink, and marten. In this, their happy hunting-ground, the Pequawkets thought themselves safe, and they would have been so for some time longer if they had not taken up the quarrel of the Norridgewocks and made bloody raids against the English border, under their war-chief, Paugus.

Not far from where their wigwams stood clustered in a bend of the Saco was the small lake now called Lovewell's Pond, named for John Lovewell of Dunstable, a Massachusetts town on the New Hampshire line. Lovewell's father, a person of consideration in the village, where he owned a "garrison house," had served in Philip's War, and taken part in the famous Narragansett Swamp Fight. The younger Lovewell, now about thirty-three years of age, lived with his wife, Hannah, and two or three children on a farm of two hundred acres. The inventory of his effects, made after his death, includes five or six cattle, one mare, two steel traps with chains, a gun, two or three books, a feather-bed and "under-bed," or mattress, along with sundry tools, pots, barrels, chests, tubs, and the like,—the equipment, in short, of a decent frontier yeoman of the time.[1] But being, like the tough veteran, his father, of a bold and adventurous disposition, he seems to have been less given to farming than to hunting and bush-fighting.

Dunstable was attacked by Indians in the autumn of 1724, and two men were carried off. Ten others went in pursuit, but fell into an ambush, and nearly all were killed, Josiah Farwell, Lovewell's brother-in-law, being, by some accounts, the only one who escaped.[2] Soon after this, a petition, styled a "Humble Memorial," was laid before the House of Representatives at Boston. It declares that in order "to kill and destroy their enemy Indians," the petitioners and forty or fifty others are ready to spend one whole year in hunting them, "provided they can meet with Encouragement suitable." The petition is signed by John Lovewell, Josiah Farwell, and Jonathan Robbins, all of Dunstable, Lovewell's name being well written, and the others after a cramped and unaccustomed fashion. The representatives accepted the proposal and voted to give each adventurer two shillings and sixpence a day,—then equal in Massachusetts currency to about one English shilling,—out of which he was to maintain himself. The men were, in addition, promised large rewards for the scalps of male Indians old enough to fight.

A company of thirty was soon raised. Lovewell was chosen captain, Farwell, lieutenant, and Robbins, ensign. They set out towards the end of November, and reappeared at Dun-

---

[1] See the inventory, in Kidder, *The Expeditions of Captain John Lovewell*, 93, 94.

[2] Other accounts say that eight of the ten were killed. The headstone of one of the number, Thomas Lund, has these words: "This man, with seven more that lies in this grave, was slew All in A day by the Indiens."

stable early in January, bringing one prisoner and one scalp. Towards the end of the month Lovewell set out again, this time with eighty-seven men, gathered from the villages of Dunstable, Groton, Lancaster, Haverhill, and Billerica. They ascended the frozen Merrimac, passed Lake Winnepesaukee, pushed nearly to the White Mountains, and encamped on a branch of the upper Saco. Here they killed a moose,—a timely piece of luck, for they were in danger of starvation, and Lovewell had been compelled by want of food to send back a good number of his men. The rest held their way, filing on snow-shoes through the deathlike solitude that gave no sign of life except the light track of some squirrel on the snow, and the brisk note of the hardy little chickadee, or black-capped titmouse, so familiar to the winter woods. Thus far the scouts had seen no human footprint; but on the 20th of February they found a lately abandoned wigwam, and following the snow-shoe tracks that led from it, at length saw smoke rising at a distance out of the gray forest. The party lay close till two o'clock in the morning; then cautiously approached, found one or more wigwams, surrounded them, and killed all the inmates, ten in number. They were warriors from Canada on a winter raid against the borders. Lovewell and his men, it will be seen, were much like hunters of wolves, catamounts, or other dangerous beasts, except that the chase of this fierce and wily human game demanded far more hardihood and skill.

They brought home the scalps in triumph, together with the blankets and the new guns furnished to the slain warriors by their Canadian friends; and Lovewell began at once to gather men for another hunt. The busy season of the farmers was at hand, and volunteers came in less freely than before. At the middle of April, however, he had raised a band of forty-six, of whom he was the captain, with Farwell and Robbins as his lieutenants. Though they were all regularly commissioned by the Governor, they were leaders rather than commanders, for they and their men were neighbors or acquaintances on terms of entire social equality. Two of the number require mention. One was Seth Wyman, of Woburn, an ensign, and the other was Jonathan Frye, of Andover, the chaplain, a youth of twenty-one, graduated at Harvard College in 1723, and now a student of theology. Chaplain though he was, he carried a gun, knife, and hatchet like the others, and not one of the party was more prompt to use them.

They began their march on April 15th. A few days afterwards, one William Cummings, of Dunstable, became so disabled by the effects of a wound received from Indians some time before, that he could not keep on with the rest, and Lovewell sent him back in charge of a kinsman, thus reducing their number to forty-four. When they reached the west shore of Lake Ossipee, Benjamin Kidder, of Nutfield, fell seriously ill. To leave him defenceless in a place so dangerous was not to be thought of; and his comrades built a small fort, or palisaded log-cabin, near the water, where they left the sick man in charge of the surgeon, together with Sergeant Woods and a guard of seven men. The rest, now reduced to thirty-four, continued their march through the forest northeastward towards Pequawket, while the savage heights of the White Mountains, still covered with snow, rose above the dismal, bare forests on their left. They seem to have crossed the Saco just below the site of Fryeburg, and in the night of May 7, as they lay in the woods near the northeast end of Lovewell's Pond, the men on guard heard sounds like Indians prowling about them. At daybreak the next morning, as they stood bareheaded, listening to a prayer from the young chaplain, they heard the report of a gun, and soon after discovered an Indian on the shore of the pond at a considerable distance. Apparently he was shooting ducks; but Lovewell, suspecting a device to lure them into an ambuscade, asked the men whether they were for pushing forward or falling back, and with one voice they called upon him to lead them on. They were then in a piece of open pine woods traversed by a small brook. He ordered them to lay down their packs and advance with extreme caution. They had moved forward for some time in this manner when they met an Indian coming towards them through the dense trees and bushes. He no sooner saw them than he fired at the leading men. His gun was charged with beaver-shot; but he was so near his mark that the effect was equal to that of a bullet, and he severely wounded Lovewell and one Whiting; on which Seth Wyman shot him dead, and the chaplain and another man scalped him. Lovewell, though believed to be mortally hurt, was still able to walk, and the party fell back to the place where they had left their packs. The packs had disappeared, and suddenly, with frightful yells, the whole body of the Pequawket warriors rushed from their hiding-places, firing as they came on. The survivors say that they were more than twice the number of the whites,—which is probably an exaggeration, though their conduct, so unusual with Indians, in rushing forward instead of firing from their ambush, shows a remarkable confidence in their numerical strength.[1] They no doubt expected to strike their enemies with a panic. Lovewell received another mortal wound; but he fired more than once on the Indians as he lay dying. His two lieutenants, Farwell and Robbins, were also badly hurt. Eight others fell; but the rest stood their ground, and pushed the Indians so hard that they drove them back to cover with heavy loss. One man played the coward, Benjamin Hassell, of Dunstable, who ran off, escaped in the confusion, and made with his best speed for the fort at Lake Ossipee.

The situation of the party was desperate, and nothing saved them from destruction but the prompt action of their surviving officers, only one of whom, Ensign Wyman, had escaped unhurt. It was probably under his direction that the men fell back steadily to the shore of the pond, which was only a few rods distant. Here the water protected their rear, so that they could not be surrounded; and now followed one of the most obstinate and deadly bush-fights in the annals of New England. It was about ten o'clock when the fight began, and it lasted till night. The Indians had the greater agility and skill in hiding and sheltering themselves, and the whites the greater steadiness and coolness in using their guns. They fought in the shade; for the forest was dense, and all alike covered themselves as they best could behind trees, bushes, or fallen trunks, where each man crouched with eyes and mind intent, firing whenever he saw, or thought he saw, the head, limbs, or body of an enemy exposed to sight for an instant. The Indians howled like wolves, yelled like enraged cougars, and made the forest ring with their whoops; while the whites

[1] Penhallow puts their number at seventy, Hutchinson at eighty, Williamson at sixty-three, and Belknap at forty-one. In such cases the smallest number is generally nearest the truth.

replied with shouts and cheers. At one time the Indians ceased firing and drew back among the trees and undergrowth, where, by the noise they made, they seemed to be holding a "pow-wow," or incantation to procure victory; but the keen and fearless Seth Wyman crept up among the bushes, shot the chief conjuror, and broke up the meeting. About the middle of the afternoon young Frye received a mortal wound. Unable to fight longer, he lay in his blood, praying from time to time for his comrades in a faint but audible voice.

Solomon Keyes, of Billerica, received two wounds, but fought on till a third shot struck him. He then crawled up to Wyman in the heat of the fight, and told him that he, Keyes, was a dead man, but that the Indians should not get his scalp if he could help it. Creeping along the sandy edge of the pond, he chanced to find a stranded canoe, pushed it afloat, rolled himself into it, and drifted away before the wind.

Soon after sunset the Indians drew off and left the field to their enemies, living and dead, not even stopping to scalp the fallen,—a remarkable proof of the completeness of their discomfiture. Exhausted with fatigue and hunger,—for, having lost their packs in the morning, they had no food,—the surviving white men explored the scene of the fight. Jacob Farrar lay gasping his last by the edge of the water. Robert Usher and Lieutenant Robbins were unable to move. Of the thirty-four men, nine had escaped without serious injury, eleven were badly wounded, and the rest were dead or dying, except the coward who had run off.

About midnight, an hour or more before the setting of the moon, such as had strength to walk left the ground. Robbins, as he lay helpless, asked one of them to load his gun, saying, "The Indians will come in the morning to scalp me, and I'll kill another of 'em if I can." They loaded the gun and left him.

To make one's way even by daylight through the snares and pitfalls of a New England forest is often a difficult task; to do so in the darkness of night and overshadowing boughs, among the fallen trees and the snarl of underbrush, was well-nigh impossible. Any but the most skilful woodsmen would have lost their way. The Indians, sick of fighting, did not molest the party. After struggling on for a mile or more, Farwell, Frye, and two other wounded men, Josiah Jones and Eleazer Davis, could go no farther, and, with their consent, the others left them, with a promise to send them help as soon as they should reach the fort. In the morning the men divided into several small bands, the better to elude pursuit. One of these parties was tracked for some time by the Indians, and Elias Barron, becoming separated from his companions, was never again heard of, though the case of his gun was afterwards found by the bank of the river Ossipee.

Eleven of the number at length reached the fort, and to their amazement found nobody there. The runaway, Hassell, had arrived many hours before them, and to excuse his flight told so frightful a story of the fate of his comrades that his hearers were seized with a panic, shamefully abandoned their post, and set out for the settlements, leaving a writing on a piece of birch bark to the effect that all the rest were killed. They had left a supply of bread and pork, and while the famished eleven rested and refreshed themselves they were joined by Solomon Keyes, the man who, after being thrice wounded, had floated away in a canoe from the place of the fight. After drifting for a considerable distance, the wind blew him ashore, when, spurred by necessity and feeling himself "wonderfully strengthened," he succeeded in gaining the fort.

Meanwhile Frye, Farwell, and their two wounded companions, Davis and Jones, after waiting vainly for the expected help, found strength to struggle forward again, till the chaplain stopped and lay down, begging the others to keep on their way, and saying to Davis, "Tell my father that I expect in a few hours to be in eternity, and am not afraid to die." They left him, and, says the old narrative, "he has not been heard of since." He had kept the journal of the expedition, which was lost with him.

Farwell died of exhaustion. The remaining two lost their way and became separated. After wandering eleven days, Davis reached the fort at Lake Ossipee, and finding food there, came into Berwick on the 27th. Jones, after fourteen days in the woods, arrived, half dead, at the village of Biddeford.

Some of the eleven who had first made their way to the fort, together with Keyes, who joined them there, came into

Dunstable during the night of the 13th, and the rest followed one or two days later. Ensign Wyman, who was now the only commissioned officer left alive, and who had borne himself throughout with the utmost intrepidity, decision, and good sense, reached the same place along with three other men on the 15th.

The runaway, Hassell, and the guard at the fort, whom he had infected with his terror, had lost no time in making their way back to Dunstable, which they seem to have reached on the evening of the 11th. Horsemen were sent in haste to carry the doleful news to Boston, on which the Governor gave orders to Colonel Tyng of the militia, who was then at Dunstable, to gather men in the border towns, march with all speed to the place of the fight, succor the wounded if any were still alive, and attack the Indians, if he could find them. Tyng called upon Hassell to go with him as a guide; but he was ill, or pretended to be so, on which one of the men who had been in the fight and had just returned offered to go in his place.

When the party reached the scene of the battle, they saw the trees plentifully scarred with bullets, and presently found and buried the bodies of Lovewell, Robbins, and ten others. The Indians, after their usual custom, had carried off or hidden their own dead; but Tyng's men discovered three of them buried together, and one of these was recognized as the war-chief Paugus, killed by Wyman, or, according to a more than doubtful tradition, by John Chamberlain.[1] Not a living Indian was to be seen.

[1] The tradition is that Chamberlain and Paugus went down to the small brook, now called Fight Brook, to clean their guns, hot and foul with frequent firing; that they saw each other at the same instant, and that the Indian said to the white man, in his broken English, "Me kill you quick!" at the same time hastily loading his piece; to which Chamberlain coolly replied, "May be not." His firelock had a large touch-hole, so that the powder could be shaken out into the pan, and the gun made to prime itself. Thus he was ready for action an instant sooner than his enemy, whom he shot dead just as Paugus pulled trigger and sent a bullet whistling over his head. The story has no good foundation, while the popular ballad, written at the time, and very faithful to the facts, says that, the other officers being killed, the English made Wyman their captain,—

"Who shot the old chief Paugus, which did the foe defeat,
Then set his men in order and brought off the retreat."

The Pequawkets were cowed by the rough handling they had met when they plainly expected a victory. Some of them joined their Abenaki kinsmen in Canada and remained there, while others returned after the peace to their old haunts by the Saco; but they never again raised the hatchet against the English.

Lovewell's Pond, with its sandy beach, its two green islands, and its environment of lonely forests, reverted for a while to its original owners,—the wolf, bear, lynx, and moose. In our day all is changed. Farms and dwellings possess those peaceful shores, and hard by, where, at the bend of the Saco, once stood, in picturesque squalor, the wigwams of the vanished Pequawkets, the village of Fryeburg preserves the name of the brave young chaplain, whose memory is still cherished, in spite of his uncanonical turn for scalping.[1] He had engaged himself to a young girl of a neighboring village, Susanna Rogers, daughter of John Rogers, minister of Boxford. It has been said that Frye's parents thought her beneath him in education and position; but this is not likely, for her father belonged to what has been called the "Brahmin caste" of New England, and, like others of his family, had had, at Harvard, the best education that the country could supply. The girl herself, though only fourteen years old, could make verses, such as they were; and she wrote an elegy on the death of her lover which, bating some grammatical lapses, deserves the modest praise of being no worse than many New England rhymes of that day.

The courage of Frye and his sturdy comrades contributed greatly to the pacification which in the next year relieved the borders from the scourge of Indian war.[2]

---

[1] The town, however, was not named for the chaplain, but for his father's cousin, General Joseph Frye, the original grantee of the land.

[2] Rev. Thomas Symmes, minister of Bradford, preached a sermon on the fate of Lovewell and his men immediately after the return of the survivors, and printed it, with a much more valuable introduction, giving a careful account of the affair, on the evidence of "the Valorous Captain Wyman and some others of good Credit that were in the Engagement." Wyman had just been made a captain, in recognition of his conduct. The narrative is followed by an attestation of its truth signed by him and two others of Lovewell's band.

A considerable number of letters relating to the expedition are preserved in the Massachusetts Archives, from Benjamin Hassell, Colonel Tyng, Governor Dummer of Massachusetts, and Governor Wentworth of New Hampshire. They give the various reports received from those in the fight, and show the action taken in consequence. The Archives also contain petitions from the survivors and the families of the slain; and the legislative Journals show that the petitioners received large grants of land. Lovewell's debts contracted in raising men for his expeditions were also paid.

The papers mentioned above, with other authentic records concerning the affair, have been printed by Kidder in his *Expeditions of Captain John Lovewell*, a monograph of thorough research. The names of all Lovewell's party, and biographical notices of some of them, are also given by Mr. Kidder. Compare Penhallow, Hutchinson, Fox, *History of Dunstable*, and Bouton, *Lovewell's Great Fight*. For various suggestions touching Lovewell's Expedition, I am indebted to Mr. C. W. Lewis, who has made it the subject of minute and careful study.

A ballad which was written when the event was fresh, and was long popular in New England, deserves mention, if only for its general fidelity to the facts. The following is a sample of its eighteen stanzas: —

> " 'T was ten o'clock in the morning when first the fight begun,
> And fiercely did continue till the setting of the sun,
> Excepting that the Indians, some hours before 't was night,
> Drew off into the bushes, and ceased awhile to fight;

> "But soon again returned in fierce and furious mood,
> Shouting as in the morning, but yet not half so loud;
> For, as we are informed, so thick and fast they fell,
> Scarce twenty of their number at night did get home well.

*   *   *

> "Our worthy Captain Lovewell among them there did die;
> They killed Lieutenant Robbins, and wounded good young Frye,
> Who was our English chaplain; he many Indians slew,
> And some of them he scalped when bullets round him flew."

Frye, as mentioned in the text, had engaged himself to Susanna Rogers, a young girl of the village of Boxford, who, after his death, wrote some untutored verses to commemorate his fate. They are entitled, *A Mournful Elegy on Mr. Jonathan Frye*, and begin thus: —

> "Assist, ye muses, help my quill,
> Whilst floods of tears does down distil;
> Not from mine eyes alone, but all
> That hears the sad and doleful fall
> Of that young student, Mr. Frye,
> Who in his blooming youth did die.
> Fighting for his dear country's good,
> He lost his life and precious blood.
> His father's only son was he;
> His mother loved him tenderly;
> And all that knew him loved him well;
> For in bright parts he did excel

> Most of his age; for he was young,—
> Just entering on twenty-one;
> A comely youth, and pious too;
> This I affirm, for him I knew."

She then describes her lover's brave deeds and sad but heroic death, alone in a howling wilderness; condoles with the bereaved parents, exhorts them to resignation, and touches modestly on her own sorrow.

In more recent times the fate of Lovewell and his companions has inspired several poetical attempts, which need not be dwelt upon. Lovewell's Fight, as Dr. Palfrey observes, was long as famous in New England as Chevy Chase on the Scottish Border.

Chapter XII

THE OUTAGAMIES AT DETROIT

The West and the Fur Trade • New York and Canada • Indian Population • The Firebrands of the West • Detroit in 1712 • Dangerous Visitors • Suspense • Timely Succors • The Outagamies attacked • Their desperate Position • Overtures • Wavering Allies • Conduct of Dubuisson • Escape of the Outagamies • Pursuit and Attack • Victory and Carnage

WE HAVE seen that the Peace of Utrecht was followed by a threefold conflict for ascendency in America,—the conflict for Acadia, the conflict for northern New England, and the conflict for the Great West; which last could not be said to take at once an international character, being essentially a competition for the fur-trade. Only one of the English colonies took an active part in it,—the province of New York. Alone among her sister communities she had a natural thoroughfare to the West, not comparable, however, with that of Canada, to whose people the St. Lawrence, the Great Lakes, and their tributary waters were a continual invitation to the vast interior.

Virginia and Pennsylvania were not yet serious rivals in the fur-trade, and New England, the most active of the British colonies, was barred out from it by the interposition of New York, which lay across her westward path, thus forcing her to turn her energies to the sea, where half a century later her achievements inspired the glowing panegyrics of Burke before the House of Commons.

New York, then, was for many years the only rival of Canada for the control of the West. It was a fatal error in the rulers of New France that they did not, in the seventeenth century, use more strenuous efforts to possess themselves, by purchase, exchange, or conquest, of this troublesome and dangerous neighbor. There was a time, under the reign of Charles II., when negotiation for the purchase of New York might have been successful; and if this failed, the conquest of the province, if attempted by forces equal to the importance of the object, would have been far from hopeless. With New York in French hands, the fate of the continent would probably have been changed. The British possessions would have been cut in two. New England, isolated and placed in constant jeopardy, would have vainly poured her unmanageable herds of raw militia against the disciplined veterans of Old France intrenched at the mouth of the Hudson. Canada would have gained complete control of her old enemies, the Iroquois, who would have been wholly dependent on her for the arms and ammunition without which they could do nothing.

The Iroquois, as the French had been accustomed to call them, were known to the English as the Five Nations,—a name which during the eighteenth century the French also adopted. Soon after the Peace of Utrecht, a kindred tribe, the Tuscaroras, was joined to the original five members of the confederacy, which thenceforward was sometimes called the Six Nations, though the Tuscaroras were never very prominent in its history; and to avoid confusion, we will keep the more familiar name of the Five Nations, which the French used to the last.

For more than two generations this league of tribes had held Canada in terror, and more than once threatened it with destruction. But now a change had come over the confederates. Count Frontenac had humbled their pride. They were crowded between the rival European nations, both of whom they distrusted. Their traditional hatred of the French would have given the English of New York a controlling influence over them if the advantage had been used with energy and tact. But a narrow and short-sighted conduct threw it away. A governor of New York, moreover, even were he as keen and far-seeing as Frontenac himself, would often have been helpless. When the Five Nations were attacked by the French, he had no troops to defend them, nor could he, like a Canadian governor, call out the forces of his province by a word, to meet the exigency. The small revenues of New York were not at his disposal. Without the votes of the frugal representatives of an impoverished people, his hands were tied. Hence the Five Nations, often left unaided when they most needed help, looked upon their Dutch and English neighbors as slothful and unwarlike.

Yet their friendship was of the greatest importance to the province, in peace as well as in war, and was indispensable in the conflict that New York was waging single-handed for the control of the Western fur-trade. The Five Nations, as we have seen,[1] acted as middlemen between the New York merchants and the tribes of the far interior, and through them English goods and English influence penetrated all the lake country, and reached even to the Mississippi.

These vast Western regions, now swarming with laborious millions, were then scantily peopled by savage hordes, whose increase was stopped by incessant mutual slaughter. This wild population had various centres or rallying points, usually about the French forts, which protected them from enemies and supplied their wants. Thus the Pottawattamies, Ottawas, and Hurons were gathered about Detroit, and the Illinois about Fort St. Louis, on the river Illinois, where Henri de Tonty and his old comrade, La Forest, with fifteen or twenty Frenchmen, held a nominal monopoly of the neighboring fur-trade. Another focus of Indian population was near the Green Bay of Lake Michigan, and on Fox River, which enters it. Here were grouped the Sacs, Winnebagoes, and Menomonies, with the Outagamies, or Foxes, a formidable tribe, the source of endless trouble to the French.

The constant aim of the Canadian authorities was to keep these Western savages at peace among themselves, while preventing their establishing relations of trade with the Five Nations, and carrying their furs to them in exchange for English goods. The position was delicate, for while a close understanding between the Western tribes and the Five Nations would be injurious to French interests, a quarrel would be still more so, since the French would then be found to side with their Western allies, and so be drawn into hostilities with the Iroquois confederacy, which of all things they most wished to avoid. Peace and friendship among the Western tribes; peace without friendship between these tribes and the Five Nations,—thus became maxims of French policy. The Canadian Governor called the Western Indians his "children," and a family quarrel among them would have been unfortu-

[1] See Chapter I.

nate, since the loving father must needs have become involved in it, to the detriment of his trading interests.

Yet to prevent such quarrels was difficult, partly because they had existed time out of mind, and partly because it was the interest of the English to promote them. Dutch and English traders, it is true, took their lives in their hands if they ventured among the Western Indians, who were encouraged by their French father to plunder and kill them, and who on occasion rarely hesitated to do so. Hence English communication with the West was largely carried on through the Five Nations. Iroquois messengers, hired for the purpose, carried wampum belts "underground,"—that is, secretly,—to such of the interior tribes as were disposed to listen with favor to the words of Corlaer, as they called the Governor of New York.

In spite of their shortcomings, the English had one powerful attraction for all the tribes alike. This was the abundance and excellence of their goods, which, with the exception of gunpowder, were better as well as cheaper than those offered by the French. The Indians, it is true, liked the taste of French brandy more than that of English rum; yet as their chief object in drinking was to get drunk, and as rum would supply as much intoxication as brandy at a lower price, it always found favor in their eyes. In the one case, to get thoroughly drunk often cost a beaver-skin; in the other, the same satisfaction could generally be had for a mink-skin.

Thus the French found that some of their Western children were disposed to listen to English seductions, look askance at their father Onontio, and turn their canoes, not towards Montreal, but towards Albany. Nor was this the worst; for there were some of Onontio's wild and unruly Western family too ready to lift their hatchets against their brethren and fill the wilderness with discord. Consequences followed most embarrassing to the French, and among them an incident prominent in the early annals of Detroit, that new establishment so obnoxious to the English, because it barred their way to the northern lakes, so that they were extremely anxious to rid themselves of it.

In the confused and tumultuous history of the savages of this continent one now and then sees some tribe or league of tribes possessed for a time with a spirit of conquest and havoc that made it the terror of its neighbors. Of this the foremost example is that of the Five Nations of the Iroquois, who, towards the middle of the seventeenth century, swept all before them and made vast regions a solitude. They were now comparatively quiet; but far in the Northwest, another people, inferior in number, organization, and mental capacity, but not in ferocity or courage, had begun on a smaller scale, and with less conspicuous success, to play a similar part. These were the Outagamies, or Foxes, with their allies, the Kickapoos and the Mascoutins, all living at the time within the limits of the present States of Wisconsin and Illinois,— the Outagamies near Fox River, and the others on Rock River.[1] The Outagamies, in particular, seem to have been seized with an access of homicidal fury. Their hand was against every man, and for twenty years and more they were the firebrands of the West, and a ceaseless peril to French interests in that region. They were, however, on good terms with the Five Nations, by means of whom, as French writers say, the Dutch and English of Albany sent them gifts and messages to incite them to kill French traders and destroy the French fort at Detroit. This is not unlikely, though the evidence on the point is far from conclusive.

Fort Ponchartrain, better known as Fort Detroit, was an enclosure of palisades, flanked by blockhouses at the corners, with an open space within to serve as a parade-ground, around which stood small wooden houses thatched with straw or meadow-grass. La Mothe-Cadillac, founder of the post, had been made governor of the new colony of Louisiana, and the Sieur Dubuisson now commanded at Detroit. There were about thirty French traders, *voyageurs*, and *coureurs de bois* in the place, but at this time no soldiers.

The village of the Pottawattamies was close to the French fort; that of the Hurons was not far distant, by the edge of the river. Their houses were those structures of bark, "very high, very long, and arched like garden arbors," which were common to all the tribes of Iroquois stock, and both villages were enclosed by strong double or triple stockades, such as Cartier had found at Hochelaga, and Champlain in the Onon-

[1] *Memoir on the Indians between Lake Erie and the Mississippi*, in *N. Y. Col. Docs.*, IX. 885.

daga country. Their neighbors, the Ottawas, who were on the east side of the river, had imitated, with imperfect success, their way of housing and fortifying themselves. These tribes raised considerable crops of peas, beans, and Indian corn; and except when engaged in their endless dances and games of ball, dressed, like the converts of the mission villages, in red or blue cloth.[1] The Hurons were reputed the most intelligent as well as the bravest of all the Western tribes, and being incensed by various outrages, they bore against the Outagamies a deadly grudge, which was shared by the other tribes, their neighbors.

All these friendly Indians were still absent on their winter hunt, when, at the opening of spring, Dubuisson and his Frenchmen were startled by a portentous visitation. Two bands of Outagamies and Mascoutins, men, women, and children, counting in all above a thousand, of whom about three hundred were warriors, appeared on the meadows behind the fort, approached to within pistol-shot of the palisades, and encamped there. It is by no means certain that they came with deliberate hostile intent. Had this been the case, they would not have brought their women and children. A paper ascribed to the engineer Léry says, moreover, that their visit was in consequence of an invitation from the late commandant, La Mothe-Cadillac, whose interest it was to attract to Detroit as many Indians as possible, in order to trade for their furs.[2] Dubuisson, however, was satisfied that they meant mischief, especially when, in spite of all his efforts to prevent them, they fortified themselves by cutting down young trees and surrounding their wigwams with a rough fence of palisades. They were rude and insolent, declared that all that country was theirs, and killed fowls and pigeons belonging to the French, who, in the absence of their friends, the Hurons and Ottawas, dared not even remonstrate. Dubuisson himself was forced to submit to their insults in silence, till a party of them came one day into the fort bent on killing two of the French, a man and a girl, against whom they had taken some offence. The commandant then ordered his men to drive them out;

[1] *Memoir on the Indians between Lake Erie and the Mississippi.*

[2] This paper is printed, not very accurately, in the *Collection de Documents relatifs à la Nouvelle France*, I. 623 (Québec, 1883).

which was done, and henceforward he was convinced that the Outagamies and Mascoutins were only watching their opportunity to burn the fort and butcher its inmates. Soon after, their excitement redoubled. News came that a band of Mascoutins, who had wintered on the river St. Joseph, had been cut off by the Ottawas and Pottawattamies, led by an Ottawa chief named Saguina; on which the behavior of the dangerous visitors became so threatening that Dubuisson hastily sent a canoe to recall the Hurons and Ottawas from their hunting-grounds, and a second to invite the friendly Ojibwas and Mississagas to come to his aid. No doubt there was good cause for alarm; yet if the dangerous strangers had resolved to strike, they would have been apt to strike at once, instead of waiting week after week, when they knew that the friends and allies of the French might arrive at any time. Dubuisson, however, felt that the situation was extremely critical, and he was confirmed in his anxiety by a friendly Outagamie, who, after the news of the massacre on the St. Joseph, told him that his tribesmen meant to burn the fort.

The church was outside the palisade, as were also several houses, one of which was stored with wheat. This the Outagamies tried to seize. The French fired on them, drove them back, and brought most of the wheat into the fort; then demolished the church and several of the houses which would have given cover to the assailants and enabled them to set fire to the palisade, close to which the buildings stood. The French worked at their task in the excitement of desperation, for they thought that all was lost.

The irritation of their savage neighbors so increased that an outbreak seemed imminent, when, on the 13th of May, the Sieur de Vincennes arrived, with seven or eight Frenchmen, from the Miami country. The reinforcement was so small that instead of proving a help it might have provoked a crisis. Vincennes brought no news of the Indian allies, who were now Dubuisson's only hope. "I did not know on what saint to call," he writes, almost in despair, when suddenly a Huron Indian came panting into the fort with the joyful news that both his people and the Ottawas were close at hand. Nor was this all. The Huron messenger announced that Makisabie, war-chief of the Pottawattamies, was then at the Huron fort, and that six hundred warriors of various tribes, deadly enemies of the Outagamies and Mascoutins, would soon arrive and destroy them all.

Here was an unlooked-for deliverance. Yet the danger was not over; for there was fear lest the Outagamies and their allies, hearing of the approaching succor, might make a desperate onslaught, burn the French fort, and kill its inmates before their friends could reach them. An interval of suspense followed, relieved at last by a French sentinel, who called to Dubuisson that a crowd of Indians was in sight. The commandant mounted to the top of a blockhouse, and, looking across the meadows behind the fort, saw a throng of savages coming out of the woods,—Pottawattamies, Sacs, Menomonies, Illinois, Missouris, and other tribes yet more remote, each band distinguished by a kind of ensign. These were the six hundred warriors promised by the Huron messenger, and with them, as it proved, came the Ottawa war-chief Saguina. Having heard during the winter that the Outagamies and Mascoutins would go to Detroit in the spring, these various tribes had combined to attack the common enemy; and they now marched with great ostentation and some show of order, not to the French fort, but to the fortified village of the Hurons, who with their neighbors, the Ottawas, had arrived just before them.

The Hurons were reputed leaders among the Western tribes, and they hated the Outagamies, not only by reason of bitter wrongs, but also through jealousy of the growing importance which these fierce upstarts had won by their sanguinary prowess. The Huron chiefs came to meet the motley crew of warriors, and urged them to instant action. "You must not stop to encamp," said the Huron spokesman; "we must all go this moment to the fort of our fathers, the French, and fight for them." Then, turning to the Ottawa war-chief: "Do you see that smoke, Saguina, rising from the camp of our enemies? They are burning three women of your village, and your wife is one of them." The Outagamies had, in fact, three Ottawa squaws in their clutches; but the burning was an invention of the crafty Huron. It answered its purpose, and wrought the hearers to fury. They ran with yells and whoops towards the French fort, the Hurons and Ottawas leading the way. A burst of answering yells rose from the camp of the enemy, and about forty of their warriors ran out in bravado, stripped naked and brandishing their weapons; but they soon fell back within their defences before the approaching multitude.

Just before the arrival of the six hundred allies, Dubuisson, whose orders were to keep the peace, if he could, among the Western tribes, had sent Vincennes to the Huron village with a proposal that they should spare the lives of the Outagamies and Mascoutins, and rest content with driving them away; to which the Hurons returned a fierce and haughty refusal. There was danger that if vexed or thwarted, the rabble of excited savages now gathered before the fort might turn from friends into enemies, and in some burst of wild caprice lift parricidal tomahawks against their French fathers. Dubuisson saw no choice but to humor them, put himself at their head, aid them in their vengeance, and even set them on. Therefore, when they called out for admittance, he did not venture to refuse it, but threw open the gate.

The savage crew poured in till the fort was full. The chiefs gathered for council on the parade, and the warriors crowded around, a living wall of dusky forms, befeathered heads, savage faces, lank snaky locks, and deep-set eyes that glittered with a devilish light. Their orator spoke briefly, but to the purpose. He declared that all present were ready to die for their French father, who had stood their friend against the bloody and perfidious Outagamies. Then he begged for food, tobacco, gunpowder, and bullets. Dubuisson replied with equal conciseness, thanked them for their willingness to die for him, said that he would do his best to supply their wants, and promised an immediate distribution of powder and bullets; to which the whole assembly answered with yells of joy.

Then the council dissolved, and the elder warriors stalked about the fort, haranguing their followers, exhorting them to fight like men and obey the orders of their father. The powder and bullets were served out, after which the whole body, white men and red, yelled the war-whoop together,—"a horrible cry, that made the earth tremble," writes Dubuisson.[1]

[1] "Cri horrible, dont la terre trembla." *Dubuisson à Vaudreuil, 15 Juin, 1712.* This is the official report of the affair.

An answering howl, furious and defiant, rose close at hand from the palisaded camp of the enemy, the firing began on both sides, and bullets and arrows filled the air.

The French and their allies outnumbered their enemies fourfold, while the Outagamie and Mascoutin warriors were encumbered with more than seven hundred women and children. Their frail defences might have been carried by assault; but the loss to the assailants must needs have been great against so brave and desperate a foe, and such a mode of attack is repugnant to the Indian genius. Instead, therefore, of storming the palisaded camp, the allies beleaguered it with vindictive patience, and wore out its defenders by a fire that ceased neither day nor night. The French raised two tall scaffolds, from which they overlooked the palisade, and sent their shot into the midst of those within, who were forced, for shelter, to dig holes in the ground four or five feet deep, and ensconce themselves there. The situation was almost hopeless, but their courage did not fail. They raised twelve red English blankets on poles as battle-flags, to show that they would fight to the death, and hung others over their palisades, calling out that they wished to see the whole earth red, like them, with blood, that they had no fathers but the English, and that the other tribes had better do as they did, and turn their backs to Onontio.

The great war-chief of the Pottawattamies now mounted to the top of one of the French scaffolds, and harangued the enemy to this effect: "Do you think, you wretches, that you can frighten us by hanging out those red blankets? If the earth is red with blood, it will be your own. You talk about the English. Their bad advice will be your ruin. They are enemies of religion, and that is why the Master of Life punishes both them and you. They are cowards, and can only defend themselves by poisoning people with their fire-water, which kills a man the instant he drinks it. We shall soon see what you will get for listening to them."

This Homeric dialogue between the chief combatants was stopped by Dubuisson, who saw that it distracted the attention of the warriors, and so enabled the besieged to run to the adjacent river for water. The firing was resumed more fiercely than ever. Before night twelve of the Indian allies were killed in the French fort, though the enemy suffered a much greater loss. One house had been left standing outside the French palisades, and the Outagamies raised a scaffold behind its bullet-proof gable, under cover of which they fired with great effect. The French at length brought two swivels to bear upon the gable, pierced it, knocked down the scaffold, killed some of the marksmen, and scattered the rest in consternation.

Famine and thirst were worse for the besieged than the bullets and arrows of the allies. Parched, starved, and fainting, they could no longer find heart for bravado, and they called out one evening from behind their defences to ask Dubuisson if they might come to speak with him. He called together the allied chiefs, and all agreed that here was an opportunity to get out of the hands of the Outagamies the three Ottawa women whom they held prisoners. The commandant, therefore, told them that if they had anything to say to their father before dying, they might come and say it in safety.

In the morning all the red blankets had disappeared, and a white flag was waving over the hostile camp. The great Outagamie chief, Pemoussa, presently came out, carrying a smaller white flag and followed by two Indian slaves. Dubuisson sent his interpreter to protect him from insult and conduct him to the parade, where all the allied chiefs presently met to hear him.

"My Father," he began, "I am a dead man. The sky is bright for you, and dark as night for me." Then he held out a belt of wampum, and continued: "By this belt I ask you, my Father, to take pity on your children and grant us two days in which our old men may counsel together to find means of appeasing your wrath." Then, offering another belt to the assembled chiefs, "This belt is to pray you to remember that you are of our kin. If you spill our blood, do not forget that it is also your own. Try to soften the heart of our father, whom we have offended so often. These two slaves are to replace some of the blood you have lost. Grant us the two days we ask, for I cannot say more till our old men have held counsel."

To which Dubuisson answered in the name of all: "If your hearts were really changed, and you honestly accepted Onontio as your father, you would have brought back the three women who are prisoners in your hands. As you have not done so, I think that your hearts are still bad. First bring them to me, if you expect me to hear you. I have no more to say."

"I am but a child," replied the envoy. "I will go back to my village, and tell our old men what you have said."

The council then broke up, and several Frenchmen conducted the chief back to his followers.

Three other chiefs soon after appeared, bearing a flag and bringing the Ottawa squaws, one of whom was the wife of the war-chief, Saguina. Again the elders met in council on the parade, and the orator of the deputation spoke thus: "My Father, here are the three pieces of flesh that you ask of us. We would not eat them, lest you should be angry. Do with them what you please, for you are the master. Now we ask that you will send away the nations that are with you, so that we may seek food for our women and children, who die of hunger every day. If you are as good a father as your other children say you are, you will not refuse us this favor."

But Dubuisson, having gained his point and recovered the squaws, spoke to them sternly, and referred them to his Indian allies for their answer. Whereupon the head chief of the Illinois, being called upon by the rest to speak in their behalf, addressed the envoys to this effect: "Listen to me, you who have troubled all the earth. We see plainly that you mean only to deceive our father. If we should leave him, as you wish, you would fall upon him and kill him. You are dogs who have always bitten him. You thought that we did not know all the messages you have had from the English, telling you to cut our father's throat, and then bring them into this our country. We will not leave him alone with you. We shall see who will be the master. Go back to your fort. We are going to fire at you again."

The envoys went back with a French escort to prevent their being murdered on the way, and then the firing began again. The Outagamies and Mascoutins gathered strength from desperation, and sent flights of fire-arrows into the fort to burn the straw-thatched houses. The flames caught in many places; but with the help of the Indians they were extinguished, though several Frenchmen were wounded, and there was great fright for a time. But the thatch was soon stripped off and the roofs covered with deer and bear skins, while mops fastened to long poles, and two large wooden canoes filled with water, were made ready for future need.

A few days after, a greater peril threatened the French. If the wild Indian has the passions of a devil, he has also the instability of a child; and this is especially true when a number of incoherent tribes or bands are joined in a common enterprise. Dubuisson's Indians became discouraged, partly at the stubborn resistance of the enemy, and partly at the scarcity of food. Some of them declared openly that they could never conquer those people, that they knew them well, and that they were braver than anybody else. In short, the French saw themselves on the point of being abandoned by their allies to a fate the most ghastly and appalling; and they urged upon the commandant the necessity of escaping to Michillimackinac before it was too late. Dubuisson appears to have met the crisis with equal resolution and address. He braced the shaken nerves of his white followers by appeals to their sense of shame, threats of the Governor's wrath, and assurances that all would yet be well; then set himself to the more difficult task of holding the Indian allies to their work. He says that he scarcely ate or slept for four days and nights, during which time he was busied without ceasing in private and separate interviews with all the young war-chiefs, persuading them, flattering them, and stripping himself of all he had to make them presents. When at last he had gained them over, he called the tribes to a general council.

"What, Children!" thus he addressed them, "when you are on the very point of destroying these wicked people, do you think of shamefully running away? How could you ever hold up your heads again? All the other nations would say: 'Are these the brave warriors who deserted the French and ran like cowards?'" And he reminded them that their enemies were already half dead with famine, and that they could easily make an end of them, thereby gaining great honor among the nations, besides the thanks and favors of Onontio, the father of all.

At this the young war-chiefs whom he had gained over interrupted him and cried out, "My Father, somebody has been lying to you. We are not cowards. We love you too much to abandon you, and we will stand by you till the last of your enemies is dead." The elder men caught the contagion, and cried, "Come on, let us show our father that those who have spoken ill of us are liars." Then they all raised the war-whoop, sang the war-song, danced the war-dance, and began to fire again.

Among the enemy were some Sakis, or Sacs, fighting for the Outagamies, while others of their tribe were among the allies of the French. Seeing the desperate turn of affairs, they escaped from time to time and came over to the winning side, bringing reports of the state of the beleaguered camp. They declared that sixty or eighty women and children were already dead from hunger and thirst, besides those killed by bullets and arrows, that the fire of the besiegers was so hot that the bodies could not be buried, and that the camp of the Outagamies and Mascoutins was a den of infection.

The end was near. The besieged savages called from their palisades to ask if they might send another deputation, and were told that they were free to do so. The chief, Pemoussa, soon appeared at the gate of the fort, naked, painted from head to foot with green earth, wearing belts of wampum about his waist, and others hanging from his shoulders, besides a kind of crown of wampum beads on his head. With him came seven women, meant as a peace-offering, all painted and adorned with wampum. Three other principal chiefs followed, each with a gourd rattle in his hand, to the cadence of which the whole party sang and shouted at the full stretch of their lungs an invocation to the spirits for help and pity. They were conducted to the parade, where the French and the allied chiefs were already assembled, and Pemoussa thus addressed them:—

"My Father, and all the Nations here present, I come to ask for life. It is no longer ours, but yours. I bring you these seven women, who are my flesh, and whom I put at your feet, to be your slaves. But do not think that I am afraid to die; it is the life of our women and children that I ask of you." He then offered six wampum belts, in token that his followers owned themselves beaten, and begged for mercy. "Tell us, I pray you,"—these were his last words,—"something that will lighten the hearts of my people when I go back to them."

Dubuisson left the answer to his allies. The appeal of the suppliant fell on hearts of stone. The whole concourse sat in fierce and sullen silence, and the envoys read their doom in the gloomy brows that surrounded them. Eight or ten of the allied savages presently came to Dubuisson, and one of them said in a low voice: "My Father, we come to ask your leave to knock these four great chiefs in the head. It is they who prevent our enemies from surrendering without conditions. When they are dead, the rest will be at our mercy."

Dubuisson told them that they must be drunk to propose such a thing. "Remember," he said, "that both you and I have given our word for their safety. If I consented to what you ask, your father at Montreal would never forgive me. Besides, you can see plainly that they and their people cannot escape you."

The would-be murderers consented to bide their time, and the wretched envoys went back with their tidings of despair.

"I confess," wrote Dubuisson to the Governor, a few days later, "that I was touched with compassion; but as war and pity do not agree well together, and especially as I understood that they were hired by the English to destroy us, I abandoned them to their fate."

The firing began once more, and the allied hordes howled round the camp of their victims like troops of ravenous wolves. But a surprise awaited them. Indians rarely set guards at night, and they felt sure now of their prey. It was the nineteenth day of the siege.[1] The night closed dark and rainy, and when morning came, the enemy were gone. All among them that had strength to move had glided away through the gloom with the silence of shadows, passed the camps of their sleeping enemies, and reached a point of land projecting into the river opposite the end of Isle au Cochon, and a few miles above the French fort. Here, knowing that they would be pursued, they barricaded themselves with trunks and branches of trees. When the astonished allies discovered their escape, they hastily followed their trail, accompanied by some of the French, led by Vincennes. In their eagerness they ran upon

---

[1] According to the paper ascribed to Léry it was only the eighth.

the barricade before seeing it, and were met by a fire that killed and wounded twenty of them. There was no alternative but to forego their revenge and abandon the field, or begin another siege. Encouraged by Dubuisson, they built their wigwams on the new scene of operations; and being supplied by the French with axes, mattocks, and two swivels, they made a wall of logs opposite the barricade, from which they galled the defenders with a close and deadly fire. The Mississagas and Ojibwas, who had lately arrived, fished and hunted for the allies, while the French furnished them with powder, ball, tobacco, Indian corn, and kettles. The enemy fought desperately for four days, and then, in utter exhaustion, surrendered at discretion.[1]

The women and children were divided among the victorious hordes, and adopted or enslaved. To the men no quarter was given. "Our Indians amused themselves," writes Dubuisson, "with shooting four or five of them every day." Here, however, another surprise awaited the conquerors and abridged their recreation, for about a hundred of these intrepid warriors contrived to make their escape, and among them was the great war-chief Pemoussa.

The Outagamies were crippled, but not disabled, for but a part of the tribe was involved in this bloody affair. The rest were wrought to fury by the fate of their kinsmen, and for many years they remained thorns in the sides of the French.

There is a disposition to assume that events like that just recounted were a consequence of the contact of white men with red; but the primitive Indian was quite able to enact such tragedies without the help of Europeans. Before French or English influence had been felt in the interior of the continent, a great part of North America was the frequent witness of scenes still more lurid in coloring, and on a larger scale of horror. In the first half of the seventeenth century the whole country, from Lake Superior to the Tennessee, and from the Alleghanies to the Mississippi, was ravaged by wars of extermination, in which tribes, large and powerful, by Indian standards, perished, dwindled into feeble remnants, or

[1] The paper ascribed to Léry says that they surrendered on a promise from Vincennes that their lives should be spared, but that the promise availed nothing.

were absorbed by other tribes and vanished from sight.
French pioneers were sometimes involved in the carnage, but
neither they nor other Europeans were answerable for it.[1]

[1] *Dubuisson à Vaudreuil, 15 Juin, 1712.* This is Dubuisson's report to the
Governor, which soon after the event he sent to Montreal by the hands of
Vincennes. He says that the great fatigue through which he had just passed
prevents him from giving every detail, and he refers Vaudreuil to the bearer
for further information. The report is, however, long and circumstantial.

*Etat de ce que M. Dubuisson a dépensé pour le service du Roy pour s'attirer les
Nations et les mettre dans ses intérêts afin de résister aux Outagamis et aux Mascoutins qui étaient payés des Anglais pour détruire le poste du Fort de Ponchartrain
du Détroit, 14 Oct. 1712.* Dubuisson reckons his outlay at 2,901 livres.

These documents, with the narrative ascribed to the engineer Léry, are the
contemporary authorities on which the foregoing account is based.

Chapter XIII

1697—1750

LOUISIANA

The Mississippi to be occupied • English Rivalry • Iberville • Bienville • Huguenots • Views of Louis XIV. • Wives for the Colony • Slaves • La Mothe-Cadillac • Paternal Government • Crozat's Monopoly • Factions • The Mississippi Company • New Orleans • The Bubble bursts • Indian Wars • The Colony firmly established • The two Heads of New France

AT THE BEGINNING of the eighteenth century an event took place that was to have a great influence on the future of French America. This was the occupation by France of the mouth of the Mississippi, and the vindication of her claim to the vast and undefined regions which La Salle had called Louisiana. La Salle's schemes had come to nought, but they were revived, seven years after his death, by his lieutenant, the gallant and faithful Henri de Tonty, who urged the seizure of Louisiana for three reasons: first, as a base of attack upon Mexico; secondly, as a dépôt for the furs and lead ore of the interior; and thirdly, as the only means of preventing the English from becoming masters of the West.[1]

Three years later, the Sieur de Rémonville, a friend of La Salle, proposed the formation of a company for the settlement of Louisiana, and called for immediate action as indispensable to anticipate the English.[2] The English were, in fact, on the point of taking possession of the mouth of the Mississippi, and were prevented only by the prompt intervention of the rival nation.

If they had succeeded, colonies would have grown up on the Gulf of Mexico after the type of those already planted along the Atlantic: voluntary immigrants would have brought to a new home their old inheritance of English freedom; would have ruled themselves by laws of their own making, through magistrates of their own choice; would have de-

[1] *Henri de Tonty à Cabart de Villermont, 11 Sept. 1694* (Margry, IV. 3).

[2] *Mémoire sur le Projet d'establir une nouvelle Colonie au Mississippi, 1697* (Margry, IV. 21).

pended on their own efforts, and not on government help, in the invigorating consciousness that their destinies were in their own hands, and that they themselves, and not others, were to gather the fruits of their toils. Out of conditions like these would have sprung communities, not brilliant, but healthy, orderly, well rooted in the soil, and of hardy and vigorous growth.

But the principles of absolutism, and not those of a regulated liberty, were to rule in Louisiana. The new French colony was to be the child of the Crown. Cargoes of emigrants, willing or unwilling, were to be shipped by authority to the fever-stricken banks of the Mississippi,—cargoes made up in part of those whom fortune and their own defects had sunk to dependence; to whom labor was strange and odious, but who dreamed of gold mines and pearl fisheries, and wealth to be won in the New World and spent in the Old; who wore the shackles of a paternal despotism which they were told to regard as of divine institution; who were at the mercy of military rulers set over them by the King, and agreeing in nothing except in enforcing the mandates of arbitrary power and the withering maxim that the labor of the colonist was due, not to himself, but to his masters. It remains to trace briefly the results of such conditions.

The before-mentioned scheme of Rémonville for settling the Mississippi country had no result. In the next year the gallant Le Moyne d'Iberville, who has been called the Cid, or, more fitly, the Jean Bart, of Canada, offered to carry out the schemes of La Salle and plant a colony in Louisiana.[1] One thing had become clear,—France must act at once, or lose the Mississippi. Already there was a movement in London to seize upon it, under a grant to two noblemen. Iberville's offer was accepted; he was ordered to build a fort at the mouth of the great river, and leave a garrison to hold it.[2] He sailed with two frigates, the "Badine" and the "Marin," and towards the end of January, 1699, reached Pensacola. Here he found two Spanish ships, which would not let him enter the harbor. Spain, no less than England, was bent on making good her claim to the Mississippi and the Gulf of Mexico, and the two

[1] *Iberville au Ministre, 18 Juin, 1698* (Margry, IV. 51).
[2] *Mémoire pour servir d'Instruction au Sieur d'Iberville* (Margry, IV. 72).

ships had come from Vera Cruz on this errand. Three hundred men had been landed, and a stockade fort was already built. Iberville left the Spaniards undisturbed and unchallenged, and felt his way westward along the coasts of Alabama and Mississippi, exploring and sounding as he went. At the beginning of March his boats were caught in a strong muddy current of fresh water, and he saw that he had reached the object of his search, the "fatal river" of the unfortunate La Salle. He entered it, encamped, on the night of the 3d, twelve leagues above its mouth, climbed a solitary tree, and could see nothing but broad flats of bushes and canebrakes.[1]

Still pushing upward against the current, he reached in eleven days a village of the Bayagoula Indians, where he found the chief attired in a blue capote, which was probably put on in honor of the white strangers, and which, as the wearer declared, had been given him by Henri de Tonty, on his descent of the Mississippi in search of La Salle, thirteen years before. Young Le Moyne de Bienville, who accompanied his brother Iberville in a canoe, brought him, some time after, a letter from Tonty which the writer had left in the hands of another chief, to be delivered to La Salle in case of his arrival, and which Bienville had bought for a hatchet. Iberville welcomed it as convincing proof that the river he had entered was in truth the Mississippi.[2] After pushing up the stream till the 24th, he returned to the ships by way of lakes Maurepas and Ponchartrain.

Iberville now repaired to the harbor of Biloxi, on the coast of the present State of Mississippi. Here he built a small stockade fort, where he left eighty men, under the Sieur de Sauvolle, to hold the country for Louis XIV.; and this done, he sailed for France. Thus the first foundations of Louisiana were laid in Mississippi.

Bienville, whom his brother had left at Biloxi as second in command, was sent by Sauvolle on an exploring expedition

[1] *Journal d'Iberville* (Margry, IV. 131).

[2] This letter, which D'Iberville gives in his Journal, is dated "Du Village des Quinipissas, le 20 Avril, 1685." Iberville identifies the Quinipissas with the Bayagoulas. The date of the letter was evidently misread, as Tonty's journey was in 1686. See *La Salle and the Discovery of the Great West*, 1027, *note*. Iberville's lieutenant, Sugères, commanding the "Marin," gives the date correctly. *Journal de la Frégate le Marin, 1698, 1699* (Margry, IV.).

up the Mississippi with five men in two canoes. At the bend of the river now called English Turn,— *Tour à l'Anglais*,— below the site of New Orleans, he found an English corvette of ten guns, having, as passengers, a number of French Protestant families taken on board from the Carolinas, with the intention of settling on the Mississippi. The commander, Captain Louis Bank, declared that his vessel was one of three sent from London by a company formed jointly of Englishmen and Huguenot refugees for the purpose of founding a colony.[1] Though not quite sure that they were upon the Mississippi, they were on their way up the stream to join a party of Englishmen said to be among the Chickasaws, with whom they were trading for Indian slaves. Bienville assured Bank that he was not upon the Mississippi, but on another river belonging to King Louis, who had a strong fort there and several settlements. "The too-credulous Englishman," says a French writer, "believed these inventions and turned back."[2] First, however, a French engineer in the service of Bank contrived to have an interview with Bienville, and gave him a petition to the King of France, signed by four hundred Huguenots who had taken refuge in the Carolinas after the revocation of the Edict of Nantes. The petitioners begged that they might have leave to settle in Louisiana, with liberty of conscience, under the French Crown. In due time they got their answer. The King replied, through the minister, Ponchartrain, that he had not expelled heretics from France in order that they should set up a republic in America.[3] Thus, by the bigotry that had been the bane of Canada and of France herself, Louis XIV. threw away the opportunity of establishing a firm and healthy colony at the mouth of the Mississippi.

[1] *Journal du Voyage du Chevalier d'Iberville sur le Vaisseau du Roy la Renommée en 1699* (Margry, IV. 395).

[2] Gayarré, *Histoire de la Louisiane* (1846), I. 69. Bénard de la Harpe, *Journal historique* (1831), 20. Coxe says, in the preface to his *Description of Carolana* (1722), that "the present proprietor of Carolana, my honour'd Father, . . . was the author of this English voyage to the Mississippi, having in the year 1698 equipp'd and fitted out Two Ships for Discovery by Sea, and also for building a Fortification and settling a Colony by land; there being in both vessels, besides Sailors and Common Men, above Thirty English and French Volunteers." Coxe adds that the expedition would have succeeded if one of the commanders had not failed to do his duty.

[3] Gayarré, *Histoire de la Louisiane* (1846), I. 69.

So threatening was the danger that England would seize the country that Iberville had scarcely landed in France when he was sent back with a reinforcement. The colonial views of the King may be gathered from his instructions to his officer. Iberville was told to seek out diligently the best places for establishing pearl-fisheries, though it was admitted that the pearls of Louisiana were uncommonly bad. He was also to catch bison calves, make a fenced park to hold them, and tame them for the sake of their wool, which was reputed to be of value for various fabrics. Above all, he was to look for mines, the finding of which the document declares to be "la grande affaire."[1]

On the 8th of January, Iberville reached Biloxi, and soon after went up the Mississippi to that remarkable tribe of sun-worshippers, the Natchez, whose villages were on and near the site of the city that now bears their name. Some thirty miles above, he found a kindred tribe, the Taensas, whose temple took fire during his visit, when, to his horror, he saw five living infants thrown into the flames by their mothers to appease the angry spirits.[2]

Retracing his course, he built a wooden redoubt near one of the mouths of the Mississippi to keep out the dreaded English.

In the next year he made a third voyage, and ordered the feeble establishment at Biloxi to be moved to the bay of Mobile. This drew a protest from the Spaniards, who rested their claims to the country on the famous bull of Pope Alexander VI. The question was referred to the two Crowns. Louis XIV., a stanch champion of the papacy when his duties as a Catholic did not clash with his interests as a king, refused submission to the bull, insisted that the Louisiana country was his, and declared that he would hold fast to it because he was bound, as a son of Holy Church, to convert the Indians and keep out the English heretics.[3] Spain was then at peace with France, and her new king, the Duc d'Anjou, grandson

---

[1] *Mémoire pour servir d'Instruction au Sieur d'Iberville* (Margry, IV. 348).

[2] *Journal du Voyage du Chevalier d'Iberville sur le Vaisseau du Roy la Renom-mée, 1699, 1700.*

[3] *Mémoire de la Junte de Guerre des Indes. Le Ministre de la Marine au Duc d'Harcourt* (Margry, IV. 553, 568).

of Louis XIV., needed the support of his powerful kinsman; hence his remonstrance against French encroachment was of the mildest.[1]

Besides Biloxi and Mobile Bay, the French formed a third establishment at Dauphin Island. The Mississippi itself, which may be called the vital organ of the colony, was thus far neglected, being occupied by no settlement and guarded only by a redoubt near one of its mouths.

Of the emigrants sent out by the court to the new land of promise, the most valuable by far were a number of Canadians who had served under Iberville at Hudson Bay. The rest were largely of the sort who are described by that officer as "beggars sent out to enrich themselves," and who expected the government to feed them while they looked for pearls and gold mines. The paternal providence of Versailles, mindful of their needs, sent them, in 1704, a gift of twenty marriageable girls, described as "nurtured in virtue and piety, and accustomed to work." Twenty-three more came in the next year from the same benignant source, besides seventy-five soldiers, five priests, and two nuns. Food, however, was not sent in proportion to the consumers; and as no crops were raised in Louisiana, famine and pestilence followed, till the starving colonists were forced to live on shell-fish picked up along the shores.

Disorder and discord filled the land of promise. Nicolas de la Salle, the *commissaire ordonnateur*, an official answering to the Canadian intendant, wrote to the minister Ponchartrain, that Iberville and his brothers, Bienville and Chateauguay, were "thieves and knaves."[2] La Vente, curé of Mobile, joined in the cry against Bienville, and stirred soldiers and settlers to disaffection; but the bitterest accuser of that truly valuable officer was the worthy matron who held the unenviable post of directress of the "King's girls,"—that is, the young women sent out as wives for the colonists. It seems that she had matrimonial views for herself as well as for her charge; and she

---

[1] Iberville wrote in 1701 a long memorial, in which he tried to convince the Spanish court that it was for the interest of Spain that the French should form a barrier between her colonies and those of England, which, he says, were about to seize the country as far as the Mississippi and beyond it.

[2] *Nicolas de la Salle au Ministre, 7 Sept. 1706.*

wrote to Ponchartrain that Major Boisbriant, commander of
the garrison, would certainly have married her if Bienville had
not interfered and dissuaded him. "It is clear," she adds, "that
M. de Bienville has not the qualities necessary for governing
the colony."[1]

Bienville was now chief in authority. Charges of peculation
and other offences poured in against him, and at last, though
nothing was proved, one De Muys was sent to succeed him,
with orders to send him home a prisoner if on examination
the accusations should prove to be true. De Muys died on the
voyage. Artaguette, the new intendant, proceeded to make
the inquiry, but refused to tell Bienville the nature of the
charges against him, saying that he had orders not to do so.
Nevertheless, when he had finished his investigation he reported to the minister that the accused was innocent; on
which Nicolas de la Salle, whom he had supplanted as intendant, wrote to Ponchartrain that Artaguette had deceived
him, being no better than Bienville himself. La Salle further
declared that Barrot, the surgeon of the colony, was an igno-
ramus, and that he made money by selling the medicines supplied by the King to cure his Louisianian subjects. Such were
the transatlantic workings of the paternalism of Versailles.

Bienville, who had been permitted to resume his authority,
paints the state of the colony to his masters, and tells them
that the inhabitants are dying of hunger,—not all, however,
for he mentions a few exceptional cases of prosperity. These
were certain thrifty colonists from Rochelle, who, says Bienville, have grown rich by keeping dram-shops, and now want
to go back to France; but he has set a watch over them, thinking it just that they should be forced to stay in the colony.[2]
This was to add the bars of a prison to the other attractions
of the new home.

As the colonists would not work, there was an attempt to
make Indian slaves work for them; but as these continually
ran off, Bienville proposed to open a barter with the French
West Indies, giving three red slaves for two black ones,—an

---

[1] "Il est clair que M. de Bienville n'a pas les qualités nécessaires pour bien
gouverner la colonie." Gayarré found this curious letter in the Archives de la
Marine.

[2] *Dépêche de Bienville, 12 Oct. 1708.*

exchange which he thought would be mutually advantageous, since the Indians, being upon islands, could no longer escape. The court disapproved the plan, on the ground that the West Indians would give only their worst negroes in exchange, and that the only way to get good ones was to fetch them from Guinea.

Complaints against Bienville were renewed till the court sent out La Mothe-Cadillac to succeed him, with orders to examine the charges against his predecessor, whom it was his interest to condemn, in order to keep the governorship. In his new post, Cadillac displayed all his old faults, began by denouncing the country in unmeasured terms, and wrote in his usual sarcastic vein to the colonial minister: "I have seen the garden on Dauphin Island, which had been described to me as a terrestrial paradise. I saw there three seedling pear-trees, three seedling apple-trees, a little plum-tree about three feet high, with seven bad plums on it, a vine some thirty feet long, with nine bunches of grapes, some of them withered or rotten and some partly ripe, about forty plants of French melons, and a few pumpkins. This is M. d'Artaguette's terrestrial paradise, M. de Rémonville's Pomona, and M. de Mandeville's Fortunate Islands. Their stories are mere fables." Then he slanders the soil, which, he declares, will produce neither grain nor vegetables.

D'Artaguette, no longer fancying himself in Eden, draws a dismal picture of the state of the colony. There are, he writes, only ten or twelve families who cultivate the soil. The inhabitants, naturally lazy, are ruined by the extravagance of their wives. "It is necessary to send out girls and laboring-men. I am convinced that we shall easily discover mines when persons are sent us who understand that business."[1]

The colonists felt no confidence in the future of Louisiana. The King was its sole support, and if, as was likely enough, he should tire of it, their case would be deplorable. When Bienville ruled over them, they had used him as their scapegoat; but that which made the colony languish was not he, but the vicious system it was his business to enforce. The royal edicts and arbitrary commands that took the place of

[1] D'Artaguette in Gayarré, *Histoire de la Louisiane*. This valuable work consists of a series of documents, connected by a thread of narrative.

law proceeded from masters thousands of miles away, who knew nothing of the country, could not understand its needs, and scarcely tried to do so.

In 1711, though the mischievous phantom of gold and silver mines still haunted the colony, we find it reported that the people were beginning to work, and were planting tobacco. The King, however, was losing patience with a dependency that cost him endless expense and trouble, and brought little or nothing in return,—and this at a time when he had a costly and disastrous war on his hands, and was in no mood to bear supernumerary burdens. The plan of giving over a colony to a merchant, or a company of merchants, was not new. It had been tried in other French colonies with disastrous effect. Yet it was now tried again. Louisiana was farmed out for fifteen years to Antoine Crozat, a wealthy man of business. The countries made over to him extended from the British colonies on the east, to New Mexico on the west, and the Rio del Norte on the south, including the entire region watered by the Mississippi, the Missouri, the Ohio, and their tributaries, as far north as the Illinois. In comparison with this immense domain, which was all included under the name of Louisiana, the present State so called is but a small patch on the American map.

To Crozat was granted a monopoly of the trade, wholesale and retail, domestic and foreign, of all these countries, besides the product of all mines, after deducting one-fourth reserved for the King. He was empowered to send one vessel a year to Guinea for a cargo of slaves. The King was to pay the Governor and other Crown officers, and during the first nine years the troops also; though after that time Crozat was to maintain them till the end of his term.

In consideration of these and other privileges, the grantee was bound to send to Louisiana a specified number of settlers every year. His charter provided that the royal edicts and the *Coutume de Paris* should be the law of the colony, to be administered by a council appointed by the King.

When Louisiana was thus handed over to a speculator for a term of years, it needed no prophet to foretell that he would get all he could out of it, and put as little into it as possible. When Crozat took possession of the colony, the French court had been thirteen years at work in building it up. The result of its labors was a total population, including troops, government officials, and clergy, of 380 souls, of whom 170 were in the King's pay. Only a few of the colonists were within the limits of the present Louisiana. The rest lived in or around the feeble stockade forts at Mobile, Biloxi, Ship Island, and Dauphin Island. This last station had been partially abandoned; but some of the colonists proposed to return to it, in order to live by fishing, and only waited, we are told, for help from the King. This incessant dependence on government relaxed the fibres of the colony and sapped its life-blood.

The King was now exchanged for Crozat and his grinding monopoly. The colonists had carried on a modest trade with the Spaniards at Pensacola in skins, fowls, Indian corn, and a few other articles, bringing back a little money in return. This, their only source of profit, was now cut off; they could sell nothing, even to each other. They were forbidden to hold meetings without permission; but some of them secretly drew up a petition to La Mothe-Cadillac, who was still the official chief of the colony, begging that the agents of Crozat should be restricted to wholesale dealings, and that the inhabitants might be allowed to trade at retail. Cadillac denounced the petition as seditious, threatened to hang the bearer of it, and deigned no other answer.

He resumed his sarcasms against the colony. "In my opinion this country is not worth a straw (*ne vaut pas un fêtu*). The inhabitants are eager to be taken out of it. The soldiers are always grumbling, and with reason." As to the council, which was to be the only court of justice, he says that no such thing is possible, because there are no proper persons to compose it; and though Duclos, the new intendant, has proposed two candidates, the first of these, the Sieur de Lafresnière, learned to sign his name only four months ago, and the other, being chief surgeon of the colony, is too busy to serve.[1]

Between Bienville, the late governor, and La Mothe-Cadillac, who had supplanted him, there was a standing quarrel; and the colony was split into hostile factions, led by the two disputants. The minister at Versailles was beset by their mutual accusations, and Bienville wrote that his refusal to marry

[1] *La Mothe-Cadillac au Ministre*, in Gayarré, I. 104, 105.

Cadillac's daughter was the cause of the spite the Governor bore him.[1]

The indefatigable curé De la Vente sent to Ponchartrain a memorial, in the preamble of which he says that since Monsieur le Ministre wishes to be informed exactly of the state of things in Louisiana, he, La Vente, has the honor, with malice to nobody, to make known the pure truth; after which he goes on to say that the inhabitants "are nearly all drunkards, gamblers, blasphemers, and enemies of everything good;" and he proceeds to illustrate the statement with many particulars.[2]

As the inhabitants were expected to work for Crozat, and not for themselves, it naturally followed that they would not work at all; and idleness produced the usual results.

The yearly shipment of girls continued; but there was difficulty in finding husbands for them. The reason was not far to seek. Duclos, the intendant, reports the arrival of an invoice of twelve of them, "so ugly that the inhabitants are in no hurry to take them."[3] The Canadians, who formed the most vigorous and valuable part of the population, much preferred Indian squaws. "It seems to me," pursues the Intendant, "that in the choice of girls, good looks should be more considered than virtue." This latter requisite seems, at the time, to have found no more attention than the other, since the candidates for matrimony were drawn from the Parisian hospitals and houses of correction, from the former of which Crozat was authorized to take one hundred girls a year, "in order to increase the population." These hospitals were compulsory asylums for the poor and vagrant of both sexes, of whom the great Hôpital Général of Paris contained at one time more than six thousand.[4]

---

[1] "Que si M. de Lamothe-Cadillac lui portoit tant d'animositié, c'étoit à cause du refus qu'il avoit fait d'épouser sa fille." Bienville in Gayarré, I. 116.

[2] *Mémoire du Curé de la Vente, 1714.*

[3] The earlier cargoes of girls seem to have been better chosen, and there was no difficulty in mating them. Serious disputes sometimes rose from the competition of rival suitors. Dumont, *Mémoires historiques de la Louisiane*, chap. v.

[4] Prominent officials of the colony are said to have got wives from these sources. Nicolas de la Salle is reported to have had two in succession, both from the hospitals. Bénard de la Harpe, 107 (ed. 1831).

Crozat had built his chief hopes of profit on a trade, contraband or otherwise, with the Mexican ports; but the Spanish officials, faithful instruments of the exclusive policy of their government, would not permit it, and were so vigilant that he could not elude them. At the same time, to his vexation, he found that the King's officers in Louisiana, with more address or better luck, and in contempt of his monopoly, which it was their business to protect, carried on, for their own profit, a small smuggling trade with Vera Cruz. He complained that they were always thwarting his agents and conspiring against his interests. At last, finding no resource left but an unprofitable trade with the Indians, he gave up his charter, which had been a bane to the colony and a loss to himself. Louisiana returned to the Crown, and was soon passed over to the new Mississippi Company, called also the Western Company.[1]

That charlatan of genius, the Scotchman John Law, had undertaken, with the eager support of the Regent Duke of Orleans, to deliver France from financial ruin through a prodigious system of credit, of which Louisiana, with its imaginary gold mines, was made the basis. The government used every means to keep up the stock of the Mississippi Company. It was ordered that the notes of the royal bank and all certificates of public debt should be accepted at par in payment for its shares. Powers and privileges were lavished on it. It was given the monopoly of the French slave trade, the monopoly of tobacco, the profits of the royal mint, and the farming of the revenues of the kingdom. Ingots of gold, pretending to have come from the new Eldorado of Louisiana, were displayed in the shop-windows of Paris. The fever of speculation rose to madness, and the shares of the company were inflated to monstrous and insane proportions.

When Crozat resigned his charter, Louisiana, by the highest estimates, contained about seven hundred souls, including soldiers, but not blacks or Indians. Crozat's successors, however, say that the whole number of whites, men, women, and children, was not above four hundred.[2] When the Mississippi

---

[1] *Lettres patentes en forme d'Edit portant établissement de la Compagnie d'Occident*, in Le Page du Pratz, *Histoire de la Louisiane*, I. 47.

[2] *Règlement de Régie, 1721.*

Company took the colony in charge, it was but a change of despots. Louisiana was a prison. But while no inhabitant could leave it without permission of the authorities, all Jews were expelled, and all Protestants excluded. The colonists could buy nothing except from the agents of the company, and sell nothing except to the same all-powerful masters, always at prices fixed by them. Foreign vessels were forbidden to enter any part of Louisiana, on pain of confiscation.

The coin in circulation was nearly all Spanish, and in less than two years the Company, by a series of decrees, made changes of about eighty per cent in its value. Freedom of conscience, freedom of speech, of trade, and of action, were alike denied. Hence voluntary immigration was not to be expected; "but," says the Duc de Saint-Simon, "the government wished to establish effective settlements in these vast countries, after the example of the English, and therefore, in order to people them, vagabonds and beggars, male and female, including many women of the town, were seized for the purpose both in Paris and throughout France."[1] Saint-Simon approves these proceedings in themselves, as tending at once to purge France and people Louisiana, but thinks the business was managed in a way to cause needless exasperation among the lower classes.

In 1720 it was ordered by royal edict that no more vagabonds or criminals should be sent to Louisiana. The edict, it seems, touched only one sex, for in the next year eighty girls were sent to the colony from the Parisian House of Correction called the Salpetrière. There had been a more or less constant demand for wives, as appears by letters still preserved in the archives of Paris, the following extract from one of which is remarkable for the freedom with which the writer, a M. de Chassin, takes it upon him to address a minister of state in a court where punctilio reigned supreme. "You see, Monseigneur, that nothing is wanting now to make a solid settlement in Louisiana but a certain piece of furniture which one often repents having got, and with which I shall dispense, like the rest, till the Company sends us girls who have at least some show of virtue. If there happens to be any young woman of your acquaintance who wants to make the voyage

[1] Saint-Simon, *Mémoires* (ed. Chéruel), XVII. 461.

for love of me, I should be much obliged to her, and would do my best to show her my gratitude."[1]

The Company, which was invested with sovereign powers, began its work by sending to Louisiana three companies of soldiers and sixty-nine colonists. Its wisest act was the removal of the Governor, L'Epinay, who had supplanted La Mothe-Cadillac, and the reappointment of Bienville in his place. Bienville immediately sought out a spot for establishing a permanent station on the Mississippi. Fifty men were sent to clear the ground, and in spite of an inundation which overflowed it for a time, the feeble foundations of New Orleans were laid. Louisiana, hitherto diffused through various petty cantonments, far and near, had at last a capital, or the germ of one.

It was the 6th of September, 1717, when the charter of the Mississippi Company was entered in the registers of the Parliament of Paris; and from that time forward, before the offices of the Company in the Rue Quincampoix, crowds of crazed speculators jostled and fought from morning till night to get their names inscribed among the stockholders. Within five years after, the huge glittering bubble had burst. The shares, each one of which had seemed a fortune, found no more purchasers, and in its fall the Company dragged down with it its ally and chief creditor, the bank. All was dismay and despair, except in those who had sold out in time, and turned delusive paper into solid values. John Law, lately the idol and reputed savior of France, fled for his life, amid a howl of execration.

Yet the interests of the kingdom required that Louisiana should be sustained. The illusions that had given to the Mississippi Company a morbid and intoxicated vitality were gone, but the Company lingered on, and the government still lent it a helping hand. A French writer remarks that the few Frenchmen who were famishing on the shores of the Mississippi and the Gulf of Mexico had cost the King, since the colony began, more than 150,000 livres a year. The directors of the Company reported that they had shipped 7,020 persons to the colony, besides four hundred already there when they took possession, and that 5,420 still remained, the rest having

[1] *De Chassin au Ministre, 1 Juillet, 1722*, in Gayarré, I. 190.

died or escaped.[1] Besides this importation of whites, they had also brought six hundred slaves from Guinea. It is reckoned that the King, Crozat, and the Mississippi Company had spent among them about eight million livres on Louisiana, without any return.[2]

The bursting of the Mississippi bubble did not change the principles of administration in Louisiana. The settlers, always looking to France to supply their needs and protect them against their own improvidence, were in the habit of butchering for food the live-stock sent them for propagation. The remedy came in the shape of a royal edict forbidding any colonist to kill, without permission of the authorities, any cow, sheep, or lamb belonging to himself, on pain of a fine of three hundred livres; or to kill any horse, cow, or bull belonging to another, on pain of death.

Authority and order were the watchwords, and disorder was the rule. The agents of power quarrelled among themselves, except when they leagued together to deceive their transatlantic masters and cover their own misdeeds. Each maligned the other, and it was scarcely possible for the King or the Company to learn the true state of affairs in their distant colony.

Accusations were renewed against Bienville, till in 1724 he was ordered to France to give account of his conduct, and the Sieur Perier was sent out to take his place. Perier had no easy task. The Natchez Indians, among whom the French had made a settlement and built a fort called Fort Rosalie, suddenly rose on their white neighbors and massacred nearly all of them.[3] Then followed a long course of Indian wars. The French believed that there was a general conspiracy among the Southern tribes for their destruction,—though this was evidently an exaggeration of the danger, which, however, was serious. The Chickasaws, a brave and warlike people, living chiefly in what is now western Tennessee and Kentucky,

[1] A considerable number of the whites brought to Louisiana in the name of the Company had been sent at the charge of persons to whom it had granted lands in various parts of the colony. Among these was John Law himself, who had the grant of large tracts on the Arkansas.

[2] Bénard de la Harpe, 371 (ed. 1831).

[3] *Lettre du Père le Petit*, in *Lettres Edifiantes*; Dumont, *Mémoires historiques*, chap. xxvii.

made common cause with the Natchez, while the more numerous Choctaws, most of whose villages were in the present
State of Mississippi, took part with the French. More than a
thousand soldiers had been sent to Louisiana; but Perier pronounced them "so bad that they seem to have been made on
purpose for the colony."[1] There were also about eight
hundred militia. Perier showed little vigor, and had little success. His chief resource was to set the tribes against each
other. He reports that his Indian allies had brought him a
number of Natchez prisoners, and that he had caused six of
them, four men and two women, to be burned alive, and had
sent the rest as slaves to St. Domingo. The Chickasaws, aided
by English traders from the Carolinas, proved formidable adversaries, and when attacked, ensconced themselves in stockade forts so strong that, as the Governor complains, there
was no dislodging the defenders without cannon and heavy
mortars.

In this state of things the directors of the Mississippi Company, whose affairs had gone from bad to worse, declared
that they could no longer bear the burden of Louisiana, and
begged the King to take it off their hands. The colony was
therefore transferred from the mercantile despotism of the
Company to the paternal despotism of the Crown, and it profited by the change. Commercial monopoly was abolished.
Trade between France and Louisiana was not only permitted,
but encouraged by bounties and exemption from duties; and
instead of paying to the Company two hundred per cent of
profit on indispensable supplies, the colonists now got them
at a reasonable price.

Perier was removed, and again Bienville was made governor. Diron d'Artaguette, who came with him as intendant,
reported that the colonists were flying the country to escape
starvation, and Bienville adds that during the past year they
had subsisted for three months on the seed of reeds and wild
grasses.[2] The white population had rather diminished than increased during the last twelve years, while the blacks, who
had lately conspired to massacre all the French along the Mis-

[1]"Nos soldats, qui semblent être faits exprès pour la colonie, tant ils sont
mauvais." *Dépêche de Perier, 18 Mars, 1730.*

[2] *Mémoire de Bienville, 1730.*

sissippi, had multiplied to two thousand.[1] A French writer says: "There must have been a worm gnawing the root of the tree that had been transplanted into so rich a soil, to make it wither instead of growing. What it needed was the air of liberty." But the air of liberty is malaria to those who have not learned to breathe it. The English colonists throve in it because they and their forefathers had been trained in a school of self-control and self-dependence; and what would have been intoxication for others, was vital force to them.

Bienville found the colony again threatened with a general rising, or, as he calls it, a revolt, of the Indian tribes. The Carolina traders, having no advantage of water-ways, had journeyed by land with pack-horses through a thousand miles of wilderness, and with the aid of gifts had instigated the tribes to attack the French. The Chickasaws especially, friends of the English and arch-enemies of Louisiana, became so threatening that a crushing blow against them was thought indispensable. The forces of the colony were mustered to attempt it; the enterprise was mismanaged, and failed completely.[2] Bienville tried to explain the disaster; but his explanation was ill-received at court, he was severely rebuked, reproved at the same time for permitting two families to emigrate to St. Domingo, and sharply ordered to suffer nobody to leave Louisiana without express license from Versailles. Deeply wounded, he offered his resignation, and it was accepted. Whatever his failings, he had faithfully served the colony, and gained from posterity the title of Father of Louisiana.

With the help of industrious nursing,—or, one might almost say, in spite of it,—Louisiana began at last to strike roots into the soil and show signs of growth, though feebly as compared with its sturdy rivals along the Atlantic seaboard, which had cost their King nothing, and had been treated, for the most part, with the coolest neglect. Cavelier de la Salle's dream of planting a firm settlement at the mouth of the Mississippi, and utilizing, by means of it, the resources of the vast

[1] For a curious account of the discovery of this negro plot, see Le Page du Pratz, III. 304.

[2] *Dépêche de Bienville, 6 Mai, 1740.* Compare Le Page du Pratz, III., chap. xxiv.

interior, was, after half a century, in some measure realized. New France (using that name in its broadest geographical sense) had now two heads,—Canada and Louisiana; one looking upon the Gulf of St. Lawrence, and the other upon the Gulf of Mexico. Canada was not without jealousy of her younger and weaker sister, lest she might draw away, as she had begun to do at the first, some of the most active and adventurous elements of the Canadian population; lest she might prove a competitor in the fur-trade; and lest she should encroach on the Illinois and other western domains, which the elder and stronger sister claimed as her own. These fears were not unfounded; yet the vital interests of the two French colonies were the same, and each needed the help of the other in the prime and all-essential task of keeping the British colonies in check. The chiefs of Louisiana looked forward to a time when the great Southern tribes, Creeks, Cherokees, Choctaws, and even the dreaded Chickasaws, won over by French missionaries to the Church, and therefore to France, should be turned against the encroaching English to stop their westward progress and force them back to the borders of the Atlantic. Meanwhile the chiefs of Canada were maturing the plan—pursued with varying assiduity, but always kept in view—of connecting the two vital extremities of New France by a chain of forts to control the passes of the West, keep communications open, and set English invasion at defiance.

Chapter XIV

1700—1732

THE OUTAGAMIE WAR

The Western Posts • Detroit • The Illinois • Perils of the West • The Outagamies • Their Turbulence • English Instigation • Louvigny's Expedition • Defeat of Outagamies • Hostilities renewed • Lignery's Expedition • Outagamies attacked by Villiers • By Hurons and Iroquois • La Butte des Morts • The Sacs and Foxes

---

THE RULERS of Canada labored without ceasing in their perplexing task of engrossing the fur-trade of the West and controlling the Western tribes to the exclusion of the English. Every day made it clearer that to these ends the Western wilderness must be held by forts and trading-posts; and this policy of extension prevailed more and more, in spite of the league of merchants who wished to draw the fur-trade to Montreal, in spite of the Jesuits, who felt that their influence over the remoter tribes would be compromised by the presence among them of officers, soldiers, and traders, and in spite of the King himself, who feared that the diffusion of the colony would breed disorder and insubordination.

Detroit, the most important of the Western posts, struggled through a critical infancy, in the charge of its founder, La Mothe-Cadillac, till, by a choice not very judicious, he was made governor of Louisiana. During his rule the population had slowly increased to about two hundred souls; but after he left the place it diminished to a point that seemed to threaten the feeble post with extinction. About 1722 it revived again; *voyageurs* and discharged soldiers settled about the fort, and the parish register shows six or eight births in the course of the year.[1]

Meanwhile, on the banks of the Mississippi another settlement was growing up which did not owe its birth to official patronage, and yet was destined to become the most noteworthy offspring of Canada in the West. It was known to the French as "the Illinois," from the name of the group of tribes

[1] Rameau, *Notes historiques sur la Colonie Canadienne du Detroit.*

belonging to that region. La Salle had occupied the banks of the river Illinois in 1682; but the curious Indian colony which he gathered about his fort on the rock of St. Louis[1] dispersed after his death, till few or none were left except the Kaskaskias, a sub-tribe of the Illinois. These still lived on the meadow below Fort St. Louis, where the Jesuits Marquette, Allouez, Rale, Gravier, and Marest labored in turn for their conversion, till, in 1700, they or some of them followed Marest to the Mississippi and set up their wigwams where the town of Kaskaskia now stands, near the mouth of the little river which bears the same name. Charlevoix, who was here in 1721, calls this the oldest settlement of the Illinois,[2] though there is some reason to believe that the village of Cahokia, established as a mission by the Jesuit Pinet, sixty miles or more above Kaskaskia, and nearly opposite the present city of St. Louis, is, by a few weeks, the elder of the two. The *voyageurs*, *coureurs de bois*, and other roving Canadians made these young settlements their resort, took to wife converted squaws,[3] and ended with making the Illinois their home. The missions turned to parishes, the missionaries to curés, and the wigwams to those compact little Canadian houses that cause one to marvel at the ingenuity which can store so multitudinous a progeny within such narrow limits.

White women from Canada or Louisiana began to find their way to these wilderness settlements, which with every generation grew more French and less Indian. The river Mississippi was at once their friend and their enemy. It carried their produce to New Orleans, but undermined their rich alluvial shores, cut away fields and meadows, and swept them in its turbid eddies thirteen hundred miles southward, as a contribution to the mud-banks of the delta.

When the Mississippi Company came into power, the Illinois, hitherto a dependency of Canada, was annexed to Louisiana. Pierre Dugué de Boisbriant was sent to take command of it, and under his direction a fort was built on the bank of

---

[1] See *La Salle and the Discovery of the Great West*, 934.

[2] "Ce poste, le premier de tous par droit d'antiquité." *Journal historique*, 403 (ed. 1744).

[3] The old parish registers of Kaskaskia are full of records of these mixed marriages. See Edward G. Mason, *Illinois in the Eighteenth Century*.

the Mississippi sixteen miles above Kaskaskia. It was named Fort Chartres, in honor of the Duc de Chartres, son of the Regent, who had himself once borne the same title. This work, built at first of wood and earth, was afterwards rebuilt of stone, and became one of the chief links in the chain of military communication between Canada and Louisiana.

Here, with the commandant at its head, sat the council of three which ruled over the little settlement.[1] Here too was a garrison to enforce the decrees of the council, keep order among the settlers, and give them a protection which they greatly needed, since they were within striking distance of the formidable Chickasaws, the effects of whose hostility appear year after year on the parish register of deaths at Kaskaskia. Worse things were in store, for the gallant young Pierre d'Artaguette, who was appointed to the command in 1734, and who marched against the Chickasaws with a band of Frenchmen and Indians, was defeated, captured, and burned alive, astonishing his torturers by the fortitude with which he met his fate. The settlement had other foes not less dangerous. These were the Outagamies, or Foxes, between whom and the tribes of the Illinois there was a deadly feud. We have seen how, in 1712, a band of Outagamies, with their allies, the Mascoutins, appeared at Detroit and excited an alarm, which, after a savage conflict, was ended with their ruin. In 1714 the Outagamies made a furious attack upon the Illinois, and killed or carried off seventy-seven of them.[2] A few years later they made another murderous onslaught in the same quarter. They were the scourge of the West, and no white man could travel between Canada and Louisiana except at the risk of his life.

In vain the French parleyed with them; threats and blandishments were useless alike. Their chiefs would promise, sometimes in good faith, to keep the peace and no more offend their Father Onontio; but nearly all the tribes of the Lake country were their hereditary enemies, and some bloody

---

[1] The two other members were La Loire des Ursins, director of the Mississippi Company, and Michel Chassin, its commissary,—he who wrote the curious letter to Ponchartrain, asking for a wife, quoted in the last chapter, pp. 546–47.

[2] *Vaudreuil au Ministre, 16 Sept. 1714.*

revenge for ancient wrongs would excite their young warriors
to a fury which the elders could not restrain. Thus, in 1722
the Saginaws, a fierce Algonkin band on the eastern borders
of Michigan, killed twenty-three Outagamies; the tribesmen
of the slain returned the blow, other tribes joined the fray,
and the wilderness was again on fire.[1]

The Canadian authorities were sorely perplexed, for this
fierce inter-tribal war threatened their whole system of Western trade. Meanwhile the English and Dutch of New York
were sending wampum belts to the Indians of the upper
Lakes, inviting them to bring their furs to Albany; and Ramesay, governor of Montreal, complains that they were all disposed to do so. "Twelve of the upper tribes," says Lord
Cornbury, "have come down this year to trade at Albany;"
but he adds that as the Indians have had no presents for
above six years, he is afraid "we shall lose them before next
summer."[2] The Governor of Canada himself is said to have
been in collusion with the English traders for his own profit.[3]
The Jesuits denied the charge, and Father Marest wrote to
the Governor, after the disaster to Walker's fleet on its way
to attack Quebec, "The protection you have given to the missions has drawn on you and the colony the miraculous protection of God."[4]

Whether his accusers did him wrong or not, Vaudreuil felt
the necessity of keeping the peace among the Western Indians
and suppressing the Outagamie incendiaries. In fact, nothing
would satisfy him but their destruction. "They are the common enemies of all the Western tribes," he writes. "They have
lately murdered three Frenchmen and five Hurons at Detroit.
The Hurons ask for our help against them, and we must give
it, or all the tribes will despise us."[5]

He put his chief trust in Louvigny, formerly commandant
at Michillimackinac. That officer proposed to muster the
friendly tribes and march on the Outagamies just as their corn

[1] *Idem, 2 Oct. 1723.*

[2] *N. Y. Col. Docs.*, V. 65.

[3] *Mémoire présenté au Comte de Ponchartrain par M. d'Auteuil, procureur-
général du Roy, 1708.*

[4] *Marest à Vaudreuil, 21 Jan. 1712.*

[5] *Vaudreuil et Bégon au Ministre, 15 Nov. 1713.*

was ripening, fight them if they stood their ground, or if not, destroy their crops, burn their wigwams, and encamp on the spot till winter; then send out parties to harass them as they roamed the woods seeking a meagre subsistence by hunting. In this way he hoped to cripple, if not destroy them.[1]

The Outagamies lived at this time on the Fox River of Green Bay,—a stream which owes its name to them.[2] Their chief village seems to have been between thirty and forty miles from the mouth of the river, where it creeps through broad tracts of rushes, willows, and wild rice. In spite of their losses at Detroit in 1712, their strength was far from being broken.

During two successive summers preparations were made to attack them; but the march was delayed, once by the tardiness of the Indian allies, and again by the illness of Louvigny. At length, on the 1st of May, 1716, he left Montreal with two hundred and twenty-five Frenchmen, while two hundred more waited to join him at Detroit and Michillimackinac, where the Indian allies were also to meet him. To save expense in pay and outfit, the Canadians recruited for the war were allowed to take with them goods for trading with the Indians. Hence great disorder and insubordination, especially as more than forty barrels of brandy were carried in the canoes, as a part of these commercial ventures, in consequence of which we hear that when French and Indians were encamped together, "hell was thrown open."[3]

The Outagamies stood their ground. Louvigny says, with probable exaggeration, that when he made his attack their village held five hundred warriors, and no less than three thousand women,—a disparity of sexes no doubt due to the inveterate fighting habits of the tribe. The wigwams were enclosed by a strong fence, consisting of three rows of heavy oaken palisades. This method of fortification was used also by tribes farther southward. When Bienville attacked the Chickasaws, he was foiled by the solid wooden wall that resisted

[1] *Vaudreuil au Ministre, 16 Sept. 1714.*

[2] "Les Renards [Outagamies] sont placez sur une rivière qui tombe dans la Baye des Puants [Green Bay]." *Registre du Conseil de la Marine, 28 Mars, 1716.*

[3] "Où il y a des François et des sauvages, c'est un enfer ouvert." *Registre du Conseil de Marine, 28 Mars, 1716.*

his cannon, being formed of trunks of trees as large as a man's body, set upright, close together, and made shot-proof by smaller trunks, planted within so as to close the interstices of the outer row.[1]

The fortified village of the Outagamies was of a somewhat different construction. The defences consisted of three rows of palisades, those of the middle row being probably planted upright, and the other two set aslant against them. Below, along the inside of the triple row, ran a sort of shallow trench or rifle-pit, where the defenders lay ensconced, firing through interstices left for the purpose between the palisades.[2]

Louvigny had brought with him two cannon and a mortar; but being light, they had little effect on the wooden wall, and as he was provided with mining tools, he resolved to attack the Outagamie stronghold by regular approaches, as if he were besieging a fortress of Vauban. Covered by the fire of three pieces of artillery and eight hundred French and Indian small-arms, he opened trenches during the night within seventy yards of the palisades, pushed a sap sixty feet nearer before morning, and on the third night burrowed to within about twenty-three yards of the wall. His plan was to undermine and blow up the palisades.

The Outagamies had made a furious resistance, in which their women took part with desperation; but dreading the threatened explosion, and unable to resist the underground approaches of their enemy, they asked for a parley, and owned themselves beaten. Louvigny demanded that they should make peace with all tribes friendly to the French, give up all prisoners, and make war on distant tribes, such as the Pawnees, in order to take captives who should supply the place of those they had killed among the allies of the French; that they should pay, in furs, the costs of the war, and give

[1] Le Page du Pratz.

[2] *Louvigny au Ministre, 14 Oct. 1716.* Louvigny's account of the Outagamie defences is short, and not very clear. La Mothe-Cadillac, describing similar works at Michillimackinac, says that the palisades of the innermost row alone were set close together, those of the two other rows being separated by spaces of six inches or more, through which the defenders fired from their loopholes. The plan seems borrowed from the Iroquois.

six chiefs, or sons of chiefs, as hostages for the fulfilment of these conditions.[1]

On the 12th of October Louvigny reached Quebec in triumph, bringing with him the six hostages.

The Outagamie question was settled for a time. The tribe remained quiet for some years, and in 1718 sent a deputation to Montreal and renewed their submission, which the Governor accepted, though they had evaded the complete fulfilment of the conditions imposed on them. Yet peace was not secure for a moment. The Kickapoos and Mascoutins would not leave their neighbors, the Illinois, at rest; the Saginaws made raids on the Miamis; and a general war seemed imminent. "The difficulty is inconceivable of keeping these Western tribes quiet," writes the Governor, almost in despair.[2]

At length the crisis came. The Illinois captured the nephew of Oushala, the principal Outagamie war-chief, and burned him alive; on which the Outagamies attacked them, drove them for refuge to the top of the rock on which La Salle's fort of St. Louis had been built, and held them there at mercy. They would have starved to death, had not the victors, dreading the anger of the French, suffered them to escape.[3] For this they took to themselves great credit, not without reason, in view of the provocation. At Versailles, however, their attack on the Illinois seemed an unpardonable offence, and the next ship from France brought a letter from the colonial minister declaring that the Outagamies must be effectually put down, and that "his Majesty will reward the officer who will reduce, or rather destroy, them."[4]

The authorities of Canada were less truculent than their masters at the court, or were better able to count the costs of another war. Longueuil, the provisional governor, persisted in measures of peace, and the Sieur de Lignery called a council of the Outagamies and their neighbors, the Sacs and Winnebagoes, at Green Bay. He told them that the Great Onontio, the King, ordered them, at their peril, to make no more attacks on the Illinois; and they dutifully promised to

---

[1] *Dépêche de Vaudreuil, 14 Oct. 1716.*

[2] *Vaudreuil au Conseil de Marine, 28 Oct. 1719.*

[3] *Paroles des Renards* [Outagamies] *dans un Conseil tenu le 6 Sept. 1722.*

[4] *Réponse du Ministre à la lettre du Marquis de Vaudreuil du 11 Oct. 1723.*

obey, while their great chief, Oushala, begged that a French officer might be sent to his village to help him keep his young warriors from the war-path.[1] The pacific policy of Longueuil was not approved by Desliettes, then commanding in the Illinois country; and he proposed to settle accounts with the Outagamies by exterminating them. "This is very well," observes a writer of the time; "but to try to exterminate them and fail would be disastrous."[2]

The Marquis de Beauharnois, who came out as governor of Canada in 1726, was averse to violent measures, since if an attempt to exterminate the offending tribe should be made without success, the life of every Frenchman in the West would be in jeopardy.[3] Lignery thought that if the Outagamies broke the promises they had made him at Green Bay, the forces of Canada and Louisiana should unite to crush them. The missionary, Chardon, advised that they should be cut off from all supplies of arms, ammunition, and merchandise of any kind, and that all the well-disposed Western tribes should then be set upon them,—which, he thought, would infallibly bring them to reason.[4]

The new Governor, perplexed by the multitude of counsellors, presently received a missive from the King, directing him not to fight the Outagamies if he could help it, "since the consequences of failure would be frightful."[5] On the other hand, Beauharnois was told that the English had sent messages to the Lake tribes urging them to kill the French in their country, and that the Outagamies had promised to do so. "This," writes the Governor, "compels us to make war in earnest. It will cost sixty thousand livres."[6]

Dupuy, the intendant, had joined with Beauharnois in this letter to the minister; but being at the time in a hot quarrel with the Governor, he soon after sent a communication of his own to Versailles, in which he declares that the war against the Outagamies was only a pretext of Beauharnois for spend-

[1] *Mémoire sur les Renards, 27 Avril, 1727.*

[2] *Mémoire concernant la Paix que M. de Lignery a faite avec les Chefs des Renards, Sakis* [Sacs] *et Puants* [Winnebagoes], *7 Juin, 1726.*

[3] *Mémoire sur les Renards, 27 Avril, 1727.*

[4] *Ibid.*

[5] *Mémoire du Roy, 29 Avril, 1727.*

[6] *Beauharnois et Dupuy au Ministre, 25 Oct. 1727.*

ing the King's money and enriching himself by buying up all the furs of the countries traversed by the army.[1]

Whatever the motives of the expedition, it left Montreal in June, under the Sieur de Lignery, followed the rugged old route of the Ottawa, and did not reach Michillimackinac till after midsummer. Thence, in a flotilla of birch canoes carrying about a thousand Indians and five hundred French, the party set out for the fort at the head of Green Bay.[2] Here they caught one Outagamie warrior and three Winnebagoes, whom the Indian allies tortured to death. Then they paddled their canoes up Fox River, reached a Winnebago village on the 24th of August, followed the channel of the stream, a ribbon of lazy water twisting in a vague, perplexing way through the broad marsh of wild rice and flags, till they saw the chief village of the Outagamies on a tract of rising ground a little above the level of the bog.[3] It consisted of bark wigwams, without palisades or defences of any kind. Its only inmates were three squaws and one old man. These were all seized, and, to the horror of Père Crespel, the chaplain, were given to the Indian allies, who kept the women as slaves, and burned the old man at a slow fire.[4] Then, after burning the village and destroying the crop of maize, peas, beans, and squashes that surrounded it, the whole party returned to Michillimackinac.[5]

The expedition was not a success. Lignery had hoped to surprise the enemy; but the alert and nimble savages had escaped him. Beauharnois makes the best of the miscarriage, and writes that "the army did good work;" but says a few weeks later that something must be done to cure the contempt which the Western allies of the French have conceived for them "since the last affair."[6]

---

[1] *Mémoire de Dupuy, 1728.*

[2] Desliettes came to meet them, by way of Chicago, with five hundred Illinois warriors and twenty Frenchmen. *La Perrière et La Fresnière à Beauharnois, 10 Sept. 1728.*

[3] *Guignas à Beauharnois, 29 Mai, 1728.*

[4] *Dépêche de Beauharnois, 1 Sept. 1728.*

[5] The best account of this expedition is that of Père Emanuel Crespel. Lignery made a report which seems to be lost, as it does not appear in the Archives.

[6] *Beauharnois au Ministre, 15 Mai, 1729; Ibid., 21 Juillet, 1729.*

Two years after Lignery's expedition, there was another attempt to humble the Outagamies. Late in the autumn of 1730 young Coulon de Villiers, who twenty-four years later defeated Washington at Fort Necessity, appeared at Quebec with news that the Sieur de Villiers, his father, who commanded the post on the St. Joseph, had struck the Outagamies a deadly blow and killed two hundred of their warriors, besides six hundred of their women and children. The force under Villiers consisted of a body of Frenchmen gathered from various Western posts, another body from the Illinois, led by the Sieurs de Saint-Ange, father and son, and twelve or thirteen hundred Indian allies from many friendly tribes.[1]

The accounts of this affair are obscure and not very trustworthy. It seems that the Outagamies began the fray by an attack on the Illinois at La Salle's old station of Le Rocher, on the river Illinois. On hearing of this, the French commanders mustered their Indian allies, hastened to the spot, and found the Outagamies intrenched in a grove which they had surrounded with a stockade. They defended themselves with their usual courage, but being hard pressed by hunger and thirst, as well as by the greatly superior numbers of their assailants, they tried to escape during a dark night, as their tribesmen had done at Detroit in 1712. The French and their allies pursued, and there was a great slaughter, in which many warriors and many more women and children were the victims.[2]

The offending tribe must now, one would think, have ceased to be dangerous; but nothing less than its destruction would content the French officials. To this end, their best

---

[1] *Beauharnois et Hocquart au Ministre, 2 Nov. 1730.* An Indian tradition says that about this time there was a great battle between the Outagamies and the French, aided by their Indian allies, at the place called Little Butte des Morts, on the Fox River. According to the story, the Outagamies were nearly destroyed. Perhaps this is a perverted version of the Villiers affair. See *Wisconsin Historical Collections*, VIII. 207. Beauharnois also reports, under date of 6 May, 1730, that a party of Outagamies, returning from a buffalo hunt, were surprised by two hundred Ottawas, Ojibwas, Menomonies, and Winnebagoes, who killed eighty warriors and three hundred women and children.

[2] Some particulars of this affair are given by Ferland, *Cours d'Histoire du Canada*, II. 437; but he does not give his authority. I have found no report of it by those engaged.

resource was in their Indian allies, among whom the Outagamies had no more deadly enemy than the Hurons of Detroit, who, far from relenting in view of their disasters, were
more eager than ever to wreak their ire on their unfortunate
foe. Accordingly, they sent messengers to the converted Iroquois at the Mission of Two Mountains, and invited them to
join in making an end of the Outagamies. The invitation was
accepted, and in the autumn of 1731 forty-seven warriors from
the Two Mountains appeared at Detroit. The party was soon
made up. It consisted of seventy-four Hurons, forty-six Iroquois, and four Ottawas. They took the trail to the mouth of
the river St. Joseph, thence around the head of Lake Michigan to the Chicago portage, and thence westward to Rock
River. Here were the villages of the Kickapoos and Mascoutins, who had been allies of the Outagamies, but having lately
quarrelled with them, received the strangers as friends and
gave them guides. The party now filed northward, by forests
and prairies, towards the Wisconsin, to the banks of which
stream the Outagamies had lately removed their villages. The
warriors were all on snow-shoes, for the weather was cold and
the snow deep. Some of the elders, overcome by the hardships of the way, called a council and proposed to turn back;
but the juniors were for pushing on at all risks, and a young
warrior declared that he would rather die than go home without killing somebody. The result was a division of the party;
the elders returned to Chicago, and the younger men, forty
Hurons and thirty Iroquois, kept on their way. At last, as
they neared the Wisconsin, they saw on an open prairie three
Outagamies, who ran for their lives. The Hurons and Iroquois gave chase, till from the ridge of a hill they discovered
the principal Outagamie village, consisting, if we may believe
their own story, of forty-six wigwams, near the bank of the
river. The Outagamie warriors came out to meet them, in
number, as they pretended, much greater than theirs; but the
Huron and Iroquois chiefs reminded their followers that they
had to do with dogs who did not believe in God, on which
they fired two volleys against the enemy, then dropped their
guns and charged with the knife in one hand and the war-
club in the other. According to their own story, which shows
every sign of mendacity, they drove back the Outagamies into

their village, killed seventy warriors, and captured fourteen more, without counting eighty women and children killed, and a hundred and forty taken prisoners. In short, they would have us believe that they destroyed the whole village, except ten men, who escaped entirely naked, and soon froze to death. They declared further that they sent one of their prisoners to the remaining Outagamie villages, ordering him to tell the inhabitants that they had just devoured the better part of the tribe, and meant to stay on the spot two days; that the tribesmen of the slain were free to attack them if they chose, but in that case, they would split the heads of all the women and children prisoners in their hands, make a breastwork of the dead bodies, and then finish it by piling upon it those of the assailants.[1]

Nothing is more misleading than Indian tradition, which is of the least possible value as evidence. It may be well, however, to mention another story, often repeated, touching these dark days of the Outagamies. It is to the effect that a French trader named Marin, whom they had incensed by levying blackmail from him, raised a party of Indians, with whose aid he surprised and defeated the unhappy tribe at the Little Butte des Morts, that they retired to the Great Butte des Morts, higher up Fox River, and that Marin here attacked them again, killing or capturing the whole. Extravagant as the story seems, it may have some foundation, though various dates, from 1725 to 1746, are assigned to the alleged exploit, and contemporary documents are silent concerning it. It is certain that the Outagamies were not destroyed, as the tribe exists to this day.[2]

---

[1] *Relation de la Défaite des Renards par les Sauvages Hurons et Iroquois, le 28 Fév. 1732.* (Archives de la Marine.)

[2] The story is told in Snelling, *Tales of the Northwest* (1830), under the title of *La Butte des Morts*, and afterwards, with variations, by the aged Augustus Grignon, in his *Recollections*, printed in the *Collections of the Wisconsin Historical Society*, III.; also by Judge M. L. Martin and others. Grignon, like all the rest, was not born till after the time of the alleged event. The nearest approach to substantial evidence touching it is in a letter of Beauharnois, who writes in 1730 that the Sieur Dubuisson was to attack the Outagamies with fifty Frenchmen and five hundred and fifty Indians, and that Marin, commander at Green Bay, was to join him. *Beauharnois au Ministre, 25 Juin, 1730.*

In 1736 it was reported that sixty or eighty Outagamie warriors were still alive.[1] Their women, who when hard pushed would fight like furies, were relatively numerous and tolerably prolific, and their villages were full of sturdy boys, likely to be dangerous in a few years. Feeling their losses and their weakness, the survivors of the tribe incorporated themselves with their kindred and neighbors, the Sacs, Sakis, or Saukies, the two forming henceforth one tribe, afterwards known to the Americans as the Sacs and Foxes. Early in the nineteenth century they were settled on both banks of the upper Mississippi. Brave and restless like their forefathers, they were a continual menace to the American frontiersmen, and in 1832 they rose in open war, under their famous chief, Blackhawk, displaying their hereditary prowess both on foot and on horseback, and more than once defeating superior numbers of American mounted militia. In the next year that excellent artist, Charles Bodmer, painted a group of them from life,— grim-visaged savages, armed with war-club, spear, or rifle, and wrapped in red, green, or brown blankets, their heads close shaven except the erect and bristling scalplock, adorned with long eagle-plumes, while both heads and faces are painted with fantastic figures in blue, white, yellow, black, and vermilion.[2]

Three or four years after, a party of their chiefs and warriors was conducted through the country by order of the Washington government, in order to impress them with the number and power of the whites. At Boston they danced a war-dance on the Common in full costume, to the delight of the boy spectators, of whom I was one.

[1] *Mémoire sur le Canada, 1736.*

[2] Charles Bodmer was the artist who accompanied Prince Maximilian of Wied in his travels in the interior of North America.

The name Outagamie is Algonkin for a fox. Hence the French called the tribe Renards, and the Americans, Foxes. They called themselves Musquawkies, which is said to mean "red earth," and to be derived from the color of the soil near one of their villages.

Chapter XV

1697—1741

FRANCE IN THE FAR WEST

French Explorers • Le Sueur on the St. Peter's • Canadians on the Missouri • Juchereau de Saint-Denis • Bénard de la Harpe on Red River • Adventures of Du Tisné • Bourgmont visits the Comanches • The Brothers Mallet in Colorado and New Mexico • Fabry de la Bruyère

T HE OCCUPATION by France of the lower Mississippi gave a strong impulse to the exploration of the West, by supplying a base for discovery, stimulating enterprise by the longing to find gold mines, open trade with New Mexico, and get a fast hold on the countries beyond the Mississippi in anticipation of Spain; and to these motives was soon added the hope of finding an overland way to the Pacific. It was the Canadians, with their indomitable spirit of adventure, who led the way in the path of discovery.

As a bold and hardy pioneer of the wilderness, the Frenchman in America has rarely found his match. His civic virtues withered under the despotism of Versailles, and his mind and conscience were kept in leading-strings by an absolute Church; but the forest and the prairie offered him an unbridled liberty, which, lawless as it was, gave scope to his energies, till these savage wastes became the field of his most noteworthy achievements.

Canada was divided between two opposing influences. On the one side were the monarchy and the hierarchy, with their principles of order, subordination, and obedience; substantially at one in purpose, since both wished to keep the colony within manageable bounds, domesticate it, and tame it to soberness, regularity, and obedience. On the other side was the spirit of liberty, or license, which was in the very air of this wilderness continent, reinforced in the chiefs of the colony by a spirit of adventure inherited from the Middle Ages, and by a spirit of trade born of present opportunities; for every official in Canada hoped to make a profit, if not a fortune, out of beaver-skins. Kindred impulses, in ruder forms, possessed the humbler colonists, drove them into the forest, and made them hardy woodsmen and skilful bush-fighters, though turbulent and lawless members of civilized society.

Time, the decline of the fur-trade, and the influence of the Canadian Church gradually diminished this erratic spirit, and at the same time impaired the qualities that were associated with it. The Canadian became a more stable colonist and a steadier farmer; but for forest journeyings and forest warfare he was scarcely his former self. At the middle of the eighteenth century we find complaints that the race of *voyageurs* is growing scarce. The taming process was most apparent in the central and lower parts of the colony, such as the Côte de Beaupré and the opposite shore of the St. Lawrence, where the hands of the government and of the Church were strong; while at the head of the colony,—that is, about Montreal and its neighborhood,—which touched the primeval wilderness, an uncontrollable spirit of adventure still held its own. Here, at the beginning of the century, this spirit was as strong as it had ever been, and achieved a series of explorations and discoveries which revealed the plains of the Far West long before an Anglo-Saxon foot had pressed their soil.

The expedition of one Le Sueur to what is now the State of Minnesota may be taken as the starting-point of these enterprises. Le Sueur had visited the country of the Sioux as early as 1683. He returned thither in 1689 with the famous *voyageur* Nicolas Perrot.[1] Four years later, Count Frontenac sent him to the Sioux country again. The declared purpose of the mission was to keep those fierce tribes at peace with their neighbors; but the Governor's enemies declared that a contraband trade in beaver was the true object, and that Frontenac's secretary was to have half the profits.[2] Le Sueur returned after two years, bringing to Montreal a Sioux chief and his squaw,—the first of the tribe ever seen there. He then went to France, and represented to the court that he had built a fort at Lake Pepin, on the upper Mississippi; that he was the only white man who knew the languages of that region; and that if the French did not speedily seize upon it, the English, who were already trading upon the Ohio, would be sure to

[1] *Journal historique de l'Etablissement des Français à la Louisiane*, 43.
[2] *Champigny au Ministre, 4 Nov. 1693.*

do so. Thereupon he asked for the command of the upper Mississippi, with all its tributary waters, together with a monopoly of its fur-trade for ten years, and permission to work its mines, promising that if his petition were granted, he would secure the country to France without expense to the King. The commission was given him. He bought an outfit and sailed for Canada, but was captured by the English on the way. After the peace he returned to France and begged for a renewal of his commission. Leave was given him to work the copper and lead mines, but not to trade in beaver-skins. He now formed a company to aid him in his enterprise, on which a cry rose in Canada that under pretence of working mines he meant to trade in beaver,—which is very likely, since to bring lead and copper in bark canoes to Montreal from the Mississippi and Lake Superior would cost far more than the metal was worth. In consequence of this clamor his commission was revoked.

Perhaps it was to compensate him for the outlays into which he had been drawn that the colonial minister presently authorized him to embark for Louisiana and pursue his enterprise with that infant colony, instead of Canada, as his base of operations. Thither, therefore, he went; and in April, 1700, set out for the Sioux country with twenty-five men, in a small vessel of the kind called a "felucca," still used in the Mediterranean. Among the party was an adventurous youth named Penecaut, a ship-carpenter by trade, who had come to Louisiana with Iberville two years before, and who has left us an account of his voyage with Le Sueur.[1]

The party slowly made their way, with sail and oar, against the muddy current of the Mississippi, till they reached the Arkansas, where they found an English trader from Carolina. On the 10th of June, spent with rowing, and half starved, they stopped to rest at a point fifteen leagues above the mouth of the Ohio. They had staved off famine with the buds and leaves of trees; but now, by good luck, one of them killed a bear, and, soon after, the Jesuit Limoges arrived from the neighboring mission of the Illinois, in a canoe well stored

[1] *Relation de Penecaut.* In my possession is a contemporary manuscript of this narrative, for which I am indebted to the kindness of General J. Meredith Reade.

with provisions. Thus refreshed, they passed the mouth of the Missouri on the 13th of July, and soon after were met by three Canadians, who brought them a letter from the Jesuit Marest, warning them that the river was infested by war-parties. In fact, they presently saw seven canoes of Sioux warriors, bound against the Illinois; and not long after, five Canadians appeared, one of whom had been badly wounded in a recent encounter with a band of Outagamies, Sacs, and Winnebagoes bound against the Sioux. To take one another's scalps had been for ages the absorbing business and favorite recreation of all these Western tribes. At or near the expansion of the Mississippi called Lake Pepin, the voyagers found a fort called Fort Perrot, after its builder;[1] and on an island near the upper end of the lake, another similar structure, built by Le Sueur himself on his last visit to the place. These forts were mere stockades, occupied from time to time by the roving fur-traders as their occasions required.

Towards the end of September, Le Sueur and his followers reached the mouth of the St. Peter, which they ascended to Blue Earth River. Pushing a league up this stream, they found a spot well suited to their purpose, and here they built a fort, of which there was great need, for they were soon after joined by seven Canadian traders, plundered and stripped to the skin by the neighboring Sioux. Le Sueur named the new post Fort l'Huillier. It was a fence of pickets, enclosing cabins for the men. The neighboring plains were black with buffalo, of which the party killed four hundred, and cut them into quarters, which they placed to freeze on scaffolds within the enclosure. Here they spent the winter, subsisting on the frozen meat, without bread, vegetables, or salt, and, according to Penecaut, thriving marvellously, though the surrounding wilderness was buried five feet deep in snow.

Band after band of Sioux appeared, with their wolfish dogs

---

[1] Penecaut, *Journal*. *Procès-verbal de la Prise de Possession du Pays des Nadouessioux, etc., par Nicolas Perrot, 1689*. Fort Perrot seems to have been built in 1685, and to have stood near the outlet of the lake, probably on the west side. Perrot afterwards built another fort, called Fort St. Antoine, a little above, on the east bank. The position of these forts has been the subject of much discussion, and cannot be ascertained with precision. It appears by the *Prise de Possession*, cited above, that there was also, in 1689, a temporary French post near the mouth of the Wisconsin.

and their sturdy and all-enduring squaws burdened with the heavy hide coverings of their teepees, or buffalo-skin tents. They professed friendship and begged for arms. Those of one band had blackened their faces in mourning for a dead chief, and calling on Le Sueur to share their sorrow, they wept over him, and wiped their tears on his hair. Another party of warriors arrived with yet deeper cause of grief, being the remnant of a village half exterminated by their enemies. They, too, wept profusely over the French commander, and then sang a dismal song, with heads muffled in their buffalo-robes.[1] Le Sueur took the needful precautions against his dangerous visitors, but got from them a large supply of beaver-skins in exchange for his goods.

When spring opened, he set out in search of mines, and found, not far above the fort, those beds of blue and green earth to which the stream owes its name. Of this his men dug out a large quantity, and selecting what seemed the best, stored it in their vessel as a precious commodity. With this and good store of beaver-skins, Le Sueur now began his return voyage for Louisiana, leaving a Canadian named D'Éraque and twelve men to keep the fort till he should come back to reclaim it, promising to send him a canoe-load of ammunition from the Illinois. But the canoe was wrecked, and D'Éraque, discouraged, abandoned Fort l'Huillier, and followed his commander down the Mississippi.[2]

Le Sueur, with no authority from government, had opened relations of trade with the wild Sioux of the Plains, whose westward range stretched to the Black Hills, and perhaps to the Rocky Mountains. He reached the settlements of Louisiana in safety, and sailed for France with four thousand pounds of his worthless blue earth.[3] Repairing at once to Versailles, he begged for help to continue his enterprise. His petition seems to have been granted. After long delay, he

[1] This weeping over strangers was a custom with the Sioux of that time mentioned by many early writers. La Mothe-Cadillac marvels that a people so brave and warlike should have such a fountain of tears always at command.

[2] In 1702 the geographer De l'Isle made a remarkable MS. map entitled *Carte de la Rivière du Mississippi, dressée sur les Mémoires de M. Le Sueur*.

[3] According to the geologist Featherstonhaugh, who examined the locality, this earth owes its color to a bluish-green silicate of iron.

sailed again for Louisiana, fell ill on the voyage, and died soon after landing.[1]

Before 1700, the year when Le Sueur visited the St. Peter, little or nothing was known of the country west of the Mississippi, except from the report of Indians. The romances of La Hontan and Matthieu Sagean were justly set down as impostures by all but the most credulous. In this same year we find Le Moyne d'Iberville projecting journeys to the upper Missouri, in hopes of finding a river flowing to the Western Sea. In 1703, twenty Canadians tried to find their way from the Illinois to New Mexico, in hope of opening trade with the Spaniards and discovering mines.[2] In 1704 we find it reported that more than a hundred Canadians are scattered in small parties along the Mississippi and the Missouri;[3] and in 1705 one Laurain appeared at the Illinois, declaring that he had been high up the Missouri and had visited many tribes on its borders.[4] A few months later, two Canadians told Bienville a similar story. In 1708 Nicolas de la Salle proposed an expedition of a hundred men to explore the same mysterious river; and in 1717 one Hubert laid before the Council of Marine a scheme for following the Missouri to its source, since, he says, "not only may we find the mines worked by the Spaniards, but also discover the great river that is said to rise in the mountains where the Missouri has its source, and is believed to flow to the Western Sea." And he advises that a hundred and fifty men be sent up the river in wooden canoes, since bark canoes would be dangerous, by reason of the multitude of snags.[5]

In 1714 Juchereau de Saint-Denis was sent by La Mothe-Cadillac to explore western Louisiana, and pushed up Red River to a point sixty-eight leagues, as he reckons, above Natchitoches. In the next year, journeying across country to-

[1] Besides the long and circumstantial *Relation de Penecaut*, an account of the earlier part of Le Sueur's voyage up the Mississippi is contained in the *Mémoire du Chevalier de Beaurain*, which, with other papers relating to this explorer, including portions of his Journal, will be found in Margry, VI. See also *Journal historique de l'Etablissement des Français à la Louisiane*, 38–71.

[2] *Iberville à ——, 15 Fév. 1703* (Margry, VI. 180).

[3] *Bienville au Ministre, 6 Sept. 1704.*

[4] Beaurain, *Journal historique*.

[5] Hubert, *Mémoire envoyé au Conseil de la Marine.*

wards the Spanish settlements, with a view to trade, he was seized near the Rio Grande and carried to the city of Mexico. The Spaniards, jealous of French designs, now sent priests and soldiers to occupy several points in Texas. Juchereau, however, was well treated, and permitted to marry a Spanish girl with whom he had fallen in love on the way; but when, in the autumn of 1716, he ventured another journey to the Mexican borders, still hoping to be allowed to trade, he and his goods were seized by order of the Mexican viceroy, and, lest worse should befall him, he fled empty handed, under cover of night.[1]

In March, 1719, Bénard de la Harpe left the feeble little French post at Natchitoches with six soldiers and a sergeant.[2] His errand was to explore the country, open trade if possible with the Spaniards, and establish another post high up Red River. He and his party soon came upon that vast entanglement of driftwood, or rather of uprooted forests, afterwards known as the Red River raft, which choked the stream and forced them to make their way through the inundated jungle that bordered it. As they pushed or dragged their canoes through the swamp, they saw with disgust and alarm a good number of snakes, coiled about twigs and boughs on the right and left, or sometimes over their heads. These were probably the deadly water-moccason, which in warm weather is accustomed to crawl out of its favorite element and bask itself in the sun, precisely as described by La Harpe. Their nerves were further discomposed by the splashing and plunging of alligators lately wakened from their wintry torpor. Still, they pushed painfully on, till they reached navigable water again, and at the end of the month were, as they thought, a hundred and eight leagues above Natchitoches. In four days more they reached the Nassonites.

These savages belonged to a group of stationary tribes, only one of which, the Caddoes, survives to our day as a separate community. Their enemies the Chickasaws, Osages, Arkansas, and even the distant Illinois, waged such deadly war

---

[1] Penecaut, *Relation*, chaps. xvii., xviii. Le Page du Pratz, *Histoire de la Louisiane*, I. 13–22. Various documents in Margry, VI. 193–202.

[2] For an interesting contemporary map of the French establishment at Natchitoches, see Thomassy, *Géologie pratique de la Louisiane*.

against them that, according to La Harpe, the unfortunate Nassonites were in the way of extinction, their numbers having fallen, within ten years, from twenty-five hundred souls to four hundred.[1]

La Harpe stopped among them to refresh his men, and build a house of cypress-wood as a beginning of the post he was ordered to establish; then, having heard that a war with Spain had ruined his hopes of trade with New Mexico, he resolved to pursue his explorations.

With him went ten men, white, red, and black, with twenty-two horses bought from the Indians, for his journeyings were henceforth to be by land. The party moved in a northerly and westerly course, by hills, forests, and prairies, passed two branches of the Wichita, and on the 3d of September came to a river which La Harpe calls the southwest branch of the Arkansas, but which, if his observation of latitude is correct, must have been the main stream, not far from the site of Fort Mann. Here he was met by seven Indian chiefs, mounted on excellent horses saddled and bridled after the Spanish manner. They led him to where, along the plateau of the low, treeless hills that bordered the valley, he saw a string of Indian villages, extending for a league and belonging to nine several bands, the names of which can no longer be recognized, and most of which are no doubt extinct. He says that they numbered in all six thousand souls; and their dwellings were high, dome-shaped structures, built of clay mixed with reeds and straw, resting, doubtless, on a frame of bent poles.[2] With them were also some of the roving Indians of the plains, with their conical teepees of dressed buffalo-skin.

The arrival of the strangers was a great and amazing event for these savages, few of whom had ever seen a white man. On the day after their arrival the whole multitude gathered to receive them and offer them the calumet, with a profusion of songs and speeches. Then warrior after warrior recounted his

---

[1] Bénard de la Harpe, in Margry, VI. 264.

[2] Beaurain says that each of these bands spoke a language of its own. They had horses in abundance, descended from Spanish stock. Among them appear to have been the Ouacos, or Huecos, and the Wichitas,—two tribes better known as the Pawnee Picts. See Marcy, *Exploration of Red River*.

exploits and boasted of the scalps he had taken. From eight in the morning till two hours after midnight the din of drums, songs, harangues, and dances continued without relenting, with a prospect of twelve hours more; and La Harpe, in desperation, withdrew to rest himself on a buffalo-robe, begging another Frenchman to take his place. His hosts left him in peace for a while; then the chiefs came to find him, painted his face blue, as a tribute of respect, put a cap of eagle-feathers on his head, and laid numerous gifts at his feet. When at last the ceremony ended, some of the performers were so hoarse from incessant singing that they could hardly speak.[1]

La Harpe was told by his hosts that the Spanish settlements could be reached by ascending their river; but to do this was at present impossible. He began his backward journey, fell desperately ill of a fever, and nearly died before reaching Natchitoches.

Having recovered, he made an attempt, two years later, to explore the Arkansas in canoes, from its mouth, but accomplished little besides killing a good number of buffalo, bears, deer, and wild turkeys. He was confirmed, however, in the belief that the Comanches and the Spaniards of New Mexico might be reached by this route.

In the year of La Harpe's first exploration, one Du Tisné went up the Missouri to a point six leagues above Grand River, where stood the village of the Missouris. He wished to go farther, but they would not let him. He then returned to the Illinois, whence he set out on horseback with a few followers across what is now the State of Missouri, till he reached the village of the Osages, which stood on a hill high up the river Osage. At first he was well received; but when they found him disposed to push on to a town of their enemies, the Pawnees, forty leagues distant, they angrily refused to let him go. His firmness and hardihood prevailed, and at last they gave him leave. A ride of a few days over rich prairies brought him to the Pawnees, who, coming as he did from the hated Osages, took him for an enemy and threatened to kill him. Twice they raised the tomahawk over his head; but

[1] Compare the account of La Harpe with that of the Chevalier de Beaurain; both are in Margry, VI. There is an abstract in *Journal historique*.

when the intrepid traveller dared them to strike, they began
to treat him as a friend. When, however, he told them that
he meant to go fifteen days' journey farther, to the Padoucas,
or Comanches, their deadly enemies, they fiercely forbade
him; and after planting a French flag in their village, he returned as he had come, guiding his way by compass, and
reaching the Illinois in November, after extreme hardships.[1]

Early in 1721 two hundred mounted Spaniards, followed by
a large body of Comanche warriors, came from New Mexico
to attack the French at the Illinois, but were met and routed
on the Missouri by tribes of that region.[2] In the next year,
Bienville was told that they meant to return, punish those
who had defeated them, and establish a post on the river Kansas; whereupon he ordered Boisbriant, commandant at the
Illinois, to anticipate them by sending troops to build a
French fort at or near the same place. But the West India
Company had already sent one Bourgmont on a similar errand, the object being to trade with the Spaniards in time of
peace, and stop their incursions in time of war.[3] It was hoped
also that, in the interest of trade, peace might be made between the Comanches and the tribes of the Missouri.[4]

Bourgmont was a man of some education, and well acquainted with these tribes, among whom he had traded for
years. In pursuance of his orders he built a fort, which he
named Fort Orléans, and which stood on the Missouri not
far above the mouth of Grand River. Having thus accomplished one part of his mission, he addressed himself to the
other, and prepared to march for the Comanche villages.

Leaving a sufficient garrison at the fort, he sent his ensign,
Saint-Ange, with a party of soldiers and Canadians, in
wooden canoes, to the villages of the Kansas higher up the
stream, and on the 3d of July set out by land to join him,
with a hundred and nine Missouri Indians and sixty-eight

[1] *Relation de Bénard de la Harpe. Autre Relation du même. Du Tisné à Bienville.* Margry, VI. 309, 310, 313.

[2] *Bienville au Conseil de Régence, 20 Juillet, 1721.*

[3] *Instructions au Sieur de Bourgmont, 17 Jan. 1722.* Margry, VI. 389.

[4] The French had at this time gained a knowledge of the tribes of the Missouri as far up as the Arickaras, who were not, it seems, many days' journey
below the Yellowstone, and who told them of "prodigiously high mountains,"—evidently the Rocky Mountains. *Mémoire de la Renaudière, 1723.*

Osages in his train. A ride of five days brought him again to the banks of the Missouri, opposite a Kansas town. Saint-Ange had not yet arrived, the angry and turbid current, joined to fevers among his men, having retarded his progress. Meanwhile Bourgmont drew from the Kansas a promise that their warriors should go with him to the Comanches. Saint-Ange at last appeared, and at daybreak of the 24th the tents were struck and the pack-horses loaded. At six o'clock the party drew up in battle array on a hill above the Indian town, and then, with drum beating and flag flying, began their march. "A fine prairie country," writes Bourgmont, "with hills and dales and clumps of trees to right and left." Sometimes the landscape quivered under the sultry sun, and sometimes thunder bellowed over their heads, and rain fell in floods on the steaming plains.

Renaudière, engineer of the party, one day stood by the side of the path and watched the whole procession as it passed him. The white men were about twenty in all. He counted about three hundred Indian warriors, with as many squaws, some five hundred children, and a prodigious number of dogs, the largest and strongest of which dragged heavy loads. The squaws also served as beasts of burden; and, says the journal, "they will carry as much as a dog will drag." Horses were less abundant among these tribes than they afterwards became, so that their work fell largely upon the women.

On the sixth day the party was within three leagues of the river Kansas, at a considerable distance above its mouth. Bourgmont had suffered from dysentery on the march, and an access of the malady made it impossible for him to go farther. It is easy to conceive the regret with which he saw himself compelled to return to Fort Orléans. The party retraced their steps, carrying their helpless commander on a litter.

First, however, he sent one Gaillard on a perilous errand. Taking with him two Comanche slaves bought for the purpose from the Kansas, Gaillard was ordered to go to the Comanche villages with the message that Bourgmont had been on his way to make them a friendly visit, and though stopped by illness, hoped soon to try again, with better success.

Early in September, Bourgmont, who had arrived safely at
Fort Orléans, received news that the mission of Gaillard had
completely succeeded; on which, though not wholly recovered from his illness, he set out again on his errand of peace,
accompanied by his young son, besides Renaudière, a surgeon, and nine soldiers. On reaching the great village of the
Kansas he found there five Comanche chiefs and warriors,
whom Gaillard had induced to come thither with him. Seven
chiefs of the Otoes presently appeared, in accordance with an
invitation of Bourgmont; then six chiefs of the Iowas and the
head chief of the Missouris. With these and the Kansas chiefs
a solemn council was held around a fire before Bourgmont's
tent; speeches were made, the pipe of peace was smoked, and
presents were distributed.

On the 8th of October the march began, the five Comanches and the chiefs of several other tribes, including the Omahas, joining the cavalcade. Gaillard and another Frenchman
named Quesnel were sent in advance to announce their approach to the Comanches, while Bourgmont and his followers moved up the north side of the river Kansas till the
eleventh, when they forded it at a point twenty leagues from
its mouth, and took a westward and southwestward course,
sometimes threading the grassy valleys of little streams, sometimes crossing the dry upland prairie, covered with the short,
tufted dull-green herbage since known as "buffalo grass."
Wild turkeys clamored along every watercourse; deer were
seen on all sides, buffalo were without number, sometimes in
grazing droves, and sometimes dotting the endless plain as far
as the eye could reach. Ruffian wolves, white and gray, eyed
the travellers askance, keeping a safe distance by day, and
howling about the camp all night. Of the antelope and the
elk the journal makes no mention. Bourgmont chased a buffalo on horseback and shot him with a pistol,—which is
probably the first recorded example of that way of hunting.

The stretches of high, rolling, treeless prairie grew more
vast as the travellers advanced. On the 17th, they found an
abandoned Comanche camp. On the next day as they stopped
to dine, and had just unsaddled their horses, they saw a distant smoke towards the west, on which they set the dry grass
on fire as an answering signal. Half an hour later a body of

wild horsemen came towards them at full speed, and among them were their two couriers, Gaillard and Quesnel, waving a French flag. The strangers were eighty Comanche warriors, with the grand chief of the tribe at their head. They dashed up to Bourgmont's bivouac and leaped from their horses, when a general shaking of hands ensued, after which white men and red seated themselves on the ground and smoked the pipe of peace. Then all rode together to the Comanche camp, three leagues distant.[1]

Bourgmont pitched his tents at a pistol-shot from the Comanche lodges, whence a crowd of warriors presently came to visit him. They spread buffalo-robes on the ground, placed upon them the French commander, his officers, and his young son; then lifted each, with its honored load, and carried them all, with yells of joy and gratulation, to the lodge of the Great Chief, where there was a feast of ceremony lasting till nightfall.

On the next day Bourgmont displayed to his hosts the marvellous store of gifts he had brought for them,—guns, swords, hatchets, kettles, gunpowder, bullets, red cloth, blue cloth, hand-mirrors, knives, shirts, awls, scissors, needles, hawks' bells, vermilion, beads, and other enviable commodities, of the like of which they had never dreamed. Two hundred savages gathered before the French tents, where Bourgmont, with the gifts spread on the ground before him, stood with a French flag in his hand, surrounded by his officers and the Indian chiefs of his party, and harangued the admiring auditors.

He told them that he had come to bring them a message from the King, his master, who was the Great Chief of all the nations of the earth, and whose will it was that the Comanches should live in peace with his other children,—the Missouris, Osages, Kansas, Otoes, Omahas, and Pawnees,—with whom they had long been at war; that the chiefs of these

[1] This meeting took place a little north of the Arkansas, apparently where that river makes a northward bend, near the 22d degree of west longitude. The Comanche villages were several days' journey to the southwest. This tribe is always mentioned in the early French narratives as the Padoucas,—a name by which the Comanches are occasionally known to this day. See Whipple and Turner, *Reports upon Indian Tribes*, in *Explorations and Surveys for the Pacific Railroad* (Senate Doc., 1853, 1854).

tribes were now present, ready to renounce their old enmities; that the Comanches should henceforth regard them as friends, share with them the blessing of alliance and trade with the French, and give to these last free passage through their country to trade with the Spaniards of New Mexico. Bourgmont then gave the French flag to the Great Chief, to be kept forever as a pledge of that day's compact. The chief took the flag, and promised in behalf of his people to keep peace inviolate with the Indian children of the King. Then, with unspeakable delight, he and his tribesmen took and divided the gifts.

The next two days were spent in feasts and rejoicings. "Is it true that you are men?" asked the Great Chief. "I have heard wonders of the French, but I never could have believed what I see this day." Then, taking up a handful of earth, "The Spaniards are like this; but you are like the sun." And he offered Bourgmont, in case of need, the aid of his two thousand Comanche warriors. The pleasing manners of his visitors, and their unparalleled generosity, had completely won his heart.

As the object of the expedition was accomplished, or seemed to be so, the party set out on their return. A ride of ten days brought them again to the Missouri; they descended in canoes to Fort Orléans, and sang Te Deum in honor of the peace.[1]

No farther discovery in this direction was made for the next fifteen years. Though the French had explored the Missouri as far as the site of Fort Clark and the Mandan villages, they were possessed by the idea—due, perhaps, to Indian reports concerning the great tributary river, the Yellowstone—that in its upper course the main stream bent so far southward as to form a water-way to New Mexico, with which it was the constant desire of the authorities of Louisiana to open trade. A way thither was at last made known by two brothers named Mallet, who with six companions went up the Platte to its South Fork, which they called River of the Padoucas,—a name given it on some maps down to the middle of this century. They followed the South Fork for some distance, and then, turning southward and southwestward, crossed the

---

[1] *Relation du Voyage du Sieur de Bourgmont, Juin–Nov., 1724*, in Margry, VI. 398. Le Page du Pratz, III. 141.

plains of Colorado. Here the dried dung of the buffalo was their only fuel; and it has continued to feed the camp-fire of the traveller in this treeless region within the memory of many now living. They crossed the upper Arkansas, and apparently the Cimarron, passed Taos, and on the 22d of July reached Santa Fé, where they spent the winter. On the 1st of May, 1740, they began their return journey, three of them crossing the plains to the Pawnee villages, and the rest descending the Arkansas to the Mississippi.[1]

The bold exploit of the brothers Mallet attracted great attention at New Orleans, and Bienville resolved to renew it, find if possible a nearer and better way to Santa Fé, determine the nature and extent of these mysterious western regions, and satisfy a lingering doubt whether they were not contiguous to China and Tartary.[2] A naval officer, Fabry de la Bruyère, was sent on this errand, with the brothers Mallet and a few soldiers and Canadians. He ascended the Canadian Fork of the Arkansas, named by him the St. André, became entangled in the shallows and quicksands of that difficult river, fell into disputes with his men, and after protracted efforts, returned unsuccessful.[3]

While French enterprise was unveiling the remote Southwest, two indomitable Canadians were pushing still more noteworthy explorations into more northern regions of the continent.

[1] *Journal du Voyage des Frères Mallet, présenté à MM. de Bienville et Salmon.* This narrative is meagre and confused, but serves to establish the main points. *Copie du Certificat donné à Santa Fé aux sept* [huit] *Français par le Général Hurtado, 24 Juillet, 1739. Père Rébald au Père de Beaubois, sans date. Bienville et Salmon au Ministre, 30 Avril, 1741,* in Margry, VI. 455–468.

[2] *Instructions données par Jean-Baptiste de Bienville à Fabry de la Bruyère, 1 Juin, 1741.* Bienville was behind his time in geographical knowledge. As early as 1724 Bénard de la Harpe knew that in ascending the Missouri or the Arkansas one was moving towards the "Western Sea,"—that is, the Pacific,—and might, perhaps, find some river flowing into it. See *Routes qu'on peut tenir pour se rendre à la Mer de l'Ouest,* in *Journal historique,* 387.

[3] *Extrait des Lettres du Sieur Fabry.*

Chapter XVI

SEARCH FOR THE PACIFIC

The Western Sea • Schemes for reaching it • Journey of Charlevoix • The Sioux Mission • Varennes de la Vérendrye • His Enterprise • His Disasters • Visits the Mandans • His Sons • Their Search for the Western Sea • Their Adventures • The Snake Indians • A great War-Party • The Rocky Mountains • A Panic • Return of the Brothers • Their Wrongs and their Fate

---

IN THE DISASTROUS last years of Louis XIV. the court gave little thought to the New World; but under the regency of the Duke of Orléans interest in American affairs revived. Plans for reaching the Mer de l'Ouest, or Pacific Ocean, were laid before the Regent in 1716. It was urged that the best hope was in sending an expedition across the continent, seeing that every attempt to find a westward passage by Hudson Bay had failed. As starting-points and bases of supply for the expedition, it was proposed to establish three posts, one on the north shore of Lake Superior, at the mouth of the river Kaministiguia, another at Lac des Cristineaux, now called Lake of the Woods, and the third at Lake Winnipeg,—the last being what in American phrase is called the "jumping-off place," or the point where the expedition was to leave behind the last trace of civilization. These posts were to cost the Crown nothing; since by a device common in such cases, those who built and maintained them were to be paid by a monopoly of the fur-trade in the adjacent countries. It was admitted, however, that the subsequent exploration must be at the charge of the government, and would require fifty good men, at 300 francs a year each, besides equipment and supplies. All things considered, it was reckoned that an overland way to the Pacific might be found for about 50,000 francs, or 10,000 dollars.[1]

The Regent approved the scheme so far as to order the

---

[1] *Mémoire fait et arresté par le Conseil de Marine, 3 Fév. 1717; Mémoire du Roy, 26 Juin, 1717.*

preliminary step to be taken by establishing the three posts, and in this same year, Lieutenant La Noue, of the colony troops, began the work by building a stockade at the mouth of the Kaministiguia. Little more was done in furtherance of the exploration till three years later, when the celebrated Jesuit, Charlevoix, was ordered by the Duke of Orléans to repair to America and gain all possible information concerning the Western Sea and the way to it.[1]

In the next year he went to the Upper Lakes, and questioned missionaries, officers, *voyageurs*, and Indians. The results were not satisfactory. The missionaries and the officers had nothing to tell; the voyagers and Indians knew no more than they, but invented confused and contradictory falsehoods to hide their ignorance. Charlevoix made note of everything, and reported to the Comte de Toulouse that the Pacific probably formed the western boundary of the country of the Sioux, and that some Indians told him that they had been to its shores and found white men there different from the French.

Believing that these stories were not without foundation, Charlevoix reported two plans as likely to lead to the coveted discovery. One was to ascend the Missouri, "the source of which is certainly not far from the sea, as all the Indians I have met have unanimously assured me;" and the other was to establish a mission among the Sioux, from whom after thoroughly learning their language, the missionaries could, as he thinks, gain all the desired information.[2]

The Regent approved the plan of the mission; but the hostile disposition of the Sioux and the Outagamies prevented its execution for several years. In 1727 the scheme was revived, and the colonial minister at Versailles ordered the Governor of Canada to send two missionaries to the Sioux. But the mission required money, and the King would not give it. Hence the usual expedient was adopted. A company was

[1] *Charlevoix au Comte de Morville, 1 Avril, 1723.*

[2] The valuable journal of Charlevoix's western travels, written in the form of letters, was published in connection with his *Histoire de la Nouvelle France*. After his visit to the Lakes, he went to New Orleans, intending to return in the spring and continue his inquiries for the Western Sea; but being unable to do this, he went back to France at the end of 1722. The official report of his mission is contained in a letter to the Comte de Toulouse, 20 Jan. 1723.

formed, and invested with a monopoly of the Sioux fur-trade, on condition of building a fort, mission-house, and chapel, and keeping an armed force to guard them. It was specially provided that none but pious and virtuous persons were to be allowed to join the Company, "in order," says the document, "to attract the benediction of God upon them and their business."[1] The prospects of the Company were thought good, and the Governor himself was one of the shareholders. While the mission was given the most conspicuous place in the enterprise, its objects were rather secular than spiritual,— to attach the Sioux to the French interest by the double ties of religion and trade, and utilize their supposed knowledge to reach the Pacific.[2]

Father Guignas was made the head of the mission, and Boucher de la Perrière the military chief. The party left Montreal in June, and journeying to the Mississippi by way of Michillimackinac, Green Bay, Fox River, and the Wisconsin, went up the great river to Lake Pepin, where the adventurous Nicolas Perrot had built two trading-posts more than forty years before. Even if his time-worn tenements were still standing, La Perrière had no thought of occupying them. On the north, or rather west, side of the lake his men found a point of land that seemed fit for their purpose, disembarked, cut down trees, and made a square stockade enclosing the necessary buildings. It was near the end of October before they were all well housed. A large band of Sioux presently appeared, and set up their teepees hard by. When the birthday of the Governor came, the party celebrated it with a display of fireworks and vociferous shouts of *Vive le Roi, Vive Charles de Beauharnois*, while the Indians yelped in fright and amazement at the pyrotechnics, or stood pressing their hands upon their mouths in silent amazement. The French called their fort Fort Beauharnois, and invited the aid of Saint Michael the Archangel by naming the mission in his honor. All went well till April, when the water rose with the spring floods and filled fort, chapel, and houses to the depth of nearly three feet,

[1] *Traité de la Compagnie des Sioux, 6 Juin, 1727.*

[2] On this scheme, *Vaudreuil et Bégon au Ministre, 4 Oct. 1723*; *Longueuil et Bégon au Ministre, 31 Oct. 1725*; *Beauharnois et Dupuy au Ministre, 25 Sept. 1727.*

ejecting the whole party, and forcing them to encamp on higher ground till the deluge subsided.[1]

Worse enemies than the floods soon found them out. These were the irrepressible Outagamies, who rose against the intruding French and incited the Sioux to join them. There was no profit for the Company, and no safety for its agents. The stockholders became discouraged, and would not support the enterprise. The fort was abandoned, till in 1731 a new arrangement was made, followed by another attempt.[2] For a time a prosperous trade was carried on; but, as commonly happened in such cases, the adventurers seem to have thought more of utilizing their monopoly than of fulfilling the terms on which they had received it. The wild Sioux of the plains, instead of being converted and turned into Frenchmen, proved such dangerous neighbors that in 1737 Legardeur de Saint-Pierre, who then commanded the post, found himself forced to abandon it.[3] The enterprise had failed in both its aims. The Western Sea was still a mystery, and the Sioux were not friends, but enemies. Legardeur de Saint-Pierre recommended that they should be destroyed,—benevolent advice easy to give, and impossible to execute.[4]

René Gaultier de Varennes, lieutenant in the regiment of Carignan, married at Three Rivers, in 1667, the daughter of Pierre Boucher, governor of that place; the age of the bride, Demoiselle Marie Boucher, being twelve years, six months, and eighteen days. Varennes succeeded his father-in-law as governor of Three Rivers, with a salary of twelve hundred francs, to which he added the profits of a farm of forty acres; and on these modest resources, reinforced by an illicit trade in furs, he made shift to sustain the dignity of his office. His wife became the mother of numerous offspring, among whom was Pierre, born in 1685,—an active and hardy youth, who, like the rest of the poor but vigorous Canadian *noblesse*, seemed born for the forest and the fur-trade. When, however, the War of the Spanish Succession broke out, the young man

---

[1] *Guignas à Beauharnois, 28 Mai, 1728.*

[2] *Beauharnois et Hocquart au Ministre, 25 Oct. 1729; Idem, 12 Oct. 1731.*

[3] *Relation du Sieur de Saint-Pierre, 14 Oct. 1737.*

[4] "Cet officier [Saint-Pierre] a ajouté qu'il seroit avantageux de detruire cette nation." *Mémoire de Beauharnois, 1738.*

crossed the sea, obtained the commission of lieutenant, and was nearly killed at the battle of Malplaquet, where he was shot through the body, received six sabre-cuts, and was left for dead on the field. He recovered, and returned to Canada, when, finding his services slighted, he again took to the woods. He had assumed the designation of La Vérendrye, and thenceforth his full name was Pierre Gaultier de Varennes de la Vérendrye.[1]

In 1728, he was in command of a small post on Lake Nipegon, north of Lake Superior. Here an Indian chief from the River Kaministiguia told him of a certain great lake which discharged itself by a river flowing westward. The Indian further declared that he had descended this river till he reached water that ebbed and flowed, and terrified by the strange phenomenon, had turned back, though not till he had heard of a great salt lake, bordered with many villages. Other Indians confirmed and improved the story. "These people," said La Vérendrye to the Jesuit Degonnor, "are great liars, but now and then they tell the truth."[2] It seemed to him likely that their stories of a western river flowing to a western sea were not totally groundless, and that the true way to the Pacific was not, as had been supposed, through the country of the Sioux, but farther northward, through that of the Cristineaux and Assinniboins, or, in other words, through the region now called Manitoba. In this view he was sustained by his friend Degonnor, who had just returned from the ill-starred Sioux mission.

La Vérendrye, fired with the zeal of discovery, offered to search for the Western Sea if the King would give him one hundred men and supply canoes, arms, and provisions.[3] But, as was usual in such cases, the King would give nothing; and though the Governor, Beauharnois, did all in his power to promote the enterprise, the burden and the risk were left to

[1] M. Benjamin Sulte has traced out the family history of the Varennes in the parish registers of Three Rivers and other trustworthy sources. See *Revue Canadienne*, X. 781, 849, 935.

[2] *Relation du Père Degonnor, Jésuite, Missionnaire des Sioux, adressée à M. le Marquis de Beauharnois.*

[3] *Relation de Degonnor; Beauharnois au Ministre, 1 Oct. 1731.*

the adventurer himself. La Vérendrye was authorized to find a way to the Pacific at his own expense, in consideration of a monopoly of the fur-trade in the regions north and west of Lake Superior. This vast and remote country was held by tribes who were doubtful friends of the French, and perpetual enemies of each other. The risks of the trade were as great as its possible profits, and to reap these, vast outlays must first be made: forts must be built, manned, provisioned, and stocked with goods brought through two thousand miles of difficult and perilous wilderness. There were other dangers, more insidious, and perhaps greater. The exclusive privileges granted to La Vérendrye would inevitably rouse the intensest jealousy of the Canadian merchants, and they would spare no effort to ruin him. Intrigue and calumny would be busy in his absence. If, as was likely, his patron, Beauharnois, should be recalled, the new governor might be turned against him, his privileges might be suddenly revoked, the forts he had built passed over to his rivals, and all his outlays turned to their profit, as had happened to La Salle on the recall of his patron, Frontenac. On the other hand, the country was full of the choicest furs, which the Indians had hitherto carried to the English at Hudson Bay, but which the proposed trading-posts would secure to the French. La Vérendrye's enemies pretended that he thought of nothing but beaver-skins, and slighted the discovery which he had bound himself to undertake; but his conduct proves that he was true to his engagements, and that ambition to gain honorable distinction in the service of the King had a large place among the motives that impelled him.

As his own resources were of the smallest, he took a number of associates on conditions most unfavorable to himself. Among them they raised money enough to begin the enterprise, and on the 8th of June, 1731, La Vérendrye and three of his sons, together with his nephew, La Jemeraye, the Jesuit Messager, and a party of Canadians, set out from Montreal. It was late in August before they reached the great portage of Lake Superior, which led across the height of land separating the waters of that lake from those flowing to Lake Winnipeg. The way was long and difficult. The men, who had perhaps been tampered with, mutinied, and refused to go farther.[1] Some of them, with much ado, consented at last to proceed, and, under the lead of La Jemeraye, made their way by an intricate and broken chain of lakes and streams to Rainy Lake, where they built a fort and called it Fort St. Pierre. La Vérendrye was forced to winter with the rest of the party at the river Kaministiguia, not far from the great portage. Here months were lost, during which a crew of useless mutineers had to be fed and paid; and it was not till the next June that he could get them again into motion towards Lake Winnipeg.

This ominous beginning was followed by a train of disasters. His associates abandoned him; the merchants on whom he depended for supplies would not send them, and he found himself, in his own words "destitute of everything." His nephew, La Jemeraye, died. The Jesuit Auneau, bent on returning to Michillimackinac, set out with La Vérendrye's eldest son and a party of twenty Canadians. A few days later, they were all found on an island in the Lake of the Woods, murdered and mangled by the Sioux.[2] The Assinniboins and Cristineaux, mortal foes of that fierce people, offered to join the French and avenge the butchery; but a war with the Sioux would have ruined La Vérendrye's plans of discovery, and exposed to torture and death the French traders in their country. Therefore he restrained himself and declined the proffered aid, at the risk of incurring the contempt of those who offered it.

Beauharnois twice appealed to the court to give La Vérendrye some little aid, urging that he was at the end of his resources, and that a grant of 30,000 francs, or 6,000 dollars, would enable him to find a way to the Pacific. All help was refused, but La Vérendrye was told that he might let out his forts to other traders, and so raise means to pursue the discovery.

In 1740 he went for the third time to Montreal, where, instead of aid, he found a lawsuit. "In spite," he says, "of the

---

[1] *Mémoire du Sieur de la Vérendrye du Sujet des Etablissements pour parvenir à la Découverte de la Mer de l'Ouest*, in Margry, VI. 585.

[2] *Beauharnois au Ministre, 14 Oct. 1736; Relation du Massacre au Lac des Bois, en Juin, 1736; Journal de la Vérendrye, joint à la lettre de M. de Beauharnois du — Oct. 1737.*

derangement of my affairs, the envy and jealousy of various persons impelled them to write letters to the court insinuating that I thought of nothing but making my fortune. If more than forty thousand livres of debt which I have on my shoulders are an advantage, then I can flatter myself that I am very rich. In all my misfortunes, I have the consolation of seeing that M. de Beauharnois enters into my views, recognizes the uprightness of my intentions, and does me justice in spite of opposition."[1]

Meanwhile, under all his difficulties, he had explored a vast region hitherto unknown, diverted a great and lucrative fur-trade from the English at Hudson Bay, and secured possession of it by six fortified posts,—Fort St. Pierre, on Rainy Lake; Fort St. Charles, on the Lake of the Woods; Fort Maurepas, at the mouth of the river Winnipeg; Fort Bourbon, on the eastern side of Lake Winnipeg; Fort La Reine, on the Assinniboin; Fort Dauphin, on Lake Manitoba. Besides these he built another post, called Fort Rouge, on the site of the city of Winnipeg; and, some time after, another, at the mouth of the River Poskoiac, or Saskatchawan, neither of which, however, was long occupied. These various forts were only stockade works flanked with block-houses; but the difficulty of building and maintaining them in this remote wilderness was incalculable.[2]

He had inquired on all sides for the Pacific. The Assinniboins could tell him nothing. Nor could any information be expected from them, since their relatives and mortal enemies, the Sioux, barred their way to the West. The Cristineaux were equally ignorant; but they supplied the place of knowledge by invention, and drew maps, some of which seem to have been made with no other intention than that of amusing them-

[1] *Mémoire du Sieur de la Vérendrye au sujet des Etablissements pour parvenir à la Découverte de la Mer de l'Ouest.*

[2] *Mémoire en abrégé de la Carte qui représente les Etablissements faits par le Sieur de la Vérendrye et ses Enfants* (Margry, VI. 616); *Carte des Nouvelles Découvertes dans l'Ouest du Canada dressée sur les Mémoires de M. de la Vérandrie et donnée au Dépôt de la Marine par M. de la Galissonnière, 1750;* Bellin, *Remarques sur la Carte de l'Amérique, 1755;* Bougainville, *Mémoire sur l'Etat de la Nouvelle France, 1757.*

Most of La Vérendrye's forts were standing during the Seven Years' War, and were known collectively as *Postes de la Mer de l'Ouest.*

selves by imposing on the inquirer. They also declared that some of their number had gone down a river called White River, or River of the West, where they found a plant that shed drops like blood, and saw serpents of prodigious size. They said further that on the lower part of this river were walled towns, where dwelt white men who had knives, hatchets, and cloth, but no firearms.[1]

Both Assinniboins and Cristineaux declared that there was a distant tribe on the Missouri, called Mantannes (Mandans), who knew the way to the Western Sea, and would guide him to it. Lured by this assurance, and feeling that he had sufficiently secured his position to enable him to begin his Western exploration, La Vérendrye left Fort La Reine in October, 1738, with twenty men, and pushed up the River Assinniboin till its rapids and shallows threatened his bark canoes with destruction. Then, with a band of Assinniboin Indians who had joined him, he struck across the prairie for the Mandans, his Indian companions hunting buffalo on the way. They approached the first Mandan village on the afternoon of the 3d of December, displaying a French flag and firing three volleys as a salute. The whole population poured out to see the marvellous visitors, who were conducted through the staring crowd to the lodge of the principal chief,—a capacious structure so thronged with the naked and greasy savages that the Frenchmen were half smothered. What was worse, they lost the bag that held all their presents for the Mandans, which was snatched away in the confusion, and hidden in one of the *caches*, called cellars by La Vérendrye, of which the place was full. The chief seemed much discomposed at this mishap, and explained it by saying that there were many rascals in the village. The loss was serious, since without the presents nothing could be done. Nor was this all; for in the morning La Vérendrye missed his interpreter, and was told that he had fallen in love with an Assinniboin girl and gone off in pursuit of her. The French were now without any means of communicating with the Mandans, from whom, however, before the disappearance of the interpreter, they had already received a variety of questionable information, chiefly touching white men

[1] *Journal de la Vérendrye joint à la Lettre de M. de Beauharnois du —* *Oct. 1737.*

cased in iron who were said to live on the river below at the distance of a whole summer's journey. As they were impervious to arrows,—so the story ran,—it was necessary to shoot their horses, after which, being too heavy to run, they were easily caught. This was probably suggested by the armor of the Spaniards, who had more than once made incursions as far as the lower Missouri; but the narrators drew on their imagination for various additional particulars.

The Mandans seem to have much declined in numbers during the century that followed this visit of La Vérendrye. He says that they had six villages on or near the Missouri, of which the one seen by him was the smallest, though he thinks that it contained a hundred and thirty houses.[1] As each of these large structures held a number of families, the population must have been considerable. Yet when Prince Maximilian visited the Mandans in 1833, he found only two villages, containing jointly two hundred and forty warriors and a total population of about a thousand souls. Without having seen the statements of La Vérendrye, he speaks of the population as greatly reduced by wars and the small-pox,—a disease which a few years later nearly exterminated the tribe.[2]

La Vérendrye represents the six villages as surrounded with ditches and stockades, flanked by a sort of bastion,—defences which, he says, had nothing savage in their construction. In later times the fortifications were of a much ruder kind, though Maximilian represents them as having pointed salients to serve as bastions. La Vérendrye mentions some peculiar customs of the Mandans which answer exactly to those described by more recent observers.

[1] *Journal de la Vérendrye, 1738, 1739.* This journal, which is ill-written and sometimes obscure, is printed in Brymner, *Report on Canadian Archives, 1889.*

[2] Le Prince Maximilien de Wied-Neuwied, *Voyage dans l'Intérieur de l'Amérique du Nord*, II. 371, 372 (Paris, 1843). When Captains Lewis and Clark visited the Mandans in 1804, they found them in two villages, with about three hundred and fifty warriors. They report that, about forty years before, they lived in nine villages, the ruins of which the explorers saw about eighty miles below the two villages then occupied by the tribe. The Mandans had moved up the river in consequence of the persecutions of the Sioux and the small-pox, which had made great havoc among them. *Expedition of Lewis and Clark*, I. 129 (ed. Philadelphia, 1814). These nine villages seem to have been above Cannon-ball River, a tributary of the Missouri.

He had intended to winter with the tribe; but the loss of the presents and the interpreter made it useless to stay, and leaving two men in the village to learn the language, he began his return to Fort La Reine. "I was very ill," he writes, "but hoped to get better on the way. The reverse was the case, for it was the depth of winter. It would be impossible to suffer more than I did. It seemed that nothing but death could release us from such miseries." He reached Fort La Reine on the 11th of February, 1739.

His iron constitution seems to have been severely shaken; but he had sons worthy of their father. The two men left among the Mandans appeared at Fort La Reine in September. They reported that they had been well treated, and that their hosts had parted from them with regret. They also declared that at the end of spring several Indian tribes, all well supplied with horses, had come, as was their yearly custom, to the Mandan villages to barter embroidered buffalo hides and other skins for corn and beans; that they had encamped, to the number of two hundred lodges, on the farther side of the Missouri, and that among them was a band said to have come from a distant country towards the sunset, where there were white men who lived in houses built of bricks and stones.

The two Frenchmen crossed over to the camp of these Western strangers, among whom they found a chief who spoke, or professed to speak, the language of the mysterious white men, which to the two Frenchmen was unintelligible. Fortunately, he also spoke the language of the Mandans, of which the Frenchmen had learned a little during their stay, and hence were able to gather that the white men in question had beards, and that they prayed to the Master of Life in great houses, built for the purpose, holding books, the leaves of which were like husks of Indian corn, singing together and repeating *Jésus, Marie*. The chief gave many other particulars, which seemed to show that he had been in contact with Spaniards,—probably those of California; for he described their houses as standing near the great lake, of which the water rises and falls and is not fit to drink. He invited the two Frenchmen to go with him to this strange country, saying that it could be reached before winter, though a wide circuit must be made, to avoid a fierce and dangerous tribe called Snake Indians (*Gens du Serpent*).[1]

On hearing this story, La Vérendrye sent his eldest son, Pierre, to pursue the discovery with two men, ordering him to hire guides among the Mandans and make his way to the Western Sea. But no guides were to be found, and in the next summer the young man returned from his bootless errand.[2]

Undaunted by this failure, Pierre set out again in the next spring, 1742, with his younger brother, the Chevalier de la Vérendrye. Accompanied only by two Canadians, they left Fort La Reine on the 29th of April, and following, no doubt, the route of the Assinniboin and Mouse River, reached the chief village of the Mandans in about three weeks.

Here they found themselves the welcome guests of this singularly interesting tribe, ruined by the small-pox nearly half a century ago, but preserved to memory by the skilful pencil of the artist Charles Bodmer, and the brush of the painter George Catlin, both of whom saw them at a time when they were little changed in habits and manners since the visit of the brothers La Vérendrye.[3]

Thus, though the report of the two brothers is too concise and brief, we know what they saw when they entered the central area, or public square, of the village. Around stood the Mandan lodges, looking like round flattened hillocks of earth, forty or fifty feet wide. On examination they proved to be framed of strong posts and poles, covered with a thick matting of intertwined willow-branches, over which was laid a bed of well-compacted clay or earth two or three feet thick.

[1] *Journal du Sieur de la Vérendrye, 1740*, in Archives de la Marine.
[2] *Mémoire du Sieur de la Vérendrye, joint à sa lettre du 31 Oct. 1744.*
[3] Prince Maximilian spent the winter of 1832–33 near the Mandan villages. His artist, with the instinct of genius, seized the characteristics of the wild life before him, and rendered them with admirable vigor and truth. Catlin spent a considerable time among the Mandans soon after the visit of Prince Maximilian, and had unusual opportunities of studying them. He was an indifferent painter, a shallow observer, and a garrulous and windy writer; yet his enthusiastic industry is beyond praise, and his pictures are invaluable as faithful reflections of aspects of Indian life which are gone forever.

Beauharnois calls the Mandans *Blancs Barbus*, and says that they have been hitherto unknown. *Beauharnois au Ministre, 14 Août, 1739.* The name Mantannes, or Mandans, is that given them by the Assinniboins.

This heavy roof was supported by strong interior posts.[1] The open place which the dwellings enclosed served for games, dances, and the ghastly religious or magical ceremonies practised by the tribe. Among the other structures was the sacred "medicine lodge," distinguished by three or four tall poles planted before it, each surmounted by an effigy looking much like a scarecrow, and meant as an offering to the spirits.

If the two travellers had been less sparing of words, they would doubtless have told us that as they entered the village square the flattened earthen domes that surrounded it were thronged with squaws and children,—for this was always the case on occasions of public interest,—and that they were forced to undergo a merciless series of feasts in the lodges of the chiefs. Here, seated by the sunken hearth in the middle, under the large hole in the roof that served both for window and chimney, they could study at their ease the domestic economy of their entertainers. Each lodge held a *gens*, or family connection, whose beds of raw buffalo hide, stretched on poles, were ranged around the circumference of the building, while by each stood a post on which hung shields, lances, bows, quivers, medicine-bags, and masks formed of the skin of a buffalo's head, with the horns attached, to be used in the magic buffalo dance.

Every day had its sports to relieve the monotony of savage existence, the game of the stick and the rolling ring, the archery practice of boys, horse-racing on the neighboring prairie, and incessant games of chance; while every evening, in contrast to these gayeties, the long, dismal wail of women rose from the adjacent cemetery, where the dead of the village, sewn fast in buffalo hides, lay on scaffolds above the reach of wolves.

The Mandans did not know the way to the Pacific, but they told the brothers that they expected a speedy visit from a tribe or band called Horse Indians, who could guide them thither. It is impossible to identify this people with any certainty.[2]

[1] The Minnetarees and other tribes of the Missouri built their lodges in a similar way.

[2] The Cheyennes have a tradition that they were the first tribe of this region to have horses. This may perhaps justify a conjecture that the northern division of this brave and warlike people were the Horse Indians of La Vérendrye; though an Indian tradition, unless backed by well-established facts, can never be accepted as substantial evidence.

The two travellers waited for them in vain till after midsummer, and then, as the season was too far advanced for longer delay, they hired two Mandans to conduct them to their customary haunts.

They set out on horseback, their scanty baggage and their stock of presents being no doubt carried by pack-animals. Their general course was west-southwest, with the Black Hills at a distance on their left, and the upper Missouri on their right. The country was a rolling prairie, well covered for the most part with grass, and watered by small alkaline streams creeping towards the Missouri with an opaque, whitish current. Except along the watercourses, there was little or no wood. "I noticed," says the Chevalier de la Vérendrye, "earths of different colors, blue, green, red, or black, white as chalk, or yellowish like ochre." This was probably in the "bad lands" of the Little Missouri, where these colored earths form a conspicuous feature in the bare and barren bluffs, carved into fantastic shapes by the storms.[1]

For twenty days the travellers saw no human being, so scanty was the population of these plains. Game, however, was abundant. Deer sprang from the tall, reedy grass of the river bottoms; buffalo tramped by in ponderous columns, or dotted the swells of the distant prairie with their grazing thousands; antelope approached, with the curiosity of their species, to gaze at the passing horsemen, then fled like the wind; and as they neared the broken uplands towards the Yellowstone, they saw troops of elk and flocks of mountain-sheep. Sometimes, for miles together, the dry plain was studded thick with the earthen mounds that marked the burrows of the curious marmots, called prairie-dogs, from their squeaking bark. Wolves, white and gray, howled about the camp at night, and their cousin, the coyote, seated in the dusk of evening upright on the grass, with nose turned to the sky, saluted them with a complication of yelpings, as if a score of petulant voices were pouring together from the throat of one small beast.

On the 11th of August, after a march of about three weeks, the brothers reached a hill, or group of hills, apparently west of the Little Missouri, and perhaps a part of the Powder

[1] A similar phenomenon occurs farther west on the face of the perpendicular bluffs that, in one place, border the valley of the river Rosebud.

River Range. It was here that they hoped to find the Horse Indians, but nobody was to be seen. Arming themselves with patience, they built a hut, made fires to attract by the smoke any Indians roaming near, and went every day to the tops of the hills to reconnoitre. At length, on the 14th of September, they descried a spire of smoke on the distant prairie.

One of their Mandan guides had left them and gone back to his village. The other, with one of the Frenchmen, went towards the smoke, and found a camp of Indians, whom the journal calls Les Beaux Hommes, and who were probably Crows, or Apsaroka, a tribe remarkable for stature and symmetry, who long claimed that region as their own. They treated the visitors well, and sent for the other Frenchmen to come to their lodges, where they were received with great rejoicing. The remaining Mandan, however, became frightened, —for the Beaux Hommes were enemies of his tribe,—and he soon followed his companion on his solitary march homeward.

The brothers remained twenty-one days in the camp of the Beaux Hommes, much perplexed for want of an interpreter. The tribes of the plains have in common a system of signs by which they communicate with each other, and it is likely that the brothers had learned it from the Sioux or Assinniboins, with whom they had been in familiar intercourse. By this or some other means they made their hosts understand that they wished to find the Horse Indians; and the Beaux Hommes, being soothed by presents, offered some of their young men as guides. They set out on the 9th of October, following a south-southwest course.[1]

In two days they met a band of Indians, called by them the Little Foxes, and on the 15th and 17th two villages of another unrecognizable horde, named Pioya. From La Vérendrye's time to our own, this name "villages" has always been given to the encampments of the wandering people of the plains. All these nomadic communities joined them, and they moved together southward, till they reached at last the lodges of the

---

[1] *Journal du Voyage fait par le Chevalier de la Vérendrye en 1742.* The copy before me is from the original in the Dépôt des Cartes de la Marine. A duplicate, in the Archives des Affaires Etrangères, is printed by Margry. It gives the above date as November 9th instead of October 9th. The context shows the latter to be correct.

long-sought Horse Indians. They found them in the extremity of distress and terror. Their camp resounded with howls and wailings; and not without cause, for the Snakes, or Shoshones,—a formidable people living farther westward,—had lately destroyed most of their tribe. The Snakes were the terror of that country. The brothers were told that the year before they had destroyed seventeen villages, killing the warriors and old women, and carrying off the young women and children as slaves.

None of the Horse Indians had ever seen the Pacific; but they knew a people called Gens de l'Arc, or Bow Indians, who, as they said, had traded not far from it. To the Bow Indians, therefore, the brothers resolved to go, and by dint of gifts and promises they persuaded their hosts to show them the way. After marching southwestward for several days, they saw the distant prairie covered with the pointed buffalo-skin lodges of a great Indian camp. It was that of the Bow Indians, who may have been one of the bands of the western Sioux,—the predominant race in this region. Few or none of them could ever have seen a white man, and we may imagine their amazement at the arrival of the strangers, who, followed by staring crowds, were conducted to the lodge of the chief. "Thus far," says La Vérendrye, "we had been well received in all the villages we had passed; but this was nothing compared with the courteous manners of the great chief of the Bow Indians, who, unlike the others, was not self-interested in the least, and who took excellent care of everything belonging to us."

The first inquiry of the travellers was for the Pacific; but neither the chief nor his tribesmen knew anything of it, except what they had heard from Snake prisoners taken in war. The Frenchmen were surprised at the extent of the camp, which consisted of many separate bands. The chief explained that they had been summoned from far and near for a grand war-party against that common foe of all,—the Snakes.[1] In

[1]The enmity between the Sioux and the Snakes lasted to our own time. When the writer lived among the western Sioux, one of their chiefs organized a war-party against the Snakes, and numerous bands came to join the expedition from a distance in some cases of three hundred miles. Quarrels broke out among them, and the scheme was ruined.

fact, the camp resounded with war-songs and war-dances. "Come with us," said their host; "we are going towards the mountains, where you can see the great water that you are looking for."

At length the camp broke up. The squaws took down the lodges, and the march began over prairies dreary and brown with the withering touch of autumn. The spectacle was such as men still young have seen in these Western lands, but which no man will see again. The vast plain swarmed with the moving multitude. The tribes of the Missouri and the Yellowstone had by this time abundance of horses, the best of which were used for war and hunting, and the others as beasts of burden. These last were equipped in a peculiar manner. Several of the long poles used to frame the teepees, or lodges, were secured by one end to each side of a rude saddle, while the other end trailed on the ground. Crossbars lashed to the poles just behind the horse kept them three or four feet apart, and formed a firm support, on which was laid, compactly folded, the buffalo-skin covering of the lodge. On this, again, sat a mother with her young family, sometimes stowed for safety in a large open willow basket, with the occasional addition of some domestic pet,—such as a tame raven, a puppy, or even a small bear cub. Other horses were laden in the same manner with wooden bowls, stone hammers, and other utensils, along with stores of dried buffalo-meat packed in cases of rawhide whitened and painted. Many of the innumerable dogs—whose manners and appearance strongly suggested their relatives the wolves, to whom, however, they bore a mortal grudge—were equipped in a similar way, with shorter poles and lighter loads. Bands of naked boys, noisy and restless, roamed the prairie, practising their bows and arrows on any small animal they might find. Gay young squaws—adorned on each cheek with a spot of ochre or red clay, and arrayed in tunics of fringed buckskin embroidered with porcupine quills—were mounted on ponies, astride like men; while lean and tattered hags—the drudges of the tribe, unkempt and hideous—scolded the lagging horses, or screeched at the disorderly dogs, with voices not unlike the yell of the great horned owl. Most of the warriors were on horseback, armed with round, white shields of bull-hide, feathered lances, war-clubs, bows, and quivers filled with stone-headed arrows; while a few of the elders, wrapped in robes of buffalo-hide, stalked along in groups with a stately air, chatting, laughing, and exchanging unseemly jokes.[1]

"We continued our march," says La Vérendrye, "sometimes south-southwest, and now and then northwest; our numbers constantly increasing by villages of different tribes which joined us." The variations of their course were probably due to the difficulties of the country, which grew more rugged as they advanced, with broken hills, tracts of dingy green sage-bushes, and bright, swift streams, edged with cottonwood and willow, hurrying northward to join the Yellowstone. At length, on the 1st of January, 1743, they saw what was probably the Bighorn Range of the Rocky Mountains, a hundred and twenty miles east of the Yellowstone Park.

A council of all the allied bands was now called, and the Frenchmen were asked to take part in it. The questions discussed were how to dispose of the women and children, and how to attack the enemy. Having settled their plans, the chiefs begged their white friends not to abandon them; and the younger of the two, the Chevalier, consented to join the warriors, and aid them with advice, though not with arms.

The tribes of the Western plains rarely go on war-parties in winter, and this great expedition must have been the result of unusual exasperation. The object was to surprise the Snakes in the security of their winter camp, and strike a deadly blow, which would have been impossible in summer.

On the 8th of January the whole body stopped to encamp, choosing, no doubt, after the invariable winter custom of Western Indians, a place sheltered from wind, and supplied with water and fuel. Here the squaws and children were to remain, while most of the warriors advanced against the enemy. By pegging the lower edge of the lodge-skin to the ground, and piling a ridge of stones and earth upon it to keep out the air, fastening with wooden skewers the flap of hide that covered the entrance, and keeping a constant fire, they

[1] The above descriptive particulars are drawn from repeated observation of similar scenes at a time when the primitive condition of these tribes was essentially unchanged, though with the difference that the concourse of savages counted by hundreds, and not by thousands.

could pass a winter endurable to Indians, though smoke, filth, vermin, bad air, the crowd, and the total absence of privacy, would make it a purgatory to any civilized white man.

The Chevalier left his brother to watch over the baggage of the party, which was stored in the lodge of the great chief, while he himself, with his two Canadians, joined the advancing warriors. They were on horseback, marching with a certain order, and sending watchmen to reconnoitre the country from the tops of the hills.[1] Their movements were so slow that it was twelve days before they reached the foot of the mountains, which, says La Vérendrye, "are for the most part well wooded, and seem very high."[2] He longed to climb their great snow-encumbered peaks, fancying that he might then see the Pacific, and never dreaming that more than eight hundred miles of mountains and forests still lay between him and his goal.

Through the whole of the present century the villages of the Snakes were at a considerable distance west of the Bighorn Range, and some of them were even on the upper waters of the Pacific slope. It is likely that they were so in 1743, in which case the war-party would not only have reached the Bighorn Mountains, but have pushed farther on to within sight of the great Wind River Range. Be this as it may, their scouts reached the chief winter camp of the Snakes, and found it abandoned, with lodges still standing, and many household possessions left behind. The enemy had discovered their approach, and fled. Instead of encouraging the allies, this news filled them with terror, for they feared that the Snake warriors might make a circuit to the rear, and fall upon the camp where they had left their women and children. The great chief spent all his eloquence in vain, nobody would listen to him; and with characteristic fickleness they gave over the enterprise, and retreated in a panic. "Our advance was made in good order; but not so our retreat," says the Chevalier's journal. "Everybody fled his own way. Our horses,

---

[1] At least this was done by a band of Sioux with whom the writer once traversed a part of the country ranged by these same Snakes, who had lately destroyed an entire Sioux village.

[2] The Bighorn Range, below the snow line, is in the main well timbered with pine, fir, oak, and juniper.

though good, were very tired, and got little to eat." The Chevalier was one day riding with his friend, the great chief, when, looking behind him, he missed his two French attendants. Hastening back in alarm, he found them far in the rear, quietly feeding their horses under the shelter of a clump of trees. He had scarcely joined them when he saw a party of fifteen hostile Indians stealthily creeping forward, covered by their bull-hide shields. He and his men let them approach, and then gave them a few shots; on which they immediately ran off, firearms being to them an astounding novelty.

The three Frenchmen now tried to rejoin the great chief and his band, but the task was not easy. The prairie, bare of snow and hard as flint, showed no trace of foot or hoof; and it was by rare good fortune that they succeeded, on the second day, not in overtaking the chief, but in reaching the camp where the women and children had been left. They found them all in safety; the Snakes had not attacked them, and the panic of the warriors was needless. It was the 9th of February. They were scarcely housed when a blizzard set in, and on the night of the 10th the plains were buried in snow. The great chief had not appeared. With such of his warriors as he could persuade to follow him, he had made a wide circuit to find the trail of the lost Frenchmen, but, to his great distress, had completely failed. It was not till five days after the arrival of the Chevalier and his men that the chief reached the camp, "more dead than alive," in the words of the journal. All his hardships were forgotten when he found his white friends safe, for he had given them up for lost. "His sorrow turned to joy, and he could not give us attention and caresses enough."

The camp broke up, and the allied bands dispersed. The great chief and his followers moved slowly through the snowdrifts towards the east-southeast, accompanied by the Frenchmen. Thus they kept on till the 1st of March, when the two brothers, learning that they were approaching the winter village of a people called Gens de la Petite Cerise, or Choke-Cherry Indians, sent one of their men, with a guide, to visit them. The man returned in ten days, bringing a message from the Choke-Cherry Indians, inviting the Frenchmen to their lodges.

The great chief of the Bow Indians, who seems to have regarded his young friends with mingled affection, respect, and wonder, was grieved at the thought of losing them, but took comfort when they promised to visit him again, provided that he would make his abode near a certain river which they pointed out. To this he readily agreed, and then, with mutual regret, they parted.[1] The Frenchmen repaired to the village of the Choke-Cherry Indians, who, like the Bow Indians, were probably a band of Sioux.[2] Hard by their lodges, which stood near the Missouri, the brothers buried a plate of lead graven with the royal arms, and raised a pile of stones in honor of the Governor of Canada. They remained at this place till April; then, mounting their horses again, followed the Missouri upward to the village of the Mandans, which they reached on the 18th of May. After spending a week here, they joined a party of Assinniboins, journeyed with them towards Fort La Reine, and reached it on the 2d of July,—to the great relief of their father, who was waiting in suspense, having heard nothing of them for more than a year.

Sixty-two years later, when the vast western regions then called Louisiana had just been ceded to the United States, Captains Lewis and Clark left the Mandan villages with thirty-two men, traced the Missouri to the mountains, penetrated the wastes beyond, and made their way to the Pacific. The first stages of that remarkable exploration were anticipated by the brothers La Vérendrye. They did not find the Pacific, but they discovered the Rocky Mountains, or at least the part of them to which the name properly belongs; for the southern continuation of the great range had long been known to the Spaniards. Their bold adventure was achieved,

[1] The only two tribes of this region who were a match for the Snakes were the Sioux and the Blackfeet. It is clear that the Bow Indians could not have been Blackfeet, as in that case, after the war-party broke up, they would have moved northward towards their own country, instead of east-southeast into the country of their enemies. Hence I incline to think the Bow Indians a band of Sioux, or Dakota,—a people then, as since, predominant in that country.

The banks of the Missouri, in the part which La Vérendrye would have reached in following an east-southeast course, were occupied by numerous bands or sub-tribes of Sioux, such as the Minneconjou, Yankton, Oncpapa, Brulé, and others, friends and relatives of the Bow Indians, supposing these to have been Sioux.

[2] The Sioux, Cheyennes, and other prairie tribes use the small astringent wild cherry for food. The squaws pound it, stones and all, and then dry it for winter use.

not at the charge of a government, but at their own cost and that of their father,—not with a band of well-equipped men, but with only two followers.

The fur-trading privilege which was to have been their compensation had proved their ruin. They were still pursued without ceasing by the jealousy of rival traders and the ire of disappointed partners. "Here in Canada more than anywhere else," the Chevalier wrote, some years after his return, "envy is the passion *à la mode*, and there is no escaping it."[1] It was the story of La Salle repeated. Beauharnois, however, still stood by them, encouraged and defended them, and wrote in their favor to the colonial minister.[2] It was doubtless through his efforts that the elder La Vérendrye was at last promoted to a captaincy in the colony troops. Beauharnois was succeeded in the government by the sagacious and able Galissonière, and he too befriended the explorers. "It seems to me," he wrote to the minister, "that what you have been told touching the Sieur de la Vérendrye, to the effect that he has been more busy with his own interests than in making discoveries, is totally false, and, moreover, that any officers employed in such work will always be compelled to give some of their attention to trade, so long as the King allows them no other means of subsistence. These discoveries are very costly, and more fatiguing and dangerous than open war."[3] Two years later, the elder La Vérendrye received the cross of the Order of St. Louis,—an honor much prized in Canada, but which he did not long enjoy; for he died at Montreal in the following December, when on the point of again setting out for the West.

His intrepid sons survived, and they were not idle. One of them, the Chevalier, had before discovered the river Saskatchawan, and ascended it as far as the forks.[4] His intention was to follow it to the mountains, build a fort there, and thence push westward in another search for the Pacific; but a disastrous event ruined all his hopes. La Galissonière returned

---

[1] *Le Chevalier de la Vérendrye au Ministre, 30 Sept. 1750.*

[2] *La Vérendrye père au Ministre, 1 Nov. 1746,* in Margry VI. 611.

[3] *La Galissonière au Ministre, 23 Oct. 1747.*

[4] *Mémoire en abrégé des Établissements et Découvertes faits par le Sieur de la Vérendrye et ses Enfants.*

to France, and the Marquis de la Jonquière succeeded him, with the notorious François Bigot as intendant. Both were greedy of money,—the one to hoard, and the other to dissipate it. Clearly there was money to be got from the fur-trade of Manitoba, for La Vérendrye had made every preparation and incurred every expense. It seemed that nothing remained but to reap where he had sown. His commission to find the Pacific, with the privileges connected with it, was refused to his sons, and conferred on a stranger. La Jonquière wrote to the minister: "I have charged M. de Saint-Pierre with this business. He knows these countries better than any officer in all the colony."[1] On the contrary, he had never seen them. It is difficult not to believe that La Jonquière, Bigot, and Saint-Pierre were partners in a speculation of which all three were to share the profits.

The elder La Vérendrye, not long before his death, had sent a large quantity of goods to his trading-forts. The brothers begged leave to return thither and save their property from destruction. They declared themselves happy to serve under the orders of Saint-Pierre, and asked for the use of only a single fort of all those which their father had built at his own cost. The answer was a flat refusal. In short, they were shamefully robbed. The Chevalier writes: "M. le Marquis de la Jonquière, being pushed hard, and as I thought even touched, by my representations, told me at last that M. de Saint-Pierre wanted nothing to do with me or my brothers." "I am a ruined man," he continues. "I am more than two thousand livres in debt, and am still only a second ensign. My elder brother's grade is no better than mine. My younger brother is only a cadet. This is the fruit of all that my father, my brothers, and I have done. My other brother, whom the Sioux murdered some years ago, was not the most unfortunate among us. We must lose all that has cost us so much, unless M. de Saint-Pierre should take juster views, and prevail on the Marquis de la Jonquière to share them. To be thus shut out from the West is to be most cruelly robbed of a sort of inheritance which we had all the pains of acquiring, and of which others will get all the profit."[2]

[1] *La Jonquière au Ministre, 27 Fév. 1750.*
[2] *Le Chevalier de la Vérendrye au Ministre, 30 Sept. 1750.*

His elder brother writes in a similar strain: "We spent our youth and our property in building up establishments so advantageous to Canada; and after all, we were doomed to see a stranger gather the fruit we had taken such pains to plant." And he complains that their goods left in the trading-posts were wasted, their provisions consumed, and the men in their pay used to do the work of others.[1]

They got no redress. Saint-Pierre, backed by the Governor and the Intendant, remained master of the position. The brothers sold a small piece of land, their last remaining property, to appease their most pressing creditors.[2]

Saint-Pierre set out for Manitoba on the 5th of June, 1750. Though he had lived more or less in the woods for thirty-six years, and though La Jonquière had told the minister that he knew the countries to which he was bound better than anybody else, it is clear from his own journal that he was now visiting them for the first time. They did not please him. "I was told," he says, "that the way would grow harder and more dangerous as we advanced, and I found, in fact, that one must risk life and property every moment." Finding himself and his men likely to starve, he sent some of them, under an ensign named Niverville, to the Saskatchawan. They could not reach it, and nearly perished on the way. "I myself was no more fortunate," says Saint-Pierre. "Food was so scarce that I sent some of my people into the woods among the Indians,—which did not save me from a fast so rigorous that it deranged my health and put it out of my power to do anything towards accomplishing my mission. Even if I had had strength enough, the war that broke out among the Indians would have made it impossible to proceed."

Niverville, after a winter of misery, tried to fulfil an order which he had received from his commander. When the Indians guided the two brothers La Vérendrye to the Rocky Mountains, the course they took tended so far southward that the Chevalier greatly feared it might lead to Spanish settle-

[1] *Mémoire des Services de Pierre Gautier de la Vérendrye l'aisné, présenté à Mgr. Rouillé, ministre et secrétaire d'Etat.*

[2] Legardeur de Saint-Pierre, in spite of his treatment of the La Vérendrye brothers, had merit as an officer. It was he who received Washington at Fort Le Bœuf in 1754. He was killed in 1755, at the battle of Lake George. See *Montcalm and Wolfe*, I. 1053.

ments; and he gave it as his opinion that the next attempt to find the Pacific should be made farther towards the north. Saint-Pierre had agreed with him, and had directed Niverville to build a fort on the Saskatchawan, three hundred leagues above its mouth. Therefore, at the end of May, 1751, Niverville sent ten men in two canoes on this errand, and they ascended the Saskatchawan to what Saint-Pierre calls the "Rock Mountain." Here they built a small stockade fort and called it Fort La Jonquière. Niverville was to have followed them; but he fell ill, and lay helpless at the mouth of the river in such a condition that he could not even write to his commander.

Saint-Pierre set out in person from Fort La Reine for Fort La Jonquière, over ice and snow, for it was late in November. Two Frenchmen from Niverville met him on the way, and reported that the Assinniboins had slaughtered an entire band of friendly Indians on whom Saint-Pierre had relied to guide him. On hearing this he gave up the enterprise, and returned to Fort La Reine. Here the Indians told him idle stories about white men and a fort in some remote place towards the west; but, he observes, "nobody could reach it without encountering an infinity of tribes more savage than it is possible to imagine."

He spent most of the winter at Fort La Reine. Here, towards the end of February, 1752, he had with him only five men, having sent out the rest in search of food. Suddenly, as he sat in his chamber, he saw the fort full of armed Assinniboins, extremely noisy and insolent. He tried in vain to quiet them, and they presently broke into the guard-house and seized the arms. A massacre would have followed, had not Saint-Pierre, who was far from wanting courage, resorted to an expedient which has more than once proved effective on such occasions. He knocked out the heads of two barrels of gunpowder, snatched a firebrand, and told the yelping crowd that he would blow up them and himself together. At this they all rushed in fright out of the gate, while Saint-Pierre ran after them, and bolted it fast. There was great anxiety for the hunters, but they all came back in the evening, without having met the enemy. The men, however, were so terrified by the adventure that Saint-Pierre was compelled to abandon the fort, after recommending it to the care of another band of

Assinniboins, who had professed great friendship. Four days after he was gone they burned it to the ground.

He soon came to the conclusion that farther discovery was impossible, because the English of Hudson Bay had stirred up the Western tribes to oppose it. Therefore he set out for the settlements, and, reaching Quebec in the autumn of 1753, placed the journal of his futile enterprise in the hands of Duquesne, the new governor.[1]

Canada was approaching her last agony. In the death-struggle of the Seven Years' War there was no time for schemes of Western discovery. The brothers La Vérendrye sank into poverty and neglect. A little before the war broke out, we find the eldest at the obscure Acadian post of Beauséjour, where he wrote to the colonial minister a statement of his services, which appears to have received no attention. After the fall of Canada, the Chevalier de la Vérendrye, he whose eyes first beheld the snowy peaks of the Rocky Mountains, perished in the wreck of the ship "Auguste," on the coast of Cape Breton, in November, 1761.[2]

[1] *Journal sommaire du Voyage de Jacques Legardeur de Saint-Pierre, chargé de la Découverte de la Mer de l'Ouest* (British Museum).

[2] The above narrative rests mainly on contemporary documents, official in character, of which the originals are preserved in the archives of the French Government. These papers have recently been printed by M. Pierre Margry, late custodian of the Archives of the Marine and Colonies at Paris, in the sixth volume of his *Découvertes et Établissements des Français dans l'Amérique Septentrionale*,—a documentary collection of great value, published at the expense of the American Government. It was M. Margry who first drew attention to the achievements of the family of La Vérendrye, by an article in the *Moniteur* in 1852. I owe to his kindness the opportunity of using the above-mentioned documents in advance of publication. I obtained copies from duplicate originals of some of the principal among them from the Dépôt des Cartes de la Marine, in 1872. These answer closely, with rare and trivial variations, to the same documents as printed from other sources by M. Margry. Some additional papers preserved in the Archives of the Marine and Colonies have also been used.

My friends, Hon. William C. Endicott, then Secretary of War, and Captain John G. Bourke, Third Cavalry, U. S. A., kindly placed in my hands a valuable collection of Government maps and surveys of the country between the Missouri and the Rocky Mountains visited by the brothers La Vérendrye; and I have received from Captain Bourke, and also from Mr. E. A. Snow, formerly of the Third Cavalry, much information concerning the same region, repeatedly traversed by them in peace and war.

Chapter XVII

1700—1750

THE CHAIN OF POSTS

Opposing Claims • Attitude of the Rival Nations • America a French Continent • England a Usurper • French Demands • Magnanimous Proposals • Warlike Preparation • Niagara • Oswego • Crown Point • The Passes of the West secured

---

WE HAVE seen that the contest between France and England in America divided itself, after the Peace of Utrecht, into three parts,—the Acadian contest; the contest for northern New England; and last, though greatest, the contest for the West. Nothing is more striking than the difference, or rather contrast, in the conduct and methods of the rival claimants to this wild but magnificent domain. Each was strong in its own qualities, and utterly wanting in the qualities that marked its opponent.

On maps of British America in the earlier part of the eighteenth century, one sees the eastern shore, from Maine to Georgia, garnished with ten or twelve colored patches, very different in shape and size, and defined, more or less distinctly, by dividing-lines which, in some cases, are prolonged westward till they touch the Mississippi, or even cross it and stretch indefinitely towards the Pacific. These patches are the British provinces, and the westward prolongation of their boundary lines represents their several claims to vast interior tracts, founded on ancient grants, but not made good by occupation, or vindicated by any exertion of power.

These English communities took little thought of the region beyond the Alleghanies. Each lived a life of its own, shut within its own limits, not dreaming of a future collective greatness to which the possession of the West would be a necessary condition. No conscious community of aims and interests held them together, nor was there any authority capable of uniting their forces and turning them to a common object. Some of the servants of the Crown had urged the necessity of joining them all under a strong central government, as the only means of making them loyal subjects and arresting the encroachments of France; but the scheme was plainly impracticable. Each province remained in jealous isolation, busied with its own work, growing in strength, in the capacity of self-rule and the spirit of independence, and stubbornly resisting all exercise of authority from without. If the English-speaking populations flowed westward, it was in obedience to natural laws, for the King did not aid the movement, the royal governors had no authority to do so, and the colonial assemblies were too much engrossed with immediate local interests. The power of these colonies was that of a rising flood slowly invading and conquering, by the unconscious force of its own growing volume, unless means be found to hold it back by dams and embankments within appointed limits.

In the French colonies all was different. Here the representatives of the Crown were men bred in an atmosphere of broad ambition and masterful and far-reaching enterprise. Achievement was demanded of them. They recognized the greatness of the prize, studied the strong and weak points of their rivals, and with a cautious forecast and a daring energy set themselves to the task of defeating them.

If the English colonies were comparatively strong in numbers, their numbers could not be brought into action; while if the French forces were small, they were vigorously commanded, and always ready at a word. It was union confronting division, energy confronting apathy, military centralization opposed to industrial democracy; and, for a time, the advantage was all on one side.

The demands of the French were sufficiently comprehensive. They repented of their enforced concessions at the Treaty of Utrecht, and in spite of that compact, maintained that, with a few local and trivial exceptions, the whole North American continent, except Mexico, was theirs of right; while their opponents seemed neither to understand the situation, nor see the greatness of the stakes at issue.

In 1720 Father Bobé, priest of the Congregation of Missions, drew up a paper in which he sets forth the claims of France with much distinctness, beginning with the declaration that "England has usurped from France nearly everything that she possesses in America," and adding that the plenipotentiaries at Utrecht did not know what they were about when they made such concessions to the enemy; that, among other blunders, they gave Port Royal to England when it belonged to France, who should "insist vigorously" on its being given back to her.

He maintains that the voyages of Verrazzano and Ribaut made France owner of the whole continent, from Florida northward; that England was an interloper in planting colonies along the Atlantic coast, and will admit as much if she is honest, since all that country is certainly a part of New France. In this modest assumption of the point at issue, he ignores John Cabot and his son Sebastian, who discovered North America more than twenty-five years before the voyage of Verrazzano, and more than sixty years before that of Ribaut.

When the English, proceeds Father Bobé, have restored Port Royal to us, which they are bound to do, though we ceded it by the treaty, a French governor should be at once set over it, with a commission to command as far as Cape Cod, which would include Boston. We should also fortify ourselves, "in a way to stop the English, who have long tried to seize on French America, of which they know the importance, and of which," he observes with much candor, "they would make a better use than the French do.[1] . . . The Atlantic coast, as far as Florida, was usurped from the French, to whom it belonged then, and to whom it belongs now." England, as he thinks, is bound in honor to give back these countries to their true owner; and it is also the part of wisdom to do so, since by grasping at too much, one often loses all. But France, out of her love of peace, will cede to England the countries along the Atlantic, from the Kennebec in New France to the Jordan[2] in Carolina, on condition that England will restore to her all that she gave up by the Treaty of Utrecht. When this is done, France, always generous, will consent to accept as boundary a line drawn from the mouth

---

[1] "De manière qu'on puisse arrêter les Anglois, qui depuis longtems tachent de s'emparer de l'Amérique françoise, dont ils conoissent l'importance et dont ils feroient un meillieur usage que celuy qui les françois en font."

[2] On the river Jordan, so named by Vasquez de Ayllon, see *Pioneers of France in the New World*, pp. 26, 46 *note*. It was probably the Broad River of South Carolina.

of the Kennebec, passing thence midway between Schenectady and Lake Champlain and along the ridge of the Alleghanies to the river Jordan, the country between this line and the sea to belong to England, and the rest of the continent to France.

If England does not accept this generous offer, she is to be told that the King will give to the Compagnie des Indes (Law's Mississippi Company) full authority to occupy "all the countries which the English have usurped from France;" and, pursues Father Bobé, "it is certain that the fear of having to do with so powerful a company will bring the English to our terms." The company that was thus to strike the British heart with terror was the same which all the tonics and stimulants of the government could not save from predestined ruin. But, concludes this ingenious writer, whether England accepts our offers or not, France ought not only to take a high tone (*parler avec hauteur*), but also to fortify diligently, and make good her right by force of arms.[1]

Three years later we have another document, this time of an official character, and still more radical in its demands. It admits that Port Royal and a part of the Nova Scotian peninsula, under the name of Acadia, were ceded to England by the treaty, and consents that she shall keep them, but requires her to restore the part of New France that she has wrongfully seized,—namely, the whole Atlantic coast from the Kennebec to Florida; since France never gave England this country, which is hers by the discovery of Verrazzano in 1524. Here, again, the voyages of the Cabots, in 1497 and 1498, are completely ignored.

"It will be seen," pursues this curious document, "that our kings have always preserved sovereignty over the countries between the 30th and the 50th degrees of north latitude. A time will come when they will be in a position to assert their rights, and then it will be seen that the dominions of a king of France cannot be usurped with impunity. What we demand now is that the English make immediate restitution." No doubt, the paper goes on to say, they will pretend to have prescriptive rights, because they have settled the country and

---

[1] *Second Mémoire concernant les Limites des Colonies présenté en 1720 par Bobé, prêtre de la Congrégation de la Mission* (Archives Nationales).

built towns and cities in it; but this plea is of no avail, because all that country is a part of New France, and because England rightfully owns nothing in America except what we, the French, gave her by the Treaty of Utrecht, which is merely Port Royal and Acadia. She is bound in honor to give back all the vast countries she has usurped; but, continues the paper, "the King loves the English nation too much, and wishes too much to do her kindness, and is too generous to exact such a restitution. Therefore, provided that England will give us back Port Royal, Acadia, and everything else that France gave her by the Treaty of Utrecht, the King will forego his rights, and grant to England the whole Atlantic coast from the 32d degree of latitude to the Kennebec, to the extent inland of twenty French leagues [about fifty miles], on condition that she will solemnly bind herself never to overstep these limits or encroach in the least on French ground."

Thus, through the beneficence of France, England, provided that she renounced all pretension to the rest of the continent, would become the rightful owner of an attenuated strip of land reaching southward from the Kennebec along the Atlantic seaboard. The document containing this magnanimous proposal was preserved in the Château St. Louis at Quebec till the middle of the eighteenth century, when, the boundary dispute having reached a crisis, and commissioners of the two powers having been appointed to settle it, a certified copy of the paper was sent to France for their instruction.[1]

Father Bobé had advised that France should not trust solely to the justice of her claims, but should back right with might, and build forts on the Niagara, the Ohio, the Tennessee, and the Alabama, as well as at other commanding points, to shut out the English from the West. Of these positions, Niagara was the most important, for the possession of it would close the access to the Upper Lakes, and stop the Western tribes on their way to trade at Albany. The Five Nations and the Governor of New York were jealous of the French designs, which, however, were likely enough to succeed, through the prevailing apathy and divisions in the British colonies. "If

[1] *Demandes de la France, 1723* (Archives des Affaires Etrangères).

those not immediately concerned," writes a member of the New York council, "only stand gazing on while the wolff is murthering other parts of the flock, it will come to every one's turn at last." The warning was well founded, but it was not heeded. Again: "It is the policy of the French to attack one colony at a time, and the others are so besotted as to sit still."[1]

For gaining the consent of the Five Nations to the building of a French fort at Niagara, Vaudreuil trusted chiefly to his agent among the Senecas, the bold, skilful, and indefatigable Joncaire, who was naturalized among that tribe, the strongest of the confederacy. Governor Hunter of New York sent Peter Schuyler and Philip Livingston to counteract his influence. The Five Nations, who, conscious of declining power, seemed ready at this time to be all things to all men, declared that they would prevent the French from building at Niagara, which, as they said, would "shut them up as in a prison."[2] Not long before, however, they had sent a deputation to Montreal to say that the English made objection to Joncaire's presence among them, but that they were masters of their land, and hoped that the French agent would come as often as he pleased; and they begged that the new King of France would take them under his protection.[3] Accordingly, Vaudreuil sent them a present, with a message to the effect that they might plunder such English traders as should come among them.[4]

Yet so jealous were the Iroquois of a French fort at Niagara that they sent three Seneca chiefs to see what was going on there. The chiefs found a few Frenchmen in a small blockhouse, or loopholed storehouse, which they had just built near Lewiston Heights. The three Senecas requested them to demolish it and go away, which the Frenchmen refused to do; on which the Senecas asked the English envoys, Schuyler and Livingston, to induce the Governor of New York to destroy the obnoxious building. In short, the Five Nations wavered

---

[1] *Colonel Heathcote to Governor Hunter, 8 July, 1715. Ibid., to Townshend, 12 July, 1715.*

[2] *Journal of Schuyler and Livingston, 1720.*

[3] *Vaudreuil au Conseil de Marine, 24 Oct. 1717.*

[4] *Vaudreuil et Bégon au Conseil de Marine, 26 Oct. 1719.*

incessantly between their two European neighbors, and changed their minds every day. The skill and perseverance of the French emissaries so far prevailed at last that the Senecas consented to the building of a fort at the mouth of the Niagara, where Denonville had built one in 1687; and thus that important pass was made tolerably secure.

Meanwhile the English of New York, or rather Burnet, their governor, were not idle. Burnet was on ill terms with his Assembly, which grudged him all help in serving the province whose interests it was supposed to represent. Burnet's plan was to build a fortified trading-house at Oswego, on Lake Ontario, in the belief that the Western Indians, who greatly preferred English goods and English prices, would pass Niagara and bring their furs to the new post. He got leave from the Five Nations to execute his plan, bought canoes, hired men, and built a loopholed house of stone on the site of the present city of Oswego. As the Assembly would give no money, Burnet furnished it himself; and though the object was one of the greatest importance to the province, he was never fully repaid.[1] A small garrison for the new post was drawn from the four independent companies maintained in the province at the charge of the Crown.

The establishment of Oswego greatly alarmed and incensed the French, and a council of war at Quebec resolved to send two thousand men against it; but Vaudreuil's successor, the Marquis de Beauharnois, learning that the court was not prepared to provoke a war, contented himself with sending a summons to the commanding officer to abandon and demolish the place within a fortnight.[2] To this no attention was given; and as Burnet had foreseen, Oswego became the great centre of Indian trade, while Niagara, in spite of its more favorable position, was comparatively slighted by the Western tribes. The chief danger rose from the obstinate prejudice of the Assembly, which, in its disputes with the Royal Gover-

---

[1] "I am ashamed to confess that he built the fort at his private expense, and that a balance of above £56 remains due to his estate to this very day." Smith, *History of New York*, 267 (ed. 1814).

[2] *Mémoire de Dupuy, 1728.* Dupuy was intendant of Canada. The King approved the conduct of Beauharnois in not using force. *Dépêche du Roy, 14 Mai, 1728.*

nor, would give him neither men nor money to defend the new post.

The Canadian authorities, who saw in Oswego an intrusion on their domain and a constant injury and menace, could not attack it without bringing on a war, and therefore tried to persuade the Five Nations to destroy it,—an attempt which completely failed.[1] They then established a trading-post at Toronto, in the vain hope of stopping the Northern tribes on their way to the more profitable English market, and they built two armed vessels at Fort Frontenac to control the navigation of Lake Ontario.

Meanwhile, in another quarter the French made an advance far more threatening to the English colonies than Oswego was to their own. They had already built a stone fort at Chambly, which covered Montreal from any English attack by way of Lake Champlain. As that lake was the great highway between the rival colonies, the importance of gaining full mastery of it was evident. It was rumored in Canada that the English meant to seize and fortify the place called Scalp Point (*Pointe à la Chevelure*) by the French, and Crown Point by the English, where the lake suddenly contracts to the proportions of a river, so that a few cannon would stop the passage.

As early as 1726 the French made an attempt to establish themselves on the east side of the lake opposite Crown Point, but were deterred by the opposition of Massachusetts. This eastern shore was, however, claimed not only by Massachusetts, but by her neighbor, New Hampshire, with whom she presently fell into a dispute about the ownership, and, as a writer of the time observes, "while they were quarrelling for the bone, the French ran away with it."[2]

At length, in 1731, the French took post on the western side of the lake, and began to intrench themselves at Crown Point, which was within the bounds claimed by New York; but that province, being then engrossed, not only by her chronic dispute with her Governor, but by a quarrel with her next neighbor, New Jersey, slighted the danger from the common

---

[1] When urged by the younger Longueuil to drive off the English from Oswego, the Indians replied, "Drive them off thyself." "*Chassez-les toi-même.*" *Longueuil fils au Ministre, 19 Oct. 1728.*

[2] Mitchell, *Contest in America*, 22.

enemy, and left the French to work their will. It was Saint-Luc de la Corne, Lieutenant du Roy at Montreal, who pointed out the necessity of fortifying this place,[1] in order to anticipate the English, who, as he imagined, were about to do so,—a danger which was probably not imminent, since the English colonies, as a whole, could not and would not unite for such a purpose, while the individual provinces were too much absorbed in their own internal affairs and their own jealousies and disputes to make the attempt. La Corne's suggestion found favor at court, and the Governor of Canada was ordered to occupy Crown Point. The Sieur de la Fresnière was sent thither with troops and workmen, and a fort was built, and named Fort Frédéric. It contained a massive stone tower, mounted with cannon to command the lake, which is here but a musket-shot wide. Thus was established an advanced post of France,—a constant menace to New York and New England, both of which denounced it as an outrageous encroachment on British territory, but could not unite to rid themselves of it.[2]

While making this bold push against their neighbors of the South, the French did not forget the West; and towards the middle of the century they had occupied points controlling all the chief waterways between Canada and Louisiana. Niagara held the passage from Lake Ontario to Lake Erie. Detroit closed the entrance to Lake Huron, and Michillimackinac guarded the point where Lake Huron is joined by Lakes Michigan and Superior; while the fort called La Baye, at the head of Green Bay, stopped the way to the Mississippi by Marquette's old route of Fox River and the Wisconsin. Another route to the Mississippi was controlled by a post on the Maumee to watch the carrying-place between that river and the Wabash, and by another on the Wabash where Vincennes now stands. La Salle's route, by way of the Kankakee and the Illinois, was barred by a fort on the St. Joseph; and even if, in spite of these obstructions, an enemy should reach the Mississippi by any of its northern affluents, the cannon of Fort Chartres would prevent him from descending it.

[1] *La Corne au Ministre, 15 Oct. 1730.*

[2] On the establishment of Crown Point, *Beauharnois et Hocquart au Roy, 10 Oct. 1731; Beauharnois et Hocquart au Ministre, 14 Nov. 1731.*

These various Western forts, except Fort Chartres and Fort Niagara, which were afterwards rebuilt, the one in stone and the other in earth, were stockades of no strength against cannon. Slight as they were, their establishment was costly; and as the King, to whom Canada was a yearly loss, grudged every franc spent upon it, means were contrived to make them self-supporting. Each of them was a station of the fur-trade, and the position of most of them had been determined more or less with a view to that traffic. Hence they had no slight commercial value. In some of them the Crown itself carried on trade through agents who usually secured a lion's share of the profits. Others were farmed out to merchants at a fixed sum. In others, again, the commanding-officer was permitted to trade on condition of maintaining the post, paying the soldiers, and supporting a missionary; while in one case, at least, he was subjected to similar obligations, though not permitted to trade himself, but only to sell trading licenses to merchants. These methods of keeping up forts and garrisons were of course open to prodigious abuses, and roused endless jealousies and rivalries.

France had now occupied the valley of the Mississippi, and joined with loose and uncertain links her two colonies of Canada and Louisiana. But the strength of her hold on these regions of unkempt savagery bore no proportion to the vastness of her claims or the growing power of the rivals who were soon to contest them.[1]

---

[1] On the claim of France that all North America, except the Spanish colonies of Mexico and Florida, belonged to her, *see* Appendix A.

Chapter XVIII

1744, 1745

A MAD SCHEME

War of the Austrian Succession • The French seize Canseau and attack Annapolis • Plan of Reprisal • William Vaughan • Governor Shirley • He advises an Attack on Louisbourg • The Assembly refuses, but at last consents • Preparation • William Pepperrell • George Whitefield • Parson Moody • The Soldiers • The Provincial Navy • Commodore Warren • Shirley as an Amateur Soldier • The Fleet sails

T HE PEACE OF UTRECHT left unsettled the perilous questions of boundary between the rival powers in North America, and they grew more perilous every day. Yet the quarrel was not yet quite ripe; and though the French Governor, Vaudreuil, and perhaps also his successor, Beauharnois, seemed willing to precipitate it, the courts of London and Versailles still hesitated to appeal to the sword. Now, as before, it was a European, and not an American, quarrel that was to set the world on fire. The War of the Austrian Succession broke out in 1744. When Frederic of Prussia seized Silesia and began that bloody conflict, it meant that packs of howling savages would again spread fire and carnage along the New England border.

News of the declaration of war reached Louisbourg some weeks before it reached Boston, and the French military Governor, Duquesnel, thought he saw an opportunity to strike an unexpected blow for the profit of France and his own great honor.

One of the French inhabitants of Louisbourg has left us a short sketch of Duquesnel, whom he calls "capricious, of an uncertain temper, inclined to drink, and when in his cups neither reasonable nor civil."[1] He adds that the Governor had offended nearly every officer in the garrison, and denounces him as the "chief cause of our disasters." When Duquesnel heard of the declaration of war, his first thought was to strike

[1] *Lettre d'un Habitant de Louisbourg contenant une Relation exacte et circonstanciée de la Prise de l'Isle Royale par les Anglois.*

some blow before the English were warned. The fishing-station of Canseau was a tempting prize, being a near and an inconvenient neighbor, at the southern end of the Strait of Canseau, which separates the Acadian peninsula from the island of Cape Breton, or Isle Royale, of which Louisbourg was the place of strength. Nothing was easier than to seize Canseau, which had no defence but a wooden redoubt built by the fishermen, and occupied by about eighty Englishmen thinking no danger. Early in May, Duquesnel sent Captain Duvivier against it, with six hundred, or, as the English say, nine hundred soldiers and sailors, escorted by two small armed vessels. The English surrendered, on condition of being sent to Boston, and the miserable hamlet, with its wooden citadel, was burned to the ground.

Thus far successful, the Governor addressed himself to the capture of Annapolis,—which meant the capture of all Acadia. Duvivier was again appointed to the command. His heart was in the work, for he was a descendant of La Tour, feudal claimant of Acadia in the preceding century. Four officers and ninety regular troops were given him,[1] and from three to four hundred Micmac and Malecite Indians joined him on the way. The Micmacs, under command, it is said, of their missionary, Le Loutre, had already tried to surprise the English fort, but had only succeeded in killing two unarmed stragglers in the adjacent garden.[2]

Annapolis, from the neglect and indifference of the British ministry, was still in such a state of dilapidation that its sandy ramparts were crumbling into the ditches, and the cows of the garrison walked over them at their pleasure. It was held by about a hundred effective men under Major Mascarene, a French Protestant whose family had been driven into exile by the persecutions that followed the revocation of the Edict of Nantes. Shirley, governor of Massachusetts, sent him a small reinforcement of militia; but as most of these came without arms, and as Mascarene had few or none to give them, they proved of doubtful value.

[1] *Lettre d'un Habitant de Louisbourg.*

[2] *Mascarene to the Besiegers, 3 July, 1744.* Duquesnel had written to all the missionaries "d'engager les sauvages à faire quelque coup important sur le fort" (Annapolis). *Duquesnel à Beauharnois, 1 Juin, 1744.*

Duvivier and his followers, white and red, appeared before the fort in August, made their camp behind the ridge of a hill that overlooked it, and marched towards the rampart; but being met by a discharge of cannon-shot, they gave up all thoughts of an immediate assault, began a fusillade under cover of darkness, and kept the garrison on the alert all night.

Duvivier had looked for help from the Acadians of the neighboring village, who were French in blood, faith, and inclination. They would not join him openly, fearing the consequences if his attack should fail; but they did what they could without committing themselves, and made a hundred and fifty scaling-ladders for the besiegers. Duvivier now returned to his first plan of an assault, which, if made with vigor, could hardly have failed. Before attempting it, he sent Mascarene a flag of truce to tell him that he hourly expected two powerful armed ships from Louisbourg, besides a reinforcement of two hundred and fifty regulars, with cannon, mortars, and other enginery of war. At the same time he proposed favorable terms of capitulation, not to take effect till the French war-ships should have appeared. Mascarene refused all terms, saying that when he saw the French ships, he would consider what to do, and meanwhile would defend himself as he could.

The expected ships were the "Ardent" and the "Caribou," then at Louisbourg. A French writer says that when Duquesnel directed their captains to sail for Annapolis and aid in its capture, they refused, saying that they had no orders from the court.[1] Duvivier protracted the parley with Mascarene, and waited in vain for the promised succor. At length the truce was broken off, and the garrison, who had profited by it to get rest and sleep, greeted the renewal of hostilities with three cheers.

Now followed three weeks of desultory attacks; but there was no assault, though Duvivier had boasted that he had the means of making a successful one. He waited for the ships which did not come, and kept the Acadians at work in making ladders and fire-arrows. At length, instead of aid from Louisbourg, two small vessels appeared from Boston, bringing Mascarene a reinforcement of fifty Indian rangers. This discouraged the besiegers, and towards the end of September they suddenly decamped and vanished. "The expedition was

[1] *Lettre d'un Habitant de Louisbourg.*

a failure," writes the *Habitant de Louisbourg*, "though one might have bet everything on its success, so small was the force that the enemy had to resist us."

This writer thinks that the seizure of Canseau and the attack of Annapolis were sources of dire calamity to the French. "Perhaps," he says, "the English would have let us alone if we had not first insulted them. It was the interest of the people of New England to live at peace with us, and they would no doubt have done so, if we had not taken it into our heads to waken them from their security. They expected that both parties would merely stand on the defensive, without taking part in this cruel war that has set Europe in a blaze."

Whatever might otherwise have been the disposition of the "Bastonnais," or New England people, the attacks on Canseau and Annapolis alarmed and exasperated them, and engendered in some heated brains a project of wild audacity. This was no less than the capture of Louisbourg, reputed the strongest fortress, French or British, in North America, with the possible exception of Quebec, which owed its chief strength to nature, and not to art.

Louisbourg was a standing menace to all the Northern British colonies. It was the only French naval station on the continent, and was such a haunt of privateers that it was called the American Dunkirk. It commanded the chief entrance of Canada, and threatened to ruin the fisheries, which were nearly as vital to New England as was the fur-trade to New France. The French government had spent twenty-five years in fortifying it, and the cost of its powerful defences— constructed after the system of Vauban—was reckoned at thirty million livres.

This was the fortress which William Vaughan of Damariscotta advised Governor Shirley to attack with fifteen hundred raw New England militia.[1] Vaughan was born at Portsmouth in 1703, and graduated at Harvard College nineteen years

[1] Smollett says that the proposal came from Robert Auchmuty, judge of admiralty in Massachusetts. Hutchinson, Douglas, Belknap, and other well-informed writers ascribe the scheme to Vaughan, while Pepperrell says that it originated with Colonel John Bradstreet. In the Public Record Office there is a letter from Bradstreet, written in 1753, but without address, in which he declares that he not only planned the siege, but "was the Principal Person in conducting it,"—assertions which may pass for what they are worth, Bradstreet being much given to self-assertion.

later. His father, also a graduate of Harvard, was for a time lieutenant-governor of New Hampshire. Soon after leaving college, the younger Vaughan—a youth of restless and impetuous activity—established a fishing-station on the island of Matinicus, off the coast of Maine, and afterwards became the owner of most of the land on both sides of the little river Damariscotta, where he built a garrison-house, or wooden fort, established a considerable settlement, and carried on an extensive trade in fish and timber. He passed for a man of ability and force, but was accused of a headstrong rashness, a self-confidence that hesitated at nothing, and a harebrained contempt of every obstacle in his way. Once, having fitted out a number of small vessels at Portsmouth for his fishing at Matinicus, he named a time for sailing. It was a gusty and boisterous March day, the sea was rough, and old sailors told him that such craft could not carry sail. Vaughan would not listen, but went on board and ordered his men to follow. One vessel was wrecked at the mouth of the river; the rest, after severe buffeting, came safe, with their owner, to Matinicus.

Being interested in the fisheries, Vaughan was doubly hostile to Louisbourg,—their worst enemy. He found a willing listener in the Governor, William Shirley. Shirley was an English barrister who had come to Massachusetts in 1731 to practise his profession and seek his fortune. After filling various offices with credit, he was made governor of the province in 1741, and had discharged his duties with both tact and talent. He was able, sanguine, and a sincere well-wisher to the province, though gnawed by an insatiable hunger for distinction. He thought himself a born strategist, and was possessed by a propensity for contriving military operations, which finally cost him dear. Vaughan, who knew something of Louisbourg, told him that in winter the snow-drifts were often banked so high against the rampart that it could be mounted readily, if the assailants could but time their arrival at the right moment. This was not easy, as that rocky and tempestuous coast was often made inaccessible by fogs and surf; Shirley therefore preferred a plan of his own contriving. But nothing could be done without first persuading his Assembly to consent.

On the 9th of January the General Court of Massachusetts—a convention of grave city merchants and solemn rustics from the country villages—was astonished by a message from the Governor to the effect that he had a communication to make, so critical that he wished the whole body to swear secrecy. The request was novel, but being then on good terms with Shirley, the Representatives consented, and took the oath. Then, to their amazement, the Governor invited them to undertake forthwith the reduction of Louisbourg. The idea of an attack on that redoubtable fortress was not new. Since the autumn, proposals had been heard to petition the British ministry to make the attempt, under a promise that the colonies would give their best aid. But that Massachusetts should venture it alone, or with such doubtful help as her neighbors might give, at her own charge and risk, though already insolvent, without the approval or consent of the ministry, and without experienced officers or trained soldiers, was a startling suggestion to the sober-minded legislators of the General Court. They listened, however, with respect to the Governor's reasons, and appointed a committee of the two houses to consider them. The committee deliberated for several days, and then made a report adverse to the plan, as was also the vote of the Court.

Meanwhile, in spite of the oath, the secret had escaped. It is said that a country member, more pious than discreet, prayed so loud and fervently, at his lodgings, for light to guide him on the momentous question, that his words were overheard, and the mystery of the closed doors was revealed. The news flew through the town, and soon spread through all the province.

After his defeat in the Assembly, Shirley returned, vexed and disappointed, to his house in Roxbury. A few days later, James Gibson, a Boston merchant, says that he saw him "walking slowly down King Street, with his head bowed down, as if in a deep study." "He entered my counting-room," pursues the merchant, "and abruptly said, 'Gibson, do you feel like giving up the expedition to Louisbourg?'" Gibson replied that he wished the House would reconsider their vote. "You are the very man I want!" exclaimed the Governor.[1] They then drew up

---

[1] Gibson, *Journal of the Siege of Louisbourg.*

a petition for reconsideration, which Gibson signed, promising to get also the signatures of merchants, not only of Boston, but of Salem, Marblehead, and other towns along the coast. In this he was completely successful, as all New England merchants looked on Louisbourg as an arch-enemy.

The petition was presented, and the question came again before the Assembly. There had been much intercourse between Boston and Louisbourg, which had largely depended on New England for provisions.[1] The captured militia-men of Canseau, who, after some delay, had been sent to Boston, according to the terms of surrender, had used their opportunities to the utmost, and could give Shirley much information concerning the fortress. It was reported that the garrison was mutinous, and that provisions were fallen short, so that the place could not hold out without supplies from France. These, however, could be cut off only by blockading the harbor with a stronger naval force than all the colonies together could supply. The Assembly had before reached the reasonable conclusion that the capture of Louisbourg was beyond the strength of Massachusetts, and that the only course was to ask the help of the mother-country.[2]

The reports of mutiny, it was urged, could not be depended on; raw militia in the open field were no match for disciplined troops behind ramparts; the expense would be enormous, and the credit of the province, already sunk low, would collapse under it; we should fail, and instead of sympathy, get nothing but ridicule. Such were the arguments of the opposition, to which there was little to answer, except that if Massachusetts waited for help from England, Louisbourg would be reinforced and the golden opportunity lost. The impetuous and irrepressible Vaughan put forth all his energy; the plan was carried by a single vote. And even this result was said to be due to the accident of a member in opposition falling and breaking a leg as he was hastening to the House.

The die was cast, and now doubt and hesitation vanished. All alike set themselves to push on the work. Shirley wrote to all the colonies, as far south as Pennsylvania, to ask for co-

[1] *Lettre d'un Habitant de Louisbourg.*

[2] *Report of Council, 12 Jan. 1745.*

operation. All excused themselves except Connecticut, New Hampshire, and Rhode Island, and the whole burden fell on the four New England colonies. These, and Massachusetts above all, blazed with pious zeal; for as the enterprise was directed against Roman Catholics, it was supposed in a peculiar manner to commend itself to Heaven. There were prayers without ceasing in churches and families, and all was ardor, energy, and confidence; while the other colonies looked on with distrust, dashed with derision. When Benjamin Franklin, in Philadelphia, heard what was afoot, he wrote to his brother in Boston, "Fortified towns are hard nuts to crack, and your teeth are not accustomed to it; but some seem to think that forts are as easy taken as snuff."[1] It has been said of Franklin that while he represented some of the New England qualities, he had no part in that enthusiasm of which our own time saw a crowning example when the cannon opened at Fort Sumter, and which pushes to its end without reckoning chances, counting costs, or heeding the scoffs of ill-wishers.

The prevailing hope and faith were, it is true, born largely of ignorance, aided by the contagious zeal of those who first broached the project; for as usual in such cases, a few individuals supplied the initiate force of the enterprise. Vaughan the indefatigable rode express to Portsmouth with a letter from Shirley to Benning Wentworth, governor of New Hampshire. That pompous and self-important personage admired the Massachusetts Governor, who far surpassed him in talents and acquirements, and who at the same time knew how to soothe his vanity. Wentworth was ready to do his part, but his province had no money, and the King had ordered him to permit the issue of no more paper currency. The same prohibition had been laid upon Shirley; but he, with sagacious forecast, had persuaded his masters to relent so far as to permit the issue of £50,000 in what were called bills of credit to meet any pressing exigency of war. He told this to Wentworth, and succeeded in convincing him that his province might stretch her credit like Massachusetts, in case of similar military need. New Hampshire was thus enabled to raise a

[1] Sparks, *Works of Franklin*, VII. 16.

regiment of five hundred men out of her scanty population, with the condition that a hundred and fifty of them should be paid and fed by Massachusetts.[1]

Shirley was less fortunate in Rhode Island. The Governor of that little colony called Massachusetts "our avowed enemy, always trying to defame us."[2] There was a grudge between the neighbors, due partly to notorious ill-treatment by the Massachusetts Puritans of Roger Williams, founder of Rhode Island, and partly to one of those boundary disputes which often produced ill-blood among the colonies. The Representatives of Rhode Island, forgetting past differences, voted to raise a hundred and fifty men for the expedition, till, learning that the project was neither ordered nor approved by the Home Government, they prudently reconsidered their action. They voted, however, that the colony sloop "Tartar," carrying fourteen cannon and twelve swivels, should be equipped and manned for the service, and that the Governor should be instructed to find and commission a captain and a lieutenant to command her.[3]

Connecticut promised five hundred and sixteen men and officers, on condition that Roger Wolcott, their commander, should have the second rank in the expedition. Shirley accordingly commissioned him as major-general. As Massachusetts was to supply above three thousand men, or more than three quarters of the whole force, she had a natural right to name a commander-in-chief.

It was not easy to choose one. The colony had been at peace for twenty years, and except some grizzled Indian fighters of the last war, and some survivors of the Carthagena expedition, nobody had seen service. Few knew well what a fortress was, and nobody knew how to attack one. Courage, energy, good sense, and popularity were the best qualities to be hoped for in the leader. Popularity was indispensable, for the soldiers were all to be volunteers, and they would not enlist under a commander whom they did not like. Shirley's

---

[1] Correspondence of Shirley and Wentworth, in *Belknap Papers. Provincial Papers of New Hampshire*, V.

[2] *Governor Wanton to the Agent of Rhode Island, 20 Dec. 1745*, in *Colony Records of Rhode Island*, V.

[3] *Colony Records of Rhode Island*, V. (*Feb. 1745*).

choice was William Pepperrell, a merchant of Kittery. Knowing that Benning Wentworth thought himself the man for the place, he made an effort to placate him, and wrote that he would gladly have given him the chief command, but for his gouty legs. Wentworth took fire at the suggestion, forgot his gout, and declared himself ready to serve his country and assume the burden of command. The position was awkward, and Shirley was forced to reply, "On communicating your offer to two or three gentlemen in whose judgment I most confide, I found them clearly of opinion that any alteration of the present command would be attended with great risk, both with respect to our Assembly and the soldiers being entirely disgusted."[1]

The painter Smibert has left us a portrait of Pepperrell,—a good bourgeois face, not without dignity, though with no suggestion of the soldier. His spacious house at Kittery Point still stands, sound and firm, though curtailed in some of its proportions. Not far distant is another noted relic of colonial times, the not less spacious mansion built by the disappointed Wentworth at Little Harbor. I write these lines at a window of this curious old house, and before me spreads the scene familiar to Pepperrell from childhood. Here the river Piscataqua widens to join the sea, holding in its gaping mouth the large island of Newcastle, with attendant groups of islets and island rocks, battered with the rack of ages, studded with dwarf savins, or half clad with patches of whortleberry bushes, sumac, and the shining wax-myrtle, green in summer, red with the touch of October. The flood tide pours strong and full around them, only to ebb away and lay bare a desolation of rocks and stones buried in a shock of brown drenched seaweed, broad tracts of glistening mud, sand-banks black with mussel-beds, and half-submerged meadows of eel-grass, with myriads of minute shell-fish clinging to its long lank tresses. Beyond all these lies the main, or northern channel, more than deep enough, even when the tide is out, to float a line-of-battle-ship. On its farther bank stands the old house of the Pepperrells, wearing even now an air of dingy respectability. Looking through its small, quaint window-

---

[1] *Shirley to Wentworth, 16 Feb. 1745.*

panes, one could see across the water the rude dwellings of fishermen along the shore of Newcastle, and the neglected earthwork called Fort William and Mary, that feebly guarded the river's mouth. In front, the Piscataqua, curving southward, widened to meet the Atlantic between rocky headlands and foaming reefs, and in dim distance the Isles of Shoals seemed floating on the pale gray sea.

Behind the Pepperrell house was a garden, probably more useful than ornamental, and at the foot of it were the owner's wharves, with storehouses for salt-fish, naval stores, and imported goods for the country trade.

Pepperrell was the son of a Welshman[1] who migrated in early life to the Isles of Shoals, and thence to Kittery, where by trade, ship-building, and the fisheries, he made a fortune, most of which he left to his son William. The young Pepperrell learned what little was taught at the village school, supplemented by a private tutor, whose instructions, however, did not perfect him in English grammar. In the eyes of his self-made father, education was valuable only so far as it could make a successful trader; and on this point he had reason to be satisfied, as his son passed for many years as the chief merchant in New England. He dealt in ships, timber, naval stores, fish, and miscellaneous goods brought from England; and he also greatly prospered by successful land purchases, becoming owner of the greater part of the growing towns of Saco and Scarborough. When scarcely twenty-one, he was made justice of the peace, on which he ordered from London what his biographer calls a law library, consisting of a law dictionary, Danvers' "Abridgment of the Common Law," the "Complete Solicitor," and several other books. In law as in war, his best qualities were good sense and good will. About the time when he was made a justice, he was commissioned captain of militia, then major, then lieutenant-colonel, and at last colonel, commanding all the militia of Maine. The town of Kittery chose him to represent her in the General Court, Maine being then a part of Massachusetts. Finally, he was made a member of the Governor's Council,—a post which

---

[1] "A native of Ravistock Parish, in Wales." Parsons, *Life of Pepperrell*. Mrs. Adelaide Cilley Waldron, a descendant of Pepperrell, assures me, however, that his father, the emigrant, came, not from Wales, but from Devonshire.

he held for thirty-two years, during eighteen of which he was president of the board.

These civil dignities served him as educators better than tutor or village school; for they brought him into close contact with the chief men of the province; and in the Massachusetts of that time, so different from our own, the best education and breeding were found in the official class. At once a provincial magnate and the great man of a small rustic village, his manners are said to have answered to both positions,—certainly they were such as to make him popular. But whatever he became as a man, he learned nothing to fit him to command an army and lay siege to Louisbourg. Perhaps he felt this, and thought, with the Governor of Rhode Island, that "the attempt to reduce that prodigiously strong town was too much for New England, which had not one officer of experience, nor even an engineer."[1] Moreover, he was unwilling to leave his wife, children, and business. He was of a religious turn of mind, and partial to the clergy, who, on their part, held him in high favor. One of them, the famous preacher, George Whitefield, was a guest at his house when he heard that Shirley had appointed him to command the expedition against Louisbourg. Whitefield had been the leading spirit in the recent religious fermentation called the Great Awakening, which, though it produced bitter quarrels among the ministers, besides other undesirable results, was imagined by many to make for righteousness. So thought the Reverend Thomas Prince, who mourned over the subsiding delirium of his flock as a sign of backsliding. "The heavenly shower was over," he sadly exclaims; "from fighting the devil they must turn to fighting the French." Pepperrell, always inclined to the clergy, and now in great perplexity and doubt, asked his guest Whitefield whether or not he had better accept the command. Whitefield gave him cold comfort, told him that the enterprise was not very promising, and that if he undertook it, he must do so "with a single eye," prepared for obloquy if he failed, and envy if he succeeded.[2]

Henry Sherburn, commissary of the New Hampshire regiment, begged Whitefield to furnish a motto for the flag. The

---

[1] *Governor Wanton to the Agent of Rhode Island in London, 20 Dec. 1745.*
[2] Parsons, *Life of Pepperrell*, 51.

preacher, who, zealot as he was, seemed unwilling to mix himself with so madcap a business, hesitated at first, but at length consented, and suggested the words, *Nil desperandum Christo duce*, which, being adopted, gave the enterprise the air of a crusade. It had, in fact, something of the character of one. The cause was imagined to be the cause of Heaven, crowned with celestial benediction. It had the fervent support of the ministers, not only by prayers and sermons, but, in one case, by counsels wholly temporal. A certain pastor, much esteemed for benevolence, proposed to Pepperrell, who had at last accepted the command, a plan, unknown to Vauban, for confounding the devices of the enemy. He advised that two trustworthy persons should cautiously walk together along the front of the French ramparts under cover of night, one of them carrying a mallet, with which he was to hammer the ground at short intervals. The French sentinels, it seems to have been supposed, on hearing this mysterious thumping, would be so bewildered as to give no alarm. While one of the two partners was thus employed, the other was to lay his ear to the ground, which, as the adviser thought, would return a hollow sound if the artful foe had dug a mine under it; and whenever such secret danger was detected, a mark was to be set on the spot, to warn off the soldiers.[1]

Equally zealous, after another fashion, was the Reverend Samuel Moody, popularly known as Father Moody, or Parson Moody, minister of York and senior chaplain of the expedition. Though about seventy years old, he was amazingly tough and sturdy. He still lives in the traditions of York as the spiritual despot of the settlement and the uncompromising guardian of its manners and doctrine, predominating over it like a rough little village pope. The comparison would have kindled his burning wrath, for he abhorred the Holy Father as an embodied Antichrist. Many are the stories told of him by the descendants of those who lived under his rod, and sometimes felt its weight; for he was known to have corrected offending parishioners with his cane.[2] When some one of his flock, nettled by his strictures from the pulpit, walked in dudgeon towards the church door, Moody would shout after

---

[1] Belknap, *Hist. New Hampshire*, II. 208.
[2] Tradition told me at York by Mr. N. Marshall.

him, "Come back, you graceless sinner, come back!" or if any ventured to the alehouse of a Saturday night, the strenuous pastor would go in after them, collar them, drag them out, and send them home with rousing admonition.[1] Few dared gainsay him, by reason both of his irritable temper and of the thick-skinned insensibility that encased him like armor of proof. And while his pachydermatous nature made him invulnerable as a rhinoceros, he had at the same time a rough and ready humor that supplied keen weapons for the warfare of words and made him a formidable antagonist. This commended him to the rude borderers, who also relished the sulphurous theology of their spiritual dictator, just as they liked the raw and fiery liquors that would have scorched more susceptible stomachs. What they did not like was the pitiless length of his prayers, which sometimes kept them afoot above two hours shivering in the polar cold of the unheated meeting-house, and which were followed by sermons of equal endurance; for the old man's lungs were of brass, and his nerves of hammered iron. Some of the sufferers ventured to remonstrate; but this only exasperated him, till one parishioner, more worldly wise than the rest, accompanied his modest petition for mercy with the gift of a barrel of cider, after which the Parson's ministrations were perceptibly less exhausting than before. He had an irrepressible conscience and a highly aggressive sense of duty, which made him an intolerable meddler in the affairs of other people, and which, joined to an underlying kindness of heart, made him so indiscreet in his charities that his wife and children were often driven to vain protest against the excesses of his almsgiving. The old Puritan fanaticism was rampant in him; and when he sailed for Louisbourg, he took with him an axe, intended, as he said, to hew down the altars of Antichrist and demolish his idols.[2]

Shirley's choice of a commander was perhaps the best that could have been made; for Pepperrell joined to an unusual

[1] Lecture of Ralph Waldo Emerson, quoted by Cabot, *Memoir of Emerson*, I. 10.

[2] Moody found sympathizers in his iconoclastic zeal. Deacon John Gray of Biddeford wrote to Pepperrell: "Oh that I could be with you and dear Parson Moody in that church [at Louisbourg] to destroy the images there set up, and hear the true Gospel of our Lord and Saviour there preached!"

popularity as little military incompetency as anybody else who could be had. Popularity, we have seen, was indispensable, and even company officers were appointed with an eye to it. Many of these were well-known men in rustic neighborhoods, who had raised companies in the hope of being commissioned to command them. Others were militia officers recruiting under orders of the Governor. Thus, John Storer, major in the Maine militia, raised in a single day, it is said, a company of sixty-one, the eldest being sixty years old, and the youngest sixteen.[1] They formed about a quarter of the fencible population of the town of Wells, one of the most exposed places on the border. Volunteers offered themselves readily everywhere; though the pay was meagre, especially in Maine and Massachusetts, where in the new provincial currency it was twenty-five shillings a month,—then equal to fourteen shillings sterling, or less than sixpence a day,[2] the soldier furnishing his own clothing and bringing his own gun. A full third of the Massachusetts contingent, or more than a thousand men, are reported to have come from the hardy population of Maine, whose entire fighting force, as shown by the muster-rolls, was then but 2,855.[3] Perhaps there was not one officer among them whose experience of war extended beyond a drill on muster day and the sham fight that closed the performance, when it generally happened that the rustic warriors were treated with rum at the charge of their captain, to put them in good humor, and so induce them to obey the word of command.

As the three provinces contributing soldiers recognized no common authority nearer than the King, Pepperrell received three several commissions as lieutenant-general,—one from the Governor of Massachusetts, and the others from the Governors of Connecticut and New Hampshire; while Wolcott, commander of the Connecticut forces, was commissioned as major-general by both the Governor of his own province and that of Massachusetts. When the levies were complete, it was

---

[1] Bourne, *Hist. of Wells and Kennebunk*, 371.

[2] Gibson, *Journal; Records of Rhode Island*, V. Governor Wanton, of that province, says, with complacency, that the pay of Rhode Island was twice that of Massachusetts.

[3] Parsons, *Life of Pepperrell*, 54.

found that Massachusetts had contributed about 3,300 men, Connecticut 516, and New Hampshire 304 in her own pay, besides 150 paid by her wealthier neighbor.[1] Rhode Island had lost faith and disbanded her 150 men; but afterwards raised them again, though too late to take part in the siege.

Each of the four New England colonies had a little navy of its own, consisting of from one to three or four small armed vessels; and as privateering—which was sometimes a euphemism for piracy where Frenchmen and Spaniards were concerned—was a favorite occupation, it was possible to extemporize an additional force in case of need. For a naval commander, Shirley chose Captain Edward Tyng, who had signalized himself in the past summer by capturing a French privateer of greater strength than his own. Shirley authorized him to buy for the province the best ship he could find, equip her for fighting, and take command of her. Tyng soon found a brig to his mind, on the stocks nearly ready for launching. She was rapidly fitted for her new destination, converted into a frigate, mounted with 24 guns, and named the "Massachusetts." The rest of the naval force consisted of the ship "Cæsar," of 20 guns; a vessel called the "Shirley," commanded by Captain Rous, and also carrying 20 guns; another, of the kind called a "snow," carrying 16 guns; one sloop of 12 guns, and two of 8 guns each; the "Boston Packet," of 16 guns; two sloops from Connecticut of 16 guns each; a privateer hired in Rhode Island, of 20 guns; the government sloop "Tartar," of the same colony, carrying 14 carriage guns and 12 swivels; and, finally, the sloop of 14 guns which formed the navy of New Hampshire.[2]

It was said, with apparent reason, that one or two heavy French ships-of-war—and a number of such was expected in the spring—would outmatch the whole colonial squadron, and, after mastering it, would hold all the transports at mercy; so that the troops on shore, having no means of return and no hope of succor, would be forced to surrender or starve. The danger was real and serious, and Shirley felt the necessity of help from a few British ships-of-war. Commo-

---

[1] Of the Massachusetts contingent, three hundred men were raised and maintained at the charge of the merchant James Gibson.

[2] The list is given by Williamson, II. 227.

dore Peter Warren was then with a small squadron at Antigua. Shirley sent an express boat to him with a letter stating
the situation and asking his aid. Warren, who had married an
American woman and who owned large tracts of land on the
Mohawk, was known to be a warm friend to the provinces.
It is clear that he would gladly have complied with Shirley's
request; but when he laid the question before a council of
officers, they were of one mind that without orders from the
Admiralty he would not be justified in supporting an attempt
made without the approval of the King.[1] He therefore saw
no choice but to decline. Shirley, fearing that his refusal
would be too discouraging, kept it secret from all but Pepperrell and General Wolcott, or, as others say, Brigadier
Waldo. He had written to the Duke of Newcastle in the preceding autumn that Acadia and the fisheries were in great
danger, and that ships-of-war were needed for their protection. On this, the Duke had written to Warren, ordering him
to sail for Boston and concert measures with Shirley "for the
annoyance of the enemy, and his Majesty's service in North
America."[2] Newcastle's letter reached Warren only two or
three days after he had sent back his refusal of Shirley's request. Thinking himself now sufficiently authorized to give
the desired aid, he made all sail for Boston with his three
ships, the "Superbe," "Mermaid," and "Launceston." On the
way he met a schooner from Boston, and learned from its
officers that the expedition had already sailed; on which, detaining the master as a pilot, he changed his course and made
directly for Canseau,—the place of rendezvous of the expedition,—and at the same time sent orders by the schooner
that any King's ships that might arrive at Boston should immediately join him.

Within seven weeks after Shirley issued his proclamation
for volunteers, the preparations were all made, and the unique
armament was afloat. Transports, such as they were, could be
had in abundance; for the harbors of Salem and Marblehead
were full of fishing-vessels thrown out of employment by the

[1] *Memoirs of the Principal Transactions of the Last War*, 44.
[2] *Ibid.*, 46. *Letters of Shirley* (Public Record Office).

war. These were hired and insured by the province for the security of the owners. There was a great dearth of cannon. The few that could be had were too light, the heaviest being of twenty-two-pound calibre. New York lent ten eighteen-pounders to the expedition. But the adventurers looked to the French for their chief supply. A detached work near Louisbourg, called the Grand, or Royal, Battery, was known to be armed with thirty heavy pieces; and these it was proposed to capture and turn against the town,—which, as Hutchinson remarks, was "like selling the skin of the bear before catching him."

It was clear that the expedition must run for luck against risks of all kinds. Those whose hopes were highest, based them on a belief in the special and direct interposition of Providence; others were sanguine through ignorance and provincial self-conceit. As soon as the troops were embarked, Shirley wrote to the ministers of what was going on, telling them that, accidents apart, four thousand New England men would land on Cape Breton in April, and that, even should they fail to capture Louisbourg, he would answer for it that they would lay the town in ruins, retake Canseau, do other good service to his Majesty, and then come safe home.[1] On receiving this communication, the Government resolved to aid the enterprise if there should yet be time, and accordingly ordered several ships-of-war to sail for Louisbourg.

The sarcastic Dr. Douglas, then living at Boston, writes that the expedition had a lawyer for contriver, a merchant for general, and farmers, fishermen, and mechanics for soldiers. In fact, it had something of the character of broad farce, to which Shirley himself, with all his ability and general good sense, was a chief contributor. He wrote to the Duke of Newcastle that though the officers had no experience and the men no discipline, he would take care to provide against these defects,—meaning that he would give exact directions how to take Louisbourg. Accordingly, he drew up copious instructions to that effect. These seem to have undergone a process

---

[1] *Shirley to Newcastle, 24 March, 1745.* The ministry was not wholly unprepared for this announcement, as Shirley had before reported to it the vote of his Assembly consenting to the expedition. *Shirley to Newcastle, 1 Feb. 1745.*

of evolution, for several distinct drafts of them are preserved.[1] The complete and final one is among the Pepperrell Papers, copied entire in the neat, commercial hand of the General himself.[2] It seems to assume that Providence would work a continued miracle, and on every occasion supply the expedition with weather precisely suited to its wants. "It is thought," says this singular document, "that Louisbourg may be surprised if they [the French] have no advice of your coming. To effect it you must time your arrival about nine of the clock in the evening, taking care that the fleet be far enough in the offing to prevent their being seen from the town in the daytime." He then goes on to prescribe how the troops are to land, after dark, at a place called Flat Point Cove, in four divisions, three of which are to march to the back of certain hills a mile and a half west of the town, where two of the three "are to halt and keep a profound silence;" the third continuing its march "under cover of the said hills," till it comes opposite the Grand Battery, which it will attack at a concerted signal; while one of the two divisions behind the hills assaults the west gate, and the other moves up to support the attack.

While this is going on, the soldiers of the fourth division are to march with all speed along the shore till they come to a certain part of the town wall, which they are to scale; then proceed "as fast as can be" to the citadel and "secure the windows of the Governor's apartments." After this follow page after page of complicated details which must have stricken the General with stupefaction. The rocks, surf, fogs, and gales of that tempestuous coast are all left out of the account; and so, too, is the nature of the country, which consists of deep

[1] The first draft of Shirley's instructions for taking Louisbourg is in the large manuscript volume entitled *Siege of Louisbourg*, in the library of the Massachusetts Historical Society. The document is called *Mem° for the attacking of Louisbourg this Spring by Surprise*. After giving minute instructions for every movement, it goes on to say that, as the surprise may possibly fail, it will be necessary to send two small mortars and twelve cannon carrying nine-pound balls, "so as to bombard them and endeavour to make Breaches in their walls and then to Storm them." Shirley was soon to discover the absurdity of trying to breach the walls of Louisbourg with nine-pounders.

[2] It is printed in the first volume of the *Collections of the Massachusetts Historical Society*. Shirley was so well pleased with it that he sent it to the Duke of Newcastle enclosed in his letter of 1 Feb. 1745 (Public Record Office).

marshes, rocky hills, and hollows choked with evergreen thickets. Yet a series of complex and mutually dependent operations, involving long marches through this rugged and pathless region, was to be accomplished, in the darkness of one April night, by raw soldiers who knew nothing of the country. This rare specimen of amateur soldiering is redeemed in some measure by a postscript in which the Governor sets free the hands of the General, thus: "Notwithstanding the instructions you have received from me, I must leave you to act, upon unforeseen emergencies, according to your best discretion."

On the 24th of March, the fleet, consisting of about ninety transports, escorted by the provincial cruisers, sailed from Nantasket Roads, followed by prayers and benedictions, and also by toasts drunk with cheers, in bumpers of rum punch.[1]

[1] The following letter from John Payne of Boston to Colonel Robert Hale, of the Essex regiment, while it gives no sign of the prevailing religious feeling, illustrates the ardor of the New England people towards their rash adventure: —

BOSTON, Apr. 24, 1745.

SIR,

I hope this will find you at Louisbourg with a Bowl of Punch a Pipe and a P—k of C—ds in your hand and whatever else you desire (I had forgot to mention a Pretty French Madammoselle). We are very Impatiently expecting to hear from you, your Friend Luke has lost several Beaver Hatts already concerning the Expedition, he is so very zealous about it that he has turned Poor Boutier out of his House for saying he believed you would not Take the Place.——Damn his Blood says Luke, let him be an Englishman or a Frenchman and not pretend to be an Englishman when he is a Frenchman in his Heart. If drinking to your success would Take Cape Briton, you must be in Possession of it now, for it 's a standing Toast. I think the least thing you Military Gent[n] can do is to send us some arrack when you take ye Place to celebrate your Victory and not to force us to do it in Rum Punch or Luke's bad wine or sour cyder.

To Collonell Robert Hale
    at (or near) Louisbourg.

I am indebted for a copy of this curious letter to Robert Hale Bancroft, Esq., a descendant of Colonel Hale.

Chapter XIX

1745

LOUISBOURG BESIEGED

Seth Pomeroy • The Voyage • Canseau • Unexpected Succors •
Delays • Louisbourg • The Landing • The Grand Battery taken
• French Cannon turned on the Town • Weakness of Duchambon
• Sufferings of the Besiegers • Their Hardihood • Their Irregular
Proceedings • Joseph Sherburn • Amateur Gunnery • Camp
Frolics • Sectarian Zeal • Perplexities of Pepperrell

O N BOARD one of the transports was Seth Pomeroy, gunsmith at Northampton, and now major of Willard's Massachusetts regiment. He had a turn for soldiering, and fought, ten years later, in the battle of Lake George. Again, twenty years later still, when Northampton was astir with rumors of war from Boston, he borrowed a neighbor's horse, rode a hundred miles, reached Cambridge on the morning of the battle of Bunker Hill, left his borrowed horse out of the way of harm, walked over Charlestown Neck, then swept by the fire of the ships-of-war, and reached the scene of action as the British were forming for the attack. When Israel Putnam, his comrade in the last war, saw from the rebel breastwork the old man striding, gun in hand, up the hill, he shouted, "By God, Pomeroy, you here! A cannon-shot would waken you out of your grave!"

But Pomeroy, with other landsmen, crowded in the small and malodorous fishing-vessels that were made to serve as transports, was now in the gripe of the most unheroic of maladies. "A terrible northeast storm" had fallen upon them, and, he says, "we lay rolling in the seas, with our sails furled, among prodigious waves." "Sick, day and night," writes the miserable gunsmith, "so bad that I have not words to set it forth."[1] The gale increased and the fleet was scattered, there being, as a Massachusetts private soldier writes in his diary, "a very fierse Storm of Snow, som Rain and very Dangerous

[1] Diary of Major Seth Pomeroy. I owe the copy before me to the kindness of his descendant, Theodore Pomeroy, Esq.

weather to be so nigh ye Shore as we was; but we escaped the Rocks, and that was all."[1]

On Friday, April 5th, Pomeroy's vessel entered the harbor of Canseau, about fifty miles from Louisbourg. Here was the English fishing-hamlet, the seizure of which by the French had first provoked the expedition. The place now quietly changed hands again. Sixty-eight of the transports lay here at anchor, and the rest came dropping in from day to day, sorely buffeted, but all safe. On Sunday there was a great concourse to hear Parson Moody preach an open-air sermon from the text, "Thy people shall be willing in the day of thy power," concerning which occasion the soldier diarist observes,— "Several sorts of Busnesses was Going on, Som a Exercising, Som a Hearing Preaching." The attention of Parson Moody's listeners was, in fact, distracted by shouts of command and the awkward drill of squads of homespun soldiers on the adjacent pasture.

Captain Ammi Cutter, with two companies, was ordered to remain at Canseau and defend it from farther vicissitudes; to which end a blockhouse was also built, and mounted with eight small cannon. Some of the armed vessels had been sent to cruise off Louisbourg, which they did to good purpose, and presently brought in six French prizes, with supplies for the fortress. On the other hand, they brought the ominous news that Louisbourg and the adjoining bay were so blocked with ice that landing was impossible. This was a serious misfortune, involving long delay, and perhaps ruin to the expedition, as the expected ships-of-war might arrive meanwhile from France. Indeed, they had already begun to appear. On Thursday, the 18th, heavy cannonading was heard far out at sea, and again on Friday "the cannon," says Pomeroy, "fired at a great rate till about 2 of the clock." It was the provincial cruisers attacking a French frigate, the "Renommée," of thirty-six guns. As their united force was too much for her, she kept up a running fight, outsailed them, and escaped after a chase of more than thirty hours, being, as Pomeroy quaintly observes, "a smart ship." She carried despatches to the Governor of Louisbourg, and being unable to deliver

[1] Diary of a Massachusetts soldier in Captain Richardson's company (Papers of Dr. Belknap).

them, sailed back for France to report what she had seen.

On Monday, the 22d, a clear, cold, windy day, a large ship, under British colors, sailed into the harbor, and proved to be the frigate "Eltham," escort to the annual mast fleet from New England. On orders from Commander Warren she had left her charge in waiting, and sailed for Canseau to join the expedition, bringing the unexpected and welcome news that Warren himself would soon follow. On the next day, to the delight of all, he appeared in the ship "Superbe," of sixty guns, accompanied by the "Launceston" and the "Mermaid," of forty guns each. Here was force enough to oppose any ships likely to come to the aid of Louisbourg; and Warren, after communicating with Pepperrell, sailed to blockade the port, along with the provincial cruisers, which, by order of Shirley, were placed under his command.

The transports lay at Canseau nearly three weeks, waiting for the ice to break up. The time was passed in drilling the raw soldiers and forming them into divisions of four and six hundred each, according to the directions of Shirley. At length, on Friday, the 27th, they heard that Gabarus Bay was free from ice, and on the morning of the 29th, with the first fair wind, they sailed out of Canseau harbor, expecting to reach Louisbourg at nine in the evening, as prescribed in the Governor's receipt for taking Louisbourg "while the enemy were asleep."[1] But a lull in the wind defeated this plan; and after sailing all day, they found themselves becalmed towards night. It was not till the next morning that they could see the town,—no very imposing spectacle, for the buildings, with a few exceptions, were small, and the massive ramparts that belted them round rose to no conspicuous height.

Louisbourg stood on a tongue of land which lay between its harbor and the sea, and the end of which was prolonged eastward by reefs and shoals that partly barred the entrance to the port, leaving a navigable passage not half a mile wide. This passage was commanded by a powerful battery called the "Island Battery," being upon a small rocky island at the west side of the channel, and was also secured by another detached work called the "Grand," or "Royal Battery," which stood on the shore of the harbor, opposite the entrance, and more than

[1] The words quoted are used by General Wolcott in his journal.

a mile from the town. Thus a hostile squadron trying to force its way in would receive a flank fire from the one battery, and a front fire from the other. The strongest line of defence of the fortress was drawn across the base of the tongue of land from the harbor on one side to the sea on the other,—a distance of about twelve hundred yards. The ditch was eighty feet wide and from thirty to thirty-six feet deep; and the rampart, of earth faced with masonry, was about sixty feet thick. The glacis sloped down to a vast marsh, which formed one of the best defences of the place. The fortress, without counting its outworks, had embrasures for one hundred and forty-eight cannon; but the number in position was much less, and is variously stated. Pomeroy says that at the end of the siege a little above ninety were found, with "a great number of swivels;" others say seventy-six.[1] In the Grand and Island batteries there were sixty heavy pieces more. Against this formidable armament the assailants had brought thirty-four cannon and mortars, of much inferior weight, to be used in bombarding the fortress, should they chance to fail of carrying it by surprise, "while the enemy were asleep."[2] Apparently they distrusted the efficacy of their siege-train, though it was far stronger than Shirley had at first thought sufficient; for they brought with them good store of balls of forty-two pounds, to be used in French cannon of that calibre which they expected to capture, their own largest pieces being but twenty-two-pounders.

According to the *Habitant de Louisbourg*, the garrison consisted of five hundred and sixty regular troops, of whom several companies were Swiss, besides some thirteen or fourteen hundred militia, inhabitants partly of the town, and partly of neighboring settlements.[3] The regulars were in bad condi-

---

[1] Brown, *Cape Breton*, 183. Parsons, *Life of Pepperrell*, 103. An anonymous letter, dated Louisbourg, 4 July, 1745, says that eighty-five cannon and six mortars have been found in the town.

[2] *Memoirs of the Principal Transactions of the Last War*, 40.

[3] "On fit venir cinq ou six cens Miliciens aux Habitans des environs; ce que, avec ceux de la Ville, pouvoit former treize à quatorze cens hommes." —*Lettre d'un Habitant de Louisbourg*. This writer says that three or four hundred more might have been had from Niganiche and its neighborhood, if they had been summoned in time. The number of militia just after the siege is set by English reports at 1,310. Parsons, 103.

tion. About the preceding Christmas they had broken into mutiny, being discontented with their rations and exasperated with getting no extra pay for work on the fortifications. The affair was so serious that though order was restored, some of the officers lost all confidence in the soldiers; and this distrust proved most unfortunate during the siege. The Governor, Chevalier Duchambon, successor of Duquesnel, who had died in the autumn, was not a man to grapple with a crisis, being deficient in decision of character, if not in capacity.

He expected an attack. "We were informed of the preparations from the first," says the *Habitant de Louisbourg*. Some Indians, who had been to Boston, carried to Canada the news of what was going on there; but it was not believed, and excited no alarm.[1] It was not so at Louisbourg, where, says the French writer just quoted, "we lost precious moments in useless deliberations and resolutions no sooner made than broken. Nothing to the purpose was done, so that we were as much taken by surprise as if the enemy had pounced upon us unawares."

It was about the 25th of March[2] when the garrison first saw the provincial cruisers hovering off the mouth of the harbor. They continued to do so at intervals till daybreak of the 30th of April, when the whole fleet of transports appeared standing towards Flat Point, which projects into Gabarus Bay, three miles west of the town.[3] On this, Duchambon sent Morpain, captain of a privateer, or "corsair," to oppose the landing. He had with him eighty men, and was to be joined by forty more, already on the watch near the supposed point of disembarkation.[4] At the same time cannon were fired and alarm bells rung in Louisbourg, to call in the militia of the neighborhood.

Pepperrell managed the critical work of landing with creditable skill. The rocks and the surf were more dangerous than the enemy. Several boats, filled with men, rowed towards Flat

[1] *Shirley to Newcastle, 17 June, 1745*, citing letters captured on board a ship from Quebec.

[2] 14 March, old style.

[3] Gabarus Bay, sometimes called "Chapeau Rouge" Bay, is a spacious outer harbor, immediately adjoining Louisbourg.

[4] *Bigot au Ministre, 1 Août, 1745*.

Point; but on a signal from the flagship "Shirley," rowed back again, Morpain flattering himself that his appearance had frightened them off. Being joined by several other boats, the united party, a hundred men in all, pulled for another landing-place called Fresh-water Cove, or Anse de la Cormorandière, two miles farther up Gabarus Bay. Morpain and his party ran to meet them; but the boats were first in the race, and as soon as the New England men got ashore, they rushed upon the French, killed six of them, captured as many more, including an officer named Boularderie, and put the rest to flight, with the loss, on their own side, of two men slightly wounded.[1] Further resistance to the landing was impossible, for a swarm of boats pushed against the rough and stony beach, the men dashing through the surf, till before night about two thousand were on shore.[2] The rest, or about two thousand more, landed at their leisure on the next day.

On the 2d of May Vaughan led four hundred men to the hills near the town, and saluted it with three cheers,—somewhat to the discomposure of the French, though they describe the unwelcome visitors as a disorderly crowd. Vaughan's next proceeding pleased them still less. He marched behind the hills, in rear of the Grand Battery, to the northeast arm of the harbor, where there were extensive magazines of naval stores. These his men set on fire, and the pitch, tar, and other combustibles made a prodigious smoke. He was returning, in the morning, with a small party of followers behind the hills, when coming opposite the Grand Battery, and observing it from the ridge, he saw neither flag on the flagstaff, nor smoke from the barrack chimneys. One of his party was a Cape Cod Indian. Vaughan bribed him with a flask of brandy which he had in his pocket,—though, as the clerical historian takes pains to assure us, he never used it himself,—and the Indian, pretending to be drunk, or, as some say, mad, staggered towards the battery to reconnoitre.[3]

---

[1] *Pepperrell to Shirley, 12 May 1745. Shirley to Newcastle, 28 Oct. 1745. Journal of the Siege*, attested by Pepperrell and four other chief officers (London, 1746).

[2] Bigot says six thousand, or two thousand more than the whole New England force, which was constantly overestimated by the French.

[3] Belknap, II.

All was quiet. He clambered in at an embrasure, and found the place empty. The rest of the party followed, and one of them, William Tufts, of Medford, a boy of eighteen, climbed the flagstaff, holding in his teeth his red coat, which he made fast at the top, as a substitute for the British flag,—a proceeding that drew upon him a volley of unsuccessful cannon-shot from the town batteries.[1]

Vaughan then sent this hasty note to Pepperrell: "May it please your Honour to be informed that by the grace of God and the courage of 13 men, I entered the Royal Battery about 9 o'clock, and am waiting for a reinforcement and a flag." Soon after, four boats, filled with men, approached from the town to re-occupy the battery,—no doubt in order to save the munitions and stores, and complete the destruction of the cannon. Vaughan and his thirteen men, standing on the open beach, under the fire of the town and the Island Battery, plied the boats with musketry, and kept them from landing, till Lieutenant-Colonel Bradstreet appeared with a reinforcement, on which the French pulled back to Louisbourg.[2]

The English supposed that the French in the battery, when the clouds of smoke drifted over them from the burning storehouses, thought that they were to be attacked in force, and abandoned their post in a panic. This was not the case. "A detachment of the enemy," writes the *Habitant de Louisbourg*, "advanced to the neighborhood of the Royal Battery." This was Vaughan's four hundred on their way to burn the storehouses. "At once we were all seized with fright," pursues this candid writer, "and on the instant it was proposed to abandon this magnificent battery, which would have been our best defence, if one had known how to use it. Various councils were held, in a tumultuous way. It would be hard to tell the reasons for such a strange proceeding. Not one shot had yet been fired at the battery, which the enemy could not take, except by making regular approaches, as if against the town

---

[1] John Langdon Sibley, in *N. E. Hist. and Gen. Register*, XXV. 377. The *Boston Gazette* of 3 June, 1771, has a notice of Tufts's recent death, with an exaggerated account of his exploit, and an appeal for aid to his destitute family.

[2] Vaughan's party seems to have consisted in all of sixteen men, three of whom took no part in this affair.

itself, and by besieging it, so to speak, in form. Some persons remonstrated, but in vain; and so a battery of thirty cannon, which had cost the King immense sums, was abandoned before it was attacked."

Duchambon says that soon after the English landed, he got a letter from Thierry, the captain in command of the Royal Battery, advising that the cannon should be spiked and the works blown up. It was then, according to the Governor, that the council was called, and a unanimous vote passed to follow Thierry's advice, on the ground that the defences of the battery were in bad condition, and that the four hundred men posted there could not stand against three or four thousand.[1] The engineer, Verrier, opposed the blowing up of the works, and they were therefore left untouched. Thierry and his garrison came off in boats, after spiking the cannon in a hasty way, without stopping to knock off the trunnions or burn the carriages. They threw their loose gunpowder into the well, but left behind a good number of cannon cartridges, two hundred and eighty large bombshells, and other ordnance stores, invaluable both to the enemy and to themselves. Brigadier Waldo was sent to occupy the battery with his regiment, and Major Seth Pomeroy, the gunsmith, with twenty soldier-mechanics, was set at drilling out the spiked touch-holes of the cannon. These were twenty-eight forty-two-pounders, and two eighteen-pounders.[2] Several were ready for use the next morning, and immediately opened on the town,— which, writes a soldier in his diary, "damaged the houses and made the women cry." "The enemy," says the *Habitant de Louisbourg*, "saluted us with our own cannon, and made a terrific fire, smashing everything within range."

[1] *Duchambon au Ministre, 2 Sept. 1745.* This is the Governor's official report. "Four hundred men" is perhaps a copyist's error, the actual number in the battery being not above two hundred.

[2] *Waldo to Shirley, 12 May, 1745.* Some of the French writers say twenty-eight thirty-six-pounders, while all the English call them forty-twos,—which they must have been, as the forty-two-pound shot brought from Boston fitted them.

Mr. Theodore Roosevelt draws my attention to the fact that cannon were differently rated in the French and English navies of the seventeenth century, and that a French thirty-six carried a ball as large as an English forty-two, or even a little larger.

The English occupation of the Grand Battery may be called the decisive event of the siege. There seems no doubt that the French could have averted the disaster long enough to make it of little help to the invaders. The water-front of the battery was impregnable. The rear defences consisted of a loopholed wall of masonry, with a ditch ten feet deep and twelve feet wide, and also a covered way and glacis, which General Wolcott describes as unfinished. In this he mistook. They were not unfinished, but had been partly demolished, with a view to reconstruction. The rear wall was flanked by two towers, which, says Duchambon, were demolished; but General Wolcott declares that swivels were still mounted on them,[1] and he adds that "two hundred men might hold the battery against five thousand without cannon." The English landed their cannon near Flat Point; and before they could be turned against the Grand Battery, they must be dragged four miles over hills and rocks, through spongy marshes and jungles of matted evergreens. This would have required a week or more. The alternative was an escalade, in which the undisciplined assailants would no doubt have met a bloody rebuff. Thus this Grand Battery, which, says Wolcott, "is in fact a fort," might at least have been held long enough to save the munitions and stores, and effectually disable the cannon, which supplied the English with the only artillery they had, competent to the work before them. The hasty abandonment of this important post was not Duchambon's only blunder, but it was the worst of them all.

On the night after their landing, the New England men slept in the woods, wet or dry, with or without blankets, as the case might be, and in the morning set themselves to encamping with as much order as they were capable of. A brook ran down from the hills and entered the sea two miles or more from the town. The ground on each side, though rough, was high and dry, and here most of the regiments made their quarters,—Willard's, Moulton's, and Moore's on the east side, and Burr's and Pepperrell's on the west. Those on the east, in some cases, saw fit to extend themselves towards Louisbourg as far as the edge of the intervening marsh;

---

[1] *Journal of Major-General Wolcott.*

but were soon forced back to a safer position by the cannon-balls of the fortress, which came bowling amongst them. This marsh was that green, flat sponge of mud and moss that stretched from this point to the glacis of Louisbourg.

There was great want of tents, for material to make them was scarce in New England. Old sails were often used instead, being stretched over poles,—perhaps after the fashion of a Sioux teepee. When these could not be had, the men built huts of sods, with roofs of spruce-boughs overlapping like a thatch; for at that early season, bark would not peel from the trees. The landing of guns, munitions, and stores was a for-midable task, consuming many days and destroying many boats, as happened again when Amherst landed his cannon at this same place. Large flat boats, brought from Boston, were used for the purpose, and the loads were carried ashore on the heads of the men, wading through ice-cold surf to the waist, after which, having no change of clothing, they slept on the ground through the chill and foggy nights, reckless of future rheumatisms.[1]

A worse task was before them. The cannon were to be dragged over the marsh to Green Hill, a spur of the line of rough heights that half encircled the town and harbor. Here the first battery was to be planted; and from this point other guns were to be dragged onward to more advanced sta-tions,—a distance in all of more than two miles, thought by the French to be impassable. So, in fact, it seemed; for at the first attempt, the wheels of the cannon sank to the hubs in mud and moss, then the carriage, and finally the piece itself slowly disappeared. Lieutenant-Colonel Meserve, of the New Hampshire regiment, a ship-builder by trade, presently over-came the difficulty. By his direction sledges of timber were made, sixteen feet long and five feet wide; a cannon was placed on each of these, and it was then dragged over the marsh by a team of two hundred men, harnessed with rope-

[1] The author of *The Importance and Advantage of Cape Breton* says: "When the hardships they were exposed to come to be considered, the behaviour of these men will hardly gain credit. They went ashore wet, had no [dry] clothes to cover them, were exposed in this condition to cold, foggy nights, and yet cheerfully underwent these difficulties for the sake of executing a project they had voluntarily undertaken."

traces and breast-straps, and wading to the knees. Horses or oxen would have foundered in the mire. The way had often to be changed, as the mossy surface was soon churned into a hopeless slough along the line of march. The work could be done only at night or in thick fog, the men being completely exposed to the cannon of the town. Thirteen years after, when General Amherst besieged Louisbourg again, he dragged his cannon to the same hill over the same marsh; but having at his command, instead of four thousand militiamen, eleven thousand British regulars, with all appliances and means to boot, he made a road, with prodigious labor, through the mire, and protected it from the French shot by an epaulement, or lateral earthwork.[1]

Pepperrell writes in ardent words of the cheerfulness of his men "under almost incredible hardships." Shoes and clothing failed, till many were in tatters and many barefooted;[2] yet they toiled on with unconquerable spirit, and within four days had planted a battery of six guns on Green Hill, which was about a mile from the King's Bastion of Louisbourg. In another week they had dragged four twenty-two-pound cannon and ten coehorns—gravely called "cowhorns" by the bucolic Pomeroy—six or seven hundred yards farther, and planted them within easy range of the citadel. Two of the cannon burst, and were replaced by four more and a large mortar, which burst in its turn, and Shirley was begged to send another. Meanwhile a battery, chiefly of coehorns, had been planted on a hillock four hundred and forty yards from the West Gate, where it greatly annoyed the French; and on the next night an advanced battery was placed just opposite the same gate, and scarcely two hundred and fifty yards from it. This West Gate, the principal gate of Louisbourg, opened upon the tract of high, firm ground that lay on the left of the besiegers, between the marsh and the harbor, an arm of which here extended westward beyond the town, into what was called the Barachois, a salt pond formed by a projecting spit of sand. On the side of the Barachois farthest from the town was a hillock on which stood the house of an *habitant* named Martissan. Here, on the 20th of May, a fifth battery

[1] See *Montcalm and Wolfe*, chap. xix.
[2] *Pepperrell to Newcastle, 28 June, 1745.*

was planted, consisting of two of the French forty-two-pounders taken in the Grand Battery, to which three others were afterwards added. Each of these heavy pieces was dragged to its destination by a team of three hundred men over rough and rocky ground swept by the French artillery. This fifth battery, called the Northwest, or Titcomb's, proved most destructive to the fortress.[1]

All these operations were accomplished with the utmost ardor and energy, but with a scorn of rule and precedent that astonished and bewildered the French. The raw New England men went their own way, laughed at trenches and zigzags, and persisted in trusting their lives to the night and the fog. Several writers say that the English engineer Bastide tried to teach them discretion; but this could hardly be, for Bastide, whose station was Annapolis, did not reach Louisbourg till the 5th of June, when the batteries were finished and the siege was nearly ended. A recent French writer makes the curious assertion that it was one of the ministers, or army chaplains, who took upon him the vain task of instruction in the art of war on this occasion.[2]

This ignorant and self-satisfied recklessness might have cost the besiegers dear if the French, instead of being perplexed and startled at the novelty of their proceedings, had taken advantage of it; but Duchambon and some of his officers, remembering the mutiny of the past winter, feared to make sorties, lest the soldiers might desert or take part with the enemy. The danger of this appears to have been small. Warren speaks with wonder in his letters of the rarity of desertions, of which there appear to have been but three during the siege,—one being that of a half-idiot, from whom no information could be got. A bolder commander would not have stood idle while his own cannon were planted by the enemy to batter down his walls; and whatever the risks of a sortie, the risks of not making one were greater. "Both troops and militia eagerly demanded it, and I believe it would have suc-

---

[1] *Journal of the Siege*, appended to Shirley's report to Newcastle; *Duchambon au Ministre, 2 Sept. 1745*; *Lettre d'un Habitant*; Pomeroy, etc.

[2] Ferland, *Cours d'Histoire du Canada*, II. 477. "L'ennemi ne nous attaquoit point dans les formes, et ne pratiquoit point aucun retranchement pour se couvrir." *Habitant de Louisbourg*.

ceeded," writes the Intendant, Bigot.[1] The attempt was actually made more than once in a half-hearted way,—notably on the 8th of May, when the French attacked the most advanced battery, and were repulsed, with little loss on either side.

The *Habitant de Louisbourg* says: "The enemy did not attack us with any regularity, and made no intrenchments to cover themselves." This last is not exact. Not being wholly demented, they made intrenchments, such as they were,—at least at the advanced battery;[2] as they would otherwise have been swept out of existence, being under the concentred fire of several French batteries, two of which were within the range of a musket shot.

The scarcity of good gunners was one of the chief difficulties of the besiegers. As privateering, and piracy also, against Frenchmen and Spaniards was a favorite pursuit in New England, there were men in Pepperrell's army who knew how to handle cannon; but their number was insufficient, and the General sent a note to Warren, begging that he would lend him a few experienced gunners to teach their trade to the raw hands at the batteries. Three or four were sent, and they found apt pupils.

Pepperrell placed the advanced battery in charge of Captain Joseph[3] Sherburn, telling him to enlist as many gunners as he could. On the next day Sherburn reported that he had found six, one of whom seems to have been sent by Warren. With these and a number of raw men he repaired to his perilous station, where "I found," he says, "a very poor intrenchment. Our best shelter from the French fire, which was very hot, was hogsheads filled with earth." He and his men made the West Gate their chief mark; but before they could get a fair sight of it, they were forced to shoot down the fish-flakes, or stages for drying cod, that obstructed the view. Some of their party were soon killed,—Captain Pierce by a cannon-ball, Thomas Ash by a "bumb," and others by musketry. In the night they improved their defences, and mounted on them

---

[1] *Bigot au Ministre, 1 Août, 1745.*

[2] *Diary of Joseph Sherburn, Captain at the Advanced Battery.*

[3] He signs his name Jos. Sherburn; but in a list of the officers of the New Hampshire Regiment it appears in full as Joseph.

three more guns, one of eighteen-pound calibre, and the others of forty-two,—French pieces dragged from the Grand Battery, a mile and three quarters round the Barachois.

The cannon could be loaded only under a constant fire of musketry, which the enemy briskly returned. The French practice was excellent. A soldier who in bravado mounted the rampart and stood there for a moment, was shot dead with five bullets. The men on both sides called to each other in scraps of bad French or broken English; while the French drank ironical healths to the New England men, and gave them bantering invitations to breakfast.

Sherburn continues his diary. "Sunday morning. Began our fire with as much fury as possible, and the French returned it as warmly from the Citidale [citadel], West Gate, and North East Battery with Cannon, Mortars, and continual showers of musket balls; but by 11 o'clock we had beat them all from their guns." He goes on to say that at noon his men were forced to stop firing from want of powder, that he went with his gunners to get some, and that while they were gone, somebody, said to be Mr. Vaughan, brought a supply, on which the men loaded the forty-two-pounders in a bungling way, and fired them. One was dismounted, and the other burst; a barrel and a half-barrel of powder blew up, killed two men, and injured two more. Again: "Wednesday. Hot fire on both sides, till the French were beat from all their guns. May 29th went to 2 Gun [Titcomb's] Battery to give the gunners some directions; then returned to my own station, where I spent the rest of the day with pleasure, seeing our Shott Tumble down their walls and Flagg Staff."

The following is the Intendant Bigot's account of the effect of the New England fire: "The enemy established their batteries to such effect that they soon destroyed the greater part of the town, broke the right flank of the King's Bastion, ruined the Dauphin Battery with its spur, and made a breach at the Porte Dauphine [West Gate], the neighboring wall, and the sort of redan adjacent."[1] Duchambon says in addition that the cannon of the right flank of the King's Bastion could not be served, by reason of the continual fire of the enemy, which broke the embrasures to pieces; that when he had them re-

[1] *Bigot au Ministre, 1 Août, 1745.*

paired, they were broken to pieces (*démantibulés*) again,— and nobody could keep his ground behind the wall of the quay, which was shot through and through and completely riddled.[1] The town was ploughed with cannon-balls, the streets were raked from end to end, nearly all the houses damaged, and the people driven for refuge into the stifling casemates. The results were creditable to novices in gunnery.

The repeated accidents from the bursting of cannon were no doubt largely due to unskilful loading and the practice of double-shotting, to which the over-zealous artillerists are said to have often resorted.[2]

It is said, in proof of the orderly conduct of the men, that not one of them was punished during all the siege; but this shows the mild and conciliating character of the General quite as much as any peculiar merit of the soldiers. The state of things in and about the camp was compared by the caustic Dr. Douglas to "a Cambridge Commencement," which academic festival was then attended by much rough frolic and boisterous horseplay among the disorderly crowds, white and black, bond and free, who swarmed among the booths on Cambridge Common. The careful and scrupulous Belknap, who knew many who took part in the siege, says: "Those who were on the spot have frequently, in my hearing, laughed at the recital of their own irregularities, and expressed their admiration when they reflected on the almost miraculous preservation of the army from destruction." While the cannon bellowed in the front, frolic and confusion reigned at the camp, where the men raced, wrestled, pitched quoits, fired at marks,—though there was no ammunition to spare,—and ran after the French cannon-balls, which were carried to the batteries, to be returned to those who sent them. Nor were calmer recreations wanting. "Some of our men went a fishing, about 2 miles off," writes Lieutenant

---

[1] *Duchambon au Ministre, 2 Sept. 1745.*

[2] "Another forty-two-pound gun burst at the Grand Battery. All the guns are in danger of going the same way, by double-shotting them, unless under better regulation than at present." *Waldo to Pepperrell, 20 May, 1745.*

Waldo had written four days before: "Captain Hale, of my regiment, is dangerously hurt by the bursting of another gun. He was our mainstay for gunnery since Captain Rhodes's misfortune" (also caused by the bursting of a cannon). *Waldo to Pepperrell, 16 May, 1745.*

Benjamin Cleaves in his diary: "caught 6 Troutts." And, on the same day, "Our men went to catch Lobsters: caught 30." In view of this truant disposition, it is not surprising that the besiegers now and then lost their scalps at the hands of prowling Indians who infested the neighborhood. Yet through all these gambols ran an undertow of enthusiasm, born in brains still fevered from the "Great Awakening." The New England soldier, a growth of sectarian hotbeds, fancied that he was doing the work of God. The army was Israel, and the French were Canaanitish idolaters. Red-hot Calvinism, acting through generations, had modified the transplanted Englishman; and the descendant of the Puritans was never so well pleased as when teaching their duty to other people, whether by pen, voice, or bombshells. The ragged artillery-men, battering the walls of papistical Louisbourg, flattered themselves with the notion that they were champions of gospel truth.

Barefoot and tattered, they toiled on with indomitable pluck and cheerfulness, doing the work which oxen could not do, with no comfort but their daily dram of New England rum, as they plodded through the marsh and over rocks, dragging the ponderous guns through fog and darkness. Their spirit could not save them from the effects of excessive fatigue and exposure. They were ravaged with diarrhœa and fever, till fifteen hundred men were at one time on the sick-list, and at another, Pepperrell reported that of the four thousand only about twenty-one hundred were fit for duty.[1] Nearly all at last recovered, for the weather was unusually good; yet the number fit for service was absurdly small. Pepperrell begged for reinforcements, but got none till the siege was ended.

It was not his nature to rule with a stiff hand,—and this, perhaps, was fortunate. Order and discipline, the sinews of an army, were out of the question; and it remained to do as well as might be without them, keep men and officers in good-humor, and avoid all that could dash their ardor. For this, at least, the merchant-general was well fitted. His popularity had helped to raise the army, and perhaps it helped now to make it efficient. His position was no bed of roses. Worries, small

[1] *Pepperrell to Warren, 28 May, 1745.*

and great, pursued him without end. He made friends of his officers, kept a bountiful table at his tent, and labored to soothe their disputes and jealousies, and satisfy their complaints. So generous were his contributions to the common cause that according to a British officer who speaks highly of his services, he gave to it, in one form or another, £10,000 out of his own pocket.[1]

His letter-books reveal a swarm of petty annoyances, which may have tried his strength and patience as much as more serious cares. The soldiers complained that they were left without clothing, shoes, or rum; and when he implored the Committee of War to send them, Osborne, the chairman, replied with explanations why it could not be done. Letters came from wives and fathers entreating that husbands and sons who had gone to the war should be sent back. At the end of the siege a captain "humble begs leave for to go home," because he lives in a very dangerous country, and his wife and children are "in a declining way" without him. Then two entire companies raised on the frontier offered the same petition on similar grounds. Sometimes Pepperrell was beset with prayers for favors and promotion; sometimes with complaints from one corps or another that an undue share of work had been imposed on it. One Morris, of Cambridge, writes a moving petition that his slave "Cuffee," who had joined the army, should be restored to him, his lawful master. One John Alford sends the General a number of copies of the Reverend Mr. Prentice's late sermon, for distribution, assuring him that "it will please your whole army of volunteers, as he has shown them the way to gain by their gallantry the hearts and affections of the Ladys." The end of the siege brought countless letters of congratulation, which, whether lay or clerical, never failed to remind him, in set phrases, that he was but an instrument in the hands of Providence.

One of his most persistent correspondents was his son-in-law, Nathaniel Sparhawk, a thrifty merchant, with a constant eye to business, who generally began his long-winded epistles with a bulletin concerning the health of "Mother Pepperrell," and rarely ended them without charging his father-in-law

[1] *Letter from an Officer of Marines*, appended to *A particular Account of the Taking of Cape Breton* (London, 1745).

with some commission, such as buying for him the cargo of a French prize, if he could get it cheap. Or thus: "If you would procure for me a hogshead of the best Clarett, and a hogshead of the best white wine, at a reasonable rate, it would be very grateful to me." After pestering him with a few other commissions, he tells him that "Andrew and Bettsy [children of Pepperrell] send their proper compliments," and signs himself, with the starched flourish of provincial breeding, "With all possible Respect, Honoured Sir, Your Obedient Son and Servant."[1] Pepperrell was much annoyed by the conduct of the masters of the transports, of whom he wrote: "The unaccountable irregular behaviour of these fellows is the greatest fatigue I meet with;" but it may be doubted whether his son-in-law did not prove an equally efficient persecutor.

[1] *Sparhawk to Pepperrell, —June, 1745.* This is but one of many letters from Sparhawk.

Chapter XX

1745

LOUISBOURG TAKEN

A Rash Resolution • The Island Battery • The Volunteers • The Attack • The Repulse • Capture of the "Vigilant" • A Sortie • Skirmishes • Despondency of the French • English Camp threatened • Pepperrell and Warren • Warren's Plan • Preparation for a General Attack • Flag of Truce • Capitulation • State of the Fortress • Parson Moody • Soldiers dissatisfied • Disorders • Army and Navy • Rejoicings • England repays Provincial Outlays

---

FREQUENT councils of war were held in solemn form at headquarters. On the 7th of May a summons to surrender was sent to Duchambon, who replied that he would answer with his cannon. Two days after, we find in the record of the council the following startling entry: "Advised unanimously that the Town of Louisbourg be attacked by storm this Night." Vaughan was a member of the board, and perhaps his impetuous rashness had turned the heads of his colleagues. To storm the fortress at that time would have been a desperate attempt for the best-trained and best-led troops. There was as yet no breach in the walls, nor the beginning of one; and the French were so confident in the strength of their fortifications that they boasted that women alone could defend them. Nine in ten of the men had no bayonets,[1] many had no shoes, and it is said that the scaling-ladders they had brought from Boston were ten feet too short.[2] Perhaps it was unfortunate for the French that the army was more prudent than its leaders; and another council being called on the same day, it was "Advised, That, inasmuch as there appears a great Dissatisfaction in many of the officers and Soldiers at the designed attack of the Town by Storm this Night, the said Attack be deferred for the present."[3]

Another plan was adopted, hardly less critical, though it found favor with the army. This was the assault of the Island

[1] *Shirley to Newcastle, 7 June, 1745.*
[2] Douglas, *Summary*, I. 347.
[3] *Record of the Council of War, 9 May, 1745.*

654

Battery, which closed the entrance of the harbor to the British squadron, and kept it open to ships from France. Nobody knew precisely how to find the two landing-places of this formidable work, which were narrow gaps between rocks lashed with almost constant surf; but Vaughan would see no difficulties, and wrote to Pepperrell that if he would give him the command and leave him to manage the attack in his own way, he would engage to send the French flag to headquarters within forty-eight hours.[1] On the next day he seems to have thought the command assured to him, and writes from the Grand Battery that the carpenters are at work mending whaleboats and making paddles, asking at the same time for plenty of pistols and one hundred hand-grenades, with men who know how to use them.[2] The weather proved bad, and the attempt was deferred. This happened several times, till Warren grew impatient, and offered to support the attack with two hundred sailors.

At length, on the 23d, the volunteers for the perilous enterprise mustered at the Grand Battery, whence the boats were to set out. Brigadier Waldo, who still commanded there, saw them with concern and anxiety, as they came dropping in in small squads, without officers, noisy, disorderly, and, in some cases, more or less drunk. "I doubt," he told the General, "whether straggling fellows, three, four, or seven out of a company, ought to go on such a service."[3] A bright moon and northern lights again put off the attack. The volunteers remained at the Grand Battery, waiting for better luck. "They seem to be impatient for action," writes Waldo. "If there were a more regular appearance, it would give me greater sattysfaction."[4] On the 26th their wish for action was fully gratified. The night was still and dark, and the boats put out from the battery towards twelve o'clock, with about three hundred men on board.[5] These were to be joined by a hundred or a hundred and fifty more from Gorham's regiment, then sta-

---

[1] *Vaughan to Pepperell, 11 May, 1745.*

[2] *Ibid., 12 May, 1745.*

[3] *Waldo to Pepperell, 23 May, 1745.*

[4] *Ibid., 26 May, 1745.*

[5] "There is scarce three hundred men on this atact [attack], so there will be a sufficient number of Whail boats." *Ibid., 26 May, 10½ p.m.*

tioned at Lighthouse Point. The commander was not Vaughan, but one Brooks,—the choice of the men themselves, as were also his subordinates.[1] They moved slowly, the boats being propelled, not by oars, but by paddles, which, if skilfully used, would make no noise. The wind presently rose; and when they found a landing-place, the surf was lashing the rocks with even more than usual fury. There was room for but three boats at once between the breakers on each hand. They pushed in, and the men scrambled ashore with what speed they might.

The Island Battery was a strong work, walled in on all sides, garrisoned by a hundred and eighty men, and armed with thirty cannon, seven swivels, and two mortars.[2] It was now a little after midnight. Captain d'Aillebout, the commandant, was on the watch, pacing the battery platform; but he seems to have seen nothing unusual till about a hundred and fifty men had got on shore, when they had the folly to announce their presence by three cheers. Then, in the words of General Wolcott, the battery "blazed with cannon, swivels, and small-arms." The crowd of boats, dimly visible through the darkness, as they lay just off the landing, waiting their turn to go in, were at once the target for volleys of grape-shot, langrage-shot, and musket-balls, of which the men on shore had also their share. These succeeded, however, in planting twelve scaling-ladders against the wall.[3] It is said that some of them climbed into the place, and the improbable story is told that Brooks, their commander, was hauling down the French flag when a Swiss grenadier cut him down with a cutlass.[4] Many of the boats were shattered or sunk, while

[1] The list of a company of forty-two "subscribers to go voluntarily upon an attack against the Island Battery" is preserved. It includes a negro called "Ruben." The captain, chosen by the men, was Daniel Bacon. The fact that neither this name nor that of Brooks, the chief commander, is to be found in the list of commissioned officers of Pepperrell's little army (see Parsons, *Life of Pepperell, Appendix*) suggests the conclusion that the "subscribers" were permitted to choose officers from their own ranks. This list, however is not quite complete.

[2] *Journal of the Siege*, appended to Shirley's report.

[3] *Duchambon au Ministre, 2 Sept. 1745. Bigot au Ministre, 1 Août, 1745.*

[4] The exploit of the boy William Tufts in climbing the French flagstaff and hanging his red coat at the top as a substitute for the British flag, has also been said to have taken place on this occasion. It was, as before mentioned, at the Grand Battery.

those in the rear, seeing the state of things, appear to have sheered off. The affair was soon reduced to an exchange of shots between the garrison and the men who had landed, and who, standing on the open ground without the walls, were not wholly invisible, while the French, behind their ramparts, were completely hidden. "The fire of the English," says Bigot, "was extremely obstinate, but without effect, as they could not see to take aim." They kept it up till daybreak, or about two hours and a half; and then, seeing themselves at the mercy of the French, surrendered to the number of one hundred and nineteen, including the wounded, three or more of whom died almost immediately. By the most trustworthy accounts the English loss in killed, drowned, and captured was one hundred and eighty-nine; or, in the words of Pepperrell, "nearly half our party."[1] Disorder, precipitation, and weak leadership ruined what hopes the attempt ever had.

As this was the only French success during the siege, Duchambon makes the most of it. He reports that the battery was attacked by a thousand men, supported by eight hundred more, who were afraid to show themselves; and, farther, that there were thirty-five boats, all of which were destroyed or sunk,[2] —though he afterwards says that two of them got away with thirty men, being all that were left of the thousand. Bigot, more moderate, puts the number of assailants at five hundred, of whom he says that all perished, except the one hundred and nineteen who were captured.[3]

At daybreak Louisbourg rang with shouts of triumph. It was plain that a disorderly militia could not capture the Island Battery. Yet captured or silenced it must be; and orders were given to plant a battery against it at Lighthouse Point, on the eastern side of the harbor's mouth, at the distance of a short half mile. The neighboring shore was rocky and almost inaccessible. Cannon and mortars were carried in boats to the nearest landing-place, hauled up a steep cliff, and dragged

---

[1] Douglas makes it a little less. "We lost in this mad frolic sixty men killed and drowned, and one hundred and sixteen prisoners." *Summary*, i. 353.

[2] "Toutes les barques furent brisées ou coulées à fond; le feu fut continuel depuis environ minuit jusqu'à trois heures du matin." *Duchambon au Ministre, 2 Sept. 1745.*

[3] *Bigot au Ministre, 1 Août, 1745.*

a mile and a quarter to the chosen spot, where they were planted under the orders of Colonel Gridley, who thirty years after directed the earthworks on Bunker Hill. The new battery soon opened fire with deadly effect.

The French, much encouraged by their late success, were plunged again into despondency by a disaster which had happened a week before the affair of the Island Battery, but did not come to their knowledge till some time after. On the 19th of May a fierce cannonade was heard from the harbor, and a large French ship-of-war was seen hotly engaged with several vessels of the squadron. She was the "Vigilant," carrying 64 guns and 560 men, and commanded by the Marquis de la Maisonfort. She had come from France with munitions and stores, when on approaching Louisbourg she met one of the English cruisers,—some say the "Mermaid," of 40 guns, and others the "Shirley," of 20. Being no match for her, the British or provincial frigate kept up a running fight and led her towards the English fleet. The "Vigilant" soon found herself beset by several other vessels, and after a gallant resistance and the loss of eighty men, struck her colors. Nothing could be more timely for the New England army, whose ammunition and provisions had sunk perilously low. The French prize now supplied their needs, and drew from the *Habitant de Louisbourg* the mournful comment, "We were victims devoted to appease the wrath of Heaven, which turned our own arms into weapons for our enemies."

Nor was this the last time when the defenders of Louisbourg supplied the instruments of their own destruction; for ten cannon were presently unearthed at low tide from the flats near the careening wharf in the northeast arm of the harbor, where they had been hidden by the French some time before. Most of them proved sound; and being mounted at Lighthouse Point, they were turned against their late owners at the Island Battery.

When Gorham's regiment first took post at Lighthouse Point, Duchambon thought the movement so threatening that he forgot his former doubts, and ordered a sortie against it, under the Sieur de Beaubassin. Beaubassin landed, with a hundred men, at a place called Lorembec, and advanced to surprise the English detachment; but was discovered by an outpost of forty men, who attacked and routed his party.[1] Being then joined by eighty Indians, Beaubassin had several other skirmishes with English scouting-parties, till, pushed by superior numbers, and their leader severely wounded, his men regained Louisbourg by sea, escaping with difficulty from the guard-boats of the squadron. The Sieur de la Vallière, with a considerable party of men, tried to burn Pepperrell's storehouses, near Flat Point Cove; but ten or twelve of his followers were captured, and nearly all the rest wounded. Various other petty encounters took place between English scouting-parties and roving bands of French and Indians, always ending, according to Pepperrell, in the discomfiture of the latter. To this, however, there was at least one exception. Twenty English were waylaid and surrounded near Petit Lorembec by forty or fifty Indians, accompanied by two or three Frenchmen. Most of the English were shot down, several escaped, and the rest surrendered on promise of life; upon which the Indians, in cold blood, shot or speared some of them, and atrociously tortured others.

This suggested to Warren a device which had two objects,—to prevent such outrages in future, and to make known to the French that the ship "Vigilant," the mainstay of their hopes, was in English hands. The treatment of the captives was told to the Marquis de la Maisonfort, late captain of the "Vigilant," now a prisoner on board the ship he had commanded, and he was requested to lay the facts before Duchambon. This he did with great readiness, in a letter containing these words: "It is well that you should be informed that the captains and officers of this squadron treat us, not as their prisoners, but as their good friends, and take particular pains that my officers and crew should want for nothing; therefore it seems to me just to treat them in like manner, and to punish those who do otherwise and offer any insult to the prisoners who may fall into your hands."

Captain M'Donald, of the marines, carried this letter to Duchambon under a flag-of-truce. Though familiar with the French language, he spoke to the Governor through an interpreter, so that the French officers present, who hitherto had only known that a large ship had been taken, expressed to

[1] *Journal of the Siege*, appended to Shirley's report. Pomeroy, *Journal*.

each other without reserve their discouragement and dismay when they learned that the prize was no other than the "Vigilant." Duchambon replied to La Maisonfort's letter that the Indians alone were answerable for the cruelties in question, and that he would forbid such conduct for the future.[1]

The besiegers were now threatened by a new danger. We have seen that in the last summer the Sieur Duvivier had attacked Annapolis. Undaunted by ill-luck, he had gone to France to beg for help to attack it again; two thousand men were promised him, and in anticipation of their arrival the Governor of Canada sent a body of French and Indians, under the noted partisan Marin, to meet and co-operate with them. Marin was ordered to wait at Les Mines till he heard of the arrival of the troops from France; but he grew impatient, and resolved to attack Annapolis without them. Accordingly, he laid siege to it with the six or seven hundred whites and Indians of his party, aided by the so-called Acadian neutrals. Mascarene, the governor, kept them at bay till the 24th of May, when, to his surprise, they all disappeared. Duchambon had sent them an order to make all haste to the aid of Louisbourg. As the report of this reached the besiegers, multiplying Marin's force four-fold, they expected to be attacked by numbers more than equal to those of their own effective men. This wrought a wholesome reform. Order was established in the camp, which was now fenced with palisades and watched by sentinels and scouting-parties.

Another tribulation fell upon the General. Shirley had enjoined it upon him to keep in perfect harmony with the naval commander, and the injunction was in accord with Pepperrell's conciliating temper. Warren was no less earnest than he for the success of the enterprise, lent him ammunition in time of need, and offered every aid in his power, while Pepperrell in letters to Shirley and Newcastle praised his colleague without stint. But in habits and character the two men differed widely. Warren was in the prime of life, and the ardor of youth still burned in him. He was impatient at the slow movement of the siege. Prisoners told him of a squadron expected from Brest, of which the "Vigilant" was the forerun-

---

[1] *De la Maisonfort à Duchambon, 18 Juin* (new style), *1745. Duchambon à de la Maisonfort, 19 Juin* (new style), *1745.*

ner; and he feared that even if it could not defeat him, it might elude the blockade, and with the help of the continual fogs, get into Louisbourg in spite of him, thus making its capture impossible. Therefore he called a council of his captains on board his flagship, the "Superbe," and proposed a plan for taking the place without further delay. On the same day he laid it before Pepperrell. It was to the effect that all the king's ships and provincial cruisers should enter the harbor, after taking on board sixteen hundred of Pepperrell's men, and attack the town from the water side, while what was left of the army should assault it by land.[1] To accept the proposal would have been to pass over the command to Warren, only about twenty-one hundred of the New England men being fit for service at the time, while of these the General informs Warren that "six hundred are gone in quest of two bodies of French and Indians, who, we are informed, are gathering, one to the eastward, and the other to the westward."[2]

To this Warren replies, with some appearance of pique, "I am very sorry that no one plan of mine, though approved by all my captains, has been so fortunate as to meet your approbation or have any weight with you." And to show his title to consideration, he gives an extract from a letter written to him by Shirley, in which that inveterate flatterer hints his regret that, by reason of other employments, Warren could not take command of the whole expedition,—"which I doubt not," says the Governor, "would be a most happy event for his Majesty's service."[3]

Pepperrell kept his temper under this thrust, and wrote to the commodore with invincible courtesy: "Am extremely sorry the fogs prevent me from the pleasure of waiting on you on board your ship," adding that six hundred men should be furnished from the army and the transports to man the "Vigilant," which was now the most powerful ship in the squadron. In short, he showed every disposition to meet Warren half way. But the Commodore was beginning to feel some doubts as to the expediency of the bold action he had

[1] *Report of a Consultation of Officers on board his Majesty's ship "Superbe,"* enclosed in a letter of *Warren to Pepperrell, 24 May, 1745.*

[2] *Pepperrell to Warren, 28 May, 1745.*

[3] *Warren to Pepperrell, 29 May, 1745.*

proposed, and informed Pepperrell that his pilots thought it impossible to go into the harbor until the Island Battery was silenced. In fact, there was danger that if the ships got in while that battery was still alive and active, they would never get out again, but be kept there as in a trap, under the fire from the town ramparts.

Gridley's artillery at Lighthouse Point had been doing its best, dropping bombshells with such precision into the Island Battery that the French soldiers were sometimes seen running into the sea to escape the explosions. Many of the Island guns were dismounted, and the place was fast becoming untenable. At the same time the English batteries on the land side were pushing their work of destruction with relentless industry, and walls and bastions crumbled under their fire. The French labored with energy under cover of night to repair the mischief; closed the shattered West Gate with a wall of stone and earth twenty feet thick, made an epaulement to protect what was left of the formidable Circular Battery,—all but three of whose sixteen guns had been dismounted,—stopped the throat of the Dauphin's Bastion with a barricade of stone, and built a cavalier, or raised battery, on the King's Bastion,— where, however, the English fire soon ruined it. Against that near and peculiarly dangerous neighbor, the advanced battery, or, as they called it, the *Batterie de Francœur*, they planted three heavy cannon to take it in flank. "These," says Duchambon, "produced a marvellous effect, dismounted one of the cannon of the Bastonnais, and damaged all their embrasures,—which," concludes the Governor, "did not prevent them from keeping up a constant fire; and they repaired by night the mischief we did them by day."[1]

Pepperrell and Warren at length came to an understanding as to a joint attack by land and water. The Island Battery was by this time crippled, and the town batteries that commanded the interior of the harbor were nearly destroyed. It was agreed that Warren, whose squadron was now increased by recent arrivals to eleven ships, besides the provincial cruisers, should enter the harbor with the first fair wind, cannonade the town and attack it in boats, while Pepperrell stormed it from the land side. Warren was to hoist a Dutch flag under

[1] *Duchambon au Ministre, 2 Sept. 1745.*

his pennant, at his main-top-gallant mast-head, as a signal that he was about to sail in; and Pepperrell was to answer by three columns of smoke, marching at the same time towards the walls with drums beating and colors flying.[1]

The French saw with dismay a large quantity of fascines carried to the foot of the glacis, ready to fill the ditch, and their scouts came in with reports that more than a thousand scaling-ladders were lying behind the ridge of the nearest hill. Toil, loss of sleep, and the stifling air of the casemates, in which they were forced to take refuge, had sapped the strength of the besieged. The town was a ruin; only one house was untouched by shot or shell. "We could have borne all this," writes the Intendant, Bigot; "but the scarcity of powder, the loss of the 'Vigilant,' the presence of the squadron, and the absence of any news from Marin, who had been ordered to join us with his Canadians and Indians, spread terror among troops and inhabitants. The townspeople said that they did not want to be put to the sword, and were not strong enough to resist a general assault."[2] On the 15th of June they brought a petition to Duchambon, begging him to capitulate.[3]

On that day Captain Sherburn, at the advanced battery, wrote in his diary: "By 12 o'clock we had got all our platforms laid, embrazures mended, guns in order, shot in place, cartridges ready, dined, gunners quartered, matches lighted to return their last favours, when we heard their drums beat a parley; and soon appeared a flag of truce, which I received midway between our battery and their walls, conducted the officer to Green Hill, and delivered him to Colonel Richman [Richmond]."

La Perelle, the French officer, delivered a note from Duchambon, directed to both Pepperrell and Warren, and asking for a suspension of arms to enable him to draw up proposals for capitulation.[4] Warren chanced to be on shore when the note came; and the two commanders answered jointly that it had come in good time, as they had just resolved on a general

---

[1] *Warren to Pepperrell, 11 June, 1745. Pepperrell to Warren, 13 June, 1745.*

[2] *Bigot au Ministre, 1 Août, 1745.*

[3] *Duchambon au Ministre, 2 Sept. 1745.*

[4] *Duchambon à Pepperrell et Warren, 26 Juin* (new style), *1745.*

attack, and that they would give the Governor till eight o'clock of the next morning to make his proposals.[1]

They came in due time, but were of such a nature that Pepperrell refused to listen to them, and sent back Bonaventure, the officer who brought them, with counter-proposals. These were the terms which Duchambon had rejected on the 7th of May, with added conditions; as, among others, that no officer, soldier, or inhabitant of Louisbourg should bear arms against the King of England or any of his allies for the space of a year. Duchambon stipulated, as the condition of his acceptance, that his troops should march out of the fortress with their arms and colors.[2] To this both the English commanders consented, Warren observing to Pepperrell "the uncertainty of our affairs, that depend so much on wind and weather, makes it necessary not to stickle at trifles."[3] The articles were signed on both sides, and on the 17th the ships sailed peacefully into the harbor, while Pepperrell with a part of his ragged army entered the south gate of the town. "Never was a place more mal'd [mauled] with cannon and shells," he writes to Shirley; "neither have I red in History of any troops behaving with greater courage. We gave them about nine thousand cannon-balls and six hundred bombs."[4] Thus this unique military performance ended in complete and astonishing success.

According to English accounts, the French had lost about three hundred men during the siege; but their real loss seems to have been not much above a third of that number. On the side of the besiegers, the deaths from all causes were only a hundred and thirty, about thirty of which were from disease. The French used their muskets to good purpose; but their mortar practice was bad, and close as was the advanced battery to their walls, they often failed to hit it, while the ground on both sides of it looked like a ploughed field, from the bursting of their shells. Their surrender was largely determined by want of ammunition, as, according to one account, the French had but thirty-seven barrels of gunpowder left,[5]

---

[1] *Warren and Pepperrell to Duchambon, 15 June, 1745.*

[2] *Duchambon à Warren et Pepperrell, 27 Juin* (new style), *1745.*

[3] *Pepperrell to Warren, 16 June, 1745. Warren to Pepperrell, 16 June, 1745.*

[4] *Pepperrell to Shirley, 18 June* (old style,) *1745. Ibid., 4 July, 1745.*

[5] *Habitant de Louisbourg.*

—in which particular the besiegers fared little better.[1]

The New England men had been full of confidence in the result of the proposed assault, and a French writer says that the timely capitulation saved Louisbourg from a terrible catastrophe;[2] yet, ill-armed and disorderly as the besiegers were, it may be doubted whether the quiet ending of the siege was not as fortunate for them as for their foes. The discouragement of the French was increased by greatly exaggerated ideas of the force of the "Bastonnais." The *Habitant de Louisbourg* places the land-force alone at eight or nine thousand men, and Duchambon reports to the minister D'Argenson that he was attacked in all by thirteen thousand. His mortifying position was a sharp temptation to exaggerate; but his conduct can only be explained by a belief that the force of his enemy was far greater than it was in fact.

Warren thought that the proposed assault would succeed, and wrote to Pepperrell that he hoped they would "soon keep a good house together, and give the Ladys of Louisbourg a Gallant Ball."[3] During his visit to the camp on the day when the flag of truce came out, he made a speech to the New England soldiers, exhorting them to behave like true Englishmen; at which they cheered lustily. Making a visit to the Grand Battery on the same day, he won high favor with the regiment stationed there by the gift of a hogshead of rum to drink his health.

Whether Warren's "gallant ball" ever took place in Louisbourg does not clearly appear. Pepperrell, on his part, celebrated the victory by a dinner to the commodore and his officers. As the redoubtable Parson Moody was the general's chaplain and the oldest man in the army, he expected to ask a blessing at the board, and was, in fact, invited to do so,—to the great concern of those who knew his habitual prolixity, and dreaded its effect on the guests. At the same time, not one of them dared rasp his irritable temper by any suggestion

[1] Pepperrell more than once complains of a total want of both powder and balls. Warren writes to him on May 29th: "It is very lucky that we could spare you some powder; I am told you had not a grain left."

[2] "C'est par une protection visible de la Providence que nous avons prévenu une journée qui nous auroit été si funeste." *Lettre d'un Habitant de Louisbourg*.

[3] *Warren to Pepperrell, 10 June, 1745.*

of brevity; and hence they came in terror to the feast, expecting an invocation of a good half-hour, ended by open revolt of the hungry Britons; when, to their surprise and relief, Moody said: "Good Lord, we have so much to thank thee for, that time will be too short, and we must leave it for eternity. Bless our food and fellowship upon this joyful occasion, for the sake of Christ our Lord, Amen." And with that he sat down.[1]

It is said that he had been seen in the French church hewing at the altar and images with the axe that he had brought for that purpose; and perhaps this iconoclastic performance had eased the high pressure of his zeal.[2]

Amazing as their triumph was, Pepperrell's soldiers were not satisfied with the capitulation, and one of them utters his disapproval in his diary thus: "Sabbath Day, ye 16th June. They came to Termes for us to enter ye Sitty to morrow, and Poore Termes they Bee too."

The occasion of discontent was the security of property assured to the inhabitants, "by which means," says that dull chronicler, Niles, "the poor soldiers lost all their hopes and just demerit [desert] of plunder promised them." In the meagreness of their pay they thought themselves entitled to the plunder of Louisbourg, which they imagined to be a seat of wealth and luxury. Nathaniel Sparhawk, Pepperrell's thrifty son-in-law, shared this illusion, and begged the General to get for him (at a low price) a handsome service of silver plate. When the volunteers exchanged their wet and dreary camp for what they expected to be the comfortable quarters of the town, they were disgusted to see the houses still occupied by the owners, and to find themselves forced to stand guard at the doors, to protect them.[3] "A great Noys and hubbub a mongst ye Solders a bout ye Plunder; Som Cursing, som a Swarein," writes one of the disgusted victors.

They were not, and perhaps could not be, long kept in

---

[1] *Collections of Mass. Hist. Society*, I. 49.

[2] A descendant of Moody, at the village of York, told me that he was found in the church busy in the work of demolition.

[3] "Thursday, ye 21st. Ye French keep possession yet, and we are forsed to stand at their Dores to gard them." *Diary of a Soldier, anonymous.*

order; and when, in accordance with the capitulation, the inhabitants had been sent on board vessels for transportation to France, discipline gave way, and General Wolcott records that, while Moody was preaching on a Sunday in the garrison-chapel, there was "excessive stealing in every part of the town." Little, however, was left to steal.

But if the army found but meagre gleanings, the navy reaped a rich harvest. French ships, instead of being barred out of the harbor, were now lured to enter it. The French flag was kept flying over the town, and in this way prizes were entrapped to the estimated value of a million sterling, half of which went to the Crown, and the rest to the British officers and crews, the army getting no share whatever.

Now rose the vexed question of the relative part borne by the colonies and the Crown, the army and the navy, in the capture of Louisbourg; and here it may be well to observe the impressions of a French witness of the siege. "It was an enterprise less of the English nation and its King than of the inhabitants of New England alone. This singular people have their own laws and administration, and their governor plays the sovereign. Admiral [Commodore] Warren had no authority over the troops sent by the Governor of Boston, and he was only a spectator. . . . Nobody would have said that their sea and land forces were of the same nation and under the same prince. No nation but the English is capable of such eccentricities (*bizarreries*),—which, nevertheless, are a part of the precious liberty of which they show themselves so jealous."[1]

The French writer is correct when he says that the land and sea forces were under separate commands, and it is equally true that but for the conciliating temper of Pepperrell, harmony could not have been preserved between the two chiefs; but when he calls Warren a mere spectator, he does glaring injustice to that gallant officer, whose activity and that of his captains was incessant, and whose services were invaluable. They maintained, with slight lapses, an almost impossible blockade, without which the siege must have failed. Two or three small vessels got into the harbor; but the capture of the

---

[1] *Lettre d'un Habitant de Louisbourg.*

"Vigilant," more than any other event of the siege, discouraged the French and prepared them for surrender.

Several English writers speak of Warren and the navy as the captors of Louisbourg, and all New England writers give the chief honor to Pepperrell and the army. Neither army nor navy would have been successful without the other. Warren and his officers, in a council of war, had determined that so long as the Island Battery and the water batteries of the town remained in an efficient state, the ships could not enter the harbor; and Warren had personally expressed the same opinion.[1] He did not mean to enter till all the batteries which had made the attempt impracticable, including the Circular Battery, which was the most formidable of all, had been silenced or crippled by the army, and by the army alone. The whole work of the siege fell upon the land forces; and though it had been proposed to send a body of marines on shore, this was not done.[2] Three or four gunners, "to put your men in the way of loading cannon,"[3] was Warren's contribution to the operations of the siege; though the fear of attack by the ships, jointly with the land force, no doubt hastened the surrender. Beauharnois, governor of Canada, ascribes the defeat to the extreme activity with which the New England men pushed their attacks.

The *Habitant de Louisbourg* says that each of the two commanders was eager that the keys of the fortress should be delivered to him, and not to his colleague; that before the surrender, Warren sent an officer to persuade the French that

[1] *Report of Consultation on board the "Superbe," 7 June, 1745.* "Commodore Warren did say publickly that before the Circular Battery was reduced he would not venture in here with three times ye sea force he had with him, and, through divine assistance, we tore that [battery] and this city almost to pieces." *Pepperrell to Shirley, 4 July, 1745.*

[2] Warren had no men to spare. He says: "If it should be thought necessary to join your troops with any men from our ships, it should only be done for some sudden attack that may be executed in one day or night." *Warren to Pepperrell, 11 May, 1745.* No such occasion arose.

[3] *Ibid., 13 May, 1745.* On the 19th of May, 1746, Warren made a parting speech to the New England men at Louisbourg, in which he tells them that it was they who conquered the country, and expresses the hope that should the French try to recover it, "the same Spirit that induced you to make this Conquest will prompt you to protect it." See the speech in *Beamish-Murdock*, II. 100–102.

it would be for their advantage to make their submission to him rather than to Pepperrell; and that it was in fact so made. Wolcott, on the other hand, with the best means of learning the truth, says in his diary that Pepperrell received the keys at the South Gate. The report that it was the British commodore, and not their own general, to whom Louisbourg surrendered, made a prodigious stir among the inhabitants of New England, who had the touchiness common to small and ambitious peoples; and as they had begun the enterprise and borne most of its burdens and dangers, they thought themselves entitled to the chief credit of it. Pepperrell was blamed as lukewarm for the honor of his country because he did not demand the keys and reject the capitulation if they were refused. After all this ebullition it appeared that the keys were in his hands, for when, soon after the siege, Shirley came to Louisbourg, Pepperrell formally presented them to him, in presence of the soldiers.

Warren no doubt thought that he had a right to precedence, as being an officer of the King in regular standing, while Pepperrell was but a civilian, clothed with temporary rank by the appointment of a provincial governor. Warren was an impetuous sailor accustomed to command, and Pepperrell was a merchant accustomed to manage and persuade. The difference appears in their correspondence during the siege. Warren is sometimes brusque and almost peremptory; Pepperrell is forbearing and considerate to the last degree. He liked Warren, and, to the last, continued to praise him highly in letters to Shirley and other provincial governors;[1] while Warren, on occasion of Shirley's arrival at Louisbourg, made a speech highly complimentary to both the General and his soldiers.

The news that Louisbourg was taken, reached Boston at one o'clock in the morning of the 3d of July by a vessel sent express. A din of bells and cannon proclaimed it to the slumbering townsmen, and before the sun rose, the streets were filled with shouting crowds. At night every window shone with lamps, and the town was ablaze with fireworks and bon-

[1] See extracts in Parson, 105, 106. The *Habitant de Louisbourg* extols Warren, but is not partial to Pepperrell, whom he calls, incorrectly, "the son of a Boston shoemaker."

fires. The next Thursday was appointed a day of general thanksgiving for a victory believed to be the direct work of Providence. New York and Philadelphia also hailed the great news with illuminations, ringing of bells, and firing of cannon.

In England the tidings were received with astonishment and a joy that was dashed with reflections on the strength and mettle of colonists supposed already to aspire to independence. Pepperrell was made a baronet, and Warren an admiral. The merchant soldier was commissioned colonel in the British army; a regiment was given him, to be raised in America and maintained by the King, while a similar recognition was granted to the lawyer Shirley.[1]

A question vital to Massachusetts worried her in the midst of her triumph. She had been bankrupt for many years, and of the large volume of her outstanding obligations, a part was not worth eightpence in the pound. Added to her load of debt, she had spent £183,649 sterling on the Louisbourg expedition. That which Smollett calls "the most important achievement of the war" would never have taken place but for her, and Old England, and not New, was to reap the profit; for Louisbourg, conquered by arms, was to be restored by diplomacy. If the money she had spent for the mother-country were not repaid, her ruin was certain. William Bollan, English by birth and a son-in-law of Shirley, was sent out to urge the just claim of the province, and after long and vigorous solicitation, he succeeded. The full amount, in sterling value, was paid to Massachusetts, and the expenditures of New Hampshire, Connecticut, and Rhode Island were also reimbursed.[2] The people of Boston saw twenty-seven of those long, unwieldy trucks which many elders of the place still remember as used in their youth, rumbling up King Street to the treasury, loaded with 217 chests of Spanish dollars, and a hundred barrels of copper coin. A pound sterling was worth eleven pounds of the old-tenor currency of

[1] To Rous, captain of a provincial cruiser, whom Warren had commended for conduct and courage, was given the command of a ship in the royal navy.

"Tell your Council and Assembly, in his Majesty's name," writes Newcastle to Shirley, "that their conduct will always entitle them, in a particular manner, to his royal favor and protection." *Newcastle to Shirley, 10 Aug. 1745.*

[2] £183,649 to Massachusetts; £16,355 to New Hampshire; £28,863 to Connecticut; £6,332 to Rhode Island.

Massachusetts, and thirty shillings of the new-tenor. Those beneficent trucks carried enough to buy in at a stroke nine tenths of the old-tenor notes of the province,—nominally worth above two millions. A stringent tax, laid on by the Assembly, paid the remaining tenth, and Massachusetts was restored to financial health.[1]

[1] Palfrey, *New England*, V. 101–109; Shirley, *Report to the Board of Trade. Bollan to Secretary Willard*, in *Coll. Mass. Hist. Soc.*, I. 53; Hutchinson, *Hist. Mass.*, II. 391–395. *Letters of Bollan* in Massachusetts Archives.

It was through the exertions of the much-abused Thomas Hutchinson, Speaker of the Assembly and historian of Massachusetts, that the money was used for the laudable purpose of extinguishing the old debt.

Shirley did his utmost to support Bollan in his efforts to obtain compensation, and after highly praising the zeal and loyalty of the people of his province, he writes to Newcastle: "Justice, as well as the affection which I bear to 'em, constrains me to beseech your Grace to recommend their Case to his Majesty's paternal Care & Tenderness in the Strongest manner." *Shirley to Newcastle, 6 Nov. 1745.*

The English documents on the siege of Louisbourg are many and voluminous. The Pepperrell Papers and the Belknap Papers, both in the library of the Massachusetts Historical Society, afford a vast number of contemporary letters and documents on the subject. The large volume entitled *Siege of Louisbourg*, in the same repository, contains many more, including a number of autograph diaries of soldiers and others. To these are to be added the journals of General Wolcott, James Gibson, Benjamin Cleaves, Seth Pomeroy, and several others, in print or manuscript, among which is especially to be noted the journal appended to Shirley's Letter to the Duke of Newcastle of Oct. 28, 1745, and bearing the names of Pepperrell, Brigadier Waldo, Colonel Moore, and Lieutenant-Colonels Lothrop and Gridley, who attest its accuracy. Many papers have also been drawn from the Public Record Office of London.

Accounts of this affair have hitherto rested, with but slight exceptions, on English sources alone. The archives of France have furnished useful material to the foregoing narrative, notably the long report of the Governor, Duchambon, to the Minister of War, and the letter of the Intendant, Bigot, to the same personage, within about six weeks after the surrender. But the most curious French evidence respecting the siege is the *Lettre d'un Habitant de Louisbourg contenant une Relation exacte & circonstanciée de la Prise de l'Isle-Royale par les Anglois. A Québec, chez Guillaume le Sincère, à l'Image de la Vérité, 1745.* This little work, of eighty-one printed pages, is extremely rare. I could study it only by having a *literatim* transcript made from the copy in the Bibliothèque Nationale, as it was not in the British Museum. It bears the signature B. L. N., and is dated *à . . . ce 28 Août, 1745.* The imprint of Québec, etc., is certainly a mask, the book having no doubt been printed in France. It severely criticises Duchambon, and makes him mainly answerable for the disaster.

For French views of the siege of Louisbourg, *see* Appendix B.

Louisbourg after the Conquest • Mutiny • Pestilence • Stephen Williams • His Diary • Scheme of conquering Canada • New-castle's Promises • Alarm in Canada • Promises broken • Plan against Crown Point • Startling News • D'Anville's Fleet • Louisbourg to be avenged • Disasters of D'Anville • Storm • Pestilence • Famine • Death of D'Anville • Suicide of the Vice-Admiral • Ruinous Failure • Return Voyage • Defeat of La Jonquière

THE TROOPS and inhabitants of Louisbourg were all em-barked for France, and the town was at last in full pos-session of the victors. The serious-minded among them—and there were few who did not bear the stamp of hereditary Pu-ritanism—now saw a fresh proof that they were the peculiar care of an approving Providence. While they were in camp the weather had been favorable; but they were scarcely housed when a cold, persistent rain poured down in floods that would have drenched their flimsy tents and turned their huts of turf into mud-heaps, robbing the sick of every hope of recovery. Even now they got little comfort from the shat-tered tenements of Louisbourg. The siege had left the town in so filthy a condition that the wells were infected and the water was poisoned.

The soldiers clamored for discharge, having enlisted to serve only till the end of the expedition; and Shirley insisted that faith must be kept with them, or no more would enlist.[1] Pepperrell, much to the dissatisfaction of Warren, sent home about seven hundred men, some of whom were on the sick list, while the rest had families in distress and danger on the exposed frontier. At the same time he begged hard for rein-forcements, expecting a visit from the French and a desperate attempt to recover Louisbourg. He and Warren governed the place jointly, under martial law, and they both passed half their time in holding courts-martial; for disorder reigned

---

[1] *Shirley to Newcastle, 27 Sept. 1745.*

among the disgusted militia, and no less among the crowd of hungry speculators, who flocked like vultures to the conquered town to buy the cargoes of captured ships, or seek for other prey. The Massachusetts soldiers, whose pay was the smallest, and who had counted on being at their homes by the end of July, were the most turbulent; but all alike were on the brink of mutiny. Excited by their ringleaders, they one day marched in a body to the parade and threw down their arms; but probably soon picked them up again, as in most cases the guns were hunting-pieces belonging to those who carried them. Pepperrell begged Shirley to come to Louisbourg and bring the mutineers back to duty. Accordingly, on the 16th of August he arrived in a ship-of-war, accompanied by Mrs. Shirley and Mrs. Warren, wife of the Commodore. The soldiers duly fell into line to receive him. As it was not his habit to hide his own merits, he tells the Duke of Newcastle that nobody but he could have quieted the malcontents,—which is probably true, as nobody else had power to raise their pay. He made them a speech, promised them forty shillings in Massachusetts new-tenor currency a month, instead of twenty-five, and ended with ordering for each man half a pint of rum to drink the King's health. Though potations so generous might be thought to promise effects not wholly sedative, the mutineers were brought to reason, and some even consented to remain in garrison till the next June.[1]

Small reinforcements came from New England to hold the place till the arrival of troops from Gibraltar, promised by the ministry. The two regiments raised in the colonies, and commanded by Shirley and Pepperrell, were also intended to form a part of the garrison; but difficulty was found in filling the ranks, because, says Shirley, some commissions have been given to Englishmen, and men will not enlist here except under American officers.

Nothing could be more dismal than the condition of Louisbourg, as reflected in the diaries of soldiers and others who spent there the winter that followed its capture. Among these diaries is that of the worthy Benjamin Crafts, private in Hale's Essex regiment, who to the entry of each day adds a pious

---

[1] *Shirley to Newcastle, 4 Dec. 1745.*

invocation, sincere in its way, no doubt, though hackneyed, and sometimes in strange company. Thus, after noting down Shirley's gift of half a pint of rum to every man to drink the King's health, he adds immediately: "The Lord Look upon us and enable us to trust in him & may he prepare us for his holy Day." On "September ye 1, being Sabath," we find the following record: "I am much out of order. This forenoon heard Mr. Stephen Williams preach from ye 18 Luke 9 verse in the afternoon from ye 8 of Ecles: 8 verse: Blessed be the Lord that has given us to enjoy another Sabath and opertunity to hear his Word Dispensed." On the next day, "being Monday," he continues, "Last night I was taken very Bad: the Lord be pleased to strengthen my inner man that I may put my whole Trust in him. May we all be prepared for his holy will. Red part of plunder, 9 small tooth combs." Crafts died in the spring, of the prevailing distemper, after doing good service in the commissary department of his regiment.

Stephen Williams, the preacher whose sermons had comforted Crafts in his trouble, was a son of Rev. John Williams, captured by the Indians at Deerfield in 1704, and was now minister of Long Meadow, Massachusetts. He had joined the anti-papal crusade as one of its chaplains, and passed for a man of ability,—a point on which those who read his diary will probably have doubts. The lot of the army chaplains was of the hardest. A pestilence had fallen upon Louisbourg, and turned the fortress into a hospital. "After we got into the town," says the sarcastic Dr. Douglas, whose pleasure it is to put everything in its worst light, "a sordid indolence or sloth, for want of discipline, induced putrid fevers and dysenteries, which at length in August became contagious, and the people died like rotten sheep." From fourteen to twenty-seven were buried every day in the cemetery behind the town, outside the Maurepas Gate, by the old lime-kiln, on Rochefort Point; and the forgotten bones of above five hundred New England men lie there to this day under the coarse, neglected grass. The chaplain's diary is little but a dismal record of sickness, death, sermons, funerals, and prayers with the dying ten times a day. "Prayed at Hospital;—Prayed at Citadel;—Preached at Grand Batery;—Visited Capt. [illegible], very sick;—One of Capt. ——'s company dy^d—Am but poorly myself, but able to keep about." Now and then there is a momentary change of note, as when he writes: "July 29th. One of ye Captains of ye men of war caind a soldier who struck ye capt. again. A great tumult. Swords were drawn; no life lost, but great uneasiness is caused." Or when he sets down the "say" of some Briton, apparently a naval officer, "that he had tho't ye New England men were Cowards—but now he tho't yt if they had a pick axe & spade, they w'd dig ye way to Hell & storm it."[1]

Williams was sorely smitten with homesickness, but he sturdily kept his post, in spite of grievous yearnings for family and flock. The pestilence slowly abated, till at length the burying-parties that passed the Maurepas Gate counted only three or four a day. At the end of January five hundred and sixty-one men had died, eleven hundred were on the sick list, and about one thousand fit for duty.[2] The promised regiments from Gibraltar had not come. Could the French have struck then, Louisbourg might have changed hands again. The Gibraltar regiments had arrived so late upon that rude coast that they turned southward to the milder shores of Virginia, spent the winter there, and did not appear at Louisbourg till April. They brought with them a commission for Warren as governor of the fortress. He made a speech of thanks to the New England garrison, now reduced to less than nineteen hundred men, sick and well, and they sailed at last for home, Louisbourg being now thought safe from any attempt of France.

To the zealous and energetic Shirley the capture of the fortress was but a beginning of greater triumphs. Scarcely had the New England militia sailed from Boston on their desperate venture, when he wrote to the Duke of Newcastle that should the expedition succeed, all New England would be on fire to attack Canada, and the other colonies would take part with them, if ordered to do so by the ministry.[3] And, some

---

[1] The autograph diary of Rev. Stephen Williams is in my possession. The handwriting is detestable.

[2] On May 10th, 1746, Shirley writes to Newcastle that eight hundred and ninety men had died during the winter. The sufferings of the garrison from cold were extreme.

[3] *Shirley to Newcastle, 4 April, 1745.*

months later, after Louisbourg was taken, he urged the policy of striking while the iron was hot, and invading Canada at once. The colonists, he said, were ready, and it would be easier to raise ten thousand men for such an attack than one thousand to lie idle in garrison at Louisbourg or anywhere else. France and England, he thinks, cannot live on the same continent. If we were rid of the French, he continues, England would soon control America, which would make her first among the nations; and he ventures what now seems the modest prediction that in one or two centuries the British colonies would rival France in population. Even now, he is sure that they would raise twenty thousand men to capture Canada, if the King required it of them, and Warren would be an acceptable commander for the naval part of the expedition; "but," concludes the Governor, "I will take no step without orders from his Majesty."[1]

The Duke of Newcastle was now at the head of the Government. Smollett and Horace Walpole have made his absurdities familiar, in anecdotes which, true or not, do no injustice to his character; yet he had talents that were great in their way, though their way was a mean one. They were talents, not of the statesman, but of the political manager, and their object was to win office and keep it.

Newcastle, whatever his motives, listened to the counsels of Shirley, and directed him to consult with Warren as to the proposed attack on Canada. At the same time he sent a circular letter to the governors of the provinces from New England to North Carolina, directing them, should the invasion be ordered, to call upon their assemblies for as many men as they would grant.[2] Shirley's views were cordially supported by Warren, and the levies were made accordingly, though not in proportion to the strength of the several colonies; for those south of New York felt little interest in the plan. Shirley was told to "dispose Massachusetts to do its part;" but neither he nor his province needed prompting. Taking his cue from the Roman senator, he exclaimed to his Assembly, "*Delenda est Canada*;" and the Assembly responded by voting to raise

[1] *Shirley to Newcastle, 29 Oct. 1745.*

[2] *Newcastle to the Provincial Governors, 14 March, 1746; Shirley to Newcastle, 31 May, 1746; Proclamation of Shirley, 2 June, 1746.*

thirty-five hundred men, and offering a bounty equivalent to £4 sterling to each volunteer, besides a blanket for every one, and a bed for every two. New Hampshire contributed five hundred men, Rhode Island three hundred, Connecticut one thousand, New York sixteen hundred, New Jersey five hundred, Maryland three hundred, and Virginia one hundred. The Pennsylvania Assembly, controlled by Quaker non-combatants, would give no soldiers; but, by a popular movement, the province furnished four hundred men, without the help of its representatives.[1]

As usual in the English attempts against Canada, the campaign was to be a double one. The main body of troops, composed of British regulars and New England militia, was to sail up the St. Lawrence and attack Quebec, while the levies of New York and the provinces farther south, aided, it was hoped, by the warriors of the Iroquois, were to advance on Montreal by way of Lake Champlain.

Newcastle promised eight battalions of British troops under Lieutenant-General Saint Clair. They were to meet the New England men at Louisbourg, and all were then to sail together for Quebec, under the escort of a squadron commanded by Warren. Shirley also was to go to Louisbourg, and arrange the plan of the campaign with the General and the Admiral. Thus, without loss of time, the captured fortress was to be made a base of operations against its late owners.

Canada was wild with alarm at reports of English preparation. There were about fifty English prisoners in barracks at Quebec, and every device was tried to get information from them; but being chiefly rustics caught on the frontiers by Indian war-parties, they had little news to give, and often refused to give even this. One of them, who had been taken long before and gained over by the French,[2] was used as an agent to extract information from his countrymen, and was called "*notre homme de confiance*." At the same time the prisoners were freely supplied with writing materials, and their

---

[1] Hutchinson, II. 381, *note*. Compare *Memoirs of the Principal Transactions of the Late War*.

[2] "Un ancien prisonnier affidé que l'on a mis dans nos interests."

letters to their friends being then opened, it appeared that they were all in expectation of speedy deliverance.[1]

In July a report came from Acadia that from forty to fifty thousand men were to attack Canada; and on the 1st of August a prisoner lately taken at Saratoga declared that there were thirty-two war-ships at Boston ready to sail against Quebec, and that thirteen thousand men were to march at once from Albany against Montreal. "If all these stories are true," writes the Canadian journalist, "all the English on this continent must be in arms."

Preparations for defence were pushed with feverish energy. Fireships were made ready at Quebec, and fire-rafts at Isle-aux-Coudres; provisions were gathered, and ammunition was distributed; reconnoitring parties were sent to watch the Gulf and the River; and bands of Canadians and Indians lately sent to Acadia were ordered to hasten back.

Thanks to the Duke of Newcastle, all these alarms were needless. The Massachusetts levies were ready within six weeks, and Shirley, eager and impatient, waited in vain for the squadron from England and the promised eight battalions of regulars. They did not come; and in August he wrote to Newcastle that it would now be impossible to reach Quebec before October, which would be too late.[2] The eight battalions had been sent to Portsmouth for embarkation, ordered on board the transports, then ordered ashore again, and finally sent on an abortive expedition against the coast of France. There were those who thought that this had been their destination from the first, and that the proposed attack on Canada was only a pretence to deceive the enemy. It was not till the next spring that Newcastle tried to explain the miscarriage to Shirley. He wrote that the troops had been detained by head-winds till General Saint Clair and Admiral Lestock thought it too late; to which he added that the demands of the European war made the Canadian expedition impracticable, and that Shirley was to stand on the defensive and attempt no further conquests. As for the provincial sol-

---

[1] *Extrait en forme de Journal de ce qui s'est passé dans la Colonie depuis . . . le 1 Déc. 1745, jusqu'au 9 Nov. 1746, signé Beauharnois et Hocquart.*

[2] *Shirley to Newcastle, 22 Aug. 1746.*

diers, who this time were in the pay of the Crown, he says that they were "very expensive," and orders the Governor to get rid of them "as cheap as possible."[1] Thus, not for the first time, the hopes of the colonies were brought to nought by the failure of the British ministers to keep their promises.

When, in the autumn of 1746, Shirley said that for the present Canada was to be let alone, he bethought him of a less decisive conquest, and proposed to employ the provincial troops for an attack on Crown Point, which formed a half-way station between Albany and Montreal, and was the constant rendezvous of war-parties against New York, New Hampshire, and Massachusetts, whose discords and jealousies had prevented them from combining to attack it. The Dutch of Albany, too, had strong commercial reasons for not coming to blows with the Canadians. Of late, however, Massachusetts and New York had suffered so much from this inconvenient neighbor that it was possible to unite them against it; and as Clinton, governor of New York, was scarcely less earnest to get possession of Crown Point than was Shirley himself, a plan of operations was soon settled. By the middle of October fifteen hundred Massachusetts troops were on their way to join the New York levies, and then advance upon the obnoxious post.[2]

Even this modest enterprise was destined to fail. Astounding tidings reached New England, and startled her like a thunder-clap from dreams of conquest. It was reported that a great French fleet and army were on their way to retake Louisbourg, reconquer Acadia, burn Boston, and lay waste the other seaboard towns. The Massachusetts troops marching for Crown Point were recalled, and the country militia were mustered in arms. In a few days the narrow, crooked streets of the Puritan capital were crowded with more than eight thousand armed rustics from the farms and villages of Middlesex, Essex, Norfolk, and Worcester, and Connecticut promised six thousand more as soon as the hostile fleet should appear. The defences of Castle William were enlarged and strengthened, and cannon were planted on the islands at the mouth of the harbor; hulks were sunk in the channel, and

[1] *Newcastle to Shirley, 30 May, 1747.*
[2] *Memoirs of the Principal Transactions of the Last War.*

a boom was laid across it under the guns of the castle.[1] The alarm was compared to that which filled England on the approach of the Spanish Armada.[2]

Canada heard the news of the coming armament with an exultation that was dashed with misgiving as weeks and months passed and the fleet did not appear. At length in September a vessel put in to an Acadian harbor with the report that she had met the ships in mid-ocean, and that they counted a hundred and fifty sail. Some weeks later the Governor and Intendant of Canada wrote that on the 14th of October they received a letter from Chibucto with "the agreeable news" that the Duc d'Anville and his fleet had arrived there about three weeks before. Had they known more, they would have rejoiced less.

That her great American fortress should have been snatched from her by a despised militia was more than France could bear; and in the midst of a burdensome war she made a crowning effort to retrieve her honor and pay the debt with usury. It was computed that nearly half the French navy was gathered at Brest under command of the Duc d'Anville. By one account his force consisted of eleven ships of the line, twenty frigates, and thirty-four transports and fireships, or sixty-five in all. Another list gives a total of sixty-six, of which ten were ships of the line, twenty-two were frigates and fireships, and thirty-four were transports.[3] These last carried the regiment of Ponthieu, with other veteran troops, to the number in all of three thousand one hundred and fifty. The fleet was to be joined at Chibucto, now Halifax, by four heavy ships-of-war lately sent to the West Indies under M. de Conflans.

From Brest D'Anville sailed for some reason to Rochelle, and here the ships were kept so long by head-winds that it was the 20th of June before they could put to sea. From the first the omens were sinister. The Admiral was beset with

---

[1] *Shirley to Newcastle, 29 Sept. 1746.* Shirley says that though the French may bombard the town, he does not think they could make a landing, as he shall have fifteen thousand good men within call to oppose them.

[2] Hutchinson, II. 382.

[3] This list is in the journal of a captured French officer called by Shirley M. Rebateau.

questions as to the destination of the fleet, which was known to him alone; and when, for the sake of peace, he told it to his officers, their discontent redoubled. The Bay of Biscay was rough and boisterous, and spars, sails, and bowsprits were carried away. After they had been a week at sea, some of the ships, being dull sailers, lagged behind, and the rest were forced to shorten sail and wait for them. In the longitude of the Azores there was a dead calm, and the whole fleet lay idle for days. Then came a squall, with lightning. Several ships were struck. On one of them six men were killed, and on the seventy-gun ship "Mars" a box of musket and cannon cartridges blew up, killed ten men, and wounded twenty-one. A store-ship which proved to be sinking was abandoned and burned. Then a pestilence broke out, and in some of the ships there were more sick than in health.

On the 14th of September they neared the coast of Nova Scotia, and were in dread of the dangerous shoals of Sable Island, the position of which they did not exactly know. They groped their way in fogs till a fearful storm, with thunder and lightning, fell upon them. The journalist of the voyage, a captain in the regiment of Ponthieu, says, with the exaggeration common in such cases, that the waves ran as high as the masts; and such was their violence that a transport, dashing against the ship "Amazone," immediately went down, with all on board. The crew of the "Prince d'Orange," half blinded by wind and spray, saw the great ship "Caribou," without bowsprit or main-topmast, driving towards them before the gale, and held their breath in expectation of the shock as she swept close alongside and vanished in the storm.[1] The tempest raged all night, and the fleet became so scattered that there was no more danger of collision. In the morning the journalist could see but five sail; but as the day advanced the rest began to reappear, and at three o'clock he counted thirty-one from the deck of the "Prince d'Orange." The gale was subsiding, but its effects were seen in hencoops, casks, and chests floating on the surges and telling the fate of one or more of the fleet. The "Argonaut" was rolling helpless, without masts

---

[1] *Journal historique du Voyage de la Flotte commandée par M. le Duc d'Enville.* The writer was on board the "Prince d'Orange," and describes what he saw (Archives du Séminaire de Québec; printed in *Le Canada Français*).

or rudder; the "Caribou" had thrown overboard all the star-board guns of her upper deck; and the vice-admiral's ship, the "Trident," was in scarcely better condition.

On the 23d they were wrapped in thick fog and lay firing guns, ringing bells, and beating drums to prevent collisions. When the weather cleared, they looked in vain for the Admiral's ship, the "Northumberland."[1] She was not lost, however, but with two other ships was far ahead of the fleet and near Chibucto, though in great perplexity, having no pilot who knew the coast. She soon after had the good fortune to capture a small English vessel with a man on board well acquainted with Chibucto harbor. D'Anville offered him his liberty and a hundred louis if he would pilot the ship in. To this he agreed; but when he rejoined his fellow-prisoners they called him a traitor to his country, on which he retracted his promise. D'Anville was sorely perplexed; but Duperrier, captain of the "Northumberland," less considerate of the prisoner's feelings, told him that unless he kept his word he should be thrown into the sea, with a pair of cannon-balls made fast to his feet. At this his scruples gave way, and before night the "Northumberland" was safe in Chibucto Bay. D'Anville had hoped to find here the four ships of Conflans which were to have met him from the West Indies at this, the appointed rendezvous; but he saw only a solitary transport of his own fleet. Hills covered with forests stood lonely and savage round what is now the harbor of Halifax. Conflans and his four ships had arrived early in the month, and finding nobody, though it was nearly three months since D'Anville left Rochelle, he cruised among the fogs for a while, and then sailed for France a few days before the Admiral's arrival.

D'Anville was ignorant of the fate of his fleet; but he knew that the two ships which had reached Chibucto with him were full of sick men, that their provisions were nearly spent, and that there was every reason to believe such of the fleet as the storm might have spared to be in no better case. An officer of the expedition describes D'Anville as a man "made to command and worthy to be loved," and says that he had borne the disasters of the voyage with the utmost fortitude

[1] The "Northumberland" was an English prize captured by Captains Serier and Conflans in 1744.

and serenity.[1] Yet suspense and distress wrought fatally upon him, and at two o'clock in the morning of the 27th he died— of apoplexy, by the best accounts; though it was whispered among the crews that he had ended his troubles by poison.[2]

At six o'clock in the afternoon of the same day D'Estournel, the vice-admiral, with such ships as remained with him, entered the harbor and learned what had happened. He saw with dismay that he was doomed to bear the burden of command over a ruined enterprise and a shattered fleet. The long voyage had consumed the provisions, and in some of the ships the crews were starving. The pestilence grew worse, and men were dying in numbers every day. On the 28th, D'Anville was buried without ceremony on a small island in the harbor. The officers met in council, and the papers of the dead commander were examined. Among them was a letter from the King in which he urged the recapture of Louisbourg as the first object of the expedition; but this was thought impracticable, and the council resolved to turn against Annapolis all the force that was left. It is said that D'Estournel opposed the attempt, insisting that it was hopeless, and that there was no alternative but to return to France. The debate was long and hot, and the decision was against him.[3] The council dissolved, and he was seen to enter his cabin in evident distress and agitation. An unusual sound was presently heard, followed by groans. His door was fastened by two bolts, put on the evening before by his order. It was burst open, and the unfortunate commander was found lying in a pool of blood, transfixed with his own sword. Enraged and mortified, he had thrown himself upon it in a fit of desperation. The surgeon drew out the blade, but it was only on the urgent persuasion of two Jesuits that the dying man would permit the wound to be dressed. He then ordered all the captains to the side of his berth, and said, "Gentlemen, I beg pardon of God and the King for what I have done, and I protest to the King that my

[1] *Journal historique du Voyage.*

[2] *Declaration of H. Kannan and D. Deas, 23 Oct. 1746. Deposition of Joseph Foster, 24 Oct. 1746, sworn to before Jacob Wendell, J. P.* These were prisoners in the ships at Chibucto.

[3] This is said by all the writers except the author of the *Journal historique*, who merely states that the council decided to attack Annapolis, and to detach some soldiers to the aid of Quebec. This last vote was reconsidered.

only object was to prevent my enemies from saying that I had not executed his orders;" and he named M. de la Jonquière to command in his place. In fact, La Jonquière's rank entitled him to do so. He was afterwards well known as governor of Canada, and was reputed a brave and able sea-officer.

La Jonquière remained at Chibucto till late in October. Messengers were sent to the Acadian settlements to ask for provisions, of which there was desperate need; and as payment was promised in good metal, and not in paper, the Acadians brought in a considerable supply. The men were encamped on shore, yet the pestilence continued its ravages. Two English prisoners were told that between twenty-three and twenty-four hundred men had been buried by sea or land since the fleet left France; and another declares that eleven hundred and thirty-five burials took place while he was at Chibucto.[1] The survivors used the clothing of the dead as gifts to the neighboring Indians, who in consequence were attacked with such virulence by the disease that of the band at Cape Sable three fourths are said to have perished. The English, meanwhile, learned something of the condition of their enemies. Towards the end of September Captain Sylvanus Cobb, in a sloop from Boston, boldly entered Chibucto Harbor, took note of the ships lying there, and though pursued, ran out to sea and carried the results of his observations to Louisbourg.[2] A more thorough reconnoissance was afterwards made by a vessel from Louisbourg bringing French prisoners for exchange under a flag of truce; and it soon became evident that the British colonies had now nothing to fear.

La Jonquière still clung to the hope of a successful stroke at Annapolis, till in October an Acadian brought him the report that the garrison of that place had received a reinforcement of twelve hundred men. The reinforcement consisted in reality of three small companies of militia sent from Boston by Shirley. La Jonquière called a secret council, and the result seems to have been adverse to any further attempt. The journalist reports that only a thousand men were left in fighting condition, and that even of these some were dying every day.

[1] *Declaration of Kannan and Deas. Deposition of Joseph Foster.*
[2] *Report of Captain Cobb*, in *Shirley to Newcastle, 13 Oct. 1746.*

La Jonquière, however, would not yet despair. The troops were re-embarked; five hospital ships were devoted to the sick; the "Parfait," a fifty-gun ship no longer serviceable, was burned, as were several smaller vessels, and on the 4th of October what was left of the fleet sailed out of Chibucto Harbor and steered for Annapolis, piloted by Acadians. The flag of truce from Louisbourg was compelled for a time to bear them company, and Joseph Foster of Beverly, an exchanged prisoner on board of her, deposed that as the fleet held its way, he saw "a great number of dead persons" dropped into the sea every day. Ill-luck still pursued the French. A storm off Cape Sable dispersed the ships, two of which some days later made their way to Annapolis Basin in expectation of finding some of their companions there. They found instead the British fifty-gun ship "Chester" and the Massachusetts frigate "Shirley" anchored before the fort, on which the two Frenchmen retired as they had come; and so ended the last aggressive movement on the part of the great armament.

The journalist reports that on the night of the 27th there was a council of officers on board the "Northumberland," at which it was resolved that no choice was left but to return to France with the ships that still kept together. On the 4th of November there was another storm, and when it subsided, the "Prince d'Orange" found herself with but nine companions, all of which were transports. These had on board eleven companies of soldiers, of whom their senior officer reports that only ninety-one were in health. The pestilence made such ravages among the crews that four or five corpses were thrown into the sea every day, and there was fear that the vessels would be left helpless in mid-ocean for want of sailors to work them.[1] At last, on the 7th of December, after narrowly escaping an English squadron, they reached Port Louis in Brittany, where several ships of the fleet had arrived before them. Among these was the frigate "La Palme." "Yesterday," says the journalist, "I supped with M. Destrahoudal, who commands this frigate; and he told me things which from anybody else would have been incredible. This is his story, exactly as I had it from him." And he goes on to the following effect.

[1] *Journal historique.*

After the storm of the 14th of September, provisions being almost spent, it was thought that there was no hope for "La Palme" and her crew but in giving up the enterprise and making all sail at once for home, since France now had no port of refuge on the western continent nearer than Quebec. Rations were reduced to three ounces of biscuit and three of salt meat a day; and after a time half of this pittance was cut off. There was diligent hunting for rats in the hold; and when this game failed, the crew, crazed with famine, demanded of their captain that five English prisoners who were on board should be butchered to appease the frenzy of their hunger. The captain consulted his officers, and they were of opinion that if he did not give his consent, the crew would work their will without it. The ship's butcher was accordingly ordered to bind one of the prisoners, carry him to the bottom of the hold, put him to death, and distribute his flesh to the men in portions of three ounces each. The captain, walking the deck in great agitation all night, found a pretext for deferring the deed till morning, when a watchman sent aloft at daylight cried, "A sail!" The providential stranger was a Portuguese ship; and as Portugal was neutral in the war, she let the frigate approach to within hailing distance. The Portuguese captain soon came alongside in a boat, "accompanied," in the words of the narrator, "by five sheep." These were eagerly welcomed by the starving crew as agreeable substitutes for the five Englishmen; and being forthwith slaughtered, were parcelled out among the men, who would not wait till the flesh was cooked, but devoured it raw. Provisions enough were obtained from the Portuguese to keep the frigate's company alive till they reached Port Louis.[1]

There are no sufficient means of judging how far the disasters of D'Anville's fleet were due to a neglect of sanitary precautions or to deficient seamanship. Certain it is that there were many in self-righteous New England who would have held it impious to doubt that God had summoned the pestilence and the storm to fight the battles of his modern Israel.

Undaunted by disastrous failure, the French court equipped another fleet, not equal to that of D'Anville, yet still

[1] *Relation du Voyage de Retour de M. Destrahoudal après la Tempête du 14 Septembre*, in *Journal historique*.

formidable, and placed it under La Jonquière, for the conquest of Acadia and Louisbourg. La Jonquière sailed from Rochelle on the 10th of May, 1747, and on the 14th was met by an English fleet stronger than his own and commanded by Admirals Anson and Warren. A fight ensued, in which, after brave resistance, the French were totally defeated. Six ships-of-war, including the flag-ship, were captured, with a host of prisoners, among whom was La Jonquière himself.[1]

[1] *Relation du Combat rendu le 14 Mai* (new style), *par l'Escadre du Roy commandée par M. de la Jonquière*, in *Le Canada Français, Supplément de Documents inédits*, 33. *Newcastle to Shirley, 30 May, 1747.*

Chapter XXII

ACADIAN CONFLICTS

Efforts of France • Apathy of Newcastle • Dilemma of Acadians • Their Character • Danger of the Province • Plans of Shirley • Acadian Priests • Political Agitators • Noble's Expedition • Ramesay at Beaubassin • Noble at Grand Pré • A Winter March • Defeat and Death of Noble • Grand Pré re-occupied by the English • Threats of Ramesay against the Acadians • The British Ministry will not protect them

---

S INCE the capture of Louisbourg, France had held constantly in view, as an object of prime importance, the recovery of her lost colony of Acadia. This was one of the chief aims of D'Anville's expedition, and of that of La Jonquière in the next year. And to make assurance still more sure, a large body of Canadians, under M. de Ramesay, had been sent to Acadia to co-operate with D'Anville's force; but the greater part of them had been recalled to aid in defending Quebec against the expected attack of the English. They returned when the news came that D'Anville was at Chibucto, and Ramesay, with a part of his command, advanced upon Port Royal, or Annapolis, in order to support the fleet in its promised attack on that place. He encamped at a little distance from the English fort, till he heard of the disasters that had ruined the fleet,[1] and then fell back to Chignecto, on the neck of the Acadian peninsula, where he made his quarters, with a force which, including Micmac, Malecite, and Penobscot Indians, amounted, at one time, to about sixteen hundred men.

If France was bent on recovering Acadia, Shirley was no less resolved to keep it, if he could. In his belief, it was the key of the British American colonies, and again and again he urged the Duke of Newcastle to protect it. But Newcastle seems scarcely to have known where Acadia was, being ignorant of most things except the art of managing the House of

[1] *Journal de Beaujeu*, in *Le Canada Français, Documents*, 53.

Commons, and careless of all things that could not help his party and himself. Hence Shirley's hyperboles, though never without a basis of truth, were lost upon him. Once, it is true, he sent three hundred men to Annapolis; but one hundred and eighty of them died on the voyage, or lay helpless in Boston hospitals, and the rest could better have been spared, some being recruits from English jails, and others Irish Catholics, several of whom deserted to the French, with information of the state of the garrison.

The defence of Acadia was left to Shirley and his Assembly, who in time of need sent companies of militia and rangers to Annapolis, and thus on several occasions saved it from returning to France. Shirley was the most watchful and strenuous defender of British interests on the continent; and in the present crisis British and colonial interests were one. He held that if Acadia were lost, the peace and safety of all the other colonies would be in peril; and in spite of the immense efforts made by the French court to recover it, he felt that the chief danger of the province was not from without, but from within. "If a thousand French troops should land in Nova Scotia," he writes to Newcastle, "all the people would rise to join them, besides all the Indians."[1] So, too, thought the French officials in America. The Governor and Intendant of Canada wrote to the colonial minister: "The inhabitants, with few exceptions, wish to return under the French dominion, and will not hesitate to take up arms as soon as they see themselves free to do so; that is, as soon as we become masters of Port Royal, or they have powder and other munitions of war, and are backed by troops for their protection against the resentment of the English."[2] Up to this time, however, though they had aided Duvivier in his attack on Annapolis so far as was possible without seeming to do so, they had not openly taken arms, and their refusal to fight for the besiegers is one among several causes to which Mascarene ascribes the success of his defence. While the greater part remained attached to France, some leaned to the English, who bought their produce and paid them in ready coin. Money was rare with the Acadians, who loved it, and were so addicted to hoarding it

[1] *Shirley to Newcastle, 29 Oct. 1745.*
[2] *Beauharnois et Hocquart au Ministre, 12 Sept. 1745.*

that the French authorities were led to speculate as to what might be the object of these careful savings.[1]

Though the Acadians loved France, they were not always ready to sacrifice their interests to her. They would not supply Ramesay's force with provisions in exchange for his promissory notes, but demanded hard cash.[2] This he had not to give, and was near being compelled to abandon his position in consequence. At the same time, in consideration of specie payment, the inhabitants brought in fuel for the English garrison at Louisbourg, and worked at repairing the rotten *chevaux de frise* of Annapolis.[3]

Mascarene, commandant at that place, being of French descent, was disposed at first to sympathize with the Acadians and treat them with a lenity that to the members of his council seemed neither fitting nor prudent. He wrote to Shirley: "The French inhabitants are certainly in a very perilous situation, those who pretend to be their friends and old masters having let loose a parcel of banditti to plunder them; whilst, on the other hand, they see themselves threatened with ruin if they fail in their allegiance to the British Government."[4]

This unhappy people were in fact between two fires. France claimed them on one side, and England on the other, and each demanded their adhesion, without regard to their feelings or their welfare. The banditti of whom Mascarene speaks were the Micmac Indians, who were completely under the control of their missionary, Le Loutre, and were used by him to terrify the inhabitants into renouncing their English allegiance and actively supporting the French cause. By the Treaty of Utrecht France had transferred Acadia to Great Britain, and the inhabitants had afterwards taken an oath of fidelity to King George. Thus they were British subjects; but as their oath had been accompanied by a promise, or at least a clear understanding, that they should not be required to take arms against Frenchmen or Indians, they had become

[1] *Beauharnois et Hocquart au Ministre, 12 Sept. 1745.*
[2] *Ibid.*
[3] *Admiral Knowles à —— 1746.* Mascarene in *Le Canada Français, Documents,* 82.
[4] Mascarene, in *Le Canada Français, Documents,* 81.

known as the "Neutral French." This name tended to perplex them, and in their ignorance and simplicity they hardly knew to which side they owed allegiance. Their illiteracy was extreme. Few of them could sign their names, and a contemporary well acquainted with them declares that he knew but a single Acadian who could read and write.[1] This was probably the notary, Le Blanc, whose compositions are crude and illiterate. Ignorant of books and isolated in a wild and remote corner of the world, the Acadians knew nothing of affairs, and were totally incompetent to meet the crisis that was soon to come upon them. In activity and enterprise they were far behind the Canadians, who looked on them as inferiors. Their pleasures were those of the humblest and simplest peasants; they were contented with their lot, and asked only to be let alone. Their intercourse was unceremonious to such a point that they never addressed each other, or, it is said, even strangers, as *monsieur*. They had the social equality which can exist only in the humblest conditions of society, and presented the phenomenon of a primitive little democracy, hatched under the wing of an absolute monarchy. Each was as good as his neighbor; they had no natural leaders, nor any to advise or guide them, except the missionary priest, who in every case was expected by his superiors to influence them in the interest of France, and who, in fact, constantly did so. While one observer represents them as living in a state of primeval innocence, another describes both men and women as extremely foul of speech; from which he draws inferences unfavorable to their domestic morals,[2] which, nevertheless, were commendable. As is usual with a well-fed and unambitious peasantry, they were very prolific, and are said to have doubled their number every sixteen years. In 1748 they counted in the peninsula of Nova Scotia between twelve and thirteen thousand souls.[3] The English rule had been of the lightest,—so light that it could scarcely be felt; and this was not surprising, since the only instruments for enforcing it over a population wholly French were some two

---

[1] Moïse des Derniers, in *Le Canada Français*, I. 118.

[2] *Journal de Franquet*, Part II.

[3] *Description de l'Acadie, avec le Nom des Paroisses et le Nombre des Habitants, 1748.*

hundred disorderly soldiers in the crumbling little fort of Annapolis; and the province was left, perforce, to take care of itself.

The appearance of D'Anville's fleet caused great excitement among the Acadians, who thought that they were about to pass again under the Crown of France. Fifty of them went on board the French ships at Chibucto to pilot them to the attack of Annapolis, and to their dismay found that no attack was to be made. When Ramesay, with his Canadians and Indians, took post at Chignecto and built a fort at Baye Verte, on the neck of the peninsula of Nova Scotia, the English power in that part of the colony seemed at an end. The inhabitants cut off all communication with Annapolis, and detained the officers whom Mascarene sent for intelligence.

From the first outbreak of the war it was evident that the French built their hopes of recovering Acadia largely on a rising of the Acadians against the English rule, and that they spared no efforts to excite such a rising. Early in 1745 a violent and cruel precaution against this danger was suggested. William Shirreff, provincial secretary, gave it as his opinion that the Acadians ought to be removed, being a standing menace to the colony.[1] This is the first proposal of such a nature that I find. Some months later, Shirley writes that, on a false report of the capture of Annapolis by the French, the Acadians sang *Te Deum*, and that every sign indicates that there will be an attempt in the spring to capture Annapolis, with their help.[2] Again, Shirley informs Newcastle that the French will get possession of Acadia unless the most dangerous of the inhabitants are removed, and English settlers put in their place.[3] He adds that there are not two hundred and twenty soldiers at Annapolis to defend the province against the whole body of Acadians and Indians, and he tells the minister that unless the expedition against Canada should end in the conquest of that country, the removal of some of the Acadians will be a necessity. He means those of Chignecto, who were kept in a threatening attitude by the presence of Ramesay and his Canadians, and who, as he thinks, had forfeited

---

[1] *Shirreff to K. Gould, agent of Phillips's Regiment, March, 1745.*
[2] *Shirley to Newcastle, 14 Dec. 1745.*
[3] *Ibid., 10 May, 1746.*

their lands by treasonable conduct. Shirley believes that families from New England might be induced to take their place, and that these, if settled under suitable regulations, would form a military frontier to the province of Nova Scotia "strong enough to keep the Canadians out," and hold the Acadians to their allegiance.[1] The Duke of Bedford thinks the plan a good one, but objects to the expense.[2] Commodore Knowles, then governor of Louisbourg, who, being threatened with consumption and convinced that the climate was killing him, vented his feelings in strictures against everything and everybody, was of opinion that the Acadians, having broken their neutrality, ought to be expelled at once, and expresses the amiable hope that should his Majesty adopt this plan, he will charge him with executing it.[3]

Shirley's energetic nature inclined him to trenchant measures, and he had nothing of modern humanitarianism; but he was not inhuman, and he shrank from the cruelty of forcing whole communities into exile. While Knowles and others called for wholesale expatriation, he still held that it was possible to turn the greater part of the Acadians into safe subjects of the British Crown;[4] and to this end he advised the planting of a fortified town where Halifax now stands, and securing by forts and garrisons the neck of the Acadian peninsula, where the population was most numerous and most disaffected. The garrisons, he thought, would not only impose respect, but would furnish the Acadians with what they wanted most,—ready markets for their produce,—and thus bind them to the British by strong ties of interest. Newcastle

[1] *Ibid., 8 July, 1747.*

[2] *Bedford to Newcastle, 11 Sept. 1747.*

[3] *Knowles to Newcastle, 8 Nov. 1746.*

[4] Shirley says that the indiscriminate removal of the Acadians would be "unjust" and "too rigorous." Knowles had proposed to put Catholic Jacobites from the Scotch Highlands into their place. Shirley thinks this inexpedient, but believes that Protestants from Germany and Ulster might safely be trusted. The best plan of all, in his opinion, is that of "treating the Acadians as subjects, confining their punishment to the most guilty and dangerous among 'em, and keeping the rest in the country and endeavoring to make them useful members of society under his Majesty's Government." *Shirley to Newcastle, 21 Nov. 1746.* If the Newcastle Government had vigorously carried his recommendations into effect, the removal of the Acadians in 1755 would not have taken place.

thought the plan good, but wrote that its execution must be deferred to a future day. Three years later it was partly carried into effect by the foundation of Halifax; but at that time the disaffection of the Acadians had so increased, and the hope of regaining the province for France had risen so high, that this partial and tardy assertion of British authority only spurred the French agents to redoubled efforts to draw the inhabitants from the allegiance they had sworn to the Crown of England.

Shirley had also other plans in view for turning the Acadians into good British subjects. He proposed, as a measure of prime necessity, to exclude French priests from the province. The free exercise of their religion had been insured to the inhabitants by the Treaty of Utrecht, and on this point the English authorities had given no just cause of complaint. A priest had occasionally been warned, suspended, or removed; but without a single exception, so far as appears, this was in consequence of conduct which tended to excite disaffection, and which would have incurred equal or greater penalties in the case of a layman.[1] The sentence was directed, not against the priest, but against the political agitator. Shirley's plan of excluding French priests from the province would not have violated the provisions of the treaty, provided that the inhabitants were supplied with other priests, not French subjects, and therefore not politically dangerous; but though such a measure was several times proposed by the provincial authorities, the exasperating apathy of the Newcastle Government gave no hope that it could be accomplished.

[1] There was afterwards sharp correspondence between Shirley and the Governor of Canada touching the Acadian priests. Thus, Shirley writes: "I can't avoid now, Sir, expressing great surprise at the other parts of your letter, whereby you take upon you to call Mr. Mascarene to account for expelling the missionary from Minas for being guilty of such treasonable practices within His Majesty's government as merited a much severer Punishment." *Shirley à Galissonière, 9 Mai, 1749.*

Shirley writes to Newcastle that the Acadians "are greatly under the influence of their priests, who continually receive their directions from the Bishop of Quebec, and are the instruments by which the Governor of Canada makes all his attempts for the reduction of the province to the French Crown." *Shirley to Newcastle, 20 Oct. 1747.* He proceeds to give facts in proof of his assertion. Compare *Montcalm and Wolfe,* I. 917, 918, 1027, *note.*

The influences most dangerous to British rule did not proceed from love of France or sympathy of race, but from the power of religion over a simple and ignorant people, trained in profound love and awe of their Church and its ministers, who were used by the representatives of Louis XV. as agents to alienate the Acadians from England.

The most strenuous of these clerical agitators was Abbé Le Loutre, missionary to the Micmacs, and after 1753 vicar-general of Acadia. He was a fiery and enterprising zealot, inclined by temperament to methods of violence, detesting the English, and restrained neither by pity nor scruple from using threats of damnation and the Micmac tomahawk to frighten the Acadians into doing his bidding. The worst charge against him, that of exciting the Indians of his mission to murder Captain Howe, an English officer, has not been proved; but it would not have been brought against him by his own countrymen if his character and past conduct had gained him their esteem.

The other Acadian priests were far from sharing Le Loutre's violence; but their influence was always directed to alienating the inhabitants from their allegiance to King George. Hence Shirley regarded the conversion of the Acadians to Protestantism as a political measure of the first importance, and proposed the establishment of schools in the province to that end. Thus far his recommendations are perfectly legitimate; but when he adds that rewards ought to be given to Acadians who renounce their faith, few will venture to defend him.

Newcastle would trouble himself with none of his schemes, and Acadia was left to drift with the tide, as before. "I shall finish my troubleing your Grace upon the affairs of Nova Scotia with this letter," writes the persevering Shirley. And he proceeds to ask, "as a proper Scheme for better securing the Subjection of the French inhabitants and Indians there," that the Governor and Council at Annapolis have special authority and direction from the King to arrest and examine such Acadians as shall be "most obnoxious and dangerous to his Majesty's Government;" and if found guilty of treasonable correspondence with the enemy, to dispose of them and their estates in such manner as his Majesty shall order, at the same time promising indemnity to the rest for past offences, upon their taking or renewing the oath of allegiance.[1]

To this it does not appear that Newcastle made any answer except to direct Shirley, eight or nine months later, to tell the Acadians that so long as they were peaceable subjects, they should be protected in property and religion.[2] Thus left to struggle unaided with a most difficult problem, entirely outside of his functions as governor of Massachusetts, Shirley did what he could. The most pressing danger, as he thought, rose from the presence of Ramesay and his Canadians at Chignecto; for that officer spared no pains to induce the Acadians to join him in another attempt against Annapolis, telling them that if they did not drive out the English, the English would drive them out. He was now at Mines, trying to raise the inhabitants in arms for France. Shirley thought it necessary to counteract him, and force him and his Canadians back to the isthmus whence they had come; but as the ministry would give no soldiers, he was compelled to draw them from New England. The defence of Acadia was the business of the Home Government, and not of the colonies; but as they were deeply interested in the preservation of the endangered province, Massachusetts gave five hundred men in response to Shirley's call, and Rhode Island and New Hampshire added, between them, as many more. Less than half of these levies reached Acadia. It was the stormy season. The Rhode Island vessels were wrecked near Martha's Vineyard. A New Hampshire transport sloop was intercepted by a French armed vessel, and ran back to Portsmouth. Four hundred and seventy men from Massachusetts, under Colonel Arthur Noble, were all who reached Annapolis, whence they sailed for Mines, accompanied by a few soldiers of the garrison. Storms, drifting ice, and the furious tides of the Bay of Fundy made their progress so difficult and uncertain that Noble resolved to finish the journey by land; and on the 4th of December he disembarked near the place now called French Cross, at the foot

[1] *Shirley to Newcastle, 15 Aug. 1746.*

[2] *Newcastle to Shirley, 30 May, 1747.* Shirley had some time before directed Mascarene to tell the Acadians that while they behave peaceably and do not correspond with the enemy, their property will be safe, but that such as turn traitors will be treated accordingly. *Shirley to Mascarene, 16 Sept. 1746.*

of the North Mountain,—a lofty barrier of rock and forest extending along the southern shore of the Bay of Fundy. Without a path and without guides, the party climbed the snow-encumbered heights and toiled towards their destination, each man carrying provisions for fourteen days in his haversack. After sleeping eight nights without shelter among the snowdrifts, they reached the Acadian village of Grand Pré, the chief settlement of the district of Mines. Ramesay and his Canadians were gone. On learning the approach of an English force, he had tried to persuade the Acadians that they were to be driven from their homes, and that their only hope was in joining with him to meet force by force; but they trusted Shirley's recent assurance of protection, and replied that they would not break their oath of fidelity to King George. On this, Ramesay retreated to his old station at Chignecto, and Noble and his men occupied Grand Pré without opposition.

The village consisted of small, low wooden houses, scattered at intervals for the distance of a mile and a half, and therefore ill fitted for defence. The English had the frame of a blockhouse, or, as some say, of two blockhouses, ready to be set up on their arrival; but as the ground was hard frozen it was difficult to make a foundation, and the frames were therefore stored in outbuildings of the village, with the intention of raising them in the spring. The vessels which had brought them, together with stores, ammunition, five small cannon, and a good supply of snow-shoes, had just arrived at the landing-place,—and here, with incredible fatuity, were allowed to remain, with most of their indispensable contents still on board. The men, meanwhile, were quartered in the Acadian houses.

Noble's position was critical, but he was assured that he could not be reached from Chignecto in such a bitter season; and this he was too ready to believe, though he himself had just made a march, which, if not so long, was quite as arduous. Yet he did not neglect every precaution, but kept out scouting-parties to range the surrounding country, while the rest of his men took their ease in the Acadian houses, living on the provisions of the villagers, for which payment was afterwards made. Some of the inhabitants, who had openly favored Ramesay and his followers, fled to the woods, in fear of the consequences; but the greater part remained quietly in the village.

At the head of the Bay of Fundy its waters form a fork, consisting of Chignecto Bay on the one hand, and Mines Basin on the other. At the head of Chignecto Bay was the Acadian settlement of Chignecto, or Beaubassin, in the houses of which Ramesay had quartered his Canadians. Here the neck of the Acadian peninsula is at its narrowest, the distance across to Baye Verte, where Ramesay had built a fort, being little more than twelve miles. Thus he controlled the isthmus,—from which, however, Noble hoped to dislodge him in the spring.

In the afternoon of the 8th of January an Acadian who had been sent to Mines by the missionary Germain, came to Beaubassin with the news that two hundred and twenty English were at Grand Pré, and that more were expected.[1] Ramesay instantly formed a plan of extraordinary hardihood, and resolved, by a rapid march and a night attack, to surprise the new-comers. His party was greatly reduced by disease, and to recruit it he wrote to La Corne, Récollet missionary at Miramichi, to join him with his Indians; writing at the same time to Maillard, former colleague of Le Loutre at the mission of Shubenacadie, and to Girard, priest of Cobequid, to muster Indians, collect provisions, and gather information concerning the English. Meanwhile his Canadians busied themselves with making snow-shoes and dog-sledges for the march.

Ramesay could not command the expedition in person, as an accident to one of his knees had disabled him from marching. This was less to be regretted, in view of the quality of his officers, for he had with him the flower of the warlike Canadian *noblesse*,—Coulon de Villiers, who, seven years later, defeated Washington at Fort Necessity; Beaujeu, the future hero of the Monongahela, in appearance a carpet knight, in reality a bold and determined warrior; the Chevalier de la Corne, a model of bodily and mental hardihood; Saint-Pierre, Lanaudière, Saint-Ours, Desligneris, Courtemanche, Repentigny, Boishébert, Gaspé, Colombière, Marin, Lusignan,—all

[1] Beaujeu, *Journal de la Campagne du Détachement de Canada à l'Acadie*, in *Le Canada Français*, II. *Documents*, 16.

adepts in the warfare of surprise and sudden onslaught in which the Canadians excelled.

Coulon de Villiers commanded in Ramesay's place; and on the 21st of January he and the other officers led their men across the isthmus from Beaubassin to Baye Verte, where they all encamped in the woods, and where they were joined by a party of Indians and some Acadians from Beaubassin and Isle St. Jean.[1] Provisions, ammunition, and other requisites were distributed, and at noon of the 23d they broke up their camp, marched three leagues, and bivouacked towards evening. On the next morning they marched again at daybreak. There was sharp cold, with a storm of snow, — not the large, moist, lazy flakes that fall peacefully and harmlessly, but those small crystalline particles that drive spitefully before the wind, and prick the cheek like needles. It was the kind of snow-storm called in Canada *la poudrerie*. They had hoped to make a long day's march; but feet and faces were freezing, and they were forced to stop, at noon, under such shelter as the thick woods of pine, spruce, and fir could supply. In the morning they marched again, following the border of the sea, their dog-teams dragging provisions and baggage over the broken ice of creeks and inlets, which they sometimes avoided by hewing paths through the forest. After a day of extreme fatigue they stopped at the small bay where the town of Wallace now stands. Beaujeu says: "While we were digging out the snow to make our huts, there came two Acadians with letters from MM. Maillard and Girard." The two priests sent a mixture of good and evil news. On one hand the English were more numerous than had been reported; on the other, they had not set up the blockhouses they had brought with them. Some Acadians of the neighboring settlement joined the party at this camp, as also did a few Indians.

On the next morning, January 27th, the adventurers stopped at the village of Tatmagouche, where they were again joined by a number of Acadians. After mending their broken sledges they resumed their march, and at five in the afternoon reached a place called Bacouel, at the beginning of the portage that led some twenty-five miles across the country to

[1] *Mascarene to Shirley, 8 Feb. 1746* (1747, new style).

Cobequid, now Truro, at the head of Mines Basin. Here they were met by Girard, priest of Cobequid, from whom Coulon exacted a promise to meet him again at that village in two days. Girard gave the promise unwillingly, fearing, says Beaujeu, to embroil himself with the English authorities. He reported that the force at Grand Pré counted at least four hundred and fifty, or, as some said, more than five hundred. This startling news ran through the camp; but the men were not daunted. "The more there are," they said, "the more we shall kill."

The party spent the 28th in mending their damaged sledges, and in the afternoon they were joined by more Acadians and Indians. Thus reinforced, they marched again, and towards evening reached a village on the outskirts of Cobequid. Here the missionary Maillard joined them,—to the great satisfaction of Coulon, who relied on him and his brother priest Girard to procure supplies of provisions. Maillard promised to go himself to Grand Pré with the Indians of his mission.

The party rested for a day, and set out again on the 1st of February, stopped at Maillard's house in Cobequid for the provisions he had collected for them, and then pushed on towards the river Shubenacadie, which runs from the south into Cobequid Bay, the head of Mines Basin. When they reached the river they found it impassable from floating ice, which forced them to seek a passage at some distance above. Coulon was resolved, however, that at any risk a detachment should cross at once, to stop the roads to Grand Pré, and prevent the English from being warned of his approach; for though the Acadians inclined to the French, and were eager to serve them when the risk was not too great, there were some of them who, from interest or fear, were ready to make favor with the English by carrying them intelligence. Boishébert, with ten Canadians, put out from shore in a canoe, and were near perishing among the drifting ice; but they gained the farther shore at last, and guarded every path to Grand Pré. The main body filed on snow-shoes up the east bank of the Shubenacadie, where the forests were choked with snow and encumbered with fallen trees, over which the sledges were to be dragged, to their great detriment. On this day, the 3d, they made five leagues; on the next only two, which brought them within half a league of Le Loutre's Micmac mission. Not far from this place the river was easily passable on the ice, and they continued their march westward across the country to the river Kennetcook by ways so difficult that their Indian guide lost the path, and for a time led them astray. On the 7th, Boishébert and his party rejoined them, and brought a reinforcement of sixteen Indians, whom the Acadians had furnished with arms. Provisions were failing, till on the 8th, as they approached the village of Pisiquid, now Windsor, the Acadians, with great zeal, brought them a supply. They told them, too, that the English at Grand Pré were perfectly secure, suspecting no danger.

On the 9th, in spite of a cold, dry storm of snow, they reached the west branch of the river Avon. It was but seven French leagues to Grand Pré, which they hoped to reach before night; but fatigue compelled them to rest till the 10th. At noon of that day, the storm still continuing, they marched again, though they could hardly see their way for the driving snow. They soon came to a small stream, along the frozen surface of which they drew up in order, and, by command of Coulon, Beaujeu divided them all into ten parties, for simultaneous attacks on as many houses occupied by the English. Then, marching slowly, lest they should arrive too soon, they reached the river Gaspereau, which enters Mines Basin at Grand Pré. They were now but half a league from their destination. Here they stopped an hour in the storm, shivering and half frozen, waiting for nightfall. When it grew dark they moved again, and soon came to a number of houses on the river-bank. Each of the ten parties took possession of one of these, making great fires to warm themselves and dry their guns.

It chanced that in the house where Coulon and his band sought shelter, a wedding-feast was going on. The guests were much startled at this sudden irruption of armed men; but to the Canadians and their chief the festival was a stroke of amazing good luck, for most of the guests were inhabitants of Grand Pré, who knew perfectly the houses occupied by the English, and could tell with precision where the officers were quartered. This was a point of extreme importance. The English were distributed among twenty-four houses, scattered, as before mentioned, for the distance of a mile and a half.[1] The assailants were too few to attack all these houses at once; but if those where the chief officers lodged could be surprised and captured with their inmates, the rest could make little resistance. Hence it was that Coulon had divided his followers into ten parties, each with one or more chosen officers; these officers were now called together at the house of the interrupted festivity, and the late guests having given full information as to the position of the English quarters and the military quality of their inmates, a special object of attack was assigned to the officer of each party, with Acadian guides to conduct him to it. The principal party, consisting of fifty, or, as another account says, of seventy-five men, was led by Coulon himself, with Beaujeu, Desligneris, Mercier, Léry, and Lusignan as his officers. This party was to attack a stone house near the middle of the village, where the main guard was stationed,—a building somewhat larger than the rest, and the only one at all suited for defence. The second party, of forty men, commanded by La Corne, with Rigauville, Lagny, and Villemont, was to attack a neighboring house, the quarters of Colonel Noble, his brother, Ensign Noble, and several other officers. The remaining parties, of twenty-five men each according to Beaujeu, or twenty-eight according to La Corne, were to make a dash, as nearly as possible at the same time, at other houses which it was thought most important to secure. All had Acadian guides, whose services in that capacity were invaluable; though Beaujeu complains that they were of no use in the attack. He says that the united force was about three hundred men, while the English Captain Goldthwait puts it, including Acadians and Indians, at from five to six hundred. That of the English was a little above five hundred in all. Every arrangement being made, and his part assigned to each officer, the whole body was drawn up in the storm, and the chaplain pronounced a general absolution. Then each of the ten parties, guided by one or more Acadians, took the path for its destination, every man on snow-shoes, with the lock of his gun well sheltered under his capote.

[1] *Goldthwait to Shirley, 2 March, 1746* (1747). Captain Benjamin Goldthwait was second in command of the English detachment.

The largest party, under Coulon, was, as we have seen, to attack the stone house in the middle of the village; but their guide went astray, and about three in the morning they approached a small wooden house not far from their true object. A guard was posted here, as at all the English quarters. The night was dark and the snow was still falling, as it had done without ceasing for the past thirty hours. The English sentinel descried through the darkness and the storm what seemed the shadows of an advancing crowd of men. He cried, "Who goes there?" and then shouted, "To arms!" A door was flung open, and the guard appeared in the entrance. But at that moment the moving shadows vanished from before the eyes of the sentinel. The French, one and all, had thrown themselves flat in the soft, light snow, and nothing was to be seen or heard. The English thought it a false alarm, and the house was quiet again. Then Coulon and his men rose and dashed forward. Again, in a loud and startled voice, the sentinel shouted, "To arms!" A great light, as of a blazing fire, shone through the open doorway, and men were seen within in hurried movement. Coulon, who was in the front, said to Beaujeu, who was close at his side, that the house was not the one they were to attack. Beaujeu replied that it was no time to change, and Coulon dashed forward again. Beaujeu aimed at the sentinel and shot him dead. There was the flash and report of muskets from the house, and Coulon dropped in the snow, severely wounded. The young cadet, Lusignan, was hit in the shoulder; but he still pushed on, when a second shot shattered his thigh. "Friends," cried the gallant youth, as he fell by the side of his commander, "don't let two dead men discourage you." The Canadians, powdered from head to foot with snow, burst into the house. Within ten minutes, all resistance was overpowered. Of twenty-four Englishmen, twenty-one were killed, and three made prisoners.[1]

Meanwhile, La Corne, with his party of forty men, had attacked the house where were quartered Colonel Noble and his brother, with Captain Howe and several other officers. Noble had lately transferred the main guard to the stone house, but had not yet removed thither himself, and the guard in the house which he occupied was small. The French

[1] Beaujeu, *Journal*.

burst the door with axes, and rushed in. Colonel Noble, startled from sleep, sprang from his bed, receiving two musketballs in the body as he did so. He seems to have had pistols, for he returned the fire several times. His servant, who was in the house, testified that the French called to the Colonel through a window and promised him quarter if he would surrender; but that he refused, on which they fired again, and a bullet, striking his forehead, killed him instantly. His brother, Ensign Noble, was also shot down, fighting in his shirt. Lieutenants Pickering and Lechmere lay in bed dangerously ill, and were killed there. Lieutenant Jones, after, as the narrator says, "ridding himself of some of the enemy," tried to break through the rest and escape, but was run through the heart with a bayonet. Captain Howe was severely wounded and made prisoner.

Coulon and Lusignan, disabled by their wounds, were carried back to the houses on the Gaspereau, where the French surgeon had remained. Coulon's party, now commanded by Beaujeu, having met and joined the smaller party under Lotbinière, proceeded to the aid of others who might need their help; for while they heard a great noise of musketry from far and near, and could discern bodies of men in motion here and there, they could not see whether these were friends or foes, or discern which side fortune favored. They presently met the party of Marin, composed of twenty-five Indians, who had just been repulsed with loss from the house which they had attacked. By this time there was a gleam of daylight, and as they plodded wearily over the snow-drifts, they no longer groped in darkness. The two parties of Colombière and Boishébert soon joined them, with the agreeable news that each had captured a house; and the united force now proceeded to make a successful attack on two buildings where the English had stored the frames of their blockhouses. Here the assailants captured ten prisoners. It was now broad day, but they could not see through the falling snow whether the enterprise, as a whole, had prospered or failed. Therefore Beaujeu sent Marin to find La Corne, who, in the absence of Coulon, held the chief command. Marin was gone two hours. At length he returned, and reported that the English in the houses which had not been attacked, together with such others as had not been killed or captured, had drawn together at the stone house in the middle of the village, that La Corne was blockading them there, and that he ordered Beaujeu and his party to join him at once. When Beaujeu reached the place he found La Corne posted at the house where Noble had been killed, and which was within easy musket-shot of the stone house occupied by the English, against whom a spattering fire was kept up by the French from the cover of neighboring buildings. Those in the stone house returned the fire; but no great harm was done on either side, till the English, now commanded by Captain Goldthwait, attempted to recapture the house where La Corne and his party were posted. Two companies made a sally; but they had among them only eighteen pairs of snow-shoes, the rest having been left on board the two vessels which had brought the stores of the detachment from Annapolis, and which now lay moored hard by, in the power of the enemy, at or near the mouth of the Gaspereau. Hence the sallying party floundered helpless among the drifts, plunging so deep in the dry snow that they could not use their guns and could scarcely move, while bullets showered upon them from La Corne's men in the house and others hovering about them on snow-shoes. The attempt was hopeless, and after some loss the two companies fell back. The firing continued, as before, till noon, or, according to Beaujeu, till three in the afternoon, when a French officer, carrying a flag of truce, came out of La Corne's house. The occasion of the overture was this.

Captain Howe, who, as before mentioned, had been badly wounded at the capture of this house, was still there, a prisoner, without surgical aid, the French surgeon being at the houses on the Gaspereau, in charge of Coulon and other wounded men. "Though," says Beaujeu, "M. Howe was a firm man, he begged the Chevalier La Corne not to let him bleed to death for want of aid, but permit him to send for an English surgeon." To this La Corne, after consulting with his officers, consented, and Marin went to the English with a white flag and a note from Howe explaining the situation. The surgeon was sent, and Howe's wound was dressed, Marin remaining as a hostage. A suspension of arms took place till the surgeon's return; after which it was prolonged till nine o'clock of the next morning, at the instance, according to French accounts, of the English, and, according to English accounts, of the French. In either case, the truce was welcome to both sides. The English, who were in the stone house to the number of nearly three hundred and fifty, crowded to suffocation, had five small cannon, two of which were four-pounders, and three were swivels; but these were probably not in position, as it does not appear that any use was made of them. There was no ammunition except what the men had in their powder-horns and bullet-pouches, the main stock having been left, with other necessaries, on board the schooner and sloop now in the hands of the French. It was found, on examination, that they had ammunition for eight shots each, and provisions for one day. Water was only to be had by bringing it from a neighboring brook. As there were snow-shoes for only about one man in twenty, sorties were out of the question; and the house was commanded by high ground on three sides.

Though their number was still considerable, their position was growing desperate. Thus it happened that when the truce expired, Goldthwait, the English commander, with another officer, who seems to have been Captain Preble, came with a white flag to the house where La Corne was posted, and proposed terms of capitulation, Howe, who spoke French, acting as interpreter. La Corne made proposals on his side, and as neither party was anxious to continue the fray, they soon came to an understanding.

It was agreed that within forty-eight hours the English should march for Annapolis with the honors of war; that the prisoners taken by the French should remain in their hands; that the Indians, who had been the only plunderers, should keep the plunder they had taken; that the English sick and wounded should be left, till their recovery, at the neighboring settlement of Rivière-aux-Canards, protected by a French guard, and that the English engaged in the affair at Grand Pré should not bear arms during the next six months within the district about the head of the Bay of Fundy, including Chignecto, Grand Pré, and the neighboring settlements.

Captain Howe was released on parole, with the condition that he should send back in exchange one Lacroix, a French prisoner at Boston,—"which," says La Corne, "he faithfully did."

Thus ended one of the most gallant exploits in French-Canadian annals. As respects the losses on each side, the French and English accounts are irreconcilable; nor are the statements of either party consistent with themselves. Mascarene reports to Shirley that seventy English were killed, and above sixty captured; though he afterwards reduces these numbers, having, as he says, received farther information. On the French side he says that four officers and about forty men were killed, and that many wounded were carried off in carts during the fight. Beaujeu, on the other hand, sets the English loss at one hundred and thirty killed, fifteen wounded, and fifty captured; and the French loss at seven killed and fifteen wounded. As for the numbers engaged, the statements are scarcely less divergent. It seems clear, however, that when Coulon began his march from Baye Verte, his party consisted of about three hundred Canadians and Indians, without reckoning some Acadians who had joined him from Beaubassin and Isle St. Jean. Others joined him on the way to Grand Pré, counting a hundred and fifty according to Shirley,—which appears to be much too large an estimate. The English, by their own showing, numbered five hundred, or five hundred and twenty-five. Of eleven houses attacked, ten were surprised and carried, with the help of the darkness and storm and the skilful management of the assailants.

"No sooner was the capitulation signed," says Beaujeu, "than we became in appearance the best of friends." La Corne directed military honors to be rendered to the remains of the brothers Noble; and in all points the Canadians, both officers and men, treated the English with kindness and courtesy. "The English commandant," again says Beaujeu, "invited us all to dine with him and his officers, so that we might have the pleasure of making acquaintance over a bowl of punch." The repast being served after such a fashion as circumstances permitted, victors and vanquished sat down together; when, says Beaujeu, "we received on the part of our hosts many compliments on our polite manners and our skill in making war." And the compliments were well deserved.

At eight o'clock on the morning of the 14th of February

the English filed out of the stone house, and with arms shouldered, drums beating, and colors flying, marched between two ranks of the French, and took the road for Annapolis. The English sick and wounded were sent to the settlement of Rivière-aux-Canards, where, protected by a French guard and attended by an English surgeon, they were to remain till able to reach the British fort.

La Corne called a council of war, and in view of the scarcity of food and other reasons it was resolved to return to Beaubassin. Many of the French had fallen ill. Some of the sick and wounded were left at Grand Pré, others at Cobequid, and the Acadians were required to supply means of carrying the rest. Coulon's party left Grand Pré on the 23d of February, and on the 8th of March reached Beaubassin.[1]

Ramesay did not fail to use the success at Grand Pré to influence the minds of the Acadians. He sent a circular letter to the inhabitants of the various districts, and especially to those of Mines, in which he told them that their country had been reconquered by the arms of the King of France, to whom he commanded them to be faithful subjects, holding no intercourse with the English under any pretence whatever, on pain of the severest punishment. "If," he concludes, "we have withdrawn our soldiers from among you, it

[1] The dates are of the new style, which the French had adopted, while the English still clung to the old style.

By far the best account of this French victory at Mines is that of Beaujeu, in his *Journal de la Campagne du Détachement de Canada à l'Acadie et aux Mines en 1746–47*. It is preserved in the Archives de la Marine et des Colonies, and is printed in the documentary supplement of *Le Canada Français*, Vol. II. It supplies the means of correcting many errors and much confusion in some recent accounts of the affair. The report of Chevalier de la Corne, also printed in *Le Canada Français*, though much shorter, is necessary to a clear understanding of the matter. Letters of Lusignan fils to the minister Maurepas, 10 Oct. 1747, of Bishop Pontbriand (to Maurepas ?), 10 July, 1747, and of Lusignan père to Maurepas, 10 Oct. 1747, give some additional incidents. The principal document on the English side is the report of Captain Benjamin Goldthwait, who succeeded Noble in command. A copy of the original, in the Public Record Office, is before me. The substance of it is correctly given in *The Boston Post Boy* of 2 March, 1747, and in *N. E. Hist. Gen. Reg.*, X. 108. Various letters from Mascarene and Shirley (Public Record Office) contain accounts derived from returned officers and soldiers. The *Notice of Colonel Arthur Noble*, by William Goold (*Collections Maine Historical Soc.*, 1881), may also be consulted.

is for reasons known to us alone, and with a view to your advantage."[1]

Unfortunately for the effect of this message, Shirley had no sooner heard of the disaster at Grand Pré than he sent a body of Massachusetts soldiers to reoccupy the place.[2] This they did in April. The Acadians thus found themselves, as usual, between two dangers; and unable to see which horn of the dilemma was the worse, they tried to avoid both by conciliating French and English alike, and assuring each of their devoted attachment. They sent a pathetic letter to Ramesay, telling him that their hearts were always French, and begging him at the same time to remember that they were a poor, helpless people, burdened with large families, and in danger of expulsion and ruin if they offended their masters, the English.[3] They wrote at the same time to Mascarene at Annapolis, sending him, to explain the situation, a copy of Ramesay's threatening letter to them;[4] begging him to consider that they could not without danger dispense with answering it; at the same time they protested their entire fidelity to King George.[5]

Ramesay, not satisfied with the results of his first letter, wrote again to the Acadians, ordering them, in the name of the Governor-General of New France, to take up arms against the English, and enclosing for their instruction an extract

[1] *Ramesay aux Députés et Habitants des Mines, 31 Mars, 1747.* At the end is written "A true copy, with the misspellings: signed W. Shirley."

[2] *Shirley to Newcastle, 24 Aug. 1747.*

[3] "Ainsis Monsieur nous vous prions de regarder notre bon Coeur et en meme Temps notre Impuissance pauvre Peuple chargez la plus part de familles nombreuse point de Recours sil falois evacuer a quoy nous sommes menacez tous les jours qui nous tien dans une Crainte perpetuelle en nous voyant a la proximitet de nos maitre depuis un sy grand nombre dannes" (printed *literatim*). *Députés des Mines à Ramesay, 24 Mai, 1747.*

[4] This probably explains the bad spelling of the letter, the copy before me having been made from the Acadian transcript sent to Mascarene, and now in the Public Record Office.

[5] *Les Habitants a l'honorable gouverneur au for d'anapolisse royal* [sic], *Mai* (?), *1747.*

On the 27th of June the inhabitants of Cobequid wrote again to Mascarene: "Monsieur nous prenons la Liberte de vous recrire celle icy pour vous assurer de nos tres humble Respect et d'un entiere Sou-mission a vos Ordres" (*literatim*).

from a letter of the French Governor. "These," says Ramesay, "are his words: 'We consider ourself as master of Beaubassin and Mines, since we have driven off the English. Therefore there is no difficulty in forcing the Acadians to take arms for us; to which end we declare to them that they are discharged from the oath that they formerly took to the English, by which they are bound no longer, as has been decided by the authorities of Canada and Monseigneur our Bishop.' "[1]

"In view of the above," continues Ramesay, "we order all the inhabitants of Memeramcook to come to this place [Beaubassin] as soon as they see the signal-fires lighted, or discover the approach of the enemy; and this on pain of death, confiscation of all their goods, burning of their houses, and the punishment due to rebels against the King."[2]

The position of the Acadians was deplorable. By the Treaty of Utrecht, France had transferred them to the British Crown; yet French officers denounced them as rebels and threatened them with death if they did not fight at their bidding against England; and English officers threatened them with expulsion from the country if they broke their oath of allegiance to King George. It was the duty of the British ministry to occupy the province with a force sufficient to protect the inhabitants against French terrorism, and leave no doubt that the King of England was master of Acadia in fact as well as in name. This alone could have averted the danger of Acadian revolt, and the harsh measures to which it afterwards gave rise. The ministry sent no aid, but left to Shirley and Massachusetts the task of keeping the province for King

[1] "Nous nous regardons aujourdhuy Maistre de Beaubassin et des Mines puisque nous en avons Chassé les Anglois; ainsi il ny a aucune difficulté de forcer les Accadiens à prendre les armes pour nous, et de les y Contraindre; leur declarons à cet effèt qu'ils sont dechargé [*sic*] du Serment preté, cy devant, à l'Anglois, auquel ils ne sont plus obligé [*sic*] comme il y a été decidé par nos puissances de Canada et de Monseigneur notre Evesque" (*literatim*).

[2] *Ramesay aux Habitants de Chignecto, etc., 25 Mai, 1747.*

A few months later, the deputies of Rivière-aux-Canards wrote to Shirley, thanking him for kindness which they said was undeserved, promising to do their duty thenceforth, but begging him to excuse them from giving up persons who had acted "contraire aux Interests de leur devoire," representing the difficulty of their position, and protesting "une Soumission parfaite et en touts Respects." The letter is signed by four deputies, of whom one writes his name, and three sign with crosses.

George. Shirley and Massachusetts did what they could; but they could not do all that the emergency demanded.

Shirley courageously spoke his mind to the ministry, on whose favor he was dependent. "The fluctuating state of the inhabitants of Acadia," he wrote to Newcastle, "seems, my lord, naturally to arise from their finding a want of due protection from his Majesty's Government."[1]

[1] *Shirley to Newcastle, 29 April, 1747.*
On Shirley's relations with the Acadians, *see* Appendix C.

Chapter XXIII

WAR AND POLITICS

Governor and Assembly • Saratoga destroyed • William Johnson •
Border Ravages • Upper Ashuelot • French "Military Movements"
• Number Four • Niverville's Attack • Phineas Stevens •
The French repulsed

FROM the East we turn to the West, for the province of New York passed for the West at that day. Here a vital question was what would be the attitude of the Five Nations of the Iroquois towards the rival European colonies, their neighbors. The Treaty of Utrecht called them British subjects. What the word "subjects" meant, they themselves hardly knew. The English told them that it meant children; the French that it meant dogs and slaves. Events had tamed the fierce confederates; and now, though, like all savages, unstable as children, they leaned in their soberer moments to a position of neutrality between their European neighbors, watching with jealous eyes against the encroachments of both. The French would gladly have enlisted them and their tomahawks in the war; but seeing little hope of this, were generally content if they could prevent them from siding with the English, who on their part regarded them as their Indians, and were satisfied with nothing less than active alliance.

When Shirley's plan for the invasion of Canada was afoot, Clinton, governor of New York, with much ado succeeded in convening the deputies of the confederacy at Albany, and by dint of speeches and presents induced them to sing the war-song and take up the hatchet for England. The Iroquois were disgusted when the scheme came to nought, their warlike ardor cooled, and they conceived a low opinion of English prowess.

The condition of New York as respects military efficiency was deplorable. She was divided against herself, and, as usual in such cases, party passion was stronger than the demands of war. The province was in the midst of one of those disputes with the representative of the Crown, which, in one degree or another, crippled or paralyzed the military activity of nearly all the British colonies. Twenty years or more earlier, when Massachusetts was at blows with the Indians on her borders, she suffered from the same disorders; but her Governor and Assembly were of one mind as to urging on the war, and quarrelled only on the questions in what way and under what command it should be waged. But in New York there was a strong party that opposed the war, being interested in the contraband trade long carried on with Canada. Clinton, the governor, had, too, an enemy in the person of the Chief Justice, James de Lancey, with whom he had had an after-dinner dispute, ending in a threat on the part of De Lancey that he would make the Governor's seat uncomfortable. To marked abilities, better education, and more knowledge of the world than was often found in the provinces, ready wit, and conspicuous social position, the Chief Justice joined a restless ambition and the arts of a demagogue.

He made good his threat, headed the opposition to the Governor, and proved his most formidable antagonist. If either Clinton or Shirley had had the independent authority of a Canadian governor, the conduct of the war would have been widely different. Clinton was hampered at every turn. The Assembly held him at advantage; for it was they, and not the King, who paid his salary, and they could withhold or retrench it when he displeased them. The people sympathized with their representatives and backed them in opposition,—at least when not under the stress of imminent danger.

A body of provincials, in the pay of the King, had been mustered at Albany for the proposed Canada expedition; and after that plan was abandoned, Clinton wished to use them for protecting the northern frontier and capturing that standing menace to the province, Crown Point. The Assembly, bent on crossing him at any price, refused to provide for transporting supplies farther than Albany. As the furnishing of provisions and transportation depended on that body, they could stop the movement of troops and defeat the Governor's military plans at their pleasure. In vain he told them, "If you deny me the necessary supplies, all my endeavors must become fruitless; I must wash my own hands, and leave at your doors the blood of the innocent people."[1]

He urged upon them the necessity of building forts on the two carrying-places between the Hudson and Lakes George and Champlain, thus blocking the path of war-parties from Canada. They would do nothing, insisting that the neighboring colonies, to whom the forts would also be useful, ought to help in building them; and when it was found that these colonies were ready to do their part, the Assembly still refused. Passionate opposition to the royal Governor seemed to blind them to the interests of the province. Nor was the fault all on their side; for the Governor, though he generally showed more self-control and moderation than could have been expected, sometimes lost temper and betrayed scorn for his opponents, many of whom were but the instruments of leaders urged by personal animosities and small but intense ambitions. They accused him of treating them with contempt, and of embezzling public money; while he retorted by charging them with encroaching on the royal prerogative and treating the representative of the King with indecency. Under such conditions an efficient conduct of the war was out of the question.

Once, when the frontier was seriously threatened, Clinton, as commander-in-chief, called out the militia to defend it; but they refused to obey, on the ground that no Act of the Assembly required them to do so.[2]

Clinton sent home bitter complaints to Newcastle and the Lords of Trade. "They [the Assembly] are selfish, jealous of the power of the Crown, and of such levelling principles that they are constantly attacking its prerogative. . . . I find that neither dissolutions nor fair means can produce from them such Effects as will tend to a publick good or their own preservation. They will neither act for themselves nor assist their neighbors. . . . Few but hirelings have a seat in the Assembly, who protract time for the sake of their wages, at a great expence to the Province, without contributing anything material for its welfare, credit, or safety." And he declares that unless Parliament takes them in hand he can do nothing for the service of the King or the good of the province,[3] for

---

[1] *Extract from the Governor's Message*, in Smith, *History of New York*, II. 124 (1830).

[2] *Clinton to the Lords of Trade, 10 Nov. 1747.*

[3] *Clinton to the Lords of Trade, 30 Nov. 1745.*

they want to usurp the whole administration, both civil and military.[1]

At Saratoga there was a small settlement of Dutch farmers, with a stockade fort for their protection. This was the farthest outpost of the colony, and the only defence of Albany in the direction of Canada. It was occupied by a sergeant, a corporal, and ten soldiers, who testified before a court of inquiry that it was in such condition that in rainy weather neither they nor their ammunition could be kept dry. As neither the Assembly nor the merchants of Albany would make it tenable, the garrison was withdrawn before winter by order of the Governor.[2]

Scarcely was this done when five hundred French and Indians, under the partisan Marin, surprised the settlement in the night of the 28th of November, burned fort, houses, mills, and stables, killed thirty persons, and carried off about a hundred prisoners.[3] Albany was left uncovered, and the Assembly voted £150 in provincial currency to rebuild the ruined fort. A feeble palisade work was accordingly set up, but it was neglected like its predecessor. Colonel Peter Schuyler was stationed there with his regiment in 1747, but was forced to abandon his post for want of supplies. Clinton then directed Colonel Roberts, commanding at Albany, to examine the fort, and if he found it indefensible, to burn it,—which he did, much to the astonishment of a French war-party, who visited the place soon after, and found nothing but ashes.[4]

The burning of Saratoga, first by the French and then by its own masters, made a deep impression on the Five Nations,

[1] *Remarks on the Representation of the Assembly of New York, May, 1747*, in *N. Y. Col. Docs.*, VI. 365. On the disputes of the Governor and Assembly, see also Smith, *History of New York*, II. (1830), and Stone, *Life and Times of Sir William Johnson*, I. *N. Y. Colonial Documents*, VI., contains many papers on the subject, chiefly on the Governor's side.

[2] *Examinations at a Court of Inquiry at Albany, 11 Dec. 1745*, in *N. Y. Col. Docs.*, VI. 374.

[3] The best account of this affair is in the journal of a French officer in Schuyler, *Colonial New York*, II. 115. The dates, being in new style, differ by eleven days from those of the English accounts. The Dutch hamlet of Saratoga, surprised by Marin, was near the mouth of the Fish Kill, on the west side of the Hudson. There was also a small fort on the east side, a little below the mouth of the Batten Kill.

[4] Schuyler, *Colonial New York*, II. 121.

and a few years later they taunted their white neighbors with these shortcomings in no measured terms. "You burned your own fort at Seraghtoga and ran away from it, which was a shame and a scandal to you."[1] Uninitiated as they were in party politics and faction quarrels, they could see nothing in this and other military lapses but proof of a want of martial spirit, if not of cowardice. Hence the difficulty of gaining their active alliance against the French was redoubled. Fortunately for the province, the adverse influence was in some measure counteracted by the character and conduct of one man. Up to this time the French had far surpassed the rival nation in the possession of men ready and able to deal with the Indians and mould them to their will. Eminent among such was Joncaire, French emissary among the Senecas in western New York, who, with admirable skill, held back that powerful member of the Iroquois league from siding with the English. But now, among the Mohawks of eastern New York, Joncaire found his match in the person of William Johnson, a vigorous and intelligent young Irishman, nephew of Admiral Warren, and his agent in the management of his estates on the Mohawk. Johnson soon became intimate with his Indian neighbors, spoke their language, joined in their games and dances, sometimes borrowed their dress and their paint, and whooped, yelped, and stamped like one of themselves. A white man thus playing the Indian usually gains nothing in the esteem of those he imitates; but, as before in the case of the redoubtable Count Frontenac, Johnson's adoption of their ways increased their liking for him and did not diminish their respect. The Mohawks adopted him into their tribe and made him a war-chief. Clinton saw his value; and as the Albany commissioners hitherto charged with Indian affairs had proved wholly inefficient, he transferred their functions to Johnson; whence arose more heart-burnings. The favor of the Governor cost the new functionary the support of the Assembly, who refused the indispensable presents to the Indians, and thus vastly increased the difficulty of his task. Yet the Five Nations promised to take up the hatchet against the French, and their orator said, in a conference at Albany, "Should any

---

[1] *Report of a Council with the Indians at Albany, 28 June, 1754.*

French priests now dare to come among us, we know no use for them but to roast them."[1] Johnson's present difficulties, however, sprang more from Dutch and English traders than from French priests, and he begs that an Act may be passed against the selling of liquor to the Indians, "as it is impossible to do anything with them while there is such a plenty to be had all round the neighborhood, being forever drunk." And he complains especially of one Clement, who sells liquor within twenty yards of Johnson's house, and immediately gets from the Indians all the bounty money they receive for scalps, "which leaves them as poor as ratts," and therefore refractory and unmanageable. Johnson says further: "There is another grand villain, George Clock, who lives by Conajoharie Castle, and robs the Indians of all their cloaths, etc." The chiefs complained, "upon which I wrote him twice to give over that custom of selling liquor to the Indians; the answer was he gave the bearer, I might hang myself."[2] Indian affairs, it will be seen, were no better regulated then than now.

Meanwhile the French Indians were ravaging the frontiers and burning farm-houses to within sight of Albany. The Assembly offered rewards for the scalps of the marauders, but were slow in sending money to pay them,—to the great discontent of the Mohawks, who, however, at Johnson's instigation, sent out various war-parties, two of which, accompanied by a few whites, made raids as far as the island of Montreal, and somewhat checked the incursions of the mission Indians by giving them work near home. The check was but momentary. Heathen Indians from the West joined the Canadian converts, and the frontiers of New York and New England, from the Mohawk to beyond the Kennebec, were stung through all their length by innumerable nocturnal surprises and petty attacks. The details of this murderous though ineffective partisan war would fill volumes, if they were worth recording. One or two examples will show the nature of all.

In the valley of the little river Ashuelot, a New Hampshire affluent of the Connecticut, was a rude border-settlement

---

[1] *Answer of the Six [Five] Nations to His Excellency the Governor at Albany, 23 Aug. 1746.*
[2] *Johnson to Clinton, 7 May, 1747.*

which later years transformed into a town noted in rural New England for kindly hospitality, culture without pretence, and good-breeding without conventionality.[1] In 1746 the place was in all the rawness and ugliness of a backwoods hamlet. The rough fields, lately won from the virgin forest, showed here and there, among the stumps, a few log-cabins, roofed with slabs of pine, spruce, or hemlock. Near by was a wooden fort, made, no doubt, after the common frontier pattern, of a stockade fence ten or twelve feet high, enclosing cabins to shelter the settlers in case of alarm, and furnished at the corners with what were called flankers, which were boxes of thick plank large enough to hold two or more men, raised above the ground on posts, and pierced with loopholes, so that each face of the stockade could be swept by a flank fire. One corner of this fort at Ashuelot was, however, guarded by a solid blockhouse, or, as it was commonly called, a "mount."

On the 23d of April a band of sixty, or, by another account, a hundred Indians, approached the settlement before daybreak, and hid in the neighboring thickets to cut off the men in the fort as they came out to their morning work. One of the men, Ephraim Dorman, chanced to go out earlier than the rest. The Indians did not fire on him, but, not to give an alarm, tried to capture or kill him without noise. Several of them suddenly showed themselves, on which he threw down his gun in pretended submission. One of them came up to him with hatchet raised; but the nimble and sturdy borderer suddenly struck him with his fist a blow in the head that knocked him flat, then snatched up his own gun, and, as some say, the blanket of the half-stunned savage also, sprang off, reached the fort unhurt, and gave the alarm. Some of the families of the place were living in the fort; but the bolder or more careless still remained in their farm-houses, and if nothing were done for their relief, their fate was sealed. Therefore the men sallied in a body, and a sharp fight ensued, giving the frightened settlers time to take refuge within the stockade. It was not too soon, for the work of havoc had already begun. Six houses and a barn were on fire, and twenty-three

[1] Keene, originally called Upper Ashuelot. On the same stream, a few miles below, was a similar settlement, called Lower Ashuelot, — the germ of the present Swanzey. This, too, suffered greatly from Indian attacks.

cattle had been killed. The Indians fought fiercely, killed John Bullard and captured Nathan Blake, but at last retreated; and after they were gone, the charred remains of several of them were found among the ruins of one of the burned cabins, where they had probably been thrown to prevent their being scalped.

Before Dorman had given the alarm, an old woman, Mrs. McKenney, went from the fort to milk her cow in a neighboring barn. As she was returning, with her full milk-pail, a naked Indian was seen to spring from a clump of bushes, plunge a long knife into her back, and dart away without stopping to take the gray scalp of his victim. She tried feebly to reach the fort; but from age, corpulence, and a mortal wound she moved but slowly, and when a few steps from the gate, fell and died.

Ten days after, a party of Indians hid themselves at night by this same fort, and sent one of their number to gain admission under pretence of friendship, intending, no doubt, to rush in when the gate should be opened; but the man on guard detected the trick, and instead of opening the gate, fired through it, mortally wounding the Indian, on which his confederates made off. Again, at the same place, Deacon Josiah Foster, who had taken refuge in the fort, ventured out on a July morning to drive his cows to pasture. A gunshot was heard; and the men who went out to learn the cause, found the Deacon lying in the wood-road, dead and scalped. An ambushed Indian had killed him and vanished. Such petty attacks were without number.

There is a French paper, called a record of "military movements," which gives a list of war-parties sent from Montreal against the English border between the 29th of March, 1746, and the 21st of June in the same year. They number thirty-five distinct bands, nearly all composed of mission Indians living in or near the settled parts of Canada,—Abenakis, Iroquois of the Lake of Two Mountains and of Sault St. Louis (Caughnawaga), Algonkins of the Ottawa, and others, in parties rarely of more than thirty, and often of no more than six, yet enough for waylaying travellers or killing women in kitchens or cow-sheds, and solitary laborers in the fields. This record is accompanied by a list of wild Western Indians who came down to Montreal in the summer of 1746 to share in these "military movements."[1]

No part of the country suffered more than the western borders of Massachusetts and New Hampshire, and here were seen too plainly the evils of the prevailing want of concert among the British colonies. Massachusetts claimed extensive tracts north of her present northern boundary, and in the belief that her claim would hold good, had built a small wooden fort, called Fort Dummer, on the Connecticut, for the protection of settlers. New Hampshire disputed the title, and the question, being referred to the Crown, was decided in her favor. On this, Massachusetts withdrew the garrison of Fort Dummer and left New Hampshire to defend her own. This the Assembly of that province refused to do, on the ground that the fort was fifty miles from any settlement made by New Hampshire people, and was therefore useless to them, though of great value to Massachusetts as a cover to Northfield and other of her settlements lower down the Connecticut, to protect[2] which was no business of New Hampshire. But some years before, in 1740, three brothers, Samuel, David, and Stephen Farnsworth, natives of Groton, Massachusetts, had begun a new settlement on the Connecticut about forty-five miles north of the Massachusetts line and on ground which was soon to be assigned to New Hampshire. They were followed by five or six others. They acted on the belief that their settlement was within the jurisdiction of Massachusetts, and that she could and would protect them. The place was one of extreme exposure, not only from its isolation, far from help, but because it was on the banks of a wild and lonely river, the customary highway of war-parties on their descent from Canada. Number Four—for so the new settlement was called, because it was the fourth in a range of townships recently marked out along the Connecticut, but, with one or two exceptions, wholly unoccupied as yet—was a rude little outpost of civilization, buried in forests that spread unbroken to the banks of the St. Lawrence, while its nearest

[1] *Extrait sur les différents Mouvements Militaires qui se sont faits à Montréal à l'occasion de la Guerre, 1745, 1746.* There is a translation in *N. Y. Col. Docs.*

[2] *Journal of the Assembly of New Hampshire*, quoted in Saunderson, *History of Charlestown, N. H.*, 20.

English neighbor was nearly thirty miles away. As may be supposed, it grew slowly, and in 1744 it had but nine or ten families. In the preceding year, when war seemed imminent, and it was clear that neither Massachusetts nor New Hampshire would lend a helping hand, the settlers of Number Four, seeing that their only resource was in themselves, called a meeting to consider the situation and determine what should be done. The meeting was held at the house, or log-cabin, of John Spafford, Jr., and being duly called to order, the following resolutions were adopted: that a fort be built at the charge of the proprietors of the said township of Number Four; that John Hastings, John Spafford, and John Avery be a committee to direct the building; that each carpenter be allowed nine shillings, old tenor, a day, each laborer seven shillings, and each pair of oxen three shillings and sixpence; that the proprietors of the township be taxed in the sum of three hundred pounds, old tenor, for building the fort; that John Spafford, Phineas Stevens, and John Hastings be assessors to assess the same, and Samuel Farnsworth collector to collect it.[1] And to the end that their fort should be a good and creditable one, they are said to have engaged the services of John Stoddard, accounted the foremost man of western Massachusetts, Superintendent of Defence, Colonel of Militia, Judge of Probate, Chief Justice of the Court of Common Pleas, a reputed authority in the construction of backwoods fortifications, and the admired owner of the only gold watch in Northampton.

Timber was abundant and could be had for the asking; for the frontiersman usually regarded a tree less as a valuable possession than as a natural enemy, to be got rid of by fair means or foul. The only cost was the labor. The fort rose rapidly. It was a square enclosing about three quarters of an acre, each side measuring a hundred and eighty feet. The wall was not of palisades, as was more usual, but of squared logs laid one upon another, and interlocked at the corners after the fashion of a log-cabin. Within were several houses, which had been built close together, for mutual protection, before the fort was begun, and which belonged to Stevens, Spafford, and

[1] Extracts from the Town Record, in Saunderson, *History of Charlestown, N. H.* (*Number Four*), 17, 18.

other settlers. Apparently they were small log-cabins; for they were valued at only from eight to thirty-five pounds each, in old tenor currency wofully attenuated by depreciation; and these sums being paid to the owners out of the three hundred pounds collected for building the fort, the cabins became public property. Either they were built in a straight line, or they were moved to form one, for when the fort was finished, they all backed against the outer wall, so that their low roofs served to fire from. The usual flankers completed the work, and the settlers of Number Four were so well pleased with it that they proudly declared their fort a better one than Fort Dummer, its nearest neighbor, which had been built by public authority at the charge of the province.

But a fort must have a garrison, and the ten or twelve men of Number Four would hardly be a sufficient one. Sooner or later an attack was certain; for the place was a backwoods Castle Dangerous, lying in the path of war-parties from Canada, whether coming down the Connecticut from Lake Memphremagog, or up Otter Creek from Lake Champlain, then over the mountains to Black River, and so down that stream, which would bring them directly to Number Four. New Hampshire would do nothing for them, and their only hope was in Massachusetts, of which most of them were natives, and which had good reasons for helping them to hold their ground, as a cover to its own settlements below. The Governor and Assembly of Massachusetts did, in fact, send small parties of armed men from time to time to defend the endangered outpost, and the succor was timely; for though, during the first year of the war, Number Four was left in peace, yet from the 19th of April to the 19th of June, 1746, it was attacked by Indians five times, with some loss of scalps, and more of cattle, horses, and hogs. On the last occasion there was a hot fight in the woods, ending in the retreat of the Indians, said to have numbered a hundred and fifty, into a swamp, leaving behind them guns, blankets, hatchets, spears, and other things, valued at forty pounds, old tenor,—which, says the chronicle, "was reckoned a great booty for such beggarly enemies."[1]

---

[1] Saunderson, *History of Charlestown, N. H.*, 29. Doolittle, *Narrative of Mischief done by the Indian Enemy*,—a contemporary chronicle.

But Massachusetts grew tired of defending lands that had been adjudged to New Hampshire, and as the season drew towards an end, Number Four was left again to its own keeping. The settlers saw no choice but to abandon a place which they were too few to defend, and accordingly withdrew to the older settlements, after burying such of their effects as would bear it, and leaving others to their fate. Six men, a dog, and a cat remained to keep the fort. Towards midwinter the human part of the garrison also withdrew, and the two uncongenial quadrupeds were left alone.

When the authorities of Massachusetts saw that a place so useful to bear the brunt of attack was left to certain destruction, they repented of their late withdrawal, and sent Captain Phineas Stevens, with thirty men, to re-occupy it. Stevens, a native of Sudbury, Massachusetts, one of the earliest settlers of Number Four, and one of its chief proprietors, was a bold, intelligent, and determined man, well fitted for the work before him. He and his band reached the fort on the 27th of March, 1747, and their arrival gave peculiar pleasure to its tenants, the dog and cat, the former of whom met them with lively demonstrations of joy. The pair had apparently lived in harmony, and found means of subsistence, as they are reported to have been in tolerable condition.

Stevens had brought with him a number of other dogs,— animals found useful for detecting the presence of Indians and tracking them to their lurking-places. A week or more after the arrival of the party, these canine allies showed great uneasiness and barked without ceasing; on which Stevens ordered a strict watch to be kept, and great precaution to be used in opening the gate of the fort. It was time, for the surrounding forest concealed what the New England chroniclers call an "army," commanded by General Debeline. It scarcely need be said that Canada had no General Debeline, and that no such name is to be found in Canadian annals. The "army" was a large war-party of both French and Indians, and a French record shows that its commander was Boucher de Niverville, ensign in the colony troops.[1]

The behavior of the dogs was as yet the only sign of dan-

[1] *Extrait en forme de Journal de ce qui s'est passé d'intéressant dans la Colonie à l'occasion des Mouvements de Guerre, etc., 1746, 1747.*

ger, when, about nine o'clock on the morning of the 7th of April, one of Stevens's men took it upon him to go out and find what was amiss. Accompanied by two or three of the dogs, he advanced, gun in hand, into the clearing, peering at every stump, lest an Indian should lurk behind it. When about twenty rods from the gate, he saw a large log, or trunk of a fallen tree, not far before him, and approached it cautiously, setting on the dogs, or, as Stevens whimsically phrases it, "saying *Choboy!*" to them. They ran forward barking, on which several heads appeared above the log, and several guns were fired at him. He was slightly wounded, but escaped to the fort. Then, all around, the air rang with warwhoops, and a storm of bullets flew from the tangle of bushes that edged the clearing, and rapped spitefully, but harmlessly, against the wooden wall. At a little distance on the windward side was a log-house, to which, with adjacent fences, the assailants presently set fire, in the hope that, as the wind was strong, the flames would catch the fort. When Stevens saw what they were doing, he set himself to thwart them; and while some of his men kept them at bay with their guns, the rest fell to work digging a number of short trenches under the wall, on the side towards the fire. As each trench was six or seven feet deep, a man could stand in it outside the wall, sheltered from bullets, and dash buckets of water, passed to him from within, against the scorching timbers. Eleven such trenches were dug, and eleven men were stationed in them, so that the whole exposed front of the wall was kept wet.[1] Thus, though clouds of smoke drifted over the fort, and burning cinders showered upon it, no harm was done, and the enemy was forced to other devices. They found a wagon, which they protected from water and bullets by a shield of planks,—for there was a saw-mill hard by,—and loaded it with dry fagots, thinking to set them on fire and push the blazing machine against a dry part of the fort wall; but the

[1] "Those who were not employed in firing at the enemy were employed in digging trenches under the bottom of the fort. We dug no less than eleven of them, so deep that a man could go and stand upright on the outside and not endanger himself; so that when these trenches were finished, we could wet all the outside of the fort, which we did, and kept it wet all night. We drew some hundreds of barrels of water; and to undergo all this hard service there were but thirty men." *Stevens to Colonel W. Williams, — April, 1747.*

task proved too dangerous, "for," says Stevens, "instead of performing what they threatened and seemed to be immediately going to undertake, they called to us and desired a cessation of arms till sunrise the next morning, which was granted, at which time they said they would come to a parley." In fact, the French commander, with about sixty of his men, came in the morning with a flag of truce, which he stuck in the ground at a musket-shot from the fort, and, in the words of Stevens, "said, if we would send three men to him, he would send as many to us." Stevens agreed to this, on which two Frenchmen and an Indian came to the fort, and three soldiers went out in return. The two Frenchmen demanded, on the part of their commander, that the garrison should surrender, under a promise of life, and be carried prisoners to Quebec; and they farther required that Stevens should give his answer to the French officer in person.

Wisely or unwisely, Stevens went out at the gate, and was at once joined by Niverville, attended, no doubt, by an interpreter. "Upon meeting the Monsieur," says the English captain, "he did not wait for me to give him an answer," but said, in a manner sufficiently peremptory, that he had seven hundred men with him, and that if his terms were refused, he would storm the fort, "run over it," burn it to the ground, and if resistance were offered, put all in it to the sword; adding that he would have it or die, and that Stevens might fight or not as he pleased, for it was all one to him. His terms being refused, he said, as Stevens reports, "Well, go back to your fort and see if your men dare fight any more, and give me an answer quickly; for my men want to be fighting." Stevens now acted as if he had been the moderator of a townmeeting. "I went into the fort and called the men together, and informed them what the General said, and then put it to vote whether they would fight or resign; and they voted to a man to stand it out, and also declared that they would fight as long as they had life."[1]

Answer was made accordingly, but Niverville's promise to storm the fort and "run over it" was not kept. Stevens says that his enemies had not the courage to do this, or even to bring up their "fortification," meaning their fire-wagon with

[1] *Stevens to Colonel William Williams, — April, 1747.*

its shield of planks. In fact, an open assault upon a fortified place was a thing unknown in this border warfare, whether waged by Indians alone, or by French and Indians together. The assailants only raised the war-whoop again, and fired, as before, from behind stumps, logs, and bushes. This amusement they kept up from two o'clock till night, when they grew bolder, approached nearer, and shot flights of fire-arrows into the fort, which, water being abundant, were harmless as their bullets. At daylight they gave over this exercise, called out "Good morning!" to the garrison, and asked for a suspension of arms for two hours. This being agreed to, another flag of truce presently appeared, carried by two Indians, who planted it in the ground within a stone's throw of the fort, and asked that two men should be sent out to confer with them. This was done, and the men soon came back with a proposal that Stevens should sell provisions to his besiegers, under a promise on their part that they would give him no farther trouble. He answered that he would not sell them provisions for money, but would exchange them for prisoners, and give five bushels of Indian corn for every hostage placed in his hands as security for the release of an English captive in Canada. To this their only answer was firing a few shots against the fort, after which they all disappeared, and were seen no more. The garrison had scarcely eaten or slept for three days. "I believe men were never known to hold out with better resolution," writes Stevens; and "though there were some thousands of guns shot at us, we had but two men slightly wounded, John Brown and Joseph Ely."[1]

Niverville and his party, disappointed and hungry, now made a tour among the scattered farms and hamlets of the country below, which, incapable of resisting such an inroad, were abandoned at their approach. Thus they took an easy revenge for their rebuff at Number Four, and in a march of thirty or forty leagues, burned five small deserted forts or stockaded houses, "three meeting-houses, several fine barns, about one hundred dwellings, mostly of two stories, furnished even to chests of drawers, and killed five to six hundred sheep and hogs, and about thirty horned cattle. This

---

[1] *Stevens to Colonel W. Williams, — April, 1747.*

devastation is well worth a few prisoners or scalps."[1] It is curious to find such exploits mentioned with complacency, as evidence of prowess.

The successful defence of the most exposed place on the frontier was welcome news throughout New England, and Commodore Charles Knowles, who was then at Boston, sent Stevens a silver-hilted sword in recognition of his conduct. The settlers of Number Four, who soon returned to their backwoods home, were so well pleased with this compliment to one of their fellows that they gave to the settlement the baptismal name of the Commodore, and the town that has succeeded the hamlet of Number Four is Charlestown to this day.[2]

[1] *N. Y. Col. Docs.*, X. 97.

[2] Just after the withdrawal of the French and Indians, Stevens wrote two letters giving an account of the affair, one to Governor Shirley, and the other to Colonel William Williams, who seems to have been his immediate military superior. At most points they are substantially the same; but that to Williams contains some passages not found in the other. The letter to Shirley is printed in Saunderson, *History of Charlestown, N. H.*, 34–37, and that to Williams in *Collections of the New Hampshire Historical Society*, IV. 109–113. Stevens also kept a diary, which was long in possession of his descendants. One of these, Mr. B. F. Stevens, kindly made a search for it, at my request, and learned that it had been unfortunately destroyed by fire, in 1856. Doolittle, in his *Narrative of Mischief*, and Hoyt, in his *Antiquarian Researches*, give other accounts. The French notices of the affair are few and short, as usual in cases of failure. For the principal one, see *N. Y. Col. Docs.*, X. 97. It is here said that Stevens asked for a parley, in order to capitulate; but all the English accounts say that the French made the first advances.

Chapter XXIV

1745–1748

FORT MASSACHUSETTS

Frontier Defence • Northfield and its Minister • Military Criticisms of Rev. Benjamin Doolittle • Rigaud de Vaudreuil • His Great War-Party • He attacks Fort Massachusetts • Sergeant Hawks and his Garrison • A Gallant Defence • Capitulation • Humanity of the French • Ravages • Return to Crown Point • Peace of Aix-la-Chapelle

---

SINCE the last war, the settlements of Massachusetts had pushed westward and begun to invade the beautiful region of mountains and valleys that now forms Berkshire. Villages, or rudiments of villages, had grown up on the Housatonic, and an establishment had been attempted at Pontoosuc, now Pittsfield, on the extreme western limits of the province. The position of these new settlements was critical, for the enemy could reach them with little difficulty by way of Lake Champlain and Wood Creek. The Massachusetts Government was not unmindful of them, and when war again broke out, three wooden forts were built for their protection, forming a line of defence westward from Northfield on the northern frontier of the province. One of these forts was in the present town of Heath, and was called Fort Shirley; another, named Fort Pelham, was in the present town of Rowe; while the third, Fort Massachusetts, was farther westward, in what is now the town of Adams, then known as East Hoosac. Two hundred men from the militia were taken into pay to hold these posts and patrol the intervening forests. Other defensive works were made here and there, sometimes by the votes of town meetings, and sometimes by individuals, at their own cost. These works consisted of a fence of palisades enclosing a farm-house, or sometimes of a blockhouse of timber or heavy planks. Thus, at Northfield, Deacon Ebenezer Alexander, a veteran of sixty who had served at Louisbourg, built a "mount," or blockhouse, on the knoll behind his house, and carried a stockade from it to enclose the dwelling, shed, and barn, the whole at the cost of thirty-six pounds, one shilling, and sixpence, in Massachusetts currency,[1] which the town repaid him, his fortifications being of public utility as a place of refuge for families in case of attack. Northfield was a place notoriously dangerous, and military methods were in vogue there in season and out of season. Thus, by a vote of the town, the people were called to the Sunday sermon by beat of drum, and Eleazer Holton was elected to sound the call in consideration of one pound and ten shillings a year, the drum being hired of Ensign Field, its fortunate possessor, for the farther sum of three shillings. This was in the earlier days of Northfield. In 1734 the Sunday drum-beat was stopped, and the worshippers were summoned by the less obstreperous method of "hanging out a flagg," for the faithful discharge of which function Daniel Wright received in 1744 one pound and five shillings.[2]

The various fortifications, public and private, were garrisoned, sometimes by the owner and his neighbors, sometimes by men in pay of the provincial Assembly. As was to be expected from a legislative body undertaking warlike operations, the work of defence was but indifferently conducted. John Stoddard, the village magnate of Northampton, was charged, among the rest of his multifarious employments, with the locating and construction of forts; Captain Ephraim Williams was assigned to the general command on the western frontier, with headquarters at Fort Shirley and afterwards at Fort Massachusetts; and Major Israel Williams, of Hatfield, was made commissary.

At Northfield dwelt the Reverend Benjamin Doolittle, minister, apothecary, physician, and surgeon of the village; for he had studied medicine no less than theology. His parishioners thought that his cure of bodies encroached on his cure of souls, and requested him to confine his attention to his spiritual charge; to which he replied that he could not afford it, his salary as minister being seventy-five pounds in irredeemable Massachusetts paper, while his medical and surgical practice brought him full four hundred a year. He offered to

[1] Temple and Sheldon, *History of Northfield*, 237, give the items from the original account. This is one of the best of the innumerable town-histories of New England.
[2] Temple and Sheldon, *History of Northfield*, 218.

comply with the wishes of his flock if they would add that amount to his salary,—which they were not prepared to do, and the minister continued his heterogeneous labors as before.

As the position of his house on the village street seems to have been regarded as strategic, the town voted to fortify it with a blockhouse and a stockade, for the benefit both of the occupant and of all the villagers. This was accordingly done, at the cost of eighteen pounds, seven shillings, and sixpence for the blockhouse, and a farther charge for the stockade; and thenceforth Mr. Doolittle could write his sermons and mix his doses in peace. To his other callings he added that of historiographer. When, after a ministry of thirty-six years, the thrifty pastor was busied one day with hammer and nails in mending the fence of his yard, he suddenly dropped dead from a stroke of heart-disease,—to the grief of all Northfield; and his papers being searched, a record was found in his handwriting of the inroads of the enemy that had happened in his time on or near the Massachusetts border. Being rightly thought worthy of publication, it was printed at Boston in a dingy pamphlet, now extremely rare, and much prized by antiquarians.[1]

Appended to it are the remarks of the author on the conduct of the war. He complains that plans are changed so often that none of them take effect; that terms of enlistment are so short that the commissary can hardly serve out provisions to the men before their time is expired; that neither bread, meat, shoes, nor blankets are kept on hand for an emergency, so that the enemy escape while the soldiers are getting ready to pursue them; that the pay of a drafted man is so small that

---

[1] *A short Narrative of Mischief done by the French and Indian Enemy, on the Western Frontiers of the Province of the Massachusetts Bay; from the Beginning of the French War, proclaimed by the King of France, March 15th, 1743–4; and by the King of Great Britain, March 29th, 1744, to August 2nd, 1748. Drawn up by the Rev. Mr. Doolittle, of Northfield, in the County of Hampshire; and found among his Manuscripts after his Death. And at the Desire of some is now Published, with some small Additions to render it more perfect. Boston; Printed and sold by S. Kneeland, in Queen Street. MDCCL.*

The facts above given concerning Mr. Doolittle are drawn from the excellent *History of Northfield* by Temple and Sheldon, and the introduction to the *Particular History of the Five Years' French and Indian War*, by S. G. Drake.

twice as much would not hire a laborer to take care of his farm in his absence; and that untried and unfit persons are commissioned as officers: in all of which strictures there is no doubt much truth.

Mr. Doolittle's rueful narrative treats mainly of miscellaneous murders and scalpings, interesting only to the sufferers and their friends; but he also chronicles briefly a formidable inroad that still holds a place in New England history.

It may be remembered that Shirley had devised a plan for capturing Fort Frédéric, or Crown Point, built by the French at the narrows of Lake Champlain, and commanding ready access for war-parties to New York and New England.

The approach of D'Anville's fleet had defeated the plan; but rumors of it had reached Canada, and excited great alarm. Large bodies of men were ordered to Lake Champlain to protect the threatened fort. The two brothers De Muy were already on the lake with a numerous party of Canadians and Indians, both Christian and heathen, and Rigaud de Vaudreuil, town-major of Three Rivers, was ordered to follow with a still larger force, repel any English attack, or, if none should be made, take the offensive and strike a blow at the English frontier. On the 3d of August, Rigaud[1] left Montreal with a fleet of canoes carrying what he calls his army, and on the 12th he encamped on the east side of the lake, at the mouth of Otter Creek. There was rain, thunder, and a violent wind all night; but the storm ceased at daybreak, and, embarking again, they soon saw the octagonal stone tower of Fort Frédéric.

The party set up their tents and wigwams near the fort, and on the morning of the 16th the elder De Muy arrived with a reinforcement of sixty Frenchmen and a band of Indians. They had just returned from an incursion towards Albany, and reported that all was quiet in those parts, and that Fort Frédéric was in no danger. Now, to their great satisfaction, Rigaud and his band saw themselves free to take the offensive. The question was, where to strike. The Indians held council after council, made speech after speech, and agreed

---

[1]French writers always call him Rigaud, to distinguish him from his brother, Pierre Rigaud de Vaudreuil-Cavagnal, afterwards governor of Canada, who is usually mentioned as Vaudreuil.

on nothing. Rigaud gave them a wampum-belt, and told them that he meant to attack Corlaer,—that is, Schenectady; at which they seemed well pleased, and sang war-songs all night. In the morning they changed their minds, and begged him to call the whole army to a council for debating the question. It appeared that some of them, especially the Iroquois converts of Caughnawaga, disapproved of attacking Schenectady, because some of their Mohawk relatives were always making visits there, and might be inadvertently killed by the wild Western Indians of Rigaud's party. Now all was doubt again, for as Indians are unstable as water, it was no easy task to hold them to any plan of action.

The Abenakis proposed a solution of the difficulty. They knew the New England border well, for many of them had lived upon it before the war, on terms of friendly intercourse with the settlers. They now drew upon the floor of the council-room a rough map of the country, on which was seen a certain river, and on its upper waters a fort which they recommended as a proper object of attack. The river was that eastern tributary of the Hudson which the French called the Kaskékouké, the Dutch the Schaticook, and the English the Hoosac. The fort was Fort Massachusetts, the most westerly of the three posts lately built to guard the frontier. "My Father," said the Abenaki spokesman to Rigaud, "it will be easy to take this fort, and make great havoc on the lands of the English. Deign to listen to your children and follow our advice."[1] One Cadenaret, an Abenaki chief, had been killed near Fort Massachusetts in the last spring, and his tribesmen were keen to revenge him. Seeing his Indians pleased with the proposal to march for the Hoosac, Rigaud gladly accepted it; on which whoops, yelps, and war-songs filled the air. Hardly, however, was the party on its way when the Indians changed their minds again, and wanted to attack Saratoga; but Rigaud told them that they had made their choice and must abide by it, to which they assented, and gave him no farther trouble.

On the 20th of August they all embarked and paddled southward, passed the lonely promontory where Fort Ticon-

---

[1] *Journal de la Campagne de Rigaud de Vaudreuil en 1746 . . . présenté à Monseigneur le Comte de Maurepas, Ministre et Secrétaire d'Etat* (written by Rigaud).

deroga was afterwards built, and held their course till the lake dwindled to a mere canal creeping through the weedy marsh then called the Drowned Lands. Here, nine summers later, passed the flotilla of Baron Dieskau, bound to defeat and ruin by the shores of Lake George. Rigaud stopped at a place known as East Bay, at the mouth of a stream that joins Wood Creek, just north of the present town of Whitehall. Here he left the younger De Muy, with thirty men, to guard the canoes. The rest of the party, guided by a brother of the slain Cadenaret, filed southward on foot along the base of Skene Mountain, that overlooks Whitehall. They counted about seven hundred men, of whom five hundred were French, and a little above two hundred were Indians.[1] Some other French reports put the whole number at eleven hundred, or even twelve hundred,[2] while several English accounts make it eight hundred or nine hundred. The Frenchmen of the party included both regulars and Canadians, with six regular officers and ten cadets, eighteen militia officers, two chaplains, —one for the whites and one for the Indians,—and a surgeon.[3]

After a march of four days, they encamped on the 26th by a stream which ran into the Hudson, and was no doubt the Batten Kill, known to the French as *la rivière de Saratogue*. Being nearly opposite Saratoga, where there was then a garrison, they changed their course, on the 27th, from south to southeast, the better to avoid scouting-parties, which might discover their trail and defeat their plan of surprise. Early on the next day they reached the Hoosac, far above its mouth; and now their march was easier, "for," says Rigaud, "we got out of the woods and followed a large road that led up the river." In fact, there seem to have been two roads, one on each side of the Hoosac; for the French were formed into two brigades, one of which, under the Sieur de la Valterie, filed along the right bank of the stream, and the other, under the Sieur de Sabrevois, along the left; while the Indians marched on the front, flanks, and rear. They passed deserted houses

---

[1] "Le 19, ayant fait passer l'armée en Revue qui se trouva de 700 hommes, scavoir 500 françois environ et 200 quelques sauvages." *Journal de Rigaud.*

[2] See *N. Y. Col. Docs.*, X. 103, 132.

[3] *Ibid.*, X. 35.

and farms belonging to Dutch settlers from the Hudson; for the Hoosac, in this part of its course, was in the province of New York.[1] They did not stop to burn barns and houses, but they killed poultry, hogs, a cow, and a horse, to supply themselves with meat. Before night they had passed the New York line, and they made their camp in or near the valley where Williamstown and Williams College now stand. Here they were joined by the Sieurs Beaubassin and La Force, who had gone forward, with eight Indians, to reconnoitre. Beaubassin had watched Fort Massachusetts from a distance, and had seen a man go up into the watch-tower, but could discover no other sign of alarm. Apparently, the fugitive Dutch farmers had not taken pains to warn the English garrison of the coming danger, for there was a coolness between the neighbors.

Before breaking up camp in the morning, Rigaud called the Indian chiefs together and said to them: "My children, the time is near when we must get other meat than fresh pork, and we will all eat it together." "Meat," in Indian parlance, meant prisoners; and as these were valuable by reason of the ransoms paid for them, and as the Indians had suspected that the French meant to keep them all, they were well pleased with this figurative assurance of Rigaud that they should have their share.[2]

The chaplain said mass, and the party marched in a brisk rain up the Williamstown valley, till after advancing about ten miles they encamped again. Fort Massachusetts was only three or four miles distant. Rigaud held a talk with the Abenaki chiefs who had acted as guides, and it was agreed that the party should stop in the woods near the fort, make scaling-ladders, battering-rams to burst the gates, and other things needful for a grand assault, to take place before daylight; but

[1] These Dutch settlements on the Hoosac were made under what was called the "Hoosac Patent," granted by Governor Dongan of New York in 1688. The settlements were not begun till nearly forty years after the grant was made. For evidence on this point I am indebted to Professor A. L. Perry, of Williams College.

[2] "Mes enfans, leur dis-je, le temps approche où il faut faire d'autre viande que le porc frais; au reste, nous les mangerons tous ensemble; ce mot les flatta dans la crainte qu'ils avoient qu'après la prise du fort nous ne nous réservâmes tous les prisonniers." *Journal de Rigaud.*

their plan came to nought through the impetuosity of the young Indians and Canadians, who were so excited at the first glimpse of the watch-tower of the fort that they dashed forward, as Rigaud says, "like lions." Hence one might fairly expect to see the fort assaulted at once; but by the maxims of forest war this would have been reprehensible rashness, and nothing of the kind was attempted. The assailants spread to right and left, squatted behind stumps, and opened a distant and harmless fire, accompanied with unearthly yells and howlings.

Fort Massachusetts was a wooden enclosure formed, like the fort at Number Four, of beams laid one upon another, and interlocked at the angles. This wooden wall seems to have rested, not immediately upon the ground, but upon a foundation of stone, designated by Mr. Norton, the chaplain, as the "underpinning,"—a name usually given in New England to foundations of the kind. At the northwest corner was a blockhouse,[1] crowned with the watch-tower, the sight of which had prematurely kindled the martial fire of the Canadians and Indians. This wooden structure, at the apex of the blockhouse, served as a lookout, and also supplied means of throwing water to extinguish fire-arrows shot upon the roof. There were other buildings in the enclosure, especially a large log-house on the south side, which seems to have overlooked the outer wall, and was no doubt loopholed for musketry. On the east side there was a well, furnished probably with one of those long well-sweeps universal in primitive New England. The garrison, when complete, consisted of fifty-one men under Captain Ephraim Williams, who has left his name to Williamstown and Williams College, of the latter of which he was the founder. He was born at Newton, near Boston; was a man vigorous in body and mind; better acquainted with the world than most of his countrymen, having followed the seas in his youth, and visited England, Spain, and Holland; frank and agreeable in manners, well fitted for such a command,

[1] The term "blockhouse" was loosely used, and was even sometimes applied to an entire fort when constructed of hewn logs, and not of palisades. The true blockhouse of the New England frontier was a solid wooden structure about twenty feet high, with a projecting upper story and loopholes above and below.

and respected and loved by his men.[1] When the proposed invasion of Canada was preparing, he and some of his men went to take part in it, and had not yet returned. The fort was left in charge of a sergeant, John Hawks, of Deerfield, with men too few for the extent of the works, and a supply of ammunition nearly exhausted. Canada being then put on the defensive, the frontier forts were thought safe for a time. On the Saturday before Rigaud's arrival, Hawks had sent Thomas Williams, the surgeon, brother of the absent captain, to Deerfield, with a detachment of fourteen men, to get a supply of powder and lead. This detachment reduced the entire force, including Hawks himself and Norton, the chaplain, to twenty-two men, half of whom were disabled with dysentery, from which few of the rest were wholly free.[2] There were also in the fort three women and five children.[3]

The site of Fort Massachusetts is now a meadow by the banks of the Hoosac. Then it was a rough clearing, encumbered with the stumps and refuse of the primeval forest, whose living hosts stood grimly around it, and spread, untouched by the axe, up the sides of the neighboring Saddleback Mountain. The position of the fort was bad, being commanded by high ground, from which, as the chaplain tells us, "the enemy could shoot over the north side into the mid-

[1] See the notice of Williams in *Mass. Hist. Coll.*, VIII. 47. He was killed in the bloody skirmish that preceded the Battle of Lake George in 1755. *Montcalm and Wolfe*, chap. ix.

[2] "Lord's Day and Monday . . . the sickness was very distressing. . . . Eleven of our men were sick, and scarcely one of us in perfect health; almost every man was troubled with the griping and flux." Norton, *The Redeemed Captive*.

[3] Rigaud erroneously makes the garrison a little larger. "La garnison se trouva de 24 hommes, entre lesquels il y avoit un ministre, 3 femmes, et 5 enfans." The names and residence of all the men in the fort when the attack began are preserved. Hawks made his report to the provincial government under the title *"An Account of the Company in his Majesty's Service under the command of Serg! John Hawks . . . at Fort Massachusetts, Aug. 20 [31, new style], 1746."* The roll is attested on oath "Before William Williams, *Just. Pacis.*" The number of men is 22, including Hawks and Norton. Each man brought his own gun. I am indebted to the kindness of Professor A. L. Perry for a copy of Hawks's report, which is addressed to "the Honble. Spencer Phipps, Esq., Lieut. Gov! and Commander in Chief [and] the Honble his Majesty's Council and House of Representatives in General Court assembled."

dle of the parade,"—for which serious defect, John Stoddard, of Northampton, legist, capitalist, colonel of militia, and "Superintendent of Defence," was probably answerable. These frontier forts were, however, often placed on low ground with a view to an abundant supply of water, fire being the most dreaded enemy in Indian warfare.[1]

Sergeant Hawks, the provisional commander, was, according to tradition, a tall man with sunburnt features, erect, spare, very sinewy and strong, and of a bold and resolute temper. He had need to be so, for counting every man in the fort, lay and clerical, sick and well, he was beset by more than thirty times his own number; or, counting only his effective men, by more than sixty times,—and this at the lowest report of the attacking force. As there was nothing but a log fence between him and his enemy, it was clear that they could hew or burn a way through it, or climb over it with no surprising effort of valor. Rigaud, as we have seen, had planned a general assault under cover of night, but had been thwarted by the precipitancy of the young Indians and Canadians. These now showed no inclination to depart from the cautious maxims of forest warfare. They made a terrific noise, but when they came within gunshot of the fort, it was by darting from stump to stump with a quick, zigzag movement that made them more difficult to hit than birds on the wing. The best moment for a shot was when they reached a stump, and stopped for an instant to duck and hide behind it. By seizing this fleeting opportunity, Hawks himself put a bullet into the breast of an Abenaki chief from St. Francis,—"which ended his days," says the chaplain. In view of the nimbleness of the assailants, a charge of buckshot was found more to the purpose than a bullet. Besides the slain Abenaki, Rigaud reports sixteen Indians and Frenchmen wounded,[2]—which, under the circumstances, was good execution for ten farmers and a minister; for Chaplain Norton loaded and fired with the rest.

[1] When I visited the place as a college student, no trace of the fort was to be seen except a hollow, which may have been the remains of a cellar, and a thriving growth of horse-radish,—a relic of the garrison garden. My friend Dr. D. D. Slade has given an interesting account of the spot in the *Magazine of American History* for October, 1888.

[2] "L'Ennemi me tua un abenakis et me blessa 16 hommes, tant Iroquois qu'Abenaquis, nipissings et françois." *Journal de Rigaud.*

Rigaud himself was one of the wounded, having been hit in the arm and sent to the rear, as he stood giving orders on the rocky hill about forty rods from the fort. Probably it was a chance shot, since, though rifles were invented long before, they were not yet in general use, and the yeoman garrison were armed with nothing but their own smooth-bore hunting-pieces, not to be trusted at long range. The supply of ammunition had sunk so low that Hawks was forced to give the discouraging order not to fire except when necessary to keep the enemy in check, or when the chance of hitting him should be unusually good. Such of the sick men as were strong enough aided the defence by casting bullets and buckshot.

The outrageous noise lasted till towards nine in the evening, when the assailants greeted the fort with a general war-whoop, and repeated it three or four times; then a line of sentinels was placed around it to prevent messengers from carrying the alarm to Albany or Deerfield. The evening was dark and cloudy. The lights of a camp could be seen by the river towards the southeast, and those of another near the swamp towards the west. There was a sound of axes, as if the enemy were making scaling-ladders for a night assault; but it was found that they were cutting fagots to burn the wall. Hawks ordered every tub and bucket to be filled with water, in preparation for the crisis. Two men, John Aldrich and Jonathan Bridgman, had been wounded, thus farther reducing the strength of the defenders. The chaplain says: "Of those that were in health, some were ordered to keep the watch, and some lay down and endeavored to get some rest, lying down in our clothes with our arms by us. . . . We got little or no rest; the enemy frequently raised us by their hideous outcries, as though they were about to attack us. The latter part of the night I kept the watch."

Rigaud spent the night in preparing for a decisive attack, "being resolved to open trenches two hours before sunrise, and push them to the foot of the palisade, so as to place fagots against it, set them on fire, and deliver the fort a prey to the fury of the flames."[1] It began to rain, and he determined

[1] "Je passay la nuit à conduire l'ouvrage auquel j'avois destiné le jour précédent, résolu à faire ouvrir la tranchée deux heures avant le lever du soleil, et de la pousser jusqu'au pied de la palissade, pour y placer les fascines, y appli-

to wait till morning. That the commander of seven hundred French and Indians should resort to such elaborate devices to subdue a sergeant, seven militia-men, and a minister,—for this was now the effective strength of the besieged,—was no small compliment to the spirit of the defence.

The firing was renewed in the morning, but there was no attempt to open trenches by daylight. Two men were sent up into the watch-tower, and about eleven o'clock one of them, Thomas Knowlton, was shot through the head. The number of effectives was thus reduced to eight, including the chaplain. Up to this time the French and English witnesses are in tolerable accord; but now there is conflict of evidence. Rigaud says that when he was about to carry his plan of attack into execution, he saw a white flag hung out, and sent the elder De Muy, with Montigny and D'Auteuil, to hear what the English commandant—whose humble rank he nowhere mentions—had to say. On the other hand, Norton, the chaplain, says that about noon the French "desired to parley," and that "we agreed to it." He says farther that the sergeant, with himself and one or two others, met Rigaud outside the gate, and that the French commander promised "good quarter" to the besieged if they would surrender, with the alternative of an assault if they would not. This account is sustained by Hawks, who says that at twelve o'clock an Indian came forward with a flag of truce, and that he, Hawks, with two or three others, went to meet Rigaud, who then offered honorable terms of capitulation.[1] The sergeant promised an answer within two hours; and going back to the fort with his companions, examined their means of defence. He found that they had left but three or four pounds of gunpowder, and about as much lead. Hawks called a council of his effective men. Norton prayed for divine aid and guidance, and then they fell to considering the situation. "Had we all been in health, or had there been only those eight of us that were in

---

quer l'artifice, et livrer le fort en proye à la fureur du feu." *Journal de Rigaud.* He mistakes in calling the log wall of the fort a palisade.

[1] *Journal of Sergeant Hawks,* cited by William L. Stone, *Life and Times of Sir William Johnson,* I. 227. What seems conclusive is that the French permitted Norton to nail to a post of the fort a short account of its capture, in which it is plainly stated that the first advances were made by Rigaud.

health, I believe every man would willingly have stood it out to the last. For my part, I should," writes the manful chaplain. But besides the sick and wounded, there were three women and five children, who, if the fort were taken by assault, would no doubt be butchered by the Indians, but who might be saved by a capitulation. Hawks therefore resolved to make the best terms he could. He had defended his post against prodigious odds for twenty-eight hours. Rigaud promised that all in the fort should be treated with humanity as prisoners of war, and exchanged at the first opportunity. He also promised that none of them should be given to the Indians, though he had lately assured his savage allies that they should have their share of the prisoners.

At three o'clock the principal French officers were admitted into the fort, and the French flag was raised over it. The Indians and Canadians were excluded; on which some of the Indians pulled out several of the stones that formed the foundation of the wall, crawled through, opened the gate, and let in the whole crew. They raised a yell when they saw the blood of Thomas Knowlton trickling from the watch-tower where he had been shot, then rushed up to where the corpse lay, brought it down, scalped it, and cut off the head and arms. The fort was then plundered, set on fire, and burned to the ground.

The prisoners were led to the French camp; and here the chaplain was presently accosted by one Doty, Rigaud's interpreter, who begged him to persuade some of the prisoners to go with the Indians. Norton replied that it had been agreed that they should all remain with the French; and that to give up any of them to the Indians would be a breach of the capitulation. Doty then appealed to the men themselves, who all insisted on being left with the French, according to the terms stipulated. Some of them, however, were given to the Indians, who, after Rigaud's promise to them, could have been pacified in no other way. His fault was in making a stipulation that he could not keep. Hawks and Norton, with all the women and children, remained in the French camp.

Hearing that men were expected from Deerfield to take the places of the sick, Rigaud sent sixty Indians to cut them off. They lay in wait for the English reinforcement, which consisted of nineteen men, gave them a close fire, shot down fifteen of them, and captured the rest.[1] This or another party of Rigaud's Indians pushed as far as Deerfield and tried to waylay the farmers as they went to their work on a Monday morning. The Indians hid in a growth of alder-bushes along the edge of a meadow where men were making hay, accompanied by some children. One Ebenezer Hawks, shooting partridges, came so near the ambushed warriors that they could not resist the temptation of killing and scalping him. This alarmed the haymakers and the children, who ran for their lives towards a mill on a brook that entered Deerfield River, fiercely pursued by about fifty Indians, who caught and scalped a boy named Amsden. Three men, Allen, Sadler, and Gillet, got under the bank of the river and fired on the pursuers. Allen and Gillet were soon killed, but Sadler escaped unhurt to an island. Three children of Allen—Eunice, Samuel, and Caleb—were also chased by the Indians, who knocked down Eunice with a tomahawk, but were in too much haste to stop and scalp her, and she lived to a good old age. Her brother Samuel was caught and dragged off, but Caleb ran into a field of tall maize, and escaped.

The firing was heard in the village, and a few armed men, under Lieutenant Clesson, hastened to the rescue; but when they reached the spot the Indians were gone, carrying the boy Samuel Allen with them, and leaving two of their own number dead. Clesson, with such men as he had, followed their trail up Deerfield River, but could not overtake the light-footed savages.

Meanwhile, the prisoners at Fort Massachusetts spent the first night, well guarded, in the French and Indian camps. In the morning, Norton, accompanied by a Frenchman and several Indians, was permitted to nail to one of the charred posts of the fort a note to tell what had happened to him and his companions.[2] The victors then marched back as they had

---

[1] One French account says that the Indians failed to meet the English party. *N. Y. Col. Docs.*, X. 35.

[2] The note was as follows: "August 20 [31, new style], 1746. These are to inform you that yesterday, about 9 of the clock, we were besieged by, as they say, seven hundred French and Indians. They have wounded two men and killed one Knowlton. The General de Vaudreuil desired capitulations, and

come, along the Hoosac road. They moved slowly, encumbered as they were by the sick and wounded. Rigaud gave the Indians presents, to induce them to treat their prisoners with humanity. Norton was in charge of De Muy, and after walking four miles sat down with him to rest in Williamstown valley. There was a yell from the Indians in the rear. "I trembled," writes Norton, "thinking they had murdered some of our people, but was filled with admiration when I saw all our prisoners come up with us, and John Aldrich carried on the back of his Indian master." Aldrich had been shot in the foot, and could not walk. "We set out again, and had gone but a little way before we came up with Josiah Reed." Reed was extremely ill, and could go no farther. Norton thought that the Indians would kill him, instead of which one of them carried him on his back. They were said to have killed him soon after, but there is good reason to think that he died of disease. "I saw John Perry's wife," pursues the chaplain; "she complained that she was almost ready to give out." The Indians threatened her, but Hawks spoke in her behalf to Rigaud, who remonstrated with them, and they afterwards treated her well. The wife of another soldier, John Smead, was near her time, and had lingered behind. The French showed her great kindness. "Some of them made a seat for her to sit upon, and brought her to the camp, where, about ten o'clock, she was graciously delivered of a daughter, and was remarkably well. . . . Friday: this morning I baptized John Smead's child. He called its name *Captivity*." The French made a litter of poles, spread over it a deer-skin and a bear-skin, on which they placed the mother and child, and so carried them forward. Three days after, there was a heavy rain, and the mother was completely drenched, but suffered no harm, though "Miriam, the wife of Moses Scott, hereby catched a grievous cold." John Perry was relieved of his pack, so that he might help his wife and carry her when her strength failed. Several horses were found at the farms along the way, and the sick Benjamin Simons and the wounded John Aldrich were allowed to use two of them. Rarely, in-

we were so distressed that we complied with his terms. We are the French's prisoners, and have it under the general's hand that every man, woman, and child shall be exchanged for French prisoners."

deed, in these dismal border-raids were prisoners treated so humanely; and the credit seems chiefly due to the efforts of Rigaud and his officers. The hardships of the march were shared by the victors, some of whom were sorely wounded; and four Indians died within a few days.

"I divided my army between the two sides of the Kaské-kouké" (Hoosac), says Rigaud, "and ordered them to do what I had not permitted to be done before we reached Fort Massachusetts. Every house was set on fire, and numbers of domestic animals of all sorts were killed. French and Indians vied with each other in pillage, and I made them enter the [valleys of all the] little streams that flow into the Kaskékouké and lay waste everything there. . . . Wherever we went we made the same havoc, laid waste both sides of the river, through twelve leagues of fertile country, burned houses, barns, stables, and even a meeting-house,—in all, above two hundred establishments,—killed all the cattle, and ruined all the crops. Such, Monseigneur, was the damage I did our enemies during the eight or nine days I was in their country."[1] As the Dutch settlers had escaped, there was no resistance.

The French and their allies left the Hoosac at the point where they had reached it, and retraced their steps northward through the forest, where there was an old Indian trail. Recrossing the Batten Kill, or "River of Saratoga," and some branches of Wood Creek, they reached the place where they had left their canoes, and found them safe. Rigaud says: "I gave leave to the Indians, at their request, to continue their fighting and ravaging, in small parties, towards Albany, Schenectady, Deerfield, Saratoga, or wherever they pleased, and I even gave them a few officers and cadets to lead them." These small ventures were more or less successful, and produced, in due time, a good return of scalps.

The main body, now afloat again, sailed and paddled northward till they reached Crown Point. Rigaud rejoiced at finding a haven of refuge, for his wounded arm was greatly inflamed: "and it was time I should reach a place of repose." He and his men encamped by the fort and remained there for some time. An epidemic, apparently like that at Fort Massachusetts, had broken out among them, and great numbers were seriously ill.

[1] *Journal de Rigaud.*

Norton was lodged in a French house on the east side of the lake, at what is now called Chimney Point; and one day his guardian, De Muy, either thinking to impress him with the strength of the place, or with an amusing confidence in the minister's incapacity for making inconvenient military observations, invited him to visit the fort. He accepted the invitation, crossed over with the courteous officer, and reports the ramparts to have been twenty feet thick, about twenty feet high, and mounted with above twenty cannon. The octagonal tower which overlooked the ramparts, and answered in some sort to the donjon of a feudal castle, was a bomb-proof structure in vaulted masonry, of the slaty black limestone of the neighborhood, three stories in height, and armed with nine or ten cannon, besides a great number of patereroes,—a kind of pivot-gun much like a swivel.[1]

In due time the prisoners reached Montreal, whence they were sent to Quebec; and in the course of the next year those who remained alive were exchanged and returned to New England.[2] Mrs. Smead and her infant daughter "Captivity" died in Canada, and, by a singular fatality, her husband had scarcely returned home when he was waylaid and killed by Indians. Fort Massachusetts was soon rebuilt by the province, and held its own thenceforth till the war was over. Sergeant Hawks became a lieutenant-colonel, and took a creditable part in the last French war.

For two years after the incursion of Rigaud the New England borders were scourged with partisan warfare, bloody, monotonous, and futile, with no event that needs recording, and no result beyond a momentary check to the progress of settlement. At length, in July, 1748, news came that the chief contending powers in Europe had come to terms of agreement, and in the next October the Peace of Aix-la-Chapelle was signed. Both nations were tired of the weary and barren conflict, with its enormous cost and its vast entail of debt. It

[1] Kalm also describes the fort and its tower. Little trace of either now remains. Amherst demolished them in 1759, when he built the larger fort, of which the ruins still stand on the higher ground behind the site of its predecessor.

[2] Of the twenty-two men in the fort when attacked, one, Knowlton, was killed by a bullet; one, Reed, died just after the surrender; ten died in Canada, and ten returned home. *Report of Sergeant Hawks.*

was agreed that conquests should be mutually restored. The chief conquest of England was Louisbourg, with the island of Cape Breton,—won for her by the farmers and fishermen of New England. When the preliminaries of peace were under discussion, Louis XV. had demanded the restitution of the lost fortress; and George II. is said to have replied that it was not his to give, having been captured by the people of Boston.[1] But his sense of justice was forced to yield to diplomatic necessity, for Louisbourg was the indispensable price of peace. To the indignation of the Northern provinces, it was restored to its former owners. "The British ministers," says Smollett, "gave up the important island of Cape Breton in exchange for a petty factory in the East Indies" (Madras), and the King deigned to send two English noblemen to the French court as security for the bargain.

Peace returned to the tormented borders; the settlements advanced again, and the colonists found a short breathing space against the great conclusive struggle of the Seven Years' War.

[1] *N. Y. Col. Docs.*, X. 147.

APPENDIX

A

Chapter XVII. England Has No Rightful Titles to North America, Except Those Which May Be Granted Her by France

Second Memoire concernant les limites des Colonies presenté en 1720, par Bobé prêtre de la congregation de la Mission. à Versailles. Archives Nationales.

(*Extracts, printed literatim.*)

"L'année Dernier 1719 je presenté un Memoire Concernant les prétensions reciproques de la grande bretagne et de la france par Raport aux Colonies des deux Nations dans L'Amerique, et au Reglement des limites des dites Colonies.

"Je ne repete pas ce que j'ay dit dans ce memoire, je prie seulement que l'on pese bien tout ce que j'y dis pour Aneantir les prétensions des Anglois, et pour les Convaincre, s'ils veullent être de bonne foy, qu'elles sont des plus mal fondées, trés Exorbitantes, et mêmes injustes, qu'ayant usurpé sur La france presque tout ce qu'ils possedent en Amerique, ils deveroient luy rendre au lieu de luy demander, et qu'ils deveroient estimer Comme un tres grand avantage pour Eux, la Compensation que j'y propose pour finir cette affaire, laqu'elle, sans cette Compensation, renaitra toujours jusqu'a ce qu'enfin la france soit rentrée en paisible possession de tout ce qui luy appartient légitimement, et dont on ne L'a depoüilleé que par la force et La malheureuse Conjoncture des tems, qui sans doute tôt ou tard luy seront plus favorables.

"Il Est surprenant que les Anglois entendus Comme ils sont par Raport à leurs Interests, ne fassent pas attention qu'il Leurs est infiniment plus Avantageux de s'assurer, par un traité raisonnable, la tranquille et perpetuelle possession des payis ou ils etoient établis avant la paix D'utrecht, que de vouloir profiter des Conjonctures pour oster aux françois des payis qu'ils ne Cederont jamais de bon Coeur, et dont ils se rempareront quand ils trouveront l'occasion favorable pour Cela, se persuadant qu'il leur sera alors permis de reprendre par force, ce que par force on leurs à pris, et ce qu'ils ont été obligé de Ceder a Utrecht; et meme de reprendre au moins une partie des payis que l'angleterre à usurpez sur la france, qui ne les à jamais cedez par aucun traité que je scache. . . .

"Jean Verazan par ordre de françois 1.ᵉʳ. fit La decouverte de tous les payis et Costes qui sont Entre le 33.ᵉ et le 47.ᵉ Degre de latitude, et y fit deux voyages dont le dernier fut en 1523 et par ordre et au nom du dit Roy francois 1.ᵉʳ il prit possession de toute cette Coste et de tous ces payis, bien long tems avant que les Anglois y Eussent Eté.

"L'an 1562 Les françois s'établirent dans La Caroline. Champlain à La fin de la relation de ses voyages fait un chapitre exprez Dans lequel il prouve.

"1°. Que La france a pris possession de toutes les Costes et payis depuis la floride inclusivement jusqu'au fleuve S.ᵗ Laurent inclusivem.ᵗ, avant tout autre prince chrêtien.

2°. Que nos roys ont eu, dez le Commancement des decouvertes des lieutenans generaux Dans ces payis et Costes.

3°. Que Les françois les ont habitez avant les Anglois.

4°. Que Les prétensions des Anglois sont Mal fondées.

"La Lecture De ce chapitre fait voir que Champlain prouve invinciblement tous ces chefs, et de maniere que les Anglois n'ont rien de bon à y repondre, de sorte que s'ils veullent être de bonne foy, ils doivent Convenir que tous ces payis appartiennent Légitimement à la france qu'ils s'en sont emparez et qu'ils les Retiennent Contre toute justice. . . .

"Il Est A Remarquer que quoyque par le traité de S.ᵗ germain l'angleterre dut restituer tout ce qu'elle Avoit occupé dans la Nouvelle france, et par Consequent toute la Coste depuis baston jusqu'a la virginie inclusivement (car alors les Anglois ne s'etoient pas encore emparez de la Caroline) laqu'elle Coste est Certainement partie de la Nouvelle france, les Anglois ne l'ont pas Cependant restituée et la gardent encore a present Contre la teneur du traité de S.ᵗ Germain, quoy que la france ne L'ait point Cedée a L'angleterre ni par le dit traité ni par Aucun Autre que je scache.

"Cecy Merite La plus serieuse attention de la france, et qu'elle fasse Entendre serieusement aux Anglois que par le traité de S.ᵗ germain ils se sont obligez de luy rendre toutte cette Coste, qui incontestablement est partie de la Nouvelle france, Comme je L'ay prouvé cy devant et encore plus au long dans mon 1.ᵉ memoire et Comme le prouvent Verazan, Champlain, Denis, et toutes les plus ancienes Cartes de l'amerique septentrionale. . . .

"Or Le Commun Consentement de toute l'Europe est de depeindre la Nouvelle france S'étendant au moins au 35.ᵉ et 36.ᵉ degrez de latitude Ainsy qu'il appert par les mappemondes imprimées en Espagne, Italie, hollande, flandres, allemagne Et Angleterre même, Sinon depuis que les Anglois se sont Emparez des Costes de la Nouvelle france, ou est L'Acadie, Etechemains L'almouchicois, et la grande riviere de S.ᵗ l'aurens, ou ils ont imposé a leur fantaisie des Noms de nouvelle Angleterre, Ecosse, et autres, mais il est mal aisé de pouvoir Effacer une chose qui est Connué De toute la Chretienteé D'ou je Conclus,

"1°. Quavant L'Usurpation faite par les Anglois, toute Cette Coste jusqu'au 35.ᵉ Degre s'appelloit Nouvelle france, laquelle Comprenoit outre plusieurs autres provinces, l'Etechemains, L'almouchicois, et L'acadie. . . .

"Les Anglois Doivent remettre à La france le Port Royal, et La france doit insister vigoureusement sur cette restitution, et ordonner aux françois de Port Royal, Des Mines, et de Beaubassin, et autres lieux De reconaitre sa Majesté tres Chretiene pour leur Souverain, et leur deffendre d'obeir a aucun autre; de plus Commander a tous ces lieux et payis, et a toute la partie Septentrionale de la Peninsule, ainsi qu'aux payis des Almouchicois et des Etechemains [*Maine, New Hampshire, and Massachusetts*], de Reconaitre le gouverneur de l'isle Royale pour leur Gouverneur.

"Il Est même apropos De Comprendre Dans le Brevet de gouverneur de L'isle Royale tous ces payis jusqu'au Cap Cod. . . .

"Que La france ne doit point souffrir que les Anglois s'etablissent Dans les payis qu'elle n'a pas Cedez.

"Qu'elle Doit incessament s'en remettre en possession, y Envoyer quantite D'habitans, et s'y fortifier de maniere qu'on puisse Arrêter les Anglois que depuis long tems tachent de s'emparer de l'amerique francoise dont ils Conaissent L'importance, et dont ils feroient un meilleur usage que celuy que les francois en font. . . .

"Si les Anglois disent que les payis qui sont entre les rivieres de quinibequi [*Kennebec*] et de Ste Croix font partie de
la Nouvelle Angleterre.

JE LEURS REPONS

"1°. Qu'ils scavent bien le Contraire, que Ces payis ont toujours fait partie de la Nouvelle france, que Les francois les ont
toujours possedez et habitez, que Monsr De St Castin gentilhomme francois a toujours eu, et a encore son habitation
entre la Riviere de Quinibequi et celle de Pentagoet [*Penobscot*] (que même depuis les usurpations des anglois et leurs
etablissements, dans leur Prétenduë Nouvelle Angleterre) les
francois ont toujours prétendu que la Nouvelle france s'etend
jusqu'au Cap Cod et qu'il en est fait mention dans toutes les
patentes de gouverneurs francois.

"2° Que De L'aveu même des Anglois, la Nouvelle Angleterre a une tres petite Etenduë du Costé de L'est, il est facile
de le prouver par eux mêmes.

"J'ay Lu une description de la Nouvelle Angleterre et des
autres Colonies Angloises, Composée par un Anglois, tra-
duite en francois, imprimée à Paris en 1674 par Loüis Billaine,
voicy les propres termes de Cet autheur Anglois, La Nouvelle
Angleterre est au Septentrion de Marylande, au raport du
Capitaine Smith, elle a prez de 25 Lieuës de Coste de mer.

"Ainsi selon les Anglois qui sont de Bonne foy, la Nouvelle
Angleterre, qui n'a que prez de 25 lieuës de Coste de mer, ne
scauroit s'etendre jusqu'e á La Riviere de Quinebequi. C'est
tout au plus si elle s'etend jusqu'a deux ou trois lieuës à l'est
De Baston.

"Il Semble même que les Anglois ont basti Baston, et en
ont fait une ville Considerable à l'extremeté de leur pretenduë
Nouvelle Angleterre.

"1° Pour être a portée et en Etat de s'emparer sur les francois de tout ce qui est à L'est de Baston.

"2° Pour être en Etat d'Empecher les francois de s'etablir
sur toute Cette Coste jusqu à La Karoline inclusivement, laquelle Coste etant de Notorieté publique de la Nouvelle
france, à eté usurpez sur La france a qui elle appartenoit alors,

et luy appartient Encore, ne L'ayant jamais cedeé. C'est ce que je vais prouver.

"Apres Avoir Invinciblement Convaincu les Anglois que tout ce qui est a L'est de quinibequi a Toujours appartenu et appartient encore a La france, excepté L'Acadie selon ses Ancienes limites, qu'elle a Cedée par force a L'Angleterre par La paix d'utrecht.

"Il faut Que Presentement je prouve que toute La Coste depuis la Riviere quinibequi jusqu' à La Caroline inclusivement appartient par toutes sortes de droits à La france. Sur qui les Anglois L'ont usurpeé, voicy une partie de mes preuves.

"Les françois ont decouvert tous ces payis Avant les Anglois, et en ont pris possession avant Eux. Les Roys de france ont nommé ces payis Caroline et Nouvelle france avant que les Anglois leurs eussent donné des Noms á leur mode pour faire oublier les Noms que les francois Leurs avoient imposez. Et que ces payis Appartenoient à La france.

"Les Roys de france ont Donné des lettres patentes à leurs sujets pour posseder et habiter ces payis, avant que Jacques 1. et Charles 1. Roys d'Angleterre en eussent donne à Leurs sujets.

"Pour Convaincre les Anglois de ces veritées il faut Lire avec attention ce qu'en ont Ecrit Jean verazan, Champlain, Laet, Denis.

"Les traitez faits Entre La france et L'Angleterre, et Le memoire que j'ay presenté L'anneé Dernier 1719.

"On y Trouvera tant de Choses, lesquelles il seroit trop long de Copier icy, qui prouvent que ces payis ont toujours appartenu de droit a La france, et que les Anglois s'en sont emparez par force, que La france ne les a jamais Cedez à l'angleterre par aucun traité, que je scache.

"Et Partant que La france Conserve toujours son droit sur tous ces payis, et qu'elle a droit de les redemander à l'Angleterre. Comme elle les redemande présentement, ou Bien un Equivalent.

"L'Equivalent que la france demande et dont elle veut bien se Contenter, C'est la restitution de tout ce qu'elle a Cedéé par force à L'Angleterre par Le traité D'utrecht.

"Il Est De l'honeur et de l'interest de l'angleterre d'accorder à la france cette Equivalent.

"1° Parceque n'y ayant point D'honeur à profiter des Malheurs D'un Roy pour Luy faire Ceder par force les payis qui luy appartiennent, il est de l'honeur de L'Angleterre de rendre a la france, ce qu'elle a eté Contrainte de luy ceder, et qu'elle ne possede qu'a ce mauvais tiltre.

"2° Il est aussi Contre la justice et l'honeur de l'angleterre de posseder sans aucun Tiltre, et Contre toute justice les payis qui sont depuis la Riviere de quinibequi jusqu'à la Caroline inclusivement.

"3° Il N'est pas moins de l'honeur et de l'interest de l'angleterre de profiter du moyen que la france veut bien luy presenter, pour sassurer a perpetuite toute Cette Coste, et pour la posseder justem! par la Cession que la france en fera, et de tous ses droits sur ces payis moyennant L'Equivalent proposé.

"4° Parceque L'Angleterre doit Craindre que la france, dont elle ne Doit mepriser ni le Ressentiment ni la puissance, ne trouve une Conjoncture favorable pour faire valoir ses pretensions et ses droits, et pour Rentrer en possession de tout ce que L'Angleterre Luy a usurpée, et de tout ce qu'elle l'a obligé par force de luy Ceder.

"5° Quand on veut trop avoir, souvent on n'a Rien, et meme on perd ce que L'on Avoit. Il est donc de la sagesse Et de l'interest de l'Angleterre de ne pas pousser trop loin ses demandes, et de Convenir avec La france de sorte qu'elle puisse posseder Avec justice et tranquillement des payis que la france Aura toujours droit de reprendre jusqu'a ce qu'elle en ait fait une Cession libre et volontaire, et qu'il paroisse que L'Angleterre En faveur de Cette Cession luy ait donné un Equivalent.

"La france s'offre donc pour vivre en paix avec l'Angleterre de luy Ceder tous ses droits sur toute la Coste qui est entre la riviere de quinibequi dans la Nouvelle france jusqu'a la Riviere Jourdain, dans la Caroline, de sorte que ces deux rivieres servent de limites aux francois et aux Anglois.

"La france Demande pour Equivalent de la Cession de tant de payis, si grands, si beaux, et si a sa biensceance que l'Angleterre luy rende Et restituë tout ce qu'elle luy à cedé par le traité Dutrecht.

"Si La france ne peut pas engager L'Angleterre à convenir de Cet Equivalent, Elle pouroit (mais Ce ne doit être qu'a L'extremité) Ceder Encore à l'Angleterre la Caroline francoise, C'est a dire, ce qui est au sud de la Riviere Jourdain, Ou bien Ce qui est Entre la Riviere quinibequi, et Celle de Pentagoet. Ou bien leur offrir une somme D'argent.

"Il Semble que L'Angleterre doive estimer Comme un grand Avantage pour Elle, que La france veuille bien Convenir de Cet Equivalent, qui Assure Aux Anglois et leur rend legitime La possession de Cette grande etenduë de Costes qu'ils ont usurpez sur La france, qui ne les a jamais Cedez, qui ne les Cedera jamais, et sur lesqu'elles elle Conservera toujours ses legitimes droit et pretensions, jusqu'a ce qu'elle les ait Cédeés a L'angleterre moyennant un Equivalent raisonnable tel qu'est la Restitution de tout ce que La France luy a Cedé par force a Utrecht.

Limites

"Suposeé L'acceptation de Cet Equivalent par L'une et l'autre Nation.

"La france toujours genereuse Consentira pour vivre en paix avec les Anglois, qu'une ligne tirée depuis l'embouchure de la Riviere de quinibequi, ou bien, depuis l'embouchure de la Riviere de Pentagoet, qui ira tout droit passer á egale distance entre Corlard [*Schenectady*] et les lacs de Champlain et du Saint Sacrement, et joindre la ligne par laqu'elle le sieur de L'isle geographe termine les terres Angloises, jusqu'a la Riviere Jourdain, ou bien jusqu'a La Caroline inclusivem^r. La france dis-je Consentira que cette ligne serve De borne et limites aux terres des deux Nations, de sorte que tous les payis et terres qui sont entre Cette ligne et la mer appartiendront à L'Angleterre, et que tout ce qui sera au dela de cette ligne appartiendra a La france.

"Dans Le fond il est avantageux a la france de faire incessament regler les limites, tant pour Empecher les Anglois d'empieter toujours de plus en plus sous pretexte de limites Non regleés, que parcequ'il est assuré que si le droit de la france est bien soutenu le réglement lui sera Avantageux, aussi bien que l'equivalent que j'ay proposé.

"Mais il pouroit arriver que les Anglois qui ont demandé le Reglement des limites, voyant qu'il ne doit pas leur etre favorable s'il est fait selon la justice, pourroient bien eux mêmes l'eloigner, afin de pouvoir toujours empieter sur les francois sous pretexte de limites non regleés, et de se mettre toujours en possession des payis Appartenans à la france.

"En ce Cas et aussi au Cas que les Anglois ne veullent pas restituer a la france leur Nouvelle Angleterre et autres payis jusqu'a la Caroline inclusivement qu'ils luy out usurpez, ou bien leur rendre L'Acadie &^{c} pour l'equivalent Dont j'ay parlé.

"1° Il faut que la france mette incessament quantité d'habitans dans le payis qui est entre la riviere de quinibequi et Celle de Ste Croix, lequel payis qui selon les Anglois N'est point en Litige, ni partie de la pretenduë Nouvelle Ecosse, même, selon l'etenduë imaginaire que luy á donnée leur Roy Jacques 1^r qui ne la fait Commancer qu'a La riviere Ste Croix, et Celle de quinibequi N'ayant jamais eté Cedé ni par le traite D'utrecht ni par Aucun autre que je scache, et ce payis Ayant toujours appartenu a La france, et eté par elle possedez et habité, M^r de St Castin gentilhomme francois ayant son habitation entre la riviere de Pentagoet et Celle de quinibequi comme je l'ay Deja dit.

"2° On peut même faire entendre a L'Angleterre que Le Roy donnera Ce payis a la Compagnie des Indes qui scaura bien le deffendre et le faire valoir.

"Que Le Roy donnera aussi a la Compagnie des Indes la Caroline francoise, Comme depandance et province de la loüisiane, a Condition qu'elle y mettera des habitans, et y fera bâtir de bons forts, et une bonne Citadelle pour soutenir et deffendre ce beau payis Contre les Anglois.

"Il Est Certain que si le Roy fait entendre serieusement qu'il est resolu de donner à la Compagnie des Indes non seulement La Caroline francoise, et le payis qui est entre les Rivieres de quinibequi et de Ste Croix, mais aussi de luy Ceder et abandonner tous ses droits sur tous les payis que les Anglois ont usurpez sur la france.

"Il Est Certain Dis je, que les Anglois, Crainte D'Avoir affaire avec une Compagnie si puissante, se resoudront au Reglement des limites, tel que je l'ay proposé, et à rendre a la france toute la Nouvelle Ecosse ou Acadie selon ses Anciènes limites, Enfin tout ce que la france leur à Cedez a Utrecht, moyennant une somme D'Argent, ou bien L'equivalent que j'ay Aussi proposé.

"Je finis Ce memoire en priant de faire une tres serieuse attention aux Exorbitantes prétensions des Anglois et a tout ce qu'ils ont fait Et font encore pour se rendre maitres de la pesche la Moluë, et de L'Amerique francoise.

"En Effet il est tres important que quand on traitera du reglement des limites, La france attaque les Anglois au lieu d'etre sur La defensive, C'est a dire, qu'elle doit demander aux Anglois tout ce qu'ils ont usurpez sur Elle, et le demander vigoureusement.

"C'est peut être le meilleur moyen de les mettre a la Raison, il est même apropos qu'elle les presse de finir Cette affaire, Dont sans doute La Conclusion luy sera Avantageuse, si on luy rend justice."

II
DEMANDES DE LA FRANCE (1723)

Archives du Ministère des Affaires Etrangères
(*Literatim.*)

"Pour tous les Raisons deduites cy devant La france demande a Langleterre.

"1° Qu'Elle laisse jouir Tranquillement la france de Tous les pays qui sont a L'Est de la riviere Quinibequi ou de Celle de S.ᵗ Georges excepté de la seulle ville de Port Royal avec sa banlieüe et de L'accadie selon ses anciennes Limites, C'Est a dire La partie Meridionale de la Peninsule depuis le Cap fourchu jusqua Camseau Exclusivement, Que la france a cedée par la traite d'Utrecht, Tout le reste qui est a L'Est de Quinibequi [*Kennebec*], appartenant a La France en tout souveraineté depuis L'an 1524. Laquélle ne la jamais cedé ny par le Traitté d'Utrecht ny par aucun autre traitté.

"2° Que les Anglois Laissent Vivre Tranquillement sous la domination du Roy les nations Sauvages qui sont dans Les payis a L'Est de Quinibequi et qu'ils Ninquietent point les Missionnaires qui demeureront Chés les d. Nations Ny les françois qui Iront Chés Elles.

"3° Que Les Anglois restituent a la france ce qu'ils ont occupé a L'Est de Quinibequi et qu'ils ne Trouvent pas mauvais que les françois prennent detruisent ou gardent les forts Postes et habitations, que les Anglois ont Etablis, ou Etabliront dans tous les Pays a L'Est de Quinibiqui, ou de la Rivierre Sr Georges Car quand même il ne Seroist pas sure que Ces d. Païs appartiennent a La France, il suffit qu'ils sont Contesté pour rendre injuste et Violente L'occupation qu'En feroient les Anglois avant que la Contestation fut finie.

"4° Que Les Anglois restituent tout ce qu'ils Occupent dans la Nouvelle france depuis Le 30e degré jusqua Quinibequi ou jusqua La Rivierre S^r georges Comme Elle y est obligeé par Le traitté de S^t germain En Laye En 1632. La france ne luy ayant jamais cedé par aucun Traitté aucune partie de toute La Nouvelle france, sinon La Ville de Port Royal avec sa Banlieüe et lacadie selon ses anciennes Limittes.

"Si les Anglois disent que la France ne s'est point opposeé aux occupations qu'ils ont fait dans la Nouvelle france.

"Je Leur repons que la france sy est toujours opposeé et qu'elle s'Est Toujours Maintenuë dans la souveraineté de toute la Nouvelle france, soit en donnant tout ses Païs en concession, soit en y envoyant des gouverneurs généraux, soit en Nommant Vice Roys de la Nouvelle france Les plus grands Seigneurs du Roÿaume, Tels Ont esté M. Le Comte de Soissons, M. Le Prince de Condé, M. de Montmorency, M. Le Duc de Vantadour, M. Le Cardinal de Richelieu etc. qui des les premiers tems ont este successivement Viceroys de la Nouvelle france et Terres Circonvoisines, par la Lecture de leurs patentes On verra que Nos Roys se sont Toujours Conservé la Souveraineté des pays qui sont Entre le 30e et Le 50e degré, et qu'ils Nont jamais Consenty que les Anglois y fissent aucun Etablissement et que sy-ils y en ont fait çá esté Malgré la france, que avoit trop d'affaires en Europe pour pouvoir les Empecher, Se reservant Toujours ses droits et la Volonté de les faire Valoir quand Elle en Trouveroit une occasion favorable, ce qui pourroit bien arriver un jour, alors on Verroit que L'on ne s'Empare pas Impunement et par Violence, des Domaines d'un Roy de france et qu'il est assés puissant pour se remettre en pocession Tost ou tard de ce qu'on a Usurpé sur luy, C'est a quoy les Anglois deveroient faire attention, et ce qui devroit les obliger de ne pas mepriser Ny maltraitter La France Comme Ils font.

"La france s'Est encore opposeé aux Usurpations des Anglois Les ayant obligé par le traitté de St Germain En 1632, de restituer a la france Tout ce qu'ils avoient jusqual'ors occupe dans la Nouvelle france, Ils Nont pas cependant Encore fait cette restitution, Mais on leur demande présentement qu'ils la fassent incessammant N'Etant pas juste qu'ils retiennent plus Longtems ce qui ne leur appartient pas, et qu'ils ont promis solennellement de restituer a la france.

"Mais disent Les Anglois Nous sommes Etablis dans La Nouvelle france depuis la Caroline Inclusivement jusqua Quinibequi depuis 1585, jusqua presant 1723. Nous y avons mis quantiteé d'habitans et bastis plusieurs grandes villes. Navons Nous pas prescrit Contre La france par une sy Longue procession."

REPONSE

"Non parce que La france sy est Toujours opposeé par les Lettres pattentes qu'Elle a donneés aux Concésionnaires Generaux, aux Lieutenants generaux et aux Viceroys de la Nouvelle france.

"Non parce que La france obligea en 1632, par Le traitté de St Germain, Langleterre de luy restituer tous les lieux occupés dans la Nouvelle france par les Anglois, Et que le traitté de Breda en 1667, celuy de Neutralité en 1686, et celuy d'Utrecht en 1713, ne disent rien d'ou on puisse Inferer que la france ait cedé a Langleterre aucune partie de la Nouvelle france, sinon la province de la Cadie selon ses anciennes Limittes, et la seule ville de Port Royal avec ses dépendances ou Banlieüe. Je dis encore que Cette longue possession des anglois, ces Villes baties et ce grand Nombre d'habitans mis par eux dans ces pays Nanéantissent point le droit de la france pour les redemander. . . . .

"Il y avoit Environ 150 ans que les françois avoient abandonné les postes qu'ils avoient alors sur la Coste du Bresil les Portuguais sy Etablirent aussitost y Mirent quantité d'habitans et y batirent de grandes Villes. Ils ne Croyoient pas cependant que pour cela la france fut dechüe de ses droits de proprieté et de souveraineté sur ces pays abandonnés par Elle depuis 150 ans, puisqua Utrecht en 1713 Le Roy de Portugal demanda au Roy qu'il luy abandonnat ses droits sur ces pays, ce qui Le Roy fit en Consideration du Portugal.

"Les Anglois possedoient depuis longues anneés La Jamaique yavoient quantité d'habitans, de forts et de riches Villes, persuadés cependant que les droits de l'Espagne subsisteroient Tant quelle Ny auroit pas renoncé en leur faveur. Ils demanderent a Utrecht Cette renonciation au Roy d'Espagne et il la leur accorda.

"Si les Anglois avoient demandé a la france une Cession de tous ces droits sur les pays occupés par Eux dans la Nouvelle france Il y a apparance que le Roy leur auroit fait cession a des Conditions raisonnables. Ils nont pas demandés cette cession, ou sy ils lont demandeé, elle ne leur a pas esté accordeé les droits de la france subsistent donc Toujours et Elle pretend presentement que les Anglois qui en usent sy mal avec Elle, luy restituënt Tout ce quelle a usurpé dans la Nouvelle france depuis le 30.ᵉ jusquau 50.ᵉ degré."

"Mais disent les Anglois Commant pouvoir restituer un sy vaste pays ou nous avons une Infinité d'habitans et un trés grand nombre de belles et riches villes? Une Telle restitution N'Est pas practicable."

RESPONSE

"Javouë qu'il est bien difficile de sy resoudre même aux personnes qui font profession d'aimer L'Equité et La Justice.

"Mais Le Roy aime trop la nation Angloise, a trop de Consideration pour Elle, desire trop luy faire plaisir, et est trop généreux pour exiger d'Elle une Telle restitution Voulant luy donner Un Exemple de la moderation dont il souhaite que Langleterre use a son Egard.

"Il se désistera Volontiers de tous ces droits et consentira que Toute la Coste jusqua 20 Lieuës dans l'Enfoncement des Terres Depuis le 32.ᵉ degré jusqua la Rivierre de Quinibequi demeure en toute proprieté et souveraineté a perpetuité a Langleterre a condition quelle Sobligera par un traitté solennel et décisif de ne jamais passer ces limites. Que la france ne

sera jamais Inquieté par Langleterre dans la Jouissance en proprieté et souveraineté de Ce qui est au dela de ces 20 lieuës
dans lenfoncement des terres et de Tous les pays qui sont a
L'Est de la rivierre de Quinibequi, qui de Ce Costé la servira
de Limites aux deux Nations, et que Langleterre rendra a la
france Le port Royal et la Cadie avec leurs dependances, Enfin Tout ce que la france luy a Cedé par le traité d'Utrecht
sans en rien Excepter.

"Cet offre du Roy doit estre agreable a Langleterre et luy
faire plaisir, parceque sy elle l'accepte elle possedera a juste
Titre cette grande partie de la Nouvelle france, qu'Elle possedera Toujours injustement sy Elle Naccepte pas un offre sy
raisonnable que Luy fait Le Roy qui sans cette acceptation
Ne renoncera jamais a ses droits de souveraineté sur une sy
grande et sy belle partie de la Nouvelle France, droits que les
anglois doivent Craindre qu'il Ne fasse Valoir Tost ou tard,
Car si puissante que soit Langleterre, Ils ne doivent pas croire
que la france ne luy cede rien en puissance ny en quoy que ce
soit, et qu'on ne la meprise et maltraitte pas Impunement.

"Sy Les Anglois ont quelques autres titres et quelques
autres raysons a alleguer en leur faveur, sy on me veut faire
L'honneur de me les Communiquer, Je moffre d'y repondre
d'une maniere a les obliger d' avouër qu'ils ont tort, sils sont
de bonne foy et si ils aiment La justice et la paix.

ADDITION

"On vient de me faire voire une carte de la nouvelle france
presenté au Roy par les Anglois sur la quelle est tracé par une
ligne tout ce qu'ils pretendent en vertu du traitté d'Utrecht.

"Ils y etendent sy loin leurs pretentions dans Les terres,
qu'il y a tout lieu de Croire que cette Ligne na pas eté traceé,
Ny Cette carte presenteé par ordre et au scû du Sage et judi-
cieux ministre dangleterre, mais par quelqu'Un que donne a
penser qu'il veut broüiller L'angleterre avec La france.

"Ce qui donne encore plus de lieu a avoir de luy cette pen-
seé C'est que le traitté d'Utrecht ayant determiné les Limites
des deux Nations pour la pesche, par desairs de vent, quoyque
par toutes les nations les airs de vent se tracent en Ligne
droite, il les a tracé en Ceintre a L'Est de Lisle de Sable, en

quoy il semble avoir Intention de se mocquer de la france et de L'Irriter.

"La prise d'un vaisseau françois dans Le passage de Camceau, La Construction d'un fort a Canceau, Le nom d'albanie donné a la partye de la Nouvelle France qui est entre quinibequi et la ville de Port Royal pays qui n'a point esté Cedé par le traitté d'Utrecht, Les forts Construits, et Les Concessions donneés, Les Nations sauvages, et Les missionnaires maltraités dans ce pays appartenant a la france, ou du moins pretendu et Contesté par Elle.

"Tout cela pourroit bien Venir de quelque Anglois qui voudroit broüiller les deux Nations. C'est aux Anglois pacifiques a le punir et a la france a sopposer a de telles entreprises jusqu ce que les Limites soient regleés d'Une Maniere Equitable.

"Collationné et figuré sur une Copie de Mémoire ou notte en papier non Signeé ni dattée estant au Secrétariat du Chateau S.ᵗ Louis de Quebec ou elle est resteé Par Le Notaire Royal en la prevosté de Quebec y resident soussigné ce jourdhuy Vingt cinq Juillet mil sept cent cinquante.

Du Laurent.

"François Bigot, Conseiller du Roy en ses Conseils, Intendant de justice, Police, finances et de la marine en la Nouvelle france.

"Certifions a tousqu'il appartiendra que M.ʳ Dulaurent qui a signé la Collation de L'autre part Est notaire Royal en la prevosté de Quebec Et que foy doit Estre ajouteé a sa signature En la d.ᵉ qualité; En temoin de quoy nous avons signeé et fait Contresigner ces presentes par nôtre secretaire et a Icelles fait apposer le Cachet de nos armes. fait en nôtre hotel a Quebec Le p.ᵉʳ Aoust, mil sept cent Cinquante.

Bigot

Par monseigneur
Deschenaux."

Endorsed. "Envoyé par M.ʳ Bigot Intend.ᵗ du Canada avec sa lettre au M.ⁱˢ de Puyzieulx du 1.ᵉʳ aoust 1750. No 25, 1723."

B

Chapters XIX., XX., XXI. The Siege of Louisbourg
as Described by French Witnesses

Lettre d'un Habitant de Louisbourg contenant une Relation exacte et circonstanciée de la Prise de l'Isle Royale par les Anglois. À Québec, chez Guillaume le Sincère, à l'Image de la Vérité. MDCCXLV. [*Extraits.*]

[*Literatim.*]

". . . Le mauvais succès dont cette entreprise (*against Annapolis*) a été suivie, est envisagé, avec raison, comme la cause de notre perte. Les Anglois ne nous auroient peut-être point inquietés, si nous n'eussions été les premiers à les insulter. Notre qualité d'aggresseurs nous a été funeste; je l'ai oüi conter à plus d'un ennemi, & je n'y vois que trop d'apparence. Les habitans de la nouvelle Angleterre étoient interressés à vivre en paix avec nous. Ils l'eussent sans doute fait, si nous ne nous étions point avisés mal à propos de les tirer de cette sécurité où ils etoient à notre égard. Ils comptoient que de part & d'autre, on ne prendroit aucun parti dans cette cruelle guerre qui a mis l'Europe en feu, et que nous nous tiendrions comme eux sur la seule défensive. La prudence le dictoit; mais elle n'est pas toujours la régle des actions des hommes: nous l'avons plus éprouvé que qui que ce soit. . . .

". . . L'expedition de l'Acadie manquée, quoiqu'il y eût tout à parier qu'il reuissiroit par le peu de forces que les ennemis avoient pour nous résister, leur fit faire de serieuses réflexions sur notre crainte, ou notre faiblesse. Selon tous les apparences, ils en conclurent qu'ils devoient profiter d'une aussi favorable circonstance, puisque dès-lors ils travaillerent avec ardeur à l'armement qui leur était necessaire. Ils ne firent pas comme nous: ils se prêterent un secours mutuel: on arma dans tous leurs Ports, depuis l'Acadie jusqu'au bas de la Côte: on dépêcha en Angleterre, & on envoya, dit on, jusqu'à *la Jamaïque* afin d'en tirer tous les secours qu'il seroit possible. Cette entreprise fut concertée avec prudence, et l'on travailla tout l'hiver pour être prêt au premier beau tems.

"Les préparatifs n'en pouvaient être si secrets, qu'il n'en transpirât quelque chose. Nous en avions été informés dès les

premiers instans, & assez à tems pour en pouvoir donner avis
à la Cour. . . .

"Nous eumes tout l'hiver à nous, c'était plus qu'il n'en falloit pour nous mettre en état de défense; mais la terreur s'étoit
emparée des esprits: on tenait des conseils, dont le résultat
n'avoit rien que de bizarre et de puérile; cependant le tems
s'écoulait, nous perdions de precieux momens en déliberations inutiles, & en résolutions presque aussitôt détruites que
prises. Quelques ouvrages demandoient qu'on les parachevât:
il en falloit renforcer quelques-uns, augmenter quelques
autres, pourvoir à des postes, visiter tous ceux de l'Isle, voir
où la descente étoit plus facile, faire le denombrement des
personnes en état de porter les armes, assigner à chacun son
poste; enfin se donner tous les soins et les mouvemens ordi-
naires en pareil cas; rien de tout cela ne se faisoit; de sorte
que nous avons été surpris, comme si l'ennemi fût venu
fondre sur nous à l'improviste. Nous aurions eu même assez
de tems pour nous precautionner mieux qu'on ne l'a fait, depuis le jour où nous vimes paroître les premiers Navires qui
nous ont bloqués; car ils n'y sont venues que les uns après les
autres, ainsi que je le dirai dans la suite. La négligence & la
déraison avoient conjuré la perte de notre malheureuse
Isle. . . .

"Ce fut le quatorze [Mars], que nous vimes les premiers
Navires ennemis; ils n'étoient encore que deux, & nous les
primes d'abord pour des Vaisseaux François; mais nous fumes
bien tôt détrompés par leur manœuvre. Le nombre en augmentoit de jour à autre, il en arriva jusqu'à la fin de Mai. Ils
croiserent long-tems, sans rien tenter. Le rendezvous général
étoit devant notre Isle, où ils arrivoient de tous côtez; car on
avoit armé à l'Acadie, Plaisance, Baston, & dans toute l'Amerique Anglaise. Les secours d'Europe ne vinrent qu'en Juin.
C'étoit moins une entreprise formée par la Nation ou par le
Roi, que par les seuls habitans de la nouvelle Angleterre. Ces
peuples singuliers ont des Lois & une Police qui leur sont
particulières, & leur Gouverneur tranche du Souverain. Cela
est si vrai, que, quoiqu'il y eût guerre déclarée entre les deux
Couronnes, il nous la déclara lui de son chef & en son nom,
comme s'il avoit fallu qu'il eût autorisé son maître. Sa declaration portoit, qu'il nous déclaroit la guerre pour lui, & pour

tous ses amis & alliés; il entendoit parler apparemment des Sauvages qui leur sont soumis, qu'on appelle *Indiens*, & que l'on distingue des Sauvages qui obéissent à la France. On verra que l'Amiral *Warren* n'avoit rien à commander aux troupes envoyées par le Gouverneur de Baston, & que cet Amiral n'a été que Spectateur, quoique ce soit à lui que nous nous soyons rendus. Il nous en avoit fait solliciter. Ce qui marque bien l'independance qu'il y avoit entre l'armée de terre & celle de mer que l'on nous a toujours distinguées comme si elles eussent été de differentes Nations. Quelle Monarchie s'est jamais gouvernée de la sorte?

"La plus grande partie des Bâtimens de transport étant arrivés dans le commencement de Mai, nous les apperçûmes le onze en ordre de bataille, au nombre de quatre-vingt seize venant du côté de Canceaux & dirigeant leur route vers la Pointe plate de la Baye de *Gabarus*. Nous ne doutames plus qu'ils n'y fissent leur descente. C'est alors qu'on vit la nécessité des precautions que nous aurions dû prendre. On y envoya à la hâte un détachement de cent hommes, tirés de la garnison & des Milices, sous le commandement du sieur *Morpain*, Capitaine de Port. Mais que pouvait un aussi faible corps, contre la multitude que les ennemis debarquoient! Cela n'aboutit qu'à faire tuer une partie des nôtres. Le sieur *Morpain* trouva déjà près de deux milles hommes débarqués; il en tua quelques-uns & se retira.

"L'Ennemi s'empare de toute la campagne, & un détachement s'avance jusques auprès de la batterie Royale. Pour le coup, la frayeur nous saisit tous; on parla dès l'instant d'abandonner cette magnifique batterie, qui auroit été notre plus grande défense, si l'on eût sçu en faire usage. On tint tumultuairement divers Conseils là-dessus. Il seroit bien difficile de dire les raisons qui portoient à un aussi étrange procédé; si ce n'est une terreur panique, que ne nous a plus quitté de tout le Siège. Il n'y avoit pas eu encore un seul coup de fusil tiré sur cette batterie, que les ennemis ne pouvoient prendre qu'en faisant leurs approches comme pour la Ville, & l'assiégeant, pour ainsi dire, dans les régles. On en a dit sourdement une raison sur laquelle je ne suis point en état de décider; je l'ai pourtant entendu assurer par une personne qui était dans la batterie; mais mon poste étant en Ville, il y avoit long-tems que je n'étois allé à la batterie Royale: C'est que ce qui détermina à un abandon si criminel, est qu'il y avoit deux brêches qui n'avoient point été réparées. Si cela est, le crime est encore plus grand, parce que nous avions eu plus de loisir qu'il n'en falloit, pour mettre ordre à tout.

"Quoiqu'il en soit, la résolution fut prise de renoncer à ce puissant boulevard, malgré les représentations de quelques gens sages, qui gémissoient de voir commettre une si lourde faute. Ils ne purent se faire écouter. Inutilement remontrèrent-ils que ce seroit témoigner notre foiblesse aux ennemis, qui ne manqueroient point de profiter d'une aussi grande étourderie, & qui tourneroient cette même batterie contre nous; que pour faire bonne contenance & ne point réchauffer le courage à l'ennemi, en lui donnant dès le premier jour, une si grande espérance de réussir, il falloit se maintenir dans ce poste important le plus que l'on pourroit: qu'il étoit évident qu'on s'y conserveroit plus de quinze jours, & que ce délai pouvoit être employé à retirer tous les canons dans la Ville. On répondit que le Conseil l'avoit résolu autrement; ainsi donc par ordre du Conseil, on abandonna le 13 sans avoir essuyé le moindre feu, une batterie de trente pièces de canon, qui avoit couté au Roi des sommes immenses. Cet abandon se fit avec tant de précipitation, qu'on ne se donna pas le temps d'enclouër les canons de la manière que cela se pratique; aussi les ennemis s'en servirent-ils dès le lendemain. Cependant on se flatoit du contraire; je fus sur le point de gager qu'ils ne tarderoient guères á nous en battre. On étoit si peu à soi, qu'avant de se retirer de la batterie, le feu prit à un baril de poudre, qui pensa faire sauter plusieurs personnes, & brûla la robe d'un Religieux Récolet. Ce n'étoit pas de ce moment que l'imprudence caracterisoit nos actions, il y avoit longtems qu'elle s'étoit refugiée parmi nous.

"Ce que j'avois prévu arriva. Dès le quatorze les ennemis nous saluèrent avec nos propres Canons, dont ils firent un feu épouvantable. Nous leur répondimes de dessus les murs; mais nous ne pouvions leur rendre le mal qu'ils nous faisoient, rasant nos maisons, & foudroyant tout ce qui étoit à leur portée.

"Tandis que les Anglois nous chauffoient de la batterie Royale, ils établissoient une Plate-forme de Mortiers sur la hauteur de Rabasse proche le Barachois du côté de l'Ouest, qui tirerent le seize jour où a commencé le bombardement. Ils avoient des Mortiers dans toutes les batteries qu'ils éleverent. Les bombes nous ont beaucoup incommodé. . . .

"Les ennemis paroissoient avoir envie de pousser vigoureusement le Siège. Ils établirent une batterie auprès de la Plaine de *Brissonnet*, qui commença à tirer le dix-sept, & travaillerent encore à une autre, pour battre directement la Porte Dauphine, entre les maisons du nommé *la Roche & Lescenne*, Canonier. Ils ne s'en tinrent point à ces batteries, quoiqu'elles nous battissent en brêche; mais ils en dresserent de nouvelles pour soutenir les premières. La Plaine marécageuse du bord de la Mer à la Pointe blanche, les incommodoit fort, & empêchoit qu'ils ne poussassent leurs travaux comme ils l'auroient souhaité: pour y rémédier, ils pratiquerent divers boyaux, afin de couper cette Plaine; étant venus à bout de la dessécher, ils y firent deux batteries qui ne tirerent que quelques jours après. Il y en avoit une au dessus de l'habitation de *Martissance*, composée de sept pièces de canon, prises en partie de la Batterie Royale & de la Pointe plate ou s'etait fait le débarquement. On la destinoit à miner le Bastion Dauphin; ces deux dernières batteries ont presque rasé la Porte Dauphine.

"Le dix-huit nous vîmes paroître un Navire, avec Pavillon Français, qui cherchoit à donner dans le Port. Il fut reconnu pour être effectivement de notre Nation, & afin de favoriser son entrée, nous fimes un feu continuel sur la Batterie Royale. Les Anglais ne pouvant resister à la vivacité de notre feu, qui ne discontinuoit point, ne purent empêcher ce Navire d'entrer, qu'il leur eut été facile sans cela de couler à fond. Ce petit refraichissement nous fit plaisir; c'étoit un Navire Basque: il nous en étoit venu un autre dans le courant d'Avril.

"Nous n'eumes pas le même bonheur pour un Navire de Granville, qui se présenta aussi pour entrer, quelques jours après; mais qui ayant été poursuivi, fut contraient de s'echouer, & se battit long-tems. Celui qui le commandoit, nomme *Daguenet*, étoit un brave homme, lequel ne se rendit qu'à la dernière extrêmité, & après avoir été accablé par le nombre. Il avoit transporté tous les Canons d'un même côté, & en fit un feu si terrible, que les ennemis n'eurent pas bon marché de lui. Il fallut armer presque toutes leurs Chaloupes pour le prendre. Nous avons sçu de ce Capitaine, qu'il avoit rencontré *le Vigilant*, & que c'étoit de ce malheureux Vaisseau, qu'il avoit apris que l'Isle Royale étoit bloquée. Cette circonstance importe au récit que je vais faire.

"Vous êtes persuadés, en France, que la prise de ce Vaisseau de guerre a occasionné la notre, cela est vraie en quelque sorte, mais nous eussions pu nous soutenir sans lui si nous n'avions pas entassé fautes sur fautes, ainsi que vous avez dû vous en apercevoir jusqu'à présent. Il est vrai que, graces à nos imprudences, lors que ce puissant secours nous arrivoit, nous commencions à être sans espérance. S'il fût entré, comme il le pouvoit, nous serions encore dans nos biens, & les Anglais eussent été forcés de se retirer.

"*Le Vigilant* parut le vingt-huit ou le vingt-neuf de Mai, à environ une lieue et demie de distance de *Santarge* [*sic*]. Le vent était pour lors Nord-Est, & par conséquent bon pour entrer. Il laissoit la Flotte Anglaise à deux lieues & demi sous le vent. Rien ne pouvoit donc l'empêcher d'entrer; & c'est par la plus grande de toutes les fatalités qu'il est devenu la proye de nos Vainqueurs. Témoins de sa manœuvre, il n'étoit personne de nous qui ne donnât des malédictions à une manœuvre si mal concertée & si imprudente.

"Le Vaisseau, commandé par M. *de la Maisonfort*, au lieu de suivre sa route, ou d'envoyer sa chaloupe à terre pour prendre langue, ainsi que le requéroit la prudence, s'amusa à poursuivre un Corsaire monté en Senault qu'il rencontra malheureusement sous la terre. Ce Corsaire, que commandoit un nommé *Brousse* (Rous) manœuvre d'une autre manière que le Vaisseau Français. Il se battit toujours en retraite, forçant de voiles et attirant son ennemi vers l'Escadre Angloise; ce qui lui réussit; car le Vigilant se trouva tellement engagé, qu'il ne lui fut plus possible de se sauver, quand on eut vu le danger. Deux Frégates l'attaquerent d'abord; M. de la Maisonfort leur répondit par un feu très vif, qui en mit bien-tôt une hors de combat; elle fut démâtée de son grand mât, désemparée de toutes les manœuvres, et contrainte de se retirer. Mais il vint cinq autres Frégates qui chaufferent le Vigilant de toutes parts; le combat que nous voyons à découvert, dura depuis cinq heures du soir jusqu'à dix. Enfin il fallut céder à la force, & se rendre. Les ennemis ont beaucoup perdu dans ce combat, & le commandant Français eut quatre-vingts hommes tués ou blessés; le Vaisseau n'a été que fort peu endommagé.

"On doit dire, à la gloire de M. de la Maisonfort, qu'il a fait preuve d'une extrême valeur dans ce combat; mais il auroit mieux valu qu'il eût suivi sa destination; c'étoit tout ce que les intérêts du Roi exigeoient. Le Ministre ne l'envoyoit pas pour donner la chasse à aucun Vaisseau ennemi; chargé de munitions de guerre & de bouche, son Vaisseau étoit uniquement destiné à ravitailler notre malheureuse Place, qui n'auroit jamais été en effet emportée, si nous eussions pû recevoir un si grand secours; mais nous étions des victimes dévouées à la colère du Ciel, qui a voulu faire servir contre nous jusqu'à nos propres forces. Nous avons sçu des Anglais, depuis notre reddition, qu'ils commençoient à manquer de munitions de guerre, & que la poudre étoit encore plus rare dans leur armée que parmi nous. Ils avoient même tenu quelques Conseils pour lever le Siége. La poudre trouvée dans le Vigilant fit bientôt évanouir cette idée; nous nous apperçumes que leur feu avoit depuis beaucoup augmenté.

"Je sçai que le Commandant de cet infortuné Vaisseau dira, pour se justifier, qu'il étoit important pour lui d'enlever le Corsaire, afin de se régler sur les nouvelles qu'il en auroit appris. Mais cela ne l'excuse point; il sçavoit que Louisbourg étoit bloqué, c'en étoit assez; qu'avoit-il besoin d'en sçavoir davantage? S'il craignoit que les Anglais n'eussent été maîtres de la Place, il étoit aisé de s'en instruire, en envoyant son canot ou sa chaloupe, & sacrifiant quelques hommes pour sa sûreté; la batterie Royale ne devoit point l'inquiéter, nous en aurions agi comme avec le Navire Basque, dont nous facilitâmes l'entrée par un feu excessif. La perte d'un secours si considerable ralentit le courage de ceux qui avoient le plus conservé de fermeté; il n'étoit pas difficile de juger que nous serions contraints d'implorer la clémence des Anglais, & plusieurs personnes furent d'avis qu'il falloit dès-lors demander à capituler. Nous avons cependant tenu un mois au-delà; c'est plus qu'on n'auroit pu exiger dans l'abbatement où venoit de nous jetter un si triste spectacle.

"L'Ennemi s'occupa à nous canoner & à nous bombarder toute le reste du mois, sans faire des progrès bien sensibles, & qui lui pussent donner de l'espoir. Comme il ne nous atta-

quoit point dans les formes; qu'il n'avoit pratiqué aucuns retranchemens pour se couvrir, il n'osoit s'aprocher de trop
près; tous nos coups portoient; au lieu que la plûpart des
siens étoient perdus: aussi ne tirons-nous que lorsque nous le
jugions nécessaire. Il tiroit, lui, plus de cinq à six cens coups
de canon par jour, contre nous vingt; à la verité, le peu de
poudre que nous avions, obligeoit à n'en user que sobrement.
La mousqueterie étoit peu d'usage.

"J'ai oublié de dire que, dès les premiers jours du siége, les
ennemis nous avoient fait sommer de nous rendre; mais nous
répondîmes selon ce que le devoir nous prescrivoit; l'Officier,
deputé pour nous en faire la proposition, voyant que nous
rejettions ses offres, proposa de faire sortir les Dames, avec
assurance qu'elles ne seroient point insultées, et qu'on les feroit garder dans les maisons qui subsistoient encore en petit
nombre; car l'ennemi, en débarquant, avoit presque tout
brûlé ou détruit dans la campagne. Nous remerçiâmes cet officier, parceque nos femmes & nos enfans étoient sûrement
dans les logemens que nous leur avions faits. On avoit mis sur
les casemates de longues piéces de bois, placées en biais, qui,
en amortissant le coup de la bombe, la rejettent, & empêchent
l'effet de son poids. C'est là dessous que nous les avions en-
terrés.

"Au commencement de Juin les Assiégeans parurent reprendre une nouvelle vigueur; n'étant pas contens du peu de
succès qu'ils avoient eu jusques-là, ils s'attacherent à d'autres
entreprises, & voulurent essayer de nous attaquer par le côté
de la mer. Pour réussir, ils tenterent de nous surprendre la
batterie de l'entrée: un Détachement d'environ cinq cens
hommes s'y étant transporté pendant la nuit du six au sept,
fut taillé en pièces par le sieur *Daillebout*, Capitaine de Compagnie, qui y commandoit, & qui tira sur eux à mitraille; plus
de trois cens resterent sur la place, & il n'y eut de sauvés que
ceux qui demandoient quartier, les blessés furent transférés
dans nos hôpitaux. Nous fîmes en cette occasion cent dix-neuf
prisonniers, & n'eûmes que trois hommes de tués ou blessés;
mais nous perdîmes un Canonier, qui fut fort regretté. . . .

"Pour sur croit d'infortune, il arrive aux Anglois le 15 une
Escadre de six Vaisseaux de guerre, venant de Londres. Ces
Vaisseaux croiserent devant la Ville, avec les Frégattes sans

tirer un seul coup. Mais nous avons sçu depuis que, si nous eussions tarder à capituler, tous les Vaisseaux se seroient embossés, et nous auroient fait essuyer le feu le plus vif. Leurs dispositions n'ont point eté ignorée, je rapporterai l'ordre qu'ils devoient tenir.

"Les ennemis ne s'étoient encore point avisés de tirer à boulets rouges; ils le firent le dix-huit & le dix-neuf, avec un succès qui auroit eté plus grand, sans le prompt secours qui y fut apporté. Le feu prit à trois ou quatre maisons, mais on l'eut bientôt éteint. La promptitude en ces sortes d'occasions, est la seul ressource que l'on puisse avoir.

"L'Arrivée de l'Escadre étoit, sans doute, l'objet de ce nouveau salut de la part de l'Armée de terre; son Général qui vouloit avoir l'honneur de notre conquête, étant bien aisé de nous forcer à nous soumettre avant que l'Escadre se fût mise en devoir de nous y contraindre.

"L'Amiral de son côté songeoit à se procurer l'honneur de nous reduire. Un Officier vint pour cet effet, le vingt-un, nous proposer de sa part, que si nous avions à nous rendre, il seroit plus convenable de le faire à lui, qui auroit des égards que nous ne trouverions peut être pas dans le Commandant de terre. Tout cela marquoit peu d'intelligence entre les deux Généraux, & verifie assés la remarque que j'ai ci-devant faite: on n'eut jamais dit en effet que ces troupes fussent de la même Nation & sous l'obéissance du même Prince. Les Anglais sont les seuls peuples capables de ces bizarreries, qui font cependant partie de cette précieuse liberté dont ils se montrent si jaloux.

"Nous répondîmes à l'Officier, par qui l'Amiral Warren nous avoit fait donner cet avis, que nous n'avions point de réponse à lui faire, & que quand nous en serions à cette extrémité, nous verrions le parti qu'il conviendroit d'embrasser. Cette fanfaronade eût fait rire quiconque auroit été témoin de notre embarras en particulier; il ne pouvoit être plus grand: cet Officier dût s'en appercevoir, malgré la bonne contenance que nous affections. Il est difficile que le visage ne décéle les mouvements du cœur. Les Conseils étoient plus frequens que jamais, mais non plus salutaires; on s'assembloit sans trop sçavoir pourquoi, aussi ne sçavoit-on que résoudre. J'ai souvent ri de ces assemblées, où il ne se passoit rien que de ridicule,

& qui n'annonçat le trouble & l'indécision. Le soin de notre défense n'étoit plus ce qui occupoit. Si les Anglois eussent sçu profiter de notre épouvante il y auroit eu longtems qu'ils nous auroient emportés, l'épée en main. Mais il faut convenir à leur louange, qu'ils avoient autant de peur que nous. Cela m'a plusieurs fois rappellé la fable du Liévre & des Grenouilles.

"Le but de nos frequens Conseils étoit de dresser des articles de capitulation. On y employa jusqu'au vingt sept, que le sieur Lopinot, Officier, sortit pour les porter au Commandant de terre. L'on se flatoit de les lui faire mieux goûter qu'à l'Amiral. Mais ils étoient si extraordinaires, que malgré l'envie que ce Général avoit de nous voir rendre à lui, il se donna à peine la patience de les écouter. Je me souviens que nous demandions par un article, cinq piéces de canon, & deux mortiers de fonte. De pareilles propositions ne quadroient guéres avec notre situation.

"Afin de réussir d'un côté ou d'autre, on envoya proposer les mêmes conditions à l'Amiral. Cette négociation avoit été confiée au sieur *Bonaventure*, Capitaine de Compagnie, qui s'intrigua beaucoup auprès de M. Warren, & qui, quoique la plûpart de nos articles fussent rejettez, en obtint pourtant d'assés honorables. On arrêta donc la Capitulation telle que les nouvelles publiques l'ont raportée. Elle nous fut annoncée par deux coups de canon tirés à bord de l'Amiral, ainsi qu'on en avoit donné l'ordre au Sieur *Bonaventure*. A cette nouvelle, nous reprimes un peu de tranquillité; car nous avions sujet d'apprehender le sort le plus triste. Nous craignons à tout moment, que les ennemis, sortant de leur aveuglement, ne se présentassent pour nous enlever d'assaut. Tout les y convioit; il y avoit deux bréches de la longueur d'environ cinquante pieds chacune, l'une à la porte Dauphine, & l'autre à l'Eperon, qui est vis-à-vis. Ils nous ont dit depuis que la resolution en avoit été prise, & l'exécution renvoyée au lendemain. Les Navires devoient les favoriser, & s'embosser de la maniere suivante.

"Quatre Vaisseaux & quatre Frégattes étoient destinés pour le bastion Dauphin: un egal nombre de Vaisseaux & de Frégattes, parmi lesquels étoit le Vigilant, devoit attaquer la piéce de la Grave: & trois autres Vaisseaux & autant de Frégattes avoient ordre de s'attacher à l'Isle de l'entree. Nous n'eussions jamais pû repondre au feu de tous ces Vaisseaux & défendre en même tems nos brêches; de façon qu'il auroit fallu succomber, quelques efforts que nous eussions pû faire, & nous voir réduits à recourir à la clémence d'un vainqueur, de la générosité duquel il y avoit à se défier. L'Armée de terre n'étoit composée que de gens ramassés, sans subordination ni discipline, qui nous auroit fait éprouver tout ce que l'insolence & la rage ont de plus furieux. La capitulation n'a point empêché qu'ils ne nous ayent bien fait du mal.

"C'est donc par une protection visible de la Providence, que nous avons prévenu une journée qui nous auroit été si funeste. Ce qui nous y a le plus déterminé, est le peu de poudre qui nous restoit: je puis assurer que nous n'en avions pas pour faire trois décharges. C'est ici le point critique & sur lequel on cherche le plus à en imposer au public mal instruit: on voudroit lui persuader qu'il nous en restoit encore vingt milliers. Fausseté insigne! Je n'ai aucune interêt à déguiser la vérité; on doit d'autant plus m'en croire, que je ne prétends pas par-là justifier entierement nos Officiers. S'ils n'ont pas capitulé trop tôt ils avoient commis assez d'autres fautes, pour ne les pas laver du blâme qu'ils ont encouru. Il est constant que nous n'avions plus que trent-sept barils de poudre, à cent livres chacun; voilà ce qui est veritable, & non pas tout ce qu'on raconte de contraire. Nous n'en trouvions même d'abord que trente-cinq; mais les recherches qu'on fit nous en procurerent deux autres, cachés apparemment par les Canoniers, qu'on sçait être partout accoutumés à ce larcin."

II

"Lettre de Monsieur Du Chambon au Ministre, à Rochefort, le 2 Septembre, 1745. *Archives de la Marine.*

"Monseigneur.

"J'ai l'honneur de vous rendre compte de l'attaque et reddition de Louisbourg, ainsy que vous me l'avez ordonné par votre lettre du 20 de ce mois.

"Nous eûmes connaissance d'un battiment le quatorze mars dernier parmy les glaces qui étaient détachées du golfe; ce battiment parut à 3 ou 4 lieues devant le port et drivait vers la partie du sud-ouest, et il nous disparut l'après-midi.

"Le 19 du d. nous vîmes encore en dehors les glaces un senaux qui couroit le long de la banquise qui était etendue depuis Escartary jusques au St Esprit, plusieurs chasseurs et soldats, hivernant dans le bois, m'informèrent qu'ils avaient vu, les uns deux battiments qui avoient viré de bord à Menadou, et d'autres qu'ils avoient entendu du canon du côté du St Esprit, ce qui fit que j'ordonnai aux habitans des ports de l'isle, qui étaient à portée de la ville, de se renger aux signaux qui leur seroient faits.

"Je fis en outre rassembler les habitans de la ville et port de Louisbourg, je formai de ceux de la ville quatre compagnies, et je donnai ordre à ceux du port de se renger à la batterie Royale, et à celle de l'isle de l'entrée, au signaux que je leur fit donner.

"Le 9 avril nous aperçûmes à l'éclaircy de la brume, et parmi les glaces vers la Pointe Blanche, quatre battimens, le premier ayant tiré quelques coups de canon, l'islot lui répondit d'un coup, et le battiment l'ayant rendu sur le champ, cela nous confirma dans l'idée que c'étoient des François qui cherchoient à forcer les glaces pour entrer dans le port. D'ailleurs ils profitoient des éclaircis pour s'y enfourner vers le port, et cela nous assuroit pour ainsi dire, que ce n'étoit pas des corsaires, mais bien des François.

"Etant dans le doute si c'étoit des basttiments François ou Anglois, j'envoyai ordre à Monsieur Benoit, officier commandant au port Toulouse, de dettacher quelqu'un de confiance à Canceau, pour apprendre s'il y avoit des basttiments, et si on y travailloit, ou s'il y avoit apparance de quelque entreprise sur l'isle Royale.

"Monsieur Benoit dettacha le nommé Jacob Coste, habitant, avec un soldat de la garnison et un Sauvage, pour faire quelques prisonniers au dit lieu. Ces trois envoyés mirent pied à terre à la Grande Terre du costé de Canceau; ils eurent le bonheur de faire quatre prisonniers anglois; et revenant avec eux, les prisonniers se rendirent maitres de nos trois François, un soir qu'ils étaient endormis, et nous n'avons pu apprendre aucune nouvelle ni des envoyés ni de l'ennemy.

"Je fus informé, le 22, par deux hommes, venus par terre du port de Toulouse, qu'on entendait tirer du canon à Canceau, et qu'ils travailloient au rétablissement de cette isle, et un troisième arrivé le soir, m'assura avoir été témoin d'un grand combat sur le navire *St-Esprit*, qu'il avoit vu venir du large trois vaisseaux sur quatre qui étoient pour lors à cette coste, et que le feu ayant commencé après la Jonction de ces bastimens, il avoit duré bien avant dans la nuit, ce qui nous engageoit à nous flatter que nous avions des vaisseaux sur la coste.

"Le 30 du d. nous vîmes sept vaisseaux parmy les glaces, dont il y avoit quatre vaisseaux, deux corvettes et un brigantin, et ils se sont tenus ce jour vers les isles à Dion, sans pavillon, ni flamme.

"Ces battiments continuèrent à se faire voir pendant quelques jours, depuis la Pointe Blanche jusques à Port de Noue, sous pavillon blanc, et les glaces s'étant écartées de la coste, nous apperçûmes, le 7 mai, un navire qui faisait route pour le port; il y entra heureusement; ce navire venoit de St Jean de Luz, commandé par le Sieur Janson Dufoure; il nous apprit qu'il avoit été poursuivi la veille par trois vaisseaux, qu'une frégatte de 24 canons l'avoit joint, et qu'il s'estoit sauvé, après un combat de trois volées de canon et de mousquetterie.

"Le 8 à la pointe du jour, nous eûmes connaissance de tous les vaisseaux au vent du port dans la partie du sud-ouest, ce qui nous occasionna une alerte, les signaux ayant été faits, les habitans de Lorembec et de la Baleine, qui étoient les plus proches de la ville, s'y rangèrent aux postes qui leur étoient destinés, ainsi que les habitans de la ville et du port, le même jour ces vaisseaux prirent à notre vue deux caboteurs frettés par le Roy et qui venoient du port de Toulouse chargés de bois de corde pour le chauffage des troupes et des corps de garde, ils prirent aussy une chaloupe qui venoit des Isles Madame chargée de gibier.

"Comme nous doutions toujours si ces vaisseaux étoient anglois ou françois jusqu'à ce jour, les glaces empêchant l'entrée du port depuis qu'ils avoient paru ensemble, j'avois eu la précaution d'arrêter, conjointement avec monsieur Bigot, deux battiments pour les faire partir en cas de nécessité pour la France, pour porter les nouvelles à Sa Grandeur de la situation où se trouvoit la colonie, et sitôt que nous fûmes confirmés par le prise de ces caboteurs que c'étoit des vaisseaux anglois et qu'il y en avoit d'autres à Canceau, au rapport des équipages qui s'étoient sauvés, nous fîmes partir à la faveur de la brume et de la nuit obscure du 10 mai, *La Société*, capitaine Subtil, avec nos lettres pour Monseigneur, pour lui apprendre l'état de la colonie avec les circonstances de vaisseaux qui bloquèrent le port; quand à l'autre bâtiment qui avoit été fretté, nous avons été obligé de la faire couler, après la descente faite par l'ennemy, étant impossible de la faire sortir.

"Les vaisseaux ennemis qui étoient au devant du port, se servant de la chaloupe qu'ils avoient prise chargée de gibier pour descendre et mettre pied à terre à Gabarrus, à notre vue, je fis partir, le 9, un détachement de 20 soldats sous le commandement du sieur de Lavallière pour aller par terre à Gabarrus, et un autre de 39 hommes d'habitans, sous le commandement du sieur Daccarrette dans un charroye pour s'emparer de cette chaloupe, mais ces deux détachements ne purent joindre cette chaloupe; celui de terre y resta deux jours et ne rentra en ville que le onze du soir, et celui du sieur Daccarrette rentra le 12 au matin, ayant été obligé d'abandonner le charroye à fourché où il avoit été à la sortie de Gabarrus.

"Le 11, à trois ou quatre heures du matin, nous eûmes connoissance de dessus les remparts de la ville, d'environ 100 voiles qui parurent du côté de fourché, derrière les isles à Dion, les vents étant de la partie de nord-ouest, ces battiments s'approchoient à vue d'œil, je ne doute pas que ce ne fussent des bastiments de transport, je fis tirer les signaux qui avoient été ordonnés, plusieurs habitans et particuliers n'ont pu s'y rendre, et entr'autres ceux des havres éloignés, la campagne étant investie de l'ennemy, et même plusieurs ont été faits prisonniers voulant se rendre en ville.

"Je fis aussy commander un détachement pour s'opposer à la descente de l'ennemy, et ce détachement au nombre de 80 hommes et 30 soldats, le surplus habitans, partit sous le commandement de Monsieur Morpain et du Sieur Mesilac, il se transporta au-dessous de la Pointe Blanche, â l'endroit où l'ennemy avoit commencé à faire sa descente, il le fit rembarquer dans les voitures, mais pendant le temps qu'il étoit en cet endroit à repousser l'ennemy, celui-cy fit faire une autre descente plus considérable de troupes de débarquement à l'anse de la Cormorandière, entre la Pointe-Plate et Gabarrus.

"Il s'y transporta avec ses troupes, sitôt qu'il en eût connoissance, mais l'ennemy avoit mis pied à terre et s'étoit emparé des lieux les plus propres qu'il jugea pour sa défense, cela n'empêcha pas ce détachement d'aller l'attaquer, mais l'ennemy étant beaucoup plus supérieur en nombre, il fut contraint de se retirer dans le bois; nous avons eu à cette occasion 4 ou 5 soldats tués ou faits prisonniers, ainsy que 4 ou 5 habitans ou particuliers du nombre desquels fut Monsieur Laboularderie; nous eûmes encore 3 ou 4 blessés qui rentrèrent en ville.

"Depuis la retraite de ce détachement l'ennemy acheva son débarquement au nombre de 4 à 500 hommes, ainsy que des planches et autres matériaux, au rapport de ceux du détachement qui rentrèrent les derniers en ville.

"L'ennemy ayant avancé dans la campagne, se fit voir en grand nombre, mais sans ordre, à la portée du canon de la pointe Dauphine et du bastion du Roy.

"Les montagnes qui commandent cette porte étoient couvertes de monde: à deux heures après-midi les canons, qui étoient sur la Barbette, tirèrent sur plusieurs pelotons qui paroissoient défiler du côté du fond de la baye, nous nous aperçûmes aussy qu'ils défiloient en quantité le long du bois vers la batterie royale, je fis fermer les portes et je fis pourvoir sur le champ à la sûreté de la ville et placer environ 1100 hommes qui s'y sont trouvés pour la défendre.

"Sur le soir, monsieur Thiery, capitaine de compagnie qui commandoit à la batterie royale, m'écrivit une lettre par laquelle il me marquoit le mauvois état de son poste, que cela pourroit donner de grande facilités à l'ennemy s'il s'en emparoit, qu'il croyoit pour le bien du service qu'il seroit à propos de travailler à le faire sauter après avoir encloué les canons.

"Je fis à cette occasion assembler le conseil de guerre, monsieur Verrier, ingénieur en chef, ayant aussi été appelé, fit son rapport que cette batterie avoit ses épaulements du costé de la terre démolis dès l'année dernière, que les chemins couverts n'étoient pas palissadés, et qu'il étoit hors d'état de résister à une attaque par terre de trois à quatre mille homme avec 400 hommes qu'il y avoit dedans pour la défense.

"Sur ce rapport le conseil de guerre décida unanimement qu'il convenoit pour la sûreté de la ville, manquant de monde pour la défendre, de l'abandonner après en avoir encloué les canons et enlevé le plus de munitions de guerre et de bouche qu'on pourroit.

"Je ne dois pas oublier de vous informer que le même conseil de guerre vouloit faire sauter cette batterie; mais que monsieur Verrier, s'y étant opposé fortement, on la laissa subsister.

"J'envoyai l'ordre en conséquence à monsieur Thiery pour abandonner la dite batterie, après qu'il auroit encloué les canons, et enlevé le plus de munitions de guerre et de bouche qu'il pourroit; cet officier travailla le soir à faire enclouer tous les canons; il fit transporter partie des vivres et des munitions et se retira à la ville avec sa troupe vers minuit.

"La dite batterie n'ayant pas été entiérement évacuée ce soir, je fis partir le lendemain les Sieurs St. Etienne, lieutenant, et Souvigny, enseigne, avec une vingtaine d'hommes pour parachever la dite évacuation, ce qu'ils firent à l'exception de tous les boulets de canon et bombes qui y sont restés, n'ayant pas pu les emporter.

"Ayant jugé nécessaire conjointement avec monsieur Bigot de faire couler tous les bastiments qui étoient armés dans le port, pour empêcher l'ennemy de s'en emparer, je commandai, le 12, le sieur Verger, enseigne, avec 5 soldats et des matelots pour faire couler ceux qui etoient vis-à-vis la ville, et le sieur Bellemont, enseigne, avec la même opération au fond de la baye, et retirer l'huile de la tour de la lanterne, ce qu'ils exécutèrent.

"Le 13, je fis sortir toutes les compagnies de milice avec des haches et des engins pour démolir les maisons qui étoient à la porte Dauphine jusqu'au Barruchois, et pour enlever le bois en ville pour le chauffage de la garnison, n'en ayant pas, et pour faire brûler toutes celles qu'on ne pourroit pas démolir, afin d'empêcher l'ennemy de s'y loger.

"Je fis soutenir ces travailleurs par 80 soldats François et Suisses commandé par monsieur Deganne, capitaine, et Rasser, officier Suisse.

"Comme ils finissaient et qu'ils étoient au moment de se retirer en ville, il parut au Barruchois et dans les vallons des hauteurs plusieurs pelotons de l'armée ennemie, il y eût même quelques coups de fusils de tirés par ceux qui étoient les plus près; nous n'eûmes personne de tué ni de blessé, et nos gens virent tomber deux hommes de l'ennemy.

"L'ennemy s'est emparé de la batterie Royale, le 13, et le lendemain il tira sur la ville plusieurs coups de canon de deux qu'il avoit désencloué.

"Le même jour l'ennemy commença aussi à nous tirer plusieurs bombes de 12 pouches, pesant 180 l. et de 9 pouces d'une batterie de quatre mortiers qu'il avoient estably sur la hauteur derrière les plaines, vis-à-vis le bastion du Roy.

"Cette batterie de mortiers n'a pas cessé de tirer de distance en distance, ainsi que douze mortiers à grenades royales que l'ennemy y avoit placés, et deux autres canons qu'ils ont désencloués à la batterie royale, mais ce feu n'a fait aucun progrès jusqu'au 18, et n'a tué ni blessé personne.

"Le 16, je fis partir un exprès en chaloupe pour porter une lettre à monsieur Marin, officier de Canada, qui commandoit un détachement de Canadiens et des Sauvages à l'Acadie, avec ordre de partir pour se rendre en toute diligence à Louisbourg, avec son détachement; c'étoit une course de 20 à 25 jours au plus, s'il avoit été aux mines, ainsi que l'on m'avoit assuré; mais ce detachement étoit parti pour le port Royal lorsque l'exprès y arriva.

"Cet exprès fut obligé d'y aller: il lui remit la lettre dont il étoit chargé, il tint conseil, plusieurs de son party ne voulurent pas le suivre, mais lui s'étant mis en chemin avec ceux de bonne volonté qui voulurent le suivre, il eût toutes les peines imaginables, à ce qu'on m'a assuré, de trouver des voitures dans toute l'Acadie, propres pour son transport.

"Ils s'y embarquèrent environ 3 à 400 dans un bateau de 25 tonneaux et dans environ une centaine de canots. Comme ils étoient dans la baie à doubler une pointe, ils furent attaqués par un bateau corsaire de 14 canons et autant de pierriers; cet officier soutint l'attaque avec vigueur, et dans le temps qu'il étoit au moment d'aborder le corsaire pour l'enlever, un autre corsaire de la même force vint au secours de son camarade, ce qui obligea le dit Sieur Marin d'abandonner la partie et de faire côte.

"Cette rencontre lui a fait perdre plusieurs jours et il n'a pu se rendre sur les terres de l'Isle Royale qu'au commencement de juillet, après que Louisbourg a été rendu; si ce détachement s'étoit rendu quinze ou vingt jours avant la reddition de la ville, je suis plus que persuadé que l'ennemy auroit été contraint de lever le siège de terre, par la terreur qu'il avoit de ce détachement qu'il pensoit être au nombre de plus de 2500.

"Je dois aussi informer Sa Grandeur que ce détachement a tué et pris, comme il se retiroit du passage de Fronsac, pour aller à l'Acadie, après notre départ, treize hommes d'un corsaire anglois qui étoit à leur passage pour les empêcher de passer, ces hommes ayant été avec leurs canots pour faire de l'eau, ils sont tombés entre les mains de ceux de ce détachement.

"Le 18, messieurs les généraux anglois me sommèrent de rendre la ville, forteresses et terres en dépendant, avec l'artillerie, les armes et les munitions de guerre qui en dépendent sous l'obéissance de la Grande Bretagne, en conséquence de quoy, promettoient de traiter humainement tous les sujets du Roy mon maître qui y étoient dedans, que leurs biens leur seroient assurés, et qu'ils auraient la liberté de se transporter avec leurs effets dans quelque partie de la domination du Roy de France, en Europe, qu'ils jugeroit à propos.

"Je répondis sur le champ à cette sommation que le Roy mon maître m'ayant confié la défense de la place, je ne pouvois qu'après la plus rigoureuse attaque écouter une semblable proposition, et que je n'avois d'autre réponse à faire à cette demande que par les bouches des canons.

"L'ennemy commença à établir, le 19, une batterie de sept pièces de canon dans les plaines et derrière un petit étang, vis-à-vis la face du bastion du Roy, laquelle batterie n'a pas cessé de tirer des boulets de 12, 18 et 24 depuis ce jour jusqu'à la reddition de la place, sur le casernes, le mur du bastion du Roy et sur la ville; cette batterie étoit, Monseigneur, la plus dangereuse de l'ennemy pour détruire le monde; tous les boulets enfiloient toutes les rues jusqu'à la porte Maurepas et au mur crénelé; personne ne pouvoit rester dans la ville, soit dans les maisons ou dans les rues.

"Aussy pour éteindre le feu de l'ennemy, je fis établir deux pièces de canon de 18 sur le cavalier du dit Bastion du Roy: on fit pour cet effet deux coffres en planches qu'on remplit de fascines et de terres qui formoient deux embrasures par le moyen desquelles les canonniers et ceux qui servirent ces canons étoient à l'abry du feu de l'ennemy.

"Je fis aussy percer en même temps deux embrasures au mur du parapet de la face droite du dit bastion; on y mit deux autre canons de 24.

"Ces quatre canons ont été si bien servis que le feu de l'ennemy de la dite batterie de la plaine a été éteint, puis-qu'ils ne tiroient lors de la reddition de la place qu'un canon, et qu'ils ont eu les autres démontés à la dite batterie, ainsy que ceux de nos gens qui ont été voir cette batterie, après la reddition de la place, m'en ont rendu compte.

"Le matin du 20, je fis assembler messieurs les capitaines des compagnies pour prendre un party s'il convenoit de faire des sorties sur l'ennemy. Il fut résolu que la ville étoit entièrement dénuée de monde, qu'il étoit préjudiciable d'en faire, qu'à peine on pourroit garder les remparts avec les 1300 hommes qu'il y avoit dans la ville y compris les deux cent de la batterie royale.

"Je fis masquer la porte Dauphine en pierre de taille, fascines et terre de l'épaisseur d'environ dix-huit pieds, ainsi que les deux corps de garde qui sont joints. Sans cet ouvrage l'ennemy auroit pu entrer en ville dés le lendemain qu'il auroit tiré de la batterie de Francœur; cette porte n'etoit pas plus forte que celle d'une porte cochère, les murs de la dite porte et des corps de garde n'avoient que trois pieds ou environ d'épaisseur. La dite porte n'étoit pas non plus flanquée et n'avoit pour toute défense que quelques créneaux aux corps de garde, desquels on ne pouvoit plus se servir sitôt qu'on étoit obligé de garnir les dits corps de garde de pierres, de terre.

"J'ordonnai qu'on fit des embrasures de gazon et de terre, n'ayant pas le temps d'en faire de pierre, aux quatre canons qui étoient sur la batterie du bastion Dauphin, sur le corps de garde des soldats, joignant la porte du dit bastion, afin d'empêcher l'ennemy en ses travaux sur les hauteurs qui étoient devant la dite porte; lesquelles embrasures furent faites.

"Tous les flancs des bastions de la ville furent aussy garnis des canons des corsaires et autres qui se sont trouvés en ville.

"L'ennemy ayant calfeutré une goelette qui étoit échouée au fond de la baye depuis l'année dernière, il l'a remplit de bois, goudron et autres matières combustibles, et à la faveur d'une nuit obscure et d'un vent frais du nord-nord-est qu'il fit le 24, il nous l'envoya en brûlot sur la ville.

"Tout le monde passoit toutes les nuits sur les remparts, nous attendions de pied ferme l'ennemy, plustôt que des artifices de cette nature, et ce brûlot ayant été s'échouer au dehors de la ville vis-à-vis du terrain du Sr Ste Marie ne fit pas l'effet que l'ennemy s'attendoit.

"L'ennemy s'étant emparé de la hauteur de Francœur qui est à la queue du glacis de la porte Dauphine, il a commencé à ouvrir des boyaux et former deux batteries malgré le feu continuel de nos canons de la barbette et du bastion Dauphin et du flanc droit du bastion du Roy et de la mousqueterie, et ces deux batteries n'ont point cessé de tirer depuis le 29 jusqu'à la reddition de la place des boulets de 18, 24, 36 et 42, pour battre en brèche la porte Dauphine et la flanc droit du bastion du Roy.

"L'ennemy, faisant plusieurs mouvements au fond de la baye et à la hauteur de la Lanterne, monsieur Vallé, lieutenant de la Compagnie des Canonniers, vint m'avertir que l'ennemy pourroit faire ces mouvements à l'occasion de plusieurs canons de dix-huit et de vingt-quatre qui avoient été mis au carénage pour servir de corps de garde depuis environ dix ans. Que parmy ces canons il y en avoit plusieurs en état de servir, qu'il avoit informé les Gouverneurs de cy-devant plusieurs fois que l'ennemy pourroit les transporter à la tour, établir une batterie pour battre l'isle de l'entree et les vaisseaux qui voudroient entrer.

"Sur un avis aussy important, et l'ennemy ayant aboré pavillon à la tour de la Lanterne, je fis faire un détachement de cinq cent jeunes gens du pays et autres de la milice et des flibustiers, sous les ordres du Sieur de Beaubassin, pour aller voir si cela étoit vrai, tâcher de suprendre l'ennemy ou empêcher de faire leurs travaux en cet endroit.

"Ce dêtachement partit en trois chaloupes le 27 may avec chacun douze jours de vivres et les munitions de guerre nécessaires qui leur furent fournies des magasins du Roy; il mit pied à terre au grand Lorembec.

"Le lendemain, faisant son approche à la tour, il fut découvert par l'ennemy qui étoit au nombre d'environ 300.

"Ils se tirèrent quelques volées de mousqueterye, et se séparèrent, ce détachement ne voyant pas son avantage et plusieurs ayant lâché le pied, il fut contraint de se retirer dans le bois, pour brûler s'il lui étoit possible les magasins qu'il y avoit, on l'avoit assuré que cela étoit aisé, que l'ennemy dormoit avec sécurité en cet endroit.

"Koller qui étoit second du dit Sieur de Beaubassin, venant de St. Pierre par terre, quelques jours auparavant, avait été dans une des barraques du dit camp et avoit emporté une chaudière sans être découvert, ce détachement, dis-je, étoit à un demi quart de lieue à l'habitation du dit Koller, il avoit envoyé des découvreurs en attendant la nuit, mais ils eurent le malheur dêtre découverts par une douzaine d'Anglois qui se trouvèrent aux environs, ce qui fit que l'ennemy détacha un party considérable qui fut pour les attaquer. Le sieur de Beaubassin fut encore obligé de se retirer après quelques coups tirés de part et d'autre: l'ennemy, depuis lors cherchoit partout ce détachement, et plusieurs de ceux-ci ayant été obligés de jeter leurs vivres pour se sauver, ils étoient sans vivres pour passer leur douze jours, et plusieurs qui étoient des havres voisins l'avoient abandonné et s'étoient retirés chez eux; il se trouvoit par conséquent sans vivres et trop faibles pour résister à l'ennemy.

"Il fut donc obligé d'aller au petit Lorembec pour prendre des chaloupes afin de rentrer dans la ville; il se trouva en ce havre environ 40 Sauvages de la colonie qui avoient détruit, il y avoit deux ou trois jours, 18 à 20 Anglois qu'ils avoient trouvés qui pillaient ce havre.

"Comme ils étaient à même d'embarquer dans les chaloupes, il leur tomba un détachement de 2 à 300 Anglois. Les Sauvages se joignèrent à ce détachement et ces deux corps faisaient environ 120 hommes qui tinrent pied ferme à l'ennemy.

"Le feu commença de part et d'autre vers les deux heures et dura pendant plus de quatre, les Anglois avoient même été repoussés deux fois et ils auroient été défaits si dès le commencement de l'action, ceux-ci n'avoient pas envoyé avertir de leurs gens qui étoient à la batterie royale et à la tour et s'il ne leur étoit pas venu à l'entrée de la nuit un party considérable qui commença à vouloir l'entourer.

"Notre détachement voyant qu'il n'y avoit pas moyen de

résister et manquant de munitions, plusieurs ayant tiré jusqu'à leur dernier coup, il se retira dans les bois, l'ennemy, supérieur comme il étoit, les poursuivit une partie de la nuit, notre detachement fut contraint de se retirer à Miré et de passer la rivière.

"Nous avons eu en cette occasion deux hommes de tués et environ 20 de blessés ou prisonniers. Monsieur de Beaubassin fut du nombre des blessés, il reçut une balle au gras de la jambre et après une heure et demie de combat, ne pouvant résister à sa blessure, il se retira. Le sieur Koller continua le combat jusqu'à la fin.

"Le dit sieur de Beaubassin, s'étant rendu en ville quelques jours après sixième dans une pirogue, m'informa de ce qui s'étoit passé à l'occasion de son détachement, que le surplus étoit refugié à Miré où il l'avait laissé sous la conduite de Koller, qu'il lui manquoit des vivres et des munitions de guerre ainsy qu'aux Sauvages.

"Sur ce rapport je fis partir une chaloupe avec 20 quarts de farine et autres vivres et des munitions, tant pour ce détachement, celui de monsieur Marin que j'attendois tous les jours, que pour les Sauvages.

"On trouva Koller avec ses gens, monsieur Marin n'y étoit pas et les Sauvages s'étoient retirés à leur village.

"Koller rentra en ville le 14 juin en chaloupe avec ceux de son détachement et les quelques autres qu'il trouva à Miré, il eût bien de la peine à passer la nuit parmy bâtiments de l'ennemy qui croisoient depuis Gabarrus jusqu'à Escatary.

"Nous avons appris depuis la reddition de la place, par des personnes de probité, que l'ennemy avoit eu au moins 150 homme de tués, et 90 de blessés au choc du petit Lorembec.

"Les canons de la porte Dauphin et ceux du flanc droit du Bastion du Roy, ne joignant pas bien la batterie que l'ennemy avoit fait sur les hauteurs de Francœur à la porte Dauphine, on perça trois embrâsures à la courtine de la grave pour battre à revers la batterie de l'ennemy de la hauteur de Francœur. Ces trois embrâsures où on avoit placé du canon de 36 furent ouvertes les 30 mai, et firent un effet merveilleux; le premier jour on leur démonta un de leurs canons, et leurs embrâsures furent toutes labourées, cela n'empêcha pas le feu continuel de l'ennemy, et quant à la batterie ce que nous défaisions le jour, ils le refaisoit la nuit.

"Le même jour, sur les trois heurs, nous eûmes connoissance d'un gros vaisseau qui donnoit chasse à un senau et ensuite qui se battoit avec le dit senau et une frégatte à environ 4 lieues du fort vers le sud-est, en même tems trois vaisseaux ennemis, qui étoient en passe vers le Cap Noir et la pointe Blanche, coururent dessus; le gros vaisseau après s'être battu longtems prit la chasse sans doute quand il eut connoissance des trois qui courroient sur lui, et nous avons entendu tirer du canon jusque vers les 9 à 10 heures du soir, nous avons appris depuis que ce vaisseau étoit le *Vigilant*.

"J'ordonnai qu'on tirât de la poudrière du Bastion Dauphin les poudres qui y étoient et les fis transporter sous la poterne de la courtine qui est entre le Bastion du Roy et celui de la Reine.

"Comme l'ennemy avait coupé par les boulets de la batterie de Francœur, les chaines du pont levi de la porte Dauphine, j'ordonnay aussy de couper le pont de la dite porte.

"Le canon de l'ennemy de la batterie de Francœur qui battoit le flanc droit du bastion du Roy, faisant beaucoup de progrès et entr'autres aux embrasures, je fis commencer à faire percer le mur de la face du bastion Dauphin de deux embrasures, pour y mettre deux canons, cet ouvrage malgré la mousqueterie que l'ennemy tiroit toujours, fut mis en état et notre canon a tiré et fut servi autant qu'on pouvoit désirer sur celui de l'ennemy.

"L'ennemy a aussi étably une batterie de cinq canons sur les hauteurs des Mortissans et a commencé à tirer le 2 juin des boulets de 36 et 42, en brèche sur le bastion Dauphin et sur l'éperon. La guérite a été jetée à bas, et une partie de l'angle saillant, le même jour. Cette batterie a déboulé l'éperon de la porte Dauphine en ses embrasures, lesquelles ont été racommodées plusieurs fois, autant bien qu'on pouvoit, à pierre sèche, avec des pierres de taille et des sacs de terre.

"Le même jour l'escadre ennemye s'augmenta par l'arrivée d'un vaisseau d'environ 40 à 50 canons, et nous vismes aussy, parmy cette escadre, un vaisseau désemparé, qu'on nous a dit depuis être celui que nous avions vu se battre le 30 may.

"Le 5 l'ennemy a envoyé vers les deux heures du matin de

la batterie royale, un brulot qui s'est échoué à la calle Frédéric
où il a brûlé sur une göelette, il n'a pas fait d'autre mal, quoiqu'il fut chargé de matières combustibles et de bombes qui
firent leur effet; toutes les batteries de l'ennemy ne cessèrent
point de tirer, pendant ce temps nos gens étoient comme de
coutume tout le long des remparts et du quay, à essuyer ce
feu avec intrépidité.

"La nuit du 6 au 7 nous eumes une alarme générale de l'isle
de l'entrée; l'ennemy, voulant enlever cette batterie, s'embar-
qua au nombre de 1000 sur 35 barques, 800 autres venant derrière devoient les soutenir. La nuit étoit très obscure et faisoit
une petite brume.

"Ces premiers furent mettre pied à terre, les uns à la Pointe
à Peletier, les autres vis-à-vis le corps des casernes, et le surplus au débarquement de la dite isle; l'ennemy en debarquant
commença à crier *hourrah* par trois fois; ils attachèrent même
environ 12 échelles aux embrasures afin de les escalader, mais
Monsieur D'Aillebout, qui commandoit à cette batterie, les
reçut à merveille; le canon et la mousqueterie de ceux de l'isle
fut servi au mieux, toutes les barques, furent toutes brisées ou
coulées à fond; le feu fut continuel depuis environ minuit
jusqu'à trois heures du matin.

"Le dit S D'Ailleboust ainsy que les Srs Duchambon, son
Lieutenant, et Eurry de la Perrelle, son enseigne, étoient les
premiers à monter sur les embrasures et faire feu sur les ennemis pour montrer à leurs soldats l'exemple, et aux autres
qui étoient avec eux à la dite batterie.

"Les soldats firent même plusieurs fois descendre leurs officiers des embrasures, leur alléguant qu'ils ne devoient point
ainsi s'exposer, qu'ils n'avoient qu'à les commander et qu'ils
en viendroient à bout; à la fin l'ennemy fut contraint de demander quartier. Les huit cents qui devoient soutenir les premiers n'osèrent pas s'approcher et s'en furent: on fit 119
prisonniers, plusieurs blessés sont morts la même journée, et
l'ennemy a eu plus de 250 de tués, noyés ou de blessés, ne
s'étant sauvés, au rapport de nos prisonniers qui étoient à la
batterie royale, que dans deux barges qui pouvoient contenir
environ 30 hommes, parmy lesquels il y avoit plusieurs de
blessés.

"L'ennemy pouvant attaquer la ville avec des barges par le

quay, j'ordonnay une estacade de mâts qui prenoit depuis l'eperon du bastion Dauphin jusques à la pièce de grave, et cette estacade a été parachevée le 11 juin. L'ennemy qui s'étoit aperçu de cet ouvrage, n'a pas cessé de tirer des canons de ses batteries, sur les travaillants, mais inutilement.

"Les ennemis ayant toujours continué leurs travaux à la tour de la Lanterne, malgré le feu continuel de bombes et de canons de la batterie de l'isle de L'entrée, il fut décidé qu'il étoit nécessaire de blinder les casernes et la boulangerie de la dite isle, et le bois manquant pour cet ouvrage le magasin du Sieur Dacarrette fut démoli pour cela.

"Le feu continuel des batteries de l'ennemy ayant démoly les embrasures du flanc droit du bastion du Roy, où nous avions six canons de dix-huit et de vingt-quatre qui tiroient continuellement, et ces canons ne pouvant pas être servis, j'ordonnay qu'on fit aussy des contremerlons et des embrasures en bois, à quoi on y travailla avec toute la diligence possible, et ces embrasures étant parachevées le 19 juin, le canon tira toujours; mais ces mêmes embrasures n'ont pas laissé d'être démantibulées aussy par le canon de l'ennemy.

"Depuis que la batterie de martissan a été établie, elle n'a pas cessé de tirer en brèche sur la porte Dauphin et sur l'éperon. L'éperon a été tout démantibulé et racommodée plusieurs fois, ainsy que je l'ai dit ci-devant; les embrasures qui battent le long du quay ont aussy été démantelées, par cette batterie et celle de Francœur, et personne ne pouvoit rester derrière le mur du quay qui a été tout criblé, les boulets de 24, 36 et 42 le perçant d'outre en outre.

"Le 18, messieurs les généraux anglois m'envoyèrent un officier avec pavillon, portant une lettre de monsieur Warren chef de l'escadre et une autre de Monsieur de la Maisonfort, capitaine de vaisseau. Par la première ce général se plaignait des cruautés que nos François et Sauvages avoient exerceés sur ceux de sa nation, et que si, à l'avenir, pareille chose arrivoit, il ne pourroit pas empêcher ses gens d'en agir de même.

"Monsieur de la Maisonfort m'apprenoit sa prise, le 30 mai, et qu'il avoit tout lieu d'être satisfait du traitement qu'on lui faisoit, ainsy qu'à ses officiers et matelots, et de punir sévèrement, etc.

"Je répondis à celle de monsieur Warren qu'il n'y avoit

point de François parmy les Sauvages qui avoient usé ainsi qu'il disoit de cruauté, comme de fait il n'y en avoit pas, qu'il devoit être persuadé que je négligeray rien pour arrêter le cours des cruautés des Sauvages autant qu'il me seroit possible de communiquer avec eux, etc.

"A celle de monsieur de la Maisonfort, que je ferai défendre aux Sauvages, lorsque je pourrai avoir communication avec eux, d'en user mieux [*sic*] par la suite, qu'il n'y avoit aucun des François avec eux lorsqu'ils ont usé de cruautés, etc., et l'officier porteur de ces lettres partit sur le champ.

"Le 21, la batterie que les ennemis ont établie à la tour de la Lanterne de 7 canons et un mortier a commencé à tirer sur celle de l'isle de L'entrée avec des boulets de 18 et un mortier de 12 pouces, pesant 180 l. et le feu de la dite batterie n'a pas cessé de tirer jusqu'à la reddition de la place, malgré le feu continuel de celle de l'isle.

"Les batteries de l'ennemy faisant un progrès considérable, malgré notre feu des canons du bastion du Roy, bastion Dauphin, de la pièce de la grave, et de la mousqueterie à la brèche de la porte Dauphine et aux corps de garde joignants, j'ordonnai à Monsieur Verrier, ingénieur, de faire un retranchement dans le bastion Dauphin pour défendre l'assaut que l'ennemy pourrait donner par la brèche. Cet ouvrage qui prenoit depuis le quay jusqu'au parapet de la face du bastion Dauphin, fut mis en état le 24 après bien des travaux de nuit.

"Il se fit le même jour une jonction de 4 vaisseaux, dont deux de 60, un de 50 et l'autre de 40 canons, avec ceux qui bloquoient le port. Ces vaisseaux sitôt qu'ils eurent tiré les signaux de reconnaissance s'assemblèrent et après s'être parlés, ils furent vers la baye de Gabarrus.

"Le lendemain les vaisseaux ennemis au nombre de 13 mouillèrent en ligne vers la Pointe Blanche à environ 2 lieues du port de Louisbourg. L'ennemy fit faire en même temps et le lendemain trois piles de bois pour des signaux sur les hauteurs qui sont à l'ouest du port de Louisbourg.

"Je ne puis pas m'empêcher d'informer Sa Grandeur et de lui dire avec vérité que toutes les batteries de l'ennemy soit de mortier ou de canon n'ont pas cessé de tirer depuis les jours qu'ils les ont établis, de même que la mousqueterie, sans discontinuer, de la batterie de Francœur; que toutes les maisons de la ville ont toutes été écrasées, criblées et mises hors d'état d'être logées; que le flanc du bastion du Roy a été tout démoli, ainsy que les embrasures en bois qu'on y avoit remplacées; qu'ils ont fait brèche à la porte Dauphine, le corps de garde joignant, et qu'il étoit praticable au moyen des fascines qu'ils avoient transporté pendant deux jours à la batterie de Francœur; que l'eperon joignant le corps de garde de l'officier de la porte Dauphine étoit tout demantelé, ainsi que les embrasures du quai, malgré le feu continuel de tous les canons, mortiers et mousqueterie que nous tirions de la ville et qui étoient servis avec toute la vigueur et l'activité qu'on pouvoit espérer en pareille occasion.

"La preuve en est assez évidente, Monseigneur, puisque de 67 milliers de poudre que nous avions au commencement du siège, il nous n'en restoit, le 27 juin, que 47 barils en ville, laquelle quantité m'étoit absolument nécessaire pour pouvoir capituler; nous avons aussi tiré toutes les bombes de 12 pouces que nous avions et presque toutes celles de 9 pouces.

"Je dois rendre justice à tous les officiers de la garnison, aux soldats et aux habitans qui ont défendu la place, ils ont tous en général supporté la fatigue de ce siège avec une intrépidité sans égale, pendant les 116 [?] jours qu'il a duré.

"Passant toutes les nuits au chemin couvert de la porte Dauphine, depuis que l'ennemy avoit commencé à battre en brèche cet endroit, à soutenir les travaillants qui otoient les décombres sur les remparts aux portes qui leur étoient destinées, sans se reposer aucune nuit et pour le jour n'ayant pas un seul endroit pour sommeiller sans courir risque d'être emporté par les canons de l'ennemy qui commandoient toute la ville.

"Aussy tout le monde étoit fatigué de travail et d'insomnie, et de 1300 que nous étions au commencement du siège, 50 ont été tués, 95 blessés hors d'état de rendre service, plusieurs étoient tombés malades par la fatigue, aussy les remparts qui n'étoient au commencement du siège garnis que de 5 à 5 pieds, se trouvoient presque tous dégarnis le 26 de juin lorsque les habitans de la ville me présentèrent leur requête tendant à ce que les forces de l'ennemy soit de terre et de mer, augmentant tous les jours, sans qu'ils nous parvint aucun secours ni apparence d'en avoir d'assez fort pour forcer l'ennemy, il me plût capituler avec les généraux afin de leur conserver le peu qu'il leur restoit.

"Cette requête, Monseigneur, me toucha jusqu'au plus vif de mon âme. D'un côte je voyois une place telle que Louisbourg et qui a coûte bien des sommes au Roi, au moment d'être enlevée par la force de l'ennemy qui avoit une brèche assez practicable pour cela et des vaisseaux en ligne qui s'installoient depuis deux jours.

"D'autre côté, il me paroissoit un nombre d'habitans, tous chargés de familles, au moment de périr, perdre par conséquent le fruit de leurs travaux depuis le commencement de l'etablissement de la colonie.

"Dans une conjoncture aussy délicate, je fis rendre compte à monsieur Verrier, ingénieur en chef, de l'état des fortifications de la Place, et à monsieur de Ste Marie, capitaine chargé de l'artillerie, de celui des munitions de guerre; l'un et l'autre me firent leur rapport, je fis tenir conseil de guerre qui décida unanimement que vu les forces de l'ennemy et l'état de la Place il convenoit de capituler.

"J'écrivis une lettre à le sortie du Conseil à messieurs les généraux anglois, je leur demanday une suspension d'armes, pour le temps qu'il me seroit convenable pour leur faire des articles de capitulation aux conditions desquelles je leur remettrois la Place.

"Monsieur de Laperelle, fils, qui étoit porteur de cette lettre, me rapporta le même soir leur réponse par laquelle ils me donnoient le temps jusques au lendemain à huit heures du matin, et que si pendant ce temps, je me déterminois à me rendre prisonnier de guerre, je pouvois compter que je serois traité avec toute la générosité possible.

"Je ne m'attendois pas à une telle réponse, aussy le lendemain 27, je leur envoyai par Monsieur de Bonnaventure les articles de capitulation avec une seconde lettre, par laquelle je leur mandai que les conditions faites la veille étoient trop dures, que je ne pouvois les accepter et que c'étoit à ceux que je faisois par mes propositions que je consentirois à leur remettre la place [*sic*].

"Messieurs les généraux ne voulurent pas répondre par apostille à ces propositions, mais ils me renvoyèrent leur réponse séparée par le dit Sieur de Bonnaventure; cette réponse m'accordoit partie des articles que j'avois demandés, mais ceux qui m'étoient le plus sensible et glorieux, qui étoient ceux de sortir de la Place, avec les honneurs de la guerre, avec arme et bagage, tambour battant et drapeaux déployés, ne s'y trouvoient pas insérés, aussy je leur écrivis sur le champ deux lettres, l'une au chef d'escadre et l'autre au général de terre, que je ne pouvois consentir à laisser sortir les troupes de la place sans ces articles qui étoient des honneurs dûs à des troupes qui avoient fait leur devoir, que cela accordé je consentois aux articles.

"Messieurs les généraux m'écrivirent en réponse qu'ils accordoient cet article et monsieur Warren augmenta des conditions pour la reddition de l'Isle et de la Place.

"Les ratifications ont été signées de part et d'autre, mais messieurs les généraux Anglois bien loin d'avoir exécuté de leur part la dite capitulation, ainsy que j'ai fait du mien en tout son contenu, ils ont manqué en plusieurs articles.

"Au premier article il est dit que tous les effets mobiliers de tous les sujets du Roy de France qui étoient dans Louisbourg leur seroient laissés et qu'ils auroient la liberté de les emporter avec eux dans tels ports d'Europe de la domination de leur Roy qu'ils jugeront à propos.

"Tous les battiments qui étoient dans le port appartenant aux particuliers, faisaient partie de leurs effets mobiliers, cependant les Anglois s'en sont emparés et les ont garde pour eux.

"Tous les particuliers généralement quelconques qui ont passé en France n'ont pu emporter aucune armoire, chaise, fauteuil, table, bureau, chenets et autres meubles de cette nature, ny même aucune grosse marchandise, messieurs les généraux n'ayant point fourni des battiments pour cela nécessaires, ils n'ont pas été pillés, mais à bien examiner la chose, ne pouvant pas emporter le peu de meubles qu'ils avoient faute de battiments, ils ont éte obligés de les laisser, ce qu'ils ont laissé à Louisbourg est tout comme si on leur avait pillé, à moins que Sa Grandeur ne fasse faire raison par la cour d'Angleterre.

"Ils ont encore manqué à cet article, pendant le temps que j'étois à la colonie; ils ont fait partir à mon insu 436 matelots et particuliers pour Baston; ils étoient embarqués ainsi que les troupes sur des vaisseaux de guerre jusqu'à leur embarquement pour la France, mais un matin le vaisseau dans lequel ils étoient eut ordre de partir pour Baston, et fit voile.

"J'en fus informé, j'en portai ma plainte, mais cela n'aboutit à autre chose sinon qu'ils n'avoient pu faire autrement faute de vivres et de battiment et qu'on les feroit repasser de Baston en France.

"Ces matelots n'ont pas été les seuls, j'ai été informé que depuis mon départ, ils ont agi de même à l'égard des familles qui n'avoient pu être placées sur les bâtiments de transport qu'ils avoient destiné pour la France, si les généraux anglois avoient voulu, les bâtiments qui ont transporté ces familles à Boston les auroient transportées pour France, ils avoient des vivres en magazin beaucoup plus que pour la traversée; mais ils n'ont agi ainsi qu'afin de disperser la colonie.

"Le 2ᵉ article regarde les battiments qui étoient dans le port et ceux qu'ils devoient fournir en cas que les premiers ne fussent pas suffisants pour faire le transport.

"J'ay fait mes remarques à ceci au précédent article, c'est un des plus considérables par rapport à la valeur des choses, y ayant quantité de battiments dans le port qui étoient coulés ou échoués, et dont l'ennemy ne pouvoit en faire sortir aucun du port ny faire aucun usage tant que nos batteries auroient existé.

"Au surplus si plusieurs particuliers de la ville n'avoient pas acheté des battiments les Anglois auroient profité de tous les effets qu'ils y ont chargés, ainsi qu'ils ont fait de ceux qui n'avoient pas le moyen d'en acheter, ces familles auroient été contraintes, ainsi que celles qui se sont embarquées en payant de gros frets, de passer à Boston.

"A l'égard du dernier article des armes, tous les habitans avoient les leurs et les ont remises en dépôt sitôt la reddition de la place; ces armes étoient partie de leurs effets, les ennemis n'ont pas voulu les rendre, je m'en suis plaint, ils m'ont fait réponse, lorsqu'ils ont envoyé les 436 matelots, qu'ils leur enverroient leurs armes, les autres habitans sont dans le même cas.

"Je crois devoir vous informer, Monseigneur, qu'ils se sont aussy emparés de tous les effets et ustensils de l'hôpital et des magasins du Roi: par la reddition de la Place ils n'ont que la ville avec les fortifications et batteries, avec toute l'artillerie armes et ustensils de guerre qui y étoient et non pas les autres effets; cependant ils s'en sont emparés, disant que c'étoit au Roy, Monsieur Bigot leur a fait ses representations qui n'ont eu aucun fruit, il vous rendra compte à ce sujet.

"Monsieur Bigot a bien voulu se charger lorsqu'il est parti de l'isle d'Aix pour vous rendre compte de ma lettre du 15 de ce mois avec tous les originaux des papiers, concernant tout ce qui s'est passé à l'occasion du siège de Louisbourg; je suis persuadé qu'ils les aura remis à sa grandeur et qu'après l'examen qu'elle en a fait, elle me rendra assez de justice que j'ay fait tout mon possible pour la défense de cette place, et que je ne l'ay rendue qu'a la dernière extrémité.

"J'oubliois d'informer monseigneur, que messieurs de la Tressillière et Souvigny, enseignes, et Lopinot, fils cadet, sont du nombre de ceux qui ont été tués pendant le siege.

"La garnison de Canceau avoit été faite prisonnière au dit lieu le 24 may de l'année dernière; elle ne devoit pas porter les armes contre le Roy pendant l'an et jour; monsieur Duquesnel donna la liberté à tous les officiers de cette garnison d'aller sur leur parole d'honneur à Baston et de passer au dit lieu le temps porté par leur capitulation.

"Le Sieur Jean Blastrick, officier, étoit du nombre, il a manqué à sa parole, puisqu'il les a prises au mois de mars dernier, c'étoit un des chefs de ceux qui ont brûlé Toulouse-Port et qui ont fait la descente à Gabarrus le 11 may.

"Il étoit colonel général de la milice de Baston, et il est entré en ville à la tête de cette milice, le lendemain de la reddition de la place."

C

Chapter XXII. Shirley and the Acadians

All the following correspondence is from the Public Record Office: America and West Indies.

Shirley to Newcastle, 14 Dec., 1745.
(Extract.)

". . . Having lately procur'd from Fort Major Phillips of Annapolis Royal the late Lieutenant Governour Armstrong's Original Instrument mention'd in my late State of the Province of Nova Scotia to be given by him to the French Inhabitants of that Province, by virtue of which and of another of the same tenour given 'em by him in 1730, they claim an Exemption from bearing Arms in defence of his Majesty's Government, I inclose your Grace a Copy of it. Mr. Phillips in his letter inclosing this Instrument to me observes that the 'Inhabitants of Nova Scotia at the first news of Louisbourg's being surrendred were in great Consternation and at Minas in particular they appear'd in Tears in the Publick Places, where nine months before they had assisted in singing Te Deum, on a false report that Annapolis Royal was surrendred to Monsieur Duvivier.' He goes on to say that a report was spread there that Monsieur Duvivier was arriv'd at Canada with rigging for two Men of War, and the Renommée a French thirty gun Ship with two Prizes at Quebec. And all the Nova Scotia Priests were gone to Canada for Instructions; and give out that there are 2000 Canadeans at Chignecto waiting ready for another attempt against his Majesty's Garrison. To which I would beg leave to subjoin that it seems to me far from being improbable that the French will Attempt the reduction of Nova Scotia early in the Spring, by gaining which they will have a fine provision Country to assemble 8 or 10,000 fighting men and all the tribes of Indians ready to join in an attempt against Louisbourg at a few days Warning as I observ'd to your Grace in a late Letter; But if they should not attempt Louisbourg they would irresistably break up all the Eastern Settlements of this Province and I doubt not the whole Province of New Hampshire it self, which would make 'em masters of all Mast Country and Naval Stores and of a rich Soil for Corn as well as Cattle and this would also enable 'em to make deep impressions on all the Western frontier of this Province, New York and Connecticut, and, how far they might penetrate is not Certain but so far at least as might make it very difficult to dislodge 'em and give 'em such an hold of the Continent as to make 'em think in time of pushing with the assistance of the Indians for the Mastery of it, which is richly worth contending for with all their might as it would in their hands lay the surest foundation for an Universal Monarchy by Sea and Land that ever a people had. This train of Consequences from the Enemies being Masters of Nova Scotia may seem remote, my Lord, but they are not impossible, and it may be very difficult for the French to regain Louisbourg at least without being Masters of Nova Scotia, and that seems under the present Circumstances of the Garrison where no recruits are yet Arriv'd from England and the Inhabitants of the Country Surrounding it are Enemies in their hearts no difficult acquisition and to be made with a small Train of Artillery in three weeks at farthest. I would submit it to your Grace's consideration whether the Garrison should not be reinforc'd as soon as may be. And the Inhabitants should not be forthwith put upon a good foot of Subjection and fidelity. Thus in obedience to your Grace's Direction I have troubled you with my whole sentiments concerning the Province of Nova Scotia which as I can't think it probable that the French will sleep the next year after the blow we have given 'em at Louisbourg (which, if they don't recover it soon by retaking Cape Breton or getting Nova Scotia will prove their Death wound in North America) seems to be most likely to be attack'd by 'em of any place in these parts, and I hope your Grace will excuse my Repetition of the Danger of it.

"I am with the most Dutiful Regards
"My Lord Duke,
"Your Grace's most Obed!
"and most Devoted Servant
"W. SHIRLEY."

SHIRLEY TO NEWCASTLE, 11 FEB. 1746.
(*Extract.*)

"MY LORD DUKE.

"Since my last to your Grace I have received the Inclos'd packett from Mr. Mascarene Containing a Representation of the State of Nova Scotia from himself and his Majesty's Council of that Province with a copy of a Letter from him to me, Showing the reasons of his late Conduct towards the French Inhabitants; Your Grace will perceive that this representation is drawn up in Stronger Terms against the Inhabitants than mine; I could wish the Gentlemen had been more Explicit in what they would Recommend as the most adviseable Method of Securing his Majesty's Government within the Province and against the French Inhabitants— But as that is not done except in Short hints, And Mr. Little, to whom both Mr. Mascarene and Mr. Secretary Shirreff referr me for a Larger Account of the Sentiments of the Gentlemen of the Garrison concerning these Matters, Offers his Service to go with my dispatches to England and return directly with any Orders his Majesty may be pleased to give thereupon, I have sent him to wait upon your Grace, and it is possible that when he is upon the Spot ready to Answer any Questions, it may be of Service— Having before troubled your Grace So Largely upon this head, I will beg leave to referr to my former Letters, Mr. Little Mr. Agent Kilby and Mr. Bollan, which two last can, I believe, give Considerable Light on the affair; And shall only add that the Spring before last the Garrison was very narrowly Saved from the Enemy by the Arrival of the New England Auxiliaries, and the last Spring, by the Expedition against Cape Breton, that the preservation of it this Spring will be of the Utmost Importance to his Majesty's Service in America, and that nothing will more effectually Secure that than putting the Inhabitants upon a proper foot of Subjection, in the most Speedy Manner, to prevent their Revolt, which Cannot be done without his Majesty's Special directions for that purpose; for the procuring of which, I find Mr. Mascarene, and his whole Council have a dependance upon me; the Language of their Several Letters being that they *Commit themselves to my Care*; and will take no step without my Advice or approbation, which has been the Case for above these last two years, And I mention to your Grace in Excuse for my being So importunate in the Affairs of another Government, which the Gentlemen of the Garrison lay me Under a Necessity of being; And I am further Urg'd to this by the late Accounts, w.ch Mr. Mascarene and the other Gentlemen have sent me of the Appearance of four hundred Indians well Cloathed, Arm'd, and Supply'd with Stores from Canada near St. Johns River, Seventeen French Officers being Seen among 'em, and another Body of French in the Neighbourhood of the Province, and Reports that Mr. Duvivier in the Parfaite Man of Warr, and another Ship of Force were at Qubec with Stores, and another was seen to put into St. Johns Island; That the Priests who went to Canada for Instructions are returned with Supplies and large promises to the Indians (before well dispos'd and upon the point of putting themselves under Our protection on the taking of Louisbourg) and Encouragements for the Inhabitants to depend upon a powerfull force against the Fort at Annapolis Royal this Spring. These alarms indeed have been Something Allay'd by Letters from the Deputies of Minas and other Districts to Mr. Mascarene, which for my own part I have no great dependance upon.

"But it seems plain upon the whole, that the French are making the Utmost Efforts to retain the Indians of those parts in their Interest, and gaining over the Inhabitants of Nova Scotia, So that the Taking of Speedy measures for Securing these last and gaining over the former which will depend upon that, as the preservation of Nova Scotia does upon both, is a Matter of the Highest Consequence.

"Upon this Occasion it seems necessary for me to apprise your Grace, that Mr. Mascarene and his Council have not So good an harmony Subsisting between them as could be wish'd, and that all the Officers have of late differ'd in Sentiments with him particularly upon the Behaviour of the French Inhabitants, Concerning whom he indeed has himself alter'd his Opinion in Some measure; But I think there may be Still danger of too much tenderness towards 'em on his part, and perhaps rigour on theirs in carrying any Orders of his Majesty's into Execution; So that by their Jarring, the Execution of the Orders may possibly be Obstructed, if they are left to themselves;

"Wherefore if their Chief Governour's Age and health, and other Circumstances would have permitted him to have been Upon the Spott, and Assisted in this Service, it would I believe have been for the Advantage of it, for him to have made 'em a short Visit at least this year, And if it could have been repeated for the two or three proceeding years it would have been still more so. . . ."

SHIRLEY TO NEWCASTLE, 10TH MAY, 1746.
(*Extract.*)

". . . I think it my indispensable duty to suggest again to

Your Grace my Fears that the Enemy will soon find an opportunity of snatching Accadie by some Sudden Stroke from
his Majesty's Government unless the danger is remov'd out
of the Heart of it there by a Removal of the most dangerous
of the french Inhabitants from thence, & transplanting English Families there in their room, which I think very practicable from hence, having lately found means of transplanting
upwards, I believe, of an hundred Families from the Province
to Louisbourg towards the Settlement of it, which yet I dont
esteem of such Importance to be immediately done as the Settlement of Nova Scotia with faithful Subjects.

"In the meanwhile 'till this can be happily effected & the
Indians in those parts secur'd in the English Interest, I have
propos'd to Mr. Warren that a Detachment of 100 Men
should be sent from Louisbourg to reinforce the garrison at
Annapolis Royal, since the late Miscarriage of 182 out of 302
of the Recruits designed for Annapolis in their Passage from
England to the garrison there. Ninety-six of the Remainder
of 'em, which came in here, I with difficulty have got recovered in his Majesty's Castle William & at the Hospital in Boston, & sent a month ago to Annapolis where I hear they are
safely arriv'd, and twenty more who are in a fair way of being
serviceable, I shall send from the Hospital within three days;
But the Garrison will still be weak as Mr. Mascarene has dismiss'd most of the New England Auxiliaries, and they have
not, I am informed, 220 effective private men left besides their
Artificers & Workmen: I have also recommended to Mr. Warren the frequent Sending of a Ship of War to look into the
Bason of Annapolis & make the Garrison there a short Visit
in order to prevent a Surprise; & by his Opinion in Concurrence with Sir Willm Pepperrell's, Mr. Mascarene's & my own
a Sloop has been hir'd & employ'd for about these last four
Months to attend upon that garrison, & carry Intelligence between Annapolis Royal, Louisbourg & Boston concerning
the State of it & the Enemy's Motions which we conceiv'd
necessary to be done for its Security, and hope your Grace
will not disapprove of.

"What Mr. Frontenac observed some years ago to M^r
Pontchartrain concerning the french King's recovering of Accadie & making himself absolute Master of the great Bank [of

Newfoundland] as in the inclos'd Extract of his Letter, seems
so seasonable to be consider'd at this time, that I would beg
leave to observe to your Grace upon it, that his Maj$^{ty's}$ holding the Possession of Annapolis Royal & Newfoundland (already conceded to his Crown by the Treaty of Utrecht) with
his late Acquisition of Cape Breton, will put the whole Cod
Fishery more in his Power than Mr Frontenac's Scheme could
have put it into the French Kings, and that besides what M^r
Frontenac calls a Commerce more advantageous than the
Conquest of the Indies, and computes the Returns of at
twenty Millions (I suppose french Livres) per annum, it
would furnish his Majesty with as good a Nursery of Seamen
for the Royal Navy as the Colliery in England does, not to
mention the great consumption of British Manufactures
which must be occasioned in carrying the Fishery on;—that
the holding of Annapolis Royal in particular will be establishing to his Majesty the Mastery of the Northern Part of this
Continent against the French, Secure to him inexhaustible
Nurseries of Masts, Yards, Bowsprits & other Stores for his
Navy, & Timber for Ship building within his Northern Colonies independent of any foreign State to be purchased with
British Manufactures & transported in British Vessels—that
the Inhabitants of the Northern Colonies would in time make
such an Addition of Subjects to the Crown of Great Britain
as would make their number Superior to that of any Prince's
upon the Continent of Europe; and in the meanwhile the
Vent of Woolen & other British Manufactures, & all Kinds
of European Commodities imported into the Colonies from
Great Britain must increase in proportion to the Increase of
their Inhabitants: by all which means the main Sources of
Wealth, & a larger Extent of Power by Sea & Land than any
State in Christendom at present enjoys, seems capable of
being secur'd to his Maj$^{ty's}$ Dominions; But which will in the
End otherwise be in all human Probability the Lot of the
french Dominions; And I would in particular observe to your
Grace the most practicable Step the Enemy can attempt making towards their obtaining that seems clearly to be their
rendring themselves Masters of Nova Scotia, the Consequences of wch would give 'em so strong an hold upon this
Continent as would make it difficult to dislodge 'em & put it

very much in their Power to harrass & annoy his Maj^{tys} Colonies both by Land & Sea, in such manner as to weaken 'em
extremely, if not by degrees finally subdue 'em.

> "I am with the most dutiful Regards,
> "My Lord Duke,
> "Your Grace's most devoted
> "and obedient Servant
> "W. SHIRLEY."

SHIRLEY TO NEWCASTLE, 31 MAY, 1746.
(Extract.)

". . . I would beg Leave to observe to your Grace, y^t the
Danger to his Majesty's garrison arises chiefly from within
the heart of the government itself, the Inhabitants & neighboring Indians whose Numbers are sufficient of themselves
with a small assistance from Canada & the help of a proper
Train of Artillery, slipt up the Bay in small Vessells (w^{ch}
would give 'em great Encouragement to take up Arms ag^t the
garrison) to reduce it. However while the Attempt against
Canada is depending, that will certainly go far towards holding the Inhabitants of Nova Scotia in suspense, till the success
of it is known; & I hope by next Spring they may either be
put upon a better foot of Subjection, or the most dangerous
among 'em removed. . . ."

SHIRLEY TO NEWCASTLE, 18 JUNE, 1746.
(Extract.)

". . . I may assure your Grace y^t one of the principal motives I had to desire I might succeed General Phillips in his
Command, was the hopes I have of it's putting it in my
power to promote his Majesty's Service in his Province of
Acadie, or Nova Scotia by securing the fidelity & Allegiance
of the Inhabitants there to his Majesty's Government in the
best manner, and thereby preventing the French from making
themselves masters of it, the Acquisition of wch to them with
the help of the Indians would likewise endanger the Loss of
the Province of New Hampshire & the Mast Country to his

Majesty with the Fishery of the Acadie or Cape Sable's Shoar, including that of Canso, to his Subjects here in present, & should not Canada be reduc'd, would enable the enemy to harrass & Diminish all his Majesty's Colonies & on the Continent, & have an inevitable Tendency to make themselves masters of the whole of it in time; not to mention the Continual Danger, wch their possession of Nova Scotia would at the same time expose Cape Breton & even Newfoundland to.

"The Considerations have induc'd me to take the Liberty of submitting it to your Grace, whether it might not be for his Majesty's Service, that before the six Regiments to be employ'd ag^t Canada return to England, orders may be sent that such part of 'em as shall be thought necessary to assist in removing the most obnoxious of the French Inhabitants of Nova Scotia from thence, should be employ'd in that Service, wch would not take up much time; I am not certain whether a sufficient Strength might not be spar'd from the Garrison at Louisbourg a short time for this purpose, wch if it could, would make the Assistance of any other Troops needless.

"And I would particularly submit it to your Grace's Consideration, whether in case of any Disappointment in the present Attempt for the reduction of Canada, the immediate removal of some at least of the French Inhabitants of Nova Scotia, & securing the province in the best manner would not be . . . adviseable and even necessary.

"If your Grace should think this deserves so much of your Attention there will be time enough for transmitting his Majesty's Commands to me upon it before the present Expedition is over.

> "I am with the most Dutifull Regard
> "My Lord Duke
> "Your Grace's most Devoted
> "& most obedient Servant
> "W. SHIRLEY."

SHIRLEY TO NEWCASTLE, 28 JULY, 1746.
(Extract.)

"I must acknowledge I should rather apprehend the french

Fleet (if it is design'd for North America) is order'd to Canada; or else to Annapolis Royal, where the Enemy may depend that upon the Apperance of such an Armament the french Inhabitants of Nova Scotia (to the Amount of between 5 & 6000 fighting men) and a considerable Number of Indians & some Canadeans, would immediately join 'em, and they would have a most convenient Country to rendezvous in within a very few days sail of Chappeaurouge Bay at Cape Breton, and be not far from Canada, than that they should attempt to enter Louisbourg Harbour with their Ships; and I am the more inclin'd to this Opinion from the Accounts I have receiv'd lately from Mr Mascarene, and the Officers of the Garrison at Annapolis Royal which inform me that the french Inhabitants at Menis & Schiegneto (in Nova Scotia) have cut off all communication with the garrison for these last five Weeks, and have stop'd the Messengers sent from thence by Mr Mascarene for Intelligence; being in Expectation of an Armament from France; And indeed it seems probable that this will for ever be the Case; and that the Province of Nova Scotia will never be out of Danger, whilst the french Inhabitants are suffer'd to remain in Nova Scotia upon their present Foot of Subjection."

Shirley to Newcastle, 15 Aug., 1746.
(Extract.)

"I shall finish my troubleing your Grace upon the Affairs of Nova Scotia with this Letter after having once more Submitted it to your Grace's Consideration as a proper Scheme for better securing the Subjection of the French Inhabitants and Indians there; that the Governour & Council or such other Person or Persons as his Majesty shall think fitt to join with 'em, should have a special authority and directions from his Majesty, forthwith to Apprehend & Examine a convenient number of such of the Inhabitants, as shall be by them judg'd to be most obnoxious & Dangerous to his Majesty's Government, & upon finding 'em guilty of holding any treasonable Correspondence with the Enemy &c to dispose of them & their Estates in such manner, as his Majesty shall order by his Commissions and to promise his Majesty's Gracious Pardon

& a general Indemnity to the Rest for what is past upon their taking the Oaths of Allegiance to his Majesty; And to Cause either two strong Blockhouses (or small Forts) capable of holding 100 Men each to be Built, one in Menis & the other in Schiegnecto, which may be Garrison'd out of Phillip's Regiment when Compleated, or else that at least one Blockhouse (or small Fort) should be Built at Menis capable of holding 150 men; and a trading house be kept at the Fort at Menis or some other part of the Province well Stock'd with all proper Supplies for the Indians to be sold or barter'd to 'em for Furrs &c at the most reasonable Rates, and some presents annually distributed to 'em: by which means and removing the Romish Priests out of the Province, & introducing Protestant English Schools, and French Protestant Ministers, and due encouragement given to such of the Inhabitants, as shall Conform to the Protestant Religion, and send their Children to the English Schools, the present Inhabitants might probably at least be kept in Subjection to his Majesty's Government, and from treasonable Correspondencies with the Canadians; and the next Generation in a great measure become true Protestant Subjects; and the Indians there soon Reclaim'd to an entire dependance upon & subjection to his Majesty; which might also have an happy Influence upon some of the Tribes now in the French Interest.

    "Your Grace will be pleas'd to Excuse all
      "Incorrectness in this rough Sketch.
        "I am with the most Dutifull Regard,
          "My Lord Duke,
            "Your Grace's most Devoted &
            "Most Obedient Servant
                    "W. SHIRLEY."

SHIRLEY TO MASCARENE, BOSTON, SEPT.[R] 16, 1746.

"SIR,

    "Having been inform'd that the french Inhabitants of Nova Scotia entertain some Jealousy of a Design in the English Government to remove them with their Families from their Settlements, & transport them to France or elsewhere; I desire (if you think it may be for his Majesty's Service) that you would be pleas'd to signify to 'em, that it is probable if his Majesty had declar'd such Intention I might have heard of the same, but that I am perfectly unaquainted with any such Design, and am perswaded there is no just Ground for this Jealousy; And be pleas'd to assure 'em that I shall use my best Endeavours by a proper Representation of their Case to be laid before his Majesty, to obtain the Continuance of his Royal Favour & Protection to such of them, as shall behave dutifully, & refuse to hold any Correspondence with his Enemies; and I doubt not but that all such of 'em will be protected by his Majesty in the Possession of their Estates & Settlements in Nova Scotia.

"And I desire you would also be pleas'd to inform them that it is expected from his Maj^{tys} french Subjects in that Province, who have for so long time enjoyed the same Privileges with his natural born Subjects there, & have been under a much easier Government than any of the french King's Subjects are in the neighbouring Province of Canada & other Parts of the french King's Dominions, that their Interest as well as their Duty and Gratitude should bind them to a strict Fidelity & Obedience to his Majesty and His Government; But on the contrary if any of the Inhabitants of the said Province shall join with the Enemy (especially those that have been sent from Canada to seduce them from their Duty to his Majesty & Attachment to the English Interest) they must expect to be treated in the same manner as his Majesty's English Subjects would be under the like Provocations.

"I am with great regard

"Sir,

"Your most obedient

"humble servant

"W. SHIRLEY."

SHIRLEY TO NEWCASTLE, BOSTON, SEPTEMBER 19, 1746.

"MY LORD DUKE,

"I express'd some hopes in my last but one to your Grace, that I should not be oblig'd to add to my former Accounts of the imminent danger, his Majesty's Province of Nova Scotia was in of being surpriz'd by the Enemy; But find my self under a Necessity of doing it from the Advices which I have since receiv'd from M.ʳ Mascarene, and the Intelligence contain'd in three Declarations upon Oath, Copies of all which are inclos'd.

"Upon the Receipt of M.ʳ Mascarene's Letter, the Contents of which are confirm'd to me by other authentick Accounts, it appear'd to me that there was no room to doubt but that a considerable Body of French and Indians from Canada was assembled in Nova Scotia, with Expectations of a Reinforcement from France; and if they fail'd of that this Year a Design of at least wintering in Minas or some other Part of the Country, by which means they would have an Opportunity of fortifying themselves in it, transporting their great artillery (which there was then the utmost reason to believe they had landed either at Bay Verte or Chebucto Harbour) to Annapolis, and work upon the French Inhabitants already ripe for a Revolt to join 'em in attacking his Majesty's Garrison there so early in the Spring that it would be extremely difficult if not impracticable to relieve it by any Succours either from Louisbourg or the Colonies on the Continent. Whereupon I immediately sent M.ʳ Mascarene an Assurance that I would send him as soon as possible 300 of the new Levies from this Province, 200 of 'em (which seems to be as many as the Garrison can hold at present besides the Troops already there) for the Reinforcement of it, and 100 of 'em to be employ'd in two Sloops up the Bay in the manner M.ʳ Mascarene proposes in his Letter to me, and that I would do the utmost in my Power to make the number up 2000 soon afterwards, in order to dislodge the Enemy, & prevent 'em from wintering in the Province; And in the mean time upon my advising with Rear Admiral Warren (who is still here) he immediately sent his Majesty's Ship Chester a 50 Gun Ship to Annapolis Royal for the further Countenance & Protection of the Garrison there.

"Some Days after this I receiv'd Information that a Fleet of upwards of 30 Sail were discover'd about 15 Leagues to the Westward of Chibucto Harbour, which lies upon the Cape Sable Shoar (the Coast of Accadie or Nova Scotia) about 150 Leagues to the Eastward of Boston, and about 60 Leagues Westward of Louisbourg, & about 80 distant from Annapolis

Royal according to Champions inclos'd Deposition, which
was confirm'd by another of the same Tenour made by one
Thornton sent me from Piscataqua, upon which I dispatched
an arm'd Brigantine with orders to look into Chibucto Harbour, & if the Master should discover any thing to proceed
directly to Louisbourg, & give Vice Admiral Townsend &
Govern.ʳ Knowles Intelligence of it, & to send me Advice of
it Express by some fishing Vessel taken up at Sea; But the
Brigantine return'd in less than 24 hours with one Stanwood
a Fisherman on board, whose Vessel fell in with the Fleet on
the 9.ᵗʰ day of Sept.ʳ about 10 Leagues to the Westward of
Chibucto, the particulars of which are contain'd in his inclos'd
Deposition; and the day after Stanwood's falling in with this
Fleet, Haskell another Master of a fishing Vessel discover'd it
standing a right course for Chibucto about 8 Leagues to the
Westw.ᵈ of it, & was chas'd by one of 'em according to the
inclos'd Deposition; which Series of Intelligence, as no Vessel
has arriv'd here yet from this Fleet (which must in all probability have happen'd had it come from England) compar'd
with the Accounts in the English News Papers of the Brest
Fleet's sailing, & the Intelligence gain'd from a french Prize
lately taken by one of M.ʳ Townsend's Squadron near the
Mouth of S.ᵗ Lawrence, that she came out with the Brest
Squadron & sail'd in Company with it eight days; the Account we had of two large french Ships being seen to go into
Chibucto Harbour about two Months ago; the behavior of
the French in Nova Scotia, & their declar'd Expectations of a
large French Armament about this time, seems to make it
very probable that these Ships may be part of the Brest
Squadron, & that they have an immediate design upon Nova
Scotia at least.—Hereupon I sent an Express Boat to Louisbourg to apprize Admiral Townsend & M.ʳ Knowles of it, &
another to Annapolis Royal to give M.ʳ Mascarene Advice of
it, & to let him know that I was embarking 300 Men for the
Reinforcement of the Garrison under his Command (which
is done & part of 'em sail'd) with a Promise of farther Succours, and to apprize him that from the publick Accounts in
the English Prints we had reason to depend upon the speedy
Arrival of Lieut.ᵗ General S.ᵗ Clair with the British Troops under his Command, & a Squadron of his Majesty's Ships with

'em at Louisbourg; And as I have reason to think that an Apprehension generally prevails among the french Inhabitants of Nova Scotia, that they shall all of 'em soon be remov'd from their Settlements there without Distinction, which may have a bad Influence upon 'em in favour of the Enemy at this critical Time. I have wrote M.ʳ Mascarene a Letter (a copy of which I inclose to your Grace) which is translated into French, & printed, in order to be dispers'd among the french Inhabitants, if M.ʳ Mascarene (to whose Discretion I have submitted it either to make Use of or suppress the printed Copies) shall be of Opinion that the Publication of it among 'em may be for his Majesty's Service.

"If the Fleet discover'd on the Cape Sable Coast should be Part of that from Brest, doubtless their visit to Nova Scotia has been encourag'd by the general Disposition of the Inhabitants, & the strength they will add to 'em for the Reduction of that Province, & afterwards for an Attempt upon Louisbourg (if they should think it adviseable to make one) as also for the defence of Canada. Should they succeed in an immediate Attempt upon Nova Scotia (which I should not be surpriz'd at) & General S.ᵗ Clair with the Squadron expected from England should arrive in time for that purpose, I should propose attempting the immediate recovery of it out of the Enemy's hands this Year; For their holding that Province till they can fortify it and farther strengthen themselves there must be attended with very bad Consequences to his Majesty's Service, worse than may be immediately apprehended, & create no inconsiderable Perplexities; at least it seems a clear point to me, that if the French should hold the Possession of Nova Scotia in Addition to Canada, the fate of Affairs in his Majesty's Northern Colonies will be suddenly alter'd in a surprizing manner & it will then soon be discern'd that the Mastery of the Northern Parts of this Continent, together with the Sources of Wealth & Power depending upon it, will be in a very fair way of being finally transfer'd to the Enemy.

"Upwards of two Months ago upon receiving Intelligence of the Appearance of two large French Ships being seen to go into Chibucto Harbour, M.ʳ Warren & I sent M.ʳ Townsend notice of it; But as we had not learn'd whether any Vessell had been sent from Louisbourg to look into that

Harbour, I sent an arm'd Brigantine to make Discoveries there, which was hinder'd from proceeding thither as is before mention'd; & I have now sent a Schooner thither with a Person who has undertaken to go into it in a Whale boat high enough to make an exact discovery of the Enemy's strength (if any of their Ships are there) & to carry the Account to Louisbourg; But it seems possible if any of 'em have been there, that after landing some Troops and Stores at Chibucto, & getting what Intelligence they can from the Nova Scotians, their Ships may be gone to Canada; for which Place we have been inform'd that sixteen french Vessels, some of 'em Ships of War, had some time ago pass'd up the River of S.ʳ Laurence; & since that six other Vessels with Stores; so that it is very probable that Quebec is much better prepar'd to receive a Visit from his Majesty's Land & Sea Forces now than it was a little time ago."

SHIRLEY TO NEWCASTLE, 23 OCT. 1746.
(*Extract.*)

"It is agreed by all the Prisoners that the French have not fortify'd at Chebucto, nor sent any Troops from thence by Land to join the Canadeans; as also that M.ʳ Destonnel the chief D'escadre & Commandant upon the Death of the Duke D'Anville, who was of Opinion, to return to France after the Admiral's Death without attempting any thing, upon being over rul'd in a Council of War & having his Flagg struck, fell upon his Sword, & dy'd of his Wound as all of 'em say, except Sanders.

"It seems very observable from Sander's Declaration how ready a Disposition the Nova Scotians show'd to afford Refreshm.ᵗˢ & Pilots to the Enemy, & that they had signified to the french Ministry their readiness to join with any force they should send for the Reduction of his Majes.ᵗʸˢ Garrison at Annapolis Royal. Also from the number of Engineers the French had with 'em that their Scheme was to hold & fortify Annapolis, for w.ᶜʰ Purpose it seems to be that the 50 brass Cannon were brought, rather than for raising Batteries against the Fort: and that from the Number of their small Arms, which they had with 'em to arm the Nova Scotians (doubtless) as well as the Indians, they had a dependance upon being join'd by them. Likewise the Apprehensions which prevail among the Nova Scotians that they are at present rather Neutrals than Subjects to the Crown of Great Britain. And I think it is not to be doubted now but that the principal Part of the french Scheme was the Reduction of Nova Scotia in the first Place.

"Upon the whole the sickly State of the French Fleet, wch is extremely ill mann'd, the hurry & Uneasiness they discover'd upon seeing the Contents of the Packets which fell into their hands, & precipitate departure from Chebucto, with their detaining the Flag of Truce & English Prisoners 'till they were got 30 Leagues from Chebucto, & then dismissing 'em with a Notion that their Fleet was going up the Bay of Fundy to Annapolis (instead of carrying 'em up there with 'em to prevent that's being known to us) makes it seem probable that the Enemy is making the best of their way to France or the West Indies, & was afraid of even Mr Townsend's following 'em.

"I am with the most dutiful Regard
"My Lord Duke,
"Your Grace's most Devoted
"and most Obedient Servant
"W. SHIRLEY."

SHIRLEY TO NEWCASTLE, BOSTON, 21 NOV. 1746.
(*Extracts.*)

"MY LORD DUKE,

"I am afraid your Grace will think, from my incessant Representations of the State of Nova Scotia, that I imagine that Province should be the sole Object of your Attention: Nothing could induce me to be so importunate with your Grace upon this Subject, but the fullest perswasion of the very great Importance of that Place to the Crown, & the British Subject, of the immediate bad Consequences of the Loss of it to his majesty's Service, & the imminent danger of its being lost, unless something is forthwith done for the effectual Security of it.

"The inclos'd Extract from Mr Mascarene's Letter & Copy of Lieut^t Colonel Gorham's will disclose in a great Measure to your Grace their Apprehensions, & the Condition of the Province: The number of the Enemy, are increas'd at Menis; they have again stop't all Communication between the Inhabitants & the Garrison, & are likely to keep footing there this Winter; and particularly from Col? Gorham's Letter your Grace will perceive what Pains the Canadeans and Malecontents among the Inhabitants take to prevent my Letter lately dispers'd among 'em, in order to setle the Minds of the Inhabitants, (a Copy of which I have before sent your Grace) from having its proper Influence; & how the Nova Scotians are alarm'd at the Rumour of a design to remove 'em from their Settlements; And it appears to me by what I farther learn from Captain Fotheringham to whom M.ʳ Mascarene refers me in his Letter, that unless something vigorous, as that Letter intimates, is done by the Middle of April at farthest, the greatest Part of the Province at least will be in the hands of the Canadeans, and it will be too late then to attempt to reclaim the Inhabitants.

*   *   *

"For the securing Nova Scotia from its present dangers I would further humbly propose it as my Opinion to be consider'd by your Grace, that if his Majesty should be pleas'd as soon as possibly might be after the Receipt of this, to cause it to be signified to the Inhabitants of Nova Scotia, that the Assurances lately given 'em by me of his Royal Protection to such of 'em as should behave dutifully and avoid all traiterous Correspondence with the Enemy at this Juncture (or to that Effect) were approv'd of by him, and should be made good to 'em, it would have a great Tendency to remove their present Apprehensions of being sent off with their Families from their Settlements in Nova Scotia, which seems to distress & perplex 'em; & effectually to prevent 'em from being drawn over to take up Arms against his Majesty, unless it should be some of the most obnoxious of 'em; which if his Majesty would be pleas'd to send over at the same time his special directions to apprehend, and proceed against, such a Proceeding against the Delinquents and gracious Declaration towards the others, would, I dare say, have a proper Effect for securing the general Fidelity of the Inhabitants, at least so far as to keep 'em from joining with the Enemy; And least the Succours now sent to Annapolis should not be a sufficient force to dislodge the Enemy this Winter, I would farther humbly propose it for your Graces' Consideration, that his Majesty's Orders should be forthwith sent to myself and the other three Governments of New England, that in case the Canadeans should not be withdrawn out of Nova Scotia, they should immediately cause the Soldiers rais'd in their respective Colonies & Provinces for his Majesty's Service in the Expedition against Canada to be transported to Annapolis Royal, as their Place of Rendezvous instead of Louisbourg, & to be employed in driving the Canadeans out of Nova Scotia, and be farther subjected to such Orders as his Majesty shall be pleas'd to signify in those Directions; and if this Order was to extend to the Governour of New York, it might not be an unnecessary Caution. I am apprehensive if such Orders are not sent, that the Attention of the several Governm.ts to the Reduction of Crown Point might very much interfere with the Preservation of Nova Scotia, which is of infinitely more Consequence.

"These are the things which occur to me at present, & which I would submit to your Grace's Consideration, as what seems to require more immediate Dispatch; As to the danger of the french Fleet's early Return from the West Indies to Nova Scotia and what Strergth of Ships may be necessary to protect that Province, Cape Breton, and the other Colonies against that Fleet, or any other french Armament which may be sent from Europe in the Spring to visit these Parts, I leave to Admiral Warren, who now goes to England in the Chester, and with whom, pursuant to the Directions of your Grace's two Letters to me in March & April last, I have acted in Concert upon all such Occasions as requir'd my consulting him with the greatest Satisfaction and Harmony, having had the Pleasure to find my own Sentiments agreable to his in all Matters of Consequence, and a most hearty Disposition in him for his Majesty's Service, and to whom I have often talk'd over the Affairs of Nova Scotia.

*   *   *

"I will avoid repeating what I have particularly mention'd

to your Grace in late Letters concerning fortifying of Chebucto Harbour and building a Blockhouse or small Fort for
150 Men at Menis, with a Trading House there for the Indians, and a Blockhouse only at Canso for 100 Men, instead of
new building and enlarging that at Annapolis Royal, and
erecting a larger Fortification at Canso; which in my humble
Opinion would greatly strengthen that Province, and together with the introducing of french Protestant Ministers,
and English Schools, & some small Encouragement by Privileges to such as should conform to the Prtestant Religion,
or send their Children to the English Schools, and Presents
to the Indians with Supplies of all necessaries for 'em at the
most reasonable Rates, in Exchange for their Furrs &.^{c}; the
Disallowance of the publick Exercise of the Roman Catholic
Religion, at least after a short Term of Years, & forbidding
Romish Priests under severe Penalties to come into the Country either among the Inhabitants or Indians; and if it might
be consistent with his Majesty's Pleasure, a Civil Government
to be in due time introduc'd among the Inhabitants; These
things, I say, my Lord together with making Examples of the
most obnoxious among the Inhabitants, and his Majesty's extending his Clemency and the Continuance of his Protection
to the rest upon taking the proper Oath of Allegiance, seem
to me to have the most promising Aspect for making good
Subjects of the present Generation of Inhabitants, at least better than they are now and good Protestants of the next Generation of 'em; especially if there was to be a Mixture of
English or other Protestants introduc'd among 'em, which the
Invitation of a Civil Government to be set up among 'em
would bid fair for doing: and the Trading House would create in the Indians a firm Dependance upon, and Attachment
to his Majesty's Government, especially if a proper Protestant
Missionary or two was supported to live among 'em at their
head Quarters, as is the Method of the french Priests; by w^{ch}.
means they gain so great an Ascendency over them.

"Just as I had finished the last Paragraph a Letter from
Governor Knowles to Admiral Warren & myself, dated the
10th Instant, was deliver'd to me, in which he informs me that
'he has given his Opinion in his Letters to your Grace, that it
will be necessary to drive *all the French* (I suppose he means

Inhabitants) out of Accadie (Nova Scotia) in the Spring, and 'that he hopes he shall have Orders to assist in doing it, if 'Admiral Warren does not go upon the Expedition to Que-'beck, which he apprehends is rendred more difficult than it 'was, by such a Number of Ships being got safe up to Que-'beck this Year, as no doubt they have carried all manner of 'warlike Stores.' And in his Letter to me of the 24th. of October he says 'if his Majesty should be pleas'd to transport the Reb-'els who are Objects of his Mercy, & encourage other High-'land Families to come over, he thinks the Colony of Nova 'Scotia would soon be repeopled;' which it is possible he may have also propos'd to your Grace as in his Opinion the best Method for peopling that Colony, after the present french Inhabitants are drove off.

"As the Sentiments, which I have taken the Liberty to offer to your Grace upon this Subject, happen to be something different from Mr. Knowles's, I think it may not only be proper but my Duty to mention the Reasons of my preferring the Scheme for attempting to make the present french Inhab-itants good Subjects to his Majesty, and keeping 'em in the Country, to that of driving 'em off & introducing some of the Rebels and other Highlanders in their Room.

"It seems very difficult to drive all the Inhabitants of Acca-die out of so large a Province as that is, and which consists chiefly of Woods; It is most probable that many of the har-diest Men would retire (for some time at least) with their Cattle into the Woods, & form Parties with the Indians; and the remainder would doubtless retreat with their Families to Canada: Those, who are acquainted with the Indian Manner of Life & making War know that one hundred of 'em under Cover of the Woods can confine a very large Frontier within their Garrisons, even tho' they have Companies continually scouting between one Garrison and another: this is at present the Case of this Province & the other Colonies of New En-gland & New York, tho' the People there are us'd to the Woods, & the Skulking of the Indians behind the Bushes & in Ditches with their other Wiles, & have large numbers of the Militia constantly upon Guard for their Protection; their Cattle is continually destroy'd; if any of 'em venture out into their Fields, they are frequently kill'd & scalp'd; and sometimes not only single Families or Garrisons are surpriz'd and cut off, as has happen'd lately in this Province, but even whole Villages, as was the Case of Sarahtoga in New York a few Months ago; so that those of the french Inhabitants, who should mix with the Indians in the Woods, would have it in their Power to put his Majesty's Garrison under such Circumstances as that it could not possibly subsist longer in the Country than they could do it without fresh Provisions, Wood & other Materials & Supplies from thence; from all which they would be wholly cut off, when the Inhabitants were drove away; And as to such of the Inhabitants, who should go with their Families to Canada, it must be expected that a very large Body of the Men would return arm'd next Spring with some Canadeans to join the Indians; from all which it seems justly to be apprehended that an Attempt to drive all the french Inhabitants from their Settlements, should it succeed, would in Effect be driving 5 or 6000 Men to take up Arms against his Majesty's Government there every Year during the War; make the reclaiming of the Indians of Nova Scotia impracticable, & render it impossible for his Majesty's Garrison there to subsist long in the Country in time of War even with the Indians only; Besides, the Addition of about 6000 fighting Men with their Families to Canada, which would greatly strengthen the French upon this Continent, and would entail upon the Posterity of those who are thus expell'd (for several Generations at least) a Desire of recovering their former Possessions in Nova Scotia, seems to be no inconsiderable Matter, but what next to the Loss of the Country itself should be avoided on the Part of his Majesty, & is I dare say an Event, which the French next to their Acquisition of this Colony would desire: It is indeed now to be wish'd that General Nicholson had upon the first Reduction of the Colony to the Obedience to the Crown of Great Britain, remov'd the french Inhabitants, when they were but a few, out of the Country, as was done at Louisbourg; and that during the Interval of Peace the Colony had been planted with Protestant Subjects; But after their having remain'd so long in the Country upon the foot of British Subjects under the Sanction of the treaty of Utrecht, and making Improvements on their Lands for one or two Generations, and being

grown up into such a Number of Families, to drive 'em all
off their Settlements without farther Inquiry seems to be liable to many Objections. Among others it may be doubted
whether under the Circumstances of these Inhabitants it
would clearly appear to be a just Usage of 'em; it is true that
the Notion of their Neutrality (which seems to have been entertain'd for some time by the English as well as themselves)
is ill-grounded, and does not comport with the Terms of their
Allegiance to his Majesty, to which such of 'em as chose to
remain in the Province are bound by the treaty of Utrecht;
whereby the french King yielded up the Inhabitants as well
as the Soil of Accadie, and together with their Persons transferred their Allegiance to the Crown of Great Britain; But if
it is consider'd that this Notion was founded upon an Act of
the late Lieut.! Governour Armstrong then the residing Commander in Chief of the Province, whereby he took upon himself to grant 'em by a Writing under his Hand an Exemption
from bearing Arms upon any Account whatever, on their
consenting to take an Oath of Allegiance to his present Majesty, which, whether it was done by him with, or without
Authority, appear'd at least to them to be authentick; it may
perhaps be deem'd too rigorous a Punishment for their behavior grounded on such a Mistake, to involve the innocent
with the Guilty in the Loss of their Estates, and the Expulsion
of their Families out of the Country; it is not improbable but
that there may be many among 'em who would even prefer
his Majesty's Governm.! to a french one, & have done nothing
to deserve such a Forfeiture; Some Allowances may likewise
be made for their bad Situation between the Canadeans, Indians & English, the Ravages of all which they have felt by
Turns in the Course of the War; during which they seem to
have been continually plac'd between two fires, the force and
Menaces of the Canadeans & Indians plundering 'em of whatever they wanted, & deterring 'em in the strongest manner
from having any Communication with his Majesty's Garrison, on the one hand; and the Resentm.ts of the Garrison for
their withholding their Intelligence & Supplies on the other,
tho' at the same time it was not in a Condition to protect 'em
from the Enemy; Wherefore it seems a Matter worthy of your
Grace's Consideration, whether under such doubtful Circum-

stances the driving all the French Inhabitants of Nova Scotia off their Settlements, and thereby very greatly strengthening the Enemy upon this Continent, not only against the Garrison in present, but finally against all the British Colonies there, and depopulating one of his Majesty's Provinces for some time (how long may be uncertain) is more eligible than treating 'em as Subjects, confining their Punishm.ᵗ to the most guilty & dangerous among 'em, & keeping the rest in the Country, and endeavouring to make them & their Posterity useful Members of Society under his Majesty's Government: I can't omit likewise observing to your Grace, that it would be exceeding difficult to fill up the Chasm which driving off the Inhabitants would make in the Country; During the Rupture with France it would certainly be impracticable, and I doubt whether it would not be so when Peace shall be made with France, if the Indians should continue at War with us; For what Number of Families can be propos'd to begin a Settlemᵗ in the Country, after the Expulsion of the French Inhabitants, with safety against the Indians, & which would be continually expos'd to be destroyed by 'em, whilst they were carrying on their Settlements; They must expect no Protection against the Indians from within the Garrison, out of the Reach of their great Guns; the Company of Rangers, which live without the Walls of the Fort, would afford more of that than a thousand Garrison Soldiers would do: Whereas if the Stock of french Inhabitants was continued in the Country, an Accommodation with the Indians would be more easily brought about and preserv'd, they would be a Cover for any Number of Families that might be introduc'd among 'em whilst they were carrying on Settlements; & secure to the Garrison its necessary Supplies of fresh Provisions, Fuel, Materials for repairing the Works, & Stores of Sorts that the Country affords.

"As to repeopling the Province with some of the late Rebels and other Highland Families, it seems much to be doubted whether it might not be too hazardous to fill that Colony, wᶜʰ should be the Barrier of all his Majesty's Colonies upon this Continent, with a Set of poor, ignorant, deluded Wretches just come out of a most unnatural Rebellion; that from their Neighbourhood to Canada would be continually expos'd to the Artifices and Attempts of french Romish Priests upon 'em who it is reasonable to think would not fail to instill the same Notions into 'em in America, which seduc'd 'em from their Allegiance in Great Britain, with a Promise of more effectual Support & Protection from the French here, than they had in the Highlands; Indeed, my Lord, this seems to be a dangerous experiment, and what might produce the worst of Consequences.

"I beg leave to submit it to your Grace's Consideration, whether the most staunch Protestants, & Families the most zealously affected to his Majesty's Government, a Number at least of such, should not rather, if possible, be transplanted there as soon as may be; I could wish four or five hundred of 'em could be induc'd to go from some Part of New England; I think from the Experience I had of the Inhabitants of this Province at least upon the late Alarm given by the french Fleet, I might safely venture to be answerable to his Majesty, that if I had suggested in my late Orders for assembling a Body of 'em under Arms in Boston from all Parts of this Province to oppose any Attempt of the Enemy, that there was a design of landing a Son of the Pretender's here, it would not have been possible to have kept any one Man, who was capable of marching hither, from appearing under Arms with the most determin'd Resolution of hazarding his Life to the utmost in defence of his Majesty's Governm:; And as the late Appearances of a fondness for removing from hence to Cape Breton seem to be quite vanished at present, I should not be without hopes of some families removing from these Parts to Nova Scotia upon due Encouragement; Protestants likewise from among the Swiss Cantons, & other Northern Parts in Germany, who are generally bred up in the Exercise of arms, and make sober and industrious Settlers, might be safely trusted in Accadie; Great Numbers of 'em yearly flock into Pensilvania, whereby the Inhabitants of that Province are almost incredibly increas'd within these twenty Years; And from the behavior of the Irish coming out of the Northern Parts of Ireland hither, a Number of which is setled in the Eastern Parts of this Province, I should think they too might be safely trusted in Nova Scotia; and it is certain that these poor unhappy Highlanders (I mean such of 'em as may be design'd to be transported into the Plantations) would be more safely dispos'd of among the four Governm.^{ts} of New England, or in New York & the Jerseys, where they would not be in danger either of corrupting the Inhabitants, or being again seduc'd themselves, but might make useful Subjects to his Majesty.

"I hope, my Lord, I shall be excus'd if I have gone beyond my Line in submitting these Observations to your Grace, at a time when the fate of one of his Majesty's Northern Colonies, the most important of 'em all to the Crown in many respects, as I apprehend, and which will be in the hands of the french the Key to all the other British Colonies upon this Continent, & even to Cape Breton, And in his Majesty's Possession the Barrier of 'em against the Enemy seems to come to a Crisis."

SHIRLEY TO NEWCASTLE, BOSTON, NEW ENGLAND, 27 FEBRUARY, 1747.

"MY LORD DUKE,

"I am sorry that I am now to Acquaint your Grace with the Advices I receiv'd last night by Express from Nova Scotia giving me an Account that the Detachment of Troops under the Command of Lieu.^{t} Colonel Noble, which I Inform'd your Grace in my last of the 21st. instant had taken possession of Minas, and had kept it near two months, was for want of a proper Security for the Men and Intelligence from the Inhabitants surpriz'd on the 31st. of January last at three o'Clock in the morning by between 5 & 600 Canadeans & Indians in which Lieu.^{t} Col.^{o} Noble with four Officers more and about 80 men were killed, and three Officers and about 60 Men were wounded and taken prisoners before it was light enough for our people to get together; they however obliged the Enemy, upwards of 20 of whom were kill'd, and about 15 wounded, to allow 'em an honourable Capitulation, a Copy of which I inclose to your Grace together with the Account given of this Affair by the Officer who was Commandant of the Detachment at the time of the Capitulation, & Extracts from Lieu.^{t} Governour Mascarene's Letter to me upon this Subject, from whence I choose your Grace should receive the Acco.^{t} in the same light it has been Conveyed to me in, and which upon the best Inquiry I can make, seems to be a just one. I also Inclose to your Grace an Extract from Col. Noble's Letter to me dated two days before his death, giving me an Account of the Situation of Affairs then at Minas; from whence your Grace will perceive that even then he was in Expectation of being Join'd by the Rhode Island Forces & the Company from this Province, which had the Misfortune to be Shipreck'd; and that, had they arriv'd at Annapolis, and the New Hampshire Companies had not return'd home without acting, the Enemy would in all probability have been drove out of Nova Scotia, and every good purpose, which I had propos'd, been answer'd before this time. As it is I shall use my best Endeavours forthwith to fit out a sufficient force by Sea to destroy M.ʳ Ramsay's Vessels at Schiegnecto, and recover our own by Spring, & to send M.ʳ Mascarene such a Reinforcement of Troops as may still drive the Enemy out of Nova Scotia by the same time and prevent any bad Consequences from the late Accident there, which seems necessary to be done (if possible) and I shall hope to succeed in, if the neighbouring Governments of New England will assist in, which I shall urge 'em to do.

"I likewise inclose the Answer of the Inhabitants of Minas to the French Letter which I some time ago Inform'd your Grace I sent M.ʳ Mascarene last Fall, and a Paragraph out of one of his Letters to me upon the same matter; whereby your Grace will perceive that that Letter seems to have had an happy Effect upon the Inhabitants at a most critical Conjuncture.

"The late Secresy of the Inhabitants of Minas with regard to the Enemys Motions, and the very certain Intelligence which the Enemy gain'd of the particular Quarters of the English Officers, notwithstanding their Supplying the King's Troops with Provisions, and the Curtesy of their Behavior to 'em before this Surprize, and their professions of being sorry for it afterwards seems to shew the necessity of his Majesty's Keeping a strong Blockhouse there with a Garrison of 150 men; And the constant ill behavior of the Inhabitants of Schiegnecto seems to make another Blockhouse with a like Garrison there equally necessary, as I at first propos'd to your Grace from Louisbourg; and these two with a Fort and Garrison at Chebucto of 300 Men at least, and the continuance of a Garrison of 300 at Annapolis Royal as it is at present, with a strong Blockhouse at Canso garrison'd with 100 Men would through the constant Correspondence that might be kept up between the several Garrisons be an effectual Security to the Province against the Enemy, and oblige the Inhabitants in a little time to contribute towards the protection & Expence of the Government, and for ever frustrate any hopes the French could Entertain of making themselves Masters of it, by their constant Endeavours to Seduce the Inhabitants from their Allegiance; all which would make Nova Scotia really His Majesty's which it seems scarcely to have been yet: And I would Submit it to your Grace's Consideration whether a Company of Rangers consisting of 100 Indians, or rather two Companies, consisting of 50 each, one to be posted at the Blockhouse at Minas, and the other in Schiegnecto would not be of the greatest Service, in Scouting thro' every part of the Province and in the Woods upon all Emergencies (for which the Regular Troops are by no means fit) and particularly in preventing the French from Introducing Men from Canada into the Province by the Bay Vert; I think the great Service which Lieuᵗ Colonel Gorham's Company of Rangers has been of to the Garrison at Annapolis Royal, is a demonstration of the Usefulness of such a Corps, besides that it may be a means of bringing Indians out of the French Interest into his Majesty's Service, and go far towards reclaiming 'em in general; especially if (as I have before propos'd for your Grace's Consideration) two Trading or Truck Houses were to be maintain'd one at Minas, and the other at Chiegnecto, for supplying the Indians with all necessaries in Exchange for furrs, and proper presents were made to 'em in the manner which the French use to Keep 'em in their Interest.

"And if your Grace would allow me the Freedom to offer my Sentiments concerning what appears to me to be farther necessary for putting this important Province of Nova Scotia (I think I may justly call it the most important to the Crown of any upon this Continent) in Security, I sho'd propose one of His Majesty's Arm'd Sloops (or Snows) with a Tender to be constantly employ'd in the Bay of Fundy for visiting all parts of it upon every occasion, as well as the several Har-

bours on the Cape Sable Coast; and one of his Majesty's
Frigates to be employ'd for the protection of the Fishery at
Canso (as was always usual in time of peace) which together
with a Tender would also be of great Service in duly attending the Bay Verte, upon every Occasion, and likewise visiting
the Coast of Accadie (or Cape Sables) besides protecting the
Fishery.

"Since writing the last Paragraph I have heard of some
other particular circumstances, which make it very suspicious
that several of the Inhabitants at least of Minas knew of the
Enemy's Motions, & I find that it is the general Opinion of
the Officers that they did.

"I am with the most dutiful Regard,

"My Lord Duke,

"Your Grace's most devoted,

"& most humble Servant

"W. SHIRLEY"

SHIRLEY TO NEWCASTLE, BOSTON, APRIL 29TH, 1747.

(*Extract.*)

"MY LORD DUKE,

"Since finishing Governour Knowles's, & my joint Letter
to your Grace, I have learn'd from one of the English Prisoners just Arriv'd from Schiegnecto in Exchange for one of
the French Prisoners sent by me from Boston, and who was
carry'd Captive from Minas, where he was taken by the Enemy in the late Surprize, that when the Canadeans went from
Minas to Schiegnecto they march'd out of the Grand Prè
about 500, but were reduc'd to about 350 before they reach'd
Schiegnecto, by several of their party's leaving 'em at every
great Village in Minas, thro' which they pass'd which makes
it Evident that 150 of the Inhabitants of that District had
Join'd the Canadeans in their late Attack upon the English at
Grand Prè, and may Serve farther to shew your Grace the
imminent Danger of all the Inhabitants of Minas's still Joining the Enemy, unless speedy measures are taken for driving
the Canadeans out of the Country, and Securing the fidelity
of the Inhabitants in some better manner than it is at present;
and how opportunely the forces sent last Winter from hence

to Annapolis, and the Assurances I took the liberty of sending the Nova Scotians that those, who behav'd as good Subjects, sho'd have His Majesty's protection in their Estates, arriv'd there for saving the whole District of Minas from an open Revolt.

"This fluctuating State of the Inhabitants of Accadie seems, my Lord, naturally to arise from their finding a want of due protection from His Majesty's Government; and their Apprehensions that the French will soon be Masters of the Province, which their repeated Attempts every year for the Reduction of His Majesty's Fort at Annapolis Royal, and the Appearance of the late Duke D'Anville's Squadron from France upon their Coast with that View strongly Impress upon 'em, as does also the Residence of the Enemy in the Province, and the Sollicitations of their own Priests; and to this, I believe, may be added some Jealousy, which the Enemy and Priests are for ever instilling into 'em, that the English want only a safe Opportunity of driving all the French Inhabitants off their Settlements; which tho' M.ʳ Mascarene assures me that his communicating to 'em my printed Letter promising 'em His Majesty's protection, had so far allay'd as together with the Arrival of the late Detachment of Soldiers sent from hence in the Winter for the Defence & protection of the Province, to disappoint M.ʳ de Ramsay's Attempt upon the Inhabitants of Minas for bringing 'em to an open Revolt, and to make him retire from Minas to Schiegnecto, yet as the hopes my Letter may have made 'em entertain have not been yet Confirm'd by Assurances of His Majesty's Royal protection directly from England I cant but think, there is a most apparant danger of Nova Scotia's being soon lost, if the Expedition against Canada should not proceed this year, nor any Measures be taken, or particular Orders be sent by His Majesty for Securing the Province against the Enemy & strengthening his Government among the Inhabitants, For I perceive that the General Assembly of this Province, from whence only the Succours & Support which His Majesty's Garrison at Annapolis Royal has hitherto received for the Protection & Defence of Nova Scotia, have been sent, are tir'd of having 'em drawn wholly from their own people, and despair of its being effectual without His Majesty's more immediate Interposition for the protection of that province; And I look upon it as a very happy Incident, that I had it in my power to send M.ʳ Mascarene the Support, I did the last Winter, and beginning of the Spring, out of the Levies rais'd for the Expedition against Canada, which I insisted upon doing as they were in His Majesty's Pay (tho' rais'd for another Service) but should not have been able to do it (I believe) had it depended wholly upon the Consent of the Assembly, tho' generally well dispos'd for His Majesty's Service."

NEWCASTLE TO SHIRLEY, 30 MAY, 1747.
(*Extract.*)

"As you and M.ʳ Warren have represented, That an Opinion prevailed amongst the Inhabitants of Nova Scotia, That It was intended to remove Them from their Settlements and Habitations in that Province; And as that Report may probably have been artfully spread amongst Them in order to induce Them to withdraw Themselves from their Allegiance to His Majesty, and to take Part with the Enemy; His Majesty thinks it necessary, That proper measures should be taken, to remove any such ill-grounded Suggestions; and, for that Purpose, It is the King's Pleasure, That you should declare in some publick and authentick manner to His Majesty's Subjects, Inhabitants of that Province, That there is not the least Foundation for any Apprehension of that nature; But That, on the contrary, It is His Majesty's Resolution to protect, and maintain, all such of Them as shall continue in their Duty, and Allegiance to His Majesty, in the quiet & peaceable Possession of their respective Habitations, and Settlements And That They shall continue to enjoy the free Exercise of their Religion.

"His Majesty did propose to have signed a Proclamation to the purport above mentioned and to have transmitted it to you, to have been published in Nova Scotia; But as the Advices, that have been received here, of a Body of the New England Troops, which were advanced to Menis having been surprised by a Party of the French Canadeans and their Indians, and having been either cut off, or taken Prisoners; And the great Probability there is, That this Misfortune could not have happened to that Body of Troops, without the Assistance or, at least, Connivance of the Inhabitants of Nova Scotia; make it very difficult to fix the Terms of the intended Proclamation; His Majesty thinks it more advisable to leave it to you to make such a Declaration in His Name, as you shall be of Opinion, the present Circumstances of the Province may require."

SHIRLEY TO NEWCASTLE, 8 JUNE, 1747.
(Extract.)

"I have nothing to add to my Letters, which I have lately transmitted to your Grace, except that M.ʳ de Ramsay is still at Chiegnecto with his party in Expectation of a Reinforcement from Canada, and the Arrival of an Armament from France, and that he has not thought fit to venture again to Manis [*Mines*], but insists in his Messages to the Inhabitants there that they should look upon themselves as Subjects to the French King since the New England Troops were oblig'd to retire out of their District by Capitulation, but that this has had no Effect upon the Inhabitants, the Reinforcement, which I sent there afterwards, having taken repossession of Manis, and hoisted the King's Flagg there, and the Deputies of Manis having thereupon renew'd their Oaths of Fidelity to His Majesty at Annapolis Royal; I continue the last Reinforcement at the Garrison still for the Security of that and Manis; But it is not strong enough to drive the French from Schiegnecto, it being suspected that the Inhabitants of that District, who were ever refractory to His Majesty's Government, would not scruple to Join the Enemy in case of an attack upon 'em; And I could not think it adviseable for me to send all the Forces, which I had rais'd for the Expedition against Canada within this Government upon another Service (as I must have done to have been strong enough to force the Enemy out of Schiegnecto after the Action at Minas) when I was in daily Expectation of receiving His Majesty's Commands concerning the prosecution of the intended expedition, and besides, the Assembly, which has been at a great Expence for the raising of the men for the service of the Expedition only, strongly insisted upon my reserving 1500 of 'em to go against Crown Point, as your Grace will perceive by the inclos'd Copy of their Answer to my Message; However the several Reinforcements, which I did send to Annapolis, have preserv'd the Garrison and province from falling into the Enemys hands the last year, and not only made the Enemy quit Manis, but still Confine 'em to Schiegnecto; and had the Rhode Island & New Hampshire Troops Join'd the Massachusetts Forces at Manis, as was propos'd, and both those Governments promis'd me they should, and one of the Massachusetts Companies had not been lost in their passage, we should have been strong enough (I am perswaded) to have drove the Enemy the last Winter quite out of the Province of Nova Scotia: As it is, I doubt not, if no Armament arrives from France, we shall be able to keep 'em out of Annapolis and Manis till I receive His Majesty's Commands, which I am in daily Expectation of, and will, I hope, Enable me to take effectual Measures for getting rid of the Enemy and Securing the Province against their Attempts for the future."

SHIRLEY TO NEWCASTLE, BOSTON, 25 JUNE, 1747.
(Extract.)

"MY LORD DUKE,

"Since my last to your Grace, I have Accounts from Nova Scotia, that the French have rais'd a Battery of Nine Guns on the back of Schiegnecto to oppose the landing of Forces from Bay Verte, that they were also building a Fort & had landed Cannon & Mortars there, which they were now hawling by Land, and may use either for Fortifying that District, or transport from thence to Annapolis Royal for the Reduction of his Majesty's Garrison; There has been likewise further Accounts from thence that the Inhabitants were in Expectation of 1000 Men from Canada, which together with the Indians & People of Schiegnecto, & some of Manis, it is said, would make up M.ʳ De Ramsay's Party 5000, who were then to proceed against Annapolis; and that three large French Ships of Force had been seen in Bay Verte, viz.ᵗ two from Canada & one from France and landed Troops & Stores. These Accounts gain Credit the more easily as it seems not to be doubted, but that the French have the Reduction of Nova

Scotia extremely at heart, and will be continually making some Attempt or other against it, whilst the Warr lasts; and I am sorry to find by a Message lately sent me from the Assembly desiring I would recall the Soldiers, I last sent to Annapolis, that they seem out of heart about the effectual Preservation of it from the Enemy. Should the French gain it by any sudden Stroke, I am perswaded, they would be so strong there by the Addition of all the Inhabitants to their other Forces, as well as the Numbers they would draw from Canada, & by immediate Fortifications of it, that it would require a very considerable Armament & Number of Troops to recover it from 'em; which makes me think it my Indispensable Duty to trouble your Grace with so frequent a Repetition of my Apprehensions concerning it. The enemy may indeed be now look'd upon as Masters of Scheignecto which Place it is evident they are busy in fortifying; & would have been so likewise of Manis by this time, had they not been oblig'd to withdraw their Troops from thence last Fall by the Arrival of the Detachments, I sent there."

SHIRLEY TO NEWCASTLE, 8 JULY, 1747.
(*Extract.*)

"I shall now take the Liberty to submit to your Grace's Consideration the most practicable Scheme, that occurs to me at present for effectually driving & keeping the Canadeans out of Nova Scotia; viz! if M!. Knowles when the Season is too far advanc'd for the French to make an Attempt from France against Louisbourg, should detach 1000 Men out of that Garrison to be join'd by 2000 from New England at Annapolis Royal, and from thence to proceed to Schiegnecto; that Force would, I apprehend, drive the Enemy off, and easily make us Masters of all the Inhabitants of that District, who seem to have ever been so deeply engaged on the Side of the Enemy as to make 'em forfeit all pretence of right to hold their Possessions; and if the 2000 New England Men were to share among 'em that District upon Condition of their setling there with their Families in such a defensible manner as they should be directed to do, and the french Inhabitants of that District were to be transplanted into New England, and distributed among the four Governments there; That I apprehend might be a Settlement of the District of Schiegnecto strong enough to keep the Canadeans out, and to defend themselves against the Indians; and the Inhabitants of the two other Districts of Nova Scotia, viz.ᵗ Menis & Annapolis, being thus lock'd up between the Settlement in Schiegnecto at one End, and his Majesty's Garrison at the other, and aw'd by the removal of the french Inhabitants of Schiegnecto from off their Lands, would be constantly held to their good behaviour, and by Intermarriages & the spreading of the English Settlement from Schiegnecto, the whole Province, or at least the greatest part of it, might in two or three Generations become English Protestants— I would add that such an Exchange of the present Inhabitants of Schiegnecto for New England Men, would make up to the four Colonies of New England the Loss of the Families propos'd to be remov'd from thence to Nova Scotia upon this Occasion, hinder Canada's being strengthened by the Expulsion of the French from their Possessions, & prevent the English Settlement at Schiegnecto from being harrass'd by their continual Attempts to recover their former Lands; And the Encouragement given to the New England Men by the propos'd Distribution of the Lands among 'em would besides make the raising of 2000 Men for this Service much more practicable, & less expensive to the Crown.

"Upon the whole, my Lord, if the War continues, unless some measures are very suddenly taken for the better Security of Nova Scotia, there seems to be great danger that that Province will not long remain his Majesty's.

"I am with the most dutiful regard,

"My Lord Duke,

"Your Grace's most devoted and

"most Obedient Servant

"W Shirley."

Shirley to Newcastle, 24 August, 1747.

"My Lord Duke,

"The French Declaration, of which the inclos'd is a Copy, did not come to my hands till I had finished the letter, wᶜʰ accompanies it: And I send it your Grace, as it may serve to shew the Views of the French with respect to Accadie, the Dependance they have upon the Dispositions of the Inhabitants, what advantage they propos'd to themselves from the New England Levies under the Command of the late Lieuten. Col. Noble's quitting Menis by Capitulation, and the necessity there was of my sending the last Detachment of soldiers to M. Mascarene to take repossession of Menis, and make the Inhabitants of it renew their oath of fidelity to his Majesty; which had its desir'd Effect.

"I am with the most Dutifull regard
"My Lord Duke,
"Your Grace's Most Devoted,
"and Most Obedient Humble Servant
"W SHIRLEY."

SHIRLEY TO NEWCASTLE, 20 OCT. 1747.
(*Extract.*)

"The general Inclination which, the french Inhabitants of Nova Scotia have to the french Interest, proceeds from their Ties of Consanguinity to the French of Canada, but more especially from those of their Religion, which last seems to put 'em greatly under the Influence of their Priests, who continually receive their Directions from the Bishop of Quebeck, & are the Instruments, by which the Governour of Canada makes all his Attempts for the Reduction of the Province to the french Crown, & Keeps the Indians of Nova Scotia (commonly called the Cape Sable Indians) in their Dependence upon him; particular Instances of which may be given in the first Body of French & Indians, which attack'd the King's Garrison soon after the Declaration of the present War's being headed by a Priest of Nova Scotia; and the principal Part in giving Intelligence to the Enemy, maintaining the Correspondence between Canada and Nova Scotia, assembling Cape Sable Indians, & influencing such of the Inhabitants as had joined with or assisted the Enemy, has been manag'd by another Priest of that Province; Other Instances of this Kind might be given, as particularly the Attempt to bring the Inhabitants into Revolt soon after the late Surprize at Menis by endeavouring to influence 'em with the Authority of the Bishop of Quebeck pronouncing 'em to be free from their Oath of Allegiance to his Majesty. But I shall content myself with observing to your Grace only one piece of Policy made use of by the french Priests in Nova Scotia for preserving the whole Body of the People intirely french, and Roman Catholick's, viz. forbidding all Intermarriages with the English under Pain of Excommunication, (of which I am informed there has been one or two late Instances in actual Excommunication upon this Occasion) & which has had so general an Effect as to prevent the Settlement of any one English Family within the Province, from the first Reduction of it to the present time, tho' some have attempted to setle in the Country; & to Keep out Inter-marriages between the French & his Majesty's English Subjects, as that I never heard of any one Instance besides the before mentioned ones; And I would humbly submit it to your Grace's Consideration if the free Exercise of the Roman Catholick Religion and an unlimited Toleration of Roman Priests in Nova Scotia should continue to have the same Effect in that Colony for the next succeeding forty years, as it has had within these last forty; the Inhabitants there are suffer'd to remain a distinct Body of French in the Neighbourhood of Canada, with the Ties of Consanguinity & Religion between *them* & the Canadeans still growing stronger, untill they double or perhaps treble their Number (the French of Canada likewise at the same time increasing their Strength & Numbers) whether it may not prove in the End cherishing a Colony of Inhabitants for the subversion of the King's Government in it, & the strengthening of the french Interest upon the Continent.

"The Treaty of Utrecht, my Lord, by which the cession of Accadie (or Nova Scotia) with its Inhabitants was made to the Crown of Great Britain does not seem to lay his Majesty under an Obligation to allow the french Inhabitants the Exercise of the Roman Catholick Religion; and as his Majesty is as yet under no Promise to do it, I should hope that Methods might be found for weakening the Ties of Consanguinity & Religion between even the present Generation of the french inhabitants of Nova Scotia & those of Canada, by beginning new ones between his Majesty's English & french subjects there, and at the same time controuling the pernicious Power

of the Romish Priests over the french Inhabitants & the Indians of that Province, which may possibly be cut off or at
least obstructed by his Majesty's making a Promise to continue the french Inhabitants in the free Exercise of their Religion.

"Wherefore as his Majesty has been pleas'd to refer it to my
Opinion to fix the Terms of the Declaration, which he has
commanded me to make in his Name to the Inhabitants of
Nova Scotia; whereby it became my Duty to avoid every
thing in it, which appear'd to me to have a Tendency to dis-
serve his Government within that Province, I have taken the
Liberty to suspend promising 'em the free Exercise of the
Romish Religion, tho' it is mention'd in your Grace's Letter
to have been part of what was at first propos'd to have been
included in his Majesty's intended Proclamation, till I could
transmit my Sentiments to your Grace, and I should have his
Majesty's farther Directions upon it; & have in the mean time
made a Declaration of such Points, as seem'd necessary to be
ascertained to the Inhabitants for quieting their Minds, &
would not admit of Delay.

"I might mention to your Grace some local Reasons for my
Omitting in the Declaration what I have done, but shall not
presume to trouble you with any but what I thought it my
indispensable Duty to lay before your Grace.

"I am with the most dutiful Regard
       "My Lord Duke,
            "Your Grace's most Devoted
                "and most Obedient Servant
                                "W Shirley."

MONTCALM AND WOLFE

Part I

Contents

Preface 841

Introduction 843

CHAPTER I 1745–1755
THE COMBATANTS
 *England in the Eighteenth Century • Her Political and Social
Aspects • Her Military Condition • France • Her Power and
Importance • Signs of Decay • The Court, the Nobles, the
Clergy, the People • The King and Pompadour • The Philoso-
phers • Germany • Prussia • Frederic II. • Russia • State
of Europe • War of the Austrian Succession • American Colo-
nies of France and England • Contrasted Systems and their
Results • Canada • Its Strong Military Position • French
Claims to the Continent • British Colonies • New England •
Virginia • Pennsylvania • New York • Jealousies, Divisions,
Internal Disputes, Military Weakness* 847

CHAPTER II 1749–1752
CÉLORON DE BIENVILLE
 *La Galissonière • English Encroachment • Mission of Céloron
• The Great West • Its European Claimants • Its Indian
Population • English Fur-Traders • Céloron on the Alleghany
• His Reception • His Difficulties • Descent of the Ohio •
Covert Hostility • Ascent of the Miami • La Demoiselle •
Dark Prospects for France • Christopher Gist • George
Croghan • Their Western Mission • Pickawillany • English
Ascendency • English Dissension and Rivalry • The Key of the
Great West* 870

CHAPTER III 1749–1753
CONFLICT FOR THE WEST
 *The Five Nations • Caughnawaga • Abbé Piquet • His
Schemes • His Journey • Fort Frontenac • Toronto • Niag-
ara • Oswego • Success of Piquet • Detroit • La Jonquière •
His Intrigues • His Trials • His Death • English Intrigues •
Critical State of the West • Pickawillany Destroyed • Du-
quesne • His Grand Enterprise* 888

Chapter IV 1710–1754
CONFLICT FOR ACADIA

Acadia ceded to England • *Acadians swear Fidelity* • *Halifax founded* • *French Intrigue* • *Acadian Priests* • *Mildness of English Rule* • *Covert Hostility of Acadians* • *The New Oath* • *Treachery of Versailles* • *Indians incited to War* • *Clerical Agents of Revolt* • *Abbé Le Loutre* • *Acadians impelled to emigrate* • *Misery of the Emigrants* • *Humanity of Cornwallis and Hopson* • *Fanaticism and Violence of Le Loutre* • *Capture of the "St. François"* • *The English at Beaubassin* • *Le Loutre drives out the Inhabitants* • *Murder of Howe* • *Beauséjour* • *Insolence of Le Loutre* • *His Harshness to the Acadians* • *The Boundary Commission* • *Its Failure* • *Approaching War* 906

Chapter V 1753, 1754
WASHINGTON

The French occupy the Sources of the Ohio • *Their Sufferings* • *Fort Le Bœuf* • *Legardeur de Saint-Pierre* • *Mission of Washington* • *Robert Dinwiddie* • *He opposes the French* • *His Dispute with the Burgesses* • *His Energy* • *His Appeals for Help* • *Fort Duquesne* • *Death of Jumonville* • *Washington at the Great Meadows* • *Coulon de Villiers* • *Fort Necessity* 932

Chapter VI 1754, 1755
THE SIGNAL OF BATTLE

Troubles of Dinwiddie • *Gathering of the Burgesses* • *Virginian Society* • *Refractory Legislators* • *The Quaker Assembly* • *It refuses to resist the French* • *Apathy of New York* • *Shirley and the General Court of Massachusetts* • *Short-sighted Policy* • *Attitude of Royal Governors* • *Indian Allies waver* • *Convention at Albany* • *Scheme of Union* • *It fails* • *Dinwiddie and Glen* • *Dinwiddie calls on England for Help* • *The Duke of Newcastle* • *Weakness of the British Cabinet* • *Attitude of France* • *Mutual Dissimulation* • *Both Powers send Troops to America* • *Collision* • *Capture of the "Alcide" and the "Lis"* 955

Chapter VII 1755
BRADDOCK

Arrival of Braddock • *His Character* • *Council at Alexandria* • *Plan of the Campaign* • *Apathy of the Colonists* • *Rage of Braddock* • *Franklin* • *Fort Cumberland* • *Composi-*

tion of the Army • Offended Friends • The March • The
French Fort • Savage Allies • The Captive • Beaujeu • He
goes to meet the English • Passage of the Monongahela • The
Surprise • The Battle • Rout of Braddock • His Death • Indian Ferocity • Reception of the Ill News • Weakness of Dunbar • The Frontier abandoned 972

CHAPTER VIII 1755–1763
REMOVAL OF THE ACADIANS

State of Acadia • Threatened Invasion • Peril of the English
• Their Plans • French Forts to be attacked • Beauséjour and
its Occupants • French Treatment of the Acadians • John
Winslow • Siege and Capture of Beauséjour • Attitude of
Acadians • Influence of their Priests • They refuse the Oath of
Allegiance • Their Condition and Character • Pretended
Neutrals • Moderation of English Authorities • The Acadians
persist in their Refusal • Enemies or Subjects? • Choice of the
Acadians • The Consequence • Their Removal determined •
Winslow at Grand Pré • Conference with Murray • Sum-
mons to the Inhabitants • Their Seizure • Their Embarkation
• Their Fate • Their Treatment in Canada • Misapprehen-
sion concerning them 1006

CHAPTER IX 1755
DIESKAU

Expedition against Crown Point • William Johnson • Vau-
dreuil • Dieskau • Johnson and the Indians • The Provincial
Army • Doubts and Delays • March to Lake George • Sun-
day in Camp • Advance of Dieskau • He changes Plan •
Marches against Johnson • Ambush • Rout of Provincials •
Battle of Lake George • Rout of the French • Rage of the
Mohawks • Peril of Dieskau • Inaction of Johnson • The
Homeward March • Laurels of Victory 1041

CHAPTER X 1755, 1756
SHIRLEY—BORDER WAR

The Niagara Campaign • Albany • March to Oswego •
Difficulties • The Expedition abandoned • Shirley and John-
son • Results of the Campaign • The Scourge of the Border •
Trials of Washington • Misery of the Settlers • Horror of their
Situation • Philadelphia and the Quakers • Disputes with the
Penns • Democracy and Feudalism • Pennsylvanian Popula-

tion • Appeals from the Frontier • Quarrel of Governor and
Assembly • Help refused • Desperation of the Borderers • Fire
and Slaughter • The Assembly alarmed • They pass a mock
Militia Law • They are forced to yield   1063

CHAPTER XI   1712–1756
MONTCALM
War declared • State of Europe • Pompadour and Maria
Theresa • Infatuation of the French Court • The European
War • Montcalm to command in America • His early Life •
An intractable Pupil • His Marriage • His Family • His
Campaigns • Preparation for America • His Associates •
Lévis, Bourlamaque, Bougainville • Embarkation • The Voy-
age • Arrival • Vaudreuil • Forces of Canada • Troops of
the Line, Colony Troops, Militia, Indians • The Military Situ-
ation • Capture of Fort Bull • Montcalm at Ticonderoga   1085

CHAPTER XII   1756
OSWEGO
The new Campaign • Untimely Change of Commanders •
Eclipse of Shirley • Earl of Loudon • Muster of Provincials •
New England Levies • Winslow at Lake George • Johnson
and the Five Nations • Bradstreet and his Boatmen • Fight
on the Onondaga • Pestilence at Oswego • Loudon and the
Provincials • New England Camps • Army Chaplains • A
sudden Blow • Montcalm attacks Oswego • Its Fall   1104

CHAPTER XIII   1756, 1757
PARTISAN WAR
Failure of Shirley's Plan • Causes • Loudon and Shirley •
Close of the Campaign • The Western Border • Armstrong
destroys Kittanning • The Scouts of Lake George • War Par-
ties from Ticonderoga • Robert Rogers • The Rangers •
Their Hardihood and Daring • Disputes as to Quarters of
Troops • Expedition of Rogers • A Desperate Bush-fight •
Enterprise of Vaudreuil • Rigaud attacks Fort William Henry   1128

CHAPTER XIV   1757
MONTCALM AND VAUDREUIL
The Seat of War • Social Life at Montreal • Familiar Corre-
spondence of Montcalm • His Employments • His Impressions

*of Canada • His Hospitalities • Misunderstandings with the
Governor • Character of Vaudreuil • His Accusations •
Frenchmen and Canadians • Foibles of Montcalm • The
opening Campaign • Doubts and Suspense • Loudon's Plan •
His Character • Fatal Delays • Abortive Attempt against
Louisbourg • Disaster to the British Fleet*   1152

CHAPTER XV   1757
FORT WILLIAM HENRY
*Another Blow • The War-song • The Army at Ticonderoga •
Indian Allies • The War-feast • Treatment of Prisoners •
Cannibalism • Surprise and Slaughter • The War Council
• March of Lévis • The Army embarks • Fort William Henry •
Nocturnal Scene • Indian Funeral • Advance upon the Fort
• General Webb • His Difficulties • His Weakness • The
Siege begun • Conduct of the Indians • The Intercepted
Letter • Desperate Position of the Besieged • Capitulation •
Ferocity of the Indians • Mission of Bougainville • Murder
of Wounded Men • A Scene of Terror • The Massacre •
Efforts of Montcalm • The Fort burned*   1166

CHAPTER XVI   1757, 1758
A WINTER OF DISCONTENT
*Boasts of Loudon • A Mutinous Militia • Panic • Accusa-
tions of Vaudreuil • His Weakness • Indian Barbarities •
Destruction of German Flats • Discontent of Montcalm • Fes-
tivities at Montreal • Montcalm's Relations with the Governor
• Famine • Riots • Mutiny • Winter at Ticonderoga • A
desperate Bush-fight • Defeat of the Rangers • Adventures of
Roche and Pringle*   1197

CHAPTER XVII   1753–1760
BIGOT
*His Life and Character • Canadian Society • Official Festivi-
ties • A Party of Pleasure • Hospitalities of Bigot • Desperate
Gambling • Château Bigot • Canadian Ladies • Cadet • La
Friponne • Official Rascality • Methods of Peculation • Cruel
Frauds on the Acadians • Military Corruption • Péan • Love
and Knavery • Varin and his Partners • Vaudreuil and the
Peculators • He defends Bigot; praises Cadet and Péan • Ca-
nadian Finances • Peril of Bigot • Threats of the Minister •
Evidence of Montcalm • Impending Ruin of the Confederates*   1208

CHAPTER XVIII   1757, 1758
PITT

*Frederic of Prussia • The Coalition against him • His desper-
ate Position • Rossbach • Leuthen • Reverses of England •
Weakness of the Ministry • A Change • Pitt and Newcastle •
Character of Pitt • Sources of his Power • His Aims • Louis
XV. • Pompadour • She controls the Court, and directs the
War • Gloomy Prospects of England • Disasters • The New
Ministry • Inspiring Influence of Pitt • The Tide turns •
British Victories • Pitt's Plans for America • Louisbourg, Ti-
conderoga, Duquesne • New Commanders • Naval Battles*   1222

CHAPTER XIX   1758
LOUISBOURG

*Condition of the Fortress • Arrival of the English • Gallantry
of Wolfe • The English Camp • The Siege begun • Progress
of the Besiegers • Sallies of the French • Madame Drucour •
Courtesies of War • French Ships destroyed • Conflagration •
Fury of the Bombardment • Exploit of English Sailors • The
End near • The White Flag • Surrender • Reception of the
News in England and America • Wolfe not satisfied • His
Letters to Amherst • He destroys Gaspé • Returns to England*   1231

CHAPTER XX   1758
TICONDEROGA

*Activity of the Provinces • Sacrifices of Massachusetts • The
Army at Lake George • Proposed Incursion of Lévis • Perplexities of Montcalm • His Plan of Defence • Camp of Abercromby • His Character • Lord Howe • His Popularity •
Embarkation of Abercromby • Advance down Lake George •
Landing • Forest Skirmish • Death of Howe • Its Effects •
Position of the French • The Lines of Ticonderoga • Blunders
of Abercromby • The Assault • A Frightful Scene • Incidents
of the Battle • British Repulse • Panic • Retreat • Triumph
of Montcalm*   1253

CHAPTER XXI   1758
FORT FRONTENAC

*The Routed Army • Indignation at Abercromby • John
Cleaveland and his Brother Chaplains • Regulars and Provin-*

cials • Provincial Surgeons • French Raids • Rogers defeats
Marin • Adventures of Putnam • Expedition of Bradstreet •
Capture of Fort Frontenac   1275

CHAPTER XXII 1758
FORT DUQUESNE
Dinwiddie and Washington • Brigadier Forbes • His Army •
Conflicting Views • Difficulties • Illness of Forbes • His Suf-
ferings • His Fortitude • His Difference with Washington •
Sir John Sinclair • Troublesome Allies • Scouting Parties •
Boasts of Vaudreuil • Forbes and the Indians • Mission of
Christian Frederic Post • Council of Peace • Second Mission of
Post • Defeat of Grant • Distress of Forbes • Dark Prospects
• Advance of the Army • Capture of the French Fort • The
Slain of Braddock's Field • Death of Forbes   1286

CHAPTER XXIII 1758, 1759
THE BRINK OF RUIN
Jealousy of Vaudreuil • He asks for Montcalm's Recall • His
Discomfiture • Scene at the Governor's House • Disgust of
Montcalm • The Canadians Despondent • Devices to encour-
age them • Gasconade of the Governor • Deplorable State of
the Colony • Mission of Bougainville • Duplicity of Vaudreuil
• Bougainville at Versailles • Substantial Aid refused to Can-
ada • A Matrimonial Treaty • Return of Bougainville •
Montcalm abandoned by the Court • His Plans of Defence •
Sad News from Candiac • Promises of Vaudreuil   1308

CHAPTER XXIV 1758, 1759
WOLFE
The Exiles of Fort Cumberland • Relief • The Voyage to
Louisbourg • The British Fleet • Expedition against Quebec •
Early Life of Wolfe • His Character • His Letters to his Par-
ents • His Domestic Qualities • Appointed to command the
Expedition • Sails for America   1320

CHAPTER XXV 1759
WOLFE AT QUEBEC
French Preparation • Muster of Forces • Gasconade of Vaudreuil • Plan of Defence • Strength of Montcalm • Advance
of Wolfe • British Sailors • Landing of the English • Difficulties before them • Storm • Fireships • Confidence of

French Commanders • Wolfe occupies Point Levi • A Futile
Night Attack • Quebec bombarded • Wolfe at the Montmorenci • Skirmishes • Danger of the English Position • Effects
of the Bombardment • Desertion of Canadians • The English
above Quebec • Severities of Wolfe • Another Attempt to burn
the Fleet • Desperate Enterprise of Wolfe • The Heights of
Montmorenci • Repulse of the English   1331

CHAPTER XXVI   1759
AMHERST—NIAGARA
Amherst on Lake George • Capture of Ticonderoga and
Crown Point • Delays of Amherst • Niagara Expedition •
La Corne attacks Oswego • His Repulse • Niagara besieged •
Aubry comes to its Relief • Battle • Rout of the French • The
Fort taken • Isle-aux-Noix • Amherst advances to attack it •
Storm • The Enterprise abandoned • Rogers attacks St. Fran-
cis • Destroys the Town • Sufferings of the Rangers   1359

CHAPTER XXVII   1759
THE HEIGHTS OF ABRAHAM
Elation of the French • Despondency of Wolfe • The Parishes
laid waste • Operations above Quebec • Illness of Wolfe • A
New Plan of Attack • Faint Hope of Success • Wolfe's Last
Despatch • Confidence of Vaudreuil • Last Letters of Mont-
calm • French Vigilance • British Squadron at Cap-Rouge •
Last Orders of Wolfe • Embarkation • Descent of the St.
Lawrence • The Heights scaled • The British Line • Last
Night of Montcalm • The Alarm • March of French Troops •
The Battle • The Rout • The Pursuit • Fall of Wolfe and of
Montcalm   1375

CHAPTER XXVIII   1759
FALL OF QUEBEC
After the Battle • Canadians resist the Pursuit • Arrival of
Vaudreuil • Scene in the Redoubt • Panic • Movements of
the Victors • Vaudreuil's Council of War • Precipitate Retreat of the French Army • Last Hours of Montcalm • His
Death and Burial • Quebec abandoned to its Fate • Despair
of the Garrison • Lévis joins the Army • Attempts to relieve
the Town • Surrender • The British occupy Quebec • Slan-

ders of Vaudreuil • Reception in England of the News of
Wolfe's Victory and Death • Prediction of Jonathan Mayhew   1402

Chapter XXIX   1759, 1760
SAINTE-FOY
   Quebec after the Siege • Captain Knox and the Nuns • Es-
   cape of French Ships • Winter at Quebec • Threats of Lévis •
   Attacks • Skirmishes • Feat of the Rangers • State of the
   Garrison • The French prepare to retake Quebec • Advance of
   Lévis • The Alarm • Sortie of the English • Rash Determi-
   nation of Murray • Battle of Ste.-Foy • Retreat of the English
   • Lévis besieges Quebec • Spirit of the Garrison • Peril of
   their Situation • Relief • Quebec saved • Retreat of Lévis •
   The News in England   1421

Chapter XXX   1760
FALL OF CANADA
   Desperate Situation • Efforts of Vaudreuil and Lévis • Plans
   of Amherst • A Triple Attack • Advance of Murray • Advance of Haviland • Advance of Amherst • Capitulation of
   Montreal • Protest of Lévis • Injustice of Louis XV. • Joy in
   the British Colonies • Character of the War   1443

Chapter XXXI   1758–1763
THE PEACE OF PARIS
   Exodus of Canadian Leaders • Wreck of the "Auguste"
   • Trial of Bigot and his Confederates • Frederic of Prussia •
   His Triumphs • His Reverses • His Peril • His Fortitude •
   Death of George II. • Change of Policy • Choiseul • His
   Overtures of Peace • The Family Compact • Fall of Pitt •
   Death of the Czarina • Frederic saved • War with Spain •
   Capture of Havana • Negotiations • Terms of Peace • Shall
   Canada be restored? • Speech of Pitt • The Treaty signed •
   End of the Seven Years War   1458

Chapter XXXII   1763–1884
CONCLUSION
   Results of the War • Germany • France • England • Can-
   ada • The British Provinces   1475

APPENDIX

A. Chapter III. Conflict for the West 1480
B. Chapter IV. Acadia 1481
C. Chapter V. Washington 1484
D. Chapter VII. Braddock 1485
E. Chapter XIV. Montcalm 1488
F. Chapter XV. Fort William Henry 1489
G. Chapter XX. Ticonderoga 1492
H. Chapter XXV. Wolfe at Quebec 1497
I. Chapter XXVII. The Heights of Abraham 1498
J. Chapter XXVIII. Fall of Quebec 1500
K. Chapter XXIX. Sainte-Foy 1502

Illustrations

Montcalm, aged 29 846
British Colonies and Northern New France, 1750–1760 850–51
Acadia with Adjacent Islands, 1755 908
Sketches of the Field of Battle, July 9 978–79
The Region of Lake George from surveys made in 1762 1170
Siege of Fort William Henry, 1757 1171
Wolfe, aged 16 1196
Siege of Louisbourg, 1758 1236
Sketch of the Country round Tyconderoga 1254
Wolfe, aged 32 1324
Siege of Quebec, 1759 1334

Preface

T HE NAMES on the titlepage stand as representative of the
two nations whose final contest for the control of North
America is the subject of the book.

A very large amount of unpublished material has been used
in its preparation, consisting for the most part of documents
copied from the archives and libraries of France and England,
especially from the Archives de la Marine et des Colonies, the
Archives de la Guerre, and the Archives Nationales at Paris,
and the Public Record Office and the British Museum at London. The papers copied for the present work in France alone
exceed six thousand folio pages of manuscript, additional and
supplementary to the "Paris Documents" procured for the
State of New York under the agency of Mr. Brodhead. The
copies made in England form ten volumes, besides many English documents consulted in the original manuscript. Great
numbers of autograph letters, diaries, and other writings of
persons engaged in the war have also been examined on this
side of the Atlantic.

I owe to the kindness of the present Marquis de Montcalm
the permission to copy all the letters written by his ancestor,
General Montcalm, when in America, to members of his family in France. General Montcalm, from his first arrival in Canada to a few days before his death, also carried on an active
correspondence with one of his chief officers, Bourlamaque,
with whom he was on terms of intimacy. These autograph
letters are now preserved in a private collection. I have examined them, and obtained copies of the whole. They form
an interesting complement to the official correspondence of
the writer, and throw the most curious side-lights on the persons and events of the time.

Besides manuscripts, the printed matter in the form of
books, pamphlets, contemporary newspapers, and other publications relating to the American part of the Seven Years'
War, is varied and abundant; and I believe I may safely say
that nothing in it of much consequence has escaped me. The
liberality of some of the older States of the Union, especially

New York and Pennsylvania, in printing the voluminous records of their colonial history, has saved me a deal of tedious labor.

The whole of this published and unpublished mass of evidence has been read and collated with extreme care, and more than common pains have been taken to secure accuracy of statement. The study of books and papers, however, could not alone answer the purpose. The plan of the work was formed in early youth; and though various causes have long delayed its execution, it has always been kept in view. Meanwhile, I have visited and examined every spot where events of any importance in connection with the contest took place, and have observed with attention such scenes and persons as might help to illustrate those I meant to describe. In short, the subject has been studied as much from life and in the open air as at the library table.

These two volumes are a departure from chronological sequence. The period between 1700 and 1748 has been passed over for a time. When this gap is filled, the series of "France and England in North America" will form a continuous history of the French occupation of the continent.

The portrait in the first volume is from a photograph of the original picture in possession of the Marquis de Montcalm; that in the second, from a photograph of the original picture in possession of Admiral Warde.

BOSTON, *Sept. 16, 1884.*

Introduction

IT IS the nature of great events to obscure the great events that came before them. The Seven Years War in Europe is seen but dimly through revolutionary convulsions and Napoleonic tempests; and the same contest in America is half lost to sight behind the storm-cloud of the War of Independence. Few at this day see the momentous issues involved in it, or the greatness of the danger that it averted. The strife that armed all the civilized world began here. "Such was the complication of political interests," says Voltaire, "that a cannon-shot fired in America could give the signal that set Europe in a blaze." Not quite. It was not a cannon-shot, but a volley from the hunting-pieces of a few backwoodsmen, commanded by a Virginian youth, George Washington.

To us of this day, the result of the American part of the war seems a foregone conclusion. It was far from being so; and very far from being so regarded by our forefathers. The numerical superiority of the British colonies was offset by organic weaknesses fatal to vigorous and united action. Nor at the outset did they, or the mother-country, aim at conquering Canada, but only at pushing back her boundaries. Canada— using the name in its restricted sense—was a position of great strength; and even when her dependencies were overcome, she could hold her own against forces far superior. Armies could reach her only by three routes,—the Lower St. Lawrence on the east, the Upper St. Lawrence on the west, and Lake Champlain on the south. The first access was guarded by a fortress almost impregnable by nature, and the second by a long chain of dangerous rapids; while the third offered a series of points easy to defend. During this same war, Frederic of Prussia held his ground triumphantly against greater odds, though his kingdom was open on all sides to attack.

It was the fatuity of Louis XV. and his Pompadour that made the conquest of Canada possible. Had they not broken the traditionary policy of France, allied themselves to Austria, her ancient enemy, and plunged needlessly into the European war, the whole force of the kingdom would have been turned, from the first, to the humbling of England and the defence of the French colonies. The French soldiers left dead on inglorious Continental battle-fields could have saved Canada, and perhaps made good her claim to the vast territories of the West.

But there were other contingencies. The possession of Canada was a question of diplomacy as well as of war. If England conquered her, she might restore her, as she had lately restored Cape Breton. She had an interest in keeping France alive on the American continent. More than one clear eye saw, at the middle of the last century, that the subjection of Canada would lead to a revolt of the British colonies. So long as an active and enterprising enemy threatened their borders, they could not break with the mother-country, because they needed her help. And if the arms of France had prospered in the other hemisphere; if she had gained in Europe or Asia territories with which to buy back what she had lost in America, then, in all likelihood, Canada would have passed again into her hands.

The most momentous and far-reaching question ever brought to issue on this continent was: Shall France remain here, or shall she not? If, by diplomacy or war, she had preserved but the half, or less than the half, of her American possessions, then a barrier would have been set to the spread of the English-speaking races; there would have been no Revolutionary War; and for a long time, at least, no independence. It was not a question of scanty populations strung along the banks of the St. Lawrence; it was—or under a government of any worth it would have been—a question of the armies and generals of France. America owes much to the imbecility of Louis XV. and the ambitious vanity and personal dislikes of his mistress.

The Seven Years War made England what she is. It crippled the commerce of her rival, ruined France in two continents, and blighted her as a colonial power. It gave England the control of the seas and the mastery of North America and India, made her the first of commercial nations, and prepared that vast colonial system that has planted new Englands in every quarter of the globe. And while it made England what

she is, it supplied to the United States the indispensable condition of their greatness, if not of their national existence.

Before entering on the story of the great contest, we will
look at the parties to it on both sides of the Atlantic.

MONTCALM.

AGED 29.

Chapter I

1745–1755

THE COMBATANTS

England in the Eighteenth Century • Her Political and Social Aspects • Her Military Condition • France • Her Power and Importance • Signs of Decay • The Court, the Nobles, the Clergy, the People • The King and Pompadour • The Philosophers • Germany • Prussia • Frederic II. • Russia • State of Europe • War of the Austrian Succession • American Colonies of France and England • Contrasted Systems and their Results • Canada • Its Strong Military Position • French Claims to the Continent • British Colonies • New England • Virginia • Pennsylvania • New York • Jealousies, Divisions, Internal Disputes, Military Weakness

---

THE LATTER HALF of the reign of George II. was one of the most prosaic periods in English history. The civil wars and the Restoration had had their enthusiasms, religion and liberty on one side, and loyalty on the other; but the old fires declined when William III. came to the throne, and died to ashes under the House of Hanover. Loyalty lost half its inspiration when it lost the tenet of the divine right of kings; and nobody could now hold that tenet with any consistency except the defeated and despairing Jacobites. Nor had anybody as yet proclaimed the rival dogma of the divine right of the people. The reigning monarch held his crown neither of God nor of the nation, but of a parliament controlled by a ruling class. The Whig aristocracy had done a priceless service to English liberty. It was full of political capacity, and by no means void of patriotism; but it was only a part of the national life. Nor was it at present moved by political emotions in any high sense. It had done its great work when it expelled the Stuarts and placed William of Orange on the throne; its ascendency was now complete. The Stuarts had received their death-blow at Culloden; and nothing was left to the dominant party but to dispute on subordinate questions, and contend for office among themselves. The Tory squires sulked in their country-houses, hunted foxes, and grumbled against the reigning dynasty; yet hardly wished to see the nation convulsed by a counter-revolution and another return of the Stuarts.

If politics had run to commonplace, so had morals; and so too had religion. Despondent writers of the day even complained that British courage had died out. There was little sign to the common eye that under a dull and languid surface, forces were at work preparing a new life, material, moral, and intellectual. As yet, Whitefield and Wesley had not wakened the drowsy conscience of the nation, nor the voice of William Pitt roused it like a trumpet-peal.

It was the unwashed and unsavory England of Hogarth, Fielding, Smollett, and Sterne; of Tom Jones, Squire Western, Lady Bellaston, and Parson Adams; of the "Rake's Progress" and "Marriage à la Mode;" of the lords and ladies who yet live in the undying gossip of Horace Walpole, be-powdered, be-patched, and be-rouged, flirting at masked balls, playing cards till daylight, retailing scandal, and exchanging double meanings. Beau Nash reigned king over the gaming-tables of Bath; the ostrich-plumes of great ladies mingled with the peacock-feathers of courtesans in the rotunda at Ranelagh Gardens; and young lords in velvet suits and embroidered ruffles played away their patrimony at White's Chocolate-House or Arthur's Club. Vice was bolder than to-day, and manners more courtly, perhaps, but far more coarse.

The humbler clergy were thought—sometimes with reason—to be no fit company for gentlemen, and country parsons drank their ale in the squire's kitchen. The passenger-wagon spent the better part of a fortnight in creeping from London to York. Travellers carried pistols against footpads and mounted highwaymen. Dick Turpin and Jack Sheppard were popular heroes. Tyburn counted its victims by scores; and as yet no Howard had appeared to reform the inhuman abominations of the prisons.

The middle class, though fast rising in importance, was feebly and imperfectly represented in parliament. The boroughs were controlled by the nobility and gentry, or by corporations open to influence or bribery. Parliamentary corruption had been reduced to a system; and offices, sinecures, pensions, and gifts of money were freely used to keep ministers in power. The great offices of state were held by men sometimes of high ability, but of whom not a few divided their lives among politics, cards, wine, horse-racing, and women, till time and the gout sent them to the waters of Bath. The dull, pompous, and irascible old King had two ruling passions,—money, and his Continental dominions of Hanover. His elder son, the Prince of Wales, was a centre of opposition to him. His younger son, the Duke of Cumberland, a character far more pronounced and vigorous, had won the day at Culloden, and lost it at Fontenoy; but whether victor or vanquished, had shown the same vehement bull-headed courage, of late a little subdued by fast growing corpulency. The Duke of Newcastle, the head of the government, had gained power and kept it by his rank and connections, his wealth, his county influence, his control of boroughs, and the extraordinary assiduity and devotion with which he practised the arts of corruption. Henry Fox, grasping, unscrupulous, with powerful talents, a warm friend after his fashion, and a most indulgent father; Carteret, with his strong, versatile intellect and jovial intrepidity; the two Townshends, Mansfield, Halifax, and Chesterfield,—were conspicuous figures in the politics of the time. One man towered above them all. Pitt had many enemies and many critics. They called him ambitious, audacious, arrogant, theatrical, pompous, domineering; but what he has left for posterity is a loftiness of soul, undaunted courage, fiery and passionate eloquence, proud incorruptibility, domestic virtues rare in his day, unbounded faith in the cause for which he stood, and abilities which without wealth or strong connections were destined to place him on the height of power. The middle class, as yet almost voiceless, looked to him as its champion; but he was not the champion of a class. His patriotism was as comprehensive as it was haughty and unbending. He lived for England, loved her with intense devotion, knew her, believed in her, and made her greatness his own; or rather, he was himself England incarnate.

The nation was not then in fighting equipment. After the peace of Aix-la-Chapelle, the army within the three kingdoms had been reduced to about eighteen thousand men. Added to these were the garrisons of Minorca and Gibraltar, and six or seven independent companies in the American colonies. Of

BRITISH COLONIES
AND
NORTHERN NEW FRANCE
1750 – 1760.

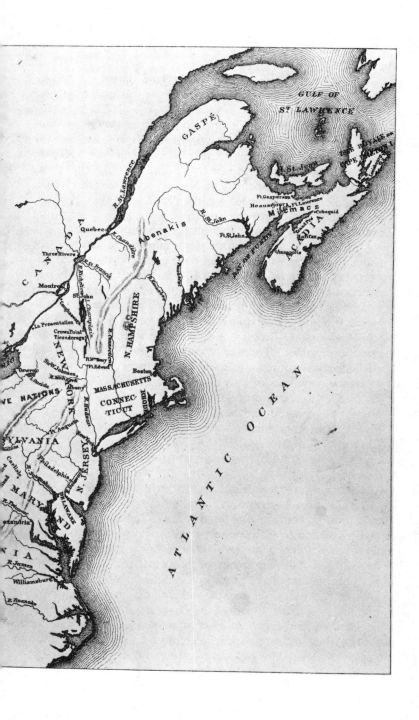

sailors, less than seventeen thousand were left in the Royal Navy. Such was the condition of England on the eve of one of the most formidable wars in which she was ever engaged.

Her rival across the Channel was drifting slowly and unconsciously towards the cataclysm of the Revolution; yet the old monarchy, full of the germs of decay, was still imposing and formidable. The House of Bourbon held the three thrones of France, Spain, and Naples; and their threatened union in a family compact was the terror of European diplomacy. At home France was the foremost of the Continental nations; and she boasted herself second only to Spain as a colonial power. She disputed with England the mastery of India, owned the islands of Bourbon and Mauritius, held important possessions in the West Indies, and claimed all North America except Mexico and a strip of sea-coast. Her navy was powerful, her army numerous, and well appointed; but she lacked the great commanders of the last reign. Soubise, Maillebois, Contades, Broglie, and Clermont were but weak successors of Condé, Turenne, Vendôme, and Villars. Marshal Richelieu was supreme in the arts of gallantry, and more famous for conquests of love than of war. The best generals of Louis XV. were foreigners. Lowendal sprang from the royal house of Denmark; and Saxe, the best of all, was one of the three hundred and fifty-four bastards of Augustus the Strong, Elector of Saxony and King of Poland. He was now, 1750, dying at Chambord, his iron constitution ruined by debaucheries.

The triumph of the Bourbon monarchy was complete. The government had become one great machine of centralized administration, with a king for its head; though a king who neither could nor would direct it. All strife was over between the Crown and the nobles; feudalism was robbed of its vitality, and left the mere image of its former self, with nothing alive but its abuses, its caste privileges, its exactions, its pride and vanity, its power to vex and oppress. In England, the nobility were a living part of the nation, and if they had privileges, they paid for them by constant service to the state; in France, they had no political life, and were separated from the people by sharp lines of demarcation. From warrior chiefs, they had changed to courtiers. Those of them who could afford it, and many who could not, left their estates to the mercy of stewards, and gathered at Versailles to revolve about the throne as glittering satellites, paid in pomp, empty distinctions, or rich sinecures, for the power they had lost. They ruined their vassals to support the extravagance by which they ruined themselves. Such as stayed at home were objects of pity and scorn. "Out of your Majesty's presence," said one of them, "we are not only wretched, but ridiculous."

Versailles was like a vast and gorgeous theatre, where all were actors and spectators at once; and all played their parts to perfection. Here swarmed by thousands this silken nobility, whose ancestors rode cased in iron. Pageant followed pageant. A picture of the time preserves for us an evening in the great hall of the Château, where the King, with piles of louis d'or before him, sits at a large oval green table, throwing the dice, among princes and princesses, dukes and duchesses, ambassadors, marshals of France, and a vast throng of courtiers, like an animated bed of tulips; for men and women alike wear bright and varied colors. Above are the frescos of Le Brun; around are walls of sculptured and inlaid marbles, with mirrors that reflect the restless splendors of the scene and the blaze of chandeliers, sparkling with crystal pendants. Pomp, magnificence, profusion, were a business and a duty at the Court. Versailles was a gulf into which the labor of France poured its earnings; and it was never full.

Here the graces and charms were a political power. Women had prodigious influence, and the two sexes were never more alike. Men not only dressed in colors, but they wore patches and carried muffs. The robust qualities of the old nobility still lingered among the exiles of the provinces, while at Court they had melted into refinements tainted with corruption. Yet if the butterflies of Versailles had lost virility, they had not lost courage. They fought as gayly as they danced. In the halls which they haunted of yore, turned now into a historical picture-gallery, one sees them still, on the canvas of Lenfant, Lepaon, or Vernet, facing death with careless gallantry, in their small three-cornered hats, powdered perukes, embroidered coats, and lace ruffles. Their valets served them with ices in the trenches, under the cannon of besieged towns. A troop of actors formed part of the army-train of Marshal Saxe. At night there was a comedy, a ballet, or a ball, and in the morning a battle. Saxe, however, himself a sturdy German, while he recognized their fighting value, and knew well how to make the best of it, sometimes complained that they were volatile, excitable, and difficult to manage.

The weight of the Court, with its pomps, luxuries, and wars, bore on the classes least able to support it. The poorest were taxed most; the richest not at all. The nobles, in the main, were free from imposts. The clergy, who had vast possessions, were wholly free, though they consented to make voluntary gifts to the Crown; and when, in a time of emergency, the minister Machault required them, in common with all others hitherto exempt, to contribute a twentieth of their revenues to the charges of government, they passionately refused, declaring that they would obey God rather than the King. The cultivators of the soil were ground to the earth by a threefold extortion,—the seigniorial dues, the tithes of the Church, and the multiplied exactions of the Crown, enforced with merciless rigor by the farmers of the revenue, who enriched themselves by wringing the peasant on the one hand, and cheating the King on the other. A few great cities shone with all that is most brilliant in society, intellect, and concentred wealth; while the country that paid the costs lay in ignorance and penury, crushed and despairing. On the inhabitants of towns, too, the demands of the tax-gatherer were extreme; but here the immense vitality of the French people bore up the burden. While agriculture languished, and intolerable oppression turned peasants into beggars or desperadoes; while the clergy were sapped by corruption, and the nobles enervated by luxury and ruined by extravagance, the middle class was growing in thrift and strength. Arts and commerce prospered, and the seaports were alive with foreign trade. Wealth tended from all sides towards the centre. The King did not love his capital; but he and his favorites amused themselves with adorning it. Some of the chief embellishments that make Paris what it is to-day—the Place de la Concorde, the Champs Élysées, and many of the palaces of the Faubourg St. Germain—date from this reign.

One of the vicious conditions of the time was the separation in sympathies and interests of the four great classes of the nation,—clergy, nobles, burghers, and peasants; and each of these, again, divided itself into incoherent fragments. France was an aggregate of disjointed parts, held together by a meshwork of arbitrary power, itself touched with decay. A disastrous blow was struck at the national welfare when the Government of Louis XV. revived the odious persecution of the Huguenots. The attempt to scour heresy out of France cost her the most industrious and virtuous part of her population, and robbed her of those most fit to resist the mocking scepticism and turbid passions that burst out like a deluge with the Revolution.

Her manifold ills were summed up in the King. Since the Valois, she had had no monarch so worthless. He did not want understanding, still less the graces of person. In his youth the people called him the "Well-beloved;" but by the middle of the century they so detested him that he dared not pass through Paris, lest the mob should execrate him. He had not the vigor of the true tyrant; but his languor, his hatred of all effort, his profound selfishness, his listless disregard of public duty, and his effeminate libertinism, mixed with superstitious devotion, made him no less a national curse. Louis XIII. was equally unfit to govern; but he gave the reins to the Great Cardinal. Louis XV. abandoned them to a frivolous mistress, content that she should rule on condition of amusing him. It was a hard task; yet Madame de Pompadour accomplished it by methods infamous to him and to her. She gained and long kept the power that she coveted: filled the Bastille with her enemies; made and unmade ministers; appointed and removed generals. Great questions of policy were at the mercy of her caprices. Through her frivolous vanity, her personal likes and dislikes, all the great departments of government—army, navy, war, foreign affairs, justice, finance—changed from hand to hand incessantly, and this at a time of crisis when the kingdom needed the steadiest and surest guidance. Few of the officers of state, except, perhaps, D'Argenson, could venture to disregard her. She turned out Orry, the comptroller-general, put her favorite, Machault, into his place, then made him keeper of the seals, and at last minister of marine. The Marquis de Puysieux, in the ministry

of foreign affairs, and the Comte de St.-Florentin, charged
with the affairs of the clergy, took their cue from her. The
King stinted her in nothing. First and last, she is reckoned to
have cost him thirty-six million francs,—answering now to
more than as many dollars.

The prestige of the monarchy was declining with the ideas
that had given it life and strength. A growing disrespect for
king, ministry, and clergy was beginning to prepare the catastrophe that was still some forty years in the future. While the
valleys and low places of the kingdom were dark with misery
and squalor, its heights were bright with a gay society,—ele-
gant, fastidious, witty,—craving the pleasures of the mind as
well as of the senses, criticising everything, analyzing everything, believing nothing. Voltaire was in the midst of it, hating, with all his vehement soul, the abuses that swarmed
about him, and assailing them with the inexhaustible shafts of
his restless and piercing intellect. Montesquieu was showing
to a despot-ridden age the principles of political freedom. Diderot and D'Alembert were beginning their revolutionary En-
cyclopædia. Rousseau was sounding the first notes of his mad
eloquence,—the wild revolt of a passionate and diseased genius against a world of falsities and wrongs. The *salons* of
Paris, cloyed with other pleasures, alive to all that was racy
and new, welcomed the pungent doctrines, and played with
them as children play with fire, thinking no danger; as time
went on, even embraced them in a genuine spirit of hope and
good-will for humanity. The Revolution began at the top,—
in the world of fashion, birth, and intellect,—and propagated
itself downwards. "We walked on a carpet of flowers," Count
Ségur afterwards said, "unconscious that it covered an abyss;"
till the gulf yawned at last, and swallowed them.

Eastward, beyond the Rhine, lay the heterogeneous patch-
work of the Holy Roman, or Germanic, Empire. The sacred
bonds that throughout the Middle Ages had held together its
innumerable fragments, had lost their strength. The Empire
decayed as a whole; but not so the parts that composed it. In
the south the House of Austria reigned over a formidable assemblage of states; and in the north the House of Brandenburg, promoted to royalty half a century before, had raised

Prussia into an importance far beyond her extent and population. In her dissevered rags of territory lay the destinies of Germany. It was the late King, that honest, thrifty, dogged, headstrong despot, Frederic William, who had made his kingdom what it was, trained it to the perfection of drill, and left it to his son, Frederic II. the best engine of war in Europe. Frederic himself had passed between the upper and nether millstones of paternal discipline. Never did prince undergo such an apprenticeship. His father set him to the work of an overseer, or steward, flung plates at his head in the family circle, thrashed him with his rattan in public, bullied him for submitting to such treatment, and imprisoned him for trying to run away from it. He came at last out of purgatory; and Europe felt him to her farthest bounds. This bookish, philosophizing, verse-making cynic and profligate was soon to approve himself the first warrior of his time, and one of the first of all time.

Another power had lately risen on the European world. Peter the Great, half hero, half savage, had roused the inert barbarism of Russia into a titanic life. His daughter Elizabeth had succeeded to his throne,—heiress of his sensuality, if not of his talents.

Over all the Continent the aspect of the times was the same. Power had everywhere left the plains and the lower slopes, and gathered at the summits. Popular life was at a stand. No great idea stirred the nations to their depths. The religious convulsions of the sixteenth and seventeenth centuries were over, and the earthquake of the French Revolution had not begun. At the middle of the eighteenth century the history of Europe turned on the balance of power; the observance of treaties; inheritance and succession; rivalries of sovereign houses struggling to win power or keep it, encroach on neighbors, or prevent neighbors from encroaching; bargains, intrigue, force, diplomacy, and the musket, in the interest not of peoples but of rulers. Princes, great and small, brooded over some real or fancied wrong, nursed some dubious claim born of a marriage, a will, or an ancient covenant fished out of the abyss of time, and watched their moment to make it good. The general opportunity came when, in 1740, the Emperor Charles VI. died and bequeathed his personal dominions of the House of Austria to his daughter, Maria Theresa. The chief Powers of Europe had been pledged in advance to sustain the will; and pending the event, the veteran Prince Eugene had said that two hundred thousand soldiers would be worth all their guaranties together. The two hundred thousand were not there, and not a sovereign kept his word. They flocked to share the spoil, and parcel out the motley heritage of the young Queen. Frederic of Prussia led the way, invaded her province of Silesia, seized it, and kept it. The Elector of Bavaria and the King of Spain claimed their share, and the Elector of Saxony and the King of Sardinia prepared to follow the example. France took part with Bavaria, and intrigued to set the imperial crown on the head of the Elector, thinking to ruin her old enemy, the House of Austria, and rule Germany through an emperor too weak to dispense with her support. England, jealous of her designs, trembling for the balance of power, and anxious for the Hanoverian possessions of her king, threw herself into the strife on the side of Austria. It was now that, in the Diet at Presburg, the beautiful and distressed Queen, her infant in her arms, made her memorable appeal to the wild chivalry of her Hungarian nobles; and, clashing their swords, they shouted with one voice: "Let us die for our king, Maria Theresa;" *Moriamur pro rege nostro, Mariâ Theresiâ,*—one of the most dramatic scenes in history; not quite true, perhaps, but near the truth. Then came that confusion worse confounded called the war of the Austrian Succession, with its Mollwitz, its Dettingen, its Fontenoy, and its Scotch episode of Culloden. The peace of Aix-la-Chapelle closed the strife in 1748. Europe had time to breathe; but the germs of discord remained alive.

THE AMERICAN COMBATANTS

The French claimed all America, from the Alleghanies to the Rocky Mountains, and from Mexico and Florida to the North Pole, except only the ill-defined possessions of the English on the borders of Hudson Bay; and to these vast regions, with adjacent islands, they gave the general name of New France.

They controlled the highways of the continent, for they held its two great rivers. First, they had seized the St. Lawrence, and then planted themselves at the mouth of the Mississippi. Canada at the north, and Louisiana at the south, were the keys of a boundless interior, rich with incalculable possibilities. The English colonies, ranged along the Atlantic coast, had no royal road to the great inland, and were, in a manner, shut between the mountains and the sea. At the middle of the century they numbered in all, from Georgia to Maine, about eleven hundred and sixty thousand white inhabitants. By the census of 1754 Canada had but fifty-five thousand.[1] Add those of Louisiana and Acadia, and the whole white population under the French flag might be something more than eighty thousand. Here is an enormous disparity; and hence it has been argued that the success of the English colonies and the failure of the French was not due to difference of religious and political systems, but simply to numerical preponderance. But this preponderance itself grew out of a difference of systems. We have said before, and it cannot be said too often, that in making Canada a citadel of the state religion,—a holy of holies of exclusive Roman Catholic orthodoxy,—the clerical monitors of the Crown robbed their country of a trans-Atlantic empire. New France could not grow with a priest on guard at the gate to let in none but such as pleased him. One of the ablest of Canadian governors, La Galissonière, seeing the feebleness of the colony compared with the vastness of its claims, advised the King to send ten thousand peasants to occupy the valley of the Ohio, and hold back the British swarm that was just then pushing its advance-guard over the Alleghanies. It needed no effort of the King to people his waste domain, not with ten thousand peasants, but with twenty times ten thousand Frenchmen of every station,—the most industrious, most instructed, most disciplined by adversity and capable of self-rule, that the country could boast. While La Galissonière was asking for colonists, the agents of the Crown, set on by priestly fanaticism, or designing selfishness masked with fanaticism, were pouring volleys of mus-

---

[1] *Censuses of Canada*, iv. 61. Rameau (*La France aux Colonies*, ii. 81) estimates the Canadian population, in 1755, at sixty-six thousand, besides *voyageurs*, Indian traders, etc. Vaudreuil, in 1760, places it at seventy thousand.

ketry into Huguenot congregations, imprisoning for life those innocent of all but their faith,—the men in the galleys, the women in the pestiferous dungeons of Aigues Mortes,—hanging their ministers, kidnapping their children, and reviving, in short, the dragonnades. Now, as in the past century, many of the victims escaped to the British colonies, and became a part of them. The Huguenots would have hailed as a boon the permission to emigrate under the fleur-de-lis, and build up a Protestant France in the valleys of the West. It would have been a bane of absolutism, but a national glory; would have set bounds to English colonization, and changed the face of the continent. The opportunity was spurned. The dominant Church clung to its policy of rule and ruin. France built its best colony on a principle of exclusion, and failed; England reversed the system, and succeeded.

I have shown elsewhere the aspects of Canada, where a rigid scion of the old European tree was set to grow in the wilderness. The military Governor, holding his miniature Court on the rock of Quebec; the feudal proprietors, whose domains lined the shores of the St. Lawrence; the peasant; the roving bushranger; the half-tamed savage, with crucifix and scalping-knife; priests; friars; nuns; and soldiers,—mingled to form a society the most picturesque on the continent. What distinguished it from the France that produced it was a total absence of revolt against the laws of its being,—an absolute conservatism, an unquestioning acceptance of Church and King. The Canadian, ignorant of everything but what the priest saw fit to teach him, had never heard of Voltaire; and if he had known him, would have thought him a devil. He had, it is true, a spirit of insubordination born of the freedom of the forest; but if his instincts rebelled, his mind and soul were passively submissive. The unchecked control of a hierarchy robbed him of the independence of intellect and character, without which, under the conditions of modern life, a people must resign itself to a position of inferiority. Yet Canada had a vigor of her own. It was not in spiritual deference only that she differed from the country of her birth. Whatever she had caught of its corruptions, she had caught nothing of its effeminacy. The mass of her people lived in a rude poverty,—not abject, like the peasant of old France, nor ground down by the tax-gatherer; while those of the higher ranks—all more or less engaged in pursuits of war or adventure, and inured to rough journeyings and forest exposures—were rugged as their climate. Even the French regular troops, sent out to defend the colony, caught its hardy spirit, and set an example of stubborn fighting which their comrades at home did not always emulate.

Canada lay ensconced behind rocks and forests. All along her southern boundaries, between her and her English foes, lay a broad tract of wilderness, shaggy with primeval woods. Innumerable streams gurgled beneath their shadows; innumerable lakes gleamed in the fiery sunsets; innumerable mountains bared their rocky foreheads to the wind. These wastes were ranged by her savage allies, Micmacs, Etechémins, Abenakis, Caughnawagas; and no enemy could steal upon her unawares. Through the midst of them stretched Lake Champlain, pointing straight to the heart of the British settlements,—a watery thoroughfare of mutual attack, and the only approach by which, without a long *détour* by wilderness or sea, a hostile army could come within striking distance of the colony. The French advanced post of Fort Frederic, called Crown Point by the English, barred the narrows of the lake, which thence spread northward to the portals of Canada guarded by Fort St. Jean. Southwestward, some fourteen hundred miles as a bird flies, and twice as far by the practicable routes of travel, was Louisiana, the second of the two heads of New France; while between lay the realms of solitude where the Mississippi rolled its sullen tide, and the Ohio wound its belt of silver through the verdant woodlands.

To whom belonged this world of prairies and forests? France claimed it by right of discovery and occupation. It was her explorers who, after De Soto, first set foot on it. The question of right, it is true, mattered little; for, right or wrong, neither claimant would yield her pretensions so long as she had strength to uphold them; yet one point is worth a moment's notice. The French had established an excellent system in the distribution of their American lands. Whoever received a grant from the Crown was required to improve it, and this within reasonable time. If he did not, the land ceased to be his, and was given to another more able or industrious.

An international extension of her own principle would have destroyed the pretensions of France to all the countries of the West. She had called them hers for three fourths of a century, and they were still a howling waste, yielding nothing to civilization but beaver-skins, with here and there a fort, trading-post, or mission, and three or four puny hamlets by the Mississippi and the Detroit. We have seen how she might have made for herself an indisputable title, and peopled the solitudes with a host to maintain it. She would not; others were at hand who both would and could; and the late claimant, disinherited and forlorn, would soon be left to count the cost of her bigotry.

The thirteen British colonies were alike, insomuch as they all had representative governments, and a basis of English law. But the differences among them were great. Some were purely English; others were made up of various races, though the Anglo-Saxon was always predominant. Some had one prevailing religious creed; others had many creeds. Some had charters, and some had not. In most cases the governor was appointed by the Crown; in Pennsylvania and Maryland he was appointed by a feudal proprietor, and in Connecticut and Rhode Island he was chosen by the people. The differences of disposition and character were still greater than those of form.

The four northern colonies, known collectively as New England, were an exception to the general rule of diversity. The smallest, Rhode Island, had features all its own; but the rest were substantially one in nature and origin. The principal among them, Massachusetts, may serve as the type of all. It was a mosaic of little village republics, firmly cemented together, and formed into a single body politic through representatives sent to the "General Court" at Boston. Its government, originally theocratic, now tended to democracy, ballasted as yet by strong traditions of respect for established worth and ability, as well as by the influence of certain families prominent in affairs for generations. Yet there were no distinct class-lines, and popular power, like popular education, was widely diffused. Practically Massachusetts was almost independent of the mother-country. Its people were purely En-

glish, of sound yeoman stock, with an abundant leaven drawn
from the best of the Puritan gentry; but their original character had been somewhat modified by changed conditions of
life. A harsh and exacting creed, with its stiff formalism and
its prohibition of wholesome recreation; excess in the pursuit
of gain,—the only resource left to energies robbed of their
natural play; the struggle for existence on a hard and barren
soil; and the isolation of a narrow village life,—joined to produce, in the meaner sort, qualities which were unpleasant, and
sometimes repulsive. Puritanism was not an unmixed blessing. Its view of human nature was dark, and its attitude towards it one of repression. It strove to crush out not only
what is evil, but much that is innocent and salutary. Human
nature so treated will take its revenge, and for every vice that
it loses find another instead. Nevertheless, while New England Puritanism bore its peculiar crop of faults, it produced
also many good and sound fruits. An uncommon vigor,
joined to the hardy virtues of a masculine race, marked the
New England type. The sinews, it is true, were hardened at
the expense of blood and flesh,—and this literally as well as
figuratively; but the staple of character was a sturdy consci-
entiousness, an undespairing courage, patriotism, public
spirit, sagacity, and a strong good sense. A great change, both
for better and for worse, has since come over it, due largely
to reaction against the unnatural rigors of the past. That mixture, which is now too common, of cool emotions with excitable brains, was then rarely seen. The New England colonies
abounded in high examples of public and private virtue,
though not always under the most prepossessing forms. They
were conspicuous, moreover, for intellectual activity, and
were by no means without intellectual eminence. Massachusetts had produced at least two men whose fame had crossed
the sea,—Edwards, who out of the grim theology of Calvin
mounted to sublime heights of mystical speculation; and
Franklin, famous already by his discoveries in electricity. On
the other hand, there were few genuine New Englanders
who, however personally modest, could divest themselves of
the notion that they belonged to a people in an especial manner the object of divine approval; and this self-righteousness,
along with certain other traits, failed to commend the Puritan

colonies to the favor of their fellows. Then, as now, New England was best known to her neighbors by her worst side.

In one point, however, she found general applause. She was regarded as the most military among the British colonies. This reputation was well founded, and is easily explained. More than all the rest, she lay open to attack. The long waving line of the New England border, with its lonely hamlets and scattered farms, extended from the Kennebec to beyond the Connecticut, and was everywhere vulnerable to the guns and tomahawks of the neighboring French and their savage allies. The colonies towards the south had thus far been safe from danger. New York alone was within striking distance of the Canadian war-parties. That province then consisted of a line of settlements up the Hudson and the Mohawk, and was little exposed to attack except at its northern end, which was guarded by the fortified town of Albany, with its outlying posts, and by the friendly and warlike Mohawks, whose "castles" were close at hand. Thus New England had borne the heaviest brunt of the preceding wars, not only by the forest, but also by the sea; for the French of Acadia and Cape Breton confronted her coast, and she was often at blows with them. Fighting had been a necessity with her, and she had met the emergency after a method extremely defective, but the best that circumstances would permit. Having no trained officers and no disciplined soldiers, and being too poor to maintain either, she borrowed her warriors from the workshop and the plough, and officered them with lawyers, merchants, mechanics, or farmers. To compare them with good regular troops would be folly; but they did, on the whole, better than could have been expected, and in the last war achieved the brilliant success of the capture of Louisbourg. This exploit, due partly to native hardihood and partly to good luck, greatly enhanced the military repute of New England, or rather was one of the chief sources of it.

The great colony of Virginia stood in strong contrast to New England. In both the population was English; but the one was Puritan with Roundhead traditions, and the other, so far as concerned its governing class, Anglican with Cavalier traditions. In the one, every man, woman, and child could read and write; in the other, Sir William Berkeley once thanked God that there were no free schools, and no prospect of any for a century. The hope had found fruition. The lower classes of Virginia were as untaught as the warmest friend of popular ignorance could wish. New England had a native literature more than respectable under the circumstances, while Virginia had none; numerous industries, while Virginia was all agriculture, with but a single crop; a homogeneous society and a democratic spirit, while her rival was an aristocracy. Virginian society was distinctly stratified. On the lowest level were the negro slaves, nearly as numerous as all the rest together; next, the indented servants and the poor whites, of low origin, good-humored, but boisterous, and sometimes vicious; next, the small and despised class of tradesmen and mechanics; next, the farmers and lesser planters, who were mainly of good English stock, and who merged insensibly into the ruling class of the great landowners. It was these last who represented the colony and made the laws. They may be described as English country squires transplanted to a warm climate and turned slave-masters. They sustained their position by entails, and constantly undermined it by the reckless profusion which ruined them at last. Many of them were well born, with an immense pride of descent, increased by the habit of domination. Indolent and energetic by turns; rich in natural gifts and often poor in book-learning, though some, in the lack of good teaching at home, had been bred in the English universities; high-spirited, generous to a fault; keeping open house in their capacious mansions, among vast tobacco-fields and toiling negroes, and living in a rude pomp where the fashions of St. James were somewhat oddly grafted on the roughness of the plantation,—what they wanted in schooling was supplied by an education which books alone would have been impotent to give, the education which came with the possession and exercise of political power, and the sense of a position to maintain, joined to a bold spirit of independence and a patriotic attachment to the Old Dominion. They were few in number; they raced, gambled, drank, and swore; they did everything that in Puritan eyes was most reprehensible; and in the day of need they gave the United Colonies a body of statesmen and orators which had no equal on the continent. A vigorous aristocracy favors the growth of personal eminence, even in those who are not of it, but only near it.

The essential antagonism of Virginia and New England was afterwards to become, and to remain for a century, an element of the first influence in American history. Each might have learned much from the other; but neither did so till, at last, the strife of their contending principles shook the continent. Pennsylvania differed widely from both. She was a conglomerate of creeds and races,—English, Irish, Germans, Dutch, and Swedes; Quakers, Lutherans, Presbyterians, Romanists, Moravians, and a variety of nondescript sects. The Quakers prevailed in the eastern districts; quiet, industrious, virtuous, and serenely obstinate. The Germans were strongest towards the centre of the colony, and were chiefly peasants; successful farmers, but dull, ignorant, and superstitious. Towards the west were the Irish, of whom some were Celts, always quarrelling with their German neighbors, who detested them; but the greater part were Protestants of Scotch descent, from Ulster; a vigorous border population. Virginia and New England had each a strong distinctive character. Pennsylvania, with her heterogeneous population, had none but that which she owed to the sober neutral tints of Quaker existence. A more thriving colony there was not on the continent. Life, if monotonous, was smooth and contented. Trade and the arts grew. Philadelphia, next to Boston, was the largest town in British America; and was, moreover, the intellectual centre of the middle and southern colonies. Unfortunately, for her credit in the approaching war, the Quaker influence made Pennsylvania non-combatant. Politically, too, she was an anomaly; for, though utterly unfeudal in disposition and character, she was under feudal superiors in the persons of the representatives of William Penn, the original grantee.

New York had not as yet reached the relative prominence which her geographical position and inherent strength afterwards gave her. The English, joined to the Dutch, the original settlers, were the dominant population; but a half-score of other languages were spoken in the province, the chief among them being that of the Huguenot French in the southern parts, and that of the Germans on the Mohawk. In religion, the province was divided between the Anglican Church, with government support and popular dislike, and numerous dissenting sects, chiefly Lutherans, Independents, Presbyterians, and members of the Dutch Reformed Church. The little city of New York, like its great successor, was the most cosmopolitan place on the continent, and probably the gayest. It had, in abundance, balls, concerts, theatricals, and evening clubs, with plentiful dances and other amusements for the poorer classes. Thither in the winter months came the great hereditary proprietors on the Hudson; for the old Dutch feudality still held its own, and the manors of Van Renselaer, Cortland, and Livingston, with their seigniorial privileges, and the great estates and numerous tenantry of the Schuylers and other leading families, formed the basis of an aristocracy, some of whose members had done good service to the province, and were destined to do more. Pennsylvania was feudal in form, and not in spirit; Virginia in spirit, and not in form; New England in neither; and New York largely in both. This social crystallization had, it is true, many opponents. In politics, as in religion, there were sharp antagonisms and frequent quarrels. They centred in the city; for in the well-stocked dwellings of the Dutch farmers along the Hudson there reigned a tranquil and prosperous routine; and the Dutch border town of Albany had not its like in America for unruffled conservatism and quaint picturesqueness.

Of the other colonies, the briefest mention will suffice: New Jersey, with its wholesome population of farmers; tobacco-growing Maryland, which, but for its proprietary government and numerous Roman Catholics, might pass for another Virginia, inferior in growth, and less decisive in features; Delaware, a modest appendage of Pennsylvania; wild and rude North Carolina; and, farther on, South Carolina and Georgia, too remote from the seat of war to take a noteworthy part in it. The attitude of these various colonies towards each other is hardly conceivable to an American of the present time. They had no political tie except a common allegiance to the British Crown. Communication between them was difficult and slow, by rough roads traced often through primeval forests. Between some of them there was less of sympathy than of jealousy kindled by conflicting interests or perpetual disputes concerning boundaries. The patriotism of the colonist was bounded by the lines of his government, except in the compact and kindred colonies of New England, which were socially united, though politically distinct. The country of the New Yorker was New York, and the country of the Virginian was Virginia. The New England colonies had once confederated; but, kindred as they were, they had long ago dropped apart. William Penn proposed a plan of colonial union wholly fruitless. James II. tried to unite all the northern colonies under one government; but the attempt came to naught. Each stood aloof, jealously independent. At rare intervals, under the pressure of an emergency, some of them would try to act in concert; and, except in New England, the results had been most discouraging. Nor was it this segregation only that unfitted them for war. They were all subject to popular legislatures, through whom alone money and men could be raised; and these elective bodies were sometimes factious and selfish, and not always either far-sighted or reasonable. Moreover, they were in a state of ceaseless friction with their governors, who represented the king, or, what was worse, the feudal proprietary. These disputes, though varying in intensity, were found everywhere except in the two small colonies which chose their own governors; and they were premonitions of the movement towards independence which ended in the war of Revolution. The occasion of difference mattered little. Active or latent, the quarrel was always present. In New York it turned on a question of the governor's salary; in Pennsylvania on the taxation of the proprietary estates; in Virginia on a fee exacted for the issue of land patents. It was sure to arise whenever some public crisis gave the representatives of the people an opportunity of extorting concessions from the representative of the Crown, or gave the representative of the Crown an opportunity to gain a point for prerogative. That is to say, the time when action was most needed was the time chosen for obstructing it.

In Canada there was no popular legislature to embarrass the central power. The people, like an army, obeyed the word of command,—a military advantage beyond all price.

Divided in government; divided in origin, feelings, and principles; jealous of each other, jealous of the Crown; the people at war with the executive, and, by the fermentation of internal politics, blinded to an outward danger that seemed remote and vague,—such were the conditions under which the British colonies drifted into a war that was to decide the fate of the continent.

This war was the strife of a united and concentred few against a divided and discordant many. It was the strife, too, of the past against the future; of the old against the new; of moral and intellectual torpor against moral and intellectual life; of barren absolutism against a liberty, crude, incoherent, and chaotic, yet full of prolific vitality.

Chapter II

CÉLORON DE BIENVILLE

*La Galissonière • English Encroachment • Mission of Céloron •
The Great West • Its European Claimants • Its Indian Population
• English Fur-Traders • Céloron on the Alleghany • His Reception
• His Difficulties • Descent of the Ohio • Covert Hostility • Ascent
of the Miami • La Demoiselle • Dark Prospects for France • Chris-
topher Gist • George Croghan • Their Western Mission • Picka-
willany • English Ascendency • English Dissension and Rivalry •
The Key of the Great West*

WHEN the peace of Aix-la-Chapelle was signed, the Marquis de la Galissonière ruled over Canada. Like all the
later Canadian governors, he was a naval officer; and, a few
years after, he made himself famous by a victory, near Minorca, over the English admiral Byng,—an achievement now
remembered chiefly by the fate of the defeated commander,
judicially murdered as the scapegoat of an imbecile ministry.
Galissonière was a humpback; but his deformed person was
animated by a bold spirit and a strong and penetrating intellect. He was the chief representative of the American policy
of France. He felt that, cost what it might, she must hold fast
to Canada, and link her to Louisiana by chains of forts strong
enough to hold back the British colonies, and cramp their
growth by confinement within narrow limits; while French
settlers, sent from the mother-country, should spread and
multiply in the broad valleys of the interior. It is true, he said,
that Canada and her dependencies have always been a burden;
but they are necessary as a barrier against English ambition;
and to abandon them is to abandon ourselves; for if we suffer
our enemies to become masters in America, their trade and
naval power will grow to vast proportions, and they will draw
from their colonies a wealth that will make them preponder-
ant in Europe.[1]

The treaty had done nothing to settle the vexed question

[1] La Galissonière, *Mémoire sur les Colonies de la France dans l'Amérique septentrionale.*

of boundaries between France and her rival. It had but staved off the inevitable conflict. Meanwhile, the English traders were crossing the mountains from Pennsylvania and Virginia, poaching on the domain which France claimed as hers, ruining the French fur-trade, seducing the Indian allies of Canada, and stirring them up against her. Worse still, English land speculators were beginning to follow. Something must be done, and that promptly, to drive back the intruders, and vindicate French rights in the valley of the Ohio. To this end the Governor sent Céloron de Bienville thither in the summer of 1749.

He was a chevalier de St. Louis and a captain in the colony troops. Under him went fourteen officers and cadets, twenty soldiers, a hundred and eighty Canadians, and a band of Indians, all in twenty-three birch-bark canoes. They left La Chine on the fifteenth of June, and pushed up the rapids of the St. Lawrence, losing a man and damaging several canoes on the way. Ten days brought them to the mouth of the Oswegatchie, where Ogdensburg now stands. Here they found a Sulpitian priest, Abbé Piquet, busy at building a fort, and lodging for the present under a shed of bark like an Indian. This enterprising father, ostensibly a missionary, was in reality a zealous political agent, bent on winning over the red allies of the English, retrieving French prestige, and restoring French trade. Thus far he had attracted but two Iroquois to his new establishment; and these he lent to Céloron.

Reaching Lake Ontario, the party stopped for a time at the French fort of Frontenac, but avoided the rival English post of Oswego, on the southern shore, where a trade in beaver skins, disastrous to French interests, was carried on, and whither many tribes, once faithful to Canada, now made resort. On the sixth of July Céloron reached Niagara. This, the most important pass of all the western wilderness, was guarded by a small fort of palisades on the point where the river joins the lake. Thence, the party carried their canoes over the portage road by the cataract, and launched them upon Lake Erie. On the fifteenth they landed on the lonely shore where the town of Portland now stands; and for the next seven days were busied in shouldering canoes and baggage up and down the steep hills, through the dense forest of beech, oak, ash, and elm, to the waters of Chautauqua Lake, eight or nine miles distant. Here they embarked again, steering southward over the sunny waters, in the stillness and solitude of the leafy hills, till they came to the outlet, and glided down the peaceful current in the shade of the tall forests that overarched it. This prosperity was short. The stream was low, in spite of heavy rains that had drenched them on the carrying place. Father Bonnecamp, chaplain of the expedition, wrote, in his Journal: "In some places—and they were but too frequent—the water was only two or three inches deep; and we were reduced to the sad necessity of dragging our canoes over the sharp pebbles, which, with all our care and precaution, stripped off large slivers of the bark. At last, tired and worn, and almost in despair of ever seeing La Belle Rivière, we entered it at noon of the 29th." The part of the Ohio, or "La Belle Rivière," which they had thus happily reached, is now called the Alleghany. The Great West lay outspread before them, a realm of wild and waste fertility.

French America had two heads,—one among the snows of Canada, and one among the cane-brakes of Louisiana; one communicating with the world through the Gulf of St. Lawrence, and the other through the Gulf of Mexico. These vital points were feebly connected by a chain of military posts,— slender, and often interrupted,—circling through the wilderness nearly three thousand miles. Midway between Canada and Louisiana lay the valley of the Ohio. If the English should seize it, they would sever the chain of posts, and cut French America asunder. If the French held it, and entrenched themselves well along its eastern limits, they would shut their rivals between the Alleghanies and the sea, control all the tribes of the West, and turn them, in case of war, against the English borders,—a frightful and insupportable scourge.

The Indian population of the Ohio and its northern tributaries was relatively considerable. The upper or eastern half of the valley was occupied by mingled hordes of Delawares, Shawanoes, Wyandots, and Iroquois, or Indians of the Five Nations, who had migrated thither from their ancestral abodes within the present limits of the State of New York, and who were called Mingoes by the English traders. Along with them were a few wandering Abenakis, Nipissings, and Ottawas. Farther west, on the waters of the Miami, the Wabash, and other neighboring streams, was the seat of a confederacy formed of the various bands of the Miamis and their kindred or affiliated tribes. Still farther west, towards the Mississippi, were the remnants of the Illinois.

France had done but little to make good her claims to this grand domain. East of the Miami she had no military post whatever. Westward, on the Maumee, there was a small wooden fort, another on the St. Joseph, and two on the Wabash. On the meadows of the Mississippi, in the Illinois country, stood Fort Chartres,—a much stronger work, and one of the chief links of the chain that connected Quebec with New Orleans. Its four stone bastions were impregnable to musketry; and, here in the depths of the wilderness, there was no fear that cannon would be brought against it. It was the centre and citadel of a curious little forest settlement, the only vestige of civilization through all this region. At Kaskaskia, extended along the borders of the stream, were seventy or eighty French houses; thirty or forty at Cahokia, opposite the site of St. Louis; and a few more at the intervening hamlets of St. Philippe and Prairie à la Roche,—a picturesque but thriftless population, mixed with Indians, totally ignorant, busied partly with the fur-trade, and partly with the raising of corn for the market of New Orleans. They communicated with it by means of a sort of row galley, of eighteen or twenty oars, which made the voyage twice a year, and usually spent ten weeks on the return up the river.[1]

The Pope and the Bourbons had claimed this wilderness for seventy years, and had done scarcely more for it than the Indians, its natural owners. Of the western tribes, even of those living at the French posts, the Hurons or Wyandots alone were Christian.[2] The devoted zeal of the early missionaries and the politic efforts of their successors had failed alike. The

---

[1] Gordon, *Journal, 1766*, appended to Pownall, *Topographical Description*. In the Dépôt des Cartes de la Marine at Paris, C. 4,040, are two curious maps of the Illinois colony, made a little after the middle of the century. In 1753 the Marquis Duquesne denounced the colonists as debauched and lazy.

[2] "De toutes les nations domiciliées dans les postes des pays d'en haut, il n'y a que les hurons du détroit qui aient embrassé la Réligion chretienne." *Mémoire du Roy pour servir d'instruction au S^r. Marquis de Lajonquière.*

savages of the Ohio and the Mississippi, instead of being tied
to France by the mild bonds of the faith, were now in a state
which the French called defection or revolt; that is, they received and welcomed the English traders.

These traders came in part from Virginia, but chiefly from
Pennsylvania. Dinwiddie, governor of Virginia, says of them:
"They appear to me to be in general a set of abandoned
wretches;" and Hamilton, governor of Pennsylvania, replies:
"I concur with you in opinion that they are a very licentious
people."[1] Indian traders, of whatever nation, are rarely models of virtue; and these, without doubt, were rough and lawless men, with abundant blackguardism and few scruples. Not
all of them, however, are to be thus qualified. Some were of
a better stamp; among whom were Christopher Gist, William
Trent, and George Croghan. These and other chief traders
hired men on the frontiers, crossed the Alleghanies with
goods packed on the backs of horses, descended into the valley of the Ohio, and journeyed from stream to stream and
village to village along the Indian trails, with which all this
wilderness was seamed, and which the traders widened to
make them practicable. More rarely, they carried their goods
on horses to the upper waters of the Ohio, and embarked
them in large wooden canoes, in which they descended the
main river, and ascended such of its numerous tributaries as
were navigable. They were bold and enterprising; and French
writers, with alarm and indignation, declare that some of
them had crossed the Mississippi and traded with the distant
Osages. It is said that about three hundred of them came over
the mountains every year.

On reaching the Alleghany, Céloron de Bienville entered
upon the work assigned him, and began by taking possession
of the country. The men were drawn up in order; Louis XV.
was proclaimed lord of all that region, the arms of France,
stamped on a sheet of tin, were nailed to a tree, a plate of
lead was buried at its foot, and the notary of the expedition
drew up a formal act of the whole proceeding. The leaden
plate was inscribed as follows: "Year 1749, in the reign of
Louis Fifteenth, King of France. We, Céloron, commanding
the detachment sent by the Marquis de la Galissonière, com-

[1] *Dinwiddie to Hamilton, 21 May, 1753. Hamilton to Dinwiddie, — May, 1753.*

mander-general of New France, to restore tranquillity in certain villages of these cantons, have buried this plate at the confluence of the Ohio and the Kanaouagon [*Conewango*], this 29th July, as a token of renewal of possession heretofore taken of the aforesaid River Ohio, of all streams that fall into it, and all lands on both sides to the source of the aforesaid streams, as the preceding Kings of France have enjoyed or ought to have enjoyed it, and which they have upheld by force of arms and by treaties, notably by those of Ryswick, Utrecht, and Aix-la-Chapelle."

This done, the party proceeded on its way, moving downward with the current, and passing from time to time rough openings in the forest, with clusters of Indian wigwams, the inmates of which showed a strong inclination to run off at their approach. To prevent this, Chabert de Joncaire was sent in advance, as a messenger of peace. He was himself half Indian, being the son of a French officer and a Seneca squaw, speaking fluently his maternal tongue, and, like his father, holding an important place in all dealings between the French and the tribes who spoke dialects of the Iroquois. On this occasion his success was not complete. It needed all his art to prevent the alarmed savages from taking to the woods. Sometimes, however, Céloron succeeded in gaining an audience; and at a village of Senecas called La Paille Coupée he read them a message from La Galissonière couched in terms sufficiently imperative: "My children, since I was at war with the English, I have learned that they have seduced you; and not content with corrupting your hearts, have taken advantage of my absence to invade lands which are not theirs, but mine; and therefore I have resolved to send you Monsieur de Céloron to tell you my intentions, which are that I will not endure the English on my land. Listen to me, children; mark well the word that I send you; follow my advice, and the sky will always be calm and clear over your villages. I expect from you an answer worthy of true children." And he urged them to stop all trade with the intruders, and send them back to whence they came. They promised compliance; "and," says the chaplain, Bonnecamp, "we should all have been satisfied if we had thought them sincere; but nobody doubted that fear had extorted their answer."

Four leagues below French Creek, by a rock scratched with Indian hieroglyphics, they buried another leaden plate. Three days after, they reached the Delaware village of Attiqué, at the site of Kittanning, whose twenty-two wigwams were all empty, the owners having fled. A little farther on, at an old abandoned village of Shawanoes, they found six English traders, whom they warned to begone, and return no more at their peril. Being helpless to resist, the traders pretended obedience; and Céloron charged them with a letter to the Governor of Pennsylvania, in which he declared that he was "greatly surprised" to find Englishmen trespassing on the domain of France. "I know," concluded the letter, "that our Commandant-General would be very sorry to be forced to use violence; but his orders are precise, to leave no foreign traders within the limits of his government."[1]

On the next day they reached a village of Iroquois under a female chief, called Queen Alequippa by the English, to whom she was devoted. Both Queen and subjects had fled; but among the deserted wigwams were six more Englishmen, whom Céloron warned off like the others, and who, like them, pretended to obey. At a neighboring town they found only two withered ancients, male and female, whose united ages, in the judgment of the chaplain, were full two centuries. They passed the site of the future Pittsburg; and some seventeen miles below approached Chiningué, called Logstown by the English, one of the chief places on the river.[2] Both English and French flags were flying over the town, and the inhabitants, lining the shore, greeted their visitors with a salute of musketry,—not wholly welcome, as the guns were charged with ball. Céloron threatened to fire on them if they did not cease. The French climbed the steep bank, and encamped on the plateau above, betwixt the forest and the village, which consisted of some fifty cabins and wigwams, grouped in picturesque squalor, and tenanted by a mixed population, chiefly of Delawares, Shawanoes, and Mingoes. Here, too, were gathered many fugitives from the deserted

---

[1] Céloron, *Journal*. Compare the letter as translated in *N. Y. Col. Docs.*, VI. 532; also *Colonial Records of Pa.*, V. 425.

[2] There was another Chiningué, the Shenango of the English, on the Alleghany.

towns above. Céloron feared a night attack. The camp was encircled by a ring of sentries; the officers walked the rounds till morning; a part of the men were kept under arms, and the rest ordered to sleep in their clothes. Joncaire discovered through some women of his acquaintance that an attack was intended. Whatever the danger may have been, the precautions of the French averted it; and instead of a battle, there was a council. Céloron delivered to the assembled chiefs a message from the Governor more conciliatory than the former, "Through the love I bear you, my children, I send you Monsieur de Céloron to open your eyes to the designs of the English against your lands. The establishments they mean to make, and of which you are certainly ignorant, tend to your complete ruin. They hide from you their plans, which are to settle here and drive you away, if I let them. As a good father who tenderly loves his children, and though far away from them bears them always in his heart, I must warn you of the danger that threatens you. The English intend to rob you of your country; and that they may succeed, they begin by corrupting your minds. As they mean to seize the Ohio, which belongs to me, I send to warn them to retire."

The reply of the chiefs, though sufficiently humble, was not all that could be wished. They begged that the intruders might stay a little longer, since the goods they brought were necessary to them. It was in fact, these goods, cheap, excellent, and abundant as they were, which formed the only true bond between the English and the Western tribes. Logstown was one of the chief resorts of the English traders; and at this moment there were ten of them in the place. Céloron warned them off. "They agreed," says the chaplain, "to all that was demanded, well resolved, no doubt, to do the contrary as soon as our backs were turned."

Having distributed gifts among the Indians, the French proceeded on their way, and at or near the mouth of Wheeling Creek buried another plate of lead. They repeated the same ceremony at the mouth of the Muskingum. Here, half a century later, when this region belonged to the United States, a party of boys, bathing in the river, saw the plate protruding from the bank where the freshets had laid it bare, knocked it down with a long stick, melted half of it into bullets, and gave what remained to a neighbor from Marietta, who, hearing of this mysterious relic, inscribed in an unknown tongue, came to rescue it from their hands.[1] It is now in the cabinet of the American Antiquarian Society.[2] On the eighteenth of August, Céloron buried yet another plate, at the mouth of the Great Kenawha. This, too, in the course of a century, was unearthed by the floods, and was found in 1846 by a boy at play, by the edge of the water.[3] The inscriptions on all these plates were much alike, with variations of date and place.

The weather was by turns rainy and hot; and the men, tired and famished, were fast falling ill. On the twenty-second they approached Scioto, called by the French St. Yotoc, or Sini-oto, a large Shawanoe town at the mouth of the river which bears the same name. Greatly doubting what welcome awaited them, they filled their powder-horns and prepared for the worst. Joncaire was sent forward to propitiate the inhab-itants; but they shot bullets through the flag that he carried, and surrounded him, yelling and brandishing their knives. Some were for killing him at once; others for burning him alive. The interposition of a friendly Iroquois saved him; and at length they let him go. Céloron was very uneasy at the reception of his messenger. "I knew," he writes, "the weak-ness of my party, two thirds of which were young men who had never left home before, and would all have run at the sight of ten Indians. Still, there was nothing for me but to keep on; for I was short of provisions, my canoes were badly damaged, and I had no pitch or bark to mend them. So I embarked again, ready for whatever might happen. I had good officers, and about fifty men who could be trusted."

As they neared the town, the Indians swarmed to the shore, and began the usual salute of musketry. "They fired," says Céloron, "full a thousand shots; for the English give them powder for nothing." He prudently pitched his camp on the farther side of the river, posted guards, and kept close watch. Each party distrusted and feared the other. At length, after

[1] O. H. Marshall, in *Magazine of American History, March, 1878.*

[2] For papers relating to it, see *Trans. Amer. Antiq. Soc.*, II.

[3] For a fac-simile of the inscription on this plate, see *Olden Time*, I. 288. Céloron calls the Kenawha, *Chinodahichetha.* The inscriptions as given in his Journal correspond with those on the plates discovered.

much ado, many debates, and some threatening movements
on the part of the alarmed and excited Indians, a council took
place at the tent of the French commander; the chiefs apologized for the rough treatment of Joncaire, and Céloron replied with a rebuke, which would doubtless have been less
mild, had he felt himself stronger. He gave them also a message from the Governor, modified, apparently, to suit the circumstances; for while warning them of the wiles of the
English, it gave no hint that the King of France claimed mastery of their lands. Their answer was vague and unsatisfactory. It was plain that they were bound to the enemy by
interest, if not by sympathy. A party of English traders were
living in the place; and Céloron summoned them to withdraw, on pain of what might ensue. "My instructions," he
says, "enjoined me to do this, and even to pillage the English;
but I was not strong enough; and as these traders were established in the village and well supported by the Indians, the
attempt would have failed, and put the French to shame."
The assembled chiefs having been regaled with a cup of
brandy each,—the only part of the proceeding which seemed
to please them,—Céloron reimbarked, and continued his
voyage.

On the thirtieth they reached the Great Miami, called by
the French, Rivière à la Roche; and here Céloron buried the
last of his leaden plates. They now bade farewell to the Ohio,
or, in the words of the chaplain, to "La Belle Rivière,—that
river so little known to the French, and unfortunately too
well known to the English." He speaks of the multitude of
Indian villages on its shores, and still more on its northern
branches. "Each, great or small, has one or more English
traders, and each of these has hired men to carry his furs.
Behold, then, the English well advanced upon our lands, and,
what is worse, under the protection of a crowd of savages
whom they have drawn over to them, and whose number increases daily."

The course of the party lay up the Miami; and they toiled
thirteen days against the shallow current before they reached
a village of the Miami Indians, lately built at the mouth of
the rivulet now called Loramie Creek. Over it ruled a chief to
whom the French had given the singular name of La Demoi-

selle, but whom the English, whose fast friend he was, called Old Britain. The English traders who lived here had prudently withdrawn, leaving only two hired men in the place. The object of Céloron was to induce the Demoiselle and his band to leave this new abode and return to their old villages near the French fort on the Maumee, where they would be safe from English seduction. To this end, he called them to a council, gave them ample gifts, and made them an harangue in the name of the Governor. The Demoiselle took the gifts, thanked his French father for his good advice, and promised to follow it at a more convenient time.[1] In vain Céloron insisted that he and his tribesmen should remove at once. Neither blandishments nor threats would prevail, and the French commander felt that his negotiation had failed.

He was not deceived. Far from leaving his village, the Demoiselle, who was Great Chief of the Miami Confederacy, gathered his followers to the spot, till, less than two years after the visit of Céloron, its population had increased eightfold. Pique Town, or Pickawillany, as the English called it, became one of the greatest Indian towns of the West, the centre of English trade and influence, and a capital object of French jealousy.

Céloron burned his shattered canoes, and led his party across the long and difficult portage to the French post on the Maumee, where he found Raymond, the commander, and all his men, shivering with fever and ague. They supplied him with wooden canoes for his voyage down the river; and, early in October, he reached Lake Erie, where he was detained for a time by a drunken debauch of his Indians, who are called by the chaplain "a species of men made to exercise the patience of those who have the misfortune to travel with them." In a month more he was at Fort Frontenac; and as he descended thence to Montreal, he stopped at the Oswegatchie, in obedience to the Governor, who had directed him to report the progress made by the Sulpitian, Abbé Piquet, at his new mission. Piquet's new fort had been burned by Indians, prompted, as he thought, by the English of Oswego; but the

[1] Céloron, *Journal*. Compare *A Message from the Twightwees* (Miamis) in *Colonial Records of Pa.*, V. 437, where they say that they refused the gifts.

priest, buoyant and undaunted, was still resolute for the glory of God and the confusion of the heretics.

At length Céloron reached Montreal; and, closing his Journal, wrote thus: "Father Bonnecamp, who is a Jesuit and a great mathematician, reckons that we have travelled twelve hundred leagues; I and my officers think we have travelled more. All I can say is, that the nations of these countries are very ill-disposed towards the French, and devoted entirely to the English."[1] If his expedition had done no more, it had at least revealed clearly the deplorable condition of French interests in the West.

While Céloron was warning English traders from the Ohio, a plan was on foot in Virginia for a new invasion of the French domain. An association was formed to settle the Ohio country; and a grant of five hundred thousand acres was procured from the King, on condition that a hundred families should be established upon it within seven years, a fort built, and a garrison maintained. The Ohio Company numbered among its members some of the chief men of Virginia, including two brothers of Washington; and it had also a London partner, one Hanbury, a person of influence, who acted as its agent in England. In the year after the expedition of Céloron, its governing committee sent the trader Christopher Gist to explore the country and select land. It must be "good level land," wrote the Committee; "we had rather go quite down to the Mississippi than take mean, broken land."[2] In November Gist reached Logstown, the Chiningué of Céloron, where he found what he calls a "parcel of reprobate Indian traders." Those whom he so stigmatizes were Pennsylvanians, chiefly Scotch-Irish, between whom and the traders from Virginia there was great jealousy. Gist was told that he "should never go home safe." He declared himself the bearer of a message from the King. This imposed respect, and

[1] *Journal de la Campagne que moy Céloron, Chevalier de l'Ordre Royal et Militaire de St. Louis, Capitaine Commandant un détachement envoyé dans la Belle Rivière par les ordres de M. le Marquis de La Galissonière*, etc.

Relation d'un voyage dans la Belle Rivière sous les ordres de M. de Céloron, par le Père Bonnecamp, en 1749.

[2] Instructions to Gist, in appendix to Pownall, *Topographical Description of North America.*

he was allowed to proceed. At the Wyandot village of Muskingum he found the trader George Croghan, sent to the Indians by the Governor of Pennsylvania, to renew the chain of
friendship.[1] "Croghan," he says, "is a mere idol among his
countrymen, the Irish traders;" yet they met amicably, and
the Pennsylvanian had with him a companion, Andrew Montour, the interpreter, who proved of great service to Gist. As
Montour was a conspicuous person in his time, and a type of
his class, he merits a passing notice. He was the reputed
grandson of a French governor and an Indian squaw. His
half-breed mother, Catharine Montour, was a native of Canada, whence she was carried off by the Iroquois, and adopted
by them. She lived in a village at the head of Seneca Lake,
and still held the belief, inculcated by the guides of her youth,
that Christ was a Frenchman crucified by the English.[2] Her
son Andrew is thus described by the Moravian Zinzendorf,
who knew him: "His face is like that of a European, but
marked with a broad Indian ring of bear's-grease and paint
drawn completely round it. He wears a coat of fine cloth of
cinnamon color, a black necktie with silver spangles, a red
satin waistcoat, trousers over which hangs his shirt, shoes and
stockings, a hat, and brass ornaments, something like the handle of a basket, suspended from his ears."[3] He was an excellent interpreter, and held in high account by his Indian
kinsmen.

After leaving Muskingum, Gist, Croghan, and Montour
went together to a village on White Woman's Creek, — so
called from one Mary Harris, who lived here. She was born
in New England, was made prisoner when a child forty years
before, and had since dwelt among her captors, finding such
comfort as she might in an Indian husband and a family of
young half-breeds. "She still remembers," says Gist, "that they

[1] *Mr. Croghan's Transactions with the Indians*, in *N. Y. Col. Docs.*, VII. 267;
Croghan to Hamilton, 16 Dec. 1750.

[2] This is stated by Count Zinzendorf, who visited her among the Senecas.
Compare *Frontenac and New France under Louis XIV.*, p. 271. In a plan of
the "Route of the Western Army," made in 1779, and of which a tracing is
before me, the village where she lived is still called "French Catharine's
Town."

[3] Journal of Zinzendorf, quoted in Schweinitz, *Life of David Zeisberger*, 112,
note.

used to be very religious in New England, and wonders how white men can be so wicked as she has seen them in these woods." He and his companions now journeyed southwestward to the Shawanoe town at the mouth of the Scioto, where they found a reception very different from that which had awaited Céloron. Thence they rode northwestward along the forest path that led to Pickawillany, the Indian town on the upper waters of the Great Miami. Gist was delighted with the country; and reported to his employers that "it is fine, rich, level land, well timbered with large walnut, ash, sugar trees and cherry trees; well watered with a great number of little streams and rivulets; full of beautiful natural meadows, with wild rye, blue-grass, and clover, and abounding with turkeys, deer, elks, and most sorts of game, particularly buffaloes, thirty or forty of which are frequently seen in one meadow." A little farther west, on the plains of the Wabash and the Illinois, he would have found them by thousands.

They crossed the Miami on a raft, their horses swimming after them; and were met on landing by a crowd of warriors, who, after smoking with them, escorted them to the neighboring town, where they were greeted by a fusillade of welcome. "We entered with English colors before us, and were kindly received by their king, who invited us into his own house and set our colors upon the top of it; then all the white men and traders that were there came and welcomed us." This "king" was Old Britain, or La Demoiselle. Great were the changes here since Céloron, a year and a half before, had vainly enticed him to change his abode, and dwell in the shadow of the fleur-de-lis. The town had grown to four hundred families, or about two thousand souls; and the English traders had built for themselves and their hosts a fort of pickets, strengthened with logs.

There was a series of councils in the long house, or townhall. Croghan made the Indians a present from the Governor of Pennsylvania; and he and Gist delivered speeches of friendship and good advice, which the auditors received with the usual monosyllabic plaudits, ejected from the depths of their throats. A treaty of peace was solemnly made between the English and the confederate tribes, and all was serenity and joy; till four Ottawas, probably from Detroit, arrived with a

French flag, a gift of brandy and tobacco, and a message from the French commandant inviting the Miamis to visit him. Whereupon the great war-chief rose, and, with "a fierce tone and very warlike air," said to the envoys: "Brothers the Ottawas, we let you know, by these four strings of wampum, that we will not hear anything the French say, nor do anything they bid us." Then addressing the French as if actually present: "Fathers, we have made a road to the sun-rising, and have been taken by the hand by our brothers the English, the Six Nations, the Delawares, Shawanoes, and Wyandots.[1] We assure you, in that road we will go; and as you threaten us with war in the spring, we tell you that we are ready to receive you." Then, turning again to the four envoys: "Brothers the Ottawas, you hear what I say. Tell that to your fathers the French, for we speak it from our hearts." The chiefs then took down the French flag which the Ottawas had planted in the town, and dismissed the envoys with their answer of defiance.

On the next day the town-crier came with a message from the Demoiselle, inviting his English guests to a "feather dance," which Gist thus describes: "It was performed by three dancing-masters, who were painted all over of various colors, with long sticks in their hands, upon the ends of which were fastened long feathers of swans and other birds, neatly woven in the shape of a fowl's wing; in this disguise they performed many antic tricks, waving their sticks and feathers about with great skill, to imitate the flying and fluttering of birds, keeping exact time with their music." This music was the measured thumping of an Indian drum. From time to time a warrior would leap up, and the drum and the dancers would cease as he struck a post with his tomahawk, and in a loud voice recounted his exploits. Then the music and the dance began anew, till another warrior caught the martial fire, and bounded into the circle to brandish his tomahawk and vaunt his prowess.

On the first of March Gist took leave of Pickawillany, and returned towards the Ohio. He would have gone to the Falls,

[1] Compare *Message of Miamis and Hurons to the Governor of Pennsylvania* in *N. Y. Col. Docs.*, VI. 594; and *Report of Croghan* in *Colonial Records of Pa.*, V. 522, 523.

where Louisville now stands, but for a band of French Indians reported to be there, who would probably have killed him. After visiting a deposit of mammoth bones on the south shore, long the wonder of the traders, he turned eastward, crossed with toil and difficulty the mountains about the sources of the Kenawha, and after an absence of seven months reached his frontier home on the Yadkin, whence he proceeded to Roanoke with the report of his journey.[1]

All looked well for the English in the West; but under this fair outside lurked hidden danger. The Miamis were hearty in the English cause, and so perhaps were the Shawanoes; but the Delawares had not forgotten the wrongs that drove them from their old abodes east of the Alleghanies, while the Mingoes, or emigrant Iroquois, like their brethren of New York, felt the influence of Joncaire and other French agents, who spared no efforts to seduce them.[2] Still more baneful to British interests were the apathy and dissensions of the British colonies themselves. The Ohio Company had built a trading-house at Will's Creek, a branch of the Potomac, to which the Indians resorted in great numbers; whereupon the jealous traders of Pennsylvania told them that the Virginians meant to steal away their lands. This confirmed what they had been taught by the French emissaries, whose intrigues it powerfully aided. The governors of New York, Pennsylvania, and Virginia saw the importance of Indian alliances, and felt their own responsibility in regard to them; but they could do nothing without their assemblies. Those of New York and Pennsylvania were largely composed of tradesmen and farmers, absorbed in local interests, and possessed by two motives, — the saving of the people's money, and opposition to the governor, who stood for the royal prerogative. It was Hamilton, of Pennsylvania, who had sent Croghan to the Miamis to "renew the chain of friendship;" and when the envoy returned, the Assembly rejected his report. "I was condemned," he says, "for bringing expense on the Government, and the Indians

---

[1] *Journal of Christopher Gist*, in appendix to Pownall, *Topographical Description*. *Mr. Croghan's Transactions with the Indians* in *N. Y. Col. Docs.*, VII. 267.

[2] Joncaire made anti-English speeches to the Ohio Indians under the eyes of the English themselves, who did not molest him. *Journal of George Croghan, 1751*, in *Olden Time*, I. 136.

were neglected."[1] In the same year Hamilton again sent him
over the mountains, with a present for the Mingoes and Delawares. Croghan succeeded in persuading them that it would
be for their good if the English should build a fortified trading-house at the fork of the Ohio, where Pittsburg now
stands; and they made a formal request to the Governor that
it should be built accordingly. But, in the words of Croghan,
the Assembly "rejected the proposal, and condemned me for
making such a report." Yet this post on the Ohio was vital to
English interests. Even the Penns, proprietaries of the province, never lavish of their money, offered four hundred
pounds towards the cost of it, besides a hundred a year towards its maintenance; but the Assembly would not listen.[2]
The Indians were so well convinced that a strong English
trading-station in their country would add to their safety and
comfort, that when Pennsylvania refused it, they repeated the
proposal to Virginia; but here, too, it found for the present
little favor.

The question of disputed boundaries had much to do with
this most impolitic inaction. A large part of the valley of the
Ohio, including the site of the proposed establishment, was
claimed by both Pennsylvania and Virginia; and each feared
that whatever money it might spend there would turn to the
profit of the other. This was not the only evil that sprang
from uncertain ownership. "Till the line is run between the
two provinces," says Dinwiddie, governor of Virginia, "I cannot appoint magistrates to keep the traders in good order."[3]
Hence they did what they pleased, and often gave umbrage
to the Indians. Clinton, of New York, appealed to his Assembly for means to assist Pennsylvania in "securing the fidelity
of the Indians on the Ohio," and the Assembly refused.[4] "We

[1] *Mr. Croghan's Transactions with the Indians*, N. Y. Col. Docs., VII. 267.

[2] *Colonial Records of Pa.*, V. 515, 529, 547. At a council at Logstown (1751),
the Indians said to Croghan: "The French want to cheat us out of our country; but we will stop them, and, Brothers the English, you must help us. We
expect that you will build a strong house on the River Ohio, that in case of
war we may have a place to secure our wives and children, likewise our
brothers that come to trade with us." *Report of Treaty at Logstown, Ibid.*, V.
538.

[3] *Dinwiddie to the Lords of Trade, 6 Oct. 1752.*

[4] *Journals of New York Assembly*, II. 283, 284. *Colonial Records of Pa.*, V. 466.

will take care of our Indians, and they may take care of theirs:" such was the spirit of their answer. He wrote to the various provinces, inviting them to send commissioners to meet the tribes at Albany, "in order to defeat the designs and intrigues of the French." All turned a deaf ear except Massachusetts, Connecticut, and South Carolina, who sent the commissioners, but supplied them very meagrely with the indispensable presents.[1] Clinton says further: "The Assembly of this province have not given one farthing for Indian affairs, nor for a year past have they provided for the subsistence of the garrison at Oswego, which is the key for the commerce between the colonies and the inland nations of Indians."[2]

In the heterogeneous structure of the British colonies, their clashing interests, their internal disputes, and the misplaced economy of penny-wise and short-sighted assembly-men, lay the hope of France. The rulers of Canada knew the vast numerical preponderance of their rivals; but with their centralized organization they felt themselves more than a match for any one English colony alone. They hoped to wage war under the guise of peace, and to deal with the enemy in detail; and they at length perceived that the fork of the Ohio, so strangely neglected by the English, formed, together with Niagara, the key of the Great West. Could France hold firmly these two controlling passes, she might almost boast herself mistress of the continent.

NOTE.—The Journal of Céloron (Archives de la Marine) is very long and circumstantial, including the *procès verbaux*, and reports of councils with Indians. The Journal of the chaplain, Bonnecamp (Dépôt de la Marine), is shorter, but is the work of an intelligent and observing man. The author, a Jesuit, was skilled in mathematics, made daily observations, and constructed a map of the route, still preserved at the Dépôt de la Marine. Concurrently with these French narratives, one may consult the English letters and documents bearing on the same subjects, in the Colonial Records of Pennsylvania, the Archives of Pennsylvania, and the Colonial Documents of New York.

Three of Céloron's leaden plates have been found,—the two mentioned in the text, and another which was never buried, and which the Indians, who regarded these mysterious tablets as "bad medicine," procured by a trick from Joncaire, or, according to Governor Clinton, stole from him. A Cayuga chief brought it to Colonel Johnson, on the Mohawk, who interpreted the "Devilish writing" in such a manner as best to inspire horror of French designs.

[1] *Clinton to Hamilton, 18 Dec. 1750. Clinton to Lords of Trade, 13 June, 1751; Ibid., 17 July, 1751.*
[2] *Clinton to Bedford, 30 July, 1750.*

Chapter III

CONFLICT FOR THE WEST

*The Five Nations • Caughnawaga • Abbé Piquet • His Schemes
• His Journey • Fort Frontenac • Toronto • Niagara • Oswego •
Success of Piquet • Detroit • La Jonquière • His Intrigues • His
Trials • His Death • English Intrigues • Critical State of the West
• Pickawillany Destroyed • Duquesne • His Grand Enterprise*

T HE IROQUOIS, or Five Nations, sometimes called Six Nations after the Tuscaroras joined them, had been a power
of high importance in American international politics. In a
certain sense they may be said to have held the balance between their French and English neighbors; but their relative
influence had of late declined. So many of them had emigrated and joined the tribes of the Ohio, that the centre of
Indian population had passed to that region. Nevertheless,
the Five Nations were still strong enough in their ancient
abodes to make their alliance an object of the utmost consequence to both the European rivals. At the western end of
their "Long House," or belt of confederated villages, Joncaire
intrigued to gain them for France; while in the east he was
counteracted by the young colonel of militia, William Johnson, who lived on the Mohawk, and was already well skilled
in managing Indians. Johnson sometimes lost his temper; and
once wrote to Governor Clinton to complain of the "confounded wicked things the French had infused into the Indians' heads; among the rest that the English were determined,
the first opportunity, to destroy them all. I assure your Excellency I had hard work to beat these and several other cursed
villanous things, told them by the French, out of their
heads."[1]

In former times the French had hoped to win over the Five
Nations in a body, by wholesale conversion to the Faith; but
the attempt had failed. They had, however, made within their
own limits an asylum for such converts as they could gain,

[1] *Johnson to Clinton, 28 April, 1749.*

whom they collected together at Caughnawaga, near Montreal, to the number of about three hundred warriors.[1] These could not be trusted to fight their kinsmen, but willingly made forays against the English borders. Caughnawaga, like various other Canadian missions, was divided between the Church, the army, and the fur-trade. It had a chapel, fortifications, and storehouses; two Jesuits, an officer, and three chief traders. Of these last, two were maiden ladies, the Demoiselles Desauniers; and one of the Jesuits, their friend Father Tournois, was their partner in business. They carried on by means of the Mission Indians, and in collusion with influential persons in the colony, a trade with the Dutch at Albany, illegal, but very profitable.[2]

Besides this Iroquois mission, which was chiefly composed of Mohawks and Oneidas, another was now begun farther westward, to win over the Onondagas, Cayugas, and Senecas. This was the establishment of Father Piquet, which Céloron had visited in its infancy when on his way to the Ohio, and again on his return. Piquet was a man in the prime of life, of an alert, vivacious countenance, by no means unprepossessing;[3] an enthusiastic schemer, with great executive talents; ardent, energetic, vain, self-confident, and boastful. The enterprise seems to have been of his own devising; but it found warm approval from the Government.[4] La Présentation, as he called the new mission, stood on the bank of the River Oswegatchie where it enters the St. Lawrence. Here the rapids ceased, and navigation was free to Lake Ontario. The place commanded the main river, and could bar the way to hostile war-parties or contraband traders. Rich meadows, forests, and abundance of fish and game, made it attractive to Indians, and the Oswegatchie gave access to the Iroquois

---

[1] The estimate of a French official report, 1736, and of Sir William Johnson, 1763.

[2] *La Jonquière au Ministre, 27 Fév. 1750. Ibid., 29 Oct. 1751. Ordres du Roy et Dépêches des Ministres, 1751. Notice biographique de la Jonquière.* La Jonquière, governor of Canada, at last broke up their contraband trade, and ordered Tournois to Quebec.

[3] I once saw a contemporary portrait of him at the mission of Two Mountains, where he had been stationed.

[4] *Rouillé à la Jonquière, 1749.* The Intendant Bigot gave him money and provisions. *N. Y. Col. Docs.*, X. 204.

towns. Piquet had chosen his site with great skill. His activity was admirable. His first stockade was burned by Indian incendiaries; but it rose quickly from its ashes, and within a year or two the mission of La Présentation had a fort of palisades flanked with blockhouses, a chapel, a storehouse, a barn, a stable, ovens, a saw-mill, broad fields of corn and beans, and three villages of Iroquois, containing, in all, forty-nine bark lodges, each holding three or four families, more or less converted to the Faith; and, as time went on, this number increased. The Governor had sent a squad of soldiers to man the fort, and five small cannon to mount upon it. The place was as safe for the new proselytes as it was convenient and agreeable. The Pennsylvanian interpreter, Conrad Weiser, was told at Onondaga, the Iroquois capital, that Piquet had made a hundred converts from that place alone; and that, "having clothed them all in very fine clothes, laced with silver and gold, he took them down and presented them to the French Governor at Montreal, who received them very kindly, and made them large presents."[1]

Such were some of the temporal attractions of La Présentation. The nature of the spiritual instruction bestowed by Piquet and his fellow-priests may be partly inferred from the words of a proselyte warrior, who declared with enthusiasm that he had learned from the Sulpitian missionary that the King of France was the eldest son of the wife of Jesus Christ.[2] This he of course took in a literal sense, the mystic idea of the Church as the spouse of Christ being beyond his savage comprehension. The effect was to stimulate his devotion to the Great Onontio beyond the sea, and to the lesser Onontio who represented him as Governor of Canada.

Piquet was elated by his success; and early in 1752 he wrote to the Governor and Intendant: "It is a great miracle that, in spite of envy, contradiction, and opposition from nearly all the Indian villages, I have formed in less than three years one of the most flourishing missions in Canada. I find myself in a position to extend the empire of my good masters, Jesus Christ and the King, even to the extremities of this new

[1] *Journal of Conrad Weiser, 1750.*

[2] Lalande, *Notice de l'Abbé Piquet,* in *Lettres Édifiantes.* See also Tassé in *Revue Canadienne, 1870,* p. 9.

world; and, with some little help from you, to do more than France and England have been able to do with millions of money and all their troops."[1]

The letter from which this is taken was written to urge upon the Government a scheme in which the zealous priest could see nothing impracticable. He proposed to raise a war-party of thirty-eight hundred Indians, eighteen hundred of whom were to be drawn from the Canadian missions, the Five Nations, and the tribes of the Ohio, while the remaining two thousand were to be furnished by the Flatheads, or Choctaws, who were at the same time to be supplied with missionaries. The united force was first to drive the English from the Ohio, and next attack the Dog Tribe, or Cherokees, who lived near the borders of Virginia, with the people of which they were on friendly terms. "If," says Piquet, "the English of Virginia give any help to this last-named tribe,— which will not fail to happen,—they [*the war-party*] will do their utmost against them, through a grudge they bear them by reason of some old quarrels." In other words, the missionary hopes to set a host of savages to butchering English settlers in time of peace![2] His wild project never took effect, though the Governor, he says, at first approved it.

In the preceding year the "Apostle of the Iroquois," as he was called, made a journey to muster recruits for his mission, and kept a copious diary on the way. By accompanying him, one gets a clear view of an important part of the region in dispute between the rival nations. Six Canadians paddled him up the St. Lawrence, and five Indian converts followed in another canoe. Emerging from among the Thousand Islands, they stopped at Fort Frontenac, where Kingston now stands. Once the place was a great resort of Indians; now none were here, for the English post of Oswego, on the other side of the lake, had greater attractions. Piquet and his company found the pork and bacon very bad, and he complains that

---

[1] *Piquet à la Jonquière et Bigot, 8 Fév. 1752.* See Appendix A. In spite of Piquet's self-laudation, and in spite also of the detraction of the author of the *Mémoires sur le Canada, 1749–1760*, there can be no doubt of his practical capacity and his fertility of resource. Duquesne, when governor of the colony, highly praises "ses talents et son activité pour le service de Sa Majesté."

[2] Appendix A.

"there was not brandy enough in the fort to wash a wound."
They crossed to a neighboring island, where they were soon
visited by the chaplain of the fort, the storekeeper, his wife,
and three young ladies, glad of an excursion to relieve the
monotony of the garrison. "My hunters," says Piquet, "had
supplied me with means of giving them a pretty good entertainment. We drank, with all our hearts, the health of the
authorities, temporal and ecclesiastical, to the sound of our
musketry, which was very well fired, and delighted the islanders." These islanders were a band of Indians who lived here.
Piquet gave them a feast, then discoursed of religion, and at
last persuaded them to remove to the new mission.

During eight days he and his party coasted the northern
shore of Lake Ontario, with various incidents, such as an encounter between his dog Cerberus and a wolf, to the disadvantage of the latter, and the meeting with "a very fine negro
of twenty-two years, a fugitive from Virginia." On the
twenty-sixth of June they reached the new fort of Toronto,
which offered a striking contrast to their last stopping-place.
"The wine here is of the best; there is nothing wanting in this
fort; everything is abundant, fine, and good." There was reason for this. The Northern Indians were flocking with their
beaver-skins to the English of Oswego; and in April, 1749, an
officer named Portneuf had been sent with soldiers and workmen to build a stockaded trading-house at Toronto, in order
to intercept them,—not by force, which would have been
ruinous to French interests, but by a tempting supply of
goods and brandy.[1] Thus the fort was kept well stocked, and
with excellent effect. Piquet found here a band of Mississagas,
who would otherwise, no doubt, have carried their furs to the
English. He was strongly impelled to persuade them to migrate to La Présentation; but the Governor had told him to
confine his efforts to other tribes; and lest, he says, the ardor
of his zeal should betray him to disobedience, he reimbarked,
and encamped six leagues from temptation.

Two days more brought him to Niagara, where he was
warmly received by the commandant, the chaplain, and the
storekeeper,— the triumvirate who ruled these forest out-

[1] On Toronto, *La Jonquière et Bigot au Ministre, 1749. La Jonquière au Ministre, 30 Août, 1750. N. Y. Col. Docs.*, X. 201, 246.

posts, and stood respectively for their three vital principles, war, religion, and trade. Here Piquet said mass; and after resting a day, set out for the trading-house at the portage of the cataract, recently built, like Toronto, to stop the Indians on their way to Oswego.[1] Here he found Joncaire, and here also was encamped a large band of Senecas; though, being all drunk, men, women, and children, they were in no condition to receive the Faith, or appreciate the temporal advantages that attended it. On the next morning, finding them partially sober, he invited them to remove to La Présentation; "but as they had still something left in their bottles, I could get no answer till the following day." "I pass in silence," pursues the missionary, "an infinity of talks on this occasion. Monsieur de Joncaire forgot nothing that could help me, and behaved like a great servant of God and the King. My recruits increased every moment. I went to say my breviary while my Indians and the Senecas, without loss of time, assembled to hold a council with Monsieur de Joncaire." The result of the council was an entreaty to the missionary not to stop at Oswego, lest evil should befall him at the hands of the English. He promised to do as they wished, and presently set out on his return to Fort Niagara, attended by Joncaire and a troop of his new followers. The journey was a triumphal progress. "Whenever we passed a camp or a wigwam, the Indians saluted me by firing their guns, which happened so often that I thought all the trees along the way were charged with gunpowder; and when we reached the fort, Monsieur de Becancour received us with great ceremony and the firing of cannon, by which my savages were infinitely flattered."

His neophytes were gathered into the chapel for the first time in their lives, and there rewarded with a few presents. He now prepared to turn homeward, his flock at the mission being left in his absence without a shepherd; and on the sixth of July he embarked, followed by a swarm of canoes. On the twelfth they stopped at the Genesee, and went to visit the Falls, where the city of Rochester now stands. On the way, the Indians found a populous resort of rattlesnakes, and attacked the gregarious reptiles with great animation, to the

[1] *La Jonquière au Ministre, 23 Fév. 1750. Ibid., 6 Oct. 1751.* Compare *Colonial Records of Pa.*, V. 508.

alarm of the missionary, who trembled for his bare-legged retainers. His fears proved needless. Forty-two dead snakes, as he avers, requited the efforts of the sportsmen, and not one of them was bitten. When he returned to camp in the afternoon he found there a canoe loaded with kegs of brandy. "The English," he says, "had sent it to meet us, well knowing that this was the best way to cause disorder among my new recruits and make them desert me. The Indian in charge of the canoe, who had the look of a great rascal, offered some to me first, and then to my Canadians and Indians. I gave out that it was very probably poisoned, and immediately embarked again."

He encamped on the fourteenth at Sodus Bay, and strongly advises the planting of a French fort there. "Nevertheless," he adds, "it would be still better to destroy Oswego, and on no account let the English build it again." On the sixteenth he came in sight of this dreaded post. Several times on the way he had met fleets of canoes going thither or returning, in spite of the rival attractions of Toronto and Niagara. No English establishment on the continent was of such ill omen to the French. It not only robbed them of the fur-trade, by which they lived, but threatened them with military and political, no less than commercial, ruin. They were in constant dread lest ships of war should be built here, strong enough to command Lake Ontario, thus separating Canada from Louisiana, and cutting New France asunder. To meet this danger, they soon after built at Fort Frontenac a large three-masted vessel, mounted with heavy cannon; thus, as usual, forestalling their rivals by promptness of action.[1] The ground on which Oswego stood was claimed by the Province of New York, which alone had control of it; but through the purblind apathy of the Assembly, and their incessant quarrels with the Governor, it was commonly left to take care of itself. For some time they would vote no money to pay the feeble little garrison; and Clinton, who saw the necessity of maintaining it, was forced to do so on his own personal credit.[2] "Why can't your Gov-

[1] *Lieutenant Lindesay to Johnson, July, 1751.*
[2] *Clinton to Lords of Trade, 30 July, 1750.*

ernor and your great men [*the Assembly*] agree?" asked a Mohawk chief of the interpreter, Conrad Weiser.[1]

Piquet kept his promise not to land at the English fort; but
he approached in his canoe, and closely observed it. The
shores, now covered by the city of Oswego, were then a desolation of bare hills and fields, studded with the stumps of
felled trees, and hedged about with a grim border of forests.
Near the strand, by the mouth of the Onondaga, were the
houses of some of the traders; and on the higher ground behind them stood a huge block-house with a projecting upper
story. This building was surrounded by a rough wall of stone,
with flankers at the angles, forming what was called the fort.[2]
Piquet reconnoitred it from his canoe with the eye of a soldier. "It is commanded," he says, "on almost every side; two
batteries, of three twelve-pounders each, would be more than
enough to reduce it to ashes." And he enlarges on the evils
that arise from it. "It not only spoils our trade, but puts the
English into communication with a vast number of our Indians, far and near. It is true that they like our brandy better
than English rum; but they prefer English goods to ours, and
can buy for two beaver-skins at Oswego a better silver brace-
let than we sell at Niagara for ten."

The burden of these reflections was lightened when he approached Fort Frontenac. "Never was reception more solemn.
The Nipissings and Algonkins, who were going on a war-
party with Monsieur Belêtre, formed a line of their own accord, and saluted us with three volleys of musketry, and cries
of joy without end. All our little bark vessels replied in the
same way. Monsieur de Verchères and Monsieur de Valtry
ordered the cannon of the fort to be fired; and my Indians,
transported with joy at the honor done them, shot off their
guns incessantly, with cries and acclamations that delighted
everybody." A goodly band of recruits joined him, and he
pursued his voyage to La Présentation, while the canoes of
his proselytes followed in a swarm to their new home; "that
establishment"—thus in a burst of enthusiasm he closes his
Journal—"that establishment which I began two years ago,

[1] *Journal of Conrad Weiser, 1750.*
[2] Compare *Doc. Hist. N. Y.*, I. 463.

in the midst of opposition; that establishment which may be regarded as a key of the colony; that establishment which officers, interpreters, and traders thought a chimæra,—that establishment, I say, forms already a mission of Iroquois savages whom I assembled at first to the number of only six, increased last year to eighty-seven, and this year to three hundred and ninety-six, without counting more than a hundred and fifty whom Monsieur Chabert de Joncaire is to bring me this autumn. And I certify that thus far I have received from His Majesty—for all favor, grace, and assistance—no more than a half pound of bacon and two pounds of bread for daily rations; and that he has not yet given a pin to the chapel, which I have maintained out of my own pocket, for the greater glory of my masters, God and the King."[1]

In his late journey he had made the entire circuit of Lake Ontario. Beyond lay four other inland oceans, to which Fort Niagara was the key. As that all-essential post controlled the passage from Ontario to Erie, so did Fort Detroit control that from Erie to Huron, and Fort Michillimackinac that from Huron to Michigan; while Fort Ste. Marie, at the outlet of Lake Superior, had lately received a garrison, and changed from a mission and trading-station to a post of war.[2] This immense extent of inland navigation was safe in the hands of France so long as she held Niagara. Niagara lost, not only the lakes, but also the Valley of the Ohio was lost with it. Next in importance was Detroit. This was not a military post alone, but also a settlement; and, except the hamlets about Fort Chartres, the only settlement that France owned in all the West. There were, it is true, but a few families; yet the hope of growth seemed good; for to such as liked a wilderness home, no spot in America had more attraction. Father Bonnecamp stopped here for a day on his way back from the expedition of Céloron. "The situation," he says, "is charming. A fine river flows at the foot of the fortifications; vast mead-

---

[1] *Journal qui peut servir de Mémoire et de Relation du Voyage que j'ay fait sur le Lac Ontario pour attirer au nouvel Établissement de La Présentation les Sauvages Iroquois des Cinq Nations, 1751.* The last passage given above is condensed in the rendering, as the original is extremely involved and ungrammatical.

[2] *La Jonquière au Ministre, 24 Août, 1750.*

ows, asking only to be tilled, extend beyond the sight. Nothing can be more agreeable than the climate. Winter lasts hardly two months. European grains and fruits grow here far better than in many parts of France. It is the Touraine and Beauce of Canada."[1] The white flag of the Bourbons floated over the compact little palisaded town, with its population of soldiers and fur-traders; and from the block-houses which served as bastions, one saw on either hand the small solid dwellings of the *habitants*, ranged at intervals along the margin of the water; while at a little distance three Indian villages—Ottawa, Pottawattamie, and Wyandot—curled their wigwam smoke into the pure summer air.[2]

When Céloron de Bienville returned from the Ohio, he went, with a royal commission, sent him a year before, to command at Detroit.[3] His late chaplain, the very intelligent Father Bonnecamp, speaks of him as fearless, energetic, and full of resource; but the Governor calls him haughty and insubordinate. Great efforts were made, at the same time, to build up Detroit as a centre of French power in the West. The methods employed were of the debilitating, paternal character long familiar to Canada. All emigrants with families were to be carried thither at the King's expense; and every settler was to receive in free gift a gun, a hoe, an axe, a ploughshare, a scythe, a sickle, two augers, large and small, a sow, six hens, a cock, six pounds of powder, and twelve pounds of lead; while to these favors were added many others. The result was that twelve families were persuaded to go, or about a twentieth part of the number wanted.[4] Detroit was expected to furnish supplies to the other posts for five hundred miles around, control the neighboring Indians,

[1] *Relation du Voiage de la Belle Rivière, 1749.*

[2] A plan of Detroit is before me, made about this time by the engineer Léry.

[3] *Le Ministre à la Jonquière et Bigot, 14 Mai, 1749. Le Ministre à Céloron, 23 Mai, 1749.*

[4] *Ordonnance du 2 Jan. 1750. La Jonquière et Bigot au Ministre, 1750.* Forty-six persons of all ages and both sexes had been induced by La Galissonière to go the year before. *Lettres communes de la Jonquière et Bigot, 1749.* The total fixed population of Detroit and its neighborhood in 1750 is stated at four hundred and eighty-three souls. In the following two years, a considerable number of young men came of their own accord, and Céloron wrote to Montreal to ask for girls to marry them.

thwart English machinations, and drive off English interlopers.

La Galissonière no longer governed Canada. He had been
honorably recalled, and the Marquis de la Jonquière sent in
his stead.[1] La Jonquière, like his predecessor, was a naval officer of high repute; he was tall and imposing in person, and
of undoubted capacity and courage; but old and, according
to his enemies, very avaricious.[2] The Colonial Minister gave
him special instructions regarding that thorn in the side of
Canada, Oswego. To attack it openly would be indiscreet, as
the two nations were at peace; but there was a way of dealing
with it less hazardous, if not more lawful. This was to attack
it vicariously by means of the Iroquois. "If Abbé Piquet succeeds in his mission," wrote the Minister to the new Governor, "we can easily persuade these savages to destroy
Oswego. This is of the utmost importance; but act with great
caution."[3] In the next year the Minister wrote again: "The
only means that can be used for such an operation in time of
peace are those of the Iroquois. If by making these savages
regard such an establishment [Oswego] as opposed to their
liberty, and, so to speak, a usurpation by which the English
mean to get possession of their lands, they could be induced
to undertake its destruction, an operation of the sort is not to
be neglected; but M. le Marquis de la Jonquière should feel
with what circumspection such an affair should be conducted,
and he should labor to accomplish it in a manner not to commit himself."[4] To this La Jonquière replies that it will need
time; but that he will gradually bring the Iroquois to attack
and destroy the English post. He received stringent orders to
use every means to prevent the English from encroaching, but
to act towards them at the same time "with the greatest politeness."[5] This last injunction was scarcely fulfilled in a cor-

---

[1] *Le Ministre à la Galissonière, 14 Mai, 1749.*

[2] *Mémoires sur le Canada, 1749 –1760.* The charges made here and elsewhere
are denied, somewhat faintly, by a descendant of La Jonquière in his elaborate *Notice biographique* of his ancestor.

[3] *Le Ministre à La Jonquière, Mai, 1749.* The instructions given to La Jonquière before leaving France also urge the necessity of destroying Oswego.

[4] *Ordres du Roy et Dépêches des Ministres; à MM. de la Jonquière et Bigot, 15
Avril, 1750.* See Appendix A. for original.

[5] *Ordres du Roy et Dépêches des Ministres, 1750.*

respondence which he had with Clinton, governor of New York, who had written to complain of the new post at the Niagara portage as an invasion of English territory, and also of the arrest of four English traders in the country of the Miamis. Niagara, like Oswego, was in the country of the Five Nations, whom the treaty of Utrecht declared "subject to the dominion of Great Britain."[1] This declaration, preposterous in itself, was binding on France, whose plenipotentiaries had signed the treaty. The treaty also provided that the subjects of the two Crowns "shall enjoy full liberty of going and coming on account of trade," and Clinton therefore demanded that La Jonquière should disavow the arrest of the four traders and punish its authors. The French Governor replied with great asperity, spurned the claim that the Five Nations were British subjects, and justified the arrest.[2] He presently went further. Rewards were offered by his officers for the scalps of Croghan and of another trader named Lowry.[3] When this reached the ears of William Johnson, on the Mohawk, he wrote to Clinton in evident anxiety for his own scalp: "If the French go on so, there is no man can be safe in his own house; for I can at any time get an Indian to kill any man for a small matter. Their going on in that manner is worse than open war."

The French on their side made counter-accusations. The captive traders were examined on oath before La Jonquière, and one of them, John Patton, is reported to have said that Croghan had instigated Indians to kill Frenchmen.[4] French officials declared that other English traders were guilty of the same practices; and there is very little doubt that the charge was true.

The dispute with the English was not the only source of trouble to the Governor. His superiors at Versailles would not adopt his views, and looked on him with distrust. He advised the building of forts near Lake Erie, and his advice was rejected. "Niagara and Detroit," he was told, "will secure

[1] Chalmers, *Collection of Treaties*, I. 382.
[2] *La Jonquière à Clinton, 10 Août, 1751.*
[3] Deposition of Morris Turner and Ralph Kilgore, in *Colonial Records of Pa.*, V. 482. The deponents had been prisoners at Detroit.
[4] *Précis des Faits, avec leurs Pièces justificatives*, 100.

forever our communications with Louisiana."[1] "His Majesty," again wrote the Colonial Minister, "thought that expenses would diminish after the peace; but, on the contrary, they have increased. There must be great abuses. You and the Intendant must look to it."[2] Great abuses there were; and of the money sent to Canada for the service of the King the larger part found its way into the pockets of peculators. The colony was eaten to the heart with official corruption; and the centre of it was François Bigot, the intendant. The Minister directed La Jonquière's attention to certain malpractices which had been reported to him; and the old man, deeply touched, replied: "I have reached the age of sixty-six years, and there is not a drop of blood in my veins that does not thrill for the service of my King. I will not conceal from you that the slightest suspicion on your part against me would cut the thread of my days."[3]

Perplexities increased; affairs in the West grew worse and worse. La Jonquière ordered Céloron to attack the English at Pickawillany; and Céloron could not or would not obey. "I cannot express," writes the Governor, "how much this business troubles me; it robs me of sleep; it makes me ill." Another letter of rebuke presently came from Versailles. "Last year you wrote that you would soon drive the English from the Ohio; but private letters say that you have done nothing. This is deplorable. If not expelled, they will seem to acquire a right against us. Send force enough at once to drive them off, and cure them of all wish to return."[4] La Jonquière answered with bitter complaints against Céloron, and then begged to be recalled. His health, already shattered, was ruined by fatigue and vexation; and he took to his bed. Before spring he was near his end.[5] It is said that, though very rich, his habits of thrift so possessed his last hours that, seeing wax-candles burning in his chamber, he ordered others of tallow to be brought instead, as being good enough to die by.

---

[1] *Ordres du Roy et Dépêches des Ministres, 1750.*

[2] *Ibid., 6 Juin, 1751.*

[3] *La Jonquière au Ministre, 19 Oct. 1751.*

[4] *Ordres du Roy et Dépêches des Ministres, 1751.*

[5] He died on the sixth of March, 1752 (*Bigot au Ministre, 6 Mai*); not on the seventeenth of May, as stated in the *Mémoires sur le Canada, 1749–1760.*

Thus frugally lighted on its way, his spirit fled; and the Baron de Longueuil took his place till a new governor should arrive.

Sinister tidings came thick from the West. Raymond, commandant at the French fort on the Maumee, close to the centre of intrigue, wrote: "My people are leaving me for Detroit. Nobody wants to stay here and have his throat cut. All the tribes who go to the English at Pickawillany come back loaded with gifts. I am too weak to meet the danger. Instead of twenty men, I need five hundred. . . . We have made peace with the English, yet they try continually to make war on us by means of the Indians; they intend to be masters of all this upper country. The tribes here are leaguing together to kill all the French, that they may have nobody on their lands but their English brothers. This I am told by Coldfoot, a great Miami chief, whom I think an honest man, if there is any such thing among Indians. . . . If the English stay in this country we are lost. We must attack, and drive them out." And he tells of war-belts sent from tribe to tribe, and rumors of plots and conspiracies far and near.

Without doubt, the English traders spared no pains to gain over the Indians by fair means or foul; sold them goods at low rates, made ample gifts, and gave gunpowder for the asking. Saint-Ange, who commanded at Vincennes, wrote that a storm would soon burst on the heads of the French. Joncaire reported that all the Ohio Indians sided with the English. Longueuil informed the Minister that the Miamis had scalped two soldiers; that the Piankishaws had killed seven Frenchmen; and that a squaw who had lived with one of the slain declared that the tribes of the Wabash and Illinois were leaguing with the Osages for a combined insurrection. Every letter brought news of murder. Small-pox had broken out at Detroit. "It is to be wished," says Longueuil, "that it would spread among our rebels; it would be fully as good as an army. . . . We are menaced with a general outbreak, and even Toronto is in danger. . . . Before long the English on the Miami will gain over all the surrounding tribes, get possession of Fort Chartres, and cut our communications with Louisiana."[1]

[1] *Dépêches de Longueuil; Lettres de Raymond; Benoit de Saint-Clerc à la Jonquière, Oct. 1751.*

The moving spirit of disaffection was the chief called Old Britain, or the Demoiselle, and its focus was his town of Pickawillany, on the Miami. At this place it is said that English traders sometimes mustered to the number of fifty or more. "It is they," wrote Longueuil, "who are the instigators of revolt and the source of all our woes."[1] Whereupon the Colonial Minister reiterated his instructions to drive them off and plunder them, which he thought would "effectually disgust them," and bring all trouble to an end.[2]

La Jonquière's remedy had been more heroic, for he had ordered Céloron to attack the English and their red allies alike; and he charged that officer with arrogance and disobedience because he had not done so. It is not certain that obedience was easy; for though, besides the garrison of regulars, a strong body of militia was sent up to Detroit to aid the stroke,[3] the Indians of that post, whose co-operation was thought necessary, proved half-hearted, intractable, and even touched with disaffection. Thus the enterprise languished till, in June, aid came from another quarter. Charles Langlade, a young French trader married to a squaw at Green Bay, and strong in influence with the tribes of that region, came down the lakes from Michillimackinac with a fleet of canoes manned by two hundred and fifty Ottawa and Ojibwa warriors; stopped a while at Detroit; then embarked again, paddled up the Maumee to Raymond's fort at the portage, and led his greased and painted rabble through the forest to attack the Demoiselle and his English friends. They approached Pickawillany at about nine o'clock on the morning of the twenty-first. The scared squaws fled from the cornfields into the town, where the wigwams of the Indians clustered about the fortified warehouse of the traders. Of these there were at the time only eight in the place. Most of the Indians also were gone on their summer hunt, though the Demoiselle remained with a band of his tribesmen. Great was the screeching of war-whoops and clatter of guns. Three of the traders were caught outside the fort. The remaining five closed the gate, and stood on their defence. The fight was soon over. Four-

[1] *Longueuil au Ministre, 21 Avril, 1752.*

[2] *Le Ministre à la Jonquière, 1752. Le Ministre à Duquesne, 9 Juillet, 1752.*

[3] *La Jonquière à Céloron, 1 Oct. 1751.*

teen Miamis were shot down, the Demoiselle among the rest. The five white men held out till the afternoon, when three of them surrendered, and two, Thomas Burney and Andrew McBryer, made their escape. One of the English prisoners being wounded, the victors stabbed him to death. Seventy years of missionaries had not weaned them from cannibalism, and they boiled and eat the Demoiselle.[1]

The captive traders, plundered to the skin, were carried by Langlade to Duquesne, the new governor, who highly praised the bold leader of the enterprise, and recommended him to the Minister for such reward as befitted one of his station. "As he is not in the King's service, and has married a squaw, I will ask for him only a pension of two hundred francs, which will flatter him infinitely."

The Marquis Duquesne, sprung from the race of the great naval commander of that name, had arrived towards midsummer; and he began his rule by a general review of troops and militia. His lofty bearing offended the Canadians; but he compelled their respect, and, according to a writer of the time, showed from the first that he was born to command. He presently took in hand an enterprise which his predecessor would probably have accomplished, had the Home Government encouraged him. Duquesne, profiting by the infatuated neglect of the British provincial assemblies, prepared to occupy the upper waters of the Ohio, and secure the passes with forts and garrisons. Thus the Virginian and Pennsylvanian traders would be debarred all access to the West, and the tribes of that region, bereft henceforth of English guns, knives, hatchets, and blankets, English gifts and English cajoleries, would be thrown back to complete dependence on the French. The moral influence, too, of such a movement would be incalculable; for the Indian respects nothing so much as a display of vigor and daring, backed by force. In short, the intended enterprise was a master-stroke, and laid the axe to the very root of disaffection. It is true that, under the treaty, commissioners had been long in session at Paris to settle the question of American boundaries; but there was no

[1]On the attack of Pickawillany, *Longueuil au Ministre, 18 Août, 1752*; *Duquesne au Ministre, 25 Oct. 1752*; *Colonial Records of Pa.*, V. 599; *Journal of William Trent, 1752*. Trent was on the spot a few days after the affair.

likelihood that they would come to agreement; and if France would make good her Western claims, it behooved her, while there was yet time, to prevent her rival from fastening a firm grasp on the countries in dispute.

Yet the Colonial Minister regarded the plan with distrust. "Be on your guard," he wrote to Duquesne, "against new undertakings; private interests are generally at the bottom of them. It is through these that new posts are established. Keep only such as are indispensable, and suppress the others. The expenses of the colony are enormous; and they have doubled since the peace." Again, a little later: "Build on the Ohio such forts as are absolutely necessary, but no more. Remember that His Majesty suspects your advisers of interested views."[1]

No doubt there was justice in the suspicion. Every military movement, and above all the establishment of every new post, was an opportunity to the official thieves with whom the colony swarmed. Some band of favored knaves grew rich; while a much greater number, excluded from sharing the illicit profits, clamored against the undertaking, and wrote charges of corruption to Versailles. Thus the Minister was kept tolerably well informed; but was scarcely the less helpless, for with the Atlantic between, the disorders of Canada defied his control. Duquesne was exasperated by the opposition that met him on all hands, and wrote to the Minister: "There are so many rascals in this country that one is forever the butt of their attacks."[2]

It seems that unlawful gain was not the only secret spring of the movement. An officer of repute says that the Intendant, Bigot, enterprising in his pleasures as in his greed, was engaged in an intrigue with the wife of Chevalier Péan; and wishing at once to console the husband and to get rid of him, sought for him a high command at a distance from the colony. Therefore while Marin, an able officer, was made first in rank, Péan was made second. The same writer hints that Duquesne himself was influenced by similar motives in his appointment of leaders.[3]

---

[1] *Ordres du Roy et Dépêches des Ministres, 1753.*

[2] *Duquesne au Ministre, 29 Sept. 1754.*

[3] Pouchot, *Mémoire sur la dernière Guerre de l'Amérique septentrionale* (*ed. 1781*), I. 8.

He mustered the colony troops, and ordered out the Canadians. With the former he was but half satisfied; with the latter he was delighted; and he praises highly their obedience and alacrity. "I had not the least trouble in getting them to march. They came on the minute, bringing their own guns, though many people tried to excite them to revolt; for the whole colony opposes my operations." The expedition set out early in the spring of 1753. The whole force was not much above a thousand men, increased by subsequent detachments to fifteen hundred; but to the Indians it seemed a mighty host; and one of their orators declared that the lakes and rivers were covered with boats and soldiers from Montreal to Presquisle.[1] Some Mohawk hunters by the St. Lawrence saw them as they passed, and hastened home to tell the news to Johnson, whom they wakened at midnight, "whooping and hollowing in a frightful manner."[2] Lieutenant Holland at Oswego saw a fleet of canoes upon the lake, and was told by a roving Frenchman that they belonged to an army of six thousand men going to the Ohio, "to cause all the English to quit those parts."[3]

The main body of the expedition landed at Presquisle, on the southeastern shore of Lake Erie, where the town of Erie now stands; and here for a while we leave them.

[1] *Duquesne au Ministre, 27 Oct. 1753.*
[2] *Johnson to Clinton, 20 April, 1753,* in *N. Y. Col. Docs.,* VI. 778.
[3] *Holland to Clinton, 15 May, 1753,* in *N. Y. Col. Docs.,* VI. 780.

Chapter IV

CONFLICT FOR ACADIA

Acadia ceded to England • Acadians swear Fidelity • Halifax founded • French Intrigue • Acadian Priests • Mildness of English Rule • Covert Hostility of Acadians • The New Oath • Treachery of Versailles • Indians incited to War • Clerical Agents of Revolt • Abbé Le Loutre • Acadians impelled to emigrate • Misery of the Emigrants • Humanity of Cornwallis and Hopson • Fanaticism and Violence of Le Loutre • Capture of the "St. François" • The English at Beaubassin • Le Loutre drives out the Inhabitants • Murder of Howe • Beauséjour • Insolence of Le Loutre • His Harshness to the Acadians • The Boundary Commission • Its Failure • Approaching War

W HILE in the West all the signs of the sky foreboded storm, another tempest was gathering in the East, less in extent, but not less in peril. The conflict in Acadia has a melancholy interest, since it ended in a catastrophe which prose and verse have joined to commemorate, but of which the causes have not been understood.

Acadia—that is to say, the peninsula of Nova Scotia, with the addition, as the English claimed, of the present New Brunswick and some adjacent country—was conquered by General Nicholson in 1710, and formally transferred by France to the British Crown, three years later, by the treaty of Utrecht. By that treaty it was "expressly provided" that such of the French inhabitants as "are willing to remain there and to be subject to the Kingdom of Great Britain, are to enjoy the free exercise of their religion according to the usage of the Church of Rome, as far as the laws of Great Britain do allow the same;" but that any who choose may remove, with their effects, if they do so within a year. Very few availed themselves of this right; and after the end of the year those who remained were required to take an oath of allegiance to King George. There is no doubt that in a little time they would have complied, had they been let alone; but the French authorities of Canada and Cape Breton did their utmost to prevent them, and employed agents to keep them hostile to England. Of these the most efficient were the French priests, who, in spite of the treaty, persuaded their flocks that they were still subjects of King Louis. Hence rose endless perplexity to the English commanders at Annapolis, who more than suspected that the Indian attacks with which they were harassed were due mainly to French instigation.[1] It was not till seventeen years after the treaty that the Acadians could be brought to take the oath without qualifications which made it almost useless. The English authorities seem to have shown throughout an unusual patience and forbearance. At length, about 1730, nearly all the inhabitants signed by crosses, since few of them could write, an oath recognizing George II. as sovereign of Acadia, and promising fidelity and obedience to him.[2] This restored comparative quiet till the war of 1745, when some of the Acadians remained neutral, while some took arms against the English, and many others aided the enemy with information and supplies.

English power in Acadia, hitherto limited to a feeble garrison at Annapolis and a feebler one at Canseau, received at this time a great accession. The fortress of Louisbourg, taken by the English during the war, had been restored by the treaty; and the French at once prepared to make it a military and naval station more formidable than ever. Upon this the British Ministry resolved to establish another station as a counterpoise; and the harbor of Chebucto, on the south coast of Acadia, was chosen as the site of it. Thither in June, 1749, came a fleet of transports loaded with emigrants, tempted by offers of land and a home in the New World. Some were mechanics, tradesmen, farmers, and laborers; others were sailors, soldiers, and subaltern officers thrown out of employment by the peace. Including women and children, they counted in all about twenty-five hundred. Alone of all the British colonies on the continent, this new settlement was the offspring, not

[1] See the numerous papers in *Selections from the Public Documents of the Province of Nova Scotia* (Halifax, 1869), pp. 1–165; a Government publication of great value.

[2] The oath was *literatim* as follows: "Je Promets et Jure Sincerement en Foi de Chrétien que Je serai entierement Fidele, et Obeierai Vraiment Sa Majesté Le Roy George Second, qui (*sic*) Je reconnoi pour Le Souvrain Seigneur de l'Accadie ou Nouvelle Ecosse. Ainsi Dieu me Soit en Aide."

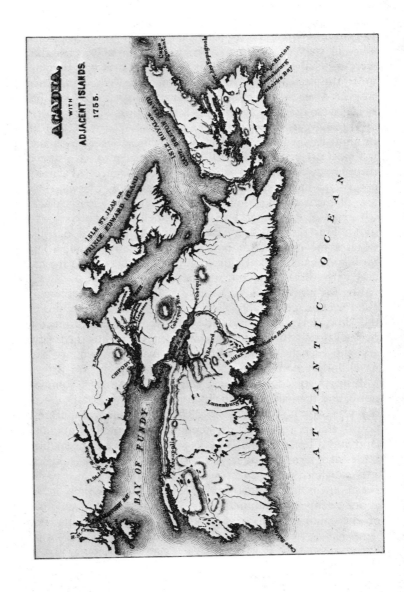

ACADIA,
WITH
ADJACENT ISLANDS.
1755.

of private enterprise, but of royal authority. Yet it was free like the rest, with the same popular representation and local self-government. Edward Cornwallis, uncle of Lord Cornwallis of the Revolutionary War, was made governor and commander-in-chief. Wolfe calls him "a man of approved courage and fidelity;" and even the caustic Horace Walpole speaks of him as "a brave, sensible young man, of great temper and good nature."

Before summer was over, the streets were laid out, and the building-lot of each settler was assigned to him; before winter closed, the whole were under shelter, the village was fenced with palisades and defended by redoubts of timber, and the battalions lately in garrison at Louisbourg manned the wooden ramparts. Succeeding years brought more emigrants, till in 1752 the population was above four thousand. Thus was born into the world the city of Halifax. Along with the crumbling old fort and miserably disciplined garrison at Annapolis, besides six or seven small detached posts to watch the Indians and Acadians, it comprised the whole British force on the peninsula; for Canseau had been destroyed by the French.

The French had never reconciled themselves to the loss of Acadia, and were resolved, by diplomacy or force, to win it back again; but the building of Halifax showed that this was to be no easy task, and filled them at the same time with alarm for the safety of Louisbourg. On one point, at least, they saw their policy clear. The Acadians, though those of them who were not above thirty-five had been born under the British flag, must be kept French at heart, and taught that they were still French subjects. In 1748 they numbered eighty-eight hundred and fifty communicants, or from twelve to thirteen thousand souls; but an emigration, of which the causes will soon appear, had reduced them in 1752 to but little more than nine thousand.[1] These were divided into six principal parishes, one of the largest being that of Annapolis. Other centres of population were Grand Pré, on the basin of Mines; Beaubassin, at the head of Chignecto Bay; Pisiquid, now Windsor; and Cobequid, now Truro. Their priests, who were missionaries

[1] *Description de l'Acadie, avec le Nom des Paroisses et le Nombre des Habitants, 1748. Mémoire à présenter à la Cour sur la Necessité de fixer les Limites de l'Acadie,* par l'Abbé de l'Isle-Dieu, 1753 (1754?). Compare the estimates in *Censuses of Canada* (Ottawa, 1876).

controlled by the diocese of Quebec, acted also as their magistrates, ruling them for this world and the next. Being subject to a French superior, and being, moreover, wholly French at heart, they formed in this British province a wheel within a wheel, the inner movement always opposing the outer.

Although, by the twelfth article of the treaty of Utrecht, France had solemnly declared the Acadians to be British subjects, the Government of Louis XV. intrigued continually to turn them from subjects into enemies. Before me is a mass of English documents on Acadian affairs from the peace of Aix-la-Chapelle to the catastrophe of 1755, and above a thousand pages of French official papers from the archives of Paris, memorials, reports, and secret correspondence, relating to the same matters. With the help of these and some collateral lights, it is not difficult to make a correct diagnosis of the political disease that ravaged this miserable country. Of a multitude of proofs, only a few can be given here; but these will suffice.

It was not that the Acadians had been ill-used by the English; the reverse was the case. They had been left in free exercise of their worship, as stipulated by treaty. It is true that, from time to time, there were loud complaints from French officials that religion was in danger, because certain priests had been rebuked, arrested, brought before the Council at Halifax, suspended from their functions, or required, on pain of banishment, to swear that they would do nothing against the interests of King George. Yet such action on the part of the provincial authorities seems, without a single exception, to have been the consequence of misconduct on the part of the priest, in opposing the Government and stirring his flock to disaffection. La Jonquière, the determined adversary of the English, reported to the bishop that they did not oppose the ecclesiastics in the exercise of their functions, and an order of Louis XV. admits that the Acadians have enjoyed liberty of religion.[1] In a long document addressed in 1750 to the Colonial Minister at Versailles, Roma, an officer at Louisbourg, testifies thus to the mildness of British rule, though he ascribes it to interested motives. "The fear that the Acadians

---

[1] *La Jonquière à l'Évêque de Québec, 14 Juin, 1750. Mémoire du Roy pour servir d'Instruction au Comte de Raymond, commandant pour Sa Majesté à l'Isle Royale* [Cape Breton], *24 Avril, 1751.*

have of the Indians is the controlling motive which makes them side with the French. The English, having in view the conquest of Canada, wished to give the French of that colony, in their conduct towards the Acadians, a striking example of the mildness of their government. Without raising the fortune of any of the inhabitants, they have supplied them for more than thirty-five years with the necessaries of life, often on credit and with an excess of confidence, without troubling their debtors, without pressing them, without wishing to force them to pay. They have left them an appearance of liberty so excessive that they have not intervened in their disputes or even punished their crimes. They have allowed them to refuse with insolence certain moderate rents payable in grain and lawfully due. They have passed over in silence the contemptuous refusal of the Acadians to take titles from them for the new lands which they chose to occupy.[1]

"We know very well," pursues Roma, "the fruits of this conduct in the last war; and the English know it also. Judge then what will be the wrath and vengeance of this cruel nation." The fruits to which Roma alludes were the hostilities, open or secret, committed by the Acadians against the English. He now ventures the prediction that the enraged conquerors will take their revenge by drafting all the young Acadians on board their ships of war, and there destroying them by slow starvation. He proved, however, a false prophet. The English Governor merely required the inhabitants to renew their oath of allegiance, without qualification or evasion.

It was twenty years since the Acadians had taken such an oath; and meanwhile a new generation had grown up. The old oath pledged them to fidelity and obedience; but they averred that Phillips, then governor of the province, had given them, at the same time, assurance that they should not be required to bear arms against either French or Indians. In fact, such service had not been demanded of them, and they would have lived in virtual neutrality, had not many of them broken their oaths and joined the French war-parties. For this reason Cornwallis thought it necessary that, in renewing the pledge, they should bind themselves to an allegiance as complete as that required of other British subjects. This spread

[1] See Appendix B.

general consternation. Deputies from the Acadian settlements appeared at Halifax, bringing a paper signed with the marks of a thousand persons. The following passage contains the pith of it. "The inhabitants in general, sir, over the whole extent of this country are resolved not to take the oath which your Excellency requires of us; but if your Excellency will grant us our old oath, with an exemption for ourselves and our heirs from taking up arms, we will accept it."[1] The answer of Cornwallis was by no means so stern as it has been represented.[2] After the formal reception he talked in private with the deputies; and "they went home in good humor, promising great things."[3]

The refusal of the Acadians to take the required oath was not wholly spontaneous, but was mainly due to influence from without. The French officials of Cape Breton and Isle St. Jean, now Prince Edward Island, exerted themselves to the utmost, chiefly through the agency of the priests, to excite the people to refuse any oath that should commit them fully to British allegiance. At the same time means were used to induce them to migrate to the neighboring islands under French rule, and efforts were also made to set on the Indians to attack the English. But the plans of the French will best appear in a despatch sent by La Jonquière to the Colonial Minister in the autumn of 1749.

"Monsieur Cornwallis issued an order on the tenth of the said month [*August*], to the effect that if the inhabitants will remain faithful subjects of the King of Great Britain, he will allow them priests and public exercise of their religion, with the understanding that no priest shall officiate without his permission or before taking an oath of fidelity to the King of Great Britain. Secondly, that the inhabitants shall not be exempted from defending their houses, their lands, and the Government. Thirdly, that they shall take an oath of fidelity to the King of Great Britain, on the twenty-sixth of this month, before officers sent them for that purpose."

La Jonquière proceeds to say that on hearing these conditions the Acadians were filled with perplexity and alarm, and

---

[1] *Public Documents of Nova Scotia*, 173.

[2] See *Ibid.*, 174, where the answer is printed.

[3] *Cornwallis to the Board of Trade, 11 Sept. 1749.*

that he, the governor, had directed Boishébert, his chief officer on the Acadian frontier, to encourage them to leave their homes and seek asylum on French soil. He thus recounts the steps he has taken to harass the English of Halifax by means of their Indian neighbors. As peace had been declared, the operation was delicate; and when three of these Indians came to him from their missionary, Le Loutre, with letters on the subject, La Jonquière was discreetly reticent. "I did not care to give them any advice upon the matter, and confined myself to a promise that I would on no account abandon them; and I have provided for supplying them with everything, whether arms, ammunition, food, or other necessaries. It is to be desired that these savages should succeed in thwarting the designs of the English, and even their settlement at Halifax. They are bent on doing so; and if they can carry out their plans, it is certain that they will give the English great trouble, and so harass them that they will be a great obstacle in their path. These savages are to act alone; neither soldier nor French inhabitant is to join them; everything will be done of their own motion, and without showing that I had any knowledge of the matter. This is very essential; therefore I have written to the Sieur de Boishébert to observe great prudence in his measures, and to act very secretly, in order that the English may not perceive that we are providing for the needs of the said savages.

"It will be the missionaries who will manage all the negotiation, and direct the movements of the savages, who are in excellent hands, as the Reverend Father Germain and Monsieur l'Abbé Le Loutre are very capable of making the most of them, and using them to the greatest advantage for our interests. They will manage their intrigue in such a way as not to appear in it."

La Jonquière then recounts the good results which he expects from these measures: first, the English will be prevented from making any new settlements; secondly, we shall gradually get the Acadians out of their hands; and lastly, they will be so discouraged by constant Indian attacks that they will renounce their pretensions to the parts of the country belonging to the King of France. "I feel, Monseigneur,"—thus the Governor concludes his despatch,—"all the delicacy of this negotiation; be assured that I will conduct it with such precaution that the English will not be able to say that my orders had any part in it."[1]

He kept his word, and so did the missionaries. The Indians gave great trouble on the outskirts of Halifax, and murdered many harmless settlers; yet the English authorities did not at first suspect that they were hounded on by their priests, under the direction of the Governor of Canada, and with the privity of the Minister at Versailles. More than this; for, looking across the sea, we find royalty itself lending its august countenance to the machination. Among the letters read before the King in his cabinet in May, 1750, was one from Desherbiers, then commanding at Louisbourg, saying that he was advising the Acadians not to take the oath of allegiance to the King of England; another from Le Loutre, declaring that he and Father Germain were consulting together how to disgust the English with their enterprise of Halifax; and a third from the Intendant, Bigot, announcing that Le Loutre was using the Indians to harass the new settlement, and that he himself was sending them powder, lead, and merchandise, "to confirm them in their good designs."[2]

To this the Minister replies in a letter to Desherbiers: "His Majesty is well satisfied with all you have done to thwart the English in their new establishment. If the dispositions of the savages are such as they seem, there is reason to hope that in the course of the winter they will succeed in so harassing the settlers that some of them will become disheartened." Desherbiers is then told that His Majesty desires him to aid English deserters in escaping from Halifax.[3] Supplies for the Indians are also promised; and he is informed that twelve medals are sent him by the frigate "La Mutine," to be given to the chiefs who shall most distinguish themselves. In another letter Desherbiers is enjoined to treat the English authorities with great politeness.[4]

[1] *La Jonquière au Ministre, 9 Oct. 1749.* See Appendix B.

[2] *Resumé des Lettres lues au Travail du Roy, Mai, 1750.*

[3] In 1750 nine captured deserters from Phillips's regiment declared on their trial that the French had aided them and supplied them all with money. *Public Documents of Nova Scotia,* 193.

[4] *Le Ministre à Desherbiers, 23 Mai, 1750; Ibid., 31 Mai, 1750.*

When Count Raymond took command at Louisbourg, he was instructed, under the royal hand, to give particular attention to the affairs of Acadia, especially in two points,—the management of the Indians, and the encouraging of Acadian emigration to countries under French rule. "His Majesty," says the document, "has already remarked that the savages have been most favorably disposed. It is of the utmost importance that no means be neglected to keep them so. The missionaries among them are in a better position than anybody to contribute to this end, and His Majesty has reason to be satisfied with the pains they take therein. The Sieur de Raymond will excite these missionaries not to slacken their efforts; but he will warn them at the same time so to contain their zeal as not to compromise themselves with the English, and give just occasion of complaint."[1] That is, the King orders his representative to encourage the missionaries in instigating their flocks to butcher English settlers, but to see that they take care not to be found out. The injunction was hardly needed. "Monsieur Desherbiers," says a letter of earlier date, "has engaged Abbé Le Loutre to distribute the usual presents among the savages, and Monsieur Bigot has placed in his hands an additional gift of cloth, blankets, powder, and ball, to be given them in case they harass the English at Halifax. This missionary is to induce them to do so."[2] In spite of these efforts, the Indians began to relent in their hostilities; and when Longueuil became provisional governor of Canada, he complained to the Minister that it was very difficult to prevent them from making peace with the English, though Father Germain was doing his best to keep them on the warpath.[3] La Jonquière, too, had done his best, even to the point of departing from his original policy of allowing no soldier or Acadian to take part with them. He had sent a body of troops under La Corne, an able partisan officer, to watch the English frontier; and in the same vessel was sent a supply of "merchandise, guns, and munitions for the savages and the Acadians who may take up arms with them; and the whole is

---

[1] *Mémoire du Roy pour servir d'Instruction au Comte de Raymond, 24 Avril, 1751.*

[2] *Lettre commune de Desherbiers et Bigot au Ministre, 15 Août, 1749.*

[3] *Longueuil au Ministre, 26 Avril, 1752.*

sent under pretext of trading in furs with the savages."[1] On another occasion La Jonquière wrote: "In order that the savages may do their part courageously, a few Acadians, dressed and painted in their way, could join them to strike the English. I cannot help consenting to what these savages do, because we have our hands tied [*by the peace*], and so can do nothing ourselves. Besides, I do not think that any inconvenience will come of letting the Acadians mingle among them, because if they [*the Acadians*] are captured, we shall say that they acted of their own accord."[2] In other words, he will encourage them to break the peace; and then, by means of a falsehood, have them punished as felons. Many disguised Acadians did in fact join the Indian war-parties; and their doing so was no secret to the English. "What we call here an Indian war," wrote Hopson, successor of Cornwallis, "is no other than a pretence for the French to commit hostilities on His Majesty's subjects."

At length the Indians made peace, or pretended to do so. The chief of Le Loutre's mission, who called himself Major Jean-Baptiste Cope, came to Halifax with a deputation of his tribe, and they all affixed their totems to a solemn treaty. In the next summer they returned with ninety or a hundred warriors, were well entertained, presented with gifts, and sent homeward in a schooner. On the way they seized the vessel and murdered the crew. This is told by Prévost, intendant at Louisbourg, who does not say that French instigation had any part in the treachery.[3] It is nevertheless certain that the Indians were paid for this or some contemporary murder; for Prévost, writing just four weeks later, says: "Last month the savages took eighteen English scalps, and Monsieur Le Loutre was obliged to pay them eighteen hundred livres, Acadian money, which I have reimbursed him."[4]

From the first, the services of this zealous missionary had been beyond price. Prévost testifies that, though Cornwallis

---

[1] *Bigot au Ministre, 1749.*

[2] *Dépêches de la Jonquière, 1 Mai, 1751.* See Appendix B.

[3] *Prévost au Ministre, 12 Mars, 1753; Ibid., 17 July, 1753.* Prévost was *ordonnateur*, or intendant, at Louisbourg. The treaty will be found in full in *Public Documents of Nova Scotia*, 683.

[4] *Prévost au Ministre, 16 Août, 1753.*

does his best to induce the Acadians to swear fidelity to King George, Le Loutre keeps them in allegiance to King Louis, and threatens to set his Indians upon them unless they declare against the English. "I have already," adds Prévost, "paid him 11,183 livres for his daily expenses; and I never cease advising him to be as economical as possible, and always to take care not to compromise himself with the English Government."[1] In consequence of "good service to religion and the state," Le Loutre received a pension of eight hundred livres, as did also Maillard, his brother missionary on Cape Breton. "The fear is," writes the Colonial Minister to the Governor of Louisbourg, "that their zeal may carry them too far. Excite them to keep the Indians in our interest, but do not let them compromise us. Act always so as to make the English appear as aggressors."[2]

All the Acadian clergy, in one degree or another, seem to have used their influence to prevent the inhabitants from taking the oath, and to persuade them that they were still French subjects. Some were noisy, turbulent, and defiant; others were too tranquil to please the officers of the Crown. A missionary at Annapolis is mentioned as old, and therefore inefficient; while the curé at Grand Pré, also an elderly man, was too much inclined to confine himself to his spiritual functions. It is everywhere apparent that those who chose these priests, and sent them as missionaries into a British province, expected them to act as enemies of the British Crown. The maxim is often repeated that duty to religion is inseparable from duty to the King of France. The Bishop of Quebec desired the Abbé de l'Isle-Dieu to represent to the Court the need of more missionaries to keep the Acadians Catholic and French; but, he adds, there is danger that they (the mission-

[1] *Ibid.*, 22 *Juillet*, 1750.

[2] *Le Ministre au Comte de Raymond, 21 Juillet, 1752.* It is curious to compare these secret instructions, given by the Minister to the colonial officials, with a letter which the same Minister, Rouillé, wrote ostensibly to La Jonquière, but which was really meant for the eye of the British Minister at Versailles, Lord Albemarle, to whom it was shown in proof of French good faith. It was afterwards printed, along with other papers, in a small volume called *Précis des Faits, avec leurs Pièces justificatives* which was sent by the French Government to all the courts of Europe to show that the English alone were answerable for the war. The letter, it is needless to say, breathes the highest sentiments of international honor.

aries) will be required to take an oath to do nothing contrary to the interests of the King of Great Britain.[1] It is a wonder that such a pledge was not always demanded. It was exacted in a few cases, notably in that of Girard, priest at Cobequid, who, on charges of instigating his flock to disaffection, had been sent prisoner to Halifax, but released on taking an oath in the above terms. Thereupon he wrote to Longueuil at Quebec that his parishioners wanted to submit to the English, and that he, having sworn to be true to the British King, could not prevent them. "Though I don't pretend to be a casuist," writes Longueuil, "I could not help answering him that he is not obliged to keep such an oath, and that he ought to labor in all zeal to preserve and increase the number of the faithful." Girard, to his credit, preferred to leave the colony, and retired to Isle St. Jean.[2]

Cornwallis soon discovered to what extent the clergy stirred their flocks to revolt; and he wrote angrily to the Bishop of Quebec: "Was it you who sent Le Loutre as a missionary to the Micmacs? and is it for their good that he excites these wretches to practise their cruelties against those who have shown them every kindness? The conduct of the priests of Acadia has been such that by command of His Majesty I have published an Order declaring that if any one of them presumes to exercise his functions without my express permission he shall be dealt with according to the laws of England."[3]

The English, bound by treaty to allow the Acadians the exercise of their religion, at length conceived the idea of replacing the French priests by others to be named by the Pope at the request of the British Government. This, becoming known to the French, greatly alarmed them, and the Intendant at Louisbourg wrote to the Minister that the matter required serious attention.[4] It threatened, in fact, to rob them of their chief agents of intrigue; but their alarm proved needless, as the plan was not carried into execution.

The French officials would have been better pleased had the conduct of Cornwallis been such as to aid their efforts to

---

[1] L'Isle-Dieu, *Mémoire sur l'État actuel des Missions*, 1753 (1754?).

[2] *Longueuil au Ministre*, 27 *Avril*, 1752.

[3] *Cornwallis to the Bishop of Quebec*, 1 *Dec.* 1749.

[4] *Daudin, prêtre, à Prévost*, 23 *Oct.* 1753. *Prévost au Ministre*, 24 *Nov.* 1753.

alienate the Acadians; and one writer, while confessing the "favorable treatment" of the English towards the inhabitants, denounces it as a snare.[1] If so, it was a snare intended simply to reconcile them to English rule. Nor was it without effect. "We must give up altogether the idea of an insurrection in Acadia," writes an officer of Cape Breton. "The Acadians cannot be trusted; they are controlled by fear of the Indians, which leads them to breathe French sentiments, even when their inclinations are English. They will yield to their interests; and the English will make it impossible that they should either hurt them or serve us, unless we take measures different from those we have hitherto pursued."[2]

During all this time, constant efforts were made to stimulate Acadian emigration to French territory, and thus to strengthen the French frontier. In this work the chief agent was Le Loutre. "This priest," says a French writer of the time, "urged the people of Les Mines, Port Royal [*Annapolis*], and other places, to come and join the French, and promised to all, in the name of the Governor, to settle and support them for three years, and even indemnify them for any losses they might incur; threatening if they did not do as he advised, to abandon them, deprive them of their priests, have their wives and children carried off, and their property laid waste by the Indians."[3] Some passed over the isthmus to the shores of the gulf, and others made their way to the Strait of Canseau. Vessels were provided to convey them, in the one case to Isle St. Jean, now Prince Edward Island, and in the other to Isle Royale, called by the English, Cape Breton. Some were eager to go; some went with reluctance; some would scarcely be persuaded to go at all. "They leave their homes with great regret," reports the Governor of Isle St. Jean, speaking of the people of Cobequid, "and they began to move their luggage only when the savages compelled them."[4] These savages were the flock of Abbé Le Loutre, who was on the spot to direct the emigration. Two thousand Acadians are reported to have left the peninsula before the end of 1751, and many more fol-

---

[1] *Mémoire à présenter à la Cour, 1753.*
[2] *Roma au Ministre, 11 Mars, 1750.*
[3] *Mémoires sur le Canada, 1749 –1760.*
[4] *Bonaventure à Desherbiers, 26 Juin, 1751.*

lowed within the next two years. Nothing could exceed the misery of a great part of these emigrants, who had left perforce most of their effects behind. They became disheartened and apathetic. The Intendant at Louisbourg says that they will not take the trouble to clear the land, and that some of them live, like Indians, under huts of spruce-branches.[1] The Governor of Isle St. Jean declares that they are dying of hunger.[2] Girard, the priest who had withdrawn to this island rather than break his oath to the English, writes: "Many of them cannot protect themselves day or night from the severity of the cold. Most of the children are entirely naked; and when I go into a house they are all crouched in the ashes, close to the fire. They run off and hide themselves, without shoes, stockings, or shirts. They are not all reduced to this extremity but nearly all are in want."[3] Mortality among them was great, and would have been greater but for rations supplied by the French Government.

During these proceedings, the English Governor, Cornwallis, seems to have justified the character of good temper given him by Horace Walpole. His attitude towards the Acadians remained on the whole patient and conciliatory. "My friends," he replied to a deputation of them asking a general permission to leave the province, "I am not ignorant of the fact that every means has been used to alienate the hearts of the French subjects of His Britannic Majesty. Great advantages have been promised you elsewhere, and you have been made to imagine that your religion was in danger. Threats even have been resorted to in order to induce you to remove to French territory. The savages are made use of to molest you; they are to cut the throats of all who remain in their native country, attached to their own interests and faithful to the Government. You know that certain officers and missionaries, who came from Canada last autumn, have been the cause of all our trouble during the winter. Their conduct has been horrible, without honor, probity, or conscience. Their aim is to embroil you with the Government. I will not believe that they are authorized to do so by the Court of France, that

---

[1] *Prévost au Ministre, 25 Nov. 1750.*

[2] *Bonaventure, ut supra.*

[3] *Girard à (Bonaventure?), 27 Oct. 1753.*

being contrary to good faith and the friendship established between the two Crowns."

What foundation there was for this amiable confidence in the Court of Versailles has been seen already. "When you declared your desire to submit yourselves to another Government," pursues Cornwallis, "our determination was to hinder nobody from following what he imagined to be his interest. We know that a forced service is worth nothing, and that a subject compelled to be so against his will is not far from being an enemy. We confess, however, that your determination to go gives us pain. We are aware of your industry and temperance, and that you are not addicted to any vice or debauchery. This province is your country. You and your fathers have cultivated it; naturally you ought yourselves to enjoy the fruits of your labor. Such was the design of the King, our master. You know that we have followed his orders. You know that we have done everything to secure to you not only the occupation of your lands, but the ownership of them forever. We have given you also every possible assurance of the free and public exercise of the Roman Catholic religion. But I declare to you frankly that, according to our laws, nobody can possess lands or houses in the province who shall refuse to take the oath of allegiance to his King when required to do so. You know very well that there are ill-disposed and mischievous persons among you who corrupt the others. Your inexperience, your ignorance of the affairs of government, and your habit of following the counsels of those who have not your real interests at heart, make it an easy matter to seduce you. In your petitions you ask for a general leave to quit the province. The only manner in which you can do so is to follow the regulations already established, and provide yourselves with our passport. And we declare that nothing shall prevent us from giving such passports to all who ask for them, the moment peace and tranquillity are re-established."[1] He declares as his reason for not giving them at once, that on crossing the frontier "you will have to pass the French detachments and savages assembled there, and that they compel all the inhabitants who go there to take up arms"

[1] The above passages are from two addresses of Cornwallis, read to the Acadian deputies in April and May, 1750. The combined extracts here given convey the spirit of the whole. See *Public Documents of Nova Scotia*, 185–190.

against the English. How well this reason was founded will soon appear.

Hopson, the next governor, described by the French themselves as a "mild and peaceable officer," was no less considerate in his treatment of the Acadians; and at the end of 1752 he issued the following order to his military subordinates: "You are to look on the French inhabitants in the same light as the rest of His Majesty's subjects, as to the protection of the laws and government; for which reason nothing is to be taken from them by force, or any price set upon their goods but what they themselves agree to. And if at any time the inhabitants should obstinately refuse to comply with what His Majesty's service may require of them, you are not to redress yourself by military force or in any unlawful manner, but to lay the case before the Governor and wait his orders thereon."[1] Unfortunately, the mild rule of Cornwallis and Hopson was not always maintained under their successor, Lawrence.

Louis Joseph Le Loutre, vicar-general of Acadia and missionary to the Micmacs, was the most conspicuous person in the province, and more than any other man was answerable for the miseries that overwhelmed it. The sheep of which he was the shepherd dwelt, at a day's journey from Halifax, by the banks of the River Shubenacadie, in small cabins of logs, mixed with wigwams of birch-bark. They were not a docile flock; and to manage them needed address, energy, and money,—with all of which the missionary was provided. He fed their traditional dislike of the English, and fanned their fanaticism, born of the villanous counterfeit of Christianity which he and his predecessors had imposed on them. Thus he contrived to use them on the one hand to murder the English, and on the other to terrify the Acadians; yet not without cost to the French Government; for they had learned the value of money, and, except when their blood was up, were slow to take scalps without pay. Le Loutre was a man of boundless egotism, a violent spirit of domination, an intense hatred of the English, and a fanaticism that stopped at nothing. Towards the Acadians he was a despot; and this simple and superstitious people, extremely susceptible to the influ-

[1] *Public Documents of Nova Scotia*, 197.

ence of their priests, trembled before him. He was scarcely less masterful in his dealings with the Acadian clergy; and, aided by his quality of the Bishop's vicar-general, he dragooned even the unwilling into aiding his schemes. Three successive governors of New France thought him invaluable, yet feared the impetuosity of his zeal, and vainly tried to restrain it within safe bounds. The Bishop, while approving his objects, thought his medicines too violent, and asked in a tone of reproof: "Is it right for you to refuse the Acadians the sacraments, to threaten that they shall be deprived of the services of a priest, and that the savages shall treat them as enemies?"[1] "Nobody," says a French Catholic contemporary, "was more fit than he to carry discord and desolation into a country."[2] Cornwallis called him "a good-for-nothing scoundrel," and offered a hundred pounds for his head.[3]

The authorities at Halifax, while exasperated by the perfidy practised on them, were themselves not always models of international virtue. They seized a French vessel in the Gulf of St. Lawrence, on the charge—probably true—that she was carrying arms and ammunition to the Acadians and Indians. A less defensible act was the capture of the armed brig "St. François," laden with supplies for a fort lately re-established by the French, at the mouth of the River St. John, on ground claimed by both nations. Captain Rous, a New England officer commanding a frigate in the Royal Navy, opened fire on the "St. François," took her after a short cannonade, and carried her into Halifax, where she was condemned by the court. Several captures of small craft, accused of illegal acts, were also made by the English. These proceedings, being all of an overt nature, gave the officers of Louis XV. precisely what they wanted,—an occasion for uttering loud complaints, and denouncing the English as breakers of the peace.

But the movement most alarming to the French was the English occupation of Beaubassin,—an act perfectly lawful in

[1] *L'Évêque de Québec à Le Loutre*; translation in *Public Documents of Nova Scotia*, 240.

[2] *Mémoires sur le Canada, 1749–1760*.

[3] On Le Loutre, compare *Public Documents of Nova Scotia*, 178–180, *note*, with authorities there cited; *N. Y. Col. Docs.*, X. 11; *Mémoires sur le Canada, 1749–1760* (Quebec, 1838).

itself, since, without reasonable doubt, the place was within the limits of Acadia, and therefore on English ground.[1] Beaubassin was a considerable settlement on the isthmus that joins the Acadian peninsula to the mainland. Northwest of the settlement lay a wide marsh, through which ran a stream called the Missaguash, some two miles beyond which rose a hill called Beauséjour. On and near this hill were stationed the troops and Canadians sent under Boishébert and La Corne to watch the English frontier. This French force excited disaffection among the Acadians through all the neighboring districts, and constantly helped them to emigrate. Cornwallis therefore resolved to send an English force to the spot; and accordingly, towards the end of April, 1750, Major Lawrence landed at Beaubassin with four hundred men. News of their approach had come before them, and Le Loutre was here with his Micmacs, mixed with some Acadians whom he had persuaded or bullied to join him. Resolved that the people of Beaubassin should not live under English influence, he now with his own hand set fire to the parish church, while his white and red adherents burned the houses of the inhabitants, and thus compelled them to cross to the French side of the river.[2] This was the first forcible removal of the Acadians. It was as premature as it was violent; since Lawrence, being threatened by La Corne, whose force was several times greater than his own, presently reimbarked. In the following September he returned with seventeen small vessels and about seven hundred men, and again attempted to land on the strand of Beaubassin. La Jonquière says that he could only be resisted indirectly, because he was on the English side of the river. This indirect resistance was undertaken by Le Loutre, who had thrown up a breastwork along the shore and manned it with his Indians and his painted and be-feathered

---

[1] La Jonquière himself admits that he thought so. "Cette partie là étant, à ce que je crois, dépendante de l'Acadie." *La Jonquière au Ministre, 3 Oct. 1750.*

[2] It has been erroneously stated that Beaubassin was burned by its own inhabitants. "Laloutre, ayant vu que les Acadiens ne paroissoient pas fort pressés d'abandonner leurs biens, avoit lui-même mis le feu à l'Église, et l'avoit fait mettre aux maisons des habitants par quelques-uns de ceux qu'il avoit gagnés," etc. *Mémoires sur le Canada, 1749–1760.* "Les sauvages y mirent le feu." *Précis des Faits,* 85. "Les savauges mirent le feu aux maisons." *Prévost au Ministre, 22 Juillet, 1750.*

Acadians. Nevertheless the English landed, and, with some loss, drove out the defenders. Le Loutre himself seems not to have been among them; but they kept up for a time a helter-skelter fight, encouraged by two other missionaries, Germain and Lalerne, who were near being caught by the English.[1] Lawrence quickly routed them, took possession of the ceme-tery, and prepared to fortify himself. The village of Beaubas-sin, consisting, it is said, of a hundred and forty houses, had been burned in the spring; but there were still in the neigh-borhood, on the English side, many hamlets and farms, with barns full of grain and hay. Le Loutre's Indians now threat-ened to plunder and kill the inhabitants if they did not take arms against the English. Few complied, and the greater part fled to the woods.[2] On this the Indians and their Acadian allies set the houses and barns on fire, and laid waste the whole district, leaving the inhabitants no choice but to seek food and shelter with the French.[3]

The English fortified themselves on a low hill by the edge of the marsh, planted palisades, built barracks, and named the new work Fort Lawrence. Slight skirmishes between them and the French were frequent. Neither party respected the dividing line of the Missaguash, and a petty warfare of aggression and reprisal began, and became chronic. Before the end of the autumn there was an atrocious act of treachery. Among the English officers was Captain Edward Howe, an intelligent and agreeable person, who spoke French fluently, and had been long stationed in the province. Le Loutre de-tested him; dreading his influence over the Acadians, by many of whom he was known and liked. One morning, at about eight o'clock, the inmates of Fort Lawrence saw what seemed an officer from Beauséjour, carrying a flag, and followed by several men in uniform, wading through the sea of grass that stretched beyond the Missaguash. When the tide was out, this river was but an ugly trench of reddish mud gashed across the

[1] La Vallière, *Journal de ce qui s'est passé à Chenitou* [Chignecto] *et autres parties des Frontières de l'Acadie, 1750–1751.* La Vallière was an officer on the spot.

[2] *Prévost au Ministre, 27 Sept. 1750.*

[3] "Les sauvages et Accadiens mirent le feu dans toutes les maisons et granges, pleines de bled et de fourrages, ce qui a causé une grande disette." La Vallière, *ut supra.*

face of the marsh, with a thread of half-fluid slime lazily crawling along the bottom; but at high tide it was filled to the brim with an opaque torrent that would have overflowed, but for the dikes thrown up to confine it. Behind the dike on the farther bank stood the seeming officer, waving his flag in sign that he desired a parley. He was in reality no officer, but one of Le Loutre's Indians in disguise, Étienne Le Bâtard, or, as others say, the great chief, Jean-Baptiste Cope. Howe, carrying a white flag, and accompanied by a few officers and men, went towards the river to hear what he had to say. As they drew near, his looks and language excited their suspicion. But it was too late; for a number of Indians, who had hidden behind the dike during the night, fired upon Howe across the stream, and mortally wounded him. They continued their fire on his companions, but could not prevent them from carrying the dying man to the fort. The French officers, indignant at this villany, did not hesitate to charge it upon Le Loutre; "for," says one of them, "what is not a wicked priest capable of doing?" But Le Loutre's brother missionary, Maillard, declares that it was purely an effect of religious zeal on the part of the Micmacs, who, according to him, bore a deadly grudge against Howe because, fourteen years before, he had spoken words disrespectful to the Holy Virgin.[1] Maillard adds that the Indians were much pleased with what they had done. Finding, however, that they could effect little against the English troops, they changed their field of action, repaired to the outskirts of Halifax, murdered about thirty settlers, and carried off eight or ten prisoners.

Strong reinforcements came from Canada. The French began a fort on the hill of Beauséjour, and the Acadians were required to work at it with no compensation but rations. They were thinly clad, some had neither shoes nor stockings, and winter was begun. They became so dejected that it was found absolutely necessary to give them wages enough to

---

[1] Maillard, *Les Missions Micmaques*. On the murder of Howe, *Public Documents of Nova Scotia*, 194, 195, 210; *Mémoires sur le Canada, 1749–1760*, where it is said that Le Loutre was present at the deed; La Vallière, *Journal*, who says that some Acadians took part in it; *Dépêches de la Jonquière*, who says "les sauvages de l'Abbé le Loutre l'ont tué par trahison;" and *Prévost au Ministre, 27 Oct. 1750*.

supply their most pressing needs. In the following season Fort Beauséjour was in a state to receive a garrison. It stood on the crown of the hill, and a vast panorama stretched below and around it. In front lay the Bay of Chignecto, winding along the fertile shores of Chipody and Memeramcook. Far on the right spread the great Tantemar marsh; on the left lay the marsh of the Missaguash; and on a knoll beyond it, not three miles distant, the red flag of England waved over the palisades of Fort Lawrence, while hills wrapped in dark forests bounded the horizon.

How the homeless Acadians from Beaubassin lived through the winter is not very clear. They probably found shelter at Chipody and its neighborhood, where there were thriving settlements of their countrymen. Le Loutre, fearing that they would return to their lands and submit to the English, sent some of them to Isle St. Jean. "They refused to go," says a French writer; "but he compelled them at last, by threatening to make the Indians pillage them, carry off their wives and children, and even kill them before their eyes. Nevertheless he kept about him such as were most submissive to his will."[1] In the spring after the English occupied Beaubassin, La Jonquière issued a strange proclamation. It commanded all Acadians to take forthwith an oath of fidelity to the King of France, and to enroll themselves in the French militia, on pain of being treated as rebels.[2] Three years after, Lawrence, who then governed the province, proclaimed in his turn that all Acadians who had at any time sworn fidelity to the King of England, and who should be found in arms against him, would be treated as criminals.[3] Thus were these unfortunates ground between the upper and nether millstones. Le Loutre replied to this proclamation of Lawrence by a letter in which he outdid himself. He declared that any of the inhabitants who had crossed to the French side of the line, and who should presume to return to the English, would be treated as enemies by his Micmacs; and in the name of these, his Indian adherents, he demanded that the entire eastern half of the Acadian peninsula, including the ground on which Fort Law-

---

[1] *Mémoires sur le Canada, 1749–1760.*
[2] *Ordonnance du 12 Avril, 1751.*
[3] *Écrit donné aux Habitants réfugiés à Beauséjour, 10 Août, 1754.*

rence stood, should be at once made over to their sole use and sovereign ownership,[1] — "which being read and considered," says the record of the Halifax Council, "the contents appeared too insolent and absurd to be answered."

The number of Acadians who had crossed the line and were collected about Beauséjour was now large. Their countrymen of Chipody began to find them a burden, and they lived chiefly on Government rations. Le Loutre had obtained fifty thousand livres from the Court in order to dike in, for their use, the fertile marshes of Memeramcook; but the relief was distant, and the misery pressing. They complained that they had been lured over the line by false assurances, and they applied secretly to the English authorities to learn if they would be allowed to return to their homes. The answer was that they might do so with full enjoyment of religion and property, if they would take a simple oath of fidelity and loyalty to the King of Great Britain, qualified by an oral intimation that they would not be required for the present to bear arms.[2] When Le Loutre heard this, he mounted the pulpit, broke into fierce invectives, threatened the terrified people with excommunication, and preached himself into a state of exhaustion.[3] The military commandant at Beauséjour used gentler means of prevention; and the Acadians, unused for generations to think or act for themselves, remained restless, but indecisive, waiting till fate should settle for them the question, under which king?

Meanwhile, for the past three years, the commissioners appointed under the treaty of Aix-la-Chapelle to settle the question of boundaries between France and England in America had been in session at Paris, waging interminable war on paper; La Galissonière and Silhouette for France, Shirley and Mildmay for England. By the treaty of Utrecht, Acadia belonged to England; but what was Acadia? According to the English commissioners, it comprised not only the peninsula

[1] *Copie de la Lettre de M. l'Abbé Le Loutre, Prêtre Missionnaire des Sauvages de l'Accadie, à M. Lawrence à Halifax, 26 Août, 1754.* There is a translation in *Public Documents of Nova Scotia.*

[2] *Public Documents of Nova Scotia*, 205, 209.

[3] Compare *Mémoires, 1749–1760*, and *Public Documents of Nova Scotia*, 229, 230.

now called Nova Scotia, but all the immense tract of land between the River St. Lawrence on the north, the Gulf of the same name on the east, the Atlantic on the south, and New England on the west.[1] The French commissioners, on their part, maintained that the name Acadia belonged of right only to about a twentieth part of this territory, and that it did not even cover the whole of the Acadian peninsula, but only its southern coast, with an adjoining belt of barren wilderness. When the French owned Acadia, they gave it boundaries as comprehensive as those claimed for it by the English commissioners; now that it belonged to a rival, they cut it down to a paring of its former self. The denial that Acadia included the whole peninsula was dictated by the need of a winter communication between Quebec and Cape Breton, which was possible only with the eastern portions in French hands. So new was this denial that even La Galissonière himself, the foremost in making it, had declared without reservation two years before that Acadia was the entire peninsula.[2] "If," says a writer on the question, "we had to do with a nation more tractable, less grasping, and more conciliatory, it would be well to insist also that Halifax should be given up to us." He thinks that, on the whole, it would be well to make the demand in any case, in order to gain some other point by yielding this one.[3] It is curious that while denying that the country was Acadia, the French invariably called the inhabitants Acadians. Innumerable public documents, commissions, grants, treaties, edicts, signed by French kings and ministers, had recognized Acadia as extending over New Brunswick and a part of Maine. Four censuses of Acadia while it belonged to the French had recognized the mainland as included in it; and so do also the early French maps. Its prodigious shrinkage was simply the consequence of its possession by an alien.

Other questions of limits, more important and equally per-

---

[1] The commission of De Monts, in 1603, defines Acadia as extending from the fortieth to the forty-sixth degrees of latitude, — that is, from central New Brunswick to southern Pennsylvania. Neither party cared to produce the document.

[2] "L'Acadie suivant ses anciennes limites est la presquisle bornée par son isthme." *La Galissonnière au Ministre, 25 Juillet, 1749*. The English commissioners were, of course, ignorant of this admission.

[3] *Mémoire de l'Abbé de l'Isle-Dieu, 1753* (1754?).

ilous, called loudly for solution. What line should separate
Canada and her western dependencies from the British colonies? Various principles of demarcation were suggested, of
which the most prominent on the French side was a geographical one. All countries watered by streams falling into
the St. Lawrence, the Great Lakes, and the Mississippi were
to belong to her. This would have planted her in the heart of
New York and along the crests of the Alleghanies, giving her
all the interior of the continent, and leaving nothing to England but a strip of sea-coast. Yet in view of what France had
achieved; of the patient gallantry of her explorers, the zeal of
her missionaries, the adventurous hardihood of her bush-
rangers, revealing to civilized mankind the existence of this
wilderness world, while her rivals plodded at their workshops,
their farms, or their fisheries,—in view of all this, her pretensions were moderate and reasonable compared with those of
England. The treaty of Utrecht had declared the Iroquois, or
Five Nations, to be British subjects; therefore it was insisted
that all countries conquered by them belonged to the British
Crown. But what was an Iroquois conquest? The Iroquois
rarely occupied the countries they overran. Their military expeditions were mere raids, great or small. Sometimes, as in
the case of the Hurons, they made a solitude and called it
peace; again, as in the case of the Illinois, they drove off the
occupants of the soil, who returned after the invaders were
gone. But the range of their war-parties was prodigious; and
the English laid claim to every mountain, forest, or prairie
where an Iroquois had taken a scalp. This would give them
not only the country between the Alleghanies and the Mississippi, but also that between Lake Huron and the Ottawa,
thus reducing Canada to the patch on the American map now
represented by the province of Quebec,—or rather, by a part
of it, since the extension of Acadia to the St. Lawrence would
cut off the present counties of Gaspé, Rimouski, and Bonaventure. Indeed among the advocates of British claims there
were those who denied that France had any rights whatever
on the south side of the St. Lawrence.[1] Such being the atti-

---

[1] The extent of British claims is best shown on two maps of the time,
Mitchell's *Map of the British and French Dominions in North America*, and
Huske's *New and Accurate Map of North America*; both are in the British

tude of the two contestants, it was plain that there was no resort but the last argument of kings. Peace must be won with the sword.

The commissioners at Paris broke up their sessions, leaving as the monument of their toils four quarto volumes of allegations, arguments, and documentary proofs.[1] Out of the discussion rose also a swarm of fugitive publications in French, English, and Spanish; for the question of American boundaries had become European. There was one among them worth notice from its amusing absurdity. It is an elaborate disquisition, under the title of *Roman politique*, by an author faithful to the traditions of European diplomacy, and inspired at the same time by the new philosophy of the school of Rousseau. He insists that the balance of power must be preserved in America as well as in Europe, because "Nature," "the aggrandizement of the human soul," and the "felicity of man" are unanimous in demanding it. The English colonies are more populous and wealthy than the French; therefore the French should have more land, to keep the balance. Nature, the human soul, and the felicity of man require that France should own all the country beyond the Alleghanies and all Acadia but a strip of the south coast, according to the "sublime negotiations" of the French commissioners, of which the writer declares himself a "religious admirer."[2]

We know already that France had used means sharper than negotiation to vindicate her claim to the interior of the continent; had marched to the sources of the Ohio to entrench herself there, and hold the passes of the West against all comers. It remains to see how she fared in her bold enterprise.

Museum. Dr. John Mitchell, in his *Contest in America* (London, 1757) pushes the English claim to its utmost extreme, and denies that the French were rightful owners of anything in North America except the town of Quebec and the trading-post of Tadoussac. Besides the claim founded on the subjection of the Iroquois to the British Crown, the English somewhat inconsistently advanced others founded on titles obtained by treaty from these same tribes, and others still, founded on the original grants of some of the colonies, which ran indefinitely westward across the continent.

[1] *Mémoires des Commissaires de Sa Majesté Très Chrétienne et de ceux de Sa Majesté Brittanique*. Paris, 1755. Several editions appeared.

[2] *Roman politique sur l'État présent des Affaires de l'Amérique* (Amsterdam, 1756). For extracts from French Documents, see Appendix B.

Chapter V

WASHINGTON

The French occupy the Sources of the Ohio • Their Sufferings • Fort Le Bœuf • Legardeur de Saint-Pierre • Mission of Washington • Robert Dinwiddie • He opposes the French • His Dispute with the Burgesses • His Energy • His Appeals for Help • Fort Duquesne • Death of Jumonville • Washington at the Great Meadows • Coulon de Villiers • Fort Necessity

---

TOWARDS THE END of spring the vanguard of the expedition sent by Duquesne to occupy the Ohio landed at Presquisle, where Erie now stands. This route to the Ohio, far better than that which Céloron had followed, was a new discovery to the French; and Duquesne calls the harbor "the finest in nature." Here they built a fort of squared chestnut logs, and when it was finished they cut a road of several leagues through the woods to Rivière aux Bœufs, now French Creek. At the farther end of this road they began another wooden fort and called it Fort Le Bœuf. Thence, when the water was high, they could descend French Creek to the Alleghany, and follow that stream to the main current of the Ohio.

It was heavy work to carry the cumbrous load of baggage across the portages. Much of it is said to have been superfluous, consisting of velvets, silks, and other useless and costly articles, sold to the King at enormous prices as necessaries of the expedition.[1] The weight of the task fell on the Canadians, who worked with cheerful hardihood, and did their part to admiration. Marin, commander of the expedition, a gruff, choleric old man of sixty-three, but full of force and capacity, spared himself so little that he was struck down with dysentery, and, refusing to be sent home to Montreal, was before long in a dying state. His place was taken by Péan, of whose private character there is little good to be said, but whose conduct as an officer was such that Duquesne calls him a

[1] Pouchot, *Mémoires sur la dernière Guerre de l'Amérique Septentrionale*, I. 8.

prodigy of talents, resources, and zeal.[1] The subalterns deserve no such praise. They disliked the service, and made no secret of their discontent. Rumors of it filled Montreal; and Duquesne wrote to Marin: "I am surprised that you have not told me of this change. Take note of the sullen and discouraged faces about you. This sort are worse than useless. Rid yourself of them at once; send them to Montreal, that I may make an example of them."[2] Péan wrote at the end of September that Marin was in extremity; and the Governor, disturbed and alarmed, for he knew the value of the sturdy old officer, looked anxiously for a successor. He chose another veteran, Legardeur de Saint-Pierre, who had just returned from a journey of exploration towards the Rocky Mountains,[3] and whom Duquesne now ordered to the Ohio.

Meanwhile the effects of the expedition had already justified it. At first the Indians of the Ohio had shown a bold front. One of them, a chief whom the English called the Half-King, came to Fort Le Bœuf and ordered the French to leave the country; but was received by Marin with such contemptuous haughtiness that he went home shedding tears of rage and mortification. The Western tribes were daunted. The Miamis, but yesterday fast friends of the English, made humble submission to the French, and offered them two English scalps to signalize their repentance; while the Sacs, Pottawattamies, and Ojibwas were loud in professions of devotion.[4] Even the Iroquois, Delawares, and Shawanoes on the Alleghany had come to the French camp and offered their help in carrying the baggage. It needed but perseverance and success in the enterprise to win over every tribe from the mountains to the Mississippi. To accomplish this and to curb the English, Duquesne had planned a third fort, at the junction of French Creek with the Alleghany, or at some point lower down; then, leaving the three posts well garrisoned, Péan was

---

[1] *Duquesne au Ministre, 2 Nov. 1753*; compare *Mémoire pour Michel-Jean Hugues Péan.*

[2] *Duquesne à Marin, 27 Août, 1753.*

[3] *Mémoire ou Journal sommaire du Voyage de Jacques Legardeur de Saint-Pierre.*

[4] *Rapports de Conseils avec les Sauvages à Montreal, Juillet, 1753. Duquesne au Ministre, 31 Oct. 1753.* Letter of Dr. Shuckburgh in *N. Y. Col. Docs.*, VI. 806.

to descend the Ohio with the whole remaining force, impose terror on the wavering tribes, and complete their conversion. Both plans were thwarted; the fort was not built, nor did Péan descend the Ohio. Fevers, lung diseases, and scurvy made such deadly havoc among troops and Canadians, that the dying Marin saw with bitterness that his work must be left half done. Three hundred of the best men were kept to garrison Forts Presquisle and Le Bœuf; and then, as winter approached, the rest were sent back to Montreal. When they arrived, the Governor was shocked at their altered looks. "I reviewed them, and could not help being touched by the pitiable state to which fatigues and exposures had reduced them. Past all doubt, if these emaciated figures had gone down the Ohio as intended, the river would have been strewn with corpses, and the evil-disposed savages would not have failed to attack the survivors, seeing that they were but spectres."[1]

Legardeur de Saint-Pierre arrived at the end of autumn, and made his quarters at Fort Le Bœuf. The surrounding forests had dropped their leaves, and in gray and patient desolation bided the coming winter. Chill rains drizzled over the gloomy "clearing," and drenched the palisades and log-built barracks, raw from the axe. Buried in the wilderness, the military exiles resigned themselves as they might to months of monotonous solitude; when, just after sunset on the eleventh of December, a tall youth came out of the forest on horseback, attended by a companion much older and rougher than himself, and followed by several Indians and four or five white men with packhorses. Officers from the fort went out to meet the strangers; and, wading through mud and sodden snow, they entered at the gate. On the next day the young leader of the party, with the help of an interpreter, for he spoke no French, had an interview with the commandant, and gave him a letter from Governor Dinwiddie. Saint-Pierre and the officer next in rank, who knew a little English, took it to another room to study it at their ease; and in it, all unconsciously, they read a name destined to stand one of the noblest in the annals of mankind; for it introduced Major

[1] *Duquesne au Ministre, 29 Nov. 1753.* On this expedition, compare the letter of Duquesne in *N. Y. Col. Docs.*, X. 255, and the deposition of Stephen Coffen, *Ibid.*, VI. 835.

George Washington, Adjutant-General of the Virginia militia.[1]

Dinwiddie, jealously watchful of French aggression, had learned through traders and Indians that a strong detachment from Canada had entered the territories of the King of England, and built forts on Lake Erie and on a branch of the Ohio. He wrote to challenge the invasion and summon the invaders to withdraw; and he could find none so fit to bear his message as a young man of twenty-one. It was this rough Scotchman who launched Washington on his illustrious career.

Washington set out for the trading station of the Ohio Company on Will's Creek; and thence, at the middle of November, struck into the wilderness with Christopher Gist as a guide, Vanbraam, a Dutchman, as French interpreter, Davison, a trader, as Indian interpreter, and four woodsmen as servants. They went to the forks of the Ohio, and then down the river to Logstown, the Chiningué of Céloron de Bienville. There Washington had various parleys with the Indians; and thence, after vexatious delays, he continued his journey towards Fort Le Bœuf, accompanied by the friendly chief called the Half-King and by three of his tribesmen. For several days they followed the traders' path, pelted with unceasing rain and snow, and came at last to the old Indian town of Venango, where French Creek enters the Alleghany. Here there was an English trading-house; but the French had seized it, raised their flag over it, and turned it into a military outpost.[2] Joncaire was in command, with two subalterns; and nothing could exceed their civility. They invited the strangers to supper; and, says Washington, "the wine, as they dosed themselves pretty plentifully with it, soon banished the restraint which at first appeared in their conversation, and gave a license to their tongues to reveal their sentiments more freely. They told me that it was their absolute design to take possession of the Ohio, and, by G—, they would do it; for that although they were sensible the English could raise two men

[1] *Journal of Major Washington. Journal of Mr. Christopher Gist.*
[2] Marin had sent sixty men in August to seize the house, which belonged to the trader Fraser. *Dépêches de Duquesne.* They carried off two men whom they found here. Letter of Fraser in *Colonial Records of Pa.*, V. 659.

for their one, yet they knew their motions were too slow and
dilatory to prevent any undertaking of theirs."[1]

With all their civility, the French officers did their best to
entice away Washington's Indians; and it was with extreme
difficulty that he could persuade them to go with him.
Through marshes and swamps, forests choked with snow, and
drenched with incessant rain, they toiled on for four days
more, till the wooden walls of Fort Le Bœuf appeared at last,
surrounded by fields studded thick with stumps, and half-en-
circled by the chill current of French Creek, along the banks
of which lay more than two hundred canoes, ready to carry
troops in the spring. Washington describes Legardeur de
Saint-Pierre as "an elderly gentleman with much the air of a
soldier." The letter sent him by Dinwiddie expressed astonishment that his troops should build forts upon lands "so notoriously known to be the property of the Crown of Great
Britain." "I must desire you," continued the letter, "to acquaint me by whose authority and instructions you have
lately marched from Canada with an armed force, and invaded the King of Great Britain's territories. It becomes my
duty to require your peaceable departure; and that you would
forbear prosecuting a purpose so interruptive of the harmony
and good understanding which His Majesty is desirous to
continue and cultivate with the Most Christian King. I persuade myself you will receive and entertain Major Washington with the candor and politeness natural to your nation;
and it will give me the greatest satisfaction if you return him
with an answer suitable to my wishes for a very long and
lasting peace between us."

Saint-Pierre took three days to frame the answer. In it he
said that he should send Dinwiddie's letter to the Marquis
Duquesne and wait his orders; and that meanwhile he should
remain at his post, according to the commands of his general.
"I made it my particular care," so the letter closed, "to receive
Mr. Washington with a distinction suitable to your dignity as
well as his own quality and great merit."[2] No form of courtesy had, in fact, been wanting. "He appeared to be extremely

---

[1] *Journal of Washington*, as printed at Williamsburg, just after his return.
[2] "La Distinction qui convient à votre Dignitté à sa Qualité et à son grand
Mérite." Copy of original letter sent by Dinwiddie to Governor Hamilton.

complaisant," says Washington, "though he was exerting every artifice to set our Indians at variance with us. I saw that every stratagem was practised to win the Half-King to their interest." Neither gifts nor brandy were spared; and it was only by the utmost pains that Washington could prevent his red allies from staying at the fort, conquered by French blandishments.

After leaving Venango on his return, he found the horses so weak that, to arrive the sooner, he left them and their drivers in charge of Vanbraam and pushed forward on foot, accompanied by Gist alone. Each was wrapped to the throat in an Indian "matchcoat," with a gun in his hand and a pack at his back. Passing an old Indian hamlet called Murdering Town, they had an adventure which threatened to make good the name. A French Indian, whom they met in the forest, fired at them, pretending that his gun had gone off by chance. They caught him, and Gist would have killed him; but Washington interposed, and they let him go.[1] Then, to escape pursuit from his tribesmen, they walked all night and all the next day. This brought them to the banks of the Alleghany. They hoped to have found it dead frozen; but it was all alive and turbulent, filled with ice sweeping down the current. They made a raft, shoved out into the stream, and were soon caught helplessly in the drifting ice. Washington, pushing hard with his setting-pole, was jerked into the freezing river; but caught a log of the raft, and dragged himself out. By no efforts could they reach the farther bank, or regain that which they had left; but they were driven against an island, where they landed, and left the raft to its fate. The night was excessively cold, and Gist's feet and hands were badly frost-bitten. In the morning, the ice had set, and the river was a solid floor. They crossed it, and succeeded in reaching the house of the trader Fraser, on the Monongahela. It was the middle of January when Washington arrived at Williamsburg and made his report to Dinwiddie.

Robert Dinwiddie was lieutenant-governor of Virginia, in place of the titular governor, Lord Albemarle, whose post was a sinecure. He had been clerk in a government office in the West Indies; then surveyor of customs in the "Old Domin-

[1] *Journal of Mr. Christopher Gist*, in *Mass. Hist. Coll., 3rd Series*, V.

ion,"—a position in which he made himself cordially disliked; and when he rose to the governorship he carried his unpopularity with him. Yet Virginia and all the British colonies owed him much; for, though past sixty, he was the most watchful sentinel against French aggression and its most strenuous opponent. Scarcely had Marin's vanguard appeared at Presquisle, when Dinwiddie warned the Home Government of the danger, and urged, what he had before urged in vain on the Virginian Assembly, the immediate building of forts on the Ohio. There came in reply a letter, signed by the King, authorizing him to build the forts at the cost of the Colony, and to repel force by force in case he was molested or obstructed. Moreover, the King wrote, "If you shall find that any number of persons shall presume to erect any fort or forts within the limits of our province of Virginia, you are first to require of them peaceably to depart; and if, notwithstanding your admonitions, they do still endeavor to carry out any such unlawful and unjustifiable designs, we do hereby strictly charge and command you to drive them off by force of arms."[1]

The order was easily given; but to obey it needed men and money, and for these Dinwiddie was dependent on his Assembly, or House of Burgesses. He convoked them for the first of November, sending Washington at the same time with the summons to Saint-Pierre. The burgesses met. Dinwiddie exposed the danger, and asked for means to meet it.[2] They seemed more than willing to comply; but debates presently arose concerning the fee of a pistole, which the Governor had demanded on each patent of land issued by him. The amount was trifling, but the principle was doubtful. The aristocratic republic of Virginia was intensely jealous of the slightest encroachment on its rights by the Crown or its representative. The Governor defended the fee. The burgesses replied that "subjects cannot be deprived of the least part of their property without their consent," declared the fee unlawful, and called

[1] *Instructions to Our Trusty and Well-beloved Robert Dinwiddie, Esq., 28 Aug. 1753.*

[2] *Address of Lieutenant-Governor Dinwiddie to the Council and Burgesses, 1 Nov. 1753.*

on Dinwiddie to confess it to be so. He still defended it. They saw in his demand for supplies a means of bringing him to terms, and refused to grant money unless he would recede from his position. Dinwiddie rebuked them for "disregarding the designs of the French, and disputing the rights of the Crown;" and he "prorogued them in some anger."[1]

Thus he was unable to obey the instructions of the King. As a temporary resource, he ventured to order a draft of two hundred men from the militia. Washington was to have command, with the trader, William Trent, as his lieutenant. His orders were to push with all speed to the forks of the Ohio, and there build a fort; "but in case any attempts are made to obstruct the works by any persons whatsoever, to restrain all such offenders, and, in case of resistance, to make prisoners of, or kill and destroy them."[2] The Governor next sent messengers to the Catawbas, Cherokees, Chickasaws, and Iroquois of the Ohio, inviting them to take up the hatchet against the French, "who, under pretence of embracing you, mean to squeeze you to death." Then he wrote urgent letters to the governors of Pennsylvania, the Carolinas, Maryland, and New Jersey, begging for contingents of men, to be at Wills Creek in March at the latest. But nothing could be done without money; and trusting for a change of heart on the part of the burgesses, he summoned them to meet again on the fourteenth of February. "If they come in good temper," he wrote to Lord Fairfax, a nobleman settled in the colony, "I hope they will lay a fund to qualify me to send four or five hundred men more to the Ohio, which, with the assistance of our neighboring colonies, may make some figure."

The session began. Again, somewhat oddly, yet forcibly, the Governor set before the Assembly the peril of the situation, and begged them to postpone less pressing questions to the exigency of the hour.[3] This time they listened; and voted ten thousand pounds in Virginia currency to defend the frontier. The grant was frugal, and they jealously placed its expen-

---

[1] *Dinwiddie Papers.*

[2] *Ibid. Instructions to Major George Washington, January, 1754.*

[3] *Speech of Lieutenant-Governor Dinwiddie to the Council and Burgesses, 14 Feb., 1754.*

diture in the hands of a committee of their own.[1] Dinwiddie, writing to the Lords of Trade, pleads necessity as his excuse for submitting to their terms. "I am sorry," he says, "to find them too much in a republican way of thinking." What vexed him still more was their sending an agent to England to complain against him on the irrepressible question of the pistole fee; and he writes to his London friend, the merchant Hanbury: "I have had a great deal of trouble from the factious disputes and violent heats of a most impudent, troublesome party here in regard to that silly fee of a pistole. Surely every thinking man will make a distinction between a fee and a tax. Poor people! I pity their ignorance and narrow, ill-natured spirits. But, my friend, consider that I could by no means give up this fee without affronting the Board of Trade and the Council here who established it." His thoughts were not all of this harassing nature, and he ends his letter with the following petition: "Now, sir, as His Majesty is pleased to make me a military officer, please send for Scott, my tailor, to make me a proper suit of regimentals, to be here by His Majesty's birthday. I do not much like gayety in dress, but I conceive this necessary. I do not much care for lace on the coat, but a neat embroidered button-hole; though you do not deal that way, I know you have a good taste, that I may show my friend's fancy in that suit of clothes; a good laced hat and two pair stockings, one silk, the other fine thread."[2]

If the Governor and his English sometimes provoke a smile, he deserves admiration for the energy with which he opposed the public enemy, under circumstances the most discouraging. He invited the Indians to meet him in council at Winchester, and, as bait to attract them, coupled the message with a promise of gifts. He sent circulars from the King to the neighboring governors, calling for supplies, and wrote letter upon letter to rouse them to effort. He wrote also to the more distant governors, Delancey of New York, and Shirley of Massachusetts, begging them to make what he called a "faint" against Canada, to prevent the French from sending so large a force to the Ohio. It was to the nearer colonies, from New Jersey to South Carolina, that he looked for direct

[1] See the bill in Hening, *Statutes of Virginia*, VI. 417.
[2] *Dinwiddie to Hanbury, 12 March, 1754; Ibid., 10 May, 1754.*

aid; and their several governors were all more or less active to procure it; but as most of them had some standing dispute with their assemblies, they could get nothing except on terms with which they would not, and sometimes could not, comply. As the lands invaded by the French belonged to one of the two rival claimants, Virginia and Pennsylvania, the other colonies had no mind to vote money to defend them. Pennsylvania herself refused to move. Hamilton, her governor, could do nothing against the placid obstinacy of the Quaker non-combatants and the stolid obstinacy of the German farmers who chiefly made up his Assembly. North Carolina alone answered the appeal, and gave money enough to raise three or four hundred men. Two independent companies maintained by the King in New York, and one in South Carolina, had received orders from England to march to the scene of action; and in these, with the scanty levies of his own and the adjacent province, lay Dinwiddie's only hope. With men abundant and willing, there were no means to put them into the field, and no commander whom they would all obey.

From the brick house at Williamsburg pompously called the Governor's Palace, Dinwiddie despatched letters, orders, couriers, to hasten the tardy reinforcements of North Carolina and New York, and push on the raw soldiers of the Old Dominion, who now numbered three hundred men. They were called the Virginia regiment; and Joshua Fry, an English gentleman, bred at Oxford, was made their colonel, with Washington as next in command. Fry was at Alexandria with half the so-called regiment, trying to get it into marching order; Washington, with the other half, had pushed forward to the Ohio Company's storehouse at Wills Creek, which was to form a base of operations. His men were poor whites, brave, but hard to discipline; without tents, ill armed, and ragged as Falstaff's recruits. Besides these, a band of backwoodsmen under Captain Trent had crossed the mountains in February to build a fort at the forks of the Ohio, where Pittsburg now stands,—a spot which Washington had examined when on his way to Fort Le Bœuf, and which he had reported as the best for the purpose. The hope was that Trent would fortify himself before the arrival of the French, and that Washington and Fry would join him in time to secure the position. Trent had begun the fort; but for some unexplained reason had gone back to Wills Creek, leaving Ensign Ward with forty men at work upon it. Their labors were suddenly interrupted. On the seventeenth of April a swarm of bateaux and canoes came down the Alleghany, bringing, according to Ward, more than a thousand Frenchmen, though in reality not much above five hundred, who landed, planted cannon against the incipient stockade, and summoned the ensign to surrender, on pain of what might ensue.[1] He complied, and was allowed to depart with his men. Retracing his steps over the mountains, he reported his mishap to Washington; while the French demolished his unfinished fort, began a much larger and better one, and named it Fort Duquesne.

They had acted with their usual promptness. Their Governor, a practised soldier, knew the value of celerity, and had set his troops in motion with the first opening of spring. He had no refractory assembly to hamper him; no lack of money, for the King supplied it; and all Canada must march at his bidding. Thus, while Dinwiddie was still toiling to muster his raw recruits, Duquesne's lieutenant, Contrecœur, successor of Saint-Pierre, had landed at Presquisle with a much greater force, in part regulars, and in part Canadians.

Dinwiddie was deeply vexed when a message from Washington told him how his plans were blighted; and he spoke his mind to his friend Hanbury: "If our Assembly had voted the money in November which they did in February, it's more than probable the fort would have been built and garrisoned before the French had approached; but these things cannot be done without money. As there was none in our treasury, I have advanced my own to forward the expedition; and if the independent companies from New York come soon, I am in hopes the eyes of the other colonies will be opened; and if they grant a proper supply of men, I hope we shall be able to dislodge the French or build a fort on that river. I congratulate you on the increase of your family. My wife and two girls join in our most sincere respects to good Mrs. Hanbury."[2]

The seizure of a king's fort by planting cannon against it

---

[1] See the summons in *Précis des Faits*, 101.

[2] *Dinwiddie to Hanbury, 10 May, 1754.*

and threatening it with destruction was in his eyes a beginning of hostilities on the part of the French; and henceforth both he and Washington acted much as if war had been declared. From their station at Wills Creek, the distance by the traders' path to Fort Duquesne was about a hundred and forty miles. Midway was a branch of the Monongahela called Redstone Creek, at the mouth of which the Ohio Company had built another storehouse. Dinwiddie ordered all the forces to cross the mountains and assemble at this point, until they should be strong enough to advance against the French. The movement was critical in presence of an enemy as superior in discipline as he was in numbers, while the natural obstacles were great. A road for cannon and wagons must be cut through a dense forest and over two ranges of high mountains, besides countless hills and streams. Washington set all his force to the work, and they spent a fortnight in making twenty miles. Towards the end of May, however, Dinwiddie learned that he had crossed the main ridge of the Alleghanies, and was encamped with a hundred and fifty men near the parallel ridge of Laurel Hill, at a place called the Great Meadows. Trent's backwoodsmen had gone off in disgust; Fry, with the rest of the regiment, was still far behind; and Washington was daily expecting an attack. Close upon this, a piece of good news, or what seemed such, came over the mountains and gladdened the heart of the Governor. He heard that a French detachment had tried to surprise Washington, and that he had killed or captured the whole. The facts were as follows.

Washington was on the Youghiogany, a branch of the Monongahela, exploring it in hopes that it might prove navigable, when a messenger came to him from his old comrade, the Half-King, who was on the way to join him. The message was to the effect that the French had marched from their fort, and meant to attack the first English they should meet. A report came soon after that they were already at the ford of the Youghiogany, eighteen miles distant. Washington at once repaired to the Great Meadows, a level tract of grass and bushes, bordered by wooded hills, and traversed in one part by a gully, which with a little labor the men turned into an entrenchment, at the same time cutting away the bushes and clearing what the young commander called "a charming field for an encounter." Parties were sent out to scour the woods, but they found no enemy. Two days passed; when, on the morning of the twenty-seventh, Christopher Gist, who had lately made a settlement on the farther side of Laurel Hill, twelve or thirteen miles distant, came to the camp with news that fifty Frenchmen had been at his house towards noon of the day before, and would have destroyed everything but for the intervention of two Indians whom he had left in charge during his absence. Washington sent seventy-five men to look for the party; but the search was vain, the French having hidden themselves so well as to escape any eye but that of an Indian. In the evening a runner came from the Half-King, who was encamped with a few warriors some miles distant. He had sent to tell Washington that he had found the tracks of two men, and traced them towards a dark glen in the forest, where in his belief all the French were lurking.

Washington seems not to have hesitated a moment. Fearing a stratagem to surprise his camp, he left his main force to guard it, and at ten o'clock set out for the Half-King's wigwams at the head of forty men. The night was rainy, and the forest, to use his own words, "as black as pitch." "The path," he continues, "was hardly wide enough for one man; we often lost it, and could not find it again for fifteen or twenty minutes, and we often tumbled over each other in the dark."[1] Seven of his men were lost in the woods and left behind. The rest groped their way all night, and reached the Indian camp at sunrise. A council was held with the Half-King, and he and his warriors agreed to join in striking the French. Two of them led the way. The tracks of the two French scouts seen the day before were again found, and, marching in single file, the party pushed through the forest into the rocky hollow where the French were supposed to be concealed. They were there in fact; and they snatched their guns the moment they saw the English. Washington gave the word to fire. A short fight ensued. Coulon de Jumonville, an ensign in command,

---

[1] *Journal of Washington* in *Précis des Faits*, 109. This Journal, which is entirely distinct from that before cited, was found by the French among the baggage left on the field after the defeat of Braddock in 1755, and a translation of it was printed by them as above. The original has disappeared.

was killed, with nine others; twenty-two were captured, and none escaped but a Canadian who had fled at the beginning of the fray. After it was over, the prisoners told Washington that the party had been sent to bring him a summons from Contrecœur, the commandant at Fort Duquesne.

Five days before, Contrecœur had sent Jumonville to scour the country as far as the dividing ridge of the Alleghanies. Under him were another officer, three cadets, a volunteer, an interpreter, and twenty-eight men. He was provided with a written summons, to be delivered to any English he might find. It required them to withdraw from the domain of the King of France, and threatened compulsion by force of arms in case of refusal. But before delivering the summons Jumonville was ordered to send two couriers back with all speed to Fort Duquesne to inform the commandant that he had found the English, and to acquaint him when he intended to communicate with them.[1] It is difficult to imagine any object for such an order except that of enabling Contrecœur to send to the spot whatever force might be needed to attack the English on their refusal to withdraw. Jumonville had sent the two couriers, and had hidden himself, apparently to wait the result. He lurked nearly two days within five miles of Washington's camp, sent out scouts to reconnoitre it, but gave no notice of his presence; played to perfection the part of a skulking enemy, and brought destruction on himself by conduct which can only be ascribed to a sinister motive on the one hand, or to extreme folly on the other. French deserters told Washington that the party came as spies, and were to show the summons only if threatened by a superior force. This last assertion is confirmed by the French officer Pouchot, who says that Jumonville, seeing himself the weaker party, tried to show the letter he had brought.[2]

French writers say that, on first seeing the English, Jumonville's interpreter called out that he had something to say to them; but Washington, who was at the head of his men, affirms this to be absolutely false. The French say further that Jumonville was killed in the act of reading the summons. This

[1] The summons and the instructions to Jumonville are in *Précis des Faits*.
[2] Pouchot, *Mémoire sur la dernière Guerre*.

is also denied by Washington, and rests only on the assertion of the Canadian who ran off at the outset, and on the alleged assertion of Indians who, if present at all, which is unlikely, escaped like the Canadian before the fray began. Druillon, an officer with Jumonville, wrote two letters to Dinwiddie after his capture, to claim the privileges of the bearer of a summons; but while bringing forward every other circumstance in favor of the claim, he does not pretend that the summons was read or shown either before or during the action. The French account of the conduct of Washington's Indians is no less erroneous. "This murder," says a chronicler of the time, "produced on the minds of the savages an effect very different from that which the cruel Vvasinghton had promised himself. They have a horror of crime; and they were so indignant at that which had just been perpetrated before their eyes, that they abandoned him, and offered themselves to us in order to take vengeance."[1] Instead of doing this, they boasted of their part in the fight, scalped all the dead Frenchmen, sent one scalp to the Delawares as an invitation to take up the hatchet for the English, and distributed the rest among the various Ohio tribes to the same end.

Coolness of judgment, a profound sense of public duty, and a strong self-control, were even then the characteristics of Washington; but he was scarcely twenty-two, was full of military ardor, and was vehement and fiery by nature. Yet it is far from certain that, even when age and experience had ripened him, he would have forborne to act as he did, for there was every reason for believing that the designs of the French were hostile; and though by passively waiting the event he would have thrown upon them the responsibility of striking the first blow, he would have exposed his small party to capture or destruction by giving them time to gain reinforcements from Fort Duquesne. It was inevitable that the killing of Jumonville should be greeted in France by an outcry of real or assumed horror; but the Chevalier de Lévis, second in command to Montcalm, probably expresses the true opinion of Frenchmen best fitted to judge when he calls it "a pre-

[1] Poulin de Lumina, *Histoire de la Guerre contre les Anglois*, 15.

tended assassination."[1] Judge it as we may, this obscure skirmish began the war that set the world on fire.[2]

Washington returned to the camp at the Great Meadows; and, expecting soon to be attacked, sent for reinforcements to Colonel Fry, who was lying dangerously ill at Wills Creek. Then he set his men to work at an entrenchment, which he named Fort Necessity, and which must have been of the slightest, as they finished it within three days.[3] The Half-King now joined him, along with the female potentate known as Queen Alequippa, and some thirty Indian families. A few days after, Gist came from Wills Creek with news that Fry was dead. Washington succeeded to the command of the regiment, the remaining three companies of which presently appeared and joined their comrades, raising the whole number to three hundred. Next arrived the independent company from South Carolina; and the Great Meadows became an animated scene, with the wigwams of the Indians, the camp-sheds of the rough Virginians, the cattle grazing on the tall grass or drinking at the lazy brook that traversed it; the surrounding heights and forests; and over all, four miles away, the lofty green ridge of Laurel Hill.

The presence of the company of regulars was a doubtful advantage. Captain Mackay, its commander, holding his commission from the King, thought himself above any officer

[1] Lévis, *Mémoire sur la Guerre du Canada.*

[2] On this affair, Sparks, *Writings of Washington*, II. 25–48, 447. *Dinwiddie Papers. Letter of Contrecœur* in *Précis des Faits. Journal of Washington, Ibid. Washington to Dinwiddie, 3 June, 1754.* Dussieux, *Le Canada sous la Domination Française*, 118. Gaspé, *Anciens Canadiens*, appendix, 396. The assertion of Abbé de l'Isle-Dieu, that Jumonville showed a flag of truce, is unsupported. Adam Stephen, who was in the fight, says that the guns of the English were so wet that they had to trust mainly to the bayonet. The Half-King boasted that he killed Jumonville with his tomahawk. Dinwiddie highly approved Washington's conduct.

In 1755 the widow of Jumonville received a pension of one hundred and fifty francs. In 1775 his daughter, Charlotte Aimable, wishing to become a nun, was given by the King six hundred francs for her "trousseau" on entering the convent. *Dossier de Jumonville et de sa Veuve, 22 Mars, 1755. Mémoire pour Mlle. de Jumonville, 10 Juillet, 1775. Réponse du Garde des Sceaux, 25 Juillet, 1775.*

[3] *Journal of Washington* in *Précis des Faits.*

commissioned by the Governor. There was great courtesy between him and Washington; but Mackay would take no orders, nor even the countersign, from the colonel of volunteers. Nor would his men work, except for an additional shilling a day. To give this was impossible, both from want of money, and from the discontent it would have bred in the Virginians, who worked for nothing besides their daily pay of eightpence. Washington, already a leader of men, possessed himself in a patience extremely difficult to his passionate temper; but the position was untenable, and the presence of the military drones demoralized his soldiers. Therefore, leaving Mackay at the Meadows, he advanced towards Gist's settlement, cutting a wagon road as he went.

On reaching the settlement the camp was formed and an entrenchment thrown up. Deserters had brought news that strong reinforcements were expected at Fort Duquesne, and friendly Indians repeatedly warned Washington that he would soon be attacked by overwhelming numbers. Forty Indians from the Ohio came to the camp, and several days were spent in councils with them; but they proved for the most part to be spies of the French. The Half-King stood fast by the English, and sent out three of his young warriors as scouts. Reports of attack thickened. Mackay and his men were sent for, and they arrived on the twenty-eighth of June. A council of war was held at Gist's house; and as the camp was commanded by neighboring heights, it was resolved to fall back. The horses were so few that the Virginians had to carry much of the baggage on their backs, and drag nine swivels over the broken and rocky road. The regulars, though they also were raised in the provinces, refused to give the slightest help. Toiling on for two days, they reached the Great Meadows on the first of July. The position, though perhaps the best in the neighborhood, was very unfavorable, and Washington would have retreated farther, but for the condition of his men. They were spent with fatigue, and there was no choice but to stay and fight.

Strong reinforcements had been sent to Fort Duquesne in the spring, and the garrison now consisted of about fourteen hundred men. When news of the death of Jumonville reached Montreal, Coulon de Villiers, brother of the slain officer, was sent to the spot with a body of Indians from all the tribes in the colony. He made such speed that at eight o'clock on the morning of the twenty-sixth of June he reached the fort with his motley following. Here he found that five hundred Frenchmen and a few Ohio Indians were on the point of marching against the English, under Chevalier Le Mercier; but in view of his seniority in rank and his relationship to Jumonville, the command was now transferred to Villiers. Hereupon, the march was postponed; the newly-arrived warriors were called to council, and Contrecœur thus harangued them: "The English have murdered my children; my heart is sick; to-morrow I shall send my French soldiers to take revenge. And now, men of the Saut St. Louis, men of the Lake of Two Mountains, Hurons, Abenakis, Iroquois of La Présentation, Nipissings, Algonquins, and Ottawas,—I invite you all by this belt of wampum to join your French father and help him to crush the assassins. Take this hatchet, and with it two barrels of wine for a feast." Both hatchet and wine were cheerfully accepted. Then Contrecœur turned to the Delawares, who were also present: "By these four strings of wampum I invite you, if you are true children of Onontio, to follow the example of your brethren;" and with some hesitation they also took up the hatchet.

The next day was spent by the Indians in making moccasons for the march, and by the French in preparing for an expedition on a larger scale than had been at first intended. Contrecœur, Villiers, Le Mercier, and Longueuil, after deliberating together, drew up a paper to the effect that "it was fitting (*convenable*) to march against the English with the greatest possible number of French and savages, in order to avenge ourselves and chastise them for having violated the most sacred laws of civilized nations;" that, though their conduct justified the French in disregarding the existing treaty of peace, yet, after thoroughly punishing them, and compelling them to withdraw from the domain of the King, they should be told that, in pursuance of his royal orders, the French looked on them as friends. But it was further agreed that should the English have withdrawn to their own side of the mountains, "they should be followed to their settlements to destroy them and treat them as enemies, till that nation should give ample satisfaction and completely change its conduct."[1]

The party set out on the next morning, paddled their canoes up the Monongahela, encamped, heard Mass; and on the thirtieth reached the deserted storehouse of the Ohio Company at the mouth of Redstone Creek. It was a building of solid logs, well loopholed for musketry. To please the Indians by asking their advice, Villiers called all the chiefs to council; which, being concluded to their satisfaction, he left a sergeant's guard at the storehouse to watch the canoes, and began his march through the forest. The path was so rough that at the first halt the chaplain declared he could go no farther, and turned back for the storehouse, though not till he had absolved the whole company in a body. Thus lightened of their sins, they journeyed on, constantly sending out scouts. On the second of July they reached the abandoned camp of Washington at Gist's settlement; and here they bivouacked, tired, and drenched all night by rain. At daybreak they marched again, and passed through the gorge of Laurel Hill. It rained without ceasing; but Villiers pushed his way through the dripping forest to see the place, half a mile from the road, where his brother had been killed, and where several bodies still lay unburied. They had learned from a deserter the position of the enemy, and Villiers filled the woods in front with a swarm of Indian scouts. The crisis was near. He formed his men in column, and ordered every officer to his place.

Washington's men had had a full day at Fort Necessity; but they spent it less in resting from their fatigue than in strengthening their rampart with logs. The fort was a simple square enclosure, with a trench said by a French writer to be only knee deep. On the south, and partly on the west, there was an exterior embankment, which seems to have been made, like a rifle-pit, with the ditch inside. The Virginians had but little ammunition, and no bread whatever, living chiefly on fresh beef. They knew the approach of the French,

[1] *Journal de Campagne de M. de Villiers depuis son Arrivée au Fort Duquesne jusqu' à son Retour au dit Fort.* These and other passages are omitted in the Journal as printed in *Précis des Faits.* Before me is a copy from the original in the Archives de la Marine.

who were reported to Washington as nine hundred strong, besides Indians. Towards eleven o'clock a wounded sentinel came in with news that they were close at hand; and they presently appeared at the edge of the woods, yelling, and firing from such a distance that their shot fell harmless. Washington drew up his men on the meadow before the fort, thinking, he says, that the enemy, being greatly superior in force, would attack at once; and choosing for some reason to meet them on the open plain. But Villiers had other views. "We approached the English," he writes, "as near as possible, without uselessly exposing the lives of the King's subjects;" and he and his followers made their way through the forest till they came opposite the fort, where they stationed themselves on two densely wooded hills, adjacent, though separated by a small brook. One of these was about a hundred paces from the English, and the other about sixty. Their position was such that the French and Indians, well sheltered by trees and bushes, and with the advantage of higher ground, could cross their fire upon the fort and enfilade a part of it. Washington had meanwhile drawn his followers within the entrenchment; and the firing now began on both sides. Rain fell all day. The raw earth of the embankment was turned to soft mud, and the men in the ditch of the outwork stood to the knee in water. The swivels brought back from the camp at Gist's farm were mounted on the rampart; but the gunners were so ill protected that the pieces were almost silenced by the French musketry. The fight lasted nine hours. At times the fire on both sides was nearly quenched by the showers, and the bedrenched combatants could do little but gaze at each other through a gray veil of mist and rain. Towards night, however, the fusillade revived, and became sharp again until dark. At eight o'clock the French called out to propose a parley.

Villiers thus gives his reasons for these overtures. "As we had been wet all day by the rain, as the soldiers were very tired, as the savages said that they would leave us the next morning, and as there was a report that drums and the firing of cannon had been heard in the distance, I proposed to M. Le Mercier to offer the English a conference." He says further that ammunition was falling short, and that he thought the enemy might sally in a body and attack him.[1] The English, on their side, were in a worse plight. They were half starved, their powder was nearly spent, their guns were foul, and among them all they had but two screw-rods to clean them. In spite of his desperate position, Washington declined the parley, thinking it a pretext to introduce a spy; but when the French repeated their proposal and requested that he would send an officer to them, he could hesitate no longer. There were but two men with him who knew French, Ensign Peyroney, who was disabled by a wound, and the Dutchman, Captain Vanbraam. To him the unpalatable errand was assigned. After a long absence he returned with articles of capitulation offered by Villiers; and while the officers gathered about him in the rain, he read and interpreted the paper by the glimmer of a sputtering candle kept alight with difficulty. Objection was made to some of the terms, and they were changed. Vanbraam, however, apparently anxious to get the capitulation signed and the affair ended, mistranslated several passages, and rendered the words *l'assassinat du Sieur de Jumonville* as *the death of the Sieur de Jumonville*.[2] As thus understood, the articles were signed about midnight. They provided that the English should march out with drums beating and the honors of war, carrying with them one of their swivels and all their other property; that they should be protected against insult from French or Indians; that the prisoners taken in the affair of Jumonville should be set free; and that two officers should remain as hostages for their safe return to Fort Duquesne. The hostages chosen were Vanbraam and a brave but eccentric Scotchman, Robert Stobo, an acquaintance of the novelist Smollett, said to be the original of his Lismahago.

Washington reports that twelve of the Virginians were killed on the spot, and forty-three wounded, while of the casualties in Mackay's company no returns appear. Villiers re-

[1] *Journal de Villiers*, original. Omitted in the Journal as printed by the French Government. A short and very incorrect abstract of this Journal will be found in *N. Y. Col. Docs.*, X.

[2] See Appendix C. On the fight at Great Meadows, compare Sparks, *Writings of Washington*, II. 456–468; also a letter of Colonel Innes to Governor Hamilton, written a week after the event, in *Colonial Records of Pa.*, VI. 50, and a letter of Adam Stephen in *Pennsylvania Gazette, 1754*.

ports his own loss at only twenty in all.[1] The numbers engaged are uncertain. The six companies of the Virginia regiment counted three hundred and five men and officers, and Mackay's company one hundred; but many were on the sick list, and some had deserted. About three hundred and fifty may have taken part in the fight. On the side of the French, Villiers says that the detachment as originally formed consisted of five hundred white men. These were increased after his arrival at Fort Duquesne, and one of the party reports that seven hundred marched on the expedition.[2] The number of Indians joining them is not given; but as nine tribes and communities contributed to it, and as two barrels of wine were required to give the warriors a parting feast, it must have been considerable. White men and red, it seems clear that the French force was more than twice that of the English, while they were better posted and better sheltered, keeping all day under cover, and never showing themselves on the open meadow. There were no Indians with Washington. Even the Half-King held aloof; though, being of a caustic turn, he did not spare his comments on the fight, telling Conrad Weiser, the provincial interpreter, that the French behaved like cowards, and the English like fools.[3]

In the early morning the fort was abandoned and the retreat began. The Indians had killed all the horses and cattle, and Washington's men were so burdened with the sick and wounded, whom they were obliged to carry on their backs, that most of the baggage was perforce left behind. Even then they could march but a few miles, and then encamped to wait

[1] Dinwiddie writes to the Lords of Trade that thirty in all were killed, and seventy wounded, on the English side; and the commissary Varin writes to Bigot that the French lost seventy-two killed and wounded.

[2] *A Journal had from Thomas Forbes, lately a Private Soldier in the King of France's Service.* (Public Record Office.) Forbes was one of Villiers' soldiers. The commissary Varin puts the number of French at six hundred, besides Indians.

[3] *Journal of Conrad Weiser*, in *Colonial Records of Pa.*, VI. 150. The Half-King also remarked that Washington "was a good-natured man, but had no experience, and would by no means take advice from the Indians, but was always driving them on to fight by his directions; that he lay at one place from one full moon to the other, and made no fortifications at all, except that little thing upon the meadow, where he thought the French would come up to him in open field."

for wagons. The Indians increased the confusion by plundering, and threatening an attack. They knocked to pieces the medicine-chest, thus causing great distress to the wounded, two of whom they murdered and scalped. For a time there was danger of panic; but order was restored, and the wretched march began along the forest road that led over the Alleghanies, fifty-two miles to the station at Wills Creek. Whatever may have been the feelings of Washington, he has left no record of them. His immense fortitude was doomed to severer trials in the future; yet perhaps this miserable morning was the darkest of his life. He was deeply moved by sights of suffering; and all around him were wounded men borne along in torture, and weary men staggering under the living load. His pride was humbled, and his young ambition seemed blasted in the bud. It was the fourth of July. He could not foresee that he was to make that day forever glorious to a new-born nation hailing him as its father.

The defeat at Fort Necessity was doubly disastrous to the English, since it was a new step and a long one towards the ruin of their interest with the Indians; and when, in the next year, the smouldering war broke into flame, nearly all the western tribes drew their scalping-knives for France.

Villiers went back exultant to Fort Duquesne, burning on his way the buildings of Gist's settlement and the storehouse at Redstone Creek. Not an English flag now waved beyond the Alleghanies.[1]

[1] See Appendix C.

Chapter VI

1754, 1755

THE SIGNAL OF BATTLE

Troubles of Dinwiddie • Gathering of the Burgesses • Virginian Society • Refractory Legislators • The Quaker Assembly • It refuses to resist the French • Apathy of New York • Shirley and the General Court of Massachusetts • Short-sighted Policy • Attitude of Royal Governors • Indian Allies waver • Convention at Albany • Scheme of Union • It fails • Dinwiddie and Glen • Dinwiddie calls on England for Help • The Duke of Newcastle • Weakness of the British Cabinet • Attitude of France • Mutual Dissimulation • Both Powers send Troops to America • Collision • Capture of the "Alcide" and the "Lis"

THE DEFEAT of Washington was a heavy blow to the Governor, and he angrily ascribed it to the delay of the expected reinforcements. The King's companies from New York had reached Alexandria, and crawled towards the scene of action with thin ranks, bad discipline, thirty women and children, no tents, no blankets, no knapsacks, and for munitions one barrel of spoiled gunpowder.[1] The case was still worse with the regiment from North Carolina. It was commanded by Colonel Innes, a countryman and friend of Dinwiddie, who wrote to him: "Dear James, I now wish that we had none from your colony but yourself, for I foresee nothing but confusion among them." The men were, in fact, utterly unmanageable. They had been promised three shillings a day, while the Virginians had only eightpence; and when they heard on the march that their pay was to be reduced, they mutinied, disbanded, and went home.

"You may easily guess," says Dinwiddie to a London correspondent, "the great fatigue and trouble I have had, which is more than I ever went through in my life." He rested his hopes on the session of his Assembly, which was to take place in August; for he thought that the late disaster would move them to give him money for defending the colony. These

---

[1] *Dinwiddie to the Lords of Trade, 24 July, 1754. Ibid. to Delancey, 20 June, 1754.*

meetings of the burgesses were the great social as well as political event of the Old Dominion, and gave a gathering signal
to the Virginian gentry scattered far and wide on their lonely
plantations. The capital of the province was Williamsburg, a
village of about a thousand inhabitants, traversed by a straight
and very wide street, and adorned with various public buildings, conspicuous among which was William and Mary College, a respectable structure, unjustly likened by Jefferson to
a brick kiln with a roof. The capitol, at the other end of the
town, had been burned some years before, and had just risen
from its ashes. Not far distant was the so-called Governor's
Palace, where Dinwiddie with his wife and two daughters exercised such official hospitality as his moderate salary and
Scottish thrift would permit.[1]

In these seasons of festivity the dull and quiet village was
transfigured. The broad, sandy street, scorching under a
southern sun, was thronged with coaches and chariots
brought over from London at heavy cost in tobacco, though
soon to be bedimmed by Virginia roads and negro care; rac-
ing and hard-drinking planters; clergymen of the Establishment, not much more ascetic than their boon companions of
the laity; ladies, with manners a little rusted by long seclusion; black coachmen and footmen, proud of their masters
and their liveries; young cavaliers, booted and spurred, sitting
their thoroughbreds with the careless grace of men whose
home was the saddle. It was a proud little provincial society,
which might seem absurd in its lofty self-appreciation, had it
not soon approved itself so prolific in ability and worth.[2]

The burgesses met, and Dinwiddie made them an opening
speech, inveighing against the aggressions of the French, their
"contempt of treaties," and "ambitious views for universal
monarchy;" and he concluded: "I could expatiate very largely
on these affairs, but my heart burns with resentment at their
insolence. I think there is no room for many arguments to

[1] For a contemporary account of Williamsburg, Burnaby, *Travels in North
America*, 6. Smyth, *Tour in America*, I. 17, describes it some years later.
[2] The English traveller Smyth, in his *Tour*, gives a curious and vivid picture of Virginian life. For the social condition of this and other colonies
before the Revolution, one cannot do better than to consult Lodge's *Short
History of the English Colonies*.

induce you to raise a considerable supply to enable me to defeat the designs of these troublesome people and enemies of mankind." The burgesses in their turn expressed the "highest and most becoming resentment," and promptly voted twenty thousand pounds; but on the third reading of the bill they added to it a rider which touched the old question of the pistole fee, and which, in the view of the Governor, was both unconstitutional and offensive. He remonstrated in vain; the stubborn republicans would not yield, nor would he; and again he prorogued them. This unexpected defeat depressed him greatly. "A governor," he wrote, "is really to be pitied in the discharge of his duty to his king and country, in having to do with such obstinate, self-conceited people. . . . I cannot satisfy the burgesses unless I prostitute the rules of government. I have gone through monstrous fatigues. Such wrong-headed people, I thank God, I never had to do with before."[1] A few weeks later he was comforted; for, having again called the burgesses, they gave him the money, without trying this time to humiliate him.[2]

In straining at a gnat and swallowing a camel, aristocratic Virginia was far outdone by democratic Pennsylvania. Hamilton, her governor, had laid before the Assembly a circular letter from the Earl of Holdernesse directing him, in common with other governors, to call on his province for means to repel any invasion which might be made "within the undoubted limits of His Majesty's dominion."[3] The Assembly of Pennsylvania was curiously unlike that of Virginia, as half and often more than half of its members were Quaker tradesmen in sober raiment and broad-brimmed hats; while of the rest, the greater part were Germans who cared little whether they lived under English rule or French, provided that they were left in peace upon their farms. The House replied to the Governor's call: "It would be highly presumptuous in us to pretend to judge of the undoubted limits of His Majesty's dominions;" and they added: "the Assemblies of this province are generally composed of a majority who are constitutionally principled against war, and represent a well-meaning, peace-

---

[1] *Dinwiddie to Hamilton, 6 Sept., 1754. Ibid. to J. Abercrombie, 1 Sept., 1754.*
[2] Hening, VI. 435.
[3] *The Earl of Holdernesse to the Governors in America, 28 Aug. 1753.*

able people."[1] They then adjourned, telling the Governor that, "As those our limits have not been clearly ascertained to our satisfaction, we fear the precipitate call upon us as the province invaded cannot answer any good purpose at this time."

In the next month they met again, and again Hamilton asked for means to defend the country. The question was put, Should the Assembly give money for the King's use? and the vote was feebly affirmative. Should the sum be twenty thousand pounds? The vote was overwhelming in the negative. Fifteen thousand, ten thousand, and five thousand, were successively proposed, and the answer was always, No. The House would give nothing but five hundred pounds for a present to the Indians; after which they adjourned "to the sixth of the month called May."[2] At their next meeting they voted to give the Governor ten thousand pounds; but under conditions which made them for some time independent of his veto, and which, in other respects, were contrary to his instructions from the King, as well as from the proprietaries of the province, to whom he had given bonds to secure his obedience. He therefore rejected the bill, and they adjourned. In August they passed a similar vote, with the same result. At their October meeting they evaded his call for supplies. In December they voted twenty thousand pounds, hampered with conditions which were sure to be refused, since Morris, the new governor, who had lately succeeded Hamilton, was under the same restrictions as his predecessor. They told him, however, that in the present case they felt themselves bound by no Act of Parliament, and added: "We hope the Governor, notwithstanding any penal bond he may have entered into, will on reflection think himself at liberty and find it consistent with his safety and honor to give his assent to this bill." Morris, who had taken the highest legal advice on the subject in England, declined to compromise himself, saying: "Consider, gentlemen, in what light you will appear to His Majesty while, instead of contributing towards your own defence, you are entering into an ill-timed controversy concerning the

[1] *Colonial Records of Pa.*, V. 748.

[2] *Pennsylvania Archives*, II. 235. *Colonial Records of Pa.*, VI. 22–26. *Works of Franklin*, III. 265.

validity of royal instructions which may be delayed to a more convenient time without the least injury to the rights of the people."[1] They would not yield, and told him "that they had rather the French should conquer them than give up their privileges."[2] "Truly," remarks Dinwiddie, "I think they have given their senses a long holiday."

New York was not much behind her sisters in contentious stubbornness. In answer to the Governor's appeal, the Assembly replied: "It appears that the French have built a fort at a place called French Creek, at a considerable distance from the River Ohio, which may, but does not by any evidence or information appear to us to be an invasion of any of His Majesty's colonies."[3] So blind were they as yet to "manifest destiny!" Afterwards, however, on learning the defeat of Washington, they gave five thousand pounds to aid Virginia.[4] Maryland, after long delay, gave six thousand. New Jersey felt herself safe behind the other colonies, and would give nothing. New England, on the other hand, and especially Massachusetts, had suffered so much from French war-parties that they were always ready to fight. Shirley, the governor of Massachusetts, had returned from his bootless errand to settle the boundary question at Paris. His leanings were strongly monarchical; yet he believed in the New Englanders, and was more or less in sympathy with them. Both he and they were strenuous against the French, and they had mutually helped each other to reap laurels in the last war. Shirley was cautious of giving umbrage to his Assembly, and rarely quarrelled with it, except when the amount of his salary was in question. He was not averse to a war with France; for though bred a lawyer, and now past middle life, he flattered himself with hopes of a high military command. On the present occasion, making use of a rumor that the French were seizing the carrying-place between the Chaudière and the Kennebec, he drew from the Assembly a large grant of money, and induced them to call upon him to march in person to the scene of danger. He

[1] *Colonial Records of Pa.*, VI. 215.

[2] *Morris to Penn, 1 Jan. 1755.*

[3] *Address of the Assembly to Lieutenant-Governor Delancey, 23 April, 1754. Lords of Trade to Delancey, 5 July, 1754.*

[4] *Delancey to Lords of Trade, 8 Oct. 1754.*

accordingly repaired to Falmouth (now Portland); and, though the rumor proved false, sent eight hundred men under Captain John Winslow to build two forts on the Kennebec as a measure of precaution.[1]

While to these northern provinces Canada was an old and pestilent enemy, those towards the south scarcely knew her by name; and the idea of French aggression on their borders was so novel and strange that they admitted it with difficulty. Mind and heart were engrossed in strife with their governors: the universal struggle for virtual self-rule. But the war was often waged with a passionate stupidity. The colonist was not then an American; he was simply a provincial, and a narrow one. The time was yet distant when these dissevered and jealous communities should weld themselves into one broad nationality, capable, at need, of the mightiest efforts to purge itself of disaffection and vindicate its commanding unity.

In the interest of that practical independence which they had so much at heart, two conditions were essential to the colonists. The one was a field for expansion, and the other was mutual help. Their first necessity was to rid themselves of the French, who, by shutting them between the Alleghanies and the sea, would cramp them into perpetual littleness. With France on their backs, growing while they had no room to grow, they must remain in helpless wardship, dependent on England, whose aid they would always need; but with the West open before them, their future was their own. King and Parliament would respect perforce the will of a people spread from the ocean to the Mississippi, and united in action as in aims. But in the middle of the last century the vision of the ordinary colonist rarely reached so far. The immediate victory over a governor, however slight the point at issue, was more precious in his eyes than the remote though decisive advantage which he saw but dimly.

The governors, representing the central power, saw the situation from the national point of view. Several of them, notably Dinwiddie and Shirley, were filled with wrath at the proceedings of the French; and the former was exasperated beyond measure at the supineness of the provinces. He had

---

[1] *Massachusetts Archives, 1754.* Hutchinson, III. 26. *Conduct of Major-General Shirley briefly stated. Journals of the Board of Trade, 1754.*

spared no effort to rouse them, and had failed. His instincts were on the side of authority; but, under the circumstances, it is hardly to be imputed to him as a very deep offence against human liberty that he advised the compelling of the colonies to raise men and money for their own defence, and proposed, in view of their "intolerable obstinacy and disobedience to his Majesty's commands," that Parliament should tax them half-a-crown a head. The approaching war offered to the party of authority temptations from which the colonies might have saved it by opening their purse-strings without waiting to be told.

The Home Government, on its part, was but half-hearted in the wish that they should unite in opposition to the common enemy. It was very willing that the several provinces should give money and men, but not that they should acquire military habits and a dangerous capacity of acting together. There was one kind of union, however, so obviously necessary, and at the same time so little to be dreaded, that the British Cabinet, instructed by the governors, not only assented to it, but urged it. This was joint action in making treaties with the Indians. The practice of separate treaties, made by each province in its own interest, had bred endless disorders. The adhesion of all the tribes had been so shaken, and the efforts of the French to alienate them were so vigorous and effective, that not a moment was to be lost. Joncaire had gained over most of the Senecas, Piquet was drawing the Onondagas more and more to his mission, and the Dutch of Albany were alienating their best friends, the Mohawks, by encroaching on their lands. Their chief, Hendrick, came to New York with a deputation of the tribe to complain of their wrongs; and finding no redress, went off in anger, declaring that the covenant chain was broken.[1] The authorities in alarm called William Johnson to their aid. He succeeded in soothing the exasperated chief, and then proceeded to the confederate council at Onondaga, where he found the assembled sachems full of anxieties and doubts. "We don't know what you Christians, English and French, intend," said one of their orators. "We are so hemmed in by you both that we have hardly a hunting-place left. In a little while, if we find a bear in a tree,

[1] *N. Y. Col. Docs.*, VI. 788. *Colonial Records of Pa.*, V. 625.

there will immediately appear an owner of the land to claim the property and hinder us from killing it, by which we live. We are so perplexed between you that we hardly know what to say or think."[1] No man had such power over the Five Nations as Johnson. His dealings with them were at once honest, downright, and sympathetic. They loved and trusted him as much as they detested the Indian commissioners at Albany, whom the province of New York had charged with their affairs, and who, being traders, grossly abused their office.

It was to remedy this perilous state of things that the Lords of Trade and Plantations directed the several governors to urge on their assemblies the sending of commissioners to make a joint treaty with the wavering tribes.[2] Seven of the provinces, New York, Pennsylvania, Maryland, and the four New England colonies, acceded to the plan, and sent to Albany, the appointed place of meeting, a body of men who for character and ability had never had an equal on the continent, but whose powers from their respective assemblies were so cautiously limited as to preclude decisive action. They met in the court-house of the little frontier city. A large "chain-belt" of wampum was provided, on which the King was symbolically represented, holding in his embrace the colonies, the Five Nations, and all their allied tribes. This was presented to the assembled warriors, with a speech in which the misdeeds of the French were not forgotten. The chief, Hendrick, made a much better speech in reply. "We do now solemnly renew and brighten the covenant chain. We shall take the chain-belt to Onondaga, where our council-fire always burns, and keep it so safe that neither thunder nor lightning shall break it." The commissioners had blamed them for allowing so many of their people to be drawn away to Piquet's mission. "It is true," said the orator, "that we live disunited. We have tried to bring back our brethren, but in vain; for the Governor of Canada is like a wicked, deluding spirit. You ask why we are so dispersed. The reason is that you have neglected us for these three years past." Here he took a stick and threw it behind him. "You have thus thrown us behind your back;

[1] *N. Y. Col. Docs.*, VI. 813.

[2] *Circular Letter of Lords of Trade to Governors in America, 18 Sept. 1753. Lords of Trade to Sir Danvers Osborne*, in *N. Y. Col. Docs.*, VI. 800.

whereas the French are a subtle and vigilant people, always using their utmost endeavors to seduce and bring us over to them." He then told them that it was not the French alone who invaded the country of the Indians. "The Governor of Virginia and the Governor of Canada are quarrelling about lands which belong to us, and their quarrel may end in our destruction." And he closed with a burst of sarcasm. "We would have taken Crown Point [*in the last war*], but you prevented us. Instead, you burned your own fort at Saratoga and ran away from it,—which was a shame and a scandal to you. Look about your country and see: you have no fortifications; no, not even in this city. It is but a step from Canada hither, and the French may come and turn you out of doors. You desire us to speak from the bottom of our hearts, and we shall do it. Look at the French: they are men; they are fortifying everywhere. But you are all like women, bare and open, without fortifications."[1]

Hendrick's brother Abraham now took up the word, and begged that Johnson might be restored to the management of Indian affairs, which he had formerly held; "for," said the chief, "we love him and he us, and he has always been our good and trusty friend." The commissioners had not power to grant the request, but the Indians were assured that it should not be forgotten; and they returned to their villages soothed, but far from satisfied. Nor were the commissioners empowered to take any effective steps for fortifying the frontier.

The congress now occupied itself with another matter. Its members were agreed that great danger was impending; that without wise and just treatment of the tribes, the French would gain them all, build forts along the back of the British colonies, and, by means of ships and troops from France, master them one by one, unless they would combine for mutual defence. The necessity of some form of union had at length begun to force itself upon the colonial mind. A rough woodcut had lately appeared in the *Pennsylvania Gazette*, figuring the provinces under the not very flattering image of a snake cut to pieces, with the motto, "Join, or die." A writer

[1] *Proceedings of the Congress at Albany, N. Y. Col. Docs.*, VI. 853. A few verbal changes, for the sake of brevity, are made in the above extracts.

of the day held up the Five Nations for emulation, observing
that if ignorant savages could confederate, British colonists
might do as much.[1] Franklin, the leading spirit of the congress, now laid before it his famous project of union, which
has been too often described to need much notice here.
Its fate is well known. The Crown rejected it because it gave
too much power to the colonies; the colonies, because it
gave too much power to the Crown, and because it required
each of them to transfer some of its functions of self-government to a central council. Another plan was afterwards devised by the friends of prerogative, perfectly agreeable to the
King, since it placed all power in the hands of a council of
governors, and since it involved compulsory taxation of the
colonists, who, for the same reasons, would have doggedly
resisted it, had an attempt been made to carry it into effect.[2]

Even if some plan of union had been agreed upon, long
delay must have followed before its machinery could be set in
motion; and meantime there was need of immediate action.
War-parties of Indians from Canada, set on, it was thought,
by the Governor, were already burning and murdering among
the border settlements of New York and New Hampshire. In
the south Dinwiddie grew more and more alarmed, "for the
French are like so many locusts; they are collected in bodies
in a most surprising manner; their number now on the Ohio
is from twelve hundred to fifteen hundred." He writes to
Lord Granville that, in his opinion, they aim to conquer the
continent, and that "the obstinacy of this stubborn generation" exposes the country "to the merciless rage of a rapacious
enemy." What vexed him even more than the apathy of the
assemblies was the conduct of his brother-governor, Glen of
South Carolina, who, apparently piqued at the conspicuous
part Dinwiddie was acting, wrote to him in a "very dictatorial
style," found fault with his measures, jested at his activity in
writing letters, and even questioned the right of England to
lands on the Ohio; till he was moved at last to retort: "I

---

[1] Kennedy, *Importance of gaining and preserving the Friendship of the Indians.*

[2] On the Albany plan of union, *Franklin's Works*, I. 177. Shirley thought it
"a great strain upon the prerogative of the Crown," and was for requiring
the colonies to raise money and men "without farther consulting them upon
any points whatever." *Shirley to Robinson, 24 Dec. 1754.*

cannot help observing that your letters and arguments would have been more proper from a French officer than from one of His Majesty's governors. My conduct has met with His Majesty's gracious approbation; and I am sorry it has not received yours." Thus discouraged, even in quarters where he had least reason to expect it, he turned all his hopes to the Home Government; again recommended a tax by Act of Parliament, and begged, in repeated letters, for arms, munitions, and two regiments of infantry.[1] His petition was not made in vain.

England at this time presented the phenomenon of a prime minister who could not command the respect of his own servants. A more preposterous figure than the Duke of Newcastle never stood at the head of a great nation. He had a feverish craving for place and power, joined to a total unfitness for both. He was an adept in personal politics, and was so busied with the arts of winning and keeping office that he had no leisure, even if he had had ability, for the higher work of government. He was restless, quick in movement, rapid and confused in speech, lavish of worthless promises, always in a hurry, and at once headlong, timid, and rash. "A borrowed importance and real insignificance," says Walpole, who knew him well, "gave him the perpetual air of a solicitor. . . . He had no pride, though infinite self-love. He loved business immoderately; yet was only always doing it, never did it. When left to himself, he always plunged into difficulties, and then shuddered for the consequences." Walpole gives an anecdote showing the state of his ideas on colonial matters. General Ligonier suggested to him that Annapolis ought to be defended. "To which he replied with his lisping, evasive hurry: 'Annapolis, Annapolis! Oh, yes, Annapolis must be defended; to be sure, Annapolis should be defended,—where is Annapolis?'"[2] Another contemporary, Smollett, ridicules him in his novel of *Humphrey Clinker*, and tells a similar story, which, founded in fact or not, shows in what estimation the minister was held: "Captain C. treated the Duke's character without any ceremony. 'This wiseacre,'

---

[1] *Dinwiddie Papers*; letters to Granville, Albemarle, Halifax, Fox, Holdernesse, Horace Walpole, and Lords of Trade.

[2] Walpole, *George II.*, I. 344.

said he, 'is still abed; and I think the best thing he can do is to sleep on till Christmas; for when he gets up he does nothing but expose his own folly. In the beginning of the war he told me in a great fright that thirty thousand French had marched from Acadia to Cape Breton. Where did they find transports? said I.—Transports! cried he, I tell you they marched by land.—By land to the island of Cape Breton!— What, is Cape Breton an island?—Certainly.—Ha! are you sure of that?—When I pointed it out on the map, he examined it earnestly with his spectacles; then, taking me in his arms,—My dear C., cried he, you always bring us good news. Egad! I'll go directly and tell the King that Cape Breton is an island.' "

His wealth, county influence, flagitious use of patronage, and long-practised skill in keeping majorities in the House of Commons by means that would not bear the light, made his support necessary to Pitt himself, and placed a fantastic political jobber at the helm of England in a time when she needed a patriot and a statesman. Newcastle was the growth of the decrepitude and decay of a great party, which had fulfilled its mission and done its work. But if the Whig soil had become poor for a wholesome crop, it was never so rich for toadstools.

Sir Thomas Robinson held the Southern Department, charged with the colonies; and Lord Mahon remarks of him that the Duke had achieved the feat of finding a secretary of state more incapable than himself. He had the lead of the House of Commons. "Sir Thomas Robinson lead us!" said Pitt to Henry Fox; "the Duke might as well send his jackboot to lead us." The active and aspiring Halifax was at the head of the Board of Trade and Plantations. The Duke of Cumberland commanded the army,—an indifferent soldier, though a brave one; harsh, violent, and headlong. Anson, the celebrated navigator, was First Lord of the Admiralty,—a position in which he disappointed everybody.

In France the true ruler was Madame de Pompadour, once the King's mistress, now his procuress, and a sort of feminine prime minister. Machault d'Arnouville was at the head of the Marine and Colonial Department. The diplomatic representatives of the two Crowns were more conspicuous for social than for political talents. Of Mirepoix, French ambassador at London, Marshal Saxe had once observed: "It is a good appointment; he can teach the English to dance." Walpole says concerning him: "He could not even learn to pronounce the names of our games of cards,—which, however, engaged most of the hours of his negotiation. We were to be bullied out of our colonies by an apprentice at whist!" Lord Albemarle, English ambassador at Versailles, is held up by Chesterfield as an example to encourage his son in the pursuit of the graces: "What do you think made our friend Lord Albemarle colonel of a regiment of Guards, Governor of Virginia, Groom of the Stole, and ambassador to Paris,—amounting in all to sixteen or seventeen thousand pounds a year? Was it his birth? No; a Dutch gentleman only. Was it his estate? No; he had none. Was it his learning, his parts, his political abilities and application? You can answer these questions as easily and as soon as I can ask them. What was it then? Many people wondered; but I do not, for I know, and will tell you,— it was his air, his address, his manners, and his graces."

The rival nations differed widely in military and naval strength. England had afloat more than two hundred ships of war, some of them of great force; while the navy of France counted little more than half the number. On the other hand, England had reduced her army to eighteen thousand men, and France had nearly ten times as many under arms. Both alike were weak in leadership. That rare son of the tempest, a great commander, was to be found in neither of them since the death of Saxe.

In respect to the approaching crisis, the interests of the two Powers pointed to opposite courses of action. What France needed was time. It was her policy to put off a rupture, wreathe her face in diplomatic smiles, and pose in an attitude of peace and good faith, while increasing her navy, reinforcing her garrisons in America, and strengthening her positions there. It was the policy of England to attack at once, and tear up the young encroachments while they were yet in the sap, before they could strike root and harden into stiff resistance.

When, on the fourteenth of November, the King made his opening speech to the Houses of Parliament, he congratulated them on the prevailing peace, and assured them that he should improve it to promote the trade of his subjects, "and protect those possessions which constitute one great source of their wealth." America was not mentioned; but his hearers understood him, and made a liberal grant for the service of the year.[1] Two regiments, each of five hundred men, had already been ordered to sail for Virginia, where their numbers were to be raised by enlistment to seven hundred.[2] Major-General Braddock, a man after the Duke of Cumberland's own heart, was appointed to the chief command. The two regiments—the forty-fourth and the forty-eighth—embarked at Cork in the middle of January. The soldiers detested the service, and many had deserted. More would have done so had they foreseen what awaited them.

This movement was no sooner known at Versailles than a counter expedition was prepared on a larger scale. Eighteen ships of war were fitted for sea at Brest and Rochefort, and the six battalions of La Reine, Bourgogne, Languedoc, Guienne, Artois, and Béarn, three thousand men in all, were ordered on board for Canada. Baron Dieskau, a German veteran who had served under Saxe, was made their general; and with him went the new governor of French America, the Marquis de Vaudreuil, destined to succeed Duquesne, whose health was failing under the fatigues of his office. Admiral Dubois de la Motte commanded the fleet; and lest the English should try to intercept it, another squadron of nine ships, under Admiral Macnamara, was ordered to accompany it to a certain distance from the coast. There was long and tedious delay. Doreil, commissary of war, who had embarked with Vaudreuil and Dieskau in the same ship, wrote from the harbor of Brest on the twenty-ninth of April: "At last I think we are off. We should have been outside by four o'clock this morning, if M. de Macnamara had not been obliged to ask Count Dubois de la Motte to wait till noon to mend some important part of the rigging (I don't know the name of it) which was broken. It is precious time lost, and gives the English the advantage over us of two tides. I talk of these things

[1] Entick, *Late War*, I. 118.

[2] *Robinson to Lords of the Admiralty, 30 Sept. 1754. Ibid., to Board of Ordnance, 10 Oct. 1754. Ibid., Circular Letter to American Governors, 26 Oct. 1754. Instructions to our Trusty and Well-beloved Edward Braddock, 25 Nov. 1754.*

as a blind man does of colors. What is certain is that Count Dubois de la Motte is very impatient to get away, and that the King's fleet destined for Canada is in very able and zealous hands. It is now half-past two. In half an hour all may be ready, and we may get out of the harbor before night." He was again disappointed; it was the third of May before the fleet put to sea.[1]

During these preparations there was active diplomatic correspondence between the two Courts. Mirepoix demanded why British troops were sent to America. Sir Thomas Robinson answered that there was no intention to disturb the peace or offend any Power whatever; yet the secret orders to Braddock were the reverse of pacific. Robinson asked on his part the purpose of the French armament at Brest and Rochefort; and the answer, like his own, was a protestation that no hostility was meant. At the same time Mirepoix in the name of the King proposed that orders should be given to the American governors on both sides to refrain from all acts of aggression. But while making this proposal the French Court secretly sent orders to Duquesne to attack and destroy Fort Halifax, one of the two forts lately built by Shirley on the Kennebec,—a river which, by the admission of the French themselves, belonged to the English. But, in making this attack, the French Governor was expressly enjoined to pretend that he acted without orders.[2] He was also told that, if necessary, he might make use of the Indians to harass the English.[3] Thus there was good faith on neither part; but it is clear through all the correspondence that the English expected to gain by precipitating an open rupture, and the French by postponing it. Projects of convention were proposed on both sides, but there was no agreement. The English insisted as a preliminary condition that the French

---

[1] *Lettres de Cremille, de Rostaing, et de Doreil au Ministre, Avril 18, 24, 28, 29, 1755. Liste des Vaisseaux de Guerre qui composent l'Escadre armée à Brest, 1755. Journal of M. de Vaudreuil's Voyage to Canada*, in *N. Y. Col. Docs.*, X. 297. Pouchot, I. 25.

[2] *Machault à Duquesne, 17 Fév. 1755.* The letter of Mirepoix proposing mutual abstinence from aggression, is dated on the 6th of the same month. The French dreaded Fort Halifax, because they thought it prepared the way for an advance on Quebec by way of the Chaudière.

[3] *Ibid.*

should evacuate all the western country as far as the Wabash. Then ensued a long discussion of their respective claims, as futile as the former discussion at Paris on Acadian boundaries.[1]

The British Court knew perfectly the naval and military preparations of the French. Lord Albemarle had died at Paris in December; but the secretary of the embassy, De Cosne, sent to London full information concerning the fleet at Brest and Rochefort.[2] On this, Admiral Boscawen, with eleven ships of the line and one frigate, was ordered to intercept it; and as his force was plainly too small, Admiral Holbourne, with seven more ships, was sent, nearly three weeks after, to join him if he could. Their orders were similar,—to capture or destroy any French vessels bound to North America.[3] Boscawen, who got to sea before La Motte, stationed himself near the southern coast of Newfoundland to cut him off; but most of the French squadron eluded him, and safely made their way, some to Louisbourg, and the others to Quebec. Thus the English expedition was, in the main, a failure. Three of the French ships, however, lost in fog and rain, had become separated from the rest, and lay rolling and tossing on an angry sea not far from Cape Race. One of them was the "Alcide," commanded by Captain Hocquart; the others were the "Lis" and the "Dauphin." The wind fell; but the fogs continued at intervals; till, on the afternoon of the seventh of June, the weather having cleared, the watchman on the maintop saw the distant ocean studded with ships. It was the fleet of Boscawen. Hocquart, who gives the account, says that in the morning they were within three leagues of him, crowding all sail in pursuit. Towards eleven o'clock one of them, the "Dunkirk," was abreast of him to windward, within short speaking distance; and the ship of the Admiral, displaying a red flag as a signal to engage, was not far off. Hocquart called out: "Are we at peace, or war?" He declares that Howe, cap-

[1] This correspondence is printed among the *Pièces justificatives* of the *Précis des Faits*.

[2] Particulars in Entick, I. 121.

[3] *Secret Instructions for our Trusty and Well-beloved Edward Boscawen, Esq., Vice-Admiral of the Blue, 16 April, 1755. Most secret Instructions for Francis Holbourne, Esq., Rear-Admiral of the Blue, 9 May, 1755. Robinson to Lords of the Admiralty, 8 May, 1755.*

tain of the "Dunkirk," replied in French: "La paix, la paix." Hocquart then asked the name of the British admiral; and on hearing it said: "I know him; he is a friend of mine." Being asked his own name in return, he had scarcely uttered it when the batteries of the "Dunkirk" belched flame and smoke, and volleyed a tempest of iron upon the crowded decks of the "Alcide." She returned the fire, but was forced at length to strike her colors. Rostaing, second in command of the troops, was killed; and six other officers, with about eighty men, were killed or wounded.[1] At the same time the "Lis" was attacked and overpowered. She had on board eight companies of the battalions of La Reine and Languedoc. The third French ship, the "Dauphin," escaped under cover of a rising fog.[2]

Here at last was an end to negotiation. The sword was drawn and brandished in the eyes of Europe.

[1] *Liste des Officiers tués et blessés dans le Combat de l'Alcide et du Lis.*

[2] Hocquart's account is given in full by Pichon, *Lettres et Mémoires pour servir à l'Histoire du Cap-Breton.* The short account in *Précis des Faits*, 272, seems, too, to be drawn from Hocquart. Also *Boscawen to Robinson, 22 June, 1755. Vaudreuil au Ministre, 24 Juillet, 1755.* Entick, I. 137.

Some English accounts say that Captain Howe, in answer to the question, "Are we at peace, or war?" returned, "I don't know; but you had better prepare for war." Boscawen places the action on the 10th, instead of the 8th, and puts the English loss at seven killed and twenty-seven wounded.

Chapter VII

BRADDOCK

Arrival of Braddock • His Character • Council at Alexandria • Plan of the Campaign • Apathy of the Colonists • Rage of Braddock • Franklin • Fort Cumberland • Composition of the Army • Offended Friends • The March • The French Fort • Savage Allies • The Captive • Beaujeu • He goes to meet the English • Passage of the Monongahela • The Surprise • The Battle • Rout of Braddock • His Death • Indian Ferocity • Reception of the Ill News • Weakness of Dunbar • The Frontier abandoned

---

"I HAVE the pleasure to acquaint you that General Braddock came to my house last Sunday night," writes Dinwiddie, at the end of February, to Governor Dobbs of North Carolina. Braddock had landed at Hampton from the ship "Centurion," along with young Commodore Keppel, who commanded the American squadron. "I am mighty glad," again writes Dinwiddie, "that the General is arrived, which I hope will give me some ease; for these twelve months past I have been a perfect slave." He conceived golden opinions of his guest. "He is, I think, a very fine officer, and a sensible, considerate gentleman. He and I live in great harmony."

Had he known him better, he might have praised him less. William Shirley, son of the Governor of Massachusetts, was Braddock's secretary; and after an acquaintance of some months wrote to his friend Governor Morris: "We have a general most judiciously chosen for being disqualified for the service he is employed in in almost every respect. He may be brave for aught I know, and he is honest in pecuniary matters."[1] The astute Franklin, who also had good opportunity of knowing him, says: "This general was, I think, a brave man, and might probably have made a good figure in some European war. But he had too much self-confidence; too high an opinion of the validity of regular

[1] *Shirley the younger to Morris, 23 May, 1755.*

troops; too mean a one of both Americans and Indians."[1] Horace Walpole, in his function of gathering and immortalizing the gossip of his time, has left a sharply drawn sketch of Braddock in two letters to Sir Horace Mann, written in the summer of this year: "I love to give you an idea of our characters as they rise upon the stage of history. Braddock is a very Iroquois in disposition. He had a sister who, having gamed away all her little fortune at Bath, hanged herself with a truly English deliberation, leaving only a note upon the table with those lines: 'To die is landing on some silent shore,' etc. When Braddock was told of it, he only said: 'Poor Fanny! I always thought she would play till she would be forced to *tuck herself up*.'" Under the name of Miss Sylvia S——, Goldsmith, in his life of Nash, tells the story of this unhappy woman. She was a rash but warm-hearted creature, reduced to penury and dependence, not so much by a passion for cards as by her lavish generosity to a lover ruined by his own follies, and with whom her relations are said to have been entirely innocent. Walpole continues: "But a more ridiculous story of Braddock, and which is recorded in heroics by Fielding in his *Covent Garden Tragedy*, was an amorous discussion he had formerly with a Mrs. Upton, who kept him. He had gone the greatest lengths with her pin-money, and was still craving. One day, that he was very pressing, she pulled out her purse and showed him that she had but twelve or fourteen shillings left. He twitched it from her: 'Let me see that.' Tied up at the other end he found five guineas. He took them, tossed the empty purse in her face, saying: 'Did you mean to cheat me?' and never went near her more. Now you are acquainted with General Braddock."

"He once had a duel with Colonel Gumley, Lady Bath's brother, who had been his great friend. As they were going to engage, Gumley, who had good-humor and wit (Braddock had the latter), said: 'Braddock, you are a poor dog! Here, take my purse; if you kill me, you will be forced to run away, and then you will not have a shilling to support you.' Braddock refused the purse, insisted on the duel, was disarmed, and would not even ask his life. However, with all his brutality, he has lately been governor of Gibraltar, where he made

[1] Franklin, *Autobiography*.

himself adored, and where scarce any governor was endured before."[1]

Another story is told of him by an accomplished actress of the time, George Anne Bellamy, whom Braddock had known from girlhood, and with whom his present relations seem to have been those of an elderly adviser and friend. "As we were walking in the Park one day, we heard a poor fellow was to be chastised; when I requested the General to beg off the offender. Upon his application to the general officer, whose name was Dury, he asked Braddock how long since he had divested himself of the brutality and insolence of his manners? To which the other replied: 'You never knew me insolent to my inferiors. It is only to such rude men as yourself that I behave with the spirit which I think they deserve.'"

Braddock made a visit to the actress on the evening before he left London for America. "Before we parted," she says, "the General told me that he should never see me more; for he was going with a handful of men to conquer whole nations; and to do this they must cut their way through unknown woods. He produced a map of the country, saying at the same time: 'Dear Pop, we are sent like sacrifices to the altar,'"[2]—a strange presentiment for a man of his sturdy temper.

Whatever were his failings, he feared nothing, and his fidelity and honor in the discharge of public trusts were never questioned. "Desperate in his fortune, brutal in his behavior, obstinate in his sentiments," again writes Walpole, "he was still intrepid and capable."[3] He was a veteran in years and in service, having entered the Coldstream Guards as ensign in 1710.

The transports bringing the two regiments from Ireland all arrived safely at Hampton, and were ordered to proceed up the Potomac to Alexandria, where a camp was to be formed. Thither, towards the end of March, went Braddock himself,

---

[1] *Letters of Horace Walpole* (1866), II. 459, 461. It is doubtful if Braddock was ever governor of Gibraltar; though, as Mr. Sargent shows, he once commanded a regiment there.

[2] *Apology for the Life of George Anne Bellamy, written by herself*, II. 204 (London, 1786).

[3] Walpole, *George II.*, I. 390.

along with Keppel and Dinwiddie, in the Governor's coach; while his aide-de-camp, Orme, his secretary, Shirley, and the servants of the party followed on horseback. Braddock had sent for the elder Shirley and other provincial governors to meet him in council; and on the fourteenth of April they assembled in a tent of the newly formed encampment. Here was Dinwiddie, who thought his troubles at an end, and saw in the red-coated soldiery the near fruition of his hopes. Here, too, was his friend and ally, Dobbs of North Carolina; with Morris of Pennsylvania, fresh from Assembly quarrels; Sharpe of Maryland, who, having once been a soldier, had been made a sort of provisional commander-in-chief before the arrival of Braddock; and the ambitious Delancey of New York, who had lately led the opposition against the Governor of that province, and now filled the office himself,—a position that needed all his manifold adroitness. But, next to Braddock, the most noteworthy man present was Shirley, governor of Massachusetts. There was a fountain of youth in this old lawyer. A few years before, when he was boundary commissioner in Paris, he had had the indiscretion to marry a young Catholic French girl, the daughter of his landlord; and now, when more than sixty years old, he thirsted for military honors, and delighted in contriving operations of war. He was one of a very few in the colonies who at this time entertained the idea of expelling the French from the continent. He held that Carthage must be destroyed; and, in spite of his Parisian marriage, was the foremost advocate of the root-and-branch policy. He and Lawrence, governor of Nova Scotia, had concerted an attack on the French fort of Beauséjour; and, jointly with others in New England, he had planned the capture of Crown Point, the key of Lake Champlain. By these two strokes and by fortifying the portage between the Kennebec and the Chaudière, he thought that the northern colonies would be saved from invasion, and placed in a position to become themselves invaders. Then, by driving the enemy from Niagara, securing that important pass, and thus cutting off the communication between Canada and her interior dependencies, all the French posts in the West would die of inanition.[1] In order to commend these schemes to the Home

[1] *Correspondence of Shirley, 1754, 1755.*

Government, he had painted in gloomy colors the dangers that beset the British colonies. Our Indians, he said, will all desert us if we submit to French encroachment. Some of the provinces are full of negro slaves, ready to rise against their masters, and of Roman Catholics, Jacobites, indented servants, and other dangerous persons, who would aid the French in raising a servile insurrection. Pennsylvania is in the hands of Quakers, who will not fight, and of Germans, who are likely enough to join the enemy. The Dutch of Albany would do anything to save their trade. A strong force of French regulars might occupy that place without resistance, then descend the Hudson, and, with the help of a naval force, capture New York and cut the British colonies asunder.[1]

The plans against Crown Point and Beauséjour had already found the approval of the Home Government and the energetic support of all the New England colonies. Preparation for them was in full activity; and it was with great difficulty that Shirley had disengaged himself from these cares to attend the council at Alexandria. He and Dinwiddie stood in the front of opposition to French designs. As they both defended the royal prerogative and were strong advocates of taxation by Parliament, they have found scant justice from American writers. Yet the British colonies owed them a debt of gratitude, and the American States owe it still.

Braddock, laid his instructions before the Council, and Shirley found them entirely to his mind; while the General, on his part, fully approved the schemes of the Governor. The plan of the campaign was settled. The French were to be attacked at four points at once. The two British regiments lately arrived were to advance on Fort Duquesne; two new regiments, known as Shirley's and Pepperell's, just raised in the provinces, and taken into the King's pay, were to reduce Niagara; a body of provincials from New England, New York, and New Jersey was to seize Crown Point; and another body of New England men to capture Beauséjour and bring Acadia to complete subjection. Braddock himself was to lead the expedition against Fort Duquesne. He asked Shirley, who, though a soldier only in theory, had held the rank of colonel since the last war, to charge himself with that against Niag-

[1] *Shirley to Robinson, 24 Jan. 1755.*

ara; and Shirley eagerly assented. The movement on Crown
Point was intrusted to Colonel William Johnson, by reason
of his influence over the Indians and his reputation for energy, capacity, and faithfulness. Lastly, the Acadian enterprise
was assigned to Lieutenant-Colonel Monckton, a regular officer of merit.

To strike this fourfold blow in time of peace was a scheme
worthy of Newcastle and of Cumberland. The pretext was
that the positions to be attacked were all on British soil; that
in occupying them the French had been guilty of invasion;
and that to expel the invaders would be an act of self-defence.
Yet in regard to two of these positions, the French, if they
had no other right, might at least claim one of prescription.
Crown Point had been twenty-four years in their undisturbed
possession, while it was three quarters of a century since they
first occupied Niagara; and, though New York claimed the
ground, no serious attempt had been made to dislodge them.

Other matters now engaged the Council. Braddock, in accordance with his instructions, asked the governors to urge
upon their several assemblies the establishment of a general
fund for the service of the campaign; but the governors were
all of opinion that the assemblies would refuse,—each being
resolved to keep the control of its money in its own hands;
and all present, with one voice, advised that the colonies
should be compelled by Act of Parliament to contribute in
due proportion to the support of the war. Braddock next
asked if, in the judgment of the Council, it would not be well
to send Colonel Johnson with full powers to treat with the
Five Nations, who had been driven to the verge of an outbreak by the misconduct of the Dutch Indian commissioners
at Albany. The measure was cordially approved, as was also
another suggestion of the General, that vessels should be built
at Oswego to command Lake Ontario. The Council then dissolved.

Shirley hastened back to New England, burdened with the
preparation for three expeditions and the command of one of
them. Johnson, who had been in the camp, though not in the
Council, went back to Albany, provided with a commission
as sole superintendent of Indian affairs, and charged, besides,
with the enterprise against Crown Point; while an express

No. 1.

A Sketch of the Field of Battle of the 9th of July, upon the Monongahela, seven miles from Fort du Quesne, shewing the Disposition of the Troops when the Action began.

EXPLANATION.

⊟ British Troops; the long lines express the number of Files. ∷ French and Indians. ⚔ Cannon and Howitzers. ⊡ Waggons, Carts, and Tumbrils. I Cattle and Packhorses.

A, French and Indians when first discovered by the Guides. B, Guides and six light Horse. C, Vanguard of the advanced Party. D, Advanced Party, commanded by Lt. Col. Gage. E, Working Party, commanded by Sir Ju. St. Clair, D.Q.M.G. F, Two Field Pieces. G, Waggons with Powder and Tools. H, Rear Guard of the advanced Party. I, Light Horse leading the Convoy. K, Sailors and Pioneers, with a Tumbril of Tools, etc. L, Three Field Pieces. M, General's Guard. N, Main Body upon the Flanks of the Convoy, with the Cattle and Packhorses between them and the Flank Guards. O, Field Piece in yᵉ rear of yᵉ Convoy. P, Rear Guards. Q, Flank Guards. R, A Hollow Way. S, a Hill which the Indians did most of the Execution from. T, Frazer's House.

(Signed)   Pat. Mackellar, Engʳ.

No. 2.

A Sketch of the Field of Battle, shew-
ing the Disposition of the Troops
about 2 o'clock, when the whole of the
main Body had joined the Advanced
and Working Partys, then beat back
from the Ground they occupied as in
Plan No. I.

EXPLANATION.

A, The French and Indians skulking behind Trees, round the British. *F,* The two
Field Pieces of the advanced Party abandoned. *C, D, E, H, K, M, N, Q,* The
whole Body of the British joined with little or no Order, but endeavouring to make
Fronts towards yᵉ Enemies Fire. *L,* The
three Field Pieces of the main Body. *P,*
The rear Guard divided (round the rear of
the Convoy now closed up) behind Trees
having been attack'd by a few Indians.

N.B. The Disposition on both Sides
continued about two hours nearly as here
represented, the British endeavouring to
recover the Guns (*F*) and to gain the Hill
(*S*) to no purpose. The British were at
length beat from the Guns (*L*). The General was wounded soon after. They were
at last beat across the Hollow Way (*R*)
and made no further Stand. The Retreat
was full of Confusion and Hurry, but after
a few Miles there was a Body got to rally.

(Signed)   Patᵗ. Mackellar, Engʳ.

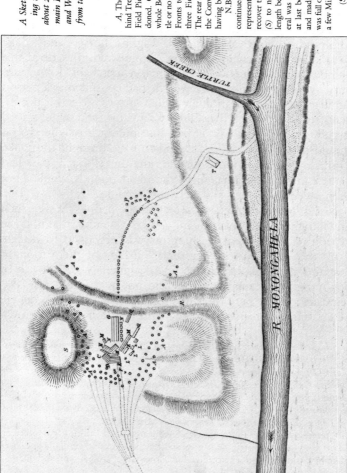

TURTLE CREEK

R. MONONGAHELA

was despatched to Monckton at Halifax, with orders to set at once to his work of capturing Beauséjour.[1]

In regard to Braddock's part of the campaign, there had been a serious error. If, instead of landing in Virginia and moving on Fort Duquesne by the long and circuitous route of Wills Creek, the two regiments had disembarked at Philadelphia and marched westward, the way would have been shortened, and would have lain through one of the richest and most populous districts on the continent, filled with supplies of every kind. In Virginia, on the other hand, and in the adjoining province of Maryland, wagons, horses, and forage were scarce. The enemies of the Administration ascribed this blunder to the influence of the Quaker merchant, John Hanbury, whom the Duke of Newcastle had consulted as a person familiar with American affairs. Hanbury, who was a prominent stockholder in the Ohio Company, and who traded largely in Virginia, saw it for his interest that the troops should pass that way; and is said to have brought the Duke to this opinion.[2] A writer of the time thinks that if they had landed in Pennsylvania, forty thousand pounds would have been saved in money, and six weeks in time.[3]

Not only were supplies scarce, but the people showed such unwillingness to furnish them, and such apathy in aiding the expedition, that even Washington was provoked to declare that "they ought to be chastised."[4] Many of them thought that the alarm about French encroachment was a device of designing politicians; and they did not awake to a full consciousness of the peril till it was forced upon them by a deluge of calamities, produced by the purblind folly of their own

[1] *Minutes of a Council held at the Camp at Alexandria, in Virginia, April 14, 1755. Instructions to Major-General Braddock, 25 Nov. 1754. Secret Instructions to Major-General Braddock, same date. Napier to Braddock, written by Order of the Duke of Cumberland, 25 Nov. 1754,* in *Précis des Faits, Pièces justificatives,* 168. Orme, *Journal of Braddock's Expedition. Instructions to Governor Shirley. Correspondence of Shirley. Correspondence of Braddock* (Public Record Office). *Johnson Papers. Dinwiddie Papers. Pennsylvania Archives,* II.

[2] *Shebbeare's Tracts,* Letter I. Dr. Shebbeare was a political pamphleteer, pilloried by one ministry, and rewarded by the next. He certainly speaks of Hanbury, though he does not give his name. Compare Sargent, 107, 162.

[3] *Gentleman's Magazine, Aug. 1755.*

[4] *Writings of Washington,* II. 78. He speaks of the people of Pennsylvania.

representatives, who, instead of frankly promoting the expedition, displayed a perverse and exasperating narrowness which chafed Braddock to fury. He praises the New England colonies, and echoes Dinwiddie's declaration that they have shown a "fine martial spirit," and he commends Virginia as having done far better than her neighbors; but for Pennsylvania he finds no words to express his wrath.[1] He knew nothing of the intestine war between proprietaries and people, and hence could see no palliation for a conduct which threatened to ruin both the expedition and the colony. Everything depended on speed, and speed was impossible; for stores and provisions were not ready, though notice to furnish them had been given months before. The quartermaster-general, Sir John Sinclair, "stormed like a lion rampant," but with small effect.[2] Contracts broken or disavowed, want of horses, want of wagons, want of forage, want of wholesome food, or sufficient food of any kind, caused such delay that the report of it reached England, and drew from Walpole the comment that Braddock was in no hurry to be scalped. In reality he was maddened with impatience and vexation.

A powerful ally presently came to his aid in the shape of Benjamin Franklin, then postmaster-general of Pennsylvania. That sagacious personage,—the sublime of common-sense, about equal in his instincts and motives of character to the respectable average of the New England that produced him, but gifted with a versatile power of brain rarely matched on earth,—was then divided between his strong desire to repel a danger of which he saw the imminence, and his equally strong antagonism to the selfish claims of the Penns, proprietaries of Pennsylvania. This last motive had determined his attitude towards their representative, the Governor, and led him into an opposition as injurious to the military good name of the province as it was favorable to its political longings. In the present case there was no such conflict of inclinations; he could help Braddock without hurting Pennsylvania. He and his son had visited the camp, and found the General waiting restlessly for the report of the agents whom he had sent to

[1] *Braddock to Robinson, 18 March, 19 April, 5 June, 1755,* etc. On the attitude of Pennsylvania, *Colonial Records of Pa.,* VI., *passim.*

[2] *Colonial Records of Pa.,* VI. 368.

collect wagons. "I stayed with him," says Franklin, "several days, and dined with him daily. When I was about to depart, the returns of wagons to be obtained were brought in, by which it appeared that they amounted only to twenty-five, and not all of these were in serviceable condition." On this the General and his officers declared that the expedition was at an end, and denounced the Ministry for sending them into a country void of the means of transportation. Franklin remarked that it was a pity they had not landed in Pennsylvania, where almost every farmer had his wagon. Braddock caught eagerly at his words, and begged that he would use his influence to enable the troops to move. Franklin went back to Pennsylvania, issued an address to the farmers appealing to their interest and their fears, and in a fortnight procured a hundred and fifty wagons, with a large number of horses.[1] Braddock, grateful to his benefactor, and enraged at everybody else, pronounced him "Almost the only instance of ability and honesty I have known in these provinces."[2] More wagons and more horses gradually arrived, and at the eleventh hour the march began.

On the tenth of May Braddock reached Wills Creek, where the whole force was now gathered, having marched thither by detachments along the banks of the Potomac. This old trading-station of the Ohio Company had been transformed into a military post and named Fort Cumberland. During the past winter the independent companies which had failed Washington in his need had been at work here to prepare a base of operations for Braddock. Their axes had been of more avail than their muskets. A broad wound had been cut in the bosom of the forest, and the murdered oaks and chestnuts turned into ramparts, barracks, and magazines. Fort Cumberland was an enclosure of logs set upright in the ground, pierced with loopholes, and armed with ten small cannon. It stood on a rising ground near the point where Wills Creek joined the Potomac, and the forest girded it like a mighty

---

[1] Franklin, *Autobiography. Advertisement of B. Franklin for Wagons; Address to the Inhabitants of the Counties of York, Lancaster, and Cumberland*, in *Pennsylvania Archives*, II. 294.

[2] *Braddock to Robinson, 5 June, 1755*. The letters of Braddock here cited are the originals in the Public Record Office.

hedge, or rather like a paling of gaunt brown stems uphold-
ing a canopy of green. All around spread illimitable woods,
wrapping hill, valley, and mountain. The spot was an oasis in
a desert of leaves,—if the name oasis can be given to anything so rude and harsh. In this rugged area, or "clearing," all
Braddock's force was now assembled, amounting, regulars,
provincials, and sailors, to about twenty-two hundred men.
The two regiments, Halket's and Dunbar's, had been completed by enlistment in Virginia to seven hundred men each.
Of Virginians there were nine companies of fifty men, who
found no favor in the eyes of Braddock or his officers. To
Ensign Allen of Halket's regiment was assigned the duty of
"making them as much like soldiers as possible,"[1]—that is,
of drilling them like regulars. The General had little hope of
them, and informed Sir Thomas Robinson that "their slothful
and languid disposition renders them very unfit for military
service,"—a point on which he lived to change his mind.
Thirty sailors, whom Commodore Keppel had lent him, were
more to his liking, and were in fact of value in many ways.
He had now about six hundred baggage-horses, besides those
of the artillery, all weakening daily on their diet of leaves; for
no grass was to be found. There was great show of discipline,
and little real order. Braddock's executive capacity seems to
have been moderate, and his dogged, imperious temper,
rasped by disappointments, was in constant irritation. "He
looks upon the country, I believe," writes Washington, "as
void of honor or honesty. We have frequent disputes on this
head, which are maintained with warmth on both sides, especially on his, as he is incapable of arguing without it, or
giving up any point he asserts, be it ever so incompatible with
reason or common sense."[2] Braddock's secretary, the younger
Shirley, writing to his friend Governor Morris, spoke thus
irreverently of his chief: "As the King said of a neighboring
governor of yours [Sharpe], when proposed for the command
of the American forces about a twelvemonth ago, and recommended as a very honest man, though not remarkably
able, 'a little more ability and a little less honesty upon the
present occasion might serve our turn better.' It is a joke to

[1] Orme, *Journal*.
[2] *Writings of Washington*, II. 77.

suppose that secondary officers can make amends for the defects of the first; the mainspring must be the mover. As to the others, I don't think we have much to boast; some are insolent and ignorant, others capable, but rather aiming at showing their own abilities than making a proper use of them. I have a very great love for my friend Orme, and think it uncommonly fortunate for our leader that he is under the influence of so honest and capable a man; but I wish for the sake of the public he had some more experience of business, particularly in America. I am greatly disgusted at seeing an expedition (as it is called), so ill-concerted originally in England, so improperly conducted since in America."[1]

Captain Robert Orme, of whom Shirley speaks, was aide-de-camp to Braddock, and author of a copious and excellent Journal of the expedition, now in the British Museum.[2] His portrait, painted at full length by Sir Joshua Reynolds, hangs in the National Gallery at London. He stands by his horse, a gallant young figure, with a face pale, yet rather handsome, booted to the knee, his scarlet coat, ample waistcoat, and small three-cornered hat all heavy with gold lace. The General had two other aides-de-camp, Captain Roger Morris and Colonel George Washington, whom he had invited, in terms that do him honor, to become one of his military family.

It has been said that Braddock despised not only provincials, but Indians. Nevertheless he took some pains to secure their aid, and complained that Indian affairs had been so ill conducted by the provinces that it was hard to gain their confidence. This was true; the tribes had been alienated by gross neglect. Had they been protected from injustice and soothed by attentions and presents, the Five Nations, Delawares, and Shawanoes would have been retained as friends. But their complaints had been slighted, and every gift begrudged. The trader Croghan brought, however, about fifty warriors, with as many women and children, to the camp at Fort Cumberland. They were objects of great curiosity to the soldiers, who gazed with astonishment on their faces, painted red, yellow, and black, their ears slit and hung with pendants, and their

---

[1] *Shirley the younger to Morris, 23 May, 1755*, in *Colonial Records of Pa.*, VI. 404.

[2] Printed by Sargent, in his excellent monograph of Braddock's Expedition.

heads close shaved, except the feathered scalp-lock at the crown. "In the day," says an officer, "they are in our camp, and in the night they go into their own, where they dance and make a most horrible noise." Braddock received them several times in his tent, ordered the guard to salute them, made them speeches, caused cannon to be fired and drums and fifes to play in their honor, regaled them with rum, and gave them a bullock for a feast; whereupon, being much pleased, they danced a war-dance, described by one spectator as "droll and odd, showing how they scalp and fight;" after which, says another, "they set up the most horrid song or cry that ever I heard."[1] These warriors, with a few others, promised the General to join him on the march; but he apparently grew tired of them, for a famous chief, called Scarroyaddy, afterwards complained: "He looked upon us as dogs, and would never hear anything that we said to him." Only eight of them remained with him to the end.[2]

Another ally appeared at the camp. This was a personage long known in Western fireside story as Captain Jack, the Black Hunter, or the Black Rifle. It was said of him that, having been a settler on the farthest frontier, in the Valley of the Juniata, he returned one evening to his cabin and found it burned to the ground by Indians, and the bodies of his wife and children lying among the ruins. He vowed undying vengeance, raised a band of kindred spirits, dressed and painted like Indians, and became the scourge of the red man and the champion of the white. But he and his wild crew, useful as they might have been, shocked Braddock's sense of military fitness; and he received them so coldly that they left him.[3]

It was the tenth of June before the army was well on its march. Three hundred axemen led the way, to cut and clear the road; and the long train of packhorses, wagons, and cannon toiled on behind, over the stumps, roots, and stones of the narrow track, the regulars and provincials marching in the forest close on either side. Squads of men were thrown out

[1] *Journal of a Naval Officer*, in Sargent. *The Expedition of Major-General Braddock, being Extracts of Letters from an Officer* (London, 1755).

[2] *Statement of George Croghan*, in Sargent, appendix iii.

[3] See several traditional accounts and contemporary letters in *Hazard's Pennsylvania Register*, IV, 389, 390, 416; V. 191.

on the flanks, and scouts ranged the woods to guard against surprise; for, with all his scorn of Indians and Canadians, Braddock did not neglect reasonable precautions. Thus, foot by foot, they advanced into the waste of lonely mountains that divided the streams flowing to the Atlantic from those flowing to the Gulf of Mexico, — a realm of forests ancient as the world. The road was but twelve feet wide, and the line of march often extended four miles. It was like a thin, long party-colored snake, red, blue, and brown, trailing slowly through the depth of leaves, creeping round inaccessible heights, crawling over ridges, moving always in dampness and shadow, by rivulets and waterfalls, crags and chasms, gorges and shaggy steeps. In glimpses only, through jagged boughs and flickering leaves, did this wild primeval world reveal itself, with its dark green mountains, flecked with the morning mist, and its distant summits pencilled in dreamy blue. The army passed the main Alleghany, Meadow Mountain, and Great Savage Mountain, and traversed the funereal pine-forest afterwards called the Shades of Death. No attempt was made to interrupt their march, though the commandant of Fort Duquesne had sent out parties for that purpose. A few French and Indians hovered about them, now and then scalping a straggler or inscribing filthy insults on trees; while others fell upon the border settlements which the advance of the troops had left defenceless. Here they were more successful, butchering about thirty persons, chiefly women and children.

It was the eighteenth of June before the army reached a place called the Little Meadows, less than thirty miles from Fort Cumberland. Fever and dysentery among the men, and the weakness and worthlessness of many of the horses, joined to the extreme difficulty of the road, so retarded them that they could move scarcely more than three miles a day. Braddock consulted with Washington, who advised him to leave the heavy baggage to follow as it could, and push forward with a body of chosen troops. This counsel was given in view of a report that five hundred regulars were on the way to reinforce Fort Duquesne. It was adopted. Colonel Dunbar was left to command the rear division, whose powers of movement were now reduced to the lowest point. The advance corps, consisting of about twelve hundred soldiers, besides officers and drivers, began its march on the nineteenth with such artillery as was thought indispensable, thirty wagons, and a large number of packhorses. "The prospect," writes Washington to his brother, "conveyed infinite delight to my mind, though I was excessively ill at the time. But this prospect was soon clouded, and my hopes brought very low indeed when I found that, instead of pushing on with vigor without regarding a little rough road, they were halting to level every mole-hill, and to erect bridges over every brook, by which means we were four days in getting twelve miles." It was not till the seventh of July that they neared the mouth of Turtle Creek, a stream entering the Monongahela about eight miles from the French fort. The way was direct and short, but would lead them through a difficult country and a defile so perilous that Braddock resolved to ford the Monongahela to avoid this danger, and then ford it again to reach his destination.

Fort Duquesne stood on the point of land where the Alleghany and the Monongahela join to form the Ohio, and where now stands Pittsburg, with its swarming population, its restless industries, the clang of its forges, and its chimneys vomiting foul smoke into the face of heaven. At that early day a white flag fluttering over a cluster of palisades and embankments betokened the first intrusion of civilized men upon a scene which, a few months before, breathed the repose of a virgin wilderness, voiceless but for the lapping of waves upon the pebbles, or the note of some lonely bird. But now the sleep of ages was broken, and bugle and drum told the astonished forest that its doom was pronounced and its days numbered. The fort was a compact little work, solidly built and strong, compared with others on the continent. It was a square of four bastions, with the water close on two sides, and the other two protected by ravelins, ditch, glacis, and covered way. The ramparts on these sides were of squared logs, filled in with earth, and ten feet or more thick. The two water sides were enclosed by a massive stockade of upright logs, twelve feet high, mortised together and loopholed. The armament consisted of a number of small cannon mounted on the bastions. A gate and drawbridge on the east side gave

access to the area within, which was surrounded by barracks
for the soldiers, officers' quarters, the lodgings of the commandant, a guard-house, and a storehouse, all built partly of
logs and partly of boards. There were no casemates, and the
place was commanded by a high woody hill beyond the Monongahela. The forest had been cleared away to the distance of
more than a musket shot from the ramparts, and the stumps
were hacked level with the ground. Here, just outside the
ditch, bark cabins had been built for such of the troops and
Canadians as could not find room within; and the rest of the
open space was covered with Indian corn and other crops.[1]

The garrison consisted of a few companies of the regular
troops stationed permanently in the colony, and to these were
added a considerable number of Canadians. Contrecœur still
held the command.[2] Under him were three other captains,
Beaujeu, Dumas, and Ligneris. Besides the troops and Canadians, eight hundred Indian warriors, mustered from far and
near, had built their wigwams and camp-sheds on the open
ground, or under the edge of the neighboring woods,—very
little to the advantage of the young corn. Some were baptized
savages settled in Canada,—Caughnawagas from Saut St.
Louis, Abenakis from St. Francis, and Hurons from Lorette,
whose chief bore the name of Anastase, in honor of that Father of the Church. The rest were unmitigated heathen,—
Pottawattamies and Ojibwas from the northern lakes under
Charles Langlade, the same bold partisan who had led them,
three years before, to attack the Miamis at Pickawillany; Shawanoes and Mingoes from the Ohio; and Ottawas from Detroit, commanded, it is said, by that most redoubtable of
savages, Pontiac. The law of the survival of the fittest had
wrought on this heterogeneous crew through countless generations; and with the primitive Indian, the fittest was the
hardiest, fiercest, most adroit, and most wily. Baptized and
heathen alike, they had just enjoyed a diversion greatly to

[1] *M'Kinney's Description of Fort Duquesne, 1756*, in *Hazard's Pennsylvania
Register*, VIII. 318. *Letters of Robert Stobo, Hostage at Fort Duquesne, 1754*, in
Colonial Records of Pa., VI. 141, 161. Stobo's *Plan of Fort Duquesne, 1754*. *Journal of Thomas Forbes, 1755*. *Letter of Captain Haslet, 1758*, in *Olden Time*, I.
184. *Plan of Fort Duquesne* in Public Record Office.
[2] See Appendix D.

their taste. A young Pennsylvanian named James Smith, a spirited and intelligent boy of eighteen, had been waylaid by three Indians on the western borders of the province and led captive to the fort. When the party came to the edge of the clearing, his captors, who had shot and scalped his companion, raised the scalp-yell; whereupon a din of responsive whoops and firing of guns rose from all the Indian camps, and their inmates swarmed out like bees, while the French in the fort shot off muskets and cannon to honor the occasion. The unfortunate boy, the object of this obstreperous rejoicing, presently saw a multitude of savages, naked, hideously bedaubed with red, blue, black, and brown, and armed with sticks or clubs, ranging themselves in two long parallel lines, between which he was told that he must run, the faster the better, as they would beat him all the way. He ran with his best speed, under a shower of blows, and had nearly reached the end of the course, when he was knocked down. He tried to rise, but was blinded by a handful of sand thrown into his face; and then they beat him till he swooned. On coming to his senses he found himself in the fort, with the surgeon opening a vein in his arm and a crowd of French and Indians looking on. In a few days he was able to walk with the help of a stick; and, coming out from his quarters one morning, he saw a memorable scene.[1]

Three days before, an Indian had brought the report that the English were approaching; and the Chevalier de la Perade was sent out to reconnoitre.[2] He returned on the next day, the seventh, with news that they were not far distant. On the eighth the brothers Normanville went out, and found that they were within six leagues of the fort. The French were in great excitement and alarm; but Contrecœur at length took a resolution, which seems to have been inspired by Beaujeu.[3] It was determined to meet the enemy on the march, and ambuscade them if possible at the crossing of the Monongahela, or

[1] *Account of Remarkable Occurrences in the Life of Colonel James Smith, written by himself.* Perhaps the best of all the numerous narratives of captives among the Indians.

[2] *Relation de Godefroy*, in Shea, *Bataille du Malangueulé* (Monongahela).

[3] Dumas, however, declares that Beaujeu adopted the plan at his suggestion. *Dumas au Ministre, 24 Juillet, 1756.*

some other favorable spot. Beaujeu proposed the plan to the Indians, and offered them the war-hatchet; but they would not take it. "Do you want to die, my father, and sacrifice us besides?" That night they held a council, and in the morning again refused to go. Beaujeu did not despair. "I am determined," he exclaimed, "to meet the English. What! will you let your father go alone?"[1] The greater part caught fire at his words, promised to follow him, and put on their war-paint. Beaujeu received the communion, then dressed himself like a savage, and joined the clamorous throng. Open barrels of gunpowder and bullets were set before the gate of the fort, and James Smith, painfully climbing the rampart with the help of his stick, looked down on the warrior rabble as, huddling together, wild with excitement, they scooped up the contents to fill their powder-horns and pouches. Then, band after band, they filed off along the forest track that led to the ford of the Monongahela. They numbered six hundred and thirty-seven; and with them went thirty-six French officers and cadets, seventy-two regular soldiers, and a hundred and forty-six Canadians, or about nine hundred in all.[2] At eight o'clock the tumult was over. The broad clearing lay lonely and still, and Contrecœur, with what was left of his garrison, waited in suspense for the issue.

It was near one o'clock when Braddock crossed the Monongahela for the second time. If the French made a stand anywhere, it would be, he thought, at the fording-place, but Lieutenant-Colonel Gage, whom he sent across with a strong advance-party, found no enemy, and quietly took possession of the farther shore. Then the main body followed. To impose on the imagination of the French scouts, who were doubtless on the watch, the movement was made with studied regularity and order. The sun was cloudless, and the men were inspirited by the prospect of near triumph. Washington afterwards spoke with admiration of the spectacle.[3] The mu-

[1] *Relation depuis le Départ des Trouppes de Québec jusqu'au 30 du Mois de Septembre, 1755.*

[2] *Liste des Officiers, Cadets, Soldats, Miliciens, et Sauvages qui composaient le Détachement qui a été au devant d'un Corps de 2,000 Anglois à 3 Lieues du Fort Duquesne, le 9 Juillet, 1755; joint à la Lettre de M. Bigot du 6 Août, 1755.*

[3] Compare the account of another eye-witness, Dr. Walker, in *Hazard's Pennsylvania Register*, VI. 104.

sic, the banners, the mounted officers, the troop of light cavalry, the naval detachment, the red-coated regulars, the blue-coated Virginians, the wagons and tumbrils, cannon, howitzers, and coehorns, the train of packhorses, and the droves of cattle, passed in long procession through the rippling shallows, and slowly entered the bordering forest. Here, when all were over, a short halt was ordered for rest and refreshment.

Why had not Beaujeu defended the ford? This was his intention in the morning; but he had been met by obstacles, the nature of which is not wholly clear. His Indians, it seems, had proved refractory. Three hundred of them left him, went off in another direction, and did not rejoin him till the English had crossed the river.[1] Hence perhaps it was that, having left Fort Duquesne at eight o'clock, he spent half the day in marching seven miles, and was more than a mile from the fording-place when the British reached the eastern shore. The delay, from whatever cause arising, cost him the opportunity of laying an ambush either at the ford or in the gullies and ravines that channelled the forest through which Braddock was now on the point of marching.

Not far from the bank of the river, and close by the British line of march, there was a clearing and a deserted house that had once belonged to the trader Fraser. Washington remembered it well. It was here that he found rest and shelter on the winter journey homeward from his mission to Fort Le Bœuf. He was in no less need of rest at this moment; for recent fever had so weakened him that he could hardly sit his horse. From Fraser's house to Fort Duquesne the distance was eight miles by a rough path, along which the troops were now beginning to move after their halt. It ran inland for a little; then curved to the left, and followed a course parallel to the river along the base of a line of steep hills that here bordered the valley. These and all the country were buried in dense and heavy forest, choked with bushes and the carcases of fallen trees. Braddock has been charged with marching blindly into an ambuscade; but it was not so. There was no ambuscade; and had there been one, he would have found it. It is true that he did not reconnoitre the woods very far in advance of the head of the column; yet, with this exception,

[1] *Relation de Godefroy*, in Shea, *Bataille du Malangueulé.*

he made elaborate dispositions to prevent surprise. Several guides, with six Virginian light horsemen, led the way. Then, a musket-shot behind, came the vanguard; then three hundred soldiers under Gage; then a large body of axemen, under Sir John Sinclair, to open the road; then two cannon with tumbrils and tool-wagons; and lastly the rear-guard, closing the line, while flanking-parties ranged the woods on both sides. This was the advance-column. The main body followed with little or no interval. The artillery and wagons moved along the road, and the troops filed through the woods close on either hand. Numerous flanking-parties were thrown out a hundred yards and more to right and left; while, in the space between them and the marching column, the pack horses and cattle, with their drivers, made their way painfully among the trees and thickets; since, had they been allowed to follow the road, the line of march would have been too long for mutual support. A body of regulars and provincials brought up the rear.

Gage, with his advance-column, had just passed a wide and bushy ravine that crossed their path, and the van of the main column was on the point of entering it, when the guides and light horsemen in the front suddenly fell back; and the engineer, Gordon, then engaged in marking out the road, saw a man, dressed like an Indian, but wearing the gorget of an officer, bounding forward along the path.[1] He stopped when he discovered the head of the column, turned, and waved his hat. The forest behind was swarming with French and savages. At the signal of the officer, who was probably Beaujeu, they yelled the war-whoop, spread themselves to right and left, and opened a sharp fire under cover of the trees. Gage's column wheeled deliberately into line, and fired several volleys with great steadiness against the now invisible assailants. Few of them were hurt; the trees caught the shot, but the noise was deafening under the dense arches of the forest. The greater part of the Canadians, to borrow the words of Dumas, "fled shamefully, crying 'Sauve qui peut!' "[2] Volley followed volley, and at the third Beaujeu dropped dead. Gage's

---

[1] *Journal of the Proceeding of the Detachment of Seamen*, in Sargent.

[2] *Dumas au Ministre, 24 Juillet, 1756. Contrecœur à Vaudreuil, 14 Juillet, 1755.* See Appendix D, where extracts are given.

two cannon were now brought to bear, on which the Indians, like the Canadians, gave way in confusion, but did not, like them, abandon the field. The close scarlet ranks of the English were plainly to be seen through the trees and the smoke; they were moving forward, cheering lustily, and shouting "God save the King!" Dumas, now chief in command, thought that all was lost. "I advanced," he says, "with the assurance that comes from despair, exciting by voice and gesture the few soldiers that remained. The fire of my platoon was so sharp that the enemy seemed astonished." The Indians, encouraged, began to rally. The French officers who commanded them showed admirable courage and address; and while Dumas and Ligneris, with the regulars and what was left of the Canadians, held the ground in front, the savage warriors, screeching their war-cries, swarmed through the forest along both flanks of the English, hid behind trees, bushes, and fallen trunks, or crouched in gullies and ravines, and opened a deadly fire on the helpless soldiery, who, themselves completely visible, could see no enemy, and wasted volley after volley on the impassive trees. The most destructive fire came from a hill on the English right, where the Indians lay in multitudes, firing from their lurking-places on the living target below. But the invisible death was everywhere, in front, flank, and rear. The British cheer was heard no more. The troops broke their ranks and huddled together in a bewildered mass, shrinking from the bullets that cut them down by scores.

When Braddock heard the firing in the front, he pushed forward with the main body to the support of Gage, leaving four hundred men in the rear, under Sir Peter Halket, to guard the baggage. At the moment of his arrival Gage's soldiers had abandoned their two cannon, and were falling back to escape the concentrated fire of the Indians. Meeting the advancing troops, they tried to find cover behind them. This threw the whole into confusion. The men of the two regiments became mixed together; and in a short time the entire force, except the Virginians and the troops left with Halket, were massed in several dense bodies within a small space of ground, facing some one way and some another, and all alike exposed without shelter to the bullets that pelted them like hail. Both men and officers were new to this blind and frightful warfare of the savage in his native woods. To charge the

Indians in their hiding-places would have been useless. They would have eluded pursuit with the agility of wildcats, and swarmed back, like angry hornets, the moment that it ceased. The Virginians alone were equal to the emergency. Fighting behind trees like the Indians themselves, they might have held the enemy in check till order could be restored, had not Braddock, furious at a proceeding that shocked all his ideas of courage and discipline, ordered them, with oaths, to form into line. A body of them under Captain Waggoner made a dash for a fallen tree lying in the woods, far out towards the lurking-places of the Indians, and, crouching behind the huge trunk, opened fire; but the regulars, seeing the smoke among the bushes, mistook their best friends for the enemy, shot at them from behind, killed many, and forced the rest to return. A few of the regulars also tried in their clumsy way to fight behind trees; but Braddock beat them with his sword, and compelled them to stand with the rest, an open mark for the Indians. The panic increased; the soldiers crowded together, and the bullets spent themselves in a mass of human bodies. Commands, entreaties, and threats were lost upon them. "We would fight," some of them answered, "if we could see anybody to fight with." Nothing was visible but puffs of smoke. Officers and men who had stood all the afternoon under fire afterwards declared that they could not be sure they had seen a single Indian. Braddock ordered Lieutenant-Colonel Burton to attack the hill where the puffs of smoke were thickest, and the bullets most deadly. With infinite difficulty that brave officer induced a hundred men to follow him; but he was soon disabled by a wound, and they all faced about. The artillerymen stood for some time by their guns, which did great damage to the trees and little to the enemy. The mob of soldiers, stupefied with terror, stood panting, their foreheads beaded with sweat, loading and firing mechanically, sometimes into the air, sometimes among their own comrades, many of whom they killed. The ground, strewn with dead and wounded men, the bounding of maddened horses, the clatter and roar of musketry and cannon, mixed with the spiteful report of rifles and the yells that rose from the indefatigable throats of six hundred unseen savages, formed a chaos of anguish and terror scarcely paralleled even in Indian war. "I cannot describe the horrors of that scene," one of Braddock's officers wrote three weeks after; "no pen could do it. The yell of the Indians is fresh on my ear, and the terrific sound will haunt me till the hour of my dissolution."[1]

Braddock showed a furious intrepidity. Mounted on horse-back, he dashed to and fro, storming like a madman. Four horses were shot under him, and he mounted a fifth. Washington seconded his chief with equal courage; he too no doubt using strong language, for he did not measure words when the fit was on him. He escaped as by miracle. Two horses were killed under him, and four bullets tore his clothes. The conduct of the British officers was above praise. Nothing could surpass their undaunted self-devotion; and in their vain attempts to lead on the men, the havoc among them was frightful. Sir Peter Halket was shot dead. His son, a lieutenant in his regiment, stooping to raise the body of his father, was shot dead in turn. Young Shirley, Braddock's secretary, was pierced through the brain. Orme and Morris, his aides-de-camp, Sinclair, the quartermaster-general, Gates and Gage, both afterwards conspicuous on opposite sides in the War of the Revolution, and Gladwin, who, eight years later, defended Detroit against Pontiac, were all wounded. Of eighty-six officers, sixty-three were killed or disabled;[2] while out of thirteen hundred and seventy-three non-commissioned officers and privates, only four hundred and fifty-nine came off unharmed.[1]

Braddock saw that all was lost. To save the wreck of his force from annihilation, he at last commanded a retreat; and as he and such of his officers as were left strove to withdraw the half-frenzied crew in some semblance of order, a bullet struck him down. The gallant bulldog fell from his horse, shot through the arm into the lungs. It is said, though on

[1] *Leslie to a Merchant of Philadelphia, 30 July, 1755*, in *Hazard's Pennsylvania Register*, V. 191. Leslie was a lieutenant of the Forty-fourth.

[2] *A List of the Officers who were present, and of those killed and wounded, in the Action on the Banks of the Monongahela, 9 July, 1755* (Public Record Office, *America and West Indies*, LXXXII.).

[3] Statement of the engineer, Mackellar. By another account, out of a total, officers and men, of 1,460, the number of all ranks who escaped was 583. Braddock's force, originally 1,200, was increased, a few days before the battle, by detachments from Dunbar.

evidence of no weight, that the bullet came from one of his own men. Be this as it may, there he lay among the bushes, bleeding, gasping, unable even to curse. He demanded to be left where he was. Captain Stewart and another provincial bore him between them to the rear.

It was about this time that the mob of soldiers, having been three hours under fire, and having spent their ammunition, broke away in a blind frenzy, rushed back towards the ford, "and when," says Washington, "we endeavored to rally them, it was with as much success as if we had attempted to stop the wild bears of the mountains." They dashed across, helter-skelter, plunging through the water to the farther bank, leaving wounded comrades, cannon, baggage, the military chest, and the General's papers, a prey to the Indians. About fifty of these followed to the edge of the river. Dumas and Ligneris, who had now only about twenty Frenchmen with them, made no attempt to pursue, and went back to the fort, because, says Contrecœur, so many of the Canadians had "retired at the first fire." The field, abandoned to the savages, was a pandemonium of pillage and murder.[1]

---

[1] "Nous prîmes le parti de nous retirer en vue de rallier notre petite armée." *Dumas au Ministre, 24 Juillet, 1755.*

On the defeat of Braddock, besides authorities already cited,— *Shirley to Robinson, 5 Nov. 1755,* accompanying the plans of the battle reproduced in this volume (Public Record Office, *America and West Indies,* LXXXII.). The plans were drawn at Shirley's request by Patrick Mackellar, chief engineer of the expedition, who was with Gage in the advance column when the fight began. They were examined and fully approved by the chief surviving officers, and they closely correspond with another plan made by the aide-de-camp Orme,—which, however, shows only the beginning of the affair.

Report of the Court of Inquiry into the Behavior of the Troops at the Monongahela. Letters of Dinwiddie. Letters of Gage. Burd to Morris, 25 July, 1755. Sinclair to Robinson, 3 Sept. Rutherford to ———, 12 July. Writings of Washington, II. 68–93. *Review of Military Operations in North America.* Entick, I. 145. *Gentleman's Magazine* (1755), 378, 426. *Letter to a Friend on the Ohio Defeat* (Boston, 1755).

Contrecœur à Vaudreuil, 14 Juillet, 1755. Estat de l'Artillerie, etc., qui se sont trouvés sur le Champ de Bataille. Vaudreuil au Ministre, 5 Août, 1755. Bigot au Ministre, 27 Août. Relation du Combat du 9 Juillet. Relation depuis le Départ des Trouppes de Québec jusqu'au 30 du Mois de Septembre. Lotbinière à d'Argenson, 24 Oct. Relation officielle imprimée au Louvre. Relation de Godefroy (Shea). *Extraits du Registre du Fort Duquesne (Ibid.). Relation de diverses Mouvements (Ibid.).* Pouchot, I. 37.

James Smith, the young prisoner at Fort Duquesne, had passed a day of suspense, waiting the result. "In the afternoon I again observed a great noise and commotion in the fort, and, though at that time I could not understand French, I found it was the voice of joy and triumph, and feared that they had received what I called bad news. I had observed some of the old-country soldiers speak Dutch; as I spoke Dutch, I went to one of them and asked him what was the news. He told me that a runner had just arrived who said that Braddock would certainly be defeated; that the Indians and French had surrounded him, and were concealed behind trees and in gullies, and kept a constant fire upon the English; and that they saw the English falling in heaps; and if they did not take the river, which was the only gap, and make their escape, there would not be one man left alive before sundown. Some time after this, I heard a number of scalp-halloos, and saw a company of Indians and French coming in. I observed they had a great number of bloody scalps, grenadiers' caps, British canteens, bayonets, etc., with them. They brought the news that Braddock was defeated. After that another company came in, which appeared to be about one hundred, and chiefly Indians; and it seemed to me that almost every one of this company was carrying scalps. After this came another company with a number of wagon-horses, and also a great many scalps. Those that were coming in and those that had arrived kept a constant firing of small arms, and also the great guns in the fort, which were accompanied with the most hideous shouts and yells from all quarters, so that it appeared to me as though the infernal regions had broke loose.

"About sundown I beheld a small party coming in with about a dozen prisoners, stripped naked, with their hands tied behind their backs and their faces and parts of their bodies blacked; these prisoners they burned to death on the bank of Alleghany River, opposite the fort. I stood on the fort wall until I beheld them begin to burn one of these men; they had him tied to a stake, and kept touching him with firebrands, red-hot irons, etc., and he screaming in a most doleful manner, the Indians in the meantime yelling like infernal spirits. As this scene appeared too shocking for me to behold, I retired to my lodging, both sore and sorry. When I came into my lodgings I saw Russel's *Seven Sermons*, which they had brought from the field of battle, which a Frenchman made a present of to me."

The loss of the French was slight, but fell chiefly on the officers, three of whom were killed, and four wounded. Of the regular soldiers, all but four escaped untouched. The Canadians suffered still less, in proportion to their numbers, only five of them being hurt. The Indians, who won the victory, bore the principal loss. Of those from Canada, twenty-seven were killed and wounded; while the casualties among the Western tribes are not reported.[1] All of these last went off the next morning with their plunder and scalps, leaving Contrecœur in great anxiety lest the remnant of Braddock's troops, reinforced by the division under Dunbar, should attack him again. His doubts would have vanished had he known the condition of his defeated enemy.

In the pain and languor of a mortal wound, Braddock showed unflinching resolution. His bearers stopped with him at a favorable spot beyond the Monongahela; and here he hoped to maintain his position till the arrival of Dunbar. By the efforts of the officers about a hundred men were collected around him; but to keep them there was impossible. Within an hour they abandoned him, and fled like the rest. Gage, however, succeeded in rallying about eighty beyond the other fording-place; and Washington, on an order from Braddock, spurred his jaded horse towards the camp of Dunbar to demand wagons, provisions, and hospital stores.

Fright overcame fatigue. The fugitives toiled on all night, pursued by spectres of horror and despair; hearing still the war-whoops and the shrieks; possessed with the one thought of escape from this wilderness of death. In the morning some order was restored. Braddock was placed on a horse; then, the pain being insufferable, he was carried on a litter, Captain Orme having bribed the carriers by the promise of a guinea and a bottle of rum apiece. Early in the succeeding night, such as had not fainted on the way reached the deserted farm of Gist. Here they met wagons and provisions, with a detachment of soldiers sent by Dunbar, whose camp was six miles

---

[1] *Liste des Officiers, Soldats, Miliciens, et Sauvages de Canada qui ont été tués et blessés le 9 Juillet, 1755.*

farther on; and Braddock ordered them to go to the relief of the stragglers left behind.

At noon of that day a number of wagoners and packhorse-drivers had come to Dunbar's camp with wild tidings of rout and ruin. More fugitives followed; and soon after a wounded officer was brought in upon a sheet. The drums beat to arms. The camp was in commotion; and many soldiers and teamsters took to flight, in spite of the sentinels, who tried in vain to stop them.[1] There was a still more disgraceful scene on the next day, after Braddock, with the wreck of his force, had arrived. Orders were given to destroy such of the wagons, stores, and ammunition as could not be carried back at once to Fort Cumberland. Whether Dunbar or the dying General gave these orders is not clear; but it is certain that they were executed with shameful alacrity. More than a hundred wagons were burned; cannon, coehorns, and shells were burst or buried; barrels of gunpowder were staved, and the contents thrown into a brook; provisions were scattered through the woods and swamps. Then the whole command began its retreat over the mountains to Fort Cumberland, sixty miles distant. This proceeding, for which, in view of the condition of Braddock, Dunbar must be held answerable, excited the utmost indignation among the colonists. If he could not advance, they thought, he might at least have fortified himself and held his ground till the provinces could send him help; thus covering the frontier, and holding French war-parties in check.

Braddock's last moment was near. Orme, who, though himself severely wounded, was with him till his death, told Franklin that he was totally silent all the first day, and at night said only, "Who would have thought it?" that all the next day he was again silent, till at last he muttered, "We shall better know how to deal with them another time," and died a few minutes after. He had nevertheless found breath to give orders at Gist's for the succor of the men who had dropped on the road. It is said, too, that in his last hours "he could not bear the sight of a red coat," but murmured praises of "the blues," or Virginians, and said that he hoped he should live

[1] *Depositions of Matthew Laird, Michael Hoover, and Jacob Hoover, Wagoners*, in *Colonial Records of Pa.*, VI. 482.

to reward them.[1] He died at about eight o'clock in the evening of Sunday, the thirteenth. Dunbar had begun his retreat that morning, and was then encamped near the Great Meadows. On Monday the dead commander was buried in the road; and men, horses, and wagons passed over his grave, effacing every sign of it, lest the Indians should find and mutilate the body.

Colonel James Innes, commanding at Fort Cumberland, where a crowd of invalids with soldiers' wives and other women had been left when the expedition marched, heard of the defeat, only two days after it happened, from a wagoner who had fled from the field on horseback. He at once sent a note of six lines to Lord Fairfax: "I have this moment received the most melancholy news of the defeat of our troops, the General killed, and numbers of our officers; our whole artillery taken. In short, the account I have received is so very bad, that as, please God, I intend to make a stand here, 't is highly necessary to raise the militia everywhere to defend the frontiers." A boy whom he sent out on horseback met more fugitives, and came back on the fourteenth with reports as vague and disheartening as the first. Innes sent them to Dinwiddie.[2] Some days after, Dunbar and his train arrived in miserable disorder, and Fort Cumberland was turned into a hospital for the shattered fragments of a routed and ruined army.

On the sixteenth a letter was brought in haste to one Buchanan at Carlisle, on the Pennsylvanian frontier:—

> SIR,—I thought it proper to let you know that I was in the battle where we were defeated. And we had about eleven hundred and fifty private men, besides officers and others. And we were attacked the ninth day about twelve o'clock, and held till about three in the afternoon, and then we were forced to retreat, when I suppose we might bring off about three hundred whole men, besides a vast many wounded. Most of our officers were either wounded or killed; General Braddock is wounded, but I hope not mortal; and Sir John Sinclair and many others, but I hope not

---

[1] *Bolling to his Son, 13 Aug. 1755.* Bolling was a Virginian gentleman whose son was at school in England.

[2] *Innes to Dinwiddie, 14 July, 1755.*

mortal. All the train is cut off in a manner. Sir Peter Halket and his son, Captain Polson, Captain Gethen, Captain Rose, Captain Tatten killed, and many others. Captain Ord of the train is wounded, but I hope not mortal. We lost all our artillery entirely, and everything else.

To Mr. John Smith and Buchannon, and give it to the next post, and let him show this to Mr. George Gibson in Lancaster, and Mr. Bingham, at the sign of the Ship, and you'll oblige,

Yours to command,

JOHN CAMPBELL, *Messenger.*[1]

The evil tidings quickly reached Philadelphia, where such confidence had prevailed that certain over-zealous persons had begun to collect money for fireworks to celebrate the victory. Two of these, brother physicians named Bond, came to Franklin and asked him to subscribe; but the sage looked doubtful. "Why, the devil!" said one of them, "you surely don't suppose the fort will not be taken?" He reminded them that war is always uncertain; and the subscription was deferred.[2] The Governor laid the news of the disaster before his Council, telling them at the same time that his opponents in the Assembly would not believe it, and had insulted him in the street for giving it currency.[3]

Dinwiddie remained tranquil at Williamsburg, sure that all would go well. The brief note of Innes, forwarded by Lord Fairfax, first disturbed his dream of triumph; but on second thought he took comfort. "I am willing to think that account was from a deserter who, in a great panic, represented what his fears suggested. I wait with impatience for another express from Fort Cumberland, which I expect will greatly contradict the former." The news got abroad, and the slaves showed signs of excitement. "The villany of the negroes on any emergency is what I always feared," continues the Governor. "An example of one or two at first may prevent these creatures entering into combinations and wicked designs."[4] And he

---

[1] *Colonial Records of Pa.*, VI. 481

[2] *Autobiography of Franklin.*

[3] *Colonial Records of Pa.*, VI. 480.

[4] *Dinwiddie to Colonel Charles Carter, 18 July, 1755.*

wrote to Lord Halifax: "The negro slaves have been very audacious on the news of defeat on the Ohio. These poor creatures imagine the French will give them their freedom. We
have too many here; but I hope we shall be able to keep them
in proper subjection." Suspense grew intolerable. "It's monstrous they should be so tardy and dilatory in sending down
any farther account." He sent Major Colin Campbell for
news; when, a day or two later, a courier brought him two
letters, one from Orme, and the other from Washington,
both written at Fort Cumberland on the eighteenth. The letter of Orme began thus: "My dear Governor, I am so extremely ill in bed with the wound I have received that I am
under the necessity of employing my friend Captain Dobson
as my scribe." Then he told the wretched story of defeat and
humiliation. "The officers were absolutely sacrificed by their
unparalleled good behavior; advancing before their men
sometimes in bodies, and sometimes separately, hoping by
such an example to engage the soldiers to follow them; but
to no purpose. Poor Shirley was shot through the head, Captain Morris very much wounded. Mr. Washington had two
horses shot under him, and his clothes shot through in several
places; behaving the whole time with the greatest courage
and resolution."

Washington wrote more briefly, saying that, as Orme was
giving a full account of the affair, it was needless for him to
repeat it. Like many others in the fight, he greatly underrated
the force of the enemy, which he placed at three hundred, or
about a third of the actual number,—a natural error, as most
of the assailants were invisible. "Our poor Virginians behaved
like men, and died like soldiers; for I believe that out of three
companies that were there that day, scarce thirty were left
alive. Captain Peronney and all his officers down to a corporal
were killed. Captain Polson shared almost as hard a fate, for
only one of his escaped. In short, the dastardly behavior of
the English soldiers exposed all those who were inclined to
do their duty to almost certain death. It is imagined (I believe
with great justice, too) that two thirds of both killed and
wounded received their shots from our own cowardly dogs
of soldiers, who gathered themselves into a body, contrary to

orders, ten and twelve deep, would then level, fire, and shoot down the men before them."[1]

To Orme, Dinwiddie replied: "I read your letter with tears in my eyes; but it gave me much pleasure to see your name at the bottom, and more so when I observed by the postscript that your wound is not dangerous. But pray, dear sir, is it not possible by a second attempt to retrieve the great loss we have sustained? I presume the General's chariot is at the fort. In it you may come here, and my house is heartily at your command. Pray take care of your valuable health; keep your spirits up, and I doubt not of your recovery. My wife and girls join me in most sincere respects and joy at your being so well, and I always am, with great truth, dear friend, your affectionate humble servant."

To Washington he is less effusive, though he had known him much longer. He begins, it is true, "Dear Washington," and congratulates him on his escape; but soon grows formal, and asks: "Pray, sir, with the number of them remaining, is there no possibility of doing something on the other side of the mountains before the winter months? Surely you must mistake. Colonel Dunbar will not march to winter-quarters in the middle of summer, and leave the frontiers exposed to the invasions of the enemy! No; he is a better officer, and I have a different opinion of him. I sincerely wish you health and happiness, and am, with great respect, sir, your obedient, humble servant."

Washington's letter had contained the astonishing announcement that Dunbar meant to abandon the frontier and march to Philadelphia. Dinwiddie, much disturbed, at once wrote to that officer, though without betraying any knowledge of his intention. "Sir, the melancholy account of the defeat of our forces gave me a sensible and real concern"—on which he enlarges for a while; then suddenly changes style: "Dear Colonel, is there no method left to retrieve the dishonor done to the British arms? As you now command all the forces that remain, are you not able, after a proper re-

---

[1] These extracts are taken from the two letters preserved in the Public Record Office, *America and West Indies*, LXXIV. LXXXII.

freshment of your men, to make a second attempt? You have four months now to come of the best weather of the year for such an expedition. What a fine field for honor will Colonel Dunbar have to confirm and establish his character as a brave officer." Then, after suggesting plans of operation, and entering into much detail, the fervid Governor concludes: "It gives me great pleasure that under our great loss and misfortunes the command devolves on an officer of so great military judgment and established character. With my sincere respect and hearty wishes for success to all your proceedings, I am, worthy sir, your most obedient, humble servant."

Exhortation and flattery were lost on Dunbar. Dinwiddie received from him in reply a short, dry note, dated on the first of August, and acquainting him that he should march for Philadelphia on the second. This, in fact, he did, leaving the fort to be defended by invalids and a few Virginians. "I acknowledge," says Dinwiddie, "I was not brought up to arms; but I think common sense would have prevailed not to leave the frontiers exposed after having opened a road over the mountains to the Ohio, by which the enemy can the more easily invade us. . . . Your great colonel," he writes to Orme, "is gone to a peaceful colony, and left our frontiers open. . . . The whole conduct of Colonel Dunbar appears to me monstrous. . . . To march off all the regulars, and leave the fort and frontiers to be defended by four hundred sick and wounded, and the poor remains of our provincial forces, appears to me absurd."[1]

He found some comfort from the burgesses, who gave him forty thousand pounds, and would, he thinks, have given a hundred thousand if another attempt against Fort Duquesne had been set afoot. Shirley, too, whom the death of Braddock had made commander-in-chief, approved the Governor's plan of renewing offensive operations, and instructed Dunbar to that effect; ordering him, however, should they prove impracticable, to march for Albany in aid of the Niagara expedition.[2] The order found him safe in Philadelphia. Here he

---

[1] Dinwiddie's view of Dunbar's conduct is fully justified by the letters of Shirley, Governor Morris, and Dunbar himself.

[2] *Orders for Colonel Thomas Dunbar, 12 Aug. 1755.* These supersede a previous order of August 6, by which Shirley had directed Dunbar to march northward at once.

lingered for a while; then marched to join the northern army, moving at a pace which made it certain that he could not arrive in time to be of the least use.

Thus the frontier was left unguarded; and soon, as Dinwiddie had foreseen, there burst upon it a storm of blood and fire.

Chapter VIII

1755–1763

REMOVAL OF THE ACADIANS

*State of Acadia • Threatened Invasion • Peril of the English •
Their Plans • French Forts to be attacked • Beauséjour and its
Occupants • French Treatment of the Acadians • John Winslow •
Siege and Capture of Beauséjour • Attitude of Acadians • Influ-
ence of their Priests • They refuse the Oath of Allegiance • Their
Condition and Character • Pretended Neutrals • Moderation of
English Authorities • The Acadians Persist in their Refusal • Ene-
mies or Subjects? • Choice of the Acadians • The Consequence •
Their Removal determined • Winslow at Grand Pré • Conference
with Murray • Summons to the Inhabitants • Their Seizure •
Their Embarkation • Their Fate • Their Treatment in Canada •
Misapprehension concerning them*

B Y THE PLAN which the Duke of Cumberland had ordained and Braddock had announced in the Council at
Alexandria, four blows were to be struck at once to force back
the French boundaries, lop off the dependencies of Canada,
and reduce her from a vast territory to a petty province. The
first stroke had failed, and had shattered the hand of the
striker; it remains to see what fortune awaited the others.

It was long since a project of purging Acadia of French
influence had germinated in the fertile mind of Shirley. We
have seen in a former chapter the condition of that afflicted
province. Several thousands of its inhabitants, wrought upon
by intriguing agents of the French Government; taught by
their priests that fidelity to King Louis was inseparable from
fidelity to God, and that to swear allegiance to the British
Crown was eternal perdition; threatened with plunder and
death at the hands of the savages whom the ferocious missionary, Le Loutre, held over them in terror,—had abandoned, sometimes willingly, but oftener under constraint,
the fields which they and their fathers had tilled, and crossing
the boundary line of the Missaguash, had placed themselves
under the French flag planted on the hill of Beauséjour.[1]

[1] See *ante*, Chapter IV.

Here, or in the neighborhood, many of them had remained, wretched and half starved; while others had been transported to Cape Breton, Isle St. Jean, or the coasts of the Gulf,—not so far, however, that they could not on occasion be used to aid in an invasion of British Acadia.[1] Those of their countrymen who still lived under the British flag were chiefly the inhabitants of the district of Mines and of the valley of the River Annapolis, who, with other less important settlements, numbered a little more than nine thousand souls. We have shown already, by the evidence of the French themselves, that neither they nor their emigrant countrymen had been oppressed or molested in matters temporal or spiritual, but that the English authorities, recognizing their value as an industrious population, had labored to reconcile them to a change of rulers which on the whole was to their advantage. It has been shown also how, with a heartless perfidy and a reckless disregard of their welfare and safety, the French Government and its agents labored to keep them hostile to the Crown of which it had acknowledged them to be subjects. The result was, that though they did not, like their emigrant countrymen, abandon their homes, they remained in a state of restless disaffection, refused to supply English garrisons with provisions, except at most exorbitant rates, smuggled their produce to the French across the line, gave them aid and intelligence, and sometimes, disguised as Indians, robbed and murdered English settlers. By the new-fangled construction of the treaty of Utrecht which the French boundary commissioners had devised,[2] more than half the Acadian peninsula, including nearly all the cultivated land and nearly all the population of French descent, was claimed as belonging to France, though England had held possession of it more than forty years. Hence, according to the political ethics adopted at the time by both

[1] Rameau (*La France aux Colonies*, I. 63), estimates the total emigration from 1748 to 1755 at 8,600 souls,—which number seems much too large. This writer, though vehemently anti-English, gives the following passage from a letter of a high French official: "que les Acadiens émigrés et en grande misère comptaient se retirer à Québec et demander des terres, mais il conviendrait mieux qu'ils restent où ils sont, afin d'avoir le voisinage de l'Acadie bien peuplé et défriché, pour approvisionner l'Isle Royale [*Cape Breton*] et tomber en cas de guerre sur l'Acadie." Rameau, I. 133.

[2] *Supra*, pp. 928–29.

nations, it would be lawful for France to reclaim it by force. England, on her part, it will be remembered, claimed vast tracts beyond the isthmus; and, on the same pretext, held that she might rightfully seize them and capture Beauséjour, with the other French garrisons that guarded them.

On the part of France, an invasion of the Acadian peninsula seemed more than likely. Honor demanded of her that, having incited the Acadians to disaffection, and so brought on them the indignation of the English authorities, she should intervene to save them from the consequences. Moreover the loss of the Acadian peninsula had been gall and wormwood to her; and in losing it she had lost great material advantages. Its possession was necessary to connect Canada with the Island of Cape Breton and the fortress of Louisbourg. Its fertile fields and agricultural people would furnish subsistence to the troops and garrisons in the French maritime provinces, now dependent on supplies illicitly brought by New England traders, and liable to be cut off in time of war when they were needed most. The harbors of Acadia, too, would be invaluable as naval stations from which to curb and threaten the northern English colonies. Hence the intrigues so assiduously practised to keep the Acadians French at heart, and ready to throw off British rule at any favorable moment. British officers believed that should a French squadron with a sufficient force of troops on board appear in the Bay of Fundy, the whole population on the Basin of Mines and along the Annapolis would rise in arms, and that the emigrants beyond the isthmus, armed and trained by French officers, would come to their aid. This emigrant population, famishing in exile, looked back with regret to the farms they had abandoned; and, prevented as they were by Le Loutre and his colleagues from making their peace with the English, they would, if confident of success, have gladly joined an invading force to regain their homes by reconquering Acadia for Louis XV. In other parts of the continent it was the interest of France to put off hostilities; if Acadia alone had been in question, it would have been her interest to precipitate them.

Her chances of success were good. The French could at any time send troops from Louisbourg or Quebec to join those maintained upon the isthmus; and they had on their side of the lines a force of militia and Indians amounting to about two thousand, while the Acadians within the peninsula had about an equal number of fighting men who, while calling themselves neutrals, might be counted on to join the invaders. The English were in no condition to withstand such an attack. Their regular troops were scattered far and wide through the province, and were nowhere more than equal to the local requirement; while of militia, except those of Halifax, they had few or none whom they dared to trust. Their fort at Annapolis was weak and dilapidated, and their other posts were mere stockades. The strongest place in Acadia was the French fort of Beauséjour, in which the English saw a continual menace.

Their apprehensions were well grounded. Duquesne, governor of Canada, wrote to Le Loutre, who virtually shared the control of Beauséjour with Vergor, its commandant: "I invite both yourself and M. Vergor to devise a plausible pretext for attacking them [*the English*] vigorously."[1] Three weeks after this letter was written, Lawrence, governor of Nova Scotia, wrote to Shirley from Halifax: "Being well informed that the French have designs of encroaching still farther upon His Majesty's rights in this province, and that they propose, the moment they have repaired the fortifications of Louisbourg, to attack our fort at Chignecto [*Fort Lawrence*], I think it high time to make some effort to drive them from the north side of the Bay of Fundy."[2] This letter was brought to Boston by Lieutenant-Colonel Monckton, who was charged by Lawrence to propose to Shirley the raising of two thousand men in New England for the attack of Beauséjour and its dependent forts. Almost at the moment when Lawrence was writing these proposals to Shirley, Shirley was writing with the same object to Lawrence, enclosing a letter from Sir Thomas Robinson, concerning which he said: "I construe the contents to be orders to us to act in concert for taking *any* advantages to drive the French of Canada out of Nova Scotia. If that is your sense of them, and your honor will be

---

[1] *Duquesne à Le Loutre, 15 Oct. 1754*; extract in *Public Documents of Nova Scotia*, 239.

[2] *Lawrence to Shirley, 5 Nov. 1754. Instructions of Lawrence to Monckton, 7 Nov. 1754.*

pleased to let me know whether you want any and what assistance to enable you to execute the orders, I will endeavor to send you such assistance from this province as you shall want."[1]

The letter of Sir Thomas Robinson, of which a duplicate had already been sent to Lawrence, was written in answer to one of Shirley informing the Minister that the Indians of Nova Scotia, prompted by the French, were about to make an attack on all the English settlements east of the Kennebec; whereupon Robinson wrote: "You will without doubt have given immediate intelligence thereof to Colonel Lawrence, and will have concerted the properest measures with him for taking all possible advantage in Nova Scotia itself from the absence of those Indians, in case Mr. Lawrence shall have force enough to attack the forts erected by the French in those parts, without exposing the English settlements; and I am particularly to acquaint you that if you have not already entered into such a concert with Colonel Lawrence, it is His Majesty's pleasure that you should immediately proceed thereupon."[2]

The Indian raid did not take place; but not the less did Shirley and Lawrence find in the Minister's letter their authorization for the attack of Beauséjour. Shirley wrote to Robinson that the expulsion of the French from the forts on the isthmus was a necessary measure of self-defence; that they meant to seize the whole country as far as Mines Basin, and probably as far as Annapolis, to supply their Acadian rebels with land; that of these they had, without reckoning Indians, fourteen hundred fighting men on or near the isthmus, and two hundred and fifty more on the St. John, with whom, aided by the garrison of Beauséjour, they could easily take Fort Lawrence; that should they succeed in this, the whole Acadian population would rise in arms, and the King would lose Nova Scotia. We should anticipate them, concludes Shirley, and strike the first blow.[3]

---

[1] *Shirley to Lawrence, 7 Nov. 1754.*

[2] *Robinson to Shirley, 5 July, 1754.*

[3] *Shirley to Robinson, 8 Dec. 1754. Ibid., 24 Jan. 1755.* The Record Office contains numerous other letters of Shirley on the subject. "I am obliged to your Honor for communicating to me the French Mémoire, which, with

He opened his plans to his Assembly in secret session, and found them of one mind with himself. Preparation was nearly complete, and the men raised for the expedition, before the Council at Alexandria, recognized it as a part of a plan of the summer campaign.

The French fort of Beauséjour, mounted on its hill between the marshes of Missaguash and Tantemar, was a regular work, pentagonal in form, with solid earthern ramparts, bomb-proofs, and an armament of twenty-four cannon and one mortar. The commandant, Duchambon de Vergor, a captain in the colony regulars, was a dull man of no education, of stuttering speech, unpleasing countenance, and doubtful character. He owed his place to the notorious Intendant, Bigot, who, it is said, was in his debt for disreputable service in an affair of gallantry, and who had ample means of enabling his friends to enrich themselves by defrauding the King. Beauséjour was one of those plague-spots of official corruption which dotted the whole surface of New France. Bigot, sailing for Europe in the summer of 1754, wrote thus to his confederate: "Profit by your place, my dear Vergor; clip and cut— you are free to do what you please—so that you can come soon to join me in France and buy an estate near me."[1] Vergor did not neglect his opportunities. Supplies in great quantities were sent from Quebec for the garrison and the emigrant Acadians. These last got but a small part of them. Vergor and his confederates sent the rest back to Quebec, or else to Louisbourg, and sold them for their own profit to the King's agents there, who were also in collusion with him.

Vergor, however, did not reign alone. Le Loutre, by force of energy, capacity, and passionate vehemence, held him in some awe, and divided his authority. The priest could count on the support of Duquesne, who had found, says a contem-

---

other reasons, puts it out of doubt that the French are determined to begin an offensive war on the peninsula as soon as ever they shall think themselves strengthened enough to venture upon it, and that they have thoughts of attempting it in the ensuing spring. I enclose your Honor extracts from two letters from Annapolis Royal, which show that the French inhabitants are in expectation of its being begun in the spring." *Shirley to Lawrence, 6 Jan. 1755.*

[1] *Mémoires sur le Canada, 1749–1760.* This letter is also mentioned in another contemporary document, *Mémoire sur les Fraudes commises dans la Colonie.*

porary, that "he promised more than he could perform, and that he was a knave," but who nevertheless felt compelled to rely upon him for keeping the Acadians on the side of France. There was another person in the fort worthy of notice. This was Thomas Pichon, commissary of stores, a man of education and intelligence, born in France of an English mother. He was now acting the part of a traitor, carrying on a secret correspondence with the commandant of Fort Lawrence, and acquainting him with all that passed at Beauséjour. It was partly from this source that the hostile designs of the French became known to the authorities of Halifax, and more especially the proceedings of "Moses," by which name Pichon always designated Le Loutre, because he pretended to have led the Acadians from the land of bondage. [1]

These exiles, who cannot be called self-exiled, in view of the outrageous means used to force most of them from their homes, were in a deplorable condition. They lived in constant dread of Le Loutre, backed by Vergor and his soldiers. The savage missionary, bad as he was, had in him an ingredient of honest fanaticism, both national and religious; though hatred of the English held a large share in it. He would gladly, if he could, have formed the Acadians into a permanent settlement on the French side of the line, not out of love for them, but in the interest of the cause with which he had identified his own ambition. His efforts had failed. There was not land enough for their subsistence and that of the older settlers; and the suffering emigrants pined more and more for their deserted farms. Thither he was resolved that they should not return. "If you go," he told them, "you will have neither priests nor sacraments, but will die like miserable wretches."[2] The assertion was false. Priests and sacraments had never been denied them. It is true that Daudin, priest of Pisiquid, had lately been sent to Halifax for using insolent language to the commandant, threatening him with an insurrection of the in-

---

[1] Pichon, called also Tyrrell from the name of his mother, was author of *Genuine Letters and Memoirs relating to Cape Breton,* — a book of some value. His papers are preserved at Halifax, and some of them are printed in the *Public Documents of Nova Scotia.*

[2] *Pichon to Captain Scott, 14 Oct. 1754,* in *Public Documents of Nova Scotia,* 229.

habitants, and exciting them to sedition; but on his promise
to change conduct, he was sent back to his parishioners.[1]
Vergor sustained Le Loutre, and threatened to put in irons
any of the exiles who talked of going back to the English.
Some of them bethought themselves of an appeal to Duquesne, and drew up a petition asking leave to return home.
Le Loutre told the signers that if they did not efface their
marks from the paper they should have neither sacraments in
this life nor heaven in the next. He nevertheless allowed two
of them to go to Quebec as deputies, writing at the same time
to the Governor, that his mind might be duly prepared. Duquesne replied: "I think that the two rascals of deputies
whom you sent me will not soon recover from the fright I
gave them, notwithstanding the emollient I administered after
my reprimand; and since I told them that they were indebted
to you for not being allowed to rot in a dungeon, they have
promised me to comply with your wishes."[2]

An entire heartlessness marked the dealings of the French
authorities with the Acadians. They were treated as mere
tools of policy, to be used, broken, and flung away. Yet, in
using them, the sole condition of their efficiency was neglected. The French Government, cheated of enormous sums
by its own ravenous agents, grudged the cost of sending a
single regiment to the Acadian border. Thus unsupported,
the Acadians remained in fear and vacillation, aiding the
French but feebly, though a ceaseless annoyance and menace
to the English.

This was the state of affairs at Beauséjour while Shirley and
Lawrence were planning its destruction. Lawrence had empowered his agent, Monckton, to draw without limit on two
Boston merchants, Apthorp and Hancock. Shirley, as commander-in-chief of the province of Massachusetts, commissioned John Winslow to raise two thousand volunteers.
Winslow was sprung from the early governors of Plymouth
colony; but, though well-born, he was ill-educated, which did
not prevent him from being both popular and influential. He
had strong military inclinations, had led a company of his
own raising in the luckless attack on Carthagena, had com-

[1] *Public Documents of Nova Scotia*, 223, 224, 226, 227, 238.
[2] *Public Documents of Nova Scotia*, 239.

manded the force sent in the preceding summer to occupy the Kennebec, and on various other occasions had left his Marshfield farm to serve his country. The men enlisted readily at his call, and were formed into a regiment, of which Shirley made himself the nominal colonel. It had two battalions, of which Winslow, as lieutenant-colonel, commanded the first, and George Scott the second, both under the orders of Monckton. Country villages far and near, from the western borders of the Connecticut to uttermost Cape Cod, lent soldiers to the new regiment. The muster-rolls preserve their names, vocations, birthplaces, and abode. Obadiah, Nehemiah, Jedediah, Jonathan, Ebenezer, Joshua, and the like Old Testament names abound upon the list. Some are set down as "farmers," "yeomen," or "husbandmen;" others as "shopkeepers," others as "fishermen," and many as "laborers;" while a great number were handicraftsmen of various trades, from blacksmiths to wig-makers. They mustered at Boston early in April, where clothing, haversacks, and blankets were served out to them at the charge of the King; and the crooked streets of the New England capital were filled with staring young rustics. On the next Saturday the following mandate went forth: "The men will behave very orderly on the Sabbath Day, and either stay on board their transports, or else go to church, and not stroll up and down the streets." The transports, consisting of about forty sloops and schooners, lay at Long Wharf; and here on Monday a grand review took place,—to the gratification, no doubt, of a populace whose amusements were few. All was ready except the muskets, which were expected from England, but did not come. Hence the delay of a month, threatening to ruin the enterprise. When Shirley returned from Alexandria he found, to his disgust, that the transports still lay at the wharf where he had left them on his departure.[1] The muskets arrived at length, and the fleet sailed on the twenty-second of May. Three small frigates, the "Success," the "Mermaid," and the "Siren," commanded by the ex-privateersman, Captain Rous, acted as convoy; and on the twenty-sixth the whole force safely reached Annapolis. Thence after some delay they sailed up the Bay of Fundy, and at sunset on the first of June anchored within five miles of the hill of Beauséjour.

[1] *Shirley to Robinson, 20 June, 1755.*

At two o'clock on the next morning a party of Acadians from Chipody roused Vergor with the news. In great alarm, he sent a messenger to Louisbourg to beg for help, and ordered all the fighting men of the neighborhood to repair to the fort. They counted in all between twelve and fifteen hundred;[1] but they had no appetite for war. The force of the invaders daunted them; and the hundred and sixty regulars who formed the garrison of Beauséjour were too few to revive their confidence. Those of them who had crossed from the English side dreaded what might ensue should they be caught in arms; and, to prepare an excuse beforehand, they begged Vergor to threaten them with punishment if they disobeyed his order. He willingly complied, promised to have them killed if they did not fight, and assured them at the same time that the English could never take the fort.[2] Three hundred of them thereupon joined the garrison, and the rest, hiding their families in the woods, prepared to wage guerilla war against the invaders.

Monckton, with all his force, landed unopposed, and encamped at night on the fields around Fort Lawrence, whence he could contemplate Fort Beauséjour at his ease. The regulars of the English garrison joined the New England men; and then, on the morning of the fourth, they marched to the attack. Their course lay along the south bank of the Missaguash to where it was crossed by a bridge called Pont-à-Buot. This bridge had been destroyed; and on the farther bank there was a large blockhouse and a breastwork of timber defended by four hundred regulars, Acadians, and Indians. They lay silent and unseen till the head of the column reached the opposite bank; then raised a yell and opened fire, causing some loss. Three field-pieces were brought up, the defenders were driven out, and a bridge was laid under a spattering fusillade from behind bushes, which continued till the English had crossed the stream. Without further opposition, they marched along the road to Beauséjour, and, turning to the right, encamped among the woody hills half a league from the fort. That night there was a grand illumination, for

[1] *Mémoires sur le Canada, 1749–1760.* An English document, *State of the English and French Forts in Nova Scotia*, says 1,200 to 1,400.

[2] *Mémoires sur le Canada, 1749–1760.*

Vergor set fire to the church and all the houses outside the ramparts.[1]

The English spent some days in preparing their camp and reconnoitring the ground. Then Scott, with five hundred provincials, seized upon a ridge within easy range of the works. An officer named Vannes came out to oppose him with a hundred and eighty men, boasting that he would do great things; but on seeing the enemy, quietly returned, to become the laughing-stock of the garrison. The fort fired furiously, but with little effect. In the night of the thirteenth, Winslow, with a part of his own battalion, relieved Scott, and planted in the trenches two small mortars, brought to the camp on carts. On the next day they opened fire. One of them was disabled by the French cannon, but Captain Hazen brought up two more, of larger size, on ox-wagons; and, in spite of heavy rain, the fire was brisk on both sides.

Captain Rous, on board his ship in the harbor, watched the bombardment with great interest. Having occasion to write to Winslow, he closed his letter in a facetious strain. "I often hear of your success in plunder, particularly a coach.[2] I hope you have some fine horses for it, at least four, to draw it, that it may be said a New England colonel [*rode in*] his coach and four in Nova Scotia. If you have any good saddle-horses in your stable, I should be obliged to you for one to ride round the ship's deck on for exercise, for I am not likely to have any other."

Within the fort there was little promise of a strong defence. Le Loutre, it is true, was to be seen in his shirt-sleeves, with a pipe in his mouth, directing the Acadians in their work of strengthening the fortifications.[3] They, on their part, thought more of escape than of fighting. Some of them vainly begged to be allowed to go home; others went off without leave,— which was not difficult, as only one side of the place was attacked. Even among the officers there were some in whom

---

[1] Winslow, *Journal and Letter Book. Mémoires sur le Canada, 1749–1760.* Letters from officers on the spot in *Boston Evening Post* and *Boston News Letter. Journal of Surgeon John Thomas.*

[2] "11 June. Capt. Adams went with a Company of Raingers, and Returned at 11 Clock with a Coach and Sum other Plunder." *Journal of John Thomas.*

[3] *Journal of Pichon,* cited by Beamish Murdoch.

interest was stronger than honor, and who would rather rob the King than die for him. The general discouragement was redoubled when, on the fourteenth, a letter came from the commandant of Louisbourg to say that he could send no help, as British ships blocked the way. On the morning of the sixteenth, a mischance befell, recorded in these words in the diary of Surgeon John Thomas: "One of our large shells fell through what they called their bomb-proof, where a number of their officers were sitting, killed six of them dead, and one Ensign Hay, which the Indians had took prisoner a few days agone and carried to the fort." The party was at breakfast when the unwelcome visitor burst in. Just opposite was a second bomb-proof, where was Vergor himself, with Le Loutre, another priest, and several officers, who felt that they might at any time share the same fate. The effect was immediate. The English, who had not yet got a single cannon into position, saw to their surprise a white flag raised on the rampart. Some officers of the garrison protested against surrender; and Le Loutre, who thought that he had everything to fear at the hands of the victors, exclaimed that it was better to be buried under the ruins of the fort than to give it up; but all was in vain, and the valiant Vannes was sent out to propose terms of capitulation. They were rejected, and others offered, to the following effect: the garrison to march out with the honors of war and to be sent to Louisbourg at the charge of the King of England, but not to bear arms in America for the space of six months. The Acadians to be pardoned the part they had just borne in the defence, "seeing that they had been compelled to take arms on pain of death." Confusion reigned all day at Beauséjour. The Acadians went home loaded with plunder. The French officers were so busy in drinking and pillaging that they could hardly be got away to sign the capitulation. At the appointed hour, seven in the evening, Scott marched in with a body of provincials, raised the British flag on the ramparts, and saluted it by a general discharge of the French cannon, while Vergor as a last act of hospitality gave a supper to the officers.[1]

[1] On the capture of Beauséjour, *Mémoires sur le Canada, 1749–1760*; Pichon, *Cape Breton*, 318; *Journal of Pichon*, cited by Murdoch; and the English accounts already mentioned.

Le Loutre was not to be found; he had escaped in disguise with his box of papers, and fled to Baye Verte to join his brother missionary, Manach. Thence he made his way to Quebec, where the Bishop received him with reproaches. He soon embarked for France; but the English captured him on the way, and kept him eight years in Elizabeth Castle, on the Island of Jersey. Here on one occasion a soldier on guard made a dash at the father, tried to stab him with his bayonet, and was prevented with great difficulty. He declared that, when he was with his regiment in Acadia, he had fallen into the hands of Le Loutre, and narrowly escaped being scalped alive, the missionary having doomed him to this fate, and with his own hand drawn a knife round his head as a beginning of the operation. The man swore so fiercely that he would have his revenge, that the officer in command transferred him to another post.[1]

Throughout the siege, the Acadians outside the fort, aided by Indians, had constantly attacked the English, but were always beaten off with loss. There was an affair of this kind on the morning of the surrender, during which a noted Micmac chief was shot, and being brought into the camp, recounted the losses of his tribe; "after which, and taking a dram or two, he quickly died," writes Winslow in his Journal.

Fort Gaspereau, at Baye Verte, twelve miles distant, was summoned by letter to surrender. Villeray, its commandant, at once complied; and Winslow went with a detachment to take possession.[2] Nothing remained but to occupy the French post at the mouth of the St. John. Captain Rous, relieved at last from inactivity, was charged with the task; and on the thirtieth he appeared off the harbor, manned his boats, and rowed for shore. The French burned their fort, and withdrew beyond his reach.[3] A hundred and fifty Indians, suddenly converted from enemies to pretended friends, stood on the strand, firing their guns into the air as a salute, and declaring themselves brothers of the English. All Acadia was now in

---

[1] Knox, *Campaigns in North America*, I. 114, *note*. Knox, who was stationed in Nova Scotia, says that Le Loutre left behind him "a most remarkable character for inhumanity."

[2] Winslow, *Journal*. *Villeray au Ministre, 20 Sept. 1755.*

[3] *Drucour au Ministre, 1 Déc. 1755.*

British hands. Fort Beauséjour became Fort Cumberland,—the second fort in America that bore the name of the royal Duke.

The defence had been of the feeblest. Two years later, on pressing demands from Versailles, Vergor was brought to trial, as was also Villeray. The Governor, Vaudreuil, and the Intendant, Bigot, who had returned to Canada, were in the interest of the chief defendant. The court-martial was packed; adverse evidence was shuffled out of sight; and Vergor, acquitted and restored to his rank, lived to inflict on New France another and a greater injury.[1]

Now began the first act of a deplorable drama. Monckton, with his small body of regulars, had pitched their tents under the walls of Beauséjour. Winslow and Scott, with the New England troops, lay not far off. There was little intercourse between the two camps. The British officers bore themselves towards those of the provincials with a supercilious coldness common enough on their part throughout the war. July had passed in what Winslow calls "an indolent manner," with prayers every day in the Puritan camp, when, early in August, Monckton sent for him, and made an ominous declaration. "The said Monckton was so free as to acquaint me that it was determined to remove all the French inhabitants out of the province, and that he should send for all the adult males from Tantemar, Chipody, Aulac, Beauséjour, and Baye Verte to read the Governor's orders; and when that was done, was determined to retain them all prisoners in the fort. And this is the first conference of a public nature I have had with the colonel since the reduction of Beauséjour; and I apprehend that no officer of either corps has been made more free with."

Monckton sent accordingly to all the neighboring settlements, commanding the male inhabitants to meet him at Beauséjour. Scarcely a third part of their number obeyed. These arrived on the tenth, and were told to stay all night under the guns of the fort. What then befell them will appear from an entry in the diary of Winslow under date of August eleventh: "This day was one extraordinary to the inhabitants of Tantemar, Oueskak, Aulac, Baye Verte, Beauséjour, and

[1] *Mémoire sur les Fraudes commises dans la Colonie, 1759. Mémoires sur le Canada, 1749–1760.*

places adjacent; the male inhabitants, or the principal of them, being collected together in Fort Cumberland to hear the sentence, which determined their property, from the Governor and Council of Halifax; which was that they were declared rebels, their lands, goods, and chattels forfeited to the Crown, and their bodies to be imprisoned. Upon which the gates of the fort were shut, and they all confined, to the amount of four hundred men and upwards." Parties were sent to gather more, but caught very few, the rest escaping to the woods.

Some of the prisoners were no doubt among those who had joined the garrison at Beauséjour, and had been pardoned for doing so by the terms of the capitulation. It was held, however, that, though forgiven this special offence, they were not exempted from the doom that had gone forth against the great body of their countrymen. We must look closely at the motives and execution of this stern sentence.

At any time up to the spring of 1755 the emigrant Acadians were free to return to their homes on taking the ordinary oath of allegiance required of British subjects. The English authorities of Halifax used every means to persuade them to do so; yet the greater part refused. This was due not only to Le Loutre and his brother priests, backed by the military power, but also to the Bishop of Quebec, who enjoined the Acadians to demand of the English certain concessions, the chief of which were that the priests should exercise their functions without being required to ask leave of the Governor, and that the inhabitants should not be called upon for military service of any kind. The Bishop added that the provisions of the treaty of Utrecht were insufficient, and that others ought to be exacted.[1] The oral declaration of the English authorities, that for the present the Acadians should not be required to bear arms, was not thought enough. They, or rather their prompters, demanded a written pledge.

The refusal to take the oath without reservation was not confined to the emigrants. Those who remained in the peninsula equally refused it, though most of them were born and had always lived under the British flag. Far from pledging themselves to complete allegiance, they showed continual

[1] *L'Évêque de Québec à Le Loutre, Nov. 1754,* in *Public Documents of Nova Scotia,* 240.

signs of hostility. In May three pretended French deserters were detected among them inciting them to take arms against the English.[1]

On the capture of Beauséjour the British authorities found themselves in a position of great difficulty. The New England troops were enlisted for the year only, and could not be kept in Acadia. It was likely that the French would make a strong effort to recover the province, sure as they were of support from the great body of its people. The presence of this disaffected population was for the French commanders a continual inducement to invasion; and Lawrence was not strong enough to cope at once with attack from without and insurrection from within.

Shirley had held for some time that there was no safety for Acadia but in ridding it of the Acadians. He had lately proposed that the lands of the district of Chignecto, abandoned by their emigrant owners, should be given to English settlers, who would act as a check and a counterpoise to the neighboring French population. This advice had not been acted upon. Nevertheless Shirley and his brother Governor of Nova Scotia were kindred spirits, and inclined to similar measures. Colonel Charles Lawrence had not the good-nature and conciliatory temper which marked his predecessors, Cornwallis and Hopson. His energetic will was not apt to relent under the softer sentiments, and the behavior of the Acadians was fast exhausting his patience. More than a year before, the Lords of Trade had instructed him that they had no right to their lands if they persisted in refusing the oath.[2] Lawrence replied, enlarging on their obstinacy, treachery, and "ingratitude for the favor, indulgence, and protection they have at all times so undeservedly received from His Majesty's Government;" declaring at the same time that, "while they remain without taking the oaths, and have incendiary French priests among them, there are no hopes of their amendment;" and that "it would be much better, if they refuse the oaths, that they were away."[3] "We were in hopes," again wrote the Lords of Trade, "that the lenity which had been shown to

[1] *Ibid.*, 242.
[2] *Lords of Trade to Lawrence, 4 March, 1754.*
[3] *Lawrence to Lords of Trade, 1 Aug. 1754.*

those people by indulging them in the free exercise of their religion and the quiet possession of their lands, would by degrees have gained their friendship and assistance, and weaned their affections from the French; but we are sorry to find that this lenity has had so little effect, and that they still hold the same conduct, furnishing them with labor, provisions, and intelligence, and concealing their designs from us." In fact, the Acadians, while calling themselves neutrals, were an enemy encamped in the heart of the province. These are the reasons which explain and palliate a measure too harsh and indiscriminate to be wholly justified.

Abbé Raynal, who never saw the Acadians, has made an ideal picture of them,[1] since copied and improved in prose and verse, till Acadia has become Arcadia. The plain realities of their condition and fate are touching enough to need no exaggeration. They were a simple and very ignorant peasantry, industrious and frugal till evil days came to discourage them; living aloof from the world, with little of that spirit of adventure which an easy access to the vast fur-bearing interior had developed in their Canadian kindred; having few wants, and those of the rudest; fishing a little and hunting in the winter, but chiefly employed in cultivating the meadows along the River Annapolis, or rich marshes reclaimed by dikes from the tides of the Bay of Fundy. The British Government left them entirely free of taxation. They made clothing of flax and wool of their own raising, hats of similar materials, and shoes or moccasons of moose and seal skin. They bred cattle, sheep, hogs, and horses in abundance; and the valley of the Annapolis, then as now, was known for the profusion and excellence of its apples. For drink, they made cider or brewed spruce-beer. French officials describe their dwellings as wretched wooden boxes, without ornaments or conveniences, and scarcely supplied with the most necessary furniture.[2] Two or more families often occupied the same house; and their way of life, though simple and virtuous, was by no means remarkable for cleanliness. Such as it was, contentment reigned among them, undisturbed by what modern America calls progress. Marriages were early, and population grew

[1] *Histoire philosophique et politique*, VI. 242 (ed. 1772).
[2] *Beauharnois et Hocquart au Comte de Maurepas, 12 Sept. 1745.*

apace. This humble society had its disturbing elements; for the Acadians, like the Canadians, were a litigious race, and neighbors often quarrelled about their boundaries. Nor were they without a bountiful share of jealousy, gossip, and back-biting, to relieve the monotony of their lives; and every village had its turbulent spirits, sometimes by fits, though rarely long, contumacious even toward the curé, the guide, counsellor, and ruler of his flock. Enfeebled by hereditary mental subjection, and too long kept in leading-strings to walk alone, they needed him, not for the next world only, but for this; and their submission, compounded of love and fear, was commonly without bounds. He was their true government; to him they gave a frank and full allegiance, and dared not disobey him if they would. Of knowledge he gave them nothing; but he taught them to be true to their wives and constant at confession and Mass, to stand fast for the Church and King Louis, and to resist heresy and King George; for, in one degree or another, the Acadian priest was always the agent of a double-headed foreign power,—the Bishop of Quebec allied with the Governor of Canada.[1]

When Monckton and the Massachusetts men laid siege to Beauséjour, Governor Lawrence thought the moment favorable for exacting an unqualified oath of allegiance from the Acadians. The presence of a superior and victorious force would help, he thought, to bring them to reason; and there were some indications that this would be the result. A number of Acadian families, who at the promptings of Le Loutre had emigrated to Cape Breton, had lately returned to Halifax, promising to be true subjects of King George if they could be allowed to repossess their lands. They cheerfully took the oath; on which they were reinstated in their old homes, and supplied with food for the winter.[2] Their example unfortunately found few imitators.

Early in June the principal inhabitants of Grand Pré and other settlements about the Basin of Mines brought a me-

---

[1] Franquet, *Journal, 1751*, says of the Acadians: "Ils aiment l'argent, n'ont dans toute leur conduite que leur intérêt pour objet, sont, indifféremment des deux sexes, d'une inconsidération dans leurs discours qui dénote de la méchanceté." Another observer, Dieréville, gives a more favorable picture.

[2] *Public Documents of Nova Scotia*, 228.

morial, signed with their crosses, to Captain Murray, the military commandant in their district, and desired him to send it to Governor Lawrence, to whom it was addressed. Murray reported that when they brought it to him they behaved with the greatest insolence, though just before they had been unusually submissive. He thought that this change of demeanor was caused by a report which had lately got among them of a French fleet in the Bay of Fundy; for it had been observed that any rumor of an approaching French force always had a similar effect. The deputies who brought the memorial were sent with it to Halifax, where they laid it before the Governor and Council. It declared that the signers had kept the qualified oath they had taken, "in spite of the solicitations and dreadful threats of another power," and that they would continue to prove "an unshaken fidelity to His Majesty, provided that His Majesty shall allow us the same liberty that he has [*hitherto*] granted us." Their memorial then demanded, in terms highly offensive to the Council, that the guns, pistols, and other weapons, which they had lately been required to give up, should be returned to them. They were told in reply that they had been protected for many years in the enjoyment of their lands, though they had not complied with the terms on which the lands were granted; "that they had always been treated by the Government with the greatest lenity and tenderness, had enjoyed more privileges than other English subjects, and had been indulged in the free exercise of their religion;" all which they acknowledged to be true. The Governor then told them that their conduct had been undutiful and ungrateful; "that they had discovered a constant disposition to assist His Majesty's enemies and to distress his subjects; that they had not only furnished the enemy with provisions and ammunition, but had refused to supply the [*English*] inhabitants or Government, and when they did supply them, had exacted three times the price for which they were sold at other markets." The hope was then expressed that they would no longer obstruct the settlement of the province by aiding the Indians to molest and kill English settlers; and they were rebuked for saying in their memorial that they would be faithful to the King only on certain conditions. The Governor added that they had some secret reason for demanding their weapons, and flattered themselves that French troops were at hand to support their insolence. In conclusion, they were told that now was a good opportunity to prove their sincerity by taking the oath of allegiance, in the usual form, before the Council. They replied that they had not made up their minds on that point, and could do nothing till they had consulted their constituents. Being reminded that the oath was personal to themselves, and that six years had already been given them to think about it, they asked leave to retire and confer together. This was granted, and at the end of an hour they came back with the same answer as before; whereupon they were allowed till ten o'clock on the next morning for a final decision.[1]

At the appointed time the Council again met, and the deputies were brought in. They persisted stubbornly in the same refusal. "They were then informed," says the record, "that the Council could no longer look on them as subjects to His Britannic Majesty, but as subjects to the King of France, and as such they must hereafter be treated; and they were ordered to withdraw." A discussion followed in the Council. It was determined that the Acadians should be ordered to send new deputies to Halifax, who should answer for them, once for all, whether they would accept the oath or not; that such as refused it should not thereafter be permitted to take it; and "that effectual measures ought to be taken to remove all such recusants out of the province."

The deputies, being then called in and told this decision, became alarmed, and offered to swear allegiance in the terms required. The answer was that it was too late; that as they had refused the oath under persuasion, they could not be trusted when they took it under compulsion. It remained to see whether the people at large would profit by their example.

"I am determined," wrote Lawrence to the Lords of Trade, "to bring the inhabitants to a compliance, or rid the province of such perfidious subjects."[2] First, in answer to the summons of the Council, the deputies from Annapolis appeared, declaring that they had always been faithful to the British Crown,

---

[1] *Minutes of Council at Halifax, 3 July, 1755*, in *Public Documents of Nova Scotia*, 247–255.

[2] *Lawrence to Lords of Trade, 18 July, 1755*.

but flatly refusing the oath. They were told that, far from having been faithful subjects, they had always secretly aided the Indians, and that many of them had been in arms against the English; that the French were threatening the province; and that its affairs had reached a crisis when its inhabitants must either pledge themselves without equivocation to be true to the British Crown, or else must leave the country. They all declared that they would lose their lands rather than take the oath. The Council urged them to consider the matter seriously, warning them that, if they now persisted in refusal, no farther choice would be allowed them; and they were given till ten o'clock on the following Monday to make their final answer.

When that day came, another body of deputies had arrived from Grand Pré and the other settlements of the Basin of Mines; and being called before the Council, both they and the former deputation absolutely refused to take the oath of allegiance. These two bodies represented nine tenths of the Acadian population within the peninsula. "Nothing," pursues the record of the Council, "now remained to be considered but what measures should be taken to send the inhabitants away, and where they should be sent to." If they were sent to Canada, Cape Breton, or the neighboring islands, they would strengthen the enemy, and still threaten the province. It was therefore resolved to distribute them among the various English colonies, and to hire vessels for the purpose with all despatch.[1]

The oath, the refusal of which had brought such consequences, was a simple pledge of fidelity and allegiance to King George II. and his successors. Many of the Acadians had already taken an oath of fidelity, though with the omission of the word "allegiance," and, as they insisted, with a saving clause exempting them from bearing arms. The effect of this was that they did not regard themselves as British subjects, and claimed, falsely as regards most of them, the character of neutrals. It was to put an end to this anomalous state

[1] *Minutes of Council, 4 July — 28 July*, in *Public Documents of Nova Scotia*, 255 – 267. Copies of these and other parts of the record were sent at the time to England, and are now in the Public Record Office, along with the letters of Lawrence.

of things that the oath without reserve had been demanded of them. Their rejection of it, reiterated in full view of the consequences, is to be ascribed partly to a fixed belief that the English would not execute their threats, partly to ties of race and kin, but mainly to superstition. They feared to take part with heretics against the King of France, whose cause, as already stated, they had been taught to regard as one with the cause of God; they were constrained by the dread of perdition. "If the Acadians are miserable, remember that the priests are the cause of it," writes the French officer Boishébert to the missionary Manach.[1]

The Council having come to a decision, Lawrence acquainted Monckton with the result, and ordered him to seize all the adult males in the neighborhood of Beauséjour; and this, as we have seen, he promptly did. It remains to observe how the rest of the sentence was carried into effect.

Instructions were sent to Winslow to secure the inhabitants on or near the Basin of Mines and place them on board transports, which, he was told, would soon arrive from Boston. His orders were stringent: "If you find that fair means will not do with them, you must proceed by the most vigorous measures possible, not only in compelling them to embark,

---

[1] On the oath and its history, compare a long note by Mr. Akin in *Public Documents of Nova Scotia*, 263–267. Winslow in his Journal gives an abstract of a memorial sent him by the Acadians, in which they say that they had refused the oath, and so forfeited their lands, from motives of religion. I have shown in a former chapter that the priests had been the chief instruments in preventing them from accepting the English government. Add the following: —

"Les malheurs des Accadiens sont beaucoup moins leur ouvrage que le fruit des sollicitations et des démarches des missionnaires." *Vaudreuil au Ministre, 6 Mai, 1760.*

"Si nous avons la guerre, et si les Accadiens sont misérables, souvenez-vous que ce sont les prêtres qui en sont la cause." *Boishébert à Manach, 21 Fév. 1760.* Both these writers had encouraged the priests in their intrigues so long as these were likely to profit the French Government, and only blamed them after they failed to accomplish what was expected of them.

"Nous avons six missionnaires dont l'occupation perpetuelle est de porter les esprits au fanatisme et à la vengeance. . . . Je ne puis supporter dans nos prêtres ces odieuses déclamations qu'ils font tous les jours aux sauvages: 'Les Anglois sont les ennemis de Dieu, les compagnons du Diable.'" Pichon, *Lettres et Mémoires pour servir à l'Histoire du Cap-Breton,* 160, 161. (La Haye, 1760.)

but in depriving those who shall escape of all means of shelter or support, by burning their houses and by destroying everything that may afford them the means of subsistence in the country." Similar orders were given to Major Handfield, the regular officer in command at Annapolis.

On the fourteenth of August Winslow set out from his camp at Fort Beauséjour, or Cumberland, on his unenviable errand. He had with him but two hundred and ninety-seven men. His mood of mind was not serene. He was chafed because the regulars had charged his men with stealing sheep; and he was doubly vexed by an untoward incident that happened on the morning of his departure. He had sent forward his detachment under Adams, the senior captain, and they were marching by the fort with drums beating and colors flying, when Monckton sent out his aide-de-camp with a curt demand that the colors should be given up, on the ground that they ought to remain with the regiment. Whatever the soundness of the reason, there was no courtesy in the manner of enforcing it. "This transaction raised my temper some," writes Winslow in his Diary; and he proceeds to record his opinion that "it is the most ungenteel, ill-natured thing that ever I saw." He sent Monckton a quaintly indignant note, in which he observed that the affair "looks odd, and will appear so in future history;" but his commander, reckless of the judgments of posterity, gave him little satisfaction.

Thus ruffled in spirit, he embarked with his men and sailed down Chignecto Channel to the Bay of Fundy. Here, while they waited the turn of the tide to enter the Basin of Mines, the shores of Cumberland lay before them dim in the hot and hazy air, and the promontory of Cape Split, like some misshapen monster of primeval chaos, stretched its portentous length along the glimmering sea, with head of yawning rock, and ridgy back bristled with forests. Borne on the rushing flood, they soon drifted through the inlet, glided under the rival promontory of Cape Blomedon, passed the red sandstone cliffs of Lyon's Cove, and descried the mouths of the rivers Canard and Des Habitants, where fertile marshes, diked against the tide, sustained a numerous and thriving population. Before them spread the boundless meadows of Grand Pré, waving with harvests or alive with grazing cattle; the green slopes behind were dotted with the simple dwellings of the Acadian farmers, and the spire of the village church rose against a background of woody hills. It was a peaceful, rural scene, soon to become one of the most wretched spots on earth. Winslow did not land for the present, but held his course to the estuary of the River Pisiquid, since called the Avon. Here, where the town of Windsor now stands, there was a stockade called Fort Edward, where a garrison of regulars under Captain Alexander Murray kept watch over the surrounding settlements. The New England men pitched their tents on shore, while the sloops that had brought them slept on the soft bed of tawny mud left by the fallen tide.

Winslow found a warm reception, for Murray and his officers had been reduced too long to their own society not to welcome the coming of strangers. The two commanders conferred together. Both had been ordered by Lawrence to "clear the whole country of such bad subjects;" and the methods of doing so had been outlined for their guidance. Having come to some understanding with his brother officer concerning the duties imposed on both, and begun an acquaintance which soon grew cordial on both sides, Winslow embarked again and retraced his course to Grand Pré, the station which the Governor had assigned him. "Am pleased," he wrote to Lawrence, "with the place proposed by your Excellency for our reception [*the village church*]. I have sent for the elders to remove all sacred things, to prevent their being defiled by heretics." The church was used as a storehouse and place of arms; the men pitched their tents between it and the graveyard; while Winslow took up his quarters in the house of the priest, where he could look from his window on a tranquil scene. Beyond the vast tract of grassland to which Grand Pré owed its name, spread the blue glistening breast of the Basin of Mines; beyond this again, the distant mountains of Cobequid basked in the summer sun; and nearer, on the left, Cape Blomedon reared its bluff head of rock and forest above the sleeping waves.

As the men of the settlement greatly outnumbered his own, Winslow set his followers to surrounding the camp with a stockade. Card-playing was forbidden, because it encouraged idleness, and pitching quoits in camp, because it spoiled the grass. Presently there came a letter from Lawrence expressing a fear that the fortifying of the camp might alarm the inhabitants. To which Winslow replied that the making of the stockade had not alarmed them in the least, since they took it as a proof that the detachment was to spend the winter with them; and he added, that as the harvest was not yet got in, he and Murray had agreed not to publish the Governor's commands till the next Friday. He concludes: "Although it is a disagreeable part of duty we are put upon, I am sensible it is a necessary one, and shall endeavor strictly to obey your Excellency's orders."

On the thirtieth, Murray, whose post was not many miles distant, made him a visit. They agreed that Winslow should summon all the male inhabitants about Grand Pré to meet him at the church and hear the King's orders, and that Murray should do the same for those around Fort Edward. Winslow then called in his three captains, — Adams, Hobbs, and Osgood, — made them swear secrecy, and laid before them his instructions and plans; which latter they approved. Murray then returned to his post, and on the next day sent Winslow a note containing the following: "I think the sooner we strike the stroke the better, therefore will be glad to see you here as soon as conveniently you can. I shall have the orders for assembling ready written for your approbation, only the day blank, and am hopeful everything will succeed according to our wishes. The gentlemen join me in our best compliments to you and the Doctor."

On the next day, Sunday, Winslow and the Doctor, whose name was Whitworth, made the tour of the neighborhood, with an escort of fifty men, and found a great quantity of wheat still on the fields. On Tuesday Winslow "set out in a whale-boat with Dr. Whitworth and Adjutant Kennedy, to consult with Captain Murray in this critical conjuncture." They agreed that three in the afternoon of Friday should be the time of assembling; then between them they drew up a summons to the inhabitants, and got one Beauchamp, a merchant, to "put it into French." It ran as follows: —

By John Winslow, Esquire, Lieutenant-Colonel and Commander of His Majesty's troops at Grand Pré, Mines, River Canard, and places adjacent.

To the inhabitants of the districts above named, as well ancients as young men and lads.

Whereas His Excellency the Governor has instructed us of his last resolution respecting the matters proposed lately to the inhabitants, and has ordered us to communicate the same to the inhabitants in general in person, His Excellency being desirous that each of them should be fully satisfied of His Majesty's intentions, which he has also ordered us to communicate to you, such as they have been given him.

We therefore order and strictly enjoin by these presents to all the inhabitants, as well of the above-named districts as of all the other districts, both old men and young men, as well as all the lads of ten years of age, to attend at the church in Grand Pré on Friday, the fifth instant, at three of the clock in the afternoon, that we may impart what we are ordered to communicate to them; declaring that no excuse will be admitted on any pretence whatsoever, on pain of forfeiting goods and chattels in default.

Given at Grand Pré, the second of September, in the twenty-ninth year of His Majesty's reign, A.D. 1755.

A similar summons was drawn up in the name of Murray for the inhabitants of the district of Fort Edward.

Captain Adams made a reconnoissance of the rivers Canard and Des Habitants, and reported "a fine country and full of inhabitants, a beautiful church, and abundance of the goods of the world." Another reconnoissance by Captains Hobbs and Osgood among the settlements behind Grand Pré brought reports equally favorable. On the fourth, another letter came from Murray: "All the people quiet, and very busy at their harvest; if this day keeps fair, all will be in here in their barns. I hope to-morrow will crown all our wishes." The Acadians, like the bees, were to gather a harvest for others to enjoy. The summons was sent out that afternoon. Powder and ball were served to the men, and all were ordered to keep within the lines.

On the next day the inhabitants appeared at the hour appointed, to the number of four hundred and eighteen men. Winslow ordered a table to be set in the middle of the church, and placed on it his instructions and the address he had prepared. Here he took his stand in his laced uniform, with one or two subalterns from the regulars at Fort Edward, and such of the Massachusetts officers as were not on guard duty; strong, sinewy figures, bearing, no doubt, more or less distinctly, the peculiar stamp with which toil, trade, and Puritanism had imprinted the features of New England. Their commander was not of the prevailing type. He was fifty-three years of age, with double chin, smooth forehead, arched eyebrows, close powdered wig, and round, rubicund face, from which the weight of an odious duty had probably banished the smirk of self-satisfaction that dwelt there at other times.[1] Nevertheless, he had manly and estimable qualities. The congregation of peasants, clad in rough homespun, turned their sunburned faces upon him, anxious and intent; and Winslow "delivered them by interpreters the King's orders in the following words," which, retouched in orthography and syntax, ran thus:—

GENTLEMEN,—I have received from His Excellency, Governor Lawrence, the King's instructions, which I have in my hand. By his orders you are called together to hear His Majesty's final resolution concerning the French inhabitants of this his province of Nova Scotia, who for almost half a century have had more indulgence granted them than any of his subjects in any part of his dominions. What use you have made of it you yourselves best know.

The duty I am now upon, though necessary, is very disagreeable to my natural make and temper, as I know it must be grievous to you, who are of the same species. But it is not my business to animadvert on the orders I have received, but to obey them; and therefore without hesitation I shall deliver to you His Majesty's instructions and commands, which are that your lands and tenements and cattle and live-stock of all kinds are forfeited to the Crown, with all your other effects, except money and household goods, and that you yourselves are to be removed from this his province.

The peremptory orders of His Majesty are that all the French inhabitants of these districts be removed; and

[1] See his portrait, at the rooms of the Massachusetts Historical Society.

through His Majesty's goodness I am directed to allow you the liberty of carrying with you your money and as many of your household goods as you can take without overloading the vessels you go in. I shall do everything in my power that all these goods be secured to you, and that you be not molested in carrying them away, and also that whole families shall go in the same vessel; so that this removal, which I am sensible must give you a great deal of trouble, may be made as easy as His Majesty's service will admit; and I hope that in whatever part of the world your lot may fall, you may be faithful subjects, and a peaceable and happy people.

I must also inform you that it is His Majesty's pleasure that you remain in security under the inspection and direction of the troops that I have the honor to command.

He then declared them prisoners of the King. "They were greatly struck," he says, "at this determination, though I believe they did not imagine that they were actually to be removed." After delivering the address, he returned to his quarters at the priest's house, whither he was followed by some of the elder prisoners, who begged leave to tell their families what had happened, "since they were fearful that the surprise of their detention would quite overcome them." Winslow consulted with his officers, and it was arranged that the Acadians should choose twenty of their number each day to revisit their homes, the rest being held answerable for their return.

A letter, dated some days before, now came from Major Handfield at Annapolis, saying that he had tried to secure the men of that neighborhood, but that many of them had escaped to the woods. Murray's report from Fort Edward came soon after, and was more favorable: "I have succeeded finely, and have got a hundred and eighty-three men into my possession." To which Winslow replied: "I have the favor of yours of this day, and rejoice at your success; and also for the smiles that have attended the party here." But he adds mournfully: "Things are now very heavy on my heart and hands." The prisoners were lodged in the church, and notice was sent to their families to bring them food. "Thus," says the Diary of the commander, "ended the memorable fifth of September, a day of great fatigue and trouble."

There was one quarter where fortune did not always smile. Major Jedediah Preble, of Winslow's battalion, wrote to him that Major Frye had just returned from Chipody, whither he had gone with a party of men to destroy the settlements and bring off the women and children. After burning two hundred and fifty-three buildings he had reimbarked, leaving fifty men on shore at a place called Peticodiac to give a finishing stroke to the work by burning the "Mass House," or church. While thus engaged, they were set upon by three hundred Indians and Acadians, led by the partisan officer Boishébert. More than half their number were killed, wounded, or taken. The rest ensconced themselves behind the neighboring dikes, and Frye, hastily landing with the rest of his men, engaged the assailants for three hours, but was forced at last to reimbark.[1] Captain Speakman, who took part in the affair, also sent Winslow an account of it, and added: "The people here are much concerned for fear your party should meet with the same fate (being in the heart of a numerous devilish crew), which I pray God avert."

Winslow had indeed some cause for anxiety. He had captured more Acadians since the fifth; and had now in charge nearly five hundred able-bodied men, with scarcely three hundred to guard them. As they were allowed daily exercise in the open air, they might by a sudden rush get possession of arms and make serious trouble. On the Wednesday after the scene in the church some unusual movements were observed among them, and Winslow and his officers became convinced that they could not safely be kept in one body. Five vessels, lately arrived from Boston, were lying within the mouth of the neighboring river. It was resolved to place fifty of the prisoners on board each of these, and keep them anchored in the Basin. The soldiers were all ordered under arms, and posted on an open space beside the church and behind the priest's house. The prisoners were then drawn up before them, ranked six deep,—the young unmarried men, as the

[1] Also *Boishébert à Drucourt, 10 Oct. 1755*, an exaggerated account. *Vaudreuil au Ministre, 18 Oct. 1755*, sets Boishébert's force at one hundred and twenty-five men.

most dangerous, being told off and placed on the left, to the number of a hundred and forty-one. Captain Adams, with eighty men, was then ordered to guard them to the vessels. Though the object of the movement had been explained to them, they were possessed with the idea that they were to be torn from their families and sent away at once; and they all, in great excitement, refused to go. Winslow told them that there must be no parley or delay; and as they still refused, a squad of soldiers advanced towards them with fixed bayonets; while he himself, laying hold of the foremost young man, commanded him to move forward. "He obeyed; and the rest followed, though slowly, and went off praying, singing, and crying, being met by the women and children all the way (which is a mile and a half) with great lamentation, upon their knees, praying." When the escort returned, about a hundred of the married men were ordered to follow the first party; and, "the ice being broken," they readily complied. The vessels were anchored at a little distance from shore, and six soldiers were placed on board each of them as a guard. The prisoners were offered the King's rations, but preferred to be supplied by their families, who, it was arranged, should go in boats to visit them every day; "and thus," says Winslow, "ended this troublesome job." He was not given to effusions of feeling, but he wrote to Major Handfield: "This affair is more grievous to me than any service I was ever employed in."[1]

Murray sent him a note of congratulation: "I am extremely pleased that things are so clever at Grand Pré, and that the poor devils are so resigned. Here they are more patient than I could have expected for people in their circumstances; and what surprises me still more is the indifference of the women, who really are, or seem, quite unconcerned. I long much to see the poor wretches embarked and our affair a little settled; and then I will do myself the pleasure of meeting you and drinking their good voyage."

This agreeable consummation was still distant. There was a long and painful delay. The provisions for the vessels which

[1] Haliburton, who knew Winslow's Journal only by imperfect extracts, erroneously states that the men put on board the vessels were sent away immediately. They remained at Grand Pré several weeks, and were then sent off at intervals with their families.

were to carry the prisoners did not come; nor did the vessels themselves, excepting the five already at Grand Pré. In vain Winslow wrote urgent letters to George Saul, the commissary, to bring the supplies at once. Murray, at Fort Edward, though with less feeling than his brother officer, was quite as impatient of the burden of suffering humanity on his hands. "I am amazed what can keep the transports and Saul. Surely our friend at Chignecto is willing to give us as much of our neighbors' company as he well can."[1] Saul came at last with a shipload of provisions; but the lagging transports did not appear. Winslow grew heartsick at the daily sight of miseries which he himself had occasioned, and wrote to a friend at Halifax: "I know they deserve all and more than they feel; yet it hurts me to hear their weeping and wailing and gnashing of teeth. I am in hopes our affairs will soon put on another face, and we get transports, and I rid of the worst piece of service that ever I was in."

After weeks of delay, seven transports came from Annapolis; and Winslow sent three of them to Murray, who joyfully responded: "Thank God, the transports are come at last. So soon as I have shipped off my rascals, I will come down and settle matters with you, and enjoy ourselves a little."

Winslow prepared for the embarkation. The Acadian prisoners and their families were divided into groups answering to their several villages, in order that those of the same village might, as far as possible, go in the same vessel. It was also provided that the members of each family should remain together; and notice was given them to hold themselves in readiness. "But even now," he writes, "I could not persuade the people I was in earnest." Their doubts were soon ended. The first embarkation took place on the eighth of October, under which date the Diary contains this entry: "Began to embark the inhabitants, who went off very solentarily [sic] and unwillingly, the women in great distress, carrying off their children in their arms; others carrying their decrepit parents in their carts, with all their goods; moving in great confusion, and appeared a scene of woe and distress."[2]

---

[1] *Murray to Winslow, 26 Sept. 1755.*

[2] In spite of Winslow's care, some cases of separation of families occurred; but they were not numerous.

Though a large number were embarked on this occasion, still more remained; and as the transports slowly arrived, the dismal scene was repeated at intervals, with more order than at first, as the Acadians had learned to accept their fate as a certainty. So far as Winslow was concerned, their treatment seems to have been as humane as was possible under the circumstances; but they complained of the men, who disliked and despised them. One soldier received thirty lashes for stealing fowls from them; and an order was issued forbidding soldiers or sailors, on pain of summary punishment, to leave their quarters without permission, "that an end may be put to distressing this distressed people." Two of the prisoners, however, while trying to escape, were shot by a reconnoitring party.

At the beginning of November Winslow reported that he had sent off fifteen hundred and ten persons, in nine vessels, and that more than six hundred still remained in his district.[1] The last of these were not embarked till late in December. Murray finished his part of the work at the end of October, having sent from the district of Fort Edward eleven hundred persons in four frightfully crowded transports.[2] At the close of that month sixteen hundred and sixty-four had been sent from the district of Annapolis, where many others escaped to the woods.[3] A detachment which was ordered to seize the inhabitants of the district of Cobequid failed entirely, finding the settlements abandoned. In the country about Fort Cumberland, Monckton, who directed the operation in person, had very indifferent success, catching in all but little more than a thousand.[4] Le Guerne, missionary priest in this neighborhood, gives a characteristic and affecting incident of the embarkation. "Many unhappy women, carried away by excessive attachment to their husbands, whom they had been allowed to see too often, and closing their ears to the voice of religion and their missionary, threw themselves blindly and despairingly into the English vessels. And now was seen the

[1] *Winslow to Monckton, 3 Nov. 1755.*

[2] *Ibid.*

[3] *Captain Adams to Winslow, 29 Nov. 1755*; see also Knox, I. 85, who exactly confirms Adams's figures.

[4] *Monckton to Winslow, 7 Oct. 1755.*

saddest of spectacles; for some of these women, solely from a religious motive, refused to take with them their grown-up sons and daughters."[1] They would expose their own souls to perdition among heretics, but not those of their children.

When all, or nearly all, had been sent off from the various points of departure, such of the houses and barns as remained standing were burned, in obedience to the orders of Lawrence, that those who had escaped might be forced to come in and surrender themselves. The whole number removed from the province, men, women, and children, was a little above six thousand. Many remained behind; and while some of these withdrew to Canada, Isle St. Jean, and other distant retreats, the rest lurked in the woods or returned to their old haunts, whence they waged, for several years a guerilla warfare against the English. Yet their strength was broken, and they were no longer a danger to the province.

Of their exiled countrymen, one party overpowered the crew of the vessel that carried them, ran her ashore at the mouth of the St. John, and escaped.[2] The rest were distributed among the colonies from Massachusetts to Georgia, the master of each transport having been provided with a letter from Lawrence addressed to the Governor of the province to which he was bound, and desiring him to receive the unwelcome strangers. The provincials were vexed at the burden imposed upon them; and though the Acadians were not in general ill-treated, their lot was a hard one. Still more so was that of those among them who escaped to Canada. The chronicle of the Ursulines of Quebec, speaking of these last, says that their misery was indescribable, and attributes it to the poverty of the colony. But there were other causes. The exiles found less pity from kindred and fellow Catholics than from the heretics of the English colonies. Some of them who had made their way to Canada from Boston, whither they had been transported, sent word to a gentleman of that place who had befriended them, that they wished to return.[3] Bougainville, the celebrated navigator, then aide-de-camp to Mont-

[1] *Le Guerne à Prévost, 10 Mars, 1756.*

[2] *Lettre commune de Drucour et Prévost au Ministre, 6 Avril, 1756. Vaudreuil au Ministre, 1 Juin, 1756.*

[3] Hutchinson, *Hist. Mass.,* III. 42, *note.*

calm, says concerning them: "They are dying by wholesale. Their past and present misery, joined to the rapacity of the Canadians, who seek only to squeeze out of them all the money they can, and then refuse them the help so dearly bought, are the cause of this mortality." "A citizen of Quebec," he says farther on, "was in debt to one of the partners of the Great Company [*Government officials leagued for plunder*]. He had no means of paying. They gave him a great number of Acadians to board and lodge. He starved them with hunger and cold, got out of them what money they had, and paid the extortioner. *Quel pays! Quels mœurs!*"[1]

Many of the exiles eventually reached Louisiana, where their descendants now form a numerous and distinct population. Some, after incredible hardship, made their way back to Acadia, where, after the peace, they remained unmolested, and, with those who had escaped seizure, became the progenitors of the present Acadians, now settled in various parts of the British maritime provinces, notably at Madawaska, on the upper St. John, and at Clare, in Nova Scotia. Others were sent from Virginia to England; and others again, after the complete conquest of the country, found refuge in France.

In one particular the authors of the deportation were disappointed in its results. They had hoped to substitute a loyal population for a disaffected one; but they failed for some time to find settlers for the vacated lands. The Massachusetts soldiers, to whom they were offered, would not stay in the province; and it was not till five years later that families of British stock began to occupy the waste fields of the Acadians. This goes far to show that a longing to become their heirs had not, as has been alleged, any considerable part in the motives for their removal.

New England humanitarianism, melting into sentimentality at a tale of woe, has been unjust to its own. Whatever judgment may be passed on the cruel measure of wholesale expatriation, it was not put in execution till every resource of patience and persuasion had been tried in vain. The agents of the French Court, civil, military, and ecclesiastical, had made some act of force a necessity. We have seen by what vile prac-

[1] Bougainville, *Journal, 1756–1758*. His statements are sustained by *Mémoires sur le Canada, 1749–1760*.

tices they produced in Acadia a state of things intolerable, and impossible of continuance. They conjured up the tempest; and when it burst on the heads of the unhappy people, they gave no help. The Government of Louis XV. began with making the Acadians its tools, and ended with making them its victims.[1]

[1] It may not be remembered that the predecessor of Louis XV., without the slightest provocation or the pretence of any, gave orders that the whole Protestant population of the colony of New York, amounting to about eighteen thousand, should be seized, despoiled of their property, placed on board his ships, and dispersed among the other British colonies in such a way that they could not reunite. Want of power alone prevented the execution of the order. See *Frontenac and New France under Louis XIV.*, 141, 142.

Chapter IX

1755

DIESKAU

Expedition against Crown Point • William Johnson • Vaudreuil • Dieskau • Johnson and the Indians • The Provincial Army • Doubts and Delays • March to Lake George • Sunday in Camp • Advance of Dieskau • He changes Plan • Marches against Johnson • Ambush • Rout of Provincials • Battle of Lake George • Rout of the French • Rage of the Mohawks • Peril of Dieskau • Inaction of Johnson • The Homeward March • Laurels of Victory

---

THE NEXT stroke of the campaign was to be the capture of Crown Point, that dangerous neighbor which, for a quarter of a century, had threatened the northern colonies. Shirley, in January, had proposed an attack on it to the Ministry; and in February, without waiting their reply, he laid the plan before his Assembly. They accepted it, and voted money for the pay and maintenance of twelve hundred men, provided the adjacent colonies would contribute in due proportion.[1] Massachusetts showed a military activity worthy of the reputation she had won. Forty-five hundred of her men, or one in eight of her adult males, volunteered to fight the French, and enlisted for the various expeditions, some in the pay of the province, and some in that of the King.[2] It remained to name a commander for the Crown Point enterprise. Nobody had power to do so, for Braddock was not yet come; but that time might not be lost, Shirley, at the request of his Assembly, took the responsibility on himself. If he had named a Massachusetts officer, it would have roused the jealousy of the other New England colonies; and he therefore appointed William Johnson of New York, thus gratifying that important province and pleasing the Five Nations, who at

---

[1] *Governor Shirley's Message to his Assembly, 13 Feb. 1755. Resolutions of the Assembly of Massachusetts, 18 Feb. 1755.* Shirley's original idea was to build a fort on a rising ground near Crown Point, in order to command it. This was soon abandoned for the more honest and more practical plan of direct attack.

[2] *Correspondence of Shirley, Feb. 1755.* The number was much increased later in the season.

this time looked on Johnson with even more than usual favor. Hereupon, in reply to his request, Connecticut voted twelve hundred men, New Hampshire five hundred, and Rhode Island four hundred, all at their own charge; while New York, a little later, promised eight hundred more. When, in April, Braddock and the Council at Alexandria approved the plan and the commander, Shirley gave Johnson the commission of major-general of the levies of Massachusetts; and the governors of the other provinces contributing to the expedition gave him similar commissions for their respective contingents. Never did general take the field with authority so heterogeneous.

He had never seen service, and knew nothing of war. By birth he was Irish, of good family, being nephew of Admiral Sir Peter Warren, who, owning extensive wild lands on the Mohawk, had placed the young man in charge of them nearly twenty years before. Johnson was born to prosper. He had ambition, energy, an active mind, a tall, strong person, a rough, jovial temper, and a quick adaptation to his surroundings. He could drink flip with Dutch boors, or Madeira with royal governors. He liked the society of the great, would intrigue and flatter when he had an end to gain, and foil a rival without looking too closely at the means; but compared with the Indian traders who infested the border, he was a model of uprightness. He lived by the Mohawk in a fortified house which was a stronghold against foes and a scene of hospitality to friends, both white and red. Here—for his tastes were not fastidious—presided for many years a Dutch or German wench whom he finally married; and after her death a young Mohawk squaw took her place. Over his neighbors, the Indians of the Five Nations, and all others of their race with whom he had to deal, he acquired a remarkable influence. He liked them, adopted their ways, and treated them kindly or sternly as the case required, but always with a justice and honesty in strong contrast with the rascalities of the commission of Albany traders who had lately managed their affairs, and whom they so detested that one of their chiefs called them "not men, but devils." Hence, when Johnson was made Indian superintendent there was joy through all the Iroquois confederacy. When, in addition, he was made a general, he assembled the warriors in council to engage them to aid the expedition.

This meeting took place at his own house, known as Fort Johnson; and as more than eleven hundred Indians appeared at his call, his larder was sorely taxed to entertain them. The speeches were interminable. Johnson, a master of Indian rhetoric, knew his audience too well not to contest with them the palm of insufferable prolixity. The climax was reached on the fourth day, and he threw down the war-belt. An Oneida chief took it up; Stevens, the interpreter, began the war-dance, and the assembled warriors howled in chorus. Then a tub of punch was brought in, and they all drank the King's health.[1] They showed less alacrity, however, to fight his battles, and scarcely three hundred of them would take the war-path. Too many of their friends and relatives were enlisted for the French.

While the British colonists were preparing to attack Crown Point, the French of Canada were preparing to defend it. Duquesne, recalled from his post, had resigned the government to the Marquis de Vaudreuil, who had at his disposal the battalions of regulars that had sailed in the spring from Brest under Baron Dieskau. His first thought was to use them for the capture of Oswego; but the letters of Braddock, found on the battle-field, warned him of the design against Crown Point; while a reconnoitring party which had gone as far as the Hudson brought back news that Johnson's forces were already in the field. Therefore the plan was changed, and Dieskau was ordered to lead the main body of his troops, not to Lake Ontario, but to Lake Champlain. He passed up the Richelieu, and embarked in boats and canoes for Crown Point. The veteran knew that the foes with whom he had to deal were but a mob of countrymen. He doubted not of putting them to rout, and meant never to hold his hand till he had chased them back to Albany.[2] "Make all haste," Vaudreuil wrote to him; "for when you return we shall send you to Oswego to execute our first design."[3]

---

[1] *Report of Conference between Major-General Johnson and the Indians, June,* 1755.

[2] *Bigot au Ministre, 27 Août, 1755. Ibid., 5 Sept. 1755.*

[3] *Mémoire pour servir d'Instruction à M. le Baron de Dieskau, Maréchal des Camps et Armées du Roy, 15 Août, 1755.*

Johnson on his part was preparing to advance. In July about three thousand provincials were encamped near Albany, some on the "Flats" above the town, and some on the meadows below. Hither, too, came a swarm of Johnson's Mohawks,—warriors, squaws, and children. They adorned the General's face with war-paint, and he danced the war-dance; then with his sword he cut the first slice from the ox that had been roasted whole for their entertainment. "I shall be glad," wrote the surgeon of a New England regiment, "if they fight as eagerly as they ate their ox and drank their wine."

Above all things the expedition needed promptness; yet everything moved slowly. Five popular legislatures controlled the troops and the supplies. Connecticut had refused to send her men till Shirley promised that her commanding officer should rank next to Johnson. The whole movement was for some time at a deadlock because the five governments could not agree about their contributions of artillery and stores.[1] The New Hampshire regiment had taken a short cut for Crown Point across the wilderness of Vermont; but had been recalled in time to save them from probable destruction. They were now with the rest in the camp at Albany, in such distress for provisions that a private subscription was proposed for their relief.[2]

Johnson's army, crude as it was, had in it good material. Here was Phineas Lyman, of Connecticut, second in command, once a tutor at Yale College, and more recently a lawyer,—a raw soldier, but a vigorous and brave one; Colonel Moses Titcomb, of Massachusetts, who had fought with credit at Louisbourg; and Ephraim Williams, also colonel of a Massachusetts regiment, a tall and portly man, who had been a captain in the last war, member of the General Court, and deputy-sheriff. He made his will in the camp at Albany, and left a legacy to found the school which has since become Williams College. His relative, Stephen Williams, was chaplain of his regiment, and his brother Thomas was its surgeon. Seth Pomeroy, gunsmith at Northampton, who, like Tit-

---

[1] *The Conduct of Major-General Shirley briefly stated* (London, 1758).

[2] *Blanchard to Wentworth, 28 Aug. 1755*, in *Provincial Papers of New Hampshire*, VI 429.

comb, had seen service at Louisbourg, was its lieutenant-colonel. He had left a wife at home, an excellent matron, to whom he was continually writing affectionate letters, mingling household cares with news of the camp, and charging her to see that their eldest boy, Seth, then in college at New Haven, did not run off to the army. Pomeroy had with him his brother Daniel; and this he thought was enough. Here, too, was a man whose name is still a household word in New England,—the sturdy Israel Putnam, private in a Connecticut regiment; and another as bold as he, John Stark, lieutenant in the New Hampshire levies, and the future victor of Bennington.

The soldiers were no soldiers, but farmers and farmers' sons who had volunteered for the summer campaign. One of the corps had a blue uniform faced with red. The rest wore their daily clothing. Blankets had been served out to them by the several provinces, but the greater part brought their own guns; some under the penalty of a fine if they came without them, and some under the inducement of a reward.[1] They had no bayonets, but carried hatchets in their belts as a sort of substitute.[2] At their sides were slung powder-horns, on which, in the leisure of the camp, they carved quaint devices with the points of their jack-knives. They came chiefly from plain New England homesteads,—rustic abodes, unpainted and dingy, with long well-sweeps, capacious barns, rough fields of pumpkins and corn, and vast kitchen chimneys, above which in winter hung squashes to keep them from frost, and guns to keep them from rust.

As to the manners and morals of the army there is conflict of evidence. In some respects nothing could be more exemplary. "Not a chicken has been stolen," says William Smith, of New York; while, on the other hand, Colonel Ephraim Williams writes to Colonel Israel Williams, then commanding on the Massachusetts frontier: "We are a wicked, profane army, especially the New York and Rhode Island troops. Nothing to be heard among a great part of them but the language of Hell. If Crown Point is taken, it will not be for our sakes, but for those good people left behind."[3] There was

---

[1] *Proclamation of Governor Shirley, 1755.*

[2] *Second Letter to a Friend on the Battle of Lake George.*

[3] *Papers of Colonel Israel Williams.*

edifying regularity in respect to form. Sermons twice a week, daily prayers, and frequent psalm-singing alternated with the much-needed military drill.[1] "Prayers among us night and morning," writes Private Jonathan Caswell, of Massachusetts, to his father. "Here we lie, knowing not when we shall march for Crown Point; but I hope not long to tarry. Desiring your prayers to God for me as I am agoing to war, I am Your Ever Dutiful Son."[2]

To Pomeroy and some of his brothers in arms it seemed that they were engaged in a kind of crusade against the myrmidons of Rome. "As you have at heart the Protestant cause," he wrote to his friend Israel Williams, "so I ask an interest in your prayers that the Lord of Hosts would go forth with us and give us victory over our unreasonable, encroaching, barbarous, murdering enemies."

Both Williams the surgeon and Williams the colonel chafed at the incessant delays. "The expedition goes on very much as a snail runs," writes the former to his wife; "it seems we may possibly see Crown Point this time twelve months." The Colonel was vexed because everything was out of joint in the department of transportation: wagoners mutinous for want of pay; ordnance stores, camp-kettles, and provisions left behind. "As to rum," he complains, "it won't hold out nine weeks. Things appear most melancholy to me." Even as he was writing, a report came of the defeat of Braddock; and, shocked at the blow, his pen traced the words: "The Lord have mercy on poor New England!"

Johnson had sent four Mohawk scouts to Canada. They returned on the twenty-first of August with the report that the French were all astir with preparation, and that eight thousand men were coming to defend Crown Point. On this a council of war was called; and it was resolved to send to the several colonies for reinforcements.[3] Meanwhile the main body had moved up the river to the spot called the Great Carrying Place, where Lyman had begun a fortified storehouse, which his men called Fort Lyman, but which was

[1] *Massachusetts Archives.*

[2] *Jonathan Caswell to John Caswell, 6 July, 1755.*

[3] *Minutes of Council of War, 22 Aug. 1755. Ephraim Williams to Benjamin Dwight, 22 Aug. 1755.*

afterwards named Fort Edward. Two Indian trails led from this point to the waters of Lake Champlain, one by way of Lake George, and the other by way of Wood Creek. There was doubt which course the army should take. A road was begun to Wood Creek; then it was countermanded, and a party was sent to explore the path to Lake George. "With submission to the general officers," Surgeon Williams again writes, "I think it a very grand mistake that the business of reconnoitring was not done months agone." It was resolved at last to march for Lake George; gangs of axemen were sent to hew out the way; and on the twenty-sixth two thousand men were ordered to the lake, while Colonel Blanchard, of New Hampshire, remained with five hundred to finish and defend Fort Lyman.

The train of Dutch wagons, guarded by the homely sol-diery, jolted slowly over the stumps and roots of the newly made road, and the regiments followed at their leisure. The hardships of the way were not without their consolations. The jovial Irishman who held the chief command made him-self very agreeable to the New England officers. "We went on about four or five miles," says Pomeroy in his Journal, "then stopped, ate pieces of broken bread and cheese, and drank some fresh lemon-punch and the best of wine with General Johnson and some of the field-officers." It was the same on the next day. "Stopped about noon and dined with General Johnson by a small brook under a tree; ate a good dinner of cold boiled and roast venison; drank good fresh lemon-punch and wine."

That afternoon they reached their destination, fourteen miles from Fort Lyman. The most beautiful lake in America lay before them; then more beautiful than now, in the wild charm of untrodden mountains and virgin forests. "I have given it the name of Lake George," wrote Johnson to the Lords of Trade, "not only in honor of His Majesty, but to ascertain his undoubted dominion here." His men made their camp on a piece of rough ground by the edge of the water, pitching their tents among the stumps of the newly felled trees. In their front was a forest of pitch-pine; on their right, a marsh, choked with alders and swamp-maples; on their left, the low hill where Fort George was afterwards built; and at their rear, the lake. Little was done to clear the forest in front, though it would give excellent cover to an enemy. Nor did Johnson take much pains to learn the movements of the French in the direction of Crown Point, though he sent scouts towards South Bay and Wood Creek. Every day stores and bateaux, or flat boats, came on wagons from Fort Lyman; and preparation moved on with the leisure that had marked it from the first. About three hundred Mohawks came to the camp, and were regarded by the New England men as nuisances. On Sunday the gray-haired Stephen Williams preached to these savage allies a long Calvinistic sermon, which must have sorely perplexed the interpreter whose business it was to turn it into Mohawk; and in the afternoon young Chaplain Newell, of Rhode Island, expounded to the New England men the somewhat untimely text, "Love your enemies." On the next Sunday, September seventh, Williams preached again, this time to the whites from a text in Isaiah. It was a peaceful day, fair and warm, with a few light showers; yet not wholly a day of rest, for two hundred wagons came up from Fort Lyman, loaded with bateaux. After the sermon there was an alarm. An Indian scout came in about sunset, and reported that he had found the trail of a body of men moving from South Bay towards Fort Lyman. Johnson called for a volunteer to carry a letter of warning to Colonel Blanchard, the commander. A wagoner named Adams offered himself for the perilous service, mounted, and galloped along the road with the letter. Sentries were posted, and the camp fell asleep.

While Johnson lay at Lake George, Dieskau prepared a surprise for him. The German Baron had reached Crown Point at the head of three thousand five hundred and seventy-three men, regulars, Canadians, and Indians.[1] He had no thought of waiting there to be attacked. The troops were told to hold themselves ready to move at a moment's notice. Officers—so ran the order—will take nothing with them but one spare shirt, one spare pair of shoes, a blanket, a bearskin, and provisions for twelve days; Indians are not to amuse themselves by taking scalps till the enemy is entirely defeated, since they

[1] *Vaudreuil au Ministre, 25 Sept. 1755.*

can kill ten men in the time required to scalp one.[1] Then Dieskau moved on, with nearly all his force, to Carillon, or Ticonderoga, a promontory commanding both the routes by which alone Johnson could advance, that of Wood Creek and that of Lake George.

The Indian allies were commanded by Legardeur de Saint-Pierre, the officer who had received Washington on his embassy to Fort Le Bœuf. These unmanageable warriors were a constant annoyance to Dieskau, being a species of humanity quite new to him. "They drive us crazy," he says, "from morning till night. There is no end to their demands. They have already eaten five oxen and as many hogs, without counting the kegs of brandy they have drunk. In short, one needs the patience of an angel to get on with these devils; and yet one must always force himself to seem pleased with them."[2]

They would scarcely even go out as scouts. At last, however, on the fourth of September, a reconnoitring party came in with a scalp and an English prisoner caught near Fort Lyman. He was questioned under the threat of being given to the Indians for torture if he did not tell the truth; but, nothing daunted, he invented a patriotic falsehood; and thinking to lure his captors into a trap, told them that the English army had fallen back to Albany, leaving five hundred men at Fort Lyman, which he represented as indefensible. Dieskau resolved on a rapid movement to seize the place. At noon of the same day, leaving a part of his force at Ticonderoga, he embarked the rest in canoes and advanced along the narrow prolongation of Lake Champlain that stretched southward through the wilderness to where the town of Whitehall now stands. He soon came to a point where the lake dwindled to a mere canal, while two mighty rocks, capped with stunted forests, faced each other from the opposing banks. Here he left an officer named Roquemaure with a detachment of troops, and again advanced along a belt of quiet water traced through the midst of a deep marsh, green at that season with sedge and water-weeds, and known to the English as the Drowned Lands. Beyond, on either hand, crags feathered

---

[1] *Livre d'Ordres, Août, Sept. 1755.*

[2] *Dieskau à Vaudreuil, 1 Sept. 1755.*

with birch and fir, or hills mantled with woods, looked down
on the long procession of canoes.[1] As they neared the site of
Whitehall, a passage opened on the right, the entrance to a
sheet of lonely water slumbering in the shadow of woody
mountains, and forming the lake then, as now, called South
Bay. They advanced to its head, landed where a small stream
enters it, left the canoes under a guard, and began their march
through the forest. They counted in all two hundred and sixteen regulars of the battalions of Languedoc and La Reine,
six hundred and eighty-four Canadians, and about six
hundred Indians.[2] Every officer and man carried provisions
for eight days in his knapsack. They encamped at night by a
brook, and in the morning, after hearing Mass, marched
again. The evening of the next day brought them near the
road that led to Lake George. Fort Lyman was but three
miles distant. A man on horseback galloped by; it was Adams,
Johnson's unfortunate messenger. The Indians shot him, and
found the letter in his pocket. Soon after, ten or twelve wagons appeared in charge of mutinous drivers, who had left the
English camp without orders. Several of them were shot, two
were taken, and the rest ran off. The two captives declared
that, contrary to the assertion of the prisoner at Ticonderoga,
a large force lay encamped at the lake. The Indians now held
a council, and presently gave out that they would not attack
the fort, which they thought well supplied with cannon, but
that they were willing to attack the camp at Lake George.
Remonstrance was lost upon them. Dieskau was not young,
but he was daring to rashness, and inflamed to emulation
by the victory over Braddock. The enemy were reported
greatly to outnumber him; but his Canadian advisers had
assured him that the English colony militia were the worst
troops on the face of the earth. "The more there are," he
said to the Canadians and Indians, "the more we shall kill;"
and in the morning the order was given to march for the
lake.

They moved rapidly on through the waste of pines, and
soon entered the rugged valley that led to Johnson's camp.

[1] I passed this way three weeks ago. There are some points where the scene
is not much changed since Dieskau saw it.
[2] *Mémoire sur l'Affaire du 8 Septembre.*

On their right was a gorge where, shadowed in bushes, gurgled a gloomy brook; and beyond rose the cliffs that buttressed the rocky heights of French Mountain, seen by glimpses between the boughs. On their left rose gradually the lower slopes of West Mountain. All was rock, thicket, and forest; there was no open space but the road along which the regulars marched, while the Canadians and Indians pushed their way through the woods in such order as the broken ground would permit.

They were three miles from the lake, when their scouts brought in a prisoner who told them that a column of English troops was approaching. Dieskau's preparations were quickly made. While the regulars halted on the road, the Canadians and Indians moved to the front, where most of them hid in the forest along the slopes of West Mountain, and the rest lay close among the thickets on the other side. Thus, when the English advanced to attack the regulars in front, they would find themselves caught in a double ambush. No sight or sound betrayed the snare; but behind every bush crouched a Canadian or a savage, with gun cocked and ears intent, listening for the tramp of the approaching column.

The wagoners who escaped the evening before had reached the camp about midnight, and reported that there was a war-party on the road near Fort Lyman. Johnson had at this time twenty-two hundred effective men, besides his three hundred Indians.[1] He called a council of war in the morning, and a resolution was taken which can only be explained by a complete misconception as to the force of the French. It was determined to send out two detachments of five hundred men each, one towards Fort Lyman, and the other towards South Bay, the object being, according to Johnson, "to catch the enemy in their retreat."[2] Hendrick, chief of the Mohawks, a brave and sagacious warrior, expressed his dissent after a fashion of his own. He picked up a stick and broke it; then he picked up several sticks, and showed that together they could

[1] *Wraxall to Lieutenant-Governor Delancey, 10 Sept. 1755.* Wraxall was Johnson's aide-de-camp and secretary. The *Second Letter to a Friend* says twenty-one hundred whites and two hundred or three hundred Indians. Blodget, who was also on the spot, sets the whites at two thousand.

[2] *Letter to the Governors of the several Colonies, 9 Sept. 1755.*

not be broken. The hint was taken, and the two detachments were joined in one. Still the old savage shook his head. "If they are to be killed," he said, "they are too many; if they are to fight, they are too few." Nevertheless, he resolved to share their fortunes; and mounting on a gun-carriage, he harangued his warriors with a voice so animated and gestures so expressive, that the New England officers listened in admiration, though they understood not a word. One difficulty remained. He was too old and fat to go afoot; but Johnson lent him a horse, which he bestrode, and trotted to the head of the column, followed by two hundred of his warriors as fast as they could grease, paint, and befeather themselves.

Captain Elisha Hawley was in his tent, finishing a letter which he had just written to his brother Joseph; and these were the last words: "I am this minute agoing out in company with five hundred men to see if we can intercept 'em in their retreat, or find their canoes in the Drowned Lands; and therefore must conclude this letter." He closed and directed it; and in an hour received his death-wound.

It was soon after eight o'clock when Ephraim Williams left the camp with his regiment, marched a little distance, and then waited for the rest of the detachment under Lieutenant-Colonel Whiting. Thus Dieskau had full time to lay his ambush. When Whiting came up, the whole moved on together, so little conscious of danger that no scouts were thrown out in front or flank; and, in full security, they entered the fatal snare. Before they were completely involved in it, the sharp eye of old Hendrick detected some sign of an enemy. At that instant, whether by accident or design, a gun was fired from the bushes. It is said that Dieskau's Iroquois, seeing Mohawks, their relatives, in the van, wished to warn them of danger. If so, the warning came too late. The thickets on the left blazed out a deadly fire, and the men fell by scores. In the words of Dieskau, the head of the column "was doubled up like a pack of cards." Hendrick's horse was shot down, and the chief was killed with a bayonet as he tried to rise. Williams, seeing a rising ground on his right, made for it, calling on his men to follow; but as he climbed the slope, guns flashed from the bushes, and a shot through the brain laid him dead. The men in the rear pressed forward to support their comrades, when a hot fire was suddenly opened on them from the forest along their right flank. Then there was a panic; some fled outright, and the whole column recoiled. The van now became the rear, and all the force of the enemy rushed upon it, shouting and screeching. There was a moment of total confusion; but a part of Williams's regiment rallied under command of Whiting, and covered the retreat, fighting behind trees like Indians, and firing and falling back by turns, bravely aided by some of the Mohawks and by a detachment which Johnson sent to their aid. "And a very handsome retreat they made," writes Pomeroy; "and so continued till they came within about three quarters of a mile of our camp. This was the last fire our men gave our enemies, which killed great numbers of them; they were seen to drop as pigeons." So ended the fray long known in New England fireside story as the "bloody morning scout." Dieskau now ordered a halt, and sounded his trumpets to collect his scattered men. His Indians, however, were sullen and unmanageable, and the Canadians also showed signs of wavering. The veteran who commanded them all, Legardeur de Saint-Pierre, had been killed. At length they were persuaded to move again, the regulars leading the way.

About an hour after Williams and his men had begun their march, a distant rattle of musketry was heard at the camp; and as it grew nearer and louder, the listeners knew that their comrades were on the retreat. Then, at the eleventh hour, preparations were begun for defence. A sort of barricade was made along the front of the camp, partly of wagons, and partly of inverted bateaux, but chiefly of the trunks of trees hastily hewn down in the neighboring forest and laid end to end in a single row. The line extended from the southern slopes of the hill on the left across a tract of rough ground to the marshes on the right. The forest, choked with bushes and clumps of rank ferns, was within a few yards of the barricade, and there was scarcely time to hack away the intervening thickets. Three cannon were planted to sweep the road that descended through the pines, and another was dragged up to the ridge of the hill. The defeated party began to come in; first, scared fugitives both white and red; then, gangs of men bringing the wounded; and at last, an hour and a half after

the first fire was heard, the main detachment was seen marching in compact bodies down the road.

Five hundred men were detailed to guard the flanks of the
camp. The rest stood behind the wagons or lay flat behind
the logs and inverted bateaux, the Massachusetts men on the
right, and the Connecticut men on the left. Besides Indians,
this actual fighting force was between sixteen and seventeen
hundred rustics, very few of whom had been under fire before
that morning. They were hardly at their posts when they saw
ranks of white-coated soldiers moving down the road, and
bayonets that to them seemed innumerable glittering between
the boughs. At the same time a terrific burst of war-whoops
rose along the front; and, in the words of Pomeroy, "the Canadians and Indians, helter-skelter, the woods full of them,
came running with undaunted courage right down the hill
upon us, expecting to make us flee."[1] Some of the men grew
uneasy; while the chief officers, sword in hand, threatened
instant death to any who should stir from their posts.[2] If
Dieskau had made an assault at that instant, there could be
little doubt of the result.

This he well knew; but he was powerless. He had his small
force of regulars well in hand; but the rest, red and white,
were beyond control, scattering through the woods and
swamps, shouting, yelling, and firing from behind trees. The
regulars advanced with intrepidity towards the camp where
the trees were thin, deployed, and fired by platoons, till Captain Eyre, who commanded the artillery, opened on them
with grape, broke their ranks, and compelled them to take to
cover. The fusillade was now general on both sides, and soon
grew furious. "Perhaps," Seth Pomeroy wrote to his wife,
two days after, "the hailstones from heaven were never much
thicker than their bullets came; but, blessed be God! that did
not in the least daunt or disturb us." Johnson received a flesh-
wound in the thigh, and spent the rest of the day in his tent.
Lyman took command; and it is a marvel that he escaped
alive, for he was four hours in the heat of the fire, directing
and animating the men. "It was the most awful day my eyes
ever beheld," wrote Surgeon Williams to his wife; "there

[1] *Seth Pomeroy to his Wife, 10 Sept. 1755.*
[2] *Dr. Perez Marsh to William Williams, 25 Sept. 1755.*

seemed to be nothing but thunder and lightning and perpetual pillars of smoke." To him, his colleague Doctor Pynchon,
one assistant, and a young student called "Billy," fell the
charge of the wounded of his regiment. "The bullets flew
about our ears all the time of dressing them; so we thought
best to leave our tent and retire a few rods behind the shelter
of a log-house." On the adjacent hill stood one Blodget, who
seems to have been a sutler, watching, as well as bushes, trees,
and smoke would let him, the progress of the fight, of which
he soon after made and published a curious bird's-eye view.
As the wounded men were carried to the rear, the wagoners
about the camp took their guns and powder-horns, and
joined in the fray. A Mohawk, seeing one of these men still
unarmed, leaped over the barricade, tomahawked the nearest
Canadian, snatched his gun, and darted back unhurt. The
brave savage found no imitators among his tribesmen, most
of whom did nothing but utter a few war-whoops, saying
that they had come to see their English brothers fight. Some
of the French Indians opened a distant flank fire from the
high ground beyond the swamp on the right, but were driven
off by a few shells dropped among them.

Dieskau had directed his first attack against the left and
centre of Johnson's position. Making no impression here, he
tried to force the right, where lay the regiments of Titcomb,
Ruggles, and Williams. The fire was hot for about an hour.
Titcomb was shot dead, a rod in front of the barricade, firing
from behind a tree like a common soldier. At length Dieskau,
exposing himself within short range of the English line, was
hit in the leg. His adjutant, Montreuil, himself wounded,
came to his aid, and was washing the injured limb with
brandy, when the unfortunate commander was again hit in
the knee and thigh. He seated himself behind a tree, while
the Adjutant called two Canadians to carry him to the rear.
One of them was instantly shot down. Montreuil took his
place; but Dieskau refused to be moved, bitterly denounced
the Canadians and Indians, and ordered the Adjutant to leave
him and lead the regulars in a last effort against the camp.

It was too late. Johnson's men, singly or in small squads,
were already crossing their row of logs; and in a few moments the whole dashed forward with a shout, falling upon

the enemy with hatchets and the butts of their guns. The French and their allies fled. The wounded General still sat helpless by the tree, when he saw a soldier aiming at him. He signed to the man not to fire; but he pulled trigger, shot him across the hips, leaped upon him, and ordered him in French to surrender. "I said," writes Dieskau, " 'You rascal, why did you fire? You see a man lying in his blood on the ground, and you shoot him!' He answered: 'How did I know that you had not got a pistol? I had rather kill the devil than have the devil kill me.' 'You are a Frenchman?' I asked. 'Yes,' he replied; 'it is more than ten years since I left Canada;' whereupon several others fell on me and stripped me. I told them to carry me to their general, which they did. On learning who I was, he sent for surgeons, and, though wounded himself, refused all assistance till my wounds were dressed."[1]

It was near five o'clock when the final rout took place. Some time before, several hundred of the Canadians and Indians had left the field and returned to the scene of the morning fight, to plunder and scalp the dead. They were resting themselves near a pool in the forest, close beside the road, when their repose was interrupted by a volley of bullets. It was fired by a scouting party from Fort Lyman, chiefly backwoodsmen, under Captains Folsom and McGinnis. The assailants were greatly outnumbered; but after a hard fight the Canadians and Indians broke and fled. McGinnis was mortally wounded. He continued to give orders till the firing was over; then fainted, and was carried, dying, to the camp. The bodies of the slain, according to tradition, were thrown into the pool, which bears to this day the name of Bloody Pond.

The various bands of fugitives rejoined each other towards night, and encamped in the forest; then made their way round the southern shoulder of French Mountain, till, in the next evening, they reached their canoes. Their plight was deplorable; for they had left their knapsacks behind, and were spent with fatigue and famine.

---

[1] *Dialogue entre le Maréchal de Saxe et le Baron de Dieskau aux Champs Élysées*. This paper is in the Archives de la Guerre, and was evidently written or inspired by Dieskau himself. In spite of its fanciful form, it is a sober statement of the events of the campaign. There is a translation of it in *N. Y. Col. Docs.*, X. 340.

Meanwhile their captive general was not yet out of danger. The Mohawks were furious at their losses in the ambush of the morning, and above all at the death of Hendrick. Scarcely were Dieskau's wounds dressed, when several of them came into the tent. There was a long and angry dispute in their own language between them and Johnson, after which they went out very sullenly. Dieskau asked what they wanted. "What do they want?" returned Johnson. "To burn you, by God, eat you, and smoke you in their pipes, in revenge for three or four of their chiefs that were killed. But never fear; you shall be safe with me, or else they shall kill us both."[1] The Mohawks soon came back, and another talk ensued, excited at first, and then more calm; till at length the visitors, seemingly appeased, smiled, gave Dieskau their hands in sign of friendship, and quietly went out again. Johnson warned him that he was not yet safe; and when the prisoner, fearing that his presence might incommode his host, asked to be removed to another tent, a captain and fifty men were ordered to guard him. In the morning an Indian, alone and apparently unarmed, loitered about the entrance, and the stupid sentinel let him pass in. He immediately drew a sword from under a sort of cloak which he wore, and tried to stab Dieskau; but was prevented by the Colonel to whom the tent belonged, who seized upon him, took away his sword, and pushed him out. As soon as his wounds would permit, Dieskau was carried on a litter, strongly escorted, to Fort Lyman, whence he was sent to Albany, and afterwards to New York. He is profuse in expressions of gratitude for the kindness shown him by the colonial officers, and especially by Johnson. Of the provincial soldiers he remarked soon after the battle that in the morning they fought like good boys, about noon like men, and in the afternoon like devils.[2] In the spring of 1757 he sailed for England, and was for a time at Falmouth; whence Colonel Matthew Sewell, fearing that he might see and learn too much, wrote to the Earl of Holdernesse: "The Baron has great penetration and quickness of apprehension. His long service under Marshal Saxe renders him a man of

---

[1] See the story as told by Dieskau to the celebrated Diderot, at Paris, in 1760. *Mémoires de Diderot*, I. 402 (1830). Compare *N. Y. Col. Docs.*, X. 343.

[2] *Dr. Perez Marsh to William Williams, 25 Sept. 1755.*

real consequence, to be cautiously observed. His circumstances deserve compassion, for indeed they are very melancholy, and I much doubt of his being ever perfectly cured." He was afterwards a long time at Bath, for the benefit of the waters. In 1760 the famous Diderot met him at Paris, cheerful and full of anecdote, though wretchedly shattered by his wounds. He died a few years later.

On the night after the battle the yeomen warriors felt the truth of the saying that, next to defeat, the saddest thing is victory. Comrades and friends by scores lay scattered through the forest. As soon as he could snatch a moment's leisure, the overworked surgeon sent the dismal tidings to his wife: "My dear brother Ephraim was killed by a ball through his head; poor brother Josiah's wound I fear will prove mortal; poor Captain Hawley is yet alive, though I did not think he would live two hours after bringing him in." Daniel Pomeroy was shot dead; and his brother Seth wrote the news to his wife Rachel, who was just delivered of a child: "Dear Sister, this brings heavy tidings; but let not your heart sink at the news, though it be your loss of a dear husband. Monday the eighth instant was a memorable day; and truly you may say, had not the Lord been on our side, we must all have been swallowed up. My brother, being one that went out in the first engagement, received a fatal shot through the middle of the head." Seth Pomeroy found a moment to write also to his own wife, whom he tells that another attack is expected; adding, in quaintly pious phrase: "But as God hath begun to show mercy, I hope he will go on to be gracious." Pomeroy was employed during the next few days with four hundred men in what he calls "the melancholy piece of business" of burying the dead. A letter-writer of the time does not approve what was done on this occasion. "Our people," he says, "not only buried the French dead, but buried as many of them as might be without the knowledge of our Indians, to prevent their being scalped. This I call an excess of civility;" his reason being that Braddock's dead soldiers had been left to the wolves.

The English loss in killed, wounded, and missing was two hundred and sixty-two;[1] and that of the French by their own

[1] *Return of Killed, Wounded, and Missing at the Battle of Lake George.*

account, two hundred and twenty-eight,[1]—a somewhat modest result of five hours' fighting. The English loss was chiefly in the ambush of the morning, where the killed greatly outnumbered the wounded, because those who fell and could not be carried away were tomahawked by Dieskau's Indians. In the fight at the camp, both Indians and Canadians kept themselves so well under cover that it was very difficult for the New England men to pick them off, while they on their part lay close behind their row of logs. On the French side, the regular officers and troops bore the brunt of the battle and suffered the chief loss, nearly all of the former and nearly half of the latter being killed or wounded.

Johnson did not follow up his success. He says that his men were tired. Yet five hundred of them had stood still all day, and boats enough for their transportation were lying on the beach. Ten miles down the lake, a path led over a gorge of the mountains to South Bay, where Dieskau had left his canoes and provisions. It needed but a few hours to reach and destroy them; but no such attempt was made. Nor, till a week after, did Johnson send out scouts to learn the strength of the enemy at Ticonderoga. Lyman strongly urged him to make an effort to seize that important pass; but Johnson thought only of holding his own position. "I think," he wrote, "we may expect very shortly a more formidable attack." He made a solid breastwork to defend his camp; and as reinforcements arrived, set them at building a fort on a rising ground by the lake. It is true that just after the battle he was deficient in stores, and had not bateaux enough to move his whole force. It is true, also, that he was wounded, and that he was too jealous of Lyman to delegate the command to him; and so the days passed till, within a fortnight, his nimble enemy were entrenched at Ticonderoga in force enough to defy him.

The Crown Point expedition was a failure disguised under an incidental success. The northern provinces, especially Massachusetts and Connecticut, did what they could to forward it, and after the battle sent a herd of raw recruits to the scene

---

[1] *Doreil au Ministre, 20 Oct. 1755.* Surgeon Williams gives the English loss as two hundred and sixteen killed, and ninety-six wounded. Pomeroy thinks that the French lost four or five hundred. Johnson places their loss at four hundred.

of action. Shirley wrote to Johnson from Oswego; declared that his reasons for not advancing were insufficient, and urged him to push for Ticonderoga at once. Johnson replied that he had not wagons enough, and that his troops were ill-clothed, ill-fed, discontented, insubordinate, and sickly. He complained that discipline was out of the question, because the officers were chosen by popular election; that many of them were no better than the men, unfit for command, and like so many "heads of a mob."[1] The reinforcements began to come in, till, in October, there were thirty-six hundred men in the camp; and as most of them wore summer clothing and had but one thin domestic blanket, they were half frozen in the chill autumn nights.

Johnson called a council of war; and as he was suffering from inflamed eyes, and was still kept in his tent by his wound, he asked Lyman to preside,—not unwilling, perhaps, to shift the responsibility upon him. After several sessions and much debate, the assembled officers decided that it was inexpedient to proceed.[2] Yet the army lay more than a month longer at the lake, while the disgust of the men increased daily under the rains, frosts, and snows of a dreary November. On the twenty-second, Chandler, chaplain of one of the Massachusetts regiments, wrote in the interleaved almanac that served him as a diary: "The men just ready to mutiny. Some clubbed their firelocks and marched, but returned back. Very rainy night. Miry water standing in the tents. Very distressing time among the sick." The men grew more and more unruly, and went off in squads without asking leave. A difficult question arose: Who should stay for the winter to garrison the new forts, and who should command them? It was settled at last that a certain number of soldiers from each province should be assigned to this ungrateful service, and that Massachusetts should have the first officer, Connecticut the second, and New York the third. Then the camp broke up. "Thursday the 27th," wrote the chaplain in his almanac, "we set out about ten of the clock, marched in a body, about three thousand, the wagons and baggage in the centre, our colonel

[1] *Shirley to Johnson, 19 Sept. 1755. Ibid., 24 Sept. 1755. Johnson to Shirley, 22 Sept. 1755. Johnson to Phipps, 10 Oct. 1755* (Massachusetts Archives).
[2] *Reports of Council of War, 11–21 Oct. 1755.*

much insulted by the way." The soldiers dispersed to their villages and farms, where in blustering winter nights, by the blazing logs of New England hearthstones, they told their friends and neighbors the story of the campaign.

The profit of it fell to Johnson. If he did not gather the fruits of victory, at least he reaped its laurels. He was a courtier in his rough way. He had changed the name of Lac St. Sacrement to Lake George, in compliment to the King. He now changed that of Fort Lyman to Fort Edward, in compliment to one of the King's grandsons; and, in compliment to another, called his new fort at the lake, William Henry. Of General Lyman he made no mention in his report of the battle, and his partisans wrote letters traducing that brave officer; though Johnson is said to have confessed in private that he owed him the victory. He himself found no lack of eulogists; and, to quote the words of an able but somewhat caustic and prejudiced opponent, "to the panegyrical pen of his secretary, Mr. Wraxall, and the *sic volo sic jubeo* of Lieutenant-Governor Delancey, is to be ascribed that mighty renown which echoed through the colonies, reverberated to Europe, and elevated a raw, inexperienced youth into a kind of second Marlborough."[1] Parliament gave him five thousand pounds, and the King made him a baronet.

[1] *Review of Military Operations in North America, in a Letter to a Nobleman* (ascribed to William Livingston).

On the Battle of Lake George a mass of papers will be found in the *N. Y. Col. Docs.*, Vols. VI. and X. Those in Vol. VI., taken chiefly from the archives of New York, consist of official and private letters, reports, etc., on the English side. Those in Vol. X. are drawn chiefly from the archives of the French War Department, and include the correspondence of Dieskau and his adjutant Montreuil. I have examined most of them in the original. Besides these I have obtained from the Archives de la Marine and other sources a number of important additional papers, which have never been printed, including Vaudreuil's reports to the Minister of War, and his strictures on Dieskau, whom he accuses of disobeying orders by dividing his force; also the translation of an English journal of the campaign found in the pocket of a captured officer, and a long account of the battle sent by Bigot to the Minister of Marine, 4 Oct. 1755.

I owe to the kindness of Theodore Pomeroy, Esq., a copy of the Journal of Lieutenant-Colonel Seth Pomeroy, whose letters also are full of interest; as are those of Surgeon Williams, from the collection of William L. Stone, Esq. The papers of Colonel Israel Williams, in the Library of the Massachusetts Historical Society, contain many other curious letters relating to the campaign, extracts from some of which are given in the text. One of the most curious records of the battle is *A Prospective-Plan of the Battle near Lake George, with an Explanation thereof, containing a full, though short, History of that important Affair, by Samuel Blodget, occasionally at the Camp when the Battle was fought.* It is an engraving, printed at Boston soon after the fight, of which it gives a clear idea. Four years after, Blodget opened a shop in Boston, where, as appears by his advertisements in the newspapers, he sold "English Goods, also English Hatts, etc." The engraving is reproduced in the *Documentary History of New York*, IV., and elsewhere. The *Explanation thereof* is only to be found complete in the original. This, as well as the anonymous *Second Letter to a Friend*, also printed at Boston in 1755, is excellent for the information it gives as to the condition of the ground where the conflict took place, and the position of the combatants. The unpublished Archives of Massachusetts; the correspondence of Sir William Johnson; the *Review of Military Operations in North America*; Dwight, *Travels in New England and New York*, III.; and Hoyt, *Antiquarian Researches on Indian Wars*, — should also be mentioned. Dwight and Hoyt drew their information from aged survivors of the battle. I have repeatedly examined the localities.

In the odd effusion of the colonial muse called *Tilden's Poems, chiefly to Animate and Rouse the Soldiers, printed 1756*, is a piece styled *The Christian Hero, or New England's Triumph*, beginning with the invocation, —

> "O Heaven, indulge my feeble Muse,
> Teach her what numbers for to choose!"

and containing the following stanza: —

> "Their Dieskau we from them detain,
> While Canada aloud complains
> And counts the numbers of their slain
>   And makes a dire complaint;
> The Indians to their demon gods;
> And with the French there 's little odds,
> While images receive their nods,
>   Invoking rotten saints."

Chapter X

SHIRLEY—BORDER WAR

The Niagara Campaign • Albany • March to Oswego • Difficulties • The Expedition abandoned • Shirley and Johnson • Results of the Campaign • The Scourge of the Border • Trials of Washington • Misery of the Settlers • Horror of their Situation • Philadelphia and the Quakers • Disputes with the Penns • Democracy and Feudalism • Pennsylvanian Population • Appeals from the Frontier • Quarrel of Governor and Assembly • Help refused • Desperation of the Borderers • Fire and Slaughter • The Assembly alarmed • They pass a mock Militia Law • They are forced to yield

THE CAPTURE of Niagara was to finish the work of the summer. This alone would have gained for England the control of the valley of the Ohio, and made Braddock's expedition superfluous. One marvels at the short-sightedness, the dissensions, the apathy which had left this key of the interior so long in the hands of France without an effort to wrest it from her. To master Niagara would be to cut the communications of Canada with the whole system of French forts and settlements in the West, and leave them to perish like limbs of a girdled tree.

Major-General Shirley, in the flush of his new martial honors, was to try his prentice hand at the work. The lawyer-soldier could plan a campaign boldly and well. It remained to see how he would do his part towards executing it. In July he arrived at Albany, the starting-point of his own expedition as well as that of Johnson. This little Dutch city was an outpost of civilization. The Hudson, descending from the northern wilderness, connected it with the lakes and streams that formed the thoroughfare to Canada; while the Mohawk, flowing from the west, was a liquid pathway to the forest homes of the Five Nations. Before the war was over, a little girl, Anne MacVicar, daughter of a Highland officer, was left at Albany by her father, and spent several years there in the house of Mrs. Schuyler, aunt of General Schuyler of the Revolution. Long after, married and middle-aged, she wrote down her recollections of the place,—the fort on the hill behind; the great street, grassy and broad, that descended thence to the river, with market, guard-house, town hall, and two churches in the middle, and rows of quaint Dutch-built houses on both sides, each detached from its neighbors, each with its well, garden, and green, and its great overshadowing tree. Before every house was a capacious porch, with seats where the people gathered in the summer twilight; old men at one door, matrons at another, young men and girls mingling at a third; while the cows with their tinkling bells came from the common at the end of the town, each stopping to be milked at the door of its owner; and children, porringer in hand, sat on the steps, watching the process and waiting their evening meal.

Such was the quiet picture painted on the memory of Anne MacVicar, and reproduced by the pen of Mrs. Anne Grant.[1] The patriarchal, semi-rural town had other aspects, not so pleasing. The men were mainly engaged in the fur-trade, sometimes legally with the Five Nations, and sometimes illegally with the Indians of Canada,—an occupation which by no means tends to soften the character. The Albany Dutch traders were a rude, hard race, loving money, and not always scrupulous as to the means of getting it. Coming events, too, were soon to have their effect on this secluded community. Regiments, red and blue, trumpets, drums, banners, artillery trains, and all the din of war transformed its peaceful streets, and brought some attaint to domestic morals hitherto commendable; for during the next five years Albany was to be the principal base of military operations on the continent.

Shirley had left the place, and was now on his way up the Mohawk. His force, much smaller than at first intended, consisted of the New Jersey regiment, which mustered five hundred men, known as the Jersey Blues, and of the fiftieth and fifty-first regiments, called respectively Shirley's and Pepperell's. These, though paid by the King and counted as regulars, were in fact raw provincials, just raised in the colonies, and wearing their gay uniforms with an awkward, unaccus-

---

[1] *Memoirs of an American Lady* (Mrs. Schuyler), Chap. VI. A genuine picture of colonial life, and a charming book, though far from being historically trustworthy. Compare the account of Albany in Kalm, II. 102.

tomed air. How they gloried in them may be gathered from a letter of Sergeant James Gray, of Pepperell's, to his brother John: "I have two Holland shirts, found me by the King, and two pair of shoes and two pair of worsted stockings; a good silver-laced hat (the lace I could sell for four dollars); and my clothes is as fine scarlet broadcloth as ever you did see. A sergeant here in the King's regiment is counted as good as an ensign with you; and one day in every week we must have our hair or wigs powdered."[1] Most of these gorgeous warriors were already on their way to Oswego, their first destination.

Shirley followed, embarking at the Dutch village of Schenectady, and ascending the Mohawk with about two hundred of the so-called regulars in bateaux. They passed Fort Johnson, the two villages of the Mohawks, and the Palatine settlement of German Flats; left behind the last trace of civilized man, rowed sixty miles through a wilderness, and reached the Great Carrying Place, which divided the waters that flow to the Hudson from those that flow to Lake Ontario. Here now stands the city which the classic zeal of its founders has adorned with the name of Rome. Then all was swamp and forest, traversed by a track that led to Wood Creek,—which is not to be confounded with the Wood Creek of Lake Champlain. Thither the bateaux were dragged on sledges and launched on the dark and tortuous stream, which, fed by a decoction of forest leaves that oozed from the marshy shores, crept in shadow through depths of foliage, with only a belt of illumined sky gleaming between the jagged tree-tops. Tall and lean with straining towards the light, their rough, gaunt stems trickling with perpetual damps, stood on either hand the silent hosts of the forest. The skeletons of their dead, barkless, blanched, and shattered, strewed the mudbanks and shallows; others lay submerged, like bones of drowned mammoths, thrusting lank, white limbs above the sullen water; and great trees, entire as yet, were flung by age or storms athwart the current,—a bristling barricade of matted boughs. There was work for the axe as well as for the oar; till at length Lake Oneida opened before them, and they rowed all day over its sunny breast, reached the outlet, and drifted down

[1] *James Gray to John Gray, 11 July, 1755.*

the shallow eddies of the Onondaga, between walls of verdure, silent as death, yet haunted everywhere with ambushed
danger. It was twenty days after leaving Schenectady when
they neared the mouth of the river; and Lake Ontario greeted
them, stretched like a sea to the pale brink of the northern
sky, while on the bare hill at their left stood the miserable
little fort of Oswego.

Shirley's whole force soon arrived; but not the needful provisions and stores. The machinery of transportation and the
commissariat was in the bewildered state inevitable among a
peaceful people at the beginning of a war; while the news of
Braddock's defeat produced such an effect on the boatmen
and the draymen at the carrying-places, that the greater part
deserted. Along with these disheartening tidings, Shirley
learned the death of his eldest son, killed at the side of Braddock. He had with him a second son, Captain John Shirley,
a vivacious young man, whom his father and his father's
friends in their familiar correspondence always called "Jack."
John Shirley's letters give a lively view of the situation.

"I have sat down to write to you,"—thus he addresses
Governor Morris, of Pennsylvania, who seems to have had a
great liking for him,—"because there is an opportunity of
sending you a few lines; and if you will promise to excuse
blots, interlineations, and grease (for this is written in the
open air, upon the head of a pork-barrel, and twenty people
about me), I will begin another half-sheet. We are not more
than about fifteen hundred men fit for duty; but that, I am
pretty sure, if we can go in time in our sloop, schooner, row-
galleys, and whale-boats, will be sufficient to take Frontenac;
after which we may venture to go upon the attack of Niagara,
but not before. I have not the least doubt with myself of
knocking down both these places yet this fall, if we can get
away in a week. If we take or destroy their two vessels at
Frontenac, and ruin their harbor there, and destroy the two
forts of that and Niagara, I shall think we have done great
things. Nobody holds it out better than my father and myself.
We shall all of us relish a good house over our heads, being
all encamped, except the General and some few field-officers,
who have what are called at Oswego houses; but they would
in other countries be called only sheds, except the fort, where

my father is. Adieu, dear sir; I hope my next will be directed from Frontenac. Yours most affectionately, John Shirley."[1]

Fort Frontenac lay to the northward, fifty miles or more across the lake. Niagara lay to the westward, at the distance of four or five days by boat or canoe along the south shore. At Frontenac there was a French force of fourteen hundred regulars and Canadians.[2] They had vessels and canoes to cross the lake and fall upon Oswego as soon as Shirley should leave it to attack Niagara; for Braddock's captured papers had revealed to them the English plan. If they should take it, Shirley would be cut off from his supplies and placed in desperate jeopardy, with the enemy in his rear. Hence it is that John Shirley insists on taking Frontenac before attempting Niagara. But the task was not easy; for the French force at the former place was about equal in effective strength to that of the English at Oswego. At Niagara, too, the French had, at the end of August, nearly twelve hundred Canadians and Indians from Fort Duquesne and the upper lakes.[3] Shirley was but imperfectly informed by his scouts of the unexpected strength of the opposition that awaited him; but he knew enough to see that his position was a difficult one. His movement on Niagara was stopped, first by want of provisions, and secondly because he was check-mated by the troops at Frontenac. He did not despair. Want of courage was not among his failings, and he was but too ready to take risks. He called a council of officers, told them that the total number of men fit for duty was thirteen hundred and seventy-six,

[1] The young author of this letter was, like his brother, a victim of the war.

"Permit me, good sir, to offer you my hearty condolence upon the death of my friend Jack, whose worth I admired, and feel for him more than I can express. . . . Few men of his age had so many friends." *Governor Morris to Shirley, 27 Nov. 1755.*

"My heart bleeds for Mr. Shirley. He must be overwhelmed with Grief when he hears of Capt. John Shirley's Death, of which I have an Account by the last Post from New York, where he died of a Flux and Fever that he had contracted at Oswego. The loss of Two Sons in one Campaign scarcely admits of Consolation. I feel the Anguish of the unhappy Father, and mix my Tears very heartily with his. I have had an intimate Acquaintance with Both of Them for many Years, and know well their inestimable Value." *Morris to Dinwiddie, 29 Nov. 1755.*

[2] *Bigot au Ministre, 27 Août, 1755.*

[3] *Ibid., 5 Sept. 1755.*

and that as soon as provisions enough should arrive he would embark for Niagara with six hundred soldiers and as many Indians as possible, leaving the rest to defend Oswego against the expected attack from Fort Frontenac.[1]

"All I am uneasy about is our provisions," writes John Shirley to his friend Morris; "our men have been upon half allowance of bread these three weeks past, and no rum given to 'em. My father yesterday called all the Indians together and made 'em a speech on the subject of General Johnson's engagement, which he calculated to inspire them with a spirit of revenge." After the speech he gave them a bullock for a feast, which they roasted and ate, pretending that they were eating the Governor of Canada! Some provisions arriving, orders were given to embark on the next day; but the officers murmured their dissent. The weather was persistently bad, their vessels would not hold half the party, and the bateaux, made only for river navigation, would infallibly founder on the treacherous and stormy lake. "All the field-officers," says John Shirley, "think it too rash an attempt; and I have heard so much of it that I think it my duty to let my father know what I hear." Another council was called; and the General, reluctantly convinced of the danger, put the question whether to go or not. The situation admitted but one reply. The council was of opinion that for the present the enterprise was impracticable; that Oswego should be strengthened, more vessels built, and preparation made to renew the attempt as soon as spring opened.[2] All thoughts of active operations were now suspended, and during what was left of the season the troops exchanged the musket for the spade, saw, and axe. At the end of October, leaving seven hundred men at Oswego, Shirley returned to Albany, and narrowly escaped drowning on the way, while passing a rapid in a whale-boat, to try the fitness of that species of craft for river navigation.[3]

Unfortunately for him, he had fallen out with Johnson, whom he had made what he was, but who now turned

---

[1] *Minutes of a Council of War at Oswego, 18 Sept. 1755.*

[2] *Ibid., 27 Sept. 1755.*

[3] On the Niagara expedition, *Braddock's Instructions to Major-General Shirley. Correspondence of Shirley, 1755. Conduct of Major-General Shirley* (London, 1758). Letters of John Shirley in *Pennsylvania Archives*, II. *Bradstreet to Shirley,*

against him,—a seeming ingratitude not wholly unprovoked. Shirley had diverted the New Jersey regiment, destined originally for Crown Point, to his own expedition against Niagara. Naturally inclined to keep all the reins in his own hands, he had encroached on Johnson's new office of Indian superintendent, held conferences with the Five Nations, and employed agents of his own to deal with them. These agents were persons obnoxious to Johnson, being allied with the clique of Dutch traders at Albany, who hated him because he had supplanted them in the direction of Indian affairs; and in a violent letter to the Lords of Trade, he inveighs against their "licentious and abandoned proceedings," "villanous conduct," "scurrilous falsehoods," and "base and insolent behavior."[1] "I am considerable enough," he says, "to have enemies and to be envied;"[2] and he declares he has proof that Shirley told the Mohawks that he, Johnson, was an upstart of his creating, whom he had set up and could pull down. Again, he charges Shirley's agents with trying to "debauch the Indians from joining him;" while Shirley, on his side, retorts the same complaint against his accuser.[3] When, by the death of Braddock, Shirley became commander-in-chief, Johnson grew so restive at being subject to his instructions that he declined to hold the management of Indian affairs unless it was made independent of his rival. The dispute became mingled with the teapot-tempest of New York provincial politics. The Lieutenant-Governor, Delancey, a politician of restless ambition and consummate dexterity, had taken umbrage at Shirley, of whose rising honors, not borne with remarkable humility, he appears to have been jealous. Delancey had hitherto favored the Dutch faction in the Assembly, hostile to Johnson; but he now changed attitude, and joined hands with him against the object of their common dislike. The one was strong in the prestige of a loudly-trumpeted victory, and the other had means of

---

17 *Aug. 1755*. MSS. in Massachusetts Archives. *Review of Military Operations in North America. Gentleman's Magazine*, 1757, p. 73. *London Magazine*, 1759, p. 594. Trumbull, *Hist. Connecticut*, II. 370.

[1] *Johnson to the Lords of Trade, 3 Sept. 1755.*

[2] *Ibid., 17 Jan. 1756.*

[3] *John Shirley to Governor Morris, 12 Aug. 1755.*

influence over the Ministry. Their coalition boded ill to Shirley, and he soon felt its effects.[1]

The campaign was now closed,—a sufficiently active one,
seeing that the two nations were nominally at peace. A disastrous rout on the Monongahela, failure at Niagara, a barren
victory at Lake George, and three forts captured in Acadia,
were the disappointing results on the part of England. Nor
had her enemies cause to boast. The Indians, it is true, had
won a battle for them: but they had suffered mortifying defeat from a raw militia; their general was a prisoner; and they
had lost Acadia past hope.

The campaign was over; but not its effects. It remains to
see what befell from the rout of Braddock and the unpardonable retreat of Dunbar from the frontier which it was his duty
to defend. Dumas had replaced Contrecœur in the command
of Fort Duquesne; and his first care was to set on the Western
tribes to attack the border settlements. His success was triumphant. The Delawares and Shawanoes, old friends of the
English, but for years past tending to alienation through
neglect and ill-usage, now took the lead against them. Many
of the Mingoes, or Five Nation Indians on the Ohio, also
took up the hatchet, as did various remoter tribes. The West
rose like a nest of hornets, and swarmed in fury against the
English frontier. Such was the consequence of the defeat of
Braddock aided by the skilful devices of the French commander. "It is by means such as I have mentioned," says Dumas,
"varied in every form to suit the occasion, that I have succeeded in ruining the three adjacent provinces, Pennsylvania,
Maryland, and Virginia, driving off the inhabitants, and
totally destroying the settlements over a tract of country
thirty leagues wide, reckoning from the line of Fort Cumberland. M. de Contrecœur had not been gone a week before
I had six or seven different war-parties in the field at once,
always accompanied by Frenchmen. Thus far, we have lost
only two officers and a few soldiers; but the Indian villages
are full of prisoners of every age and sex. The enemy has

[1] On this affair, see various papers in *N. Y. Col. Docs.*, VI., VII. Smith,
Hist. New York, Part II., Chaps. IV. V. *Review of Military Operations in North
America*. Both Smith and Livingston, the author of the *Review*, were person-
ally cognizant of the course of the dispute.

lost far more since the battle than on the day of his defeat."[1]

Dumas, required by the orders of his superiors to wage a detestable warfare against helpless settlers and their families, did what he could to temper its horrors, and enjoined the officers who went with the Indians to spare no effort to prevent them from torturing prisoners.[2] The attempt should be set down to his honor; but it did not avail much. In the record of cruelties committed this year on the borders, we find repeated instances of children scalped alive. "They kill all they meet," writes a French priest; "and after having abused the women and maidens, they slaughter or burn them."[3]

Washington was now in command of the Virginia regiment, consisting of a thousand men, raised afterwards to fifteen hundred. With these he was to protect a frontier of three hundred and fifty miles against more numerous enemies, who could choose their time and place of attack. His headquarters were at Winchester. His men were an ungovernable crew, enlisted chiefly on the turbulent border, and resenting every kind of discipline as levelling them with negroes; while the sympathizing House of Burgesses hesitated for months to pass any law for enforcing obedience, lest it should trench on the liberties of free white men. The service was to the last degree unpopular. "If we talk of obliging men to serve their country," wrote Landon Carter, "we are sure to hear a fellow mumble over the words 'liberty' and 'property' a thousand times."[4] The people, too, were in mortal fear of a slave insurrection, and therefore dared not go far from home.[5] Meanwhile a panic reigned along the border. Captain Waggoner, passing a gap in the Blue Ridge, could hardly make his way for the crowd of fugitives. "Every day," writes Washington, "we have accounts of such cruelties and bar-

---

[1] *Dumas au Ministre, 24 Juillet, 1756.*

[2] *Mémoires de Famille de l'Abbé Casgrain*, cited in *Le Foyer Canadien*, III. 26, where an extract is given from an order of Dumas to Baby, a Canadian officer. Orders of Contrecœur and Ligneris to the same effect are also given. A similar order, signed by Dumas, was found in the pocket of Douville, an officer killed by the English on the frontier. *Writings of Washington*, II. 137, note.

[3] *Rev. Claude Godefroy Cocquard, S. J., à son Frère, Mars* (?), *1757.*

[4] Extract in *Writings of Washington*, II. 145, *note.*

[5] *Letters of Dinwiddie, 1755.*

barities as are shocking to human nature. It is not possible to conceive the situation and danger of this miserable country. Such numbers of French and Indians are all around that no road is safe."

These frontiers had always been at peace. No forts of refuge had thus far been built, and the scattered settlers had no choice but flight. Their first impulse was to put wife and children beyond reach of the tomahawk. As autumn advanced, the invading bands grew more and more audacious. Braddock had opened a road for them by which they could cross the mountains at their ease; and scouts from Fort Cumberland reported that this road was beaten by as many feet as when the English army passed last summer. Washington was beset with difficulties. Men and officers alike were unruly and mutinous. He was at once blamed for their disorders and refused the means of repressing them. Envious detractors published slanders against him. A petty Maryland captain, who had once had a commission from the King, refused to obey his orders, and stirred up factions among his officers. Dinwiddie gave him cold support. The temper of the old Scotchman, crabbed at the best, had been soured by disappointment, vexation, weariness, and ill-health. He had, besides, a friend and countryman, Colonel Innes, whom, had he dared, he would gladly have put in Washington's place. He was full of zeal in the common cause, and wanted to direct the defence of the borders from his house at Williamsburg, two hundred miles distant. Washington never hesitated to obey; but he accompanied his obedience by a statement of his own convictions and his reasons for them, which, though couched in terms the most respectful, galled his irascible chief. The Governor acknowledged his merit; but bore him no love, and sometimes wrote to him in terms which must have tried his high temper to the utmost. Sometimes, though rarely, he gave words to his emotion.

"Your Honor," he wrote in April, "may see to what unhappy straits the distressed inhabitants and myself are reduced. I see inevitable destruction in so clear a light, that unless vigorous measures are taken by the Assembly, and speedy assistance sent from below, the poor inhabitants that are now in forts must unavoidably fall, while the remainder are flying before the barbarous foe. In fine, the melancholy situation of the people; the little prospect of assistance; the gross and scandalous abuse cast upon the officers in general, which is reflecting upon me in particular for suffering misconduct of such extraordinary kinds; and the distant prospect, if any, of gaining honor and reputation in the service,—cause me to lament the hour that gave me a commission, and would induce me at any other time than this of imminent danger to resign, without one hesitating moment, a command from which I never expect to reap either honor or benefit, but, on the contrary, have almost an absolute certainty of incurring displeasure below, while the murder of helpless families may be laid to my account here.

"The supplicating tears of the women and moving petitions of the men melt me into such deadly sorrow, that I solemnly declare, if I know my own mind, I could offer myself a willing sacrifice to the butchering enemy, provided that would contribute to the people's ease."[1]

In the turmoil around him, patriotism and public duty seemed all to be centred in the breast of one heroic youth. He was respected and generally beloved, but he did not kindle enthusiasm. His were the qualities of an unflagging courage, an all-enduring fortitude, and a deep trust. He showed an astonishing maturity of character, and the kind of mastery over others which begins with mastery over self. At twenty-four he was the foremost man, and acknowledged as such, along the whole long line of the western border.

To feel the situation, the nature of these frontiers must be kept in mind. Along the skirts of the southern and middle colonies ran for six or seven hundred miles a loose, thin, dishevelled fringe of population, the half-barbarous pioneers of advancing civilization. Their rude dwellings were often miles apart. Buried in woods, the settler lived in an appalling loneliness. A low-browed cabin of logs, with moss stuffed in the chinks to keep out the wind, roof covered with sheets of bark, chimney of sticks and clay, and square holes closed by a shutter in place of windows; an unkempt matron, lean with hard work, and a brood of children with bare heads and tattered

[1] *Writings of Washington*, II. 143.

garments eked out by deerskin,—such was the home of the pioneer in the remoter and wilder districts. The scene around bore witness to his labors. It was the repulsive transition from savagery to civilization, from the forest to the farm. The victims of his axe lay strewn about the dismal "clearing" in a chaos of prostrate trunks, tangled boughs, and withered leaves, waiting for the fire that was to be the next agent in the process of improvement; while around, voiceless and grim, stood the living forest, gazing on the desolation, and biding its own day of doom. The owner of the cabin was miles away, hunting in the woods for the wild turkey and venison which were the chief food of himself and his family till the soil could be tamed into the bearing of crops.

Towards night he returned; and as he issued from the forest shadows he saw a column of blue smoke rising quietly in the still evening air. He ran to the spot; and there, among the smouldering logs of his dwelling, lay, scalped and mangled, the dead bodies of wife and children. A war-party had passed that way. Breathless, palpitating, his brain on fire, he rushed through the thickening night to carry the alarm to his nearest neighbor, three miles distant.

Such was the character and the fate of many incipient settlements of the utmost border. Farther east, they had a different aspect. Here, small farms with well-built log-houses, cattle, crops of wheat and Indian corn, were strung at intervals along some woody valley of the lower Alleghanies: yesterday a scene of hardy toil; to-day swept with destruction from end to end. There was no warning; no time for concert, perhaps none for flight. Sudden as the leaping panther, a pack of human wolves burst out of the forest, did their work, and vanished.

If the country had been an open one, like the plains beyond the Mississippi, the situation would have been less frightful; but the forest was everywhere, rolled over hill and valley in billows of interminable green,—a leafy maze, a mystery of shade, a universal hiding-place, where murder might lurk unseen at its victim's side, and Nature seemed formed to nurse the mind with wild and dark imaginings. The detail of blood is set down in the untutored words of those who saw and felt it. But there was a suffering that had no record,—the mortal fear of women and children in the solitude of their wilderness homes, haunted, waking and sleeping, with nightmares of horror that were but the forecast of an imminent reality. The country had in past years been so peaceful, and the Indians so friendly, that many of the settlers, especially on the Pennsylvanian border, had no arms, and were doubly in need of help from the Government. In Virginia they had it, such as it was. In Pennsylvania they had for months none whatever; and the Assembly turned a deaf ear to their cries.

Far to the east, sheltered from danger, lay staid and prosperous Philadelphia, the home of order and thrift. It took its stamp from the Quakers, its original and dominant population, set apart from the other colonists not only in character and creed, but in the outward symbols of a peculiar dress and a daily sacrifice of grammar on the altar of religion. The even tenor of their lives counteracted the effects of climate, and they are said to have been perceptibly more rotund in feature and person than their neighbors. Yet, broad and humanizing as was their faith, they were capable of extreme bitterness towards opponents, clung tenaciously to power, and were jealous for the ascendency of their sect, which had begun to show signs of wavering. On other sects they looked askance; and regarded the Presbyterians in particular with a dislike which in moments of crisis rose to detestation.[1] They held it sin to fight, and above all to fight against Indians.

Here was one cause of military paralysis. It was reinforced by another. The old standing quarrel between governor and assembly had grown more violent than ever; and this as a direct consequence of the public distress, which above all things demanded harmony. The dispute turned this time on a single issue,—that of the taxation of the proprietary estates. The estates in question consisted of vast tracts of wild land, yielding no income, and at present to a great extent worthless, being overrun by the enemy.[2] The Quaker Assembly had refused to protect them; and on one occasion had rejected an offer of the proprietaries to join them in paying the cost of

[1] See a crowd of party pamphlets, Quaker against Presbyterian, which appeared at Philadelphia in 1764, abusively acrimonious on both sides.

[2] The productive estates of the proprietaries were taxed through the tenants.

their defence.[1] But though they would not defend the land, they insisted on taxing it; and farther insisted that the taxes upon it should be laid by the provincial assessors. By a law of the province, these assessors were chosen by popular vote; and in consenting to this law, the proprietaries had expressly provided that their estates should be exempted from all taxes to be laid by officials in whose appointment they had no voice.[2] Thomas and Richard Penn, the present proprietaries, had debarred their deputy, the Governor, both by the terms of his commission and by special instruction, from consenting to such taxation, and had laid him under heavy bonds to secure his obedience. Thus there was another side to the question than that of the Assembly; though our American writers have been slow to acknowledge it.

Benjamin Franklin was leader in the Assembly and shared its views. The feudal proprietorship of the Penn family was odious to his democratic nature. It was, in truth, a pestilent anomaly, repugnant to the genius of the people; and the disposition and character of the present proprietaries did not tend to render it less vexatious. Yet there were considerations which might have tempered the impatient hatred with which the colonists regarded it. The first proprietary, William Penn, had used his feudal rights in the interest of a broad liberalism; and through them had established the popular institutions and universal tolerance which made Pennsylvania the most democratic province in America, and nursed the spirit of liberty which now revolted against his heirs. The one absorbing passion of Pennsylvania was resistance to their deputy, the Governor. The badge of feudalism, though light, was insufferably irritating; and the sons of William Penn were moreover detested by the Quakers as renegades from the faith of their father. Thus the immediate political conflict engrossed mind and heart; and in the rancor of their quarrel with the proprietaries, the Assembly forgot the French and Indians.

---

[1] The proprietaries offered to contribute to the cost of building and maintaining a fort on the spot where the French soon after built Fort Duquesne. This plan, vigorously executed, would have saved the province from a deluge of miseries. One of the reasons assigned by the Assembly for rejecting it was that it would irritate the enemy. See *supra*, pp. 885–86.

[2] *A Brief View of the Conduct of Pennsylvania for the year 1755.*

In Philadelphia and the eastern districts the Quakers could ply their trades, tend their shops, till their farms, and discourse at their ease on the wickedness of war. The midland counties, too, were for the most part tolerably safe. They were occupied mainly by crude German peasants, who nearly equalled in number all the rest of the population, and who, gathered at the centre of the province, formed a mass politically indigestible. Translated from servitude to the most ample liberty, they hated the thought of military service, which reminded them of former oppression, cared little whether they lived under France or England, and, thinking themselves out of danger, had no mind to be taxed for the defence of others. But while the great body of the Germans were sheltered from harm, those of them who lived farther westward were not so fortunate. Here, mixed with Scotch Irish Presbyterians and Celtic Irish Catholics, they formed a rough border population, the discordant elements of which could rarely unite for common action; yet, though confused and disjointed, they were a living rampart to the rest of the colony. Against them raged the furies of Indian war; and, maddened with distress and terror, they cried aloud for help.

Petition after petition came from the borders for arms and ammunition, and for a militia law to enable the people to organize and defend themselves. The Quakers resisted. "They have taken uncommon pains," writes Governor Morris to Shirley, "to prevent the people from taking up arms."[1] Braddock's defeat, they declared, was a just judgment on him and his soldiers for molesting the French in their settlements on the Ohio.[2] A bill was passed by the Assembly for raising fifty thousand pounds for the King's use by a tax which included the proprietary lands. The Governor, constrained by his instructions and his bonds, rejected it. "I can only say," he told them, "that I will readily pass a bill for striking any sum in paper money the present exigency may require, provided funds are established for sinking the same in five years." Messages long and acrimonious were exchanged between the parties. The Assembly, had they chosen, could easily have raised money enough by methods not involving the point in dis-

[1] *Morris to Shirley, 16 Aug. 1755.*
[2] *Morris to Sir Thomas Robinson, 28 Aug. 1755.*

pute; but they thought they saw in the crisis a means of forcing the Governor to yield. The Quakers had an alternative motive: if the Governor gave way, it was a political victory; if he stood fast, their non-resistance principles would triumph, and in this triumph their ascendency as a sect would be confirmed. The debate grew every day more bitter and unmannerly. The Governor could not yield; the Assembly would not. There was a complete deadlock. The Assembly requested the Governor "not to make himself the hateful instrument of reducing a free people to the abject state of vassalage."[1] As the raising of money and the control of its expenditure was in their hands; as he could not prorogue or dissolve them, and as they could adjourn on their own motion to such time as pleased them; as they paid his support, and could withhold it if he offended them,—which they did in the present case,—it seemed no easy task for him to reduce them to vassalage. "What must we do," pursued the Assembly, "to please this kind governor, who takes so much pains to render us obnoxious to our sovereign and odious to our fellow-subjects? If we only tell him that the difficulties he meets with are not owing to the causes he names,—which indeed have no existence,—but to his own want of skill and abilities for his station, he takes it extremely amiss, and says 'we forget all decency to those in authority.' We are apt to think there is likewise some decency due to the Assembly as a part of the government; and though we have not, like the Governor, had a courtly education, but are plain men, and must be very imperfect in our politeness, yet we think we have no chance of improving by his example."[2] Again, in another Message, the Assembly, with a thrust at Morris himself, tell him that colonial governors have often been "transient persons, of broken fortunes, greedy of money, destitute of all concern for those they govern, often their enemies, and endeavoring not only to oppress, but to defame them."[3] In such unseemly fashion was the battle waged. Morris, who was

[1] *Colonial Records of Pa.*, VI. 584.

[2] *Message of the Assembly to the Governor, 29 Sept. 1755* (written by Franklin), in *Colonial Records of Pa.*, VI. 631, 632.

[3] *Writings of Franklin*, III. 447. The Assembly at first suppressed this paper, but afterwards printed it.

himself a provincial, showed more temper and dignity; though there was not too much on either side. "The Assembly," he wrote to Shirley, "seem determined to take advantage of the country's distress to get the whole power of government into their own hands." And the Assembly proclaimed on their part that the Governor was taking advantage of the country's distress to reduce the province to "Egyptian bondage."

Petitions poured in from the miserable frontiersmen. "How long will those in power, by their quarrels, suffer us to be massacred?" demanded William Trent, the Indian trader. "Two and forty bodies have been buried on Patterson's Creek; and since they have killed more, and keep on killing."[1] Early in October news came that a hundred persons had been murdered near Fort Cumberland. Repeated tidings followed of murders on the Susquehanna; then it was announced that the war-parties had crossed that stream, and were at their work on the eastern side. Letter after letter came from the sufferers, bringing such complaints as this: "We are in as bad circumstances as ever any poor Christians were ever in; for the cries of widowers, widows, fatherless and motherless children, are enough to pierce the most hardest of hearts. Likewise it's a very sorrowful spectacle to see those that escaped with their lives with not a mouthful to eat, or bed to lie on, or clothes to cover their nakedness, or keep them warm, but all they had consumed into ashes. These deplorable circumstances cry aloud for your Honor's most wise consideration; for it is really very shocking for the husband to see the wife of his bosom her head cut off, and the children's blood drunk like water, by these bloody and cruel savages."[2]

Morris was greatly troubled. "The conduct of the Assembly," he wrote to Shirley, "is to me shocking beyond parallel." "The inhabitants are abandoning their plantations, and we are in a dreadful situation," wrote John Harris from the east bank of the Susquehanna. On the next day he wrote again: "The Indians are cutting us off every day, and I had a certain account of about fifteen hundred Indians, besides French, being on their march against us and Virginia, and now close on our borders, their scouts scalping our families on our frontiers

---

[1] *Trent to James Burd, 4 Oct. 1755.*
[2] *Adam Hoops to Governor Morris, 3 Nov. 1755.*

daily." The report was soon confirmed; and accounts came that the settlements in the valley called the Great Cove had been completely destroyed. All this was laid before the Assembly. They declared the accounts exaggerated, but confessed that outrages had been committed; hinted that the fault was with the proprietaries; and asked the Governor to explain why the Delawares and Shawanoes had become unfriendly. "If they have suffered wrongs," said the Quakers, "we are resolved to do all in our power to redress them, rather than entail upon ourselves and our posterity the calamities of a cruel Indian war." The Indian records were searched, and several days spent in unsuccessful efforts to prove fraud in a late land-purchase.

Post after post still brought news of slaughter. The upper part of Cumberland County was laid waste. Edward Biddle wrote from Reading: "The drum is beating and bells ringing, and all the people under arms. This night we expect an attack. The people exclaim against the Quakers." "We seem to be given up into the hands of a merciless enemy," wrote John Elder from Paxton. And he declares that more than forty persons have been killed in that neighborhood, besides numbers carried off. Meanwhile the Governor and Assembly went on fencing with words and exchanging legal subtleties; while, with every cry of distress that rose from the west, each hoped that the other would yield.

On the eighth of November the Assembly laid before Morris for his concurrence a bill for emitting bills of credit to the amount of sixty thousand pounds, to be sunk in four years by a tax including the proprietary estates.[1] "I shall not," he replied, "enter into a dispute whether the proprietaries ought to be taxed or not. It is sufficient for me that they have given me no power in that case; and I cannot think it consistent either with my duty or safety to exceed the powers of my commission, much less to do what that commission expressly prohibits."[2] He stretched his authority, however, so far as to propose a sort of compromise by which the question should be referred to the King; but they refused it; and the quarrel

[1] *Colonial Records of Pa.*, VI. 682.
[2] *Message of the Governor to the Assembly, 8 Nov. 1755*, in *Colonial Records of Pa.*, VI. 684.

and the murders went on as before. "We have taken," said the Assembly, "every step in our power, consistent with the just rights of the freemen of Pennsylvania, for the relief of the poor distressed inhabitants; and we have reason to believe that they themselves would not wish us to go farther. Those who would give up essential liberty to purchase a little temporary safety deserve neither liberty nor safety."[1] Then the borderers deserved neither; for, rather than be butchered, they would have let the proprietary lands lie untaxed for another year. "You have in all," said the Governor, "proposed to me five money bills, three of them rejected because contrary to royal instructions; the other two on account of the unjust method proposed for taxing the proprietary estate. If you are disposed to relieve your country, you have many other ways of granting money to which I shall have no objection. I shall put one proof more both of your sincerity and mine in our professions of regard for the public, by offering to agree to any bill in the present exigency which it is consistent with my duty to pass; lest, before our present disputes can be brought to an issue, we should neither have a privilege to dispute about, nor a country to dispute in."[2] They stood fast; and with an obstinacy for which the Quakers were chiefly answerable, insisted that they would give nothing, except by a bill taxing real estate, and including that of the proprietaries.

But now the Assembly began to feel the ground shaking under their feet. A paper, called a "Representation," signed by some of the chief citizens, was sent to the House, calling for measures of defence. "You will forgive us, gentlemen," such was its language, "if we assume characters somewhat higher than that of humble suitors praying for the defence of our lives and properties as a matter of grace or favor on your side. You will permit us to make a positive and immediate demand of it."[3] This drove the Quakers mad. Preachers, male and female, harangued in the streets, denouncing the iniquity of war. Three of the sect from England, two women and a

---

[1] *Message of the Assembly to the Governor, 11 Nov. Ibid.*, VI. 692. The words are Franklin's.

[2] *Message of the Governor to the Assembly, 22 Nov. 1755, in Colonial Records of Pa.*, VI. 714.

[3] *Pennsylvania Archives*, II. 485.

man, invited their brethren of the Assembly to a private house, and fervently exhorted them to stand firm. Some of the principal Quakers joined in an address to the House, in which they declared that any action on its part "inconsistent with the peaceable testimony we profess and have borne to the world appears to us in its consequences to be destructive of our religious liberties."[1] And they protested that they would rather "suffer" than pay taxes for such ends. Consistency, even in folly, has in it something respectable; but the Quakers were not consistent. A few years after, when heated with party-passion and excited by reports of an irruption of incensed Presbyterian borderers, some of the pacific sectaries armed for battle; and the streets of Philadelphia beheld the curious conjunction of musket and broad-brimmed hat.[2]

The mayor, aldermen, and common council next addressed the Assembly, adjuring them, "in the most solemn manner, before God and in the name of all our fellow-citizens," to provide for defending the lives and property of the people.[2] A deputation from a band of Indians on the Susquehanna, still friendly to the province, came to ask whether the English meant to fight or not; for, said their speaker, "if they will not stand by us, we will join the French." News came that the settlement of Tulpehocken, only sixty miles distant, had been destroyed; and then that the Moravian settlement of Gnadenhütten was burned, and nearly all its inmates massacred. Colonel William Moore wrote to the Governor that two thousand men were coming from Chester County to compel him and the Assembly to defend the province; and Conrad Weiser wrote that more were coming from Berks on the same errand. Old friends of the Assembly began to cry out against them. Even the Germans, hitherto their fast allies, were roused from their attitude of passivity, and four hundred of them came in procession to demand measures of war. A band of frontiersmen presently arrived, bringing in a wagon the bodies of friends and relatives lately murdered, displaying them at the doors of the Assembly, cursing the Quakers, and threatening vengeance.[4]

[1] *Ibid.*, II. 487.
[2] See *Conspiracy of Pontiac*, II. 143, 152.
[3] *A Remonstrance*, etc., in *Colonial Records of Pa.*, VI. 734.
[4] Mante, 47; Entick, I. 377.

Finding some concession necessary, the House at length passed a militia law, — probably the most futile ever enacted. It specially exempted the Quakers, and constrained nobody; but declared it lawful, for such as chose, to form themselves into companies and elect officers by ballot. The company officers thus elected might, if they saw fit, elect, also by ballot, colonels, lieutenant-colonels, and majors. These last might then, in conjunction with the Governor, frame articles of war; to which, however, no officer or man was to be subjected unless, after three days' consideration, he subscribed them in presence of a justice of the peace, and declared his willingness to be bound by them.[1]

This mockery could not appease the people; the Assembly must raise money for men, arms, forts, and all the detested appliances of war. Defeat absolute and ignominious seemed hanging over the House, when an incident occurred which gave them a decent pretext for retreat. The Governor informed them that he had just received a letter from the proprietaries, giving to the province five thousand pounds sterling to aid in its defence, on condition that the money should be accepted as a free gift, and not as their proportion of any tax that was or might be laid by the Assembly. They had not learned the deplorable state of the country, and had sent the money in view of the defeat of Braddock and its probable consequences. The Assembly hereupon yielded, struck out from the bill before them the clause taxing the proprietary estates, and, thus amended, presented it to the Governor, who by his signature made it a law.[2]

The House had failed to carry its point. The result disappointed Franklin, and doubly disappointed the Quakers. His maxim was: Beat the Governor first, and then beat the enemy; theirs: Beat the Governor, and let the enemy alone. The measures that followed, directed in part by Franklin himself, held the Indians in check, and mitigated the distress of the western counties; yet there was no safety for them through-

---

[1] This remarkable bill, drawn by Franklin, was meant for political rather than military effect. It was thought that Morris would refuse to pass it, and could therefore be accused of preventing the province from defending itself; but he avoided the snare by signing it.

[2] *Minutes of Council, 27 Nov. 1755.*

out the two or three years when France was cheering on her hell-hounds against this tormented frontier.

As in Pennsylvania, so in most of the other colonies there was conflict between assemblies and governors, to the unspeakable detriment of the public service. In New York, though here no obnoxious proprietary stood between the people and the Crown, the strife was long and severe. The point at issue was an important one,—whether the Assembly should continue their practice of granting yearly supplies to the Governor, or should establish a permanent fund for the ordinary expenses of government,—thus placing him beyond their control. The result was a victory for the Assembly.

Month after month the great continent lay wrapped in snow. Far along the edge of the western wilderness men kept watch and ward in lonely blockhouses, or scoured the forest on the track of prowling war-parties. The provincials in garrison at forts Edward, William Henry, and Oswego dragged out the dreary winter; while bands of New England rangers, muffled against the piercing cold, caps of fur on their heads, hatchets in their belts, and guns in their mittened hands, glided on skates along the gleaming ice-floor of Lake George, to spy out the secrets of Ticonderoga, or seize some careless sentry to tell them tidings of the foe. Thus the petty war went on; but the big war was frozen into torpor, ready, like a hibernating bear, to wake again with the birds, the bees, and the flowers.[1]

---

[1] On Pennsylvanian disputes,— *A Brief State of the Province of Pennsylvania* (London, 1755). *A Brief View of the Conduct of Pennsylvania* (London, 1756). These are pamphlets on the Governor's side, by William Smith, D.D., Provost of the College of Pennsylvania. *An Answer to an invidious Pamphlet, intituled a Brief State*, etc. (London, 1755). Anonymous. *A True and Impartial State of the Province of Pennsylvania* (Philadelphia, 1759). Anonymous. The last two works attack the first two with great vehemence. The *True and Impartial State* is an able presentation of the case of the Assembly, omitting, however, essential facts. But the most elaborate work on the subject is the *Historical Review of the Constitution and Government of Pennsylvania*, inspired and partly written by Franklin. It is hotly partisan, and sometimes sophistical and unfair. Articles on the quarrel will also be found in the provincial newspapers, especially the *New York Mercury*, and in the *Gentleman's Magazine* for 1755 and 1756. But it is impossible to get any clear and just view of it without wading through the interminable documents concerning it in the *Colonial Records of Pennsylvania* and the *Pennsylvania Archives*.

Chapter XI

1712-1756

MONTCALM

War declared • State of Europe • Pompadour and Maria Theresa • Infatuation of the French Court • The European War • Montcalm to command in America • His early Life • An intractable Pupil • His Marriage • His Family • His Campaigns • Preparation for America • His Associates • Lévis, Bourlamaque, Bougainville • Embarkation • The Voyage • Arrival • Vaudreuil • Forces of Canada • Troops of the Line, Colony Troops, Militia, Indians • The Military Situation • Capture of Fort Bull • Montcalm at Ticonderoga

---

ON THE EIGHTEENTH of May, 1756, England, after a year of open hostility, at length declared war. She had attacked France by land and sea, turned loose her ships to prey on French commerce, and brought some three hundred prizes into her ports. It was the act of a weak Government, supplying by spasms of violence what it lacked in considerate resolution. France, no match for her amphibious enemy in the game of marine depredation, cried out in horror; and to emphasize her complaints and signalize a pretended good faith which her acts had belied, ostentatiously released a British frigate captured by her cruisers. She in her turn declared war on the ninth of June: and now began the most terrible conflict of the eighteenth century; one that convulsed Europe and shook America, India, the coasts of Africa, and the islands of the sea.

In Europe the ground was trembling already with the coming earthquake. Such smothered discords, such animosities, ambitions, jealousies, possessed the rival governments; such entanglements of treaties and alliances, offensive or defensive, open or secret,—that a blow at one point shook the whole fabric. Hanover, like the heel of Achilles, was the vulnerable part for which England was always trembling. Therefore she made a defensive treaty with Prussia, by which each party bound itself to aid the other, should its territory be invaded. England thus sought a guaranty against France, and Prussia against Russia. She had need. Her King, Frederic the Great, had drawn upon himself an avalanche. Three women—two empresses and a concubine—controlled the forces of the three great nations, Austria, Russia, and France; and they all hated him: Elizabeth of Russia, by reason of a distrust fomented by secret intrigue and turned into gall by the biting tongue of Frederic himself, who had jibed at her amours, compared her to Messalina, and called her "*infâme catin du Nord*;" Maria Theresa of Austria, because she saw in him a rebellious vassal of the Holy Roman Empire, and, above all, because he had robbed her of Silesia; Madame de Pompadour, because when she sent him a message of compliment, he answered, "*Je ne la connais pas*," forbade his ambassador to visit her, and in his mocking wit spared neither her nor her royal lover. Feminine pique, revenge, or vanity had then at their service the mightiest armaments of Europe.

The recovery of Silesia and the punishment of Frederic for his audacity in seizing it, possessed the mind of Maria Theresa with the force of a ruling passion. To these ends she had joined herself in secret league with Russia; and now at the prompting of her minister Kaunitz she courted the alliance of France. It was a reversal of the hereditary policy of Austria; joining hands with an old and deadly foe, and spurning England, of late her most trusty ally. But France could give powerful aid against Frederic; and hence Maria Theresa, virtuous as she was high-born and proud, stooped to make advances to the all-powerful mistress of Louis XV., wrote her flattering letters, and addressed her, it is said, as "*Ma chère cousine*." Pompadour was delighted, and could hardly do enough for her imperial friend. She ruled the King, and could make and unmake ministers at will. They hastened to do her pleasure, disguising their subserviency by dressing it out in specious reasons of state. A conference at her summer-house, called Babiole, "Bawble," prepared the way for a treaty which involved the nation in the anti-Prussian war, and made it the instrument of Austria in the attempt to humble Frederic,— an attempt which if successful would give the hereditary enemy of France a predominance over Germany. France engaged to aid the cause with twenty-four thousand men; but in the zeal of her rulers began with a hundred thousand. Thus the three great Powers stood leagued against Prussia. Sweden and Saxony joined them; and the Empire itself, of which Prussia was a part, took arms against its obnoxious member.

Never in Europe had power been more centralized, and never in France had the reins been held by persons so pitiful, impelled by motives so contemptible. The levity, vanity, and spite of a concubine became a mighty engine to influence the destinies of nations. Louis XV., enervated by pleasures and devoured by *ennui*, still had his emotions; he shared Pompadour's detestation of Frederic, and he was tormented at times by a lively fear of damnation. But how damn a king who had entered the lists as champion of the Church? England was Protestant, and so was Prussia; Austria was supremely Catholic. Was it not a merit in the eyes of God to join her in holy war against the powers of heresy? The King of the Parc-aux-Cerfs would propitiate Heaven by a new crusade.

Henceforth France was to turn her strength against her European foes; and the American war, the occasion of the universal outbreak, was to hold in her eyes a second place. The reasons were several: the vanity of Pompadour, infatuated by the advances of the Empress-Queen, and eager to secure her good graces; the superstition of the King; the anger of both against Frederic; the desire of D'Argenson, minister of war, that the army, and not the navy, should play the foremost part; and the passion of courtiers and nobles, ignorant of the naval service, to win laurels in a continental war,—all conspired to one end. It was the interest of France to turn her strength against her only dangerous rival; to continue as she had begun, in building up a naval power that could face England on the seas and sustain her own rising colonies in America, India, and the West Indies: for she too might have multiplied herself, planted her language and her race over all the globe, and grown with the growth of her children, had she not been at the mercy of an effeminate profligate, a mistress turned procuress, and the favorites to whom they delegated power.

Still, something must be done for the American war; at least there must be a new general to replace Dieskau. None of the Court favorites wanted a command in the backwoods, and the minister of war was free to choose whom he would.

His choice fell on Louis Joseph, Marquis de Montcalm-Gozon de Saint-Véran.

Montcalm was born in the south of France, at the Château of Candiac, near Nîmes, on the twenty-ninth of February, 1712. At the age of six he was placed in the charge of one Dumas, a natural son of his grandfather. This man, a conscientious pedant, with many theories of education, ruled his pupil stiffly; and, before the age of fifteen, gave him a good knowledge of Latin, Greek, and history. Young Montcalm had a taste for books, continued his reading in such intervals of leisure as camps and garrisons afforded, and cherished to the end of his life the ambition of becoming a member of the Academy. Yet, with all his liking for study, he sometimes revolted against the sway of the pedagogue who wrote letters of complaint to his father protesting against the "judgments of the vulgar, who, contrary to the experience of ages, say that if children are well reproved they will correct their faults." Dumas, however, was not without sense, as is shown by another letter to the elder Montcalm, in which he says that the boy had better be ignorant of Latin and Greek "than know them as he does without knowing how to read, write, and speak French well." The main difficulty was to make him write a good hand,—a point in which he signally failed to the day of his death. So refractory was he at times, that his master despaired. "M. de Montcalm," Dumas informs the father, "has great need of docility, industry, and willingness to take advice. What will become of him?" The pupil, aware of these aspersions, met them by writing to his father his own ideas of what his aims should be. "First, to be an honorable man, of good morals, brave, and a Christian. Secondly, to read in moderation; to know as much Greek and Latin as most men of the world; also the four rules of arithmetic, and something of history, geography, and French and Latin *belles-lettres*, as well as to have a taste for the arts and sciences. Thirdly, and above all, to be obedient, docile, and very submissive to your orders and those of my dear mother; and also to defer to the advice of M. Dumas. Fourthly, to fence and ride as well as my small abilities will permit."[1]

If Louis de Montcalm failed to satisfy his preceptor, he had

[1] This passage is given by Somervogel from the original letter.

a brother who made ample amends. Of this infant prodigy it is related that at six years he knew Latin, Greek, and Hebrew, and had some acquaintance with arithmetic, French history, geography, and heraldry. He was destined for the Church, but died at the age of seven; his precocious brain having been urged to fatal activity by the exertions of Dumas.

Other destinies and a more wholesome growth were the lot of young Louis. At fifteen he joined the army as ensign in the regiment of Hainaut. Two years after, his father bought him a captaincy, and he was first under fire at the siege of Philipsbourg. His father died in 1735, and left him heir to a considerable landed estate, much embarrassed by debt. The Marquis de la Fare, a friend of the family, soon after sought for him an advantageous marriage to strengthen his position and increase his prospects of promotion; and he accordingly espoused Mademoiselle Angélique Louise Talon du Boulay,— a union which brought him influential alliances and some property. Madame de Montcalm bore him ten children, of whom only two sons and four daughters were living in 1752. "May God preserve them all," he writes in his autobiography, "and make them prosper for this world and the next! Perhaps it will be thought that the number is large for so moderate a fortune, especially as four of them are girls; but does God ever abandon his children in their need?

> " 'Aux petits des oiseaux il donne la pâture,
>   Et sa bonté s'étend sur toute la nature.' "

He was pious in his soldierly way, and ardently loyal to Church and King.

His family seat was Candiac; where, in the intervals of campaigning, he found repose with his wife, his children, and his mother, who was a woman of remarkable force of character and who held great influence over her son. He had a strong attachment to this home of his childhood; and in after years, out of the midst of the American wilderness, his thoughts turned longingly towards it. *"Quand reverrai-je mon cher Candiac!"*

In 1741 Montcalm took part in the Bohemian campaign. He was made colonel of the regiment of Auxerrois two years

later, and passed unharmed through the severe campaign of
1744. In the next year he fought in Italy under Maréchal de
Maillebois. In 1746, at the disastrous action under the walls
of Piacenza, where he twice rallied his regiment, he received
five sabre-cuts,—two of which were in the head,—and was
made prisoner. Returning to France on parole, he was promoted in the year following to the rank of brigadier; and
being soon after exchanged, rejoined the army, and was again
wounded by a musket-shot. The peace of Aix-la-Chapelle now
gave him a period of rest.[1] At length, being on a visit to Paris
late in the autumn of 1755, the minister, D'Argenson, hinted
to him that he might be appointed to command the troops in
America. He heard no more of the matter till, after his return
home, he received from D'Argenson a letter dated at Versailles the twenty-fifth of January, at midnight. "Perhaps,
Monsieur," it began, "you did not expect to hear from me
again on the subject of the conversation I had with you the
day you came to bid me farewell at Paris. Nevertheless I have
not forgotten for a moment the suggestion I then made you;
and it is with the greatest pleasure that I announce to you
that my views have prevailed. The King has chosen you to
command his troops in North America, and will honor you
on your departure with the rank of major-general."

The Chevalier de Lévis, afterwards Marshal of France, was
named as his second in command, with the rank of brigadier,
and the Chevalier de Bourlamaque as his third, with the rank
of colonel; but what especially pleased him was the appointment of his eldest son to command a regiment in France. He
set out from Candiac for the Court, and occupied himself on
the way with reading Charlevoix. "I take great pleasure in it,"
he writes from Lyons to his mother; "he gives a pleasant account of Quebec. But be comforted; I shall always be glad to
come home." At Paris he writes again: "Don't expect any
long letter from me before the first of March; all my business

---

[1] The account of Montcalm up to this time is chiefly from his unpublished
autobiography, preserved by his descendants, and entitled *Mémoires pour servir à l'Histoire de ma Vie*. Somervogel, *Comme on servait autrefois*; Bonne-
chose, *Montcalm et le Canada*; Martin, *Le Marquis de Montcalm*; *Éloge de
Montcalm*; *Autre Éloge de Montcalm*; *Mémoires sur le Canada, 1749–1760*, and
other writings in print and manuscript have also been consulted.

will be done by that time, and I shall begin to breathe again. I have not yet seen the Chevalier de Montcalm [*his son*]. Last night I came from Versailles, and am going back to-morrow. The King gives me twenty-five thousand francs a year, as he did to M. Dieskau, besides twelve thousand for my equipment, which will cost me above a thousand crowns more; but I cannot stop for that. I embrace my dearest and all the family." A few days later his son joined him. "He is as thin and delicate as ever, but grows prodigiously tall."

On the second of March he informs his mother, "My affairs begin to get on. A good part of the baggage went off the day before yesterday in the King's wagons; an assistant-cook and two liverymen yesterday. I have got a good cook. Estève, my secretary, will go on the eighth; Joseph and Déjean will follow me. To-morrow evening I go to Versailles till Sunday, and will write from there to Madame de Montcalm [*his wife*]. I have three aides-de-camp; one of them, Bougainville, a man of parts, pleasant company. Madame Mazade was happily delivered on Wednesday; in extremity on Friday with a malignant fever; Saturday and yesterday, reports favorable. I go there twice a day, and am just going now. She has a girl. I embrace you all." Again, on the fifteenth: "In a few hours I set out for Brest. Yesterday I presented my son, with whom I am well pleased, to all the royal family. I shall have a secretary at Brest, and will write more at length." On the eighteenth he writes from Rennes to his wife: "I arrived, dearest, this morning, and stay here all day. I shall be at Brest on the twenty-first. Everything will be on board on the twenty-sixth. My son has been here since yesterday for me to coach him and get him a uniform made, in which he will give thanks for his regiment at the same time that I take leave in my embroidered coat. Perhaps I shall leave debts behind. I wait impatiently for the bills. You have my will; I wish you would get it copied, and send it to me before I sail."

Reaching Brest, the place of embarkation, he writes to his mother: "I have business on hand still. My health is good, and the passage will be a time of rest. I embrace you, and my dearest, and my daughters. Love to all the family. I shall write up to the last moment."

No translation can give an idea of the rapid, abrupt, elliptical style of this familiar correspondence, where the meaning is sometimes suggested by a single word, unintelligible to any but those for whom it is written.

At the end of March Montcalm, with all his following, was ready to embark; and three ships of the line, the "Léopard," the "Héros," and the "Illustre," fitted out as transports, were ready to receive the troops; while the General, with Lévis and Bourlamaque, were to take passage in the frigates "Licorne," "Sauvage," and "Sirène." "I like the Chevalier de Lévis," says Montcalm, "and I think he likes me." His first aide-de-camp, Bougainville, pleased him, if possible, still more. This young man, son of a notary, had begun life as an advocate in the Parliament of Paris, where his abilities and learning had already made him conspicuous, when he resigned the gown for the sword, and became a captain of dragoons. He was destined in later life to win laurels in another career, and to become one of the most illustrious of French navigators. Montcalm, himself a scholar, prized his varied talents and accomplishments, and soon learned to feel for him a strong personal regard.

The troops destined for Canada were only two battalions, one belonging to the regiment of La Sarre, and the other to that of Royal Roussillon. Louis XV. and Pompadour sent a hundred thousand men to fight the battles of Austria, and could spare but twelve hundred to reinforce New France. These troops marched into Brest at early morning, breakfasted in the town, and went at once on board the transports, "with an incredible gayety," says Bougainville. "What a nation is ours! Happy he who commands it, and commands it worthily!"[1] Montcalm and he embarked in the "Licorne," and sailed on the third of April, leaving Lévis and Bourlamaque to follow a few days after.[2]

The voyage was a rough one. "I have been fortunate," writes Montcalm to his wife, "in not being ill nor at all incommoded by the heavy gale we had in Holy Week. It was not so with those who were with me, especially M. Estève, my secretary, and Joseph, who suffered cruelly,—seventeen

---

[1] *Journal de Bougainville.* This is a fragment; his Journal proper begins a few weeks later.

[2] *Lévis à ——, 5 Avril, 1756.*

days without being able to take anything but water. The season was very early for such a hard voyage, and it was fortunate that the winter has been so mild. We had very favorable weather till Monday the twelfth; but since then till Saturday evening we had rough weather, with a gale that lasted ninety hours, and put us in real danger. The forecastle was always under water, and the waves broke twice over the quarter-deck. From the twenty-seventh of April to the evening of the fourth of May we had fogs, great cold, and an amazing quantity of icebergs. On the thirtieth, when luckily the fog lifted for a time, we counted sixteen of them. The day before, one drifted under the bowsprit, grazed it, and might have crushed us if the deck-officer had not called out quickly, *Luff.* After speaking of our troubles and sufferings, I must tell you of our pleasures, which were fishing for cod and eating it. The taste is exquisite. The head, tongue, and liver are morsels worthy of an epicure. Still, I would not advise anybody to make the voyage for their sake. My health is as good as it has been for a long time. I found it a good plan to eat little and take no supper; a little tea now and then, and plenty of lemonade. Nevertheless I have taken very little liking for the sea, and think that when I shall be so happy as to rejoin you I shall end my voyages there. I don't know when this letter will go. I shall send it by the first ship that returns to France, and keep on writing till then. It is pleasant, I know, to hear particulars about the people one loves, and I thought that my mother and you, my dearest and most beloved, would be glad to read all these dull details. We heard Mass on Easter Day. All the week before, it was impossible, because the ship rolled so that I could hardly keep my legs. If I had dared, I think I should have had myself lashed fast. I shall not soon forget that Holy Week."

This letter was written on the eleventh of May, in the St. Lawrence, where the ship lay at anchor, ten leagues below Quebec, stopped by ice from proceeding farther. Montcalm made his way to the town by land, and soon after learned with great satisfaction that the other ships were safe in the river below. "I see," he writes again, "that I shall have plenty of work. Our campaign will soon begin. Everything is in motion. Don't expect details about our operations; generals never speak of movements till they are over. I can only tell you that the winter has been quiet enough, though the savages have made great havoc in Pennsylvania and Virginia, and carried off, according to their custom, men, women, and children. I beg you will have High Mass said at Montpellier or Vauvert to thank God for our safe arrival and ask for good success in future."[1]

Vaudreuil, the governor-general, was at Montreal, and Montcalm sent a courier to inform him of his arrival. He soon went thither in person, and the two men met for the first time. The new general was not welcome to Vaudreuil, who had hoped to command the troops himself, and had represented to the Court that it was needless and inexpedient to send out a general officer from France.[2] The Court had not accepted his views;[3] and hence it was with more curiosity than satisfaction that he greeted the colleague who had been assigned him. He saw before him a man of small stature, with a lively countenance, a keen eye, and, in moments of animation, rapid, vehement utterance, and nervous gesticulation. Montcalm, we may suppose, regarded the Governor with no less attention. Pierre François Rigaud, Marquis de Vaudreuil, was son of Philippe de Vaudreuil, who had governed Canada early in the century; and he himself had been governor of Louisiana. He had not the force of character which his position demanded, lacked decision in times of crisis; and though tenacious of authority, was more jealous in asserting than self-reliant in exercising it. One of his traits was a sensitive egotism, which made him forward to proclaim his own part in every success, and to throw on others the burden of every failure. He was facile by nature, and capable of being led by such as had skill and temper for the task. But the impetuous Montcalm was not of their number; and the fact that he was born in France would in itself have thrown obstacles in his way to the good graces of the Governor. Vaudreuil, Canadian by birth, loved the colony and its people, and distrusted Old France and all that came out of it. He had been bred, more-

---

[1] These extracts are translated from copies of the original letters, in possession of the present Marquis de Montcalm.

[2] *Vaudreuil au Ministre, 30 Oct. 1755.*

[3] *Ordres du Roy et Dépêches des Ministres, Fév. 1756.*

over, to the naval service; and, like other Canadian governors, his official correspondence was with the minister of marine, while that of Montcalm was with the minister of war. Even had Nature made him less suspicious, his relations with the General would have been critical. Montcalm commanded the regulars from France, whose very presence was in the eyes of Vaudreuil an evil, though a necessary one. Their chief was, it is true, subordinate to him in virtue of his office of governor;[1] yet it was clear that for the conduct of the war the trust of the Government was mainly in Montcalm; and the Minister of War had even suggested that he should have the immediate command, not only of the troops from France, but of the colony regulars and the militia. An order of the King to this effect was sent to Vaudreuil, with instructions to communicate it to Montcalm or withhold it, as he should think best.[2] He lost no time in replying that the General "ought to concern himself with nothing but the command of the troops from France;" and he returned the order to the minister who sent it.[3] The Governor and the General represented the two parties which were soon to divide Canada,—those of New France and of Old.

A like antagonism was seen in the forces commanded by the two chiefs. These were of three kinds,—the *troupes de terre*, troops of the line, or regulars from France; the *troupes de la marine*, or colony regulars; and lastly the militia. The first consisted of the four battalions that had come over with Dieskau and the two that had come with Montcalm, comprising in all a little less than three thousand men.[4] Besides these,

[1] *Le Ministre à Vaudreuil, 15 Mars, 1756. Commission du Marquis de Montcalm. Mémoire du Roy pour servir d'Instruction au Marquis de Montcalm.*

[2] *Ordres du Roy et Dépêches des Ministres, 1756. Le Ministre à Vaudreuil, 15 Mars, 1756.*

[3] *Vaudreuil au Ministre, 16 Juin, 1756.* "Qu'il ne se mêle que du commandement des troupes de terre."

[4] Of about twelve hundred who came with Montcalm, nearly three hundred were now in hospital. The four battalions that came with Dieskau are reported at the end of May to have sixteen hundred and fifty-three effective men. *État de la Situation actuelle des Bataillons*, appended to Montcalm's despatch of 12 June. Another document, *Détail de ce qui s'est passé en Canada, Juin, 1755, jusqu'à Juin, 1756,* sets the united effective strength of the battalions in Canada at twenty-six hundred and seventy-seven, which was increased by recruits which arrived from France about midsummer.

the battalions of Artois and Bourgogne, to the number of eleven hundred men, were in garrison at Louisbourg. All these troops wore a white uniform, faced with blue, red, yellow, or violet,[1] a black three-cornered hat, and gaiters, generally black, from the foot to the knee. The subaltern officers in the French service were very numerous, and were drawn chiefly from the class of lesser nobles. A well-informed French writer calls them "a generation of *petits-maîtres*, dissolute, frivolous, heedless, light-witted; but brave always, and ready to die with their soldiers, though not to suffer with them."[2] In fact the course of the war was to show plainly that in Europe the regiments of France were no longer what they had once been. It was not so with those who fought in America. Here, for enduring gallantry, officers and men alike deserve nothing but praise.

The *troupes de la marine* had for a long time formed the permanent military establishment of Canada. Though attached to the naval department, they served on land, and were employed as a police within the limits of the colony, or as garrisons of the outlying forts, where their officers busied themselves more with fur-trading than with their military duties. Thus they had become ill-disciplined and inefficient, till the hard hand of Duquesne restored them to order. They originally consisted of twenty-eight independent companies, increased in 1750 to thirty companies, at first of fifty, and afterwards of sixty-five men each, forming a total of nineteen hundred and fifty rank and file. In March, 1757, ten more companies were added. Their uniform was not unlike that of the troops attached to the War Department, being white, with black facings. They were enlisted for the most part in France; but when their term of service expired, and even before, in time of peace, they were encouraged to become settlers in the colony as was also the case with their officers, of whom a great part were of European birth. Thus the relations of the *troupes de la marine* with the colony were close; and they formed a sort of connecting link between the troops of the line and the

[1] Except, perhaps, the battalion of Béarn, which formerly wore, and possibly wore still, a uniform of light blue.

[2] Susane, *Ancienne Infanterie Française*. In the atlas of this work are colored plates of the uniforms of all the regiments of foot.

native militia.[1] Besides these colony regulars, there was a company of colonial artillery, consisting this year of seventy men, and replaced in 1757 by two companies of fifty men each.

All the effective male population of Canada, from fifteen years to sixty, was enrolled in the militia, and called into service at the will of the Governor. They received arms, clothing, equipment, and rations from the King, but no pay; and instead of tents they made themselves huts of bark or branches. The best of them were drawn from the upper parts of the colony, where habits of bushranging were still in full activity. Their fighting qualities were much like those of the Indians, whom they rivalled in endurance and in the arts of forest war. As bush-fighters they had few equals; they fought well behind earthworks, and were good at a surprise or sudden dash; but for regular battle on the open field they were of small account, being disorderly, and apt to break and take to cover at the moment of crisis. They had no idea of the great operations of war. At first they despised the regulars for their ignorance of woodcraft, and thought themselves able to defend the colony alone; while the regulars regarded them in turn with a contempt no less unjust. They were excessively given to gasconade, and every true Canadian boasted himself a match for three Englishmen at least. In 1750 the militia of all ranks counted about thirteen thousand; and eight years later the number had increased to about fifteen thousand.[1] Until the last two years of the war, those employed in actual warfare were but few. Even in the critical year 1758 only about eleven hundred were called to arms, except for two or three weeks in summer;[2] though about four thousand were employed in transporting troops and supplies, for which service they received pay.

[1] On the *troupes de la marine,—Mémoire pour servir d'Instruction à MM. Jonquière et Bigot, 30 Avril, 1749. Ordres du Roy et Dépêches des Ministres, 1750. Ibid., 1755. Ibid., 1757. Instruction pour Vaudreuil, 22 Mars, 1755. Ordonnance pour l'Augmentation de Soldats dans les Compagnies de Canada, 14 Mars, 1755. Duquesne au Ministre, 26 Oct. 1753. Ibid., 30 Oct. 1753. Ibid., 29 Fév. 1754. Duquesne à Marin, 27 Août, 1753. Atlas de Susane.*

[2] *Récapitulation des Milices du Gouvernement de Canada, 1750. Dénombrement des Milices, 1758, 1759.* On the militia, see also Bougainville in Margry, *Relations et Mémoires inédits*, 60, and *N. Y. Col. Docs.*, X. 680.

[3] *Montcalm au Ministre, 1 Sept. 1758.*

To the white fighting force of the colony are to be added the red men. The most trusty of them were the Mission Indians, living within or near the settled limits of Canada, chiefly the Hurons of Lorette, the Abenakis of St. Francis and Batiscan, the Iroquois of Caughnawaga and La Présentation, and the Iroquois and Algonkins at the Two Mountains on the Ottawa. Besides these, all the warriors of the west and north, from Lake Superior to the Ohio, and from the Alleghanies to the Mississippi, were now at the beck of France. As to the Iroquois or Five Nations who still remained in their ancient seats within the present limits of New York, their power and pride had greatly fallen; and crowded as they were between the French and the English, they were in a state of vacillation, some leaning to one side, some to the other, and some to each in turn. As a whole, the best that France could expect from them was neutrality.

Montcalm at Montreal had more visits than he liked from his red allies. "They are *vilains messieurs*," he informs his mother, "even when fresh from their toilet, at which they pass their lives. You would not believe it, but the men always carry to war, along with their tomahawk and gun, a mirror to daub their faces with various colors, and arrange feathers on their heads and rings in their ears and noses. They think it a great beauty to cut the rim of the ear and stretch it till it reaches the shoulder. Often they wear a laced coat, with no shirt at all. You would take them for so many masqueraders or devils. One needs the patience of an angel to get on with them. Ever since I have been here, I have had nothing but visits, harangues, and deputations of these gentry. The Iroquois ladies, who always take part in their government, came also, and did me the honor to bring me belts of wampum, which will oblige me to go to their village and sing the war-song. They are only a little way off. Yesterday we had eighty-three warriors here, who have gone out to fight. They make war with astounding cruelty, sparing neither men, women, nor children, and take off your scalp very neatly,—an operation which generally kills you.

"Everything is horribly dear in this country; and I shall find it hard to make the two ends of the year meet, with the twenty-five thousand francs the King gives me. The Chevalier de Lévis did not join me till yesterday. His health is excellent. In a few days I shall send him to one camp, and M. de Bourlamaque to another; for we have three of them: one at Carillon, eighty leagues from here, towards the place where M. de Dieskau had his affair last year; another at Frontenac, sixty leagues; and the third at Niagara, a hundred and forty leagues. I don't know when or whither I shall go myself; that depends on the movements of the enemy. It seems to me that things move slowly in this new world; and I shall have to moderate my activity accordingly. Nothing but the King's service and the wish to make a career for my son could prevent me from thinking too much of my expatriation, my distance from you, and the dull existence here, which would be duller still if I did not manage to keep some little of my natural gayety."

The military situation was somewhat perplexing. Iroquois spies had brought reports of great preparations on the part of the English. As neither party dared offend these wavering tribes, their warriors could pass with impunity from one to the other, and were paid by each for bringing information, not always trustworthy. They declared that the English were gathering in force to renew the attempt made by Johnson the year before against Crown Point and Ticonderoga, as well as that made by Shirley against forts Frontenac and Niagara. Vaudreuil had spared no effort to meet the double danger. Lotbinière, a Canadian engineer, had been busied during the winter in fortifying Ticonderoga, while Pouchot, a captain in the battalion of Béarn, had rebuilt Niagara, and two French engineers were at work in strengthening the defences of Frontenac. The Governor even hoped to take the offensive, anticipate the movements of the English, capture Oswego, and obtain the complete command of Lake Ontario. Early in the spring a blow had been struck which materially aided these schemes.

The English had built two small forts to guard the Great Carrying Place on the route to Oswego. One of these, Fort Williams, was on the Mohawk; the other, Fort Bull, a mere collection of storehouses surrounded by a palisade, was four miles distant, on the bank of Wood Creek. Here a great quantity of stores and ammunition had imprudently been collected against the opening campaign. In February Vaudreuil sent Léry, a colony officer, with three hundred and sixty-two picked men, soldiers, Canadians, and Indians, to seize these two posts. Towards the end of March, after extreme hardship, they reached the road that connected them, and at half-past five in the morning captured twelve men going with wagons to Fort Bull. Learning from them the weakness of that place, they dashed forward to surprise it. The thirty provincials of Shirley's regiment who formed the garrison had barely time to shut the gate, while the assailants fired on them through the loopholes, of which they got possession in the tumult. Léry called on the defenders to yield; but they refused, and pelted the French for an hour with bullets and hand-grenades. The gate was at last beat down with axes, and they were summoned again; but again refused, and fired hotly through the opening. The French rushed in, shouting *Vive le roi*, and a frightful struggle followed. All the garrison were killed, except two or three who hid themselves till the slaughter was over; the fort was set on fire and blown to atoms by the explosion of the magazines; and Léry then withdrew, not venturing to attack Fort Williams. Johnson, warned by Indians of the approach of the French, had pushed up the Mohawk with reinforcements; but came too late.[1]

Vaudreuil, who always exaggerates any success in which he has had part, says that besides bombs, bullets, cannon-balls, and other munitions, forty-five thousand pounds of gunpowder were destroyed on this occasion. It is certain that damage enough was done to retard English operations in the direction of Oswego sufficiently to give the French time for securing all their posts on Lake Ontario. Before the end of June this was in good measure done. The battalion of Béarn lay encamped before the now strong fort of Niagara, and the battalions of Guienne and La Sarre, with a body of Canadians, guarded Frontenac against attack. Those of La Reine and

[1] *Bigot au Ministre, 12 Avril, 1756. Vaudreuil au Ministre, 1 Juin, 1756. Ibid., 8 Juin, 1756. Journal de ce qui s'est passé en Canada depuis le Mois d'Octobre, 1755, jusqu'au Mois de Juin, 1756. Shirley to Fox, 7 May, 1756. Conduct of Major General-Shirley briefly stated. Information of Captain John Vicars, of the Fiftieth (Shirley's) Regiment.* Eastburn, *Faithful Narrative.* Entick, I. 471. The French accounts place the number of English at sixty or eighty.

Languedoc had been sent to Ticonderoga, while the Governor, with Montcalm and Lévis, still remained at Montreal watching the turn of events.[1] Hither, too, came the intendant François Bigot, the most accomplished knave in Canada, yet indispensable for his vigor and executive skill; Bougainville, who had disarmed the jealousy of Vaudreuil, and now stood high in his good graces; and the Adjutant-General, Montreuil, clearly a vain and pragmatic personage, who, having come to Canada with Dieskau the year before, thought it behooved him to give the General the advantage of his experience. "I like M. de Montcalm very much," he writes to the minister, "and will do the impossible to deserve his confidence. I have spoken to him in the same terms as to M. Dieskau; thus: 'Trust only the French regulars for an expedition, but use the Canadians and Indians to harass the enemy. Don't expose yourself; send me to carry your orders to points of danger.' The colony officers do not like those from France. The Canadians are independent, spiteful, lying, boastful; very good for skirmishing, very brave behind a tree, and very timid when not under cover. I think both sides will stand on the defensive. It does not seem to me that M. de Montcalm means to attack the enemy; and I think he is right. In this country a thousand men could stop three thousand."[2]

"M. de Vaudreuil overwhelms me with civilities," Montcalm writes to the Minister of War. "I think that he is pleased with my conduct towards him, and that it persuades him there are general officers in France who can act under his orders without prejudice or ill-humor."[3] "I am on good terms with him," he says again; "but not in his confidence, which he never gives to anybody from France. His intentions are good, but he is slow and irresolute."[4]

Indians presently brought word that ten thousand English were coming to attack Ticonderoga. A reinforcement of colony regulars was at once despatched to join the two battalions

---

[1] *Correspondance de Montcalm, Vaudreuil, et Lévis.*

[2] *Montreuil au Ministre, 12 Juin, 1756.* The original is in cipher.

[3] *Montcalm au Ministre, 12 Juin, 1756.*

[4] *Ibid., 19 Juin, 1756.* "Je suis bien avec luy, sans sa confiance, qu'il ne donne jamais à personne de la France." Erroneously rendered in *N. Y. Col. Docs.*, X. 421.

already there; a third battalion, Royal Roussillon, was sent
after them. The militia were called out and ordered to follow
with all speed, while both Montcalm and Lévis hastened to
the supposed scene of danger.[1] They embarked in canoes on
the Richelieu, coasted the shore of Lake Champlain, passed
Fort Frederic or Crown Point, where all was activity and bus-
tle, and reached Ticonderoga at the end of June. They found
the fort, on which Lotbinière had been at work all winter,
advanced towards completion. It stood on the crown of the
promontory, and was a square with four bastions, a ditch,
blown in some parts out of the solid rock, bomb-proofs, barracks of stone, and a system of exterior defences as yet only
begun. The rampart consisted of two parallel walls ten feet
apart, built of the trunks of trees, and held together by trans-
verse logs dovetailed at both ends, the space between being
filled with earth and gravel well packed.[2] Such was the first
Fort Ticonderoga, or Carillon,—a structure quite distinct
from the later fort of which the ruins still stand on the same
spot. The forest had been hewn away for some distance
around, and the tents of the regulars and huts of the Canadians had taken its place; innumerable bark canoes lay along the
strand, and gangs of men toiled at the unfinished works.

Ticonderoga was now the most advanced position of the
French, and Crown Point, which had before held that perilous honor, was in the second line. Lévis, to whom had been
assigned the permanent command of this post of danger, set
out on foot to explore the neighboring woods and mountains, and slept out several nights before he reappeared at the
camp. "I do not think," says Montcalm, "that many high officers in Europe would have occasion to take such tramps as
this. I cannot speak too well of him. Without being a man of
brilliant parts, he has good experience, good sense, and a
quick eye; and, though I had served with him before, I never
should have thought that he had such promptness and efficiency. He has turned his campaigns to good account."[3] Lévis
writes of his chief with equal warmth. "I do not know if the

---

[1] *Montcalm au Ministre, 26 Juin, 1756. Détail de ce qui s'est passé, Oct. 1755–
Juin, 1756.*

[2] *Lotbinière au Ministre, 31 Oct. 1756. Montcalm au Ministre, 20 Juillet, 1756.*

[3] *Montcalm au Ministre, 20 Juillet, 1756.*

Marquis de Montcalm is pleased with me, but I am sure that I am very much so with him, and shall always be charmed to serve under his orders. It is not for me, Monseigneur, to speak to you of his merit and his talents. You know him better than anybody else; but I may have the honor of assuring you that he has pleased everybody in this colony, and manages affairs with the Indians extremely well."[1]

The danger from the English proved to be still remote, and there was ample leisure in the camp. Duchat, a young captain in the battalion of Languedoc, used it in writing to his father a long account of what he saw about him,—the forests full of game; the ducks, geese, and partridges; the prodigious flocks of wild pigeons that darkened the air; the bears, the beavers; and above all the Indians, their canoes, dress, ball-play, and dances. "We are making here," says the military prophet, "a place that history will not forget. The English colonies have ten times more people than ours; but these wretches have not the least knowledge of war, and if they go out to fight, they must abandon wives, children, and all that they possess. Not a week passes but the French send them a band of *hairdressers*, whom they would be very glad to dispense with. It is incredible what a quantity of scalps they bring us. In Virginia they have committed unheard-of cruelties, carried off families, burned a great many houses, and killed an infinity of people. These miserable English are in the extremity of distress, and repent too late the unjust war they began against us. It is a pleasure to make war in Canada. One is troubled neither with horses nor baggage; the King provides everything. But it must be confessed that if it costs no money, one pays for it in another way, by seeing nothing but pease and bacon on the mess-table. Luckily the lakes are full of fish, and both officers and soldiers have to turn fishermen."[2]

Meanwhile, at the head of Lake George, the raw bands of ever-active New England were mustering for the fray.

[1] *Lévis au Ministre, 17 Juillet, 1756.*
[2] *Relation de M. Duchat, Capitaine au Régiment de Languedoc, écrite au Camp de Carillon, 15 Juillet, 1756.*

Chapter XII

1756

OSWEGO

The new Campaign • Untimely Change of Commanders • Eclipse of Shirley • Earl of Loudon • Muster of Provincials • New England Levies • Winslow at Lake George • Johnson and the Five Nations • Bradstreet and his Boatmen • Fight on the Onondaga • Pestilence at Oswego • Loudon and the Provincials • New England Camps • Army Chaplains • A sudden Blow • Montcalm attacks Oswego • Its Fall

W HEN, at the end of the last year, Shirley returned from his bootless Oswego campaign, he called a council of war at New York and laid before it his scheme for the next summer's operations. It was a comprehensive one: to master Lake Ontario by an overpowering naval force and seize the French forts upon it, Niagara, Frontenac, and Toronto; attack Ticonderoga and Crown Point on the one hand, and Fort Duquesne on the other, and at the same time perplex and divide the enemy by an inroad down the Chaudière upon the settlements about Quebec.[1] The council approved the scheme; but to execute it the provinces must raise at least sixteen thousand men. This they refused to do. Pennsylvania and Virginia would take no active part, and were content with defending themselves. The attack on Fort Duquesne was therefore abandoned, as was also the diversion towards Quebec. The New England colonies were discouraged by Johnson's failure to take Crown Point, doubtful of the military abilities of Shirley, and embarrassed by the debts of the last campaign; but when they learned that Parliament would grant a sum of money in partial compensation for their former sacrifices,[2] they plunged into new debts without hesita-

[1] *Minutes of Council of War held at New York, 12 and 13 Dec. 1755. Shirley to Robinson, 19 Dec. 1755. The Conduct of Major-General Shirley briefly stated. Review of Military Operations in North America.*

[2] *Lords of Trade to Lords of the Treasury, 12 Feb. 1756. Fox to American Governors, 13 March, 1756. Shirley to Phipps, 15 June, 1756.* The sum was £115,000, divided in proportion to the expense incurred by the several colonies; Mas-

tion, and raised more men than the General had asked; though, with their usual jealousy, they provided that their soldiers should be employed for no other purpose than the attack on Ticonderoga and Crown Point. Shirley chose John Winslow to command them, and gave him a commission to that effect; while he, to clinch his authority, asked and obtained supplementary commissions from every government that gave men to the expedition.[1] For the movement against the forts of Lake Ontario, which Shirley meant to command in person, he had the remains of his own and Pepperell's regiments, the two shattered battalions brought over by Braddock, the "Jersey Blues," four provincial companies from North Carolina, and the four King's companies of New York. His first care was to recruit their ranks and raise them to their full complement; which, when effected, would bring them up to the insufficient strength of about forty-four hundred men.

While he was struggling with contradictions and cross purposes, a withering blow fell upon him; he learned that he was superseded in the command. The cabal formed against him, with Delancey at its head, had won over Sir Charles Hardy, the new governor of New York, and had painted Shirley's conduct in such colors that the Ministry removed him. It was essential for the campaign that a successor should be sent at once, to form plans on the spot and make preparations accordingly. The Ministry were in no such haste. It was presently announced that Colonel Daniel Webb would be sent to America, followed by General James Abercromby; who was to be followed in turn by the Earl of Loudon, the destined commander-in-chief. Shirley was to resign his command to Webb, Webb to Abercromby, and Abercromby to Loudon.[2] It chanced that the two former arrived in June at about the same time, while the Earl came in July; and meanwhile it devolved on Shirley to make ready for them. Unable to divine what their plans would be, he prepared the campaign in accordance with his own.

---

sachusetts having £54,000, Connecticut £26,000, and New York £15,000, the rest being given to New Hampshire, Rhode Island, and New Jersey.

[1] *Letter and Order Books of General Winslow, 1756.*

[2] *Fox to Shirley, 13 March, 1756. Ibid., 31 March, 1756. Order to Colonel Webb, 31 March, 1756. Order to Major-General Abercromby, 1 April, 1756. Halifax to Shirley, 1 April, 1756. Shirley to Fox, 13 June, 1756.*

His star, so bright a twelvemonth before, was now miserably dimmed. In both his public and private life he was the butt
of adversity. He had lost two promising sons; he had made
a mortifying failure as a soldier; and triumphant enemies
were rejoicing in his fall. It is to the credit of his firmness
and his zeal in the cause that he set himself to his task with as
much vigor as if he, and not others, were to gather the fruits.
His chief care was for his favorite enterprise in the direction
of Lake Ontario. Making Albany his headquarters, he rebuilt
the fort at the Great Carrying Place destroyed in March by
the French, sent troops to guard the perilous route to Oswego,
and gathered provisions and stores at the posts along the way.

Meanwhile the New England men, strengthened by the levies of New York, were mustering at Albany for the attack of
Crown Point. At the end of May they moved a short distance
up the Hudson, and encamped at a place called Half-Moon,
where the navigation was stopped by rapids. Here and at the
posts above were gathered something more than five thousand men, as raw and untrained as those led by Johnson in
the summer before.[1] The four New England colonies were
much alike in their way of raising and equipping men, and
the example of Massachusetts may serve for them all. The Assembly or "General Court" voted the required number, and
chose a committee of war authorized to impress provisions,
munitions, stores, clothing, tools, and other necessaries, for
which fair prices were to be paid within six months. The Governor issued a proclamation calling for volunteers. If the full
number did not appear within the time named, the colonels
of militia were ordered to muster their regiments, and immediately draft out of them men enough to meet the need. A
bounty of six dollars was offered this year to stimulate enlistment, and the pay of a private soldier was fixed at one pound
six shillings a month, Massachusetts currency. If he brought
a gun, he had an additional bounty of two dollars. A powder-
horn, bullet-pouch, blanket, knapsack, and "wooden bottle,"
or canteen, were supplied by the province; and if he brought
no gun of his own, a musket was given him, for which, as for
the other articles, he was to account at the end of the cam-

---

[1] *Letter and Order Books of Winslow, 1756.*

paign. In the next year it was announced that the soldier should receive, besides his pay, "a coat and soldier's hat." The coat was of coarse blue cloth, to which breeches of red or blue were afterwards added. Along with his rations, he was promised a gill of rum each day, a privilege of which he was extremely jealous, deeply resenting every abridgment of it. He was enlisted for the campaign, and could not be required to serve above a year at farthest.

The complement of a regiment was five hundred, divided into companies of fifty; and as the men and officers of each were drawn from the same neighborhood, they generally knew each other. The officers, though nominally appointed by the Assembly, were for the most part the virtual choice of the soldiers themselves, from whom they were often indistinguishable in character and social standing. Hence discipline was weak. The pay—or, as it was called, the wages—of a colonel was twelve pounds sixteen shillings, Massachusetts currency, a month; that of a captain, five pounds eight shillings,—an advance on the pay of the last year; and that of a chaplain, six pounds eight shillings.[1] Penalties were enacted against "irreligion, immorality, drunkenness, debauchery, and profaneness." The ordinary punishments were the wooden horse, irons, or, in bad cases, flogging.

Much difficulty arose from the different rules adopted by the various colonies for the regulation of their soldiers. Nor was this the only source of trouble. Besides its war committee, the Assembly of each of the four New England colonies chose another committee "for clothing, arming, paying, victualling, and transporting" its troops. They were to go to the scene of operations, hire wagons, oxen, and horses, build boats and vessels, and charge themselves with the conveyance of all supplies belonging to their respective governments. They were to keep in correspondence with the committee of war at home, to whom they were responsible; and the officer commanding the contingent of their colony was required to furnish them with guards and escorts. Thus four independent committees were engaged in the work of transportation at the same time, over the same roads, for the same object. Each

---

[1] *Vote of General Court, 26 Feb. 1756.*

colony chose to keep the control of its property in its own hands. The inconveniences were obvious. "I wish to God," wrote Lord Loudon to Winslow, "you could persuade your people to go all one way." The committees themselves did not always find their task agreeable. One of their number, John Ashley, of Massachusetts, writes in dudgeon to Governor Phipps: "Sir, I am apt to think that things have been misrepresented to your Honor, or else I am certain I should not suffer in my character, and be styled a damned rascal, and ought to be put in irons, etc., when I am certain I have exerted myself to the utmost of my ability to expedite the business assigned me by the General Court." At length, late in the autumn, Loudon persuaded the colonies to forego this troublesome sort of independence, and turn over their stores to the commissary-general, receipts being duly given.[1]

From Winslow's headquarters at Half-Moon a road led along the banks of the Hudson to Stillwater, whence there was water carriage to Saratoga. Here stores were again placed in wagons and carried several miles to Upper Falls; thence by boat to Fort Edward; and thence, fourteen miles across country, to Fort William Henry at Lake George, where the army was to embark for Ticonderoga. Each of the points of transit below Fort Edward was guarded by a stockade and two or more companies of provincials. They were much pestered by Indians, who now and then scalped a straggler, and escaped with their usual nimbleness. From time to time strong bands of Canadians and Indians approached by way of South Bay or Wood Creek, and threatened more serious mischief. It is surprising that some of the trains were not cut off, for the escorts were often reckless and disorderly to the last degree. Sometimes the invaders showed great audacity. Early in June Colonel Fitch at Albany scrawls a hasty note to Winslow: "Friday, 11 o'clock: Sir, about half an hour since, a party of

[1] The above particulars are gathered from the voluminous papers in the State House at Boston, *Archives, Military*, Vols. LXXV., LXXVI. These contain the military acts of the General Court, proclamations, reports of committees, and other papers relating to military affairs in 1755 and 1756. The *Letter and Order Books of Winslow*, in the Library of the Massachusetts Historical Society, have supplied much concurrent matter. See also *Colonial Records of R. I.*, V., and *Provincial Papers of N. H.*, VI.

near fifty French and Indians had the impudence to come down to the river opposite to this city and captivate two men;" and Winslow replies with equal quaintness: "We daily discover the Indians about us; but not yet have been so happy as to obtain any of them."[1]

Colonel Jonathan Bagley commanded at Fort William Henry, where gangs of men were busied under his eye in building three sloops and making several hundred whaleboats to carry the army to Ticonderoga. The season was advancing fast, and Winslow urged him to hasten on the work; to which the humorous Bagley answered: "Shall leave no stone un-turned; every wheel shall go that rum and human flesh can move."[2] A fortnight after he reports: "I must really confess I have almost wore the men out, poor dogs. Pray where are the committee, or what are they about?" He sent scouts to watch the enemy, with results not quite satisfactory. "There is a vast deal of news here; every party brings abundance, but all dif-ferent." Again, a little later: "I constantly keep out small scouting parties to the eastward and westward of the lake, and make no discovery but the tracks of small parties who are plaguing us constantly; but what vexes me most, we can't catch one of the sons of ———. I have sent out skulking parties some distance from the sentries in the night, to lie still in the bushes to intercept them; but the flies are so plenty, our people can't bear them."[3] Colonel David Wooster, at Fort Edward, was no more fortunate in his attempts to take satis-faction on his midnight visitors; and reports that he has not thus far been able "to give those villains a dressing."[4] The English, however, were fast learning the art of forest war, and the partisan chief, Captain Robert Rogers, began already to be famous. On the seventeenth of June he and his band lay hidden in the bushes within the outposts of Ticonderoga, and made a close survey of the fort and surrounding camps.[5] His

---

[1] Vaudreuil, in his despatch of 12 August, gives particulars of these raids, with an account of the scalps taken on each occasion. He thought the results disappointing.

[2] *Bagley to Winslow, 2 July, 1756.*

[3] *Ibid., 15 July, 1756.*

[4] *Wooster to Winslow, 2 June, 1756.*

[5] *Report of Rogers, 19 June, 1756.* Much abridged in his published *Journals.*

report was not cheering. Winslow's so-called army had now grown to nearly seven thousand men; and these, it was plain, were not too many to drive the French from their stronghold.

While Winslow pursued his preparations, tried to settle disputes of rank among the colonels of the several colonies, and strove to bring order out of the little chaos of his command, Sir William Johnson was engaged in a work for which he was admirably fitted. This was the attaching of the Five Nations to the English interest. Along with his patent of baronetcy, which reached him about this time, he received, direct from the Crown, the commission of "Colonel, Agent, and Sole Superintendent of the Six Nations and other Northern Tribes."[1] Henceforth he was independent of governors and generals, and responsible to the Court alone. His task was a difficult one. The Five Nations would fain have remained neutral, and let the European rivals fight it out; but, on account of their local position, they could not. The exactions and lies of the Albany traders, the frauds of land-speculators, the contradictory action of the different provincial governments, joined to English weakness and mismanagement in the last war, all conspired to alienate them and to aid the efforts of the French agents, who cajoled and threatened them by turns. But for Johnson these intrigues would have prevailed. He had held a series of councils with them at Fort Johnson during the winter, and not only drew from them a promise to stand by the English, but persuaded all the confederated tribes, except the Cayugas, to consent that the English should build forts near their chief towns, under the pretext of protecting them from the French.[1]

In June he went to Onondaga, well escorted, for the way was dangerous. This capital of the Confederacy was under a cloud. It had just lost one Red Head, its chief sachem; and first of all it behooved the baronet to condole their affliction. The ceremony was long, with compliments, lugubrious speeches, wampum-belts, the scalp of an enemy to replace the departed, and a final glass of rum for each of the assembled

[1] *Fox to Johnson, 13 March, 1756. Papers of Sir William Johnson.*

[2] *Conferences between Sir William Johnson and the Indians, Dec. 1755, to Feb. 1756,* in *N. Y. Col. Docs.,* VII. 44–74. *Account of Conferences held and Treaties made between Sir William Johnson, Bart., and the Indian Nations of North America* (London, 1756).

mourners. The conferences lasted a fortnight; and when Johnson took his leave, the tribes stood pledged to lift the hatchet for the English.[1]

When he returned to Fort Johnson a fever seized him, and he lay helpless for a time; then rose from his sick bed to meet another congregation of Indians. These were deputies of the Five Nations, with Mohegans from the Hudson, and Delawares and Shawanoes from the Susquehanna, whom he had persuaded to visit him in hope that he might induce them to cease from murdering the border settlers. All their tribesmen were in arms against the English; but he prevailed at last, and they accepted the war-belt at his hands. The Delawares complained that their old conquerors, the Five Nations, had forced them "to wear the petticoat," that is, to be counted not as warriors but as women. Johnson, in presence of all the Assembly, now took off the figurative garment, and pronounced them henceforth men. A grand war-dance followed. A hundred and fifty Mohawks, Oneidas, Onondagas, Delawares, Shawanoes, and Mohegans stamped, whooped, and yelled all night.[2] In spite of Piquet, the two Joncaires, and the rest of the French agents, Johnson had achieved a success. But would the Indians keep their word? It was more than doubtful. While some of them treated with him on the Mohawk, others treated with Vaudreuil at Montreal.[3] A display of military vigor on the English side, crowned by some signal victory, would alone make their alliance sure.

It was not the French only who thwarted the efforts of Johnson; for while he strove to make friends of the Delawares and Shawanoes, Governor Morris of Pennsylvania declared war against them, and Governor Belcher of New Jersey followed his example; though persuaded at last to hold his hand till the baronet had tried the virtue of pacific measures.[4]

What Shirley longed for was the collecting of a body of

[1] *Minutes of Councils at Onondaga, 19 June to 3 July, 1756*, in *N. Y. Col. Docs.*, VII. 134–150.

[2] *Minutes of Councils at Fort Johnson, 9 July to 12 July*, in *N. Y. Col. Docs.*, VII. 152–160.

[3] *Conferences between M. de Vaudreuil and the Five Nations, 28 July to 20 Aug.*, in *N. Y. Col. Docs.*, X. 445–453.

[4] *Johnson to Lords of Trade, 28 May, 1756. Ibid., 17 July, 1756. Johnson to Shirley, 24 April, 1756. Colonial Records of Pa.*, VII. 75, 88, 194.

Five Nation warriors at Oswego to aid him in his cherished enterprise against Niagara and Frontenac. The warriors had promised him to come; but there was small hope that they would do so. Meanwhile he was at Albany pursuing his preparations, posting his scanty force in the forts newly built on the Mohawk and the Great Carrying Place, and sending forward stores and provisions. Having no troops to spare for escorts, he invented a plan which, like everything he did, was bitterly criticised. He took into pay two thousand boatmen, gathered from all parts of the country, including many whalemen from the eastern coasts of New England, divided them into companies of fifty, armed each with a gun and a hatchet, and placed them under the command of Lieutenant-Colonel John Bradstreet.[1] Thus organized, they would, he hoped, require no escort. Bradstreet was a New England officer who had been a captain in the last war, somewhat dogged and self-opinioned, but brave, energetic, and well fitted for this kind of service.

In May Vaudreuil sent Coulon de Villiers with eleven hundred soldiers, Canadians, and Indians, to harass Oswego and cut its communications with Albany.[2] Nevertheless Bradstreet safely conducted a convoy of provisions and military stores to the garrison; and on the third of July set out on his return with the empty boats. The party were pushing their way up the river in three divisions. The first of these, consisting of a hundred boats and three hundred men, with Bradstreet at their head, were about nine miles from Oswego, when, at three in the afternoon, they received a heavy volley from the forest on the east bank. It was fired by a part of Villiers' command, consisting, by English accounts, of about seven hundred men. A considerable number of the boatmen were killed or disabled, and the others made for the shelter of the western shore. Some prisoners were taken in the confusion; and if the French had been content to stop here, they might fairly have claimed a kind of victory: but, eager to push their advantage, they tried to cross under cover of an island just above. Bradstreet saw the movement, and landed on the

---

[1] *Shirley to Fox, 7 May, 1756. Shirley to Abercromby, 27 June, 1756. Loudon to Fox, 19 Aug. 1756.*

[2] *Détail de ce qui s'est passé en Canada, Oct. 1755–Juin, 1756.*

island with six or eight followers, among whom was young Captain Schuyler, afterwards General Schuyler of the Revolution. Their fire kept the enemy in check till others joined them, to the number of about twenty. These a second and a third time beat back the French, who now gave over the attempt, and made for another ford at some distance above. Bradstreet saw their intention; and collecting two hundred and fifty men, was about to advance up the west bank to oppose them, when Dr. Kirkland, a surgeon, came to tell him that the second division of boats had come up, and that the men had landed. Bradstreet ordered them to stay where they were, and defend the lower crossing: then hastened forward; but when he reached the upper ford, the French had passed the river, and were ensconced in a pine-swamp near the shore. Here he attacked them; and both parties fired at each other from behind trees for an hour, with little effect. Bradstreet at length encouraged his men to make a rush at the enemy, who were put to flight and driven into the river, where many were shot or drowned as they tried to cross. Another party of the French had meanwhile passed by a ford still higher up to support their comrades; but the fight was over before they reached the spot, and they in their turn were set upon and driven back across the stream. Half an hour after, Captain Patten arrived from Onondaga with the grenadiers of Shirley's regiment; and late in the evening two hundred men came from Oswego to reinforce the victors. In the morning Bradstreet prepared to follow the French to their camp, twelve miles distant; but was prevented by a heavy rain which lasted all day. On the Monday following, he and his men reached Albany, bringing two prisoners, eighty French muskets, and many knapsacks picked up in the woods. He had lost between sixty and seventy killed, wounded, and taken.[1]

This affair was trumpeted through Canada as a victory of the French. Their notices of it are discordant, though very

---

[1] *Letter of J. Choate, Albany, 12 July, 1756*, in Massachusetts Archives, LV. *Three Letters from Albany, July, Aug. 1756*, in *Doc. Hist. of N. Y.*, I. 482. *Review of Military Operations. Shirley to Fox, 26 July, 1756. Abercromby to Sir Charles Hardy, 11 July, 1756*. Niles, in *Mass. Hist. Coll., Fourth Series*, V. 417. Lossing, *Life of Schuyler*, I. 131 (1860). Mante, 60. Bradstreet's conduct on this occasion afterwards gained for him the warm praises of Wolfe.

brief. One of them says that Villiers had four hundred men.
Another gives him five hundred, and a third eight hundred,
against fifteen hundred English, of whom they killed eight
hundred, or an Englishman apiece. A fourth writer boasts
that six hundred Frenchmen killed nine hundred English. A
fifth contents himself with four hundred; but thinks that forty
more would have been slain if the Indians had not fired too
soon. He says further that there were three hundred boats;
and presently forgetting himself, adds that five hundred were
taken or destroyed. A sixth announces a great capture of
stores and provisions, though all the boats were empty. A
seventh reports that the Canadians killed about three
hundred, and would have killed more but for the bad quality
of their tomahawks. An eighth, with rare modesty, puts the
English loss at fifty or sixty. That of Villiers is given in every
proportion of killed or wounded, from one up to ten. Thus
was Canada roused to martial ardor, and taught to look for
future triumphs cheaply bought.[1]

The success of Bradstreet silenced for a time the enemies of
Shirley. His cares, however, redoubled. He was anxious for
Oswego, as the two prisoners declared that the French meant
to attack it, instead of waiting to be attacked from it. Nor
was the news from that quarter reassuring. The engineer,
Mackellar, wrote that the works were incapable of defence;
and Colonel Mercer, the commandant, reported general discontent in the garrison.[2] Captain John Vicars, an invalid officer of Shirley's regiment, arrived at Albany with yet more
deplorable accounts. He had passed the winter at Oswego,
where he declared the dearth of food to have been such that
several councils of war had been held on the question of
abandoning the place from sheer starvation. More than half
his regiment died of hunger or disease; and, in his own
words, "had the poor fellows lived they must have eaten one

[1] *Nouvelles du Camp établi au Portage de Chouaguen, première Relation.
Ibid., Séconde Relation, 10 Juillet, 1756.* Bougainville, *Journal*, who gives the
report as he heard it. *Lettre du R. P. Cocquard, S. J., 1756. Vaudreuil au
Ministre, 10 Juillet, 1756. Ursulines de Québec*, II. 292. *N. Y. Col. Docs.*, X. 434,
467, 477, 483. Some prisoners taken in the first attack were brought to Montreal, where their presence gave countenance to these fabrications.

[2] *Mackellar to Shirley, June, 1756. Mercer to Shirley, 2 July, 1756.*

another." Some of the men were lodged in barracks, though without beds, while many lay all winter in huts on the bare ground. Scurvy and dysentery made frightful havoc. "In January," says Vicars, "we were informed by the Indians that we were to be attacked. The garrison was then so weak that the strongest guard we proposed to mount was a subaltern and twenty men; but we were seldom able to mount more than sixteen or eighteen, and half of those were obliged to have sticks in their hands to support them. The men were so weak that the sentries often fell down on their posts, and lay there till the relief came and lifted them up." His own company of fifty was reduced to ten. The other regiment of the garrison, Pepperell's, or the fifty-first, was quartered at Fort Ontario, on the other side of the river; and being better sheltered, suffered less.

The account given by Vicars of the state of the defences was scarcely more flattering. He reported that the principal fort had no cannon on the side most exposed to attack. Two pieces had been mounted on the trading-house in the centre; but as the concussion shook down stones from the wall whenever they were fired, they had since been removed. The second work, called Fort Ontario, he had not seen since it was finished, having been too ill to cross the river. Of the third, called New Oswego, or "Fort Rascal," he testifies thus: "It never was finished, and there were no loopholes in the stockades; so that they could not fire out of the fort but by opening the gate and firing out of that."[1]

Through the spring and early summer Shirley was gathering recruits, often of the meanest quality, and sending them to Oswego to fill out the two emaciated regiments. The place must be defended at any cost. Its fall would ruin not only the enterprise against Niagara and Frontenac, but also that against Ticonderoga and Crown Point; since, having nothing more to fear on Lake Ontario, the French could unite their whole force on Lake Champlain, whether for defence or attack.

Towards the end of June Abercromby and Webb arrived at

[1] *Information of Captain John Vicars, of the Fiftieth (Shirley's) Regiment*, enclosed with a despatch of Lord Loudon. Vicars was a veteran British officer who left Oswego with Bradstreet on the third of July. *Shirley to Loudon, 5 Sept. 1756.*

Albany, bringing a reinforcement of nine hundred regulars, consisting of Otway's regiment, or a part of it, and a body of Highlanders. Shirley resigned his command, and Abercromby requested him to go to New York, wait there till Lord Loudon arrived, and lay before him the state of affairs.[1] Shirley waited till the twenty-third of July, when the Earl at length appeared. He was a rough Scotch lord, hot and irascible; and the communications of his predecessor, made, no doubt, in a manner somewhat pompous and self-satisfied, did not please him. "I got from Major-General Shirley," he says, "a few papers of very little use; only he insinuated to me that I would find everything prepared, and have nothing to do but to pull laurels; which I understand was his constant conversation before my arrival."[2]

Loudon sailed up the Hudson in no placid mood. On reaching Albany he abandoned the attempt against Niagara and Frontenac; and had resolved to turn his whole force against Ticonderoga, when he was met by an obstacle that both perplexed and angered him. By a royal order lately issued, all general and field officers with provincial commissions were to take rank only as eldest captains when serving in conjunction with regular troops.[3] Hence the whole provincial army, as Winslow observes, might be put under the command of any British major.[4] The announcement of this regulation naturally caused great discontent. The New England officers held a meeting, and voted with one voice that in their belief its enforcement would break up the provincial army and prevent the raising of another. Loudon, hearing of this, desired Winslow to meet him at Albany for a conference on the subject. Thither Winslow went with some of his chief officers. The Earl asked them to dinner, and there was much talk, with no satisfactory result; whereupon, somewhat chafed, he required Winslow to answer in writing, yes or no, whether the provincial officers would obey the commander-in-chief and act in conjunction with the regulars. Thus forced to choose

---

[1] *Shirley to Fox, 4 July, 1756.*

[2] *Loudon (to Fox?), 19 Aug. 1756.*

[3] *Order concerning the Rank of Provincial General and Field Officers in North America. Given at our Court at Kensington, 12 May, 1756.*

[4] *Winslow to Shirley, 21 Aug. 1756.*

between acquiescence and flat mutiny, they declared their submission to his orders, at the same time asking as a favor that they might be allowed to act independently; to which Loudon gave for the present an unwilling assent. Shirley, who, in spite of his removal from command, had the good of the service deeply at heart, was much troubled at this affair, and wrote strong letters to Winslow in the interest of harmony.[1]

Loudon next proceeded to examine the state of the provincial forces, and sent Lieutenant-Colonel Burton, of the regulars, to observe and report upon it. Winslow by this time had made a forward movement, and was now at Lake George with nearly half his command, while the rest were at Fort Edward under Lyman, or in detachments at Saratoga and the other small posts below. Burton found Winslow's men encamped with their right on what are now the grounds of Fort William Henry Hotel, and their left extending southward between the mountain in their front and the marsh in their rear. "There are here," he reports, "about twenty-five hundred men, five hundred of them sick, the greatest part of them what they call poorly; they bury from five to eight daily, and officers in proportion; extremely indolent, and dirty to a degree." Then, in vernacular English, he describes the infectious condition of the fort, which was full of the sick. "Their camp," he proceeds, "is nastier than anything I could conceive; their ——, kitchens, graves, and places for slaughtering cattle all mixed through their encampment; a great waste of provisions, the men having just what they please; no great command kept up. Colonel Gridley governs the general; not in the least alert; only one advanced guard of a subaltern and twenty-four men. The cannon and stores in great confusion." Of the camp at Fort Edward he gives a better account. "It is much cleaner than at Fort William Henry, but not sufficiently so to keep the men healthy; a much better command kept up here. General Lyman very ready to order out to work and to assist the engineers with any number of men they require, and keeps a succession of scouting-parties out towards Wood Creek and South Bay."[2]

[1] *Correspondence of Loudon, Abercromby, and Shirley, July, Aug. 1756. Record of Meeting of Provincial Officers, July, 1756. Letter and Order Books of Winslow.*
[2] *Burton to Loudon, 27 Aug. 1756.*

The prejudice of the regular officer may have colored the picture, but it is certain that the sanitary condition of the provincial camps was extremely bad. "A grievous sickness among the troops," writes a Massachusetts surgeon at Fort Edward; "we bury five or six a day. Not more than two thirds of our army fit for duty. Long encampments are the bane of New England men."[1] Like all raw recruits, they did not know how to take care of themselves; and their officers had not the experience, knowledge, or habit of command to enforce sanitary rules. The same evils were found among the Canadians when kept long in one place. Those in the camp of Villiers are reported at this time as nearly all sick.[2]

Another penman, very different from the military critic, was also on the spot, noting down every day what he saw and felt. This was John Graham, minister of Suffield, in Connecticut, and now chaplain of Lyman's regiment. His spirit, by nature far from buoyant, was depressed by bodily ailments, and still more by the extremely secular character of his present surroundings. It appears by his Diary that he left home "under great exercise of mind," and was detained at Albany for a time, being, as he says, taken with an ague-fit and a quinsy; but at length he reached the camp at Fort Edward, where deep despondency fell upon him. "Labor under great discouragements," says the Diary, under date of July twenty-eighth; "for find my business but mean in the esteem of many, and think there's not much for a chaplain to do." Again, Tuesday, August seventeenth: "Breakfasted this morning with the General. But a graceless meal; never a blessing asked, nor thanks given. At the evening sacrifice a more open scene of wickedness. The General and head officers, with some of the regular officers, in General Lyman's tent, within four rods of the place of public prayers. None came to prayers; but they fixed a table without the door of the tent, where a head colonel was posted to make punch in the sight of all, they within drinking, talking, and laughing during the whole of the service, to the disturbance and disaffection of most present. This was not only a bare neglect, but an open contempt, of the

<hr />

[1] *Dr. Thomas Williams to Colonel Israel Williams, 28 Aug. 1756.*
[2] Bougainville, *Journal.*

worship of God by the heads of this army. 'T was but last Sabbath that General Lyman spent the time of divine service in the afternoon in his tent, drinking in company with Mr. Gordon, a regular officer. I have oft heard cursing and swearing in his presence by some provincial field-officers, but never heard a reproof nor so much as a check to them come from his mouth, though he never uses such language himself. Lord, what is man! Truly, the May-game of Fortune! Lord, make me know my duty, and what I ought to do!"

That night his sleep was broken and his soul troubled by angry voices under his window, where one Colonel Glasier was berating, in unhallowed language, the captain of the guard; and here the chaplain's Journal abruptly ends.[1]

A brother minister, bearing no likeness to the worthy Graham, appeared on the same spot some time after. This was Chaplain William Crawford, of Worcester, who, having neglected to bring money to the war, suffered much annoyance, aggravated by what he thought a want of due consideration for his person and office. His indignation finds vent in a letter to his townsman, Timothy Paine, member of the General Court: "No man can reasonably expect that I can with any propriety discharge the duty of a chaplain when I have nothing either to eat or drink, nor any conveniency to write a line other than to sit down upon a stump and put a piece of paper upon my knee. As for Mr. Weld [*another chaplain*], he is easy and silent whatever treatment he meets with, and I suppose they thought to find me the same easy and ductile person; but may the wide yawning earth devour me first! The state of the camp is just such as one at home would guess it to be,— nothing but a hurry and confusion of vice and wickedness, with a stygian atmosphere to breathe in."[2] The vice and

---

[1] I owe to my friend George S. Hale, Esq., the opportunity of examining the autograph Journal; it has since been printed in the *Magazine of American History* for March, 1882.

[2] The autograph letter is in Massachusetts Archives, LVI. no. 142. The same volume contains a letter from Colonel Frye, of Massachusetts, in which he speaks of the forlorn condition in which Chaplain Weld reached the camp. Of Chaplain Crawford, he says that he came decently clothed, but without bed or blanket, till he, Frye, lent them to him, and got Captain Learned to take him into his tent. Chaplains usually had a separate tent, or shared that of the colonel.

wickedness of which he complains appear to have consisted in a frequent infraction of the standing order against "Curse-ing and Swareing," as well as of that which required atten-dance on daily prayers, and enjoined "the people to appear in a decent manner, clean and shaved," at the two Sunday sermons.[1]

At the beginning of August Winslow wrote to the commit-tees of the several provinces: "It looks as if it won't be long before we are fit for a remove,"—that is, for an advance on Ticonderoga. On the twelfth Loudon sent Webb with the forty-fourth regiment and some of Bradstreet's boatmen to reinforce Oswego.[2] They had been ready for a month; but confusion and misunderstanding arising from the change of command had prevented their departure.[3] Yet the utmost anxiety had prevailed for the safety of that important post, and on the twenty-eighth Surgeon Thomas Williams wrote: "Whether Oswego is yet ours is uncertain. Would hope it is, as the reverse would be such a terrible shock as the country never felt, and may be a sad omen of what is coming upon poor sinful New England. Indeed we can't expect anything but to be severely chastened till we are humbled for our pride and haughtiness."[4]

His foreboding proved true. Webb had scarcely reached the Great Carrying Place, when tidings of disaster fell upon him like a thunderbolt. The French had descended in force upon Oswego, taken it with all its garrison; and, as report ran, were advancing into the province, six thousand strong. Wood Creek had just been cleared, with great labor, of the trees that choked it. Webb ordered others to be felled and thrown into the stream to stop the progress of the enemy; then, with shameful precipitation, he burned the forts of the Carrying Place, and retreated down the Mohawk to German Flats. Loudon ordered Winslow to think no more of Ticonderoga, but to stay where he was and hold the French in check. All was astonishment and dismay at the sudden blow. "Oswego

---

[1] *Letter and Order Books of Winslow.*

[2] *Loudon (to Fox?), 19 Aug. 1756.*

[3] *Conduct of Major-General Shirley briefly stated. Shirley to Loudon, 4 Sept. 1756. Shirley to Fox, 16 Sept. 1756.*

[4] *Thomas Williams to Colonel Israel Williams, 28 Aug. 1756.*

has changed masters, and I think we may justly fear that the whole of our country will soon follow, unless a merciful God prevent, and awake a sinful people to repentance and reformation." Thus wrote Dr. Thomas Williams to his wife from the camp at Fort Edward. "Such a shocking affair has never found a place in English annals," wrote the surgeon's young relative, Colonel William Williams. "The loss is beyond account; but the dishonor done His Majesty's arms is infinitely greater."[1] It remains to see how the catastrophe befell.

Since Vaudreuil became chief of the colony he had nursed the plan of seizing Oswego, yet hesitated to attempt it. Montcalm declares that he confirmed the Governor's wavering purpose; but Montcalm himself had hesitated. In July, however, there came exaggerated reports that the English were moving upon Ticonderoga in greatly increased numbers; and both Vaudreuil and the General conceived that a feint against Oswego would draw off the strength of the assailants, and, if promptly and secretly executed, might even be turned successfully into a real attack. Vaudreuil thereupon recalled Montcalm from Ticonderoga.[2] Leaving that post in the keeping of Lévis and three thousand men, he embarked on Lake Champlain, rowed day and night, and reached Montreal on the nineteenth. Troops were arriving from Quebec, and Indians from the far west. A band of Menomonies from beyond Lake Michigan, naked, painted, plumed, greased, stamping, uttering sharp yelps, shaking feathered lances, brandishing tomahawks, danced the war-dance before the Governor, to the thumping of the Indian drum. Bougainville looked on astonished, and thought of the Pyrrhic dance of the Greeks.

Montcalm and he left Montreal on the twenty-first, and reached Fort Frontenac in eight days. Rigaud, brother of the Governor, had gone thither some time before, and crossed with seven hundred Canadians to the south side of the lake, where Villiers was encamped at Niaouré Bay, now Sackett's Harbor, with such of his detachment as war and disease had spared. Rigaud relieved him, and took command of the united bands. With their aid the engineer, Descombles, reconnoitred the English forts, and came back with the report

[1] *Colonel William Williams to Colonel Israel Williams, 30 Aug. 1756.*
[2] *Vaudreuil au Ministre, 12 Août, 1756. Montcalm à sa Femme, 20 Juillet, 1756.*

that success was certain.[1] It was but a confirmation of what had already been learned from deserters and prisoners, who declared that the main fort was but a loopholed wall held by six or seven hundred men, ill fed, discontented, and mutinous.[2] Others said that they had been driven to desert by the want of good food, and that within a year twelve hundred men had died of disease at Oswego.[3]

The battalions of La Sarre, Guienne, and Béarn, with the colony regulars, a body of Canadians, and about two hundred and fifty Indians, were destined for the enterprise. The whole force was a little above three thousand, abundantly supplied with artillery. La Sarre and Guienne were already at Fort Frontenac. Béarn was at Niagara, whence it arrived in a few days, much buffeted by the storms of Lake Ontario. On the fourth of August all was ready. Montcalm embarked at night with the first division, crossed in darkness to Wolf Island, lay there hidden all day, and embarking again in the evening, joined Rigaud at Niaouré Bay at seven o'clock in the morning of the sixth. The second division followed, with provisions, hospital train, and eighty artillery boats; and on the eighth all were united at the bay. On the ninth Rigaud, covered by the universal forest, marched in advance to protect the landing of the troops. Montcalm followed with the first division; and, coasting the shore in bateaux, landed at midnight of the tenth within half a league of the first English fort. Four cannon were planted in battery upon the strand, and the men bivouacked by their boats. So skilful were the assailants and so careless the assailed that the English knew nothing of their danger, till in the morning, a reconnoitring canoe discovered the invaders. Two armed vessels soon came to cannonade them; but their light guns were no match for the heavy artillery of the French, and they were forced to keep the offing.

Descombles, the engineer, went before dawn to reconnoitre the fort, with several other officers and a party of Indians. While he was thus employed, one of these savages,

---

[1] *Vaudreuil au Ministre, 4 Août, 1756. Vaudreuil à Bourlamaque, — Juin,* 1756.

[2] Bougainville, *Journal.*

[3] *Vaudreuil au Ministre, 10 Juillet, 1756. Résumé des Nouvelles du Canada,* Sept. 1756.

hungry for scalps, took him in the gloom for an Englishman, and shot him dead. Captain Pouchot, of the battalion of Béarn, replaced him; and the attack was pushed vigorously. The Canadians and Indians, swarming through the forest, fired all day on the fort under cover of the trees. The second division came up with twenty-two more cannon; and at night the first parallel was marked out at a hundred and eighty yards from the rampart. Stumps were grubbed up, fallen trunks shoved aside, and a trench dug, sheltered by fascines, gabions, and a strong abattis.

Fort Ontario, counted as the best of the three forts at Oswego, stood on a high plateau at the east or right side of the river where it entered the lake. It was in the shape of a star, and was formed of trunks of trees set upright in the ground, hewn flat on two sides, and closely fitted together,—an excellent defence against musketry or swivels, but worthless against cannon. The garrison, three hundred and seventy in all, were the remnant of Pepperell's regiment, joined to raw recruits lately sent up to fill the places of the sick and dead. They had eight small cannon and a mortar, with which on the next day, Friday, the thirteenth, they kept up a brisk fire till towards night; when, after growing more rapid for a time, it ceased, and the fort showed no sign of life. Not a cannon had yet opened on them from the trenches; but it was certain that with the French artillery once in action, their wooden rampart would be shivered to splinters. Hence it was that Colonel Mercer, commandant at Oswego, thinking it better to lose the fort than to lose both fort and garrison, signalled to them from across the river to abandon their position and join him on the other side. Boats were sent to bring them off; and they passed over unmolested, after spiking their cannon and firing off their ammunition or throwing it into the well.

The fate of Oswego was now sealed. The principal work, called Old Oswego, or Fort Pepperell, stood at the mouth of the river on the west side, nearly opposite Fort Ontario, and less than five hundred yards distant from it. The trading-house, which formed the centre of the place, was built of rough stone laid in clay, and the wall which enclosed it was of the same materials; both would crumble in an instant at the touch of a twelve-pound shot. Towards the west and south they had been protected by an outer line of earthworks, mounted with cannon, and forming an entrenched camp; while the side towards Fort Ontario was left wholly exposed, in the rash confidence that this work, standing on the opposite heights, would guard against attack from that quarter. On a hill, a fourth of a mile beyond Old Oswego, stood the unfinished stockade called New Oswego, Fort George, or, by reason of its worthlessness, Fort Rascal. It had served as a cattle pen before the French appeared, but was now occupied by a hundred and fifty Jersey provincials. Old Oswego with its outwork was held by Shirley's regiment, chiefly invalids and raw recruits, to whom were now joined the garrison of Fort Ontario and a number of sailors, boatmen, and laborers.

Montcalm lost no time. As soon as darkness set in he began a battery at the brink of the height on which stood the captured fort. His whole force toiled all night, digging, setting gabions, and dragging up cannon, some of which had been taken from Braddock. Before daybreak twenty heavy pieces had been brought to the spot, and nine were already in position. The work had been so rapid that the English imagined their enemies to number six thousand at least. The battery soon opened fire. Grape and round shot swept the intrenchment and crashed through the rotten masonry. The English, says a French officer, "were exposed to their shoe-buckles." Their artillery was pointed the wrong way, in expectation of an attack, not from the east, but from the west. They now made a shelter of pork-barrels, three high and three deep, planted cannon behind them, and returned the French fire with some effect.

Early in the morning Montcalm had ordered Rigaud to cross the river with the Canadians and Indians. There was a ford three quarters of a league above the forts;[1] and here they passed over unopposed, the English not having discovered the movement.[2] The only danger was from the river. Some of the men were forced to swim, others waded to the waist, and others to the neck; but they all crossed safely, and presently showed themselves at the edge of the woods, yelling and

[1] Bougainville, *Journal.*
[2] Pouchot, I. 76.

firing their guns, too far for much execution, but not too far to discourage the garrison.

The garrison were already disheartened. Colonel Mercer, the soul of the defence, had just been cut in two by a cannon-shot while directing the gunners. Up to this time the defenders had behaved with spirit; but despair now seized them, increased by the screams and entreaties of the women, of whom there were more than a hundred in the place. There was a council of officers, and then the white flag was raised. Bougainville went to propose terms of capitulation. "The cries, threats, and hideous howlings of our Canadians and Indians," says Vaudreuil, "made them quickly decide." "This," observes the Reverend Father Claude Godefroy Cocquard, "reminds me of the fall of Jericho before the shouts of the Israelites." The English surrendered prisoners of war, to the number, according to the Governor, of sixteen hundred,[1] which included the sailors, laborers, and women. The Canadians and Indians broke through all restraint, and fell to plundering. There was an opening of rum-barrels and a scene of drunkenness, in which some of the prisoners had their share; while others tried to escape in the confusion, and were tomahawked by the excited savages. Many more would have been butchered, but for the efforts of Montcalm, who by unstinted promises succeeded in appeasing his ferocious allies, whom he dared not offend. "It will cost the King," he says, "eight or ten thousand livres in presents."[2]

The loss on both sides is variously given. By the most trustworthy accounts, that of the English did not reach fifty killed, and that of the French was still less. In the forts and vessels were found above a hundred pieces of artillery, most of them swivels and other light guns, with a large quantity of powder,

[1] *Vaudreuil au Ministre, 20 Août, 1756.* He elsewhere makes the number somewhat greater. That the garrison, exclusive of civilians, did not exceed at the utmost fourteen hundred, is shown by *Shirley to Loudon, 5 Sept. 1756.* Loudon had charged Shirley with leaving Oswego weakly garrisoned; and Shirley replies by alleging that the troops there were in number as above. It was of course his interest to make them appear as numerous as possible. In the printed *Conduct of Major-General Shirley briefly stated*, they are put at only ten hundred and fifty.

[2] Several English writers say, however, that fifteen or twenty young men were given up to the Indians to be adopted in place of warriors lately killed.

shot, and shell. The victors burned the forts and the vessels on the stocks, destroyed such provisions and stores as they could not carry away, and made the place a desert. The priest Piquet, who had joined the expedition, planted amid the ruin a tall cross, graven with the words, *In hoc signo vincunt*; and near it was set a pole bearing the arms of France, with the inscription, *Manibus date lilia plenis*. Then the army decamped, loaded with prisoners and spoil, descended to Montreal, hung the captured flags in the churches, and sang Te Deum in honor of their triumph.

It was the greatest that the French arms had yet achieved in America. The defeat of Braddock was an Indian victory; this last exploit was the result of bold enterprise and skilful tactics. With its laurels came its fruits. Hated Oswego had been laid in ashes, and the would-be assailants forced to a vain and hopeless defence. France had conquered the undisputed command of Lake Ontario, and her communications with the West were safe. A small garrison at Niagara and another at Frontenac would now hold those posts against any effort that the English could make this year; and the whole French force could concentrate at Ticonderoga, repel the threatened attack, and perhaps retort it by seizing Albany. If the English, on the other side, had lost a great material advantage, they had lost no less in honor. The news of the surrender was received with indignation in England and in the colonies. Yet the behavior of the garrison was not so discreditable as it seemed. The position was indefensible, and they could have held out at best but a few days more. They yielded too soon; but unless Webb had come to their aid, which was not to be expected, they must have yielded at last.

The French had scarcely gone, when two English scouts, Thomas Harris and James Conner, came with a party of Indians to the scene of desolation. The ground was strewn with broken casks and bread sodden with rain. The remains of burnt bateaux and whaleboats were scattered along the shore. The great stone trading-house in the old fort was a smoking ruin; Fort Rascal was still burning on the neighboring hill; Fort Ontario was a mass of ashes and charred logs, and by it stood two poles on which were written words which the visitors did not understand. They went back to Fort Johnson with their story; and Oswego reverted for a time to the bears, foxes, and wolves.[1]

[1]On the capture of Oswego, the authorities examined here have been very numerous, and only the best need be named. *Livre d'Ordres, Campagne de 1756,* contains all orders from headquarters. *Mémoire pour servir d'Instruction à M. le Marquis de Montcalm, 21 Juillet, 1756, signé Vaudreuil.* Bougainville, *Journal. Vaudreuil au Ministre, 15 Juin, 1756* (designs against Oswego). *Ibid., 13 Août, 1755. Ibid., 30 Août.* Pouchot, I. 67–81. *Relation de la Prise des Forts de Chouaguen. Bigot au Ministre, 3 Sept. 1756. Journal du Siége de Chouaguen. Précis des Événements, 1756. Montcalm au Ministre, 20 Juillet, 1756. Ibid., 28 Août, 1756. Desandrouins à ——, même date. Montcalm à sa Femme, 30 Août.* Translations of several of the above papers, along with others less important, will be found in *N. Y. Col. Docs.,* X., and *Doc. Hist. N. Y.,* I.

State of Facts relating to the Loss of Oswego, in *London Magazine* for 1757, p. 14. *Correspondence of Shirley. Correspondence of Loudon. Littlehales to Loudon, 30 Aug. 1756. Hardy to Lords of Trade, 5 Sept. 1756. Conduct of Major-General Shirley briefly stated. Declaration of some Soldiers of Shirley's Regiment,* in *N. Y. Col. Docs.,* VII. 126. Letter from an officer present, in *Boston Evening Post* of 16 May, 1757. The published plans and drawings of Oswego at this time are very inexact.

Chapter XIII

1756, 1757

PARTISAN WAR

Failure of Shirley's Plan • Causes • Loudon and Shirley • Close of the Campaign • The Western Border • Armstrong destroys Kittanning • The Scouts of Lake George • War Parties from Ticonderoga • Robert Rogers • The Rangers • Their Hardihood and Daring • Disputes as to Quarters of Troops • Expedition of Rogers • A Desperate Bush-fight • Enterprise of Vaudreuil • Rigaud attacks Fort William Henry

---

S HIRLEY'S grand scheme for cutting New France in twain had come to wreck. There was an element of boyishness in him. He made bold plans without weighing too closely his means of executing them. The year's campaign would in all likelihood have succeeded if he could have acted promptly; if he had had ready to his hand a well-trained and well-officered force, furnished with material of war and means of transportation, and prepared to move as soon as the streams and lakes of New York were open, while those of Canada were still sealed with ice. But timely action was out of his power. The army that should have moved in April was not ready to move till August. Of the nine discordant semi-republics whom he asked to join in the work, three or four refused, some of the others were lukewarm, and all were slow. Even Massachusetts, usually the foremost, failed to get all her men into the field till the season was nearly ended. Having no military establishment, the colonies were forced to improvise a new army for every campaign. Each of them watched its neighbors, or, jealous lest it should do more than its just share, waited for them to begin. Each popular assembly acted under the eye of a frugal constituency, who, having little money, were as chary of it as their descendants are lavish; and most of them were shaken by internal conflicts, more absorbing than the great question on which hung the fate of the continent. Only the four New England colonies were fully earnest for the war, and one, even of these, was ready to use the crisis as a means of extorting concessions from its Governor in return for grants of money and men. When the lagging contingents came together at last, under a commander whom none of them trusted, they were met by strategical difficulties which would have perplexed older soldiers and an abler general; for they were forced to act on the circumference of a vast semicircle, in a labyrinth of forests, without roads, and choked with every kind of obstruction.

Opposed to them was a trained army, well organized and commanded, focused at Montreal, and moving for attack or defence on two radiating lines,—one towards Lake Ontario, and the other towards Lake Champlain,—supported by a martial peasantry, supplied from France with money and material, dependent on no popular vote, having no will but that of its chief, and ready on the instant to strike to right or left as the need required. It was a compact military absolutism confronting a heterogeneous group of industrial democracies, where the force of numbers was neutralized by diffusion and incoherence. A long and dismal apprenticeship waited them before they could hope for success; nor could they ever put forth their full strength without a radical change of political conditions and an awakened consciousness of common interests and a common cause. It was the sense of powerlessness arising from the want of union that, after the fall of Oswego, spread alarm through the northern and middle colonies, and drew these desponding words from William Livingston, of New Jersey: "The colonies are nearly exhausted, and their funds already anticipated by expensive unexecuted projects. Jealous are they of each other; some ill-constituted, others shaken with intestine divisions, and, if I may be allowed the expression, parsimonious even to prodigality. Our assemblies are diffident of their governors, governors despise their assemblies; and both mutually misrepresent each other to the Court of Great Britain." Military measures, he proceeds, demand secrecy and despatch; but when so many divided provinces must agree to join in them, secrecy and despatch are impossible. In conclusion he exclaims: "Canada must be demolished,—*Delenda est Carthago*,—or we are undone."[1]

---

[1] *Review of Military Operations*, 187, 189 (Dublin, 1757).

But Loudon was not Scipio, and cis-Atlantic Carthage was to stand for some time longer.

The Earl, in search of a scapegoat for the loss of Oswego, naturally chose Shirley, attacked him savagely, told him that he was of no use in America, and ordered him to go home to England without delay.[1] Shirley, who was then in Boston, answered this indecency with dignity and effect.[2] The chief fault was with Loudon himself, whose late arrival in America had caused a change of command and of plans in the crisis of the campaign. Shirley well knew the weakness of Oswego; and in early spring had sent two engineers to make it defensible, with particular instructions to strengthen Fort Ontario.[3] But they, thinking that the chief danger lay on the west and south, turned all their attention thither, and neglected Ontario till it was too late. Shirley was about to reinforce Oswego with a strong body of troops when the arrival of Abercromby took the control out of his hands and caused ruinous delay. He cannot, however, be acquitted of mismanagement in failing to supply the place with wholesome provisions in the preceding autumn, before the streams were stopped with ice. Hence came the ravages of disease and famine which, before spring, reduced the garrison to a hundred and forty effective men. Yet there can be no doubt that the change of command was a blunder. This is the view of Franklin, who knew Shirley well, and thus speaks of him: "He would in my opinion, if continued in place, have made a much better campaign than that of Loudon, which was frivolous, expensive, and disgraceful to our nation beyond conception. For though Shirley was not bred a soldier, he was sensible and sagacious in himself, and attentive to good advice from others, capable of forming judicious plans, and quick and active in carrying them into execution."[4] He sailed for England in the autumn, disappointed and poor; the bullheaded Duke of Cumberland had been deeply prejudiced

[1] *Loudon to Shirley, 6 Sept. 1756.*

[2] The correspondence on both sides is before me, copied from the originals in the Public Record Office.

[3] "The principal thing for which I sent Mr. Mackellar to Oswego was to strengthen Fort Ontario as much as he possibly could." *Shirley to Loudon, 4 Sept. 1756.*

[4] *Works of Franklin*, I. 220.

against him, and it was only after long waiting that this strenuous champion of British interests was rewarded in his old
age with the petty government of the Bahamas.

Loudon had now about ten thousand men at his command,
though not all fit for duty. They were posted from Albany to
Lake George. The Earl himself was at Fort Edward, while
about three thousand of the provincials still lay, under Winslow, at the lake. Montcalm faced them at Ticonderoga, with
five thousand three hundred regulars and Canadians, in a position where they could defy three times their number.[1] "The
sons of Belial are too strong for me," jocosely wrote Winslow;[2] and he set himself to intrenching his camp; then had
the forest cut down for the space of a mile from the lake to
the mountains, so that the trees, lying in what he calls a "pro-
miscuous manner," formed an almost impenetrable abatis. An
escaped prisoner told him that the French were coming to
visit him with fourteen thousand men;[3] but Montcalm
thought no more of stirring than Loudon himself; and each
stood watching the other, with the lake between them, till the
season closed.

Meanwhile the western borders were still ravaged by the
tomahawk. New York, New Jersey, Pennsylvania, Maryland,
and Virginia all writhed under the infliction. Each had made
a chain of blockhouses and wooden forts to cover its frontier,
and manned them with disorderly bands, lawless, and almost
beyond control.[4] The case was at the worst in Pennsylvania,
where the tedious quarrelling of Governor and Assembly,
joined to the doggedly pacific attitude of the Quakers, made
vigorous defence impossible. Rewards were offered for prisoners and scalps, so bountiful that the hunting of men would
have been a profitable vocation, but for the extreme wariness
and agility of the game.[5] Some of the forts were well built

[1] "Nous sommes tant à Carillon qu'aux postes avancés 5,300 hommes."
Bougainville, *Journal*.

[2] *Winslow to Loudon, 29 Sept. 1756.*

[3] *Examination of Sergeant James Archibald.*

[4] In the Public Record Office, *America and West Indies*, LXXXII., is a manuscript map showing the positions of such of these posts as were north of
Virginia. They are thirty-five in number, from the head of James River to a
point west of Esopus, on the Hudson.

[5] *Colonial Records of Pa.*, VII. 76.

stockades; others were almost worthless; but the enemy rarely molested even the feeblest of them, preferring to ravage the lonely and unprotected farms. There were two or three exceptions. A Virginian fort was attacked by a war-party under an officer named Douville, who was killed, and his followers were put to flight.[1] The assailants were more fortunate at a small stockade called Fort Granville, on the Juniata. A large body of French and Indians attacked it in August while most of the garrison were absent protecting the farmers at their harvest; they set it on fire, and, in spite of a most gallant resistance by the young lieutenant left in command, took it, and killed all but one of the defenders.[2]

What sort of resistance the Pennsylvanian borderers would have made under political circumstances less adverse may be inferred from an exploit of Colonel John Armstrong, a settler of Cumberland. After the loss of Fort Granville the Governor of the province sent him with three hundred men to attack the Delaware town of Kittanning, a populous nest of savages on the Alleghany, between the two French posts of Duquesne and Venango. Here most of the war-parties were fitted out, and the place was full of stores and munitions furnished by the French. Here, too, lived the redoubted chief called Captain Jacobs, the terror of the English border. Armstrong set out from Fort Shirley, the farthest outpost, on the last of August, and, a week after, was within six miles of the Indian town. By rapid marching and rare good luck, his party had escaped discovery. It was ten o'clock at night, with a bright moon. The guides were perplexed, and knew neither the exact position of the place nor the paths that led to it. The adventurers threaded the forest in single file, over hills and through hollows, bewildered and anxious, stopping to watch and listen. At length they heard in the distance the beating of an Indian drum and the whooping of warriors in the war-dance. Guided by the sounds, they cautiously moved forward, till those in the front, scrambling down a rocky hill, found themselves on the banks of the Alleghany, about a hundred rods below Kittanning. The moon was near setting; but they could dimly see the town beyond a great intervening field of corn.

[1] *Washington to Morris,—April, 1756.*
[2] *Colonial Records of Pa.*, VII. 232, 242; *Pennsylvania Archives*, II. 744.

"At that moment," says Armstrong, "an Indian whistled in a very singular manner, about thirty perches from our front, in the foot of the cornfield." He thought they were discovered; but one Baker, a soldier well versed in Indian ways, told him that it was only some village gallant calling to a young squaw. The party then crouched in the bushes, and kept silent. The moon sank behind the woods, and fires soon glimmered through the field, kindled to drive off mosquitoes by some of the Indians who, as the night was warm, had come out to sleep in the open air. The eastern sky began to redden with the approach of day. Many of the party, spent with a rough march of thirty miles, had fallen asleep. They were now cautiously roused; and Armstrong ordered nearly half of them to make their way along the ridge of a bushy hill that overlooked the town, till they came opposite to it, in order to place it between two fires. Twenty minutes were allowed them for the movement; but they lost their way in the dusk, and reached their station too late. When the time had expired, Armstrong gave the signal to those left with him, who dashed into the cornfield, shooting down the astonished savages or driving them into the village, where they turned and made desperate fight.

It was a cluster of thirty log-cabins, the principal being that of the chief, Jacobs, which was loopholed for musketry, and became the centre of resistance. The fight was hot and stubborn. Armstrong ordered the town to be set on fire, which was done, though not without loss; for the Delawares at this time were commonly armed with rifles, and used them well. Armstrong himself was hit in the shoulder. As the flames rose and the smoke grew thick, a warrior in one of the houses sang his death-song, and a squaw in the same house was heard to cry and scream. Rough voices silenced her, and then the inmates burst out, but were instantly killed. The fire caught the house of Jacobs, who, trying to escape through an opening in the roof, was shot dead. Bands of Indians were gathering beyond the river, firing from the other bank, and even crossing to help their comrades; but the assailants held to their work till the whole place was destroyed. "During the burning of the houses," says Armstrong, "we were agreeably entertained by the quick succession of charged guns, gradually firing off as reached by the fire; but much more so with the vast explosion of sundry bags and large kegs of gunpowder, wherewith almost every house abounded; the prisoners afterwards informing us that the Indians had frequently said they had a sufficient stock of ammunition for ten years' war with the English."

These prisoners were eleven men, women, and children, captured in the border settlements, and now delivered by their countrymen. The day was far spent when the party withdrew, carrying their wounded on Indian horses, and moving perforce with extreme slowness, though expecting an attack every moment. None took place; and they reached the settlements at last, having bought their success with the loss of seventeen killed and thirteen wounded.[1] A medal was given to each officer, not by the Quaker-ridden Assembly, but by the city council of Philadelphia.

The report of this affair made by Dumas, commandant at Fort Duquesne, is worth noting. He says that Attiqué, the French name of Kittanning, was attacked by "le Général Wachinton," with three or four hundred men on horseback; that the Indians gave way; but that five or six Frenchmen who were in the town held the English in check till the fugitives rallied; that Washington and his men then took to flight, and would have been pursued but for the loss of some barrels of gunpowder which chanced to explode during the action. Dumas adds that several large parties are now on the track of the enemy, and he hopes will cut them to pieces. He then asks for a supply of provisions and merchandise to replace those which the Indians of Attiqué had lost by a fire.[2] Like other officers of the day, he would admit nothing but successes in the department under his command.

Vaudreuil wrote singular despatches at this time to the minister at Versailles. He takes credit to himself for the number of war-parties that his officers kept always at work, and

---

[1] *Report of Armstrong to Governor Denny, 14 Sept. 1756*, in *Colonial Records of Pa.*, VII. 257,—a modest yet very minute account. *A List of the Names of the Persons killed, wounded, and missing in the late Expedition against the Kittanning.* Hazard, *Pennsylvania Register*, I. 366.

[2] *Dumas à Vaudreuil, 9 Sept. 1756*, cited in *Bigot au Ministre, 6 Oct. 1756*, and in Bougainville, *Journal.*

fills page after page with details of the *coups* they had struck; how one brought in two English scalps, another three, another one, and another seven. He owns that they committed frightful cruelties, mutilating and sometimes burning their prisoners; but he expresses no regret, and probably felt none, since he declares that the object of this murderous warfare was to punish the English till they longed for peace.[1]

The waters and mountains of Lake George, and not the western borders, were the chief centre of partisan war. Ticonderoga was a hornet's nest, pouring out swarms of savages to infest the highways and byways of the wilderness. The English at Fort William Henry, having few Indians, could not retort in kind; but they kept their scouts and rangers in active movement. What they most coveted was prisoners, as sources of information. One Kennedy, a lieutenant of provincials, with five followers, white and red, made a march of rare audacity, passed all the French posts, took a scalp and two prisoners on the Richelieu, and burned a magazine of provisions between Montreal and St. John. The party were near famishing on the way back; and Kennedy was brought into Fort William Henry in a state of temporary insanity from starvation.[2] Other provincial officers, Peabody, Hazen, Waterbury, and Miller, won a certain distinction in this adventurous service, though few were so conspicuous as the blunt and sturdy Israel Putnam. Winslow writes in October that he has just returned from the best "scout" yet made, and that, being a man of strict truth, he may be entirely trusted.[3] Putnam had gone with six followers down Lake George in a whaleboat to a point on the east side, opposite the present village of Hague, hid the boat, crossed northeasterly to Lake Champlain, three miles from the French fort, climbed the mountain that overlooks it, and made a complete reconnoissance; then approached it, chased three Frenchmen, who escaped within the lines, climbed the mountain again, and moving westward along the ridge, made a minute survey of every outpost between the fort and Lake George.[4] These adventures were not

[1] *Dépêches de Vaudreuil, 1756.*

[2] *Minute of Lieutenant Kennedy's Scout. Winslow to Loudon, 20 Sept. 1756.*

[3] *Winslow to Loudon, 16 Oct. 1756.*

[4] *Report of a Scout to Ticonderoga, Oct. 1756*, signed Israel Putnam.

always fortunate. On the nineteenth of September Captain
Hodges and fifty men were ambushed a few miles from Fort
William Henry by thrice their number of Canadians and In-
dians, and only six escaped. Thus the record stands in the
Letter Book of Winslow.[1] By visiting the encampments of Ti-
conderoga, one may learn how the blow was struck.

After much persuasion, much feasting, and much consumption of tobacco and brandy, four hundred Indians, Christians
from the Missions and heathen from the far west, were persuaded to go on a grand war-party with the Canadians. Of
these last there were a hundred, — a wild crew, bedecked and
bedaubed like their Indian companions. Perière, an officer of
colony regulars, had nominal command of the whole; and
among the leaders of the Canadians was the famous bushfighter, Marin. Bougainville was also of the party. In the evening
of the sixteenth they all embarked in canoes at the French
advance-post commanded by Contrecœur, near the present
steamboat-landing, passed in the gloom under the bare steeps
of Rogers Rock, paddled a few hours, landed on the west
shore, and sent scouts to reconnoitre. These came back with
their reports on the next day, and an Indian crier called the
chiefs to council. Bougainville describes them as they stalked
gravely to the place of meeting, wrapped in colored blankets,
with lances in their hands. The accomplished young aide-de-
camp studied his strange companions with an interest not unmixed with disgust. "Of all caprice," he says, "Indian caprice
is the most capricious." They were insolent to the French,
made rules for them which they did not observe themselves,
and compelled the whole party to move when and whither
they pleased. Hiding the canoes, and lying close in the forest
by day, they all held their nocturnal course southward, by the
lofty heights of Black Mountain, and among the islets of the
Narrows, till the eighteenth. That night the Indian scouts reported that they had seen the fires of an encampment on the
west shore; on which the whole party advanced to the attack,
an hour before dawn, filing silently under the dark arches of
the forest, the Indians nearly naked, and streaked with their
war-paint of vermilion and soot. When they reached the spot,

[1] Compare Massachusetts Archives, LXXVI. 81.

they found only the smouldering fires of a deserted bivouac. Then there was a consultation; ending, after much dispute, with the choice by the Indians of a hundred and ten of their most active warriors to attempt some stroke in the neighborhood of the English fort. Marin joined them with thirty Canadians, and they set out on their errand; while the rest encamped to await the result. At night the adventurers returned, raising the death-cry and firing their guns; somewhat depressed by losses they had suffered, but boasting that they had surprised fifty-three English, and killed or taken all but one. It was a modest and perhaps an involuntary exaggeration. "The very recital of the cruelties they committed on the battle-field is horrible," writes Bougainville. "The ferocity and insolence of these black-souled barbarians makes one shudder. It is an abominable kind of war. The air one breathes is contagious of insensibility and hardness."[1] This was but one of many such parties sent out from Ticonderoga this year.

Early in September a band of New England rangers came to Winslow's camp, with three prisoners taken within the lines of Ticonderoga. Their captain was Robert Rogers, of New Hampshire,—a strong, well-knit figure, in dress and appearance more woodsman than soldier, with a clear, bold eye, and features that would have been good but for the ungainly proportions of the nose.[2] He had passed his boyhood in the rough surroundings of a frontier village. Growing to manhood, he engaged in some occupation which, he says, led him to frequent journeyings in the wilderness between the French and English settlements, and gave him a good knowledge of both.[3] It taught him also to speak a little French. He does not disclose the nature of this mysterious employment; but there can be little doubt that it was a smuggling trade with Canada. His character leaves much to be desired. He had been charged with forgery, or complicity in it, seems to have had no scruple in matters of business, and after the war was accused of treasonable dealings with the French and Span-

[1] Bougainville, *Journal.*

[2] A large engraved portrait of him, nearly at full length, is before me, printed at London in 1776.

[3] Rogers, *Journals, Introduction* (1765).

iards in the west.[1] He was ambitious and violent, yet able in
more ways than one, by no means uneducated, and so skilled
in woodcraft, so energetic and resolute, that his services were
invaluable. In recounting his own adventures, his style is direct, simple, without boasting, and to all appearance without
exaggeration. During the past summer he had raised a band
of men, chiefly New Hampshire borderers, and made a series
of daring excursions which gave him a prominent place in this
hardy byplay of war. In the spring of the present year he
raised another company, and was commissioned as its captain,
with his brother Richard as his first lieutenant, and the intrepid John Stark as his second. In July still another company
was formed, and Richard Rogers was promoted to command
it. Before the following spring there were seven such; and
more were afterwards added, forming a battalion dispersed on
various service, but all under the orders of Robert Rogers,
with the rank of major.[2] These rangers wore a sort of woodland uniform, which varied in the different companies, and
were armed with smooth-bore guns, loaded with buckshot,
bullets, or sometimes both.

The best of them were commonly employed on Lake
George; and nothing can surpass the adventurous hardihood
of their lives. Summer and winter, day and night, were alike
to them. Embarked in whaleboats or birch-canoes, they
glided under the silent moon or in the languid glare of a
breathless August day, when islands floated in dreamy haze,
and the hot air was thick with odors of the pine; or in the
bright October, when the jay screamed from the woods,
squirrels gathered their winter hoard, and congregated blackbirds chattered farewell to their summer haunts; when gay
mountains basked in light, maples dropped leaves of rustling
gold, sumachs glowed like rubies under the dark green of the
unchanging spruce, and mossed rocks with all their painted
plumage lay double in the watery mirror: that festal evening
of the year, when jocund Nature disrobes herself, to wake

[1] *Provincial Papers of New Hampshire*, VI. 364. *Correspondence of Gage, 1766.*
N. Y. Col. Docs., VII. 990. Caleb Stark, *Memoir and Correspondence of John
Stark*, 386.
[2] Rogers, *Journals. Report of the Adjutant-General of New Hampshire* (1866),
II. 158, 159.

again refreshed in the joy of her undying spring. Or, in the tomb-like silence of the winter forest, with breath frozen on his beard, the ranger strode on snow-shoes over the spotless drifts; and, like Dürer's knight, a ghastly death stalked ever at his side. There were those among them for whom this stern life had a fascination that made all other existence tame.

Rogers and his men had been in active movement since midwinter. In January they skated down Lake George, passed Ticonderoga, hid themselves by the forest-road between that post and Crown Point, intercepted two sledges loaded with provisions, and carried the drivers to Fort William Henry. In February they climbed a hill near Crown Point and made a plan of the works; then lay in ambush by the road from the fort to the neighboring village, captured a prisoner, burned houses and barns, killed fifty cattle, and returned without loss. At the end of the month they went again to Crown Point, burned more houses and barns, and reconnoitred Ticonderoga on the way back. Such excursions were repeated throughout the spring and summer. The reconnoissance of Ticonderoga and the catching of prisoners there for the sake of information were always capital objects. The valley, four miles in extent, that lay between the foot of Lake George and the French fort, was at this time guarded by four distinct outposts or fortified camps. Watched as it was at all points, and ranged incessantly by Indians in the employ of France, Rogers and his men knew every yard of the ground. On a morning in May he lay in ambush with eleven followers on a path between the fort and the nearest camp. A large body of soldiers passed; the rangers counted a hundred and eighteen, and lay close in their hiding-place. Soon after came a party of twenty-two. They fired on them, killed six, captured one, and escaped with him to Fort William Henry. In October Rogers was passing with twenty men in two whaleboats through the seeming solitude of the Narrows when a voice called to them out of the woods. It was that of Captain Shepherd, of the New Hampshire regiment, who had been captured two months before, and had lately made his escape. He told them that the French had the fullest information of the numbers and movements of the English; that letters often reached them from within the English lines; and that Lydius, a Dutch trader at Albany, was their principal correspondent.[1] Arriving at Ticonderoga, Rogers cautiously approached the fort, till, about noon, he saw a sentinel on the road leading thence to the woods. Followed by five of his men, he walked directly towards him. The man challenged, and Rogers answered in French. Perplexed for a moment, the soldier suffered him to approach; till, seeing his mistake, he called out in amazement, "*Qui êtes vous?*" "Rogers," was the answer; and the sentinel was seized, led in hot haste to the boats, and carried to the English fort, where he gave important information.

An exploit of Rogers towards midsummer greatly perplexed the French. He embarked at the end of June with fifty men in five whaleboats, made light and strong, expressly for this service, rowed about ten miles down Lake George, landed on the east side, carried the boats six miles over a gorge of the mountains, launched them again in South Bay, and rowed down the narrow prolongation of Lake Champlain under cover of darkness. At dawn they were within six miles of Ticonderoga. They landed, hid their boats, and lay close all day. Embarking again in the evening, they rowed with muffled oars under the shadow of the eastern shore, and passed so close to the French fort that they heard the voices of the sentinels calling the watchword. In the morning they had left it five miles behind. Again they hid in the woods; and from their lurking-place saw bateaux passing, some northward, and some southward, along the narrow lake. Crown Point was ten or twelve miles farther on. They tried to pass it after nightfall, but the sky was too clear and the stars too bright; and as they lay hidden the next day, nearly a hundred boats passed before them on the way to Ticonderoga. Some other boats which appeared about noon landed near them, and they watched the soldiers at dinner, within a musket-shot of their lurking-place. The next night was more favorable. They embarked at nine in the evening, passed Crown Point unseen, and hid themselves as before, ten miles below. It was the seventh of July. Thirty boats and a schooner

---

[1] *Letter and Order Books of Winslow.* "One Lydiass . . . whom we suspect for a French spy; he lives better than anybody, without any visible means, and his daughters have had often presents from Mr. Vaudreuil." *Loudon* (*to Fox?*), *19 Aug. 1756.*

passed them, returning towards Canada. On the next night they rowed fifteen miles farther, and then sent men to reconnoitre, who reported a schooner at anchor about a mile off. They were preparing to board her, when two sloops appeared, coming up the lake at but a short distance from the land. They gave them a volley, and called on them to surrender; but the crews put off in boats and made for the opposite shore. They followed and seized them. Out of twelve men their fire had killed three and wounded two, one of whom, says Rogers in his report, "could not march, therefore we put an end to him, to prevent discovery."[1] They sank the vessels, which were laden with wine, brandy, and flour, hid their boats on the west shore, and returned on foot with their prisoners.[2]

Some weeks after, Rogers returned to the place where he had left the boats, embarked in them, reconnoitred the lake nearly to St. John, hid them again eight miles north of Crown Point, took three prisoners near that post, and carried them to Fort William Henry. In the next month the French found several English boats in a small cove north of Crown Point. Bougainville propounds five different hypotheses to account for their being there; and exploring parties were sent out in the vain attempt to find some water passage by which they could have reached the spot without passing under the guns of two French forts.[3]

The French, on their side, still kept their war-parties in motion, and Vaudreuil faithfully chronicled in his despatches every English scalp they brought in. He believed in Indians, and sent them to Ticonderoga in numbers that were sometimes embarrassing. Even Pottawattamies from Lake Michigan were prowling about Winslow's camp and silently killing his sentinels with arrows, while their "medicine men" remained at Ticonderoga practising sorcery and divination to

---

[1] *Report of Rogers to Sir William Johnson, July, 1756.* This incident is suppressed in the printed *Journals*, which merely say that the man "soon died."

[2] *Rogers, Journals*, 20. *Shirley to Fox, 26 July, 1756.* "This afternoon Capt. Rogers came down with 4 scalps and 8 prisoners which he took on Lake Champlain, between 20 and 30 miles beyond Crown Point." *Surgeon Williams to his Wife, 16 July, 1756.*

[3] Bougainville, *Journal.*

aid the warriors or learn how it fared with them. Bougainville writes in his Journal on the fifteenth of October: "Yesterday the old Pottawattamies who have stayed here 'made medicine' to get news of their brethren. The lodge trembled, the sorcerer sweated drops of blood, and the devil came at last and told him that the warriors would come back with scalps and prisoners. A sorcerer in the medicine lodge is exactly like the Pythoness on the tripod or the witch Canidia invoking the shades." The diviner was not wholly at fault. Three days after, the warriors came back with a prisoner.[1]

Till November, the hostile forces continued to watch each other from the opposite ends of Lake George. Loudon repeated his orders to Winslow to keep the defensive, and wrote sarcastically to the Colonial Minister: "I think I shall be able to prevent the provincials doing anything very rash, without their having it in their power to talk in the language of this country that they could have taken all Canada if they had not been prevented by the King's servants." Winslow tried to console himself for the failure of the campaign, and wrote in his odd English to Shirley: "Am sorry that this year's performance has not succeeded as was intended; have only to say I pushed things to the utmost of my power to have been sooner in motion, which was the only thing that should have carried us to Crown Point; and though I am sensible that we are doing our duty in acting on the defensive, yet it makes no *eclate* [*sic*], and answers to little purpose in the eyes of my constituents."

On the first of the month the French began to move off towards Canada, and before many days Ticonderoga was left in the keeping of five or six companies.[2] Winslow's men followed their example. Major Eyre, with four hundred regulars, took possession of Fort William Henry, and the provincials marched for home, their ranks thinned by camp diseases and small-pox.[3] In Canada the regulars were quartered on the inhabitants, who took the infliction as a matter of course. In the English provinces the question was not so simple. Most

[1] This kind of divination was practised by Algonkin tribes from the earliest times. See *Pioneers of France in the New World*, 254.

[2] Bougainville, *Journal*. Malartic, *Journal*.

[3] *Letter and Order Books of Winslow. Winslow to Halifax, 30 Dec. 1756.*

of the British troops were assigned to Philadelphia, New York, and Boston; and Loudon demanded free quarters for them, according to usage then prevailing in England during war. Nor was the demand in itself unreasonable, seeing that the troops were sent over to fight the battles of the colonies. In Philadelphia lodgings were given them in the public-houses, which, however, could not hold them all. A long dispute followed between the Governor, who seconded Loudon's demand, and the Assembly, during which about half the soldiers lay on straw in outhouses and sheds till near mid-winter, many sickening, and some dying from exposure. Loudon grew furious, and threatened, if shelter were not provided, to send Webb with another regiment and billet the whole on the inhabitants; on which the Assembly yielded, and quarters were found.[1]

In New York the privates were quartered in barracks, but the officers were left to find lodging for themselves. Loudon demanded that provision should be made for them also. The city council hesitated, afraid of incensing the people if they complied. Cruger, the mayor, came to remonstrate. "God damn my blood!" replied the Earl; "if you do not billet my officers upon free quarters this day, I'll order here all the troops in North America, and billet them myself upon this city." Being no respecter of persons, at least in the provinces, he began with Oliver Delancey, brother of the late acting Governor, and sent six soldiers to lodge under his roof. Delancey swore at the unwelcome guests, on which Loudon sent him six more. A subscription was then raised among the citizens, and the required quarters were provided.[2] In Boston there was for the present less trouble. The troops were lodged in the barracks of Castle William, and furnished with blankets, cooking utensils, and other necessaries.[3]

Major Eyre and his soldiers, in their wilderness exile by the

---

[1] *Loudon to Denny, 28 Oct. 1756. Colonial Records of Pa., VII. 358–380. Loudon to Pitt, 10 March, 1757. Notice of Colonel Bouquet,* in *Pennsylvania Magazine,* III. 124. *The Conduct of a Noble Commander in America impartially reviewed* (1758).

[2] Smith, *Hist. of N. Y.,* Part II. 242. *William Corry to Johnson, 15 Jan., 1757,* in Stone, *Life of Sir William Johnson,* II. 24, note. *Loudon to Hardy, 21 Nov. 1756.*

[3] Massachusetts Archives, LXXVI. 153.

borders of Lake George, whiled the winter away with few
other excitements than the evening howl of wolves from the
frozen mountains, or some nocturnal savage shooting at a
sentinel from behind a stump on the moonlit fields of snow.
A livelier incident at last broke the monotony of their lives.
In the middle of January Rogers came with his rangers from
Fort Edward, bound on a scouting party towards Crown
Point. They spent two days at Fort William Henry in making
snow-shoes and other preparation, and set out on the seventeenth. Captain Spikeman was second in command, with
Lieutenants Stark and Kennedy, several other subalterns, and
two gentlemen volunteers enamoured of adventure. They
marched down the frozen lake and encamped at the Narrows.
Some of them, unaccustomed to snow-shoes, had become unfit for travel, and were sent back, thus reducing the number
to seventy-four. In the morning they marched again, by ici-
cled rocks and icebound waterfalls, mountains gray with naked woods and fir-trees bowed down with snow. On the
nineteenth they reached the west shore, about four miles
south of Rogers Rock, marched west of north eight miles,
and bivouacked among the mountains. On the next morning
they changed their course, marched east of north all day,
passed Ticonderoga undiscovered, and stopped at night some
five miles beyond it. The weather was changing, and rain was
coming on. They scraped away the snow with their snow-
shoes, piled it in a bank around them, made beds of spruce-
boughs, built fires, and lay down to sleep, while the sentinels
kept watch in the outer gloom. In the morning there was a
drizzling rain, and the softened snow stuck to their snow-
shoes. They marched eastward three miles through the dripping forest, till they reached the banks of Lake Champlain,
near what is now called Five Mile Point, and presently saw a
sledge, drawn by horses, moving on the ice from Ticonderoga
towards Crown Point. Rogers sent Stark along the shore to
the left to head it off, while he with another party, covered
by the woods, moved in the opposite direction to stop its
retreat. He soon saw eight or ten more sledges following the
first, and sent a messenger to prevent Stark from showing
himself too soon; but Stark was already on the ice. All the
sledges turned back in hot haste. The rangers ran in pursuit

and captured three of them, with seven men and six horses, while the rest escaped to Ticonderoga. The prisoners, being separately examined, told an ominous tale. There were three hundred and fifty regulars at Ticonderoga; two hundred Canadians and forty-five Indians had lately arrived there, and more Indians were expected that evening,—all destined to waylay the communications between the English forts, and all prepared to march at a moment's notice. The rangers were now in great peril. The fugitives would give warning of their presence, and the French and Indians, in overwhelming force, would no doubt cut off their retreat.

Rogers at once ordered his men to return to their last night's encampment, rekindle the fires, and dry their guns, which were wet by the rain of the morning. Then they marched southward in single file through the snow-encumbered forest, Rogers and Kennedy in the front, Spikeman in the centre, and Stark in the rear. In this order they moved on over broken and difficult ground till two in the afternoon, when they came upon a valley, or hollow, scarcely a musket-shot wide, which ran across their line of march, and, like all the rest of the country, was buried in thick woods. The front of the line had descended the first hill, and was mounting that on the farther side, when the foremost men heard a low clicking sound, like the cocking of a great number of guns; and in an instant a furious volley blazed out of the bushes on the ridge above them. Kennedy was killed outright, as also was Gardner, one of the volunteers. Rogers was grazed in the head by a bullet, and others were disabled or hurt. The rest returned the fire, while a swarm of French and Indians rushed upon them from the ridge and the slopes on either hand, killing several more, Spikeman among the rest, and capturing others. The rangers fell back across the hollow and regained the hill they had just descended. Stark with the rear, who were at the top when the fray began, now kept the assailants in check by a brisk fire till their comrades joined them. Then the whole party, spreading themselves among the trees that covered the declivity, stubbornly held their ground and beat back the French in repeated attempts to dislodge them. As the assailants were more than two to one, what Rogers had most to dread was a movement to outflank him and get into his rear. This they tried twice, and were twice repulsed by a party held in reserve for the purpose. The fight lasted several hours, during which there was much talk between the combatants. The French called out that it was a pity so many brave men should be lost, that large reinforcements were expected every moment, and that the rangers would then be cut to pieces without mercy; whereas if they surrendered at once they should be treated with the utmost kindness. They called to Rogers by name, and expressed great esteem for him. Neither threats nor promises had any effect, and the firing went on till darkness stopped it. Towards evening Rogers was shot through the wrist; and one of the men, John Shute, used to tell in his old age how he saw another ranger trying to bind the captain's wound with the ribbon of his own queue.

As Ticonderoga was but three miles off, it was destruction to stay where they were; and they withdrew under cover of night, reduced to forty-eight effective and six wounded men. Fourteen had been killed, and six captured. Those that were left reached Lake George in the morning, and Stark, with two followers, pushed on in advance to bring a sledge for the wounded. The rest made their way to the Narrows, where they encamped, and presently descried a small dark object on the ice far behind them. It proved to be one of their own number, Sergeant Joshua Martin, who had received a severe wound in the fight, and was left for dead; but by desperate efforts had followed on their tracks, and was now brought to camp in a state of exhaustion. He recovered, and lived to an advanced age. The sledge sent by Stark came in the morning, and the whole party soon reached the fort. Abercromby, on hearing of the affair, sent them a letter of thanks for gallant conduct.

Rogers reckons the number of his assailants at about two hundred and fifty in all. Vaudreuil says that they consisted of eighty-nine regulars and ninety Canadians and Indians. With his usual boastful exaggeration, he declares that forty English were left dead on the field, and that only three reached Fort William Henry alive. He says that the fight was extremely hot and obstinate, and admits that the French lost thirty-seven killed and wounded. Rogers makes the number much greater.

That it was considerable is certain, as Lusignan, commandant at Ticonderoga, wrote immediately for reinforcements.[1]

The effects of his wound and an attack of small-pox kept Rogers quiet for a time. Meanwhile the winter dragged slowly away, and the ice of Lake George, cracking with change of temperature, uttered its strange cry of agony, heralding that dismal season when winter begins to relax its gripe, but spring still holds aloof; when the sap stirs in the sugar-maples, but the buds refuse to swell, and even the catkins of the willows will not burst their brown integuments; when the forest is patched with snow, though on its sunny slopes one hears in the stillness the whisper of trickling waters that ooze from the half-thawed soil and saturated beds of fallen leaves; when clouds hang low on the darkened mountains, and cold mists entangle themselves in the tops of the pines; now a dull rain, now a sharp morning frost, and now a storm of snow powdering the waste, and wrapping it again in the pall of winter.

In this cheerless season, on St. Patrick's Day, the seventeenth of March, the Irish soldiers who formed a part of the garrison of Fort William Henry were paying homage to their patron saint in libations of heretic rum, the product of New England stills; and it is said that John Stark's rangers forgot theological differences in their zeal to share the festivity. The story adds that they were restrained by their commander, and

[1] Rogers, *Journals*, 38–44. Caleb Stark, *Memoir and Correspondence of John Stark*, 18, 412. *Return of Killed, Wounded, and Missing in the Action near Ticonderoga, Jan. 1757*; all the names are here given. James Abercromby, aide-de-camp to his uncle, General Abercromby, wrote to Rogers from Albany: "You cannot imagine how all ranks of people here are pleased with your conduct and your men's behavior."

The accounts of the French writers differ from each other, but agree in placing the English force at from seventy to eighty, and their own much higher. The principal report is that of *Vaudreuil au Ministre, 19 Avril, 1757* (his second letter of this date). Bougainville, Montcalm, Malartic, and Montreuil all speak of the affair, placing the English loss much higher than is shown by the returns. The story, repeated in most of the French narratives, that only three of the rangers reached Fort William Henry, seems to have arisen from the fact that Stark with two men went thither in advance of the rest. As regards the antecedents of the combat, the French and English accounts agree.

that their enforced sobriety proved the saving of the fort. This
may be doubted; for without counting the English soldiers of
the garrison who had no special call to be drunk that day, the
fort was in no danger till twenty-four hours after, when the
revellers had had time to rally from their pious carouse.
Whether rangers or British soldiers, it is certain that watchmen were on the alert during the night between the eighteenth and nineteenth, and that towards one in the morning
they heard a sound of axes far down the lake, followed by the
faint glow of a distant fire. The inference was plain, that an
enemy was there, and that the necessity of warming himself
had overcome his caution. Then all was still for some two
hours, when, listening in the pitchy darkness, the watchers
heard the footsteps of a great body of men approaching on
the ice, which at the time was bare of snow. The garrison
were at their posts, and all the cannon on the side towards
the lake vomited grape and round-shot in the direction of the
sound, which thereafter was heard no more.

Those who made it were a detachment, called by Vaudreuil
an army, sent by him to seize the English fort. Shirley had
planned a similar stroke against Ticonderoga a year before;
but the provincial levies had come in so slowly, and the ice
had broken up so soon, that the scheme was abandoned. Vaudreuil was more fortunate. The whole force, regulars, Canadians, and Indians, was ready to his hand. No pains were
spared in equipping them. Overcoats, blankets, bearskins to
sleep on, tarpaulins to sleep under, spare moccasons, spare
mittens, kettles, axes, needles, awls, flint and steel, and many
miscellaneous articles were provided, to be dragged by the
men on light Indian sledges, along with provisions for twelve
days. The cost of the expedition is set at a million francs,
answering to more than as many dollars of the present time.
To the disgust of the officers from France, the Governor
named his brother Rigaud for the chief command; and before
the end of February the whole party was on its march along
the ice of Lake Champlain. They rested nearly a week at Ticonderoga, where no less than three hundred short scaling-
ladders, so constructed that two or more could be joined in
one, had been made for them; and here, too, they received a
reinforcement, which raised their number to sixteen hundred.

Then, marching three days along Lake George, they neared the fort on the evening of the eighteenth, and prepared for a general assault before daybreak.

The garrison, including rangers, consisted of three hundred and forty-six effective men.[1] The fort was not strong, and a resolute assault by numbers so superior must, it seems, have overpowered the defenders; but the Canadians and Indians who composed most of the attacking force were not suited for such work; and, disappointed in his hope of a surprise, Rigaud withdrew them at daybreak, after trying in vain to burn the buildings outside. A few hours after, the whole body reappeared, filing off to surround the fort, on which they kept up a brisk but harmless fire of musketry. In the night they were heard again on the ice, approaching as if for an assault; and the cannon, firing towards the sound, again drove them back. There was silence for a while, till tongues of flame lighted up the gloom, and two sloops, ice-bound in the lake, and a large number of bateaux on the shore were seen to be on fire. A party sallied to save them; but it was too late. In the morning they were all consumed, and the enemy had vanished.

It was Sunday, the twentieth. Everything was quiet till noon, when the French filed out of the woods and marched across the ice in procession, ostentatiously carrying their scaling-ladders, and showing themselves to the best effect. They stopped at a safe distance, fronting towards the fort, and several of them advanced, waving a red flag. An officer with a few men went to meet them, and returned bringing Le Mercier, chief of the Canadian artillery, who, being led blindfold into the fort, announced himself as bearer of a message from Rigaud. He was conducted to the room of Major Eyre, where all the British officers were assembled; and, after mutual compliments, he invited them to give up the place peaceably, promising the most favorable terms, and threatening a general assault and massacre in case of refusal. Eyre said that he should defend himself to the last; and the envoy, again blindfolded, was led back to whence he came.

---

[1] *Strength of the Garrison of Fort William Henry when the Enemy came before it*, enclosed in the letter of *Major Eyre to Loudon, 26 March, 1757*. There were also one hundred and twenty-eight invalids.

The whole French force now advanced as if to storm the works, and the garrison prepared to receive them. Nothing came of it but a fusillade, to which the British made no reply. At night the French were heard advancing again, and each man nerved himself for the crisis. The real attack, however, was not against the fort, but against the buildings outside, which consisted of several storehouses, a hospital, a saw-mill, and the huts of the rangers, besides a sloop on the stocks and piles of planks and cord-wood. Covered by the night, the assailants crept up with fagots of resinous sticks, placed them against the farther side of the buildings, kindled them, and escaped before the flame rose; while the garrison, straining their ears in the thick darkness, fired wherever they heard a sound. Before morning all around them was in a blaze, and they had much ado to save the fort barracks from the shower of burning cinders. At ten o'clock the fires had subsided, and a thick fall of snow began, filling the air with a restless chaos of large moist flakes. This lasted all day and all the next night, till the ground and the ice were covered to a depth of three feet and more. The French lay close in their camps till a little before dawn on Tuesday morning, when twenty volunteers from the regulars made a bold attempt to burn the sloop on the stocks, with several storehouses and other structures, and several hundred scows and whaleboats which had thus far escaped. They were only in part successful; but they fired the sloop and some buildings near it, and stood far out on the ice watching the flaming vessel, a superb bonfire amid the wilderness of snow. The spectacle cost the volunteers a fourth of their number killed and wounded.

On Wednesday morning the sun rose bright on a scene of wintry splendor, and the frozen lake was dotted with Rigaud's retreating followers toiling towards Canada on snowshoes. Before they reached it many of them were blinded for a while by the insufferable glare, and their comrades led them homewards by the hand.[1]

[1] *Eyre to Loudon, 24 March, 1757. Ibid., 25 March*, enclosed in Loudon's despatch of 25 April, 1757. *Message of Rigaud to Major Eyre, 20 March, 1757. Letter from Fort William Henry, 26 March, 1757*, in *Boston Gazette, No. 106*, and *Boston Evening Post, No. 1,128. Abstract of Letters from Albany*, in *Boston News Letter, No. 2,860*. Caleb Stark, *Memoir and Correspondence of John Stark*, 22, a curious

mixture of truth and error. *Relation de la Campagne sur le Lac St. Sacrement pendant l'Hiver, 1757.* Bougainville, *Journal.* Malartic, *Journal. Montcalm au Ministre, 24 Avril, 1757. Montreuil au Ministre, 23 Avril, 1757. Montcalm à sa Mère, 1 Avril, 1757. Mémoires sur le Canada, 1749 –1760.*

The French loss in killed and wounded is set by Montcalm at eleven. That of the English was seven, slightly wounded, chiefly in sorties. They took three prisoners. Stark was touched by a bullet, for the only time in his adventurous life.

Chapter XIV

1757

MONTCALM AND VAUDREUIL

The Seat of War • Social Life at Montreal • Familiar Correspondence of Montcalm • His Employments • His Impressions of Canada • His Hospitalities • Misunderstandings with the Governor • Character of Vaudreuil • His Accusations • Frenchmen and Canadians • Foibles of Montcalm • The opening Campaign • Doubts and Suspense • Loudon's Plan • His Character • Fatal Delays • Abortive Attempt against Louisbourg • Disaster to the British Fleet

S PRING CAME at last, and the Dutch burghers of Albany heard, faint from the far height, the clamor of the wild-fowl, streaming in long files northward to their summer home. As the aërial travellers winged their way, the seat of war lay spread beneath them like a map. First the blue Hudson, slumbering among its forests, with the forts along its banks, Half-Moon, Stillwater, Saratoga, and the geometric lines and earthen mounds of Fort Edward. Then a broad belt of dingy evergreen; and beyond, released from wintry fetters, the glistening breast of Lake George, with Fort William Henry at its side, amid charred ruins and a desolation of prostrate forests. Hence the lake stretched northward, like some broad river, trenched between mountain ranges still leafless and gray. Then they looked down on Ticonderoga, with the flag of the Bourbons, like a flickering white speck, waving on its ramparts; and next on Crown Point with its tower of stone. Lake Champlain now spread before them, widening as they flew: on the left, the mountain wilderness of the Adirondacks, like a stormy sea congealed; on the right, the long procession of the Green Mountains; and, far beyond, on the dim verge of the eastern sky, the White Mountains throned in savage solitude. They passed over the bastioned square of Fort St. John, Fort Chambly guarding the rapids of the Richelieu, and the broad belt of the St. Lawrence, with Montreal seated on its bank. Here we leave them, to build their nests and hatch their brood among the fens of the lonely North.

Montreal, the military heart of Canada, was in the past winter its social centre also, where were gathered conspicuous representatives both of Old France and of New; not men only, but women. It was a sparkling fragment of the reign of Louis XV. dropped into the American wilderness. Montcalm was here with his staff and his chief officers, now pondering schemes of war, and now turning in thought to his beloved Château of Candiac, his mother, children, and wife, to whom he sent letters with every opportunity. To his wife he writes: "Think of me affectionately; give love to my girls. I hope next year I may be with you all. I love you tenderly, dearest." He says that he has sent her a packet of marten-skins for a muff; "and another time I shall send some to our daughter; but I should like better to bring them myself." Of this eldest daughter he writes in reply to a letter of domestic news from Madame de Montcalm: "The new gown with blonde trimmings must be becoming, for she is pretty." Again, "There is not an hour in the day when I do not think of you, my mother and my children." He had the tastes of a country gentleman, and was eager to know all that was passing on his estate. Before leaving home he had set up a mill to grind olives for oil, and was well pleased to hear of its prosperity. "It seems to be a good thing, which pleases me very much. Bougainville and I talk a great deal about the oil-mill." Some time after, when the King sent him the coveted decoration of the *cordon rouge*, he informed Madame de Montcalm of the honor done him, and added: "But I think I am better pleased with what you tell me of the success of my oil-mill."

To his mother he writes of his absorbing occupations, and says: "You can tell my dearest that I have no time to occupy myself with the ladies, even if I wished to." Nevertheless he now and then found leisure for some little solace in his banishment; for he writes to Bourlamaque, whom he had left at Quebec, after a visit which he had himself made there early in the winter: "I am glad you sometimes speak of me to the three ladies in the Rue du Parloir; and I am flattered by their remembrance, especially by that of one of them, in whom I find at certain moments too much wit and too many charms for my tranquillity." These ladies of the Rue du Parloir are several times mentioned in his familiar correspondence with Bourlamaque.

His station obliged him to maintain a high standard of living, to his great financial detriment, for Canadian prices were inordinate. "I must live creditably, and so I do; sixteen persons at table every day. Once a fortnight I dine with the Governor-General and with the Chevalier de Lévis, who lives well too. He has given three grand balls. As for me, up to Lent I gave, besides dinners, great suppers, with ladies, three times a week. They lasted till two in the morning; and then there was dancing, to which company came uninvited, but sure of a welcome from those who had been at supper. It is very expensive, not very amusing, and often tedious. At Quebec, where we spent a month, I gave receptions or parties, often at the Intendant's house. I like my gallant Chevalier de Lévis very much. Bourlamaque was a good choice; he is steady and cool, with good parts. Bougainville has talent, a warm head, and warm heart; he will ripen in time. Write to Madame Cornier that I like her husband; he is perfectly well, and as impatient for peace as I am. Love to my daughters, and all affection and respect to my mother. I live only in the hope of joining you all again. Nevertheless, Montreal is as good a place as Alais even in time of peace, and better now, because the Government is here; for the Marquis de Vaudreuil, like me, spent only a month at Quebec. As for Quebec, it is as good as the best cities of France, except ten or so. Clear sky, bright sun; neither spring nor autumn, only summer and winter. July, August, and September, hot as in Languedoc: winter insupportable; one must keep always indoors. The ladies *spirituelles*, *galantes*, *dévotes*. Gambling at Quebec, dancing and conversation at Montreal. My friends the Indians, who are often unbearable, and whom I treat with perfect tranquillity and patience, are fond of me. If I were not a sort of general, though very subordinate to the Governor, I could gossip about the plans of the campaign, which it is likely will begin on the tenth or fifteenth of May. I worked at the plan of the last affair [*Rigaud's expedition to Fort William Henry*], which might have turned out better, though good as it was. I wanted only eight hundred men. If I had had my way, Monsieur de Lévis or Monsieur de Bougainville would have had charge of it. However, the thing was all right, and in good hands. The Governor, who is extremely civil to me, gave it to his brother; he thought him more used to winter marches. Adieu, my heart; I adore and love you!"

To meet his manifold social needs, he sends to his wife orders for prunes, olives, anchovies, muscat wine, capers, sausages, confectionery, cloth for liveries, and many other such items; also for scent-bags of two kinds, and perfumed pomatum for presents; closing in postscript with an injunction not to forget a dozen pint-bottles of English lavender. Some months after, he writes to Madame de Saint-Véran: "I have got everything that was sent me from Montpellier except the sausages. I have lost a third of what was sent from Bordeaux. The English captured it on board the ship called 'La Superbe;' and I have reason to fear that everything sent from Paris is lost on board 'La Liberté.' I am running into debt here. Pshaw! I must live. I do not worry myself. Best love to you, my mother."

When Rigaud was about to march with his detachment against Fort William Henry, Montcalm went over to La Prairie to see them. "I reviewed them," he writes to Bourlamaque, "and gave the officers a dinner, which, if anybody else had given it, I should have said was a grand affair. There were two tables, for thirty-six persons in all. On Wednesday there was an Assembly at Madame Varin's; on Friday the Chevalier de Lévis gave a ball. He invited sixty-five ladies, and got only thirty, with a great crowd of men. Rooms well lighted, excellent order, excellent service, plenty of refreshments of every sort all through the night; and the company stayed till seven in the morning. As for me, I went to bed early. I had had that day eight ladies at a supper given to Madame Varin. Tomorrow I shall have half-a-dozen at another supper, given to I don't know whom, but incline to think it will be La Roche Beaucour. The gallant Chevalier is to give us still another ball."

Lent put a check on these festivities. "To-morrow," he tells Bourlamaque, "I shall throw myself into devotion with might and main (*à corps perdu*). It will be easier for me to detach myself from the world and turn heavenward here at Montreal than it would be at Quebec." And, some time after, "Bougainville spent Monday delightfully at Isle Ste. Hélène, and Tuesday devoutly with the Sulpitian Fathers at the Mountain. I was there myself at four o'clock, and did them the civility to sup in their refectory at a quarter before six."

In May there was a complete revival of social pleasures, and Montcalm wrote to Bourlamaque: "Madame de Beaubassin's supper was very gay. There were toasts to the Rue du Parloir and to the General. To-day I must give a dinner to Madame de Saint-Ours, which will be a little more serious. Péan is gone to establish himself at La Chine, and will come back with La Barolon, who goes thither with a husband of hers, bound to the Ohio with Villejoin and Louvigny. The Chevalier de Lévis amuses himself very much here. He and his friends spend all their time with Madame de Lenisse."

Under these gayeties and gallantries there were bitter heart-burnings. Montcalm hints at some of them in a letter to Bourlamaque, written at the time of the expedition to Fort William Henry, which, in the words of Montcalm, who would have preferred another commander, the Governor had ordered to march "under the banners of brother Rigaud." "After he got my letter on Sunday evening," says the disappointed General, "Monsieur de Vaudreuil sent me his secretary with the instructions he had given his brother," which he had hitherto withheld. "This gave rise after dinner to a long conversation with him; and I hope for the good of the service that his future conduct will prove the truth of his words. I spoke to him with frankness and firmness of the necessity I was under of communicating to him my reflections; but I did not name any of the persons who, to gain his good graces, busy themselves with destroying his confidence in me. I told him that he would always find me disposed to aid in measures tending to our success, even should his views, which always ought to prevail, be different from mine; but that I dared flatter myself that he would henceforward communicate his plans to me sooner; for, though his knowledge of the country gave greater weight to his opinions, he might rest satisfied that I should second him in methods and details. This explanation passed off becomingly enough, and ended with a proposal to dine on a moose's nose [*an estimed morsel*] the day after to-morrow. I burn your letters, Monsieur, and I beg you to do the same with mine, after making a note of anything you may want to keep." But Bourlamaque kept all the letters, and bound them in a volume, which still exists.[1]

Montcalm was not at this time fully aware of the feeling of Vaudreuil towards him. The touchy egotism of the Governor and his jealous attachment to the colony led him to claim for himself and the Canadians the merit of every achievement and to deny it to the French troops and their general. Before the capture of Oswego was known, he wrote to the naval minister that Montcalm would never have dared attack that place if he had not encouraged him and answered his timid objections.[2] "I am confident that I shall reduce it," he adds; "my expedition is sure to succeed if Monsieur de Montcalm follows the directions I have given him." When the good news came he immediately wrote again, declaring that the victory was due to his brother Rigaud and the Canadians, who, he says, had been ill-used by the General, and not allowed either to enter the fort or share the plunder, any more than the Indians, who were so angry at the treatment they had met that he had great difficulty in appeasing them. He hints that the success was generally ascribed to him. "There has been a great deal of talk here; but I will not do myself the honor of repeating it to you, especially as it relates to myself. I know how to do violence to my self-love. The measures I took assured our victory, in spite of opposition. If I had been less vigilant and firm, Oswego would still be in the hands of the English. I cannot sufficiently congratulate myself on the zeal which my brother and the Canadians and Indians showed on this occasion; for without them my orders would have been given in vain. The hopes of His Britannic Majesty have vanished, and will hardly revive again; for I shall take care to crush them in the bud."[3]

The pronouns "I" and "my" recur with monotonous frequency in his correspondence. "I have laid waste all the British provinces." "By promptly uniting my forces at Carillon, I

---

[1] The preceding extracts are from *Lettres de Montcalm à Madame de Saint-Véran, sa Mère, et à Madame de Montcalm, sa Femme, 1756, 1757 (Papiers de Famille)*; and *Lettres de Montcalm à Bourlamaque, 1757*. See Appendix E.

[2] *Vaudreuil au Ministre de la Marine, 13 Août, 1756.*

[3] *Vaudreuil au Ministre de la Marine, 1 Sept. 1756.*

have kept General Loudon in check, though he had at his disposal an army of about twenty thousand men;"[1] and so without end, in all varieties of repetition. It is no less characteristic that he here assigns to his enemies double their actual force.

He has the faintest of praise for the troops from France. "They are generally good, but thus far they have not absolutely distinguished themselves. I do justice to the firmness they showed at Oswego; but it was only the colony troops, Canadians, and Indians who attacked the forts. Our artillery was directed by the Chevalier Le Mercier and M. Frémont [*colony officers*], and was served by our colony troops and our militia. The officers from France are more inclined to defence than attack. Far from spending the least thing here, they lay by their pay. They saved the money allowed them for refreshments, and had it in pocket at the end of the campaign. They get a profit, too, out of their provisions, by having certificates made under borrowed names, so that they can draw cash for them on their return. It is the same with the soldiers, who also sell their provisions to the King and get paid for them. In conjunction with M. Bigot, I labor to remedy all these abuses; and the rules we have established have saved the King a considerable expense. M. de Montcalm has complained very much of these rules." The Intendant Bigot, who here appears as a reformer, was the centre of a monstrous system of public fraud and robbery; while the charges against the French officers are unsupported. Vaudreuil, who never loses an opportunity of disparaging them, proceeds thus: —

"The troops from France are not on very good terms with our Canadians. What can the soldiers think of them when they see their officers threaten them with sticks or swords? The Canadians are obliged to carry these gentry on their shoulders, through the cold water, over rocks that cut their feet; and if they make a false step they are abused. Can anything be harder? Finally, Monsieur de Montcalm is so quick-tempered that he goes to the length of striking the Canadians. How can he restrain his officers when he cannot restrain himself? Could any example be more contagious? This is the way our Canadians are treated. They deserve something better."

[1] *Ibid.*, 6 Nov. 1756.

He then enlarges on their zeal, hardihood, and bravery, and adds that nothing but their blind submission to his commands prevents many of them from showing resentment at the usage they had to endure. The Indians, he goes on to say, are not so gentle and yielding; and but for his brother Rigaud and himself, might have gone off in a rage. "After the campaign of Oswego they did not hesitate to tell me that they would go wherever I sent them, provided I did not put them under the orders of M. de Montcalm. They told me positively that they could not bear his quick temper. I shall always maintain the most perfect union and understanding with M. le Marquis de Montcalm, but I shall be forced to take measures which will assure to our Canadians and Indians treatment such as their zeal and services merit."[1]

To the subject of his complaints Vaudreuil used a different language; for Montcalm says, after mentioning that he had had occasion to punish some of the Canadians at Oswego: "I must do Monsieur de Vaudreuil the justice to say that he approved my proceedings." He treated the General with the blandest politeness. "He is a good-natured man," continues Montcalm, "mild, with no character of his own, surrounded by people who try to destroy all his confidence in the general of the troops from France. I am praised excessively, in order to make him jealous, excite his Canadian prejudices, and prevent him from dealing with me frankly, or adopting my views when he can help it."[2] He elsewhere complains that Vaudreuil gave to both him and Lévis orders couched in such equivocal terms that he could throw the blame on them in case of reverse.[1] Montcalm liked the militia no better than the Governor liked the regulars. "I have used them with good effect, though not in places exposed to the enemy's fire. They know neither discipline nor subordination, and think themselves in all respects the first nation on earth." He is sure, however, that they like him: "I have gained the utmost confidence of the Canadians and Indians; and in the eyes of the former, when I travel or visit their camps, I have the air of a

---

[1] *Vaudreuil au Ministre de la Marine, 23 Oct. 1756.* The above extracts are somewhat condensed in the translation. See the letter in Dussieux, 279.

[2] *Montcalm au Ministre de la Guerre, 11 Juillet, 1757.*

[3] *Ibid., 1 Nov. 1756.*

tribune of the people."[1] "The affection of the Indians for me is so strong that there are moments when it astonishes the Governor."[2] "The Indians are delighted with me," he says in another letter; "the Canadians are pleased with me; their officers esteem and fear me, and would be glad if the French troops and their general could be dispensed with; and so should I."[3] And he writes to his mother: "The part I have to play is unique: I am a general-in-chief subordinated; sometimes with everything to do, and sometimes nothing; I am esteemed, respected, beloved, envied, hated; I pass for proud, supple, stiff, yielding, polite, devout, gallant, etc.; and I long for peace."[4]

The letters of the Governor and those of the General, it will be seen, contradict each other flatly at several points. Montcalm is sustained by his friend Bougainville, who says that the Indians had a great liking for him, and that he "knew how to manage them as well as if he had been born in their wigwams."[5] And while Vaudreuil complains that the Canadians are ill-used by Montcalm, Bougainville declares that the regulars are ill-used by Vaudreuil. "One must be blind not to see that we are treated as the Spartans treated the Helots." Then he comments on the jealous reticence of the Governor. "The Marquis de Montcalm has not the honor of being consulted; and it is generally through public rumor that he first hears of Monsieur de Vaudreuil's military plans." He calls the Governor "a timid man, who can neither make a resolution nor keep one;" and he gives another trait of him, illustrating it, after his usual way, by a parallel from the classics: "When V. produces an idea he falls in love with it, as Pygmalion did with his statue. I can forgive Pygmalion, for what he produced was a masterpiece."[6]

The exceeding touchiness of the Governor was sorely tried by certain indiscretions on the part of the General, who in his rapid and vehement utterances sometimes forgot the rules of

[1] *Ibid.*, *18 Sept. 1757.*

[2] *Ibid.*, *4 Nov. 1757.*

[3] *Ibid.*, *28 Août, 1756.*

[4] *Montcalm à Madame de Saint-Véran, 23 Sept. 1757.*

[5] *Bougainville à Saint-Laurens, 19 Août, 1757.*

[6] Bougainville, *Journal.*

prudence. His anger, though not deep, was extremely impetuous; and it is said that his irritation against Vaudreuil sometimes found escape in the presence of servants and soldiers.[1]
There was no lack of reporters, and the Governor was told
everything. The breach widened apace, and Canada divided
itself into two camps: that of Vaudreuil with the colony officers, civil and military, and that of Montcalm with the officers
from France. The principal exception was the Chevalier de
Lévis. This brave and able commander had an easy and adapt-
able nature, which made him a sort of connecting link between the two parties. "One should be on good terms with
everybody," was a maxim which he sometimes expressed, and
on which he shaped his conduct with notable success. The
Intendant Bigot also, an adroit and accomplished person, had
the skill to avoid breaking with either side.

But now the season of action was near, and domestic strife
must give place to efforts against the common foe. "God or
devil!" Montcalm wrote to Bourlamaque, "we must do something and risk a fight. If we succeed, we can, all three of us
[*you, Lévis, and I*], ask for promotion. Burn this letter." The
prospects, on the whole, were hopeful. The victory at Oswego had wrought marvels among the Indians, inspired the
faithful, confirmed the wavering, and daunted the ill-disposed. The whole West was astir, ready to pour itself again
in blood and fire against the English border; and even the
Cherokees and Choctaws, old friends of the British colonies,
seemed on the point of turning against them.[2] The Five Nations were half won for France. In November a large deputation of them came to renew the chain of friendship at
Montreal. "I have laid Oswego in ashes," said Vaudreuil; "the
English quail before me. Why do you nourish serpents in
your bosom? They mean only to enslave you." The deputies
trampled under foot the medals the English had given them,
and promised the "Devourer of Villages," for so they styled
the Governor, that they would never more lift the hatchet
against his children. The chief difficulty was to get rid of
them; for, being clothed and fed at the expense of the King,
they were in no haste to take leave; and learning that New

[1] *Événements de la Guerre en Canada, 1759, 1760.*
[2] *Vaudreuil au Ministre de la Marine, 19 Avril, 1757.*

Year's Day was a time of visits, gifts, and health-drinking, they declared that they would stay to share its pleasures; which they did, to their own satisfaction and the annoyance of those who were forced to entertain them and their squaws.[1] An active siding with France was to be expected only from the western bands of the Confederacy. Neutrality alone could be hoped for from the others, who were too near the English safely to declare against them; while from one of the tribes, the Mohawks, even neutrality was doubtful.

Vaudreuil, while disliking the French regulars, felt that he could not dispense with them, and had asked for a reinforcement. His request was granted; and the Colonial Minister informed him that twenty-four hundred men had been ordered to Canada to strengthen the colony regulars and the battalions of Montcalm.[2] This, according to the estimate of the Minister, would raise the regular force in Canada to sixty-six hundred rank and file.[3] The announcement was followed by another, less agreeable. It was to the effect that a formidable squadron was fitting out in British ports. Was Quebec to be attacked, or Louisbourg? Louisbourg was beyond reach of succor from Canada; it must rely on its own strength and on help from France. But so long as Quebec was threatened, all the troops in the colony must be held ready to defend it, and the hope of attacking England in her own domains must be abandoned. Till these doubts were solved, nothing could be done; and hence great activity in catching prisoners for the sake of news. A few were brought in, but they knew no more of the matter than the French themselves; and Vaudreuil and Montcalm rested for a while in suspense.

The truth, had they known it, would have gladdened their hearts. The English preparations were aimed at Louisbourg. In the autumn before, Loudon, prejudiced against all plans of his predecessor, Shirley, proposed to the Ministry a scheme

[1] *Montcalm au Ministre de la Guerre, 24 Avril, 1757; Relation de l'Ambassade des Cinq Nations à Montreal, jointe à la lettre précédente. Procès-verbal de différentes Entrevues entre M. de Vaudreuil et les Députés des Nations sauvages du 13 au 30 Déc. 1756.* Malartic, *Journal. Montcalm à Madame de Saint-Véran, 1 Avril, 1757.*

[2] *Ordres du Roy et Dépêches des Ministres, Mars, 1757.*

[3] *Ministerial Minute on the Military Force in Canada, 1757,* in N. Y. Col. Docs., X. 523.

of his own, involving a possible attack on Quebec, but with the reduction of Louisbourg as its immediate object,—an important object, no doubt, but one that had no direct bearing on the main question of controlling the interior of the continent. Pitt, then for a brief space at the head of the Government, accepted the suggestion, and set himself to executing it; but he was hampered by opposition, and early in April was forced to resign. Then followed a contest of rival claimants to office; and the war against France was made subordinate to disputes of personal politics. Meanwhile one Florence Hensey, a spy at London, had informed the French Court that a great armament was fitting out for America, though he could not tell its precise destination. Without loss of time three French squadrons were sent across the Atlantic, with orders to rendezvous at Louisbourg, the conjectured point of attack.

The English were as tardy as their enemies were prompt. Everything depended on speed; yet their fleet, under Admiral Holbourne, consisting of fifteen ships of the line and three frigates, with about five thousand troops on board, did not get to sea till the fifth of May, when it made sail for Halifax, where Loudon was to meet it with additional forces.

Loudon had drawn off the best part of the troops from the northern frontier, and they were now at New York waiting for embarkation. That the design might be kept secret, he laid an embargo on colonial shipping,—a measure which exasperated the colonists without answering its purpose. Now ensued a long delay, during which the troops, the provincial levies, the transports destined to carry them, and the ships of war which were to serve as escort, all lay idle. In the interval Loudon showed great activity in writing despatches and other avocations more or less proper to a commander, being always busy, without, according to Franklin, accomplishing anything. One Innis, who had come with a message from the Governor of Pennsylvania, and had waited above a fortnight for the General's reply, remarked of him that he was like St. George on a tavern sign, always on horseback, and never riding on.[1] Yet nobody longed more than he to reach the ren-

---

[1] *Works of Franklin,* I. 219. Franklin intimates that while Loudon was constantly writing, he rarely sent off despatches. This is a mistake; there is abundance of them, often tediously long, in the Public Record Office.

dezvous at Halifax. He was waiting for news of Holbourne, and he waited in vain. He knew only that a French fleet had been seen off the coast strong enough to overpower his escort and sink all his transports.[1] But the season was growing late; he must act quickly if he was to act at all. He and Sir Charles Hardy agreed between them that the risk must be run; and on the twentieth of June the whole force put to sea. They met no enemy, and entered Halifax harbor on the thirtieth. Holbourne and his fleet had not yet appeared; but his ships soon came straggling in, and before the tenth of July all were at anchor before the town. Then there was more delay. The troops, nearly twelve thousand in all, were landed, and weeks were spent in drilling them and planting vegetables for their refreshment. Sir Charles Hay was put under arrest for saying that the nation's money was spent in sham battles and raising cabbages. Some attempts were made to learn the state of Louisbourg; and Captain Gorham, of the rangers, who reconnoitred it from a fishing vessel, brought back an imperfect report, upon which, after some hesitation, it was resolved to proceed to the attack. The troops were embarked again, and all was ready, when, on the fourth of August, a sloop came from Newfoundland, bringing letters found on board a French vessel lately captured. From these it appeared that all three of the French squadrons were united in the harbor of Louisbourg, to the number of twenty-two ships of the line, besides several frigates, and that the garrison had been increased to a total force of seven thousand men, ensconced in the strongest fortress of the continent. So far as concerned the naval force, the account was true. La Motte, the French admiral, had with him a fleet carrying an aggregate of thirteen hundred and sixty cannon, anchored in a sheltered harbor under the guns of the town. Success was now hopeless, and the costly enterprise was at once abandoned. Loudon with his troops sailed back for New York, and Admiral Holbourne, who had been joined by four additional ships, steered for Louisbourg, in hopes that the French fleet would come out and fight him. He cruised off the port; but La Motte did not accept the challenge.

The elements declared for France. A September gale, of

[1] *Loudon to Pitt, 30 May, 1757.* He had not learned Pitt's resignation.

fury rare even on that tempestuous coast, burst upon the British fleet. "It blew a perfect hurricane," says the unfortunate Admiral, "and drove us right on shore." One ship was dashed on the rocks, two leagues from Louisbourg. A shifting of the wind in the nick of time saved the rest from total wreck. Nine were dismasted; others threw their cannon into the sea. Not one was left fit for immediate action; and had La Motte sailed out of Louisbourg, he would have had them all at his mercy.

Delay, the source of most of the disasters that befell England and her colonies at this dismal epoch, was the ruin of the Louisbourg expedition. The greater part of La Motte's fleet reached its destination a full month before that of Holbourne. Had the reverse taken place, the fortress must have fallen. As it was, the ill-starred attempt, drawing off the British forces from the frontier, where they were needed most, did for France more than she could have done for herself, and gave Montcalm and Vaudreuil the opportunity to execute a scheme which they had nursed since the fall of Oswego.[1]

[1] *Despatches of Loudon, Feb. to Aug. 1757.* Knox, *Campaigns in North America*, I. 6–28. Knox was in the expedition. *Review of Mr. Pitt's Administration* (London, 1763). *The Conduct of a Noble Commander in America impartially reviewed* (London, 1758). Beatson, *Naval and Military Memoirs*, II. 49–59. *Answer to the Letter to two Great Men* (London, 1760). Entick, II. 168, 169. *Holbourne to Loudon, 4 Aug. 1757. Holbourne to Pitt, 29 Sept. 1757. Ibid., 30 Sept. 1757. Holbourne to Pownall, 2 Nov. 1757.* Mante, 86, 97. *Relation du Désastre arrivé à la Flotte Anglaise commandée par l'Amiral Holbourne.* Chevalier Johnstone, *Campaign of Louisbourg. London Magazine*, 1757, 514. *Gentleman's Magazine*, 1757, 463, 476. *Ibid.*, 1758, 168–173.

It has been said that Loudon was scared from his task by false reports of the strength of the French at Louisbourg. This was not the case. The *Gazette de France*, 621, says that La Motte had twenty-four ships of war. Bougainville says that as early as the ninth of June there were twenty-one ships of war, including five frigates, at Louisbourg. To this the list given by Knox closely answers.

Chapter XV

1757

FORT WILLIAM HENRY

Another Blow • The War-song • The Army at Ticonderoga • Indian Allies • The War-feast • Treatment of Prisoners • Cannibalism • Surprise and Slaughter • The War Council • March of Lévis • The Army embarks • Fort William Henry • Nocturnal Scene • Indian Funeral • Advance upon the Fort • General Webb • His Difficulties • His Weakness • The Siege begun • Conduct of the Indians • The Intercepted Letter • Desperate Position of the Besieged • Capitulation • Ferocity of the Indians • Mission of Bougainville • Murder of Wounded Men • A Scene of Terror • The Massacre • Efforts of Montcalm • The Fort burned

---

I AM GOING on the ninth to sing the war-song at the Lake of Two Mountains, and on the next day at Saut St. Louis,—a long, tiresome ceremony. On the twelfth I am off; and I count on having news to tell you by the end of this month or the beginning of next." Thus Montcalm wrote to his wife from Montreal early in July. All doubts had been solved. Prisoners taken on the Hudson and despatches from Versailles had made it certain that Loudon was bound to Louisbourg, carrying with him the best of the troops that had guarded the New York frontier. The time was come, not only to strike the English on Lake George, but perhaps to seize Fort Edward and carry terror to Albany itself. Only one difficulty remained, the want of provisions. Agents were sent to collect corn and bacon among the inhabitants; the curés and militia captains were ordered to aid in the work; and enough was presently found to feed twelve thousand men for a month.[1]

The emissaries of the Governor had been busy all winter among the tribes of the West and North; and more than a thousand savages, lured by the prospect of gifts, scalps, and plunder, were now encamped at Montreal. Many of them had never visited a French settlement before. All were eager to see

[1] Vaudreuil, *Lettres circulaires aux Curés et aux Capitaines de Milice des Paroisses du Gouvernement de Montreal, 16 Juin, 1757.*

Montcalm, whose exploit in taking Oswego had inflamed their imagination; and one day, on a visit of ceremony, an orator from Michillimackinac addressed the General thus: "We wanted to see this famous man who tramples the English under his feet. We thought we should find him so tall that his head would be lost in the clouds. But you are a little man, my Father. It is when we look into your eyes that we see the greatness of the pine-tree and the fire of the eagle."[1]

It remained to muster the Mission Indians settled in or near the limits of the colony; and it was to this end that Montcalm went to sing the war-song with the converts of the Two Mountains. Rigaud, Bougainville, young Longueuil, and others were of the party; and when they landed, the Indians came down to the shore, their priests at their head, and greeted the General with a volley of musketry; then received him after dark in their grand council-lodge, where the circle of wild and savage visages, half seen in the dim light of a few candles, suggested to Bougainville a midnight conclave of wizards. He acted vicariously the chief part in the ceremony. "I sang the war-song in the name of M. de Montcalm, and was much applauded. It was nothing but these words: 'Let us trample the English under our feet,' chanted over and over again, in cadence with the movements of the savages." Then came the war-feast, against which occasion Montcalm had caused three oxen to be roasted.[2] On the next day the party went to Caughnawaga, or Saut St. Louis, where the ceremony was repeated; and Bougainville, who again sang the war-song in the name of his commander, was requited by adoption into the clan of the Turtle. Three more oxen were solemnly devoured, and with one voice the warriors took up the hatchet.

Meanwhile troops, Canadians and Indians, were moving by detachments up Lake Champlain. Fleets of bateaux and canoes followed each other day by day along the capricious lake, in calm or storm, sunshine or rain, till, towards the end

[1] Bougainville, *Journal*.

[2] Bougainville describes a ceremony in the Mission Church of the Two Mountains in which warriors and squaws sang in the choir. Ninety-nine years after, in 1856, I was present at a similar ceremony on the same spot, and heard the descendants of the same warriors and squaws sing like their ancestors. Great changes have since taken place at this old mission.

of July, the whole force was gathered at Ticonderoga, the base of the intended movement. Bourlamaque had been there since May with the battalions of Béarn and Royal Roussillon, finishing the fort, sending out war-parties, and trying to discover the force and designs of the English at Fort William Henry.

Ticonderoga is a high rocky promontory between Lake Champlain on the north and the mouth of the outlet of Lake George on the south. Near its extremity and close to the fort were still encamped the two battalions under Bourlamaque, while bateaux and canoes were passing incessantly up the river of the outlet. There were scarcely two miles of navigable water, at the end of which the stream fell foaming over a high ledge of rock that barred the way. Here the French were building a saw-mill; and a wide space had been cleared to form an encampment defended on all sides by an abattis, within which stood the tents of the battalions of La Reine, La Sarre, Languedoc, and Guienne, all commanded by Lévis. Above the cascade the stream circled through the forest in a series of beautiful rapids, and from the camp of Lévis a road a mile and a half long had been cut to the navigable water above. At the end of this road there was another fortified camp, formed of colony regulars, Canadians, and Indians, under Rigaud. It was scarcely a mile farther to Lake George, where on the western side there was an outpost, chiefly of Canadians and Indians; while advanced parties were stationed at Bald Mountain, now called Rogers Rock, and elsewhere on the lake, to watch the movements of the English. The various encampments just mentioned were ranged along a valley extending four miles from Lake Champlain to Lake George, and bordered by mountains wooded to the top.

Here was gathered a martial population of eight thousand men, including the brightest civilization and the darkest barbarism: from the scholar-soldier Montcalm and his no less accomplished aide-de-camp; from Lévis, conspicuous for graces of person; from a throng of courtly young officers, who would have seemed out of place in that wilderness had they not done their work so well in it; from these to the foulest man-eating savage of the uttermost northwest.

Of Indian allies there were nearly two thousand. One of

their tribes, the Iowas, spoke a language which no interpreter understood; and they all bivouacked where they saw fit: for no man could control them. "I see no difference," says Bougainville, "in the dress, ornaments, dances, and songs of the various western nations. They go naked, excepting a strip of cloth passed through a belt, and paint themselves black, red, blue, and other colors. Their heads are shaved and adorned with bunches of feathers, and they wear rings of brass wire in their ears. They wear beaver-skin blankets, and carry lances, bows and arrows, and quivers made of the skins of beasts. For the rest they are straight, well made, and generally very tall. Their religion is brute paganism. I will say it once for all, one must be the slave of these savages, listen to them day and night, in council and in private, whenever the fancy takes them, or whenever a dream, a fit of the vapors, or their perpetual craving for brandy, gets possession of them; besides which they are always wanting something for their equipment, arms, or toilet, and the general of the army must give written orders for the smallest trifle,—an eternal, wearisome detail, of which one has no idea in Europe."

It was not easy to keep them fed. Rations would be served to them for a week; they would consume them in three days, and come for more. On one occasion they took the matter into their own hands, and butchered and devoured eighteen head of cattle intended for the troops; nor did any officer dare oppose this "St. Bartholomew of the oxen," as Bougainville calls it. "Their paradise is to be drunk," says the young officer. Their paradise was rather a hell; for sometimes, when mad with brandy, they grappled and tore each other with their teeth like wolves. They were continually "making medicine," that is, consulting the Manitou, to whom they hung up offerings, sometimes a dead dog, and sometimes the belt-cloth which formed their only garment.

The Mission Indians were better allies than these heathen of the west; and their priests, who followed them to the war, had great influence over them. They were armed with guns, which they well knew how to use. Their dress, though savage, was generally decent, and they were not cannibals; though in other respects they retained all their traditional ferocity and most of their traditional habits. They held frequent war-feasts,

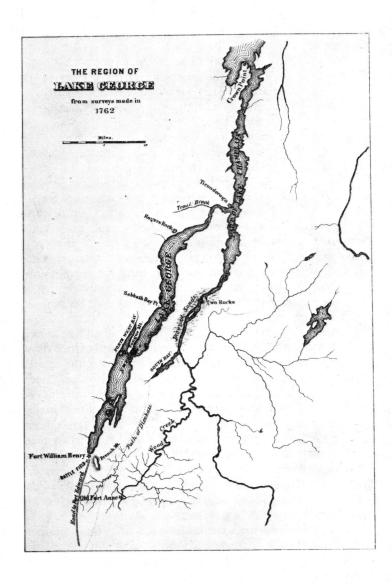

THE REGION OF
LAKE GEORGE
from surveys made in
1762

Miles.

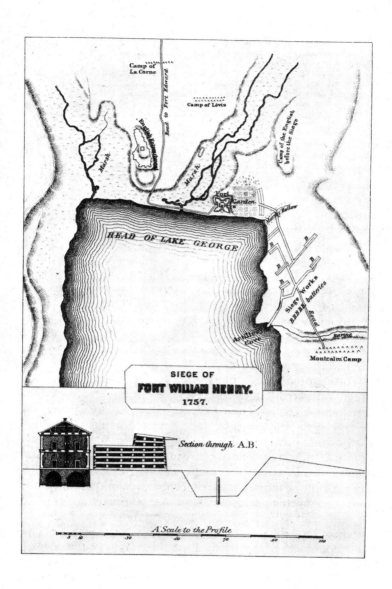

Camp of
La Corne

Camp of Lévis

Road to Fort Edward

Camp of the English
before the Siege

English Entrenched Camp

Marsh

Marsh

Fort
Garden

Nagus Hollow

HEAD OF LAKE GEORGE

B   B

B

B

B

Siege Works
B B B B batteries

Ravine

Artillery Cove

Road

Montcalm Camp

SIEGE OF
FORT WILLIAM HENRY.
1757.

Section through A.B.

A Scale to the Profile

5   10   30   50   70   90   110

one of which is described by Roubaud, Jesuit missionary of
the Abenakis of St. Francis, whose flock formed a part of
the company present.

"Imagine," says the father, "a great assembly of savages
adorned with every ornament most suited to disfigure them
in European eyes, painted with vermilion, white, green, yellow, and black made of soot and the scrapings of pots. A
single savage face combines all these different colors, method-
ically laid on with the help of a little tallow, which serves for
pomatum. The head is shaved except at the top, where there
is a small tuft, to which are fastened feathers, a few beads of
wampum, or some such trinket. Every part of the head has its
ornament. Pendants hang from the nose and also from the
ears, which are split in infancy and drawn down by weights
till they flap at last against the shoulders. The rest of the
equipment answers to this fantastic decoration: a shirt bedaubed with vermilion, wampum collars, silver bracelets, a
large knife hanging on the breast, moose-skin moccasons, and
a belt of various colors always absurdly combined. The sachems and war-chiefs are distinguished from the rest: the latter by a gorget, and the former by a medal, with the King's
portrait on one side, and on the other Mars and Bellona joining hands, with the device, *Virtus et Honor*."

Thus attired, the company sat in two lines facing each
other, with kettles in the middle filled with meat chopped for
distribution. To a dignified silence succeeded songs, sung by
several chiefs in succession, and compared by the narrator to
the howling of wolves. Then followed a speech from the chief
orator, highly commended by Roubaud, who could not help
admiring this effort of savage eloquence. "After the harangue," he continues, "they proceeded to nominate the
chiefs who were to take command. As soon as one was named
he rose and took the head of some animal that had been
butchered for the feast. He raised it aloft so that all the company could see it, and cried: 'Behold the head of the enemy!'
Applause and cries of joy rose from all parts of the assembly.
The chief, with the head in his hand, passed down between
the lines, singing his war-song, bragging of his exploits,
taunting and defying the enemy, and glorifying himself beyond all measure. To hear his self-laudation in these moments

of martial transport one would think him a conquering hero ready to sweep everything before him. As he passed in front of the other savages, they would respond by dull broken cries jerked up from the depths of their stomachs, and accompanied by movements of their bodies so odd that one must be well used to them to keep countenance. In the course of his song the chief would utter from time to time some grotesque witticism; then he would stop, as if pleased with himself, or rather to listen to the thousand confused cries of applause that greeted his ears. He kept up his martial promenade as long as he liked the sport; and when he had had enough, ended by flinging down the head of the animal with an air of contempt, to show that his warlike appetite craved meat of another sort."[1] Others followed with similar songs and pantomime, and the festival was closed at last by ladling out the meat from the kettles, and devouring it.

Roubaud was one day near the fort, when he saw the shore lined with a thousand Indians, watching four or five English prisoners, who, with the war-party that had captured them, were approaching in a boat from the farther side of the water. Suddenly the whole savage crew broke away together and ran into the neighboring woods, whence they soon emerged, yelling diabolically, each armed with a club. The wretched prisoners were to be forced to "run the gauntlet," which would probably have killed them. They were saved by the chief who commanded the war-party, and who, on the persuasion of a French officer, claimed them as his own and forbade the game; upon which, according to rule in such cases, the rest abandoned it. On this same day the missionary met troops of Indians conducting several bands of English prisoners along the road that led through the forest from the camp of Lévis. Each of the captives was held by a cord made fast about the neck; and the sweat was starting from their brows in the extremity of their horror and distress. Roubaud's tent was at this time in the camp of the Ottawas. He presently saw a large number of them squatted about a fire, before which meat was roasting on sticks stuck in the ground; and, approaching, he saw that it was the flesh of an Englishman,

[1] *Lettre du Père . . .* (Roubaud), *Missionnaire chez les Abnakis, 21 Oct. 1757,* in *Lettres Edifiantes et Curieuses,* VI. 189 (1810).

other parts of which were boiling in a kettle, while near by sat eight or ten of the prisoners, forced to see their comrade devoured. The horror-stricken priest began to remonstrate; on which a young savage fiercely replied in broken French: "You have French taste; I have Indian. This is good meat for me;" and the feasters pressed him to share it.

Bougainville says that this abomination could not be prevented; which only means that if force had been used to stop it, the Ottawas would have gone home in a rage. They were therefore left to finish their meal undisturbed. Having eaten one of their prisoners, they began to treat the rest with the utmost kindness, bringing them white bread, and attending to all their wants,—a seeming change of heart due to the fact that they were a valuable commodity, for which the owners hoped to get a good price at Montreal. Montcalm wished to send them thither at once, to which after long debate the Indians consented, demanding, however, a receipt in full, and bargaining that the captives should be supplied with shoes and blankets.[1]

These unfortunates belonged to a detachment of three hundred provincials, chiefly New Jersey men, sent from Fort William Henry under command of Colonel Parker to reconnoitre the French outposts. Montcalm's scouts discovered them; on which a band of Indians, considerably more numerous, went to meet them under a French partisan named Corbière, and ambushed themselves not far from Sabbath Day Point. Parker had rashly divided his force; and at daybreak of the twenty-sixth of July three of his boats fell into the snare, and were captured without a shot. Three others followed, in ignorance of what had happened, and shared the fate of the first. When the rest drew near, they were greeted by a deadly volley from the thickets, and a swarm of canoes darted out upon them. The men were seized with such a panic that some of them jumped into the water to escape, while the Indians leaped after them and speared them with their lances like fish. "Terrified," says Bougainville, "by the sight of these monsters, their agility, their firing, and their yells, they surrendered almost without resistance." About a hundred, however, made

---

[1] *Journal de l'Expédition contre le Fort George* [William Henry] *du 12 Juillet au 16 Août, 1757.* Bougainville, *Journal. Lettre du P. Roubaud.*

their escape. The rest were killed or captured, and three of the bodies were eaten on the spot. The journalist adds that the victory so elated the Indians that they became insupportable; "but here in the forests of America we can no more do without them than without cavalry on the plain."[1]

Another success at about the same time did not tend to improve their manners. A hundred and fifty of them, along with a few Canadians under Marin, made a dash at Fort Edward, killed or drove in the pickets, and returned with thirty-two scalps and a prisoner. It was found, however, that the scalps were far from representing an equal number of heads, the Indians having learned the art of making two or three out of one by judicious division.[2]

Preparations were urged on with the utmost energy. Provisions, camp equipage, ammunition, cannon, and bateaux were dragged by gangs of men up the road from the camp of Lévis to the head of the rapids. The work went on through heat and rain, by day and night, till, at the end of July, all was done. Now, on the eve of departure, Montcalm, anxious for harmony among his red allies, called them to a grand council near the camp of Rigaud. Forty-one tribes and subtribes, Christian and heathen, from the east and from the west, were represented in it. Here were the mission savages,—Iroquois of Caughnawaga, Two Mountains, and La Présentation; Hurons of Lorette and Detroit; Nipissings of Lake Nipissing; Abenakis of St. Francis, Becancour, Missisqui, and the Penobscot; Algonkins of Three Rivers and Two Mountains; Micmacs and Malecites from Acadia: in all eight hundred chiefs and warriors. With these came the heathen of the west,—Ottawas of seven distinct bands; Ojibwas from Lake Superior, and Mississagas from the region of Lakes Erie and Huron; Pottawattamies and Menomonies from Lake Michigan; Sacs, Foxes, and Winnebagoes from Wisconsin;

[1] Bougainville, *Journal*. Malartic, *Journal*. *Montcalm à Vaudreuil, 27 Juillet, 1757*. *Webb to Loudon, 1 Aug. 1757*. *Webb to Delancey, 30 July, 1757*. *Journal de l'Expédition contre le Fort George*. *London Magazine*, 1757, 457. Niles, *French and Indian Wars*. *Boston Gazette*, 15 Aug. 1757.

[2] This affair was much exaggerated at the time. I follow Bougainville, who had the facts from Marin. According to him, the thirty-two scalps represented eleven killed; which exactly answers to the English loss as stated by Colonel Frye in a letter from Fort Edward.

Miamis from the prairies of Illinois, and Iowas from the
banks of the Des Moines: nine hundred and seventy-nine
chiefs and warriors, men of the forests and men of the plains,
hunters of the moose and hunters of the buffalo, bearers of
steel hatchets and stone war-clubs, of French guns and of
flint-headed arrows. All sat in silence, decked with ceremonial
paint, scalp-locks, eagle plumes, or horns of buffalo; and the
dark and wild assemblage was edged with white uniforms of
officers from France, who came in numbers to the spectacle.
Other officers were also here, all belonging to the colony.
They had been appointed to the command of the Indian allies, over whom, however, they had little or no real authority.
First among them was the bold and hardy Saint-Luc de la
Corne, who was called general of the Indians; and under him
were others, each assigned to some tribe or group of tribes,—
the intrepid Marin; Charles Langlade, who had left his squaw
wife at Michillimackinac to join the war; Niverville, Langis,
La Plante, Hertel, Longueuil, Herbin, Lorimier, Sabrevois,
and Fleurimont; men familiar from childhood with forests
and savages. Each tribe had its interpreter, often as lawless as
those with whom he had spent his life; and for the converted
tribes there were three missionaries,—Piquet for the Iroquois, Mathevet for the Nipissings, who were half heathen,
and Roubaud for the Abenakis.[1]

There was some complaint among the Indians because they
were crowded upon by the officers who came as spectators.
This difficulty being removed, the council opened, Montcalm
having already explained his plans to the chiefs and told them
the part he expected them to play.

Pennahouel, chief of the Ottawas, and senior of all the Assembly, rose and said: "My father, I, who have counted more
moons than any here, thank you for the good words you have
spoken. I approve them. Nobody ever spoke better. It is the
Manitou of War who inspires you."

Kikensick, chief of the Nipissings, rose in behalf of the

---

[1] The above is chiefly from *Tableau des Sauvages qui se trouvent à l'Armée
du Marquis de Montcalm, le 28 Juillet, 1757*. Forty-one tribes and sub-tribes are
here named, some, however, represented by only three or four warriors. Besides those set down under the head of Christians, it is stated that a few of
the Ottawas of Detroit and Michillimackinac still retained the faith.

Christian Indians, and addressed the heathen of the west. "Brothers, we thank you for coming to help us defend our lands against the English. Our cause is good. The Master of Life is on our side. Can you doubt it, brothers, after the great blow you have just struck? It covers you with glory. The lake, red with the blood of Corlaer [*the English*] bears witness forever to your achievement. We too share your glory, and are proud of what you have done." Then, turning to Montcalm: "We are even more glad than you, my father, who have crossed the great water, not for your own sake, but to obey the great King and defend his children. He has bound us all together by the most solemn of ties. Let us take care that nothing shall separate us."

The various interpreters, each in turn, having explained this speech to the Assembly, it was received with ejaculations of applause; and when they had ceased, Montcalm spoke as follows: "Children, I am delighted to see you all joined in this good work. So long as you remain one, the English cannot resist you. The great King has sent me to protect and defend you; but above all he has charged me to make you happy and unconquerable, by establishing among you the union which ought to prevail among brothers, children of one father, the great Onontio." Then he held out a prodigious wampum belt of six thousand beads: "Take this sacred pledge of his word. The union of the beads of which it is made is the sign of your united strength. By it I bind you all together, so that none of you can separate from the rest till the English are defeated and their fort destroyed."

Pennahouel took up the belt and said: "Behold, brothers, a circle drawn around us by the great Onontio. Let none of us go out from it; for so long as we keep in it, the Master of Life will help all our undertakings." Other chiefs spoke to the same effect, and the council closed in perfect harmony.[1] Its various members bivouacked together at the camp by the lake, and by their carelessness soon set it on fire; whence the place became known as the Burned Camp. Those from the missions confessed their sins all day; while their heathen brothers hung an old coat and a pair of leggings on a pole as tribute to the Manitou. This greatly embarrassed the three priests, who

[1] Bougainville, *Journal.*

were about to say Mass, but doubted whether they ought to say it in presence of a sacrifice to the devil. Hereupon they took counsel of Montcalm. "Better say it so than not at all," replied the military casuist. Brandy being prudently denied them, the allies grew restless; and the greater part paddled up the lake to a spot near the place where Parker had been defeated. Here they encamped to wait the arrival of the army, and amused themselves meantime with killing rattlesnakes, there being a populous "den" of those reptiles among the neighboring rocks.

Montcalm sent a circular letter to the regular officers, urging them to dispense for a while with luxuries, and even comforts. "We have but few bateaux, and these are so filled with stores that a large division of the army must go by land;" and he directed that everything not absolutely necessary should be left behind, and that a canvas shelter to every two officers should serve them for a tent, and a bearskin for a bed. "Yet I do not forbid a mattress," he adds. "Age and infirmities may make it necessary to some; but I shall not have one myself, and make no doubt that all who can will willingly imitate me."[1]

The bateaux lay ready by the shore, but could not carry the whole force; and Lévis received orders to march by the side of the lake with twenty-five hundred men, Canadians, regulars, and Iroquois. He set out at daybreak of the thirtieth of July, his men carrying nothing but their knapsacks, blankets, and weapons. Guided by the unerring Indians, they climbed the steep gorge at the side of Rogers Rock, gained the valley beyond, and marched southward along a Mohawk trail which threaded the forest in a course parallel to the lake. The way was of the roughest; many straggled from the line, and two officers completely broke down. The first destination of the party was the mouth of Ganouskie Bay, now called Northwest Bay, where they were to wait for Montcalm, and kindle three fires as a signal that they had reached the rendezvous.[2]

Montcalm left a detachment to hold Ticonderoga; and then, on the first of August, at two in the afternoon, he em-

[1] *Circulaire du Marquis de Montcalm, 25 Juillet, 1757.*
[2] *Guerre du Canada, par le Chevalier de Lévis.* This manuscript of Lévis is largely in the nature of a journal.

barked at the Burned Camp with all his remaining force. Including those with Lévis, the expedition counted about seven thousand six hundred men, of whom more than sixteen hundred were Indians.[1] At five in the afternoon they reached the place where the Indians, having finished their rattlesnake hunt, were smoking their pipes and waiting for the army. The red warriors embarked, and joined the French flotilla; and now, as evening drew near, was seen one of those wild pageantries of war which Lake George has often witnessed. A restless multitude of birch canoes, filled with painted savages, glided by shores and islands, like troops of swimming waterfowl. Two hundred and fifty bateaux came next, moved by sail and oar, some bearing the Canadian militia, and some the battalions of Old France in trim and gay attire: first, La Reine and Languedoc; then the colony regulars; then La Sarre and Guienne; then the Canadian brigade of Courtemanche; then the cannon and mortars, each on a platform sustained by two bateaux lashed side by side, and rowed by the militia of Saint-Ours; then the battalions of Béarn and Royal Roussillon; then the Canadians of Gaspé, with the provision-bateaux and the field-hospital; and, lastly, a rear guard of regulars closed the line. So, under the flush of sunset, they held their course along the romantic lake, to play their part in the historic drama that lends a stern enchantment to its fascinating scenery. They passed the Narrows in mist and darkness; and when, a little before dawn, they rounded the high promontory of Tongue Mountain, they saw, far on the right, three fiery sparks shining through the gloom. These were the signal-fires of Lévis, to tell them that he had reached the appointed spot.[2]

Lévis had arrived the evening before, after his hard march through the sultry midsummer forest. His men had now rested for a night, and at ten in the morning he marched

[1] *État de l'Armée Française devant le Fort George, autrement Guillaume-Henri, le 3 Août, 1757. Tableau des Sauvages qui se trouvent à l'Armée du Marquis de Montcalm, le 28 Juillet, 1757.* This gives a total of 1,799 Indians, of whom some afterwards left the army. *État de l'Armée du Roi en Canada, sur le Lac St. Sacrement et dans les Camps de Carillon, le 29 Juillet, 1757.* This gives a total of 8,019 men, of whom about four hundred were left in garrison at Ticonderoga.

[2] The site of the present village of Bolton.

again. Montcalm followed at noon, and coasted the western shore, till, towards evening, he found Lévis waiting for him by the margin of a small bay not far from the English fort, though hidden from it by a projecting point of land. Canoes and bateaux were drawn up on the beach, and the united forces made their bivouac together.

The earthen mounds of Fort William Henry still stand by the brink of Lake George; and seated at the sunset of an August day under the pines that cover them, one gazes on a scene of soft and soothing beauty, where dreamy waters reflect the glories of the mountains and the sky. As it is to-day, so it was then; all breathed repose and peace. The splash of some leaping trout, or the dipping wing of a passing swallow, alone disturbed the summer calm of that unruffled mirror.

About ten o'clock at night two boats set out from the fort to reconnoitre. They were passing a point of land on their left, two miles or more down the lake, when the men on board descried through the gloom a strange object against the bank; and they rowed towards it to learn what it might be. It was an awning over the bateaux that carried Roubaud and his brother missionaries. As the rash oarsmen drew near, the bleating of a sheep in one of the French provision-boats warned them of danger; and turning, they pulled for their lives towards the eastern shore. Instantly more than a thousand Indians threw themselves into their canoes and dashed in hot pursuit, making the lake and the mountains ring with the din of their war-whoops. The fugitives had nearly reached land when their pursuers opened fire. They replied; shot one Indian dead, and wounded another; then snatched their oars again, and gained the beach. But the whole savage crew was upon them. Several were killed, three were taken, and the rest escaped in the dark woods.[1] The prisoners were brought before Montcalm, and gave him valuable information of the strength and position of the English.[2]

[1] *Lettre du Père Roubaud, 21 Oct. 1757.* Roubaud, who saw the whole, says that twelve hundred Indians joined the chase, and that their yells were terrific.

[2] The remains of Fort William Henry are now—1882—crowded between a hotel and the wharf and station of a railway. While I write, a scheme is on foot to level the whole for other railway structures. When I first knew the place the ground was in much the same state as in the time of Montcalm.

The Indian who was killed was a noted chief of the Nipis-sings; and his tribesmen howled in grief for their bereave-ment. They painted his face with vermilion, tied feathers in his hair, hung pendants in his ears and nose, clad him in a resplendent war-dress, put silver bracelets on his arms, hung a gorget on his breast with a flame colored ribbon, and seated him in state on the top of a hillock, with his lance in his hand, his gun in the hollow of his arm, his tomahawk in his belt, and his kettle by his side. Then they all crouched about him in lugubrious silence. A funeral harangue followed; and next a song and solemn dance to the booming of the Indian drum. In the gray of the morning they buried him as he sat, and placed food in the grave for his journey to the land of souls.[1]

As the sun rose above the eastern mountains the French camp was all astir. The column of Lévis, with Indians to lead the way, moved through the forest towards the fort, and Montcalm followed with the main body; then the artillery boats rounded the point that had hid them from the sight of the English, saluting them as they did so with musketry and cannon; while a host of savages put out upon the lake, ranged their canoes abreast in a line from shore to shore, and ad-vanced slowly, with measured paddle-strokes and yells of de-fiance.

The position of the enemy was full in sight before them. At the head of the lake, towards the right, stood the fort, close to the edge of the water. On its left was a marsh; then the rough piece of ground where Johnson had encamped two years before; then a low, flat, rocky hill, crowned with an entrenched camp; and, lastly, on the extreme left, another marsh. Far around the fort and up the slopes of the western mountain the forest had been cut down and burned, and the ground was cumbered with blackened stumps and charred carcasses and limbs of fallen trees, strewn in savage disorder one upon another.[2] This was the work of Winslow in the autumn before. Distant shouts and war-cries, the clatter of musketry, white puffs of smoke in the dismal clearing and along the scorched edge of the bordering forest, told that Lévis' Indians were skirmishing with parties of the English,

[1] *Lettre du Père Roubaud.*
[2] *Précis des Événements de la Campagne de 1757 en la Nouvelle France.*

who had gone out to save the cattle roaming in the neighborhood, and burn some out-buildings that would have favored
the besiegers. Others were taking down the tents that stood
on a plateau near the foot of the mountain on the right, and
moving them to the entrenchment on the hill. The garrison
sallied from the fort to support their comrades, and for a time
the firing was hot.

Fort William Henry was an irregular bastioned square,
formed by embankments of gravel surmounted by a rampart
of heavy logs, laid in tiers crossed one upon another, the interstices filled with earth. The lake protected it on the north,
the marsh on the east, and ditches with *chevaux-de-frise* on the
south and west. Seventeen cannon, great and small, besides
several mortars and swivels, were mounted upon it;[1] and a
brave Scotch veteran, Lieutenant-Colonel Monro, of the
thirty-fifth regiment, was in command.

General Webb lay fourteen miles distant at Fort Edward,
with twenty-six hundred men, chiefly provincials. On the
twenty-fifth of July he had made a visit to Fort William
Henry, examined the place, given some orders, and returned
on the twenty-ninth. He then wrote to the Governor of New
York, telling him that the French were certainly coming, begging him to send up the militia, and saying: "I am determined
to march to Fort William Henry with the whole army under
my command as soon as I shall hear of the farther approach
of the enemy." Instead of doing so he waited three days, and
then sent up a detachment of two hundred regulars under
Lieutenant-Colonel Young, and eight hundred Massachusetts
men under Colonel Frye. This raised the force at the lake to
two thousand and two hundred, including sailors and mechanics, and reduced that of Webb to sixteen hundred, besides half as many more distributed at Albany and the
intervening forts.[2] If, according to his spirited intention, he
should go to the rescue of Monro, he must leave some of his
troops behind him to protect the lower posts from a possible
French inroad by way of South Bay. Thus his power of aiding

[1] *État des Effets et Munitions de Guerre qui se sont trouvés au Fort Guillaume-
Henri.* There were six more guns in the entrenched camp.

[2] Frye, *Journal of the Attack of Fort William Henry. Webb to Loudon, 1 Aug.
1757. Ibid., 5 Aug. 1757.*

Monro was slight, so rashly had Loudon, intent on Louisbourg, left this frontier open to attack. The defect, however, was as much in Webb himself as in his resources. His conduct in the past year had raised doubts of his personal courage; and this was the moment for answering them. Great as was the disparity of numbers, the emergency would have justified an attempt to save Monro at any risk. That officer sent him a hasty note, written at nine o'clock on the morning of the third, telling him that the French were in sight on the lake; and, in the next night, three rangers came to Fort Edward, bringing another short note, dated at six in the evening, announcing that the firing had begun, and closing with the words: "I believe you will think it proper to send a reinforcement as soon as possible." Now, if ever, was the time to move, before the fort was invested and access cut off. But Webb lay quiet, sending expresses to New England for help which could not possibly arrive in time. On the next night another note came from Monro to say that the French were upon him in great numbers, well supplied with artillery, but that the garrison were all in good spirits. "I make no doubt," wrote the hard-pressed officer, "that you will soon send us a reinforcement;" and again on the same day: "We are very certain that a part of the enemy have got between you and us upon the high road, and would therefore be glad (if it meets with your approbation) the whole army was marched."[1] But Webb gave no sign.[2]

When the skirmishing around the fort was over, La Corne, with a body of Indians, occupied the road that led to Fort Edward, and Lévis encamped hard by to support him, while Montcalm proceeded to examine the ground and settle his plan of attack. He made his way to the rear of the entrenched camp and reconnoitred it, hoping to carry it by assault; but it had a breastwork of stones and logs, and he thought the attempt too hazardous. The ground where he stood was that

[1] *Copy of four Letters from Lieutenant-Colonel Monro to Major-General Webb, enclosed in the General's Letter of the fifth of August to the Earl of Loudon.*

[2] "The number of troops remaining under my Command at this place [*Fort Edward*], excluding the Posts on Hudson's River, amounts to but sixteen hundred men fit for duty, with which Army, so much inferior to that of the enemy, I did not think it prudent to pursue my first intentions of Marching to their Assistance." *Webb to Loudon, 5 Aug. 1757.*

where Dieskau had been defeated; and as the fate of his predecessor was not of flattering augury, he resolved to besiege the fort in form.

He chose for the site of his operations the ground now covered by the village of Caldwell. A little to the north of it was a ravine, beyond which he formed his main camp, while Lévis occupied a tract of dry ground beside the marsh, whence he could easily move to intercept succors from Fort Edward on the one hand, or repel a sortie from Fort William Henry on the other. A brook ran down the ravine and entered the lake at a small cove protected from the fire of the fort by a point of land; and at this place, still called Artillery Cove, Montcalm prepared to debark his cannon and mortars.

Having made his preparations, he sent Fontbrune, one of his aides-de-camp, with a letter to Monro. "I owe it to humanity," he wrote, "to summon you to surrender. At present I can restrain the savages, and make them observe the terms of a capitulation, as I might not have power to do under other circumstances; and an obstinate defence on your part could only retard the capture of the place a few days, and endanger an unfortunate garrison which cannot be relieved, in consequence of the dispositions I have made. I demand a decisive answer within an hour." Monro replied that he and his soldiers would defend themselves to the last. While the flags of truce were flying, the Indians swarmed over the fields before the fort; and when they learned the result, an Abenaki chief shouted in broken French: "You won't surrender, eh! Fire away then, and fight your best; for if I catch you, you shall get no quarter." Monro emphasized his refusal by a general discharge of his cannon.

The trenches were opened on the night of the fourth,—a task of extreme difficulty, as the ground was covered by a profusion of half-burned stumps, roots, branches, and fallen trunks. Eight hundred men toiled till daylight with pick, spade, and axe, while the cannon from the fort flashed through the darkness, and grape and round-shot whistled and screamed over their heads. Some of the English balls reached the camp beyond the ravine, and disturbed the slumbers of the officers off duty, as they lay wrapped in their blankets and bear-skins. Before daybreak the first parallel was made; a battery was nearly finished on the left, and another was begun on the right. The men now worked under cover, safe in their burrows; one gang relieved another, and the work went on all day.

The Indians were far from doing what was expected of them. Instead of scouting in the direction of Fort Edward to learn the movements of the enemy and prevent surprise, they loitered about the camp and in the trenches, or amused themselves by firing at the fort from behind stumps and logs. Some, in imitation of the French, dug little trenches for themselves, in which they wormed their way towards the rampart, and now and then picked off an artillery-man, not without loss on their own side. On the afternoon of the fifth, Montcalm invited them to a council, gave them belts of wampum, and mildly remonstrated with them. "Why expose yourselves without necessity? I grieve bitterly over the losses that you have met, for the least among you is precious to me. No doubt it is a good thing to annoy the English; but that is not the main point. You ought to inform me of everything the enemy is doing, and always keep parties on the road between the two forts." And he gently hinted that their place was not in his camp, but in that of Lévis, where missionaries were provided for such of them as were Christians, and food and ammunition for them all. They promised, with excellent docility, to do everything he wished, but added that there was something on their hearts. Being encouraged to relieve themselves of the burden, they complained that they had not been consulted as to the management of the siege, but were expected to obey orders like slaves. "We know more about fighting in the woods than you," said their orator; "ask our advice, and you will be the better for it."[1]

Montcalm assured them that if they had been neglected, it was only through the hurry and confusion of the time; expressed high appreciation of their talents for bush-fighting, promised them ample satisfaction, and ended by telling them that in the morning they should hear the big guns. This greatly pleased them, for they were extremely impatient for the artillery to begin. About sunrise the battery of the left opened with eight heavy cannon and a mortar, joined, on the next morning, by the battery of the right, with eleven pieces

[1] Bougainville, *Journal*.

more. The fort replied with spirit. The cannon thundered all
day, and from a hundred peaks and crags the astonished wilderness roared back the sound. The Indians were delighted.
They wanted to point the guns; and to humor them, they
were now and then allowed to do so. Others lay behind logs
and fallen trees, and yelled their satisfaction when they saw
the splinters fly from the wooden rampart.

Day after day the weary roar of the distant cannonade fell
on the ears of Webb in his camp at Fort Edward. "I have not
yet received the least reinforcement," he writes to Loudon;
"this is the disagreeable situation we are at present in. The
fort, by the heavy firing we hear from the lake, is still in our
possession; but I fear it cannot long hold out against so warm
a cannonading if I am not reinforced by a sufficient number
of militia to march to their relief." The militia were coming;
but it was impossible that many could reach him in less than
a week. Those from New York alone were within call, and
two thousand of them arrived soon after he sent Loudon the
above letter. Then, by stripping all the forts below, he could
bring together forty-five hundred men; while several French
deserters assured him that Montcalm had nearly twelve thousand. To advance to the relief of Monro with a force so inferior, through a defile of rocks, forests, and mountains, made
by nature for ambuscades,—and this too with troops who
had neither the steadiness of regulars nor the bush-fighting
skill of Indians,—was an enterprise for firmer nerve than his.

He had already warned Monro to expect no help from him.
At midnight of the fourth, Captain Bartman, his aide-de-
camp, wrote: "The General has ordered me to acquaint you
he does not think it prudent to attempt a junction or to assist
you till reinforced by the militia of the colonies, for the immediate march of which repeated expresses have been sent."
The letter then declared that the French were in complete
possession of the road between the two forts, that a prisoner
just brought in reported their force in men and cannon to be
very great, and that, unless the militia came soon, Monro had
better make what terms he could with the enemy.[1]

---

[1] Frye, in his *Journal*, gives the letter in full. A spurious translation of it is
appended to a piece called *Jugement impartial sur les Opérations militaires en
Canada*.

The chance was small that this letter would reach its destination; and in fact the bearer was killed by La Corne's Indians, who, in stripping the body, found the hidden paper, and carried it to the General. Montcalm kept it several days, till the English rampart was half battered down; and then, after saluting his enemy with a volley from all his cannon, he sent it with a graceful compliment to Monro. It was Bougainville who carried it, preceded by a drummer and a flag. He was met at the foot of the glacis, blindfolded, and led through the fort and along the edge of the lake to the entrenched camp, where Monro was at the time. "He returned many thanks," writes the emissary in his Diary, "for the courtesy of our nation, and protested his joy at having to do with so generous an enemy. This was his answer to the Marquis de Montcalm. Then they led me back, always with eyes blinded; and our batteries began to fire again as soon as we thought that the English grenadiers who escorted me had had time to re-enter the fort. I hope General Webb's letter may induce the English to surrender the sooner."[1]

By this time the sappers had worked their way to the angle of the lake, where they were stopped by a marshy hollow, beyond which was a tract of high ground, reaching to the fort and serving as the garden of the garrison.[2] Logs and fascines in large quantities were thrown into the hollow, and hurdles were laid over them to form a causeway for the cannon. Then the sap was continued up the acclivity beyond, a trench was opened in the garden, and a battery begun, not two hundred and fifty yards from the fort. The Indians, in great number, crawled forward among the beans, maize, and cabbages, and lay there ensconced. On the night of the seventh, two men came out of the fort, apparently to reconnoitre, with a view to a sortie, when they were greeted by a general volley and a burst of yells which echoed among the mountains; followed by responsive whoops pealing through the darkness from the various camps and lurking-places of the savage warriors far and near.

The position of the besieged was now deplorable. More

[1] Bougainville, *Journal. Bougainville au Ministre, 19 Août, 1757.*

[2] Now (1882) the site of Fort William Henry Hotel, with its grounds. The hollow is partly filled by the main road of Caldwell.

than three hundred of them had been killed and wounded; small-pox was raging in the fort; the place was a focus of infection, and the casemates were crowded with the sick. A sortie from the entrenched camp and another from the fort had been repulsed with loss. All their large cannon and mortars had been burst, or disabled by shot; only seven small pieces were left fit for service;[1] and the whole of Montcalm's thirty-one cannon and fifteen mortars and howitzers would soon open fire, while the walls were already breached, and an assault was imminent. Through the night of the eighth they fired briskly from all their remaining pieces. In the morning the officers held a council, and all agreed to surrender if honorable terms could be had. A white flag was raised, a drum was beat, and Lieutenant-Colonel Young, mounted on horseback, for a shot in the foot had disabled him from walking, went, followed by a few soldiers, to the tent of Montcalm.

It was agreed that the English troops should march out with the honors of war, and be escorted to Fort Edward by a detachment of French troops; that they should not serve for eighteen months; and that all French prisoners captured in America since the war began should be given up within three months. The stores, munitions, and artillery were to be the prize of the victors, except one field-piece, which the garrison were to retain in recognition of their brave defence.

Before signing the capitulation Montcalm called the Indian chiefs to council, and asked them to consent to the conditions, and promise to restrain their young warriors from any disorder. They approved everything and promised everything. The garrison then evacuated the fort, and marched to join their comrades in the entrenched camp, which was included in the surrender. No sooner were they gone than a crowd of Indians clambered through the embrasures in search of rum and plunder. All the sick men unable to leave their beds were instantly butchered.[2] "I was witness of this spectacle," says the missionary Roubaud; "I saw one of these barbarians come out of the casemates with a human head in his hand, from which the blood ran in streams, and which he paraded as if he had got the finest prize in the world." There was little left

[1] Frye, *Journal*.
[2] *Attestation of William Arbuthnot, Captain in Frye's Regiment.*

to plunder; and the Indians, joined by the more lawless of the Canadians, turned their attention to the entrenched camp, where all the English were now collected.

The French guard stationed there could not or would not keep out the rabble. By the advice of Montcalm the English stove their rum-barrels; but the Indians were drunk already with homicidal rage, and the glitter of their vicious eyes told of the devil within. They roamed among the tents, intrusive, insolent, their visages besmirched with war-paint; grinning like fiends as they handled, in anticipation of the knife, the long hair of cowering women, of whom, as well as of children, there were many in the camp, all crazed with fright. Since the last war the New England border population had regarded Indians with a mixture of detestation and horror. Their mysterious warfare of ambush and surprise, their midnight onslaughts, their butcheries, their burnings, and all their nameless atrocities, had been for years the theme of fireside story; and the dread they excited was deepened by the distrust and dejection of the time. The confusion in the camp lasted through the afternoon. "The Indians," says Bougainville, "wanted to plunder the chests of the English; the latter resisted; and there was fear that serious disorder would ensue. The Marquis de Montcalm ran thither immediately, and used every means to restore tranquillity: prayers, threats, caresses, interposition of the officers and interpreters who have some influence over these savages."[1] "We shall be but too happy if we can prevent a massacre. Detestable position! of which nobody who has not been in it can have any idea, and which makes victory itself a sorrow to the victors. The Marquis spared no efforts to prevent the rapacity of the savages and, I must say it, of certain persons associated with them, from resulting in something worse than plunder. At last, at nine o'clock in the evening, order seemed restored. The Marquis even induced the Indians to promise that, besides the escort agreed upon in the capitulation, two chiefs for each tribe should accompany the English on their way to Fort Edward."[2] He also ordered La Corne and the other Canadian officers attached to

[1] *Bougainville au Ministre, 19 Août, 1757.*
[2] Bougainville, *Journal.*

the Indians to see that no violence took place. He might well have done more. In view of the disorders of the afternoon, it would not have been too much if he had ordered the whole body of regular troops, whom alone he could trust for the purpose, to hold themselves ready to move to the spot in case of outbreak, and shelter their defeated foes behind a hedge of bayonets.

Bougainville was not to see what ensued; for Montcalm now sent him to Montreal, as a special messenger to carry news of the victory. He embarked at ten o'clock. Returning daylight found him far down the lake; and as he looked on its still bosom flecked with mists, and its quiet mountains sleeping under the flush of dawn, there was nothing in the wild tranquillity of the scene to suggest the tragedy which even then was beginning on the shore he had left behind.

The English in their camp had passed a troubled night, agitated by strange rumors. In the morning something like a panic seized them; for they distrusted not the Indians only, but the Canadians. In their haste to be gone they got together at daybreak, before the escort of three hundred regulars had arrived. They had their muskets, but no ammunition; and few or none of the provincials had bayonets. Early as it was, the Indians were on the alert; and, indeed, since midnight great numbers of them had been prowling about the skirts of the camp, showing, says Colonel Frye, "more than usual malice in their looks." Seventeen wounded men of his regiment lay in huts, unable to join the march. In the preceding afternoon Miles Whitworth, the regimental surgeon, had passed them over to the care of a French surgeon, according to an agreement made at the time of the surrender; but, the Frenchman being absent, the other remained with them attending to their wants. The French surgeon had caused special sentinels to be posted for their protection. These were now removed, at the moment when they were needed most; upon which, about five o'clock in the morning, the Indians entered the huts, dragged out the inmates, and tomahawked and scalped them all, before the eyes of Whitworth, and in presence of La Corne and other Canadian officers, as well as of a French guard stationed within forty feet of the spot; and, declares the surgeon under oath, "none, either officer or soldier, protected the said wounded men."[1] The opportune butchery relieved them of a troublesome burden.

A scene of plundering now began. The escort had by this time arrived, and Monro complained to the officers that the capitulation was broken; but got no other answer than advice to give up the baggage to the Indians in order to appease them. To this the English at length agreed; but it only increased the excitement of the mob. They demanded rum; and some of the soldiers, afraid to refuse, gave it to them from their canteens, thus adding fuel to the flame. When, after much difficulty, the column at last got out of the camp and began to move along the road that crossed the rough plain between the entrenchment and the forest, the Indians crowded upon them, impeded their march, snatched caps, coats, and weapons from men and officers, tomahawked those that resisted, and, seizing upon shrieking women and children, dragged them off or murdered them on the spot. It is said that some of the interpreters secretly fomented the disorder.[1] Suddenly there rose the screech of the war-whoop. At this signal of butchery, which was given by Abenaki Christians from the mission of the Penobscot,[2] a mob of savages rushed upon the New Hampshire men at the rear of the column, and killed or dragged away eighty of them.[3] A frightful tumult ensued, when Montcalm, Lévis, Bourlamaque, and many other French officers, who had hastened from their camp on the first news of disturbance, threw themselves among the Indians, and by promises and threats tried to allay their frenzy. "Kill me, but spare the English who are under my protection," exclaimed Montcalm. He took from one of them a young officer whom the savage had seized; upon which several other Indians immediately tomahawked their

---

[1] *Affidavit of Miles Whitworth*. See Appendix F.

[2] This is stated by Pouchot and Bougainville; the latter of whom confirms the testimony of the English witnesses, that Canadian officers present did nothing to check the Indians.

[3] See note, end of chapter.

[4] Belknap, *History of New Hampshire*, says that eighty were killed. Governor Wentworth, writing immediately after the event, says "killed or captivated."

prisoners, lest they too should be taken from them. One writer says that a French grenadier was killed and two wounded in attempting to restore order; but the statement is doubtful. The English seemed paralyzed, and fortunately did not attempt a resistance, which, without ammunition as they were, would have ended in a general massacre. Their broken column straggled forward in wild disorder, amid the din of whoops and shrieks, till they reached the French advance-guard, which consisted of Canadians; and here they demanded protection from the officers, who refused to give it, telling them that they must take to the woods and shift for themselves. Frye was seized by a number of Indians, who, brandishing spears and tomahawks, threatened him with death and tore off his clothing, leaving nothing but breeches, shoes, and shirt. Repelled by the officers of the guard, he made for the woods. A Connecticut soldier who was present says of him that he leaped upon an Indian who stood in his way, disarmed and killed him, and then escaped; but Frye himself does not mention the incident. Captain Burke, also of the Massachusetts regiment, was stripped, after a violent struggle, of all his clothes; then broke loose, gained the woods, spent the night shivering in the thick grass of a marsh, and on the next day reached Fort Edward. Jonathan Carver, a provincial volunteer, declares that, when the tumult was at its height, he saw officers of the French army walking about at a little distance and talking with seeming unconcern. Three or four Indians seized him, brandished their tomahawks over his head, and tore off most of his clothes, while he vainly claimed protection from a sentinel, who called him an English dog, and violently pushed him back among his tormentors. Two of them were dragging him towards the neighboring swamp, when an English officer, stripped of everything but his scarlet breeches, ran by. One of Carver's captors sprang upon him, but was thrown to the ground; whereupon the other went to the aid of his comrade and drove his tomahawk into the back of the Englishman. As Carver turned to run, an English boy, about twelve years old, clung to him and begged for help. They ran on together for a moment, when the boy was seized, dragged from his protector, and, as Carver judged by his shrieks, was murdered. He himself escaped to the forest, and after three days of famine reached Fort Edward.

The bonds of discipline seem for the time to have been completely broken; for while Montcalm and his chief officers used every effort to restore order, even at the risk of their lives, many other officers, chiefly of the militia, failed atrociously to do their duty. How many English were killed it is impossible to tell with exactness. Roubaud says that he saw forty or fifty corpses scattered about the field. Lévis says fifty; which does not include the sick and wounded before murdered in the camp and fort. It is certain that six or seven hundred persons were carried off, stripped, and otherwise maltreated. Montcalm succeeded in recovering more than four hundred of them in the course of the day; and many of the French officers did what they could to relieve their wants by buying back from their captors the clothing that had been torn from them. Many of the fugitives had taken refuge in the fort, whither Monro himself had gone to demand protection for his followers; and here Roubaud presently found a crowd of half-frenzied women, crying in anguish for husbands and children. All the refugees and redeemed prisoners were afterwards conducted to the entrenched camp, where food and shelter were provided for them and a strong guard set for their protection until the fifteenth, when they were sent under an escort to Fort Edward. Here cannon had been fired at intervals to guide those who had fled to the woods, whence they came dropping in from day to day, half dead with famine.

On the morning after the massacre the Indians decamped in a body and set out for Montreal, carrying with them their plunder and some two hundred prisoners, who, it is said, could not be got out of their hands. The soldiers were set to the work of demolishing the English fort; and the task occupied several days. The barracks were torn down, and the huge pine-logs of the rampart thrown into a heap. The dead bodies that filled the casemates were added to the mass, and fire was set to the whole. The mighty funeral pyre blazed all night. Then, on the sixteenth, the army reimbarked. The din of ten thousand combatants, the rage, the terror, the agony, were gone; and no living thing was left but the wolves that gathered from the mountains to feast upon the dead.[1]

[1] The foregoing chapter rests largely on evidence never before brought to light, including the minute *Journal* of Bougainville,—a document which can hardly be commended too much,—the correspondence of Webb, a letter of Colonel Frye, written just after the massacre, and a journal of the siege, sent by him to Governor Pownall as his official report. Extracts from these, as well as from the affidavit of Dr. Whitworth, which is also new evidence, are given in Appendix F.

The Diary of Malartic and the correspondence of Montcalm, Lévis, Vaudreuil, and Bigot, also throw light on the campaign, as well as numerous reports of the seige, official and semi-official. The long letter of the Jesuit Roubaud, printed anonymously in the *Lettres Édifiantes et Curieuses*, gives a remarkably vivid account of what he saw. He was an intelligent person, who may be trusted where he has no motive for lying. Curious particulars about him will be found in a paper called, *The deplorable Case of Mr. Roubaud*, printed in the *Historical Magazine, Second Series*, VIII. 282. Compare Verreau, *Report on Canadian Archives, 1874.*

Impressions of the massacre at Fort William Henry have hitherto been derived chiefly from the narrative of Captain Jonathan Carver, in his *Travels*. He has discredited himself by his exaggeration of the number killed; but his account of what he himself saw tallies with that of the other witnesses. He is outdone in exaggeration by an anonymous French writer of the time, who seems rather pleased at the occurrence, and affirms that all the English were killed except seven hundred, these last being captured, so that none escaped (*Nouvelles du Canada envoyées de Montréal, Août, 1757*). Carver puts killed and captured together at fifteen hundred. Vaudreuil, who always makes light of Indian barbarities, goes to the other extreme, and avers that no more than five or six were killed. Lévis and Roubaud, who saw everything, and were certain not to exaggerate the number, give the most trustworthy evidence on this point. The capitulation, having been broken by the allies of France, was declared void by the British Government.

The Signal of Butchery. Montcalm, Bougainville, and several others say that the massacre was begun by the Abenakis of Panaouski. Father Martin, in quoting the letter in which Montcalm makes this statement, inserts the word *idolâtres*, which is not in the original. Dussieux and O'Callaghan give the passage correctly. This Abenaki band, ancestors of the present Penobscots, were no idolaters, but had been converted more than half a century. In the official list of the Indian allies they are set down among the Christians. Roubaud, who had charge of them during the expedition, speaks of these and other converts with singular candor: "Vous avez dû vous apercevoir . . . que nos sauvages, pour être Chrétiens, n'en sont pas plus irrépréhensibles dans leur conduite."

MONTCALM AND WOLFE

Part II

WOLFE.

AGED 16.

Chapter XVI

1757, 1758

A WINTER OF DISCONTENT

Boasts of Loudon • A Mutinous Militia • Panic • Accusations of Vaudreuil • His Weakness • Indian Barbarities • Destruction of German Flats • Discontent of Montcalm • Festivities at Montreal • Montcalm's Relations with the Governor • Famine • Riots • Mutiny • Winter at Ticonderoga • A desperate Bush-fight • Defeat of the Rangers • Adventures of Roche and Pringle

---

LOUDON, on his way back from Halifax, was at sea off the coast of Nova Scotia when a despatch-boat from Governor Pownall of Massachusetts startled him with news that Fort William Henry was attacked; and a few days after he learned by another boat that the fort was taken and the capitulation "inhumanly and villanously broken." On this he sent Webb orders to hold the enemy in check without risking a battle till he should himself arrive. "I am on the way," these were his words, "with a force sufficient to turn the scale, with God's assistance; and then I hope we shall teach the French to comply with the laws of nature and humanity. For although I abhor barbarity, the knowledge I have of Mr. Vaudreuil's behavior when in Louisiana, from his own letters in my possession, and the murders committed at Oswego and now at Fort William Henry, will oblige me to make those gentlemen sick of such inhuman villany whenever it is in my power." He reached New York on the last day of August, and heard that the French had withdrawn. He nevertheless sent his troops up the Hudson, thinking, he says, that he might still attack Ticonderoga; a wild scheme, which he soon abandoned, if he ever seriously entertained it.[1]

Webb had remained at Fort Edward in mortal dread of

[1] *Loudon to Webb, 20 Aug. 1757. Loudon to Holdernesse, Oct. 1757. Loudon to Pownall, 16 [18?] Aug. 1757.* A passage in this last letter, in which Loudon says that he shall, if prevented by head-winds from getting into New York, disembark the troops on Long Island, is perverted by that ardent partisan, William Smith, the historian of New York, into the absurd declaration "that he should encamp on Long Island for the defence of the continent."

attack. Johnson had joined him with a band of Mohawks; and on the day when Fort William Henry surrendered there had been some talk of attempting to throw succors into it by night. Then came the news of its capture; and now, when it was too late, tumultuous mobs of militia came pouring in from the neighboring provinces. In a few days thousands of them were bivouacked on the fields about Fort Edward, doing nothing, disgusted and mutinous, declaring that they were ready to fight, but not to lie still without tents, blankets, or kettles. Webb writes on the fourteenth that most of those from New York had deserted, threatening to kill their officers if they tried to stop them. Delancey ordered them to be fired upon. A sergeant was shot, others were put in arrest, and all was disorder till the seventeenth; when Webb, learning that the French were gone, sent them back to their homes.[1]

Close on the fall of Fort William Henry came crazy rumors of disaster, running like wildfire through the colonies. The number and ferocity of the enemy were grossly exaggerated; there was a cry that they would seize Albany and New York itself;[2] while it was reported that Webb, as much frightened as the rest, was for retreating to the Highlands of the Hudson.[3] This was the day after the capitulation, when a part only of the militia had yet appeared. If Montcalm had seized the moment, and marched that afternoon to Fort Edward, it is not impossible that in the confusion he might have carried it by a *coup-de-main*.

Here was an opportunity for Vaudreuil, and he did not fail to use it. Jealous of his rival's exploit, he spared no pains to tarnish it; complaining that Montcalm had stopped half way on the road to success, and, instead of following his instructions, had contented himself with one victory when he should have gained two. But the Governor had enjoined upon him as a matter of the last necessity that the Canadians should be at their homes before September to gather the crops, and he would have been the first to complain had the injunction been disregarded. To besiege Fort Edward was impossible, as

[1] *Delancey to* [*Holdernesse?*], *24 Aug. 1757.*

[2] *Captain Christie to Governor Wentworth, 11 Aug. 1757. Ibid., to Governor Pownall, same date.*

[3] Smith, *Hist. N. Y.*, Part II. 254.

Montcalm had no means of transporting cannon thither; and to attack Webb without them was a risk which he had not the rashness to incur.

It was Bougainville who first brought Vaudreuil the news of the success on Lake George. A day or two after his arrival, the Indians, who had left the army after the massacre, appeared at Montreal, bringing about two hundred English prisoners. The Governor rebuked them for breaking the capitulation, on which the heathen savages of the West declared that it was not their fault, but that of the converted Indians, who, in fact, had first raised the war-whoop. Some of the prisoners were presently bought from them at the price of two kegs of brandy each; and the inevitable consequences followed.

"I thought," writes Bougainville, "that the Governor would have told them they should have neither provisions nor presents till all the English were given up; that he himself would have gone to their huts and taken the prisoners from them; and that the inhabitants would be forbidden, under the severest penalties, from selling or giving them brandy. I saw the contrary; and my soul shuddered at the sights my eyes beheld. On the fifteenth, at two o'clock, in the presence of the whole town, they killed one of the prisoners, put him into the kettle, and forced his wretched countrymen to eat of him." The Intendant Bigot, the friend of the Governor, confirms this story; and another French writer says that they "compelled mothers to eat the flesh of their children."[1] Bigot declares that guns, canoes, and other presents were given to the Western tribes before they left Montreal; and he adds, "they must be sent home satisfied at any cost." Such were the pains taken to preserve allies who were useful chiefly through the terror inspired by their diabolical cruelties. This time their ferocity cost them dear. They had dug up and scalped the corpses in the graveyard of Fort William Henry, many of which were

[1] "En chemin faisant et même en entrant à Montréal ils les ont mangés et fait manger aux autres prisonniers." *Bigot au Ministre, 24 Août, 1757*.

"Des sauvages ont fait manger aux mères la chair de leurs enfants." *Jugement impartial sur les Opérations militaires en Canada*. A French diary kept in Canada at this time, and captured at sea, is cited by Hutchinson as containing similar statements.

remains of victims of the small-pox; and the savages caught the disease, which is said to have made great havoc among them.[1]

Vaudreuil, in reporting what he calls "my capture of Fort William Henry," takes great credit to himself for his "generous procedures" towards the English prisoners; alluding, it seems, to his having bought some of them from the Indians with the brandy which was sure to cause the murder of others.[2] His obsequiousness to his red allies did not cease with permitting them to kill and devour before his eyes those whom he was bound in honor and duty to protect. "He let them do what they pleased," says a French contemporary; "they were seen roaming about Montreal, knife in hand, threatening everybody, and often insulting those they met. When complaint was made, he said nothing. Far from it; instead of reproaching them, he loaded them with gifts, in the belief that their cruelty would then relent."[3]

Nevertheless, in about a fortnight all, or nearly all, the surviving prisoners were bought out of their clutches; and then, after a final distribution of presents and a grand debauch at La Chine, the whole savage rout paddled for their villages.

The campaign closed in November with a partisan exploit on the Mohawk. Here, at a place called German Flats, on the farthest frontier, there was a thriving settlement of German peasants from the Palatinate, who were so ill-disposed towards the English that Vaudreuil had had good hope of stirring them to revolt, while at the same time persuading their neighbors, the Oneida Indians, to take part with France.[4] As his measures to this end failed, he resolved to attack them. Therefore, at three o'clock in the morning of the twelfth of November, three hundred colony troops, Canadians and Indians, under an officer named Belêtre, wakened the unhappy peasants by a burst of yells, and attacked the small picket forts which they had built as places of refuge. These were taken

[1] One of these corpses was that of Richard Rogers, brother of the noted partisan Robert Rogers. He had died of small-pox some time before. Rogers, *Journals*, 55, *note*.

[2] *Vaudreuil au Ministre, 15 Sept. 1757.*

[3] *Mémoires sur le Canada, 1749–1760.*

[4] *Dépêches de Vaudreuil, 1757.*

one by one and set on fire. The sixty dwellings of the settlement, with their barns and outhouses, were all burned, forty
or fifty of the inhabitants were killed, and about three times
that number, chiefly women and children, were made prisoners, including Johan Jost Petrie, the magistrate of the place.
Fort Herkimer was not far off, with a garrison of two
hundred men under Captain Townshend, who at the first
alarm sent out a detachment too weak to arrest the havoc;
while Belêtre, unable to carry off his booty, set on his followers to the work of destruction, killed a great number of hogs,
sheep, cattle, and horses, and then made a hasty retreat. Lord
Howe, pushing up the river from Schenectady with troops
and militia, found nothing but an abandoned slaughter-field.
Vaudreuil reported the affair to the Court, and summed up
the results with pompous egotism: "I have ruined the plans
of the English; I have disposed the Five Nations to attack
them; I have carried consternation and terror into all those
parts."[1]

Montcalm, his summer work over, went to Montreal; and
thence in September to Quebec, a place more to his liking.
"Come as soon as you can," he wrote to Bourlamaque, "and
I will tell a certain fair lady how eager you are." Even Quebec
was no paradise for him; and he writes again to the same
friend: "My heart and my stomach are both ill at ease, the
latter being the worse." To his wife he says: "The price of
everything is rising. I am ruining myself; I owe the treasurer
twelve thousand francs. I long for peace and for you. In spite
of the public distress, we have balls and furious gambling."
In February he returned to Montreal in a sleigh on the ice of
the St. Lawrence,—a mode of travelling which he describes
as cold but delicious. Montreal pleased him less than ever,

---

[1] *Loudon to Pitt, 14 Feb. 1758. Vaudreuil au Ministre, 12 Fév. 1758. Ibid., 28
Nov. 1758.* Bougainville, *Journal. Summary of M. de Belêtre's Campaign,* in
N. Y. Col. Docs., X. 672. Extravagant reports of the havoc made were sent to
France. It was pretended that three thousand cattle, three thousand sheep
(Vaudreuil says four thousand), and from five hundred to fifteen hundred
horses were destroyed, with other personal property to the amount of
1,500,000 livres. These official falsehoods are contradicted in a letter from
Quebec, *Daine au Maréchal de Belleisle, 19 Mai, 1758.* Lévis says that the whole
population of the settlement, men, women, and children, was not above three
hundred.

especially as he was not in favor at what he calls the Court, meaning the circle of the Governor-General. "I find this place so amusing," he writes ironically to Bourlamaque, "that I wish Holy Week could be lengthened, to give me a pretext for neither making nor receiving visits, staying at home, and dining there almost alone. Burn all my letters, as I do yours." And in the next week: "Lent and devotion have upset my stomach and given me a cold; which does not prevent me from having the Governor-General at dinner to-day to end his lenten fast, according to custom here." Two days after he announces: "To-day a grand dinner at Martel's; twenty-three persons, all big-wigs (*les grosses perruques*); no ladies. We still have got to undergo those of Péan, Deschambault, and the Chevalier de Lévis. I spend almost every evening in my chamber, the place I like best, and where I am least bored."

With the opening spring there were changes in the modes of amusement. Picnics began, Vaudreuil and his wife being often of the party, as too was Lévis. The Governor also made visits of compliment at the houses of the seigniorial proprietors along the river; "very much," says Montcalm, as "Henri IV. did to the bourgeois notables of Paris. I live as usual, fencing in the morning, dining, and passing the evening at home or at the Governor's. Péan has gone up to La Chine to spend six days with the reigning sultana [*Péan's wife, mistress of Bigot*]. As for me, my *ennui* increases. I don't know what to do, or say, or read, or where to go; and I think that at the end of the next campaign I shall ask bluntly, blindly, for my recall, only because I am bored."[1]

His relations with Vaudreuil were a constant annoyance to him, notwithstanding the mask of mutual civility. "I never," he tells his mother, "ask for a place in the colony troops for anybody. You need not be an Œdipus to guess this riddle. Here are four lines from Corneille: —

" 'Mon crime véritable est d'avoir aujourd'hui
    Plus de nom que . . . [*Vaudreuil*], plus de vertus que lui,
    Et c'est de là que part cette secrète haine
    Que le temps ne rendra que plus forte et plus pleine.'

---

[1] *Montcalm à Bourlamaque, 22 Mai, 1758.*

Nevertheless I live here on good terms with everybody, and do my best to serve the King. If they could but do without me; if they could but spring some trap on me, or if I should happen to meet with some check!"

Vaudreuil meanwhile had written to the Court in high praise of Lévis, hinting that he, and not Montcalm, ought to have the chief command.[1]

Under the hollow gayeties of the ruling class lay a great public distress, which broke at last into riot. Towards mid-winter no flour was to be had in Montreal; and both soldiers and people were required to accept a reduced ration, partly of horse-flesh. A mob gathered before the Governor's house, and a deputation of women beset him, crying out that the horse was the friend of man, and that religion forbade him to be eaten. In reply he threatened them with imprisonment and hanging; but with little effect, and the crowd dispersed, only to stir up the soldiers quartered in the houses of the town. The colony regulars, ill-disciplined at the best, broke into mutiny, and excited the battalion of Béarn to join them. Vaudreuil was helpless; Montcalm was in Quebec; and the task of dealing with the mutineers fell upon Lévis, who proved equal to the crisis, took a high tone, threatened death to the first soldier who should refuse horse-flesh, assured them at the same time that he ate it every day himself, and by a characteristic mingling of authority and tact, quelled the storm.[2]

The prospects of the next campaign began to open. Captain Pouchot had written from Niagara that three thousand savages were waiting to be let loose against the English borders. "What a scourge!" exclaims Bougainville. "Humanity groans at being forced to use such monsters. What can be done against an invisible enemy, who strikes and vanishes, swift as the lightning? It is the destroying angel." Captain Hebecourt kept watch and ward at Ticonderoga, begirt with snow and ice, and much plagued by English rangers, who sometimes got into the ditch itself.[3] This was to reconnoitre the place in

[1] *Vaudreuil au Ministre de la Marine, 16 Sept. 1757. Ibid., au Ministre de la Guerre, même date.*

[2] Bougainville, *Journal. Montcalm à Mirepoix, 20 Avril, 1758.* Lévis, *Journal de la Guerre du Canada.*

[3] *Montcalm à Bourlamaque, 28 Mars, 1758.*

preparation for a winter attack which Loudon had planned, but which, like the rest of his schemes, fell to the ground.[1] Towards midwinter a band of these intruders captured two soldiers and butchered some fifteen cattle close to the fort, leaving tied to the horns of one of them a note addressed to the commandant in these terms: "I am obliged to you, sir, for the rest you have allowed me to take and the fresh meat you have sent me. I shall take good care of my prisoners. My compliments to the Marquis of Montcalm." Signed, Rogers.[2]

A few weeks later Hebecourt had his revenge. About the middle of March a report came to Montreal that a large party of rangers had been cut to pieces a few miles from Ticonderoga, and that Rogers himself was among the slain. This last announcement proved false; but the rangers had suffered a crushing defeat. Colonel Haviland, commanding at Fort Edward, sent a hundred and eighty of them, men and officers, on a scouting party towards Ticonderoga; and Captain Pringle and Lieutenant Roche, of the twenty-seventh regiment, joined them as volunteers, no doubt through a love of hardy adventure, which was destined to be fully satisfied. Rogers commanded the whole. They passed down Lake George on the ice under cover of night, and then, as they neared the French outposts, pursued their way by land behind Rogers Rock and the other mountains of the western shore. On the preceding day, the twelfth of March, Hebecourt had received a reinforcement of two hundred Mission Indians and a body of Canadians. The Indians had no sooner arrived than, though nominally Christians, they consulted the spirits, by whom they were told that the English were coming. On this they sent out scouts, who came back breathless, declaring that they had found a great number of snow-shoe tracks. The superhuman warning being thus confirmed, the whole body of Indians, joined by a band of Canadians and a number of volunteers from the regulars, set out to meet the approaching enemy, and took their way up the valley of Trout Brook, a mountain gorge that opens from the west upon the valley of Ticonderoga.

[1] *Loudon to Pitt, 14 Feb. 1758.*

[2] *Journal de ce qui s'est passé en Canada, 1757, 1758.* Compare Rogers, *Journals,* 72–75.

Towards three o'clock on the afternoon of that day Rogers had reached a point nearly west of the mountain that bears his name. The rough and rocky ground was buried four feet in snow, and all around stood the gray trunks of the forest, bearing aloft their skeleton arms and tangled intricacy of leafless twigs. Close on the right was a steep hill, and at a little distance on the left was the brook, lost under ice and snow. A scout from the front told Rogers that a party of Indians was approaching along the bed of the frozen stream, on which he ordered his men to halt, face to that side, and advance cautiously. The Indians soon appeared, and received a fire that killed some of them and drove back the rest in confusion.

Not suspecting that they were but an advance-guard, about half the rangers dashed in pursuit, and were soon met by the whole body of the enemy. The woods rang with yells and musketry. In a few minutes some fifty of the pursuers were shot down, and the rest driven back in disorder upon their comrades. Rogers formed them all on the slope of the hill; and here they fought till sunset with stubborn desperation, twice repulsing the overwhelming numbers of the assailants, and thwarting all their efforts to gain the heights in the rear. The combatants were often not twenty yards apart, and sometimes they were mixed together. At length a large body of Indians succeeded in turning the right flank of the rangers. Lieutenant Phillips and a few men were sent by Rogers to oppose the movement; but they quickly found themselves surrounded, and after a brave defence surrendered on a pledge of good treatment. Rogers now advised the volunteers, Pringle and Roche, to escape while there was time, and offered them a sergeant as guide; but they gallantly resolved to stand by him. Eight officers and more than a hundred rangers lay dead and wounded in the snow. Evening was near and the forest was darkening fast, when the few survivors broke and fled. Rogers with about twenty followers escaped up the mountain; and gathering others about him, made a running fight against the Indian pursuers, reached Lake George, not without fresh losses, and after two days of misery regained Fort Edward with the remnant of his band. The enemy on their part suffered heavily, the chief loss falling on the

Indians; who, to revenge themselves, murdered all the wounded and nearly all the prisoners, and tying Lieutenant Phillips and his men to trees, hacked them to pieces.

Captain Pringle and Lieutenant Roche had become separated from the other fugitives; and, ignorant of woodcraft, they wandered by moonlight amid the desolation of rocks and snow, till early in the night they met a man whom they knew as a servant of Rogers, and who said that he could guide them to Fort Edward. One of them had lost his snow-shoes in the fight; and, crouching over a miserable fire of broken sticks, they worked till morning to make a kind of substitute with forked branches, twigs, and a few leather strings. They had no hatchet to cut firewood, no blankets, no overcoats, and no food except part of a Bologna sausage and a little ginger which Pringle had brought with him. There was no game; not even a squirrel was astir; and their chief sustenance was juniper-berries and the inner bark of trees. But their worst calamity was the helplessness of their guide. His brain wandered; and while always insisting that he knew the country well, he led them during four days hither and thither among a labyrinth of nameless mountains, clambering over rocks, wading through snowdrifts, struggling among fallen trees, till on the fifth day they saw with despair that they had circled back to their own starting-point. On the next morning, when they were on the ice of Lake George, not far from Rogers Rock, a blinding storm of sleet and snow drove in their faces. Spent as they were, it was death to stop; and bending their heads against the blast, they fought their way forward, now on the ice, and now in the adjacent forest, till in the afternoon the storm ceased, and they found themselves on the bank of an unknown stream. It was the outlet of the lake; for they had wandered into the valley of Ticonderoga, and were not three miles from the French fort. In crossing the torrent Pringle lost his gun, and was near losing his life. All three of the party were drenched to the skin; and, becoming now for the first time aware of where they were, they resolved on yielding themselves prisoners to save their lives. Night, however, again found them in the forest. Their guide became delirious, saw visions of Indians all around, and, murmuring incoherently, straggled off a little way, seated himself in the snow, and was soon dead. The two officers, themselves but half alive, walked all night round a tree to keep the blood in motion. In the morning, again toiling on, they presently saw the fort across the intervening snowfields, and approached it, waving a white handkerchief. Several French officers dashed towards them at full speed, and reached them in time to save them from the clutches of the Indians, whose camps were near at hand. They were kindly treated, recovered from the effects of their frightful ordeal, and were afterwards exchanged. Pringle lived to old age, and died in 1800, senior major-general of the British army.[1]

[1] Rogers, two days after reaching Fort Edward, made a detailed report of the fight, which was printed in the *New Hampshire Gazette* and other provincial papers. It is substantially incorporated in his published *Journals*, which also contain a long letter from Pringle to Colonel Haviland, dated at Carillon (Ticonderoga), 28 March, and giving an excellent account of his and Roche's adventures. It was sent by a flag of truce, which soon after arrived from Fort Edward with a letter for Vaudreuil. The French accounts of the fight are *Hebecourt à [Vaudreuil?], 15 Mars, 1758. Montcalm au Ministre de la Guerre, 10 Avril, 1758. Doreil à Belleisle, 30 Avril, 1758.* Bougainville, *Journal. Relation de l'Affaire de Roger, 19 Mars, 1758. Autre Relation, même date.* Lévis, *Journal.* According to Lévis, the French force consisted of 250 Indians and Canadians, and a number of officers, cadets, and soldiers. Rogers puts it at 700. Most of the French writers put the force of the rangers, correctly, at about 180. Rogers reports his loss at 125. None of the wounded seem to have escaped, being either murdered after the fight, or killed by exposure in the woods. The Indians brought in 144 scalps, having no doubt divided some of them, after their ingenious custom. Rogers threw off his overcoat during the fight, and it was found on the field, with his commission in the pocket; whence the report of his death. There is an unsupported tradition that he escaped by sliding on his snow-shoes down a precipice of Rogers Rock.

Chapter XVII

1753—1760

BIGOT

*His Life and Character • Canadian Society • Official Festivities •
A Party of Pleasure • Hospitalities of Bigot • Desperate Gambling
• Château Bigot • Canadian Ladies • Cadet • La Friponne •
Official Rascality • Methods of Peculation • Cruel Frauds on the
Acadians • Military Corruption • Péan • Love and Knavery •
Varin and his Partners • Vaudreuil and the Peculators • He de-
fends Bigot; praises Cadet and Péan • Canadian Finances • Peril
of Bigot • Threats of the Minister • Evidence of Montcalm • Im-
pending Ruin of the Confederates*

AT THIS STORMY epoch of Canadian history the sinister figure of the Intendant Bigot moves conspicuous on the
scene. Not that he was answerable for all the manifold corruption that infected the colony, for much of it was rife before his time, and had a vitality of its own; but his office and
character made him the centre of it, and, more than any other
man, he marshalled and organized the forces of knavery.

In the dual government of Canada the Governor represented the King and commanded the troops; while the Intendant was charged with trade, finance, justice, and all other
departments of civil administration.[1] In former times the two
functionaries usually quarrelled; but between Vaudreuil and
Bigot there was perfect harmony.

François Bigot, in the words of his biographer, was "born
in the bosom of the magistracy," both his father and his
grandfather having held honorable positions in the parliament
of Bordeaux.[2] In appearance he was not prepossessing,
though his ugly, pimpled face was joined with easy and agreeable manners. In spite of indifferent health, he was untiring
both in pleasure and in work, a skilful man of business, of
great official experience, energetic, good-natured, free-
handed, ready to oblige his friends and aid them in their

[1] See *Old Régime in Canada.*

[2] *Procès de Bigot, Cadet, et autres, Mémoire pour Messire François Bigot, accusé,
contre Monsieur le Procureur-Général du Roi, accusateur.*

needs at the expense of the King, his master; fond of social enjoyments, lavish in hospitality.

A year or two before the war began, the engineer Franquet was sent from France to strengthen Louisbourg and inspect the defences of Canada. He kept a copious journal, full of curious observation, and affording bright glimpses not only of the social life of the Intendant, but of Canadian society in the upper or official class. Thus, among various matters of the kind, he gives us the following. Bigot, who was in Quebec, had occasion to go to Montreal to meet the Governor; and this official journey was turned into a pleasure excursion, of which the King paid all the costs. Those favored with invitations, a privilege highly prized, were Franquet, with seven or eight military officers and a corresponding number of ladies, including the wife of Major Péan, of whom Bigot was enamoured. A chief steward, cooks, servants, and other attendants, followed the party. The guests had been requested to send their portmanteaus to the Intendant's Palace six days before, that they might be sent forward on sledges along with bedding, table service, cooking utensils, and numberless articles of comfort and luxury. Orders were given to the inhabitants along the way, on pain of imprisonment, to level the snowdrifts and beat the road smooth with ox-teams, as also to provide relays of horses. It is true that they were well paid for this last service; so well that the hire of a horse to Montreal and back again would cost the King the entire value of the animal. On the eighth of February the party met at the palace; and after a grand dinner set out upon their journey in twenty or more sleighs, some with two guests and a driver, and the rest with servants and attendants. The procession passed at full trot along St. Vallier street amid the shouts of an admiring crowd, stopped towards night at Pointe-aux-Trembles, where each looked for lodging; and then they all met and supped with the Intendant. The militia captain of the place was ordered to have fresh horses ready at seven in the morning, when Bigot regaled his friends with tea, coffee, and chocolate, after which they set out again, drove to Cap-Santé, and stopped two hours at the house of the militia captain to breakfast and warm themselves. In the afternoon they reached Ste. Anne-de-la-Pérade, when Bigot gave them a supper at the house in which he lodged, and they spent the evening at cards.

The next morning brought them to Three Rivers, where Madame Marin, Franquet's travelling companion, wanted to stop to see her sister, the wife of Rigaud, who was then governor of the place. Madame de Rigaud, being ill, received her visitors in bed, and ordered an ample dinner to be provided for them; after which they returned to her chamber for coffee and conversation. Then they all set out again, saluted by the cannon of the fort.

Their next stopping-place was Isle-au-Castor, where, being seated at cards before supper, they were agreeably surprised by the appearance of the Governor, who had come down from Montreal to meet them with four officers, Duchesnaye, Marin, Le Mercier, and Péan. Many were the embraces and compliments; and in the morning they all journeyed on together, stopping towards night at the largest house they could find, where their servants took away the partitions to make room, and they sat down to a supper, followed by the inevitable game of cards. On the next night they reached Montreal and were lodged at the intendency, the official residence of the hospitable Bigot. The succeeding day was spent in visiting persons of eminence and consideration, among whom are to be noted the names, soon to become notorious, of Varin, naval commissary, Martel, King's storekeeper, Antoine Penisseault, and François Maurin. A succession of festivities followed, including the benediction of three flags for a band of militia on their way to the Ohio. All persons of quality in Montreal were invited on this occasion, and the Governor gave them a dinner and a supper. Bigot, however, outdid him in the plenitude of his hospitality, since, in the week before Lent, forty guests supped every evening at his table, and dances, masquerades, and cards consumed the night.[1]

His chief abode was at Quebec, in the capacious but somewhat ugly building known as the Intendant's Palace. Here it was his custom during the war to entertain twenty persons at dinner every day; and there was also a hall for dancing, with a gallery to which the citizens were admitted as spectators.[2]

[1] Franquet, *Journal*.
[2] De Gaspé, *Mémoires*, 119.

The bounteous Intendant provided a separate dancing-hall for the populace; and, though at the same time he plundered and ruined them, his gracious demeanor long kept him a place in their hearts. Gambling was the chief feature of his entertainments, and the stakes grew deeper as the war went on. He played desperately himself, and early in 1758 lost two hundred and four thousand francs, — a loss which he well knew how to repair. Besides his official residence on the banks of the St. Charles, he had a country house about five miles distant, a massive old stone building in the woods at the foot of the mountain of Charlesbourg; its ruins are now known as Château Bigot. In its day it was called the Hermitage; though the uses to which it was applied savored nothing of asceticism. Tradition connects it and its owner with a romantic, but more than doubtful, story of love, jealousy, and murder.

The chief Canadian families were so social in their habits and so connected by intermarriage that, along with the French civil and military officers of the colonial establishment, they formed a society whose members all knew each other, like the corresponding class in Virginia. There was among them a social facility and ease rare in democratic communities; and in the ladies of Quebec and Montreal were often seen graces which visitors from France were astonished to find at the edge of a wilderness. Yet this small though lively society had anomalies which grew more obtrusive towards the close of the war. Knavery makes strange companions; and at the tables of high civil officials and colony officers of rank sat guests as boorish in manners as they were worthless in character.

Foremost among these was Joseph Cadet, son of a butcher at Quebec, who at thirteen went to sea as a pilot's boy, then kept the cows of an inhabitant of Charlesbourg, and at last took up his father's trade and prospered in it.[1] In 1756 Bigot got him appointed commissary-general, and made a contract with him which flung wide open the doors of peculation. In the next two years Cadet and his associates, Péan, Maurin, Corpron, and Penisseault, sold to the King, for about twenty-three million francs, provisions which cost them eleven mil-

---

[1] *Procès de Bigot, Cadet, et autres, Mémoire pour Messire François Bigot.* Compare *Mémoires sur le Canada, 1749–1760.*

lions, leaving a net profit of about twelve millions. It was not legally proved that the Intendant shared Cadet's gains; but there is no reasonable doubt that he did so. Bigot's chief profits rose, however, from other sources. It was his business to see that the King's storehouses for the supply of troops, militia, and Indians were kept well stocked. To this end he and Bréard, naval comptroller at Quebec, made a partnership with the commercial house of Gradis and Son at Bordeaux. He next told the Colonial Minister that there were stores enough already in Canada to last three years, and that it would be more to the advantage of the King to buy them in the colony than to take the risk of sending them from France.[1] Gradis and Son then shipped them to Canada in large quantities, while Bréard or his agent declared at the custom-house that they belonged to the King, and so escaped the payment of duties. They were then, as occasion rose, sold to the King at a huge profit, always under fictitious names. Often they were sold to some favored merchant or speculator, who sold them in turn to Bigot's confederate, the King's storekeeper; and sometimes they passed through several successive hands, till the price rose to double or triple the first cost, the Intendant and his partners sharing the gains with friends and allies. They would let nobody else sell to the King; and thus a grinding monopoly was established, to the great profit of those who held it.[2]

Under the name of a trader named Claverie, Bigot, some time before the war, set up a warehouse on land belonging to the King and not far from his own palace. Here the goods shipped from Bordeaux were collected, to be sold in retail to the citizens, and in wholesale to favored merchants and the King. This establishment was popularly known as La Friponne, or The Cheat. There was another Friponne at Montreal, which was leagued with that of Quebec, and received goods from it.

Bigot and his accomplices invented many other profitable frauds. Thus he was charged with the disposal of the large quantity of furs belonging to his master, which it was his

[1] *Bigot au Ministre, 8 Oct. 1749.*

[2] *Procès de Bigot, Cadet, et autres. Mémoire sur les Fraudes commises dans la Colonie.* Compare *Mémoires sur le Canada, 1749–1760.*

duty to sell at public auction, after due notice, to the highest bidder. Instead of this, he sold them privately at a low price to his own confederates. It was also his duty to provide transportation for troops, artillery, provisions, and stores, in which he made good profit by letting to the King, at high prices, boats or vessels which he had himself bought or hired for the purpose.[1]

Yet these and other illicit gains still left him but the second place as public plunderer. Cadet, the commissary-general, reaped an ampler harvest, and became the richest man in the colony. One of the operations of this scoundrel, accomplished with the help of Bigot, consisted in buying for six hundred thousand francs a quantity of stores belonging to the King, and then selling them back to him for one million four hundred thousand.[2] It was further shown on his trial that in 1759 he received 1,614,354 francs for stores furnished at the post of Miramichi, while the value of those actually furnished was but 889,544 francs; thus giving him a fraudulent profit of more than seven hundred and twenty-four thousand.[3] Cadet's chief resource was the falsification of accounts. The service of the King in Canada was fenced about by rigid formalities. When supplies were wanted at any of the military posts, the commandant made a requisition specifying their nature and quantity, while, before pay could be drawn for them, the King's storekeeper, the local commissary, and the inspector must set their names as vouchers to the list, and finally Bigot must sign it.[4] But precautions were useless where all were leagued to rob the King. It appeared on Cadet's trial that by gifts of wine, brandy, or money he had bribed the officers, both civil and military, at all the principal forts to attest the truth of accounts in which the supplies furnished by him were set at more than twice their true amount. Of the many frauds charged against him there was one peculiarly odious. Large numbers of refugee Acadians were to be supplied with rations to keep them alive. Instead of wholesome food, mouldered and unsalable salt cod was sent them, and paid for by the

[1] *Jugement rendu souverainement dans l'Affaire du Canada.*

[2] *Procès de Bigot, Cadet, et autres, Requête du Procureur-Général, 19 Déc. 1761.*

[3] *Procès de Bigot, Cadet, et autres, Mémoire pour Messire François Bigot.*

[4] *Mémoire sur le Canada* (Archives Nationales).

King at inordinate prices.[1] It was but one of many heartless outrages practised by Canadian officials on this unhappy people.

Cadet told the Intendant that the inhabitants were hoarding their grain, and got an order from him requiring them to sell it at a low fixed price, on pain of having it seized. Thus nearly the whole fell into his hands. Famine ensued; and he then sold it at a great profit, partly to the King, and partly to its first owners. Another of his devices was to sell provisions to the King which, being sent to the outlying forts, were falsely reported as consumed; on which he sold them to the King a second time. Not without reason does a writer of the time exclaim: "This is the land of abuses, ignorance, prejudice, and all that is monstrous in government. Peculation, monopoly, and plunder have become a bottomless abyss."[2]

The command of a fort brought such opportunities of making money that, according to Bougainville, the mere prospect of appointment to it for the usual term of three years was thought enough for a young man to marry upon. It was a favor in the gift of the Governor, who was accused of sharing the profits. These came partly from the fur-trade, and still more from frauds of various kinds. For example, a requisition was made for supplies as gifts to the Indians in order to keep them friendly or send them on the war-path; and their number was put many times above the truth in order to get more goods, which the commandant and his confederates then bartered for furs on their own account, instead of giving them as presents. "And," says a contemporary, addressing the Colonial Minister, "those who treat the savages so basely are officers of the King, depositaries of his authority, ministers of that Great Onontio whom they call their father."[3] At the post of Green Bay, the partisan officer Marin, and Rigaud, the Governor's brother, made in a short time a profit of three hundred and twelve thousand francs.[4] "Why is it," asks Bougainville, "that of all which the King sends to the Indians two

[1] *Mémoires sur le Canada, 1749–1760.*

[2] *Considérations sur l'État présent du Canada.*

[3] *Ibid.*

[4] *Mémoire sur les Fraudes commises dans la Colonie.* Bougainville, *Mémoire sur l'État de la Nouvelle France.*

thirds are stolen, and the rest sold to them instead of being given?"[1]

The transportation of military stores gave another opportunity of plunder. The contractor would procure from the Governor or the local commandant an order requiring the inhabitants to serve him as boatmen, drivers, or porters, under a promise of exemption that year from duty as soldiers. This saved him his chief item of expense, and the profits of his contract rose in proportion.

A contagion of knavery ran through the official life of the colony; and to resist it demanded no common share of moral robustness. The officers of the troops of the line were not much within its influence; but those of the militia and colony regulars, whether of French or Canadian birth, shared the corruption of the civil service. Seventeen of them, including six chevaliers of St. Louis and eight commandants of forts, were afterwards arraigned for fraud and malversation, though some of the number were acquitted. Bougainville gives the names of four other Canadian officers as honorable exceptions to the general demoralization,—Benoît, Repentigny, Lainé, and Le Borgne; "not enough," he observes, "to save Sodom."

Conspicuous among these military thieves was Major Péan, whose qualities as a soldier have been questioned, but who nevertheless had shown almost as much vigor in serving the King during the Ohio campaign of 1753 as he afterwards displayed effrontery in cheating him. "Le petit Péan" had married a young wife, Mademoiselle Desméloizes, Canadian like himself, well born, and famed for beauty, vivacity, and wit. Bigot, who was near sixty, became her accepted lover; and the fortune of Péan was made. His first success seems to have taken him by surprise. He had bought as a speculation a large quantity of grain, with money of the King lent him by the Intendant. Bigot, officially omnipotent, then issued an order raising the commodity to a price far above that paid by Péan, who thus made a profit of fifty thousand crowns.[2] A few years later his wealth was estimated at from two to four million francs. Madame Péan became a power in Canada, the dis-

[1] Bougainville, *Journal*.

[2] *Mémoires sur le Canada, 1749–1760. Mémoire sur les Fraudes*, etc. Compare Pouchot, I. 8.

penser of favors and offices; and all who sought opportunity
to rob the King hastened to pay her their court. Péan, jilted
by his own wife, made prosperous love to the wife of his
partner, Penisseault; who, though the daughter of a Montreal
tradesman, had the air of a woman of rank, and presided with
dignity and grace at a hospitable board where were gathered
the clerks of Cadet and other lesser lights of the administrative hierarchy. It was often honored by the presence of the
Chevalier de Lévis, who, captivated by the charms of the
hostess, condescended to a society which his friends condemned as unworthy of his station. He succeeded Péan in the
graces of Madame Penisseault, and after the war took her
with him to France; while the aggrieved husband found consolation in the wives of the small functionaries under his orders.[1]

Another prominent name on the roll of knavery was that
of Varin, commissary of marine, and Bigot's deputy at Montreal, a Frenchman of low degree, small in stature, sharp
witted, indefatigable, conceited, arrogant, headstrong, capricious, and dissolute. Worthless as he was, he found a
place in the Court circle of the Governor, and aspired to supplant Bigot in the intendancy. To this end, as well as to save
himself from justice, he had the fatuity to turn informer and
lay bare the sins of his confederates, though forced at the
same time to betray his own. Among his comrades and allies
may be mentioned Deschenaux, son of a shoemaker at Quebec, and secretary to the Intendant; Martel, King's storekeeper at Montreal; the humpback Maurin, who is not to be
confounded with the partisan officer Marin; and Corpron, a
clerk whom several tradesmen had dismissed for rascality, but
who was now in the confidence of Cadet, to whom he made
himself useful, and in whose service he grew rich.

Canada was the prey of official jackals,—true lion's provid-
ers, since they helped to prepare a way for the imperial beast,
who, roused at last from his lethargy, was gathering his
strength to seize her for his own. Honesty could not be expected from a body of men clothed with arbitrary and ill-
defined powers, ruling with absolute sway an unfortunate
people who had no voice in their own destinies, and answer-

[1] *Mémoires sur le Canada, 1749 –1760.*

able only to an apathetic master three thousand miles away. Nor did the Canadian Church, though supreme, check the corruptions that sprang up and flourished under its eye. The Governor himself was charged with sharing the plunder; and though he was acquitted on his trial, it is certain that Bigot had him well in hand, that he was intimate with the chief robbers, and that they found help in his weak compliances and wilful blindness. He put his stepson, Le Verrier, in command at Michillimackinac, where, by fraud and the connivance of his stepfather, the young man made a fortune.[1] When the Colonial Minister berated the Intendant for maladministration, Vaudreuil became his advocate, and wrote thus in his defence: "I cannot conceal from you, Monseigneur, how deeply M. Bigot feels the suspicions expressed in your letters to him. He does not deserve them, I am sure. He is full of zeal for the service of the King; but as he is rich, or passes as such, and as he has merit, the ill-disposed are jealous, and insinuate that he has prospered at the expense of His Majesty. I am certain that it is not true, and that nobody is a better citizen than he, or has the King's interest more at heart."[2] For Cadet, the butcher's son, the Governor asked a patent of nobility as a reward for his services.[3] When Péan went to France in 1758, Vaudreuil wrote to the Colonial Minister: "I have great confidence in him. He knows the colony and its needs. You can trust all he says. He will explain everything in the best manner. I shall be extremely sensible to any kindness you may show him, and hope that when you know him you will like him as much as I do."[4]

Administrative corruption was not the only bane of Canada. Her financial condition was desperate. The ordinary circulating medium consisted of what was known as card money, and amounted to only a million of francs. This being insufficient, Bigot, like his predecessor Hocquart, issued promissory notes on his own authority, and made them legal tender. They were for sums from one franc to a hundred, and were called *ordonnances*. Their issue was blamed at Versailles

[1] *Mémoires sur le Canada, 1749–1760.*
[2] *Vaudreuil au Ministre, 15 Oct. 1759.*
[3] *Ibid., 7 Nov. 1759.*
[4] *Ibid., 6 Août, 1758.*

as an encroachment on the royal prerogative, though they were recognized by the Ministry in view of the necessity of the case. Every autumn those who held them to any considerable amount might bring them to the colonial treasurer, who gave in return bills of exchange on the royal treasury in France. At first these bills were promptly paid; then delays took place, and the notes depreciated; till in 1759 the Ministry, aghast at the amount, refused payment, and the utmost dismay and confusion followed.[1]

The vast jarring, discordant mechanism of corruption grew incontrollable; it seized upon Bigot, and dragged him, despite himself, into perils which his prudence would have shunned. He was becoming a victim to the rapacity of his own confederates, whom he dared not offend by refusing his connivance and his signature to frauds which became more and more recklessly audacious. He asked leave to retire from office, in the hope that his successor would bear the brunt of the ministerial displeasure. Péan had withdrawn already, and with the fruits of his plunder bought land in France, where he thought himself safe. But though the Intendant had long been an object of distrust, and had often been warned to mend his ways,[2] yet such was his energy, his executive power, and his fertility of resource, that in the crisis of the war it was hard to dispense with him. Neither his abilities, however, nor his strong connections in France, nor an ally whom he had secured in the bureau of the Colonial Minister himself, could avail him much longer; and the letters from Versailles became appalling in rebuke and menace.

"The ship 'Britannia,'" wrote the Minister, Berryer, "laden with goods such as are wanted in the colony, was captured by a privateer from St.-Malo, and brought into Quebec. You sold the whole cargo for eight hundred thousand francs. The purchasers made a profit of two millions. You bought back a part for the King at one million, or two hundred thousand more than the price for which you sold the whole. With conduct like this it is no wonder that the expenses of the colony

[1] *Réflexions sommaires sur le Commerce qui s'est fait en Canada. État présent du Canada.* Compare Stevenson, *Card Money of Canada,* in *Transactions of the Historical Society of Quebec, 1873–1875.*

[2] *Ordres du Roy et Dépêches des Ministres, 1751–1758.*

become insupportable. The amount of your drafts on the treasury is frightful. The fortunes of your subordinates throw suspicion on your administration." And in another letter on the same day: "How could it happen that the small-pox among the Indians cost the King a million francs? What does this expense mean? Who is answerable for it? Is it the officers who command the posts, or is it the storekeepers? You give me no particulars. What has become of the immense quantity of provisions sent to Canada last year? I am forced to conclude that the King's stores are set down as consumed from the moment they arrive, and then sold to His Majesty at exorbitant prices. Thus the King buys stores in France, and then buys them again in Canada. I no longer wonder at the immense fortunes made in the colony."[1] Some months later the Minister writes: "You pay bills without examination, and then find an error in your accounts of three million six hundred thousand francs. In the letters from Canada I see nothing but incessant speculation in provisions and goods, which are sold to the King for ten times more than they cost in France. For the last time, I exhort you to give these things your serious attention, for they will not escape from mine."[2]

"I write, Monsieur, to answer your last two letters, in which you tell me that instead of sixteen millions, your drafts on the treasury for 1758 will reach twenty-four millions, and that this year they will rise to from thirty-one to thirty-three millions. It seems, then, that there are no bounds to the expenses of Canada. They double almost every year, while you seem to give yourself no concern except to get them paid. Do you suppose that I can advise the King to approve such an administration? or do you think that you can take the immense sum of thirty-three millions out of the royal treasury by merely assuring me that you have signed drafts for it? This, too, for expenses incurred irregularly, often needlessly, always wastefully; which make the fortune of everybody who has the least hand in them, and about which you know so little that after reporting them at sixteen millions, you find two months after that they will reach twenty-four. You are accused of having given the furnishing of provisions to one man, who, un-

[1] *Le Ministre à Bigot,* 19 Jan. 1759.
[2] *Ibid.,* 29 Août, 1759.

der the name of commissary-general, has set what prices he
pleased; of buying for the King at second or third hand what
you might have got from the producer at half the price; of
having in this and other ways made the fortunes of persons
connected with you; and of living in splendor in the midst of
a public misery, which all the letters from the colony agree in
ascribing to bad administration, and in charging M. de Vaudreuil with weakness in not preventing."[1]

These drastic utterances seem to have been partly due to a
letter written by Montcalm in cipher to the Maréchal de Belleisle, then minister of war. It painted the deplorable condition
of Canada, and exposed without reserve the peculations and
robberies of those intrusted with its interests. "It seems," said
the General, "as if they were all hastening to make their fortunes before the loss of the colony; which many of them perhaps desire as a veil to their conduct." He gives among other
cases that of Le Mercier, chief of Canadian artillery, who had
come to Canada as a private soldier twenty years before, and
had so prospered on fraudulent contracts that he would soon
be worth nearly a million. "I have often," continues Montcalm, "spoken of these expenditures to M. de Vaudreuil and
M. Bigot; and each throws the blame on the other."[2] And yet
at the same time Vaudreuil was assuring the Minister that
Bigot was without blame.

Some two months before Montcalm wrote this letter, the
Minister, Berryer, sent a despatch to the Governor and Intendant which filled them with ire and mortification. It ordered
them to do nothing without consulting the general of the
French regulars, not only in matters of war, but in all matters
of administration touching the defence and preservation of
the colony. A plainer proof of confidence on one hand and
distrust on the other could not have been given.[3]

One Querdisien-Tremais was sent from Bordeaux as an
agent of Government to make investigation. He played the
part of detective, wormed himself into the secrets of the confederates, and after six months of patient inquisition traced
out four distinct combinations for public plunder. Explicit or-

[1] *Le Ministre à Bigot, 29 Août, 1759* (second letter of this date).
[2] *Montcalm au Ministre de la Guerre, Lettre confidentielle, 12 Avril, 1759.*
[3] *Le Ministre à Vaudreuil et Bigot, 20 Fév. 1759.*

ders were now given to Bigot, who, seeing no other escape, broke with Cadet, and made him disgorge two millions of stolen money. The Commissary-General and his partners became so terrified that they afterwards gave up nearly seven millions more.[1] Stormy events followed, and the culprits found shelter for a time amid the tumults of war. Peculation did not cease, but a day of reckoning was at hand.

NOTE.—The printed documents of the trial of Bigot and the other peculators include the defence of Bigot, of which the first part occupies 303 quarto pages, and the second part 764. Among the other papers are the arguments for Péan, Varin, Saint-Blin, Boishébert, Martel, Joncaire-Chabert, and several more, along with the elaborate *Jugement rendu*, the *Requêtes du Procureur-Général*, the *Réponse aux Mémoires de M. Bigot et du Sieur Péan*, etc., forming together five quarto volumes, all of which I have carefully examined. These are in the Library of Harvard University. There is another set, also of five volumes, in the Library of the Historical Society of Quebec, containing most of the papers just mentioned, and, bound with them, various others in manuscript, among which are documents in defence of Vaudreuil (printed in part), Estèbe, Corpron, Penisseault, Maurin, and Bréard. I have examined this collection also. The manuscript *Ordres du Roy et Dépêches des Ministres, 1751–1760*, as well as the letters of Vaudreuil, Bougainville, Daine, Doreil, and Montcalm throw much light on the maladministration of the time; as do many contemporary documents, notably those entitled *Mémoire sur les Fraudes commises dans la Colonie*, *État présent du Canada*, and *Mémoire sur le Canada* (Archives Nationales). The remarkable anonymous work printed by the Historical Society of Quebec under the title *Mémoires sur le Canada depuis 1749 jusqu'à 1760*, is full of curious matter concerning Bigot and his associates which squares well with other evidence. This is the source from which Smith, in his *History of Canada* (Quebec, 1815), drew most of his information on the subject. A manuscript which seems to be the original draft of this valuable document was preserved at the Bastile, and, with other papers, was thrown into the street when that castle was destroyed. They were gathered up, and afterwards bought by a Russian named Dubrowski, who carried them to St. Petersburg. Lord Dufferin, when minister there, procured a copy of the manuscript in question, which is now in the keeping of Abbé H. Verreau at Montreal, to whose kindness I owe the opportunity of examining it. In substance it differs little from the printed work, though the language and the arrangement often vary from it. The author, whoever he may have been, was deeply versed in Canadian affairs of the time, and though often caustic, is generally trustworthy.

[1] *Procès de Bigot, Cadet, et autres, Mémoire pour François Bigot, 3ᵐᵉ partie.*

Chapter XVIII

1757–1758

PITT

Frederic of Prussia • The Coalition against him • His desperate Position • Rossbach • Leuthen • Reverses of England • Weakness of the Ministry • A Change • Pitt and Newcastle • Character of Pitt • Sources of his Power • His Aims • Louis XV. • Pompadour • She controls the Court and directs the War • Gloomy Prospects of England • Disasters • The new Ministry • Inspiring Influence of Pitt • The Tide turns • British Victories • Pitt's Plans for America • Louisbourg, Ticonderoga, Duquesne • New Commanders • Naval Battles

---

THE WAR kindled in the American forest was now raging in full conflagration among the kingdoms of Europe; and in the midst stood Frederic of Prussia, a veritable fire-king. He had learned through secret agents that he was to be attacked, and that the wrath of Maria Theresa with her two allies, Pompadour and the Empress of Russia, was soon to wreak itself upon him. With his usual prompt audacity he anticipated his enemies, marched into Saxony, and began the Continental war. His position seemed desperate. England, sundered from Austria, her old ally, had made common cause with him; but he had no other friend worth the counting. France, Russia, Austria, Sweden, Saxony, the collective Germanic Empire, and most of the smaller German States had joined hands for his ruin, eager to crush him and divide the spoil, parcelling out his dominions among themselves in advance by solemn mutual compact. Against the five millions of Prussia were arrayed populations of more than a hundred millions. The little kingdom was open on all sides to attack, and her enemies were spurred on by the bitterest animosity. It was thought that one campaign would end the war. The war lasted seven years, and Prussia came out of it triumphant. Such a warrior as her indomitable king Europe has rarely seen. If the Seven Years War made the maritime and colonial greatness of England, it also raised Prussia to the rank of a first-class Power.

Frederic began with a victory, routing the Austrians in one of the fiercest of recorded conflicts, the battle of Prague. Then in his turn he was beaten at Kolin. All seemed lost. The hosts of the coalition were rolling in upon him like a deluge. Surrounded by enemies, in the jaws of destruction, hoping for little but to die in battle, this strange hero solaced himself with an exhaustless effusion of bad verses, sometimes mournful, sometimes cynical, sometimes indignant, and sometimes breathing a dauntless resolution; till, when his hour came, he threw down his pen to achieve those feats of arms which stamp him one of the foremost soldiers of the world.

The French and Imperialists, in overwhelming force, thought to crush him at Rossbach. He put them to shameful rout; and then, instead of bonfires and Te Deums, mocked at them in doggerel rhymes of amazing indecency. While he was beating the French, the Austrians took Silesia from him. He marched to recover it, found them strongly posted at Leuthen, eighty thousand men against thirty thousand, and without hesitation resolved to attack them. Never was he more heroic than on the eve of this, his crowning triumph. "The hour is at hand," he said to his generals. "I mean, in spite of the rules of military art, to attack Prince Karl's army, which is nearly thrice our own. This risk I must run, or all is lost. We must beat him or die, all of us, before his batteries." He burst unawares upon the Austrian right, and rolled their whole host together, corps upon corps, in a tumult of irretrievable ruin.

While her great ally was reaping a full harvest of laurels, England, dragged into the Continental war because that apple of discord, Hanover, belonged to her King, found little but humiliation. Minorca was wrested from her, and the Ministry had an innocent man shot to avert from themselves the popular indignation; while the same Ministry, scared by a phantom of invasion, brought over German troops to defend British soil. But now an event took place pregnant with glorious consequence. The reins of power fell into the hands of William Pitt. He had already held them for a brief space, forced into office at the end of 1756 by popular clamor, in spite of the Whig leaders and against the wishes of the King. But the place was untenable. Newcastle's Parliament would not support him; the Duke of Cumberland opposed him; the King hated him; and in April, 1757, he was dismissed. Then ensued eleven weeks of bickering and dispute, during which, in the midst of a great war, England was left without a government. It became clear that none was possible without Pitt; and none with him could be permanent and strong unless joined with those influences which had thus far controlled the majorities of Parliament. Therefore an extraordinary union was brought about; Lord Chesterfield acting as go-between to reconcile the ill-assorted pair. One of them brought to the alliance the confidence and support of the people; the other, Court management, borough interest, and parliamentary connections. Newcastle was made First Lord of the Treasury, and Pitt, the old enemy who had repeatedly browbeat and ridiculed him, became Secretary of State, with the lead of the House of Commons and full control of the war and foreign affairs. It was a partnership of magpie and eagle. The dirty work of government, intrigue, bribery, and all the patronage that did not affect the war, fell to the share of the old politician. If Pitt could appoint generals, admirals, and ambassadors, Newcastle was welcome to the rest. "I will borrow the Duke's majorities to carry on the government," said the new secretary; and with the audacious self-confidence that was one of his traits, he told the Duke of Devonshire, "I am sure that I can save this country, and that nobody else can." England hailed with one acclaim the undaunted leader who asked for no reward but the honor of serving her. The hour had found the man. For the next four years this imposing figure towers supreme in British history.

He had glaring faults, some of them of a sort not to have been expected in him. Vanity, the common weakness of small minds, was the most disfiguring foible of this great one. He had not the simplicity which becomes greatness so well. He could give himself theatrical airs, strike attitudes, and dart stage lightnings from his eyes; yet he was formidable even in his affectations. Behind his great intellectual powers lay a burning enthusiasm, a force of passion and fierce intensity of will, that gave redoubled impetus to the fiery shafts of his eloquence; and the haughty and masterful nature of the man had its share in the ascendency which he long held over Parliament. He would blast the labored argument of an adversary by a look of scorn or a contemptuous wave of the hand.

The Great Commoner was not a man of the people in the popular sense of that hackneyed phrase. Though himself poor, being a younger son, he came of a rich and influential family; he was patrician at heart; both his faults and his virtues, his proud incorruptibility and passionate, domineering patriotism, bore the patrician stamp. Yet he loved liberty and he loved the people, because they were the English people. The effusive humanitarianism of to-day had no part in him, and the democracy of to-day would detest him. Yet to the middle-class England of his own time, that unenfranchised England which had little representation in Parliament, he was a voice, an inspiration, and a tower of strength. He would not flatter the people; but, turning with contempt from the tricks and devices of official politics, he threw himself with a confidence that never wavered on their patriotism and public spirit. They answered him with a boundless trust, asked but to follow his lead, gave him without stint their money and their blood, loved him for his domestic virtues and his disinterestedness, believed him even in his self-contradiction, and idolized him even in his bursts of arrogant passion. It was he who waked England from her lethargy, shook off the spell that Newcastle and his fellow-enchanters had cast over her, and taught her to know herself again. A heart that beat in unison with all that was British found responsive throbs in every corner of the vast empire that through him was to become more vast. With the instinct of his fervid patriotism he would join all its far-extended members into one, not by vain assertions of parliamentary supremacy, but by bonds of sympathy and ties of a common freedom and a common cause.

The passion for power and glory subdued in him all the sordid parts of humanity, and he made the power and glory of England one with his own. He could change front through resentment or through policy; but in whatever path he moved, his objects were the same: not to curb the power of France in America, but to annihilate it; crush her navy, cripple her foreign trade, ruin her in India, in Africa, and wherever else, east or west, she had found foothold; gain for England the mastery of the seas, open to her the great high-

ways of the globe, make her supreme in commerce and colonization; and while limiting the activities of her rival to the
European continent, give to her the whole world for a sphere.

To this British Roman was opposed the pampered Sardanapalus of Versailles, with the silken favorite who by calculated adultery had bought the power to ruin France. The
Marquise de Pompadour, who began life as Jeanne Poisson,—Jane Fish,—daughter of the head clerk of a banking
house, who then became wife of a rich financier, and then, as
mistress of the King, rose to a pinnacle of gilded ignominy,
chose this time to turn out of office the two ministers who
had shown most ability and force,—Argenson, head of the
department of war, and Machault, head of the marine and
colonies; the one because he was not subservient to her will,
and the other because he had unwittingly touched the self-
love of her royal paramour. She aspired to a share in the conduct of the war, and not only made and unmade ministers
and generals, but discussed campaigns and battles with them,
while they listened to her prating with a show of obsequious
respect, since to lose her favor was to risk losing all. A few
months later, when blows fell heavy and fast, she turned a
deaf ear to representations of financial straits and military disasters, played the heroine, affected a greatness of soul superior to misfortune, and in her perfumed boudoir varied her
tiresome graces by posing as a Roman matron. In fact she
never wavered in her spite against Frederic, and her fortitude
was perfect in bearing the sufferings of others and defying
dangers that could not touch her.

When Pitt took office it was not over France, but over England that the clouds hung dense and black. Her prospects
were of the gloomiest. "Whoever is in or whoever is out,"
wrote Chesterfield, "I am sure we are undone both at home
and abroad: at home by our increasing debt and expenses;
abroad by our ill-luck and incapacity. We are no longer a nation." And his despondency was shared by many at the beginning of the most triumphant Administration in British
history. The shuffling weakness of his predecessors had left
Pitt a heritage of tribulation. From America came news of
Loudon's manifold failures; from Germany that of the miscarriage of the Duke of Cumberland, who, at the head of an

army of Germans in British pay, had been forced to sign the convention of Kloster-Zeven, by which he promised to disband them. To these disasters was added a third, of which the new Government alone had to bear the burden. At the end of summer Pitt sent a great expedition to attack Rochefort; the military and naval commanders disagreed, and the consequence was failure. There was no light except from far-off India, where Clive won the great victory of Plassey, avenged the Black Hole of Calcutta, and prepared the ruin of the French power and the undisputed ascendency of England.

If the English had small cause as yet to rejoice in their own successes, they found comfort in those of their Prussian allies. The rout of the French at Rossbach and of the Austrians at Leuthen spread joy through their island. More than this, they felt that they had found at last a leader after their own heart; and the consciousness regenerated them. For the paltering imbecility of the old Ministry they had the unconquerable courage, the iron purpose, the unwavering faith, the inextinguishable hope, of the new one. "England has long been in labor," said Frederic of Prussia, "and at last she has brought forth a man." It was not only that instead of weak commanders Pitt gave her strong ones; the same men who had served her feebly under the blight of the Newcastle Administration served her manfully and well under his robust impulsion. "Nobody ever entered his closet," said Colonel Barré, "who did not come out of it a braver man." That inspiration was felt wherever the British flag waved. Zeal awakened with the assurance that conspicuous merit was sure of its reward, and that no officer who did his duty would now be made a sacrifice, like Admiral Byng, to appease public indignation at ministerial failures. As Nature, languishing in chill vapors and dull smothering fogs, revives at the touch of the sun, so did England spring into fresh life under the kindling influence of one great man.

With the opening of the year 1758 her course of Continental victories began. The Duke of Cumberland, the King's son, was recalled in disgrace, and a general of another stamp, Prince Ferdinand of Brunswick, was placed in command of the Germans in British pay, with the contingent of English troops now added to them. The French, too, changed com-

manders. The Duke of Richelieu, a dissolute old beau, returned to Paris to spend in heartless gallantries the wealth he
had gained by plunder; and a young soldier-churchman, the
Comte de Clermont, took his place. Prince Ferdinand pushed
him hard with an inferior force, drove him out of Hanover,
and captured eleven thousand of his soldiers. Clermont was
recalled, and was succeeded by Contades, another incapable.
One of his subordinates won for him the battle of Lutterberg;
but the generalship of Ferdinand made it a barren victory,
and the campaign remained a success for the English. They
made descents on the French coasts, captured St.-Servan, a
suburb of St.-Malo, and burned three ships of the line,
twenty-four privateers, and sixty merchantmen; then entered
Cherbourg, destroyed the forts, carried off or spiked the cannon, and burned twenty-seven vessels,—a success partially
offset by a failure on the coast of Brittany, where they were
repulsed with some loss. In Africa they drove the French from
the Guinea coast, and seized their establishment at Senegal.

It was towards America that Pitt turned his heartiest efforts. His first aim was to take Louisbourg, as a step towards
taking Quebec; then Ticonderoga, that thorn in the side of
the northern colonies; and lastly Fort Duquesne, the Key of
the Great West. He recalled Loudon, for whom he had a
fierce contempt; but there were influences which he could not
disregard, and Major-General Abercromby, who was next in
order of rank, an indifferent soldier, though a veteran in
years, was allowed to succeed him, and lead in person the
attack on Ticonderoga.[1] Pitt hoped that Brigadier Lord
Howe, an admirable officer, who was joined with Abercromby, would be the real commander, and make amends for
all shortcomings of his chief. To command the Louisbourg
expedition, Colonel Jeffrey Amherst was recalled from the
German war, and made at one leap a major-general.[2] He was
energetic and resolute, somewhat cautious and slow, but with
a bulldog tenacity of grip. Under him were three brigadiers,
Whitmore, Lawrence, and Wolfe, of whom the youngest is

[1] *Order, War Office, 19 Dec. 1757.*
[2] *Pitt to Abercromby, 27 Jan. 1758. Instructions for our Trusty and Well-beloved
Jeffrey Amherst, Esq., Major-General of our Forces in North America, 3 March,
1758.*

the most noteworthy. In the luckless Rochefort expedition, Colonel James Wolfe was conspicuous by a dashing gallantry that did not escape the eye of Pitt, always on the watch for men to do his work. The young officer was ardent, headlong, void of fear, often rash, almost fanatical in his devotion to military duty, and reckless of life when the glory of England or his own was at stake. The third expedition, that against Fort Duquesne, was given to Brigadier John Forbes, whose qualities well fitted him for the task.

During his first short term of office, Pitt had given a new species of troops to the British army. These were the Scotch Highlanders, who had risen against the House of Hanover in 1745, and would rise against it again should France accomplish her favorite scheme of throwing a force into Scotland to excite another insurrection for the Stuarts. But they would be useful to fight the French abroad, though dangerous as their possible allies at home; and two regiments of them were now ordered to America.

Delay had been the ruin of the last year's attempt against Louisbourg. This time preparation was urged on apace; and before the end of winter two fleets had put to sea: one, under Admiral Boscawen, was destined for Louisbourg; while the other, under Admiral Osborn, sailed for the Mediterranean to intercept the French fleet of Admiral La Clue, who was about to sail from Toulon for America. Osborn, cruising between the coasts of Spain and Africa, barred the way to the Straits of Gibraltar, and kept his enemy imprisoned. La Clue made no attempt to force a passage; but several combats of detached ships took place, one of which is too remarkable to pass unnoticed. Captain Gardiner of the "Monmouth," a ship of four hundred and seventy men and sixty-four guns, engaged the French ship "Foudroyant," carrying a thousand men and eighty-four guns of heavier metal than those of the Englishman. Gardiner had lately been reproved by Anson, First Lord of the Admiralty, for some alleged misconduct or shortcoming, and he thought of nothing but retrieving his honor. "We must take her," he said to his crew as the "Foudroyant" hove in sight. "She looks more than a match for us, but I will not quit her while this ship can swim or I have a soul left alive;" and the sailors answered with cheers. The fight was long and furious. Gardiner was killed by a musket shot, begging his first lieutenant with his dying breath not to haul down his flag. The lieutenant nailed it to the mast. At length the "Foudroyant" ceased from thundering, struck her colors, and was carried a prize to England.[1]

The typical British naval officer of that time was a rugged sea-dog, a tough and stubborn fighter, though no more so than the politer generations that followed, at home on the quarter-deck, but no ornament to the drawing-room, by reason of what his contemporary, Entick, the strenuous chronicler of the war, calls, not unapprovingly, "the ferocity of his manners." While Osborn held La Clue imprisoned at Toulon, Sir Edward Hawke, worthy leader of such men, sailed with seven ships of the line and three frigates to intercept a French squadron from Rochefort convoying a fleet of transports with troops for America. The French ships cut their cables and ran for the shore, where most of them stranded in the mud, and some threw cannon and munitions overboard to float themselves. The expedition was broken up. Of the many ships fitted out this year for the succor of Canada and Louisbourg, comparatively few reached their destination, and these for the most part singly or by twos and threes.

Meanwhile Admiral Boscawen with his fleet bore away for Halifax, the place of rendezvous, and Amherst, in the ship "Dublin," followed in his wake.

[1] Entick, III. 56–60.

Chapter XIX

1758

LOUISBOURG

Condition of the Fortress • Arrival of the English • Gallantry of Wolfe • The English Camp • The Siege begun • Progress of the Besiegers • Sallies of the French • Madame Drucour • Courtesies of War •. French Ships destroyed • Conflagration • Fury of the Bombardment • Exploit of English Sailors • The End near • The White Flag • Surrender • Reception of the News in England and America • Wolfe not satisfied • His Letters to Amherst • He destroys Gaspé • Returns to England

---

THE STORMY coast of Cape Breton is indented by a small land-locked bay, between which and the ocean lies a tongue of land dotted with a few grazing sheep, and intersected by rows of stone that mark more or less distinctly the lines of what once were streets. Green mounds and embankments of earth enclose the whole space, and beneath the highest of them yawn arches and caverns of ancient masonry. This grassy solitude was once the "Dunkirk of America;" the vaulted caverns where the sheep find shelter from the rain were casemates where terrified women sought refuge from storms of shot and shell, and the shapeless green mounds were citadel, bastion, rampart, and glacis. Here stood Louisbourg; and not all the efforts of its conquerors, nor all the havoc of succeeding times, have availed to efface it. Men in hundreds toiled for months with lever, spade, and gunpowder in the work of destruction, and for more than a century it has served as a stone quarry; but the remains of its vast defences still tell their tale of human valor and human woe.

Stand on the mounds that were once the King's Bastion. The glistening sea spreads eastward three thousand miles, and its waves meet their first rebuff against this iron coast. Lighthouse Point is white with foam; jets of spray spout from the rocks of Goat Island; mist curls in clouds from the seething surf that lashes the crags of Black Point, and the sea boils like a caldron among the reefs by the harbor's mouth; but on the calm water within, the small fishing vessels rest tranquil at their moorings. Beyond lies a hamlet of fishermen by the edge of the water, and a few scattered dwellings dot the rough hills, bristled with stunted firs, that gird the quiet basin; while close at hand, within the precinct of the vanished fortress, stand two small farmhouses. All else is a solitude of ocean, rock, marsh, and forest.[1]

At the beginning of June, 1758, the place wore another aspect. Since the peace of Aix-la-Chapelle vast sums had been spent in repairing and strengthening it; and Louisbourg was the strongest fortress in French or British America. Nevertheless it had its weaknesses. The original plan of the works had not been fully carried out; and owing, it is said, to the bad quality of the mortar, the masonry of the ramparts was in so poor a condition that it had been replaced in some parts with fascines. The circuit of the fortifications was more than a mile and a half, and the town contained about four thousand inhabitants. The best buildings in it were the convent, the hospital, the King's storehouses, and the chapel and governor's quarters, which were under the same roof. Of the private houses, only seven or eight were of stone, the rest being humble wooden structures, suited to a population of fishermen. The garrison consisted of the battalions of Artois, Bourgogne, Cambis, and Volontaires Étrangers, with two companies of artillery and twenty-four of colony troops from Canada,—in all three thousand and eighty regular troops, besides officers;[2] and to these were added a body of armed inhabitants and a band of Indians. In the harbor were five ships of the line and seven frigates, carrying in all five hundred and forty-four guns and about three thousand men.[3] Two hundred and nineteen cannon and seventeen mortars were mounted on the walls and outworks.[4] Of these last the most

[1] Louisbourg is described as I saw it ten days before writing the above, after an easterly gale.

[2] *Journal du Siége de Louisbourg.* Twenty-nine hundred regulars were able to bear arms when the siege began. *Houllière, Commandant des Troupes, au Ministre, 6 Août, 1758.*

[3] Le Prudent, 74 guns; Entreprenant, 74; Capricieux, 64; Célèbre, 64; Bienfaisant, 64; Apollon, 50; Chèvre, 22; Biche, 18; Fidèle, 22; Écho, 26; Aréthuse, 36; Comète, 30. The Bizarre, 64, sailed for France on the eighth of June, and was followed by the Comète.

[4] *État d'Artillerie,* appended to the Journal of Drucour. There were also forty-four cannon in reserve.

important were the Grand Battery on the shore of the harbor opposite its mouth, and the Island Battery on the rocky islet at its entrance.

The strongest front of the works was on the land side, along the base of the peninsular triangle on which the town stood. This front, about twelve hundred yards in extent, reached from the sea on the left to the harbor on the right, and consisted of four bastions with their connecting curtains, the Princess's, the Queen's, the King's, and the Dauphin's. The King's Bastion formed part of the citadel. The glacis before it sloped down to an extensive marsh, which, with an adjacent pond, completely protected this part of the line. On the right, however, towards the harbor, the ground was high enough to offer advantages to an enemy, as was also the case, to a less degree, on the left, towards the sea. The best defence of Louisbourg was the craggy shore, that, for leagues on either hand, was accessible only at a few points, and even there with difficulty. All these points were vigilantly watched.

There had been signs of the enemy from the first opening of spring. In the intervals of fog, rain, and snow-squalls, sails were seen hovering on the distant sea; and during the latter part of May a squadron of nine ships cruised off the mouth of the harbor, appearing and disappearing, sometimes driven away by gales, sometimes lost in fogs, and sometimes approaching to within cannon-shot of the batteries. Their object was to blockade the port,—in which they failed; for French ships had come in at intervals, till, as we have seen, twelve of them lay safe anchored in the harbor, with more than a year's supply of provisions for the garrison.

At length, on the first of June, the southeastern horizon was white with a cloud of canvas. The long-expected crisis was come. Drucour, the governor, sent two thousand regulars, with about a thousand militia and Indians, to guard the various landing-places; and the rest, aided by the sailors, remained to hold the town.[1]

At the end of May Admiral Boscawen was at Halifax with twenty-three ships of the line, eighteen frigates and fire-ships, and a fleet of transports, on board of which were eleven thousand and six hundred soldiers, all regulars, except five

[1] *Rapport de Drucour. Journal du Siége.*

hundred provincial rangers.[1] Amherst had not yet arrived, and on the twenty-eighth, Boscawen, in pursuance of his orders and to prevent loss of time, put to sea without him; but scarcely had the fleet sailed out of Halifax, when they met the ship that bore the expected general. Amherst took command of the troops; and the expedition held its way till the second of June, when they saw the rocky shore-line of Cape Breton, and descried the masts of the French squadron in the harbor of Louisbourg.

Boscawen sailed into Gabarus Bay. The sea was rough; but in the afternoon Amherst, Lawrence, and Wolfe, with a number of naval officers, reconnoitred the shore in boats, coasting it for miles, and approaching it as near as the French batteries would permit. The rocks were white with surf, and every accessible point was strongly guarded. Boscawen saw little chance of success. He sent for his captains, and consulted them separately. They thought, like him, that it would be rash to attempt a landing, and proposed a council of war. One of them alone, an old sea officer named Ferguson, advised his commander to take the responsibility himself, hold no council, and make the attempt at every risk. Boscawen took his advice, and declared that he would not leave Gabarus Bay till he had fulfilled his instructions and set the troops on shore.[2]

West of Louisbourg there were three accessible places, Freshwater Cove, four miles from the town, and Flat Point, and White Point, which were nearer, the last being within a mile of the fortifications. East of the town there was an inlet called Lorambec, also available for landing. In order to distract the attention of the enemy, it was resolved to threaten all these places, and to form the troops into three divisions, two of which, under Lawrence and Whitmore, were to advance towards Flat Point and White Point, while a detached regiment was to make a feint at Lorambec. Wolfe, with the third division, was to make the real attack and try to force a landing at Freshwater Cove, which, as it proved, was the

---

[1] Of this force, according to Mante, only 9,900 were fit for duty. The table printed by Knox (I. 127) shows a total of 11,112, besides officers, artillery, and rangers. The *Authentic Account of the Reduction of Louisbourg, by a Spectator*, puts the force at 11,326 men, besides officers. Entick makes the whole 11,936.

[2] Entick, III. 224.

most strongly defended of all. When on shore Wolfe was an habitual invalid, and when at sea every heave of the ship made him wretched; but his ardor was unquenchable. Before leaving England he wrote to a friend: "Being of the profession of arms, I would seek all occasions to serve; and therefore have thrown myself in the way of the American war, though I know that the very passage threatens my life, and that my constitution must be utterly ruined and undone."

On the next day, the third, the surf was so high that nothing could be attempted. On the fourth there was a thick fog and a gale. The frigate "Trent" struck on a rock, and some of the transports were near being stranded. On the fifth there was another fog and a raging surf. On the sixth there was fog, with rain in the morning and better weather towards noon, whereupon the signal was made and the troops entered the boats; but the sea rose again, and they were ordered back to the ships. On the seventh more fog and more surf till night, when the sea grew calmer, and orders were given for another attempt. At two in the morning of the eighth the troops were in the boats again. At daybreak the frigates of the squadron, anchoring before each point of real or pretended attack, opened a fierce cannonade on the French intrenchments; and, a quarter of an hour after, the three divisions rowed towards the shore. That of the left, under Wolfe, consisted of four companies of grenadiers, with the light infantry and New England rangers, followed and supported by Fraser's Highlanders and eight more companies of grenadiers. They pulled for Freshwater Cove. Here there was a crescent-shaped beach, a quarter of a mile long, with rocks at each end. On the shore above, about a thousand Frenchmen, under Lieutenant-Colonel de Saint-Julien, lay behind entrenchments covered in front by spruce and fir trees, felled and laid on the ground with the tops outward.[1] Eight cannon and swivels were planted to sweep every part of the beach and its approaches, and these pieces were masked by young evergreens stuck in the ground before them.

The English were allowed to come within close range un-

[1] Drucour reports 985 soldiers as stationed here under Saint-Julien; there were also some Indians. Freshwater Cove, otherwise Kennington Cove, was called La Cormorandière by the French.

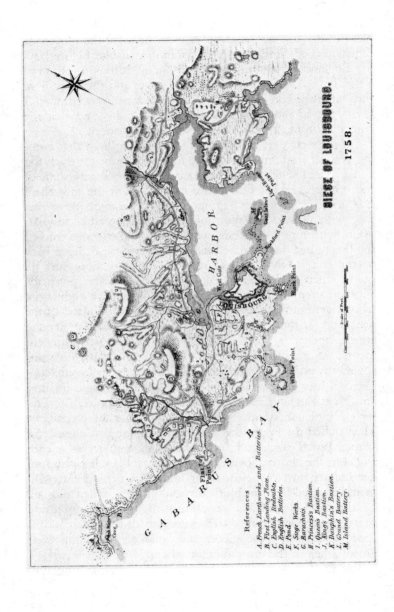

References

A. French Earthworks and Batteries.
B. First Landing Place.
C. English Redoubts.
D. English Batteries.
E. Pond.
F. Siege Works.
G. Barachois.
H. Princess Bastion.
I. Queen's Bastion.
J. King's Bastion.
K. Dauphin's Bastion.
L. Grand Batery.
M. Island Batery.

SIEGE OF LOUISBOURG.

1758.

Scale of Feet.

molested. Then the batteries opened, and a deadly storm of grape and musketry was poured upon the boats. It was clear in an instant that to advance farther would be destruction; and Wolfe waved his hand as a signal to sheer off. At some distance on the right, and little exposed to the fire, were three boats of light infantry under Lieutenants Hopkins and Brown and Ensign Grant; who, mistaking the signal or wilfully misinterpreting it, made directly for the shore before them. It was a few rods east of the beach; a craggy coast and a strand strewn with rocks and lashed with breakers, but sheltered from the cannon by a small projecting point. The three officers leaped ashore, followed by their men. Wolfe saw the movement, and hastened to support it. The boat of Major Scott, who commanded the light infantry and rangers, next came up, and was stove in an instant; but Scott gained the shore, climbed the crags, and found himself with ten men in front of some seventy French and Indians. Half his followers were killed and wounded, and three bullets were shot through his clothes; but with admirable gallantry he held his ground till others came to his aid.[1] The remaining boats now reached the landing. Many were stove among the rocks, and others were overset; some of the men were dragged back by the surf and drowned; some lost their muskets, and were drenched to the skin: but the greater part got safe ashore. Among the foremost was seen the tall, attenuated form of Brigadier Wolfe, armed with nothing but a cane, as he leaped into the surf and climbed the crags with his soldiers. As they reached the top they formed in compact order, and attacked and carried with the bayonet the nearest French battery, a few rods distant. The division of Lawrence soon came up; and as the attention of the enemy was now distracted, they made their landing with little opposition at the farther end of the beach, whither they were followed by Amherst himself. The French, attacked on right and left, and fearing, with good reason, that they would be cut off from the town, abandoned all their cannon and fled into the woods. About seventy of them were captured and fifty killed. The rest, circling among the hills and around the marshes, made their way to Louis-

[1] Pichon, *Mémoires du Cap-Breton*, 284.

bourg, and those at the intermediate posts joined their flight. The English followed through a matted growth of firs till they reached the cleared ground; when the cannon, opening on them from the ramparts, stopped the pursuit. The first move of the great game was played and won.[1]

Amherst made his camp just beyond range of the French cannon, and Flat Point Cove was chosen as the landing-place of guns and stores. Clearing the ground, making roads, and pitching tents filled the rest of the day. At night there was a glare of flames from the direction of the town. The French had abandoned the Grand Battery after setting fire to the buildings in it and to the houses and fish-stages along the shore of the harbor. During the following days stores were landed as fast as the surf would permit: but the task was so difficult that from first to last more than a hundred boats were stove in accomplishing it; and such was the violence of the waves that none of the siege-guns could be got ashore till the eighteenth. The camp extended two miles along a stream that flowed down to the Cove among the low, woody hills that curved around the town and harbor. Redoubts were made to protect its front, and blockhouses to guard its left and rear from the bands of Acadians known to be hovering in the woods.

Wolfe, with twelve hundred men, made his way six or seven miles round the harbor, took possession of the battery at Lighthouse Point which the French had abandoned, planted guns and mortars, and opened fire on the Island Battery that guarded the entrance. Other guns were placed at different points along the shore, and soon opened on the French ships. The ships and batteries replied. The artillery fight raged night and day; till on the twenty-fifth the island guns were dismounted and silenced. Wolfe then strengthened his posts, secured his communications, and returned to the main army in front of the town.

Amherst had reconnoitred the ground and chosen a hillock

[1] *Journal of Amherst*, in Mante, 117. *Amherst to Pitt, 11 June, 1758. Authentic Account of the Reduction of Louisbourg, by a Spectator*, 11. *General Orders of Amherst, 3–7 June, 1759. Letter from an Officer*, in Knox, I. 191; Entick, III. 225. The French accounts generally agree in essentials with the English. The English lost one hundred and nine, killed, wounded, and drowned.

at the edge of the marsh, less than half a mile from the ramparts, as the point for opening his trenches. A road with an epaulement to protect it must first be made to the spot; and as the way was over a tract of deep mud covered with waterweeds and moss, the labor was prodigious. A thousand men worked at it day and night under the fire of the town and ships.

When the French looked landward from their ramparts they could see scarcely a sign of the impending storm. Behind them Wolfe's cannon were playing busily from Lighthouse Point and the heights around the harbor; but, before them, the broad flat marsh and the low hills seemed almost a solitude. Two miles distant, they could descry some of the English tents; but the greater part were hidden by the inequalities of the ground. On the right, a prolongation of the harbor reached nearly half a mile beyond the town, ending in a small lagoon formed by a projecting sandbar, and known as the Barachois. Near this bar lay moored the little frigate "Aréthuse," under a gallant officer named Vauquelin. Her position was a perilous one; but so long as she could maintain it she could sweep with her fire the ground before the works, and seriously impede the operations of the enemy. The other naval captains were less venturous; and when the English landed, they wanted to leave the harbor and save their ships. Drucour insisted that they should stay to aid the defence, and they complied; but soon left their moorings and anchored as close as possible under the guns of the town, in order to escape the fire of Wolfe's batteries. Hence there was great murmuring among the military officers, who would have had them engage the hostile guns at short range. The frigate "Écho," under cover of a fog, had been sent to Quebec for aid; but she was chased and captured; and, a day or two after, the French saw her pass the mouth of the harbor with an English flag at her mast-head.

When Wolfe had silenced the Island Battery, a new and imminent danger threatened Louisbourg. Boscawen might enter the harbor, overpower the French naval force, and cannonade the town on its weakest side. Therefore Drucour resolved to sink four large ships at the entrance; and on a dark and foggy night this was successfully accomplished. Two more vessels were afterwards sunk, and the harbor was then thought safe.

The English had at last finished their preparations, and were urging on the siege with determined vigor. The landward view was a solitude no longer. They could be seen in multitudes piling earth and fascines beyond the hillock at the edge of the marsh. On the twenty-fifth they occupied the hillock itself, and fortified themselves there under a shower of bombs. Then they threw up earth on the right, and pushed their approaches towards the Barachois, in spite of a hot fire from the frigate "Aréthuse." Next they appeared on the left towards the sea about a third of a mile from the Princess's Bastion. It was Wolfe, with a strong detachment, throwing up a redoubt and opening an entrenchment. Late on the night of the ninth of July six hundred French troops sallied to interrupt the work. The English grenadiers in the trenches fought stubbornly with bayonet and sword, but were forced back to the second line, where a desperate conflict in the dark took place; and after severe loss on both sides the French were driven back. Some days before, there had been another sortie on the opposite side, near the Barachois, resulting in a repulse of the French and the seizure by Wolfe of a more advanced position.

Various courtesies were exchanged between the two commanders. Drucour, on occasion of a flag of truce, wrote to Amherst that there was a surgeon of uncommon skill in Louisbourg, whose services were at the command of any English officer who might need them. Amherst on his part sent to his enemy letters and messages from wounded Frenchmen in his hands, adding his compliments to Madame Drucour, with an expression of regret for the disquiet to which she was exposed, begging her at the same time to accept a gift of pineapples from the West Indies. She returned his courtesy by sending him a basket of wine; after which amenities the cannon roared again. Madame Drucour was a woman of heroic spirit. Every day she was on the ramparts, where her presence roused the soldiers to enthusiasm; and every day with her own hand she fired three cannon to encourage them.

The English lines grew closer and closer, and their fire more and more destructive. Desgouttes, the naval commander, withdrew the "Aréthuse" from her exposed position, where her fire had greatly annoyed the besiegers. The shot-holes in her sides were plugged up, and in the dark night of the fourteenth of July she was towed through the obstructions in the mouth of the harbor, and sent to France to report the situation of Louisbourg. More fortunate than her predecessor, she escaped the English in a fog. Only five vessels now remained afloat in the harbor, and these were feebly manned, as the greater part of their officers and crews had come ashore, to the number of two thousand, lodging under tents in the town, amid the scarcely suppressed murmurs of the army officers.

On the eighth of July news came that the partisan Boishébert was approaching with four hundred Acadians, Canadians, and Micmacs to attack the English outposts and detachments. He did little or nothing, however, besides capturing a few stragglers. On the sixteenth, early in the evening, a party of English, led by Wolfe, dashed forward, drove off a band of French volunteers, seized a rising ground called Hauteur-de-la-Potence, or Gallows Hill, and began to entrench themselves scarcely three hundred yards from the Dauphin's Bastion. The town opened on them furiously with grape-shot; but in the intervals of the firing the sound of their picks and spades could plainly be heard. In the morning they were seen throwing up earth like moles as they burrowed their way forward; and on the twenty-first they opened another parallel, within two hundred yards of the rampart. Still their sappers pushed on. Every day they had more guns in position, and on right and left their fire grew hotter. Their pickets made a lodgment along the foot of the glacis, and fired up the slope at the French in the covered way.

The twenty-first was a memorable day. In the afternoon a bomb fell on the ship "Célèbre" and set her on fire. An explosion followed. The few men on board could not save her, and she drifted from her moorings. The wind blew the flames into the rigging of the "Entreprenant," and then into that of the "Capricieux." At night all three were in full blaze; for when the fire broke out the English batteries turned on them a tempest of shot and shell to prevent it from being extinguished. The glare of the triple conflagration lighted up the town, the trenches, the harbor, and the surrounding hills, while the burning ships shot off their guns at random as they slowly drifted westward, and grounded at last near the Barachois. In the morning they were consumed to the water's edge; and of all the squadron the "Prudent" and the "Bienfaisant" alone were left.

In the citadel, of which the King's Bastion formed the front, there was a large oblong stone building containing the chapel, lodgings for men and officers, and at the southern end the quarters of the Governor. On the morning after the burning of the ships a shell fell through the roof among a party of soldiers in the chamber below, burst, and set the place on fire. In half an hour the chapel and all the northern part of the building were in flames; and no sooner did the smoke rise above the bastion than the English threw into it a steady shower of missiles. Yet soldiers, sailors, and inhabitants hastened to the spot, and labored desperately to check the fire. They saved the end occupied by Drucour and his wife, but all the rest was destroyed. Under the adjacent rampart were the casemates, one of which was crowded with wounded officers, and the rest with women and children seeking shelter in these subterranean dens. Before the entrances there was a long barrier of timber to protect them from exploding shells; and as the wind blew the flames towards it, there was danger that it would take fire and suffocate those within. They rushed out, crazed with fright, and ran hither and thither with outcries and shrieks amid the storm of iron.

In the neighboring Queen's Bastion was a large range of barracks built of wood by the New England troops after their capture of the fortress in 1745. So flimsy and combustible was it that the French writers call it a "house of cards" and "a paper of matches." Here were lodged the greater part of the garrison: but such was the danger of fire, that they were now ordered to leave it; and they accordingly lay in the streets or along the foot of the ramparts, under shelters of timber which gave some little protection against bombs. The order was well timed; for on the night after the fire in the King's Bastion, a shell filled with combustibles set this building also in flames. A fearful scene ensued. All the English batteries opened upon it. The roar of mortars and cannon, the rushing and screaming of round-shot and grape, the hissing of fuses and the explosion of grenades and bombs mingled with a storm of musketry from the covered way and trenches; while, by the glare of the conflagration, the English regiments were seen drawn up in battle array, before the ramparts, as if preparing for an assault.

Two days after, at one o'clock in the morning, a burst of loud cheers was heard in the distance, followed by confused cries and the noise of musketry, which lasted but a moment. Six hundred English sailors had silently rowed into the harbor and seized the two remaining ships, the "Prudent" and the "Bienfaisant." After the first hubbub all was silent for half an hour. Then a light glowed through the thick fog that covered the water. The "Prudent" was burning. Being aground with the low tide, her captors had set her on fire, allowing the men on board to escape to the town in her boats. The flames soon wrapped her from stem to stern; and as the broad glare pierced the illumined mists, the English sailors, reckless of shot and shell, towed her companion-ship, with all on board, to a safe anchorage under Wolfe's batteries.

The position of the besieged was deplorable. Nearly a fourth of their number were in the hospitals; while the rest, exhausted with incessant toil, could find no place to snatch an hour of sleep; "and yet," says an officer, "they still show ardor." "To-day," he again says, on the twenty-fourth, "the fire of the place is so weak that it is more like funeral guns than a defence." On the front of the town only four cannon could fire at all. The rest were either dismounted or silenced by the musketry from the trenches. The masonry of the ramparts had been shaken by the concussion of their own guns; and now, in the Dauphin's and King's bastions, the English shot brought it down in masses. The trenches had been pushed so close on the rising grounds at the right that a great part of the covered way was enfiladed, while a battery on a hill across the harbor swept the whole front with a flank fire. Amherst had ordered the gunners to spare the houses of the town; but, according to French accounts, the order had little effect, for shot and shell fell everywhere. "There is not a house in the place," says the Diary just quoted, "that has not felt the effects of this formidable artillery. From yesterday morning till seven o'clock this evening we reckon that a thousand or twelve hundred bombs, great and small, have been thrown into the town, accompanied all the time by the fire of forty pieces of cannon, served with an activity not often seen. The hospital and the houses around it, which also serve as hospitals, are attacked with cannon and mortar. The surgeon trembles as he amputates a limb amid cries of *Gare la bombe!* and leaves his patient in the midst of the operation, lest he should share his fate. The sick and wounded, stretched on mattresses, utter cries of pain, which do not cease till a shot or the bursting of a shell ends them."[1] On the twenty-sixth the last cannon was silenced in front of the town, and the English batteries had made a breach which seemed practicable for assault.

On the day before, Drucour, with his chief officers and the engineer, Franquet, had made the tour of the covered way, and examined the state of the defences. All but Franquet were for offering to capitulate. Early on the next morning a council of war was held, at which were present Drucour, Franquet, Desgouttes, naval commander, Houllière, commander of the regulars, and the several chiefs of battalions. Franquet presented a memorial setting forth the state of the fortifications. As it was he who had reconstructed and repaired them, he was anxious to show the quality of his work in the best light possible; and therefore, in the view of his auditors, he understated the effects of the English fire. Hence an altercation arose, ending in a unanimous decision to ask for terms. Accordingly, at ten o'clock, a white flag was displayed over the breach in the Dauphin's Bastion, and an officer named Loppinot was sent out with offers to capitulate. The answer was prompt and stern: the garrison must surrender as prisoners of war; a definite reply must be given within an hour; in case of refusal the place will be attacked by land and sea.[2]

Great was the emotion in the council; and one of its mem-

[1] Early in the siege Drucour wrote to Amherst asking that the hospitals should be exempt from fire. Amherst answered that shot and shell might fall on any part of so small a town, but promised to insure the sick and wounded from molestation if Drucour would send them either to the island at the mouth of the harbor, or to any of the ships, if anchored apart from the rest. The offer was declined, for reasons not stated. Drucour gives the correspondence in his Diary.

[2] Mante and other English writers give the text of this reply.

bers, D'Anthonay, lieutenant-colonel of the battalion of Volontaires Étrangers, was sent to propose less rigorous terms. Amherst would not speak with him; and jointly with Boscawen despatched this note to the Governor:—

SIR,—We have just received the reply which it has pleased your Excellency to make as to the conditions of the capitulation offered you. We shall not change in the least our views regarding them. It depends on your Excellency to accept them or not; and you will have the goodness to give your answer, yes or no, within half an hour.

We have the honor to be, etc.,

E. BOSCAWEN,

J. AMHERST.[1]

Drucour answered as follows:—

GENTLEMEN,—To reply to your Excellencies in as few words as possible, I have the honor to repeat that my position also remains the same, and that I persist in my first resolution.

I have the honor to be, etc.,

THE CHEVALIER DE DRUCOUR.

In other words, he refused the English terms, and declared his purpose to abide the assault. Loppinot was sent back to the English camp with this note of defiance. He was no sooner gone than Prévost, the intendant, an officer of functions purely civil, brought the Governor a memorial which, with or without the knowledge of the military authorities, he had drawn up in anticipation of the emergency. "The violent resolution which the council continues to hold," said this document, "obliges me, for the good of the state, the preservation of the King's subjects, and the averting of horrors shocking to humanity, to lay before your eyes the consequences that may ensue. What will become of the four thousand souls who compose the families of this town, of the thousand or twelve hundred sick in the hospitals, and the officers and crews of our unfortunate ships? They will be delivered over to carnage and the rage of an unbridled soldiery,

[1] Translated from the Journal of Drucour.

eager for plunder, and impelled to deeds of horror by pretended resentment at what has formerly happened in Canada. Thus they will all be destroyed, and the memory of their fate will live forever in our colonies. . . . It remains, Monsieur," continues the paper, "to remind you that the councils you have held thus far have been composed of none but military officers. I am not surprised at their views. The glory of the King's arms and the honor of their several corps have inspired them. You and I alone are charged with the administration of the colony and the care of the King's subjects who compose it. These gentlemen, therefore, have had no regard for them. They think only of themselves and their soldiers, whose business it is to encounter the utmost extremity of peril. It is at the prayer of an intimidated people that I lay before you the considerations specified in this memorial."

"In view of these considerations," writes Drucour, "joined to the impossibility of resisting an assault, M. le Chevalier de Courserac undertook in my behalf to run after the bearer of my answer to the English commander and bring it back." It is evident that the bearer of the note had been in no hurry to deliver it, for he had scarcely got beyond the fortifications when Courserac overtook and stopped him. D'Anthonay, with Duvivier, major of the battalion of Artois, and Loppinot, the first messenger, was then sent to the English camp, empowered to accept the terms imposed. An English spectator thus describes their arrival: "A lieutenant-colonel came running out of the garrison, making signs at a distance, and bawling out as loud as he could, '*We accept! We accept!*' He was followed by two others; and they were all conducted to General Amherst's headquarters."[1] At eleven o'clock at night they returned with the articles of capitulation and the following letter: —

Sir, — We have the honor to send your Excellency the articles of capitulation signed.

Lieutenant-Colonel D'Anthonay has not failed to speak in behalf of the inhabitants of the town; and it is nowise our intention to distress them, but to give them all the aid in our power.

[1] *Authentic Account of the Siege of Louisbourg, by a Spectator.*

Your Excellency will have the goodness to sign a duplicate of the articles and send it to us.

It only remains to assure your Excellency that we shall with great pleasure seize every opportunity to convince your Excellency that we are with the most perfect consideration,

Sir, your Excellency's most obedient servants,

E. BOSCAWEN.
J. AMHERST.

The articles stipulated that the garrison should be sent to England, prisoners of war, in British ships; that all artillery, arms, munitions, and stores, both in Louisbourg and elsewhere on the Island of Cape Breton, as well as on Isle St.-Jean, now Prince Edward's Island, should be given up intact; that the gate of the Dauphin's Bastion should be delivered to the British troops at eight o'clock in the morning; and that the garrison should lay down their arms at noon. The victors, on their part, promised to give the French sick and wounded the same care as their own, and to protect private property from pillage.

Drucour signed the paper at midnight, and in the morning a body of grenadiers took possession of the Dauphin's Gate. The rude soldiery poured in, swarthy with wind and sun, and begrimed with smoke and dust; the garrison, drawn up on the esplanade, flung down their muskets and marched from the ground with tears of rage; the cross of St. George floated over the shattered rampart; and Louisbourg, with the two great islands that depended on it, passed to the British Crown. Guards were posted, a stern discipline was enforced, and perfect order maintained. The conquerors and the conquered exchanged greetings, and the English general was lavish of courtesies to the brave lady who had aided the defence so well. "Every favor she asked was granted," says a Frenchman present.

Drucour and his garrison had made a gallant defence. It had been his aim to prolong the siege till it should be too late for Amherst to co-operate with Abercromby in an attack on Canada; and in this, at least, he succeeded.

Five thousand six hundred and thirty-seven officers, soldiers, and sailors were prisoners in the hands of the victors. Eighteen mortars and two hundred and twenty-one cannon were found in the town, along with a great quantity of arms, munitions, and stores.[1] At the middle of August such of the prisoners as were not disabled by wounds or sickness were embarked for England, and the merchants and inhabitants were sent to France. Brigadier Whitmore, as governor of Louisbourg, remained with four regiments to hold guard over the desolation they had made.

The fall of the French stronghold was hailed in England with noisy rapture. Addresses of congratulation to the King poured in from all the cities of the kingdom, and the captured flags were hung in St. Paul's amid the roar of cannon and the shouts of the populace. The provinces shared these rejoicings. Sermons of thanksgiving resounded from countless New England pulpits. At Newport there were fireworks and illuminations; and, adds the pious reporter, "We have reason to believe that Christians will make wise and religious improvement of so signal a favor of Divine Providence." At Philadelphia a like display was seen, with music and universal ringing of bells. At Boston "a stately bonfire like a pyramid was kindled on the top of Fort Hill, which made a lofty and prodigious blaze;" though here certain jealous patriots protested against celebrating a victory won by British regulars, and not by New England men. At New York there was a grand official dinner at the Province Arms in Broadway, where every loyal toast was echoed by the cannon of Fort George; and illuminations and fireworks closed the day.[2] In the camp of Abercromby at Lake George, Chaplain Cleaveland, of Bagley's Massachusetts regiment, wrote: "The General put out orders that the breastwork should be lined with troops, and to fire three rounds for joy, and give thanks to God in a religious way."[3] But nowhere did the tidings find a warmer welcome than in the small detached forts scattered through the solitudes of Nova Scotia, where the military exiles, restless from inaction, listened with greedy ears for every word from

---

[1] *Account of the Guns, Mortars, Shot, Shell, etc., found in the Town of Louisbourg upon its Surrender this day*, signed *Jeffrey Amherst, 27 July, 1758.*

[2] These particulars are from the provincial newspapers.

[3] Cleaveland, *Journal.*

the great world whence they were banished. So slow were their communications with it that the fall of Louisbourg was known in England before it had reached them all. Captain John Knox, then in garrison at Annapolis, tells how it was greeted there more than five weeks after the event. It was the sixth of September. A sloop from Boston was seen coming up the bay. Soldiers and officers ran down to the wharf to ask for news. "Every soul," says Knox, "was impatient, yet shy of asking; at length, the vessel being come near enough to be spoken to, I called out, 'What news from Louisbourg?' To which the master simply replied, and with some gravity, 'Nothing strange.' This answer, which was so coldly delivered, threw us all into great consternation, and we looked at each other without being able to speak; some of us even turned away with an intent to return to the fort. At length one of our soldiers, not yet satisfied, called out with some warmth: 'Damn you, Pumpkin, is n't Louisbourg taken yet?' The poor New England man then answered: 'Taken, yes, above a month ago, and I have been there since; but if you have never heard it before, I have got a good parcel of letters for you now.' If our apprehensions were great at first, words are insufficient to express our transports at this speech, the latter part of which we hardly waited for; but instantly all hats flew off, and we made the neighboring woods resound with our cheers and huzzas for almost half an hour. The master of the sloop was amazed beyond expression, and declared he thought we had heard of the success of our arms eastward before, and had sought to banter him."[1] At night there was a grand bonfire and universal festivity in the fort and village.

Amherst proceeded to complete his conquest by the subjection of all the adjacent possessions of France. Major Dalling was sent to occupy Port Espagnol, now Sydney. Colonel Monckton was despatched to the Bay of Fundy and the River St. John with an order "to destroy the vermin who are settled there."[2] Lord Rollo, with the thirty-fifth regiment and two battalions of the sixtieth, received the submission of Isle St.-Jean, and tried to remove the inhabitants,—with small suc-

[1] Knox, *Historical Journal*, I. 158.
[2] *Orders of Amherst to Wolfe, 15 Aug. 1758; Ibid. to Monckton, 24 Aug. 1758; Report of Monckton, 12 Nov. 1758.*

cess; for out of more than four thousand he could catch but seven hundred.[1]

The ardent and indomitable Wolfe had been the life of the siege. Wherever there was need of a quick eye, a prompt decision, and a bold dash, there his lank figure was always in the front. Yet he was only half pleased with what had been done. The capture of Louisbourg, he thought, should be but the prelude of greater conquests; and he had hoped that the fleet and army would sail up the St. Lawrence and attack Quebec. Impetuous and impatient by nature, and irritable with disease, he chafed at the delay that followed the capitulation, and wrote to his father a few days after it: "We are gathering strawberries and other wild fruits of the country, with a seeming indifference about what is doing in other parts of the world. Our army, however, on the continent wants our help." Growing more anxious, he sent Amherst a note to ask his intentions; and the General replied, "What I most wish to do is to go to Quebec. I have proposed it to the Admiral, and yesterday he seemed to think it impracticable." On which Wolfe wrote again: "If the Admiral will not carry us to Quebec, reinforcements should certainly be sent to the continent without losing a moment. This damned French garrison take up our time and attention, which might be better bestowed. The transports are ready, and a small convoy would carry a brigade to Boston or New York. With the rest of the troops we might make an offensive and destructive war in the Bay of Fundy and the Gulf of St. Lawrence. I beg pardon for this freedom, but I cannot look coolly upon the bloody inroads of those hell-hounds, the Canadians; and if nothing further is to be done, I must desire leave to quit the army."

Amherst answered that though he had meant at first to go to Quebec with the whole army, late events on the continent made it impossible; and that he now thought it best to go with five or six regiments to the aid of Abercromby. He asked Wolfe to continue to communicate his views to him, and would not hear for a moment of his leaving the army; adding, "I know nothing that can tend more to His Majesty's service than your assisting in it." Wolfe again wrote to his com-

[1] *Villejouin, commandant à l'Isle St.-Jean, au Ministre, 8 Sept. 1758.*

mander, with whom he was on terms of friendship: "An offensive, daring kind of war will awe the Indians and ruin the French. Blockhouses and a trembling defensive encourage the meanest scoundrels to attack us. If you will attempt to cut up New France by the roots, I will come with pleasure to assist."

Amherst, with such speed as his deliberate nature would permit, sailed with six regiments for Boston to reinforce Abercromby at Lake George, while Wolfe set out on an errand but little to his liking. He had orders to proceed to Gaspé, Miramichi, and other settlements on the Gulf of St. Lawrence, destroy them, and disperse their inhabitants; a measure of needless and unpardonable rigor, which, while detesting it, he executed with characteristic thoroughness. "Sir Charles Hardy and I," he wrote to his father, "are preparing to rob the fishermen of their nets and burn their huts. When that great exploit is at an end, I return to Louisbourg, and thence to England." Having finished the work, he wrote to Amherst: "Your orders were carried into execution. We have done a great deal of mischief, and spread the terror of His Majesty's arms through the Gulf, but have added nothing to the reputation of them." The destruction of property was great; yet, as Knox writes, "he would not suffer the least barbarity to be committed upon the persons of the wretched inhabitants."[1]

He returned to Louisbourg, and sailed for England to recruit his shattered health for greater conflicts.

NOTE.—Four long and minute French diaries of the siege of Louisbourg are before me. The first, that of Drucour, covers a hundred and six folio pages, and contains his correspondence with Amherst, Boscawen, and Desgouttes. The second is that of the naval captain Tourville, commander of the ship "Capricieux," and covers fifty pages. The third is by an officer of the garrison whose name does not appear. The fourth, of about a hundred pages, is by another officer of the garrison, and is also anonymous. It is an excellent record of what passed each day, and of the changing conditions, moral and physical, of the besieged. These four Journals, though clearly independent of each other, agree in nearly all essential particulars. I have also numerous letters from the principal officers, military, naval, and civil, engaged in the defence,—Drucour, Desgouttes, Houllière, Beaussier, Marolles, Tourville, Courserac, Franquet, Villejouin, Prévost, and Querdisien. These, with various other documents relating to the siege, were copied from the originals in

[1] "Les Anglais ont très-bien traités les prisonniers qu'ils ont faits dans cette partie" [*Gaspé*, etc]. *Vaudreuil au Ministre, 4 Nov. 1758.*

the Archives de la Marine. Among printed authorities on the French side may be mentioned Pichon, *Lettres et Mémoires pour servir à l'Histoire du Cap-Breton*, and the *Campaign of Louisbourg*, by the Chevalier Johnstone, a Scotch Jacobite serving under Drucour.

The chief authorities on the English side are the official Journal of Amherst, printed in the *London Magazine* and in other contemporary periodicals, and also in Mante, *History of the Late War*; five letters from Amherst to Pitt, written during the siege (Public Record Office); an excellent private Journal called *An Authentic Account of the Reduction of Louisbourg, by a Spectator*, parts of which have been copied verbatim by Entick without acknowledgment; the admirable Journal of Captain John Knox, which contains numerous letters and orders relating to the siege; and the correspondence of Wolfe contained in his Life by Wright. Before me is the Diary of a captain or subaltern in the army of Amherst at Louisbourg, found in the garret of an old house at Windsor, Nova Scotia, on an estate belonging in 1760 to Chief Justice Deschamps. I owe the use of it to the kindness of George Wiggins, Esq., of Windsor, N. S. Mante gives an excellent plan of the siege operations, and another will be found in Jefferys, *Natural and Civil History of French Dominions in North America*.

Chapter XX

1758

TICONDEROGA

*Activity of the Provinces • Sacrifices of Massachusetts • The Army
at Lake George • Proposed Incursion of Lévis • Perplexities of
Montcalm • His Plan of Defence • Camp of Abercromby • His
Character • Lord Howe • His Popularity • Embarkation of Abercromby • Advance down Lake George • Landing • Forest Skirmish
• Death of Howe • Its Effects • Position of the French • The Lines
of Ticonderoga • Blunders of Abercromby • The Assault • A
frightful Scene • Incidents of the Battle • British Repulse •
Panic • Retreat • Triumph of Montcalm*

IN THE LAST year Loudon called on the colonists for four
thousand men. This year Pitt asked them for twenty thousand, and promised that the King would supply arms, ammunition, tents, and provisions, leaving to the provinces only
the raising, clothing, and pay of their soldiers; and he added
the assurance that Parliament would be asked to make some
compensation even for these.[1] Thus encouraged, cheered by
the removal of Loudon, and animated by the unwonted vigor
of British military preparation, the several provincial assemblies voted men in abundance, though the usual vexatious delays took place in raising, equipping, and sending them to the
field.

In this connection, an able English writer has brought
against the colonies, and especially against Massachusetts,
charges which deserve attention. Viscount Bury says: "Of all
the colonies, Massachusetts was the first which discovered the
designs of the French and remonstrated against their aggressions; of all the colonies she most zealously promoted measures of union for the common defence, and made the
greatest exertions in furtherance of her views." But he adds
that there is a reverse to the picture, and that "this colony, so
high-spirited, so warlike, and apparently so loyal, would never
move hand or foot in her own defence till certain of repay-

---

[1] *Pitt to the Colonial Governors, 30 Dec. 1757.*

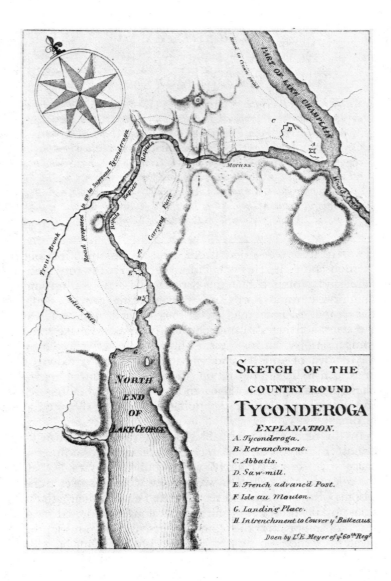

SKETCH OF THE
COUNTRY ROUND
TYCONDEROGA

EXPLANATION.

A. Tyconderoga.
B. Retranchment.
C. Abbatis.
D. Saw-mill.
E. French advanc'd Post.
F. Isle au Mouton.
G. Landing Place.
H. Intrenchment to Couver y Batteaus.

Doen by Lt E. Meyer of yͤ 60th Regt

NORTH
END
OF
LAKE GEORGE

Road to Crown point

PART OF LAKE CHAMPLAIN

Wood Creek

Morass

Carrying Place

Rapids

Road proposed to go to Surround Tyconderoga

Trout Brook

Indian Path

ment by the mother country."[1] The groundlessness of this charge is shown by abundant proofs, one of which will be enough. The Englishman Pownall, who had succeeded Shirley as royal governor of the province, made this year a report of its condition to Pitt. Massachusetts, he says, "has been the frontier and advanced guard of all the colonies against the enemy in Canada," and has always taken the lead in military affairs. In the three past years she has spent on the expeditions of Johnson, Winslow, and Loudon £242,356, besides about £45,000 a year to support the provincial government, at the same time maintaining a number of forts and garrisons, keeping up scouting-parties, and building, equipping, and manning a ship of twenty guns for the service of the King. In the first two months of the present year, 1758, she made a further military outlay of £172,239. Of all these sums she has received from Parliament a reimbursement of only £70,117, and hence she is deep in debt; yet, in addition, she has this year raised, paid, maintained, and clothed seven thousand soldiers placed under the command of General Abercromby, besides above twenty-five hundred more serving the King by land or sea; amounting in all to about one in four of her able-bodied men.

Massachusetts was extremely poor by the standards of the present day, living by fishing, farming, and a trade sorely hampered by the British navigation laws. Her contributions of money and men were not ordained by an absolute king, but made by the voluntary act of a free people. Pownall goes on to say that her present war-debt, due within three years, is 366,698 pounds sterling, and that to meet it she has imposed on herself taxes amounting, in the town of Boston, to thirteen shillings and twopence to every pound of income from real and personal estate; that her people are in distress, that she is anxious to continue her efforts in the public cause, but that without some further reimbursement she is exhausted and helpless.[2] Yet in the next year she incurred a new and heavy

---

[1] Bury, *Exodus of the Western Nations*, II. 250, 251.

[2] *Pownall to Pitt, 30 Sept. 1758* (Public Record Office, *America and West Indies*, LXXI.). "The province of Massachusetts Bay has exerted itself with great zeal and at vast expense for the public service." *Registers of Privy Council, 26 July, 1757.*

debt. In 1760 Parliament repaid her £59,575.[1] Far from being fully reimbursed, the end of the war found her on the brink of bankruptcy. Connecticut made equal sacrifices in the common cause,—highly to her honor, for she was little exposed to danger, being covered by the neighboring provinces; while impoverished New Hampshire put one in three of her able-bodied men into the field.[2]

In June the combined British and provincial force which Abercromby was to lead against Ticonderoga was gathered at the head of Lake George; while Montcalm lay at its outlet around the walls of the French stronghold, with an army not one fourth so numerous. Vaudreuil had devised a plan for saving Ticonderoga by a diversion into the valley of the Mohawk under Lévis, Rigaud, and Longueuil, with sixteen hundred men, who were to be joined by as many Indians. The English forts of that region were to be attacked, Schenectady threatened, and the Five Nations compelled to declare for France.[3] Thus, as the Governor gave out, the English would be forced to cease from aggression, leave Montcalm in peace, and think only of defending themselves.[4] "This," writes Bougainville on the fifteenth of June, "is what M. de Vaudreuil thinks will happen, because he never doubts anything. Ticonderoga, which is the point really threatened, is abandoned without support to the troops of the line and their general. It would even be wished that they might meet a reverse, if the consequences to the colony would not be too disastrous."

The proposed movement promised, no doubt, great advantages; but it was not destined to take effect. Some rangers taken on Lake George by a partisan officer named Langy declared with pardonable exaggeration that twenty-five or thirty thousand men would attack Ticonderoga in less than a fortnight. Vaudreuil saw himself forced to abandon his Mohawk

[1] *Bollan, Agent of Massachusetts, to Speaker of Assembly, 20 March, 1760.* It was her share of £200,000 granted to all the colonies in the proportion of their respective efforts.

[2] *Address to His Majesty from the Governor, Council, and Assembly of New Hampshire, Jan. 1759.*

[3] *Lévis au Ministre, 17 Juin, 1758. Doreil au Ministre, 16 Juin, 1758. Montcalm à sa Femme, 18 Avril, 1758.*

[4] *Correspondance de Vaudreuil, 1758. Livre d'Ordres, Juin, 1758.*

expedition, and to order Lévis and his followers, who had not yet left Montreal, to reinforce Montcalm.[1] Why they did not go at once is not clear. The Governor declares that there were not boats enough. From whatever cause, there was a long delay, and Montcalm was left to defend himself as he could.

He hesitated whether he should not fall back to Crown Point. The engineer, Lotbinière, opposed the plan, as did also Le Mercier.[2] It was but a choice of difficulties, and he stayed at Ticonderoga. His troops were disposed as they had been in the summer before; one battalion, that of Berry, being left near the fort, while the main body, under Montcalm himself, was encamped by the saw-mill at the Falls, and the rest, under Bourlamaque, occupied the head of the portage, with a small advanced force at the landing-place on Lake George. It remained to determine at which of these points he should concentrate them and make his stand against the English. Ruin threatened him in any case; each position had its fatal weakness or its peculiar danger, and his best hope was in the ignorance or blundering of his enemy. He seems to have been several days in a state of indecision.

In the afternoon of the fifth of July the partisan Langy, who had again gone out to reconnoitre towards the head of Lake George, came back in haste with the report that the English were embarked in great force. Montcalm sent a canoe down Lake Champlain to hasten Lévis to his aid, and ordered the battalion of Berry to begin a breastwork and abattis on the high ground in front of the fort. That they were not begun before shows that he was in doubt as to his plan of defence; and that his whole army was not now set to work at them shows that his doubt was still unsolved.

It was nearly a month since Abercromby had begun his camp at the head of Lake George. Here, on the ground where Johnson had beaten Dieskau, where Montcalm had planted his batteries, and Monro vainly defended the wooden ramparts of Fort William Henry, were now assembled more than fifteen thousand men; and the shores, the foot of the mountains, and the broken plains between them were studded thick

[1] *Bigot au Ministre, 21 Juillet, 1758.*

[2] *N. Y. Col. Docs.*, X. 893. Lotbinière's relative, Vaudreuil, confirms the statement. Montcalm had not, as has been said, begun already to fall back.

with tents. Of regulars there were six thousand three hundred and sixty-seven, officers and soldiers, and of provincials nine thousand and thirty-four.[1] To the New England levies, or at least to their chaplains, the expedition seemed a crusade against the abomination of Babylon; and they discoursed in their sermons of Moses sending forth Joshua against Amalek. Abercromby, raised to his place by political influence, was little but the nominal commander. "A heavy man," said Wolfe in a letter to his father; "an aged gentleman, infirm in body and mind," wrote William Parkman, a boy of seventeen, who carried a musket in a Massachusetts regiment, and kept in his knapsack a dingy little note-book, in which he jotted down what passed each day.[2] The age of the aged gentleman was fifty-two.

Pitt meant that the actual command of the army should be in the hands of Brigadier Lord Howe,[3] and he was in fact its real chief; "the noblest Englishman that has appeared in my time, and the best soldier in the British army," says Wolfe.[4] And he elsewhere speaks of him as "that great man." Abercromby testifies to the universal respect and love with which officers and men regarded him, and Pitt calls him "a character of ancient times; a complete model of military virtue."[5] High as this praise is, it seems to have been deserved. The young nobleman, who was then in his thirty-fourth year, had the qualities of a leader of men. The army felt him, from general to drummer-boy. He was its soul; and while breathing into it his own energy and ardor, and bracing it by stringent discipline, he broke through the traditions of the service and gave it new shapes to suit the time and place. During the past year he had studied the art of forest warfare, and joined Rogers and his rangers in their scouting-parties, sharing all their hardships and making himself one of them. Perhaps the reforms that he introduced were fruits of this rough self-imposed schooling. He made officers and men throw off all

[1] *Abercromby to Pitt, 12 July, 1758.*

[2] Great-uncle of the writer, and son of the Rev. Ebenezer Parkman, a graduate of Harvard, and minister of Westborough, Mass.

[3] Chesterfield, *Letters*, IV. 260 (ed. Mahon).

[4] *Wolfe to his Father, 7 Aug. 1758*, in Wright, 450.

[5] *Pitt to Grenville, 22 Aug. 1758*, in *Grenville Papers*, I. 262.

useless incumbrances, cut their hair close, wear leggings to protect them from briers, brown the barrels of their muskets, and carry in their knapsacks thirty pounds of meal, which they cooked for themselves; so that, according to an admiring Frenchman, they could live a month without their supply-trains.[1] "You would laugh to see the droll figure we all make," writes an officer. "Regulars as well as provincials have cut their coats so as scarcely to reach their waists. No officer or private is allowed to carry more than one blanket and a bearskin. A small portmanteau is allowed each officer. No women follow the camp to wash our linen. Lord Howe has already shown an example by going to the brook and washing his own."[2]

Here, as in all things, he shared the lot of the soldier, and required his officers to share it. A story is told of him that before the army embarked he invited some of them to dinner in his tent, where they found no seats but logs, and no carpet but bearskins. A servant presently placed on the ground a large dish of pork and peas, on which his lordship took from his pocket a sheath containing a knife and fork and began to cut the meat. The guests looked on in some embarrassment; upon which he said: "Is it possible, gentlemen, that you have come on this campaign without providing yourselves with what is necessary?" And he gave each of them a sheath, with a knife and fork, like his own.

Yet this Lycurgus of the camp, as a contemporary calls him, is described as a man of social accomplishments rare even in his rank. He made himself greatly beloved by the provincial officers, with many of whom he was on terms of intimacy, and he did what he could to break down the barriers between the colonial soldiers and the British regulars. When he was at Albany, sharing with other high officers the kindly hospitalities of Mrs. Schuyler, he so won the heart of that excellent matron that she loved him like a son; and, though not given to such effusion, embraced him with tears on the morning when he left her to lead his division to the lake.[3] In Westmin-

[1] Pouchot, *Dernière Guerre de l'Amérique*, I. 140.

[2] *Letter from Camp, 12 June, 1758*, in *Boston Evening Post*. Another, in *Boston News Letter*, contains similar statements.

[3] Mrs. Grant, *Memoirs of an American Lady*, 226 (ed. 1876).

ster Abbey may be seen the tablet on which Massachusetts pays grateful tribute to his virtues, and commemorates "the affection her officers and soldiers bore to his command."

On the evening of the fourth of July, baggage, stores, and ammunition were all on board the boats, and the whole army embarked on the morning of the fifth. The arrangements were perfect. Each corps marched without confusion to its appointed station on the beach, and the sun was scarcely above the ridge of French Mountain when all were afloat. A spectator watching them from the shore says that when the fleet was three miles on its way, the surface of the lake at that distance was completely hidden from sight.[1] There were nine hundred bateaux, a hundred and thirty-five whaleboats, and a large number of heavy flatboats carrying the artillery. The whole advanced in three divisions, the regulars in the centre, and the provincials on the flanks. Each corps had its flags and its music. The day was fair and men and officers were in the highest spirits.

Before ten o'clock they began to enter the Narrows; and the boats of the three divisions extended themselves into long files as the mountains closed on either hand upon the contracted lake. From front to rear the line was six miles long. The spectacle was superb: the brightness of the summer day; the romantic beauty of the scenery; the sheen and sparkle of those crystal waters; the countless islets, tufted with pine, birch, and fir; the bordering mountains, with their green summits and sunny crags; the flash of oars and glitter of weapons; the banners, the varied uniforms, and the notes of bugle, trumpet, bagpipe, and drum, answered and prolonged by a hundred woodland echoes. "I never beheld so delightful a prospect," wrote a wounded officer at Albany a fortnight after.

Rogers with the rangers, and Gage with the light infantry, led the way in whaleboats, followed by Bradstreet with his corps of boatmen, armed and drilled as soldiers. Then came the main body. The central column of regulars was commanded by Lord Howe, his own regiment, the fifty-fifth, in the van, followed by the Royal Americans, the twenty-

---

[1] *Letter from Lake George*, in *Boston News Letter*.

seventh, forty-fourth, forty-sixth, and eightieth infantry, and the Highlanders of the forty-second, with their major, Duncan Campbell of Inverawe, silent and gloomy amid the general cheer, for his soul was dark with foreshadowings of death.[1] With this central column came what are described as two floating castles, which were no doubt batteries to cover the landing of the troops. On the right hand and the left were the provincials, uniformed in blue, regiment after regiment, from Massachusetts, Connecticut, New York, New Jersey, and Rhode Island. Behind them all came the bateaux, loaded with stores and baggage, and the heavy flatboats that carried the artillery, while a rear-guard of provincials and regulars closed the long procession.[2]

At five in the afternoon they reached Sabbath-Day Point, twenty-five miles down the lake, where they stopped till late in the evening, waiting for the baggage and artillery, which had lagged behind; and here Lord Howe, lying on a bearskin by the side of the ranger, John Stark, questioned him as to the position of Ticonderoga and its best points of approach. At about eleven o'clock they set out again, and at daybreak entered what was then called the Second Narrows; that is to say, the contraction of the lake where it approaches its outlet. Close on their left, ruddy in the warm sunrise, rose the vast bare face of Rogers Rock, whence a French advanced party, under Langy and an officer named Trepezec, was watching their movements. Lord Howe, with Rogers and Bradstreet, went in whaleboats to reconnoitre the landing. At the place which the French called the Burnt Camp, where Montcalm had embarked the summer before, they saw a detachment of the enemy too weak to oppose them. Their men landed and drove them off. At noon the whole army was on shore. Rogers, with a party of rangers, was ordered forward to reconnoitre, and the troops were formed for the march.

From this part of the shore[3] a plain covered with forest stretched northwestward half a mile or more to the mountains behind which lay the valley of Trout Brook. On this

[1] See Appendix G.

[2] *Letter from Lake George*, in *Boston News Letter*. Even Rogers, the ranger, speaks of the beauty of the scene.

[3] Between the old and new steamboat-landings, and parts adjacent.

plain the army began its march in four columns, with the intention of passing round the western bank of the river of the outlet, since the bridge over it had been destroyed. Rogers, with the provincial regiments of Fitch and Lyman, led the way, at some distance before the rest. The forest was extremely dense and heavy, and so obstructed with undergrowth that it was impossible to see more than a few yards in any direction, while the ground was encumbered with fallen trees in every stage of decay. The ranks were broken, and the men struggled on as they could in dampness and shade, under a canopy of boughs that the sun could scarcely pierce. The difficulty increased when, after advancing about a mile, they came upon undulating and broken ground. They were now not far from the upper rapids of the outlet. The guides became bewildered in the maze of trunks and boughs; the marching columns were confused, and fell in one upon the other. They were in the strange situation of an army lost in the woods.

The advanced party of French under Langy and Trepezec, about three hundred and fifty in all, regulars and Canadians, had tried to retreat; but before they could do so, the whole English army had passed them, landed, and placed itself between them and their countrymen. They had no resource but to take to the woods. They seem to have climbed the steep gorge at the side of Rogers Rock and followed the Indian path that led to the valley of Trout Brook, thinking to descend it, and, by circling along the outskirts of the valley of Ticonderoga, reach Montcalm's camp at the saw-mill. Langy was used to bushranging; but he too became perplexed in the blind intricacies of the forest. Towards the close of the day he and his men had come out from the valley of Trout Brook, and were near the junction of that stream with the river of the outlet, in a state of some anxiety, for they could see nothing but brown trunks and green boughs. Could any of them have climbed one of the great pines that here and there reared their shaggy spires high above the surrounding forest, they would have discovered where they were, but would have gained not the faintest knowledge of the enemy. Out of the woods on the right they would have seen a smoke rising from the burning huts of the French camp at the head of the portage, which Bourlamaque had set on fire and abandoned. At a mile or more in front, the saw-mill at the Falls might perhaps have been descried, and, by glimpses between the trees, the tents of the neighboring camp where Montcalm still lay with his main force. All the rest seemed lonely as the grave; mountain and valley lay wrapped in primeval woods, and none could have dreamed that, not far distant, an army was groping its way, buried in foliage; no rumbling of wagons and artillery trains, for none were there; all silent but the cawing of some crow flapping his black wings over the sea of tree-tops.

Lord Howe, with Major Israel Putnam and two hundred rangers, was at the head of the principal column, which was a little in advance of the three others. Suddenly the challenge, *Qui vive!* rang sharply from the thickets in front. *Français!* was the reply. Langy's men were not deceived; they fired out of the bushes. The shots were returned; a hot skirmish followed; and Lord Howe dropped dead, shot through the breast. All was confusion. The dull, vicious reports of musketry in thick woods, at first few and scattering, then in fierce and rapid volleys, reached the troops behind. They could hear, but see nothing. Already harassed and perplexed, they became perturbed. For all they knew, Montcalm's whole army was upon them. Nothing prevented a panic but the steadiness of the rangers, who maintained the fight alone till the rest came back to their senses. Rogers, with his reconnoitring party, and the regiments of Fitch and Lyman, were at no great distance in front. They all turned on hearing the musketry, and thus the French were caught between two fires. They fought with desperation. About fifty of them at length escaped; a hundred and forty-eight were captured, and the rest killed or drowned in trying to cross the rapids. The loss of the English was small in numbers, but immeasurable in the death of Howe. "The fall of this noble and brave officer," says Rogers, "seemed to produce an almost general languor and consternation through the whole army." "In Lord Howe," writes another contemporary, Major Thomas Mante, "the soul of General Abercromby's army seemed to expire. From the unhappy moment the General was deprived of his advice, neither order nor discipline was observed, and a strange kind of infatuation usurped the place of resolution." The death of one man was the ruin of fifteen thousand.

The evil news was despatched to Albany, and in two or three days the messenger who bore it passed the house of Mrs. Schuyler on the meadows above the town. "In the afternoon," says her biographer, "a man was seen coming from the north galloping violently without his hat. Pedrom, as he was familiarly called, Colonel Schulyer's only surviving brother, was with her, and ran instantly to inquire, well knowing that he rode express. The man galloped on, crying out that Lord Howe was killed. The mind of our good aunt had been so engrossed by her anxiety and fears for the event impending, and so impressed with the merit and magnanimity of her favorite hero, that her wonted firmness sank under the stroke, and she broke out into bitter lamentations. This had such an effect on her friends and domestics that shrieks and sobs of anguish echoed through every part of the house."

The effect of the loss was seen at once. The army was needlessly kept under arms all night in the forest, and in the morning was ordered back to the landing whence it came.[1] Towards noon, however, Bradstreet was sent with a detachment of regulars and provincials to take possession of the saw-mill at the Falls, which Montcalm had abandoned the evening before. Bradstreet rebuilt the bridges destroyed by the retiring enemy, and sent word to his commander that the way was open; on which Abercromby again put his army in motion, reached the Falls late in the afternoon, and occupied the deserted encampment of the French.

Montcalm with his main force had held this position at the Falls through most of the preceding day, doubtful, it seems, to the last whether he should not make his final stand there. Bourlamaque was for doing so; but two old officers, Bernès and Montguy, pointed out the danger that the English would occupy the neighboring heights;[2] whereupon Montcalm at length resolved to fall back. The camp was broken up at five o'clock. Some of the troops embarked in bateaux, while others marched a mile and a half along the forest road, passed the place where the battalion of Berry was still at work on the

---

[1] *Abercromby to Pitt, 12 July, 1758.*
[2] Pouchot, I. 145.

breastwork begun in the morning, and made their bivouac a little farther on, upon the cleared ground that surrounded the fort.

The peninsula of Ticonderoga consists of a rocky plateau, with low grounds on each side, bordering Lake Champlain on the one hand, and the outlet of Lake George on the other. The fort stood near the end of the peninsula, which points towards the southeast. Thence, as one goes westward, the ground declines a little, and then slowly rises, till, about half a mile from the fort, it reaches its greatest elevation, and begins still more gradually to decline again. Thus a ridge is formed across the plateau between the steep declivities that sink to the low grounds on right and left. Some weeks before, a French officer named Hugues had suggested the defence of this ridge by means of an abattis.[1] Montcalm approved his plan; and now, at the eleventh hour, he resolved to make his stand here. The two engineers, Pontleroy and Desandrouin, had already traced the outline of the works, and the soldiers of the battalion of Berry had made some progress in constructing them. At dawn of the seventh, while Abercromby, fortunately for his enemy, was drawing his troops back to the landing-place, the whole French army fell to their task. The regimental colors were planted along the line, and the officers, stripped to the shirt, took axe in hand and labored with their men. The trees that covered the ground were hewn down by thousands, the tops lopped off, and the trunks piled one upon another to form a massive breastwork. The line followed the top of the ridge, along which it zigzagged in such a manner that the whole front could be swept by flank-fires of musketry and grape. Abercromby describes the wall of logs as between eight and nine feet high;[2] in which case there must have been a rude *banquette*, or platform to fire from, on the inner side It was certainly so high that nothing could be seen over it but the crowns of the soldiers' hats. The upper tier was formed of single logs, in which notches were cut to serve as loopholes; and in some places sods and bags of sand were piled along the

[1] *N. Y. Col. Docs.*, X. 708.

[2] *Abercromby to Barrington, 12 July, 1758.* "At least eight feet high." Rogers, *Journals*, 116.

top, with narrow spaces to fire through.[1] From the central part of the line the ground sloped away like a natural glacis; while at the sides, and especially on the left, it was undulating and broken. Over this whole space, to the distance of a musket-shot from the works, the forest was cut down, and the trees left lying where they fell among the stumps, with tops turned outwards, forming one vast abattis, which, as a Massachusetts officer says, looked like a forest laid flat by a hurricane.[2] But the most formidable obstruction was immediately along the front of the breastwork, where the ground was covered with heavy boughs, overlapping and interlaced, with sharpened points bristling into the face of the assailant like the quills of a porcupine. As these works were all of wood, no vestige of them remains. The earthworks now shown to tourists as the lines of Montcalm are of later construction; and though on the same ground, are not on the same plan.[3]

Here, then, was a position which, if attacked in front with musketry alone, might be called impregnable. But would Abercromby so attack it? He had several alternatives. He might attempt the flank and rear of his enemy by way of the low grounds on the right and left of the plateau, a movement which the precautions of Montcalm had made difficult, but not impossible. Or, instead of leaving his artillery idle on the strand of Lake George, he might bring it to the front and batter the breastwork, which, though impervious to musketry, was worthless against heavy cannon. Or he might do what Burgoyne did with success a score of years later, and plant a battery on the heights of Rattlesnake Hill, now called Mount Defiance, which commanded the position of the French, and whence the inside of their breastwork could be scoured with round-shot from end to end. Or, while threatening the French front with a part of his army, he could march the rest a short distance through the woods on his left to the road which led from Ticonderoga to Crown Point, and

[1] A Swiss officer of the Royal Americans, writing on the 14th, says that there were two, and in some parts three, rows of loopholes. See the letter in *Pennsylvania Archives*, III. 472.

[2] *Colonel Oliver Partridge to his Wife, 12 July, 1758.*

[3] A new line of works was begun four days after the battle, to replace the log breastwork. Malartic, *Journal. Travaux faits à Carillon, 1758.*

which would soon have brought him to the place called Five-Mile Point, where Lake Champlain narrows to the width of an easy rifle-shot, and where a battery of field-pieces would have cut off all Montcalm's supplies and closed his only way of retreat. As the French were provisioned for but eight days, their position would thus have been desperate. They plainly saw the danger; and Doreil declares that had the movement been made, their whole army must have surrendered.[1] Montcalm had done what he could; but the danger of his position was inevitable and extreme. His hope lay in Abercromby; and it was a hope well founded. The action of the English general answered the utmost wishes of his enemy.

Abercromby had been told by his prisoners that Montcalm had six thousand men, and that three thousand more were expected every hour. Therefore he was in haste to attack before these succors could arrive. As was the general, so was the army. "I believe," writes an officer, "we were one and all infatuated by a notion of carrying every obstacle by a mere *coup de mousqueterie*."[2] Leadership perished with Lord Howe, and nothing was left but blind, headlong valor.

Clerk, chief engineer, was sent to reconnoitre the French works from Mount Defiance; and came back with the report that, to judge from what he could see, they might be carried by assault. Then, without waiting to bring up his cannon, Abercromby prepared to storm the lines.

The French finished their breastwork and abattis on the evening of the seventh, encamped behind them, slung their kettles, and rested after their heavy toil. Lévis had not yet appeared; but at twilight one of his officers, Captain Pouchot, arrived with three hundred regulars, and announced that his commander would come before morning with a hundred more. The reinforcement, though small, was welcome, and Lévis was a host in himself. Pouchot was told that the army was half a mile off. Thither he repaired, made his report to Montcalm, and looked with amazement at the prodigious amount of work accomplished in one day.[3] Lévis himself ar-

---

[1] *Doreil au Ministre, 28 Juillet, 1758*. The Chevalier Johnstone thought that Montcalm was saved by Abercromby's ignorance of the ground. *A Dialogue in Hades* (Quebec Historical Society).

[2] See the letter in Knox, I. 148.   [3] Pouchot, I. 137.

rived in the course of the night, and approved the arrangement of the troops. They lay behind their lines till daybreak;
then the drums beat, and they formed in order of battle.[1] The
battalions of La Sarre and Languedoc were posted on the left,
under Bourlamaque, the first battalion of Berry with that of
Royal Roussillon in the centre, under Montcalm, and those
of La Reine, Béarn, and Guienne on the right, under Lévis.
A detachment of volunteers occupied the low grounds between the breastwork and the outlet of Lake George; while,
at the foot of the declivity on the side towards Lake Champlain, were stationed four hundred and fifty colony regulars
and Canadians, behind an abattis which they had made for
themselves; and as they were covered by the cannon of the
fort, there was some hope that they would check any flank
movement which the English might attempt on that side.
Their posts being thus assigned, the men fell to work again
to strengthen their defences. Including those who came with
Lévis, the total force of effective soldiers was now thirty-six
hundred.[2]

Soon after nine o'clock a distant and harmless fire of small-
arms began on the slopes of Mount Defiance. It came from a
party of Indians who had just arrived with Sir William Johnson, and who, after amusing themselves in this manner for a
time, remained for the rest of the day safe spectators of the
fight. The soldiers worked undisturbed till noon, when volleys of musketry were heard from the forest in front. It was
the English light troops driving in the French pickets. A cannon was fired as a signal to drop tools and form for battle.
The white uniforms lined the breastwork in a triple row, with
the grenadiers behind them as a reserve, and the second battalion of Berry watching the flanks and rear.

Meanwhile the English army had moved forward from its
camp by the saw-mill. First came the rangers, the light infantry, and Bradstreet's armed boatmen, who, emerging into the
open space, began a spattering fire. Some of the provincial
troops followed, extending from left to right, and opening

[1] *Livre d'Ordres, Disposition de Défense des Retranchements, 8 Juillet, 1758.*

[2] Montcalm, *Relation de la Victoire remportée à Carillon, 8 Juillet, 1758.* Vaudreuil puts the number at 4,760, besides officers, which includes the garrison
and laborers at the fort. *Vaudreuil au Ministre, 28 Juillet, 1758.*

fire in turn; then the regulars, who had formed in columns of attack under cover of the forest, advanced their solid red masses into the sunlight, and passing through the intervals between the provincial regiments, pushed forward to the assault. Across the rough ground, with its maze of fallen trees whose leaves hung withering in the July sun, they could see the top of the breastwork, but not the men behind it; when, in an instant, all the line was obscured by a gush of smoke, a crash of exploding firearms tore the air, and grapeshot and musket-balls swept the whole space like a tempest; "a damnable fire," says an officer who heard them screaming about his ears. The English had been ordered to carry the works with the bayonet; but their ranks were broken by the obstructions through which they struggled in vain to force their way, and they soon began to fire in turn. The storm raged in full fury for an hour. The assailants pushed close to the breastwork; but there they were stopped by the bristling mass of sharpened branches, which they could not pass under the murderous cross-fires that swept them from front and flank. At length they fell back, exclaiming that the works were impregnable. Abercromby, who was at the saw-mill, a mile and a half in the rear, sent orders to attack again, and again they came on as before.

The scene was frightful: masses of infuriated men who could not go forward and would not go back; straining for an enemy they could not reach, and firing on an enemy they could not see; caught in the entanglement of fallen trees; tripped by briers, stumbling over logs, tearing through boughs; shouting, yelling, cursing, and pelted all the while with bullets that killed them by scores, stretched them on the ground, or hung them on jagged branches in strange attitudes of death. The provincials supported the regulars with spirit, and some of them forced their way to the foot of the wooden wall.

The French fought with the intrepid gayety of their nation, and shouts of *Vive le Roi!* and *Vive notre Général!* mingled with the din of musketry. Montcalm, with his coat off, for the day was hot, directed the defence of the centre, and repaired to any part of the line where the danger for the time seemed greatest. He is warm in praise of his enemy, and declares that between one and seven o'clock they attacked him six

successive times. Early in the action Abercromby tried to turn
the French left by sending twenty bateaux, filled with troops,
down the outlet of Lake George. They were met by the fire
of the volunteers stationed to defend the low grounds on that
side, and, still advancing, came within range of the cannon
of the fort, which sank two of them and drove back the rest.

A curious incident happened during one of the attacks. De
Bassignac, a captain in the battalion of Royal Roussillon, tied
his handkerchief to the end of a musket and waved it over the
breastwork in defiance. The English mistook it for a sign of
surrender, and came forward with all possible speed, holding
their muskets crossed over their heads in both hands, and
crying *Quarter*. The French made the same mistake; and
thinking that their enemies were giving themselves up as prisoners, ceased firing, and mounted on the top of the breastwork to receive them. Captain Pouchot, astonished, as he says,
to see them perched there, looked out to learn the cause, and
saw that the enemy meant anything but surrender. Whereupon
he shouted with all his might: *"Tirez! Tirez! Ne voyez-vous pas
que ces gens-là vont vous enlever?"* The soldiers, still standing
on the breastwork, instantly gave the English a volley, which
killed some of them, and sent back the rest discomfited.[1]

This was set to the account of Gallic treachery. "Another
deceit the enemy put upon us," says a military letter-writer:
"they raised their hats above the breastwork, which our people fired at; they, having loopholes to fire through, and being
covered by the sods, we did them little damage, except shooting their hats to pieces."[2] In one of the last assaults a soldier
of the Rhode Island regiment, William Smith, managed to
get through all obstructions and ensconce himself close under
the breastwork, where in the confusion he remained for a
time unnoticed, improving his advantages meanwhile by
shooting several Frenchmen. Being at length observed, a soldier fired vertically down upon him and wounded him severely, but not enough to prevent his springing up, striking
at one of his enemies over the top of the wall, and braining
him with his hatchet. A British officer who saw the feat, and

---

[1] Pouchot, I. 153. Both Niles and Entick mention the incident.

[2] *Letter from Saratoga, 12 July, 1758*, in *New Hampshire Gazette*. Compare
Pennsylvania Archives, III. 474.

was struck by the reckless daring of the man, ordered two regulars to bring him off; which, covered by a brisk fire of musketry, they succeeded in doing. A letter from the camp two or three weeks later reports him as in a fair way to recover, being, says the writer, much braced and invigorated by his anger against the French, on whom he was swearing to have his revenge.[1]

Toward five o'clock two English columns joined in a most determined assault on the extreme right of the French, defended by the battalions of Guienne and Béarn. The danger for a time was imminent. Montcalm hastened to the spot with the reserves. The assailants hewed their way to the foot of the breastwork; and though again and again repulsed, they again and again renewed the attack. The Highlanders fought with stubborn and unconquerable fury. "Even those who were mortally wounded," writes one of their lieutenants, "cried to their companions not to lose a thought upon them, but to follow their officers and mind the honor of their country. Their ardor was such that it was difficult to bring them off."[2] Their major, Campbell of Inverawe, found his foreboding true. He received a mortal shot, and his clansmen bore him from the field. Twenty-five of their officers were killed or wounded, and half the men fell under the deadly fire that poured from the loopholes. Captain John Campbell and a few followers tore their way through the abattis, climbed the breastwork, leaped down among the French, and were bayoneted there.[3]

As the colony troops and Canadians on the low ground were left undisturbed, Lévis sent them an order to make a sortie and attack the left flank of the charging columns. They accordingly posted themselves among the trees along the declivity, and fired upwards at the enemy, who presently shifted their position to the right, out of the line of shot. The assault still continued, but in vain; and at six there was another effort, equally fruitless. From this time till half-past seven a lin-

---

[1] *Letter from Lake George, 26 July, 1758,* in *Boston Gazette.* The story is given, without much variation, in several other letters.

[2] *Letter of Lieutenant William Grant,* in *Maclachlan's Highlands,* II. 340 (ed. 1875).

[3] *Ibid.,* II. 339.

gering fight was kept up by the rangers and other provincials, firing from the edge of the woods and from behind the stumps, bushes, and fallen trees in front of the lines. Its only objects were to cover their comrades, who were collecting and bringing off the wounded, and to protect the retreat of the regulars, who fell back in disorder to the Falls. As twilight came on, the last combatant withdrew, and none were left but the dead. Abercromby had lost in killed, wounded, and missing, nineteen hundred and forty-four officers and men.[1] The loss of the French, not counting that of Langy's detachment, was three hundred and seventy-seven. Bourlamaque was dangerously wounded; Bougainville slightly; and the hat of Lévis was twice shot through.[2]

Montcalm, with a mighty load lifted from his soul, passed along the lines, and gave the tired soldiers the thanks they nobly deserved. Beer, wine, and food were served out to them, and they bivouacked for the night on the level ground between the breastwork and the fort. The enemy had met a terrible rebuff; yet the danger was not over. Abercromby still had more than thirteen thousand men, and he might renew the attack with cannon. But, on the morning of the ninth, a band of volunteers who had gone out to watch him brought back the report that he was in full retreat. The saw-mill at the Falls was on fire, and the last English soldier was gone. On the morning of the tenth, Lévis, with a strong detachment, followed the road to the landing-place, and found signs that a panic had overtaken the defeated troops. They had left behind several hundred barrels of provisions and a large quantity of baggage; while in a marshy place that they had crossed was found a considerable number of their shoes, which had stuck in the mud, and which they had not stopped to recover. They had embarked on the morning after the battle, and retreated to the head of the lake in a disorder and dejection wofully contrasted with the pomp of their advance. A gallant army was sacrificed by the blunders of its chief.

Montcalm announced his victory to his wife in a strain of exaggeration that marks the exaltation of his mind. "Without Indians, almost without Canadians or colony troops,—I had

[1] See Appendix G.
[2] *Lévis au Ministre, 13 Juillet, 1758.*

only four hundred,—alone with Lévis and Bourlamaque and the troops of the line, thirty-one hundred fighting men, I have beaten an army of twenty-five thousand. They repassed the lake precipitately, with a loss of at least five thousand. This glorious day does infinite honor to the valor of our battalions. I have no time to write more. I am well, my dearest, and I embrace you." And he wrote to his friend Doreil: "The army, the too-small army of the King, has beaten the enemy. What a day for France! If I had had two hundred Indians to send out at the head of a thousand picked men under the Chevalier de Lévis, not many would have escaped. Ah, my dear Doreil, what soldiers are ours! I never saw the like. Why were they not at Louisbourg?"

On the morrow of his victory he caused a great cross to be planted on the battle-field, inscribed with these lines, composed by the soldier-scholar himself,—

"Quid dux? quid miles? quid strata ingentia ligna?
En Signum! en victor! Deus hîc, Deus ipse triumphat."

"Soldier and chief and rampart's strength are nought;
Behold the conquering Cross! 'T is God the triumph wrought."[1]

[1] Along with the above paraphrase I may give that of Montcalm himself, which was also inscribed on the cross:—

"Chrétien! ce ne fut point Montcalm et la prudence,
Ces arbres renversés, ces héros, leurs exploits,
Qui des Anglais confus ont brisé l'espérance;
C'est le bras de ton Dieu, vainqueur sur cette croix."

In the same letter in which Montcalm sent these lines to his mother he says: "Je vous envoie, pour vous amuser, deux chansons sur le combat du 8 Juillet, dont l'une est en style des poissardes de Paris." One of these songs, which were written by soldiers after the battle, begins,—

"Je chante des François
La valeur et la gloire,
Qui toujours sur l'Anglois
Remportent la victoire.
Ce sont des héros,
Tous nos généraux,
Et Montcalm et Lévis,
Et Bourlamaque aussi.

> "Mars, qui les engendra
> Pour l'honneur de la France,
> D'abord les anima
> De sa haute vaillance,
> Et les transporta
> Dans le Canada,
> Où l'on voit les François
> Culbuter les Anglois."

The other effusion of the military muse is in a different strain, "en style des poissardes de Paris." The following is a specimen, given *literatim*: —

> "L'aumônier fit l'exhortation,
> Puis il donnit l'absolution;
> Aisément cela se peut croire.
> Enfants, dit-il, animez-vous!
> L'bon Dieu, sa mère, tout est pour vous.
> *S—é! j'sommes catholiques. Les Anglois sont des hérétiques.*

"Ce sont des chiens; à coups d'pieds, a coups d'poings faut leur casser la gueule et la mâchoire.

> "Soldats, officiers, généraux,
> Chacun en ce jour fut héros.
> Aisément cela se peut croire.
> Montcalm, comme défunt Annibal,
> S'montroit soldat et général.
> *S—é! sil y avoit quelqu'un qui ne l'aimît point!*

"Je veux être un chien; à coups d'pieds, a coups d'poings, j'lui cass'rai la gueule et la mâchoire."

This is an allusion to Vaudreuil. On the battle of Ticonderoga, see Appendix G.

Chapter XXI

1758

FORT FRONTENAC

The routed Army • Indignation at Abercromby • John Cleaveland and his Brother Chaplains • Regulars and Provincials • Provincial Surgeons • French Raids • Rogers defeats Marin • Adventures of Putnam • Expedition of Bradstreet • Capture of Fort Frontenac

---

THE RASHNESS of Abercromby before the fight was matched by his poltroonery after it. Such was his terror that on the evening of his defeat he sent an order to Colonel Cummings, commanding at Fort William Henry, to send all the sick and wounded and all the heavy artillery to New York without delay.[1] He himself followed so closely upon this disgraceful missive that Cummings had no time to obey it.

The defeated and humbled troops proceeded to reoccupy the ground they had left a few days before in the flush of confidence and pride; and young Colonel Williams, of Massachusetts, lost no time in sending the miserable story to his uncle Israel. His letter, which is dated "Lake George (sorrowful situation), July y⁴ 11ᵗʰ," ends thus: "I have told facts; you may put the epithets upon them. In one word, what with fatigue, want of sleep, exercise of mind, and leaving the place we went to capture, the best part of the army is unhinged. I have told enough to make you sick, if the relation acts on you as the facts have on me."

In the routed army was the sturdy John Cleaveland, minister of Ipswich, and now chaplain of Bagley's Massachusetts regiment, who regarded the retreat with a disgust that was shared by many others. "This day," he writes in his Diary, at the head of Lake George, two days after the battle, "wherever I went I found people, officers and soldiers, astonished that we left the French ground, and commenting on the strange conduct in coming off." From this time forth the provincials called their commander Mrs. Nabbycromby.[2] He thought of

---

[1] *Cunningham, aide-de-camp of Abercromby, to Cummings, 8 July, 1758.*

[2] Trumbull, *Hist. Connecticut*, II. 392. "Nabby" (Abigail) was then a common female name in New England.

nothing but fortifying himself. "Towards evening," continues the chaplain, "the General, with his Rehoboam counsellors, came over to line out a fort on the rocky hill where our breastwork was last year. Now we begin to think strongly that the grand expedition against Canada is laid aside, and a foundation made totally to impoverish our country." The whole army was soon intrenched. The chaplain of Bagley's, with his brother Ebenezer, chaplain of another regiment, one day walked round the camp and carefully inspected it. The tour proved satisfactory to the militant divines, and John Cleaveland reported to his wife: "We have built an extraordinary good breastwork, sufficient to defend ourselves against twenty thousand of the enemy, though at present we have not above a third part of that number fit for duty." Many of the troops had been sent to the Mohawk, and others to the Hudson.

In the regiment of which Cleaveland was chaplain there was a young surgeon from Danvers, Dr. Caleb Rea, who also kept a copious diary, and, being of a serious turn, listened with edification to the prayers and exhortations to which the yeoman soldiery were daily summoned. In his zeal, he made an inquest among them for singers, and chose the most melodious to form a regimental choir, "the better to carry on the daily service of singing psalms;" insomuch that the New England camp was vocal with rustic harmony, sincere, if somewhat nasal. These seemly observances were not inconsistent with a certain amount of disorder among the more turbulent spirits, who, removed from the repressive influence of tight-laced village communities, sometimes indulged in conduct which grieved the conscientious surgeon. The rural New England of that time, with its narrowness, its prejudices, its oddities, its combative energy, and rugged, unconquerable strength, is among the things of the past, or lingers in remote corners where the whistle of the locomotive is never heard. It has spread itself in swarming millions over half a continent, changing with changing conditions; and even the part of it that clings to the ancestral hive has transformed and continues to transform itself.

The provincials were happy in their chaplains, among whom there reigned a marvellous harmony, Episcopalians,

Presbyterians, and Congregationalists meeting twice a week to hold prayer-meetings together. "A rare instance indeed," says Dr. Rea, "and perhaps scarce ever was an army blessed with such a set of chaplains before." On one occasion, just before the fatal expedition, nine of them, after prayers and breakfast, went together to call upon the General. "He treated us very kindly," says the chaplain of Bagley's, "and told us that he hoped we would teach the people to do their duty and be courageous; and told us a story of a chaplain in Germany, where he was, who just before the action told the soldiers he had not time to say much, and therefore should only say: 'Be courageous; for no cowards go to heaven.' The General treated us to a bowl of punch and a bottle of wine, and then we took our leave of him."[1]

When Cleaveland and the more gifted among his brethren preached of a Sunday, officers and men of the regulars, no less than the provincials, came to listen; yet that pious Sabbatarian, Dr. Rea, saw much to afflict his conscience. "Sad, sad it is to see how the Sabbath is profaned in the camp," above all by "the horrid custom of swearing, more especially among the regulars; and I can't but charge our defeat on this sin."

It would have been well had the harmony that prevailed among the chaplains found its counterpart among the men of the sword; but between the British regular officers and those of the provinces there was anything but an equal brotherhood. It is true that Pitt, in the spirit of conciliation which he always showed towards the colonies, had procured a change in the regulations concerning the relative rank of British and provincial officers, thus putting them in a position much nearer equality; but this, while appeasing the provincials, seems to have annoyed the others. Till the campaign was nearly over, not a single provincial colonel had been asked to join in a council of war; and, complains Cleaveland, "they know no more of what is to be done than a sergeant, till the orders come out." Of the British officers, the greater part had seen but little active service. Most of them were men of fam-

[1] For the use of the Diary of Chaplain Cleaveland, as well as of his letters to his wife, I am indebted to the kindness of Miss Abby E. Cleaveland, his descendant.

ily, exceedingly prejudiced and insular, whose knowledge of
the world was limited to certain classes of their own countrymen, and who looked down on all others, whether domestic
or foreign. Towards the provincials their attitude was one of
tranquil superiority, though its tranquillity was occasionally
disturbed by what they regarded as absurd pretension on the
part of the colony officers. One of them gave vent to his feelings in an article in the *London Chronicle*, in which he advanced the very reasonable proposition that "a farmer is not
to be taken from the plough and made an officer in a day;"
and he was answered wrathfully, at great length, in the *Boston
Evening Post*, by a writer signing himself "A New England
Man." The provincial officers, on the other hand, and especially those of New England, being no less narrow and prejudiced, filled with a sensitive pride and a jealous local
patriotism, and bred up in a lofty appreciation of the merits
and importance of their country, regarded British supercil-
iousness with a resentment which their strong love for England could not overcome. This feeling was far from being
confined to the officers. A provincial regiment stationed at
Half-Moon, on the Hudson, thought itself affronted by Captain Cruikshank, a regular officer; and the men were so incensed that nearly half of them went off in a body. The
deportment of British officers in the Seven Years War no
doubt had some part in hastening on the Revolution.

What with levelling Montcalm's siege works, planting palisades, and grubbing up stumps in their bungling and laborious way, the regulars found abundant occupation. Discipline
was stiff and peremptory. The wooden horse and the whip-
ping-post were conspicuous objects in the camp, and often in
use. Caleb Rea, being tender-hearted, never went to see the
lash laid on; for, as he quaintly observes, "the cries were satisfactory to me, without the sight of the strokes." He and the
rest of the doctors found active exercise for such skill as they
had, since fever and dysentery were making scarcely less havoc
than the bullets at Ticonderoga. This came from the bad state
of the camps and unwholesome food. The provincial surgeons
seem to have been very little impressed with the importance
of sanitary regulations, and to have thought it their business
not to prevent disease, but only to cure it. The one grand

essential in their eyes was a well-stocked medicine-chest, rich in exhaustless stores of rhubarb, ipecacuanha, and calomel. Even this sometimes failed. Colonel Williams reports "the sick destitute of everything proper for them; medicine-chest empty; nothing but their dirty blankets for beds; Dr. Ashley dead, Dr. Wright gone home, low enough; Bille worn off his legs,—such is our case. I have near a hundred sick. Lost a sergeant and a private last night."[1] Chaplain Cleaveland himself, though strong of frame, did not escape; but he found solace in his trouble from the congenial society of a brother chaplain, Mr. Emerson, of New Hampshire, "a right-down hearty Christian minister, of savory conversation," who came to see him in his tent, breakfasted with him, and joined him in prayer. Being somewhat better, he one day thought to recreate himself with the apostolic occupation of fishing. The sport was poor; the fish bit slowly; and as he lay in his boat, still languid with his malady, he had leisure to reflect on the contrasted works of Providence and man,—the bright lake basking amid its mountains, a dream of wilderness beauty, and the swarms of harsh humanity on the shore beside him, with their passions, discords, and miseries. But it was with the strong meat of Calvinistic theology, and not with reveries like these, that he was accustomed to nourish his military flock.

While at one end of the lake the force of Abercromby was diminished by detachments and disease, that of Montcalm at the other was so increased by reinforcements that a forward movement on his part seemed possible. He contented himself, however, with strengthening the fort, reconstructing the lines that he had defended so well, and sending out frequent war-parties by way of Wood Creek and South Bay, to harass Abercromby's communications with Fort Edward. These parties, some of which consisted of several hundred men, were generally more or less successful; and one of them, under La Corne, surprised and destroyed a large wagon train escorted by forty soldiers. When Abercromby heard of it, he ordered Rogers, with a strong detachment of provincials, light infantry, and rangers, to go down the lake in boats, cross the mountains to the narrow waters of Lake Champlain, and cut

[1] *Colonel William Williams to Colonel Israel Williams, 4 Sept. 1758.*

off the enemy. But though Rogers set out at two in the morning, the French retreated so fast that he arrived too late. As he was on his way back, he was met by a messenger from the General with orders to intercept other French parties reported to be hovering about Fort Edward. On this he retraced his steps, marched through the forest to where Whitehall now stands, and thence made his way up Wood Creek to old Fort Anne, a relic of former wars, abandoned and falling to decay. Here, on the neglected "clearing" that surrounded the ruin, his followers encamped. They counted seven hundred in all, and consisted of about eighty rangers, a body of Connecticut men under Major Putnam, and a small regular force, chiefly light infantry, under Captain Dalzell, the brave officer who was afterwards killed by Pontiac's warriors at Detroit.

Up to this time Rogers had observed his usual caution, commanding silence on the march, and forbidding fires at night; but, seeing no signs of an enemy, he forgot himself; and on the following morning, the eighth of August, he and Lieutenant Irwin, of the light infantry, amused themselves by firing at a mark on a wager. The shots reached the ears of four hundred and fifty French and Indians under the famous partisan Marin, who at once took steps to reconnoitre and ambuscade his rash enemy. For nearly a mile from the old fort the forest had formerly been cut down and burned; and Nature had now begun to reassert herself, covering the open tract with a dense growth of bushes and saplings almost impervious to anything but a wild-cat, had it not been traversed by a narrow Indian path. Along this path the men were forced to march in single file. At about seven o'clock, when the two marksmen had decided their bet, and before the heavy dew of the night was dried upon the bushes, the party slung their packs and set out. Putnam was in the front with his Connecticut men; Dalzell followed with the regulars; and Rogers, with his rangers, brought up the rear of the long and slender line. Putnam himself led the way, shouldering through the bushes, gun in hand; and just as the bluff yeoman emerged from them to enter the forest-growth beyond, the air was rent with yells, the thickets before him were filled with Indians, and one of them, a Caughnawaga chief, sprang upon him, hatchet in hand. He had time to cock his gun and snap it at the breast of his assailant; but it missed fire, and he was instantly seized and dragged back into the forest, as were also a lieutenant named Tracy and three private men. Then the firing began. The French and Indians, lying across the path in a semicircle, had the advantage of position and surprise. The Connecticut men fell back among the bushes in disorder; but soon rallied, and held the enemy in check while Dalzell and Rogers—the latter of whom was nearly a mile behind—were struggling through briers and thickets to their aid. So close was the brushwood that it was full half an hour before they could get their followers ranged in some kind of order in front of the enemy; and even then each man was forced to fight for himself as best he could. Humphreys, the biographer of Putnam, blames Rogers severely for not coming at once to the aid of the Connecticut men; but two of their captains declare that he came with all possible speed; while a regular officer present highly praised him to Abercromby for cool and officer-like conduct.[1] As a man his deserts were small; as a bushfighter he was beyond reproach.

Another officer recounts from hearsay the remarkable conduct of an Indian, who sprang into the midst of the English and killed two of them with his hatchet; then mounted on a log and defied them all. One of the regulars tried to knock him down with the butt of his musket; but though the blow made him bleed, he did not fall, and would have killed his assailant if Rogers had not shot him dead.[2] The firing lasted about two hours. At length some of the Canadians gave way, and the rest of the French and Indians followed.[3] They broke into small parties to elude pursuit, and reuniting towards evening, made their bivouac on a spot surrounded by impervious swamps.

Rogers remained on the field and buried all his own dead, forty-nine in number. Then he resumed his march to Fort Edward, carrying the wounded on litters of branches till the

---

[1] *Letter from the Camp at Lake George, 5 Sept. 1758*, signed by Captains Maynard and Giddings, and printed in the *Boston Weekly Advertiser*. "Rogers deserves much to be commended." *Abercromby to Pitt, 19 Aug. 1758.*

[2] *Thomas Barnsley to Bouquet, 7 Sept. 1758.*

[3] *Doreil au Ministre, 31 Août, 1757.*

next day, when he met a detachment coming with wagons to his relief. A party sent out soon after for the purpose reported that they had found and buried more than a hundred French and Indians. From this time forward the war-parties from Ticonderoga greatly relented in their activity.

The adventures of the captured Putnam were sufficiently remarkable. The Indians, after dragging him to the rear, lashed him fast to a tree so that he could not move a limb, and a young savage amused himself by throwing a hatchet at his head, striking it into the wood as close as possible to the mark without hitting it. A French petty officer then thrust the muzzle of his gun violently against the prisoner's body, pretended to fire it at him, and at last struck him in the face with the butt; after which dastardly proceeding he left him. The French and Indians being forced after a time to fall back, Putnam found himself between the combatants and exposed to bullets from both sides; but the enemy, partially recovering the ground they had lost, unbound him, and led him to a safe distance from the fight. When the retreat began, the Indians hurried him along with them, stripped of coat, waistcoat, shoes, and stockings, his back burdened with as many packs of the wounded as could be piled upon it, and his wrists bound so tightly together that the pain became intense. In his torment he begged them to kill him; on which a French officer who was near persuaded them to untie his hands and take off some of the packs, and the chief who had captured him gave him a pair of moccasons to protect his lacerated feet. When they encamped at night, they prepared to burn him alive, stripped him naked, tied him to a tree, and gathered dry wood to pile about him. A sudden shower of rain interrupted their pastime; but when it was over they began again, and surrounded him with a circle of brushwood which they set on fire. As they were yelling and dancing their delight at the contortions with which he tried to avoid the rising flames, Marin, hearing what was going forward, broke through the crowd, and with a courageous humanity not too common among Canadian officers, dashed aside the burning brush, untied the prisoner, and angrily upbraided his tormentors. He then restored him to the chief who had captured him, and whose right of property in his prize the others had failed to respect.

The Caughnawaga treated him at first with kindness; but, with the help of his tribesmen, took effectual means to prevent his escape, by laying him on his back, stretching his arms and legs in the form of a St. Andrew's cross, and binding the wrists and ankles fast to the stems of young trees. This was a mode of securing prisoners in vogue among Indians from immemorial time; but, not satisfied with it, they placed brushwood upon his body, and then laid across it the long slender stems of saplings, on the ends of which several warriors lay down to sleep, so that the slightest movement on his part would rouse them. Thus he passed a night of misery, which did not prevent him from thinking of the ludicrous figure he made in the hands of the tawny Philistines.

On the next night, after a painful march, he reached Ticonderoga, where he was questioned by Montcalm, and afterwards sent to Montreal in charge of a French officer, who showed him the utmost kindness. On arriving, wofully tattered, bruised, scorched, and torn, he found a friend in Colonel Schuyler, himself a prisoner on parole, who helped him in his need, and through whose good offices the future major-general of the Continental Army was included in the next exchange of prisoners.[1]

The petty victory over Marin was followed by a more substantial success. Early in September Abercromby's melancholy camp was cheered with the tidings that the important French post of Fort Frontenac, which controlled Lake Ontario, which had baffled Shirley in his attempt against Niagara, and given Montcalm the means of conquering Oswego, had fallen into British hands. "This is a glorious piece of news, and may

[1] On Putnam's adventures, Humphreys, 57 (1818). He had the story from Putnam himself, and seems to give it with substantial correctness, though his account of the battle is at several points erroneous. The "Molang" of his account is Marin. On the battle, besides authorities already cited, *Recollections of Thomson Maxwell*, a soldier present (*Essex Institute*, VII. 97). Rogers, *Journals*, 117. Letter from camp in *Boston Gazette*, no. 117. Another in *New Hampshire Gazette*, no. 104. *Gentleman's Magazine*, 1758, p. 498. Malartic, *Journal du Régiment de Béarn*. Lévis, *Journal de la Guerre en Canada*. The French notices of the affair are few and brief. They admit a defeat, but exaggerate the force and the losses of the English, and underrate their own. Malartic, however, says that Marin set out with four hundred men, and was soon after joined by an additional number of Indians; which nearly answers to the best English accounts.

God have all the glory of the same!" writes Chaplain Cleaveland in his Diary. Lieutenant-Colonel Bradstreet had planned
the stroke long before, and proposed it first to Loudon, and
then to Abercromby. Loudon accepted it; but his successor
received it coldly, though Lord Howe was warm in its favor.
At length, under the pressure of a council of war, Abercromby consented that the attempt should be made, and gave
Bradstreet three thousand men, nearly all provincials. With
these he made his way, up the Mohawk and down the Onondaga, to the lonely and dismal spot where Oswego had once
stood. By dint of much persuasion a few Oneidas joined him;
though, like most of the Five Nations, they had been nearly
lost to the English through the effects of the defeat at Ticonderoga. On the twenty-second of August his fleet of whaleboats and bateaux pushed out on Lake Ontario; and, three
days after, landed near the French fort. On the night of the
twenty-sixth Bradstreet made a lodgment within less than two
hundred yards of it; and early in the morning De Noyan, the
commandant, surrendered himself and his followers, numbering a hundred and ten soldiers and laborers, prisoners of war.
With them were taken nine armed vessels, carrying from eight
to eighteen guns, and forming the whole French naval force
on Lake Ontario. The crews escaped. An enormous quantity
of provisions, naval stores, munitions, and Indian goods intended for the supply of the western posts fell into the hands
of the English, who kept what they could carry off, and
burned the rest. In the fort were found sixty cannon and sixteen mortars, which the victors used to batter down the walls;
and then, reserving a few of the best, knocked off the trunnions of the others. The Oneidas were bent on scalping some
of the prisoners. Bradstreet forbade it. They begged that he
would do as the French did,—turn his back and shut his
eyes; but he forced them to abstain from all violence, and
consoled them by a lion's share of the plunder. In accordance
with the orders of Abercromby, the fort was dismantled, and
all the buildings in or around it burned, as were also the vessels, except the two largest, which were reserved to carry off
some of the captured goods. Then, with boats deeply laden,
the detachment returned to Oswego; where, after unloading
and burning the two vessels, they proceeded towards Albany,

leaving a thousand of their number at the new fort which Brigadier Stanwix was building at the Great Carrying Place of the Mohawk.

Next to Louisbourg, this was the heaviest blow that the French had yet received. Their command of Lake Ontario was gone. New France was cut in two; and unless the severed parts could speedily reunite, all the posts of the interior would be in imminent jeopardy. If Bradstreet had been followed by another body of men to reoccupy and rebuild Oswego, thus recovering a harbor on Lake Ontario, all the captured French vessels could have been brought thither, and the command of this inland sea assured at once. Even as it was, the advantages were immense. A host of savage warriors, thus far inclined to France or wavering between the two belligerents, stood henceforth neutral, or gave themselves to England; while Fort Duquesne, deprived of the supplies on which it depended, could make but faint resistance to its advancing enemy.

Amherst, with five regiments from Louisbourg, came, early in October, to join Abercromby at Lake George, and the two commanders discussed the question of again attacking Ticonderoga. Both thought the season too late. A fortnight after, a deserter brought news that Montcalm was breaking up his camp. Abercromby followed his example. The opposing armies filed off each to its winter quarters, and only a few scouting parties kept alive the embers of war on the waters and mountains of Lake George.

Meanwhile Brigadier Forbes was climbing the Alleghanies, hewing his way through the forests of western Pennsylvania, and toiling inch by inch towards his goal of Fort Duquesne.[1]

[1] On the capture of Fort Frontenac, *Bradstreet to Abercromby, 31 Aug. 1758. Impartial Account of Lieutenant-Colonel Bradstreet's Expedition, by a Volunteer in the Expedition* (London, 1759). Letter from a New York officer to his colonel, in *Boston Gazette*, no. 182. Several letters from persons in the expedition, in *Boston Evening Post*, no. 1,203, *New Hampshire Gazette*, no. 104, and *Boston News Letter*, no. 2,932. *Abercromby to Pitt, 25 Nov. 1758. Lieutenant Macauley to Horatio Gates, 30 Aug. 1758. Vaudreuil au Ministre, 30 Oct. 1758.* Pouchot, I. 162. *Mémoires sur le Canada, 1749–1760.*

Chapter XXII

1758

FORT DUQUESNE

Dinwiddie and Washington • Brigadier Forbes • His Army • Conflicting Views • Difficulties • Illness of Forbes • His Sufferings • His Fortitude • His Difference with Washington • Sir John Sinclair • Troublesome Allies • Scouting Parties • Boasts of Vaudreuil • Forbes and the Indians • Mission of Christian Frederic Post • Council of Peace • Second Mission of Post • Defeat of Grant • Distress of Forbes • Dark Prospects • Advance of the Army • Capture of the French Fort • The Slain of Braddock's Field • Death of Forbes

DURING the last year Loudon, filled with vain schemes against Louisbourg, had left the French scalping-parties to their work of havoc on the western borders. In Virginia Washington still toiled at his hopeless task of defending with a single regiment a forest frontier of more than three hundred miles; and in Pennsylvania the Assembly thought more of quarrelling with their governor than of protecting the tormented settlers. Fort Duquesne, the source of all the evil, was left undisturbed. In vain Washington urged the futility of defensive war, and the necessity of attacking the enemy in his stronghold. His position, trying at the best, was made more so by the behavior of Dinwiddie. That crusty Scotchman had conceived a dislike to him, and sometimes treated him in a manner that must have been unspeakably galling to the proud and passionate young man, who nevertheless, unconquerable in his sense of public duty, curbed himself to patience, or the semblance of it.

Dinwiddie was now gone, and a new governor had taken his place. The conduct of the war, too, had changed, and in the plans of Pitt the capture of Fort Duquesne held an important place. Brigadier John Forbes was charged with it. He was a Scotch veteran, forty-eight years of age, who had begun life as a student of medicine, and who ended it as an able and faithful soldier. Though a well-bred man of the world, his tastes were simple; he detested ceremony, and dealt frankly and plainly with the colonists, who both respected and liked him. In April he was in Philadelphia waiting for his army, which as yet had no existence; for the provincials were not enlisted, and an expected battalion of Highlanders had not arrived. It was the end of June before they were all on the march; and meanwhile the General was attacked with a painful and dangerous malady, which would have totally disabled a less resolute man.

His force consisted of provincials from Pennsylvania, Virginia, Maryland, and North Carolina, with twelve hundred Highlanders of Montgomery's regiment and a detachment of Royal Americans, amounting in all, with wagoners and camp followers, to between six and seven thousand men. The Royal American regiment was a new corps raised, in the colonies, largely from among the Germans of Pennsylvania. Its officers were from Europe; and conspicuous among them was Lieutenant-Colonel Henry Bouquet, a brave and accomplished Swiss, who commanded one of the four battalions of which the regiment was composed. Early in July he was encamped with the advance-guard at the hamlet of Raystown, now the town of Bedford, among the eastern heights of the Alleghanies. Here his tents were pitched in an opening of the forest by the banks of a small stream; and Virginians in hunting-shirts, Highlanders in kilt and plaid, and Royal Americans in regulation scarlet, labored at throwing up intrenchments and palisades, while around stood the silent mountains in their mantles of green.

Now rose the question whether the army should proceed in a direct course to Fort Duquesne, hewing a new road through the forest, or march thirty-four miles to Fort Cumberland, and thence follow the road made by Braddock. It was the interest of Pennsylvania that Forbes should choose the former route, and of Virginia that he should choose the latter. The Old Dominion did not wish to see a highway cut for her rival to those rich lands of the Ohio which she called her own. Washington, who was then at Fort Cumberland with a part of his regiment, was earnest for the old road; and in an interview with Bouquet midway between that place and Raystown, he spared no effort to bring him to the same opinion. But the quartermaster-general, Sir John Sinclair, who

was supposed to know the country, had advised the Pennsylvania route; and both Bouquet and Forbes were resolved to
take it. It was shorter, and when once made would furnish
readier and more abundant supplies of food and forage; but
to make it would consume a vast amount of time and labor.
Washington foretold the ruin of the expedition unless it took
Braddock's road. Ardent Virginian as he was, there is no
cause to believe that his decision was based on any but military reasons; but Forbes thought otherwise, and found great
fault with him. Bouquet did him more justice. "Colonel
Washington," he writes to the General, "is filled with a sincere zeal to aid the expedition, and is ready to march with
equal activity by whatever way you choose."

The fate of Braddock had impressed itself on all the army,
and inspired a caution that was but too much needed; since,
except Washington's men and a few others among the provincials, the whole, from general to drummer-boy, were total
strangers to that insidious warfare of the forest in which their
enemies, red and white, had no rival. Instead of marching,
like Braddock, at one stretch for Fort Duquesne, burdened
with a long and cumbrous baggage-train, it was the plan of
Forbes to push on by slow stages, establishing fortified magazines as he went, and at last, when within easy distance of
the fort, to advance upon it with all his force, as little
impeded as possible with wagons and pack-horses. He bore
no likeness to his predecessor, except in determined resolution, and he did not hesitate to embrace military heresies
which would have driven Braddock to fury. To Bouquet, in
whom he placed a well-merited trust, he wrote, "I have been
long in your opinion of equipping numbers of our men like
the savages, and I fancy Colonel Burd, of Virginia, has most
of his best people equipped in that manner. In this country
we must learn the art of war from enemy Indians, or anybody
else who has seen it carried on here."

His provincials displeased him, not without reason; for the
greater part were but the crudest material for an army, unruly,
and recalcitrant to discipline. Some of them came to the rendezvous at Carlisle with old province muskets, the locks tied
on with a string; others brought fowling-pieces of their own,
and others carried nothing but walking-sticks; while many

had never fired a gun in their lives.[1] Forbes reported to Pitt that their officers, except a few in the higher ranks, were "an extremely bad collection of broken innkeepers, horse-jockeys, and Indian traders;" nor is he more flattering towards the men, though as to some of them he afterwards changed his mind.[2]

While Bouquet was with the advance at Raystown, Forbes was still in Philadelphia, trying to bring the army into shape, and collecting provisions, horses, and wagons; much vexed meantime by the Assembly, whose tedious disputes about taxing the proprietaries greatly obstructed the service. "No sergeant or quartermaster of a regiment," he says, "is obliged to look into more details than I am; and if I did not see to everything myself, we should never get out of this town." July had begun before he could reach the frontier village of Carlisle, where he found everything in confusion. After restoring some order, he wrote to Bouquet: "I have been and still am but poorly, with a cursed flux, but shall move day after to-morrow." He was doomed to disappointment; and it was not till the ninth of August that he sent another letter from the same place to the same military friend. "I am now able to write after three weeks of a most violent and tormenting distemper, which, thank God, seems now much abated as to pain, but has left me as weak as a new-born infant. However, I hope to have strength enough to set out from this place on Friday next." The disease was an inflammation of the stomach and other vital organs; and when he should have been in bed, with complete repose of body and mind, he was racked continually with the toils and worries of a most arduous campaign.

He left Carlisle on the eleventh, carried on a kind of litter made of a hurdle slung between two horses; and two days later he wrote from Shippensburg: "My journey here from Carlisle raised my disorder and pains to so intolerable a degree that I was obliged to stop, and may not get away for a day or two." Again, on the eighteenth: "I am better, and partly free from the excruciating pain I suffered; but still so weak that I can scarce bear motion." He lay helpless at Ship-

[1] *Correspondence of Forbes and Bouquet, July, August, 1758.*
[2] *Forbes to Pitt, 6 Sept. 1758.*

pensburg till September was well advanced. On the second he says: "I really cannot describe how I have suffered both in body and mind of late, and the relapses have been worse as the disappointment was greater;" and on the fourth, still writing to Bouquet, who in the camp at Raystown was struggling with many tribulations: "I am sorry you have met with so many cross accidents to vex you, and have such a parcel of scoundrels as the provincials to work with; *mais le vin est tiré*, and you must drop a little of the gentleman and treat them as they deserve. Seal and send off the enclosed despatch to Sir John by some sure hand. He is a very odd man, and I am sorry it has been my fate to have any concern with him. I am afraid our army will not admit of division, lest one half meet with a check; therefore I would consult Colonel Washington, though perhaps not follow his advice, as his behavior about the roads was noways like a soldier. I thank my good cousin for his letter, and have only to say that I have all my life been subject to err; but I now reform, as I go to bed at eight at night, if able to sit up so late."

Nobody can read the letters of Washington at this time without feeling that the imputations of Forbes were unjust, and that here, as elsewhere, his ruling motive was the public good.[1] Forbes himself, seeing the rugged and difficult nature of the country, began to doubt whether after all he had not better have chosen the old road of Braddock. He soon had an interview with its chief advocates, the two Virginia colonels, Washington and Burd, and reported the result to Bouquet, adding: "I told them that, whatever they thought, I had acted on the best information to be had, and could safely say for myself, and believed I might answer for you, that the good of the service was all we had at heart, not valuing provincial interests, jealousies, or suspicions one single twopence." It must be owned that, considering the slow and sure mode of advance which he had wisely adopted, the old soldier was probably right in his choice; since before the army could reach Fort Duquesne, the autumnal floods would have made the Youghiogany and the Monongahela impassable.

---

[1] Besides the printed letters, there is an autograph collection of his correspondence with Bouquet in 1758 (forming vol. 21,641, *Additional Manuscripts*, British Museum). Copies of the whole are before me.

The Sir John mentioned by Forbes was the quartermaster-general, Sir John Sinclair, who had gone forward with Virginians and other troops from the camp of Bouquet to make the road over the main range of the Alleghanies, whence he sent back the following memorandum of his requirements: "Pickaxes, crows, and shovels; likewise more whiskey. Send me the newspapers, and tell my black to send me a candlestick and half a loaf of sugar." He was extremely inefficient; and Forbes, out of all patience with him, wrote confidentially to Bouquet that his only talent was for throwing everything into confusion. Yet he found fault with everybody else, and would discharge volleys of oaths at all who met his disapproval. From this cause or some other, Lieutenant-Colonel Stephen, of the Virginians, told him that he would break his sword rather than be longer under his orders. "As I had not sufficient strength," says Sinclair, "to take him by the neck from among his own men, I was obliged to let him have his own way, that I might not be the occasion of bloodshed." He succeeded at last in arresting him, and Major Lewis, of the same regiment, took his place.

The aid of Indians as scouts and skirmishers was of the last importance to an army so weak in the arts of woodcraft, and efforts were made to engage the services of the friendly Cherokees and Catawbas, many of whom came to the camp, where their caprice, insolence, and rapacity tried to the utmost the patience of the commanders. That of Sir John Sinclair had already been overcome by his dealings with the provincial authorities; and he wrote in good French, at the tail of a letter to the Swiss colonel: "Adieu, my dear Bouquet. The greatest curse that our Lord can pronounce against the worst of sinners is to give them business to do with provincial commissioners and friendly Indians." A band of sixty warriors told Colonel Burd that they would join the army on condition that it went by Braddock's road. "This," wrote Forbes, on hearing of the proposal, "is a new system of military discipline truly, and shows that my good friend Burd is either made a cat's-foot of himself, or little knows me if he imagines that sixty scoundrels are to direct me in my measures."[1] Bouquet,

[1] The above extracts are from the *Bouquet and Haldimand Papers*, British Museum.

with a pliant tact rarely seen in the born Briton, took great pains to please these troublesome allies, and went so far as to adopt one of them as his son.[1] A considerable number joined the army; but they nearly all went off when the stock of presents provided for them was exhausted.

Forbes was in total ignorance of the strength and movements of the enemy. The Indians reported their numbers to be at least equal to his own; but nothing could be learned from them with certainty, by reason of their inveterate habit of lying. Several scouting-parties of whites were therefore sent forward, of which the most successful was that of a young Virginian officer, accompanied by a sergeant and five Indians. At a little distance from the French fort, the Indians stopped to paint themselves and practise incantations. The chief warrior of the party then took certain charms from an otter-skin bag and tied them about the necks of the other Indians. On that of the officer he hung the otter-skin itself; while to the sergeant he gave a small packet of paint from the same mystic receptacle. "He told us," reports the officer, "that none of us could be shot, for those things would turn the balls from us; and then shook hands with us, and told us to go and fight like men." Thus armed against fate, they mounted the high ground afterwards called Grant's Hill, where, covered by trees and bushes, they had a good view of the fort, and saw plainly that the reports of the French force were greatly exaggerated.[2]

Meanwhile Bouquet's men pushed on the heavy work of road-making up the main range of the Alleghanies, and, what proved far worse, the parallel mountain ridge of Laurel Hill, hewing, digging, blasting, laying fascines and gabions to support the track along the sides of steep declivities, or worming their way like moles through the jungle of swamp and forest. Forbes described the country to Pitt as an "immense uninhabited wilderness, overgrown everywhere with trees and brushwood, so that nowhere can one see twenty yards." In truth, as far as eye or mind could reach, a prodigious forest vegetation spread its impervious canopy over hill, valley, and

[1] *Bouquet to Forbes, 3 June, 1758.*

[2] *Journal of a Reconnoitring Party, Aug. 1758.* The writer seems to have been Ensign Chew, of Washington's regiment.

plain, and wrapped the stern and awful waste in the shadows of the tomb.

Having secured his magazines at Raystown, and built a fort there named Fort Bedford, Bouquet made a forward movement of some forty miles, crossed the main Alleghany and Laurel Hill, and, taking post on a stream called Loyalhannon Creek, began another depot of supplies as a base for the final advance on Fort Duquesne, which was scarcely fifty miles distant.

Vaudreuil had learned from prisoners the march of Forbes, and, with his usual egotism, announced to the Colonial Minister what he had done in consequence. "I have provided for the safety of Fort Duquesne." "I have sent reinforcements to M. de Ligneris, who commands there." "I have done the impossible to supply him with provisions, and I am now sending them in abundance, in order that the troops I may perhaps have occasion to send to drive off the English may not be delayed." "A stronger fort is needed on the Ohio; but I cannot build one till after the peace; then I will take care to build such a one as will thenceforth keep the English out of that country." Some weeks later he was less confident, and very anxious for news from Ligneris. He says that he has sent him all the succors he could, and ordered troops to go to his aid from Niagara, Detroit, and Illinois, as well as the militia of Detroit, with the Indians there and elsewhere in the West,—Hurons, Ottawas, Pottawattamies, Miamis, and other tribes. What he fears is that the English will not attack the fort till all these Indians have grown tired of waiting, and have gone home again.[1] This was precisely the intention of Forbes, and the chief object of his long delays.

He had another good reason for making no haste. There was hope that the Delawares and Shawanoes, who lived within easy reach of Fort Duquesne, and who for the past three years had spread havoc throughout the English border, might now be won over from the French alliance. Forbes wrote to Bouquet from Shippensburg: "After many intrigues with Quakers, the Provincial Commissioners, the Governor, etc., and by the downright bullying of Sir William Johnson, I hope I have now brought about a general convention of the

[1] *Vaudreuil au Ministre, Juillet, Août, Octobre 1758.*

Indians."[1] The convention was to include the Five Nations, the Delawares, the Shawanoes, and other tribes, who had accepted wampum belts of invitation, and promised to meet the Governor and Commissioners of the various provinces at the town of Easton, before the middle of September. This seeming miracle was wrought by several causes. The Indians in the French interest, always greedy for presents, had not of late got enough to satisfy them. Many of those destined for them had been taken on the way from France by British cruisers, and the rest had passed through the hands of official knaves, who sold the greater part for their own profit. Again, the goods supplied by French fur-traders were few and dear; and the Indians remembered with regret the abundance and comparative cheapness of those they had from the English before the war. At the same time it was reported among them that a British army was marching to the Ohio strong enough to drive out the French from all that country; and the Delawares and Shawanoes of the West began to waver in their attachment to the falling cause. The eastern Delawares, living at Wyoming and elsewhere on the upper Susquehanna, had made their peace with the English in the summer before; and their great chief, Teedyuscung, thinking it for his interest that the tribes of the Ohio should follow his example, sent them wampum belts, inviting them to lay down the hatchet. The Five Nations, with Johnson at one end of the Confederacy and Joncaire at the other,—the one cajoling them in behalf of England, and the other in behalf of France,—were still divided in counsel; but even among the Senecas, the tribe most under Joncaire's influence, there was a party so far inclined to England that, like the Delaware chief, they sent wampum to the Ohio, inviting peace. But the influence most potent in reclaiming the warriors of the West was of a different kind. Christian Frederic Post, a member of the Moravian brotherhood, had been sent at the instance of Forbes as an envoy to the hostile tribes from the Governor and Council of Pennsylvania. He spoke the Delaware language, knew the Indians well, had lived among them, had married a converted squaw, and, by his simplicity of character, directness, and perfect honesty, gained their full confidence. He now accepted

[1] *Forbes to Bouquet, 18 Aug. 1758.*

his terrible mission, and calmly prepared to place himself in the clutches of the tiger. He was a plain German, upheld by a sense of duty and a single-hearted trust in God; alone, with no great disciplined organization to impel and support him, and no visions and illusions such as kindled and sustained the splendid heroism of the early Jesuit martyrs. Yet his errand was no whit less perilous. And here we may notice the contrast between the mission settlements of the Moravians in Pennsylvania and those which the later Jesuits and the Sulpitians had established at Caughnawaga, St. Francis, La Présentation, and other places. The Moravians were apostles of peace, and they succeeded to a surprising degree in weaning their converts from their ferocious instincts and warlike habits; while the Mission Indians of Canada retained all their native fierceness, and were systematically impelled to use their tomahawks against the enemies of the Church. Their wigwams were hung with scalps, male and female, adult and infant; and these so-called missions were but nests of baptized savages, who wore the crucifix instead of the medicine-bag, and were encouraged by the Government for purposes of war.[1]

The Moravian envoy made his way to the Delaware town of Kushkushkee, on Beaver Creek, northwest of Fort Duquesne, where the three chiefs known as King Beaver, Shingas, and Delaware George received him kindly, and conducted him to another town on the same stream. Here his reception was different. A crowd of warriors, their faces distorted with rage, surrounded him, brandishing knives and threatening to kill him; but others took his part, and, order being at last restored, he read them his message from the Governor, which seemed to please them. They insisted, however, that he should go with them to Fort Duquesne, in order that the Indians assembled there might hear it also. Against this dangerous proposal he protested in vain. On arriving near the fort, the French demanded that he should be given

---

[1] Of the Hurons of the mission of Lorette, Bougainville says: "Ils sont toujours sauvages autant que ceux qui sont les moins apprivoisés." And yet they had been converts under Jesuit control for more than four generations. The case was no better at the other missions; and at St. Francis it seems to have been worse.

up to them, and, being refused, offered a great reward for his scalp; on which his friends advised him to keep close by the camp-fire, as parties were out with intent to kill him. "Accordingly," says Post, "I stuck to the fire as if I had been chained there. On the next day the Indians, with a great many French officers, came out to hear what I had to say. The officers brought with them a table, pens, ink, and paper. I spoke in the midst of them with a free conscience, and perceived by their looks that they were not pleased with what I said." The substance of his message was an invitation to the Indians to renew the old chain of friendship, joined with a warning that an English army was on its way to drive off the French, and that they would do well to stand neutral.

He addressed an audience filled with an inordinate sense of their own power and importance, believing themselves greater and braver than either of the European nations, and yet deeply jealous of both. "We have heard," they said, "that the French and English mean to kill all the Indians and divide the land among themselves." And on this string they harped continually. If they had known their true interest, they would have made no peace with the English, but would have united as one man to form a barrier of fire against their farther progress; for the West in English hands meant farms, villages, cities, the ruin of the forest, the extermination of the game, and the expulsion of those who lived on it; while the West in French hands meant but scattered posts of war and trade, with the native tribes cherished as indispensable allies.

After waiting some days, the three tribes of the Delawares met in council, and made their answer to the message brought by Post. It was worthy of a proud and warlike race, and was to the effect that since their brothers of Pennsylvania wished to renew the old peace-chain, they on their part were willing to do so, provided that the wampum belt should be sent them in the name, not of Pennsylvania alone, but of the rest of the provinces also.

Having now accomplished his errand, Post wished to return home; but the Indians were seized with an access of distrust, and would not let him go. This jealousy redoubled when they saw him writing in his notebook. "It is a troublesome cross and heavy yoke to draw this people," he says;

"they can punish and squeeze a body's heart to the utmost. There came some together and examined me about what I had wrote yesterday. I told them I writ what was my duty. 'Brothers, I tell you I am not afraid of you. I have a good conscience before God and man. I tell you, brothers, there is a bad spirit in your hearts, which breeds jealousy, and will keep you ever in fear.' " At last they let him go; and, eluding a party that lay in wait for his scalp, he journeyed twelve days through the forest, and reached Fort Augusta with the report of his mission.[1]

As the result of it, a great convention of white men and red was held at Easton in October. The neighboring provinces had been asked to send their delegates, and some of them did so; while belts of invitation were sent to the Indians far and near. Sir William Johnson, for reasons best known to himself, at first opposed the plan; but was afterwards led to favor it and to induce tribes under his influence to join in the grand pacification. The Five Nations, with the smaller tribes lately admitted into their confederacy, the Delawares of the Susquehanna, the Mohegans, and several kindred bands, all had their representatives at the meeting. The conferences lasted nineteen days, with the inevitable formalities of such occasions, and the weary repetition of conventional metaphors and longwinded speeches. At length, every difficulty being settled, the Governor of Pennsylvania, in behalf of all the English, rose with a wampum belt in his hand, and addressed the tawny congregation thus: "By this belt we heal your wounds; we remove your grief; we take the hatchet out of your heads; we make a hole in the earth, and bury it so deep that nobody can dig it up again." Then, laying the first belt before them, he took another, very large, made of white wampum beads, in token of peace: "By this belt we renew all our treaties; we brighten the chain of friendship; we put fresh earth to the roots of the tree of peace, that it may bear up against every storm, and live and flourish while the sun shines and the rivers run." And he gave them the belt with the request that they would send it to their friends and allies, and invite them to take hold also of the chain of friendship. Accordingly all

[1] *Journal of Christian Frederic Post, July, August, September, 1758.*

present agreed on a joint message of peace to the tribes of the Ohio.[1]

Frederic Post, with several white and Indian companions, was chosen to bear it. A small escort of soldiers that attended him as far as the Alleghany was cut to pieces on its return by a band of the very warriors to whom he was carrying his offers of friendship; and other tenants of the grim and frowning wilderness met the invaders of their domain with inhospitable greetings. "The wolves made a terrible music this night," he writes at his first bivouac after leaving Loyalhannon. When he reached the Delaware towns his reception was ominous. The young warriors said: "Anybody can see with half an eye that the English only mean to cheat us. Let us knock the messengers in the head." Some of them had attacked an English outpost, and had been repulsed; hence, in the words of Post, "They were possessed with a murdering spirit, and with bloody vengeance were thirsty and drunk. I said: 'As God has stopped the mouths of the lions that they could not devour Daniel, so he will preserve us from their fury.'" The chiefs and elders were of a different mind from their fierce and capricious young men. They met during the evening in the loghouse where Post and his party lodged; and here a French officer presently arrived with a string of wampum from the commandant, inviting them to help him drive back the army of Forbes. The string was scornfully rejected. "They kicked it from one to another as if it were a snake. Captain Peter took a stick, and with it flung the string from one end of the room to the other, and said: 'Give it to the French captain; he boasted of his fighting, now let us see him fight. We have often ventured our lives for him, and got hardly a loaf of bread in return; and now he thinks we shall jump to serve him.' Then we saw the French captain mortified to the uttermost. He looked as pale as death. The Indians discoursed and joked till midnight, and the French captain sent messengers at midnight to Fort Duquesne."

There was a grand council, at which the French officer was present; and Post delivered the peace message from the council at Easton, along with another with which Forbes had charged him. "The messages pleased all the hearers except the

[1] *Minutes of Conferences at Easton, October, 1758.*

French captain. He shook his head in bitter grief, and often changed countenance. Isaac Still [*an Indian*] ran him down with great boldness, and pointed at him, saying, 'There he sits!' They all said: 'The French always deceived us!' pointing at the French captain; who, bowing down his head, turned quite pale, and could look no one in the face. All the Indians began to mock and laugh at him. He could hold it no longer, and went out."[1]

The overtures of peace were accepted, and the Delawares, Shawanoes, and Mingoes were no longer enemies of the English. The loss was the more disheartening to the French, since, some weeks before, they had gained a success which they hoped would confirm the adhesion of all their wavering allies. Major Grant, of the Highlanders, had urged Bouquet to send him to reconnoitre Fort Duquesne, capture prisoners, and strike a blow that would animate the assailants and discourage the assailed. Bouquet, forgetting his usual prudence, consented; and Grant set out from the camp at Loyalhannon with about eight hundred men, Highlanders, Royal Americans, and provincials. On the fourteenth of September, at two in the morning, he reached the top of the rising ground thenceforth called Grant's Hill, half a mile or more from the French fort. The forest and the darkness of the night hid him completely from the enemy. He ordered Major Lewis, of the Virginians, to take with him half the detachment, descend to the open plain before the fort, and attack the Indians known to be encamped there; after which he was to make a feigned retreat to the hill, where the rest of the troops were to lie in ambush and receive the pursuers. Lewis set out on his errand, while Grant waited anxiously for the result. Dawn was near, and all was silent; till at length Lewis returned, and incensed his commander by declaring that his men had lost their way in the dark woods, and fallen into such confusion that the attempt was impracticable. The morning twilight now began, but the country was wrapped in thick fog. Grant abandoned his first plan, and sent a few Highlanders into the cleared ground to burn a warehouse that had been seen there. He was convinced that the French and their Indians were too few

[1] *Journal of Christian Frederic Post, October, November, 1758.*

to attack him, though their numbers in fact were far greater than his own.[1] Infatuated with this idea, and bent on taking prisoners, he had the incredible rashness to divide his force in such a way that the several parts could not support each other. Lewis, with two hundred men, was sent to guard the baggage two miles in the rear, where a company of Virginians, under Captain Bullitt, was already stationed. A hundred Pennsylvanians were posted far off on the right, towards the Alleghany, while Captain Mackenzie, with a detachment of Highlanders, was sent to the left, towards the Monongahela. Then, the fog having cleared a little, Captain Macdonald, with another company of Highlanders, was ordered into the open plain to reconnoitre the fort and make a plan of it, Grant himself remaining on the hill with a hundred of his own regiment and a company of Maryland men. "In order to put on a good countenance," he says, "and convince our men they had no reason to be afraid, I gave directions to our drums to beat the reveille. The troops were in an advantageous post, and I must own I thought we had nothing to fear." Macdonald was at this time on the plain, midway between the woods and the fort, and in full sight of it. The roll of the drums from the hill was answered by a burst of war-whoops, and the French came swarming out like hornets, many of them in their shirts, having just leaped from their beds. They all rushed upon Macdonald and his men, who met them with a volley that checked their advance; on which they surrounded him at a distance, and tried to cut off his retreat. The Highlanders broke through, and gained the woods, with the loss of their commander, who was shot dead. A crowd of French followed close, and soon put them to rout, driving them and Mackenzie's party back to the hill where Grant was posted. Here there was a hot fight in the forest, lasting about three quarters of an hour. At length the force of numbers, the novelty of the situation, and the appalling yells of the Canadians and Indians, completely overcame the Highlanders, so

---

[1] *Grant to Forbes, no date.* "Les rapports sur le nombre des Français varient de 3,000 à 1,200." *Bouquet à Forbes, 17 Sept. 1758.* Bigot says that 3,500 daily rations were delivered at Fort Duquesne throughout the summer. *Bigot au Ministre, 22 Nov. 1758.* In October the number had fallen to 1,180, which included Indians. *Ligneris à Vaudreuil, 18 Oct. 1758.*

intrepid in the ordinary situations of war. They broke away in a wild and disorderly retreat. "Fear," says Grant, "got the better of every other passion; and I trust I shall never again see such a panic among troops."

His only hope was in the detachment he had sent to the rear under Lewis to guard the baggage. But Lewis and his men, when they heard the firing in front, had left their post and pushed forward to help their comrades, taking a straight course through the forest; while Grant was retreating along the path by which he had advanced the night before. Thus they missed each other; and when Grant reached the spot where he expected to find Lewis, he saw to his dismay that nobody was there but Captain Bullitt and his company. He cried in despair that he was a ruined man; not without reason, for the whole body of French and Indians was upon him. Such of his men as held together were forced towards the Alleghany, and, writes Bouquet, "would probably have been cut to pieces but for Captain Bullitt and his Virginians, who kept up the fight against the whole French force till two thirds of them were killed." They were offered quarter, but refused it; and the survivors were driven at last into the Alleghany, where some were drowned, and others swam over and escaped. Grant was surrounded and captured, and Lewis, who presently came up, was also made prisoner, along with some of his men, after a stiff resistance. Thus ended this mismanaged affair, which cost the English two hundred and seventy three killed, wounded, and taken. The rest got back safe to Loyalhannon.[1]

The invalid General was deeply touched by this reverse, yet expressed himself with a moderation that does him honor. He wrote to Bouquet from Raystown: "Your letter of the seventeenth I read with no less surprise than concern, as I could

[1] On Grant's defeat, *Grant to Forbes, no date*, a long and minute report, written while a prisoner. *Bouquet à Forbes, 17 Sept. 1758. Forbes to Pitt, 20 Oct. 1758. Vaudreuil au Ministre, 1 Nov. 1758.* Letters from camp in *Boston Evening Post, Boston Weekly Advertiser, Boston News Letter*, and other provincial newspapers of the time. *List of Killed, Wounded, and Missing in the Action of Sept. 14. Gentleman's Magazine*, XXIX. 173. *Hazard's Pennsylvania Register*, VIII. 141. *Olden Time*, I. 179. Vaudreuil, with characteristic exaggeration, represents all Grant's party as killed or taken, except a few who died of starvation. The returns show that 540 came back safe, out of 813.

not believe that such an attempt would have been made without my knowledge and concurrence. The breaking in upon our fair and flattering hopes of success touches me most sensibly. There are two wounded Highland officers just now arrived, who give so lame an account of the matter that one can draw nothing from them, only that my friend Grant most certainly lost his wits, and by his thirst of fame brought on his own perdition, and ran great risk of ours."[1]

The French pushed their advantage with spirit. Early in October a large body of them hovered in the woods about the camp at Loyalhannon, drove back a detachment sent against them, approached under cover of the trees, and, though beaten off, withdrew deliberately, after burying their dead and killing great numbers of horses and cattle.[2] But, with all their courageous energy, their position was desperate. The militia of Louisiana and the Illinois left the fort in November and went home; the Indians of Detroit and the Wabash would stay no longer; and, worse yet, the supplies destined for Fort Duquesne had been destroyed by Bradstreet at Fort Frontenac. Hence Ligneris was compelled by prospective starvation to dismiss the greater part of his force, and await the approach of his enemy with those that remained.

His enemy was in a plight hardly better than his own. Autumnal rains, uncommonly heavy and persistent, had ruined the newly-cut road. On the mountains the torrents tore it up, and in the valleys the wheels of the wagons and cannon churned it into soft mud. The horses, overworked and underfed, were fast breaking down. The forest had little food for them, and they were forced to drag their own oats and corn, as well as supplies for the army, through two hundred miles of wilderness. In the wretched condition of the road this was no longer possible. The magazines of provisions formed at Raystown and Loyalhannon to support the army on its forward march were emptied faster than they could be filled. Early in October the elements relented; the clouds broke, the

[1] *Forbes to Bouquet, 23 Sept. 1758.*

[2] *Burd to Bouquet, 12 Oct. 1758. Bouquet à Forbes, 13 Oct. 1758. Forbes to Pitt, 20 Oct. 1758. Letter from Loyalhannon, 14 Oct.*, in *Olden Time*, I. 180. *Letters from camp*, in *Boston News Letter. Ligneris à Vaudreuil, 18 Oct. 1758. Vaudreuil au Ministre, 20 Nov. 1758.*

sky was bright again, and the sun shone out in splendor on mountains radiant in the livery of autumn. A gleam of hope revisited the heart of Forbes. It was but a flattering illusion. The sullen clouds returned, and a chill, impenetrable veil of mist and rain hid the mountains and the trees. Dejected Nature wept and would not be comforted. Above, below, around, all was trickling, oozing, pattering, gushing. In the miserable encampments the starved horses stood steaming in the rain, and the men crouched, disgusted, under their dripping tents, while the drenched picket-guard in the neighboring forest paced dolefully through black mire and spongy mosses. The rain turned to snow; the descending flakes clung to the many-colored foliage, or melted from sight in the trench of half-liquid clay that was called a road. The wheels of the wagons sank in it to the hub, and to advance or retreat was alike impossible.

Forbes from his sick bed at Raystown wrote to Bouquet: "Your description of the road pierces me to the very soul." And a few days later to Pitt: "I am in the greatest distress, occasioned by rains unusual at this season, which have rendered the clay roads absolutely impracticable. If the weather does not favor, I shall be absolutely locked up in the mountains. I cannot form any judgment how I am to extricate myself, as everything depends on the weather, which snows and rains frightfully." There was no improvement. In the next week he writes to Bouquet: "These four days of constant rain have completely ruined the road. The wagons would cut it up more in an hour than we could repair in a week. I have written to General Abercromby, but have not had one scrape of a pen from him since the beginning of September; so it looks as if we were either forgot or left to our fate."[1] Wasted and tortured by disease, the perplexed commander was forced to burden himself with a multitude of details which would else have been neglected, and to do the work of commissary and quartermaster as well as general. "My time," he writes, "is disagreeably spent between business and medicine."

In the beginning of November he was carried to Loyalhannon, where the whole army was then gathered. There was a

[1] *Forbes to Bouquet, 15 Oct. 1758. Ibid., 25 Oct. 1758. Forbes to Pitt, 20 Oct. 1758.*

council of officers, and they resolved to attempt nothing more that season; but, a few days later, three prisoners were brought in who reported the defenceless condition of the French, on which Forbes gave orders to advance again. The wagons and all the artillery, except a few light pieces, were left behind; and on the eighteenth of November twenty-five hundred picked men marched for Fort Duquesne, without tents or baggage, and burdened only with knapsacks and blankets. Washington and Colonel Armstrong, of the Pennsylvanians, had opened a way for them by cutting a road to within a day's march of the French fort. On the evening of the twenty-fourth, the detachment encamped among the hills of Turkey Creek; and the men on guard heard at midnight a dull and heavy sound booming over the western woods. Was it a magazine exploded by accident, or were the French blowing up their works? In the morning the march was resumed, a strong advance-guard leading the way. Forbes came next, carried in his litter; and the troops followed in three parallel columns, the Highlanders in the centre under Montgomery, their colonel, and the Royal Americans and provincials on the right and left, under Bouquet and Washington.[1] Thus, guided by the tap of the drum at the head of each column, they moved slowly through the forest, over damp, fallen leaves, crisp with frost, beneath an endless entanglement of bare gray twigs that sighed and moaned in the bleak November wind. It was dusk when they emerged upon the open plain and saw Fort Duquesne before them, with its background of wintry hills beyond the Monongahela and the Alleghany. During the last three miles they had passed the scattered bodies of those slain two months before at the defeat of Grant; and it is said that, as they neared the fort, the Highlanders were goaded to fury at seeing the heads of their slaughtered comrades stuck on poles, round which the kilts were hung derisively, in imitation of petticoats. Their rage was vain; the enemy was gone. Only a few Indians lingered about the place, who reported that the garrison, to the number of four or five hundred, had retreated, some down the Ohio, some overland towards Presquisle, and the rest, with

[1] *Letter from a British Officer in the Expedition, 25 Feb. 1759, Gentleman's Magazine*, XXIX. 171.

their commander, up the Alleghany to Venango, called by the French, Fort Machault. They had burned the barracks and storehouses, and blown up the fortifications.

The first care of the victors was to provide defence and shelter for those of their number on whom the dangerous task was to fall of keeping what they had won. A stockade was planted around a cluster of traders' cabins and soldiers' huts, which Forbes named Pittsburg, in honor of the great minister. It was not till the next autumn that General Stanwix built, hard by, the regular fortified work called Fort Pitt.[1] Captain West, brother of Benjamin West, the painter, led a detachment of Pennsylvanians, with Indian guides, through the forests of the Monongahela, to search for the bones of those who had fallen under Braddock. In the heart of the savage wood they found them in abundance, gnawed by wolves and foxes, and covered with the dead leaves of four successive autumns. Major Halket, of Forbes' staff, had joined the party; and, with the help of an Indian who was in the fight, he presently found two skeletons lying under a tree. In one of them he recognized, by a peculiarity of the teeth, the remains of his father, Sir Peter Halket, and in the other he believed that he saw the bones of a brother who had fallen at his father's side. The young officer fainted at the sight. The two skeletons were buried together, covered with a Highland plaid, and the Pennsylvanian woodsmen fired a volley over the grave. The rest of the bones were undistinguishable; and, being carefully gathered up, they were all interred in a deep trench dug in the freezing ground.[2]

The work of the new fort was pushed on apace, and the task of holding it for the winter was assigned to Lieutenant-Colonel Mercer, of the Virginians, with two hundred provincials. The number was far too small. It was certain that, unless vigorously prevented by a counter attack, the French would gather in early spring from all their nearer western posts, Niagara, Detroit, Presquisle, Le Bœuf, and Venango, to retake the place; but there was no food for a larger garrison, and the risk must be run.

The rest of the troops, with steps quickened by hunger,

[1] *Stanwix to Pitt, 20 Nov. 1759.*
[2] Galt, *Life of Benjamin West*, I. 64 (ed. 1820).

began their homeward march early in December. "We would soon make M. de Ligneris shift his quarters at Venango," writes Bouquet just after the fort was taken, "if we only had provisions; but we are scarcely able to maintain ourselves a few days here. After God, the success of this expedition is entirely due to the General, who, by bringing about the treaty with the Indians at Easton, struck the French a stunning blow, wisely delayed our advance to wait the effects of that treaty, secured all our posts and left nothing to chance, and resisted the urgent solicitation to take Braddock's road, which would have been our destruction. In all his measures he has shown the greatest prudence, firmness, and ability."[1] No sooner was his work done, than Forbes fell into a state of entire prostration, so that for a time he could neither write a letter nor dictate one. He managed, however, two days after reaching Fort Duquesne, to send Amherst a brief notice of his success, adding: "I shall leave this place as soon as I am able to stand; but God knows when I shall reach Philadelphia, if I ever do."[2] On the way back, a hut with a chimney was built for him at each stopping-place, and on the twenty-eighth of December Major Halket writes from "Tomahawk Camp:" "How great was our disappointment, on coming to this ground last night, to find that the chimney was unlaid, no fire made, nor any wood cut that would burn. This distressed the General to the greatest degree, by obliging him after his long journey to sit above two hours without any fire, exposed to a snowstorm, which had very near destroyed him entirely; but with great difficulty, by the assistance of some cordials, he was brought to."[3] At length, carried all the way in his litter, he reached Philadelphia, where, after lingering through the winter, he died in March, and was buried with military honors in the chancel of Christ Church.

If his achievement was not brilliant, its solid value was above price. It opened the Great West to English enterprise, took from France half her savage allies, and relieved the western borders from the scourge of Indian war. From southern New York to North Carolina, the frontier populations had

[1] *Bouquet to Chief Justice Allen, 25 Nov. 1758.*
[2] *Forbes to Amherst, 26 Nov. 1758.*
[3] *Halket to Bouquet, 28 Dec. 1758.*

cause to bless the memory of the steadfast and all-enduring soldier.

So ended the campaign of 1758. The centre of the French had held its own triumphantly at Ticonderoga; but their left had been forced back by the capture of Louisbourg, and their right by that of Fort Duquesne, while their entire right wing had been well nigh cut off by the destruction of Fort Frontenac. The outlook was dark. Their own Indians were turning against them. "They have struck us," wrote Doreil to the Minister of War; "they have seized three canoes loaded with furs on Lake Ontario, and murdered the men in them: sad forerunner of what we have to fear! Peace, Monseigneur, give us peace! Pardon me, but I cannot repeat that word too often."

NOTE.—The *Bouquet and Haldimand Papers* in the British Museum contain a mass of curious correspondence of the principal persons engaged in the expedition under Forbes; copies of it all are before me. The Public Record Office, *America and West Indies*, has also furnished much material, including the official letters of Forbes. The *Writings of Washington*, the *Archives* and *Colonial Records* of Pennsylvania, and the magazines and newspapers of the time may be mentioned among the sources of information, along with a variety of miscellaneous contemporary letters. The Journals of Christian Frederic Post are printed in full in the *Olden Time* and elsewhere.

Chapter XXIII

1758, 1759

THE BRINK OF RUIN

Jealousy of Vaudreuil • He asks for Montcalm's Recall • His Discomfiture • Scene at the Governor's House • Disgust of Montcalm • The Canadians despondent • Devices to encourage them • Gasconade of the Governor • Deplorable State of the Colony • Mission of Bougainville • Duplicity of Vaudreuil • Bougainville at Versailles • Substantial Aid refused to Canada • A matrimonial Treaty • Return of Bougainville • Montcalm abandoned by the Court • His Plans of Defence • Sad News from Candiac • Boasts of Vaudreuil

---

N EVER WAS general in a more critical position than I was: God has delivered me; his be the praise! He gives me health, though I am worn out with labor, fatigue, and miserable dissensions that have determined me to ask for my recall. Heaven grant that I may get it!"

Thus wrote Montcalm to his mother after his triumph at Ticonderoga. That great exploit had entailed a train of vexations, for it stirred the envy of Vaudreuil, more especially as it was due to the troops of the line, with no help from Indians, and very little from Canadians. The Governor assured the Colonial Minister that the victory would have bad results, though he gives no hint what these might be; that Montcalm had mismanaged the whole affair; that he would have been beaten but for the manifest interposition of Heaven;[1] and, finally, that he had failed to follow his (Vaudreuil's) directions, and had therefore enabled the English to escape. The real directions of the Governor, dictated, perhaps, by dread lest his rival should reap laurels, were to avoid a general engagement; and it was only by setting them at nought that Abercromby had been routed. After the battle a sharp correspondence passed between the two chiefs. The Governor, who had left Montcalm to his own resources before the crisis, sent him Canadians and Indians in abundance after it was

[1] *Vaudreuil au Ministre, 8 Août, 1758.*

over; and while he cautiously refrained from committing himself by positive orders, repeated again and again that if these reinforcements were used to harass Abercromby's communications, the whole English army would fall back to the Hudson, and leave baggage and artillery a prey to the French. These preposterous assertions and tardy succors were thought by Montcalm to be a device for giving color to the charge that he had not only failed to deserve victory, but had failed also to make use of it.[1] He did what was possible, and sent strong detachments to act in the English rear; which, though they did not, and could not, compel the enemy to fall back, caused no slight annoyance, till Rogers checked them by the defeat of Marin. Nevertheless Vaudreuil pretended on one hand that Montcalm had done nothing with the Canadians and Indians sent him, and on the other that these same Canadians and Indians had triumphed over the enemy by their mere presence at Ticonderoga. "It was my activity in sending these succors to Carillon [*Ticonderoga*] that forced the English to retreat. The Marquis de Montcalm might have made their retreat difficult; but it was in vain that I wrote to him, in vain that the colony troops, Canadians and Indians, begged him to pursue the enemy."[2] The succors he speaks of were sent in July and August, while the English did not fall back till the first of November. Neither army left its position till the season was over, and Abercromby did so only when he learned that the French were setting the example. Vaudreuil grew more and more bitter. "As the King has intrusted this colony to me, I cannot help warning you of the unhappy consequences that would follow if the Marquis de Montcalm should remain here. I shall keep him by me till I receive your orders. It is essential that they reach me early." "I pass over in silence all the infamous conduct and indecent talk he has held or countenanced; but I should be wanting in my duty to the King if I did not beg you to ask for his recall."[3]

He does not say what is meant by infamous conduct and indecent talk; but the allusion is probably to irreverent utter-

[1] Much of the voluminous correspondence on these matters will be found in *N. Y. Col. Docs.*, X.

[2] *Vaudreuil au Ministre, 8 Avril, 1759.*

[3] *Ibid.*

ances touching the Governor in which the officers from
France were apt to indulge, not always without the knowledge of their chief. Vaudreuil complained of this to Montcalm, adding, "I am greatly above it, and I despise it."[1] To
which the General replied: "You are right to despise gossip,
supposing that there has been any. For my part, though I
hear that I have been torn to pieces without mercy in your
presence, I do not believe it."[2] In these infelicities Bigot figures as peacemaker, though with no perceptible success. Vaudreuil's cup of bitterness was full when letters came from
Versailles ordering him to defer to Montcalm on all questions
of war, or of civil administration bearing upon war.[3] He had
begged hard for his rival's recall, and in reply his rival was set
over his head.

The two yokefellows were excellently fitted to exasperate
each other: Montcalm, with his southern vivacity of emotion
and an impetuous, impatient volubility that sometimes forgot
prudence; and Vaudreuil, always affable towards adherents,
but full of suspicious egotism and restless jealousy that bristled within him at the very thought of his colleague. Some of
the byplay of the quarrel may be seen in Montcalm's familiar
correspondence with Bourlamaque. One day the Governor, in
his own house, brought up the old complaint that Montcalm,
after taking Fort William Henry, did not take Fort Edward
also. The General, for the twentieth time, gave good reasons
for not making the attempt. "I ended," he tells Bourlamaque,
"by saying quietly that when I went to war I did the best I
could; and that when one is not pleased with one's lieutenants, one had better take the field in person. He was very
much moved, and muttered between his teeth that perhaps he
would; at which I said that I should be delighted to serve
under him. Madame de Vaudreuil wanted to put in her word.
I said: 'Madame, saving due respect, permit me to have the
honor to say that ladies ought not to talk war.' She kept on.
I said: 'Madame, saving due respect, permit me to have the
honor to say that if Madame de Montcalm were here, and
heard me talking war with Monsieur le Marquis de Vau-

[1] *Vaudreuil à Montcalm, 1 Août, 1758.*
[2] *Montcalm à Vaudreuil, 6 Août, 1758.*
[3] *Ordres du Roy et Dépêches des Ministres, 1758, 1759.*

dreuil, she would remain silent.' This scene was in presence of eight officers, three of them belonging to the colony troops; and a pretty story they will make of it."

These letters to Bourlamaque, in their detestable handwriting, small, cramped, confused, without stops, and sometimes almost indecipherable, betray the writer's state of mind. "I should like as well as anybody to be Marshal of France; but to buy the honor with the life I am leading here would be too much." He recounts the last news from Fort Duquesne, just before its fall. "Mutiny among the Canadians, who want to come home; the officers busy with making money, and stealing like mandarins. Their commander sets the example, and will come back with three or four hundred thousand francs; the pettiest ensign, who does not gamble, will have ten, twelve, or fifteen thousand. The Indians don't like Ligneris, who is drunk every day. Forgive the confusion of this letter; I have not slept all night with thinking of the robberies and mismanagement and folly. *Pauvre Roi, pauvre France, cara patria!*" "Oh, when shall we get out of this country! I think I would give half that I have to go home. Pardon this digression to a melancholy man. It is not that I have not still some remnants of gayety; but what would seem such in anybody else is melancholy for a Languedocian. Burn my letter, and never doubt my attachment." "I shall always say, Happy he who is free from the proud yoke to which I am bound. When shall I see my château of Candiac, my plantations, my chestnut grove, my oil-mill, my mulberry-trees? *O bon Dieu! Bon soir; brûlez ma lettre.*"[1]

Never was dispute more untimely than that between these ill-matched colleagues. The position of the colony was desperate. Thus far the Canadians had never lost heart, but had obeyed with admirable alacrity the Governor's call to arms, borne with patience the burdens and privations of the war, and submitted without revolt to the exactions and oppressions of Cadet and his crew; loyal to their native soil, loyal to their Church, loyal to the wretched government that crushed and belittled them. When the able-bodied were ordered to the war, where four fifths of them were employed in the hard and

[1] The above extracts are from letters of 5 and 27 Nov. and 9 Dec. 1758, and 18 and 23 March, 1759.

tedious work of transportation, the women, boys, and old men tilled the fields and raised a scanty harvest, which always might be, and sometimes was, taken from them in the name of the King. Yet the least destitute among them were forced every winter to lodge soldiers in their houses, for each of whom they were paid fifteen francs a month, in return for substance devoured and wives and daughters debauched.[1]

No pains had been spared to keep up the courage of the people and feed them with flattering illusions. When the partisan officer Boishébert was tried for peculation, his counsel met the charge by extolling the manner in which he had fulfilled the arduous duty of encouraging the Acadians, "putting on an air of triumph even in defeat; using threats, caresses, stratagems; painting our victories in vivid colors; hiding the strength and successes of the enemy; promising succors that did not and could not come; inventing plausible reasons why they did not come, and making new promises to set off the failure of the old; persuading a starved people to forget their misery; taking from some to give to others; and doing all this continually in the face of a superior enemy, that this country might be snatched from England and saved to France."[2] What Boishébert was doing in Acadia, Vaudreuil was doing on a larger scale in Canada. By indefatigable lying, by exaggerating every success and covering over every reverse, he deceived the people and in some measure himself. He had in abundance the Canadian gift of gasconade, and boasted to the Colonial Minister that one of his countrymen was a match for from three to ten Englishmen. It is possible that he almost believed it; for the midnight surprise of defenceless families and the spreading of panics among scattered border settlements were inseparable from his idea of war. Hence the high value he set on Indians, who in such work outdid the Canadians themselves. Sustained by the intoxication of flattering falsehoods, and not doubting that the blunders and weakness of the first years of the war gave the measure of English efficiency, the colonists had never suspected that they could be subdued.

[1] *Mémoire sur le moyen d'entretenir 10,000 Hommes de Troupes dans les Colonies, 1759.*

[2] *Procès de Bigot, Cadet, et autres, Mémoire pour le Sieur de Boishébert.*

But now there was a change. The reverses of the last campaign, hunger, weariness, and possibly some incipient sense
of atrocious misgovernment, began to produce their effect;
and some, especially in the towns, were heard to murmur that
further resistance was useless. The Canadians, though brave
and patient, needed, like Frenchmen, the stimulus of success.
"The people are alarmed," said the modest Governor, "and
would lose courage if my firmness did not rekindle their zeal
to serve the King."[1]

"Rapacity, folly, intrigue, falsehood, will soon ruin this colony which has cost the King so dear," wrote Doreil to the
Minister of War. "We must not flatter ourselves with vain
hope; Canada is lost if we do not have peace this winter." "It
has been saved by miracle in these past three years; nothing
but peace can save it now, in spite of all the efforts and the
talents of M. de Montcalm."[2] Vaudreuil himself became thoroughly alarmed, and told the Court in the autumn of 1758 that
food, arms, munitions, and everything else were fast failing,
and that without immediate peace or heavy reinforcements all
was lost.

The condition of Canada was indeed deplorable. The St.
Lawrence was watched by British ships; the harvest was
meagre; a barrel of flour cost two hundred francs; most of
the cattle and many of the horses had been killed for food.
The people lived chiefly on a pittance of salt cod or on rations
furnished by the King; all prices were inordinate; the officers
from France were starving on their pay; while a legion of
indigenous and imported scoundrels fattened on the general
distress. "What a country!" exclaims Montcalm. "Here all the
knaves grow rich, and the honest men are ruined." Yet he was
resolved to stand by it to the last, and wrote to the Minister
of War that he would bury himself under its ruins. "I asked
for my recall after the glorious affair of the eighth of July; but
since the state of the colony is so bad, I must do what I can
to help it and retard its fall." The only hope was in a strong
appeal to the Court; and he thought himself fortunate in persuading Vaudreuil to consent that Bougainville should be

[1] *Vaudreuil au Ministre, 10 Avril, 1759.*
[2] *Doreil au Ministre, 31 Juillet, 1758. Ibid. 12 Août, 1758. Ibid. 31 Août, 1758.*
Ibid. 1 Sept. 1758.

commissioned to make it, seconded by Doreil. They were to sail in different ships, in order that at least one of them might arrive safe.

Vaudreuil gave Bougainville a letter introducing him to the Colonial Minister in high terms of praise: "He is in all respects better fitted than anybody else to inform you of the state of the colony. I have given him my instructions, and you can trust entirely in what he tells you."[1] Concerning Doreil he wrote to the Minister of War: "I have full confidence in him, and he may be entirely trusted. Everybody here likes him."[2] While thus extolling the friends of his rival, the Governor took care to provide against the effects of his politic commendations, and wrote thus to his patron, the Colonial Minister: "In order to condescend to the wishes of M. de Montcalm, and leave no means untried to keep in harmony with him, I have given letters to MM. Doreil and Bougainville; but I have the honor to inform you, Monseigneur, that they do not understand the colony, and to warn you that they are creatures of M. de Montcalm."[3]

The two envoys had sailed for France. Winter was close at hand, and the harbor of Quebec was nearly empty. One ship still lingered, the last of the season, and by her Montcalm sent a letter to his mother: "You will be glad to have me write to you up to the last moment to tell you for the hundredth time that, occupied as I am with the fate of New France, the preservation of the troops, the interest of the state, and my own glory, I think continually of you all. We did our best in 1756, 1757, and 1758; and so, God helping, we will do in 1759, unless you make peace in Europe." Then, shut from the outer world for half a year by barriers of ice, he waited what returning spring might bring forth.

Both Bougainville and Doreil escaped the British cruisers and safely reached Versailles, where, in the slippery precincts of the Court, as new to him as they were treacherous, the young aide-de-camp justified all the confidence of his chief. He had interviews with the ministers, the King, and, more important than all, with Madame de Pompadour, whom he

[1] *Vaudreuil au Ministre de la Marine, 4 Nov. 1758.*
[2] *Vaudreuil au Ministre de la Guerre, 11 Oct. 1758.*
[3] *Vaudreuil au Ministre de la Marine, 3 Nov. 1758.*

succeeded in propitiating, though not, it seems, without difficulty and delay. France, unfortunate by land and sea, with finances ruined and navy crippled, had gained one brilliant victory, and she owed it to Montcalm. She could pay for it in honors, if in nothing else. Montcalm was made lieutenant-general, Lévis major-general, Bourlamaque brigadier, and Bougainville colonel and chevalier of St. Louis; while Vaudreuil was solaced with the grand cross of that order.[1] But when the two envoys asked substantial aid for the imperilled colony, the response was chilling. The Colonial Minister, Berryer, prepossessed against Bougainville by the secret warning of Vaudreuil, received him coldly, and replied to his appeal for help: "Eh, Monsieur, when the house is on fire one cannot occupy one's self with the stable." "At least, Monsieur, nobody will say that you talk like a horse," was the irreverent answer.

Bougainville laid four memorials before the Court, in which he showed the desperate state of the colony and its dire need of help. Thus far, he said, Canada has been saved by the dissensions of the English colonies; but now, for the first time, they are united against her, and prepared to put forth their strength. And he begged for troops, arms, munitions, food, and a squadron to defend the mouth of the St. Lawrence.[2] The reply, couched in a letter to Montcalm, was to the effect that it was necessary to concentrate all the strength of the kingdom for a decisive operation in Europe; that, therefore, the aid required could not be sent; and that the King trusted everything to his zeal and generalship, joined with the valor of the victors of Ticonderoga.[3] All that could be obtained was between three and four hundred recruits for the regulars, sixty engineers, sappers, and artillerymen, and gunpowder, arms, and provisions sufficient, along with the supplies brought over by the contractor, Cadet, to carry the colony through the next campaign.[4]

Montcalm had intrusted Bougainville with another mission, widely different. This was no less than the negotiating

[1] *Ordres du Roy et Dépêches des Ministres, Janvier, Février, 1759.*
[2] *Mémoire remis au Ministre par M. de Bougainville, Décembre, 1758.*
[3] *Le Ministre à Montcalm, 3 Fév. 1759.*
[4] *Ordres du Roy et Dépêches des Ministres, Février, 1759.*

of suitable marriages for the eldest son and daughter of his commander, with whom, in the confidence of friendship, he had had many conversations on the matter. "He and I," Montcalm wrote to his mother, Madame de Saint-Véran, "have two ideas touching these marriages,—the first, romantic and chimerical; the second, good, practicable."[1] Bougainville, invoking the aid of a lady of rank, a friend of the family, acquitted himself well of his delicate task. Before he embarked for Canada, in early spring, a treaty was on foot for the marriage of the young Comte de Montcalm to an heiress of sixteen; while Mademoiselle de Montcalm had already become Madame d'Espineuse. "Her father will be delighted," says the successful negotiator.[2]

Again he crossed the Atlantic and sailed up the St. Lawrence as the portentous spring of 1759 was lowering over the dissolving snows of Canada. With him came a squadron bearing the supplies and the petty reinforcement which the Court had vouchsafed. "A little is precious to those who have nothing," said Montcalm on receiving them. Despatches from the ministers gave warning of a great armament fitted out in English ports for the attack of Quebec, while a letter to the General from the Maréchal de Belleisle, minister of war, told what was expected of him, and why he and the colony were abandoned to their fate. "If we sent a large reinforcement of troops," said Belleisle, "there would be great fear that the English would intercept them on the way; and as the King could never send you forces equal to those which the English are prepared to oppose to you, the attempt would have no other effect than to excite the Cabinet of London to increased efforts for preserving its superiority on the American continent.

"As we must expect the English to turn all their force against Canada, and attack you on several sides at once, it is necessary that you limit your plans of defence to the most essential points and those most closely connected, so that, being concentrated within a smaller space, each part may be within reach of support and succor from the rest. How small soever may be the space you are able to hold, it is indispens-

[1] *Montcalm à Madame de Saint-Véran, 24 Sept. 1758.*
[2] *Lettres de Bougainville à Madame de Saint-Véran, 1758, 1759.*

able to keep a footing in North America; for if we once lose the country entirely, its recovery will be almost impossible. The King counts on your zeal, courage, and persistency to accomplish this object, and relies on you to spare no pains and no exertions. Impart this resolution to your chief officers, and join with them to inspire your soldiers with it. I have answered for you to the King; I am confident that you will not disappoint me, and that for the glory of the nation, the good of the state, and your own preservation, you will go to the utmost extremity rather than submit to conditions as shameful as those imposed at Louisbourg, the memory of which you will wipe out."[1] "We will save this unhappy colony, or perish," was the answer of Montcalm.

It was believed that Canada would be attacked with at least fifty thousand men. Vaudreuil had caused a census to be made of the governments of Montreal, Three Rivers, and Quebec. It showed a little more than thirteen thousand effective men.[2] To these were to be added thirty-five hundred troops of the line, including the late reinforcement, fifteen hundred colony troops, a body of irregulars in Acadia, and the militia and *coureurs-de-bois* of Detroit and the other upper posts, along with from one to two thousand Indians who could still be counted on. Great as was the disparity of numbers, there was good hope that the centre of the colony could be defended; for the only avenues by which an enemy could approach were barred by the rock of Quebec, the rapids of the St. Lawrence, and the strong position of Isle-aux-Noix, at the outlet of Lake Champlain. Montcalm had long inclined to the plan of concentration enjoined on him by the Minister of War. Vaudreuil was of another mind; he insisted on still occupying Acadia and the forts of the upper country: matters on which he and the General exchanged a correspondence that widened the breach between them.

Should every effort of resistance fail, and the invaders force their way into the heart of Canada, Montcalm proposed the desperate resort of abandoning the valley of the St. Lawrence, descending the Mississippi with his troops and as many as

---

[1] *Belleisle à Montcalm, 19 Fév. 1759.*

[2] *Vaudreuil au Ministre, 8 Avril, 1759.* The *Mémoires sur le Canada, 1749 – 1760,* says 15,229 effective men.

possible of the inhabitants, and making a last stand for France among the swamps of Louisiana.[1]

In April, before Bougainville's return, he wrote to his wife: "Can we hope for another miracle to save us? I trust in God; he fought for us on the eighth of July. Come what may, his will be done! I wait the news from France with impatience and dread. We have had none for eight months; and who knows if much can reach us at all this year? How dearly I have to pay for the dismal privilege of figuring two or three times in the gazettes!" A month later, after Bougainville had come: "Our daughter is well married. I think I would renounce every honor to join you again; but the King must be obeyed. The moment when I see you once more will be the brightest of my life. Adieu, my heart! I believe that I love you more than ever."

Bougainville had brought sad news. He had heard before sailing from France that one of Montcalm's daughters was dead, but could not learn which of them. "I think," says the father, "that it must be poor Mirète, who was like me, and whom I loved very much." He was never to know if this conjecture was true.

To Vaudreuil came a repetition of the detested order that he should defer to Montcalm on all questions of war; and moreover that he should not take command in person except when the whole body of the militia was called out; nor, even then, without consulting his rival.[2] His ire and vexation produced an access of jealous self-assertion, and drove him into something like revolt against the ministerial command. "If the English attack Quebec, I shall always hold myself free to go thither myself with most of the troops and all the militia and Indians I can assemble. On arriving I shall give battle to the enemy; and I shall do so again and again, till I have forced him to retire, or till he has entirely crushed me by excessive superiority of numbers. My obstinacy in opposing his landing will be the more *à propos*, as I have not the means of sustaining a siege. If I succeed as I wish, I shall next march to Carillon to arrest him there. You see, Monseigneur, that the

[1] *Mémoire sur le Canada remis au Ministre, 27 Déc. 1758.*
[2] *Ordres du Roy et Dépêches des Ministres, Lettre à Vaudreuil, 3 Fév. 1759.*

slightest change in my arrangements would have the most unfortunate consequences."[1]

Whether he made good this valorous declaration will presently be seen.

NOTE.—The Archives de la Guerre and the Archives de la Marine contain a mass of letters and documents on the subjects treated in the above chapter; these I have carefully read and collated. The other principal authorities are the correspondence of Montcalm with Bourlamaque and with his own family; the letters of Vaudreuil preserved in the Archives Nationales; and the letters of Bougainville and Doreil to Montcalm and Madame de Saint-Véran while on their mission to France. For copies of these last I am indebted to the present Marquis de Montcalm.

[1] *Vaudreuil au Ministre, 8 Avril, 1759.*

Chapter XXIV

1758, 1759

WOLFE

The Exiles of Fort Cumberland • Relief • The Voyage to Louis-
bourg • The British Fleet • Expedition against Quebec • Early
Life of Wolfe • His Character • His Letters to his Parents • His
domestic Qualities • Appointed to command the Expedition
• Sails for America

CAPTAIN JOHN KNOX, of the forty-third regiment, had
spent the winter in garrison at Fort Cumberland, on the
hill of Beauséjour. For nearly two years he and his comrades
had been exiles amid the wilds of Nova Scotia, and the monotonous inaction was becoming insupportable. The great
marsh of Tantemar on the one side, and that of Missaguash
on the other, two vast flat tracts of glaring snow, bounded by
dark hills of spruce and fir, were hateful to their sight. Shooting, fishing, or skating were a dangerous relief; for the neighborhood was infested by "vermin," as they called the Acadians
and their Micmac allies. In January four soldiers and a ranger
were waylaid not far from the fort, disabled by bullets, and
then scalped alive. They were found the next morning on the
snow, contorted in the agonies of death, and frozen like mar-
ble statues. St. Patrick's Day brought more cheerful excitements. The Irish officers of the garrison gave their comrades
a feast, having laid in during the autumn a stock of frozen
provisions, that the festival of their saint might be duly honored. All was hilarity at Fort Cumberland, where it is recorded that punch to the value of twelve pounds sterling,
with a corresponding supply of wine and beer, was consumed
on this joyous occasion.[1]

About the middle of April a schooner came up the bay,
bringing letters that filled men and officers with delight. The
regiment was ordered to hold itself ready to embark for
Louisbourg and join an expedition to the St. Lawrence, under command of Major-General Wolfe. All that afternoon the

[1] Knox, *Historical Journal*, I. 228.

soldiers were shouting and cheering in their barracks; and when they mustered for the evening roll-call, there was another burst of huzzas. They waited in expectancy nearly three weeks, and then the transports which were to carry them arrived, bringing the provincials who had been hastily raised in New England to take their place. These Knox describes as a mean-looking set of fellows, of all ages and sizes, and without any kind of discipline; adding that their officers are sober, modest men, who, though of confined ideas, talk very clearly and sensibly, and make a decent appearance in blue, faced with scarlet, though the privates have no uniform at all.

At last the forty-third set sail, the cannon of the fort saluting them, and the soldiers cheering lustily, overjoyed to escape from their long imprisonment. A gale soon began; the transports became separated; Knox's vessel sheltered herself for a time in Passamaquoddy Bay; then passed the Grand Menan, and steered southward and eastward along the coast of Nova Scotia. A calm followed the gale; and they moved so slowly that Knox beguiled the time by fishing over the stern, and caught a halibut so large that he was forced to call for help to pull it in. Then they steered northeastward, now lost in fogs, and now tossed mercilessly on those boisterous waves; till, on the twenty-fourth of May, they saw a rocky and surf-lashed shore, with a forest of masts rising to all appearance out of it. It was the British fleet in the land-locked harbor of Louisbourg.

On the left, as they sailed through the narrow passage, lay the town, scarred with shot and shell, the red cross floating over its battered ramparts; and around in a wide semicircle rose the bristling backs of rugged hills, set thick with dismal evergreens. They passed the great ships of the fleet, and anchored among the other transports towards the head of the harbor. It was not yet free from ice; and the floating masses lay so thick in some parts that the reckless sailors, returning from leave on shore, jumped from one to another to regain their ships. There was a review of troops, and Knox went to see it; but it was over before he reached the place, where he was presently told of a characteristic reply just made by Wolfe to some officers who had apologized for not having taught their men the new exercise. "Poh, poh!—new exercise—new fiddlestick. If they are otherwise well disciplined, and will fight, that 's all I shall require of them."

Knox does not record his impressions of his new commander, which must have been disappointing. He called him afterwards a British Achilles; but in person at least Wolfe bore no likeness to the son of Peleus, for never was the soul of a hero cased in a frame so incongruous. His face, when seen in profile, was singular as that of the Great Condé. The forehead and chin receded; the nose, slightly upturned, formed with the other features the point of an obtuse triangle; the mouth was by no means shaped to express resolution; and nothing but the clear, bright, and piercing eye bespoke the spirit within. On his head he wore a black three-cornered hat; his red hair was tied in a queue behind; his narrow shoulders, slender body, and long, thin limbs were cased in a scarlet frock, with broad cuffs and ample skirts that reached the knee; while on his left arm he wore a band of crape in mourning for his father, of whose death he had heard a few days before.

James Wolfe was in his thirty-third year. His father was an officer of distinction, Major-General Edward Wolfe, and he himself, a delicate and sensitive child, but an impetuous and somewhat headstrong youth, had served the King since the age of fifteen. From childhood he had dreamed of the army and the wars. At sixteen he was in Flanders, adjutant of his regiment, discharging the duties of the post in a way that gained him early promotion and, along with a painstaking assiduity, showing a precocious faculty for commanding men. He passed with credit through several campaigns, took part in the victory of Dettingen, and then went to Scotland to fight at Culloden. Next we find him at Stirling, Perth, and Glasgow, always ardent and always diligent, constant in military duty, and giving his spare hours to mathematics and Latin. He presently fell in love; and being disappointed, plunged into a variety of dissipations, contrary to his usual habits, which were far above the standard of that profligate time.

At twenty-three he was a lieutenant-colonel, commanding his regiment in the then dirty and barbarous town of Inverness, amid a disaffected and turbulent population whom it was his duty to keep in order: a difficult task, which he accomplished so well as to gain the special commendation of the King, and even the goodwill of the Highlanders themselves. He was five years among these northern hills, battling with ill-health, and restless under the intellectual barrenness of his surroundings. He felt his position to be in no way salutary, and wrote to his mother: "The fear of becoming a mere ruffian and of imbibing the tyrannical principles of an absolute commander, or giving way insensibly to the temptations of power till I became proud, insolent, and intolerable,— these considerations will make me wish to leave the regiment before next winter; that by frequenting men above myself I may know my true condition, and by discoursing with the other sex may learn some civility and mildness of carriage." He got leave of absence, and spent six months in Paris, where he was presented at Court and saw much of the best society. This did not prevent him from working hard to perfect himself in French, as well as in horsemanship, fencing, dancing, and other accomplishments, and from earnestly seeking an opportunity to study the various armies of Europe. In this he was thwarted by the stupidity and prejudice of the commander-in-chief; and he made what amends he could by extensive reading in all that bore on military matters.

His martial instincts were balanced by strong domestic inclinations. He was fond of children; and after his disappointment in love used to say that they were the only true inducement to marriage. He was a most dutiful son, and wrote continually to both his parents. Sometimes he would philosophize on the good and ill of life; sometimes he held questionings with his conscience; and once he wrote to his mother in a strain of self-accusation not to be expected from a bold and determined soldier. His nature was a compound of tenderness and fire, which last sometimes showed itself in sharp and unpleasant flashes. His excitable temper was capable almost of fierceness, and he could now and then be needlessly stern; but towards his father, mother, and friends he was a model of steady affection. He made friends readily, and kept them, and was usually a pleasant companion, though subject to sallies of imperious irritability which occasionally broke through his strong sense of good breeding. For this his

WOLFE.

Aged 32.

susceptible constitution was largely answerable, for he was a living barometer, and his spirits rose and fell with every change of weather. In spite of his impatient outbursts, the officers whom he had commanded remained attached to him for life; and, in spite of his rigorous discipline, he was beloved by his soldiers, to whose comfort he was always attentive. Frankness, directness, essential good feeling, and a high integrity atoned for all his faults.

In his own view, as expressed to his mother, he was a person of very moderate abilities, aided by more than usual diligence; but this modest judgment of himself by no means deprived him of self-confidence, nor, in time of need, of self-assertion. He delighted in every kind of hardihood; and, in his contempt for effeminacy, once said to his mother: "Better be a savage of some use than a gentle, amorous puppy, obnoxious to all the world." He was far from despising fame; but the controlling principles of his life were duty to his country and his profession, loyalty to the King, and fidelity to his own ideal of the perfect soldier. To the parent who was the confidant of his most intimate thoughts he said: "All that I wish for myself is that I may at all times be ready and firm to meet that fate we cannot shun, and to die gracefully and properly when the hour comes." Never was wish more signally fulfilled. Again he tells her: "My utmost desire and ambition is to look steadily upon danger;" and his desire was accomplished. His intrepidity was complete. No form of death had power to daunt him. Once and again, when bound on some deadly enterprise of war, he calmly counts the chances whether or not he can compel his feeble body to bear him on till the work is done. A frame so delicately strung could not have been insensible to danger; but forgetfulness of self, and the absorption of every faculty in the object before him, shut out the sense of fear. He seems always to have been at his best in the thick of battle; most complete in his mastery over himself and over others.

But it is in the intimacies of domestic life that one sees him most closely, and especially in his letters to his mother, from whom he inherited his frail constitution, without the beauty that distinguished her. "The greatest happiness that I wish for here is to see you happy." "If you stay much at home I will come and shut myself up with you for three weeks or a month, and play at piquet from morning till night; and you shall laugh at my short red hair as much as you please." The playing at piquet was a sacrifice to filial attachment; for the mother loved cards, and the son did not. "Don't trouble yourself about my room or my bedclothes; too much care and delicacy at this time would enervate me and complete the destruction of a tottering constitution. Such as it is, it must serve me now, and I'll make the best of it while it holds." At the beginning of the war his father tried to dissuade him from offering his services on board the fleet; and he replies in a letter to Mrs. Wolfe: "It is no time to think of what is convenient or agreeable; that service is certainly the best in which we are the most useful. For my part, I am determined never to give myself a moment's concern about the nature of the duty which His Majesty is pleased to order us upon. It will be a sufficient comfort to you two, as far as my person is concerned, — at least it will be a reasonable consolation, — to reflect that the Power which has hitherto preserved me may, if it be his pleasure, continue to do so; if not, that it is but a few days or a few years more or less, and that those who perish in their duty and in the service of their country die honorably." Then he proceeds to give particular directions about his numerous dogs, for the welfare of which in his absence he provides with anxious solicitude, especially for "my friend Cæsar, who has great merit and much good-humor."

After the unfortunate expedition against Rochefort, when the board of general officers appointed to inquire into the affair were passing the highest encomiums upon his conduct, his parents were at Bath, and he took possession of their house at Blackheath, whence he wrote to his mother: "I lie in your chamber, dress in the General's little parlor, and dine where you did. The most perceptible difference and change of affairs (exclusive of the bad table I keep) is the number of dogs in the yard; but by coaxing Ball [*his father's dog*] and rubbing his back with my stick, I have reconciled him with the new ones, and put them in some measure under his protection."

When about to sail on the expedition against Louisbourg, he was anxious for his parents, and wrote to his uncle, Major

Wolfe, at Dublin: "I trust you will give the best advice to my mother, and such assistance, if it should be wanted, as the distance between you will permit. I mention this because the General seems to decline apace, and narrowly escaped being carried off in the spring. She, poor woman, is in a bad state of health, and needs the care of some friendly hand. She has long and painful fits of illness, which by succession and inheritance are likely to devolve on me, since I feel the early symptoms of them." Of his friends Guy Carleton, afterwards Lord Dorchester, and George Warde, the companion of his boyhood, he also asks help for his mother in his absence.

His part in the taking of Louisbourg greatly increased his reputation. After his return he went to Bath to recruit his health; and it seems to have been here that he wooed and won Miss Katherine Lowther, daughter of an ex-Governor of Barbadoes, and sister of the future Lord Lonsdale. A betrothal took place, and Wolfe wore her portrait till the night before his death. It was a little before this engagement that he wrote to his friend Lieutenant-Colonel Rickson: "I have this day signified to Mr. Pitt that he may dispose of my slight carcass as he pleases, and that I am ready for any undertaking within the compass of my skill and cunning. I am in a very bad condition both with the gravel and rheumatism; but I had much rather die than decline any kind of service that offers. If I followed my own taste it would lead me into Germany. However, it is not our part to choose, but to obey. My opinion is that I shall join the army in America."

Pitt chose him to command the expedition then fitting out against Quebec; made him a major-general, though, to avoid giving offence to older officers, he was to hold that rank in America alone; and permitted him to choose his own staff. Appointments made for merit, and not through routine and patronage, shocked the Duke of Newcastle, to whom a man like Wolfe was a hopeless enigma; and he told George II. that Pitt's new general was mad. "Mad is he?" returned the old King; "then I hope he will bite some others of my generals."

At the end of January the fleet was almost ready, and Wolfe wrote to his uncle Walter: "I am to act a greater part in this business than I wished. The backwardness of some of the older officers has in some measure forced the Government to come down so low. I shall do my best, and leave the rest to fortune, as perforce we must when there are not the most commanding abilities. We expect to sail in about three weeks. A London life and little exercise disagrees entirely with me, but the sea still more. If I have health and constitution enough for the campaign, I shall think myself a lucky man; what happens afterwards is of no great consequence." He sent to his mother an affectionate letter of farewell, went to Spithead, embarked with Admiral Saunders in the ship "Neptune," and set sail on the seventeenth of February. In a few hours the whole squadron was at sea, the transports, the frigates, and the great line-of-battle ships, with their ponderous armament and their freight of rude humanity armed and trained for destruction; while on the heaving deck of the "Neptune," wretched with seasickness and racked with pain, stood the gallant invalid who was master of it all.

The fleet consisted of twenty-two ships of the line, with frigates, sloops-of-war, and a great number of transports. When Admiral Saunders arrived with his squadron off Louisbourg, he found the entrance blocked by ice, and was forced to seek harborage at Halifax. The squadron of Admiral Holmes, which had sailed a few days earlier, proceeded to New York to take on board troops destined for the expedition, while the squadron of Admiral Durell steered for the St. Lawrence to intercept the expected ships from France.

In May the whole fleet, except the ten ships with Durell, was united in the harbor of Louisbourg. Twelve thousand troops were to have been employed for the expedition; but several regiments expected from the West Indies were for some reason countermanded, while the accessions from New York and the Nova Scotia garrisons fell far short of the looked-for numbers. Three weeks before leaving Louisbourg, Wolfe writes to his uncle Walter that he has an army of nine thousand men. The actual number seems to have been somewhat less.[1] "Our troops are good," he informs Pitt; "and if valor can make amends for the want of numbers, we shall probably succeed."

Three brigadiers, all in the early prime of life, held command under him: Monckton, Townshend, and Murray. They

[1] See *Grenville Correspondence*, I. 305.

were all his superiors in birth, and one of them, Townshend, never forgot that he was so. "George Townshend," says Walpole, "has thrust himself again into the service; and, as far as wrongheadedness will go, is very proper for a hero."[1] The same caustic writer says further that he was of "a proud, sullen, and contemptuous temper," and that he "saw everything in an ill-natured and ridiculous light."[2] Though his perverse and envious disposition made him a difficult colleague, Townshend had both talents and energy; as also had Monckton, the same officer who commanded at the capture of Beauséjour in 1755. Murray, too, was well matched to the work in hand, in spite of some lingering remains of youthful rashness.

On the sixth of June the last ship of the fleet sailed out of Louisbourg harbor, the troops cheering and the officers drinking to the toast, "British colors on every French fort, port, and garrison in America." The ships that had gone before lay to till the whole fleet was reunited, and then all steered together for the St. Lawrence. From the headland of Cape Egmont, the Micmac hunter, gazing far out over the shimmering sea, saw the horizon flecked with their canvas wings, as they bore northward on their errand of havoc.

NOTE.—For the material of the foregoing sketch of Wolfe I am indebted to Wright's excellent Life of him and the numerous letters contained in it. Several autograph letters which have escaped the notice of Mr. Wright are preserved in the Public Record Office. The following is a characteristic passage from one of these, written on board the "Neptune," at sea, on the sixth of June, the day when the fleet sailed from Louisbourg. It is directed to a nobleman of high rank in the army, whose name does not appear, the address being lost (War Office Records: *North America, various, 1756–1763*): "I have had the honour to receive two letters from your Lordship, one of an old date, concerning my stay in this country [*after the capture of Louisbourg*], in answer to which I shall only say that the Marshal told me I was to return at the end of the campaign; and as General Amherst had no other commands than to send me to winter at Halifax under the orders of an officer [*Brigadier Lawrence*] who was but a few months before put over my head, I thought it was much better to get into the way of service and out of the way of being insulted; and as the style of your Lordship's letter is pretty strong, I must take the liberty to inform you that . . . rather than receive orders in the Government [*of Nova Scotia*] from an officer younger than myself (though a very worthy man), I should certainly have desired leave to resign my com-

[1] Horace Walpole, *Letters* III. 207 (ed. Cunningham, 1857).
[2] Ibid. *George II.*, II. 345.

mission; for as I neither ask nor expect any favour, so I never intend to submit to any ill-usage whatsoever."

Many other papers in the Public Record Office have been consulted in preparing the above chapter, including the secret instructions of the King to Wolfe and to Saunders, and the letters of Amherst to Wolfe and to Pitt. Other correspondence touching the same subjects is printed in *Selections from the Public Documents of Nova Scotia*, 441–450. Knox, Mante, and Entick are the best contemporary printed sources.

A story has gained currency respecting the last interview of Wolfe with Pitt, in which he is said to have flourished his sword and boasted of what he would achieve. This anecdote was told by Lord Temple, who was present at the interview, to Mr. Grenville, who, many years after, told it to Earl Stanhope, by whom it was made public. That the incident underwent essential changes in the course of these transmissions,—which extended over more than half a century, for Earl Stanhope was not born till 1805,—can never be doubted by one who considers the known character of Wolfe, who may have uttered some vehement expression, but who can never be suspected of gasconade.

Chapter XXV

1759

WOLFE AT QUEBEC

French Preparation • Muster of Forces • Gasconade of Vaudreuil • Plan of Defence • Strength of Montcalm • Advance of Wolfe • British Sailors • Landing of the English • Difficulties before them • Storm • Fireships • Confidence of French Commanders • Wolfe occupies Point Levi • A futile Night Attack • Quebec bombarded • Wolfe at the Montmorenci • Skirmishes • Danger of the English Position • Effects of the Bombardment • Desertion of Canadians • The English above Quebec • Severities of Wolfe • Another Attempt to burn the Fleet • Desperate Enterprise of Wolfe • The Heights of Montmorenci • Repulse of the English

---

IN EARLY spring the chiefs of Canada met at Montreal to settle a plan of defence. What at first they most dreaded was an advance of the enemy by way of Lake Champlain. Bourlamaque, with three battalions, was ordered to take post at Ticonderoga, hold it if he could, or, if overborne by numbers, fall back to Isle-aux-Noix, at the outlet of the lake. La Corne was sent with a strong detachment to intrench himself at the head of the rapids of the St. Lawrence, and oppose any hostile movement from Lake Ontario. Every able-bodied man in the colony, and every boy who could fire a gun, was to be called to the field. Vaudreuil sent a circular letter to the militia captains of all the parishes, with orders to read it to the parishioners. It exhorted them to defend their religion, their wives, their children, and their goods from the fury of the heretics; declared that he, the Governor, would never yield up Canada on any terms whatever; and ordered them to join the army at once, leaving none behind but the old, the sick, the women, and the children.[1] The Bishop issued a pastoral mandate: "On every side, dearest brethren, the enemy is making immense preparations. His forces, at least six times more numerous than ours, are already in motion. Never was Canada in a state so critical and full of peril. Never were we so

[1] *Mémoires sur le Canada, 1749 –1760.*

destitute, or threatened with an attack so fierce, so general, and so obstinate. Now, in truth, we may say, more than ever before, that our only resource is in the powerful succor of our Lord. Then, dearest brethren, make every effort to deserve it. 'Seek first the kingdom of God; and all these things shall be added unto you.' " And he reproves their sins, exhorts them to repentance, and ordains processions, masses, and prayers.[1]

Vaudreuil bustled and boasted. In May he wrote to the Minister: "The zeal with which I am animated for the service of the King will always make me surmount the greatest obstacles. I am taking the most proper measures to give the enemy a good reception whenever he may attack us. I keep in view the defence of Quebec. I have given orders in the parishes below to muster the inhabitants who are able to bear arms, and place women, children, cattle, and even hay and grain, in places of safety. Permit me, Monseigneur, to beg you to have the goodness to assure His Majesty that, to whatever hard extremity I may be reduced, my zeal will be equally ardent and indefatigable, and that I shall do the impossible to prevent our enemies from making progress in any direction, or, at least, to make them pay extremely dear for it."[2] Then he writes again to say that Amherst with a great army will, as he learns, attack Ticonderoga; that Bradstreet, with six thousand men, will advance to Lake Ontario; and that six thousand more will march to the Ohio. "Whatever progress they may make," he adds, "I am resolved to yield them nothing, but hold my ground even to annihilation." He promises to do his best to keep on good terms with Montcalm, and ends with a warm eulogy of Bigot.[3]

It was in the midst of all these preparations that Bougainville arrived from France with news that a great fleet was on its way to attack Quebec. The town was filled with consternation mixed with surprise, for the Canadians had believed that the dangerous navigation of the St. Lawrence would deter their enemies from the attempt. "Everybody," writes one of them, "was stupefied at an enterprise that seemed so bold."

---

[1] I am indebted for a copy of this mandate to the kindness of Abbé Bois. As printed by Knox, it is somewhat different, though the spirit is the same.

[2] *Vaudreuil au Ministre, 8 Mai, 1759.*

[3] *Vaudreuil au Ministre, 20 [?] Mai, 1759.*

In a few days a crowd of sails was seen approaching. They were not enemies, but friends. It was the fleet of the contractor Cadet, commanded by an officer named Kanon, and loaded with supplies for the colony. They anchored in the harbor, eighteen sail in all, and their arrival spread universal joy. Admiral Durell had come too late to intercept them, catching but three stragglers that had lagged behind the rest. Still others succeeded in eluding him, and before the first of June five more ships had come safely into port.

When the news brought by Bougainville reached Montreal, nearly the whole force of the colony, except the detachments of Bourlamaque and La Corne, was ordered to Quebec. Montcalm hastened thither, and Vaudreuil followed. The Governor-General wrote to the Minister in his usual strain, as if all the hope of Canada rested in him. Such, he says, was his activity, that, though very busy, he reached Quebec only a day and a half after Montcalm; and, on arriving, learned from his scouts that English ships-of-war had already appeared at Isle-aux-Coudres. These were the squadron of Durell. "I expect," Vaudreuil goes on, "to be sharply attacked, and that our enemies will make their most powerful efforts to conquer this colony; but there is no ruse, no resource, no means which my zeal does not suggest to lay snares for them, and finally, when the exigency demands it, to fight them with an ardor, and even a fury, which exceeds the range of their ambitious designs. The troops, the Canadians, and the Indians are not ignorant of the resolution I have taken, and from which I shall not recoil under any circumstance whatever. The burghers of this city have already put their goods and furniture in places of safety. The old men, women, and children hold themselves ready to leave town. My firmness is generally applauded. It has penetrated every heart; and each man says aloud: 'Canada, our native land, shall bury us under its ruins before we surrender to the English!' This is decidedly my own determination, and I shall hold to it inviolably." He launches into high praise of the contractor Cadet, whose zeal for the service of the King and the defence of the colony he declares to be triumphant over every difficulty. It is necessary, he adds, that ample supplies of all kinds should be sent out in the autumn, with the distribution of which Cadet offers to

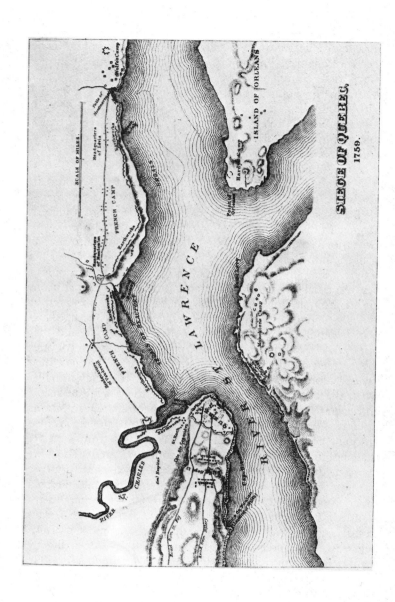

SIEGE OF QUEBEC,
1759.

charge himself, and to account for them at their first cost; but he does not say what prices his disinterested friend will compel the destitute Canadians to pay for them.[1]

Five battalions from France, nearly all the colony troops, and the militia from every part of Canada poured into Quebec, along with a thousand or more Indians, who, at the call of Vaudreuil, came to lend their scalping-knives to the defence. Such was the ardor of the people that boys of fifteen and men of eighty were to be seen in the camp. Isle-aux-Coudres and Isle d'Orléans were ordered to be evacuated, and an excited crowd on the rock of Quebec watched hourly for the approaching fleet. Days passed and weeks passed, yet it did not appear. Meanwhile Vaudreuil held council after council to settle a plan of defence. They were strange scenes: a crowd of officers of every rank, mixed pell-mell in a small room, pushing, shouting, elbowing each other, interrupting each other; till Montcalm, in despair, took each aside after the meeting was over, and made him give his opinion in writing.[2]

He himself had at first proposed to encamp the army on the plains of Abraham and the meadows of the St. Charles, making that river his line of defence;[3] but he changed his plan, and, with the concurrence of Vaudreuil, resolved to post his whole force on the St. Lawrence below the city, with his right resting on the St. Charles, and his left on the Montmorenci. Here, accordingly, the troops and militia were stationed as they arrived. Early in June, standing at the northeastern brink of the rock of Quebec, one could have seen the whole position at a glance. On the curving shore from the St. Charles to the rocky gorge of the Montmorenci, a distance of seven or eight miles, the whitewashed dwellings of the parish of Beauport stretched down the road in a double chain, and the fields on both sides were studded with tents, huts, and Indian wigwams. Along the borders of the St. Lawrence, as far as the eye could distinguish them, gangs of men were throwing up redoubts, batteries, and lines of intrenchment. About midway between the two extremities of the encamp-

---

[1] *Vaudreuil au Ministre, 28 Mai, 1759.*

[2] *Journal du Siége de Québec déposé à la Bibliothêque de Hartwell, en Angleterre.* (Printed at Quebec, 1836.)

[3] *Livre d'Ordres, Disposition pour s'opposer à la Descente.*

ment ran the little river of Beauport; and on the rising
ground just beyond it stood a large stone house, round which
the tents were thickly clustered; for here Montcalm had made
his headquarters.

A boom of logs chained together was drawn across the
mouth of the St. Charles, which was further guarded by two
hulks mounted with cannon. The bridge of boats that crossed
the stream nearly a mile above, formed the chief communication between the city and the camp. Its head towards Beauport was protected by a strong and extensive earthwork; and
the banks of the stream on the Quebec side were also intrenched, to form a second line of defence in case the position
at Beauport should be forced.

In the city itself every gate, except the Palace Gate, which
gave access to the bridge, was closed and barricaded. A
hundred and six cannon were mounted on the walls.[1] A floating battery of twelve heavy pieces, a number of gunboats,
eight fireships, and several firerafts formed the river defences.
The largest merchantmen of Kanon's fleet were sacrificed to
make the fireships; and the rest, along with the frigates that
came with them, were sent for safety up the St. Lawrence
beyond the River Richelieu, whence about a thousand of
their sailors returned to man the batteries and gunboats.

In the camps along the Beauport shore were about fourteen
thousand men, besides Indians. The regulars held the centre;
the militia of Quebec and Three Rivers were on the right,
and those of Montreal on the left. In Quebec itself there was
a garrison of between one and two thousand men under the
Chevalier de Ramesay. Thus the whole number, including Indians, amounted to more than sixteen thousand;[2] and though
the Canadians who formed the greater part of it were of little
use in the open field, they could be trusted to fight well behind intrenchments. Against this force, posted behind defensive works, on positions almost impregnable by nature, Wolfe
brought less than nine thousand men available for operations
on land.[3] The steep and lofty heights that lined the river

[1] This number was found after the siege. Knox, II. 151. Some French writers
make it much greater.
[2] See Appendix H.
[3] Ibid.

made the cannon of the ships for the most part useless, while the exigencies of the naval service forbade employing the sailors on shore. In two or three instances only, throughout the siege, small squads of them landed to aid in moving and working cannon; and the actual fighting fell to the troops alone.

Vaudreuil and Bigot took up their quarters with the army. The Governor-General had delegated the command of the land-forces to Montcalm, whom, in his own words, he authorized "to give orders everywhere, provisionally." His relations with him were more than ever anomalous and critical; for while Vaudreuil, in virtue of his office, had a right to supreme command, Montcalm, now a lieutenant-general, held a military grade far above him; and the Governor, while always writing himself down in his despatches as the head and front of every movement, had too little self-confidence not to leave the actual command in the hands of his rival.

Days and weeks wore on, and the first excitement gave way to restless impatience. Why did not the English come? Many of the Canadians thought that Heaven would interpose and wreck the English fleet, as it had wrecked that of Admiral Walker half a century before. There were processions, prayers, and vows towards this happy consummation. Food was scarce. Bigot and Cadet lived in luxury; fowls by thousands were fattened with wheat for their tables, while the people were put on rations of two ounces of bread a day.[1] Durell and his ships were reported to be still at Isle-aux-Coudres. Vaudreuil sent thither a party of Canadians, and they captured three midshipmen, who, says Montcalm, had gone ashore *pour polissonner*, that is, on a lark. These youths were brought to Quebec, where they increased the general anxiety by grossly exaggerating the English force.

At length it became known that eight English vessels were anchored in the north channel of Orleans, and on the twenty-first of June the masts of three of them could plainly be seen. One of the fireships was consumed in a vain attempt to burn them, and several firerafts and a sort of infernal machine were tried with no better success; the unwelcome visitors still held their posts.

Meanwhile the whole English fleet had slowly advanced,

[1] *Mémoires sur le Canada, 1749–1760.*

piloted by Denis de Vitré, a Canadian of good birth, captured
at sea some time before, and now compelled to serve, under
a threat of being hanged if he refused.[1] Nor was he alone; for
when Durell reached the place where the river pilots were
usually taken on board, he raised a French flag to his mast-
head, causing great rejoicings among the Canadians on shore,
who thought that a fleet was come to their rescue, and that
their country was saved. The pilots launched their canoes and
came out to the ships, where they were all made prisoners;
then the French flag was lowered, and the red cross displayed
in its stead. The spectators on shore turned from joy to despair; and a priest who stood watching the squadron with a
telescope is said to have dropped dead with the revulsion of
feeling.

Towards the end of June the main fleet was near the mountain of Cape Tourmente. The passage called the Traverse, between the Cape and the lower end of the Island of Orleans,
was reputed one of the most dangerous parts of the St. Lawrence; and as the ships successively came up, the captive pilots
were put on board to carry them safely through, on pain of
death. One of these men was assigned to the transport
"Goodwill," in which was Captain Knox, who spoke French,
and who reports thus in his Diary: "He gasconaded at a most
extravagant rate, and gave us to understand that it was much
against his will that he was become an English pilot. The
poor fellow assumed great latitude in his conversation, and
said 'he made no doubt that some of the fleet would return
to England, but they should have a dismal tale to carry with
them; for Canada should be the grave of the whole army, and
he expected in a short time to see the walls of Quebec orna-
mented with English scalps.' Had it not been in obedience to
the Admiral, who gave orders that he should not be ill-used,
he would certainly have been thrown overboard." The master
of the transport was an old sailor named Killick, who despised the whole Gallic race, and had no mind to see his ship
in charge of a Frenchman. "He would not let the pilot speak,"
continues Knox, "but fixed his mate at the helm, charged him
not to take orders from any person but himself, and going
forward with his trumpet to the forecastle, gave the necessary

[1] *Mémorial de Jean-Denis de Vitré au Très-honorable William Pitt.*

instructions. All that could be said by the commanding officer and the other gentlemen on board was to no purpose; the pilot declared we should be lost, for that no French ship ever presumed to pass there without a pilot. 'Ay, ay, my dear,' replied our son of Neptune, 'but, damn me, I'll convince you that an Englishman shall go where a Frenchman dare not show his nose.' The 'Richmond' frigate being close astern of us, the commanding officer called out to the captain and told him our case; he inquired who the master was, and was answered from the forecastle by the man himself, who told him 'he was old Killick, and that was enough.' I went forward with this experienced mariner, who pointed out the channel to me as we passed; showing me by the ripple and color of the water where there was any danger, and distinguishing the places where there were ledges of rocks (to me invisible) from banks of sand, mud, or gravel. He gave his orders with great unconcern, joked with the sounding-boats which lay off on each side with different colored flags for our guidance; and when any of them called to him and pointed to the deepest water, he answered: 'Ay, ay, my dear, chalk it down, a damned dangerous navigation, eh! If you don't make a sputter about it you'll get no credit in England.' After we had cleared this remarkable place, where the channel forms a complete zigzag, the master called to his mate to give the helm to somebody else, saying, 'Damn me if there are not a thousand places in the Thames fifty times more hazardous than this; I am ashamed that Englishmen should make such a rout about it.' The Frenchman asked me if the captain had not been there before. I assured him in the negative; upon which he viewed him with great attention, lifting at the same time his hands and eyes to heaven with astonishment and fervency."[1]

Vaudreuil was blamed for not planting cannon at a certain plateau on the side of the mountain of Cape Tourmente, where the gunners would have been inaccessible, and whence

---

[1] Others, as well as the pilot, were astonished. "The enemy passed sixty ships of war where we hardly dared risk a vessel of a hundred tons." "Notwithstanding all our precautions, the English, without any accident, by night, as well as by day, passed through it [*the Traverse*] their ships of seventy and eighty guns, and even many of them together." *Vaudreuil au Ministre, 22 Oct. 1759.*

they could have battered every passing ship with a plunging fire. As it was, the whole fleet sailed safely through. On the twenty-sixth they were all anchored off the south shore of the Island of Orleans, a few miles from Quebec; and, writes Knox, "here we are entertained with a most agreeable prospect of a delightful country on every side; windmills, watermills, churches, chapels, and compact farmhouses, all built with stone, and covered, some with wood, and others with straw. The lands appear to be everywhere well cultivated; and with the help of my glass I can discern that they are sowed with flax, wheat, barley, peas, etc., and the grounds are enclosed with wooden pales. The weather to-day is agreeably warm. A light fog sometimes hangs over the highlands, but in the river we have a fine clear air. In the curve of the river, while we were under sail, we had a transient view of a stupendous natural curiosity called the waterfall of Montmorenci."

That night Lieutenant Meech, with forty New England rangers, landed on the Island of Orleans, and found a body of armed inhabitants, who tried to surround him. He beat them off, and took possession of a neighboring farmhouse, where he remained till daylight; then pursued the enemy, and found that they had crossed to the north shore. The whole army now landed, and were drawn up on the beach. As they were kept there for some time, Knox and several brother officers went to visit the neighboring church of Saint-Laurent, where they found a letter from the parish priest, directed to "The Worthy Officers of the British Army," praying that they would protect the sacred edifice, and also his own adjoining house, and adding, with somewhat needless civility, that he wished they had come sooner, that they might have enjoyed the asparagus and radishes of his garden, now unhappily going to seed. The letter concluded with many compliments and good wishes, in which the Britons to whom they were addressed saw only "the frothy politeness so peculiar to the French." The army marched westward and encamped. Wolfe, with his chief engineer, Major Mackellar, and an escort of light infantry, advanced to the extreme point of the island.

Here he could see, in part, the desperate nature of the task he had undertaken. Before him, three or four miles away, Quebec sat perched upon her rock, a congregation of stone houses, churches, palaces, convents, and hospitals; the green trees of the Seminary garden and the spires of the Cathedral, the Ursulines, the Recollets, and the Jesuits. Beyond rose the loftier height of Cape Diamond, edged with palisades and capped with redoubt and parapet. Batteries frowned every-where; the Château battery, the Clergy battery, the Hospital battery, on the rock above, and the Royal, Dauphin's, and Queen's batteries on the strand, where the dwellings and ware-houses of the lower town clustered beneath the cliff.

Full in sight lay the far-extended camp of Montcalm, stretching from the St. Charles, beneath the city walls, to the chasm and cataract of the Montmorenci. From the cataract to the river of Beauport, its front was covered by earthworks along the brink of abrupt and lofty heights; and from the river of Beauport to the St. Charles, by broad flats of mud swept by the fire of redoubts, intrenchments, a floating bat-tery, and the city itself. Above the city, Cape Diamond hid the view; but could Wolfe have looked beyond it, he would have beheld a prospect still more disheartening. Here, mile after mile, the St. Lawrence was walled by a range of steeps, often inaccessible, and always so difficult that a few men at the top could hold an army in check; while at Cap-Rouge, about eight miles distant, the high plateau was cleft by the channel of a stream which formed a line of defence as strong as that of the Montmorenci. Quebec was a natural fortress. Bougainville had long before examined the position, and re-ported that "by the help of intrenchments, easily and quickly made, and defended by three or four thousand men, I think the city would be safe. I do not believe that the English will make any attempt against it; but they may have the madness to do so, and it is well to be prepared against surprise."

Not four thousand men, but four times four thousand, now stood in its defence; and their chiefs wisely resolved not to throw away the advantages of their position. Nothing more was heard of Vaudreuil's bold plan of attacking the in-vaders at their landing; and Montcalm had declared that he would play the part, not of Hannibal, but of Fabius. His plan was to avoid a general battle, run no risks, and protract the defence till the resources of the enemy were exhausted, or till approaching winter forced them to withdraw. Success was almost certain but for one contingency. Amherst, with a force larger than that of Wolfe, was moving against Ticonderoga. If he should capture it, and advance into the colony, Montcalm would be forced to weaken his army by sending strong detachments to oppose him. Here was Wolfe's best hope. This failing, his only chance was in audacity. The game was desperate; but, intrepid gamester as he was in war, he was a man, in the last resort, to stake everything on the cast of the dice.

The elements declared for France. On the afternoon of the day when Wolfe's army landed, a violent squall swept over the St. Lawrence, dashed the ships together, drove several ashore, and destroyed many of the flat-boats from which the troops had just disembarked. "I never saw so much distress among shipping in my whole life," writes an officer to a friend in Boston. Fortunately the storm subsided as quickly as it rose. Vaudreuil saw that the hoped-for deliverance had failed; and as the tempest had not destroyed the British fleet, he resolved to try the virtue of his fireships. "I am afraid," says Montcalm, "that they have cost us a million, and will be good for nothing after all." This remained to be seen. Vaudreuil gave the chief command of them to a naval officer named Delouche; and on the evening of the twenty-eighth, after long consultation and much debate among their respective captains, they set sail together at ten o'clock. The night was moonless and dark. In less than an hour they were at the entrance of the north channel. Delouche had been all enthusiasm; but as he neared the danger his nerves failed, and he set fire to his ship half an hour too soon, the rest following his example.[1]

There was an English outpost at the Point of Orleans; and, about eleven o'clock, the sentries descried through the gloom the ghostly outlines of the approaching ships. As they gazed, these mysterious strangers began to dart tongues of flame; fire ran like lightning up their masts and sails, and then they burst out like volcanoes. Filled as they were with pitch, tar, and every manner of combustible, mixed with fireworks, bombs, grenades, and old cannon, swivels, and muskets loaded to the

[1] Foligny, *Journal mémoratif. Vaudreuil au Ministre, 5 Oct. 1759. Journal du Siége* (Bibliothêque de Hartwell).

throat, the effect was terrific. The troops at the Point, amazed at the sudden eruption, the din of the explosions, and the showers of grapeshot that rattled among the trees, lost their wits and fled. The blazing dragons hissed and roared, spouted sheets of fire, vomited smoke in black, pitchy volumes and vast illumined clouds, and shed their infernal glare on the distant city, the tents of Montcalm, and the long red lines of the British army, drawn up in array of battle, lest the French should cross from their encampments to attack them in the confusion. Knox calls the display "the grandest fireworks that can possibly be conceived." Yet the fireships did no other harm than burning alive one of their own captains and six or seven of his sailors who failed to escape in their boats. Some of them ran ashore before reaching the fleet; the others were seized by the intrepid English sailors, who, approaching in their boats, threw grappling-irons upon them and towed them towards land, till they swung round and stranded. Here, after venting their fury for a while, they subsided into quiet conflagration, which lasted till morning. Vaudreuil watched the result of his experiment from the steeple of the church at Beauport; then returned, dejected, to Quebec.

Wolfe longed to fight his enemy; but his sagacious enemy would not gratify him. From the heights of Beauport, the rock of Quebec, or the summit of Cape Diamond, Montcalm could look down on the river and its shores as on a map, and watch each movement of the invaders. He was hopeful, perhaps confident; and for a month or more he wrote almost daily to Bourlamaque at Ticonderoga, in a cheerful, and often a jocose vein, mingling orders and instructions with pleasantries and bits of news. Yet his vigilance was unceasing. "We pass every night in bivouac, or else sleep in our clothes. Perhaps you are doing as much, my dear Bourlamaque."[1]

Of the two commanders, Vaudreuil was the more sanguine, and professed full faith that all would go well. He too corresponded with Bourlamaque, to whom he gave his opinion, founded on the reports of deserters, that Wolfe had no chance of success unless Amherst should come to his aid. This he pronounced impossible; and he expressed a strong desire that the English would attack him, "so that we may rid ourselves

[1] *Montcalm à Bourlamaque, 27 Juin, 1759.* All these letters are before me.

of them at once."[1] He was courageous, except in the immediate presence of danger, and failed only when the crisis came.

Wolfe, held in check at every other point, had one movement in his power. He could seize the heights of Point Levi, opposite the city; and this, along with his occupation of the Island of Orleans, would give him command of the Basin of Quebec. Thence also he could fire on the place across the St. Lawrence, which is here less than a mile wide. The movement was begun on the afternoon of the twenty-ninth, when, shivering in a north wind and a sharp frost, a part of Monckton's brigade was ferried over to Beaumont, on the south shore, and the rest followed in the morning. The rangers had a brush with a party of Canadians, whom they drove off, and the regulars then landed unopposed. Monckton ordered a proclamation, signed by Wolfe, to be posted on the door of the parish church. It called on the Canadians, in peremptory terms, to stand neutral in the contest, promised them, if they did so, full protection in property and religion, and threatened that, if they presumed to resist the invaders, their houses, goods, and harvests should be destroyed, and their churches despoiled. As soon as the troops were out of sight the inhabitants took down the placard and carried it to Vaudreuil.

The brigade marched along the river road to Point Levi, drove off a body of French and Indians posted in the church, and took possession of the houses and the surrounding heights. In the morning they were intrenching themselves, when they were greeted by a brisk fire from the edge of the woods. It came from a party of Indians, whom the rangers presently put to flight, and, imitating their own ferocity, scalped nine of them. Wolfe came over to the camp on the next day, went with an escort to the heights opposite Quebec, examined it with a spy-glass, and chose a position from which to bombard it. Cannon and mortars were brought ashore, fascines and gabions made, intrenchments thrown up, and batteries planted. Knox came over from the main camp, and says that he had "a most agreeable view of the city of Quebec. It is a very fair object for our artillery, particularly the lower town." But why did Wolfe wish to bombard it? Its fortifica-

[1] *Vaudreuil à Bourlamaque, 8 Juillet, 1759.*

tions were but little exposed to his fire, and to knock its houses, convents, and churches to pieces would bring him no nearer to his object. His guns at Point Levi could destroy the city, but could not capture it; yet doubtless they would have good moral effect, discourage the French, and cheer his own soldiers with the flattering belief that they were achieving something.

The guns of Quebec showered balls and bombs upon his workmen; but they still toiled on, and the French saw the fatal batteries fast growing to completion. The citizens, alarmed at the threatened destruction, begged the Governor for leave to cross the river and dislodge their assailants. At length he consented. A party of twelve or fifteen hundred was made up of armed burghers, Canadians from the camp, a few Indians, some pupils of the Seminary, and about a hundred volunteers from the regulars. Dumas, an experienced officer, took command of them; and, going up to Sillery, they crossed the river on the night of the twelfth of July. They had hardly climbed the heights of the south shore when they grew exceedingly nervous, though the enemy was still three miles off. The Seminary scholars fired on some of their own party, whom they mistook for English; and the same mishap was repeated a second and a third time. A panic seized the whole body, and Dumas could not control them. They turned and made for their canoes, rolling over each other as they rushed down the heights, and reappeared at Quebec at six in the morning, overwhelmed with despair and shame.[1]

The presentiment of the unhappy burghers proved too true. The English batteries fell to their work, and the families of the town fled to the country for safety. In a single day eighteen houses and the cathedral were burned by exploding shells; and fiercer and fiercer the storm of fire and iron hailed upon Quebec.

Wolfe did not rest content with distressing his enemy.

---

[1] *Événements de la Guerre en Canada* (Hist. Soc. Quebec, 1861). *Mémoires sur le Canada, 1749–1760*. *Vaudreuil au Ministre, 5 Oct. 1759*. *L'Abeille*, II. No. 14 (a publication of the Quebec Seminary). *Journal du Siége de Québec* (Bibliothêque de Hartwell). Panet, *Journal du Siége*. Foligny, *Journal mémoratif. Memoirs of the Siege of Quebec, by John Johnson, Clerk and Quartermaster-Sergeant to the Fifty-eighth Regiment*.

With an ardor and a daring that no difficulties could cool, he sought means to strike an effective blow. It was nothing to lay Quebec in ruins if he could not defeat the army that protected it. To land from boats and attack Montcalm in front, through the mud of the Beauport flats or up the heights along the neighboring shore, was an enterprise too rash even for his temerity. It might, however, be possible to land below the cataract of Montmorenci, cross that stream higher up, and strike the French army in flank or rear; and he had no sooner secured his positions at the points of Levi and Orleans, than he addressed himself to this attempt.

On the eighth several frigates and a bomb-ketch took their stations before the camp of the Chevalier de Lévis, who, with his division of Canadian militia, occupied the heights along the St. Lawrence just above the cataract. Here they shelled and cannonaded him all day; though, from his elevated position, with very little effect. Towards evening the troops on the Point of Orleans broke up their camp. Major Hardy, with a detachment of marines, was left to hold that post, while the rest embarked at night in the boats of the fleet. They were the brigades of Townshend and Murray, consisting of five battalions, with a body of grenadiers, light infantry, and rangers,—in all three thousand men. They landed before daybreak in front of the parish of L'Ange Gardien, a little below the cataract. The only opposition was from a troop of Canadians and Indians, whom they routed, after some loss, climbed the heights, gained the plateau above, and began to intrench themselves. A company of rangers, supported by detachments of regulars, was sent into the neighboring forest to protect the parties who were cutting fascines, and apparently, also, to look for a fording-place.

Lévis, with his Scotch-Jacobite aide-de-camp, Johnstone, had watched the movements of Wolfe from the heights across the cataract. Johnstone says that he asked his commander if he was sure there was no ford higher up on the Montmorenci, by which the English could cross. Lévis averred that there was none, and that he himself had examined the stream to its source; on which a Canadian who stood by whispered to the aide-de-camp: "The General is mistaken; there is a ford." Johnstone told this to Lévis, who would not believe it, and so browbeat the Canadian that he dared not repeat what he had said. Johnstone, taking him aside, told him to go and find somebody who had lately crossed the ford, and bring him at once to the General's quarters; whereupon he soon reappeared with a man who affirmed that he had crossed it the night before with a sack of wheat on his back. A detachment was immediately sent to the place, with orders to intrench itself, and Repentigny, lieutenant of Lévis, was posted not far off with eleven hundred Canadians.

Four hundred Indians passed the ford under the partisan Langlade, discovered Wolfe's detachment, hid themselves, and sent their commander to tell Repentigny that there was a body of English in the forest, who might all be destroyed if he would come over at once with his Canadians. Repentigny sent for orders to Lévis, and Lévis sent for orders to Vaudreuil, whose quarters were three or four miles distant. Vaudreuil answered that no risk should be run, and that he would come and see to the matter himself. It was about two hours before he arrived; and meanwhile the Indians grew impatient, rose from their hiding-place, fired on the rangers, and drove them back with heavy loss upon the regulars, who stood their ground, and at last repulsed the assailants. The Indians recrossed the ford with thirty-six scalps. If Repentigny had advanced, and Lévis had followed with his main body, the consequences to the English might have been serious; for, as Johnstone remarks, "a Canadian in the woods is worth three disciplined soldiers, as a soldier in a plain is worth three Canadians." Vaudreuil called a council of war. The question was whether an effort should be made to dislodge Wolfe's main force. Montcalm and the Governor were this time of one mind, and both thought it inexpedient to attack, with militia, a body of regular troops whose numbers and position were imperfectly known. Bigot gave his voice for the attack. He was overruled, and Wolfe was left to fortify himself in peace.[1]

His occupation of the heights of Montmorenci exposed

[1]The above is from a comparison of the rather discordant accounts of Johnstone, the *Journal tenu à l'Armée*, the *Journal* of Panet, and that of the Hartwell Library. The last says that Lévis crossed the Montmorenci. If so, he accomplished nothing. This affair should not be confounded with a somewhat similar one which took place on the 26th.

him to great risks. The left wing of his army at Point Levi was six miles from its right wing at the cataract, and Major Hardy's detachment on the Point of Orleans was between them, separated from each by a wide arm of the St. Lawrence. Any one of the three camps might be overpowered before the others could support it; and Hardy with his small force was above all in danger of being cut to pieces. But the French kept persistently on the defensive; and after the failure of Dumas to dislodge the English from Point Levi, Vaudreuil would not hear of another such attempt. Wolfe was soon well intrenched; but it was easier to defend himself than to strike at his enemy. Montcalm, when urged to attack him, is said to have answered: "Let him amuse himself where he is. If we drive him off he may go to some place where he can do us harm." His late movement, however, had a discouraging effect on the Canadians, who now for the first time began to desert. His batteries, too, played across the chasm of Montmorenci upon the left wing of the French army with an effect extremely annoying.

The position of the hostile forces was a remarkable one. They were separated by the vast gorge that opens upon the St. Lawrence; an amphitheatre of lofty precipices, their brows crested with forests, and their steep brown sides scantily feathered with stunted birch and fir. Into this abyss leaps the Montmorenci with one headlong plunge of nearly two hundred and fifty feet, a living column of snowy white, with its spray, its foam, its mists, and its rainbows; then spreads itself in broad thin sheets over a floor of rock and gravel, and creeps tamely to the St. Lawrence. It was but a gunshot across the gulf, and the sentinels on each side watched each other over the roar and turmoil of the cataract. Captain Knox, coming one day from Point Levi to receive orders from Wolfe, improved a spare hour to visit this marvel of nature. "I had very nigh paid dear for my inquisitiveness; for while I stood on the eminence I was hastily called to by one of our sentinels, when, throwing my eyes about, I saw a Frenchman creeping under the eastern extremity of their breastwork to fire at me. This obliged me to retire as fast as I could out of his reach, and, making up to the sentry to thank him for his attention, he told me the fellow had snapped his piece twice, and the second time it flashed in the pan at the instant I turned away from the Fall." Another officer, less fortunate, had a leg broken by a shot from the opposite cliffs.

Day after day went by, and the invaders made no progress. Flags of truce passed often between the hostile camps. "You will demolish the town, no doubt," said the bearer of one of them, "but you shall never get inside of it." To which Wolfe replied: "I will have Quebec if I stay here till the end of November." Sometimes the heat was intense, and sometimes there were floods of summer rain that inundated the tents. Along the river, from the Montmorenci to Point Levi, there were ceaseless artillery fights between gunboats, frigates, and batteries on shore. Bands of Indians infested the outskirts of the camps, killing sentries and patrols. The rangers chased them through the woods; there were brisk skirmishes, and scalps lost and won. Sometimes the regulars took part in these forest battles; and once it was announced, in orders of the day, that "the General has ordered two sheep and some rum to Captain Cosnan's company of grenadiers for the spirit they showed this morning in pushing those scoundrels of Indians." The Indians complained that the British soldiers were learning how to fight, and no longer stood still in a mass to be shot at, as in Braddock's time. The Canadian *coureurs-de-bois* mixed with their red allies and wore their livery. One of them was caught on the eighteenth. He was naked, daubed red and blue, and adorned with a bunch of painted feathers dangling from the top of his head. He and his companions used the scalping-knife as freely as the Indians themselves; nor were the New England rangers much behind them in this respect, till an order came from Wolfe forbidding "the inhuman practice of scalping, except when the enemy are Indians, or Canadians dressed like Indians."

A part of the fleet worked up into the Basin, beyond the Point of Orleans; and here, on the warm summer nights, officers and men watched the cannon flashing and thundering from the heights of Montmorenci on one side, and those of Point Levi on the other, and the bombs sailing through the air in fiery semicircles. Often the gloom was lighted up by the blaze of the burning houses of Quebec, kindled by incendiary shells. Both the lower and the upper town were nearly deserted by the inhabitants, some retreating into the country, and some into the suburb of St. Roch; while the Ursulines and Hospital nuns abandoned their convents to seek harborage beyond the range of shot. The city was a prey to robbers, who pillaged the empty houses, till an order came from headquarters promising the gallows to all who should be caught. News reached the French that Niagara was attacked, and that the army of Amherst was moving against Ticonderoga. The Canadians deserted more and more. They were disheartened by the defensive attitude in which both Vaudreuil and Montcalm steadily persisted; and accustomed as they were to rapid raids, sudden strokes, and a quick return to their homes, they tired of long weeks of inaction. The English patrols caught one of them as he was passing the time in fishing. "He seemed to be a subtle old rogue," says Knox, "of seventy years of age, as he told us. We plied him well with port wine, and then his heart was more open; and seeing that we laughed at the exaggerated accounts he had given us, he said he 'wished the affair was well over, one way or the other; that his countrymen were all discontented, and would either surrender, or disperse and act a neutral part, if it were not for the persuasions of their priests and the fear of being maltreated by the savages, with whom they are threatened on all occasions.'" A deserter reported on the nineteenth of July that nothing but dread of the Indians kept the Canadians in the camp.

Wolfe's proclamation, at first unavailing, was now taking effect. A large number of Canadian prisoners, brought in on the twenty-fifth, declared that their countrymen would gladly accept his offers but for the threats of their commanders that if they did so the Indians should be set upon them. The prisoners said further that "they had been under apprehension for several days past of having a body of four hundred barbarians sent to rifle their parish and habitations."[1] Such threats were not wholly effectual. A French chronicler of the time says: "The Canadians showed their disgust every day, and deserted at every opportunity, in spite of the means taken to prevent them." "The people were intimidated, seeing all our army kept in one body and solely on the defensive; while the English, though far less numerous, divided their forces,

[1] Knox, I. 347; compare pp. 339, 341, 346.

and undertook various bold enterprises without meeting resistance."[1]

On the eighteenth the English accomplished a feat which promised important results. The French commanders had thought it impossible for any hostile ship to pass the batteries of Quebec; but about eleven o'clock at night, favored by the wind, and covered by a furious cannonade from Point Levi, the ship "Sutherland," with a frigate and several small vessels, sailed safely by and reached the river above the town. Here they at once attacked and destroyed a fireship and some small craft that they found there. Now, for the first time, it became necessary for Montcalm to weaken his army at Beauport by sending six hundred men, under Dumas, to defend the accessible points in the line of precipices between Quebec and Cap-Rouge. Several hundred more were sent on the next day, when it became known that the English had dragged a fleet of boats over Point Levi, launched them above the town, and despatched troops to embark in them. Thus a new feature was introduced into the siege operations, and danger had risen on a side where the French thought themselves safe. On the other hand, Wolfe had become more vulnerable than ever. His army was now divided, not into three parts, but into four, each so far from the rest that, in case of sudden attack, it must defend itself alone. That Montcalm did not improve his opportunity was apparently due to want of confidence in his militia.

The force above the town did not lie idle. On the night of the twentieth, Colonel Carleton, with six hundred men, rowed eighteen miles up the river, and landed at Pointe-aux-Trembles, on the north shore. Here some of the families of Quebec had sought asylum; and Wolfe had been told by prisoners that not only were stores in great quantity to be found here, but also letters and papers throwing light on the French plans. Carleton and his men drove off a band of Indians who fired on them, and spent a quiet day around the parish church; but found few papers, and still fewer stores. They withdrew towards evening, carrying with them nearly a hundred women, children, and old men; and they were no sooner gone than the Indians returned to plunder the empty

[1] *Journal du Siége* (Bibliothèque de Hartwell).

houses of their unfortunate allies. The prisoners were treated
with great kindness. The ladies among them were entertained
at supper by Wolfe, who jested with them on the caution of
the French generals, saying: "I have given good chances to
attack me, and am surprised that they have not profited by
them."[1] On the next day the prisoners were all sent to Quebec under a flag of truce.

Thus far Wolfe had refrained from executing the threats he
had affixed the month before to the church of Beaumont. But
now he issued another proclamation. It declared that the Canadians had shown themselves unworthy of the offers he had
made them, and that he had therefore ordered his light troops
to ravage their country and bring them prisoners to his camp.
Such of the Canadian militia as belonged to the parishes near
Quebec were now in a sad dilemma; for Montcalm threatened
them on one side, and Wolfe on the other. They might desert
to their homes, or they might stand by their colors; in the
one case their houses were to be burned by French savages,
and in the other by British light infantry.

Wolfe at once gave orders in accord with his late proclamation; but he commanded that no church should be profaned, and no woman or child injured. The first effects of his
stern policy are thus recorded by Knox: "Major Dalling's
light infantry brought in this afternoon to our camp two
hundred and fifty male and female prisoners. Among this
number was a very respectable looking priest, and about forty
men fit to bear arms. There was almost an equal number of
black cattle, with about seventy sheep and lambs, and a few
horses. Brigadier Monckton entertained the reverend father
and some other fashionable personages in his tent, and most
humanely ordered refreshments to all the rest of the captives;
which noble example was followed by the soldiery, who gen-
erously crowded about those unhappy people, sharing their
provisions, rum, and tobacco with them. They were sent in
the evening on board of transports in the river." Again, two
days later: "Colonel Fraser's detachment returned this morning, and presented us with more scenes of distress and the
dismal consequences of war, by a great number of wretched
families, whom they brought in prisoners, with some of their

[1] *Journal tenu à l'Armée que commandoit feu M. le Marquis de Montcalm.*

effects, and near three hundred black cattle, sheep, hogs, and horses."

On the next night the attention of the excellent journalist was otherwise engaged. Vaudreuil tried again to burn the English fleet. "Late last night," writes Knox, under date of the twenty-eighth, "the enemy sent down a most formidable fire-raft, which consisted of a parcel of schooners, shallops, and stages chained together. It could not be less than a hundred fathoms in length, and was covered with grenades, old swivels, gun and pistol barrels loaded up to their muzzles, and various other inventions and combustible matters. This seemed to be their last attempt against our fleet, which happily miscarried, as before; for our gallant seamen, with their usual expertness, grappled them before they got down above a third part of the Basin, towed them safe to shore, and left them at anchor, continually repeating, *All's well*. A remarkable expression from some of these intrepid souls to their comrades on this occasion I must not omit, on account of its singular uncouthness; namely: 'Damme, Jack, didst thee ever take hell in tow before?' "

According to a French account, this aquatic infernal machine consisted of seventy rafts, boats, and schooners. Its failure was due to no shortcoming on the part of its conductors; who, under a brave Canadian named Courval, acted with coolness and resolution. Nothing saved the fleet but the courage of the sailors, swarming out in their boats to fight the approaching conflagration.

It was now the end of July. More than half the summer was gone, and Quebec seemed as far as ever beyond the grasp of Wolfe. Its buildings were in ruins, and the neighboring parishes were burned and ravaged; but its living rampart, the army of Montcalm, still lay in patient defiance along the shores of Beauport, while above the city every point where a wildcat could climb the precipices was watched and guarded, and Dumas with a thousand men held the impregnable heights of Cap-Rouge. Montcalm persisted in doing nothing that his enemy wished him to do. He would not fight on Wolfe's terms, and Wolfe resolved at last to fight him on his own; that is, to attack his camp in front.

The plan was desperate; for, after leaving troops enough to

hold Point Levi and the heights of Montmorenci, less than five thousand men would be left to attack a position of commanding strength, where Montcalm at an hour's notice could collect twice as many to oppose them. But Wolfe had a boundless trust in the disciplined valor of his soldiers, and an utter scorn of the militia who made the greater part of his enemy's force.

Towards the Montmorenci the borders of the St. Lawrence are, as we have seen, extremely high and steep. At a mile from the gorge of the cataract there is, at high tide, a strand, about the eighth of a mile wide, between the foot of these heights and the river; and beyond this strand the receding tide lays bare a tract of mud nearly half a mile wide. At the edge of the dry ground the French had built a redoubt mounted with cannon, and there were other similar works on the strand a quarter of a mile nearer the cataract. Wolfe could not see from the river that these redoubts were commanded by the musketry of the intrenchments along the brink of the heights above. These intrenchments were so constructed that they swept with cross-fires the whole face of the declivity, which was covered with grass, and was very steep. Wolfe hoped that, if he attacked one of the redoubts, the French would come down to defend it, and so bring on a general engagement; or, if they did not, that he should gain an opportunity of reconnoitring the heights to find some point where they could be stormed with a chance of success.

In front of the gorge of the Montmorenci there was a ford during several hours of low tide, so that troops from the adjoining English camp might cross to co-operate with their comrades landing in boats from Point Levi and the Island of Orleans. On the morning of the thirty-first of July, the tide then being at the flood, the French saw the ship "Centurion," of sixty-four guns, anchor near the Montmorenci and open fire on the redoubts. Then two armed transports, each of fourteen guns, stood in as close as possible to the first redoubt and fired upon it, stranding as the tide went out, till in the afternoon they lay bare upon the mud. At the same time a battery of more than forty heavy pieces, planted on the lofty promontory beyond the Montmorenci, began a furious cannonade upon the flank of the French intrenchments. It did no great harm, however, for the works were protected by a great number of traverses, which stopped the shot; and the Canadians, who manned this part of the lines, held their ground with excellent steadiness.

About eleven o'clock a fleet of boats filled with troops, chiefly from Point Levi, appeared in the river and hovered off the shore west of the parish church of Beauport, as if meaning to land there. Montcalm was perplexed, doubting whether the real attack was to be made here, or toward the Montmorenci. Hour after hour the boats moved to and fro, to increase his doubts and hide the real design; but he soon became convinced that the camp of Lévis at the Montmorenci was the true object of his enemy; and about two o'clock he went thither, greeted as he rode along the lines by shouts of *Vive notre Général!* Lévis had already made preparations for defence with his usual skill. His Canadians were reinforced by the battalions of Béarn, Guienne, and Royal Roussillon; and, as the intentions of Wolfe became certain, the right of the camp was nearly abandoned, the main strength of the army being gathered between the river of Beauport and the Montmorenci, where, according to a French writer, there were, towards the end of the afternoon, about twelve thousand men.[1]

At half-past five o'clock the tide was out, and the crisis came. The batteries across the Montmorenci, the distant batteries of Point Levi, the cannon of the "Centurion," and those of the two stranded ships, all opened together with redoubled fury. The French batteries replied; and, amid this deafening roar of artillery, the English boats set their troops ashore at the edge of the broad tract of sedgy mud that the receding river had left bare. At the same time a column of two thousand men was seen, a mile away, moving in perfect order across the Montmorenci ford. The first troops that landed from the boats were thirteen companies of grenadiers and a detachment of Royal Americans. They dashed swiftly forward; while at some distance behind came Monckton's brigade, composed of the fifteenth, or Amherst's regiment, and the seventy-eighth, or Fraser's Highlanders. The day had been fair and warm; but the sky was now thick with clouds, and large raindrops began to fall, the precursors of a summer storm.

[1] Panet, *Journal.*

With the utmost precipitation, without orders, and without waiting for Monckton's brigade to come up, the grenadiers in front made a rush for the redoubt near the foot of the hill. The French abandoned it; but the assailants had no sooner gained their prize than the thronged heights above blazed with musketry, and a tempest of bullets fell among them. Nothing daunted, they dashed forward again, reserving their fire, and struggling to climb the steep ascent; while, with yells and shouts of *Vive le Roi!* the troops and Canadians at the top poured upon them a hailstorm of musket-balls and buck-shot, and dead and wounded in numbers rolled together down the slope. At that instant the clouds burst, and the rain fell in torrents. "We could not see half way down the hill," says the Chevalier Johnstone, who was at this part of the line. Ammunition was wet on both sides, and the grassy steeps became so slippery that it was impossible to climb them. The English say that the storm saved the French; the French, with as much reason, that it saved the English.

The baffled grenadiers drew back into the redoubt. Wolfe saw the madness of persisting, and ordered a retreat. The rain ceased, and troops of Indians came down the heights to scalp the fallen. Some of them ran towards Lieutenant Peyton, of the Royal Americans, as he lay disabled by a musket-shot. With his double-barrelled gun he brought down two of his assailants, when a Highland sergeant snatched him in his arms, dragged him half a mile over the mud-flats, and placed him in one of the boats. A friend of Peyton, Captain Ochter-lony, had received a mortal wound, and an Indian would have scalped him but for the generous intrepidity of a soldier of the battalion of Guienne; who, seizing the enraged savage, held him back till several French officers interposed, and had the dying man carried to a place of safety.

The English retreated in good order, after setting fire to the two stranded vessels. Those of the grenadiers and Royal Americans who were left alive rowed for the Point of Or-leans; the fifteenth regiment rowed for Point Levi; and the Highlanders, led by Wolfe himself, joined the column from beyond the Montmorenci, placing themselves in its rear as it slowly retired along the flats and across the ford, the Indians yelling and the French shouting from the heights, while the

British waved their hats, daring them to come down and fight.

The grenadiers and the Royal Americans, who had borne the brunt of the fray, bore also nearly all the loss; which, in proportion to their numbers, was enormous. Knox reports it at four hundred and forty-three, killed, wounded, and missing, including one colonel, eight captains, twenty-one lieutenants, and three ensigns.

Vaudreuil, delighted, wrote to Bourlamaque an account of the affair. "I have no more anxiety about Quebec. M. Wolfe, I can assure you, will make no progress. Luckily for him, his prudence saved him from the consequences of his mad enterprise, and he contented himself with losing about five hundred of his best soldiers. Deserters say that he will try us again in a few days. That is what we want; he 'll find somebody to talk to (*il trouvera à qui parler*)."

NOTE. — Among the killed in this affair was Edward Botwood, sergeant in the grenadiers of the forty-seventh, or Lascelles' regiment. "Ned Botwood" was well known among his comrades as a poet; and the following lines of his, written on the eve of the expedition to Quebec, continued to be favorites with the British troops during the War of the Revolution (see *Historical Magazine*, II., First Series, 164). It may be observed here that the war produced a considerable quantity of indifferent verse on both sides. On that of the English it took the shape of occasional ballads, such as "Bold General Wolfe," printed on broadsides, or of patriotic effusions scattered through magazines and newspapers, while the French celebrated all their victories with songs.

HOT STUFF

AIR, — *Lilies of France.*

Come, each death-doing dog who dares venture his neck,
Come, follow the hero that goes to Quebec;
Jump aboard of the transports, and loose every sail,
Pay your debts at the tavern by giving leg-bail;
And ye that love fighting shall soon have enough:
Wolfe commands us, my boys; we shall give them Hot Stuff.

Up the River St. Lawrence our troops shall advance,
To the Grenadiers' March we will teach them to dance.
Cape Breton we have taken, and next we will try
At their capital to give them another black eye.
Vaudreuil, 't is in vain you pretend to look gruff, —
Those are coming who know how to give you Hot Stuff.

With powder in his periwig, and snuff in his nose,
Monsieur will run down our descent to oppose;
And the Indians will come: but the light infantry
Will soon oblige *them* to betake to a tree.
From such rascals as these may we fear a rebuff?
Advance, grenadiers, and let fly your Hot Stuff!

When the forty-seventh regiment is dashing ashore,
While bullets are whistling and cannons do roar,
Says Montcalm: "Those are Shirley's—I know the lappels."
"You lie," says Ned Botwood, "we belong to Lascelles'!
Tho' our cloathing is changed, yet we scorn a powder-puff;
So at you, ye b——s, here 's give you Hot Stuff."

On the repulse at Montmorenci, *Wolfe to Pitt, 2 Sept. 1759. Vaudreuil au Ministre, 5 Oct. 1759.* Panet, *Journal du Siége.* Johnstone, *Dialogue in Hades. Journal tenu à l'Armée,* etc. *Journal of the Siege of Quebec, by a Gentleman in an eminent Station on the Spot. Mémoires sur le Canada, 1749 –1760.* Fraser, *Journal of the Siege. Journal du Siége d'après un MS. déposé à la Bibliothêque Hartwell.* Foligny, *Journal mémoratif. Journal of Transactions at the Siege of Quebec,* in *Notes and Queries,* XX. 164. John Johnson, *Memoirs of the Siege of Quebec. Journal of an Expedition on the River St. Lawrence. An Authentic Account of the Expedition against Quebec, by a Volunteer on that Expedition. J. Gibson to Governor Lawrence, 1 Aug. 1759.* Knox, I. 354. Mante, 244.

Chapter XXVI

1759

AMHERST—NIAGARA

Amherst on Lake George • Capture of Ticonderoga and Crown Point • Delays of Amherst • Niagara Expedition • La Corne attacks Oswego • His Repulse • Niagara besieged • Aubry comes to its Relief • Battle • Rout of the French • The Fort taken • Isle-aux-Noix • Amherst advances to attack it • Storm • The Enterprise abandoned • Rogers attacks St. Francis • Destroys the Town • Sufferings of the Rangers

---

Pɪᴛᴛ had directed that, while Quebec was attacked, an attempt should be made to penetrate into Canada by way of Ticonderoga and Crown Point. Thus the two armies might unite in the heart of the colony, or, at least, a powerful diversion might be effected in behalf of Wolfe. At the same time Oswego was to be re-established, and the possession of Fort Duquesne, or Pittsburg, secured by reinforcements and supplies; while Amherst, the commander-in-chief, was further directed to pursue any other enterprise which in his opinion would weaken the enemy, without detriment to the main objects of the campaign.[1] He accordingly resolved to attempt the capture of Niagara. Brigadier Prideaux was charged with this stroke; Brigadier Stanwix was sent to conduct the operations for the relief of Pittsburg; and Amherst himself prepared to lead the grand central advance against Ticonderoga, Crown Point, and Montreal.[2]

Towards the end of June he reached that valley by the head of Lake George which for five years past had been the annual mustering-place of armies. Here were now gathered about eleven thousand men, half regulars and half provincials,[3] drilling every day, firing by platoons, firing at marks, practising manœuvres in the woods; going out on scouting parties, bathing parties, fishing parties; gathering wild herbs to serve for greens, cutting brushwood and meadow hay to make hos-

[1] *Pitt to Amherst, 23 Jan., 10 March, 1759.*
[2] *Amherst to Pitt, 19 June, 1759. Amherst to Stanwix, 6 May, 1759.*
[3] Mante, 210.

pital beds. The sick were ordered on certain mornings to repair to the surgeon's tent, there, in prompt succession, to
swallow such doses as he thought appropriate to their several
ailments; and it was further ordered that "every fair day they
that can walk be paraded together and marched down to the
lake to wash their hands and faces." Courts-martial were numerous; culprits were flogged at the head of each regiment in
turn, and occasionally one was shot. A frequent employment
was the cutting of spruce tops to make spruce beer. This innocent beverage was reputed sovereign against scurvy; and
such was the fame of its virtues that a copious supply of the
West Indian molasses used in concocting it was thought indispensable to every army or garrison in the wilderness.
Throughout this campaign it is repeatedly mentioned in general orders, and the soldiers are promised that they shall have
as much of it as they want at a halfpenny a quart.[1]

The rear of the army was well protected from insult. Fortified
posts were built at intervals of three or four miles along the road
to Fort Edward, and especially at the station called Half-way
Brook; while, for the whole distance, a broad belt of wood on
both sides was cut down and burned, to deprive a skulking enemy of cover. Amherst was never long in one place without
building a fort there. He now began one, which proved wholly
needless, on that flat rocky hill where the English made their intrenched camp during the siege of Fort William Henry. Only
one bastion of it was ever finished, and this is still shown to
tourists under the name of Fort George.

The army embarked on Saturday, the twenty-first of July.
The Reverend Benjamin Pomeroy watched their departure in
some concern, and wrote on Monday to Abigail, his wife: "I
could wish for more appearance of dependence on God than
was observable among them; yet I hope God will grant deliverance unto Israel by them." There was another military pageant, another long procession of boats and banners, among
the mountains and islands of Lake George. Night found them

[1] *Orderly Book of Commissary Wilson in the Expedition against Ticonderoga,
1759. Journal of Samuel Warner, a Massachusetts Soldier, 1759. General and Regimental Orders, Army of Major-General Amherst, 1759. Diary of Sergeant Mer-
riman, of Ruggles's Regiment, 1759.* I owe to William L. Stone, Esq., the use
of the last two curious documents.

near the outlet; and here they lay till morning, tossed unpleasantly on waves ruffled by a summer gale. At daylight they landed, beat back a French detachment, and marched by the portage road to the saw-mill at the waterfall. There was little resistance. They occupied the heights, and then advanced to the famous line of intrenchment against which the army of Abercromby had hurled itself in vain. These works had been completely reconstructed, partly of earth, and partly of logs. Amherst's followers were less numerous than those of his predecessor, while the French commander, Bourlamaque, had a force nearly equal to that of Montcalm in the summer before; yet he made no attempt to defend the intrenchment, and the English, encamping along its front, found it an excellent shelter from the cannon of the fort beyond.

Amherst brought up his artillery and began approaches in form, when, on the night of the twenty-third, it was found that Bourlamaque had retired down Lake Champlain, leaving four hundred men under Hebecourt to defend the place as long as possible. This was in obedience to an order from Vaudreuil, requiring him on the approach of the English to abandon both Ticonderoga and Crown Point, retreat to the outlet of Lake Champlain, take post at Isle-aux-Noix, and there defend himself to the last extremity;[1] a course unquestionably the best that could have been taken, since obstinacy in holding Ticonderoga might have involved the surrender of Bourlamaque's whole force, while Isle-aux-Noix offered rare advantages for defence.

The fort fired briskly; a cannon-shot killed Colonel Townshend, and a few soldiers were killed and wounded by grape and bursting shells; when, at dusk on the evening of the twenty-sixth, an unusual movement was seen among the garrison, and, about ten o'clock, three deserters came in great excitement to the English camp. They reported that Hebecourt and his soldiers were escaping in their boats, and that a match was burning in the magazine to blow Ticonderoga to atoms. Amherst offered a hundred guineas to any one of them who would point out the match, that it might be cut; but they shrank from the perilous venture. All was silent till

[1] *Vaudreuil au Ministre, 8 Nov. 1759. Instructions pour M. de Bourlamaque, 20 Mai, 1759, signé Vaudreuil. Montcalm à Bourlamaque, 4 Juin, 1759.*

eleven o'clock, when a broad, fierce glare burst on the night, and a roaring explosion shook the promontory; then came a few breathless moments, and then the fragments of Fort Ticonderoga fell with clatter and splash on the water and the land. It was but one bastion, however, that had been thus hurled skyward. The rest of the fort was little hurt, though the barracks and other combustible parts were set on fire, and by the light the French flag was seen still waving on the rampart.[1] A sergeant of the light infantry, braving the risk of other explosions, went and brought it off. Thus did this redoubted stronghold of France fall at last into English hands, as in all likelihood it would have done a year sooner, if Amherst had commanded in Abercromby's place; for, with the deliberation that marked all his proceedings, he would have sat down before Montcalm's wooden wall and knocked it to splinters with his cannon.

He now set about repairing the damaged works and making ready to advance on Crown Point; when on the first of August his scouts told him that the enemy had abandoned this place also, and retreated northward down the lake.[2] Well pleased, he took possession of the deserted fort, and, in the animation of success, thought for a moment of keeping the promise he had given to Pitt "to make an irruption into Canada with the utmost vigor and despatch."[3] Wolfe, his brother in arms and his friend, was battling with the impossible under the rocks of Quebec, and every motive, public and private, impelled Amherst to push to his relief, not counting costs, or balancing risks too nicely. He was ready enough to spur on others, for he wrote to Gage: "We must all be alert and active day and night; if we all do our parts the French must fall;"[4] but, far from doing his, he set the army to building a new fort at Crown Point, telling them that it would "give plenty, peace, and quiet to His Majesty's subjects for ages to come."[5]

[1] *Journal of Colonel Amherst* (brother of General Amherst). *Vaudreuil au Ministre, 8 Nov. 1759. Amherst to Prideaux, 28 July, 1759. Amherst to Pitt, 27 July, 1759.* Mante, 213. Knox, I., 397–403. *Vaudreuil à Bourlamaque, 19 Juin, 1759.*

[2] *Amherst to Pitt, 5 Aug. 1759.*

[3] *Ibid., 19 June, 1759.*

[4] *Amherst to Gage, 1 Aug. 1759.*

[5] *General Orders, 13 Aug. 1759.*

Then he began three small additional forts, as outworks to the first, sent two parties to explore the sources of the Hudson; one party to explore Otter Creek; another to explore South Bay, which was already well known; another to make a road across what is now the State of Vermont, from Crown Point to Charlestown, or "Number Four," on the Connecticut; and another to widen and improve the old French road between Crown Point and Ticonderoga. His industry was untiring; a great deal of useful work was done: but the essential task of making a diversion to aid the army of Wolfe was needlessly postponed.

It is true that some delay was inevitable. The French had four armed vessels on the lake, and this made it necessary to provide an equal or superior force to protect the troops on their way to Isle-aux-Noix. Captain Loring, the English naval commander, was therefore ordered to build a brigantine; and, this being thought insufficient, he was directed to add a kind of floating battery, moved by sweeps. Three weeks later, in consequence of farther information concerning the force of the French vessels, Amherst ordered an armed sloop to be put on the stocks; and this involved a long delay. The saw-mill at Ticonderoga was to furnish planks for the intended navy; but, being overtasked in sawing timber for the new works at Crown Point, it was continually breaking down. Hence much time was lost, and autumn was well advanced before Loring could launch his vessels.[1]

Meanwhile news had come from Prideaux and the Niagara expedition. That officer had been ordered to ascend the Mohawk with five thousand regulars and provincials, leave a strong garrison at Fort Stanwix, on the Great Carrying Place, establish posts at both ends of Lake Oneida, descend the Onondaga to Oswego, leave nearly half his force there under Colonel Haldimand, and proceed with the rest to attack Niagara.[2] These orders he accomplished. Haldimand remained to reoccupy the spot that Montcalm had made desolate three years before; and, while preparing to build a fort, he barri-

---

[1] *Amherst to Pitt, 22 Oct. 1759.* This letter, which is in the form of a journal, covers twenty-one folio pages.

[2] *Instructions of Amherst to Prideaux, 17 May, 1759. Prideaux to Haldimand, 30 June, 1759.*

caded his camp with pork and flour barrels, lest the enemy
should make a dash upon him from their station at the head
of the St. Lawrence Rapids. Such an attack was probable; for
if the French could seize Oswego, the return of Prideaux
from Niagara would be cut off, and when his small stock of
provisions had failed, he would be reduced to extremity.
Saint-Luc de la Corne left the head of the Rapids early in July
with a thousand French and Canadians and a body of Indians, who soon made their appearance among the stumps and
bushes that surrounded the camp at Oswego. The priest Piquet was of the party; and five deserters declared that he solemnly blessed them, and told them to give the English no
quarter.[1] Some valuable time was lost in bestowing the benediction; yet Haldimand's men were taken by surprise. Many
of them were dispersed in the woods, cutting timber for the
intended fort; and it might have gone hard with them had
not some of La Corne's Canadians become alarmed and
rushed back to their boats, oversetting Father Piquet on the
way.[2] These being rallied, the whole party ensconced itself in
a tract of felled trees so far from the English that their fire did
little harm. They continued it about two hours, and resumed
it the next morning; when, three cannon being brought to
bear on them, they took to their boats and disappeared, having lost about thirty killed and wounded, including two officers and La Corne himself, who was shot in the thigh. The
English loss was slight.

Prideaux safely reached Niagara, and laid siege to it. It was
a strong fort, lately rebuilt in regular form by an excellent
officer, Captain Pouchot, of the battalion of Béarn, who commanded it. It stood where the present fort stands, in the angle
formed by the junction of the River Niagara with Lake Ontario, and was held by about six hundred men, well supplied
with provisions and munitions of war.[3] Higher up the river,
a mile and a half above the cataract, there was another fort,
called Little Niagara, built of wood, and commanded by the

---

[1] *Journal of Colonel Amherst.*

[2] Pouchot, II. 130. Compare *Mémoires sur le Canada, 1749–1760*; *N. Y. Col. Docs.*, VII. 395; and *Letter from Oswego*, in *Boston Evening Post*, No. 1,248.

[3] Pouchot says 515, besides 60 men from Little Niagara; Vaudreuil gives a total of 589.

half-breed officer, Joncaire-Chabert, who with his brother, Joncaire-Clauzonne, and a numerous clan of Indian relatives, had so long thwarted the efforts of Johnson to engage the Five Nations in the English cause. But recent English successes had had their effect. Joncaire's influence was waning, and Johnson was now in Prideaux's camp with nine hundred Five Nation warriors pledged to fight the French. Joncaire, finding his fort untenable, burned it, and came with his garrison and his Indian friends to reinforce Niagara.[1]

Pouchot had another resource, on which he confidently relied. In obedience to an order from Vaudreuil, the French population of the Illinois, Detroit, and other distant posts, joined with troops of Western Indians, had come down the Lakes to recover Pittsburg, undo the work of Forbes, and restore French ascendency on the Ohio. Pittsburg had been in imminent danger; nor was it yet safe, though General Stanwix was sparing no effort to succor it.[2] These mixed bands of white men and red, bushrangers and savages, were now gathered, partly at Le Bœuf and Venango, but chiefly at Presquisle, under command of Aubry, Ligneris, Marin, and other partisan chiefs, the best in Canada. No sooner did Pouchot learn that the English were coming to attack him than he sent a messenger to summon them all to his aid.[3]

The siege was begun in form, though the English engineers were so incompetent that the trenches, as first laid out, were scoured by the fire of the place, and had to be made anew.[4] At last the batteries opened fire. A shell from a coehorn burst prematurely, just as it left the mouth of the piece, and a fragment striking Prideaux on the head, killed him instantly. Johnson took command in his place, and made up in energy what he lacked in skill. In two or three weeks the fort was in

[1] Pouchot, II. 52, 59. *Procès de Bigot, Cadet, et autres, Mémoire pour Daniel de Joncaire-Chabert.*

[2] *Letters of Colonel Hugh Mercer, commanding at Pittsburg, January–June, 1759. Letters of Stanwix, May–July, 1759. Letter from Pittsburg,* in *Boston News Letter,* No. 3,023. *Narrative of John Ormsby.*

[3] Pouchot, II. 46.

[4] *Rutherford to Haldimand, 14 July, 1759.* Prideaux was extremely disgusted. *Prideaux to Haldimand, 13 July, 1759.* Allan Macleane, of the Highlanders, calls the engineers "fools and blockheads, G—d d—n them." *Macleane to Haldimand, 21 July, 1759.*

extremity. The rampart was breached, more than a hundred of the garrison were killed or disabled, and the rest were exhausted with want of sleep. Pouchot watched anxiously for the promised succors; and on the morning of the twenty-fourth of July a distant firing told him that they were at hand.

Aubry and Ligneris, with their motley following, had left Presquisle a few days before, to the number, according to Vaudreuil, of eleven hundred French and two hundred Indians.[1] Among them was a body of colony troops; but the Frenchmen of the party were chiefly traders and bushrangers from the West, connecting links between civilization and savagery; some of them indeed were mere white Indians, imbued with the ideas and morals of the wigwam, wearing hunting-shirts of smoked deer-skin embroidered with quills of the Canada porcupine, painting their faces black and red, tying eagle feathers in their long hair, or plastering it on their temples with a compound of vermilion and glue. They were excellent woodsmen, skilful hunters, and perhaps the best bushfighters in all Canada.

When Pouchot heard the firing, he went with a wounded artillery officer to the bastion next the river; and as the forest had been cut away for a great distance, they could see more than a mile and a half along the shore. There, by glimpses among trees and bushes, they descried bodies of men, now advancing, and now retreating; Indians in rapid movement, and the smoke of guns, the sound of which reached their ears in heavy volleys, or a sharp and angry rattle. Meanwhile the English cannon had ceased their fire, and the silent trenches seemed deserted, as if their occupants were gone to meet the advancing foe. There was a call in the fort for volunteers to sally and destroy the works; but no sooner did they show themselves along the covered way than the seemingly abandoned trenches were thronged with men and bayonets, and the attempt was given up. The distant firing lasted half an

---

[1] "Il n'y avoit que 1,100 François et 200 sauvages." *Vaudreuil au Ministre, 30 Oct. 1759.* Johnson says "1,200 men, with a number of Indians." *Johnson to Amherst, 25 July, 1759.* Portneuf, commanding at Presquisle, wrote to Pouchot that there were 1,600 French and 1,200 Indians. Pouchot, II. 94. A letter from Aubry to Pouchot put the whole at 2,500, half of them Indians. *Historical Magazine,* V., Second Series, 199.

hour, then ceased, and Pouchot remained in suspense; till, at two in the afternoon, a friendly Onondaga, who had passed unnoticed through the English lines, came to him with the announcement that the French and their allies had been routed and cut to pieces. Pouchot would not believe him.

Nevertheless his tale was true. Johnson, besides his Indians, had with him about twenty-three hundred men, whom he was forced to divide into three separate bodies,—one to guard the bateaux, one to guard the trenches, and one to fight Aubry and his band. This last body consisted of the provincial light infantry and the pickets, two companies of grenadiers, and a hundred and fifty men of the forty-sixth regiment, all under command of Colonel Massey.[1] They took post behind an abattis at a place called La Belle Famille, and the Five Nation warriors placed themselves on their flanks. These savages had shown signs of disaffection; and when the enemy approached, they opened a parley with the French Indians, which, however, soon ended, and both sides raised the warwhoop. The fight was brisk for a while; but at last Aubry's men broke away in a panic. The French officers seem to have made desperate efforts to retrieve the day, for nearly all of them were killed or captured; while their followers, after heavy loss, fled to their canoes and boats above the cataract, hastened back to Lake Erie, burned Presquisle, Le Bœuf, and Venango, and, joined by the garrisons of those forts, retreated to Detroit, leaving the whole region of the upper Ohio in undisputed possession of the English.

At four o'clock on the day of the battle, after a furious cannonade on both sides, a trumpet sounded from the trenches, and an officer approached the fort with a summons to surrender. He brought also a paper containing the names of the captive French officers, though some of them were spelled in a way that defied recognition. Pouchot, feigning incredulity, sent an officer of his own to the English camp, who soon saw unanswerable proof of the disaster; for here, under a shelter of leaves and boughs near the tent of Johnson, sat Ligneris, severely wounded, with Aubry, Villiers, Mon-

---

[1] *Johnson to Amherst, 25 July, 1759.* Knox, II. 135. *Captain Delancey to ——, 25 July, 1759.* This writer commanded the light infantry in the fight.

tigny, Marin, and their companions in misfortune,—in all, sixteen officers, four cadets, and a surgeon.[1]

Pouchot had now no choice but surrender. By the terms of the capitulation, the garrison were to be sent prisoners to New York, though honors of war were granted them in acknowledgment of their courageous conduct. There was a special stipulation that they should be protected from the Indians, of whom they stood in the greatest terror, lest the massacre of Fort William Henry should be avenged upon them. Johnson restrained his dangerous allies, and, though the fort was pillaged, no blood was shed.

The capture of Niagara was an important stroke. Thenceforth Detroit, Michillimackinac, the Illinois, and all the other French interior posts, were severed from Canada, and left in helpless isolation; but Amherst was not yet satisfied. On hearing of Prideaux's death he sent Brigadier Gage to supersede Johnson and take command on Lake Ontario, directing him to descend the St. Lawrence, attack the French posts at the head of the rapids, and hold them if possible for the winter. The attempt was difficult; for the French force on the St. Lawrence was now greater than that which Gage could bring against it, after providing for the safety of Oswego and Niagara. Nor was he by nature prone to dashing and doubtful enterprise. He reported that the movement was impossible, much to the disappointment of Amherst, who seemed to expect from subordinates an activity greater than his own.[2]

He, meanwhile, was working at his fort at Crown Point, while the season crept away, and Bourlamaque lay ready to receive him at Isle-aux-Noix. "I wait his coming with impatience," writes the French commander, "though I doubt if he will venture to attack a post where we are intrenched to the teeth, and armed with a hundred pieces of cannon."[3] Bourlamaque now had with him thirty-five hundred men, in a position of great strength. Isle-aux-Noix, planted in mid-channel

[1] Johnson gives the names in his private *Diary*, printed in Stone, *Life of Johnson*, II. 394. Compare Pouchot, II. 105, 106. *Letter from Niagara*, in *Boston Evening Post*, No. 1,250. *Vaudreuil au Ministre, 30 Oct. 1759.*

[2] *Amherst to Gage, 28 July, 1 Aug., 14 Aug., 11 Sept. 1759. Diary of Sir William Johnson*, in Stone, *Life of Johnson*, II. 394–429.

[3] *Bourlamaque à (Bernetz?), 22 Sept. 1759.*

of the Richelieu soon after it issues from Lake Champlain, had been diligently fortified since the spring. On each side of it was an arm of the river, closed against an enemy with *chevaux-de-frise*. To attack it in front in the face of its formidable artillery would be a hazardous attempt, and the task of reducing it was likely to be a long one. The French force in these parts had lately received accessions. After the fall of Niagara the danger seemed so great, both in the direction of Lake Ontario and that of Lake Champlain, that Lévis had been sent up from Quebec with eight hundred men to command the whole department of Montreal.[1] A body of troops and militia was encamped opposite that town, ready to march towards either quarter, as need might be, while the abundant crops of the neighboring parishes were harvested by armed bands, ready at a word to drop the sickle for the gun.

Thus the promised advance of Amherst into Canada would be not without its difficulties, even when his navy, too tardily begun, should be ready to act its part. But if he showed no haste in succoring Wolfe, he at least made some attempts to communicate with him. Early in August he wrote him a letter, which Ensign Hutchins, of the rangers, carried to him in about a month by the long and circuitous route of the Kennebec, and which, after telling the news of the campaign, ended thus: "You may depend on my doing all I can for effectually reducing Canada. Now is the time!"[2] Amherst soon after tried another expedient, and sent Captains Kennedy and Hamilton with a flag of truce and a message of peace to the Abenakis of St. Francis, who, he thought, won over by these advances, might permit the two officers to pass unmolested to Quebec. But the Abenakis seized them and carried them prisoners to Montreal; on which Amherst sent Major Robert Rogers and a band of rangers to destroy their town.[3]

It was the eleventh of October before the miniature navy of Captain Loring—the floating battery, the brig, and the sloop that had been begun three weeks too late—was ready for service. They sailed at once to look for the enemy. The

---

[1] *Montcalm à Bourlamaque, 9 Août, 1759. Rigaud à Bourlamaque, 14 Août, 1759. Lévis à Bourlamaque, 25 Août, 1759.*

[2] *Amherst to Wolfe, 7 Aug. 1759.*

[3] *Amherst to Pitt, 22 Oct. 1759.* Rogers, *Journals,* 144.

four French vessels made no resistance. One of them succeeded in reaching Isle-aux-Noix; one was run aground; and
two were sunk by their crews, who escaped to the shore. Amherst, meanwhile, leaving the provincials to work at the fort,
embarked with the regulars in bateaux, and proceeded on his
northern way till, on the evening of the twelfth, a head-wind
began to blow, and, rising to a storm, drove him for shelter
into Ligonier Bay, on the west side of the lake.[1] On the thirteenth, it blew a gale. The lake raged like an angry sea, and
the frail bateaux, fit only for smooth water, could not have
lived a moment. Through all the next night the gale continued, with floods of driving rain. "I hope it will soon change,"
wrote Amherst on the fifteenth, "for I have no time to lose."
He was right. He had waited till the season of autumnal
storms, when nature was more dangerous than man. On the
sixteenth there was frost, and the wind did not abate. On the
next morning it shifted to the south, but soon turned back
with violence to the north, and the ruffled lake put on a look
of winter, "which determined me," says the General, "not to
lose time by striving to get to the Isle-aux-Noix, where I
should arrive too late to force the enemy from their post, but
to return to Crown Point and complete the works there."
This he did, and spent the remnant of the season in the congenial task of finishing the fort, of which the massive remains
still bear witness to his industry.

When Lévis heard that the English army had fallen back,
he wrote, well pleased, to Bourlamaque: "I don't know how
General Amherst will excuse himself to his Court, but I am
very glad he let us alone, because the Canadians are so backward that you could count on nobody but the regulars."[2]

Concerning this year's operations on the Lakes, it may be
observed that the result was not what the French feared, or
what the British colonists had cause to hope. If, at the end of
winter, Amherst had begun, as he might have done, the
building of armed vessels at the head of the navigable waters
of Lake Champlain, where Whitehall now stands, he would
have had a navy ready to his hand before August, and would
have been able to follow the retreating French without delay,

[1] *Orderly Book of Commissary Wilson.*
[2] *Lévis à Bourlamaque, 1 Nov. 1759.*

and attack them at Isle-aux-Noix before they had finished their fortifications. And if, at the same time, he had directed Prideaux, instead of attacking Niagara, to co-operate with him by descending the St. Lawrence towards Montreal, the prospect was good that the two armies would have united at that place, and ended the campaign by the reduction of all Canada. In this case Niagara and all the western posts would have fallen without a blow.

Major Robert Rogers, sent in September to punish the Abenakis of St. Francis, had addressed himself to the task with his usual vigor. These Indians had been settled for about three quarters of a century on the River St. Francis, a few miles above its junction with the St. Lawrence. They were nominal Christians, and had been under the control of their missionaries for three generations; but though zealous and sometimes fanatical in their devotion to the forms of Romanism, they remained thorough savages in dress, habits, and character. They were the scourge of the New England borders, where they surprised and burned farmhouses and small hamlets, killed men, women, and children without distinction, carried others prisoners to their village, subjected them to the torture of "running the gantlet," and compelled them to witness dances of triumph around the scalps of parents, children, and friends.

Amherst's instructions to Rogers contained the following: "Remember the barbarities that have been committed by the enemy's Indian scoundrels. Take your revenge, but don't forget that, though those dastardly villains have promiscuously murdered women and children of all ages, it is my order that no women or children be killed or hurt."

Rogers and his men set out in whaleboats, and, eluding the French armed vessels, then in full activity, came, on the tenth day, to Missisquoi Bay, at the north end of Lake Champlain. Here he hid his boats, leaving two friendly Indians to watch them from a distance, and inform him should the enemy discover them. He then began his march for St. Francis, when, on the evening of the second day, the two Indians overtook him with the startling news that a party of about four hundred French had found the boats, and that half of them were on his tracks in hot pursuit. It was certain that the alarm would soon be given, and other parties sent to cut him off. He took the bold resolution of outmarching his pursuers, pushing straight for St. Francis, striking it before succors could arrive, and then returning by Lake Memphremagog and the Connecticut. Accordingly he despatched Lieutenant McMullen by a circuitous route back to Crown Point, with a request to Amherst that provisions should be sent up the Connecticut to meet him on the way down. Then he set his course for the Indian town, and for nine days more toiled through the forest with desperate energy. Much of the way was through dense spruce swamps, with no dry resting-place at night. At length the party reached the River St. Francis, fifteen miles above the town, and, hooking their arms together for mutual support, forded it with extreme difficulty. Towards evening, Rogers climbed a tree, and descried the town three miles distant. Accidents, fatigue, and illness had reduced his followers to a hundred and forty-two officers and men. He left them to rest for a time, and, taking with him Lieutenant Turner and Ensign Avery, went to reconnoitre the place; left his two companions, entered it disguised in an Indian dress, and saw the unconscious savages yelling and singing in the full enjoyment of a grand dance. At two o'clock in the morning he rejoined his party, and at three led them to the attack, formed them in a semicircle, and burst in upon the town half an hour before sunrise. Many of the warriors were absent, and the rest were asleep. Some were killed in their beds, and some shot down in trying to escape. "About seven o'clock in the morning," he says, "the affair was completely over, in which time we had killed at least two hundred Indians and taken twenty of their women and children prisoners, fifteen of whom I let go their own way, and five I brought with me, namely, two Indian boys and three Indian girls. I likewise retook five English captives."

English scalps in hundreds were dangling from poles over the doors of the houses.[1] The town was pillaged and burned, not excepting the church, where ornaments of some value were found. On the side of the rangers, Captain Ogden and six men were wounded, and a Mohegan Indian from Stock-

---

[1] Rogers says "about six hundred." Other accounts say six or seven hundred. The late Abbé Maurault, missionary of the St. Francis Indians, and their historian, adopts the latter statement, though it is probably exaggerated.

bridge was killed. Rogers was told by his prisoners that a party of three hundred French and Indians was encamped on the river below, and that another party of two hundred and fifteen was not far distant. They had been sent to cut off the retreat of the invaders, but were doubtful as to their designs till after the blow was struck. There was no time to lose. The rangers made all haste southward, up the St. Francis, subsisting on corn from the Indian town; till, near the eastern borders of Lake Memphremagog, the supply failed, and they separated into small parties, the better to sustain life by hunting. The enemy followed close, attacked Ensign Avery's party, and captured five of them; then fell upon a band of about twenty, under Lieutenants Dunbar and Turner, and killed or captured nearly all. The other bands eluded their pursuers, turned southeastward, reached the Connecticut, some here, some there, and, giddy with fatigue and hunger, toiled wearily down the wild and lonely stream to the appointed rendezvous at the mouth of the Amonoosuc.

This was the place to which Rogers had requested that provisions might be sent; and the hope of finding them there had been the breath of life to the famished wayfarers. To their horror, the place was a solitude. There were fires still burning, but those who made them were gone. Amherst had sent Lieutenant Stephen up the river from Charlestown with an abundant supply of food; but finding nobody at the Amonoosuc, he had waited there two days, and then returned, carrying the provisions back with him; for which outrageous conduct he was expelled from the service. "It is hardly possible," says Rogers, "to describe our grief and consternation." Some gave themselves up to despair. Few but their indomitable chief had strength to go farther. There was scarcely any game, and the barren wilderness yielded no sustenance but a few lily bulbs and the tubers of the climbing plant called in New England the ground-nut. Leaving his party to these miserable resources, and promising to send them relief within ten days, Rogers made a raft of dry pine logs, and drifted on it down the stream, with Captain Ogden, a ranger, and one of the captive Indian boys. They were stopped on the second day by rapids, and gained the shore with difficulty. At the foot of the rapids, while Ogden and the ranger went in search of squirrels, Rogers set himself to making another raft; and, having no strength to use the axe, he burned down the trees, which he then divided into logs by the same process. Five days after leaving his party he reached the first English settlement, Charlestown, or "Number Four," and immediately sent a canoe with provisions to the relief of the sufferers, following himself with other canoes two days later. Most of the men were saved, though some died miserably of famine and exhaustion. Of the few who had been captured, we are told by a French contemporary that they "became victims of the fury of the Indian women," from whose clutches the Canadians tried in vain to save them.[1]

NOTE.—On the day after he reached "Number Four," Rogers wrote a report of his expedition to Amherst. This letter is printed in his *Journals*, in which he gives also a supplementary account, containing further particulars. The *New Hampshire Gazette*, *Boston Evening Post*, and other newspapers of the time recount the story in detail. Hoyt (*Indian Wars*, 302) repeats it, with a few additions drawn from the recollections of survivors, long after. There is another account, very short and unsatisfactory, by Thompson Maxwell, who says that he was of the party, which is doubtful. Mante (223) gives horrible details of the sufferings of the rangers. An old chief of the St. Francis Indians, said to be one of those who pursued Rogers after the town was burned, many years ago told Mr. Jesse Pennoyer, a government land surveyor, that Rogers laid an ambush for the pursuers, and defeated them with great loss. This, the story says, took place near the present town of Sherbrooke; and minute details are given, with high praise of the skill and conduct of the famous partisan. If such an incident really took place, it is scarcely possible that Rogers would not have made some mention of it. On the other hand, it is equally incredible that the Indians would have invented the tale of their own defeat. I am indebted for Pennoyer's puzzling narrative to the kindness of R. A. Ramsay, Esq., of Montreal. It was printed, in 1869, in the *History of the Eastern Townships*, by Mrs. C. M. Day. All things considered, it is probably groundless.

Vaudreuil describes the destruction of the village in a letter to the Minister dated October 26, and says that Rogers had a hundred and fifty men; that St. Francis was burned to ashes; that the head chief and others were killed; that he (Vaudreuil), hearing of the march of the rangers, sent the most active of the Canadians to oppose them, and that Longueuil sent all the Canadians and Indians he could muster to pursue them on their retreat; that forty-six rangers were killed, and ten captured; that he thinks all the rest will starve to death; and, finally, that the affair is very unfortunate.

I once, when a college student, followed on foot the route of Rogers from Lake Memphremagog to the Connecticut.

[1] *Événements de la Guerre en Canada, 1759, 1760*. Compare *N. Y. Col. Docs.*, X. 1042.

Chapter XXVII

1759

THE HEIGHTS OF ABRAHAM

Elation of the French • Despondency of Wolfe • The Parishes laid waste • Operations above Quebec • Illness of Wolfe • A new Plan of Attack • Faint Hope of Success • Wolfe's last Despatch • Confidence of Vaudreuil • Last Letters of Montcalm • French Vigilance • British Squadron at Cap-Rouge • Last Orders of Wolfe • Embarkation • Descent of the St. Lawrence • The Heights scaled • The British Line • Last Night of Montcalm • The Alarm • March of French Troops • The Battle • The Rout • The Pursuit • Fall of Wolfe and of Montcalm

---

WOLFE WAS deeply moved by the disaster at the heights of Montmorenci, and in a General Order on the next day he rebuked the grenadiers for their precipitation. "Such impetuous, irregular, and unsoldierlike proceedings destroy all order, make it impossible for the commanders to form any disposition for an attack, and put it out of the general's power to execute his plans. The grenadiers could not suppose that they could beat the French alone."

The French were elated by their success. "Everybody," says the commissary Berniers, "thought that the campaign was as good as ended, gloriously for us." They had been sufficiently confident even before their victory; and the bearer of a flag of truce told the English officers that he had never imagined they were such fools as to attack Quebec with so small a force. Wolfe, on the other hand, had every reason to despond. At the outset, before he had seen Quebec and learned the nature of the ground, he had meant to begin the campaign by taking post on the Plains of Abraham, and thence laying siege to the town; but he soon discovered that the Plains of Abraham were hardly more within his reach than was Quebec itself. Such hope as was left him lay in the composition of Montcalm's army. He respected the French commander, and thought his disciplined soldiers not unworthy of the British steel; but he held his militia in high scorn, and could he but face them in the open field, he never doubted the result. But Montcalm also distrusted them, and persisted in refusing the coveted battle.

Wolfe, therefore, was forced to the conviction that his chances were of the smallest. It is said that, despairing of any decisive stroke, he conceived the idea of fortifying Isle-aux-Coudres, and leaving a part of his troops there when he sailed for home, against another attempt in the spring. The more to weaken the enemy and prepare his future conquest, he began at the same time a course of action which for his credit one would gladly wipe from the record; for, though far from in-human, he threw himself with extraordinary intensity into whatever work he had in hand, and, to accomplish it, spared others scarcely more than he spared himself. About the middle of August he issued a third proclamation to the Canadians, declaring that as they had refused his offers of protection and "had made such ungrateful returns in practising the most unchristian barbarities against his troops on all occasions, he could no longer refrain in justice to himself and his army from chastising them as they deserved." The barbarities in question consisted in the frequent scalping and mutilating of sentinels and men on outpost duty, perpetrated no less by Canadians than by Indians. Wolfe's object was twofold: first, to cause the militia to desert, and, secondly, to exhaust the colony. Rangers, light infantry, and Highlanders were sent to waste the settlements far and wide. Wherever resistance was offered, farmhouses and villages were laid in ashes, though churches were generally spared. St. Paul, far below Quebec, was sacked and burned, and the settlements of the opposite shore were partially destroyed. The parishes of L'Ange Gardien, Château Richer, and St. Joachim were wasted with fire and sword. Night after night the garrison of Quebec could see the light of burning houses as far down as the mountain of Cape Tourmente. Near St. Joachim there was a severe skirmish, followed by atrocious cruelties. Captain Alexander Montgomery, of the forty-third regiment, who commanded the detachment, and who has been most unjustly confounded with the revolutionary general, Richard Montgomery, ordered the prisoners to be shot in cold blood, to the indignation of his own officers.[1] Robineau de Portneuf, curé of St. Joachim, placed himself at the head of thirty parishioners and took possession of a large stone house in the adjacent parish of Château Richer, where for a time he held the English at bay. At length he and his followers were drawn out into an ambush, where they were surrounded and killed; and, being disguised as Indians, the rangers scalped them all.[2]

Most of the French writers of the time mention these barbarities without much comment, while Vaudreuil loudly denounces them. Yet he himself was answerable for atrocities incomparably worse, and on a far larger scale. He had turned loose his savages, red and white, along a frontier of six hundred miles, to waste, burn, and murder at will. "Women and children," such were the orders of Wolfe, "are to be treated with humanity; if any violence is offered to a woman, the offender shall be punished with death." These orders were generally obeyed. The English, with the single exception of Montgomery, killed none but armed men in the act of resistance or attack; Vaudreuil's war-parties spared neither age nor sex.

Montcalm let the parishes burn, and still lay fast intrenched in his lines of Beauport. He would not imperil all Canada to save a few hundred farmhouses; and Wolfe was as far as ever from the battle that he coveted. Hitherto, his attacks had been made chiefly below the town; but, these having failed, he now changed his plan and renewed on a larger scale the movements begun above it in July. With every fair wind, ships and transports passed the batteries of Quebec, favored by a hot fire from Point Levi, and generally succeeded, with more or less damage, in gaining the upper river. A fleet of flatboats was also sent thither, and twelve hundred troops marched overland to embark in them, under Brigadier Murray. Admiral Holmes took command of the little fleet now gathered above the town, and operations in that quarter were systematically resumed.

To oppose them, Bougainville was sent from the camp at Beauport with fifteen hundred men. His was a most arduous

[1] Fraser, *Journal*. Fraser was an officer under Montgomery, of whom he speaks with anger and disgust.
[2] Knox, II. 32. Most of the contemporary journals mention the incident.

and exhausting duty. He must watch the shores for fifteen or twenty miles, divide his force into detachments, and subject himself and his followers to the strain of incessant vigilance and incessant marching. Murray made a descent at Pointe-aux-Trembles, and was repulsed with loss. He tried a second time at another place, was met before landing by a body of ambushed Canadians, and was again driven back, his foremost boats full of dead and wounded. A third time he succeeded, landed at Deschambault, and burned a large building filled with stores and all the spare baggage of the French regular officers. The blow was so alarming that Montcalm hastened from Beauport to take command in person; but when he arrived the English were gone.

Vaudreuil now saw his mistake in sending the French frigates up the river out of harm's way, and withdrawing their crews to serve the batteries of Quebec. Had these ships been there, they might have overpowered those of the English in detail as they passed the town. An attempt was made to retrieve the blunder. The sailors were sent to man the frigates anew and attack the squadron of Holmes. It was too late. Holmes was already too strong for them, and they were recalled. Yet the difficulties of the English still seemed insurmountable. Dysentery and fever broke out in their camps, the number of their effective men was greatly reduced, and the advancing season told them that their work must be done quickly, or not done at all.

On the other side, the distress of the French grew greater every day. Their army was on short rations. The operations of the English above the town filled the camp of Beauport with dismay, for troops and Canadians alike dreaded the cutting off of their supplies. These were all drawn from the districts of Three Rivers and Montreal; and, at best, they were in great danger, since when brought down in boats at night they were apt to be intercepted, while the difficulty of bringing them by land was extreme, through the scarcity of cattle and horses. Discipline was relaxed, disorder and pillage were rife, and the Canadians deserted so fast, that towards the end of August two hundred of them, it is said, would sometimes go off in one night. Early in the month the disheartening news came of the loss of Ticonderoga and Crown Point, the retreat of Bourlamaque, the fall of Niagara, and the expected advance of Amherst on Montreal. It was then that Lévis was despatched to the scene of danger; and Quebec was deplorably weakened by his absence. About this time the Lower Town was again set on fire by the English batteries, and a hundred and sixty-seven houses were burned in a night. In the front of the Upper Town nearly every building was a ruin. At the General Hospital, which was remote enough to be safe from the bombardment, every barn, shed, and garret, and even the chapel itself, were crowded with sick and wounded, with women and children from the town, and the nuns of the Ursulines and the Hôtel-Dieu, driven thither for refuge. Bishop Pontbriand, though suffering from a mortal disease, came almost daily to visit and console them from his lodging in the house of the curé at Charlesbourg.

Towards the end of August the sky brightened again. It became known that Amherst was not moving on Montreal, and Bourlamaque wrote that his position at Isle-aux-Noix was impregnable. On the twenty-seventh a deserter from Wolfe's army brought the welcome assurance that the invaders despaired of success, and would soon sail for home; while there were movements in the English camps and fleet that seemed to confirm what he said. Vaudreuil breathed more freely, and renewed hope and confidence visited the army of Beauport.

Meanwhile a deep cloud fell on the English. Since the siege began, Wolfe had passed with ceaseless energy from camp to camp, animating the troops, observing everything, and directing everything; but now the pale face and tall lean form were seen no more, and the rumor spread that the General was dangerously ill. He had in fact been seized by an access of the disease that had tortured him for some time past; and fever had followed. His quarters were at a French farmhouse in the camp at Montmorenci; and here, as he lay in an upper chamber, helpless in bed, his singular and most unmilitary features haggard with disease and drawn with pain, no man could less have looked the hero. But as the needle, though quivering, points always to the pole, so, through torment and languor and the heats of fever, the mind of Wolfe dwelt on the capture of Quebec. His illness, which began before the twentieth of August, had so far subsided on the twenty-fifth that Knox wrote in his Diary of that day: "His Excellency General Wolfe is on the recovery, to the inconceivable joy of the whole army." On the twenty-ninth he was able to write or dictate a letter to the three brigadiers, Monckton, Townshend, and Murray: "That the public service may not suffer by the General's indisposition, he begs the brigadiers will meet and consult together for the public utility and advantage, and consider of the best method to attack the enemy." The letter then proposes three plans, all bold to audacity. The first was to send a part of the army to ford the Montmorenci eight or nine miles above its mouth, march through the forest, and fall on the rear of the French at Beauport, while the rest landed and attacked them in front. The second was to cross the ford at the mouth of the Montmorenci and march along the strand, under the French intrenchments, till a place could be found where the troops might climb the heights. The third was to make a general attack from boats at the Beauport flats. Wolfe had before entertained two other plans, one of which was to scale the heights at St. Michel, about a league above Quebec; but this he had abandoned on learning that the French were there in force to receive him. The other was to storm the Lower Town; but this also he had abandoned, because the Upper Town, which commanded it, would still remain inaccessible.

The brigadiers met in consultation, rejected the three plans proposed in the letter, and advised that an attempt should be made to gain a footing on the north shore above the town, place the army between Montcalm and his base of supply, and so force him to fight or surrender. The scheme was similar to that of the heights of St. Michel. It seemed desperate, but so did all the rest; and if by chance it should succeed, the gain was far greater than could follow any success below the town. Wolfe embraced it at once.

Not that he saw much hope in it. He knew that every chance was against him. Disappointment in the past and gloom in the future, the pain and exhaustion of disease, toils, and anxieties "too great," in the words of Burke, "to be supported by a delicate constitution, and a body unequal to the vigorous and enterprising soul that it lodged," threw him at times into deep dejection. By those intimate with him he was heard to say that he would not go back defeated, "to be exposed to the censure and reproach of an ignorant populace." In other moods he felt that he ought not to sacrifice what was left of his diminished army in vain conflict with hopeless obstacles. But his final resolve once taken, he would not swerve from it. His fear was that he might not be able to lead his troops in person. "I know perfectly well you cannot cure me," he said to his physician; "but pray make me up so that I may be without pain for a few days, and able to do my duty: that is all I want."

In a despatch which Wolfe had written to Pitt, Admiral Saunders conceived that he had ascribed to the fleet more than its just share in the disaster at Montmorenci; and he sent him a letter on the subject. Major Barré kept it from the invalid till the fever had abated. Wolfe then wrote a long answer, which reveals his mixed dejection and resolve. He affirms the justice of what Saunders had said, but adds: "I shall leave out that part of my letter to Mr. Pitt which you object to. I am sensible of my own errors in the course of the campaign, see clearly wherein I have been deficient, and think a little more or less blame to a man that must necessarily be ruined, of little or no consequence. I take the blame of that unlucky day entirely upon my own shoulders, and I expect to suffer for it." Then, speaking of the new project of an attack above Quebec, he says despondingly: "My ill state of health prevents me from executing my own plan; it is of too desperate a nature to order others to execute." He proceeds, however, to give directions for it. "It will be necessary to run as many small craft as possible above the town, with provisions for six weeks, for about five thousand, which is all I intend to take. My letters, I hope, will be ready to-morrow, and I hope I shall have strength to lead these men to wherever we can find the enemy."

On the next day, the last of August, he was able for the first time to leave the house. It was on this same day that he wrote his last letter to his mother: "My writing to you will convince you that no personal evils worse than defeats and disappointments have fallen upon me. The enemy puts nothing to risk, and I can't in conscience put the whole army to risk. My antagonist has wisely shut himself up in inaccessible intrenchments, so that I can't get at him without spilling a torrent of blood, and that perhaps to little purpose. The Marquis de Montcalm is at the head of a great number of bad soldiers, and I am at the head of a small number of good ones, that wish for nothing so much as to fight him; but the wary old fellow avoids an action, doubtful of the behavior of his army. People must be of the profession to understand the disadvantages and difficulties we labor under, arising from the uncommon natural strength of the country."

On the second of September a vessel was sent to England with his last despatch to Pitt. It begins thus: "The obstacles we have met with in the operations of the campaign are much greater than we had reason to expect or could foresee; not so much from the number of the enemy (though superior to us) as from the natural strength of the country, which the Marquis of Montcalm seems wisely to depend upon. When I learned that succors of all kinds had been thrown into Quebec; that five battalions of regular troops, completed from the best inhabitants of the country, some of the troops of the colony, and every Canadian that was able to bear arms, besides several nations of savages, had taken the field in a very advantageous situation,—I could not flatter myself that I should be able to reduce the place. I sought, however, an occasion to attack their army, knowing well that with these troops I was able to fight, and hoping that a victory might disperse them." Then, after recounting the events of the campaign with admirable clearness, he continues: "I found myself so ill, and am still so weak, that I begged the general officers to consult together for the general utility. They are all of opinion that, as more ships and provisions are now got above the town, they should try, by conveying up a corps of four or five thousand men (which is nearly the whole strength of the army after the Points of Levi and Orleans are left in a proper state of defence), to draw the enemy from their present situation and bring them to an action. I have acquiesced in the proposal, and we are preparing to put it into execution." The letter ends thus: "By the list of disabled officers, many of whom are of rank, you may perceive that the army is much weakened. By the nature of the river, the most formidable part of this armament is deprived of the power of acting; yet we have almost the whole force of Canada to oppose. In this situation there is such a choice of difficulties that I own myself at a loss how to determine. The affairs of Great Britain, I know, require the most vigorous measures; but the courage of a handful of brave troops should be exerted only when there is some hope of a favorable event; however, you may be assured that the small part of the campaign which remains shall be employed, as far as I am able, for the honor of His Majesty and the interest of the nation, in which I am sure of being well seconded by the Admiral and by the generals; happy if our efforts here can contribute to the success of His Majesty's arms in any other parts of America."

Some days later, he wrote to the Earl of Holdernesse: "The Marquis of Montcalm has a numerous body of armed men (I cannot call it an army), and the strongest country perhaps in the world. Our fleet blocks up the river above and below the town, but can give no manner of aid in an attack upon the Canadian army. We are now here [*off Cap-Rouge*] with about thirty-six hundred men, waiting to attack them when and wherever they can best be got at. I am so far recovered as to do business; but my constitution is entirely ruined, without the consolation of doing any considerable service to the state, and without any prospect of it." He had just learned, through the letter brought from Amherst by Ensign Hutchins, that he could expect no help from that quarter.

Perhaps he was as near despair as his undaunted nature was capable of being. In his present state of body and mind he was a hero without the light and cheer of heroism. He flattered himself with no illusions, but saw the worst and faced it all. He seems to have been entirely without excitement. The languor of disease, the desperation of the chances, and the greatness of the stake may have wrought to tranquillize him. His energy was doubly tasked: to bear up his own sinking frame, and to achieve an almost hopeless feat of arms.

Audacious as it was, his plan cannot be called rash if we may accept the statement of two well-informed writers on the French side. They say that on the tenth of September the English naval commanders held a council on board the flagship, in which it was resolved that the lateness of the season required the fleet to leave Quebec without delay. They say further that Wolfe then went to the Admiral, told him that he had found a place where the heights could be scaled, that he would send up a hundred and fifty picked men to feel the way, and that if they gained a lodgment at the top, the other troops should follow; if, on the other hand, the French were there in force to oppose them, he would not sacrifice the army in a hopeless attempt, but embark them for home, consoled by the thought that all had been done that man could do. On this, concludes the story, the Admiral and his officers consented to wait the result.[1]

As Wolfe had informed Pitt, his army was greatly weakened. Since the end of June his loss in killed and wounded was more than eight hundred and fifty, including two colonels, two majors, nineteen captains, and thirty-four subalterns; and to these were to be added a greater number disabled by disease.

The squadron of Admiral Holmes above Quebec had now increased to twenty-two vessels, great and small. One of the last that went up was a diminutive schooner, armed with a few swivels, and jocosely named the "Terror of France." She sailed by the town in broad daylight, the French, incensed at her impudence, blazing at her from all their batteries; but she passed unharmed, anchored by the Admiral's ship, and saluted him triumphantly with her swivels.

Wolfe's first move towards executing his plan was the critical one of evacuating the camp at Montmorenci. This was accomplished on the third of September. Montcalm sent a strong force to fall on the rear of the retiring English. Monckton saw the movement from Point Levi, embarked two battalions in the boats of the fleet, and made a feint of landing at Beauport. Montcalm recalled his troops to repulse the threatened attack; and the English withdrew from Montmorenci unmolested, some to the Point of Orleans, others to Point Levi. On the night of the fourth a fleet of flatboats passed above the town with the baggage and stores. On the

---

[1] This statement is made by the Chevalier Johnstone, and, with some variation, by the author of the valuable *Journal tenu à l'Armée que commandoit feu M. le Marquis de Montcalm.* Bigot says that, after the battle, he was told by British officers that Wolfe meant to risk only an advance party of two hundred men, and to reimbark if they were repulsed.

fifth, Murray, with four battalions, marched up to the River Etechemin, and forded it under a hot fire from the French batteries at Sillery. Monckton and Townshend followed with three more battalions, and the united force, of about thirty-six hundred men, was embarked on board the ships of Holmes, where Wolfe joined them on the same evening.

These movements of the English filled the French commanders with mingled perplexity, anxiety, and hope. A deserter told them that Admiral Saunders was impatient to be gone. Vaudreuil grew confident. "The breaking up of the camp at Montmorenci," he says, "and the abandonment of the intrenchments there, the reimbarkation on board the vessels above Quebec of the troops who had encamped on the south bank, the movements of these vessels, the removal of the heaviest pieces of artillery from the batteries of Point Levi,—these and the lateness of the season all combined to announce the speedy departure of the fleet, several vessels of which had even sailed down the river already. The prisoners and the deserters who daily came in told us that this was the common report in their army."[1] He wrote to Bourlamaque on the first of September: "Everything proves that the grand design of the English has failed."

Yet he was ceaselessly watchful. So was Montcalm; and he, too, on the night of the second, snatched a moment to write to Bourlamaque from his headquarters in the stone house, by the river of Beauport: "The night is dark; it rains; our troops are in their tents, with clothes on, ready for an alarm; I in my boots; my horses saddled. In fact, this is my usual way. I wish you were here; for I cannot be everywhere, though I multiply myself, and have not taken off my clothes since the twenty-third of June." On the eleventh of September he wrote his last letter to Bourlamaque, and probably the last that his pen ever traced. "I am overwhelmed with work, and should often lose temper, like you, if I did not remember that I am paid by Europe for not losing it. Nothing new since my last. I give the enemy another month, or something less, to stay here." The more sanguine Vaudreuil would hardly give them a week.

Meanwhile, no precaution was spared. The force under Bougainville above Quebec was raised to three thousand

[1] *Vaudreuil au Ministre, 5 Oct. 1759.*

men.[1] He was ordered to watch the shore as far as Jacques-Cartier, and follow with his main body every movement of Holmes's squadron. There was little fear for the heights near the town; they were thought inaccessible.[2] Even Montcalm believed them safe, and had expressed himself to that effect some time before. "We need not suppose," he wrote to Vaudreuil, "that the enemy have wings;" and again, speaking of the very place where Wolfe afterwards landed, "I swear to you that a hundred men posted there would stop their whole army."[3] He was right. A hundred watchful and determined men could have held the position long enough for reinforcements to come up.

The hundred men were there. Captain de Vergor, of the colony troops, commanded them, and reinforcements were within his call; for the battalion of Guienne had been ordered to encamp close at hand on the Plains of Abraham.[4] Vergor's post, called Anse du Foulon, was a mile and a half from Quebec. A little beyond it, by the brink of the cliffs, was another post, called Samos, held by seventy men with four cannon; and, beyond this again, the heights of Sillery were guarded by a hundred and thirty men, also with cannon.[5] These were outposts of Bougainville, whose headquarters were at Cap-Rouge, six miles above Sillery, and whose troops were in continual movement along the intervening shore. Thus all was vigilance; for while the French were strong in the hope of speedy delivery, they felt that there was no safety till the tents of the invader had vanished from their shores and his ships from their river. "What we knew," says one of them, "of the character of M. Wolfe, that impetuous, bold, and intrepid warrior, prepared us for a last attack before he left us."

Wolfe had been very ill on the evening of the fourth. The troops knew it, and their spirits sank; but, after a night of torment, he grew better, and was soon among them again, rekindling their ardor, and imparting a cheer that he could

---

[1] *Journal du Siége* (Bibliothêque de Hartwell). *Journal tenu à l'Armée*, etc. *Vaudreuil au Ministre, 5 Oct. 1759.*

[2] Pontbriand, *Jugement impartial.*

[3] *Montcalm à Vaudreuil, 27 Juillet. Ibid., 29 Juillet, 1759.*

[4] Foligny, *Journal mémoratif. Journal tenu à l'Armée*, etc.

[5] *Vaudreuil au Ministre, 5 Oct. 1759.*

not share. For himself he had no pity; but when he heard of the illness of two officers in one of the ships, he sent them a message of warm sympathy, advised them to return to Point Levi, and offered them his own barge and an escort. They thanked him, but replied that, come what might, they would see the enterprise to an end. Another officer remarked in his hearing that one of the invalids had a very delicate constitution. "Don't tell me of constitution," said Wolfe; "he has good spirit, and good spirit will carry a man through everything."[1] An immense moral force bore up his own frail body and forced it to its work.

Major Robert Stobo, who, five years before, had been given as a hostage to the French at the capture of Fort Necessity, arrived about this time in a vessel from Halifax. He had long been a prisoner at Quebec, not always in close custody, and had used his opportunities to acquaint himself with the neighborhood. In the spring of this year he and an officer of rangers named Stevens had made their escape with extraordinary skill and daring; and he now returned to give his countrymen the benefit of his local knowledge.[2] His biographer says that it was he who directed Wolfe in the choice of a landing-place.[3] Be this as it may, Wolfe in person examined the river and the shores as far as Pointe-aux-Trembles; till at length, landing on the south side a little above Quebec, and looking across the water with a telescope, he descried a path that ran with a long slope up the face of the woody precipice, and saw at the top a cluster of tents. They were those of Vergor's guard at the Anse du Foulon, now called Wolfe's Cove. As he could see but ten or twelve of them, he thought that the guard could not be numerous, and might be overpowered. His hope would have been stronger if he had known that Vergor had once been tried for misconduct and cowardice in the surrender of Beauséjour, and saved from merited disgrace by the friendship of Bigot and the protection of Vaudreuil.[4]

The morning of the seventh was fair and warm, and the vessels of Holmes, their crowded decks gay with scarlet uni-

[1] Knox, II. 61, 65.
[2] Letters in *Boston Post Boy*, No. 97, and *Boston Evening Post*, No. 1,258.
[3] *Memoirs of Major Robert Stobo*. Curious, but often inexact.
[4] See *supra*, p. 1019.

forms, sailed up the river to Cap-Rouge. A lively scene awaited them; for here were the headquarters of Bougainville, and here lay his principal force, while the rest watched the banks above and below. The cove into which the little river runs was guarded by floating batteries; the surrounding shore was defended by breastworks; and a large body of regulars, militia, and mounted Canadians in blue uniforms moved to and fro, with restless activity, on the hills behind. When the vessels came to anchor, the horsemen dismounted and formed in line with the infantry; then, with loud shouts, the whole rushed down the heights to man their works at the shore. That true Briton, Captain Knox, looked on with a critical eye from the gangway of his ship, and wrote that night in his Diary that they had made a ridiculous noise. "How different!" he exclaims, "how nobly awful and expressive of true valor is the customary silence of the British troops!"

In the afternoon the ships opened fire, while the troops entered the boats and rowed up and down as if looking for a landing-place. It was but a feint of Wolfe to deceive Bougainville as to his real design. A heavy easterly rain set in on the next morning, and lasted two days without respite. All operations were suspended, and the men suffered greatly in the crowded transports. Half of them were therefore landed on the south shore, where they made their quarters in the village of St. Nicolas, refreshed themselves, and dried their wet clothing, knapsacks, and blankets.

For several successive days the squadron of Holmes was allowed to drift up the river with the flood tide and down with the ebb, thus passing and repassing incessantly between the neighborhood of Quebec on one hand, and a point high above Cap-Rouge on the other; while Bougainville, perplexed, and always expecting an attack, followed the ships to and fro along the shore, by day and by night, till his men were exhausted with ceaseless forced marches.[1]

At last the time for action came. On Wednesday, the twelfth, the troops at St. Nicolas were embarked again, and all were told to hold themselves in readiness. Wolfe, from the flagship "Sutherland," issued his last general orders. "The enemy's force is now divided, great scarcity of provisions in

[1] Joannès, Major de Québec, *Mémoire sur la Campagne de 1759.*

their camp, and universal discontent among the Canadians. Our troops below are in readiness to join us; all the light artillery and tools are embarked at the Point of Levi; and the troops will land where the French seem least to expect it. The first body that gets on shore is to march directly to the enemy and drive them from any little post they may occupy; the officers must be careful that the succeeding bodies do not by any mistake fire on those who go before them. The battalions must form on the upper ground with expedition, and be ready to charge whatever presents itself. When the artillery and troops are landed, a corps will be left to secure the landing-place, while the rest march on and endeavor to bring the Canadians and French to a battle. The officers and men will remember what their country expects from them, and what a determined body of soldiers inured to war is capable of doing against five weak French battalions mingled with a disorderly peasantry."

The spirit of the army answered to that of its chief. The troops loved and admired their general, trusted their officers, and were ready for any attempt. "Nay, how could it be otherwise," quaintly asks honest Sergeant John Johnson, of the fifty-eighth regiment, "being at the heels of gentlemen whose whole thirst, equal with their general, was for glory? We had seen them tried, and always found them sterling. We knew that they would stand by us to the last extremity."

Wolfe had thirty-six hundred men and officers with him on board the vessels of Holmes; and he now sent orders to Colonel Burton at Point Levi to bring to his aid all who could be spared from that place and the Point of Orleans. They were to march along the south bank, after nightfall, and wait further orders at a designated spot convenient for embarkation. Their number was about twelve hundred, so that the entire force destined for the enterprise was at the utmost forty-eight hundred.[1] With these, Wolfe meant to climb the heights of Abraham in the teeth of an enemy who, though much reduced, were still twice as numerous as their assailants.[2]

[1] See Note, end of chapter.

[2] Including Bougainville's command. An escaped prisoner told Wolfe, a few days before, that Montcalm still had fourteen thousand men. *Journal of an Expedition on the River St. Lawrence*. This meant only those in the town and the camps of Beauport. "I don't believe their whole army amounts to that

Admiral Saunders lay with the main fleet in the Basin of Quebec. This excellent officer, whatever may have been his views as to the necessity of a speedy departure, aided Wolfe to the last with unfailing energy and zeal. It was agreed between them that while the General made the real attack, the Admiral should engage Montcalm's attention by a pretended one. As night approached, the fleet ranged itself along the Beauport shore; the boats were lowered and filled with sailors, marines, and the few troops that had been left behind; while ship signalled to ship, cannon flashed and thundered, and shot ploughed the beach, as if to clear a way for assailants to land. In the gloom of the evening the effect was imposing. Montcalm, who thought that the movements of the English above the town were only a feint, that their main force was still below it, and that their real attack would be made there, was completely deceived, and massed his troops in front of Beauport to repel the expected landing. But while in the fleet of Saunders all was uproar and ostentatious menace, the danger was ten miles away, where the squadron of Holmes lay tranquil and silent at its anchorage off Cap-Rouge.

It was less tranquil than it seemed. All on board knew that a blow would be struck that night, though only a few high officers knew where. Colonel Howe, of the light infantry, called for volunteers to lead the unknown and desperate venture, promising, in the words of one of them, "that if any of us survived we might depend on being recommended to the General."[1] As many as were wanted—twenty-four in all— soon came forward. Thirty large bateaux and some boats belonging to the squadron lay moored alongside the vessels; and late in the evening the troops were ordered into them, the twenty-four volunteers taking their place in the foremost. They held in all about seventeen hundred men. The rest remained on board.

---

number," wrote Wolfe to Colonel Burton, on the tenth. He knew, however, that if Montcalm could bring all his troops together, the French would outnumber him more than two to one.

[1] *Journal of the Particular Transactions during the Siege of Quebec*. The writer, a soldier in the light infantry, says he was one of the first eight who came forward. See *Notes and Queries*, XX. 370.

Bougainville could discern the movement, and misjudged it, thinking that he himself was to be attacked. The tide was still flowing; and, the better to deceive him, the vessels and boats were allowed to drift upward with it for a little distance, as if to land above Cap-Rouge.

The day had been fortunate for Wolfe. Two deserters came from the camp of Bougainville with intelligence that, at ebb tide on the next night, he was to send down a convoy of provisions to Montcalm. The necessities of the camp at Beauport, and the difficulties of transportation by land, had before compelled the French to resort to this perilous means of conveying supplies; and their boats, drifting in darkness under the shadows of the northern shore, had commonly passed in safety. Wolfe saw at once that, if his own boats went down in advance of the convoy, he could turn the intelligence of the deserters to good account.

He was still on board the "Sutherland." Every preparation was made, and every order given; it only remained to wait the turning of the tide. Seated with him in the cabin was the commander of the sloop-of-war "Porcupine," his former school-fellow, John Jervis, afterwards Earl St. Vincent. Wolfe told him that he expected to die in the battle of the next day; and taking from his bosom a miniature of Miss Lowther, his betrothed, he gave it to him with a request that he would return it to her if the presentiment should prove true.[1]

Towards two o'clock the tide began to ebb, and a fresh wind blew down the river. Two lanterns were raised into the maintop shrouds of the "Sutherland." It was the appointed signal; the boats cast off and fell down with the current, those of the light infantry leading the way. The vessels with the rest of the troops had orders to follow a little later.

To look for a moment at the chances on which this bold adventure hung. First, the deserters told Wolfe that provision-boats were ordered to go down to Quebec that night; secondly, Bougainville countermanded them; thirdly, the sentries posted along the heights were told of the order, but not of the countermand;[2] fourthly, Vergor at the Anse du Foulon had permitted most of his men, chiefly Canadians from Lo-

[1] Tucker, *Life of Earl St. Vincent*, I. 19. (London, 1844.)
[2] *Journal tenu à l'Armée*, etc.

rette, to go home for a time and work at their harvesting, on condition, it is said, that they should afterwards work in a neighboring field of his own;[1] fifthly, he kept careless watch, and went quietly to bed; sixthly, the battalion of Guienne, ordered to take post on the Plains of Abraham, had, for reasons unexplained, remained encamped by the St. Charles;[2] and lastly, when Bougainville saw Holmes's vessels drift down the stream, he did not tax his weary troops to follow them, thinking that they would return as usual with the flood tide.[3] But for these conspiring circumstances New France might have lived a little longer, and the fruitless heroism of Wolfe would have passed, with countless other heroisms, into oblivion.

For full two hours the procession of boats, borne on the current, steered silently down the St. Lawrence. The stars were visible, but the night was moonless and sufficiently dark. The General was in one of the foremost boats, and near him was a young midshipman, John Robison, afterwards professor of natural philosophy in the University of Edinburgh. He used to tell in his later life how Wolfe, with a low voice, repeated Gray's *Elegy in a Country Churchyard* to the officers about him. Probably it was to relieve the intense strain of his thoughts. Among the rest was the verse which his own fate was soon to illustrate, —

"The paths of glory lead but to the grave."

"Gentlemen," he said, as his recital ended, "I would rather have written those lines than take Quebec." None were there to tell him that the hero is greater than the poet.

As they neared their destination, the tide bore them in towards the shore, and the mighty wall of rock and forest towered in darkness on their left. The dead stillness was suddenly broken by the sharp *Qui vive!* of a French sentry, invisible in the thick gloom. *France!* answered a Highland officer of Fraser's regiment from one of the boats of the light infantry. He had served in Holland, and spoke French fluently.

À quel régiment?

De la Reine, replied the Highlander. He knew that a part

[1] *Mémoires sur le Canada, 1749 –1760.*
[2] Foligny, *Journal mémoratif. Journal tenu à l'Armée*, etc.
[3] Johnstone, *Dialogue. Vaudreuil au Ministre, 5 Oct. 1759.*

of that corps was with Bougainville. The sentry, expecting the convoy of provisions, was satisfied, and did not ask for the password.

Soon after, the foremost boats were passing the heights of Samos, when another sentry challenged them, and they could see him through the darkness running down to the edge of the water, within range of a pistol-shot. In answer to his questions, the same officer replied, in French: "Provision-boats. Don't make a noise; the English will hear us."[1] In fact, the sloop-of-war "Hunter" was anchored in the stream not far off. This time, again, the sentry let them pass. In a few moments they rounded the headland above the Anse du Foulon. There was no sentry there. The strong current swept the boats of the light infantry a little below the intended landing-place.[2] They disembarked on a narrow strand at the foot of heights as steep as a hill covered with trees can be. The twenty-four volunteers led the way, climbing with what silence they might, closely followed by a much larger body. When they reached the top they saw in the dim light a cluster of tents at a short distance, and immediately made a dash at them. Vergor leaped from bed and tried to run off, but was shot in the heel and captured. His men, taken by surprise, made little resistance. One or two were caught, and the rest fled.

The main body of troops waited in their boats by the edge of the strand. The heights near by were cleft by a great ravine choked with forest trees; and in its depths ran a little brook called Ruisseau St.-Denis, which, swollen by the late rains, fell plashing in the stillness over a rock. Other than this no sound could reach the strained ear of Wolfe but the gurgle of the tide and the cautious climbing of his advance-parties as they mounted the steeps at some little distance from where he sat listening. At length from the top came a sound of musket-shots, followed by loud huzzas, and he knew that his men were masters of the position. The word was given; the troops

[1] See a note of Smollett, *History of England*, V. 56 (ed. 1805). Sergeant Johnson, Vaudreuil, Foligny, and the *Journal of Particular Transactions* give similar accounts.

[2] *Saunders to Pitt, 20 Sept. Journal of Sergeant Johnson.* Compare Knox, II. 67.

leaped from the boats and scaled the heights, some here, some there, clutching at trees and bushes, their muskets slung at their backs. Tradition still points out the place, near the mouth of the ravine, where the foremost reached the top. Wolfe said to an officer near him: "You can try it, but I don't think you'll get up." He himself, however, found strength to drag himself up with the rest. The narrow slanting path on the face of the heights had been made impassable by trenches and abattis; but all obstructions were soon cleared away, and then the ascent was easy. In the gray of the morning the long file of red-coated soldiers moved quickly upward, and formed in order on the plateau above.

Before many of them had reached the top, cannon were heard close on the left. It was the battery at Samos firing on the boats in the rear and the vessels descending from Cap-Rouge. A party was sent to silence it; this was soon effected, and the more distant battery at Sillery was next attacked and taken. As fast as the boats were emptied they returned for the troops left on board the vessels and for those waiting on the southern shore under Colonel Burton.

The day broke in clouds and threatening rain. Wolfe's battalions were drawn up along the crest of the heights. No enemy was in sight, though a body of Canadians had sallied from the town and moved along the strand towards the landing-place, whence they were quickly driven back. He had achieved the most critical part of his enterprise; yet the success that he coveted placed him in imminent danger. On one side was the garrison of Quebec and the army of Beauport, and Bougainville was on the other. Wolfe's alternative was victory or ruin; for if he should be overwhelmed by a combined attack, retreat would be hopeless. His feelings no man can know; but it would be safe to say that hesitation or doubt had no part in them.

He went to reconnoitre the ground, and soon came to the Plains of Abraham, so called from Abraham Martin, a pilot known as Maître Abraham, who had owned a piece of land here in the early times of the colony. The Plains were a tract of grass, tolerably level in most parts, patched here and there with cornfields, studded with clumps of bushes, and forming a part of the high plateau at the eastern end of which Quebec stood. On the south it was bounded by the declivities along the St. Lawrence; on the north, by those along the St. Charles, or rather along the meadows through which that lazy stream crawled like a writhing snake. At the place that Wolfe chose for his battle-field the plateau was less than a mile wide.

Thither the troops advanced, marched by files till they reached the ground, and then wheeled to form their line of battle, which stretched across the plateau and faced the city. It consisted of six battalions and the detached grenadiers from Louisbourg, all drawn up in ranks three deep. Its right wing was near the brink of the heights along the St. Lawrence; but the left could not reach those along the St. Charles. On this side a wide space was perforce left open, and there was danger of being outflanked. To prevent this, Brigadier Townshend was stationed here with two battalions, drawn up at right angles with the rest, and fronting the St. Charles. The battalion of Webb's regiment, under Colonel Burton, formed the reserve; the third battalion of Royal Americans was left to guard the landing; and Howe's light infantry occupied a wood far in the rear. Wolfe, with Monckton and Murray, commanded the front line, on which the heavy fighting was to fall, and which, when all the troops had arrived, numbered less than thirty-five hundred men.[1]

Quebec was not a mile distant, but they could not see it; for a ridge of broken ground intervened, called Buttes-à-Neveu, about six hundred paces off. The first division of troops had scarcely come up when, about six o'clock, this ridge was suddenly thronged with white uniforms. It was the battalion of Guienne, arrived at the eleventh hour from its camp by the St. Charles. Some time after there was hot firing in the rear. It came from a detachment of Bougainville's command attacking a house where some of the light infantry were posted. The assailants were repulsed, and the firing ceased. Light showers fell at intervals, besprinkling the troops as they stood patiently waiting the event.

Montcalm had passed a troubled night. Through all the evening the cannon bellowed from the ships of Saunders, and the boats of the fleet hovered in the dusk off the Beauport shore, threatening every moment to land. Troops lined the

[1] See Note, end of chapter.

intrenchments till day, while the General walked the field that adjoined his headquarters till one in the morning, accompanied by the Chevalier Johnstone and Colonel Poulariez. Johnstone says that he was in great agitation, and took no rest all night. At daybreak he heard the sound of cannon above the town. It was the battery at Samos firing on the English ships. He had sent an officer to the quarters of Vaudreuil, which were much nearer Quebec, with orders to bring him word at once should anything unusual happen. But no word came, and about six o'clock he mounted and rode thither with Johnstone. As they advanced, the country behind the town opened more and more upon their sight; till at length, when opposite Vaudreuil's house, they saw across the St. Charles, some two miles away, the red ranks of British soldiers on the heights beyond.

"This is a serious business," Montcalm said; and sent off Johnstone at full gallop to bring up the troops from the centre and left of the camp. Those of the right were in motion already, doubtless by the Governor's order. Vaudreuil came out of the house. Montcalm stopped for a few words with him; then set spurs to his horse, and rode over the bridge of the St. Charles to the scene of danger.[1] He rode with a fixed look, uttering not a word.[2]

The army followed in such order as it might, crossed the bridge in hot haste, passed under the northern rampart of Quebec, entered at the Palace Gate, and pressed on in headlong march along the quaint narrow streets of the warlike town: troops of Indians in scalplocks and war-paint, a savage glitter in their deep-set eyes; bands of Canadians whose all was at stake,—faith, country, and home; the colony regulars; the battalions of Old France, a torrent of white uniforms and gleaming bayonets, La Sarre, Languedoc, Roussillon, Béarn,—victors of Oswego, William Henry, and Ticonderoga. So they swept on, poured out upon the plain, some by the gate of St. Louis, and some by that of St. John, and hurried, breathless, to where the banners of Guienne still fluttered on the ridge.

Montcalm was amazed at what he saw. He had expected a

---

[1] Johnstone, *Dialogue.*
[2] *Malartic à Bourlamaque,* — Sept. *1759.*

detachment, and he found an army. Full in sight before him stretched the lines of Wolfe: the close ranks of the English infantry, a silent wall of red, and the wild array of the High-landers, with their waving tartans, and bagpipes screaming defiance. Vaudreuil had not come; but not the less was felt the evil of a divided authority and the jealousy of the rival chiefs. Montcalm waited long for the forces he had ordered to join him from the left wing of the army. He waited in vain. It is said that the Governor had detained them, lest the En-glish should attack the Beauport shore. Even if they did so, and succeeded, the French might defy them, could they but put Wolfe to rout on the Plains of Abraham. Neither did the garrison of Quebec come to the aid of Montcalm. He sent to Ramesay, its commander, for twenty-five field-pieces which were on the Palace battery. Ramesay would give him only three, saying that he wanted them for his own defence. There were orders and counter-orders; misunderstanding, haste, de-lay, perplexity.

Montcalm and his chief officers held a council of war. It is said that he and they alike were for immediate attack. His enemies declare that he was afraid lest Vaudreuil should arrive and take command; but the Governor was not a man to as-sume responsibility at such a crisis. Others say that his impet-uosity overcame his better judgment; and of this charge it is hard to acquit him. Bougainville was but a few miles distant, and some of his troops were much nearer; a messenger sent by way of Old Lorette could have reached him in an hour and a half at most, and a combined attack in front and rear might have been concerted with him. If, moreover, Montcalm could have come to an understanding with Vaudreuil, his own force might have been strengthened by two or three thousand additional men from the town and the camp of Beauport; but he felt that there was no time to lose, for he imagined that Wolfe would soon be reinforced, which was impossible, and he believed that the English were fortifying themselves, which was no less an error. He has been blamed not only for fighting too soon, but for fighting at all. In this he could not choose. Fight he must, for Wolfe was now in a position to cut off all his supplies. His men were full of ardor, and he resolved to attack before their ardor cooled. He spoke

a few words to them in his keen, vehement way. "I remember
very well how he looked," one of the Canadians, then a boy
of eighteen, used to say in his old age; "he rode a black or
dark bay horse along the front of our lines, brandishing his
sword, as if to excite us to do our duty. He wore a coat with
wide sleeves, which fell back as he raised his arm, and showed
the white linen of the wristband."[1]

The English waited the result with a composure which, if
not quite real, was at least well feigned. The three field-pieces
sent by Ramesay plied them with canister-shot, and fifteen
hundred Canadians and Indians fusilladed them in front and
flank. Over all the plain, from behind bushes and knolls and
the edge of cornfields, puffs of smoke sprang incessantly from
the guns of these hidden marksmen. Skirmishers were thrown
out before the lines to hold them in check, and the soldiers
were ordered to lie on the grass to avoid the shot. The firing
was liveliest on the English left, where bands of sharpshooters
got under the edge of the declivity, among thickets, and behind scattered houses, whence they killed and wounded a
considerable number of Townshend's men. The light infantry
were called up from the rear. The houses were taken and retaken, and one or more of them was burned.

Wolfe was everywhere. How cool he was, and why his followers loved him, is shown by an incident that happened
in the course of the morning. One of his captains was
shot through the lungs; and on recovering consciousness he
saw the General standing at his side. Wolfe pressed his hand,
told him not to despair, praised his services, promised him
early promotion, and sent an aide-de-camp to Monckton
to beg that officer to keep the promise if he himself should
fall.[2]

It was towards ten o'clock when, from the high ground on
the right of the line, Wolfe saw that the crisis was near. The
French on the ridge had formed themselves into three bodies,
regulars in the centre, regulars and Canadians on right and
left. Two field-pieces, which had been dragged up the heights
at Anse du Foulon, fired on them with grape-shot, and the

[1] *Recollections of Joseph Trahan*, in *Revue Canadienne*, IV. 856.
[2] Sir Denis Le Marchant, cited by Wright, 579. Le Marchant knew the captain in his old age. Monckton kept Wolfe's promise.

troops, rising from the ground, prepared to receive them. In a few moments more they were in motion. They came on rapidly, uttering loud shouts, and firing as soon as they were within range. Their ranks, ill ordered at the best, were further confused by a number of Canadians who had been mixed among the regulars, and who, after hastily firing, threw themselves on the ground to reload.[1] The British advanced a few rods; then halted and stood still. When the French were within forty paces the word of command rang out, and a crash of musketry answered all along the line. The volley was delivered with remarkable precision. In the battalions of the centre, which had suffered least from the enemy's bullets, the simultaneous explosion was afterwards said by French officers to have sounded like a cannon-shot. Another volley followed, and then a furious clattering fire that lasted but a minute or two. When the smoke rose, a miserable sight was revealed: the ground cumbered with dead and wounded, the advancing masses stopped short and turned into a frantic mob, shouting, cursing, gesticulating. The order was given to charge. Then over the field rose the British cheer, mixed with the fierce yell of the Highland slogan. Some of the corps pushed forward with the bayonet; some advanced firing. The clansmen drew their broadswords and dashed on, keen and swift as bloodhounds. At the English right, though the attacking column was broken to pieces, a fire was still kept up, chiefly, it seems, by sharpshooters from the bushes and cornfields, where they had lain for an hour or more. Here Wolfe himself led the charge, at the head of the Louisbourg grenadiers. A shot shattered his wrist. He wrapped his handkerchief about it and kept on. Another shot struck him, and he still advanced, when a third lodged in his breast. He staggered, and sat on the ground. Lieutenant Brown, of the grenadiers, one Henderson, a volunteer in the same company, and a private soldier, aided by an officer of artillery who ran to join them, carried him in their arms to the rear. He begged them to lay him down. They did so, and asked if he would have a surgeon. "There's no need," he answered; "it's all over with me."

---

[1] "Les Canadiens, qui étaient mêlés dans les bataillons, se pressèrent de tirer et, dès qu'ils l'eussent fait, de mettre ventre à terre pour charger, ce qui rompit tout l'ordre." *Malartic à Bourlamaque, 25 Sept. 1759.*

A moment after, one of them cried out: "They run; see how they run!" "Who run?" Wolfe demanded, like a man roused from sleep. "The enemy, sir. Egad, they give way everywhere!" "Go, one of you, to Colonel Burton," returned the dying man; "tell him to march Webb's regiment down to Charles River, to cut off their retreat from the bridge." Then, turning on his side, he murmured, "Now, God be praised, I will die in peace!" and in a few moments his gallant soul had fled.

Montcalm, still on horseback, was borne with the tide of fugitives towards the town. As he approached the walls a shot passed through his body. He kept his seat; two soldiers supported him, one on each side, and led his horse through the St. Louis Gate. On the open space within, among the excited crowd, were several women, drawn, no doubt, by eagerness to know the result of the fight. One of them recognized him, saw the streaming blood, and shrieked, *"O mon Dieu! mon Dieu! le Marquis est tué!"* "It's nothing, it's nothing," replied the death-stricken man; "don't be troubled for me, my good friends." (*"Ce n'est rien, ce n'est rien; ne vous affligez pas pour moi, mes bonnes amies."*)

NOTE.—There are several contemporary versions of the dying words of Wolfe. The report of Knox, given above, is by far the best attested. Knox says that he took particular pains at the time to learn them accurately from those who were with Wolfe when they were uttered.

The anecdote of Montcalm is due to the late Hon. Malcolm Fraser, of Quebec. He often heard it in his youth from an old woman, who, when a girl, was one of the group who saw the wounded general led by, and to whom the words were addressed.

Force of the English and French at the Battle of Quebec.—The tabular return given by Knox shows the number of officers and men in each corps engaged. According to this, the battalions as they stood on the Plains of Abraham before the battle varied in strength from 322 (Monckton's) to 683 (Webb's), making a total of 4,828, including officers. But another return, less specific, signed *George Townshend, Brigadier*, makes the entire number only 4,441. Townshend succeeded Wolfe in the command; and this return, which is preserved in the Public Record Office, was sent to London a few days after the battle. Some French writers present put the number lower, perhaps for the reason that Webb's regiment and the third battalion of Royal Americans took no part in the fight, the one being in the rear as a reserve, and the other also invisible, guarding the landing place. Wolfe's front line, which alone met and turned the French attack, was made up as follows, the figures including officers and men:—

Thirty-fifth Regiment............	519	Twenty-eighth Regiment	421
Fifty-eighth "	335	Forty-seventh "	360
Seventy-eighth "	662	Forty-third "	327
Louisbourg Grenadiers..........	241	Light Infantry	400

Making a total of 3,265.

The French force engaged cannot be precisely given. Knox, on information received from "an intelligent Frenchman," states the number, corps by corps, the aggregate being 7,520. This, on examination, plainly appears exaggerated. Fraser puts it at 5,000; Townshend at 4,470, including militia. Bigot says, 3,500, which may perhaps be as many as actually advanced to the attack, since some of the militia held back. Including Bougainville's command, the militia and artillerymen left in the Beauport camp, the sailors at the town batteries, and the garrison of Quebec, at least as many of the French were out of the battle as were in it; and the numbers engaged on each side seem to have been about equal.

For authorities of the foregoing chapter, see Appendix I.

Chapter XXVIII

1759

FALL OF QUEBEC

After the Battle • Canadians resist the Pursuit • Arrival of Vaudreuil • Scene in the Redoubt • Panic • Movements of the Victors • Vaudreuil's Council of War • Precipitate Retreat of the French Army • Last Hours of Montcalm • His Death and Burial • Quebec abandoned to its Fate • Despair of the Garrison • Lévis joins the Army • Attempts to relieve the Town • Surrender • The British occupy Quebec • Slanders of Vaudreuil • Reception in England of the News of Wolfe's Victory and Death • Prediction of Jonathan Mayhew

---

NEVER WAS rout more complete than that of our army," says a French official.[1] It was the more so because Montcalm held no troops in reserve, but launched his whole force at once against the English. Nevertheless there was some resistance to the pursuit. It came chiefly from the Canadians, many of whom had not advanced with the regulars to the attack. Those on the right wing, instead of doing so, threw themselves into an extensive tract of bushes that lay in front of the English left; and from this cover they opened a fire, too distant for much effect, till the victors advanced in their turn, when the shot of the hidden marksmen told severely upon them. Two battalions, therefore, deployed before the bushes, fired volleys into them, and drove their occupants out.

Again, those of the Canadians who, before the main battle began, attacked the English left from the brink of the plateau towards the St. Charles, withdrew when the rout took place, and ran along the edge of the declivity till, at the part of it called Côte Ste.-Geneviève, they came to a place where it was overgrown with thickets. Into these they threw themselves; and were no sooner under cover than they faced about to fire upon the Highlanders, who presently came up. As many of these mountaineers, according to their old custom, threw

[1] *Daine au Ministre, 9 Oct. 1759.*

down their muskets when they charged, and had no weapons but their broadswords, they tried in vain to dislodge the marksmen, and suffered greatly in the attempt. Other troops came to their aid, cleared the thickets, after stout resistance, and drove their occupants across the meadow to the bridge of boats. The conduct of the Canadians at the Côte Ste.-Geneviève went far to atone for the shortcomings of some of them on the battle-field.

A part of the fugitives escaped into the town by the gates of St. Louis and St. John, while the greater number fled along the front of the ramparts, rushed down the declivity to the suburb of St. Roch, and ran over the meadows to the bridge, protected by the cannon of the town and the two armed hulks in the river. The rout had but just begun when Vaudreuil crossed the bridge from the camp of Beauport. It was four hours since he first heard the alarm, and his quarters were not much more than two miles from the battle-field. He does not explain why he did not come sooner; it is certain that his coming was well timed to throw the blame on Montcalm in case of defeat, or to claim some of the honor for himself in case of victory. "Monsieur the Marquis of Montcalm," he says, "unfortunately made his attack before I had joined him."[1] His joining him could have done no good; for though he had at last brought with him the rest of the militia from the Beauport camp, they had come no farther than the bridge over the St. Charles, having, as he alleges, been kept there by an unauthorized order from the chief of staff, Montreuil.[2] He declares that the regulars were in such a fright that he could not stop them; but that the Canadians listened to his voice, and that it was he who rallied them at the Côte Ste.-Geneviève. Of this the evidence is his own word. From other accounts it would appear that the Canadians rallied themselves. Vaudreuil lost no time in recrossing the bridge and joining the militia in the redoubt at the farther end, where a crowd of fugitives soon poured in after him.

The aide-de-camp Johnstone, mounted on horseback, had stopped for a moment in what is now the suburb of St. John to encourage some soldiers who were trying to save a cannon

[1] *Vaudreuil au Ministre, 21 Sept. 1759.*
[2] *Ibid., 5 Oct. 1759.*

that had stuck fast in a marshy hollow; when, on spurring his horse to the higher ground, he saw within musket-shot a long line of British troops, who immediately fired upon him. The bullets whistled about his ears, tore his clothes, and wounded his horse; which, however, carried him along the edge of the declivity to a windmill, near which was a roadway to a bakehouse on the meadow below. He descended, crossed the meadow, reached the bridge, and rode over it to the great redoubt or hornwork that guarded its head.

The place was full of troops and Canadians in a wild panic. "It is impossible," says Johnstone, "to imagine the disorder and confusion I found in the hornwork. Consternation was general. M. de Vaudreuil listened to everybody, and was always of the opinion of him who spoke last. On the appearance of the English troops on the plain by the bakehouse, Montguet and La Motte, two old captains in the regiment of Béarn, cried out with vehemence to M. de Vaudreuil 'that the hornwork would be taken in an instant by assault, sword in hand; that we all should be cut to pieces without quarter; and that nothing would save us but an immediate and general capitulation of Canada, giving it up to the English.' "[1] Yet the river was wide and deep, and the hornwork was protected on the water side by strong palisades, with cannon. Nevertheless there rose a general cry to cut the bridge of boats. By doing so more than half the army, who had not yet crossed, would have been sacrificed. The axemen were already at work, when they were stopped by some officers who had not lost their wits.

"M. de Vaudreuil," pursues Johnstone, "was closeted in a house in the inside of the hornwork with the Intendant and some other persons. I suspected they were busy drafting the articles for a general capitulation, and I entered the house, where I had only time to see the Intendant, with a pen in his hand, writing upon a sheet of paper, when M. de Vaudreuil told me I had no business there. Having answered him that what he had said was true, I retired immediately, in wrath to see them intent on giving up so scandalously a dependency

[1] Confirmed by *Journal tenu à l'Armée*, etc. "Divers officiers des troupes de terre n'hésitèrent point à dire, tout haut en présence du soldat, qu'il ne nous restoit d'autre ressource que celle de capituler promptement pour toute la colonie," etc.

for the preservation of which so much blood and treasure had been expended." On going out he met Lieutenant-colonels Dalquier and Poulariez, whom he begged to prevent the apprehended disgrace; and, in fact, if Vaudreuil really meant to capitulate for the colony, he was presently dissuaded by firmer spirits than his own.

Johnstone, whose horse could carry him no farther, set out on foot for Beauport, and, in his own words, "continued sorrowfully jogging on, with a very heavy heart for the loss of my dear friend M. de Montcalm, sinking with weariness, and lost in reflection upon the changes which Providence had brought about in the space of three or four hours."

Great indeed were these changes. Montcalm was dying; his second in command, the Brigadier Senezergues, was mortally wounded; the army, routed and demoralized, was virtually without a head; and the colony, yesterday cheered as on the eve of deliverance, was plunged into sudden despair. "Ah, what a cruel day!" cries Bougainville; "how fatal to all that was dearest to us! My heart is torn in its most tender parts. We shall be fortunate if the approach of winter saves the country from total ruin."[1]

The victors were fortifying themselves on the field of battle. Like the French, they had lost two generals; for Monckton, second in rank, was disabled by a musket-shot, and the command had fallen upon Townshend at the moment when the enemy were in full flight. He had recalled the pursuers, and formed them again in line of battle, knowing that another foe was at hand. Bougainville, in fact, appeared at noon from Cap-Rouge with about two thousand men; but withdrew on seeing double that force prepared to receive him. He had not heard till eight o'clock that the English were on the Plains of Abraham; and the delay of his arrival was no doubt due to his endeavors to collect as many as possible of his detachments posted along the St. Lawrence for many miles towards Jacques-Cartier.

Before midnight the English had made good progress in their redoubts and intrenchments, had brought cannon up the heights to defend them, planted a battery on the Côte Ste.-Geneviève, descended into the meadows of the St. Charles,

[1] *Bougainville à Bourlamaque, 18 Sept. 1759.*

and taken possession of the General Hospital, with its crowds of sick and wounded. Their victory had cost them six hundred and sixty-four of all ranks, killed, wounded, and missing. The French loss is placed by Vaudreuil at about six hundred and forty, and by the English official reports at about fifteen hundred. Measured by the numbers engaged, the battle of Quebec was but a heavy skirmish; measured by results, it was one of the great battles of the world.

Vaudreuil went from the hornwork to his quarters on the Beauport road and called a council of war. It was a tumultuous scene. A letter was despatched to Quebec to ask advice of Montcalm. The dying General sent a brief message to the effect that there was a threefold choice,—to fight again, retreat to Jacques-Cartier, or give up the colony. There was much in favor of fighting. When Bougainville had gathered all his force from the river above, he would have three thousand men; and these, joined to the garrison of Quebec, the sailors at the batteries, and the militia and artillerymen of the Beauport camp, would form a body of fresh soldiers more than equal to the English then on the Plains of Abraham. Add to these the defeated troops, and the victors would be greatly outnumbered.[1] Bigot gave his voice for fighting. Vaudreuil expressed himself to the same effect; but he says that all the officers were against him. "In vain I remarked to these gentlemen that we were superior to the enemy, and should beat them if we managed well. I could not at all change their opinion, and my love for the service and for the colony made me subscribe to the views of the council. In fact, if I had attacked the English against the advice of all the principal officers, their ill-will would have exposed me to the risk of losing the battle and the colony also."[2]

[1] Bigot, as well as Vaudreuil, sets Bougainville's force at three thousand. "En réunissant le corps de M. de Bougainville, les bataillons de Montréal [*laissés au camp de Beauport*] et la garnison de la ville, il nous restoit encore près de 5,000 hommes de troupes fraîches." *Journal tenu à l'Armée*. Vaudreuil says that there were fifteen hundred men in garrison at Quebec who did not take part in the battle. If this is correct, the number of fresh troops after it was not five thousand, but more than six thousand; to whom the defeated force is to be added, making, after deducting killed and wounded, some ten thousand in all.

[2] *Vaudreuil au Ministre, 5 Oct. 1759.*

It was said at the time that the officers voted for retreat because they thought Vaudreuil unfit to command an army, and, still more, to fight a battle.[1] There was no need, however, to fight at once. The object of the English was to take Quebec, and that of Vaudreuil should have been to keep it. By a march of a few miles he could have joined Bougainville; and by then intrenching himself at or near Ste.-Foy he would have placed a greatly superior force in the English rear, where his position might have been made impregnable. Here he might be easily furnished with provisions, and from hence he could readily throw men and supplies into Quebec, which the English were too few to invest. He could harass the besiegers, or attack them, should opportunity offer, and either raise the siege or so protract it that they would be forced by approaching winter to sail homeward, robbed of the fruit of their victory.

At least he might have taken a night for reflection. He was safe behind the St. Charles. The English, spent by fighting, toil, and want of sleep, were in no condition to disturb him. A part of his own men were in deadly need of rest; the night would have brought refreshment, and the morning might have brought wise counsel. Vaudreuil would not wait, and orders were given at once for retreat.[2] It began at nine o'clock that evening. Quebec was abandoned to its fate. The cannon were left in the lines of Beauport, the tents in the encampments, and provisions enough in the storehouses to supply the army for a week. "The loss of the Marquis de Montcalm," says a French officer then on the spot, "robbed his successors of their senses, and they thought of nothing but flight; such was their fear that the enemy would attack the intrenchments the next day. The army abandoned the camp in such disorder that the like was never known."[3] "It was not a retreat," says Johnstone, who was himself a part of it, "but an abominable flight, with such disorder and confusion that, had the English known it, three hundred men sent after us would have been sufficient to cut all our army to pieces. The soldiers were all mixed, scattered, dispersed, and running as hard as they

[1] *Mémoires sur le Canada, 1749–1760.*

[2] *Livre d'Ordres, Ordre du 13 Sept. 1759.*

[3] Foligny, *Journal mémoratif.*

could, as if the English army were at their heels." They passed Charlesbourg, Lorette, and St. Augustin, till, on the fifteenth, they found rest on the impregnable hill of Jacques-Cartier, by the brink of the St. Lawrence, thirty miles from danger.

In the night of humiliation when Vaudreuil abandoned Quebec, Montcalm was breathing his last within its walls. When he was brought wounded from the field, he was placed in the house of the Surgeon Arnoux, who was then with Bourlamaque at Isle-aux-Noix, but whose younger brother, also a surgeon, examined the wound and pronounced it mortal. "I am glad of it," Montcalm said quietly; and then asked how long he had to live. "Twelve hours, more or less," was the reply. "So much the better," he returned. "I am happy that I shall not live to see the surrender of Quebec." He is reported to have said that since he had lost the battle it consoled him to have been defeated by so brave an enemy; and some of his last words were in praise of his successor, Lévis, for whose talents and fitness for command he expressed high esteem. When Vaudreuil sent to ask his opinion, he gave it; but when Ramesay, commandant of the garrison, came to receive his orders, he replied: "I will neither give orders nor interfere any further. I have much business that must be attended to, of greater moment than your ruined garrison and this wretched country. My time is very short; therefore pray leave me. I wish you all comfort, and to be happily extricated from your present perplexities." Nevertheless he thought to the last of those who had been under his command, and sent the following note to Brigadier Townshend: "Monsieur, the humanity of the English sets my mind at peace concerning the fate of the French prisoners and the Canadians. Feel towards them as they have caused me to feel. Do not let them perceive that they have changed masters. Be their protector as I have been their father."[1]

Bishop Pontbriand, himself fast sinking with mortal disease, attended his death-bed and administered the last sacraments. He died peacefully at four o'clock on the morning of the fourteenth. He was in his forty-eighth year.

In the confusion of the time no workman could be found

[1] I am indebted to Abbé Bois for a copy of this note. The last words of Montcalm, as above, are reported partly by Johnstone, and partly by Knox.

to make a coffin, and an old servant of the Ursulines, known as Bonhomme Michel, gathered a few boards and nailed them together so as to form a rough box. In it was laid the body of the dead soldier; and late in the evening of the same day he was carried to his rest. There was no tolling of bells or firing of cannon. The officers of the garrison followed the bier, and some of the populace, including women and children, joined the procession as it moved in dreary silence along the dusky street, shattered with cannon-ball and bomb, to the chapel of the Ursuline convent. Here a shell, bursting under the floor, had made a cavity which had been hollowed into a grave. Three priests of the Cathedral, several nuns, Ramesay with his officers, and a throng of townspeople were present at the rite. After the service and the chant, the body was lowered into the grave by the light of torches; and then, says the chronicle, "the tears and sobs burst forth. It seemed as if the last hope of the colony were buried with the remains of the General."[1] In truth, the funeral of Montcalm was the funeral of New France.[2]

It was no time for grief. The demands of the hour were too exigent and stern. When, on the morning after the battle, the people of Quebec saw the tents standing in the camp of Beauport, they thought the army still there to defend them.[3] Ramesay knew that the hope was vain. On the evening before, Vaudreuil had sent two hasty notes to tell him of his flight. "The position of the enemy," wrote the Governor, "becomes stronger every instant; and this, with other reasons, obliges me to retreat." "I have received all your letters. As I set out this moment, I pray you not to write again. You shall hear from me to-morrow. I wish you good evening." With these notes came the following order: "M. de Ramesay is not to wait till the enemy carries the town by assault. As soon as provisions fail, he will raise the white flag." This order was accompanied by a memorandum of terms which Ramesay was to ask of the victors.[4]

---

[1] *Ursulines de Québec*, III. 10.
[2] See Appendix J.
[3] *Mémoire du Sieur de Ramesay.*
[4] *Mémoire pour servir d'Instruction à M. de Ramesay, 13 Sept. 1759.* Appended, with the foregoing notes, to the *Mémoire de Ramesay.*

"What a blow for me," says the unfortunate commandant, "to find myself abandoned so soon by the army, which alone could defend the town!" His garrison consisted of between one and two hundred troops of the line, some four or five hundred colony troops, a considerable number of sailors, and the local militia.[1] These last were in a state of despair. The inhabitants who, during the siege, had sought refuge in the suburb of St. Roch, had returned after the battle, and there were now twenty-six hundred women and children, with about a thousand invalids and other non-combatants to be supported, though the provisions in the town, even at half rations, would hardly last a week. Ramesay had not been informed that a good supply was left in the camps of Beauport; and when he heard at last that it was there, and sent out parties to get it, they found that the Indians and the famished country people had carried it off.

"Despondency," he says again, "was complete; discouragement extreme and universal. Murmurs and complaints against the army that had abandoned us rose to a general outcry. I could not prevent the merchants, all of whom were officers of the town militia, from meeting at the house of M. Daine, the mayor. There they declared for capitulating, and presented me a petition to that effect, signed by M. Daine and all the principal citizens."

Ramesay called a council of war. One officer alone, Fiedmont, captain of artillery, was for reducing the rations still more, and holding out to the last. All the others gave their voices for capitulation.[2] Ramesay might have yielded without dishonor; but he still held out till an event fraught with new hope took place at Jacques-Cartier.

This event was the arrival of Lévis. On the afternoon of the battle Vaudreuil took one rational step; he sent a courier to Montreal to summon that able officer to his aid.[3] Lévis set out at once, reached Jacques-Cartier, and found his worst fears realized. "The great number of fugitives that I began to meet at Three Rivers prepared me for the disorder in which I

---

[1] The English returns give a total of 615 French regulars in the place besides sailors and militia.

[2] *Copie du Conseil de Guerre tenu par M. de Ramesay à Québec, 15 Sept. 1759.*

[3] *Lévis à Bourlamaque, 15 Sept. 1759.* Lévis, *Guerre du Canada.*

found the army. I never in my life knew the like of it. They left everything behind in the camp at Beauport; tents, baggage, and kettles."

He spoke his mind freely; loudly blamed the retreat, and urged Vaudreuil to march back with all speed to whence he came.[1] The Governor, stiff at ordinary times, but pliant at a crisis, welcomed the firmer mind that decided for him, consented that the troops should return, and wrote afterwards in his despatch to the Minister: "I was much charmed to find M. de Lévis disposed to march with the army towards Quebec."[2]

Lévis, on his part, wrote: "The condition in which I found the army, bereft of everything, did not discourage me, because M. de Vaudreuil told me that Quebec was not taken, and that he had left there a sufficiently numerous garrison; I therefore resolved, in order to repair the fault that had been committed, to engage M. de Vaudreuil to march the army back to the relief of the place. I represented to him that this was the only way to prevent the complete defection of the Canadians and Indians; that our knowledge of the country would enable us to approach very near the enemy, whom we knew to be intrenching themselves on the heights of Quebec and constructing batteries to breach the walls; that if we found their army ill posted, we could attack them, or, at any rate, could prolong the siege by throwing men and supplies into the town; and that if we could not save it, we could evacuate and burn it, so that the enemy could not possibly winter there."[3]

Lévis quickly made his presence felt in the military chaos about him. Bigot bestirred himself with his usual vigor to collect provisions; and before the next morning all was ready.[4] Bougainville had taken no part in the retreat, but sturdily held his ground at Cap-Rouge while the fugitive mob swept by him. A hundred of the mounted Canadians who formed part of his command were now sent to Quebec, each with a bag of biscuit across his saddle. They were to circle

[1] *Bigot au Ministre, 15 Oct. 1759. Malartic à Bourlamaque, 28 Sept. 1759.*

[2] "Je fus bien charmé," etc. *Vaudreuil au Ministre, 5 Oct. 1759.*

[3] *Lévis au Ministre, 10 Nov. 1759.*

[4] *Livre d'Ordres, Ordre du 17–18 Sept. 1759.*

round to the Beauport side, where there was no enemy, and whence they could cross the St. Charles in canoes to the town. Bougainville followed close with a larger supply. Vaudreuil sent Ramesay a message, revoking his order to surrender if threatened with assault, telling him to hold out to the last, and assuring him that the whole army was coming to his relief. Lévis hastened to be gone; but first he found time to write a few lines to Bourlamaque. "We have had a very great loss, for we have lost M. de Montcalm. I regret him as my general and my friend. I found our army here. It is now on the march to retrieve our fortunes. I can trust you to hold your position; as I have not M. de Montcalm's talents, I look to you to second me and advise me. Put a good face on it. Hide this business as long as you can. I am mounting my horse this moment. Write me all the news."[1]

The army marched that morning, the eighteenth. In the evening it reached St. Augustin; and here it was stopped by the chilling news that Quebec had surrendered.

Utter confusion had reigned in the disheartened garrison. Men deserted hourly, some to the country, and some to the English camp; while Townshend pushed his trenches nearer and nearer to the walls, in spite of the cannonade with which Fiedmont and his artillerymen tried to check them. On the evening of the seventeenth, the English ships of war moved towards the Lower Town, and a column of troops was seen approaching over the meadows of the St. Charles, as if to storm the Palace Gate. The drums beat the alarm; but the militia refused to fight. Their officers came to Ramesay in a body; declared that they had no mind to sustain an assault; that they knew he had orders against it; that they would carry their guns back to the arsenal; that they were no longer soldiers, but citizens; that if the army had not abandoned them they would fight with as much spirit as ever; but that they would not get themselves killed to no purpose. The town-major, Joannès, in a rage, beat two of them with the flat of his sword.

The white flag was raised; Joannès pulled it down, thinking, or pretending to think, that it was raised without authority; but Ramesay presently ordered him to go to the English

[1] *Lévis à Bourlamaque, 18 Sept. 1759.*

camp and get what terms he could. He went, through driving rain, to the quarters of Townshend, and, in hope of the promised succor, spun out the negotiation to the utmost, pretended that he had no power to yield certain points demanded, and was at last sent back to confer with Ramesay, under a promise from the English commander that, if Quebec were not given up before eleven o'clock, he would take it by storm. On this Ramesay signed the articles, and Joannès carried them back within the time prescribed. Scarcely had he left the town, when the Canadian horsemen appeared with their sacks of biscuit and a renewed assurance that help was near; but it was too late. Ramesay had surrendered, and would not break his word. He dreaded an assault, which he knew he could not withstand, and he but half believed in the promised succor. "How could I trust it?" he asks. "The army had not dared to face the enemy before he had fortified himself; and could I hope that it would come to attack him in an intrenched camp, defended by a formidable artillery?" Whatever may be thought of his conduct, it was to Vaudreuil, and not to him, that the loss of Quebec was due.

The conditions granted were favorable, for Townshend knew the danger of his position, and was glad to have Quebec on any terms. The troops and sailors of the garrison were to march out of the place with the honors of war, and to be carried to France. The inhabitants were to have protection in person and property, and free exercise of religion.[1]

In the afternoon a company of artillerymen with a field-piece entered the town, and marched to the place of arms, followed by a body of infantry. Detachments took post at all the gates. The British flag was raised on the heights near the top of Mountain Street, and the capital of New France passed into the hands of its hereditary foes. The question remained, should they keep, or destroy it? It was resolved to keep it at every risk. The marines, the grenadiers from Louisbourg, and some of the rangers were to reimbark in the fleet; while the ten battalions, with the artillery and one company of rangers, were to remain behind, bide the Canadian winter, and defend the ruins of Quebec against the efforts of Lévis. Monckton,

[1] *Articles de Capitulation, 18 Sept. 1759.*

the oldest brigadier, was disabled by his wound, and could not stay; while Townshend returned home, to parade his laurels and claim more than his share of the honors of victory.[1] The command, therefore, rested with Murray.

The troops were not idle. Levelling their own field-works, repairing the defences of the town, storing provisions sent ashore from the fleet, making fascines, and cutting firewood, busied them through the autumn days bright with sunshine, or dark and chill with premonition of the bitter months to come. Admiral Saunders put off his departure longer than he had once thought possible; and it was past the middle of October when he fired a parting salute, and sailed down the river with his fleet. In it was the ship "Royal William," carrying the embalmed remains of Wolfe.

Montcalm lay in his soldier's grave before the humble altar of the Ursulines, never more to see the home for which he yearned, the wife, mother, and children whom he loved, the olive-trees and chestnut-groves of his beloved Candiac. He slept in peace among triumphant enemies, who respected his memory, though they hardly knew his resting-place. It was left for a fellow-countryman—a colleague and a brother-in-arms—to belittle his achievements and blacken his name. The jealous spite of Vaudreuil pursued him even in death. Leaving Lévis to command at Jacques-Cartier, whither the army had again withdrawn, the Governor retired to Montreal, whence he wrote a series of despatches to justify himself at the expense of others, and above all of the slain general, against whom his accusations were never so bitter as now, when the lips were cold that could have answered them. First, he threw on Ramesay all the blame of the surrender of Quebec. Then he addressed himself to his chief task, the defamation of his unconscious rival. "The letter that you wrote in cipher, on the tenth of February, to Monsieur the Marquis of Montcalm and me, in common,[2] flattered his self-love to such a degree that, far from seeking conciliation, he did nothing but try to persuade the public that his authority surpassed mine. From

[1] *Letter to an Honourable Brigadier-General* [Townshend], printed in 1760. A *Refutation* soon after appeared, angry, but not conclusive. Other replies will be found in the *Imperial Magazine* for 1760.

[2] See *ante*, p. 1310.

the moment of Monsieur de Montcalm's arrival in this colony, down to that of his death, he did not cease to sacrifice everything to his boundless ambition. He sowed dissension among the troops, tolerated the most indecent talk against the government, attached to himself the most disreputable persons, used means to corrupt the most virtuous, and, when he could not succeed, became their cruel enemy. He wanted to be Governor-General. He privately flattered with favors and promises of patronage every officer of the colony troops who adopted his ideas. He spared no pains to gain over the people of whatever calling, and persuade them of his attachment; while, either by himself or by means of the troops of the line, he made them bear the most frightful yoke (*le joug le plus affreux*). He defamed honest people, encouraged insubordination, and closed his eyes to the rapine of his soldiers."

This letter was written to Vaudreuil's official superior and confidant, the Minister of the Marine and Colonies. In another letter, written about the same time to the Minister of War, who held similar relations to his rival, he declares that he "greatly regretted Monsieur de Montcalm."[1]

His charges are strange ones from a man who was by turns the patron, advocate, and tool of the official villains who cheated the King and plundered the people. Bigot, Cadet, and the rest of the harpies that preyed on Canada looked to Vaudreuil for support, and found it. It was but three or four weeks since he had written to the Court in high eulogy of Bigot and effusive praise of Cadet, coupled with the request that a patent of nobility should be given to that notorious public thief.[2] The corruptions which disgraced his government were rife, not only in the civil administration, but also among the officers of the colony troops, over whom he had complete control. They did not, as has been seen already, extend to the officers of the line, who were outside the circle of peculation. It was these who were the habitual associates of Montcalm; and when Vaudreuil charges him with "attaching to himself the most disreputable persons, and using means to corrupt the most virtuous," the true interpretation of his words is that the former were disreputable because they dis-

[1] *Vaudreuil au Ministre de la Guerre, 1 Nov. 1759.*
[2] See *ante*, p. 1217.

liked him (the Governor), and the latter virtuous because they were his partisans.

Vaudreuil continues thus: "I am in despair, Monseigneur, to be under the necessity of painting you such a portrait after death of Monsieur the Marquis of Montcalm. Though it contains the exact truth, I would have deferred it if his personal hatred to me were alone to be considered; but I feel too deeply the loss of the colony to hide from you the cause of it. I can assure you that if I had been the sole master, Quebec would still belong to the King, and that nothing is so disadvantageous in a colony as a division of authority and the mingling of troops of the line with marine [*colony*] troops. Thoroughly knowing Monsieur de Montcalm, I did not doubt in the least that unless I condescended to all his wishes, he would succeed in ruining Canada and wrecking all my plans."

He then charges the dead man with losing the battle of Quebec by attacking before he, the Governor, arrived to take command; and this, he says, was due to Montcalm's absolute determination to exercise independent authority, without caring whether the colony was saved or lost. "I cannot hide from you, Monseigneur, that if he had had his way in past years Oswego and Fort George [*William Henry*] would never have been attacked or taken; and he owed the success at Ticonderoga to the orders I had given him."[1] Montcalm, on the other hand, declared at the time that Vaudreuil had ordered him not to risk a battle, and that it was only through his disobedience that Ticonderoga was saved.

Ten days later Vaudreuil wrote again: "I have already had the honor, by my letter written in cipher on the thirtieth of last month, to give you a sketch of the character of Monsieur the Marquis of Montcalm; but I have just been informed of a stroke so black that I think, Monseigneur, that I should fail in my duty to you if I did not tell you of it." He goes on to say that, a little before his death, and "no doubt in fear of the fate that befell him," Montcalm placed in the hands of Father Roubaud, missionary at St. Francis, two packets of papers containing remarks on the administration of the colony, and especially on the manner in which the military posts were fur-

[1] *Vaudreuil au Ministre de la Marine, 30 Oct. 1759.*

nished with supplies; that these observations were accompanied by certificates; and that they involved charges against him, the Governor, of complicity in peculation. Roubaud, he continues, was to send these papers to France; "but now, Monseigneur, that you are informed about them, I feel no anxiety, and I am sure that the King will receive no impression from them without acquainting himself with their truth or falsity."

Vaudreuil's anxiety was natural; and so was the action of Montcalm in making known to the Court the outrageous abuses that threatened the King's service with ruin. His doing so was necessary, both for his own justification and for the public good; and afterwards, when Vaudreuil and others were brought to trial at Paris, and when one of the counsel for the defence charged the late general with slanderously accusing his clients, the Court ordered the charge to be struck from the record.[1] The papers the existence of which, if they did exist, so terrified Vaudreuil, have thus far escaped research. But the correspondence of the two rivals with the chiefs of the departments on which they severally depended is in large measure preserved; and while that of the Governor is filled with defamation of Montcalm and praise of himself, that of the General is neither egotistic nor abusive. The faults of Montcalm have sufficiently appeared. They were those of an impetuous, excitable, and impatient nature, by no means free from either ambition or vanity; but they were never inconsistent with the character of a man of honor. His impulsive utterances, reported by retainers and sycophants, kept Vaudreuil in a state of chronic rage; and, void as he was of all magnanimity, gnawed with undying jealousy, and mortally in dread of being compromised by the knaveries to which he had lent his countenance, he could not contain himself within the bounds of decency or sense. In another letter he had the baseness to say that Montcalm met his death in trying to escape from the English.

Among the Governor's charges are some which cannot be flatly denied. When he accuses his rival of haste and precipitation in attacking the English army, he touches a fair subject of criticism; but, as a whole, he is as false in his detraction of Montcalm as in his praises of Bigot and Cadet.

[1] *Procès de Bigot, Cadet, et autres.*

The letter which Wolfe sent to Pitt a few days before his death, written in what may be called a spirit of resolute despair, and representing success as almost hopeless, filled England with a dejection that found utterance in loud grumblings against the Ministry. Horace Walpole wrote the bad news to his friend Mann, ambassador at Florence: "Two days ago came letters from Wolfe, despairing as much as heroes can despair. Quebec is well victualled, Amherst is not arrived, and fifteen thousand men are encamped to defend it. We have lost many men by the enemy, and some by our friends; that is, we now call our nine thousand only seven thousand. How this little army will get away from a much larger, and in this season, in that country, I don't guess: yes, I do."

Hardly were these lines written when tidings came that Montcalm was defeated, Quebec taken, and Wolfe killed. A flood of mixed emotion swept over England. Even Walpole grew half serious as he sent a packet of newspapers to his friend the ambassador. "You may now give yourself what airs you please. An ambassador is the only man in the world whom bullying becomes. All precedents are on your side: Persians, Greeks, Romans, always insulted their neighbors when they took Quebec. Think how pert the French would have been on such an occasion! What a scene! An army in the night dragging itself up a precipice by stumps of trees to assault a town and attack an enemy strongly intrenched and double in numbers! The King is overwhelmed with addresses on our victories; he will have enough to paper his palace."[1]

When, in soberer mood, he wrote the annals of his time, and turned, not for the better, from the epistolary style to the historical, he thus described the impression made on the English public by the touching and inspiring story of Wolfe's heroism and death: "The incidents of dramatic fiction could not be conducted with more address to lead an audience from despondency to sudden exaltation than accident prepared to excite the passions of a whole people. They despaired, they triumphed, and they wept; for Wolfe had fallen in the hour of victory. Joy, curiosity, astonishment, was painted on every countenance. The more they inquired, the more their admi-

[1] *Letters of Horace Walpole*, III. 254, 257 (ed. Cunningham, 1857).

ration rose. Not an incident but was heroic and affecting."[1] England blazed with bonfires. In one spot alone all was dark and silent; for here a widowed mother mourned for a loving and devoted son, and the people forbore to profane her grief with the clamor of their rejoicings.

New England had still more cause of joy than Old, and she filled the land with jubilation. The pulpits resounded with sermons of thanksgiving, some of which were worthy of the occasion that called them forth. Among the rest, Jonathan Mayhew, a young but justly celebrated minister of Boston, pictured with enthusiasm the future greatness of the British-American colonies, with the continent thrown open before them, and foretold that, "with the continued blessing of Heaven, they will become, in another century or two, a mighty empire;" adding in cautious parenthesis, "*I do not mean an independent one.*" He read Wolfe's victory aright, and divined its far-reaching consequence.

NOTE.—The authorities of this chapter are, in the main, the same as those of the preceding, with some additions, the principal of which is the *Mémoire du Sieur de Ramezay, Chevalier de l'Ordre royal et militaire de St.-Louis, cy-devant Lieutenant pour le Roy commandant à Québec, au sujet de la Reddition de cette Ville, qui a été suivie de la Capitulation du 18 7ʰʳᵉ, 1759* (Archives de la Marine). To this document are appended a number of important "pièces justificatives." These, with the *Mémoire*, have been printed by the Quebec Historical Society. The letters of Vaudreuil cited in this chapter are chiefly from the Archives Nationales.

If Montcalm, as Vaudreuil says, really intrusted papers to the care of the Jesuit missionary Roubaud, he was not fortunate in his choice of a depositary. After the war Roubaud renounced his Order, abjured his faith, and went over to the English. He gave various and contradictory accounts of the documents said to be in his hands. On one occasion he declared that Montcalm's effects left with him at his mission of St. Francis had been burned to prevent their falling into the hands of the enemy (see Verreau, *Report on Canadian Archives, 1874*, p. 183). Again, he says that he had placed in the hands of the King of England certain letters of Montcalm (see *Mr. Roubaud's Deplorable Case, humbly submitted to Lord North's Consideration*, in *Historical Magazine*, Second Series, VIII. 283). Yet again, he speaks of these same letters as "pretended" (Verreau, *as above*). He complains that some of them had been published, without his consent, "by a Lord belonging to His Majesty's household" (*Mr. Roubaud's Deplorable Case*).

The allusion here is evidently to a pamphlet printed in London, in 1777, in French and English, and entitled, *Lettres de Monsieur le Marquis de Montcalm,*

[1] Walpole, *Memoirs of George II.*, II. 384.

Gouverneur-Général en Canada, à Messieurs de Berryer et de la Molé, écrites dans les Années 1757, 1758, et 1759, avec une Version Angloise. They profess to be observations by Montcalm on the English colonies, their political character, their trade, and their tendency to independence. They bear the strongest marks of being fabricated to suit the times, the colonies being then in revolt. The principal letter is one addressed to Molé, and bearing date Quebec, Aug. 24, 1759. It foretells the loss of her colonies as a consequence to England of her probable conquest of Canada. I laid before the Massachusetts Historical Society my reasons for believing this letter, like the rest, an imposture (see the *Proceedings* of that Society for 1869–1870, pp. 112–128). To these reasons it may be added that at the date assigned to the letter all correspondence was stopped between Canada and France. From the arrival of the English fleet, at the end of spring, till its departure, late in autumn, communication was completely cut off. It was not till towards the end of November, when the river was clear of English ships, that the naval commander Kanon ran by the batteries of Quebec and carried to France the first news from Canada. Some of the letters thus sent were dated a month before, and had waited in Canada till Kanon's departure.

Abbé Verreau—a high authority on questions of Canadian history—tells me a comparison of the handwriting has convinced him that these pretended letters of Montcalm are the work of Roubaud.

On the burial of Montcalm, see Appendix J.

Chapter XXIX

1759, 1760

SAINTE-FOY

Quebec after the Siege • Captain Knox and the Nuns • Escape of French Ships • Winter at Quebec • Threats of Lévis • Attacks • Skirmishes • Feat of the Rangers • State of the Garrison • The French prepare to retake Quebec • Advance of Lévis • The Alarm • Sortie of the English • Rash Determination of Murray • Battle of Ste.-Foy • Retreat of the English • Lévis besieges Quebec • Spirit of the Garrison • Peril of their Situation • Relief • Quebec saved • Retreat of Lévis • The News in England

---

THE FLEET was gone; the great river was left a solitude; and the chill days of a fitful November passed over Quebec in alternations of rain and frost, sunshine and snow. The troops, driven by cold from their encampment on the Plains, were all gathered within the walls. Their own artillery had so battered the place that it was not easy to find shelter. The Lower Town was a wilderness of scorched and crumbling walls. As you ascended Mountain Street, the Bishop's Palace, on the right, was a skeleton of tottering masonry, and the buildings on the left were a mass of ruin, where ragged boys were playing at see-saw among the fallen planks and timbers.[1] Even in the Upper Town few of the churches and public buildings had escaped. The Cathedral was burned to a shell. The solid front of the College of the Jesuits was pockmarked by numberless cannon-balls, and the adjacent church of the Order was wofully shattered. The church of the Recollets suffered still more. The bombshells that fell through the roof had broken into the pavement, and as they burst had thrown up the bones and skulls of the dead from the graves beneath.[2] Even the more distant Hôtel-Dieu was pierced by fifteen projectiles, some of which had exploded in the halls and chambers.[3]

[1] Drawings made on the spot by Richard Short. These drawings, twelve in number, were engraved and published in 1761.

[2] Short's *Views in Quebec, 1759*. Compare Pontbriand, in *N. Y. Col. Docs.*, X. 1,057.

[3] Casgrain, *Hôtel-Dieu de Québec*, 445.

The Commissary-General, Berniers, thus describes to Bourlamaque the state of the town: "Quebec is nothing but a shapeless mass of ruins. Confusion, disorder, pillage reign even among the inhabitants, for the English make examples of severity every day. Everybody rushes hither and thither, without knowing why. Each searches for his possessions, and, not finding his own, seizes those of other people. English and French, all is chaos alike. The inhabitants, famished and destitute, escape to the country. Never was there seen such a sight."[1]

Quebec swarmed with troops. There were guard-houses at twenty different points; sentinels paced the ramparts, squads of men went the rounds, soldiers off duty strolled the streets, some in mitre caps and some in black three-cornered hats; while a ceaseless rolling of drums and a rigid observance of military forms betrayed the sense of a still imminent danger. While some of the inhabitants left town, others remained, having no refuge elsewhere. They were civil to the victors, but severe towards their late ruler. "The citizens," says Knox, "particularly the females, reproach M. Vaudreuil upon every occasion, and give full scope to bitter invectives." He praises the agreeable manners and cheerful spirit of the Canadian ladies, concerning whom another officer also writes: "It is very surprising with what ease the gayety of their tempers enables them to bear misfortunes which to us would be insupportable. Families whom the calamities of war have reduced from the height of luxury to the want of common necessaries laugh, dance, and sing, comforting themselves with this reflection— *Fortune de guerre*. Their young ladies take the utmost pains to teach our officers French; with what view I know not, if it is not that they may hear themselves praised, flattered, and courted without loss of time."[2]

Knox was quartered in a small stable, with a hayloft above and a rack and manger at one end: a lodging better than fell to the lot of many of his brother officers; and, by means of a stove and some help from a carpenter, he says that he made himself tolerably comfortable. The change, however, was an

---

[1] *Berniers à Bourlamaque, 27 Sept. 1759.*

[2] *Alexander Campbell to John Lloyd, 22 Oct. 1759.* Campbell was a lieutenant of the Highlanders; Lloyd was a Connecticut merchant.

agreeable one when he was ordered for a week to the General Hospital, a mile out of the town, where he was to command the guard stationed to protect the inmates and watch the enemy. Here were gathered the sick and wounded of both armies, nursed with equal care by the nuns, of whom Knox speaks with gratitude and respect. "When our poor fellows were ill and ordered to be removed from their odious regimental hospital to this general receptacle, they were indeed rendered inexpressibly happy. Each patient has his bed, with curtains, allotted to him, and a nurse to attend him. Every sick or wounded officer has an apartment to himself, and is attended by one of these religious sisters, who in general are young, handsome, courteous, rigidly reserved, and very respectful. Their office of nursing the sick furnishes them with opportunities of taking great latitudes if they are so disposed; but I never heard any of them charged with the least levity." The nuns, on their part, were well pleased with the conduct of their new masters, whom one of them describes as the "most moderate of all conquerors."

"I lived here," Knox continues, "at the French King's table, with an agreeable, polite society of officers, directors, and commissaries. Some of the gentlemen were married, and their ladies honored us with their company. They were generally cheerful, except when we discoursed on the late revolution and the affairs of the campaign; then they seemingly gave way to grief, uttered by profound sighs, followed by an *O mon Dieu!*" He walked in the garden with the French officers, played at cards with them, and passed the time so pleasantly that his short stay at the hospital seemed an oasis in his hard life of camp and garrison.

Mère de Sainte-Claude, the Superior, a sister of Ramesay, late commandant of Quebec, one morning sent him a note of invitation to what she called an English breakfast; and though the repast answered to nothing within his experience, he says that he "fared exceedingly well, and passed near two hours most agreeably in the society of this ancient lady and her virgin sisters."

The excellent nuns of the General Hospital are to-day what their predecessors were, and the scene of their useful labors still answers at many points to that described by the careful pen of their military guest. Throughout the war they and the nuns of the Hôtel-Dieu had been above praise in their assiduous devotion to the sick and wounded.

Brigadier Murray, now in command of Quebec, was a gallant soldier, upright, humane, generous, eager for distinction, and more daring than prudent. He befriended the Canadians, issued strict orders against harming them in person or property, hanged a soldier who had robbed a citizen of Quebec, and severely punished others for slighter offences of the same sort. In general the soldiers themselves showed kindness towards the conquered people; during harvest they were seen helping them to reap their fields, without compensation, and sharing with them their tobacco and rations. The inhabitants were disarmed, and required to take the oath of allegiance. Murray reported in the spring that the whole country, from Cap-Rouge downward, was in subjection to the British Crown.[1]

Late in October it was rumored that some of the French ships in the river above Quebec were preparing to run by the batteries. This was the squadron which had arrived in the spring with supplies, and had lain all summer at Batiscan, in the Richelieu, and at other points beyond reach of the English. After nearly a month of expectancy, they at length appeared, anchored off Sillery on the twenty-first of November, and tried to pass the town on the dark night of the twenty-fourth. Seven or eight of them succeeded; four others ran aground and were set on fire by their crews, excepting one which was stranded on the south shore and abandoned. Captain Miller, with a lieutenant and above forty men, boarded her; when, apparently through their own carelessness, she blew up.[2] Most of the party were killed by the explosion, and the rest, including the two officers, were left in a horrible condition between life and death. Thus they remained till a Canadian, venturing on board in search of plunder, found them, called his neighbors to his aid, carried them to his own house, and after applying, with the utmost kindness, what simple remedies he knew, went over to Quebec and told of

[1] *Murray to Pitt, 25 May, 1760.* Murray, *Journal, 1759, 1760.*

[2] *Murray to Amherst, 25 Jan. 1760.* Not, as some believed, by a train laid by the French.

the disaster. Fortunately for themselves, the sufferers soon died.

December came, and brought the Canadian winter, with its fierce light and cold, glaring snowfields, and piercing blasts that scorch the cheek like a firebrand. The men were frost-bitten as they dug away the dry, powdery drifts that the wind had piled against the rampart. The sentries were relieved every hour; yet feet and fingers were continually frozen. The clothing of the troops was ill-suited to the climate, and, though stoves had been placed in the guard and barrack rooms, the supply of fuel constantly fell short. The cutting and dragging of wood was the chief task of the garrison for many weeks. Parties of axemen, strongly guarded, were always at work in the forest of Ste.-Foy, four or five miles from Quebec, and the logs were brought to town on sledges dragged by the soldiers. Eight of them were harnessed in pairs to each sledge; and as there was always danger from Indians and bushrangers, every man carried his musket slung at his back. The labor was prodigious; for frequent snow-storms made it necessary again and again to beat a fresh track through the drifts. The men bore their hardships with admirable good humor; and once a party of them on their return, dragging their load through the street, met a Canadian, also with a load of wood, which was drawn by a team of dogs harnessed much like themselves. They accosted them as yoke-fellows, comrades, and brothers; asked them what allowance of pork and rum they got; and invited them and their owner to mess at the regimental barracks.

The appearance of the troops on duty within the town, as described by Knox, was scarcely less eccentric. "Our guards on the grand parade make a most grotesque appearance in their different dresses; and our inventions to guard us against the extreme rigor of this climate are various beyond imagination. The uniformity as well as nicety of the clean, methodical soldier is buried in the rough, fur-wrought garb of the frozen Laplander; and we rather resemble a masquerade than a body of regular troops, insomuch that I have frequently been accosted by my acquaintances, whom, though their voices were familiar to me, I could not discover, or conceive who they were. Besides, every man seems to be in a continual hurry;

for instead of walking soberly through the streets, we are obliged to observe a running or trotting pace."

Early in January there was a storm of sleet, followed by severe frost, which glazed the streets with ice. Knox, being ordered to mount guard in the Lower Town, found the descent of Mountain Street so slippery that it was impossible to walk down with safety, especially as the muskets of the men were loaded; and the whole party, seating themselves on the ground, slid one after another to the foot of the hill. The Highlanders, in spite of their natural hardihood, suffered more from the cold than the other troops, as their national costume was but a sorry defence against the Canadian winter. A detachment of these breechless warriors being on guard at the General Hospital, the nuns spent their scanty leisure in knitting for them long woollen hose, which they gratefully accepted, though at a loss to know whether modesty or charity inspired the gift.

From the time when the English took possession of Quebec, reports had come in through deserters that Lévis meant to attack and recover it. Early in November there was a rumor that he was about to march upon it with fifteen thousand men. In December word came that he was on his way, resolved to storm it on or about the twenty-second, and dine within the walls, under the French flag, on Christmas Day. He failed to appear; but in January a deserter said that he had prepared scaling-ladders, and was training his men to use them by assaults on mock ramparts of snow. There was more tangible evidence that the enemy was astir. Murray had established two fortified outposts, one at Ste.-Foy, and the other farther on, at Old Lorette. War-parties hovered round both, and kept the occupants in alarm. A large body of French grenadiers appeared at the latter place in February, and drove off a herd of cattle; when a detachment of rangers, much inferior in number, set upon them, put them to flight, and recovered the plunder. At the same time a party of regulars, Canadians, and Indians took up a strong position near the church at Point Levi, and sent a message to the English officers that a large company of expert hairdressers were ready to wait upon them whenever they required their services. The allusion was of course to the scalp-lifting practices of the Indians and bushrangers.

The river being now hard frozen, Murray sent over a detachment of light infantry under Major Dalling. A sharp fight ensued on the snow, around the church, and in the neighboring forest, where the English soldiers, taught to use snowshoes by the rangers, routed the enemy, and killed or captured a considerable number. A third post was then established at the church and the priest's house adjacent. Some days after, the French came back in large numbers, fortified themselves with felled trees, and then attacked the English position. The firing being heard at Quebec, the light infantry went over to the scene of action, and Murray himself followed on the ice, with the Highlanders and other troops. Before he came up, the French drew off and retreated to their breastwork, where they were attacked and put to flight, the nimble Highlanders capturing a few, while the greater part made their escape.

As it became known that the French held a strong post at Le Calvaire, near St. Augustin, two days' march from Quebec, Captain Donald MacDonald was sent with five hundred men to attack it. He found the enemy behind a breastwork of logs protected by an abattis. The light infantry advanced and poured in a brisk fire; on which the French threw down their arms and fled. About eighty of them were captured; but their commander, Herbin, escaped, leaving to the victors his watch, hat and feather, wine, liquor-case, and mistress. The English had six men wounded and nearly a hundred frost-bitten.[1]

Captain Hazen and his rangers soon after had a notable skirmish. They were posted in a house not far from the station at Lorette. A scout came in with news that a large party of the enemy was coming to attack them; on which Hazen left a sergeant and fourteen men in the house, and set out for Lorette with the rest to ask a reinforcement. On the way he met the French, who tried to surround him; and he told his men to fall back to the house. They remonstrated, saying that they "felt spry," and wanted to show the regulars that provin-

[1] Knox, II. 275. Murray, *Journal*. Fraser, *Journal*. Vaudreuil, in his usual way, multiplies the English force by three.

cials could fight as well as red-coats. Thereupon they charged the enemy, gave them a close volley of buckshot and bullets, and put them to flight; but scarcely had they reloaded their guns when they were fired upon from behind. Another body of assailants had got into their rear, in order to cut them off. They faced about, attacked them, and drove them back like the first. The two French parties then joined forces, left Hazen to pursue his march, and attacked the fourteen rangers in the house, who met them with a brisk fire. Hazen and his men heard the noise; and, hastening back, fell upon the rear of the French, while those in the house sallied and attacked them in front. They were again routed; and the rangers chased them two miles, killing six of them and capturing seven. Knox, in whose eyes provincials usually find no favor, launches this time into warm commendation of "our simply honest New England men."

Fresh reports came in from time to time that the French were gathering all their strength to recover Quebec; and late in February these stories took a definite shape. A deserter from Montreal brought Murray a letter from an officer of rangers, who was a prisoner at that place, warning him that eleven thousand men were on the point of marching to attack him. Three other deserters soon after confirmed the news, but added that the scheme had met with a check; for as it was intended to carry the town by storm, a grand rehearsal had taken place, with the help of scaling-ladders planted against the wall of a church; whereupon the Canadians rushed with such zeal to the assault that numerous broken legs, arms, and heads ensued, along with ruptures, sprains, bruises, and dislocations; insomuch, said the story, that they became disgusted with the attempt. All remained quiet till after the middle of April, when the garrison was startled by repeated assurances that at the first breaking-up of the ice all Canada would be upon them. Murray accordingly ordered the French inhabitants to leave the town within three days.[1]

In some respects the temper of the troops was excellent. In the petty warfare of the past winter they had generally been successful, proving themselves a match for the bushrangers

---

[1] *Ordonnance faite à Québec le 21 Avril, 1760, par son Excellence, Jacques Murray.*

and Indians on their own ground; so that, as Sergeant John-son remarks, in his odd way, "Very often a small number of our men would put to flight a considerable party of those Cannibals." They began to think themselves invincible; yet they had the deepest cause for anxiety. The effective strength of the garrison was reduced to less than half, and of those that remained fit for duty, hardly a man was entirely free from scurvy. The rank and file had no fresh provisions; and, in spite of every precaution, this malignant disease, aided by fever and dysentery, made no less havoc among them than among the crews of Jacques Cartier at this same place two centuries before. Of about seven thousand men left at Quebec in the autumn, scarcely more than three thousand were fit for duty on the twenty-fourth of April.[1] About seven hundred had found temporary burial in the snowdrifts, as the frozen ground was impenetrable as a rock.

Meanwhile Vaudreuil was still at Montreal, where he says that he "arrived just in time to take the most judicious measures and prevent General Amherst from penetrating into the colony."[2] During the winter some of the French regulars were kept in garrison at the outposts, and the rest quartered on the inhabitants; while the Canadians were dismissed to their homes, subject to be mustered again at the call of the Governor. Both he and Lévis were full of the hope of retaking Quebec. He had spies and agents among Murray's soldiers; and though the citizens had sworn allegiance to King George, some of them were exceedingly useful to his enemies. Vaudreuil had constant information of the state of the garrison. He knew that the scurvy was his active and powerful ally, and that the hospitals and houses of Quebec were crowded with the sick. At the end of March he was informed that more than half the British were on the sick-list; and it was presently rumored that Murray had only two thousand men able to bear arms.[3] With every allowance for exaggeration in these reports, it was plain that the French could attack their invaders in overwhelming force.

[1] *Return of the present State of His Majesty's Forces in Garrison at Quebec, 24 April, 1760* (Public Record Office).
[2] *Vaudreuil au Ministre, 30 Oct. 1759.*
[3] *Vaudreuil au Ministre, 15 Avril, 1760.*

The difficulty was to find means of transportation. The depth of the snow and the want of draught animals made it necessary to wait till the river should become navigable; but preparation was begun at once. Lévis was the soul of the enterprise. Provisions were gathered from far and near; cannon, mortars, and munitions of war were brought from the frontier posts, and butcher-knives were fitted to the muzzles of guns to serve the Canadians in place of bayonets. All the workmen about Montreal were busied in making tools and gun-carriages. Stores were impressed from the merchants; and certain articles, which could not otherwise be had, were smuggled, with extraordinary address, out of Quebec itself.[1] Early in spring the militia received orders to muster for the march. There were doubts and discontent; but, says a contemporary, "sensible people dared not speak, for if they did they were set down as English." Some there were who in secret called the scheme "Lévis' folly;" yet it was perfectly rational, well conceived, and conducted with vigor and skill. Two frigates, two sloops-of-war, and a number of smaller craft still remained in the river, under command of Vauquelin, the brave officer who had distinguished himself at the siege of Louisbourg. The stores and cannon were placed on board these vessels, the army embarked in a fleet of bateaux, and on the twentieth of April the whole set out together for the scene of action. They comprised eight battalions of troops of the line and two of colony troops; with the colonial artillery, three thousand Canadians, and four hundred Indians. When they left Montreal, their effective strength, besides Indians, is said by Lévis to have been six thousand nine hundred and ten, a number which was increased as he advanced by the garrisons of Jacques-Cartier, Déschambault, and Pointe-aux-Trembles, as well as by the Canadians on both sides of the St. Lawrence below Three Rivers; for Vaudreuil had ordered the militia captains to join his standard, with all their followers, armed and equipped, on pain of death.[2] These accessions appear to have raised his force to between eight and nine thousand.

[1] *Vaudreuil au Ministre, 23 Avril, 1760.*

[2] *Vaudreuil aux Capitaines de Milice, 16 Avril, 1760.* I am indebted to Abbé H. R. Casgrain for a copy of this letter.

The ice still clung to the river banks, the weather was bad, and the navigation difficult; but on the twenty-sixth the army landed at St. Augustin, crossed the river of Cap-Rouge on bridges of their own making, and moved upon the English outpost at Old Lorette. The English abandoned it and fell back to Ste.-Foy. Lévis followed. Night came on, with a gale from the southeast, a driving rain, and violent thunder, unusual at that season. The road, a bad and broken one, led through the marsh called La Suède. Causeways and bridges broke down under the weight of the marching columns and plunged the men into water, mud, and half-thawed ice. "It was a frightful night," says Lévis; "so dark that but for the flashes of lightning we should have been forced to stop." The break of day found the vanguard at the edge of the woods bordering the farther side of the marsh. The storm had abated; and they saw before them, a few hundred yards distant, through the misty air, a ridge of rising ground on which stood the parish church of Ste.-Foy, with a row of Canadian houses stretching far to right and left. This ridge was the declivity of the plateau of Quebec; the same which as it approaches the town, some five or six miles towards the left, takes the names of Côte d'Abraham and Côte Ste.-Geneviéve. The church and the houses were occupied by British troops, who, as the French debouched from the woods, opened on them with cannon, and compelled them to fall back. Though the ridge at this point is not steep, the position was a strong one; but had Lévis known how few were as yet there to oppose him, he might have carried it by an assault in front. As it was, he resolved to wait till night, and then flank the enemy by a march to the right along the border of the wood.

It was the morning of Sunday, the twenty-seventh. Till late in the night before, Murray and the garrison of Quebec were unaware of the immediate danger; and they learned it at last through a singular stroke of fortune. Some time after midnight the watch on board the frigate "Racehorse," which had wintered in the dock at the Lower Town, heard a feeble cry of distress from the midst of the darkness that covered the St. Lawrence. Captain Macartney was at once informed of it; and, through an impulse of humanity, he ordered a boat to put out amid the drifting ice that was sweeping up the river with the tide. Guided by the faint cries, the sailors found a man lying on a large cake of ice, drenched, and half dead with cold; and, taking him with difficulty into their boat, they carried him to the ship. It was long before he was able to speak intelligibly; but at last, being revived by cordials and other remedies, he found strength to tell his benefactors that he was a sergeant of artillery in the army that had come to retake Quebec; that in trying to land a little above Cap-Rouge, his boat had been overset, his companions drowned, and he himself saved by climbing upon the cake of ice where they had discovered him; that he had been borne by the ebb tide down to the Island of Orleans, and then brought up to Quebec by the flow; and, finally, that Lévis was marching on the town with twelve thousand men at his back.

He was placed in a hammock and carried up Mountain Street to the quarters of the General, who was roused from sleep at three o'clock in the morning to hear his story. The troops were ordered under arms; and soon after daybreak Murray marched out with ten pieces of cannon and more than half the garrison. His principal object was to withdraw the advanced posts at Ste.-Foy, Cap-Rouge, Sillery, and Anse du Foulon. The storm had turned to a cold, drizzling rain, and the men, as they dragged their cannon through snow and mud, were soon drenched to the skin. On reaching Ste.-Foy, they opened a brisk fire from the heights upon the woods which now covered the whole army of Lévis; and being rejoined by the various outposts, returned to Quebec in the afternoon, after blowing up the church, which contained a store of munitions that they had no means of bringing off. When they entered Quebec a gill of rum was served out to each man; several houses in the suburb of St. Roch were torn down to supply them with firewood for drying their clothes; and they were left to take what rest they could against the morrow. The French, meanwhile, took possession of the abandoned heights; and while some filled the houses, barns, and sheds of Ste.-Foy and its neighborhood, others, chiefly Canadians, crossed the plateau to seek shelter in the village of Sillery.

Three courses were open to Murray. He could defend Quebec, fortify himself outside the walls on the Buttes-à-Neveu,

or fight Lévis at all risks. The walls of Quebec could not withstand a cannonade, and he had long intended to intrench his
army on the Buttes, as a better position of defence; but the
ground, frozen like a rock, had thus far made the plan impracticable. Even now, though the surface was thawed, the
soil beneath was still frost-bound, making the task of fortification extremely difficult, if indeed the French would give
him time for it. Murray was young in years, and younger still
in impulse. He was ardent, fearless, ambitious, and emulous
of the fame of Wolfe. "The enemy," he soon after wrote to
Pitt, "was greatly superior in number, it is true; but when I
considered that our little army was in the habit of beating that
enemy, and had a very fine train of field artillery; that shutting
ourselves at once within the walls was putting all upon the
single chance of holding out for a considerable time a
wretched fortification, I resolved to give them battle; and,
half an hour after six in the morning, we marched with all the
force I could muster, namely, three thousand men."[1] Some of
these had left the hospitals of their own accord in their eagerness to take part in the fray.

The rain had ceased; but as the column emerged from St.
Louis Gate, the scene before them was a dismal one. As yet
there was no sign of spring. Each leafless bush and tree was
dark with clammy moisture; patches of bare earth lay oozy
and black on the southern slopes: but elsewhere the ground
was still covered with snow, in some places piled in drifts,
and everywhere sodden with rain; while each hollow and
depression was full of that half-liquid, lead-colored mixture of
snow and water which New England schoolboys call "slush,"
for all drainage was stopped by the frozen subsoil. The troops
had with them two howitzers and twenty field-pieces, which
had been captured when Quebec surrendered, and had
formed a part of that very battery which Ramesay refused to
Montcalm at the battle of the autumn before. As there were
no horses, the cannon were dragged by some of the soldiers,
while others carried picks and spades; for as yet Murray seems
not to have made up his mind whether to fortify or fight.
Thus they advanced nearly half a mile; till reaching the
Buttes-à-Neveu, they formed in order of battle along their

[1] *Murray to Pitt, 25 May, 1760.*

farther slopes, on the same ground that Montcalm had occupied on the morning of his death.

Murray went forward to reconnoitre. Immediately before him was a rising ground, and, beyond it, a tract of forest called Sillery Wood, a mile or more distant. Nearer, on the left, he could see two blockhouses built by the English in the last autumn, not far from the brink of the plateau above the Anse du Foulon where Wolfe climbed the heights. On the right, at the opposite brink of the plateau, was a house and a fortified windmill belonging to one Dumont. The blockhouses, the mill, and the rising ground between them were occupied by the vanguard of Lévis' army; while, behind, he could descry the main body moving along the road from Ste.-Foy, then turning, battalion after battalion, and rapidly marching across the plateau along the edge of Sillery Wood. The two brigades of the leading column had already reached the blockhouses by the Anse du Foulon, and formed themselves as the right wing of the French line of battle; but those behind were not yet in position.

Murray, kindling at the sight, thought that so favorable a moment was not to be lost, and ordered an advance. His line consisted of eight battalions, numbering a little above two thousand. In the intervals between them the cannon were dragged through slush and mud by five hundred men; and, at a little distance behind, the remaining two battalions followed as a reserve. The right flank was covered by Dalling's light infantry; the left by Hazen's company of rangers and a hundred volunteers under Major MacDonald. They all moved forward till they were on nearly the same ground where Wolfe's army had been drawn up. Then the cannon unlimbered, and opened on the French with such effect that Lévis, who was on horseback in the middle of the field, sent orders to the corps of his left to fall back to the cover of the woods. The movement caused some disorder. Murray mistook it for retreat, and commanded a farther advance. The whole British line, extending itself towards the right, pushed eagerly forward: in doing which it lost the advantage of the favorable position it had occupied; and the battalions of the right soon found themselves on low grounds, wading in half-melted snow, which in some parts was knee deep. Here the cannon could no longer be worked with effect. Just in front, a small brook ran along the hollow, through soft mud and saturated snowdrifts, then gurgled down the slope on the right, to lose itself in the meadows of the St. Charles. A few rods before this brook stood the house and windmill of Dumont, occupied by five companies of French grenadiers. The light infantry at once attacked them. A furious struggle ensued, till at length the French gave way, and the victors dashed forward to follow up their advantage. Their ardor cost them dear. The corps on the French left, which had fallen back into the woods, now advanced again as the cannon ceased to play, rushing on without order but with the utmost impetuosity, led by a gallant old officer, Colonel Dalquier, of the battalion of Béarn. A bullet in the body could not stop him. The light infantry were overwhelmed; and such of them as were left alive were driven back in confusion upon the battalions behind them, along the front of which they remained dispersed for some minutes, preventing the troops from firing on the advancing French, who thus had time to reform their ranks. At length the light infantry got themselves out of the way and retired to the rear, where, having lost nearly all their officers, they remained during the rest of the fight. Another struggle followed for the house and mill of Dumont, of which the French again got possession, to be again driven out; and it remained, as if by mutual consent, unoccupied for some time by either party. For above an hour more the fight was hot and fierce. "We drove them back as long as we had ammunition for our cannon," says Sergeant Johnson; but now it failed, and no more was to be had, because, in the eccentric phrase of the sergeant, the tumbrils were "bogged in deep pits of snow."

While this was passing on the English right, it fared still worse with them on the left. The advance of the line was no less disastrous here than there. It brought the troops close to the woods which circled round to this point from the French rear, and from which the Canadians, covered by the trees, now poured on them a deadly fire. Here, as on the right, Lévis had ordered his troops to fall back for a time; but when the fire of the English cannon ceased, they advanced again, and their artillery, though consisting of only three pieces, played its part with good effect. Hazen's rangers and Mac-Donald's volunteers attacked and took the two adjacent blockhouses, but could not hold them. Hazen was wounded, MacDonald killed, and their party overpowered. The British battalions held their ground till the French, whose superior numbers enabled them to extend themselves on both sides beyond the English line, made a furious attack on the left wing, in front and flank. The reserves were ordered up, and the troops stood for a time in sullen desperation under the storm of bullets; but they were dropping fast in the blood-stained snow, and the order came at length to fall back. They obeyed with curses: "Damn it, what is falling back but re-treating?"[1] The right wing, also outflanked, followed the ex-ample of the left. Some of the corps tried to drag off their cannon; but being prevented by the deep mud and snow they spiked the pieces and abandoned them. The French followed close, hoping to cut off the fugitives from the gates of Que-bec; till Lévis, seeing that the retreat, though precipitate, was not entirely without order, thought best to stop the pursuit.

The fight lasted about two hours, and did credit to both sides. The Canadians not only showed their usual address and courage when under cover of woods, but they also fought well in the open field; and the conduct of the whole French force proved how completely they had recovered from the panic of the last autumn. From the first they were greatly superior in number, and at the middle and end of the affair, when they had all reached the field, they were more than two against one.[2] The English, on the other hand, besides the op-portunity of attacking before their enemies had completely formed, had a vastly superior artillery and a favorable posi-tion, both which advantages they lost after their second ad-vance.

Some curious anecdotes are told of the retreat. Colonel Fraser, of the Highlanders, received a bullet which was no doubt half spent, and which, with excellent precision, hit the base of his queue, so deadening the shock that it gave him no other inconvenience than a stiff neck. Captain Hazen, of the rangers, badly wounded, was making his way towards the

[1] Knox, II. 295.
[2] See Appendix K.

gate, supported by his servant, when he saw at a great distance a French officer leading a file of men across a rising ground; whereupon he stopped and told the servant to give him his gun. A volunteer named Thompson, who was near by and who tells the story, thought that he was out of his senses; but Hazen persisted, seated himself on the ground, took a long aim, fired, and brought down his man. Thompson congratulated him. "A chance shot may kill the devil," replied Hazen; and resigning himself again to the arms of his attendant, he reached the town, recovered from his wound, and lived to be a general of the Revolution.[1]

The English lost above a thousand, or more than a third of their whole number, killed, wounded, and missing.[2] They carried off some of their wounded, but left others behind; and the greater part of these were murdered, scalped, and mangled by the Indians, all of whom were converts from the mission villages. English writers put the French loss at two thousand and upwards, which is no doubt a gross exaggeration. Lévis declares that the number did not exceed six or eight hundred; but afterwards gives a list which makes it eight hundred and thirty-three.

Murray had left three or four hundred men to guard Quebec when the rest marched out; and adding them to those who had returned scathless from the fight, he now had about twenty-four hundred rank and file fit for duty. Yet even the troops that were rated as effective were in so bad a condition that the hyperbolical Sergeant Johnson calls them "half-starved, scorbutic skeletons." That worthy soldier, commonly a model of dutiful respect to those above him, this time so far forgets himself as to criticise his general for the "mad, enthusiastic zeal" by which he nearly lost the fruits of Wolfe's victory. In fact, the fate of Quebec trembled in the balance. "We were too few and weak to stand an assault," continues Johnson, "and we were almost in as deep a distress as we could be." At first there was some drunkenness and some plunder-

---

[1] Thompson, deceived by Hazen's baptismal name, Moses, thought that he was a Jew. (*Revue Canadienne*, IV. 865.) He was, however, of an old New England Puritan family. See the Hazen genealogy in *Historic-Genealogical Register*, XXXIII.

[2] *Return of Killed, Wounded, and Missing*, signed J. Murray.

ing of private houses; but Murray stopped the one by staving
the rum-barrels of the sutlers, and the other by hanging the
chief offender. Within three days order, subordination, hope,
and almost confidence were completely restored. Not a man
was idle. The troops left their barracks and lay in tents close
to their respective alarm posts. On the open space by St.
Louis Gate a crowd of convalescents were busy in filling sand-
bags to strengthen the defences, while the sick and wounded
in the hospitals made wadding for the cannon. The ramparts
were faced with fascines, of which a large stock had been provided in the autumn; *chevaux-de-frise* were planted in exposed
places; an outwork was built to protect St. Louis Gate; embrasures were cut along the whole length of the walls; and
the French cannon captured when the town was taken were
planted against their late owners. Every man was tasked to
the utmost of his strength; and the garrison, gaunt, worn,
besmirched with mud, looked less like soldiers than like overworked laborers.

The conduct of the officers troubled the spirit of Sergeant
Johnson. It shocked his sense of the fitness of things to see
them sharing the hard work of the private men, and he thus
gives utterance to his feelings: "None but those who were
present on the spot can imagine the grief of heart the soldiers
felt to see their officers yoked in the harness, dragging up
cannon from the Lower Town; to see gentlemen, who were
set over them by His Majesty to command and keep them to
their duty, working at the batteries with the barrow, pickaxe,
and spade." The effect, however, was admirable. The spirit of
the men rose to the crisis. Murray, no less than his officers,
had all their confidence; for if he had fallen into a fatal error,
he atoned for it now by unconquerable resolution and exhaustless fertility of resource. Deserters said that Lévis would
assault the town; and the soldiers replied: "Let him come on;
he will catch a Tartar."

Lévis and his army were no less busy in digging trenches
along the stony back of the Buttes-à-Neveu. Every day the
English fire grew hotter; till at last nearly a hundred and fifty
cannon vomited iron upon them from the walls of Quebec,
and May was well advanced before they could plant a single
gun to reply. Their vessels had landed artillery at the Anse du

Foulon; but their best hope lay in the succors they daily expected from the river below. In the autumn Lévis, with a view to his intended enterprise, had sent a request to Versailles that a ship laden with munitions and heavy siege-guns should be sent from France in time to meet him at Quebec in April; while he looked also for another ship, which had wintered at Gaspé, and which therefore might reach him as soon as navigation opened. The arrival of these vessels would have made the position of the English doubly critical; and, on the other hand, should an English squadron appear first, Lévis would be forced to raise the siege. Thus each side watched the river with an anxiety that grew constantly more intense; and the English presently descried signals along the shore which seemed to say that French ships were moving up the St. Lawrence. Meantime, while doing their best to compass each other's destruction, neither side forgot the courtesies of war. Lévis heard that Murray liked spruce-beer for his table, and sent him a flag of truce with a quantity of spruce-boughs and a message of compliment; Murray responded with a Cheshire cheese, and Lévis rejoined with a present of partridges.

Bad and scanty fare, excessive toil, and broken sleep were telling ominously on the strength of the garrison when, on the ninth of May, Murray, as he sat pondering over the fire at his quarters in St. Louis Street, was interrupted by an officer who came to tell him that there was a ship-of-war in the Basin beating up towards the town. Murray started from his revery, and directed that British colors should be raised immediately on Cape Diamond.[1] The halyards being out of order, a sailor climbed the staff and drew up the flag to its place. The news had spread; men and officers, divided between hope and fear, crowded to the rampart by the Château, where Durham Terrace now overlooks the St. Lawrence, and every eye was strained on the approaching ship, eager to see whether she would show the red flag of England or the white one of France. Slowly her colors rose to the mast-head and unfurled to the wind the red cross of St. George. It was the British frigate "Lowestoffe." She anchored before the Lower Town, and saluted the garrison with twenty-one guns. "The

[1]Thompson in *Revue Canadienne*, IV. 866.

gladness of the troops," says Knox, "is not to be expressed. Both officers and soldiers mounted the parapet in the face of the enemy and huzzaed with their hats in the air for almost an hour. The garrison, the enemy's camp, the bay, and circumjacent country resounded with our shouts and the thunder of our artillery; for the gunners were so elated that they did nothing but load and fire for a considerable time. In short, the general satisfaction is not to be conceived, except by a person who had suffered the extremities of a siege, and been destined, with his brave friends and countrymen, to the scalping-knives of a faithless conqueror and his barbarous allies." The "Lowestoffe" brought news that a British squadron was at the mouth of the St. Lawrence, and would reach Quebec in a few days.

Lévis, in ignorance of this, still clung to the hope that French ships would arrive strong enough to overpower the unwelcome stranger. His guns, being at last in position, presently opened fire upon a wall that was not built to bear the brunt of heavy shot; but an artillery better and more numerous than his own almost silenced them, and his gunners were harassed by repeated sallies. The besiegers had now no real chance of success unless they could carry the place by storm, to which end they had provided abundant scaling-ladders as well as petards to burst in the gates. They made, however, no attempt to use them. A week passed, when, on the evening of the fifteenth, the ship of the line "Vanguard" and the frigate "Diana" sailed into the harbor; and on the next morning the "Diana" and the "Lowestoffe" passed the town to attack the French vessels in the river above. These were six in all,—two frigates, two smaller armed ships, and two schooners; the whole under command of the gallant Vauquelin. He did not belie his reputation; fought his ship with persistent bravery till his ammunition was spent, refused even then to strike his flag, and being made prisoner, was treated by his captors with distinguished honor. The other vessels made little or no resistance. One of them threw her guns overboard and escaped; the rest ran ashore and were burned.

The destruction of his vessels was a death-blow to the hopes of Lévis, for they contained his stores of food and ammunition. He had passed the preceding night in great agitation; and when the cannonade on the river ceased, he hastened to raise the siege. In the evening deserters from his camp told Murray that the French were in full retreat; on which all the English batteries opened, firing at random through the darkness, and sending cannon-balls *en ricochet*, bowling by scores together, over the Plains of Abraham on the heels of the retiring enemy. Murray marched out at dawn of day to fall upon their rear; but, with a hundred and fifty cannon bellowing behind them, they had made such speed that, though he pushed over the marsh to Old Lorette, he could not overtake them; they had already crossed the river of Cap-Rouge. Why, with numbers still superior, they went off in such haste, it is hard to say. They left behind them thirty-four cannon and six mortars, with petards, scaling-ladders, tents, ammunition, baggage, intrenching tools, many of their muskets, and all their sick and wounded.

The effort to recover Quebec did great honor to the enterprise of the French; but it availed them nothing, served only to waste resources that seemed already at the lowest ebb, and gave fresh opportunity of plunder to Cadet and his crew, who failed not to make use of it.

After the battle of Ste.-Foy Murray sent the frigate "Racehorse" to Halifax with news of his defeat, and from Halifax it was sent to England. The British public were taken by surprise. "Who the deuce was thinking of Quebec?" says Horace Walpole. "America was like a book one has read and done with; but here we are on a sudden reading our book backwards." Ten days passed, and then came word that the siege was raised and that the French were gone; upon which Walpole wrote to General Conway: "Well, Quebec is come to life again. Last night I went to see the Holdernesses. I met my Lady in a triumphal car, drawn by a Manx horse, thirteen little fingers high, with Lady Emily. Mr. Milbank was walking by himself in ovation after the car, and they were going to see the bonfire at the alehouse at the corner. The whole procession returned with me; and from the Countess's dressing-room we saw a battery fired before the house, the mob crying, 'God bless the good news!' These are all the particulars I know of the siege. My Lord would have showed me the journal; but we amused ourselves much better in going to eat peaches from the new Dutch stoves [*hot-houses*]."

NOTE.—On the battle of Ste.-Foy and the subsequent siege, Lévis, *Guerre du Canada. Relation de la seconde Bataille de Québec et du Siége de cette Ville* (there are several copies of this paper, with different titles and some variation). *Murray to Amherst, 30 April, 1760.* Murray, *Journal kept at Quebec from Sept. 18, 1759, to May 17, 1760* (Public Record Office, *America and West Indies,* XCIX.). *Murray to Pitt, 25 May, 1760. Letter from an Officer of the Royal Americans at Quebec, 24 May, 1760* (in *London Magazine* and several periodical papers of the time). Fraser, *Journal* (Quebec Hist. Soc.); Johnstone, *Campaign of 1760* (Ibid.). *Relation de ce qui s'est passé au Siége de Québec, par une Réligieuse de l'Hôpital Général* (Ibid.). *Memoirs of the Siege of Quebec,* by Sergeant John Johnson. *Mémoires sur le Canada, 1749–1760.* Letters of Lévis, Bourlamaque, and Vaudreuil, May, June, 1760. Several letters from officers at Quebec in provincial newspapers. Knox, II. 292–322. *Plan of the Battle and Situation of the British and French on the Heights of Abraham, the 28th of April, 1760,*—an admirable plan, attached to the great plan of operations at Quebec before mentioned, and necessary to an understanding of the position and movements of the two armies (British Museum, King's Maps).

The narratives of Mante, Entick, Wynne, Smith, and other secondary writers give no additional light. On the force engaged on each side, see Appendix K.

Chapter XXX

1760

FALL OF CANADA

Desperate Situation • Efforts of Vaudreuil and Lévis • Plans of Amherst • A Triple Attack • Advance of Murray • Advance of Haviland • Advance of Amherst • Capitulation of Montreal • Protest of Lévis • Injustice of Louis XV. • Joy in the British Colonies • Character of the War

---

THE RETREAT of Lévis left Canada little hope but in a speedy peace. This hope was strong, for a belief widely prevailed that, even if the colony should be subdued, it would be restored to France by treaty. Its available force did not exceed eight or ten thousand men, as most of the Canadians below the district of Three Rivers had sworn allegiance to King George; and though many of them had disregarded the oath to join the standard of Lévis, they could venture to do so no longer. The French had lost the best of their artillery, their gunpowder was falling short, their provisions would barely carry them to harvest time, and no more was to be hoped for, since a convoy of ships which had sailed from France at the end of winter, laden with supplies of all kinds, had been captured by the English. The blockade of the St. Lawrence was complete. The Western Indians would not fight, and even those of the mission villages were wavering and insolent.

Yet Vaudreuil and Lévis exerted themselves for defence with an energy that does honor to them both. "Far from showing the least timidity," says the ever-modest Governor, "I have taken positions such as may hide our weakness from the enemy."[1] He stationed Rochbeaucourt with three hundred men at Pointe-aux-Trembles; Repentigny with two hundred at Jacques-Cartier; and Dumas with twelve hundred at Deschambault to watch the St. Lawrence and, if possible, prevent Murray from moving up the river. Bougainville was stationed at Isle-aux-Noix to bar the approach from Lake

[1] *Vaudreuil au Ministre, 22 Juin, 1760.*

1443

Champlain, and a force under La Corne was held ready to defend the rapids above Montreal, should the English attempt that dangerous passage. Prisoners taken by war parties near Crown Point gave exaggerated reports of hostile preparation, and doubled and trebled the forces that were mustering against Canada.

These forces were nevertheless considerable. Amherst had resolved to enter the colony by all its three gates at once, and, advancing from east, west, and south, unite at Montreal and crush it as in the jaws of a vice. Murray was to ascend the St. Lawrence from Quebec, while Brigadier Haviland forced an entrance by way of Lake Champlain, and Amherst himself led the main army down the St. Lawrence from Lake Ontario. This last route was long, circuitous, difficult, and full of danger from the rapids that obstructed the river. His choice of it for his chief line of operation, instead of the shorter and easier way of Lake Champlain, was meant, no doubt, to prevent the French army from escaping up the Lakes to Detroit and the other wilderness posts, where it might have protracted the war for an indefinite time; while the plan adopted, if successful, would make its capture certain. The plan was a critical one. Three armies advancing from three different points, hundreds of miles apart, by routes full of difficulty, and with no possibility of intercommunication, were to meet at the same place at the same time, or, failing to do so, run the risk of being destroyed in detail. If the French troops could be kept together, and if the small army of Murray or of Haviland should reach Montreal a few days before the co-operating forces appeared, it might be separately attacked and overpowered. In this lay the hope of Vaudreuil and Lévis.[1]

After the siege of Quebec was raised, Murray had an effective force of about twenty-five hundred rank and file.[2] As the spring opened the invalids were encamped on the Island of Orleans, where fresh air, fresh provisions, and the change from the pestiferous town hospitals wrought such wonders on the scorbutic patients, that in a few weeks a considerable number of them were again fit for garrison duty, if not for

[1] *Lévis à Bourlamaque, Juillet, Août, 1760.*

[2] *Return of the Present State of His Majesty's Forces in Garrison at Quebec, 21 May, 1760.*

the field. Thus it happened that on the second of July twenty-four hundred and fifty men and officers received orders to embark for Montreal; and on the fifteenth they set sail, in thirty-two vessels, with a number of boats and bateaux.[1] They were followed some time after by Lord Rollo, with thirteen hundred additional men just arrived from Louisbourg, the King having ordered that fortress to be abandoned and dismantled. They advanced slowly, landing from time to time, skirmishing with detachments of the enemy who followed them along the shore, or more frequently trading with the farmers who brought them vegetables, poultry, eggs, and fresh meat. They passed the fortified hill of Jacques-Cartier, whence they were saluted with shot and shell, stopped at various parishes, disarmed the inhabitants, administered oaths of neutrality, which were taken without much apparent reluctance, and on the fourth of August came within sight of Three Rivers, then occupied by a body of troops expecting an attack. "But," says Knox, "a delay here would be absurd, as that wretched place must share the fate of Montreal. Our fleet sailed this morning. The French troops, apparently about two thousand, lined their different works, and were in general clothed as regulars, except a very few Canadians and about fifty naked Picts or savages, their bodies being painted of a reddish color and their faces of different colors, which I plainly discerned with my glass. Their light cavalry, who paraded along shore, seemed to be well appointed, clothed in blue, faced with scarlet; but their officers had white uniforms. In fine, their troops, batteries, fair-looking houses; their situation on the banks of a delightful river; our fleet sailing triumphantly before them, with our floating batteries drawn up in line of battle; the country on both sides interspersed with neat settlements, together with the verdure of the fields and trees and the clear, pleasant weather, afforded as agreeable a prospect as the most lively imagination can conceive."

This excellent lover of the picturesque was still more delighted as the fleet sailed among the islands of St. Peter. "I think nothing could equal the beauties of our navigation this morning: the meandering course of the narrow channel; the

[1] Knox, II. 344, 348.

awfulness and solemnity of the dark forests with which these islands are covered; the fragrancy of the spontaneous fruits, shrubs, and flowers; the verdure of the water by the reflection of the neighboring woods; the wild chirping notes of the feathered inhabitants; the masts and sails of ships appearing as if among the trees, both ahead and astern: formed altogether an enchanting diversity."

The evening recalled him from dreams to realities; for towards seven o'clock they reached the village of Sorel, where they found a large body of troops and militia intrenched along the strand. Bourlamaque was in command here with two or three thousand men, and Dumas, with another body, was on the northern shore. Both had orders to keep abreast of the fleet as it advanced; and thus French and English alike drew slowly towards Montreal, where lay the main French force under Lévis, ready to unite with Bourlamaque and Dumas, and fall upon Murray at the first opportunity. Montreal was now but a few leagues distant, and the situation was becoming delicate. Murray sent five rangers towards Lake Champlain to get news of Haviland, and took measures at the same time to cause the desertion of the Canadians, who formed the largest part of the opposing force. He sent a proclamation among the parishes, advising the inhabitants to remain peacefully at home, promising that those who did so should be safe in person and property, and threatening to burn every house from which the men of the family were absent. These were not idle words. A detachment sent for the purpose destroyed a settlement near Sorel, the owners of which were in arms under Bourlamaque. "I was under the cruel necessity of burning the greatest part of these poor unhappy people's houses," wrote Murray. "I pray God this example may suffice, for my nature revolts when this becomes a necessary part of my duty."[1] On the other hand, he treated with great kindness all who left the army and returned to their families. The effect was soon felt. The Canadians came in by scores and by hundreds to give up their arms and take the oath of neutrality, till, before the end of August, half Bourlamaque's force had disappeared. Murray encamped on

[1] *Murray to Pitt, 24 Aug. 1760.*

Isle Ste.-Thérèse, just below Montreal, and watched and waited for Haviland and Amherst to appear.[1]

Vaudreuil on his part was not idle. He sent a counter-proclamation through the parishes as an antidote to that of Murray. "I have been compelled," he writes to the Minister, "to decree the pain of death to the Canadians who are so dastardly as to desert or give up their arms to the enemy, and to order that the houses of those who do not join our army shall be burned."[2] Execution was to be summary, without court-martial.[3] Yet desertion increased daily. The Canadians felt themselves doubly ruined, for it became known that the Court had refused to redeem the paper that formed the whole currency of the colony; and, in their desperation, they preferred to trust the tried clemency of the enemy rather than exasperate him by persisting in a vain defence. Vaudreuil writes in his usual strain: "I am taking the most just measures to unite our forces, and, if our situation permits, fight a battle, or several battles. It is to be feared that we shall go down before an enemy so numerous and strong; but, whatever may be the event, we will save the honor of the King's arms. I have the honor to repeat to you, Monseigneur, that if any resource were left me, whatever the progress the English might make, I would maintain myself in some part of the colony with my remaining troops, after having fought with the greatest obstinacy; but I am absolutely without the least remnant of the necessary means. In these unhappy circumstances I shall continue to use every manœuvre and device to keep the enemy in check; but if we succumb in the battles we shall fight, I shall apply myself to obtaining a capitulation which may avert the total ruin of a people who will remain forever French, and who could not survive their misfortunes but for the hope of being restored by the treaty of peace to the rule of His Most Christian Majesty. It is with this view that I shall remain in this town, the Chevalier de Lévis having represented to me that it would be an evil to the colonists past remedy if any accident should happen to me." Lévis was willing to go very far in soothing the susceptibilities of the

---

[1] Knox, II. 382, 384. Mante, 340.

[2] *Vaudreuil au Ministre, 29 Août, 1760.*

[3] *Lévis à Bourlamaque, 25 Août, 1760.*

Governor; but it may be suspected this time that he thought him more useful within four walls than in the open field.

There seemed good hope of stopping the advance of Haviland. To this end Vaudreuil had stationed Bougainville at Isle-aux-Noix with seventeen hundred men, and Roquemaure at St. John, a few miles distant, with twelve or fifteen hundred more, besides all the Indians.[1] Haviland embarked at Crown Point with thirty-four hundred regulars, provincials, and Indians.[2] Four days brought him to Isle-aux-Noix; he landed, planted cannon in the swamp, and opened fire. Major Darby with the light infantry, and Rogers with the rangers, dragged three light pieces through the forest, and planted them on the river-bank in the rear of Bougainville's position, where lay the French naval force, consisting of three armed vessels and several gunboats. The cannon were turned upon the principal ship; a shot cut her cable, and a strong west wind drove her ashore into the hands of her enemies. The other vessels and gunboats made all sail for St. John, but stranded in a bend of the river, where the rangers, swimming out with their tomahawks, boarded and took one of them, and the rest soon surrendered. It was a fatal blow to Bougainville, whose communications with St. John were now cut off. In accordance with instructions from Vaudreuil, he abandoned the island on the night of the twenty-seventh of August, and, making his way with infinite difficulty through the dark forest, joined Roquemaure at St. John, twelve miles below. Haviland followed, the rangers leading the way. Bougainville and Roquemaure fell back, abandoned St. John and Chambly, and joined Bourlamaque on the banks of the St. Lawrence, where the united force at first outnumbered that of Haviland, though fast melted away by discouragement and desertion. Haviland opened communication with Murray, and they both looked daily for the arrival of Amherst, whose approach was rumored by prisoners and deserters.[3]

[1] *Vaudreuil au Ministre, 29 Août, 1760.*

[2] *A List of the Forces employed in the Expedition against Canada, 1760.* Compare Mante, 340, Knox, II. 392, and Rogers, 188. Chevalier Johnstone, who was with Bougainville, says "about four thousand," which Vaudreuil multiplies to twelve thousand.

[3] Rogers, *Journals. Diary of a Sergeant in the Army of Haviland.* Johnstone, *Campaign of 1760. Bigot au Ministre, 29 Août, 1760.*

The army of Amherst had gathered at Oswego in July. On the tenth of August it was all afloat on Lake Ontario, to the number of ten thousand one hundred and forty-two men, besides about seven hundred Indians under Sir William Johnson.[1] Before the fifteenth the whole had reached La Présentation, otherwise called Oswegatchie or La Galette, the seat of Father Piquet's mission. Near by was a French armed brig, the "Ottawa," with ten cannon and a hundred men, threatening destruction to Amherst's bateaux and whaleboats. Five gunboats attacked and captured her. Then the army advanced again, and were presently joined by two armed vessels of their own which had lingered behind, bewildered among the channels of the Thousand Islands.

Near the head of the rapids, a little below La Galette, stood Fort Lévis, built the year before on an islet in mid-channel. Amherst might have passed its batteries with slight loss, continuing his voyage without paying it the honor of a siege; and this was what the French commanders feared that he would do. "We shall be fortunate," Lévis wrote to Bourlamaque, "if the enemy amuse themselves with capturing it. My chief anxiety is lest Amherst should reach Montreal so soon that we may not have time to unite our forces to attack Haviland or Murray." If he had better known the English commander, Lévis would have seen that he was not the man to leave a post of the enemy in his rear under any circumstances; and Amherst had also another reason for wishing to get the garrison into his hands, for he expected to find among them the pilots whom he needed to guide his boats down the rapids. He therefore invested the fort, and, on the twenty-third, cannonaded it from his vessels, the mainland, and the neighboring islands. It was commanded by Pouchot, the late commandant of Niagara, made prisoner in the last campaign, and since exchanged. As the rocky islet had but little earth, the defences, though thick and strong, were chiefly of logs, which flew in splinters under the bombardment. The French, however, made a brave resistance. The firing lasted all day, was resumed in the morning, and continued two days more; when Pouchot, whose works were in ruins, surrendered him-

[1] *A List of the Forces employed in the Expedition against Canada.* Compare Mante, 301, and Knox, II. 403.

self and his garrison. On this, Johnson's Indians prepared to kill the prisoners; and, being compelled to desist, three fourths of them went home in a rage.[1]

Now began the critical part of the expedition, the descent of the rapids. The Galops, the Rapide Plat, the Long Saut, the Côteau du Lac were passed in succession, with little loss, till they reached the Cedars, the Buisson, and the Cascades, where the reckless surges dashed and bounded in the sun, beautiful and terrible as young tigers at play. Boat after boat, borne on their foaming crests, rushed madly down the torrent. Forty-six were totally wrecked, eighteen were damaged, and eighty-four men were drowned.[2] La Corne was watching the rapids with a considerable body of Canadians; and it is difficult to see why this bold and enterprising chief allowed the army to descend undisturbed through passes so dangerous. At length the last rapid was left behind; and the flotilla, gliding in peace over the smooth breast of Lake St. Louis, landed at Isle Perrot, a few leagues from Montreal. In the morning, September sixth, the troops embarked again, landed unopposed at La Chine, nine miles from the city, marched on without delay, and encamped before its walls.

The Montreal of that time was a long, narrow assemblage of wooden or stone houses, one or two stories high, above which rose the peaked towers of the Seminary, the spires of three churches, the walls of four convents, with the trees of their adjacent gardens, and, conspicuous at the lower end, a high mound of earth, crowned by a redoubt, where a few cannon were mounted. The whole was surrounded by a shallow moat and a bastioned stone wall, made for defence against Indians, and incapable of resisting cannon.[3]

On the morning after Amherst encamped above the place,

[1] On the capture of Fort Lévis, *Amherst to Pitt, 26 Aug. 1760. Amherst to Monckton, same date.* Pouchot, II. 264–282. Knox, II. 405–413. Mante, 303–306. *All Canada in the Hands of the English* (Boston, 1760). *Journal of Colonel Nathaniel Woodhull.*

[2] *Amherst to Pitt, 8 Sept. 1760.*

[3] *An East View of Montreal, drawn on the Spot by Thomas Patten* (King's Maps, British Museum), *Plan of Montreal, 1759. A Description of Montreal,* in several magazines of the time. The recent Canadian publication called *Le Vieux Montréal,* is exceedingly incorrect as to the numbers of the British troops and the position of their camps.

Murray landed to encamp below it; and Vaudreuil, looking across the St. Lawrence, could see the tents of Haviland's little army on the southern shore. Bourlamaque, Bougainville, and Roquemaure, abandoned by all their militia, had crossed to Montreal with the few regulars that remained with them. The town was crowded with non-combatant refugees. Here, too, was nearly all the remaining force of Canada, consisting of twenty-two hundred troops of the line and some two hundred colony troops; for all the Canadians had by this time gone home. Many of the regulars, especially of the colony troops, had also deserted; and the rest were so broken in discipline that their officers were forced to use entreaties instead of commands. The three armies encamped around the city amounted to seventeen thousand men;[1] Amherst was bringing up his cannon from La Chine, and the town wall would have crumbled before them in an hour.

On the night when Amherst arrived, the Governor called a council of war.[2] It was resolved that since all the militia and many of the regulars had abandoned the army, and the Indian allies of France had gone over to the enemy, further resistance was impossible. Vaudreuil laid before the assembled officers a long paper that he had drawn up, containing fifty-five articles of capitulation to be proposed to the English; and these were unanimously approved.[3] In the morning Bougainville carried them to the tent of Amherst. He granted the greater part, modified some, and flatly refused others. That which the French officers thought more important than all the rest was the provision that the troops should march out with arms, cannon, and the honors of war; to which it was replied: "The whole garrison of Montreal and all other French troops in Canada must lay down their arms, and shall not serve during the present war." This demand was felt to be intolerable. The

[1] *A List of the Forces employed in the Expedition against Canada.* See Smith, *History of Canada*, I. Appendix xix. Vaudreuil writes to Charles Langlade, on the ninth, that the three armies amount to twenty thousand, and raises the number to thirty-two thousand in a letter to the Minister on the next day. Berniers says twenty thousand; Lévis, for obvious reasons, exaggerates the number to forty thousand.

[2] *Vaudreuil au Ministre, 10 Sept. 1760.*

[3] *Procès-verbal de la Délibération du Conseil de Guerre tenu à Montréal, 6 Sept. 1760.*

Governor sent Bougainville back to remonstrate; but Amherst was inflexible. Then Lévis tried to shake his resolution, and sent him an officer with the following note: "I send your Excellency M. de la Pause, Assistant Quartermaster-General of the Army, on the subject of the too rigorous article which you dictate to the troops by the capitulation, to which it would not be possible for us to subscribe." Amherst answered the envoy: "I am fully resolved, for the infamous part the troops of France have acted in exciting the savages to perpetrate the most horrid and unheard of barbarities in the whole progress of the war, and for other open treacheries and flagrant breaches of faith, to manifest to all the world by this capitulation my detestation of such practices;" and he dismissed La Pause with a short note, refusing to change the conditions.

On the next morning, September eighth, Vaudreuil yielded, and signed the capitulation. By it Canada and all its dependencies passed to the British Crown. French officers, civil and military, with French troops and sailors, were to be sent to France in British ships. Free exercise of religion was assured to the people of the colony, and the religious communities were to retain their possessions, rights, and privileges. All persons who might wish to retire to France were allowed to do so, and the Canadians were to remain in full enjoyment of feudal and other property, including negro and Indian slaves.[1]

The greatest alarm had prevailed among the inhabitants lest they should suffer violence from the English Indians, and Vaudreuil had endeavored to provide that these dangerous enemies should be sent back at once to their villages. This was refused, with the remark: "There never have been any cruelties committed by the Indians of our army." Strict precautions were taken at the same time, not only against the few savages whom the firm conduct of Johnson at Fort Lévis had not driven away, but also against the late allies of the French, now become a peril to them. In consequence, not a man, woman, or child was hurt. Amherst, in general orders, expressed his confidence "that the troops will not disgrace themselves by the least appearance of inhumanity, or by any unsoldierlike behavior in seeking for plunder; and that as the

---

[1] *Articles of Capitulation, 8 Sept. 1760. Amherst to Pitt, same date.*

Canadians are now become British subjects, they will feel the good effects of His Majesty's protection." They were in fact treated with a kindness that seemed to surprise them.

Lévis was so incensed at the demand that the troops should lay down their arms and serve no longer during the war that, before the capitulation was signed, he made a formal protest[1] in his own name and that of the officers from France, and insisted that the negotiation should be broken off. "If," he added, "the Marquis de Vaudreuil, through political motives, thinks himself obliged to surrender the colony at once, we ask his permission to withdraw with the troops of the line to the Island of St. Helen, in order to uphold there, on our own behalf, the honor of the King's arms." The proposal was of course rejected, as Lévis knew that it would be, and he and his officers were ordered to conform to the capitulation. When Vaudreuil reached France, three months after, he had the mortification to receive from the Colonial Minister a letter containing these words: "Though His Majesty was perfectly aware of the state of Canada, nevertheless, after the assurances you had given to make the utmost efforts to sustain the honor of his arms, he did not expect to hear so soon of the surrender of Montreal and the whole colony. But, granting that capitulation was a necessity, his Majesty was not the less surprised and ill pleased at the conditions, so little honorable, to which you submitted, especially after the representations made you by the Chevalier de Lévis."[2] The brother of Vaudreuil complained to the Minister of the terms of this letter, and the Minister replied: "I see with regret, Monsieur, that you are pained by the letter I wrote your brother; but I could not help telling him what the King did me the honor to say to me; and it would have been unpleasant for him to hear it from anybody else."[3]

It is true that Vaudreuil had in some measure drawn this reproach upon himself by his boastings about the battles he

[1] *Protêt de M. de Lévis à M. de Vaudreuil contre la Clause dans les Articles de Capitulation qui exige que les Troupes mettront bas les Armes, avec l'Ordre de M. de Vaudreuil au Chevalier de Lévis de se conformer à la Capitulation proposée. Vaudreuil au Ministre de la Marine, 10 Sept. 1760. Lévis au Ministre de la Guerre, 27 Nov. 1760.*

[2] *Le Ministre à Vaudreuil, 5 Déc. 1760.*

[3] *Le Ministre au Vicomte de Vaudreuil, Frère du Gouverneur, 21 Déc. 1760.*

would fight; yet the royal displeasure was undeserved. The Governor had no choice but to give up the colony; for Amherst had him in his power, and knew that he could exact what terms he pleased. Further resistance could only have ended in surrender at the discretion of the victor, and the protest of Lévis was nothing but a device to save his own reputation and that of his brother officers from France. Vaudreuil had served the King and the colony in some respects with ability, always with an unflagging zeal; and he loved the land of his birth with a jealous devotion that goes far towards redeeming his miserable defects. The King himself, and not the servants whom he abandoned to their fate, was answerable for the loss of New France.

Half the continent had changed hands at the scratch of a pen. Governor Bernard, of Massachusetts, proclaimed a day of thanksgiving for the great event, and the Boston newspapers recount how the occasion was celebrated with a parade of the cadets and other volunteer corps, a grand dinner in Faneuil Hall, music, bonfires, illuminations, firing of cannon, and, above all, by sermons in every church of the province; for the heart of early New England always found voice through her pulpits. Before me lies a bundle of these sermons, rescued from sixscore years of dust, scrawled on their title-pages with names of owners dead long ago, worm-eaten, dingy, stained with the damps of time, and uttering in quaint old letterpress the emotions of a buried and forgotten past. Triumph, gratulation, hope, breathe in every line, but no ill-will against a fallen enemy. Thomas Foxcroft, pastor of the "Old Church in Boston," preaches from the text, "The Lord hath done great things for us, whereof we are glad." "Long," he says, "had it been the common opinion, *Delenda est Carthago*, Canada must be conquered, or we could hope for no lasting quiet in these parts; and now, through the good hand of our God upon us, we see the happy day of its accomplishment. We behold His Majesty's victorious troops treading upon the high places of the enemy, their last fortress delivered up, and their whole country surrendered to the King of Britain in the person of his general, the intrepid, the serene, the successful Amherst."

The loyal John Mellen, pastor of the Second Church in

Lancaster, exclaims, boding nothing of the tempest to come: "Let us fear God and honor the King, and be peaceable subjects of an easy and happy government. And may the blessing of Heaven be ever upon those enemies of our country that have now submitted to the English Crown, and according to the oath they have taken lead quiet lives in all godliness and honesty." Then he ventures to predict that America, now thrown open to British colonists, will be peopled in a century and a half with sixty million souls: a prophecy likely to be more than fulfilled.

"God has given us to sing this day the downfall of New France, the North American Babylon, New England's rival," cries Eli Forbes to his congregation of sober farmers and staid matrons at the rustic village of Brookfield. Like many of his flock, he had been to the war, having served two years as chaplain of Ruggles's Massachusetts regiment; and something of a martial spirit breathes through his discourse. He passes in review the events of each campaign down to their triumphant close. "Thus God was our salvation and our strength; yet he who directs the great events of war suffered not our joy to be uninterrupted, for we had to lament the fall of the valiant and good General Wolfe, whose death demands a tear from every British eye, a sigh from every Protestant heart. Is he dead? I recall myself. Such heroes are immortal; he lives on every loyal tongue; he lives in every grateful breast; and charity bids me give him a place among the princes of heaven." Nor does he forget the praises of Amherst, "the renowned general, worthy of that most honorable of all titles, the Christian hero; for he loves his enemies, and while he subdues them he makes them happy. He transplants British liberty to where till now it was unknown. He acts the General, the Briton, the Conqueror, and the Christian. What fair hopes arise from the peaceful and undisturbed enjoyment of this good land, and the blessing of our gracious God with it! Methinks I see towns enlarged, settlements increased, and this howling wilderness become a fruitful field which the Lord hath blessed; and, to complete the scene, I see churches rise and flourish in every Christian grace where has been the seat of Satan and Indian idolatry."

Nathaniel Appleton, of Cambridge, hails the dawning of a

new era. "Who can tell what great and glorious things God is about to bring forward in the world, and in this world of America in particular? Oh, may the time come when these deserts, which for ages unknown have been regions of darkness and habitations of cruelty, shall be illuminated with the light of the glorious Gospel, and when this part of the world, which till the later ages was utterly unknown, shall be the glory and joy of the whole earth!"

On the American continent the war was ended, and the British colonists breathed for a space, as they drifted unwittingly towards a deadlier strife. They had learned hard and useful lessons. Their mutual jealousies and disputes, the quarrels of their governors and assemblies, the want of any general military organization, and the absence, in most of them, of military habits, joined to narrow views of their own interest, had unfitted them to the last degree for carrying on offensive war. Nor were the British troops sent for their support remarkable in the beginning for good discipline or efficient command. When hostilities broke out, the army of Great Britain was so small as to be hardly worth the name. A new one had to be created; and thus the inexperienced Shirley and the incompetent Loudon, with the futile Newcastle behind them, had, besides their own incapacity, the disadvantage of raw troops and half-formed officers; while against them stood an enemy who, though weak in numbers, was strong in a centralized military organization, skilful leaders armed with untrammelled and absolute authority, practised soldiers, and a population not only brave, but in good part inured to war.

The nature of the country was another cause that helped to protract the contest. "Geography," says Von Moltke, "is three fourths of military science;" and never was the truth of his words more fully exemplified. Canada was fortified with vast outworks of defence in the savage forests, marshes, and mountains that encompassed her, where the thoroughfares were streams choked with fallen trees and obstructed by cataracts. Never was the problem of moving troops, encumbered with baggage and artillery, a more difficult one. The question was less how to fight the enemy than how to get at him. If a few practicable roads had crossed this broad tract of wilderness, the war would have been shortened and its character changed.

From these and other reasons, the numerical superiority of the English was to some extent made unavailing. This superiority, though exaggerated by French writers, was nevertheless immense if estimated by the number of men called to arms; but only a part of these could be employed in offensive operations. The rest garrisoned forts and blockhouses and guarded the far reach of frontier from Nova Scotia to South Carolina, where a wily enemy, silent and secret as fate, choosing their own time and place of attack, and striking unawares at every unguarded spot, compelled thousands of men, scattered at countless points of defence, to keep unceasing watch against a few hundred savage marauders. Full half the levies of the colonies, and many of the regulars, were used in service of this kind.

In actual encounters the advantage of numbers was often with the French, through the comparative ease with which they could concentrate their forces at a given point. Of the ten considerable sieges or battles of the war, five, besides the great bushfight in which the Indians defeated Braddock, were victories for France; and in four of these—Oswego, Fort William Henry, Montmorenci, and Ste.-Foy—the odds were greatly on her side.

Yet in this the most picturesque and dramatic of American wars, there is nothing more noteworthy than the skill with which the French and Canadian leaders used their advantages; the indomitable spirit with which, slighted and abandoned as they were, they grappled with prodigious difficulties, and the courage with which they were seconded by regulars and militia alike. In spite of occasional lapses, the defence of Canada deserves a tribute of admiration.

Chapter XXXI

1758–1763

THE PEACE OF PARIS

Exodus of Canadian Leaders • Wreck of the "Auguste" • Trial of
Bigot and his Confederates • Frederic of Prussia • His Triumphs •
His Reverses • His Peril • His Fortitude • Death of George II. •
Change of Policy • Choiseul • His Overtures of Peace • The Fam-
ily Compact • Fall of Pitt • Death of the Czarina • Frederic saved
• War with Spain • Capture of Havana • Negotiations • Terms
of Peace • Shall Canada be restored? • Speech of Pitt • The Treaty
Signed • End of the Seven Years War

In accordance with the terms of the capitulation of Montreal, the French military officers, with such of the soldiers
as could be kept together, as well as all the chief civil officers
of the colony, sailed for France in vessels provided by the
conquerors. They were voluntarily followed by the principal
members of the Canadian *noblesse*, and by many of the merchants who had no mind to swear allegiance to King George.
The peasants and poorer colonists remained at home to begin
a new life under a new flag.

Though this exodus of the natural leaders of Canada was
in good part deferred till the next year, and though the number of persons to be immediately embarked was reduced by
the desertion of many French soldiers who had married Canadian wives, yet the English authorities were sorely perplexed to find vessels enough for the motley crowd of
passengers. When at last they were all on their way, a succession of furious autumnal storms fell upon them. The ship that
carried Lévis barely escaped wreck, and that which bore Vaudreuil and his wife fared little better.[1] Worst of all was the
fate of the "Auguste," on board of which was the bold but
ruthless partisan, Saint-Luc de la Corne, his brother, his children, and a party of Canadian officers, together with ladies,
merchants, and soldiers. A worthy ecclesiastical chronicler
paints the unhappy vessel as a floating Babylon, and sees in

---

[1] *Lévis à Belleisle, 27 Nov. 1760.*

1458

her fate the stern judgment of Heaven.[1] It is true that New France ran riot in the last years of her existence; but before the "Auguste" was well out of the St. Lawrence she was so tossed and buffeted, so lashed with waves and pelted with rain, that the most alluring forms of sin must have lost their charm, and her inmates passed days rather of penance than transgression. There was a violent storm as the ship entered the Gulf; then a calm, during which she took fire in the cook's galley. The crew and passengers subdued the flames after desperate efforts; but their only food thenceforth was dry biscuit. Off the coast of Cape Breton another gale rose. They lost their reckoning and lay tossing blindly amid the tempest. The exhausted sailors took, in despair, to their hammocks, from which neither commands nor blows could rouse them, while amid shrieks, tears, prayers, and vows to Heaven, the "Auguste" drove towards the shore, struck, and rolled over on her side. La Corne with six others gained the beach; and towards night they saw the ship break asunder, and counted a hundred and fourteen corpses strewn along the sand. Aided by Indians and by English officers, La Corne made his way on snow-shoes up the St. John, and by a miracle of enduring hardihood reached Quebec before the end of winter.[2]

The other ships weathered the November gales, and landed their passengers on the shores of France, where some of them found a dismal welcome, being seized and thrown into the Bastille. These were Vaudreuil, Bigot, Cadet, Péan, Bréard, Varin, Le Mercier, Penisseault, Maurin, Corpron, and others accused of the frauds and peculations that had helped to ruin Canada. In the next year they were all put on trial, whether as an act of pure justice or as a device to turn public indignation from the Government. In December, 1761, judges commissioned for the purpose began their sessions at the Châtelet, and a prodigious mass of evidence was laid before them. Cadet, with brazen effrontery, at first declared himself innocent, but ended with full and unblushing confession. Bigot denied everything till silenced point by point with papers bearing his own signature. The prisoners defended them-

[1] Faillon, *Vie de Mademoiselle Le Ber*, 363–370.
[2] *Journal du Voyage de M. Saint-Luc de la Corne*. This is his own narrative.

selves by accusing each other. Bigot and Vaudreuil brought mutual charges, while all agreed in denouncing Cadet. Vaudreuil, as before mentioned, was acquitted. Bigot was banished from France for life, his property was confiscated, and he was condemned to pay fifteen hundred thousand francs by way of restitution. Cadet was banished for nine years from Paris and required to refund six millions; while others were sentenced in sums varying from thirty thousand to eight hundred thousand francs, and were ordered to be held in prison till the money was paid. Of twenty-one persons brought to trial ten were condemned, six were acquitted, three received an admonition, and two were dismissed for want of evidence. Thirty-four failed to appear, of whom seven were sentenced in default, and judgment was reserved in the case of the rest.[1] Even those who escaped from justice profited little by their gains, for unless they had turned them betimes into land or other substantial values, they lost them in a discredited paper currency and dishonored bills of exchange.

While on the American continent the last scenes of the war were drawing to their close, the contest raged in Europe with unabated violence. England was in the full career of success; but her great ally, Frederic of Prussia, seemed tottering to his ruin. In the summer of 1758 his glory was at its height. French, Austrians, and Russians had all fled before him. But the autumn brought reverses; and the Austrian general, Daun, at the head of an overwhelming force, gained over him a partial victory, which his masterly strategy robbed of its fruits. It was but a momentary respite. His kingdom was exhausted by its own triumphs. His best generals were dead, his best soldiers killed or disabled, his resources almost spent, the very chandeliers of his palace melted into coin; and all Europe was in arms against him. The disciplined valor of the Prussian troops and the supreme leadership of their undespairing King had thus far held the invading hosts at bay; but now the end seemed near. Frederic could not be everywhere at once; and while he stopped one leak the torrent poured in at another. The Russians advanced again, defeated General Wedell, whom he sent against them, and made a junction with the

[1] *Jugement rendu souverainement et en dernier Ressort dans l'Affaire du Canada*. Papers at the Châtelet of Paris, cited by Dussieux.

Austrians. In August, 1759, he attacked their united force at Kunersdorf, broke their left wing to pieces, took a hundred and eighty cannon, forced their centre to give ground, and after hours of furious fighting was overwhelmed at last. In vain he tried to stop the rout. The bullets killed two horses under him, tore his clothes, and crushed a gold snuff-box in his waistcoat pocket. "Is there no b— of a shot that can hit me, then?" he cried in his bitterness, as his aides-de-camp forced him from the field. For a few days he despaired; then rallied to his forlorn task, and with smiles on his lip and anguish at his heart watched, manœuvred, and fought with cool and stubborn desperation. To his friend D'Argens he wrote soon after his defeat: "Death is sweet in comparison to such a life as mine. Have pity on me and it; believe that I still keep to myself a great many evil things, not wishing to afflict or disgust anybody with them, and that I would not counsel you to fly these unlucky countries if I had any ray of hope. Adieu, mon cher!" It was well for him and for Prussia that he had strong allies in the dissensions and delays of his enemies. But his cup was not yet full. Dresden was taken from him, eight of his remaining generals and twelve thousand men were defeated and captured at Maxen, and "this infernal campaign," as he calls it, closed in thick darkness.

"I wrap myself in my stoicism as best I can," he writes to Voltaire. "If you saw me you would hardly know me: I am old, broken, gray-headed, wrinkled. If this goes on there will be nothing left of me but the mania of making verses and an inviolable attachment to my duties and to the few virtuous men I know. But you will not get a peace signed by my hand except on conditions honorable to my nation. Your people, blown up with conceit and folly, may depend on this."

The same stubborn conflict with overmastering odds, the same intrepid resolution, the same subtle strategy, the same skill in eluding the blow and lightning-like quickness in retorting it, marked Frederic's campaign of 1760. At Liegnitz three armies, each equal to his own, closed round him, and he put them all to flight. While he was fighting in Silesia, the Allies marched upon Berlin, took it, and held it three days, but withdrew on his approach. For him there was no peace. "Why weary you with the details of my labors and my sorrows?" he wrote again to his faithful D'Argens. "My spirits have forsaken me; all gayety is buried with the loved noble ones to whom my heart was bound." He had lost his mother and his devoted sister Wilhelmina. "You as a follower of Epicurus put a value upon life; as for me, I regard death from the Stoic point of view. I have told you, and I repeat it, never shall my hand sign a humiliating peace. Finish this campaign I will, resolved to dare all, to succeed, or find a glorious end." Then came the victory of Torgau, the last and one of the most desperate of his battles: a success dearly bought, and bringing neither rest nor safety. Once more he wrote to D'Argens: "Adieu, dear Marquis; write to me sometimes. Don't forget a poor devil who curses his fatal existence ten times a day." "I live like a military monk. Endless business, and a little consolation from my books. I don't know if I shall outlive this war, but if I do I am firmly resolved to pass the rest of my life in solitude in the bosom of philosophy and friendship. Your nation, you see, is blinder than you thought. These fools will lose their Canada and Pondicherry to please the Queen of Hungary and the Czarina."

The campaign of 1761 was mainly defensive on the part of Frederic. In the exhaustion of his resources he could see no means of continuing the struggle. "It is only Fortune," says the royal sceptic, "that can extricate me from the situation I am in. I escape out of it by looking at the universe on the great scale like an observer from some distant planet. All then seems to be so infinitely small that I could almost pity my enemies for giving themselves so much trouble about so very little. I read a great deal, I devour my books. But for them I think hypochondria would have had me in Bedlam before now. In fine, dear Marquis, we live in troublous times and desperate situations. I have all the properties of a stage hero; always in danger, always on the point of perishing."[1] And in another mood: "I begin to feel that, as the Italians say, revenge is a pleasure for the gods. My philosophy is worn out by suffering. I am no saint, and I will own that I should die content if only I could first inflict a part of the misery that I endure."

[1] The above extracts are as translated by Carlyle in his *History of Frederick II. of Prussia*.

While Frederic was fighting for life and crown, an event took place in England that was to have great influence on the war. Walpole recounts it thus, writing to George Montagu on the twenty-fifth of October, 1760: "My man Harry tells me all the amusing news. He first told me of the late Prince of Wales's death, and to-day of the King's; so I must tell you all I know of departed majesty. He went to bed well last night, rose at six this morning as usual, looked, I suppose, if all his money was in his purse, and called for his chocolate. A little after seven he went into the closet; the German *valet-de-chambre* heard a noise, listened, heard something like a groan, ran in, and found the hero of Oudenarde and Dettingen on the floor with a gash on his right temple by falling against the corner of a bureau. He tried to speak, could not, and expired. The great ventricle of the heart had burst. What an enviable death!"

The old King was succeeded by his grandson, George III., a mirror of domestic virtues, conscientious, obstinate, narrow. His accession produced political changes that had been preparing for some time. His grandfather was German at heart, loved his Continental kingdom of Hanover, and was eager for all measures that looked to its defence and preservation. Pitt, too, had of late vigorously supported the Continental war, saying that he would conquer America in Germany. Thus with different views the King and the Minister had concurred in the same measures. But George III. was English by birth, language, and inclination. His ruling passion was the establishment and increase of his own authority. He disliked Pitt, the representative of the people. He was at heart averse to a war, the continuance of which would make the Great Commoner necessary, and therefore powerful, and he wished for a peace that would give free scope to his schemes for strengthening the prerogative. He was not alone in his pacific inclinations. The enemies of the haughty Minister, who had ridden rough-shod over men far above him in rank, were tired of his ascendency, and saw no hope of ending it but by ending the war. Thus a peace party grew up, and the young King became its real, though not at first its declared, supporter.

The Tory party, long buried, showed signs of resurrection.

There were those among its members who, even in a king of the hated line of Hanover, could recognize and admire the same spirit of arbitrary domination that had marked their fallen idols, the Stuarts; and they now joined hands with the discontented Whigs in opposition to Pitt. The horrors of war, the blessings of peace, the weight of taxation, the growth of the national debt, were the rallying cries of the new party; but the mainspring of their zeal was hostility to the great Minister. Even his own colleagues chafed under his spirit of mastery; the chiefs of the Opposition longed to inherit his power; and the King had begun to hate him as a lion in his path. Pitt held to his purpose regardless of the gathering storm. That purpose, as proclaimed by his adherents, was to secure a solid and lasting peace, which meant the reduction of France to so low an estate that she could no more be a danger to her rival. In this he had the sympathy of the great body of the nation.

Early in 1761 the King, a fanatic for prerogative, set his enginery in motion. The elections for the new Parliament were manipulated in his interest. If he disliked Pitt as the representative of the popular will, he also disliked his colleague, the shuffling and uncertain Newcastle, as the representative of a too powerful nobility. Elements hostile to both were introduced into the Cabinet and the great offices. The King's favorite, the Earl of Bute, supplanted Holdernesse as Secretary of State for the Northern Department; Charles Townshend, an opponent of Pitt, was made Secretary of War; Legge, Chancellor of the Exchequer, was replaced by Viscount Barrington, who was sure for the King; while a place in the Cabinet was also given to the Duke of Bedford, one of the few men who dared face the formidable Minister. It was the policy of the King and his following to abandon Prussia, hitherto supported by British subsidies, make friends with Austria and Russia at her expense, and conclude a separate peace with France.

France was in sore need of peace. The infatuation that had turned her from her own true interest to serve the passions of Maria Theresa and the Czarina Elizabeth had brought military humiliation and financial ruin. Abbé de Bernis, Minister of Foreign Affairs, had lost the favor of Madame de Pompadour, and had been supplanted by the Duc de Choiseul. The new Minister had gained his place by pleasing the favorite; but he kept it through his own ability and the necessities of the time. The Englishman Stanley, whom Pitt sent to negotiate with him, drew this sketch of his character: "Though he may have his superiors, not only in experience of business, but in depth and refinement as a statesman, he is a person of as bold and daring a spirit as any man whatever in our country or in his own. Madame Pompadour has ever been looked upon by all preceding courtiers and ministers as their tutelary deity, under whose auspices only they could exist, and who was as much out of their reach as if she were of a superior class of beings; but this Minister is so far from being in subordination to her influence that he seized the first opportunity of depriving her not of an equality, but of any share of power, reducing her to the necessity of applying to him even for those favors that she wants for herself and her dependents. He has effected this great change, which every other man would have thought impossible, in the interior of the Court, not by plausibility, flattery, and address, but with a high hand, with frequent railleries and sarcasms which would have ruined any other, and, in short, by a clear superiority of spirit and resolution."[1]

Choiseul was vivacious, brilliant, keen, penetrating; believing nothing, fearing nothing; an easy moralist, an uncertain ally, a hater of priests; light-minded, inconstant; yet a kind of patriot, eager to serve France and retrieve her fortunes.

He flattered himself with no illusions. "Since we do not know how to make war," he said, "we must make peace;"[2] and he proposed a congress of all the belligerent Powers at Augsburg. At the same time, since the war in Germany was distinct from the maritime and colonial war of France and England, he proposed a separate negotiation with the British Court in order to settle the questions between them as a preliminary to the general pacification. Pitt consented, and Stanley went as envoy to Versailles; while M. de Bussy came as envoy to London and, in behalf of Choiseul, offered terms of peace, the first of which was the entire abandonment of Can-

---

[1] *Stanley to Pitt, 6 Aug. 1761*, in *Grenville Correspondence*, I. 367, *note*.
[2] Flassan, *Diplomatie Française*, V. 376 (Paris, 1809).

ada to England.[1] But the offers were accompanied by the demand that Spain, which had complaints of its own against England, should be admitted as a party to the negotiation, and even hold in some measure the attitude of a mediator. Pitt spurned the idea with fierce contempt. "Time enough to treat of all that, sir, when the Tower of London is taken sword in hand."[2] He bore his part with the ability that never failed him, and with a supreme arrogance that rose to a climax in his demand that the fortress of Dunkirk should be demolished, not because it was any longer dangerous to England, but because the nation would regard its destruction "as an eternal monument of the yoke imposed on France."[3]

Choiseul replied with counter-propositions less humiliating to his nation. When the question of accepting or rejecting them came before the Ministry, the views of Pitt prevailed by a majority of one, and, to the disappointment of Bute and the King, the conferences were broken off. Choiseul, launched again on the billows of a disastrous war, had seen and provided against the event. Ferdinand VI. of Spain had died, and Carlos III. had succeeded to his throne. Here, as in England, change of kings brought change of policy. While negotiating vainly with Pitt, the French Minister had negotiated secretly and successfully with Carlos; and the result was the treaty known as the Family Compact, having for its object the union of the various members of the House of Bourbon in common resistance to the growing power of England. It provided that in any future war the Kings of France and Spain should act as one towards foreign Powers, insomuch that the enemy of either should be the enemy of both; and the Bourbon princes of Italy were invited to join in the covenant.[4] What was more to the present purpose, a special agreement was concluded on

---

[1] See the proposals in Entick, V. 161.

[2] Beatson, *Military Memoirs*, II. 434. *The Count de Fuentes to the Earl of Egremont, 25 Dec. 1761*, in Entick, V. 264.

[3] On this negotiation, see *Mémoire historique sur la Négociation de la France et de l'Angleterre* (Paris, 1761), a French Government publication containing papers on both sides. The British Ministry also published such documents as they saw fit, under the title of *Papers relating to the Rupture with Spain.* Compare Adolphus, *George III.*, I. 31–39.

[4] Flassan, *Diplomatie Française*, V. 317 (Paris, 1809).

the same day, by which Spain bound herself to declare war against England unless that Power should make peace with France before the first of May, 1762. For the safety of her colonies and her trade Spain felt it her interest to join her sister nation in putting a check on the vast expansion of British maritime power. She could bring a hundred ships of war to aid the dilapidated navy of France, and the wealth of the Indies to aid her ruined treasury.

Pitt divined the secret treaty, and soon found evidence of it. He resolved to demand at once full explanation from Spain; and, failing to receive a satisfactory reply, attack her at home and abroad before she was prepared. On the second of October he laid his plan before a Cabinet Council held at a house in St. James Street. There were present the Earl of Bute, the Duke of Newcastle, Earl Granville, Earl Temple, and others of the Ministry. Pitt urged his views with great warmth. "This," he exclaimed, "is the time for humbling the whole House of Bourbon!"[1] His brother-in-law, Temple, supported him. Newcastle kept silent. Bute denounced the proposal, and the rest were of his mind. "If these views are to be followed," said Pitt, "this is the last time I can sit at this board. I was called to the administration of affairs by the voice of the people; to them I have always considered myself as accountable for my conduct; and therefore cannot remain in a situation which makes me responsible for measures I am no longer allowed to guide." Nothing could be more offensive to George III. and his adherents.

The veteran Carteret, Earl Granville, replied angrily: "I find the gentleman is determined to leave us; nor can I say I am sorry for it, since otherwise he would certainly have compelled us to leave him. But if he is resolved to assume the office of exclusively advising His Majesty and directing the operations of the war, to what purpose are we called to this council? When he talks of being responsible to the people, he talks the language of the House of Commons, and forgets that at this board he is responsible only to the King. However, though he may possibly have convinced himself of his infallibility, still it remains that we should be equally con-

[1] Beatson, II. 438.

vinced before we can resign our understandings to his direction, or join with him in the measure he proposes."[1]

Pitt resigned, and his colleagues rejoiced.[2] Power fell to Bute and the Tories; and great was the fall. The mass of the nation was with the defeated Minister. On Lord Mayor's Day Bute and Barrington were passing St. Paul's in a coach, which the crowd mistook for that of Pitt, and cheered lustily; till one man, looking in at the window, shouted to the rest: "This is n't Pitt; it 's Bute, and be damned to him!" The cheers turned forthwith to hisses, mixed with cries of "No Bute!" "No Newcastle salmon!" "Pitt forever!" Handfuls of mud were showered against the coach, and Barrington's ruffles were besmirched with it.[3]

The fall of Pitt was like the knell of doom to Frederic of Prussia. It meant abandonment by his only ally, and the loss of the subsidy which was his chief resource. The darkness around him grew darker yet, and not a hope seemed left; when as by miracle the clouds broke, and light streamed out of the blackness. The bitterest of his foes, the Czarina Elizabeth, she whom he had called *infâme catin du Nord*, died, and was succeeded by her nephew, Peter III. Here again, as in England and Spain, a new sovereign brought new measures. The young Czar, simple and enthusiastic, admired the King of Prussia, thought him the paragon of heroes, and proclaimed himself his friend. No sooner was he on the throne than Russia changed front. From the foe of Frederic she became his ally; and in the opening campaign of 1762 the army that was to have aided in crushing him was ranged on his side. It was a turn of fortune too sharp and sudden to endure. Ill-balanced and extreme in all things, Peter plunged into headlong reforms, exasperated the clergy and the army, and alienated his wife, Catherine, who had hoped to rule in his name, and who now saw herself supplanted by his mistress. Within six months he was deposed and strangled. Catherine, one of whose lovers had borne part in the murder, reigned in

---

[1] *Annual Register, 1761*, p. 44. Adolphus, *George III.*, I. 40. Thackeray, *Life of Chatham*, I. 592.

[2] Walpole, *George III.*, I. 80, and note by Sir Denis Le Marchant, 80–82.

[3] *Nuthall to Lady Chatham, 12 Nov. 1761*, in *Chatham Correspondence*, II. 166.

his stead, conspicuous by the unbridled disorders of her life, and by powers of mind that mark her as the ablest of female sovereigns. If she did not share her husband's enthusiasm for Frederic, neither did she share Elizabeth's hatred of him. He, on his part, taught by hard experience, conciliated instead of insulting her, and she let him alone.

Peace with Russia brought peace with Sweden, and Austria with the Germanic Empire stood alone against him. France needed all her strength to hold her own against the mixed English and German force under Ferdinand of Brunswick in the Rhine countries. She made spasmodic efforts to seize upon Hanover, but the result was humiliating defeat.

In England George III. pursued his policy of strengthening the prerogative, and, jealous of the Whig aristocracy, attacked it in the person of Newcastle. In vain the old politician had played false with Pitt, and trimmed to please his young master. He was worried into resigning his place in the Cabinet, and Bute, the obsequious agent of the royal will, succeeded him as First Lord of the Treasury. Into his weak and unwilling hands now fell the task of carrying on the war; for the nation, elated with triumphs and full of fight, still called on its rulers for fresh efforts and fresh victories. Pitt had proved a true prophet, and his enemies were put to shame; for the attitude of Spain forced Bute and his colleagues to the open rupture with her which the great Minister had vainly urged upon them; and a new and formidable war was now added to the old.[1] Their counsels were weak and half-hearted; but the armies and navies of England still felt the impulsion that the imperial hand of Pitt had given and the unconquerable spirit that he had roused.

This spirit had borne them from victory to victory. In Asia they had driven the French from Pondicherry and all their Indian possessions; in Africa they had wrested from them Gorée and the Senegal country; in the West Indies they had taken Guadeloupe and Dominica; in the European seas they had captured ship after ship, routed and crippled the great fleet of Admiral Conflans, seized Belleisle, and defeated a bold attempt to invade Ireland. The navy of France was reduced to helplessness. Pitt, before his resignation, had planned a series

[1] *Declaration of War against the King of Spain, 4 Jan. 1762.*

of new operations, including an attack on Martinique, with
other West Indian islands still left to France, and then in turn
on the Spanish possessions of Havana, Panama, Manila, and
the Philippines. Now, more than ever before, the war appeared in its true character. It was a contest for maritime and
colonial ascendency; and England saw herself confronted by
both her great rivals at once.

Admiral Rodney sailed for Martinique, and Brigadier
Monckton joined him with troops from America. Before the
middle of February the whole island was in their hands; and
Grenada, St. Lucia, and St. Vincent soon shared its fate. The
Earl of Albemarle and Admiral Sir George Pococke sailed in
early spring on a more important errand, landed in June near
Havana with eleven thousand soldiers, and attacked Moro
Castle, the key of the city. The pitiless sun of the tropic midsummer poured its fierce light and heat on the parched rocks
where the men toiled at the trenches. Earth was so scarce that
hardly enough could be had to keep the fascines in place. The
siege works were little else than a mass of dry faggots; and
when, after exhausting toil, the grand battery opened on the
Spanish defences, it presently took fire, was consumed, and
had to be made anew. Fresh water failed, and the troops died
by scores from thirst; fevers set in, killed many, and disabled
nearly half the army. The sea was strewn with floating
corpses, and carrion-birds in clouds hovered over the populous graveyards and infected camps. Yet the siege went on: a
formidable sally was repulsed; Moro Castle was carried by
storm; till at length, two months and eight days after the
troops landed, Havana fell into their hands.[1] At the same
time Spain was attacked at the antipodes, and the loss of Manila and the Philippines gave her fresh cause to repent her
rash compact with France. She was hardly more fortunate
near home; for having sent an army to invade Portugal,
which was in the interest of England, a small British force,
under Brigadier Burgoyne, foiled it, and forced it to retire.

The tide of British success was checked for an instant in
Newfoundland, where a French squadron attacked St. John's
and took it, with its garrison of sixty men. The news reached

[1] *Journal of the Siege, by the Chief Engineer*, in Beatson, II. 544. Mante, 398–
465. Entick, V. 363–383.

Amherst at New York; his brother, Lieutenant-Colonel Amherst, was sent to the scene of the mishap. St. John's was retaken, and its late conquerors were made prisoners of war.

The financial condition of France was desperate. Her people were crushed with taxation; her debt grew apace; and her yearly expenditure was nearly double her revenue. Choiseul felt the need of immediate peace; and George III. and Bute were hardly less eager for it, to avert the danger of Pitt's return to power and give free scope to their schemes for strengthening the prerogative. Therefore, in September, 1762, negotiations were resumed. The Duke of Bedford was sent to Paris to settle the preliminaries, and the Duc de Nivernois came to London on the same errand. The populace were still for war. Bedford was hissed as he passed through the streets of London, and a mob hooted at the puny figure of Nivernois as he landed at Dover.

The great question was, Should Canada be restored? Should France still be permitted to keep a foothold on the North American continent? Ever since the capitulation of Montreal a swarm of pamphlets had discussed the momentous subject. Some maintained that the acquisition of Canada was not an original object of the war; that the colony was of little value and ought to be given back to its old masters; that Guadeloupe should be kept instead, the sugar trade of that island being worth far more than the Canadian fur trade; and, lastly, that the British colonists, if no longer held in check by France, would spread themselves over the continent, learn to supply all their own wants, grow independent, and become dangerous. Nor were these views confined to Englishmen. There were foreign observers who clearly saw that the adhesion of her colonies to Great Britain would be jeopardized by the extinction of French power in America. Choiseul warned Stanley that they "would not fail to shake off their dependence the moment Canada should be ceded;" while thirteen years before, the Swedish traveller Kalm declared that the presence of the French in America gave the best assurance to Great Britain that its own colonies would remain in due subjection.[1]

The most noteworthy argument on the other side was that

[1] Kalm, *Travels in North America*, I. 207.

of Franklin, whose words find a strange commentary in the
events of the next few years. He affirmed that the colonies
were so jealous of each other that they would never unite
against England. "If they could not agree to unite against the
French and Indians, can it reasonably be supposed that there
is any danger of their uniting against their own nation, which
it is well known they all love much more than they love one
another? I will venture to say union amongst them for such a
purpose is not merely improbable, it is impossible;" that is,
he prudently adds, without "the most grievous tyranny and
oppression," like the bloody rule of "Alva in the Netherlands."[1]

If Pitt had been in office he would have demanded terms
that must ruin past redemption the maritime and colonial
power of France; but Bute was less exacting. In November
the plenipotentiaries of England, France, and Spain agreed on
preliminaries of peace, in which the following were the essential points. France ceded to Great Britain Canada and all her
possessions on the North American continent east of the
River Mississippi, except the city of New Orleans and a small
adjacent district. She renounced her claims to Acadia, and
gave up to the conqueror the Island of Cape Breton, with all
other islands in the Gulf and River of St. Lawrence. Spain
received back Havana, and paid for it by the cession of Florida, with all her other possessions east of the Mississippi.
France, subject to certain restrictions, was left free to fish in
the Gulf of St. Lawrence and off a part of the coast of Newfoundland; and the two little islands of St. Pierre and Miquelon were given her as fishing stations on condition that she
should not fortify or garrison them. In the West Indies, England restored the captured islands of Guadeloupe, Marigalante, Désirade, and Martinique, and France ceded Grenada
and the Grenadines; while it was agreed that of the so-called

[1] *Interest of Great Britain in regard to her Colonies* (London, 1760).

Lord Bath argues for retaining Canada in *A Letter addressed to Two Great
Men on the Prospect of Peace* (1759). He is answered by another pamphlet called
Remarks on the Letter to Two Great Men (1760). The *Gentleman's Magazine*
for 1759 has an ironical article styled *Reasons for restoring Canada to the
French*; and in 1761 a pamphlet against the restitution appeared under the
title, *Importance of Canada considered in Two Letters to a Noble Lord*. These are
but a part of the writings on the question.

neutral islands, St. Vincent, Dominica, and Tobago should belong to England, and St. Lucia to France. In Europe, each side promised to give no more help to its allies in the German war. France restored Minorca, and England restored Belleisle; France gave up such parts of Hanoverian territory as she had occupied, and evacuated certain fortresses belonging to Prussia, pledging herself at the same time to demolish, under the inspection of English engineers, her own maritime fortress of Dunkirk. In Africa France ceded Senegal, and received back the small Island of Gorée. In India she lost everything she had gained since the peace of Aix-la-Chapelle; recovered certain trading stations, but renounced the right of building forts or maintaining troops in Bengal.

On the day when the preliminaries were signed, France made a secret agreement with Spain, by which she divested herself of the last shred of her possessions on the North American continent. As compensation for Florida, which her luckless ally had lost in her quarrel, she made over to the Spanish Crown the city of New Orleans, and under the name of Louisiana gave her the vast region spreading westward from the Mississippi towards the Pacific.

On the ninth of December the question of approving the preliminaries came up before both Houses of Parliament. There was a long debate in the Commons. Pitt was not present, confined, it was said, by gout; till late in the day the House was startled by repeated cheers from the outside. The doors opened, and the fallen Minister entered, carried in the arms of his servants, and followed by an applauding crowd. His bearers set him down within the bar, and by the help of a crutch he made his way with difficulty to his seat. "There was a mixture of the very solemn and the theatric in this apparition," says Walpole, who was present. "The moment was so well timed, the importance of the man and his services, the languor of his emaciated countenance, and the study bestowed on his dress were circumstances that struck solemnity into a patriot mind, and did a little furnish ridicule to the hardened and insensible. He was dressed in black velvet, his legs and thighs wrapped in flannel, his feet covered with buskins of black cloth, and his hands with thick gloves." Not for the first time, he was utilizing his maladies for purposes of stage effect. He spoke for about three hours, sometimes standing, and sometimes seated; sometimes with a brief burst of power, more often with the accents of pain and exhaustion. He highly commended the retention of Canada, but denounced the leaving to France a share in the fisheries, as well as other advantages tending to a possible revival of her maritime power. But the Commons listened coldly, and by a great majority approved the preliminaries of peace.

These preliminaries were embodied in the definitive treaty concluded at Paris on the tenth of February, 1763. Peace between France and England brought peace between the warring nations of the Continent. Austria, bereft of her allies, and exhausted by vain efforts to crush Frederic, gave up the attempt in despair, and signed the treaty of Hubertsburg. The Seven Years War was ended.

Chapter XXXII
1763–1884
CONCLUSION
Results of the War • Germany • France • England • Canada • The British Provinces

"THIS," said Earl Granville on his deathbed, "has been the most glorious war and the most triumphant peace that England ever knew." Not all were so well pleased, and many held with Pitt that the House of Bourbon should have been forced to drain the cup of humiliation to the dregs. Yet the fact remains that the Peace of Paris marks an epoch than which none in modern history is more fruitful of grand results. With it began a new chapter in the annals of the world. To borrow the words of a late eminent writer, "It is no exaggeration to say that three of the many victories of the Seven Years War determined for ages to come the destinies of mankind. With that of Rossbach began the re-creation of Germany; with that of Plassey the influence of Europe told for the first time since the days of Alexander on the nations of the East; with the triumph of Wolfe on the Heights of Abraham began the history of the United States."[1]

So far, however, as concerns the war in the Germanic countries, it was to outward seeming but a mad debauch of blood and rapine, ending in nothing but the exhaustion of the combatants. The havoc had been frightful. According to the King of Prussia's reckoning, 853,000 soldiers of the various nations had lost their lives, besides hundreds of thousands of noncombatants who had perished from famine, exposure, disease, or violence. And with all this waste of life not a boundary line had been changed. The rage of the two empresses and the vanity and spite of the concubine had been completely foiled. Frederic had defied them all, and had come out of the strife intact in his own hereditary dominions and master of all that he had snatched from the Empress-Queen; while Prussia, portioned out by her enemies as their spoil, lay depleted indeed,

[1] Green, *History of the English People*, IV. 193 (London, 1880).

1475

and faint with deadly striving, but crowned with glory, and with the career before her which, through tribulation and adversity, was to lead her at last to the headship of a united Germany.

Through centuries of strife and vicissitude the French monarchy had triumphed over nobles, parliaments, and people, gathered to itself all the forces of the State, beamed with illusive splendors under Louis the Great, and shone with the phosphorescence of decay under his contemptible successor; till now, robbed of prestige, burdened with debt, and mined with corruption, it was moving swiftly and more swiftly towards the abyss of ruin.

While the war hastened the inevitable downfall of the French monarchy, it produced still more notable effects. France under Colbert had embarked on a grand course of maritime and colonial enterprise, and followed it with an activity and vigor that promised to make her a great and formidable ocean power. It was she who led the way in the East, first trained the natives to fight her battles, and began that system of mixed diplomacy and war which, imitated by her rival, enabled a handful of Europeans to master all India. In North America her vast possessions dwarfed those of every other nation. She had built up a powerful navy and created an extensive foreign trade. All this was now changed. In India she was reduced to helpless inferiority, with total ruin in the future; and of all her boundless territories in North America nothing was left but the two island rocks on the coast of Newfoundland that the victors had given her for drying her codfish. Of her navy scarcely forty ships remained; all the rest were captured or destroyed. She was still great on the continent of Europe, but as a world power her grand opportunities were gone.

In England as in France the several members of the State had battled together since the national life began, and the result had been, not the unchecked domination of the Crown, but a system of balanced and adjusted forces, in which King, Nobility, and Commons all had their recognized places and their share of power. Thus in the war just ended two great conditions of success had been supplied: a people instinct

with the energies of ordered freedom, and a masterly leadership to inspire and direct them.

All, and more than all, that France had lost England had
won. Now, for the first time, she was beyond dispute the
greatest of maritime and colonial Powers. Portugal and Holland, her precursors in ocean enterprise, had long ago fallen
hopelessly behind. Two great rivals remained, and she had
humbled the one and swept the other from her path. Spain,
with vast American possessions, was sinking into the decay
which is one of the phenomena of modern history; while
France, of late a most formidable competitor, had abandoned
the contest in despair. England was mistress of the seas, and
the world was thrown open to her merchants, explorers, and
colonists. A few years after the Peace the navigator Cook began his memorable series of voyages, and surveyed the strange
and barbarous lands which after times were to transform into
other Englands, vigorous children of this great mother of nations. It is true that a heavy blow was soon to fall upon her;
her own folly was to alienate the eldest and greatest of her
offspring. But nothing could rob her of the glory of giving
birth to the United States; and, though politically severed,
this gigantic progeny were to be not the less a source of
growth and prosperity to the parent that bore them, joined
with her in a triple kinship of laws, language, and blood. The
war or series of wars that ended with the Peace of Paris secured the opportunities and set in action the forces that have
planted English homes in every clime, and dotted the earth
with English garrisons and posts of trade.

With the Peace of Paris ended the checkered story of New
France; a story which would have been a history if faults of
constitution and the bigotry and folly of rulers had not
dwarfed it to an episode. Yet it is a noteworthy one in both
its lights and its shadows: in the disinterested zeal of the
founder of Quebec, the self-devotion of the early missionary
martyrs, and the daring enterprise of explorers; in the spiritual and temporal vassalage from which the only escape was
to the savagery of the wilderness; and in the swarming corruptions which were the natural result of an attempt to rule,
by the absolute hand of a master beyond the Atlantic, a peo-

ple bereft of every vestige of civil liberty. Civil liberty was given them by the British sword; but the conqueror left their religious system untouched, and through it they have imposed upon themselves a weight of ecclesiastical tutelage that finds few equals in the most Catholic countries of Europe. Such guardianship is not without certain advantages. When faithfully exercised it aids to uphold some of the tamer virtues, if that can be called a virtue which needs the constant presence of a sentinel to keep it from escaping: but it is fatal to mental robustness and moral courage; and if French Canada would fulfil its aspirations it must cease to be one of the most priest-ridden communities of the modern world.

Scarcely were they free from the incubus of France when the British provinces showed symptoms of revolt. The measures on the part of the mother-country which roused their resentment, far from being oppressive, were less burdensome than the navigation laws to which they had long submitted; and they resisted taxation by Parliament simply because it was in principle opposed to their rights as freemen. They did not, like the American provinces of Spain at a later day, sunder themselves from a parent fallen into decrepitude; but with astonishing audacity they affronted the wrath of England in the hour of her triumph, forgot their jealousies and quarrels, joined hands in the common cause, fought, endured, and won. The disunited colonies became the United States. The string of discordant communities along the Atlantic coast has grown to a mighty people, joined in a union which the earthquake of civil war served only to compact and consolidate. Those who in the weakness of their dissensions needed help from England against the savage on their borders have become a nation that may defy every foe but that most dangerous of all foes, herself, destined to a majestic future if she will shun the excess and perversion of the principles that made her great, prate less about the enemies of the past and strive more against the enemies of the present, resist the mob and the demagogue as she resisted Parliament and King, rally her powers from the race for gold and the delirium of prosperity to make firm the foundations on which that prosperity rests, and turn some fair proportion of her vast mental forces to other objects than material progress and the game of party politics. She has tamed the savage continent, peopled the solitude, gathered wealth untold, waxed potent, imposing, redoubtable; and now it remains for her to prove, if she can, that the rule of the masses is consistent with the highest growth of the individual; that democracy can give the world a civilization as mature and pregnant, ideas as energetic and vitalizing, and types of manhood as lofty and strong, as any of the systems which it boasts to supplant.

Appendix

A
Chapter III. Conflict for the West

Piquet and his War-Party. — "Ce parti [*de guerre*] pour lequel M. le Général a donné son consentement, sera de plus de 3,800 hommes. . . . 500 hommes de nos domiciliés, 700 des Cinq nations à l'exclusion des Agniers [*Mohawks*] qui ne sont plus regardés que comme des anglais, 600 tant Iroquois que d'autres nations le long de la Belle Rivière d'où ils espèrent chasser les anglais qui y forment des Établissemens contraires au bien des guerriers, 2,000 hommes qu'ils doivent prendre aux têtes plates [*Choctaws*] où ils s'arresteront, c'est la où les deux chefs de guerre doivent proposer à l'armée l'expédition des Miamis au retour de celle contre la Nation du Chien [*Cherokees*]. Un vieux levain, quelques anciennes querelles leur feront tout entreprendre contre les anglais de la Virginie s'ils donnent encore quelques secours à cette derniere nation, ce qui ne manquera pas d'arriver. . . .

"C'est un grand miracle que malgré l'envie, les contradictions, l'opposition presque générale de tous les Villages sauvages, j'aye formé en moins de 3 ans une des plus florissantes missions du Canada. . . . Je me trouve donc, Messieurs, dans l'occasion de pouvoir étendre l'empire de Jésus Christ et du Roy mes bons maitres jusqu'aux extrémités de ce nouveau monde, et de plus faire avec quelques secours que vous me procurerez que la France et l'angleterre ne pourraient faire avec plusieurs millions et toutes leur troupes." *Copie de la Lettre écrite par M. l'Abbé Picquet, dattée à la Présentation du 8 Fév. 1752* (Archives de la Marine).

I saw in the possession of the late Jacques Viger, of Montreal, an illuminated drawing of one of Piquet's banners, said to be still in existence, in which the cross, the emblems of the Virgin and the Saviour, the fleur-de-lis, and the Iroquois totems are all embroidered and linked together by strings of wampum beads wrought into the silk.

Directions of the French Colonial Minister for the Destruction of Oswego. — "La seule voye dont on puisse faire usage en temps de paix pour une pareille opération est celle des Iroquois des cinq nations. Les terres sur lesquelles le poste a été établi leur appartiennent et ce n'est qu'avec leur consentement que les anglois s'y sont placés. Si en faisant regarder à ces sauvages un pareil établissement comme contraire à leur liberté et comme une usurpation dont les anglois prétendent faire usage pour acquérir la propriété de leur terre on pourrait les déterminer à entreprendre de les détruire, une pareille opération ne seroit pas à négliger; mais M. le Marquis de la Jonquière doit sentir avec quelle circonspection une affaire de cette espèce doit être conduite et il faut en effêt qu'il y travaille de façon à ne se point compromettre." *Le Ministre à MM. de la Jonquière et Bigot, 15 Avril, 1750* (Archives de la Marine).

B
Chapter IV. Acadia

English Treatment of Acadians.—"Les Anglois dans la vue de la Conquête du Canada ont voulu donner aux peuples françois de ces Colonies un exemple frappant de la douceur de leur gouvernement dans leur conduite à l'égard des Acadiens.

"Ils leur ont fourni pendant plus de 35 ans le simple nécessaire, sans élever la fortune d'aucun, ils leur ont fourni ce nécessaire souvent à crédit, avec un excès de confiance, sans fatiguer les débiteurs, sans les presser, sans vouloir les forcer au payement.

"Ils leur ont laissé une apparence de liberté si excessive qu'ils n'ont voulu prendre aucune différence [*sic*] de leur différents, pas même pour les crimes. . . . Ils ont souffert que les accadiens leur refusassent insolemment certains rentes de grains, modiques & très-légitimement dues.

"Ils ont dissimulé le refus méprisant que les accadiens ont fait de prendre d'eux des concessions pour les nouveaux terreins qu'ils voulaient occuper.

"Les fruits que cette conduite a produit dans la dernière guerre nous le savons [*sic*] et les anglois n'en ignorent rien. Qu'on juge là-dessus de leur ressentiment et des vues de vengeance de cette nation cruelle. . . . Je prévois notamment la dispersion des jeunes accadiens sur les vaisseaux de guerre anglois, où la seule règle pour la ration du pain suffit pour les detruire jusqu'au dernier." *Roma, Officier à l'Isle Royale à* ——, *1750*.

Indians, directed by Missionaries, to attack the English in Time of Peace.—"La lettre de M. l'Abbé Le Loutre me paroit si intéressante que j'ay l'honneur de vous en envoyer Copie. . . . Les trois sauvages qui m'ont porté ces dépêches m'ont parlé relativement à ce que M. l'Abbé Le Loutre marque dans sa lettre; je n'ay eu garde de leur donner aucun Conseil làdessus et je me suis borné à leur promettre que je ne les abandonnerai point, aussy ai-je pourvu à tout, soit pour les armes, munitions de guerre et de bouche, soit pour les autres choses nécessaires.

"Il seroit à souhaiter que ces Sauvages rassemblés pussent parvenir à traverser les anglois dans leurs entreprises, même dans celle de Chibouctou [*Halifax*], ils sont dans cette résolution et s'ils peuvent mettre à execution ce qu'ils ont projetté il est assuré qu'ils seront fort incommodes aux Anglois et que les vexations qu'ils exerceront sur eux leur seront un très grand obstacle.

"Ces sauvages doivent agir seuls, il n'y aura ny soldat ny habitant, tout se fera de leur pur mouvement, et sans qu'il paraisse que j'en eusse connoissance.

"Cela est très essentiel, aussy ai-je écrit au S.ʳ de Boishébert d'observer beaucoup de prudence dans ses démarches et de les faire très secrètement pour que les Anglois ne puissent pas s'apercevoir que nous pourvoyons aux besoins des dits sauvages.

"Ce seront les missionnaires qui feront toutes les négociations et qui dirigeront les pas des dits sauvages, ils sont en très bonnes mains, le R. P. Germain et M. l'Abbé Le Loutre étant fort au fait d'en tirer tout le party possible et le plus avantageux pour nos interêts, ils ménageront leur intrigue de façon à n'y pas paroitre. . . .

"Je sens, Monseigneur, toute la delicatesse de cette negociation, soyez persuadé que je la conduirai avec tant de précautions que les anglois ne pourront pas dire que mes ordres y ont eu part." *La Jonquière au Ministre, 9 Oct. 1749.*

Missionaries to be encouraged in their Efforts to make the Indians attack the English.—"Les sauvages . . . se distinguent, depuis la paix, dans les mouvements qu'il y a du côté de l'Acadie, et sur lesquels Sa Majesté juge à propos d'entrer dans quelques details avec le Sieur de Raymond. . . .

"Sa Majesté luy a déjà observé que les sauvages ont été jusqu'à présent dans les dispositions les plus favorables. Il est de la plus grande importance, et pour le présent et pour l'avenir, de ne rien négliger pour les y maintenir. Les missionnaires qui sont auprès d'eux sont plus à portés d'y contribuer que personne, et Sa Majesté a lieu d'être satisfaite des soins qu'ils y donnent. Le S.ᵣ de Raymond doit exciter ces missionnaires à ne point se relacher sur cela; mais en même temps il doit les avertir de contenir leur zèle de manière qu'ils ne se compromettent pas mal à propos avec les anglois et qu'ils ne donnent point de justes sujets de plaintes." *Mémoire du Roy pour servir d'Instruction au Comte de Raymond, 24 Avril, 1751.*

Acadians to join the Indians in attacking the English.—"Pour que ces Sauvages agissent avec beaucoup de Courage, quelques accadiens habillés et matachés comme les Sauvages pourront se joindre à eux pour faire coup sur les Anglois. Je ne puis éviter de consentir à ce que ces Sauvages feront puisque nous avons les bras liés et que nous ne pouvons rien faire par nous-mêmes, au surplus je ne crois pas qu'il y ait de l'inconvenient de laisser mêler les accadiens parmi les Sauvages, parceque s'ils sont pris, nous dirons qu'ils ont agi de leur propre mouvement." *La Jonquière au Ministre, 1 Mai, 1751.*

Cost of Le Loutre's Intrigues.—"J'ay déjà fait payer a M. Le Loutre depuis l'année dernière la somme de 11183*l.* 18*s.* pour acquitter les dépenses qu'il fait journellement et je ne cesse de luy recommander de s'en tenir aux indispensables en evitant toujours de rien compromettre avec le gouvernement anglois." *Prévost au Ministre, 22 Juillet, 1750.*

Payment for English Scalps in Time of Peace.—"Les Sauvages ont pris, il y a un mois, 18 chevelures angloises [*English scalps*], et M. Le Loutre a été obligé de les payer 1800*l.*, argent de l'Acadie, dont je luy ay fait le remboursement." *Ibid., 16 Août, 1753.*

Many pages might be filled with extracts like the above. These, with most of the other French documents used in Chapter IV., are taken from the Archives de la Marine et des Colonies.

C
Chapter V. Washington

Washington and the Capitulation at Fort Necessity.—Villiers, in his Journal, boasts that he made Washington sign a virtual admission that he had assassinated Jumonville. In regard to this point, a letter, of which the following is an extract, is printed in the provincial papers of the time. It is from Captain Adam Stephen, an officer in the action, writing to a friend five weeks after.

"When Mr. Vanbraam returned with the French proposals, we were obliged to take the sense of them from his mouth; it rained so heavy that he could not give us a written translation of them; we could scarcely keep the candle lighted to read them by; they were written in a bad hand, on wet and blotted paper, so that no person could read them but Vanbraam, who had heard them from the mouth of the French officer. Every officer there is ready to declare that there was no such word as *assassination* mentioned. The terms expressed were, *the death of Jumonville*. If it had been mentioned we would by all means have had it altered, as the French, during the course of the interview, seemed very condescending, and desirous to bring things to an issue." He then gives several other points in which Vanbraam had misled them.

Dinwiddie, recounting the affair to Lord Albemarle, says that Washington, being ignorant of French, was deceived by the interpreter, who, through poltroonery, suppressed the word assassination.

Captain Mackay, writing to Washington in September, after a visit to Philadelphia, says: "I had several disputes about our capitulation; but I satisfied every person that mentioned the subject as to the articles in question, that they were owing to a bad interpreter, and contrary to the translation made to us when we signed them."

At the next meeting of the burgesses they passed a vote of thanks for gallant conduct to Washington and all his officers by name, except Vanbraam and the major of the regiment, the latter being charged with cowardice, and the former with treacherous misinterpretation of the articles.

Sometime after, Washington wrote to a correspondent who had questioned him on the subject: "That we were wilfully or ignorantly deceived by our interpreter in regard to the word *assassination* I do aver, and will to my dying moment; so will every officer that was present. The interpreter was a Dutchman little acquainted with the English tongue, therefore might not advert to the tone and meaning of the word in English; but, whatever his motives for so doing, certain it is that he called it the *death* or the *loss* of the Sieur Jumonville. So we received and so we understood it, until, to our great surprise and mortification, we found it otherwise in a literal translation." Sparks, *Writings of Washington*, II. 464, 465.

D
Chapter VII. Braddock

It has been said that Beaujeu, and not Contrecœur, commanded at Fort Duquesne at the time of Braddock's expedition. Some contemporaries, and notably the chaplain of the fort, do, in fact, speak of him as in this position; but their evidence is overborne by more numerous and conclusive authorities, among them Vaudreuil, governor of Canada, and Contrecœur himself, in an official report. Vaudreuil says of him: "Ce commandant s'occupa le 8 [*Juillet*] à former un parti pour aller au devant des Anglois;" and adds that this party was commanded by Beaujeu and consisted of 250 French and 650 Indians (*Vaudreuil au Ministre, 5 Août, 1755*). In the autumn of 1756 Vaudreuil asked the Colonial Minister to procure a pension for Contrecœur and Ligneris. He says: "Le premier de ces Messieurs a commandé longtemps au fort Duquesne; c'est luy qui a ordonné et dirigé tous les mouvements qui se sont faits dans cette partie, soit pour faire abandonner le premier établissement des Anglois, soit pour les forcer à se retirer du fort Nécessité, et soit enfin pour aller au devant de

l'armée du Général Braddock qui a été entièrement défaite"
(*Vaudreuil au Ministre, 8 Nov. 1756*). Beaujeu, who had lately
arrived with a reinforcement, had been named to relieve Contrecœur (*Dumas au Ministre, 24 Juillet, 1756*), but had not yet
done so.

As the report of Contrecœur has never been printed, I give
an extract from it (*Contrecœur à Vaudreuil, 14 Juillet, 1755*, in
Archives de la Marine):—

"Le même jour [*8 Juillet*] je formai un party de tout ce que
je pouvois mettre hors du fort pour aller à leur rencontre. Il
étoit composé de 250 François et de 650 sauvages, ce qui faisoit 900 hommes. M. de Beaujeu, capitaine, le commandoit.
Il y avoit deux capitaines qui estoient Mrs Dumas et Ligneris
et plusieurs autres officiers subalternes. Ce parti se mit en
marche le 9 à 8 heures du matin, et se trouva à midi et demie
en présence des Anglois à environ 3 lieues du fort. On commença à faire feu de part et d'autre. Le feu de l'artillerie ennemie fit reculer un peu par deux fois notre parti. M. de
Beaujeu fut tué à la troisième décharge. M. Dumas prit le
commandement et s'en acquitta au mieux. Nos François,
pleins de courage, soutenus par les sauvages, quoiqu'ils n'eussent point d'artillerie, firent à leur tour plier les Anglois qui
se battirent en ordre de bataille et en bonne contenance. Et
ces derniers voyant l'ardeur de nos gens qui fonçoient avec
une vigeur infinie furent enfin obligés de plier tout à fait après
4 heures d'un grand feu. Mrs Dumas et Ligneris qui n'avoient
plus avec eux q'une vingtaine de François ne s'engagerent
point dans la poursuite. Ils rentrerent dans le fort, parceq'une
grande partie des Canadiens qui n'estoient malheureusement
que des enfants s'estoient retirés à la première décharge."

The letter of Dumas cited in the text has been equally unknown. It was written a year after the battle in order to draw
the attention of the minister to services which the writer
thought had not been duly recognized. The following is an
extract (*Dumas au Ministre, 24 Juillet, 1756*, in Archives de la
Marine):—

"M. de Beaujeu marcha donc, et sous ses ordres M. de Ligneris et moi. Il attaqua avec beaucoup d'audace mais sans
nulle disposition; notre première décharge fut faite hors de

portée; l'ennemi fit la sienne de plus près, et dans le premier instant du combat, cent miliciens, qui fasaient la moitié de nos Français lâcherent honteusement le pied en criant 'Sauve qui peut.' Deux cadets qui depuis ont été faits officiers autorisait cette fuite par leur exemple. Ce mouvement en arrière ayant encouragé l'ennemi, il fit retentir ses cris de Vive le Roi et avança sur nous à grand pas. Son artillerie s'étant preparée pendant ce temps là commença à faire feu ce qui épouvanta tellement les Sauvages que tout prit la fuite; l'ennemi faisait sa troisième décharge de mousqueterie quand M. de Beaujeu fut tué.

"Notre déroute se présenta a mes yeux sous le plus désagréable point de vue, et pour n'être point chargé de la mauvaise manœuvre d'autrui, je ne songeai plus qu'à me faire tuer. Ce fut alors, Monseigneur, qu'excitant de la voix et du geste le peu de soldats qui restait, je m'avançai avec la contenance qui donne le désespoir. Mon peloton fit un feu si vif que l'ennemi en parut étonné; il grossit insensiblement et les Sauvages voyant que mon attaque faisait cesser les cris de l'ennemi revinrent à moi. Dans ce moment j'envoyai M. le Chev.ʳ Le Borgne et M. de Rocheblave dire aux officiers qui étaient à la tête des Sauvages de prendre l'ennemi en flanc. Le canon qui battit en tête donna faveur à mes ordres. L'ennemi, pris de tous cotés, combattit avec la fermeté la plus opiniâtre. Des rangs entiers tombaient à la fois; presque tous les officiers périrent; et le désordre s'etant mis par là dans cette colonne, tout prit la fuite."

Whatever may have been the conduct of the Canadian militia, the French officers behaved with the utmost courage, and shared with the Indians the honors of the victory. The partisan chief Charles Langlade seems also to have been especially prominent. His grandson, the aged Pierre Grignon, declared that it was he who led the attack (Draper, *Recollections of Grignon*, in the *Collections of the Wisconsin Historical Society*, III.). Such evidence, taken alone, is of the least possible weight; but both the traveller Anbury and General John Burgoyne, writing many years after the event, speak of Langlade, who was then alive, as the author of Braddock's defeat. Hence there can be little doubt that he took an important part in it, though the contemporary writers do not mention his name. Compare Tassé, *Notice sur Charles Langlade*. The honors fell to Contrecœur, Dumas, and Ligneris, all of whom received the cross of the Order of St. Louis (*Ordres du Roy et Dépêches des Ministres, 1755*).

E
Chapter XIV. Montcalm

To show the style of Montcalm's familiar letters, I give a few examples. Literal translation is often impossible.

À Madame de Montcalm, à Montréal, 16 Avril, 1757.
(*Extrait.*)

"Ma santé assez bonne, malgré beaucoup de travail, surtout d'ecriture. Estève, mon secretaire, se marie. Beau caractère. Bon autographe, écrivant vite. Je lui procure un emploi et le moyen de faire fortune s'il veut. Il fait un meilleur mariage que ne lui appartient; malgré cela je crains qu'il ne la fasse pas comme un autre; fat, frivole, joueur, glorieux, petit-maître, dépensier. J'ai toujours Marcel, des soldats copistes dans le besoin. . . . Tous les soldats de Montpellier se portants bien, hors le fils de Pierre mort chez moi. Tout est hors de prix. Il faut vivre honorablement et je le fais, tous les jours seize personnes. Une fois tous les quinze jours chez M. le Gouverneur général et M.ʳ le Chev. de Lévis qui vit aussi très bien. Il a donné trois beaux grands bals. Pour moi jusqu'au carême, outre les diners, de grands soupers de dames trois fois la semaine. Le jour des devotes prudes, des concerts. Les jours des jeûnes des violons d'hazard, parcequ'on me les demandait, cela ne menait que jusqu'à deux heures du matin et il se joignait l'après-souper compagnie dansante sans être priée, mais sure d'être bien reçue à celle qui avait soupé. Fort cher, peu amusant, et souvent ennuyeux. . . . Vous connaissiez ma maison, je l'ai augmentée d'un cocher, d'un frotteur, un garçon de cuisine, et j'ai marié mon aide de cuisine; car je travaille à peupler la colonie: 80 mariages de soldats cet hiver et deux d'officiers. Germain a perdu sa fille. Il a epousé mieux que lui; bonne femme mais sans bien, comme toutes. . . ."

À Madame de Montcalm, à Montréal, 6 Juin, 1757.
(Extrait.)

"J'addresse la première de cette lettre à ma mère. Il n'y a pas une heure dans la journée que je ne songe à vous, à elle, et à mes enfants. J'embrasse ma fille; je vous adore, ma très chère, ainsi que ma mère. Mille choses à mes sœurs. Je n'ai pas le temps de leur écrire, ni à Naujac, ni aux abbesses. . . . Des compliments au château d'Arbois, aux Du Cayla, et aux Givard. P. S. N'oubliez pas d'envoyer une douzaine de bouteilles d'Angleterre de pinte d'eau de lavande; vous en mettrez quatre pour chaque envoi."

À Bourlamaque, à Montréal, 20 Février, 1757.
(Extrait.)

"Dimanche j'avais rassemblé les dames de France hors Mad. de Parfouru qui m'a fait l'honneur de me venir voir il y a trois jours et en la voyant je me suis apperçu que l'amour avait des traits de puissance dont on ne pouvait pas rendre raison, non pas par l'impression qu'elle a faite sur mon cœur, mais bien par celle qu'elle a faite sur celui de son époux. Mercredi une assemblée chez Mad. Varin. Jeudi un bal chez le Chev. de Lévis qui avait prié 65 Dames ou demoiselles; Il n'y en avait que trente—autant d'hommes qu'à la guerre. Sa salle bien éclairée, aussi grand que celle de l'Intendance, beaucoup d'ordre, beaucoup d'attention, des rafraichissements en abondance toute la nuit de tout genre et de toute espèce et on ne se retira qu'à sept heures du matin. Pour moi qui ay quitté le séjour de Québec, Je me couchai de bonne heure. J'avais eu ce jour-là huit dames à souper et ce souper était dedié à Mad. Varin. Demain j'en aurai une demi douzaine. Je ne scai encore a qui il est dedié, Je suis tenté de croire que c'est à La Roche Beaucourt Le galant Chev.ʳ nous donne encore un bal."

F

Chapter XV. Fort William Henry

Webb to Loudon, Fort Edward, 11 Aug. 1757.
Public Record Office. (Extract.)

"On leaving the Camp Yesterday Morning they [*the English soldiers*] were stript by the Indians of everything they had both Officers and Men the Women and Children drag'd from among them and most inhumanly butchered before their faces, the party of about three hundred Men which were given them as an escort were during this time quietly looking on, from this and other circumstances we are too well convinced these barbarities must have been connived at by the French, After having destroyed the women and children they fell upon the rear of our Men who running in upon the Front soon put the whole to a most precipitate flight in which confusion part of them came into this Camp about two o'Clock yesterday morning in a most distressing situation, and have continued dropping in ever since, a great many men and we are afraid several Officers were massacred."

The above is independent of the testimony of Frye, who did not reach Fort Edward till the day after Webb's letter was written.

Frye to Thomas Hubbard, Speaker of the House of Representatives of Massachusetts, Albany, 16 Aug. 1757.
Public Record Office. (Extract.)

"We did not march till ye 10th at which time the Savages were let loose upon us, Strips, Kills, & Scalps our people drove them into Disorder Rendered it impossible to Rally, the French Gaurds we were promised shou'd Escort us to Fort Edward Could or would not protect us so that there Opened the most horrid Scene of Barbarity immaginable, I was strip'd myself of my Arms & Cloathing that I had nothing left but Briches Stockings Shoes & Shirt, the Indians round me with their Tomehawks Spears &c threatening Death I flew to the Officers of the French Gaurds for Protection but they would afford me none, therefore was Oblig'd to fly and was in the woods till the 12th in the Morning of which I arriv'd at Fort Edward almost Famished . . . with what of Fatigue Starving &c I am obliged to break off but as soon as I can Recollect myself shall write to you more fully."

Frye, Journal of the Attack of Fort William Henry.
Public Record Office. (Extract.)

"*Wednesday, August 10th.*—Early this morning we were ordered to prepare for our march, but found the Indians in a worse temper (if possible) than last night, every one having a tomahawk, hatchett or some other instrument of death, and Constantly plundering from the officers their arms &ca this Col! Monro Complained of, as a breach of the Articles of Capitulation but to no effect, the french officers however told us that if we would give up the baggage of the officers and men, to the Indians, they thought it would make them easy, which at last Col° Monro Consented to but this was no sooner done, then they began to take the Officers Hatts, Swords, guns & Cloaths, stripping them all to their Shirts, and on some officers, left no shirt at all, while this was doing they killed and scalp'd all the sick and wounded before our faces and then took out from our troops, all the Indians and negroes, and Carried them off, one of the former they burnt alive afterwards.

"At last with great difficulty the troops gott from the Retrenchment, but they were no sooner out, then the savages fell upon the rear, killing & scalping, which Occasioned an order for a halt, which at last was done in great Confusion but as soon as those in the front knew what was doing in the rear they again pressed forward, and thus the Confusion continued & encreased till we came to the Advanc'd guard of the French, the savages still carrying away Officers, privates, Women and Children, some of which latter they kill'd & scalpt in the road. This horrid scene of blood and slaughter obliged our officers to apply to the Officers of the French Guard for protection, which they refus'd & told them they must take to the woods and shift for themselves which many did, and in all probability many perish't in the woods, many got into Fort Edward that day and others daily Continued coming in, but vastly fatigued with their former hardships added to this last, which threw several of them into Deliriums."

Affidavit of Miles Whitworth, Surgeon of the Massachusetts Regiment, taken before Governor Pownall 17 Oct. 1757. Public Record Office. (Extract.)

"Being duly sworn on the Holy Evangelists doth declare . . . that there were also seventeen Men of the Massachusetts

Regiment wounded unable to March under his immediate
Care in the Intrenched Camp, that according to the Capitulation he did deliver them over to the French Surgeon on the
ninth of August at two in the Afternoon . . . that the French
Surgeon received them into his Custody and placed Centinals
of the French Troops upon the said seventeen wounded. That
the French Surgeon going away to the French Camp, the said
Miles Whitworth continued with the said wounded Men till
five o'Clock on the Morn of the tenth of August, That the
Centinals were taken off and that he the said Whitworth saw
the French Indians about 5 O'Clock in the Morn of the 10th
of August dragg the said seventeen wounded men out of their
Hutts, Murder them with their Tomohawks and scalp them,
That the French Troops posted round the lines were not further than forty feet from the Hutts where the said wounded
Men lay, that several Canadian Officers particularly one La-
corne were present and that none, either Officer or Soldier,
protected the said wounded Men.

"MILES WHITWORTH.

"*Sworn before me* T. POWNALL."

G
Chapter XX. Ticonderoga

The French accounts of the battle at Ticonderoga are very
numerous, and consist of letters and despatches of Montcalm,
Lévis, Bougainville, Doreil, and other officers, besides several
anonymous narratives, one of which was printed in pamphlet
form at the time. Translations of many of them may be found
in *N. Y. Colonial Documents*, X. There are, however, various
others preserved in the archives of the War and Marine Departments at Paris which have not seen the light. I have carefully examined and collated them all. The English accounts
are by no means so numerous or so minute. Among those
not already cited, may be mentioned a letter of Colonel
Woolsey of the New York provincials, and two letters from
British officers written just after the battle and enclosed in a

letter from Alexander Colden to Major Halkett, 17 July. (*Bouquet and Haldimand Papers.*)

The French greatly exaggerated the force of the English and their losses in the battle. They place the former at from twenty thousand to thirty-one thousand, and the latter at from four thousand to six thousand. Prisoners taken at the end of the battle told them that the English had lost four thousand,—a statement which they readily accepted, though the prisoners could have known little more about the matter than they themselves. And these figures were easily magnified. The number of dead lying before the lines is variously given at from eight hundred to three thousand. Montcalm himself, who was somewhat elated by his victory, gives this last number in one of his letters, though he elsewhere says two thousand; while Lévis, in his *Journal de la Guerre*, says "about eight hundred." The truth is that no pains were taken to ascertain the exact number, which, by the English returns, was a little above five hundred, the total of killed, wounded, and missing being nineteen hundred and forty-four. A friend of Knox, writing to him from Fort Edward three weeks after the battle, gives a tabular statement which shows nineteen hundred and fifty in all, or six more than the official report. As the name of every officer killed or wounded, with the corps to which he belonged, was published at the time (*London Magazine*, 1758), it is extremely unlikely that the official return was falsified. Abercromby's letter to Pitt, on July 12, says that he retreated "with the loss of four hundred and sixty-four regulars killed, twenty-nine missing eleven hundred and seventeen wounded; and eighty-seven provincials killed, eight missing, and two hundred and thirty-nine wounded, officers of both included." In a letter to Viscount Barrington, of the same date (Public Record Office), Abercromby encloses a full detail of losses, regiment by regiment and company by company, being a total of nineteen hundred and forty-five. Several of the French writers state correctly that about fourteen thousand men (including reserves) were engaged in the attack; but they add erroneously that there were thirteen thousand more at the Falls. In fact there was only a small provincial regiment left there, and a battalion of the New York regiment, under Colonel Woolsey, at the landing.

A LEGEND OF TICONDEROGA.—Mention has been made of the death of Major Duncan Campbell of Inverawe. The following family tradition relating to it was told me in 1878 by the late Dean Stanley, to whom I am also indebted for various papers on the subject, including a letter from James Campbell, Esq., the present laird of Inverawe, and great-nephew of the hero of the tale. The same story is told, in an amplified form and with some variations, in the *Legendary Tales of the Highlands* of Sir Thomas Dick Lauder. As related by Dean Stanley and approved by Mr. Campbell, it is this:—

The ancient castle of Inverawe stands by the banks of the Awe, in the midst of the wild and picturesque scenery of the western Highlands. Late one evening, before the middle of the last century, as the laird, Duncan Campbell, sat alone in the old hall, there was a loud knocking at the gate; and, opening it, he saw a stranger, with torn clothing and kilt besmeared with blood, who in a breathless voice begged for asylum. He went on to say that he had killed a man in a fray, and that the pursuers were at his heels. Campbell promised to shelter him. "Swear on your dirk!" said the stranger; and Campbell swore. He then led him to a secret recess in the depths of the castle. Scarcely was he hidden when again there was a loud knocking at the gate, and two armed men appeared. "Your cousin Donald has been murdered, and we are looking for the murderer!" Campbell, remembering his oath, professed to have no knowledge of the fugitive; and the men went on their way. The laird, in great agitation, lay down to rest in a large dark room, where at length he fell asleep. Waking suddenly in bewilderment and terror, he saw the ghost of the murdered Donald standing by his bedside, and heard a hollow voice pronounce the words: *"Inverawe! Inverawe! blood has been shed. Shield not the murderer!"* In the morning Campbell went to the hiding-place of the guilty man and told him that he could harbor him no longer. "You have sworn on your dirk!" he replied; and the laird of Inverawe, greatly perplexed and troubled, made a compromise between conflicting duties, promised not to betray his guest, led him to the neighboring mountain, and hid him in a cave.

In the next night, as he lay tossing in feverish slumbers, the same stern voice awoke him, the ghost of his cousin Donald stood again at his bedside, and again he heard the same appalling words: *"Inverawe! Inverawe! blood has been shed. Shield not the murderer!"* At break of day he hastened, in strange agitation, to the cave; but it was empty, the stranger was gone. At night, as he strove in vain to sleep, the vision appeared once more, ghastly pale, but less stern of aspect than before. *"Farewell, Inverawe!"* it said; *"Farewell, till we meet at TICONDEROGA!"*

The strange name dwelt in Campbell's memory. He had joined the Black Watch, or Forty-second Regiment, then employed in keeping order in the turbulent Highlands. In time he became its major; and, a year or two after the war broke out, he went with it to America. Here, to his horror, he learned that it was ordered to the attack of Ticonderoga. His story was well known among his brother officers. They combined among themselves to disarm his fears; and when they reached the fatal spot they told him on the eve of the battle, "This is not Ticonderoga; we are not there yet; this is Fort George." But in the morning he came to them with haggard looks. "I have seen him! You have deceived me! He came to my tent last night! This is Ticonderoga! I shall die to-day!" and his prediction was fulfilled.

Such is the tradition. The indisputable facts are that Major Duncan Campbell of Inverawe, his arm shattered by a bullet, was carried to Fort Edward, where, after amputation, he died and was buried. (*Abercromby to Pitt, 19 August, 1758.*) The stone that marks his grave may still be seen, with this inscription: *"Here lyes the Body of Duncan Campbell of Inverawe, Esqre., Major to the old Highland Regiment, aged 55 Years, who died the 17th July, 1758, of the Wounds he received in the Attack of the Retrenchment of Ticonderoga or Carrillon, on the 8th July, 1758."*

His son, Lieutenant Alexander Campbell, was severely wounded at the same time, but reached Scotland alive, and died in Glasgow.

Mr. Campbell, the present Inverawe, in the letter mentioned above, says that forty-five years ago he knew an old man whose grandfather was foster-brother to the slain major of the forty-second, and who told him the following story while carrying a salmon for him to an inn near Inverawe. The old man's grandfather was sleeping with his son, then a lad, in the same room, but in another bed. This son, father of the narrator, "was awakened," to borrow the words of Mr. Campbell, "by some unaccustomed sound, and behold there was a bright light in the room, and he saw a figure, in full Highland regimentals, cross over the room and stoop down over his father's bed and give him a kiss. He was too frightened to speak, but put his head under his coverlet and went to sleep. Once more he was roused in like manner, and saw the same sight. In the morning he spoke to his father about it, who told him that it was Macdonnochie [*the Gaelic patronymic of the laird of Inverawe*] whom he had seen, and who came to tell him that he had been killed in a great battle in America. Sure enough, said my informant, it was on the very day that the battle of Ticonderoga was fought and the laird was killed."

It is also said that two ladies of the family of Inverawe saw a battle in the clouds, in which the shadowy forms of Highland warriors were plainly to be descried; and that when the fatal news came from America, it was found that the time of the vision answered exactly to that of the battle in which the head of the family fell.

The legend of Inverawe has within a few years found its way into an English magazine, and it has also been excellently told in the *Atlantic Monthly* of September of this year, 1884, by Miss C. F. Gordon Cumming. Her version differs a little from that given above from the recital of Dean Stanley and the present laird of Inverawe, but the essential points are the same. Miss Gordon Cumming, however, is in error when she says that Duncan Campbell was wounded in the breast, and that he was first buried at Ticonderoga. His burial-place was near Fort Edward, where he died, and where his remains still lie, though not at the same spot, as they were long after removed by a family named Gilchrist, who claimed kinship with the Campbells of Inverawe.

H
Chapter XXV. Wolfe at Quebec

Force of the French and English at the Siege of Quebec.

"Les retranchemens que j'avois fait tracer depuis la rivière St. Charles jusqu'au saut Montmorency furent occupés par plus de 14,000 hommes, 200 cavaliers dont je formai un corps aux ordres de M. de la Rochebeaucour, environ 1,000 sauvages Abenakis et des différentes nations du nord des pays d'en haut. M. de Boishébert arriva ensuite avec les Acadiens et sauvages qu'il avoit rassemblés. Je réglai la garnison de Québec à 2,000 hommes." *Vaudreuil au Ministre, 5 Oct. 1759.*

The commissary Berniers says that the whole force was about fifteen thousand men, besides Indians, which is less than the number given by Vaudreuil.

Bigot says: "Nous avions 13,000 hommes et mille à 1,200 sauvages, sans compter 2,000 hommes de garnison dans la ville." *Bigot au Ministre, 25 Oct. 1759.*

The Hartwell *Journal du Siége* says: "Il fut décidé qu'on ne laisseroit dans la place que 1,200 hommes, et que tout le reste marcheroit au camp, où l'on comptoit se trouver plus de 15,000 hommes, y compris les sauvages."

Rigaud, Vaudreuil's brother, writing from Montreal to Bourlamaque on the 23d of June, says: "Je compte que l'armée campée sous Québec sera de 17,000 hommes bien effectifs, sans les sauvages." He then gives a list of Indians who have joined the army, or are on the way, amounting to thirteen hundred.

At the end of June Wolfe had about eight thousand six hundred effective soldiers. Of these the ten battalions, commonly mentioned as regiments, supplied six thousand four hundred; detached grenadiers from Louisbourg, three hundred; artillery, three hundred; rangers, four hundred; light infantry, two hundred; marines, one thousand. The complement of the battalions was in some cases seven hundred and in others one thousand (Knox, II. 25); but their actual strength varied from five hundred to eight hundred, except the Highlanders, who mustered eleven hundred, their ranks being more than full. Fraser, in his *Journal of the Siege*, gives a tabular view of the whole. At the end of the campaign Lévis reckons the remaining English troops at about six thousand (*Lévis au Ministre, 10 Nov. 1759*), which answers to the report of General Murray: "The troops will amount to six thousand" (*Murray to Pitt, 12 Oct. 1759*). The precise number is given in the *Return of the State of His Majesty's Forces left in Garrison at Quebec*, dated 12 Oct. 1759, and signed, Robert Monckton (Public Record Office, *America and West Indies*, XCIX.). This shows the total of rank and file to have been 6,214, which the addition of officers, sergeants, and drummers raises to about seven thousand, besides 171 artillerymen.

I

Chapter XXVII. The Heights of Abraham

One of the most important unpublished documents on Wolfe's operations against Quebec is the long and elaborate *Journal mémoratif de ce qui s'est passé de plus remarquable pendant qu'a duré le Siége de la Ville de Québec* (Archives de la Marine). The writer, M. de Foligny, was a naval officer who during the siege commanded one of the principal batteries of the town. The official correspondence of Vaudreuil for 1759 (Archives Nationales) gives the events of the time from his point of view; and various manuscript letters of Bigot, Lévis, Montreuil, and others (Archives de la Marine, Archives de la Guerre) give additional particulars. The letters, generally private and confidential, written to Bourlamaque by Montcalm, Lévis, Vaudreuil, Malartic, Berniers, and others during the siege contain much that is curious and interesting.

Siége de Québec en 1759, d'après un Manuscrit déposé à la Bibliothêque de Hartwell en Angleterre. A very valuable diary, by a citizen of Quebec; it was brought from England in 1834 by the Hon. D. B. Viger, and a few copies were printed at Quebec in 1836. *Journal tenu à l'Armée que commandoit feu M. le Marquis de Montcalm*. A minute diary of an officer under Montcalm (printed by the Quebec Historical Society). *Mémoire sur la Campagne de 1759, par M. de Joannès, Major de Québec* (Archives de la Guerre). *Lettres et Dépêches de Mont-*

calm (Ibid.). These touch chiefly the antecedents of the siege. *Mémoires sur le Canada depuis 1749 jusqu'à 1760* (Quebec Historical Society). *Journal du Siége de Québec en 1759, par M. Jean Claude Panet, notaire* (Ibid.). The writer of this diary was in Quebec at the time. Several other journals and letters of persons present at the siege have been printed by the Quebec Historical Society, under the title *Événements de la Guerre en Canada durant les Années 1759 et 1760. Relation de ce qui s'est passé au Siége de Québec, par une Réligieuse de l'Hôpital Général de Québec* (Quebec Historical Society). *Jugement impartial sur les Opérations militaires de la Campagne, par M.ᵍʳ de Pontbriand, Évêque de Québec* (Ibid.). *Memoirs of the Siege of Quebec, from the Journal of a French Officer on board the Chezine Frigate, taken by His Majesty's Ship Rippon, by Richard Gardiner, Esq., Captain of Marines in the Rippon*, London, 1761.

General Wolfe's Instructions to Young Officers, Philadelphia, 1778. This title is misleading, the book being a collection of military orders. *General Orders in Wolfe's Army* (Quebec Historical Society). This collection is much more full than the foregoing, so far as concerns the campaign of 1759. *Letters of Wolfe* (in Wright's *Wolfe*), *Despatches of Wolfe, Saunders, Monckton, and Townshend* (in contemporary magazines). *A Short Authentic Account of the Expedition against Quebec, by a Volunteer upon that Expedition*, Quebec, 1872. This valuable diary is ascribed to James Thompson, a volunteer under Wolfe, who died at Quebec in 1830 at the age of ninety-eight, after holding for many years the position of overseer of works in the Engineer Department. Another manuscript, for the most part identical with this, was found a few years ago among old papers in the office of the Royal Engineers at Quebec. *Journal of the Expedition on the River St. Lawrence*. Two entirely distinct diaries bear this name. One is printed in the *New York Mercury* for December, 1759; the other was found among the papers of George Alsopp, secretary to Sir Guy Carleton, who served under Wolfe (Quebec Historical Society). Johnstone, *A Dialogue in Hades* (Ibid.). The Scotch Jacobite, Chevalier Johnstone, as aide-de-camp to Lévis, and afterwards to Montcalm, had great opportunities of acquiring information during the campaign; and the results, though produced in the fanciful form of a dialogue between the ghosts of Wolfe and Montcalm, are of substantial historical value. The *Dialogue* is followed by a plain personal narrative. Fraser, *Journal of the Siege of Quebec* (Ibid.). Fraser was an officer in the Seventy-eighth Highlanders. *Journal of the Siege of Quebec, by a Gentleman in an Eminent Station on the Spot*, Dublin, 1759. *Journal of the Particular Transactions during the Siege of Quebec* (*Notes and Queries*, XX.). The writer was a soldier or non-commissioned officer serving in the light infantry.

Memoirs of the Siege of Quebec and Total Reduction of Canada, by John Johnson, Clerk and Quarter-master Sergeant to the Fifty-eighth Regiment. A manuscript of 176 pages, written when Johnson was a pensioner at Chelsea (England). The handwriting is exceedingly neat and clear; and the style, though often grandiloquent, is creditable to a writer in his station. This curious production was found among the papers of Thomas McDonough, Esq., formerly British Consul at Boston, and is in possession of his grandson, my relative, George Francis Parkman, Esq., who, by inquiries at the Chelsea Hospital, learned that Johnson was still living in 1802.

I have read and collated with extreme care all the above authorities, with others which need not be mentioned.

Among several manuscript maps and plans showing the operations of the siege may be mentioned one entitled, *Plan of the Town and Basin of Quebec and Part of the Adjacent Country, shewing the principal Encampments and Works of the British Army commanded by Major Gen! Wolfe, and those of the French Army by Lieut. Gen! the Marquis of Montcalm.* It is the work of three engineers of Wolfe's army, and is on a scale of eight hundred feet to an inch. A fac-simile from the original in possession of the Royal Engineers is before me.

Among the "King's Maps," British Museum (CXIX. 27), is a very large colored plan of operations at Quebec in 1759, 1760, superbly executed in minute detail.

J
Chapter XXVIII. Fall of Quebec

Death and Burial of Montcalm.—Johnstone, who had every means of knowing the facts, says that Montcalm was carried after his wound to the house of the surgeon Arnoux. Yet it is not quite certain that he died there. According to Knox, his death took place at the General Hospital; according to the modern author of the *Ursulines de Québec*, at the Château St.-Louis. But the General Hospital was a mile out of the town, and in momentary danger of capture by the English; while the Château had been made untenable by the batteries of Point Levi, being immediately exposed to their fire. Neither of these places was one to which the dying general was likely to be removed, and it is probable that he was suffered to die in peace at the house of the surgeon.

It has been said that the story of the burial of Montcalm in a grave partially formed by the explosion of a bomb, rests only on the assertion in his epitaph, composed in 1761 by the Academy of Inscriptions at the instance of Bougainville. There is, however, other evidence of the fact. The naval captain Foligny, writing on the spot at the time of the burial, says in his Diary, under date of September 14: "A huit heures du soir, dans l'église des Ursulines, fut enterré dans une fosse faite sous la chaire *par le travail de la Bombe*, M. le Marquis de Montcalm, décédé du matin à 4 heures après avoir reçu tous les Sacrements. Jamais Général n'avoit été plus aimé de sa troupe et plus universellement regretté. Il étoit d'un esprit supérieur, doux, gracieux, affable, familier à tout le monde, ce qui lui avoit fait gagner la confiance de toute la Colonie: *requiescat in pace*."

The author of *Les Ursulines de Québec* says : "Un des projectiles ayant fait une large ouverture dans le plancher de bas, on en profita pour creuser la fosse du général."

The *Boston Post Boy and Advertiser*, in its issue of Dec. 3, 1759, contains a letter from "an officer of distinction" at Quebec to Messrs. Green and Russell, proprietors of the newspaper. This letter contains the following words: "He [*Montcalm*] died the next day; and, with a little Improvement, one of our 13-inch Shell-Holes served him for a Grave."

The particulars of his burial are from the *Acte Mortuaire du Marquis de Montcalm* in the registers of the Church of Notre Dame de Québec, and from that valuable chronicle, *Les Ursulines de Québec*, composed by the Superior of the convent. A nun of the sisterhood, Mère Aimable Dubé de Saint-

Ignace, was, when a child, a witness of the scene, and preserved a vivid memory of it to the age of eighty-one.

K
Chapter XXIX. Sainte-Foy

Strength of the French and English at the Battle of Ste.-Foy.

In the Public Record Office (*America and West Indies*, XCIX.) are preserved the tabular returns of the garrison of Quebec for 1759, 1760, sent by Murray to the War Office. They show the exact condition of each regiment, in all ranks, for every month of the autumn, winter, and spring. The return made out on the 24th of April, four days before the battle, shows that the total number of rank and file, exclusive of non-commissioned officers and drummers, was 6,808, of whom 2,612 were fit for duty in Quebec, and 654 at other places in Canada; that is, at Ste.-Foy, Old Lorette, and the other outposts. This gives a total of 3,266 rank and file fit for duty at or near Quebec; besides which there were between one hundred and two hundred artillerymen, and a company of rangers. This was Murray's whole available force at the time. Of the rest of the 6,808 who appear in the return, 2,299 were invalids at Quebec, and 669 in New York; 538 were on service in Halifax and New York, and 36 were absent on furlough. These figures nearly answer to the condensed statement of Fraser, and confirm the various English statements of the numbers that took part in the battle; namely, 3,140 (Knox), 3,000 (John Johnson), 3,111, and elsewhere, in round numbers, 3,000 (Murray). Lévis, with natural exaggeration, says 4,000. Three or four hundred were left in Quebec to guard the walls when the rest marched out.

I have been thus particular because a Canadian writer, Garneau, says: "Murray sortit de la ville le 28 au matin à la tête de toute la garnison, dont les seules troupes de la ligne comptaient encore 7,714 combattants, non compris les officiers." To prove this, he cites the pay-roll of the garrison; which, in fact, corresponds to the returns of the same date, if non-commissioned officers, drummers, and artillerymen are counted with the rank and file. But Garneau falls into a double error. He assumes, first, that there were no men on the sick list; and secondly, that there were none absent from Quebec; when in reality, as the returns show, considerably more than half were in one or the other of these categories. The pay-rolls were made out at the headquarters of each corps, and always included the entire number of men enlisted in it, whether sick or well, present or absent. On the same fallacious premises Garneau affirms that Wolfe, at the battle on the Plains of Abraham, had eight thousand soldiers, or a little less than double his actual force.

Having stated, as above, that Murray marched out of Quebec with at least 7,714 effective troops, Garneau, not very consistently, goes on to say that he advanced against Lévis with six thousand or seven thousand men; and he adds that the two armies were about equal, because Lévis had left some detachments behind to guard his boats and artillery. The number of the French, after they had all reached the field, was, in truth, about seven thousand; at the beginning of the fight it seems not to have exceeded five thousand. The *Relation de la seconde Bataille de Québec* says: "Notre petite armée consistoit *au moment de l'action* en 3,000 hommes de troupes reglées et 2,000 Canadiens ou sauvages." A large number of Canadians came up from Sillery while the affair went on; and as the whole French army, except the detachments mentioned by Garneau, had passed the night at no greater distance from the field than Ste.-Foy and Sillery, the last man must have reached it before the firing was half over.

Chronology

1823   Born in Boston, September 16. His father, the Reverend Francis Parkman, was pastor of the New North Church and the son of a wealthy Boston merchant. His mother, Caroline Hall Parkman, was a descendant of John Cotton. Other children were his half-sister Sarah (by his father's first marriage) and younger sisters Caroline and Mary Eliza and brother John Eliot.

1831–36   For reasons of health, lives on farm of maternal grandparents in Medford, Massachusetts. Regularly plays and hunts in nearby woods (Middlesex Fells), where he comes to love outdoor life.

1836–40   Attends Chauncy Hall School in Boston. In a shed behind his father's house, conducts chemical experiments which (he wrote later) "served little other purpose than injuring himself by confinement, poisoning him with noxious gases, and occasionally scorching him with some ill-starred explosion." Studies Greek, Latin, and English literature. Admires Scott, Cooper, and Byron. Writes in verse an account of the tournament in *Ivanhoe*.

1840   Enters Harvard College. Begins independent historical research, consulting Jared Sparks, the first Harvard professor of modern history. Already showing "symptoms of 'Injuns' on the brain" and looking ahead to his forest epic ("the whole course of the American conflict between France and England"), he spends much time horseback riding, boxing, and shooting.

1841   Makes first trip into wilderness of New Hampshire, and almost annually for several years thereafter explores White Mountains, Lake Champlain, Glens Falls, and Lake George. Trains intensely to perfect his shooting and riding, and learns to canoe.

1843–44   Suffers first breakdown and leaves college for several months. Through winter and spring travels in Italy, Switzerland, France, and the United Kingdom. His first extended observation of European priests and monks (in Rome, where he stays at convent of Passionist Fathers) both attracts him to Roman Catholicism and deepens his objections to it.

1844   Elected Phi Beta Kappa, graduates from Harvard, and enters Harvard Law School.

1845   Publishes in *Knickerbocker, or New-York Monthly Magazine* five sketches about his early vacation excursions. Conducts research on Pontiac in New York, Pennsylvania, and Michigan.

1846   Graduates from Harvard Law School in January, resisting severe visual disability by having his sister read law books to him. Travels to New York and Pennsylvania for research on Pontiac's conspiracy, but by late March he is alarmingly overwrought. Goes then with his cousin Quincy Shaw, via St. Louis and the site of Pontiac's assassination, to the California and Oregon Trail and Fort Laramie. Hunts buffalo. Lives among the Sioux for several weeks. Joins their summer hunt for buffalo and their preparations for war, although he is weakened by dysentery and his nervous disorder. Breaks down completely soon after his return to New England. While convalescing at a clinic on Staten Island, New York, dictates *The Oregon Trail* to a member of his family or to a paid secretary.

1847   Publishes "The Oregon Trail. Or a Summer's Journey Out of Bounds" serially in *Knickerbocker*, the first installment signed "A Bostonian," the others under his own name, Francis Parkman, Jr.

1848   Begins work on *The Conspiracy of Pontiac,* first of a series of volumes on Anglo-French wars in North America. Nervous ailment persists; symptoms include feeling of nervous exhaustion and an inability to bear sunlight, to write with eyes open, or to concentrate on any intellectual subject for more than a few minutes at a time. He follows the historian William H. Prescott's method: has documents read aloud to him and writes his notes and drafts of the manuscript in a box fitted with wire grids that guide his hand.

1849   Publishes *The California and Oregon Trail* ("California" added by publisher to exploit gold-rush fever), subsequently issued as *The Oregon Trail*.

1850   Marries Catherine Scollay Bigelow, daughter of well-known Boston doctor. Three children: Grace Parkman Coffin (1851-1928), Francis Parkman III (1854-1857), Katherine Parkman Coolidge (1858-1900).

1851   Publishes *The History of the Conspiracy of Pontiac* (2 volumes). Permanently hampered by ailing knee joint.

1852   Publishes admiring essay on James Fenimore Cooper's life (1789–1851) and works, in *North American Review*.

1853–56   Illness forces him to abandon historical work. Begins novel for diversion and takes up study of horticulture.

1856   Publishes *Vassall Morton*, his partly autobiographical and only novel, emphasizing the protagonist's endurance through extreme physical and emotional hardship. Visits Montreal, Ottawa, and Quebec (October–November).

1857   His son, Francis, dies.

1858   His wife dies. His nervous illness worsens; he feels as if "a steel band is tightening around his head." Consults doctors in Paris, one of whom predicts he will go mad.

1859   Returns to Boston via Nice and Genoa and lives with mother and two sisters. His daughters live with his sister-in-law. Joins Massachusetts Horticultural Society and begins to spend summers at Jamaica Pond, where he pursues his horticultural avocation.

1862–63   Enters into business partnership to sell flowers, but firm dissolves within a year. Aroused by Civil War crisis and chagrined that poor health disqualifies him for service. Writes series of letters to Boston *Daily Advertiser* on decline of political leadership.

1865   Publication of *Pioneers of France in the New World*, a popular work, establishes his reputation as a historian. Travels to Richmond to collect Confederate papers for Boston Athenaeum.

1866   Publishes *The Book of Roses*, starts life-long correspondence with Abbé Henri-Raymond Casgrain of Canada, and begins series of Canadian visits for historical research.

1867   Travels for five weeks through Iowa, Illinois, Missouri, and Minnesota, gathering material on discovery of the Mississippi. *The Jesuits in North America in the Seventeenth Century* published.

1868   Elected to Board of Overseers at Harvard. In Paris (November) to recover from illness. Consults material on Old Northwest and colonial New York, assisted by government archivist, Pierre Margry.

1869   Leaves Paris (March) for Boston. *The Discovery of the Great West* published.

1870   Publishes enlarged edition of *Pontiac* as *The Conspiracy of Pontiac and the Indian War after the Conquest of Canada*. Explores Mt. Desert, Maine. Publishes reminiscence of his stay (1844) at convent of Passionist Fathers in Rome.

1871   First meeting with Abbé Casgrain when Casgrain comes to Boston. Parkman makes brief visit to Nova Scotia and New Brunswick. Accepts professorship in horticulture at Bussey Institute (Harvard) but resigns in less than a year. After his mother dies, he shares Chestnut Street house with sister, Lizzie, for the rest of his life.

1872   In Europe (July–October) and sees Pierre Margry in Paris. Revises *The Oregon Trail*.

1873   Visits Canada for several weeks (August) to increase his knowledge of French-Canadians. Sees Casgrain. Elected to Saturday Club, which was founded by Emerson before the Civil War.

1874   *The Old Régime in Canada* published. Howells' review introduces Parkman to wider public in America and England. Visits Quebec (July).

1875   Elected to the Harvard Corporation.

1876   Reviews first volume of Pierre Margry, *Découvertes et Établissements des Français dans l'Ouest et dans le Sud de l'Amérique Septentrionale (1614–1754), Mémoires et Documents originaux*, in *The Nation*. By persuading the U.S. Congress to subsidize this edition, Parkman gains access to materials he was not allowed to see when composing *The Discovery of the Great West*. Produces a new flower, *lilium Parkmanii*, and is elected to the Royal Historical Society in London. Visits Lake Champlain and Ottawa (August–September).

1877   Publishes *Count Frontenac and New France under Louis XIV*.

1878   Articles on suffrage and democracy (1878–1880) answered by feminists and liberals. Laval University's proposal to award Parkman honorary degree blocked by Catholic opposition offended by his anti-clericalism. Visits Lake George, Fort Ticonderoga, Quebec (November).

1879   Publishes *La Salle and the Discovery of the Great West*, an enlarged and revised edition of *The Discovery of the Great West* (1869), based on documents in Margry's collection. Awarded honorary degree from McGill University. Examines Louisbourg fortress in Nova Scotia (August). *North American Review* publishes his "The Woman Question," which argues against women's suffrage.

1880   Helps to found St. Botolph Club in Boston.

1884   Publishes *Montcalm and Wolfe* ahead of its chronological place in *France and England in North America* because it has always been the most important part of the history for him and he wants to be sure to complete it before he dies.

1885   Travels through Florida to study the scenes of action described in *Pioneers of France*, places he had not been able to visit while writing *Pioneers* during the Civil War. Publishes revised edition of *Pioneers*, with new descriptions of Florida and some revisions of the section on Champlain. Awarded LL.D. by Williams College.

1887   Publishes *Some of the Reasons Against Woman Suffrage*. Travels to Europe for the last time.

1889   Awarded LL.D. by Harvard.

1890   Publishes *Our Common Schools* to defend the public schools against what he considers dangerous competition from parochial schools.

1892   Publishes *A Half-Century of Conflict*, the last two volumes of his *France and England in North America*.

1893   In June completes a new section to be added to the beginning of *The Old Régime in Canada* because he has gained access to documents that were unavailable when he published the first edition. Dies November 8, 1893, at Jamaica Pond, Boston. His *Journals* and *Letters* were published in 1947 and 1960, respectively.

Note on the Texts

This volume reprints the last three parts of Francis Parkman's seven-part history, *France and England in North America*; the four preceding parts are reprinted in the companion volume. Parkman published these seven works separately, under their individual titles, between 1865 and 1892. He referred to them as "parts" of a single enterprise. "Each work," he wrote, "is designed to be a unit in itself, independently of the rest; but the whole, taken as a series, will form a connected history of France in the New World." The three parts (or works) that make up this volume—*Count Frontenac and New France under Louis XIV., A Half-Century of Conflict*, and *Montcalm and Wolfe*—went through many reprintings during Parkman's lifetime. His publishers, Little, Brown and Co., referred to these issues as "editions," but in every case they were reprinted from the original stereotype plates.

Parkman first conceived the idea of a comprehensive history of France and England in North America while an undergraduate at Harvard in the 1840s; and as early as 1851, when he published *The Conspiracy of Pontiac*, he tried out a version of the entire narrative, from the earliest explorations through the Indian wars of the mid-1760s. He spent the following forty years gathering the materials for his study, and he traveled widely in both Europe and North America, to collect manuscripts, consult archives, and visit sites described in his history. This accumulation of data became a vital part of his project, and although his ill-health and the weakness of his eyes forced him to employ assistants to read aloud from his sources and to write from his dictation, he took great pains to insure the accuracy of his work. With the aid of readers, he corrected his own proofs and dictated changes directly to the printers.

He revised only three of the seven parts of *France and England in North America*, and the changes made in each of these volumes were designed to incorporate new material that had been originally unavailable. To approximate Parkman's own conception of *France and England in North America*, this volume reprints the texts of the first editions, or, for the three parts he materially revised, the first edition in which those changes were incorporated. Specifically, this volume reprints the first editions of *Count Frontenac and New France under Louis XIV.* (1877), *A Half-Century of Conflict* (1892), and *Montcalm and Wolfe* (1884). The text of *France and England in North America* in the edition of Parkman's *Complete Works* (1897–98) was prepared after his death and without his supervision. Collation has shown that, though the text is based on the same earlier editions chosen for inclusion here, unauthorized changes were introduced editorially in the diction, orthography, and punctuation.

Count Frontenac (Part Five) was first published in 1877 and reprinted from the original plates many times. No changes were ever made in the text of the work. The only change was the addition of a paragraph to the note on page 119. (This paragraph appears in the Notes to this volume, 119.36.) For example, though Parkman brought out a revised and retitled edition of Part Three as *La Salle and the Discovery of the Great West* in 1879, the subsequent reprintings of *Count Frontenac* continue to cite the 1869 edition, *The Discovery of the Great West.* Thus it is the first edition of *Count Frontenac* which must be considered the most authoritative text, and it is the one reprinted here.

A Half-Century of Conflict (Part Six of the series) appeared in two volumes in 1892, only a year before Parkman's death. He made no changes at all in this first edition, which provides the text reprinted here.

Montcalm and Wolfe (Part Seven) was published in two volumes in 1884, eight years before Part Six, because Parkman's health, never good, seemed to be growing worse and he feared he might not live to finish the part that had earlier given him the inspiration for the entire history. The first-edition text was never revised. A portrait of General Wolfe was added by Parkman in 1887, and is reproduced in this volume. Parkman's letters mention one other change he intended to make—the correction of the spelling of Foligny to Foligné—but that emendation was not made in subsequent reprintings. This volume, therefore, reprints as most authoritative the first edition of *Montcalm and Wolfe*, and places it as the concluding work in *France and England in North America*.

The standards for American English continue to fluctuate and in some ways were conspicuously different in earlier periods from what they are now. In nineteenth-century writings, for example, a word might be spelled in more than one way, even in the same work, and such variations might be carried into print. Commas were sometimes used expressively to suggest the movements of voice, and capitals were sometimes meant to give significances to a word beyond those it might have in its uncapitalized form. Since modernization would remove such effects, this volume has preserved the spelling, punctuation, capitalization, and wording of those editions, which, of the available texts, appear most faithful to Parkman's intentions. It has also retained the original tables of contents despite their inconsistencies with the chapter headings found in the body of the text. The present volume represents the *texts* of these editions; it does not attempt to reproduce the features of their typographic design—such as the display capitalization of chapter openings.

Some changes, however, have been made. Parkman's references to page numbers have been changed to conform to the pages in these volumes, and his three indexes have been combined to make up a single one here. Obvious typographical errors have been corrected, and they are here listed: 37.17, Fenelon; 119.32, Greenalgh's; 168.39, *Mather*; 214.31, Relation; 255.3, Malecites; 262.5, Pentegeot; 272.37, Calières; 321.21, Mascontins; 346.3, others'; 420.29, in chief; 442.14, that the; 750.13, qusqu'au; 799.21, Disappoinment; 805.18, to to; 809.11, istead; 1150.32–33, show-shoes; 1207.23, Roger; 1211.11, Charlebourg; 1211.32, Charlebourg.

Notes

In the notes below, the numbers refer to page and line of the present volume (the line count includes chapter headings). No note is made for material included in a standard desk-reference book. Notes printed at the foot of pages within the text are by the author.

COUNT FRONTENAC AND NEW FRANCE UNDER LOUIS XIV.

119.36   Parkman later added the following paragraph to the note that ends here: *The Chevalier de Baugy, aide-de-camp to Denonville, kept a journal of the expedition which has lately been discovered among the papers of his descendant, Madame de Vaveray. His account of the battle is confused and adds little to what is known from other sources.*

A HALF-CENTURY OF CONFLICT

597.37–40   The . . . thousands.]   Parkman alludes here to his adventures in the West in the summer of 1846, adventures which he described in *The Oregon Trail*, 1849.

655.35   *Pepperell*]   This inconsistent spelling appears in a number of the citations of reports, and throughout *Montcalm and Wolfe*.

MONTCALM AND WOLFE

903.7   eat]   Here Parkman uses the archaic form of the past tense, usually pronounced *et*.

1087.15–16   Parc-aux-Cerfs]   Here Parkman alludes to the notorious retreat, built at Versailles on the site of a "hunting box," where Louis XV "received and gave hospitality to young women of easy virtue." In Parkman's day, lurid tales of "an immense park . . . and a whole troop of innocent does pursued by a libidinous monarch" had not yet been discredited. See Pierre Gaxotte, *Louis XV and His Times* (Philadelphia, 1934), pp. 129–130.

1196   WOLFE]   In 1887, Parkman added the following note before the new frontispiece:

THE PORTRAIT OF WOLFE

The portrait of WOLFE in the present edition of this book was never before made known to the public. The picture from which it is taken was painted from life by Highmore, an English artist well known in the last century. When Wolfe, then a mere boy, received his first commission and was about to join the army, he caused his

likeness to be painted in uniform, and gave it, as a token of attachment, to Reverend Samuel Francis Swinden, Vicar of Greenwich,
whose pupil he had been, and whose friend he remained for life.
The descendants of this gentleman still possess it; and it is to their
kindness, and especially to that of his great-great-granddaughter,
Miss Florence Armstrong, that I owe the photograph which is here
reproduced. It is believed that Wolfe never again sat for his portrait.
After his death his mother caused a miniature to be taken from the
Highmore picture, and from this several enlarged copies were afterwards made.

The portrait in possession of Admiral Warde, hitherto supposed
to be an original, now seems to be one of these copies. It appeared
first in Wright's "Life of Wolfe," and is the same that was engraved
for the early editions of "Montcalm and Wolfe." The existence of
the present more trustworthy and interesting picture has been
known to few besides its fortunate possessors.

15 October, 1887.

1342.39 Foligny] Parkman said in a letter that he would correct this mis-
spelling of Foligné in subsequent editions, but he did not do so.

LIBRARY OF CONGRESS CATALOGING IN PUBLICATION DATA

PARKMAN, FRANCIS, 1823–1893.
    France and England in North America.

    (The Library of America)
    Edited by David Levin.
    Includes bibliographical references and indexes.
    Contents: v.1. Pioneers of France in the New World. The Jesuits in
North America in the seventeenth century. La Salle and the discovery of the
Great West. The old régime in Canada—v.2. Count Frontenac and New
France under Louis XIV. A half-century of conflict. Montcalm and Wolfe.
    1. Canada—History—To 1763 (New France) I. Levin, David,
1924– . II. Title. III. Series: Library of America.
    F1030.P24   1983   971.01   82-18658
    ISBN 0-940450-10-0 (v.1)   AACR2
    ISBN 0-940450-11-9 (v.2)

Index

Abenakis, Indians of Acadia and Maine, 162, 163, 168, 225, 265–66, 861, 873, 988, 1172, 1489–92; attack the Christian Iroquois, 172; their domain, 245; missions, 246; attack on York, 252; incited against the English colonists, 252; visit Villebon at St. John, 254; their attack on Wells, 255; is foiled, 257; are won back by the French, 260–62; treaty with the English at Pemaquid, 260; influenced by missionary priests, 269–71; active in William and Mary's War, 360; living in Maine, 360; their treacherous peace with Governor Dudley, 360–61; attack the towns of Wells, Casco, etc., 364–69; troops sent by Governor Dudley for defence against them, 369; join in an attack on Deerfield, 373; march with their captives away from Deerfield, 382–89; considered in the Treaty of Utrecht, 459; to be transported to Isle Royale, 461; burn the village of Brunswick, 494; conclude a treaty of peace, 505; join in war-parties from Montreal, 719; propose an attack upon Fort Massachusetts, to Rigaud, 732; they attack the fort, 737; their humane treatment of the prisoners, 742; their general devastation of villages in the Hoosac valley, 743; settled in Canada, 861; at Fort Duquesne, 948–49; assist the Canadian militia, 1098; called to a council of war by Montcalm, 1175–78; position of the English at Fort William Henry, 1184–85; the massacre at Fort William Henry (see *William Henry, Fort*), 1191–94, evidence concerning the massacre, 1194 *note;* their conversion to Christianity, 1194 *note;* Rogers sent to destroy one of their towns, 1369, 1371–74 *note;* seize the messengers of Amherst, 1369; the St. Francis settlement, 1371; their cruelty, 1371, 1372;

statistics of warriors at the siege of Quebec, 1497.

Abercrombie, Captain, sent with summons for the surrender of Port Royal, 438.

Abercromby, General James, 957 *note;* to supersede Webb in command of the army, 1105; to resign in favor of Earl Loudon, 1105; arrives at Albany, 1115–16; sends a letter of approbation to Rogers, 1147 *note;* Loudon recalled from office, 1228; succeeds Loudon in command, 1228; to lead the expedition against Louisbourg, 1228; Amherst prevented from co-operation with, 1247; the rejoicing at the fall of Louisbourg, 1248; Amherst plans to assist him at Lake George, 1250; expedition led by, against Ticonderoga, 1256–74 *note;* his camp at Lake George, 1257; number of his troops, 1257, 1258; his leadership, 1258; his opinion of Lord Howe, 1258; statistics of the expedition against Ticonderoga, 1260, 1492–93; the passage of Lake George, 1260–61; the army lost in the woods, 1262; effect of the death of Lord Howe upon his army, 1263–64; the army reaches the Falls, 1264; statements concerning the French defences, 1265–66; different courses of action open to, 1266; his encounter with Montcalm at Ticonderoga, 1267–72; the eve of battle, 1267; order of the assault, 1268–69; his losses, 1272, 1493; his retreat, 1272, 1275, 1308; a disgraceful order sent to Colonel Cummings, 1275; nickname given to, by the Provincials, 1275; visited by the chaplains, 1277; sends a war-party into the woods, 1279–81; receives news of the fall of Fort Frontenac, 1283; despatches Bradstreet to capture Fort Frontenac, 1284; Fort Frontenac dismantled,

1283–84; his camp broken up, 1285; joined by Amherst, 1285; neglects to assist Forbes's army, 1303; Amherst's superior leadership, 1362; his letter to Pitt, 1493.

Abraham, an Indian, 963.

Abraham Martin, his name given to the Heights of Abraham, 1394.

Abraham, the Heights of, 1375, 1475, 1498–1500; Wolfe discovers a path ascending the cliff, 1384; general belief in the safety of the heights, 1386; ascent of the troops under Wolfe's direction, 1389, 1393; statistics concerning Wolfe's army, and the action upon, 1498–1500.

Abraham, the Plains of, 1335, 1400 note, 1421, 1441, 1503; inaccessibility of, 1375; Guienne's troops not at their post, 1392; origin of the name, and description of, 1394; the fall of Quebec, 1402–19, 1419 note, 1420 note.

Acadia (Nova Scotia and westward to the Kennebec), 410, 966, 1175; exposed to inroads from New England, 92, 243; the region, 243–46; the war in, 243–65; relations with New England, 246; hostilities, 247–48; Villebon governor, border war, 251, 254–60; New England attacks, 269; a governor appointed for, 410; its people deprived of their fishing by privateers, 410; they fight the Massachusetts privateers, 411; the conquest of, 439; offers made by Louis XIV. to retain, 459; creeds and politics at, 464; neglected by England, 468, 469; population of, 468, 859, 909, 929–30, 1026, 1039; France endeavors to repossess, 469; questions of boundary, 477, 906, 929–31, 970, 1007–08, 1023; Governor Shirley urges the protection of, 688; troops sent by Governor Shirley to protect, 696; attacks made on New England, 864; ceded to England by France, 906, 909–10; conditions of residence for French subjects, 906–07; conflict for, 906–31; conquest of, by Nicholson in 1710, 906; English power in, 907; the naval station at

Chebucto, 907; determination of the French to recover it, 909–10; religion, priests, and government of, 909–10, 913, 918, 1023; six principal parishes of, 909–10; documents on the affairs, of, 910–11; attention given by Count Raymond to the affairs of, 915; wretched condition of the emigrants from, 919–20; Joseph Le Loutre, the vicar-general of, 922; Beaubassin occupied by the English, 923–27; emigration encouraged by the French, 924; need of communication between Quebec and Cape Breton, 929; the census of, 929; the question of French or English ownership, 929–30, 969–70, 1007, 1009, 1472; expedition against, to be led by Lieutenant-Colonel Monckton, 977; sad condition of the people of, 1006, 1007; questions of policy for the French and English in Acadia, 1007–10; the French use the inhabitants to carry on their war-parties, 1007; importance of her harbors, 1008; probability of French invasion, 1008; arrival of the English troops, 1014; conditions leading to the expulsion of the inhabitants from, 1018–28; removal of the inhabitants from their homes, 1019, 1026–40; encampment of the New England troops, 1029; arrival of the vessels of transport at Nova Scotia, 1034; arrival of Saul with provisions, 1036; embarkation of the Acadians, 1036–38; families of British stock settle in, 1039; return of a portion of the exiles, 1039; the act of expatriation criticised, 1039; capture of forts by the English, 1070; plans of Vaudreuil for conquest, 1317.

Acadian missionaries labor against the British Government, 469; their political work, 470; complaints of English governors against them, 470, 471.

Acadians, the, 909; their migration to Isle Royale desired, 462; their oath to Queen Anne, 463; induced to migrate, 465; their freedom of worship, 469; refuse oath of allegiance to

George I., 473; the proclamation of General Philipps concerning their oath, 473; their oath of allegiance to George II., 474; their child-like dependence, 475; divided in sentiment between their allegiance to the French or English, 689; made British subjects by the Treaty of Utrecht, 690; known as "Neutral French," 691; their illiteracy, social quality, population, etc., 691; excited at the appearance of D'Anville's fleet, 692; Governor Shirley's plan concerning them, 692–93 and *note,* 694; incited to insurrection by the French, 692; proposal of Governor Shirley to exclude French priests, 694; and convert them to Protestantism, 695; Ramesay endeavors to excite them to insurrection, 696; threatened by Ramesay against intercourse with the English, 708; endeavor to conciliate both French and English, 709 and *note;* ordered to take arms against the English, 709; their deplorable condition, 710; religious privileges accorded to, by the treaty of Utrecht, 906, 1020; required to take the oath of allegiance to England, 906, 907, 1023; form of the oath of allegiance, 907 *note,* 1026–27; influence of the French upon, 907, 909–31, 1006–08, 1011–13; the war of 1745, 907; their hostility to the English encouraged by the French priests, 907, 912–19, 922, 927, 1006, 1008, 1021, 1023, 1481–84; their religion, 907, 910, 1023, 1038; taught to love France, and to call themselves French subjects, 909–10, 1006, 1008; their condition and numbers from 1748 to 1752, 909; official papers relating to, 910–11; their fear of the Indians, 910–11, 919, 922; treatment received from the English, and mildness of their rule, 910–11, 1007, 1024, 1481–82; quotations from Roma, alluding to, 911; their neutrality, 911, 1022; their oath of allegiance to be made more binding, 911–12; deputies sent to meet Cornwallis at Halifax, 912; join the Indian war-parties of the French against the English, 912, 916, 1024–26, 1481–84; order of Cornwallis issued to, concerning the oath, 912; plans of the French to recover their possessions, 912–14; promise good behavior and a reasonable compliance, 912; their refusal to take an unqualified oath of allegiance to George II., 912; their covert war, 913–17; advised by Desherbiers and others to refuse the oath of allegiance, 914; letters from French officials showing their secret work against the English, 914; encouraged by the French to emigrate to French lands, 915, 919–20; testimony of Prévost concerning, 917; cruelly and dishonorably treated by the priest Le Loutre, 919–20, 922–28, 1006–08, 1011–13, 1482, 1483; wretchedness of the emigrants after leaving their English farms, 919–20, 927–28, 1006–08, 1012–13; speech of Cornwallis to the deputies, 920–21; French method of terrifying, by using the Micmacs, 922–23; treatment received from Hopson, 922; occupation of Beaubassin by the English, 923–28; disaffection among, 924; forcibly removed by the French from Beaubassin, and obliged to live on French ground, 924; the murder of Captain Howe, 925–26; a French fort to be built on Beauséjour, 927; contest between French and English, 927–28; ordered to swear allegiance to France, 927; proclamation of Lawrence concerning, 927; a portion of the inhabitants cross the French lines, 928; absurd demands of Le Loutre, 928; their suffering inside the French lines, 928, 1012–13; plans of Shirley to send away from Acadia all French settlers, 1006, 1021; a portion of the people transported to French settlements, 1007 and *note;* fears of the English, 1009–10; supplies sent to the emigrants, 1011; their supplies stolen by the officials, 1011; desire of, to return to their English allegiance, 1012–13; false statements of Le Loutre, 1012–13; plans of Le Loutre for the emigrants, 1012–13; an annoyance to the English, 1013; dealt with by the French with heartlessness, 1013; harsh treatment received from Governor Duquesne, 1013; prevented by Le Loutre from appealing to Duquesne, 1013; disloyalty of, 1015, 1021, 1023; join the French garrison, 1015; the siege of Beauséjour by the English, 1015–19, 1023; their terror upon the arrival of the English troops, 1015; assisted by Le Loutre at Beauséjour, 1016; capitulation of Beauséjour, 1017; condition leading to the explusion of, from Acadia, 1018–28; ordered by Monckton to meet him at Beauséjour, 1019; sentence pronounced upon, by Monckton, and prisoners taken at Fort Cumberland, 1019–20, 1027–28; again ordered to take the oath of allegiance, 1020; demands made by the priests with regard to their return to their home, 1020; explanation of the imprisonment of, 1020–28; prevented by the priests from joining the English, 1020; refuse to take the oath of allegiance to England, 1020; desire of Shirley to expel from the country, 1021; instruction sent to Governor Lawrence with regard to, 1021; to be compelled to take the oath of allegiance, 1021; depicted by Abbé Raynal, 1022; marriages among, 1022–23; their animals, 1022; their clothing, 1022; their country commonly considered as Arcadia, 1022; their food, 1022; their furniture, 1022; their houses, 1022, 1029; their means and mode of living, 1022–23; their population, 1022; their village life, 1022–23; their priests, religion, and government, 1023; only a few take the required oath, 1023; the priests assist the French Bishop and Governor of Canada, 1023; loyal to Louis XV., and untrue to George II., 1023, 1026; described by Dieréville, 1023

note; the oath of allegiance administered by George Lawrence, 1023; emigration of a small number of, to Cape Breton, 1023; they return, and take the oath of allegiance, 1023; kind treatment vouchsafed to the loyal inhabitants, 1023; memorial brought by, to Captain Murray, 1023–25; contents of their memorial sent to Governor Lawrence, 1023–25; their insolence, 1024; ordered to take the oath of allegiance to England, or to leave the country, 1025, 1026; again refuse the oath of allegiance, 1026; declare their preference to lose their lands, 1026; instructions quoted with regard to the removal of, 1027–28; instrumentality of the priests in the expulsion of, 1027 and *note*; plans of removal discussed by the English, 1027; removal of, by the English, from their homes, 1027–40; summoned to meet Winslow to hear the orders of George II., 1030–33; meet Winslow in the church at Grand Pré, 1031–34; declared prisoners of the King, 1033; arrival of the transports, 1034; number in charge of Winslow, 1034; unite with the Indians to attack the English, 1034; detention of, on the vessels, 1035 and *note;* supplies for prisoners delayed, 1035–36; cases of the separation of families, 1036, 1037; removal of, described, 1036–38; effort of the prisoners to escape, 1037; number of, embarked for the colonies, 1037–38; distribution of the exiles, 1038; exiles on one of the vessels escape to the St. John, 1038; guerilla warfare against the English, 1038; heartless outrages practised upon, in Canada, 1038–39, 1213; treatment received in the colonies, 1038; arrival of the exiles in Louisiana, 1039; progenitors of the present race, 1039; death of, 1039; sent to England, 1039; sent to France, 1039; at the siege of Louisbourg, 1238, 1241; false dealing of, Boishébert, 1312; their hostility to the English, 1320.

Acts of Parliament. See *Parliament*.

Adams (East Hoosac), Mass., 728.

Adams, a wagoner, carries a letter of warning to Fort Lyman, 1048; shot by the Indians, 1050.

Adams, Captain, 1016 *note*, 1030–31; removal of the Acadians, 1035, 1037 *note*.

Adams, Mr., of Medfield, 488 *note*.

Adams, Parson, 848.

Addison, 434.

Adirondacks, 1152.

Admiralty, Lords of the, citation from letters to, 968.

Admiralty, the position held by Anson, 966.

Africa, 1225, 1229; the French driven from Guinea, 1228; the power of England over, 1469; France cedes Senegal, 1473.

Aigues Mortes, dungeons of, 860.

Aix-la-Chapelle, the Peace of, signed, 744; the treaty of, 849, 858, 870, 875, 910, 1090, 1232, 1473; questions of boundary to be settled by commissioners, 929–31.

Akins, Mr., 476 *note*.

Alabama, 536.

Alabama River, the French propose to build forts at, 610.

Alais, 1154.

Albany, Fort, on Hudson's Bay, taken by Canadians, 103.

Albany, N.Y., 343, 369, 864, 889, 961, 1004, 1044, 1049, 1057, 1068, 1118, 1131, 1140, 1152, 1198, 1259, 1260; an Indian mart, 63; Indian council there, 73, 94; Iroquois summoned thither by Dongan, 120; by Schuyler, 287; expedition against Montreal, 181; the fur-trade carried on at, 347; a rendezvous for troops, 426; the fort at, neglected, 715; Indian ravages in vicinity of, 717; conservatism of, in the eighteenth century, 867; meeting of Indians and commissioners, 887; congress of Indians and English held, 962–63; plan of Franklin for colonial union, 964; the Dutch at, 976, 1064; the base of military operations, 1063–64; described by Mrs.

Grant, 1064; headquarters of Shirley, 1106, 1112; the Indians misled by the traders, 1110; plans of Vaudreuil, 1112; return of Bradstreet, 1113; arrival of Webb and Abercromby, 1115–16; rumors of danger from the enemy, 1126; news sent to, of the death of Lord Howe, 1264; advance of Bradstreet, 1284.

Albemarle, Duke of, aids Phips, 178.

Albemarle, Earl of, expedition of, 1470.

Albemarle, Lord, Governor of Virginia, 917 *note*, 937; English ambassador at Versailles, 967; his death, 970.

"Alcide," the, 970.

Aldrich, John, wounded in defending Fort Massachusetts, 738; on the march as a prisoner of war from Fort Massachusetts, 742.

Alembert, D', 856.

Alequippa, Queen, 947; flies from her possessions, 876.

Alexander, 1475.

Alexander VI., Pope, 538.

Alexander, Deacon Ebenezer, fortifies his house at Northfield against Indian attack, 728.

Alexandria, 941, 955, 1014; camp of Braddock at, 974; council held at the camp, 980 *note*, 1006, 1011, 1042.

Alford, John, mentioned, 652.

Algonquins, or Algonkins, the, 895; join in war-parties from Montreal, 719; at Fort Duquesne, 948–49; assist the Canadian militia, 1098; their means of divination, 1142 *note*; called to a council by Montcalm, 1175–78.

Alleghany Mountains, the, 858, 872, 885, 930–31, 943, 945, 954, 1098, 1285, 1287, 1291–92; crossed by the English traders, 874; road made through, by Braddock's forces, 986, 1290, 1291; condition of the settlers, 1074.

Alleghany River, the, 872, 932, 935, 937, 942, 987, 997, 1132, 1298, 1300–01, 1304; work of Céloron de Bienville, 874; settlement of Shenango, 876 *note*; a fort planned, 933.

Allein, ——, at Port Royal, 415.

Allen, ——, killed at Deerfield by Indians, 741.

Allen, Chief Justice, letter from Bouquet quoted, 1306 *note*.

Allen, Ensign, to train the Provincials in Braddock's expedition, 983.

Allen, Eunice, Samuel, and Caleb, children attacked by Indians at Deerfield, 741.

Allen's River, 412, 421, 437.

Alliance, triple, of Indians and English, 147.

Allison, widow, living at Deerfield, 376.

Allouez, Jesuit missionary at St. Louis, 553.

Alsopp, George, 1499.

Alton Bay, meeting of an Indian war-party at, 400.

Alva, 1472.

Amalek, 1258.

"Amazone," French war-ship, 681.

America, 984, 995 *note,* 1003 *note,* 1017, 1047, 1090, 1096, 1105, 1226, 1229, 1327, 1383, 1463, 1470; the extent of territory claimed by the British provinces of, 606; the claim of France to, 609; complication of political interests, 843–44; conditions during, and results following, the Seven Years War in Europe, 843, 858–59; the British and French possessions compared, 843–44; the War of Independence, 843; British soldiers in, 849; number of French and English inhabitants in the middle of the eighteenth century, 859; towns and colonies compared and contrasted, 862–69; plan for the increase of French settlements, 870; questions of boundaries, 871, 896–97, 899, 903, 929–31; commissioners appointed to decide upon French and English possessions in, 929–31; the balance of power, 931; conditions in the English colonies, 953–61; results of the meeting of the colonial Assemblies with their governors, 955–60; France and England compared, 967; the policy of England, 967; expedition ordered to, from France, 968–69; regiments ordered to, from England,

968; council of American governors held with Braddock, 975–77; the democracy of Pennsylvania, 1076 and *note;* conflict of the eighteenth century, 1087; holds a secondary place in the interests of France, 1087; French power in, to be sustained, 1087; money granted by Parliament to the colonies, 1104 and *note;* usefulness of Indian warriors, 1175; the power of Pitt, 1223–27; interest felt for, by Pitt, 1228–29; prophecy of John Mellen, 1454–55; and of the French and English war, 1455–57, 1460; predictions concerning the future of the British colonies, 1471.

American Antiquarian Society, the, 878; plate buried by the French in the possession of, 878; Transactions of, 878.

American colonies, their part in the War of the Spanish Succession, 339.

Amesbury, annoyed by Indians, 402.

Amherst, General Jeffrey, mentioned, 646, 648, 744 *note,* 1329 *note,* 1355, 1429; his character, 1228; promoted to be major-general, 1228; recalled from the German war, 1228; takes command of the expedition against Louisbourg, 1228–29, 1234–51; lands his troops at Freshwater Cove, 1234–38; plans of attack, 1234; his camp, 1238; roads made through marshes, 1238–39; courtesies between the commanders, 1240; his humanity, 1243, 1452; terms of capitulation extended to Louisbourg, 1244–45; capitulation of Louisbourg, 1246 and *note;* prevented from uniting with Abercromby, 1247; increases his conquests, 1249; action after the reduction of Louisbourg, 1250; orders issued to Wolfe, 1250, 1251; evidences concerning the siege of Louisbourg, 1251 *note;* joins Abercromby at Lake George, 1285; letter sent to, from General Forbes, 1306; his army moves against Ticonderoga, 1332, 1342, 1350; his ability to render aid to Wolfe, 1342–43; commander-in-chief of the troops in America,

1359; deputes Prideaux to take charge of the expedition against Niagara, 1359; on Lake George, 1359; plans of Pitt for his movements, 1359; the capture of Ticonderoga, 1359–63; forts built by, 1360; Bourlamaque retires before, 1361; Ticonderoga blown up by the French, 1361–62; advances upon Crown Point, 1362–63; Crown Point rebuilt by, 1362–63; his delay in joining Wolfe, 1362–63, 1368–69, 1383, 1418; roads built by, across Vermont, 1362–63; his navy, 1363, 1369–70; at Crown Point, 1368; sends Major Rogers to destroy the Abenakis' town, 1369, 1371; tries to pacify the Abenakis, 1369; the result of his campaign, 1370–71; unsuccessful attempt to reach Isle-aux-Noix, 1370; desired to send supplies to Rogers, 1372–73; Lieutenant Stephen sent to meet Rogers' rangers, 1373; letter from Rogers, 1374 *note;* defers his advance upon Montreal, 1379; his plans, 1444; the fall of Canada, 1444–57; attacks Fort Lévis, 1449; his army embarks for Montreal, 1449; the "Ottawa" captured, 1449; encamps near Montreal, 1450; passage of the rapids, 1450; a council of war held by Vaudreuil, 1451; articles of capitulation insisted upon by Amherst, 1451–52; number of his troops, 1451; his detestation of French cruelty, 1452; Vaudreuil obliged to surrender Montreal, 1453–54; the news of his victory received in Boston, 1454; sends his brother to recapture St. John's, 1471.

Amherst, Lieutenant-Colonel, recaptures St. John's, 1471.

Amonoosuc River, the, 1373.

Amours, councilor at Quebec, imprisoned by Frontenac, 47–48 (see 181).

Amsden, ——, a boy killed at Deerfield by Indians, 741.

Anastase, 988.

Anbury, the traveller, 1487.

Andros, Sir Edmund, appointed colonial governor, 124; his jurisdiction, 124; plunders Castine, 163; is deposed, 164; at Pentegoet, 250; mentioned, 406.

Androscoggin Indians, pretended peace with Governor Dudley, 360.

Ange, Gardien L', landing of the English before, 1346; burned by order of Wolfe, 1376.

Anglican Church, the, in New York, 866–67.

Anglicans, the, 864.

Anglo-Saxon race, the, 862.

Ann, Cape, 497.

Annapolis, Acadia, 907, 917, 965, 1010, 1036; an uprising of the Acadians at, 463; the government at, a mockery, 466; neglected by England, 468; attacked by the French under Duvivier, 617; garrison at, 907, 909; parish of, 909; Acadians encouraged to emigrate from, 919; the inhabitants of the valley, 1007; French feeling in the hearts of the inhabitants, 1008; arrival of the English force, 1014; means of living practised by the Acadians, 1022; number of Acadians sent away in the vessels, 1037; isolation of the garrison at, 1249; rejoicing at the fall of Louisbourg, 1248–49.

Annapolis River, 411, 421.

Anne, Fort, 430, 1280.

Anne, Queen, mentioned, 406, 463; receives some Mohawk chiefs, 434; concerning the emigrants at Acadia, 465.

Anse du Foulon, 1386, 1391, 1393, 1432, 1434, 1438; now called Wolfe's Cove, 1387.

Anson, Admiral of an English fleet, 687; First Lord of the Admiralty, 966, 1229.

Anthonay, D', lieutenant-colonel, sent to the English concerning the terms of capitulation for Louisbourg, 1245; empowered to accept the capitulation for Louisbourg, 1246.

Anticosti, Island of, 450.

"Apollon," the number of her guns, 1232 *note.*

Appleton, Colonal William, makes attack upon Port Royal, 421.

Appleton, Nathaniel, his utterance after the fall of Canada, 1455–56.

Apthorp, a Boston merchant, furnishes money for the English troops, 1013.

Arbuthnot, William, his attestation, 1188 *note*.

Arcadia, 1022.

Archives of Massachusetts, 375 *note*.

"Ardent," a war-ship at Louisbourg, 618.

"Aréthuse," the, 1239; number of her guns, 1232 *note;* fires upon the English, 1240; withdrawn from her position, 1241.

Argens, D', letters from Frederic II., 1461–62.

Argenson, D', Minister of War, 1743–1747, 855, 1087, 1095, 1226; writes to Montcalm of his appointment, 1090; letter to, from Montcalm, 1101.

"Argonaut," French war-ship, 681.

Arickaras, Indians on the Missouri, 574 *note*.

Arkansas Indians, 571.

Arkansas River, 567, 579.

Armstrong, Colonel John, 1132, 1304; the attack upon Kittanning, 1132–34; receives a medal from the Council of Philadelphia, 1134.

Armstrong, Lieutenant-Colonel and Governor, at Annapolis, 468; mentioned, 470; quoted concerning the Acadian missionaries, 470, 471; endeavors to persuade the Acadians to allegiance, 474.

Army, the English, matters pertaining to the troops, 1105–08; discipline in, 1278. See *English*.

Army, the French, description of French troops, 1095–99; number of troops in Canada, 1095 *note*. See *French*.

Army, the Provincial, 1044, 1045; preaching on Sunday to, 1048.

Army chaplains, 1276, 1277.

Arnold, Benedict, mentioned, 478.

Arnoux, Surgeon, 1408; Montcalm carried to his house, 1408, 1501.

Arthur's Club, 848.

Artillery Cove, 1184.

Artois, battalion of, 1096, 1232, 1246; ordered to America, 968.

Ash, Thomas, killed at siege of Louisbourg, 648.

Ashley, Dr., his death, 1279.

Ashley, John, difficulties among the war committees, 1108.

Ashuelot River, 717.

Asia, diplomatic and political position of France and England towards, 844; the power of England over, 1469.

Assagunticooks, join in a council to meet Governor Shute, 485.

Assemblies of the English colonies, the, neglect their own interests, 903; instructions from the Lords of Trade, 962; matters to be laid before, 977.

Assembly of Massachusetts, the, dealings of Governor Shirley with, 495, 959; grants money to aid the English in Maine, 959; plans of Shirley laid before, 1011; money and supplies voted by, for the expedition against Crown Point, 1041.

Assembly of New York, the, 885; opposition to the war-plans of Governor Clinton, 713; quotation from Governor Clinton concerning their neglect of New York to protect Indian trade, 886–87; apathy of, 894; address of, to Lieutenant-Governor Delancey, cited, 959; results of the meeting of, with the Governor of New York, 959; its hostility to Johnson, 1069; political difficulties, 1084.

Assembly of Pennsylvania, the, 885, 941, 1134; refuses the request of the Indians to build a trading-house on the Ohio, 886; unwilling to aid Dinwiddie, 941; letter from the Earl of Holdernesse laid before, 957; persons composing, 957; result of the meeting with the Governor, 957–59; causes of military paralysis, 1075–76; needs of the people laid before, 1075; Benjamin Franklin leader in, 1076; question of taxing proprietary lands, 1076–79, 1080–82; contentions with the Quakers and the Governor, 1077–79; quarrels with the Governor, 1077–79, 1083, 1084 *note,* 1286, 1289; relations of with Governor Morris, 1077–84; relations of, with the people, 1077–84; desires to issue bills of credit, 1080–81; anger of the Quakers, 1081–82; the paper called a "Representation" sent to the House, 1081; a militia law passed, 1082; deputations from the people and from friendly Indians seeking aid, 1082; growing unpopularity of, 1082, 1083; the proprietaries of Pennsylvania offer to raise money for defence, 1083; difficulties in quartering the troops, 1143.

Assembly of Virginia, efforts of Dinwiddie to repel the French in the West, 938–40; aid voted to Dinwiddie, 939–40, 1004; slowness of movement of, 942; speech of Dinwiddie to, 956–57; result of the meeting with Dinwiddie, 957, 1004; the distress of the people, 1072–73; the needs of Washington, 1072–73; needs of the people laid before, 1075.

Assinniboin River, 588.

Assinniboins, Indians of the West, 584, 586, 587, 588; join La Vérendrye in his search for the Pacific, 588.

Atkinson, Mr., envoy from New Hampshire to Vaudreuil, 503.

Atlantic Ocean, the, 845, 904, 929, 986, 1163, 1316, 1477; English possessions bordering on, 859; the United States, 1478.

Attiqué, village of, 876; French name for Kittanning, 1134. See *Kittanning*.

Aubry, 1365; the engagement at Niagara, 1365–68; taken prisoner, 1367.

Augsburg, 1465.

Augusta, Fort, 1297.

Augusta, Me., a stone fort built at, 483.

"Auguste," ship wrecked at Cape Breton, 605.

"Auguste," fate of the, 1458, 1459.

Augustus the Strong, 852.

Aulac, inhabitants removed from, 1019–20; the declaration of Monckton, 1019.

Auneau, Jesuit, a member of La Vérendrye's party, 586.

Austria, effects of the French alliance, 843; succession of Maria Theresa, 858; political alliances sought, 1086; a Catholic country, 1087; troops sent against, 1092; position of affairs in Europe, 1222; policy of George III., 1464; hostile to Prussia, 1469; the treaty of Hubertsburg, 1474.

Austria, House of, its rule, 856; enmity of France towards, 858.

Austrian Succession, the war of, 616, 858.

Austrians, the, 1223; the battle of Prague, 1223; routed at Leuthen, 1227; fly before Frederic, 1460.

Auteuil, attorney-general of Canada, an enemy of Frontenac, 44, 181; banished, 45.

Auxerrois, 1089.

Avaux, Count d', French envoy at London, 103.

Avery, Ensign, the expedition against the Abenakis, 1372–73.

Avery, John, on committee to protect the settlement of Number Four, 721.

Avon River, 701; the former name of, 1029.

Awe River, the, 1494.

Ayllon, Vasquez de, 608 *note*.

Babiole, 1086.

Baby, a Canadian officer, 1072 *note*.

Babylon, 1258, 1455, 1458.

Bacon, Daniel, a captain in Pepperrell's army, 656 *note*.

Bacouel, village of, 699.

"Badine," frigate, 535.

Bagley, Colonel Jonathan, 1248, 1275, 1277; commands at Fort William Henry, 1109; extracts from his letters, 1109; preparations for attacking Ticonderoga, 1109.

Bahama Islands, the, 1131.

Baker, ——, escapes from Indian captivity, 393–94.

Baker, a soldier, 1133.

Baker, Lieutenant, killed at Grand Pré, 418.

Baker, Miss Alice C., paper on John Sheldon, by, cited, 395 *note;* extracts of baptism of captives in Canada, 396 *note*.

Bald Mountain, 1168.

Ball, a dog, 1326.

Ballads, 1357 note.

Bancroft, Robert Hale, 635 note.

Bangor, 498.

Bank, Captain Louis, sent from London with French colonists, 537.

Banks, Lieutenant, secures the ransom of Elisha Plaisted from the Indians, 371.

Baptiste, Captain, a noted sea-rover, 390; released by English governor in exchange for Rev. John Williams, 394.

Barachois, 1239, 1242; a pond near Louisbourg, 646; approach of the English, 1240.

Barbadoes, Island of, 1327.

Barnard, Rev. John, chaplain in expedition, to Port Royal, 420 note; attempts a plan of the fort, 422; takes part in a skirmish, 423.

Barnsley, Thomas, 1281 note.

Barré, 1227, 1381.

Barrett, Ensign John, his personal property, 364.

Barrington, Viscount, 1468, 1493; replaces Chancellor Legge, 1464.

Barron, Elias, a member of Lovewell's expedition, 512.

Barrot, surgeon of the colony of Louisiana, 540.

Bartlett, J. R., cited, 434 note.

Basin of Mines, Acadia, concerning the migration of its people, 466.

Bassignac, De, curious incident in the attack on Montcalm, at Ticonderoga, 1270.

Bastide, ——, English engineer at Louisbourg, 647.

Bastille, the, 855, 1459; confinement of Perrot, 39–40.

"Bastonnais" (Bostonians), their trade with the Acadians, 413.

Bath, England, 848, 973, 1058, 1327.

Bath, Lady, 973.

Bath, Lord, 1472 note.

Batiscan, 1098, 1424.

Batten Kill River, on the Hudson River, 715 note; known as la rivière de Saratogue, 733.

Baugis, Chevalier de, sent by La Barre to seize Fort St. Louis, 70.

Bavaria, the Elector of, 858.

Baxter, Rev. Joseph, intended to teach the Eastern Indians, 485; his correspondence with Sebastien Rale, 488; his preaching to the Norridgewocks, 488; his mission a failure, 489.

Bay of Biscay, 681.

Bay of Fundy, 418, 696.

Bay Verte, a fort built at, 692.

Bayagoula Indians, on the Mississippi, 536.

Bean, Lieutenant, sent to attack Norridgewock, 498.

Béarn, the battalion of, 1099, 1268, 1271, 1355; ordered to America, 968; uniform of the battalion of, 1096 note; encamped before Niagara, 1100; capture of Oswego, 1122; preparations to attack Fort William Henry, 1168; advance of Montcalm upon Fort William Henry, 1179; mutiny at Montreal, 1203; attack upon Quebec, 1396.

Beaubassin (Chignecto), an Acadian settlement, 909; attacked by Colonel Church, 419; Ramesay's troops quartered at, 698; Ramesay in possession of, 710; English occupation of, 924–27; the parish fired by Le Loutre, 924; departure of Major Lawrence from, and return of, 924–25.

Beaubassin, Madame de, suppers given by, 1156.

Beaubassin, Sieur de, a French officer in Indian attack at Casco, 366, 367; quoted concerning Indian warfare, 404; sent to defend Lighthouse Point from the English invasion, 658; joins Rigaud's war-party, 734; mentioned, 780–81.

Beauchamp, merchant, 1030.

Beaucour, 218; French officer in command of a war-party, 399.

Beaucour, La Roche, 1155, 1489.

Beauharnois, Charles, Marquis de, governor of Canada, averse to attacking the Outagamies, 559; quoted, 561 note, 563 note; mentioned, 582, 601; promotes La Vérendrye's enterprise,

585, 586; succeeded by Galissonière as governor, 601; threatens the destruction of the trading-house at Oswego, 612; quoted concerning Acadia, 689.

Beauharnois, Fort, the Souix mission at, 582.

Beaujeu, Captain, journal cited, 688 *note;* in Ramesay's expedition, 698; the hero of the Monongahela, 698; assists in attack on Grand Pré, 702; commands Coulon de Villiers' party after his death, 704; renders valuable assistance to La Corne, 705; account of attentions paid by the English after the capitulation at Grand Pré, 707; reports the French and English losses at Grand Pré, 707; his account of the French victory cited, 708 *note;* at Fort Duquesne, 988, 1485; encounter of the French with the English, 989–1000; death of, 992.

Beaumont, 1352.

Beauport, River of, 1336, 1341.

Beauport, the seigniory of, 353.

Beauport, the village of, 1335, 1343, 1353, 1378, 1384, 1405; Montcalm stations his camp here at the siege of Quebec, 1335, 1336, 1341, 1397, 1401 *note,* 1406; attack of Wolfe on the French camp, 1355–57; approach of Wolfe's fleet, 1390–94; flight of the French army, 1403–04, 1407; the French supplies plundered, 1410; return of the army to Quebec, 1412.

Beaurain, Chevalier de, *Mémoire* cited, 570 *note.*

Beauséjour, Fort, 928, 1320; erected by the French, 926–27, 1006; an attack upon, planned by the English, 975–76, 980, 1008, 1009, 1010, 1013; M. Vergor commandant of, 1009, 1011; strength of the fort, 1009, 1011; official corruption at, 1011, 1012, 1013, 1016–17; encounter of the French with the English, 1015–19, 1023; capitulation offered by the French, 1017; capture of, 1018, 1021, 1329, 1387; escape of Le Loutre, 1018; became Fort Cumberland, 1019; encampment of Monckton, 1019; the declaration of Monckton, 1019; inhabitants re-

moved from, 1020–21; departure of Winslow from, 1028.

Beauséjour, hill, 924, 926.

Beaver Creek, 1295.

Beaver. See *Fur-trade.*

Beaver, King, Indian chief, 1295.

Becancour, 1175; an Abenaki mission, 480.

Becancour, M. de, 893.

Bedford, Duke of, 1464; concerning the removal of the Acadians, 693; sent to Paris to negotiate for peace, 1471.

Bedford, Fort, erection of, 1293.

Bedford, town of, 1287.

Bégon, Intendant, cited, 471 *note.*

Belcher, Governor of New Jersey, declares war against the Indians, 1111; postpones his action, 1111.

Belêtre conducts a war-party, 895; the attack at German Flats, 1200–01.

Belknap, ——, *History of New Hampshire* cited, 367 *note,* 491 *note,* 510 *note,* 619 *note,* 671 *note,* 1191 *note.*

"Bell of St. Regis," the story of, 397 *note.*

Bellamy, George Anne, story of Braddock in regard to, 974 and *note.*

Bellefonds, Maréchal de, a friend of Frontenac at court, 52.

Belleisle, 1469, 1473.

Belleisle, Madame de, at Port Royal, 415.

Belleisle, Maréchal de, minister of war, 1758–1761, 1220, 1316; double-dealing and boasting of Vaudreuil, 1312–14, 1333; his letter to Montcalm, 1316–17; plans of war enjoined upon Montcalm, 1316–17; letter from Vaudreuil to, 1415.

Bellomont, Earl of, governor of New York, 304; corresponds with Frontenac, 304–06; mentioned, 341, 342; quoted concerning the Five Nations, 344.

Bellona, 1172.

Belmont, Abbé, cited, 81 *note,* 117.

Bengal, 1473.

Bennett, Captain, 470.

Bennington, 1045.

Benoît, 1215.

Berkeley, Sir William, his opinion of education for the people, 864.

Berks, 1082.

Berkshire, Valley of, Massachusetts settlements made in, 728.

Berlin, 1461.

Bernard, Governor of Massachusetts, 1454.

Bernès, 1264.

Bernières, vicar of Laval in Canada, 38.

Berniers, commissary-general, 1375, 1498; the state of Quebec described after the siege, 1422.

Bernis, Abbé de, minister of foreign affairs, 1464.

Berry, battalion of, 1257, 1264–65, 1268.

Berryer, minister of marine and colonies, 1758–1761, 1315; official corruption in Canada, 1217–19; ministerial rebukes sent to officials in Canada, 1217–21; letters from Vaudreuil, 1293, 1314, 1414; boasting and jealousy of Vaudreuil, 1308, 1312; prepossessed against Bougainville, 1314–15; reproof given to Vaudreuil, 1453.

Berwick, Me., attacked by Indians, 368, 402.

"Biche," number of her guns, 1232 note.

Biddle, Edward, letter from Reading, 1080.

"Bienfaisant," 1242; number of her guns, 1232 note; seized by the English, 1243.

Bienville, Céloron de. See Céloron.

Bienville, François de, 210.

Bienville, Le Moyne de, with Iberville, in his exploration to Louisiana, 536; proceeds to explore the Mississippi River, 536; encounters a party of French colonists, and deceives them into abandoning their project, 537; accusations against him at Mobile, 539; governor of the colony of Louisiana, 540; succeeded by La Mothe-Cadillac, 541; reappointed governor of Louisiana, 547; recalled to France, 548; again made governor of Louisiana, 549; resignation of, 550; called the father of Louisiana, 550; his disastrous attempt at fighting the Chickasaws, 550; mentioned, 570 and note; orders a fort built on Missouri River, 574; sends a party to explore in New Mexico, 579.

Big Horn Range of Rocky Mountains, 597, 598 note.

Big Mouth, an Iroquois chief, 76, 78, 82, 89, 108; his speech in defiance of La Barre, 84–86; his power in the confederacy, 129; defiance of Denonville, 129.

Bigot, François, Intendant at Canada, 602, 760, 889 note, 891 note, 897 note, 900, 1011, 1202, 1208; quoted, 641 note, 647–48, 657 and note; quoted concerning the siege of Louisbourg, 649, 663; his official corruption, 900, 904, 1011, 1158; his plans against the English, 914; the Indians encouraged to butcher the English, 915; sails for Europe, 1011; returns to Canada, 1019; defends Vergor, 1019, 1387; his character and office, 1101, 1208, 1217–18; his popularity, 1161; relates the cruelties of the Indians, 1199, 1200; his birth, 1208; his manner of life, 1208–17, 1337; his official journeys and pleasure-excursions, 1208–10; his relations with Vaudreuil, 1208, 1415, 1417; his houses and palace, 1210, 1211; his circle of friends, 1211–17; his gambling, and frauds in trade, 1211–15; the lover of Madame Péan, 1215; promissory notes issued, 1217; receives ministerial rebukes, 1217–21; revelations of his stealings, 1219–21, 1221 note; breaks with Cadet, 1221; statistics concerning the rations at Fort Duquesne, 1300 note; the dissensions between Montcalm and Vaudreuil, 1310; the siege and reduction of Quebec, 1337; Vaudreuil holds a council of war, 1347, 1406; forces at Quebec, 1401 note, 1497; French troops available after the battle, 1406 note; returns with the army to Quebec, 1411; arrested, and thrown into the Bastille, 1459; his trial, 1459, 1460; his sentence, 1460; his letters, 1498.

Bigot, Jacques and Vincent, Jesuits, 162–63; in Acadia, 270, 273.

Billerica, joins in Lovewell's expedition, 508.

"Billy," assists Surgeon Williams, 1055; sickness in the army, 1279.

Biloxi, a fort built at, by Iberville, 536.

Bishop of Canada, see *Laval, Saint-Vallier.*

Bishop of Quebec, 465.

Bizard, Lieutenant, despatched by Frontenac to Montreal, 33.

"Bizarre," number of her guns, 1232 *note.*

Black Hills, 569, 593.

Black Hole of Calcutta, the, 1227.

Black Hunter, the, 985.

Black Mountain, 1136.

Black Point, 1231.

Black Point, Me., men murdered and captured by Indians at, 368.

Black Rifle, the, 985.

Blackhawk, chief of the Sacs and Foxes, 564.

Blake, Nathan, captured by Indians at Keene, 719.

Blanchard, Colonel, defends Fort Lyman, 1047; a letter of warning sent to, 1048.

Blenheim, 445.

Blodget, Samuel, 1051 *note;* his view of the battle at Lake George, 1055; prospective plan, etc., of the battle near Lake George, etc., 1062 *note,*

Blomedon, Cape, 1028–29.

"Bloody morning scout," the, 1053.

Bloody Pond, origin of its name, 1056.

Blue Earth River, 568.

Blue Ridge, panic among the settlers, 1071–72.

Board of Trade of New York, 342.

Bobé, Father, the claims of France to American territory as set forth by, 607–09; his advice to France towards securing territory in America, 610.

Bodmer, Charles, painted a group of Sacs and Foxes, Indians, 564 and *note.*

Bœufs, Rivière aux, 932.

Bois, Abbé, 1332 *note,* 1408 *note.*

Boisbriant, Pierre Dugué de, commander of garrison at Mobile, 540; built Fort Chartres, 553–54; commandant at the Illinois, 553, 574.

Boishébert, a French officer, 698, 1027, 1482, 1497; a member of Ramesay's expedition, guards the roads to Grand Pré, 700; assists in the attack upon Grand Pré, 704; to induce the Acadians to leave their home, 913; troops sent to watch the English frontier, 924; letter to Manach quoted, 1027; leads the attack at Peticodiac, 1034; forces of, 1034 *note;* approaches Louisbourg, 1241; his dealings with the Acadians, 1312; tried for peculation, 1312.

Boisseau, his quarrel at Quebec, 55.

Bollan, William, urges the claim of Massachusetts in England for reimbursement for the cost of taking Louisbourg, 670–71; to Secretary Willard, cited, 671 *note.*

Bolling, a Virginian gentleman, 1000 *note.*

Bolton, 1179 *note.*

Bomazeen, Captain, an Indian chief, 361, 371; his wife captured, 498–99.

Bonaventure, Captain, 930; concerning Boston traders, 408 *note;* acting governor at Port Royal, 413 and *note;* charges made against him, 414.

Bonaventure, Madame de, at breakfast of the English officers, 439.

Bonaventure, priest, 465.

Bonavista, Newfoundland, 424.

Bond, Dr., 1001.

Bonhomme, Michel, 1409.

Bonnecamp, Father, a Jesuit priest, 881; extract from his journal, 872, 875, 887 *note;* his map, 887 *note;* at Detroit, 896; his opinion of Céloron, 897.

Bonner, Captain, a pilot in Walker's expedition, 449.

Bordeaux, 1155, 1208, 1212.

Borland, an illicit trader, 408.

Boscawen, Admiral, ordered to intercept the French fleet, 970–71; takes charge of the fleet sent against Louisbourg, 1229, 1230, 1233–47;

at Halifax, 1233–34; siege and capitulation of Louisbourg, 1233–47; the correspondence with Drucour, 1245, 1246–47, 1251 *note;* unwilling to follow Amherst's wishes, 1250.

Boston, 1009, 1013, 1062 *note,* 1249, 1250; after the failure at Quebec, 207, 215, plan of attack on, 275–76; plan of Le Moyne d'Iberville to destroy, 340; plan of the French to destroy, 340; plan of Baron de Saint-Castin to attack, 341 *note;* accused of illicit trade with the French of Acadia, 408; troops encamped at, awaiting an attack on Canada, 432; arrival of British squadron at, 435; preparations for the attack on Port Royal, 435; warned of the designs of British ministry, 442; must be reduced, 443, 444 and *note;* arrival of a fleet, designed to attack Canada, 445, 446 *note;* preparations at, to join in Walker's Canada expedition, 447, 448 *note;* friends of the Indians at, 484; sends reinforcement to the fort at Annapolis, 618; the news of the surrender of Louisbourg received in, 669; arrival of the chests of money from England as payment of the cost of taking of Louisbourg, 670; alarmed at the expected coming of a French fleet, 679; relative size of, 866; departure of the English troops for Nova Scotia, 1014; rules laid down for the soldiers on the Sabbath Day, 1014; transport-vessels to be hired to convey the Acadians from Nova Scotia, 1027, 1034–35; treatment received by the Acadian exiles, 1038; winter-quarters found for the troops, 1143; taxes levied to pay the war-debt, 1255; news of the fall of Canada, 1454.

"Boston Evening Post," article upon provincial soldiery, 1278.

Boston Gazette, cited, 642 *note.*

Boston News Letter, 439 *note.*

"Boston Packet," a war-ship, 631.

Botwood, Edward, killed, 1357 *note;* "Hot Stuff," 1357–58 *note.*

Boucher, Marie, marriage of, to René Gaultier de Varennes, 583.

Boucher, Pierre, governor of Three Rivers, 583.

Bougainville, 1101, 1121, 1153; aide-de-camp to Montcalm, 1038–39, 1091; his description of the Acadian exiles, 1039; friendly relations with Montcalm, 1092, 1154, 1160; his youth, 1092; terms of capitulation proposed to the English, at Oswego, 1125; his description of the Indians and their cruelties, 1136–37, 1169, 1174–75, 1188–89, 1199, 1203, 1295; joins the war-party of Perière, 1136–37; perplexity at finding the boats of Rogers, 1141; life during Lent, 1155–56; the ships-of-war at Louisbourg, 1165 *note;* seeks to gain Indian allies, 1167; sings the war-song, 1167; the "St. Bartholomew of the oxen," 1169; his diary quoted, 1187, 1194 *note;* sent as a messenger to Montreal from Fort William Henry, 1190; evidence concerning the massacre at Fort William Henry, 1194 *note;* official knavery commented upon, 1214; extract from, concerning Vaudreuil's plans, 1256; slightly wounded, 1272; expedition of, to France, 1313–16; his efforts to gain aid for Canada, 1313–15; double-dealing of Vaudreuil, 1314; his promotion, 1315; to negotiate the marriages of the children of Montcalm, 1316; return to Canada, 1316, 1332–33; sad news brought to Montcalm, 1318; his opinion of the strength of Quebec, 1341; sent from Beauport to oppose the English, 1377–78; precautions taken to watch the shore of Quebec, 1386; at Cap-Rouge, 1386; Holmes's vessels sail up the river, 1387–88; deceived by a feint of Wolfe, 1388; deceived by the movement of Holmes's vessels, 1390; supply-boats to be sent to Montcalm, 1391; neglects to follow Holmes's vessels, 1392; danger of Wolfe's position, 1394; attacks the light infantry, 1395; repulsed, 1395; statistics of the forces at Quebec, 1401 *note;* the fall of his friends, 1405; council of war held, 1406; his forces,

1406 and *note;* question of capitulation for Quebec, 1406–07; remains at Cap-Rouge, 1411; follows the army to Quebec, 1412; at Isle-aux-Noix, 1443; the fall of Canada, 1443–57; ordered to stop Haviland's progress, 1448; articles of capitulation carried to Amherst, 1451–52; at Montreal, 1451; Montreal capitulates, 1451–52.

Boularderie, a French officer at Louisbourg, captured, 641.

Boundary, questions of, 871, 886, 898–99, 929–31, 959, 970, 1006–08, 1023; the matter discussed at Paris, 903.

Bounties on scalps, &c., 217.

Bouquet, Lieutenant-Colonel Henry, his soldiers, 1287; interview with Washington, 1287; serves in reducing Fort Duquesne, 1287, 1306; the expedition against Fort Duquesne, 1287–1307; justice of his opinion of Washington, 1288; relations with Forbes, 1288–89; extracts from his correspondence with Forbes, 1289–90, 1293, 1301–03; his tact with the Indians, 1291–92; the road over the Alleghanies, 1292; forward movement of, 1293; Grant's expedition, 1299–1302; retreat of Major Grant, 1301; sufferings of Forbes's troops, 1303; letter to Chief Justice Allen quoted, 1306 and *note.*

Bourbon, Fort, built by La Vérendrye, 587.

Bourbon, house of, 852, 873, 897, 1152, 1467, 1475; triumphs of, 852; the Family Compact, 1466.

Bourbon, Island of, 852.

Bourgmont, ——, sent by West India Company to river Missouri, 574; built Fort Orléans on river Missouri, 574; his journey to Comanche villages, 574; makes a second visit to the Comanches, and holds a council, 576; his meeting with the Comanche chiefs, 577; makes a treaty of alliance with them, 577–78; returns to Fort Orléans, 578.

Bourgogne, battalion of, 1096, 1232; ordered to America, 968.

Bourke, Captain John G., 605 *note.*

Bourlamaque, Chevalier de, 1099, 1201, 1202, 1257; named as the third officer of Montcalm, 1090; embarks for America, 1092; extracts from his correspondence with Montcalm, 1153, 1155–57, 1161, 1263, 1310, 1343, 1385, 1408, 1489, 1498; encampment of, 1168; preparations to attack Fort William Henry, 1168; his efforts to save the English, 1191; Montcalm's position near Ticonderoga, 1264; the battle of Ticonderoga, 1268; wounded, 1272; his promotion, 1315; ordered to hold Ticonderoga, 1331; troops ordered to Quebec, 1333; letter from Vaudreuil, 1357, 1385; Amherst attacks him, 1360–61; retires before Amherst, 1361; at Isle-aux-Noix, 1361, 1368, 1379; letter from Lévis quoted, 1370; retreat of, 1379; his troops advance upon Montreal, 1446; his troops thinning out, 1446–47; joined by the French, 1448; movements of Amherst, 1449; at Montreal, 1451; letter from Montcalm given in the original, 1489.

Bourne, Ed E., *History of Wells, Me.,* cited, 364 *note,* 630 *note.*

Bow Indians, Gens de L'Arc, visit of the brothers Le Vérendrye to them, 595.

Braddock, Fanny, stories of her death, 973.

Braddock, Major-General, 968, 1041, 1063; ordered to America with regiments, 968; anecdotes of, 972–74; characteristics of, 972–74; his arrival at Hampton, 972; opinion of, expressed by Dinwiddie, 972; opinions of, held by different persons, 972–74; beloved as Governor of Gibraltar, 973–74; story told of duel with Colonel Gumley, 973; interview with Dury, 974; parting visit to George Anne Bellamy, 974; doubts concerning the office held at Gibraltar, 974 *note;* position held by, in the Coldstream Guards, 974; arrival of the regiments at Hampton, 974; opinion of, held by Horace Walpole, 974; sends for the governors of the colonies to meet in council, 975–77; decisions of the Council at Alexandria, 976–77; his instructions laid before the council at Alexandria, 976; in sympathy with Shirley's plans, 976; to lead the expedition against Fort Duquesne, 976; suggestions of, approved by the Council at Alexandria, 977; matters to be laid before the colonial Assemblies, 977; suggestions of, with regard to ship-building, 977; error in regard to his campaign, 980; lands in Virginia, 980; supplies scarce, 980–81; aided by Franklin, 981–82; his expedition against Fort Duquesne, 980–1005, 1485–88; journal of his expedition, 980 *note;* his horses and wagons, 982–83; need of wagons, 982; his estimate of the provincial troops, 983; his troops, 983, 992, 995 *note;* relations with Washington, 983; invites Washington to become his aide-de-camp, 984; tries to secure the aid of Indians, 984; his scorn of Indians, 984–85; departure of his expedition for the scene of action, 985–86; his reception of Captain Jack and his company, 985; road made for his expedition, 985–87, 1287, 1290, 1306; difficulties of the march, 986; consultation with Washington, 986; his forces reach Little Meadows, 986; illness among his men, 986; his mode of advance, 986–87; fords the Monongahela, 987, 990; rumors of his approach reach Fort Duquesne, 989; nature of the country through which he passed, 991–93; destructive fire of the French and Indians, 993–94; confusion among the English troops, 993–94; horrors of the battle, 993–95; his ignorance of American warfare, 994; his defeat, 995–1001, 996 *note,* 1046, 1066, 1070, 1077, 1126, 1349, 1485–88; number of his army lost in the battle of the Monongahela, 995 and *note;* retreat of his troops, 995–1000; shot in the lungs, 995; his papers left to the Indians, 996; plans drawn by Mackellar for his expedition, 996 *note;* condition of, 998; his sufferings, 998; reinforcements for, under Dunbar, 998; confusion in his camp, 999; his death, 999–1000, 1069, 1288; panic among the troops, 999; remarks concerning the soldiery, 999–1000; buried in the road, 1000; mentioned in Campbell's letter, 1000; letter from Washington quoted, concerning, 1002; Shirley made commander-in-chief, 1004; the Council at Alexandria, 1006, 1042; letters of, warn Dieskau of danger, 1043; his dead soldiers left to the wolves, but afterwards buried, 1058, 1305; his captured papers reveal the plans of the English, 1067; his instructions to Major-General Shirley, 1068 *note;* his roads used by the invaders, 1072; his battalions, 1105; compared with Forbes, 1288.

Bradley, Joseph, the house of, attacked by Indians, 368; his wife captured, 368.

Bradstreet, at the age of eighty-seven, made governor after Andros at Boston, 164.

Bradstreet, Colonel John, proposed the attack upon Louisbourg, 619 *note;* reinforced Vaughan at Louisbourg, 642; men placed under, by Shirley, 1112; his boatmen carry provisions to Oswego, 1112; action with Villiers' forces, 1112–13; his success, 1113–14; his boatmen sent to Oswego, 1120; serves under Abercromby, 1260; reconnoitres the landing, 1260–61; his action after the death of Lord Howe, 1264; his armed boatmen, 1268; conquest of Fort Frontenac, 1283–85; troops given him to conquer Fort Frontenac, 1284; mercy shown to his prisoners, 1284; advances towards Albany, 1284; his return to Oswego, 1284; Fort Frontenac dismantled, 1284; importance of his conquest, 1285; supplies destroyed by, 1302; reported to advance upon Lake Ontario, 1332.

Brandenburg, House of, promoted to royalty, 856.

Brandon, Arthur, his wife and children killed by Indians, 368.

Brattleboro', a halting-place of the Indians on their retreat from Deerfield, 385.

Bréard, his official knavery, 1212; accused of fraud in Canada, 1459.

Brébeuf, a Jesuit mission priest, 348, 429, 479.

Brest, 968, 970, 1043, 1091; D'Anville's fleet at, 680; embarkation of Dieskau's expedition, 968–69; French armament at, 969.

Breton, Cape, 453; called Isle Royale, 460; offered to France, 460; mentioned, 605.

Bretonvilliers, superior of Jesuits, 40.

Bridgman, Jonathan, wounded in the defence of Fort Massachusetts, 738.

"Britannia," ship, captured by privateers, 1218.

British colonies. See *English colonies*.

British ministry, the, 982, 1041, 1223, 1466; the plan for building a naval station at Chebucto, 907; attitude of, toward the Indians, 961; the French forts to be attacked, 1010; hostility to Shirley in New York, 1070; the removal of Shirley from his command, 1105; ill effect of a letter from Wolfe, 1418; changes in, 1464; plans of Pitt laid before, 1467; Newcastle resigns his position, 1469.

British Museum, the, 930 *note,* 984.

British officers, how regarded in New England, 421; not pleased with the colonists at Boston, 446.

British Provinces of America, the extent of territory claimed by them, 606.

British Provinces, the, 1039.

Britons, 1340.

Broadway, 1248.

Broglie, 852.

Brookfield, annoyed by Indians, 402.

Brooks, ——, commanded the attack upon the island battery at Louisbourg, 656; attempts to haul down the French flag, 656.

Brouillan, Jacques François de, governor of Acadia, proposes a treaty with New England, 341 and *note;* appointed governor of Acadia, 410; death of, 412; the charges against him, 412.

Brown, ——, *Cape Breton,* 639 *note.*

Brown, Captain, sent to attack Norridgewock, 498.

Brown, John Carter, collection of portraits, 434 *note.*

Brown, Lieutenant, the attack on Louisbourg, 1237; aids Wolfe when shot, 1399.

Brucy, a lieutenant, agent of Perrot, his traffic with Indians, 31, 35.

Brulé Indians, a tribe of the Sioux, 600 *note.*

Brunswick, Ferdinand of, 1227, 1469.

Brunswick, Me., 481; burned in revenge by the Abenakis, 494.

Bruyas, a Jesuit interpreter, 83; an agent among the Five Nations, 344.

Bruyère, Fabry de la, sent to explore in New Mexico, 579.

Brymner's *Report,* etc., cited, 589 *note.*

Buchanan, letter to, from John Campbell, 1000–01.

Buchannon. See *Buchanan.*

Buffaloes, 883.

Buisson, the, 1450.

Bull, Fort, attacked and reduced by Léry, 1099–1100.

Bullard, John, killed in Indian attack at Keene, 719.

Bullitt, Captain, expedition of Major Grant, 1300, 1301.

Bunker Hill, battle of, 636.

Burchett, ——, Secretary of the Admiralty, 446 *note.*

Burd, Colonel, his mode of warfare, 1288; interview with Forbes, 1290; Indian allies join the army, 1291–92.

Burgesses, slow to enforce obedience among the Virginian troops, 1072.

Burghers, the, of France, 855.

Burgoyne, John, 1266; his expedition, 1470; mention made of Langlade, in connection with Braddock's defeat, 1488.

Burke, ——, 517; his remarks concerning Wolfe quoted, 1380.

Burke, Captain, cruelly treated by Indians, 1192.

Burlington, Vt., 387.

Burnaby, "Travels in North America" cited, 956 *note.*

Burned Camp, 1179, 1261; origin of name, 1177.

Burnet, Governor, built a trading-house at Oswego on Lake Ontario, 612.

Burney, Thomas, escapes from Indians, 903.

Burr, ——, his soldiers camped at Louisbourg, 644.

Burton, Lieutenant-Colonel, his encounter with the French in Braddock's expedition, 994; his report concerning the provincial camp, 1117; orders given to bring his men to the Point of Orleans, 1389; his men embark for the heights, 1394; dying command of Wolfe, 1400.

Bury, Viscount, 1253; his charges against Massachusetts refuted, 1255; his "Exodus of the Western Nations" cited, 1255 *note.*

Bussy, M. de, comes to London as envoy, 1465.

Bute, Earl of, 1464, 1467; his coming into office, 458; made secretary of state, 1464; propositions made by Choiseul to Pitt, 1466; anecdote of the dislike of the people for, 1468; comes into power, 1468; succeeds Newcastle as First Lord of the Treasury, 1469; desires peace with France, 1471; peace made between France and England, 1472.

Butler, Captain, officer in Nicholson's army, 454.

Buttes-à-Neveu, 1395, 1432–33, 1438.

Byng, Admiral, 870, 1227.

Cabinet, the. See *British Ministry.*

Cabot, ——, *Memoir of Emerson* cited, 629 *note.*

Cabot, John, mentioned, 608.

Cabot, Sebastian, mentioned, 608.

Cadenaret, an Abenaki chief, 732.

Cadet, Joseph, 1315; official knavery, 1211–16, 1415, 1441, 1459; ministerial rebukes administered to, 1217–19; oppresses the Canadians, 1311–12; relations with Vaudreuil, 1333, 1415, 1417; supply-boats sent to Quebec, 1333; his manner of living, 1337; thrown into the Bastille, 1459; his trial, 1459, 1460.

Cadillac, 234, 292; at Michillimackinac, 290–91.

"Cæsar," a war-ship, 631.

Cæsar, dog owned by Wolfe, 1326.

Cahokia, a mission on the Mississippi, 553; French settlement at, 873.

Caldwell, site of, 1184.

Callières, governor of Montreal, 115, 116; his scheme for conquering the English colonies, 140; comes to the defence of Quebec, 189, 197–98, 204 *note;* at La Prairie, 211; quarrel with the bishop, 238–39; in the Onondaga expedition, 295–96, 299; succeeds Frontenac as governor, 315; treats with the Iroquois, 315–17; conference at Montreal, 321–24; opposes the plan of Cadillac for the Indians, 353; letters cited, 355 *note,* 356 *note.*

Calvin, John, 863; his doctrines preached to the army, 1048, 1279.

Cambis, battalion of, 1232.

Cambridge, a rendezvous for troops, 436.

Campbell, Captain John, his death, 1271.

Campbell, Donald, 1494.

Campbell, Duncan, 1261; his premonitions of death, 1261, 1495; his death and burial, 1271, 1494, 1495, 1496; the legend of Inverawe, 1494–96; vision of the child, 1495, 1496.

Campbell, James, 1494; vision seen by the child, 1495, 1496.

Campbell, John, letter from, to Buchanan, quoted, 1000–01.

Campbell, Lieutenant Alexander, 1495.

Campbell, Major Colin, sent for news by Dinwiddie, 1002.

Canada, 861, 871, 872, 891 *note,* 897, 906, 920, 1009, 1063, 1067–68, 1101, 1212, 1462; character of its colonial rule, 25–26; its condition under Denonville, 123–27; Iroquois invasion, 133–36, (see 209, 214, 219); a scheme for the reduction of, 425–33; the possibilities of her conquest of New York, 517; her policy towards the Western savages and the Five Nations, 519; jealousy of the Louisiana colony, 551; endeavors to control the Western posts and secure the fur-trade, 552; the opposing influences exerted upon her pioneers, 565–66; a company formed to establish a mission among the Sioux, 581–82; a chain of French posts established from, to Louisiana, 614; Governor Shirley's proposal to capture, 675–76; the plan of the campaign, 677; alarmed, prepares for defence, 677, 678; the campaign a failure, 678–79; conquest of, by England, 843, 844; plans and political intentions of England with regard to, 843–44; French possessions in, 858, 859; Catholicism in, 859, 1478; censuses of, 859, 909 *note;* difference in the political and religious systems, from those of the English colonies, 859, 860; aspects of, under the Church and King, 860–61; lack of popular legislation in, 868; line of military posts connecting with Louisiana, 870–72, 899–900; the governors largely naval officers, 870; methods of warfare and organization, 887, 942; mission of Piquet, 890; method of building up a town, 897; La Jonquière succeeds La Galissonière as governor of, 898; Baron de Longueuil succeeds La Jonquière as governor of, 901; importance of Fort Chartres, 901; internal disorders of, 904; official knavery and stealing, 904, 1211–21, 1312, 1415–17, 1442, 1459; confines of, 930; enmity towards New England, 959–60, 964; French expedition sails for, under Dieskau, 968, 969; Governor de Vaudreuil despatched to, 968; plans of Shirley in regard to, 975, 976; plans of the English to repel the French in, 1006; importance of the possession of Acadia, 1008; conditions leading to the removal of the Acadians, 1018–28 (see *Acadia* and *Acadians*); return of Bigot, 1019; the governor of, depends on the priests for aid, 1023; the Great Company, 1039; the English victorious, 1055–56; importance of the position of Niagara, 1063, 1368; the fur-trade, 1064; growth of political parties in, 1095–96, 1161; the French troops and the militia, 1095 and *note,* 1096–98, 1162, 1317, 1443; descriptions given by Montcalm, 1098; descriptions given by Duchat, 1103; causes of the English losses, 1128–30; life at Montreal, 1153; its government, 1208–09; social and official life, 1209–11, 1215–16; financial condition, 1217–19; efforts of Massachusetts to subdue, 1253, 1275–76; mission settlements of the Jesuits, 1295; appeal made to court for assistance and troops, 1313–16; fall of Quebec, 1331–58, 1375–1444 (see *Quebec*); effect of losing Fort Niagara, 1368; the result of Amherst's campaign, 1370–71; Montcalm's position, 1377; authorities concerning the history of, 1419 *note,* 1420 *note;* English rule, 1424; its winter, 1425; passes to the British crown, 1443–57, 1465–66; Montreal capitulates, 1451–52; return of the troops to France, 1452, 1458–59; utterances from the pulpits after the fall of, 1454–56; end of the war, 1455–57; her natural defences, 1456; aided by Indians, 1457; predictions of Choiseul, 1471; question of restoration to France, 1471, 1473; retention of, by England, approved by Pitt, 1473–74; the peace signed at Paris, 1474.

Canadians, the, 860–61, 891, 1250; their missions and religion, 860–61, 889–91; sent to watch the English frontier, 924; join the expedition of Duquesne to the Ohio, 932–37, 942–54; at Fort Duquesne, 988; number of, fighting under the French flag, 990; their cowardly action, 992; losses of, at the battle of the Monongahela, 998 and *note;* a litigious race, 1023; harsh treatment of the Acadians, 1038–39; rapacity of, 1039; under Dieskau, 1048, 1050, 1053, 1055; the battle of Lake George, 1050, 1053–62; attacked by a party from Fort Lyman, 1056; troops at Fort Frontenac, 1067; political parties among, 1094–95; guard Fort Frontenac, 1100; join the expedition of Léry, 1100; mode of fighting, 1101; at Ticonderoga, 1102, 1145; harass the English, 1108, 1112; evils of long encampments, 1118; under Rigaud, 1121; capture of Oswego, 1122–27; under Montcalm, 1131; disguised as Indians, 1136; join the war-party of Perière, 1136–37; fight with Rogers' rangers, 1146; the attack upon Fort William Henry, 1147–50, 1167, 1178–94; exaggerated praise given by Vaudreuil, 1157–58; their sentiment towards Montcalm, 1160; fortified camps of, 1168; dash at Fort Edward, 1175; orders of Vaudreuil in relation to the return of, 1198; the fight at German Flats, 1200–01; join Hebecourt, 1204; official knavery, 1211–21; outrages practised upon the Acadians, 1213–14; loss of Louisbourg, 1231–51; under Montcalm at Ticonderoga, 1268; under Lévis, 1271; meet the war-party of Rogers, 1281; encounter with Major Grant, 1300–01; sent to Montcalm, 1308–09; comments of Montcalm concerning, 1310–11; their loyalty and courage, 1311–12; their sufferings, 1311–12; their alarm and discontent, 1313; siege and fall of Quebec, 1331–58, 1375–1420; first proclamation issued by Wolfe, 1344; desert the French, 1348, 1350, 1378–79, 1446–47; coureurs-de-bois, 1349; fight like Indians, 1349; their dread of the Indians, 1350; Wolfe's second proclamation, 1352; the siege of Niagara, 1364–68; the third proclamation of Wolfe to, 1376; dread of

losing their supplies, 1378; defend Cap-Rouge, 1388; last movement of Wolfe, 1388–1400; rally at Côte Ste.-Geneviève, 1402–03; panic stricken, 1404; the army to return to Quebec, 1409–12; the capitulation of Quebec, 1412; bring news to Quebec of promised help, 1413; the ladies, 1422; befriended by Murray, 1424; kindness to some wounded officers, 1424–25; threatened the English, 1426–27; encounter with Major Dalling, 1427; fresh efforts to attack Quebec, 1428, 1430–42; the winter, 1429–30; at Sainte-Foy, 1431, 1502–03; the fall of Canada, 1443–57; Murray advances upon Montreal, 1444–47; proclamation of Vaudreuil, 1447; kindly treated by the English, 1452–53; their privileges as set down in the capitulation of Canada, 1452; skilful leadership of, 1457.

Canard River, 1028; reconnoissance of, 1028–29; the inhabitants summoned by Winslow to hear the King's orders, 1030–31.

Candiac, château of, 1153; family seat of Montcalm, 1088–89, 1414; departure of Montcalm from, 1090.

Canidia, 1142.

Cannehoot, a Seneca chief, 147.

Cannibalism of the Indians, 88, 116–17, 152, 153 *note,* 291, 903, 1169, 1174–75, 1429.

Canseau, fishing-station, seizure of, by the French Governor, Duquesnel, 617; garrison at, 907; destroyed by the French, 909.

Canseau, Straits of, 919.

Canso, Nova Scotia, attacked by Indians, 497.

Canterbury, Archbishop of, 434.

Cap-Rouge, 1341, 1351, 1383, 1386, 1388, 1394, 1424, 1431, 1441; held by Dumas, 1353; defended by the French, 1388, 1390–91; the fall of Quebec, 1405; expedition of Lévis, 1432.

Cap-Santé, 1209.

Cape Breton, 864, 906, 910 *note,* 912, 917, 919, 966, 1459; restoration of, by England to France, 844; the Acadians transported to, 1007 and *note;* importance of the possession of Acadia to the French, 1008; papers and writings relating to, 1012 *note;* plans of the English with regard to the Acadians, 1026 (see *Acadia* and *Acadians*); description of, 1231–32; arrival of Boscawen's expedition, 1234; the capitulation of Louisbourg, 1247; given up to England, 1472.

"Capricieux," the, 1251 *note;* number of her guns, 1232 *note;* burned at anchor, 1241.

Captives in Canada, their experience, release, etc., 392–98; baptism and marriage of, 395.

Capuchin friars, at Port Royal, 415.

Card-playing, 1029.

Carheil, ——, Jesuit missionary, at Michillimackinac, 150; mentioned, 348, 349; his dispute with La Mothe-Cadillac, 350; deprived of his converts, 356.

"Caribou," a French war-ship, 618, 681.

Carignan, regiment of, mentioned, 583.

Carillon (see *Ticonderoga*), 1495.

Carion, an officer of Perrot, 32; arrested by Frontenac, 33.

Carleton, Sir Guy, 1327, 1499; lands at Pointe-aux-Trembles, 1351; drives the Indians from Pointe-aux-Trembles, 1351.

Carlisle, Penn., 1000, 1288; village of, 1289; departure of Forbes, 1289.

Carlos III., secret negotiations of Choiseul with, 1466; succeeds to the throne of Spain, 1466; the Family Compact, 1466.

Carolina traders, instigate the Indians against the French colonists, 550.

Carter, Colonel Charles, letter to, cited, 1001.

Carter, Ebenezer, ransomed from the Indians, 393.

Carter, Landon, quoted, concerning the service of the country, 1071.

Carter, Marah, murdered by Indians, 379.

Carteret, Earl Granville. See *Granville.*

Carthagena, attack on, 1013.

Cartier, ——, mentioned, 348.

Cartier, Jacques, 1429.

Carver, Jonathan, his version of the massacre at Fort William Henry, 1192; his narrow escape, 1192; his "Travels," 1194 *note.*

Cascades, the, 1450.

Casco (Falmouth, Me.), a council of Eastern Indians meet Governor Dudley at, 360; Indian attack upon the fort at, 365, 366; annoyed by Indians, 402.

Casco Bay, 423; garrison at, 164; defeat of Indians, 166; the garrison overcome and slaughtered, 168–70; a meeting of Indians at, to ratify the treaty, 505.

Casgrain, Abbé, cited, 466 *note,* 1071 *note,* 1430 *note.*

Casgrain, Rev. H. R., cited, 476 *note.*

Castine, town of, Maine, 362.

Castor, Isle au, 1210.

Caswell, Jonathan, his letter concerning the expedition sent against Crown Point, 1046.

Cataraqui (Fort Frontenac), 85.

Catawbas, their service sought by the English army, 1291.

Catherine II. reigns in Russia, 1468; conciliated by Frederic, 1469.

Catholicism, 889, 1089, 1478; the tithes of, 854; policy of rule held by, 859–60; in Maryland, 867; freedom of, accorded to the Acadians, 906, 921; evil influence of the priests upon the Acadians, 907, 910, 912, 915, 917–18, 1012–13, 1021, 1023–27, 1039; in the English colonies, 976; in Pennsylvania, 1077; in Europe, 1087; influence over the Indians, 1169.

Catlin, Joseph, inhabitant of Deerfield, 378.

Catlin, Mrs. John, members of her family killed by Indians, 378; her death, 378.

Caughnawaga, 1175; a mission settlement of Mohawk and Oneida Indians, 345, 889, 1295.

Caughnawagas, Indians, 861, 988, 1167, 1280, 1283; their contraband trade between New York and Canada, 346;

join in an attack on Deerfield, 373, 377; they march away from Deerfield, 382–89; join a war-party, 400.

Caulfield, deputy-governor at Annapolis, 466; tries to induce the Acadians to swear allegiance to George I., 472.

Cavaliers, the, 864.

Cayugas, 1110; efforts of the French to convert, 889.

"Célèbre," the, number of her guns, 1232 note; burned by the English, 1241.

Céloron de Bienville, 871, 897 note, 902 and note, 932, 935; at Ogdensburg and Niagara, 871; despatched to the West to hold the land for France, 871–87; leaden plates buried by, 874, 878, 879, 887 note; inscription on the plates, 874–75, 877–78, 887 note; the plates discovered, 878, 887 note; visits the Senecas, 875; drives out the English from the West, 875–81; extract from his writings, 876 note, 879–81, 887 note; encounter with Indians at Scioto, 878; name given by, to the Kenawha River, 878 note; failure of his plans with regard to La Demoiselle, 880; return of his party to Canada, 880, 881; journey to the Ohio, 889; visits the mission of Father Piquet, 889; at Detroit, 897; his character, 897; ordered to attack Pickawillany, 900; orders from La Jonquière, 902.

Celts in Pennsylvania, 866.

Census, the, taken in Acadia and Canada, 859 and note, 909 note, 929, 1317.

"Centurion," the, 1354, 1355.

Cerberus, dog belonging to Piquet, 892.

Chacornacle, ——, accompanies Cadillac to Detroit, 355.

Chamberlain, John, said to have shot the Indian chief Paugus, 513 note.

Chambly, Fort, 1152; abandoned by the French, 1448.

Chambly, the French outpost, 387; near Montreal, 430; a fort built at, by the French, 613.

Chambord, 852.

Champigny, intendant of Canada, 105, 240; his treacherous seizure of Indians at Fort Frontenac, 108–09; at Quebec, 181; at Montreal, 184; defends himself, 215–16; relations with Frontenac, 231; a champion of the Jesuits, 233, 238; reconciled to Frontenac, 308–09; opposes Callières, 315; opposes the plan of Cadillac for the Indians, 353.

Champlain, Lake, 346, 348, 387, 426, 430, 728, 843, 861, 975, 1043, 1047, 1049, 1065, 1102, 1115, 1121, 1129, 1135, 1140, 1144, 1148, 1152, 1167, 1168, 1257, 1265, 1279, 1317, 1331, 1361, 1369, 1370, 1444.

Chandler, a chaplain, his diary quoted concerning the camp at Lake George, 1060.

Chaplains, 1276–77; their pay, 1107; their accommodations, 1119 note.

Chardon, missionary, his scheme concerning the Outagamies, 559.

Charles II., 425, 517.

Charles VI., his will, 858; death of, 858; his will set aside, 858.

Charles River, 1400.

Charlesbourg, 1211, 1379, 1408.

Charlestown Neck, Mass., 636.

Charlestown, N.H., 727, 1373, 1374; road built by Amherst, 1363. See Number Four.

Charlevoix, Jesuit historian, quoted, 367, 431 note, 479, 1090; quoted concerning the siege of Port Royal, 439 note; at Kaskaskia, 553; his search for the Pacific Ocean, 581 and note.

Charters, 862.

Chartres, Duc de, mentioned, 554.

Chartres, Fort, 873, 896; enabled the French to control the upper Mississippi, 614; increasing power of the English, 901.

Chassin, Michel de, quoted concerning the wives sent to Louisiana, 546–47; in council at "the Illinois," 554 note.

Château battery, the, 1341.

Château Richer, a Jesuit mission near Quebec, 390.

Châtelet, the, 1459.

Chaudière River, 340, 477, 959, 1104; fortifications on, 975.

Chautauqua, Lake, 872.

Chebucto, plan for making a naval station by the English, 907; harbor of, 907. See *Halifax*.

Chedabucto (Nova Scotia), Frontenac's rendezvous, 141; fortifications, 244.

Chenitou (Chignecto), 925 *note*.

Cherbourg, 1228.

Cherokees, the, 891, 939, 1161, 1480; their service sought by the English army, 1291.

Chesnaye (La), a trader of Quebec, 61, 81.

Chesnaye, La, massascres at, 145, 219–20.

Chester County, 1082.

"Chester," English war-ship, 437, 449; sent to reinforce Annapolis, 685.

Chesterfield, Lord, 849; his opinion of Lord Albemarle, 967; acts as mediator, 1224; his despondency, 1226.

Chevereaux, an Acadian missionary, 469.

"Chèvre," the number of her guns, 1232 *note*.

Chevry, M. de, quoted, 404 *note*.

Chew, Ensign, 1292 *note*.

Chibucto (Halifax), 410; arrival of Duc D'Anville at, 680.

Chickasaws, Indians, 939; attack the colonists in Louisiana, 548–49; mentioned, 571.

Chignecto Bay, 909, 927.

Chignecto (Beaubassin) Acadia, 925 *note;* concerning the migration of its people, 466, 698; preparations of the French to attack, 1009; proposal to give the land to English settlers, 1021.

Chignecto Channel, 1028.

Chimney Point, on Lake Champlain, 744.

Chiningué, 876, 881, 935.

Chinodahichetha, name given by Céloron to the Kenawha River, 878 *note*.

Chipody, 927, 928, 1015, 1019; news of disaster, 1034.

Choctaws, Indians of Mississippi, 891, 1161; allies of the French, 549.

Choiseul, Duc de, his character, 1465; made minister of foreign affairs,

1465; sketch of, by Stanley, 1465; propositions made to Pitt, 1465–66; his forethought, 1466; the Family Compact, 1466; his negotiation with Pitt proves fruitless, 1466; terms of peace offered to England, 1466; desires peace with England, 1471; his predictions concerning American possessions, 1471.

Choke-Cherry Indians, a band of the Sioux, 600 and *note*.

Christ Church, Philadelphia, 1306.

Christian, a Mohawk, in the attack on Norridgewock, 500.

Christianity, Indian followers of, 873, 1175–76.

Christmas Day, 1426.

Chubb (Pascho), commands at Pemaquid, 273; which he surrenders, 274.

Church of Notre Dame de Quebec, 1501.

Church of Rome. See *Catholicism*.

Church of the Jesuits, the, after the siege, 1421.

Church, Colonel Benjamin, sent on expedition by Governor Dudley, 417; inhabitant of Deerfield, 378; his scheme of retaliation for Deerfield, 417; attacks Canadians at Passamaquoddy Bay, 418; attacks Grand Pré, 418; at Port Royal, 419.

Church, *Entertaining Passages*, cited, 419 *note*.

Cimarron River, 579.

Clare River, 1039.

Clark, Fort, on the Missouri River, 578.

Claverie, La Friponne, 1212.

Cleaveland, John, chaplain of Bagley's Massachusetts regiment, 1248; extract from his diary, 1275, 1277 *note*, 1283–84; extract from letters to his wife, 1276, 1277 *note*; report concerning the defences of Abercromby, 1276; preaching on Sunday, 1277; his illness, 1279.

Cleaveland, Miss Abby E., 1277 *note*.

Cleaves, Benjamin, his journal cited, 671 *note*.

Clement, ——, complained of for selling liquor to the Indians, 717.

Clergy, the, how considered during the reign of George II., 848; corruption of, 854; the condition of, in France, 854, 855, 856; influence of, in regard to the oath of allegiance for the Acadians, 917 *note*. See *Acadians*.

Clergy battery, the, 1341.

Clerk, engineer under Abercromby, reconnoitres the French works, 1267.

Clermont, 852; recalled, 1228.

Clinker, Humphrey, 965.

Clinton, George, Governor of New York, 905 *note;* induced the Iroquois to join in the invasion of Canada, 712; his enemy, Chief-Justice James De Lancey, 713; hampered in his war-plans by the Assembly, 713; his complaints to the Duke of Newcastle concerning the Assembly, 714; desirability of an Indian alliance, 885; quotation from, concerning the neglect of New York to protect Indian trade, 886–87; invites commissioners from the provinces to meet the Indians at Albany, 887; Johnson's complaints of the French dealings with the Indians, 888; quarrels with the Assembly of New York, 894–95; complaints concerning invasions of territory by the French, 899.

Clive, the victory of Plassey, 1227.

Clock, George, complained of for selling liquor to the Indians, 717.

Cobb, Captain Sylvanus, sails into Chibucto harbor to spy upon the French fleet, 684.

Cobequid (Truro), 918; a missionary station, 698, 700, 708; formerly the name of Truro, 910; Acadian emigration from, 919; mountains of, 1029; failure of the expedition to, 1037.

Cobequid Bay, 700.

Cocheco (Dover, N.H.), attacked, 165.

Cockerill, Thomas, 428 *note*.

Cocquard, Father Claude Godefroy, his remarks concerning the fall of Oswego, 1125.

Cod, Cape, soldiers from, for the French campaigns, 1014.

Coffen, Stephen, deposition of, 934 *note*.

Coffin, an illicit trader, 408.

Colbert, minister of Louis XIV., 339, 1476; his zeal for the French colonies, 22; despatches to Frontenac, 26, 40, 46, 52; instructions to Duchesneau, 42, 43, 49.

Colden, Alexander, 1493.

Coldfoot, a Miami chief, 901.

Coldstream Guards, the, 974.

Cole, Isaac, killed by Indians, 370.

Collections of Maine Historical Society, cited, 708 *note*.

Collections of New Hampshire Historical Society, 727 *note*.

Collections of Nova Scotia Historical Society, cited, 426 *note*, 438 *note*.

Collections of Wisconsin Historical Society, cited, 563 *note*.

College of the Jesuits, the, after the siege, 1421.

Colombière, in Ramesay's expedition, 698; assists in the attack upon Grand Pré, 704.

Colonial New York, cited, 434 *note*.

Colorado, 579.

Colton, Mrs., great-granddaughter of John Williams, 396 *note*.

Comanche Indians, join Spaniards to attack the French at the Illinois, 574; visit of Bourgmont to their village, 577; make a treaty of alliance with Bourgmont, 577–78.

"Comète," number of her guns, 1232 *note*.

Commissioners of boundary, 929–31, 1007–08; commissioners of Indian affairs, 962–64, 977.

Condé, 852, 1322.

Condé, Prince de, 756.

Conflans, M. de, commands French ships-of-war, 680, 1469; arrives at Halifax, and re-sails for France, 682.

Congregationalists in the army, 1277.

Congress at Albany, of Indians and English, 962–64.

Congress of Governors, cited, 446 *note*.

Connecticut, 887, 1014, 1042, 1045, 1054, 1118; called upon for troops, 426; assists in an attack upon Louisbourg, 623; her contribution toward the siege of Louisbourg, 631; reimbursed for expenses of taking Louisbourg, 670; contributes men to capture Canada, 677; appointment of the governor of, 862; extent of the New England border, 864; soldiers in the expedition against Crown Point, 1044–45; recruits sent to Johnson, 1059; to provide an officer for the English garrison, 1060; money granted to, from Parliament, 1104 *note;* her sacrifices in time of war, 1256; provincials under Abercromby, 1261; men serving under Putnam, 1280.

Connecticut River, 717, 1372, 1373.

Conner, James, English scout, 1126; visits Oswego, 1126; the news of the loss carried to Fort Johnson, 1127.

Contades, 852; appointed to command, 1228.

Contrecœur, 1136; succeeds Saint-Pierre in command, 942; commandant at Fort Duquesne, 945, 988, 1485; Jumonville sent on an expedition to warn the English to leave the West, 945; harangues the Indians, 949; consults with Beaujeu, 989; his resolution to despatch forces to meet Braddock, 989–90; waits at Fort Duquesne, 990; return of the troops after defeating Braddock, 996, 997; Dumas succeeds at Fort Duquesne, 1070; orders concerning prisoners, 1071 *note;* receives the cross of the Order of St. Louis, 1488.

Converts, Indians, their piety, &c., 264, 271 *note.*

Conway, General, letter from Walpole, 1441–42.

Conway, New Hampshire, 506.

Cook, his voyages, 1477.

Cope, Major Jean-Baptiste, Indian chief, signs a treaty of peace with the English, 916; the murder of Capt. Howe, 926.

Copps Hill, Boston, 446.

Corbière, Colonel Parker's company taken, 1174.

Cork, 968.

Corlaer. (See *Schenectady.*)

Corlaer, Indian word for the English, 1177.

Corlaer, the Iroquois name for the governor of New York, 74 *note* (see 86, 106, 148); origin of the name, 160 *note.*

Cornbury, Lord, quoted, 342, 375, 555; Governor of New York, 375.

Corneille, 1202.

Cornier, Madame, 1154.

Cornwallis, Edward, uncle of Lord Cornwallis, 909; made governor of Acadia, 909; opinions of Wolfe and of Horace Walpole concerning, 909, 920; makes the oath of allegiance more strict for the Acadians, 912; his successor, 916; efforts of, to compel the Acadians to swear fidelity to England, 917; angry letter written to the Bishop of Quebec, 918; discovers the treachery of the French, 918; relations with the French and Acadians, 918–20; his speech to the Acadians, 920–21; misplaced confidence in the French crown, 921; mild rule of, in Nova Scotia, 922, 1021; his opinion of Le Loutre, 923.

Cornwallis, Lord, 909.

Corpron, 1216; his official knavery, 1211–13; thrown into the Bastille, 1459.

Corse, Elizabeth, married Jean Dumontel, 395.

Cortlandt, ——, 342; manor of, 867.

Cosnan, Captain, 1349.

Costebelle, governor at Placentia, 425; his scheme for warning Massachusetts against the designs of England, 440, 442; letter commanding the evacuation of Placentia, etc., 461.

Côte d'Abraham, 1431.

Côte Ste.-Geneviève, 1402, 1403, 1431.

Côteau du Lac, the, 1450.

Coudres, Isle aux, 1333, 1376; ordered to be evacuated, 1335; Admiral Durell at, 1337.

Coulon de Villiers. (See *Villiers, Coulon de.*)

Council at Onondaga, 146–49; at Montreal, 317–24.

Council at Quebec, hostile to Frontenac, 44–47, 182–84; alarmed at rumors of attack, 181.

Courcelle, predecessor of Frontenac, 30.

Coureurs de bois, 1317, 1349; to be arrested, 32, 35; amnesty, 47; under Du Lhut, 48, 79, 99, 111, 144; their influence with Frontenac, 50–51; the king's charge regarding them, 51; at Michillimackinac, 95; deserters, 97; in the Seneca expedition, 114; their license, 137; hardihood, 154.

Courserac, 1251 *note;* sent to the English camp from Louisbourg, 1246.

Courtemanche, a French officer, escorts ransomed prisoners from Canada, 394 and *note;* in Ramesay's expedition, 698; his advance upon Fort William Henry, 1179.

Courts-martial in the English army, 1360.

Courval, the French fire-rafts commanded by, 1353.

Coxe, *Description of Carolina,* quoted, 537 *note.*

Crafts, Benjamin, a private at Louisbourg, extract from his diary, 673; death of, 674.

Craggs, Secretary, 473 *note.*

Crawford Notch, 506.

Crawford, Chaplain William, letter to Timothy Paine, 1119; his account of the provincial camp, 1119.

Creeds and politics at Acadia, 464.

Crespel, Père, chaplain of Lignery's expedition, 560.

Cristineaux, Indians of the West, 584–87; join La Vérendrye in his search for the Pacific, 587–88.

Croghan, George, 874; expedition of, to the Ohio, 882–86; Indian trader, 882; sent to the Miamis to promote friendly feelings, 885, 886 and *note;* accusations against, 899; reward offered for his scalp, 899; brings Indians to Braddock's camp, 984.

Crown Point, 861, 963, 1043, 1069, 1102, 1152, 1257, 1266; landing of Ramesay's troops at, 430; the intention of the English to seize, 613; the French build a fort and take possession, 613; the capture of, proposed by Governor Shirley, 679; capture of, planned, 975–77, 1041; expedition against, led by Colonel William Johnson, 977, 1041–62, 1099, 1104; French designs in relation to, 1043, 1046, 1048; reached by Dieskau, 1048; the battle, 1053–61; result of the expedition, 1059–60; importance of, 1102; plan of capture by Shirley, 1104–06, 1115; expeditions of Rogers' rangers, 1139–41; Winslow's regret at the failures of the English, 1142; the scouting-party of Rogers, 1144–47; captured by Amherst, 1359–62, 1378; retreat of the French, 1361; new fort built by Amherst, 1362–63, 1370; the situation between French and English, 1444.

Crozat, Antoine, the monopoly of Louisiana granted to him, 542; thwarted in his project, he resigns his charter, 545.

Cruger, Mayor, difficulty in quartering the troops in New York, 1143.

Cruikshank, Captain, affront given to a provincial regiment, 1278.

Culloden, battle of, 847, 849, 858, 1322.

Cumberland, Duke of, 977, 1019, 1224; his place as a soldier, 966; his opinion of Major-General Braddock, 968; military plans of, 1006; his prejudice against Shirley, 1130–31; miscarriage of his plans, 1226; recalled from Germany, 1227.

Cumberland, Nova Scotia, 1028.

Cumberland, Penn., 1132.

Cumberland County laid waste, 1080.

Cumberland Fort, 984, 999–1002, 1287; erection of, 982; distance from Little Meadows, 986; Colonel James Innes, commander of, 1000; name given to Beauséjour, 1019, 1020 (see *Beauséjour*), 1028, 1037, 1320; Indians attack the frontier, and murder the settlers, 1071–73, 1079; St. Patrick's Day celebrated, 1320.

Cumming, C. F. Gordon, 1496.

Cummings, Colonel, disgraceful order of Abercromby to, 1275.

Cummings, William, joined in Lovewell's expedition, 509.

Cushnoc (Augusta), 483.

Cut Nose, an Iroquois convert, 146; his speech at the Onondaga council, 147.

Cutter, Captain Ammi, left in command of defences at Canseau, 637.

D'Aillebout, Captain, commandant at the Island Battery at Louisbourg, 656, 784.

Daine, Mayor of Quebec, 1410.

Dalling, Major, sent to occupy Port Espagnol, 1249; Canadians taken prisoners, 1352; encounter with Canadians and Indians, 1427; his light infantry, 1434.

Dalquier, Lieutenant-Colonel, 1405; his leadership and bravery, 1435.

Dalzell, Captain, skirmish in the woods, 1280; his death, 1280.

D'Anjou, Duc, contests with France the Louisiana country, 538–39.

Danvers, 1298.

D'Anville, Duc, sails with his fleet for Halifax, 680; meets with severe storms, 681; arrival at Chibucto (Halifax), 682; death of, 683; return of the fleet to France, 685; the disasters to the fleet, 685–86.

Darby, Major, 1448.

D'Argenson, 665.

D'Artaguette, Diron, accompanies Bienville to Louisiana as intendant, 540, 549; quoted, 541.

D'Artaguette, Pierre, captured and killed by the Chickasaws, 554.

Daudin, priest of Pisiquid, 1012.

Daulnay, Jean, Canadian, 395.

Daulnay, Mrs. Jean (Freedom French), 395.

Daun, the Austrian general, 1460; his victory, 1460.

"Dauphin," escape of the, 970–71.

Dauphin, Fort, built by La Vérendrye, 587.

Dauphin Island, a French fort established at, 539.

Dauphin's Bastion, the, 1233; approach of Wolfe, 1241; condition of the besieged, 1243; the white flag, 1244; to be opened to British troops, 1247.

Dauphin's Battery, the, 1341.

D'Auteuil, a member of Rigaud's war-party, 739.

Davis, ——, saved the meeting-house from the Indians at Haverhill, 401.

Davis, Eleazer, in the fight at Lovewell's Pond, 512; reached the fort at Lake Ossipee, 512.

Davis, Sylvanus, a trader, commanding at Fort Loyal, Casco Bay, 168; his surrender, 170; captivity, 170–71.

Davison, a trader, 935.

Deas, D., cited, 683 note.

Debeline, General, mentioned as a commander of Canadian troops, 723.

De Cosne, 970.

Deerfield, its site, people, etc., 374; the attack of Hertel de Rouville upon, planned, 374; fears of an Indian attack, 375; the end of a winter day at, 376; the attack upon, 377; driving the enemy out of, 380; after the attack, 381; the number of killed and wounded, 381; garrisoned against further attack, 382.

Defiance, Mount, 1266–68.

De Gannes, quoted, 439 note.

Degonnor, Jesuit missionary, 584.

De Goutin recounts some gossip at Port Royal, 414.

Déjean, 1091.

Delancey, Lieutenant-Governor of New York, 1061, 1143; asked to aid in repelling the French on the Ohio, 940; council of governors held with Braddock, 975–77; the cabal against Shirley, 1069, 1105; questions at issue in New York, 1084; orders to fire upon deserters, 1198.

De Lancey, James, Chief-Justice of New York, an enemy to Governor Clinton, 713.

Delancey, Oliver, soldiers sent to lodge with, 1143.

De la Vente, quoted, 544.

Delaware, colony of, 867.

Delaware, George, Indian chief, 1295.

Delawares, the, 872, 876, 884, 886, 933, 984; attitude towards the English, 885; efforts of the English to obtain allies from, 946; at Fort Duquesne,

949; instigated to fight against the English, 1070, 1079–80; council held with Johnson, 1111; attack and reduction of Kittanning, 1132–34; convention of Indians, 1293–94; wavering allies, 1294; declare themselves allies of the English, 1296, 1297, 1299.

De Léry, his paper, *Mémoire sur la Canada*, cited, 430 *note*.

De l'Isle, the geographer, 569 *note*.

Delouche commands the fire-ships, 1342.

De Monts, commission of, 929 *note*.

De Muy, brothers, reinforce Fort Frédéric at Crown Point, 731; the younger, a member of Rigaud's war-party, 733; the elder, sent to the fort to parley with Hawks, 739.

De Muys, sent to succeed Bienville in Louisiana, 540; death of, 540.

Denmark, 852.

Denny, Governor, 1134 *note*.

Denonville, successor of La Barre as governor of Canada, 1685–1689, sails for Canada, 91; circumstances there, his character, 92; his instructions, 93; his intrigues, 94; correspondence with Dongan, 95–101; threatens to attack Albany, 99; orders Du Lhut to shoot bush-rangers and deserters, 100; plans an expedition against the Iroquois, 105; musters the Canadian militia, 106; treacherously seizes a party of Indians, 107–08; arrives at Fort Frontenac, 110; at Irondequoit Bay, 113; march for the Seneca country, 114–15; battle in the woods, 116; his report of the battle, 116–17; destroys "the Babylon of the Senecas," 117; builds a fort on the Niagara, 118; further correspondence with Dongan, 120–26; sends an envoy to Albany, 123; abandons the Niagara fort, 126; begs for the return of Indian captives, 126; his wretched condition, 127; seeks a conference with the Iroquois, 128; who deceive him, and invade Canada, 133; horrors of the invasion, 134–35; he is recalled, and succeeded by Frontenac, 136; who finds him at Montreal, 143; having ordered the destruction of Fort Frontenac, 143; orders the occupation of Detroit, 351–52.

De Noyan, commandant at Fort Frontenac, 1284.

Denys, M. de La Ronde, sent to Boston with a mission from New France, 442; his mission a failure, 443; induced the Acadians to migrate, 465; continues his mission to other settlements, 466.

"Deptford," a British frigate, 420.

D'Éraque, with Le Sueur on the Mississippi, 569; abandoned Fort l'Huillier, 569.

Deruisseau, a French scout, 430.

Desandrouin, French engineer, 1265.

Desauniers, Demoiselles, 889.

Deschambault, 1202, 1378, 1430, 1443.

Deschamps, Chief Justice, diary found in his house, 1252 *note*.

Deschenaux, M., 760; official corruption, 1216.

Descombles, French engineer, 1121; reconnoitres the fort at Oswego, 1122–23; shot by an Indian, 1122–23.

Deserters, French, demanded by Denonville, 98; sheltered by Dongan, 100–01.

Desgouttes withdraws the "Aréthuse," 1240–41; considerations in regard to capitulation, 1244–46; correspondence with Drucour, 1251 *note*.

Des Habitants River, the, 1028; reconnoissance of, 1031.

Desherbiers, commandant at Louisbourg, instructions in regard to the Acadians, 914; his treachery, 914, 915; medals sent to, 914.

Désirade Island, restored by England, 1472.

Desliettes, commandant in the Illinois country, proposes to exterminate the Outagamies, 559; joins Lignery's expedition against them, 560 and *note*.

Desligneris, in Ramesay's expedition, 698; assists in attack on Grand Pré, 701–02.

Desméloizes, Mademoiselle, wife of M. Péan, 1215.

Des Moines, 1176.

De Soto, 861.

"Despatch," one of Walker's war-ships, 451.

D'Estournel, vice-admiral of D'Anville's fleet, 683; death of, 683–84.

Destrahoudal, M., commander of warship "La Palme," 685.

Detroit, 87, 901, 988, 995, 1175, 1280, 1293, 1365; a fort built here by Du Lhut, 99; held by the French, 324; Farmer's *History of,* cited, 349 *note;* motives of both French and English for the occupation of, 351; the city of, founded by La Mothe-Cadillac, 355; an attempt at settlement by the French, 358; included in deed from the Five Nations to King William III., 358; in command of Sieur Dubuisson, 521; arrival of the Outagamies, a hostile tribe, 522; some mischief done by the Indians, 522; arrival of friendly Indians to aid Dubuisson, 524, 525; its growth under the charge of La Mothe-Cadillac, 552; importance of the post, 896, 899–900; population of, 896, 897 *note;* Céloron visits, with a royal commission, 897; plan of, 897 *note;* efforts to build up, by the French, 897; smallpox at, 901; the English to be attacked, 901; danger to Fort Duquesne, 1305; the coureurs-de-bois, 1317; retreat to, of the French forces, 1367; injured by the loss of Niagara, 1368.

Dettingen, 858, 1322, 1463.

Devonshire, Duke of, 1224.

D'Harcourt, Duc, 538 *note.*

Diamond, Cape, 1341, 1343, 1439.

"Diana," the, 1440.

Diderot, 856; meeting with Dieskau, 1057 *note,* 1058.

Dieskau, Baron, 733, 1043, 1099, 1101; letter of, quoted, 968–69; made general in Canada, 968; a letter of Braddock found, 1043; his forces, 1043, 1048, 1095; plans of, in regard to the French campaign, 1043; prepares an ambush for Johnson, 1048, 1051–53; advances through the forest, 1049–50; news of the approach of the

English, 1051; the battle of Lake George, 1052–62; success of the action against Whiting and Williams, 1053; badly wounded, 1055–56, 1058; carried to the English camp, and kindly cared for, 1056–57; his defeat, 1056, 1184, 1257; his remarks concerning his surrender, and Johnson's soldiers, 1056 and *note,* 1057; carried to Fort Lyman, 1057; his interview with Diderot, 1057 and *note,* 1058; his life threatened by the Mohawks, 1057; his life saved by Johnson, 1057; his service under Saxe, 1057; his death, 1058; his Indians tomahawk the Englishmen, 1059; succeeded by Montcalm, 1087–88; his salary, 1091.

Diet at Presburg, 858.

Dinwiddie, Robert, Lieutenant-Governor of Virginia, 874, 937–38; letter to Hamilton quoted, 874 *note;* desirability of an Indian alliance, 885; difficulties of boundary, 886; letter from, to Saint-Pierre, introducing George Washington, 934–35, 936; tries to repel the French aggression in the West, 935, 938, 939, 941, 964, 976; answer sent to, from Saint-Pierre, 936; report of Washington made to, 937; orders received from the King, 938; his dependence on the Assembly of Virginia, 938, 955; Virginia refuses to pay certain fees, 938–39; sends Washington with a party to resist the French at Fort Duquesne, 938–54; orders sent to Indian tribes on the Ohio, 939; seeks aid from other colonies, 939; letter to Lord Fairfax, 939; a fort to be built on the Ohio, 939; letters to Hanbury quoted, 940, 942 and *note;* invites the Indians to meet him at Winchester, 940; the governor's Palace, 941, 956; seeks to raise regiments, 941; plans of the English blighted, 942, 943; good news from Washington, 943; letters from Druillon, 946; the defeat of Washington, 955; letter to a London correspondent quoted, 955; speech to the Assembly of Virginia, 956–57; exasperated at the French,

960–61; letter to Lord Granville quoted, 964; correspondence with Glen, 964–65; desires aid from the home government, 965; taxes recommended, 965; his opinion of Braddock, 972; accompanies Braddock to Alexandria, 974–75; council of governors held with Braddock, 975–77; defends taxation by Parliament, 976; supplies for the army scarce, 980, 981; praises of the New England colonies, 981; greatly disturbed at the losses of the English, 1001–05; letter to Lord Halifax, 1001–02; correspondence with Orme quoted, 1002–04; correspondence with Washington, 1002–03; sends Major Colin Campbell for news, 1002; desires to renew offensive operations, 1003–04; letter to Dunbar quoted, 1003–04; his view of Dunbar's conduct justified, 1004 *note;* his fears realized, 1005; his plans of war, 1072; relations with Washington, 1286; removed from office, 1286; matters pertaining to the "assassination" of Jumonville, 1484–85.

Dobbs, Governor of North Carolina, 972; council of governors held with Braddock, 975–77.

Dobson, Captain, 1002.

Dog tribe, the, 891.

Dominica taken by England, 1469; to belong to England, 1473.

Dominique, Father, at Acadia, 462.

Dongan (an Irish Catholic), governor of New Netherland, 72; holds an Indian council at Albany, 73–74; his rivalry with Canada, 93; complaints of Denonville, 94; their correspondence, 95–99; he sends Denonville some oranges, 100; vindicates himself, 100; his pacific instructions from England, 104; his wrath at the French attack on the Indian country, 120; is recalled, and replaced by Sir Edmund Andros, 124.

Dongan, Governor, New York, granted the "Hoosac Patent" to Dutch settlers, 734 *note.*

Doolittle, *Narrative of Mischief,* etc., cited, 722 *note,* 727 *note.*

Doolittle, Rev. Benjamin, his heterogeneous labors at Northfield, 729; his record of Indian invasion, etc., 730 and *note;* death of, 730.

Dorchester, Mass., 420; a rendezvous for troops, 436.

Doreil, commissary of war, embarks with Dieskau, 968–69; letter from Montcalm to, 1273; letter to the minister of war, 1307; appeal made to France, 1313; letter concerning the state of Canada, 1313; double-dealing of Vaudreuil, 1314; matters pertaining to Ticonderoga, 1492–96.

Dorman, Ephraim, an inhabitant of Keene, surprised by the Indians, 718.

Doty, ——, interpreter in Rigaud's war-party, 740.

Doucette, deputy-governor at Annapolis, 466, 470 *note.*

Douglas, ——, cited, 619 *note.*

Douglas, Dr., quoted concerning the expedition against Louisbourg, 633, 650; estimates the loss of men at Island Battery, 657 *note;* extracts from his observations, 674.

Douville, orders concerning prisoners, 1071 *note;* killed, 1132.

Dover, 1471.

Dover, N.H. (Cocheco), attacked by Indians, 165, 399; annoyed by Indians, 402.

Downing, Joshua, killed by Indians, 370.

"Dragon," English war-ship, 427, 434 *note,* 437.

Drake, S. G., *Particular History,* etc., cited, 730 *note.*

Dresden taken from Frederic, 1461.

Drowned Lands, the, 1049, 1052.

Drucour, Governor at Louisbourg, 1233; the siege and reduction of Louisbourg, 1233–51, 1251 *note;* statistics of troops, 1235 *note;* his effort to protect the harbor of Louisbourg, 1239; courtesies between the commanders, 1240; his lodgings in flames, 1242; Amherst promises to spare the sick, 1244 *note;* terms of capitulation extended to, 1244–47; signs the capitulation, 1247.

Drucour, Madame, her heroism, 1240.

Druillon, letters sent to Dinwiddie, 946.

Dublin, 1129 *note*, 1327.

"Dublin," the ship, Amherst embarks in her, 1230.

Dubrowski, 1221 *note*.

Dubuisson, Sieur, in command at Detroit, 521; surprised by a visit from the Outagamies, 522; asks aid of friendly Indians, 523; leads an attack upon the camp of the Outagamies, 525; grants an interview to the chief of the Outagamies, 527; addresses his wavering allies, 529; the Outagamies surrender to, 532; to Vaudreuil, cited, 533 *note*; mentioned, 563 *note*.

Du Cayla, 1489.

Duchambon, Governor, at Louisbourg during the siege, 640; quoted, 643 and *note*; his blunder in deserting the Grand Battery, 644; quoted concerning the siege of Louisbourg, 649–50; refuses to surrender Louisbourg, 654; his account of the attack upon the Island Battery, 657; offers resistance to the taking of Lighthouse Point by the English, 658; receives news of the taking of the war-ship "Vigilant" by the English, 659; sends a flag of truce to Pepperrell and Warren, 663; agrees to Pepperrell's terms of capitulation, 664; his report of the surrender mentioned, 671 *note*.

Duchat, Captain, his description of Canadian life, 1103.

Duchesnaye, 1210.

Duchesneau, sent as intendant to Quebec, sides with the clergy against Frontenac, 43; dispute as to the presidency of the council, 48–51; quarrel in the council, 48; his accusations against Frontenac, 49–51; Frontenac's complaints of him, 52–54; and violence to his son, 55; Duchesneau recalled, 57.

Duclos, ——, intendant in Louisiana, 543.

Dudley, Governor Joseph, attempts a peace with Indians of Maine, 360; sends troops to defend against the Abenakis Indians, 369; quoted, 382 *note*; quoted concerning the ransom of prisoners, 393; gives leave for a raid into Canada, 403; to Lord ——, cited, 403 *note*; urges the capture of Quebec, 404; attempts a neutrality with Governor Vaudreuil, 405; sent prisoner to England, 406; a member of Parliament, 406; portrayed, 406–08; sent as governor of Massachusetts, 406; accused of illicit trade with the French, 408; a memorial for his recall refused, 409; sends Colonel Church on an expedition into Canada, 417; proposes an expedition against Port Royal, 420; appoints Colonel John March commander, 420; sends councillors to Colonel March, 423; receives the royal message for the reduction of Canada, 427; disappointed by the non-arrival of the British squadron, 433; in conference of governors concerning England's attack on Canada, 446.

Dudley, Governor Thomas, 405.

Dudley, Paul, 407.

Dudley, William, goes to Canada with Courtemanche, 394, 405; concerning the officers at Port Royal, 423; sent as ambassador to Vaudreuil, 503; interviews the Indians, 504.

Dufferin, Lord, 1221 *note*.

Dugué, ——, accompanies Cadillac to Detroit, 355.

Du Lhut, a leader of *coureurs de bois*, 48, 50, 67, 79; rivalry with English traders of Hudson's Bay, 67; intrigues with Indians, 87; builds a fort near Detroit, 99; where he has a large force of French and Indians, 111, 112; leads attack on the Senecas, 114; defeats a party of Indians on the Ottawa, 144.

Dulhut, Greysolon, occupied Detroit, 351.

Dumas, has charge of the youth of Montcalm, 1088; letter of, concerning Montcalm's education, 1088.

Dumas, Captain, at Fort Duquesne,

988; encounter with Braddock, 993–1000; returns to Fort Duquesne, 996; succeeds Contrecœur at Fort Duquesne, 1070; efforts of the French to prevent the torture of prisoners, 1071; quoted concerning his influence over the Indians, 1071; the border warfare encouraged by, 1071; commands the party to attack the English at Point Levi, 1345; his failure to dislodge the English, 1348; holds Cap-Rouge, 1353; to prevent Murray moving up the St. Lawrence, 1443; advances upon Montreal, 1446; matters relating to a pension for, 1486; receives the cross of the Order of St. Louis, 1488.

Dummer, Fort, a subject of dispute between Massachusetts and New Hampshire, 720.

Dummer, Jeremiah, 408 *note*, 424 *note*.

Dummer, William, acting governor of Massachusetts, 495; the Legislature attempt to deprive him of his prerogative of power, 496; correspondence with Vaudreuil on the death of Sebastien Rale, the missionary, 502; sends an embassy to Vaudreuil, 503.

Dumont, 1434, 1435.

Dumontel, Jean, 395.

Dumontel, Mrs. Jean (Elizabeth Corse), 395.

Dunbar, Colonel Thomas, his troops, 983, 995 *note*, 1373; to take command of the rear division of Braddock's expedition, 986; reinforcements for Braddock, 998; arrival at his camp, of a portion of Braddock's army, 999; his course of action blamed by the colonies, 999; arrival of his train at Fort Cumberland, 1000; encamped at Great Meadows, 1000; retreat of, 1000, 1071; exhorted to retrieve the English losses, 1003–04; his conduct wanting in courage, and condemned by Dinwiddie, 1003–05, 1004 *note;* letter to, from Dinwiddie, quoted, 1003–04; instructions from his superior officers neglected, 1004.

Dunkirk, fortress of, 1466; the fortress to be destroyed, 1473.

"Dunkirk," the, chases the French vessels, 970.

"Dunkirk of America," the, 1231.

Dunstable, Mass., 506; attacked by Indians, 507; joins in Lovewell's expedition, 508.

Duperrier, captain of French war-ship "Northumberland," 682.

Dupuy, intendant at Canada, 559.

Duquesne, Fort, 980, 1067, 1286; built by the French, 942, 1076 *note;* expedition of Jumonville, 945; reinforcements sent to, 948–49; French force at, 952, 986; exultant return of Villiers to, 954; Braddock to lead the expedition against, 976; Braddock's expedition against, 985–87, 991–1001, 1485–88; parties sent out to interrupt General Braddock's march, 986; situation and appearance of, 987–88; command held by Contrecœur, 988; number of Indians and Canadians at, 988; Indians and French depart from, to fight with Braddock's expedition, 990–91, 1485–88; return of the French troops, 996; desire to attack a second time, 1004; Dumas succeeds Contrecœur in command, 1070; plan of capture, 1104; the attack abandoned, 1104; importance of position, 1228; the war-policy of Pitt, 1228, 1286; expedition against, fitted out by the English, 1229, 1285; approached by General Forbes's army, 1285–88, 1290–93; French reinforcements sent to, 1293; Indians near, sought as allies by English and French, 1293, 1294; M. de Ligneris, commandant of, 1293; the missions of Frederic Post, 1294–99; Post invited to go thither, 1295; Grant's expedition, 1299–1301; statistics concerning the daily rations, 1300 *note;* desperate condition of the French, 1302; evacuated by the French, 1304–05; garrison left by the English under Lieutenant-Colonel Mercer, 1305; effect of the English victory, 1306, 1359;

letter from Montcalm referring to matters there, 1311.

Duquesne, Marquis, Governor of Canada, 873 *note,* 1009; his opinion of Piquet, 891 *note;* his character and personal appearance, 903; prepares to secure the upper part of the Ohio Valley, 903–04; influenced by unworthy motives, 904; landing of his force at Presquisle, 932; a fort to be built on French Creek, 933; instructions to Marin, 933; plans of the expedition thwarted, 933–34; return of a part of the expedition to Montreal, 934; letters of, compared with other writings, 934 *note;* Contrecœur succeeds Saint-Pierre, 942; succeeded by De Vaudreuil, 968, 1043; orders sent to, from France, 969; letters to Le Loutre concerning Acadia, 1009; relations with Le Loutre, 1009–12; his harsh treatment of the Acadians, 1013; resigns his government, 1043; his discipline over troops, 1096.

Duquesnel, governor of Canada, 617; attempts the capture of Annapolis, 617; seizes the fishing-station of Canseau, 617; death of, 640.

Durantaye, La, at Niagara, 79; with Du Lhut at Michillimackinac, 87; at Detroit, 111; captures Rooseboom and McGregory, 112; commanding at Michillimackinac, sends bad news to Montreal, 150; is replaced by Louvigny, 151.

Durell, Admiral, 1328, 1333; arrival of his fleet in the St. Lawrence, 1337–40; at Isle-aux-Coudres, 1337; ruse to obtain a pilot, 1338.

D'Urfé, Abbé, a Canadian missionary, is ill received by Frontenac, 36; carries complaints of him to France, 39, 40.

Durham Terrace, 1439.

Dury, interview with Braddock, 974.

Dussieux, 1194 *note.*

Dustan, Mrs., of Haverhill, her exploit, 278–79.

Dutch, the, 1042; in Pennsylvania, 866; trading interests at Albany, 867, 889, 976, 1064, 1069; alienate the Mohawks, 961; their language, 997; at Schenectady, 1065; hostile to Johnson, 1069.

Dutch Reformed Church, the, 867.

Dutch traders instigate Iroquois against the French, 63; pursuit of the fur trade into their country, 72.

Du Tisné, explored the Missouri River, 573; visits the Pawnees, 573; arrives at the village of the Osages, 573; returns to the Illinois, 573.

Duvivier to accept the terms of capitulation for Louisbourg, 1246–47.

Duvivier, Captain, married to Marie Muis de Poubomcoup, 415; attempted attack upon Annapolis, 617; sent to seize Canseau, 617; proposes terms of capitulation with Mascarene, 618; asks assistance of France to renew his attack upon Annapolis, 660.

Duxbury, Mass., 417.

East Bay, on Lake Champlain, 733.

Eastern Indians, called to a council by Governor Shute, 485; renew the treaty of Portsmouth with Governor Shute, 487; letter to Governor Shute cited, 491 *note.*

Easton, Indian convention at, 1294, 1297–98, 1306.

"Echo," the, number of her guns, 1232 *note;* captured by the English, 1239.

"Edgar," flag-ship of Admiral Walker, 450; blown up in the Thames River, 456.

Edict of Nantes, mentioned, 339.

Edinburgh, the University of, 1392.

Edward, Fort, in New York, 429, 1108, 1121, 1144, 1152, 1279, 1493, 1495; name given to Fort Lyman, 1046–47, 1061; winter life of the garrison, 1084; difficulties of carrying stores to, 1108; forces stationed here, 1117; its condition, 1117–18; Earl Loudon stationed at, 1131; exposed condition of, 1166, 1198; attacked by a party under Marin, 1175; position of General Webb, 1182–83, 1186, 1197; arrival of soldiers escaping from Fort William

Henry, 1192–94, 1489, 1490–91; arrival of troops to aid Monro, 1198; mutiny among the troops, 1198; omission of Montcalm to attack, after his success at Fort William Henry, 1198, 1310; commanded by Colonel Haviland, 1204; expedition of Rogers' rangers, 1204–07, 1281; fortified by the English, 1360.

Edward, Fort, in Nova Scotia, 1029–31, 1033, 1037.

Edward, grandson of George II., name given to Fort Edward, 1061.

Edwards, Jonathan, 863.

Egmont, Cape, 1329.

Elder, John, letter from, quoted, 1080.

Eliot, John, recaptures some fishing-vessels, 497.

Elizabeth Castle, 1018.

Elizabeth of Russia, 857, 1464, 1475; her hatred of Frederic the Great, 1086, 1462, 1468; her death, 1468.

"Eltham," a British frigate, 638.

Emerson, Ralph Waldo, 629 *note*.

Emerson, Rev. Mr., 1279.

Emery, Samuel, minister at Wells, Me., 363.

Endicott, Honorable William C., 605 *note*.

Engelran, a Jesuit father, 356 *note;* at Michillimackinac, confers with Denonville, 94; his dealings with the Indians, 111, 115, 318; is wounded by the Senecas, 117.

England, 891, 1057; declares war with France, 340; grants aid for the reduction of Canada, 426; her ministry sends an expedition against Canada, 445; news received of the surrender of Louisbourg, 670; "England has no rightful titles to North America," etc., 747; her possessions in America, and questions of boundary, 843–44, 859–71, 883, 892, 906–09, 929–31, 935, 954, 959, 970, 1007–08, 1012; her commerce, 844; influence of the Seven Years War, 844, 1222–30, 1460, 1475–79; restoration of Cape Breton, by, 844; result of the subjection of Canada, 844; decline of the Tory power, 847; fall of the Stuarts,

847; religion, morals, and society under George II., 847–52; conditions of, after the peace of Aix-la-Chapelle, 849–52; service rendered by Pitt, 849, 1223–28, 1466–70; the army and navy, 849, 967, 1456–57, 1469, 1477; question of the mastery of India, 852; action taken by, at the time of the succession of Maria Theresa, 858; French and English population in America in 1754, compared, 859; success of, in establishing her colonies, and their condition, 860, 862–68, 930–31, 1315–16, 1470, 1471, 1477; importance of Piquetown and of Oswego, 880, 891, 892, 894, 1067, 1115, 1126; seeks to repel the French aggressions in the West, 881, 935–41; importance of securing the Iroquois Indians as allies, 888–89, 930, 1098, 1099; neglect of the British Assemblies, of their interests, 903; conditions imposed on French inhabitants of Acadia, 906; the oath of allegiance to be taken by the Acadians, 906, 907, 911–12, 917–18, 1006, 1023, 1026–27; the possession of Acadia, 906–07, 910, 928–29, 1007, 1018–19; hostility of the Acadians and Indians encouraged by the French, 907, 910, 912–19, 1006–10, 1011–13, 1026; bound by treaty to allow the Acadians freedom in religion, 910, 918; mildness of her rule over the Acadians, 910–11, 928, 1024; pretended peace made by the Indians, 916; relations of Cornwallis with the Acadians, 918–19; commissioners appointed to decide upon the boundaries of possessions in America, 929–31; the question of the pistole fee, 938, 940; attitude and policy of the home government, 961, 965–67; the southern department held by Sir Thomas Robinson, 966; regiments ordered to America, 968; diplomatic correspondence of, 969; warlike intentions concealed from France, 969; the plans of France known to, 970–71; Braddock despatched to America to take military command, 973–74; plans of Shirley laid before the government, 975–76; supplies for Braddock's campaign scarce, 980–81; questions of policy for the French and English in Acadia, 1006–09; desire of the Acadians to return to their allegiance, 1008, 1013; conditions leading to the removal of the Acadians from their home, 1018–28, 1040 (see *Acadians*); results of the campaign of 1755, 1070–71; attitude of the population of Pennyslvania towards, 1077; declares war, 1085; political outlook, 1085–86; preys on French commerce, 1085; Protestant country, 1087; money granted by Parliament to the colonies, 1104 and *note;* an armament fitted out for the reduction of Louisbourg, 1163–64; the fleet of Holbourne wrecked, 1165; disasters and victories in Europe, 1226–28; prisoners of war sent to, 1248; rejoicing at the fall of Louisbourg, 1248–49; preparations made to attack Quebec, 1316, 1329; siege of Quebec, 1331–57, 1375–1419, 1419 *note,* 1420 *note;* news of Wolfe's death and his heroism, 1418; the fall of Canada, 1443–57; end of the war in America, 1456–57; death of George, II., 1463; succession of George III., 1463; growth of a peace party, 1463; changes among the officials, 1464; the policy of George III., 1464, 1469; terms of peace offered to, 1466; the Family Compact, 1466; the negotiations of Choiseul with Pitt, 1466; the secret treaty made by Choiseul, 1466–67; need of a peace with France, 1467; the policy of Bute, 1469; victories gained through the influence of Pitt, 1469–70; expedition against Havana, 1470; the conflict for colonial ascendency, 1470–71; negotiations with France for peace, 1471–74; cessions made by France, 1472; restores Belleisle, 1473; the treaty of peace signed at Paris, 1474, 1475; results of the war, 1475–79; the growth of the United States, 1478–79.

English colonies, designs of Louis XIV. for their destruction, 141; their individual strength, and independence of each other, 606–07; condition of, as compared with French possessions, 843–45, 859; inhabitants of, 859–60, 862; compared and examined, 862–69, 887, 930–31; government of, 862, 960–61, 1084, 1129; means of travel, 867; politics and religion in, 867–69, 938, 939, 960–61, 1083, 1129; plan of France to unite Louisiana and Canada against, 870; efforts to repel the French in the West, 938–41, 960–63; hampered by the Assemblies, 938; plan of union of Franklin, 964; council of governors held with Braddock, 974–77; slaves in, 976; the frontier left unguarded, 1000, 1003–04; distribution of the exiled Acadians, 1037–38; mode of life of the frontier settler, 1073–75; united against Canada, 1315; prediction of Mayhew for, 1419; predictions of several persons concerning their future in America, 1471; symptoms of revolt shown in, 1478.

English colonists, how they regarded the Five Nations, 712.

English colonists of New England invade Acadia, 92; their organization and policy compared with the French, 284–85; their military inefficiency, 293–94 (see *New England*).

English ministry, plans of, concerning America, 445. (See *British Ministry*).

English Turn, at the bend of the Mississippi River, 537.

English, the, 880, 882; their motives for the occupation of Detroit, 351; the condition of, at Annapolis, 463; prevented from occupying Louisiana, 534; at Grand Pré, Ramesay's expedition against, 698; plan of the attack, 701; the attack, 702–07; attempted resistance, 703–05; their position becoming desperate, 706; they capitulate, 706; the number of troops at Grand Pré during the French attack upon, 707; their losses estimated, 707; they march from

Grand Pré to Annapolis, 707–08; driven from the West by the French, 875–77, 885, 888–905; the French combine with the Indians to injure, 877, 888–89, 891, 892, 894, 901, 913, 914, 916, 917, 922, 933, 954, 961, 969, 984, 1006–09, 1483; matters of interest concerning trade and traders, 879, 892, 894–95, 899, 903, 904; orders given to the French governor with regard to, 898–901; attacked at Pickawillany, 902–03; the fortress of Louisbourg restored to France, 907; treatment of the Acadians, 907, 910 (see *Acadia* and *Acadians*); occupation of Beaubassin, 924–27; successful encounter with the French, 944–45; the fight at Great Meadows, 950–54; results of the meeting of the colonial Assemblies with their governors, 955–60; rights of, on the Ohio River, 964; to intercept the French fleet, 970; arrival of Braddock in America, 972, 974; matters pertaining to Braddock's expedition, 972, 974, 977, 980–93; expedition given in charge to Johnson, 977; the battle of the Monongahela, 992–96, 998; defeat of Braddock, and retreat of his troops, 995–1005; death and burial of Braddock, 995–96, 998–1000; Shirley made commander-in-chief of the army, 1004; loyalty of the troops, 1009; plans of, in regard to the French, 1009–10; capture of Fort Beauséjour, 1010–19; surrender of French forts, 1018–19; removal of the Acadians from their homes, 1019–20, 1026–40 (see *Acadians*); plan to increase the English population in Acadia, 1021; disaster at Peticodiac, 1034; expedition against Crown Point, 1041–62; character of the army in the expedition, 1044–46; preaching on Sunday to the army, 1048; an ambush prepared for, by Dieskau, 1051; the battle of Lake George, 1052–62; expedition of Shirley against Niagara, 1063–70; arrive at Fort Oswego, 1066; lack of supplies, 1067–68; Shirley leaves Oswego, 1068; results of the campaign against the French, 1070, 1071; border warfare encouraged by the French, 1071–84; conditions in Pennsylvania, 1075–76; forts built to guard the Great Carrying Place, 1099; prepare to attack Ticonderoga, 1101–02, 1108; the appointment of Earl Loudon as commander-in-chief, 1105; payment of troops, and other matters pertaining to soldiers, 1106–08; forest war, 1109; receive discouraging reports from Ticonderoga, 1109; action between Villiers and Bradstreet, 1112–13; royal orders concerning provincial officers, 1116; condition of the New England troops, 1117; the loss of Oswego, 1120–30; difficulties in the French war, 1125–27; the Indians butcher the prisoners, 1125; number of men under Earl Loudon, 1131; the attack made on Kittanning, 1132–34; despatches sent by Vaudreuil to France, concerning, 1134–35; at Fort William Henry, 1135; scouting-parties, 1135; the war-party of Perière, 1136–37; exploits of Rogers' rangers, 1139–41 (see *Rogers*); the difficulty in quartering the troops in winter, 1143; party sent by Vaudreuil to attack Fort William Henry, 1148–51; capture French stores, 1155; number of their antagonists, 1162; plan for the reduction of Louisbourg, 1162; delay in starting the fleet for Halifax, 1163–64; fleet of Holbourne wrecked, 1164–65; the attack and massacre of, at Fort William Henry, 1175–94, 1199, 1200, 1360, 1489–92; the tide turning, 1227; Loudon succeeded by Abercromby, in office, 1228; the siege and reduction of Louisbourg, 1228–52 *note* (see *Louisbourg*); the Scotch Highlanders join the army, 1229; the typical British naval officer, 1230; expedition fitted out against, to serve under Abercromby, 1253–74 *note*; reforms in the army introduced by Lord Howe, 1258; effect of the death of Lord Howe, 1263–64; the assault at Ticonderoga,

1267–72; matters pertaining to life in the army, 1276–79, 1425–26, 1429; gain possession of Fort Frontenac, 1283–84; the reduction of Fort Duquesne, 1286–1307; need of Indian allies, 1291–98; use of Western lands, 1296; expedition of Major Grant, 1299–1302; burial of Braddock's slain, 1305; Lieutenant-Colonel Mercer to hold Fort Duquesne, 1305; the situation in 1758, 1307; expedition fitted out to serve under General Wolfe, 1320–22, 1328–30; the siege and reduction of Quebec, 1340–58, 1375–1420 note (see Wolfe and Quebec); bravery of the sailors, 1353; capture of Ticonderoga and Crown Point by Amherst, 1359–62; Fort Edward fortified, 1360; spruce beer made in the army, 1360; their general humanity, 1377, 1408; council of war held, 1383–84; action of Holmes's squadron, 1387–88; love of the soldiers for their officers, 1389, 1398; loss of General Wolfe, 1398–1400; the precision of their fire, 1399; statistics concerning the army at the battle of Quebec, 1400–01 note, 1406 and note, 1497–98, 1502–03; rule in Canada, 1424; skirmish at Lorette, 1427–28; the battle of Sainte-Foy, 1431, 1434–42, 1502–03; the fall of Canada, 1443–57; embark for Montreal, 1444–47; passage of the rapids, 1450; numerical superiority of their troops, 1457; recapture St. John's, 1471.

"Entreprenant," the number of her guns, 1232 note; burned at anchor, 1241.

Epicurus, 1462.

Episcopalians in the army, 1276.

Erie, Lake, 351, 871, 880, 1175, 1367; the passage to Lake Huron, 896; desirability of erecting forts near, 899, 935.

Erie, town of, 905.

Esopus, 1131 note.

Espagnol, Port, 1249.

Espineuse, Madame d', 1316.

Estève, secretary of Montcalm, 1091; his voyage, 1092; his marriage, 1488.

Etechémin, River, the, 1385.

Etechémins, the, 861.

Ethier, Dr., quoted, 383 note.

Eugene, Prince, 416; remark of, concerning the result of Charles VI.'s death, 858.

Europe, 1169, 1287, 1323; complication of political interests, 843–45, 1085–87, 1315; the Seven Years War, 843, 858, 1222–23, 1460, 1473; power of the House of Bourbon, 852; rule of the House of Austria, 856; power and influence of Peter the Great, 857; power of Frederic II. of Prussia, 857; the balance of power, 857, 931; the peace of Aix-la-Chapelle, 858; the princes pledged to sustain the will of Charles VI., 858; grains and fruit of, growing in America, 897; question of American boundary, 929–31; war commenced between the powers of, 971; the peace of Paris, 1458–74; the conflict for colonial ascendency, 1470; results of the victory of Plassey, 1475; the mastery of India, 1476; Catholicism in, 1478.

Exchequer, the, 1464.

Exeter, infested by Indians, 402.

Extrait d'une Liasse de Papiers concernant le Canada, 493 note.

Eyre, Major, occupies Fort William Henry, 1142–44; party sent by Vaudreuil to reduce the fort, 1148–51; requested to give up Fort William Henry, 1149; his answer, and the result thereof, 1149–51.

Fairfax, Lord, letter from Dinwiddie, 939; letters from Colonel Innes, 1000.

Falmouth rebuilt, 483.

Falmouth, 960, 1057.

"Falmouth," English war-ship, 437.

Falmouth, Me. See Casco.

Family Compact, the, 1466.

Famine (La), on Lake Ontario, visited by La Barre, 82; the council, 82–86; treaty of, 88, 91; treacherous attack here on the Iroquois by Kondiaronk (the Rat), 130–32.

Faneuil Hall, 1454.

"Far Indians," or "Upper Nations," of what tribes they consisted, 345; their fur-trade with Canada, 346.

Fare, Marquis de la, 1089.

Farnsworth, David, forms a new settlement, 720.

Farnsworth, Samuel, of Groton, forms a new settlement, Number Four, 720.

Farnsworth, Stephen, forms a new settlement, 720.

Farrar, Jacob, killed in the fight at Lovewell's Pond, 511.

Farwell, Josiah, escapes from Indians at Dunstable, 507; signs petition to fight Indians, 507; wounded by Indians, 510; death of, 512.

Feather dance, a, description of, 884.

Featherstonhaugh, geologist, cited, 569 note.

Félix, Père, defies the power of the governor at Port Royal, 415.

Fénelon, a zealous missionary priest at Montreal, 34; arraigned at Quebec by Frontenac, 36–38; is sent to France, 38; and forbidden to return, 40–41.

Ferdinand VI. of Spain, death of, 1146.

Ferdinand, Prince of Brunswick, appointed to command, 1228; generalship of, 1228; action with Clermont, 1228.

Ferguson, 1234.

Ferland, Cours d'Histoire, 561 note; Cours d'Histoire du Canada, quoted, 647 note.

Ferryland, Newfoundland, 424.

Feudalism, 852; in Canada and in the British colonies, 860, 866–69.

"Feversham," English war-ship, 437.

"Fidèle," the, number of her guns, 1232 note.

Fiedmont, 1412.

Field, Ensign, Northfield, Mass., 729.

Fielding, 848, 973.

Fifty-eighth Regiment, the, 1401 note.

Filles de la Congrégation, at Louisbourg, 461.

Fireships, 1336; descend upon the English, 1342–43.

First Lord of the Treasury, the, 1469.

Fish Kill River, 715 note.

Fish, Jane. See Pompadour.

Fisheries of Newfoundland considered in the Treaty of Utrecht, 459.

Fisheries, the, 1472, 1476.

Fishery question, the, between New England and Acadia, 410.

Fitch, Colonel, letter to Winslow, 1108–09; his regiment, 1262; encounter with Langy in the woods, 1263.

Five Mile Point, 1144, 1267.

Five Nations, the, of the Iroquois, 871, 872, 876, 878, 891, 933, 1201, 1256; ingratitude of New York towards them, 343; the influence of the French and English agents among them, 344–45; deed a part of the Northwestern country to King William III., 358; induced to join in the reduction of Canada, 428; made British subjects, 458; the attitude of New York towards them, 518; their friendship necessary to New York for her control of the fur-trade, 519; acted as middlemen in trade between New York and the West, 520; their jealousy of the French designs upon Niagara, 610; finally give their consent to the building of a fort, 612; allow Governor Burnet to build a trading-house, 612; their attitude towards the French and English colonies, 712; induced by Governor Clinton to join in the invasion of Canada, 712; dialects of, 875; adopt Catharine Montour, 882; efforts of the French to gain as allies, and to cause the destruction of the English, 885, 888–89, 898, 984, 1098, 1161; power of Johnson over, 888, 962, 977, 1042–43, 1110–11; their influence and position, 888–89, 930, 1098–99; their missionary, 891, 1176, 1480; their country disposed of in the treaty of Utrecht, 899, 930 and note; range of their war-parties, 930 note; orders sent from Dinwiddie, 939; at Fort Duquesne, 949; the congress at Albany, 962–64; Indian commissioners treated by, 977; Johnson made Indian superintendent, 1042–43, 1110; homes of, 1063; the fur trade, 1064; conferences held with, by Shirley, 1069; border warfare, 1071; the spies, 1099; council called by Montcalm, 1175–78; join in the attack upon Fort William Henry, 1178; Indian convention, 1294; declare their alliance with the English, 1297, 1365; the fight at Niagara, 1367; their totems on a flag of Piquet, 1480.

Flanders, 1322.

Flat Point, 1234.

Flat Point Cove, a place of landing at Louisbourg, 634, 640, 1238; Pepperrell's storehouses at, 659.

Flatheads, the, 891.

Fletcher, governor of New York, his complaints of weakness and divisions, 294.

Fleurimont, 1176.

Flogging, 1360.

Florence, 1418.

Florida, 858; ceded by Spain to England, 1472–73.

Flynt, Rev. Henry, cited, 484 *note,* 489 *note.*

Foligny, M. de, his journal, 1498, 1501; matters relating to the death of Montcalm, 1501.

Folsom, Captain, 1056.

Folsom, *History of Saco, etc.,* cited, 367 *note.*

Fontbrune, aide-de-camp of General Montcalm, 1184.

Fontenoy, battle of, 849, 858.

Forbes, Brigadier John, 1229; the reduction of Fort Duquesne, 1229, 1285–1307; his early life, 1286–87; his route and plan of attack, 1287–93, 1303; compared with Braddock, 1288; his relations with Washington, 1288–90; his relations with Bouquet, 1288–89; his letters to Bouquet quoted, 1289–90, 1293, 1303; his sickness, 1289–90, 1303, 1306; letter to Pitt concerning his provincials, 1289; erects Fort Bedford, 1293; messages of peace sent to the Indians, 1294–

99; Grant's expedition, 1299–1302; finds Fort Duquesne evacuated, 1304; names the settlement of Pittsburg, 1305; letter to Amherst, 1306; leaves Fort Duquesne, 1306; the homeward march retarded by illness, 1306; effect of his expedition, 1306; his death and burial, 1306.

Forbes, Rev. Eli, pastor at Brookfield, his sermon on the fall of Canada, 1455.

Forest posts, their abuses and their value to the French, 301.

Forests in the West, the, 986.

Fort Hill, 1248.

Fort, see *Albany, Famine (La), Frontenac, Loyal, Niagara, St. Louis, Nelson.*

Fortifications of Canada, 216.

Forty-fourth Regiment, the, 995 *note.*

Forty-seventh Regiment, the, 1401 *note.*

Forty-third Regiment, the, 1321, 1401 *note.*

Foster, Deacon Josiah, killed by Indians at Keene, 719.

Foster, Joseph, of Beverly, a prisoner of war, 685; cited, 683 *note.*

"Foudroyant," the, captured by the English, 1229–30.

Fox, Henry, 849, 966.

Fox Indians, charged with cowardice, 88.

Fox River, 519, 556, 563, 582.

Foxcroft, Thomas, pastor of the "Old Church" in Boston, his sermon on the occasion of the fall of Canada, 1454.

Foxes, the, a tribe of the "Far Indians," 345; called to a council by Montcalm, 1175–78.

Fox's *History of Dunstable,* cited, 515 *note.*

France and England, their rival claims in America, 608–09.

France and Spain contest the Louisiana country, 538.

France, 852, 891, 945, 1012, 1093, 1101, 1154, 1176, 1179, 1216, 1225, 1229, 1306, 1392, 1470, 1471; the power gained by Great Britain over, 339; schemes for conquest in New England, 340;

sends her missionaries among the Acadians, 469; her claim to American territory as set forth by Father Bobé, 607–09; requires the restoration of Port Royal, Acadia, etc., 608; her designs upon the English colonies in America, 610–11; "Demandes de La France" (1723), 755; alliance with Austria, 843; her possessions in America, 843–44, 858, 861–62, 870, 872, 873, 874–75, 876, 887–90, 896, 899, 929–31, 1063, 1475, 1476; influence of the Seven Years War upon, 844, 1476; condition of, under Louis XV., 852–56; her army and navy, 852, 967, 1095–99, 1159, 1456, 1457, 1470, 1476; her commanders, 852; the persecution of the Huguenots, 855, 859–60; growing disrespect for the clergy and ministry, 856; takes part with Bavaria, 858; French and English population in America in 1754 compared, 859; rule established by, in Canada, 860; forts held by, in America, 872, 873, 896, 1063; leaden plates given to Céloron to bury in America, 874, 876, 878, 887 *note;* missions established by, among the Indians, 888–91; the treaty of Utrecht, 899; cession of Acadia to England, 906, 909; French maxims of duty to the King, 917; the Acadians ordered to swear allegiance to, 927; balance of power, 931; conditions of rule in, 966–67; diplomatic representatives of, 966–67, 969; the marine and colonial department, 966; expedition of war ordered to America, 968; her naval and military plans, 969–71; questions of policy for the French and English in Acadia, 1006–10; the Acadians French at heart, 1006–08; corruption among the officials, 1011, 1211–15, 1226, 1459, 1460; conditions leading to the expulsion of the Acadians from their home, 1018–28 (see *Acadians*); expedition fitted out against Crown Point, 1041–42; expedition sent to America under Dieskau, 1043; results of the campaign, 1070–71; attitude of Pennsylvania towards, 1077; war declared between England and, 1085; political combinations in Europe, 1085–87; alliance sought by Maria Theresa, 1086; Montcalm to succeed Dieskau, 1087–88; paucity of troops sent to America, 1092; troops sent against Austria, 1092; attitude of Governor Vaudreuil towards, 1094–95; growth of political parties in Canada, 1095; Indian allies, 1098, 1161–62, 1294, 1306, 1457; her communication with the West, 1126; causes of the English losses, 1128–30; information from England obtained through Florence Hensey, 1163; prospects at the time of Pitt, 1226; loss of Louisbourg, 1244–47; inhabitants of Louisbourg sent to, 1248; victory of Montcalm at Ticonderoga, 1273; appeals made in behalf of Canada, 1313–16; promotions of Montcalm and others, 1315; scant assistance given to Canada, 1315; the loss of Quebec, 1331–58, 1375–1420 *note;* funeral of Montcalm, 1409; Lévis sends for aid, 1439; loss of Montreal and Canada, 1452; return of the troops, 1452, 1458–59; end of the war in America, 1456–57; her victories, 1457; trial of those accused of peculation in Canada, 1459–60; political situation in 1761, 1464–66; terms of peace offered to England, 1465–66; the negotiations of Choiseul, 1466; provisions of the Family Compact, 1466; her enemies in Europe, 1469; her financial condition in 1762, 1471; negotiations with England for peace, 1471–74; possessions ceded by, 1472; privileges of fishing, 1472; the fortress of Dunkirk to be destroyed, 1473; a secret agreement made with Spain, 1473; the treaty of peace signed at Paris, 1474; her influence in the East, 1476; under Colbert, 1476; her power on the continent of Europe, 1476–77.

Francis, Dr. Convers, 488 *note,* 501 *note.*

Françoise, Marie, baptismal name of Freedom French, 395.

Franklin, Benjamin, 623, 863; his plan

of union for the colonies, 964; his relations with Braddock, 972–73, 981–82; his position in the Assembly of Pennsylvania, 981–82, 1076; account of Braddock's death, 999; the defeat of the English, 1001; bill drawn by, 1083 *note;* his policy, 1083; his opinion of Shirley and of Loudon, 1130, 1163; remark of, concerning the union of the British colonies, 1472.

Franquet, 1244; his journal, 691 *note,* 1209; sent to strengthen Louisbourg, 1209; his account of a travelling party in Canada, 1209–10.

Fraser, Colonel, his Highlanders serve under Wolfe, 1235, 1355, 1401 *note,* 1502; Canadian prisoners, 1352.

Fraser, his trading-house, 935 *note,* 991; Washington at his house, 937.

Fraser, Hon. Malcolm, anecdote of Montcalm, 1400 *note.*

Frederic II. of Prussia, 843, 857, 1222; began the War of the Austrian Succession, 616; his youth and training, 857; seizes the province of Silesia, 858; political conditions in his realm, 1086; combination against, 1087, 1222–23; the Seven Years War, 1222–23, 1475; the battle of Prague, 1223; confidence felt in Pitt, 1227; his glory in 1758, 1460; his reverses and trials, 1460–63, 1468–69; his letters to D'Argens, 1461–62; letter to Voltaire, 1461; the campaigns of 1760 and 1761, 1461–63; Russia becomes the ally of, 1469; the treaty of Hubertsburg, 1474; his dominions intact, 1475; numbers lost in the Seven Years War, 1475.

Frederic William of Prussia, 857.

Frederic, Fort, 861, 1102; built at Crown Point, 614.

French Academy, the, 1088.

French accounts of the attack on Port Royal, cited, 424 *note.*

French Canadians, their spirit of adventure and trade lead to the exploration of the West, 565, 566.

French Catharine's Town, 882 *note.*

French colonies, their desire for achievement, 607.

French colonists, how they regarded the Five Nations, 712.

French Creek, 876, 933, 935, 959; former name of, 932.

French designs of colonization and conquest, 93; policy of conquest and massacre, 267–69; colonization, compared with English, 284–86; occupation of the Great West, 324.

French explorers west of the Mississippi, 570.

French Indians, 885; narrow escape of Washington, 937.

French Mountain, 1051, 1056, 1260.

French officer, an incident of his attack upon Deerfield, 378.

French pioneers in America, their desire for discovery and trade, 565.

French Revolution, the, 857.

French River (Winooski or Onion), 387.

French, Deacon Thomas, inhabitant of Deerfield, 376 and *note;* captured at Deerfield by Indians, 395.

French, Freedom, captured by Indians, baptized as Marie Françoise, and married Jean Daulnay, 395.

French, Martha, married Jacques Roy, afterwards Jean Louis Ménard, 395.

French, the, 864; effect of the Seven Years War upon, 843–44, 1223, 1476; attacks made on New England, 864, 959; their efforts to gain and retain Indian allies, 864, 873–74, 877, 878, 884, 888–89, 933, 936, 954, 961, 963, 1070–71, 1099, 1132, 1161–62, 1168–69, 1174–76, 1199, 1200, 1296, 1298–99; fur-trade, the, 871; New France connected by forts, 872, 873; missions among the Indians, 873–74, 889; desire to control the West, 874, 881, 894–95, 903–05, 960, 964, 980, 1005, 1296; matters relating to trade, 889, 892–95, 903; methods of warfare and organization, 894, 942, 1122, 1165; the attack at Pickawillany, 902–03; conditions of residence of, in Acadia, 906; injurious influence of, upon the

Acadians, 907, 911–20, 928, 1006–08, 1012–13, 1015, 1021–22, 1026, 1027 and *note;* officials and priests aid the Indians to destroy the English, 912–19, 922–23, 1007, 1071–80, 1368, 1452, 1484; double-dealing, 915–16, 917 and *note,* 923; relations with Cornwallis, 918–19; occupation of Beaubassin by the English, 924–27; the murder of Captain Howe, 925–26; questions of boundary, 929–31, 970, 1006–08; forts erected by, 932, 942; expedition of Duquesne to the Ohio, 932–37, 942–54; efforts of Dinwiddie to repel, in the West, 935–41; prepare for war, 942, 948–50; alleged causes of Jumonville's expedition, 945–46; fight between Washington and Villiers, 948–54; opinions expressed by the Indians concerning, 961–63; aid to be expected from the Catholics, 976; try to interrupt Braddock's march, 986; the encounter with Braddock's forces, 989–1000; their method of warfare, 992–95; death of Braddock, 996, 999–1000; return of the troops, 996; treatment of their prisoners, 997; losses of, in the battle of the Monongahela, 998; their standard planted on Beauséjour, 1006, 1015; matters pertaining to the army, 1008, 1011, 1015, 1095 and *note,* 1131, 1141–42, 1159–63, 1232, 1233, 1445, 1452, 1458, 1460; hostile designs of, 1012; encounter with the English at Beauséjour, 1015–19; burn Fort St. John, 1018; conditions leading to the expulsion of the Acadians, examined, 1018–28 (see *Acadia* and *Acadians*); expedition fitted out against Crown Point, 1041–42; prepare to defend Crown Point, 1043, 1046; advance of Dieskau's forces to meet Johnson, 1048–50; the battle of Lake George, 1053–62; their losses, 1058–59, 1059 *note;* occupy Ticonderoga, 1059, 1109–10, 1145, 1168, 1267; strength of their position at Niagara, 1063, 1067; expedition of Shirley against Niagara, 1063–70; the troops at Fort

Frontenac, 1067, 1121; results of the campaign, 1070–71; building of Fort Duquesne, 1076 *note;* their settlements on the Ohio molested, 1077; on the march against Virginia, 1079; arrival of Montcalm, 1093; camps of Montcalm, 1099; Fort Bull taken by, 1100; letter of Montreuil quoted, 1101; expedition fitted out to defend Ticonderoga, 1101–02; preparations of Shirley for war, 1106; action between Villiers and Bradstreet, 1112–13; the capture of Oswego, 1114–30; their losses, 1125; rumors of attack at Lake George, 1131; reduction of Fort Granville, 1132; their war-parties, 1136–37, 1141; dealings of Rogers' rangers with, 1137–38, 1144–45, 1280–82, 1373; a war-party sent to attack Fort William Henry, 1147–51; the seat of war, 1152; their ships-of-war, 1165 *note;* the capture of Fort William Henry, 1166–94, 1490–92; officers of the Indians, 1176; circular letter sent by Montcalm to the officers, 1178; official knavery, 1211–21; routed at Rossbach, 1227; change of commanders, 1227–28; the siege and reduction of Louisbourg, 1228–52 *note* (see *Louisbourg*); their ships burned off Louisbourg, 1241–43; treatment received by prisoners from the English, 1251, 1284; expedition against Ticonderoga, 1256–74 *note* (see *Ticonderoga*); losses of, 1272; mistake occurring from the waving of a handkerchief, 1270; serve under Marin, 1280; loss of Fort Frontenac, 1283–85; vessels on Lake Ontario taken by the British, 1284; loss of the command of Lake Ontario, 1285; loss of Fort Duquesne, 1286–1307; reinforcements sent to Fort Duquesne, 1293; loss of Indian allies, 1294, 1298–99; encounter with Major Grant, 1299–1302; retreat from Fort Duquesne, 1304–05; effect of the Indian conference at Easton, 1306; effect of the loss of Fort Duquesne, 1307; the situation in 1758, 1307; letter from Doreil to the minister of war, 1307;

Montcalm desires his recall, 1309; alarming condition of Canada, 1311–13; danger to the shipping, 1313–14; siege and reduction of Quebec, 1331–58, 1375–1402, 1418, 1419 *note* (see *Quebec* and *Wolfe*); measures of defence taken by Montcalm, 1333–37; the camp, 1341; the fireships let loose upon the enemy, 1342–43; opposition to the work at Point Levi, 1345; Dumas' expedition unsuccessful, 1345; preserve the defensive, 1348; the Canadians desert their cause, 1348, 1350, 1447; Niagara attacked and captured, 1350, 1361, 1363–68; affair of the Montmorenci, 1354–57, 1375; at Isle-aux-Noix, 1361, 1363, 1368; loss of Ticonderoga, 1362, 1378; Crown Point abandoned, 1362, 1378; effort to recover Pittsburg, 1365; their fear of the Indians, 1367, 1452; parishes laid waste, 1376; barbarities of Vaudreuil, 1377; fear of losing supplies, 1378, 1397; Montcalm poorly supported, 1389 and *note,* 1397; the army routed, 1400–05, 1407, 1408; statistics concerning the army at the battle of Quebec, 1401 *note,* 1406, 1497–98; the protecting care of Montcalm, 1408; the death and burial of Montcalm, 1408–09; confusion in the army, 1410; Lévis assumes command, 1411; the army to retrace their steps, 1411, 1412; the campaign and its actors misrepresented by Vaudreuil, 1414–17; the English threatened, 1426–27; at Le Calvaire, 1427; encounter with the English under Major Dalling, 1427; skirmish at Lorette, 1427–28; efforts to renew the conflict at Quebec, 1428; the troops during the winter, 1429; Lévis's expedition to attack Quebec, 1430–42; occupy Sainte-Foy, 1432, 1502–03; the battle between Murray and Lévis, 1434–36; the English retreat, 1436–37; available force of fighting men, 1443; small resources left in Canada, 1443; fall of Canada, 1443–57; plans of Amherst, 1444; the English fleet sails for Montreal, 1444–47; advance upon Montreal, 1446; Fort Lévis captured, 1449; the articles of capitulation for Montreal, 1451–52; cruelties of the Indians encouraged by, 1452; Canada passes to the crown of England, 1452; return of the troops to France, 1452, 1458–59; fly before Frederic, 1460; driven from Pondicherry, 1469; capture St. John's, and lose it again, 1470–71; payment offered for English scalps, 1483.

Frenchmen in America, the advantage to them of holding Detroit, 351; assist in Indian attacks at Wells, etc., 365; their object in spurring the Abenakis to these attacks, 367; policy towards the Five Nations, 368, 373; motive for inducing the Indian warfare against New England, 403; incite the Abenakis against English, 492; jealousy of the trading-house at Oswego, 612; establish a trading-post at Toronto, 613; and place armed vessels at Fort Frontenac, 613; their chain of posts from Canada to Louisiana, 614; they seize Canseau, 617; the number of troops engaged in the attack on Grand Pré, 707; losses at the attack upon Grand Pré, 707.

Freneuse, Madame de, at Port Royal, 413, 414.

Freshwater Cove (Anse de la Cormorandière), 1234; a landing-place near Louisbourg, 641; attacked and taken by the English, 1235–38; known by other names, 1235 *note.*

Friponne, La, 1212.

Frontenac, Count (Louis de Buade), governor of Canada, 1672–1682, 1689–1698, at St. Fargeau, 15; his early life, 15; marriage, 16, 327; his quarrel at St. Fargeau, 17; his estate, 17–18; his vanity, 18; aids Venice at Candia, his appointment to command in New France, 19–20; at Quebec, 22; convokes the three estates, 24; his address, 24; form of government, 25; his merits and faults, 26–27; complains of the Jesuits, 27–29, 232–33; Fort Frontenac built and confided to La Salle, 30–31; dispute with Perrot, governor of Montreal, whom he throws into prison, 31–35; this leads to a quarrel with Abbé Fénelon and the priests, 36–38; Frontenac's relations with the clergy, 39; his instructions from the king and Colbert, 39–43; his hot temper, 42, 43; question of the presidency, 44–46; imprisonment of Amours, 47–48; disputes on the fur trade, and accusations of Duchesneau, 48–52; reproof from the king and Colbert, 51–52; complaints against Duchesneau, 52–54; arrest of his son, 55; relations with Perrot, 56; with the Church, 57–58; with the Indians, 58–59, 186; his recall, 57; sails for France, 60; relations at this time with the Iroquois, 64–65; Frontenac is sent again to Canada, 139; scheme of invading New York, 140; arrives at Chedabucto, 141; at Quebec and Montreal, 143; attempts to save the fort, 144; summons a conference of Indians, 145–46; the conference, 146–49; another failure, 150; message to the Lake Indians, 151; scheme of attack on English colonies, 154; Schenectady, 156–61; Pemaquid, 165; Salmon Falls, 167; Casco Bay, 168; conference with Davis, 171; defence of Quebec, 181–204; leads the war-dance, 186; reply to Phips's summons, 196; begs troops from the king, 215; expedition against the Mohawks, 225–28; appeal to Ponchartrain, 230–33, 300; jealousies against him, 231–32; complaints of Champigny, 232; scheme of coast-attack, 258; treats with the Iroquois, 286–87, 289, 302; his difficult position, 289; expedition against the Onondagas, 295–98, 302; his tardy reward, 299; his policy, 301–02; correspondence with Bellomont, 303–05; death and character, 308–14; the eulogist and the critic, 309–13; his administration, 314; account of his family, 325–27; mentioned, 349, 351, 403; sends

Le Sueur into the Sioux country, 566.

Frontenac, Fort, 30–31, 65, 871, 891, 1275, 1302; La Barre's muster of troops, 70, 79; his arrival, 81; summons a council of Indians, 108; who are treacherously seized and made prisoners, 108–10 (see 122, 126, 128); expedition against the Senecas, 112–18; sickness, 125; visit of the Rat, 132; the fort destroyed by order of Denonville, 143–44; restored, 293, 299; armed vessels placed at, by the French, 613; return of Céloron de Bienville, 880; action of the French in regard to ship-building, 894; reception offered to Father Piquet, 895; proposed capture of, 1066–67, 1099, 1104, 1112; position of, 1067; held by the French, 1099, 1100, 1126; the attack abandoned, 1116; arrival of Montcalm, 1121; taken by the British, 1283–85; dismantled, 1283–84, 1307.

Frontenac, Madame, her portrait at Versailles, 13; with Mlle. Montpensier at Orleans, 14, 17; surprised by her husband's visit, 15; dismissed by the princess, 19; her stay in Paris and death, 20, 21; serves Frontenac at the court, 232; is made his heir, 309.

Fry, Joshua, Colonel, 941, 943; despatches from Washington, 947; illness of, 947; his death, 947.

Frye, Colonel, 1119 note; disaster to the English, 1034; number killed at Fort Edward, 1175 note; sent with a detachment to Fort William Henry, 1182; the massacre at Fort William Henry, 1190, 1194 note, 1490–91.

Frye, General Joseph, granted the land of Fryeburg, 514 note.

Frye, Jonathan, Andover, joined in Lovewell's expedition as chaplain, 508; wounded, 511; death of, 512; his engagement to Susanna Rogers, 514; his name cherished at Fryeburg, 514.

Fryeburg, N.H., 506.

Fundy, Bay of, 1008, 1009, 1014, 1024, 1028, 1249, 1250; dikes on, 1022.

Fur-trade, the, 871, 873, 879, 889, 894, 897, 916, 1064, 1096, 1212, 1214, 1471;

carried on by French and English with the Indians, 346–47; to be controlled by a company, 355–56; interest of New York in the, 517; of the West, the desire of Canada to control, 552; controlled by the French posts, 615.

Fur-trade Company, complaints of the, 356–57; transfer their control to Cadillac, 358.

Gabarus Bay (Chapeau Rouge Bay), 638, 640 *note*, 1234.

Gage, Lieutenant-Colonel, 990; in Braddock's expedition, 992–93; in the battle of the Monongahela, 995; rallies his troops, 998; his infantry under Abercromby, 1260; letter from Amherst, 1362; sent to supersede Johnson, 1368.

Gaillard, sent by Bourgmont to the Comanche village, 575.

Galissonière, Comte de la, governor of Canada, 874, 875, 881 *note;* succeeded Beauharnois as governor, 601; effort to have the population of Canada increased, 859; his personal appearance, 870; his plans for uniting Canada and Louisiana, 870; message given to the Indians, 877; soldiers sent to protect Piquet's mission, 890; persons induced to settle at Detroit, 897 *note;* honorably recalled from office, 898; questions of boundary, 929.

Galley-slaves, 108–09.

Ganneious, a mission village, Indians treacherously seized, 107.

Ganouskie Bay, 1178.

Garangula, 76 (see *Big Mouth*).

Gardiner, Captain, captures the ship "Foudroyant," 1229–30; mortally wounded, 1230.

Gardner, 1145.

Gardner, ——, a militia officer at Haverhill, 401.

Garneau, 1502–03.

Garnier, Charles, a Jesuit mission priest, 429, 479.

Garrison houses described, 268.

Gasconade, 1312, 1330 *note,* 1338.

Gaspé, 930, 1179, 1251, 1439.

Gaspé, Bay of, Walker's fleet at, 450.

Gaspé, in Ramesay's expedition, 698.

Gaspereau, Fort, at Baye Verte, 1018; surrender of, to the English, 1018.

Gaspereau River, 701.

Gates wounded in battle, 995.

Gaudalie, *curé* of Mines, 475.

Gaulin, an insurgent priest at Annapolis, 463, 465; charged with incendiary conduct among Acadians, 471.

Gayarré, *Histoire de Louisiane,* cited, 537 *note.*

General Court of Massachusetts, the, 862, 1044, 1119; offers prize for Indian scalps, 369; resolves upon the reduction of Canada, 426; vote concerning an attack upon Louisbourg, 620–21; the arguments for and against the scheme, 622; at last consent to the attack, 622; method of raising troops, 1106–08.

General Hospital of Quebec, the, 1501; crowded with sick, 1379, 1406; the nuns care for the sick, 1423–24.

Genesee, 893.

Genesee Falls, 893.

George I., on the throne of England, 472, 505.

George II., King of England, 1043, 1061, 1064, 1065, 1072, 1223, 1327; his accession to the throne, 474; the Acadians protest fidelity to, 709; yielded Louisbourg to the French by the Peace of Aix-la-Chapelle, 745; society, morals, and religion during his reign, 847–52; his possessions in the West, 881, 935, 936; the oath of allegiance to be taken by the Acadians, 906–12, 1026; forts to be erected on the Ohio, 938; plans of colonial union, 964; his speech concerning America, 967–68; American regiments to be taken into his pay, 976; remark concerning Governor Sharpe, 983; the Acadians disloyal to, 1023; his orders to the Acadians, 1030, 1032–33; the Acadians declared prisoners, 1033; his name given to Lake George, 1047, 1061; the rank of provincial officers, 1116; the fall of

Louisbourg, 1248; troops called for, 1253; secret instructions to Wolfe, 1330 *note;* the victory at Quebec, 1418, 1429; the fall of Canada, 1443; Louisbourg to be abandoned, 1445; his death, 1463.

George III., succeeds to the throne of England, 1463; growth of a peace-party, 1463–64; his character and opinions, 1463–65, 1467; the negotiation with France broken off, 1466; quarrels with Newcastle, 1469; desires peace with France, 1471; resistance of the British colonies, 1478.

George, Fort, 1248, 1360; built on the Androscoggin River, 483; erection of, 1047; condition of, 1124.

George, Lake, 1047, 1048, 1103, 1108, 1117, 1131, 1144, 1147, 1149, 1152, 1204, 1205, 1206, 1248, 1251, 1275, 1285; the battle of, 1045 *note*, 1053–62, 1070; its beauty of scenery, 1047; the name given to, by Johnson, 1047, 1061; advance of Dieskau's army, 1050; conditions at the camp of, 1060; its former name, 1061; winter life of the garrisons, 1084; scouting-party sent out, 1135–36; exploits of Rogers' rangers, 1139–41; the French camp, 1142, 1168; the English camp, 1144; exposed condition of the forts, 1166; position of Ticonderoga, 1168, 1265; advance of Montcalm's forces upon Fort William Henry, 1175–80; voyage of the troops on their way to attack Ticonderoga, 1256–58, 1260–61; arrangement of Montcalm's troops, 1268; mustering-place of the armies at the head of, 1359.

Georgetown, rebuilt, 483; a council of Indians held at, by Governor Shute, 485; another Indian council held at, 490; Sebastien Rale arrives with hostile Indians at, 490–91; the fort at, attacked, 492.

Georgia, 867; English possessions, 859; distribution of the exiled Acadians, 1038.

Germain, a Jesuit father, 356 *note;* efforts against the English, 913–15; the fight at Beaubassin, 925.

German Flats, 1065, 1120; attacked by Vaudreuil, 1200–01.

German States, the, 1222–23.

German War, the, 1473.

Germanic Empire, the, 856, 1222; decay of, 856; hostile to Frederic II., 1469.

Germans, the, 1200, 1227, 1287; in Pennsylvania, 866, 957, 976, 1077, 1082; their language spoken in New York, 866.

Germany, 1277; destiny of, involved with that of Prussia, 857; intrigue formed by France, concerning, 858; the convention of Kloster-Zeven, 1227; political situation in 1761, 1463–65; recreation of, 1475; results of the Seven Years War, 1475.

Gethen, Captain, 1001.

Gibraltar, garrisons of, 849; governorship of General Braddock, 973, 974 *note.*

Gibraltar, Straits of, 1229.

Gibson, George, 1001.

Gibson, James, interested in the scheme for an attack upon Louisbourg, 621; his journal cited, 630 *note*, 671 *note;* raised men for the siege of Louisbourg, 631 *note.*

Giddings, Captain, 1281 *note.*

Gilchrist, 1496.

Gill, Charles, 398 *note.*

Gill, Samuel, taken captive by Abenaki Indians, 397; his descendants estimated, 397.

Gillet, ——, killed at Deerfield by Indians, 741.

Girard, priest at Cobequid, 698–99, 918, 1489; correspondence with Longueuil, 918; his honorable action, 918; oath required of, 918; quotation from, concerning the Acadian emigrants, 920.

Gist, Christopher, 874, 935; sent to select land for settlers, 881–86; his expedition to Ohio, 881; his description of a feather dance, 884; adventure with Indians, 937; his journal, 937 *note;* joins Washington, 944, 947; his settlement, 947, 951; council held by Washington, 948; his buildings burned, 954; reached by the retreating troops of Braddock, 998; orders given by Braddock to, 999.

Gladwin, wounded in the battle of the Monongahela, 995.

Glasgow, 1322.

Glasier, Colonel, 1119.

Glen, Governor of South Carolina, correspondence with Dinwiddie, 964–65.

Glen, John S., at Schenectady, 157–60, 160 note.

Gnadenhütten settlement destroyed by the Indians, 1082.

Goat Island, 1231.

Goddard, Captain, saves Walker's fleet from shipwreck, 450.

Godolphin, minister, 444.

Goldsmith, his Life of Nash, 973.

Goldthwait, Captain Benjamin, in command of the English detachment at Grand Pré, 702 note; attempts a defence against the French attack upon Grand Pré, 705; proposes to capitulate to La Corne, 706; mentioned, 708 note.

"Goodwill," the, 1338.

Gordon, Mr., 1119; engineer in Braddock's expedition, 992.

Gorée, Island of, 1469; restored to France, 1473.

Gorham, ——, his regiment posted at Lighthouse Point, Louisbourg, 658.

Gorham, Captain, reconnoitres Louisbourg, 1164.

Goutin, M. de, a magistrate at Port Royal, quoted concerning affairs at Port Royal, 412.

Governor's Palace, the, 941, 956.

Governors of America, the, position of, 960–61, 1038; council held with Braddock, 975–77; matter of raising money for the campaigns, 977; jealousies between the Assemblies and, 1129.

Gradis and Son, 1212; official knavery, 1212.

Graham, Rev. John of Suffield, Conn., his accounts of the condition of the provincial camp, 1118–19; his Diary quoted, 1118–19.

Grand Battery at Louisbourg, 1233; besieged, 643–44; abandoned by the French, 1238.

Grand Menan, the, 1321.

Grand Pré, the attack of Colonel Church upon, 418; the Acadian village, 697; the plan of attack upon, by Ramesay's officers, 699; the attack and its results, 702–07; the French successes at, 704; affairs becoming desperate for the English, 706; they decide to capitulate, 706; the French and English losses, 707; deserted by the English, 707–08.

Grand Pré, 909, 917, 1023, 1026; meadows of, 1028; encampment of Winslow, 1029; its inhabitants, 1029–30; origin of its name, 1029; the inhabitants summoned to hear the King's orders, 1031–34; the removal of the Acadians, 1035–37.

Grant, Ensign, the attack upon Louisbourg, 1237.

Grant, Major, his expedition, 1299–1302; surrounded and captured, 1301.

Grant, Mrs. Anne, recollections of Albany, 1064; her "Memoirs of an American Lady," cited, 1064, 1259 note.

Grant's Hill, 1292; origin of the name, 1299.

Granville, Earl, 849, 1467; letter from Dinwiddie to, quoted, 964; angry reply given to Pitt, 1467–68; remarks on his death-bed, 1475.

Granville, Fort, attacked by the French and Indians, 1132.

Gratiot, Fort, 351.

Gravier, Jesuit missionary at St. Louis, 553.

Gray, Deacon John, quoted, 629 note.

Gray, John, letter from James Gray, 1065.

Gray, Sergeant James, letter to his brother quoted, 1065.

Gray, words of Wolfe concerning the Elegy, 1392.

Great Britain gains power from the War of the Spanish Succession, 339.

Great Butte des Morts, 563.

Great Carrying Place, the, 429, 1046,

1065, 1112, 1363; guarded by the English, 1099; fort rebuilt by Shirley, 1106; the fort burned, 1120; new fort to be erected, 1285.

Great Company, the, in Canada, 1039.

Great Cove, the settlement destroyed, 1080.

Great Kenawha, the, 878; plate buried by the French near, 878.

Great Lakes, the, 896, 930.

Great Meadows, the, 943; Washington assembles his force, 944, 947, 948; the fight at, 951–54; encampment of Dunbar, 1000.

Great Miami, the, 879, 883; neighboring country described, 883.

Great Savage Mountain, the, 986.

Greeks, the, 1121, 1418.

Green and Russell, Messrs., 1501.

Green Bay, Wis., 397, 582, 902; groups of Indians near, 519; a fort built at, by the French, 614; fraudulent trade, 1214.

Green Dragon Tavern, a dinner at, 436.

Green Hill, a battery planted at, for the attack upon Louisbourg, 645.

Green Mountains, 387, 1152.

Green, his "History of the English People" cited, 1475 and note.

Grenada, 1470; ceded by France, 1472.

Grenadines, the, 1472.

Grenville, Mr., 1330 note.

Grey Lock, a noted Indian chief, 498.

Gridley, Colonel, 1117; plants a battery at Lighthouse Point, Louisbourg, 658; his effective work at Lighthouse Point, 662; mentioned, 671 note.

Grignan, Count de, 20 note.

Grignon, Augustus, Recollections, cited, 563 note.

Grignon, Pierre, 1487.

Groton, attacked by Indians, 402; joins in Lovewell's expedition, 508.

Guadeloupe, 1469; question of its comparative value with that of Canada, 1471; restored by England, 1472.

Guienne, the battalion of, 968, 1268, 1271, 1355, 1356; guards Fort Frontenac, 1100; the capture of Oswego, 1122; camp of, 1168; advances upon Fort William Henry, 1179; ordered to

encamp on the Plains of Abraham, 1386; encamps by the St. Charles, 1392, 1395–96.

Guignas, Father, a missionary to the Sioux Indians, 582.

Guillaume le Sincère, 671 note.

Guinea, the French driven from, 1228.

Gulf of Mexico, 426.

Gumley, Colonel, 973.

Habitant de Louisbourg, concerning the attack upon Louisbourg, 639–40; quoted, 665, 667.

Hadley, Mass., 374; the inhabitants go to the rescue of Deerfield, 379–80.

Hagar, a servant of Rev. —— Rolfe, 401.

Hague, 1135.

Hainaut, 1089.

Haldimand, Colonel, 1363; attacked by the French, 1363–64.

Hale, Captain ——, hurt by bursting of a gun at Louisbourg, 650 note.

Hale, Colonel Robert, letter of John Payne to, 635 note; commander in the siege of Louisbourg, 635 note.

Hale, George S., 1119 note.

Half-King, chief of the Indians on the Ohio, 933; aids and accompanies Washington, 935, 943–44, 947, 948, 953; efforts of Saint-Pierre to entice away his Indians, 936; council held with Half-King by Washington, 944; boast concerning the death of Jumonville, 947 note; his comments on the fight at Great Meadows, 953.

Half-Moon, 1106, 1152, 1278.

Haliburton, statement from, 1035 note.

Halifax, 914, 916, 918, 922, 923, 980, 1009, 1012, 1020, 1197, 1387; settlement of English at, 472; foundation and growth of, 909; meeting of deputies from Acadia with Cornwallis, 912; questions of ownership, 929; hearing given to the Acadians, 1023–26; destined port of the English fleet, 1163–64; fleet sails for, under Admiral Boscawen, 1230; departure of Boscawen's ships, 1234; arrival of Admiral Saunders, 1328.

Halifax, Fort, 969 and *note.*

Halifax, Lord, on the Board of Trade, 966; letter from Dinwiddie to, 1001–02.

Halket, Major, 1493; discovers his father's body, 1305; letter from Tomahawk Camp, 1306.

Halket, Sir Peter, attacked by the French, 993–95; shot in battle, 995, 1001; burial of his remains, 1305.

Halket, son of Sir Peter, shot in battle, 995; his remains discovered, 1305.

Hamilton, James, Governor of Pennsylvania, 882, 883; his opinion of English traders, 874; correspondence with Dinwiddie, 874 *note,* 941; receives a message from the Miamis and Hurons, 883–84 and 884 *note;* desirability of an Indian alliance, 885; tries to build a trading-house on the Ohio, 886; result of the meeting of, with the Assembly of Pennsylvania, 957–59; succeeded by Governor Morris, 958.

Hampton, arrival of Braddock, 972; arrival of regiments at, 974.

Hampton, attacks upon by Indians, 368.

Hanbury, John, 940; stockholder in the Ohio Company, 881, 980; extracts from his correspondence with Dinwiddie, 940, 942; error ascribed to, 980.

Hanbury, Mrs., 942.

Hancock, a Boston merchant, furnishes money for the English troops, 1013.

Handfield, Major, in command at Annapolis, 1028; instructions to expel the Acadians, 1028; letter from, to Winslow, 1032–33; letter of Winslow concerning the removal of the Acadians, 1035.

Hannibal, 1341.

Hanover, 847, 849, 1085, 1223, 1228, 1229, 1463, 1464, 1469; possessions of England in, 858; restorations made by France, 1473.

Harding, Stephen, escapes murder from Indians, 365.

Hardy, Major, to hold the Point of Orleans, 1346, 1348.

Hardy, Sir Charles, Governor of New York, 1105, 1164; opposition to Shirley, 1105; orders issued to scatter the Nova Scotia settlers, 1251.

Harley, ——, Lord Treasurer of England, 444.

Harmon, Captain, sent to attack Norridgewock, 498.

Harpe, Bénard de la. (See *La Harpe, B. de.*)

Harris, John, sufferings of the settlers, 1079.

Harris, Mary, story of, 882.

Harris, Thomas, English scout, 1126.

Harry, 1463.

Hartwell Library, the, 1347 *note.*

Hassell, Benjamin, a cowardly member of Lovewell's expedition, 510, 512, 513.

Hastings, John, helps form a settlement on the Connecticut called Number Four, 721; chosen on committee to protect the settlement, 721.

Hatfield, Mass., 374, 378; the inhabitants go to the rescue of Deerfield, 379–80; an intended Indian attack upon, 400.

Hauteur-de-la-Potence, 1241.

Havana, expedition of Pococke, 1470; conquered, 1470; returned to Spain, 1472.

Haverhill, attacked by Indians, 401; joins in Lovewell's expedition, 508.

Haviland, Colonel, commander at Fort Edward, 1204; the fall of Canada, 1443–57; opens communication with Murray, 1448; encamped near Montreal, 1451.

Hawke, Sir Edward, his character, 1230.

Hawks, Ebenezer, killed at Deerfield by Indians, 741.

Hawks, John, *Account of the Company at Fort Massachusetts,* 736; in charge of Fort Massachusetts, 736; considers and accepts terms of capitulation from Rigaud, 739–40; sergeant, made lieutenant-colonel, 744.

Hawley, Elisha, his wounds, 1052, 1058; his last letter to his brother quoted, 1052.

Hawley, Joseph, 1052.

Hay, Ensign, killed at Beauséjour, 1017.

Hay, Sir Charles, 1164.

Hayes, Fort (Hudson's Bay), seized, 102.

Hazen, Captain Moses, 1436–37; the encounter at Beauséjour, 1016; his courage, 1135; skirmish at Lorette, 1427–28; the battle between Lévis and Murray, 1434–36.

Heath, Joseph, an English settler at Brunswick, 481 note, 490 note; captain, burns the new village of the Penobscots, 504–05.

Heath, town of, Massachusetts, 728.

Hebecourt, Captain, stationed at Ticonderoga, 1203; receives a reinforcement of Indians, 1204; Bourlamaque leaves him in charge, 1361.

Helots, 1160.

Henderson, 1399.

Hendrick, chief of the Mohawks, 1051; his arrival at New York, 961; speech made at Albany, 961–63; encounter with Dieskau, 1051–52; his advice to Johnson, 1051; killed in battle, 1052, 1057.

Henry IV., of France, 1202; anecdotes of, 325.

Hensey, Florence, a spy at London, 1163.

Herbin, 1176; skirmish with Captain MacDonald, 1427.

Herkimer, Fort, 1201.

Hermitage, the, 1211.

"Héros," the, the ship, 1092.

Hertel, 1176.

Hertel, Fr., commands an expedition against New Hampshire, 162, 167.

Highlanders, the, 1261, 1299, 1323; their bravery, 1271, 1356; serve under Forbes, 1287–1307; their comrades exposed on poles, 1304; action at Quebec, 1356, 1376–77, 1392, 1497; the slogan, 1399; encounter with the Canadians, 1402; their costume insufficient in Canada, 1426; encounter with the French, 1427.

Hill, Fort, Boston, 446.

Hill, General John, given command of the Canada expedition, 445; his reception in Boston, 446; anxious for retreat, 452; arrives in England, 456; reaps honors, 457.

Hill, Mrs. John, 456.

Hill, Samuel, capture of his family by Indians, 365; goes to Canada to negotiate for release of prisoners, 394, 405.

Hilton, Colonel Winthrop, a commander in the expedition to Port Royal, 420; mentioned, 481.

Historical Magazine, cited, 499 note.

Hix, Jacob, death of, 386.

Hobbs, Captain, 1030, 1031.

Hobby, Sir Charles, in expedition against Port Royal, 436; at a breakfast of the English officers at Port Royal, 439.

Hochelaga, Indian defences at, 348.

Hocquart, Captain, fate of the "Alcide," 970; encounter with Captain Howe, 970–71.

Hocquart, Intendant, financial condition of Canada, 1217.

Hodges, Captain, 1136.

Hogarth, 848.

Holbourne, Admiral Francis, ordered to intercept the French fleet, 970; commands the English fleet to sail for America, 1163–64; his arrival at Halifax, 1164; approaches Louisbourg, 1164; his fleet wrecked, 1165.

Holdernesse, Earl of, 1057, 1441; letter laid before the Assembly of Pennsylvania, 957; letter from Wolfe concerning Quebec, 1383; visited by Walpole, 1441; supplanted by the Earl of Bute, 1464.

Holdernesse, Lady Emily, 1441.

Holland, 1392; her rank in maritime enterprise, 1477.

Holland, Lieutenant, his report of Duquesne's war-party, 905.

Holmes, Admiral, sails for New York, 1328; his squadron, 1377, 1384; attacked by the French, 1378; the ships carefully watched by the French, 1385–86; his fleet prepares for service, 1387–90; feint to deceive Bougainville, 1388; the final attack on Quebec, 1389.

Holton, Eleazar, Northfield, Mass., 729.

Hontan (Baron La), 82, 83, 218; at Fort Frontenac, 107; his account of the attack on Quebec, 203.

Hook, Sergeant, defends Major March against Indians at Casco, 366.

Hoosac, name given to eastern tributary of the Hudson, 732.

Hopkins, Lieutenant, the attack on Louisbourg, 1237–38.

Hopson, Governor of Acadia, 916, 1021; succeeded by Lawrence, 922.

Horse Indians of the West, 592 and *note;* visited by the brothers La Vérendrye, 595; their march against the Snake Indians, 595; they find the camp of the Snakes deserted, 598; their disbandment, 598.

Horseflesh eaten at Montreal, 1203.

Hospital battery, the, 1341.

"Hot Stuff," 1357 *note,* 1358 *note.*

Hôtel-Dieu, 1379; its condition after the siege, 1421; care of the sick, 1424.

Houllière, commander of French regulars, 1244.

Housatonic River, villages settled along the, 728.

House of Burgesses, the, 938.

House of Commons, the, 1224, 1476; influence of the Duke of Newcastle in, 966; debate concerning the peace between France and England, 1473.

House of Representatives, the, approve Lovewell's expedition against Indians, 507.

Howard, Lord (governor of Virginia), at Albany, 73.

Howard the philanthropist, 848.

Howe, Brigadier-Lord, 1228; effort made to assist the settlement at German Flats, 1200; united with Abercromby in command, 1228; his leadership, 1258; reforms introduced into the army by, 1258; his characteristics, 1258–59; the expedition against Ticonderoga, 1258–64; tablet erected to, in Westminster Abbey, 1259–60; passage of the expedition across Lake George, 1260–61; reconnoitres the landing, 1261; the meeting of the forces in the woods, 1263; effect of his death on the army, 1263–64, 1267.

Howe, Captain, 1284; the encounter with Hocquart, 970–71.

Howe, Captain, 1390; the Heights of Abraham scaled by his men, 1395.

Howe, Captain, the missionary Le Loutre charged with inciting the murder of, 695; quartered with Colonel Noble at Grand Pré, 703; wounded and taken prisoner, 704; allowed by La Corne to call an English surgeon, 705; released on parole after the capitulation, 706.

Howe, Captain Edward, an English officer, 925; treacherously murdered, 925–26.

Hoyt, ——, antiquarian, 397; *Antiquarian Researches* mentioned, 727 *note.*

Hoyt, David, inhabitant of Deerfield, 378; his wife wounded during Indian attack, 378; death of, 386.

Hubbard, Thomas, 1490.

Hubert, his scheme for exploring the Missouri, 570.

Hubertsburg, the treaty of, 1474.

Hudson Bay, 580; English possessions near, 858.

Hudson River, the, 346, 864, 976, 1043, 1063, 1065, 1106, 1108, 1111, 1152, 1197, 1276, 1278, 1309; an eastern tributary called Kaskékouké, Schaticook, and Hoosac, 732; Dutch proprietors on the, 867; parties sent to explore, 1363.

Hudson's Bay, English traders, 92; attack on their posts by Troyes, 101–03; by Iberville, 282–83.

Huguenot colonists, at Port Royal, 247; their intention to settle on the Mississippi, 537; deceived by Bienville, and abandoned the project, 537; petition the French king to allow them to settle in Louisiana, 537; persecution of, 855, 860; the language of, spoken in New York, 866.

Hugues, plan of defence proposed by, 1265.

Humble memorial, of John Lovewell and others, to destroy Indians, 507.

Hungary, appeal made to the nobles of, by Maria Theresa, 858; action of the nobles, 858.

Hungary, the Queen of, 1462.

Hunter, Governor, endeavors to prevent the building of a fort by the French at Niagara, 611.

"Hunter," the, 1393.

Huron, Lake, 351, 896, 1175.

Huron converts, 29, 63, 186; at Michillimackinac, 152.

Huron Indians, 930, 949, 988; inclined to the English, 92; at Michillimackinac, 152; join a war-party, 400; settled about Detroit, 519; the village of, 521; form a party to attack the Outagamies, 562; their account of their defeat of the Outagamies, 562–63; their Christianity, 873; assist the French, 1098, 1293; called to a council by Montcalm, 1175–78; their savagery, 1295 note.

Hurons and Ottawas, Indians settled at Michillimackinac, 349; savage and mischievous, 348.

Hurst, Benjamin, child murdered by Indians, 395–96.

Hurst, Sarah, baptized as Marie Jeanne, 395–96.

Hurtado, Général, cited, 579 note.

Huske, map of North America, 930 note.

Hutchins, Ensign, 1369, 1383.

Hutchinson, ——, cited, 402 note, 487 note, 500 note, 510 note, 515 note, 619 note.

Hutchinson, Indian cruelties, 1199 note.

Hutchinson, Thomas, History of Massachusetts, cited, 671 note.

Iberville, Le Moyne d' (the Jean Bart of Canada), plan of, to destroy Boston, 340; offered to plant a colony in Louisiana, 535; his offer accepted, 535; explores his way to the mouth of the Mississippi, 536; builds a fort at Biloxi and sails for France, 536; returned to Louisiana to protect against English intrusion, 538; re-

moves the fort from Biloxi to Mobile Bay, 538; made a voyage up the Mississippi, 538; memorial by, quoted, 539 note; his hope of discovering the Pacific, 570.

Iberville, son of Le Moyne, 102; his military career, 280; attack on Newfoundland, 281–82; at Fort Nelson, 282–83.

Illicit traders in Boston, 408–09.

Illinois, 930, 1176, 1293; French claims in, 873; two maps of, 873 note.

Illinois Indians, 65, 95; settled about Fort St. Louis, 519; aid Dubuisson at Detroit, 524; home of, 873.

Illinois River, the, 883, 901, 1302, 1365; French interests, 1368.

"Illustre," the, 1092.

Independents, the, 867.

India, 844, 1467; results of the Seven Years War, 844; the mastery of, 852; French colonies in, 1087; the power of Pitt, 1225; losses to be sustained by France, 1473, 1476.

Indian corn, 988, 1074.

Indian Old Point (Norridgewock), 481 note.

Indian Old Town, present abode of the Penobscots, 504–05.

Indian population in the West, 519.

Indian trade, the, between the English and West, 520.

Indians, the, 909, 1256; illustrations of their manners and customs, 28, 58–59, 75, 111, 113–14, 115, 118, 185–86, 321; their cannibalism, 77, 88, 116–17, 135, 153 note, 227, 903, 1169, 1174; graveyard, 117; torture, 135, 219; instigated by French, 152, 257; great conference at Montreal, 317–24; the plan of La Mothe-Cadillac for civilizing, 353; attack towns in Massachusetts and New Hampshire, 399, 402; reward offered for scalps of, 402 and note; their native warlike propensities, 532; influenced by the French to fight the English, 864, 871, 877–78, 902, 913–19, 922, 948, 954, 961, 963, 969, 990–91, 1006, 1009–10, 1098, 1111, 1139, 1161–62, 1167, 1169, 1293, 1294, 1295,

1457; population in the Ohio Valley, 872, 879, 886, 933, 939; allies of the English, 874, 1111, 1291, 1292, 1294, 1297, 1298, 1299, 1307, 1451; visited by Bienville, 875, 876; hostile encounter with Bienville, 878; village of, on Loramie Creek, 879; importance of Pique Town, 880; matters pertaining to trade and missions, 881, 887–94, 1214, 1295; councils held with Gist by Old Britain and his followers, 883–84; invite the English to a feather dance, 884; power of Sir William Johnson over, 888, 962, 977, 1042, 1110–11; at Oswego, 893–94; their treachery, 898–99; rumors of plots among, 901–02; attacked at Pickawillany, 902; relations with the Acadians, 911, 912–19, 1026, 1482, 1483; plans of the French in Duquesne's expedition, thwarted, 933–34; parleys, held with Washington, 935; assist Washington, 943–45, 947; account of the conduct of Washington's band, 946; at Great Meadows, 947; under Coulon de Villiers, 949, 950; harangued by Contrecœur, 949; tribes at Fort Duquesne, 949, 988; sent out as scouts by the French, 950; attack Washington, 951–54; attitude of the British cabinet towards, 961; complaints of the Mohawks, 961; commissioners at Albany, 962; their opinions of the French, 962–63; meeting at Albany for conference, 962–64; estimate of, held by Braddock, 972–73; Johnson made sole superintendent of the Northern Tribes, 977, 1110; join Braddock's expedition, 984–85; try to interrupt General Braddock's march, 986; tribes at Fort Duquesne, 988; cruelties practised by, on prisoners and others, 989, 996–97; depart from Fort Duquesne to fight the English, 990; their mode of warfare, 992–95, 1288; the encounter with Braddock, 993–1000, 1457; the battle of Beauséjour, 1015; attack the English at Peticodiac, 1034; speeches made by, 1043; sent as scouts to Canada, 1046;

under Dieskau, 1048, 1050; demands made by, 1049; forces under Sir William Johnson, 1051, 1268, 1449; the battle of Lake George, 1051–59; the fur-trade, 1064; under Governor Shirley, 1068; cruelties of, 1071–73, 1077, 1079, 1082, 1098, 1103, 1131, 1132, 1173–74, 1188–94, 1194 note, 1199, 1200, 1205, 1282–83, 1312, 1347, 1350, 1356, 1367, 1374, 1377, 1426–27, 1437, 1452, 1483, 1489–92; efforts of the French to prevent the prisoners being tortured, 1071; feelings of the Quakers towards, 1075, 1077, 1080; petition sent to the Assembly of Pennsylvania, 1082; policy of Franklin, 1083; described by Montcalm, 1098, 1154, 1159–60; relations of Montcalm with, 1098, 1103, 1159–60, 1166–67; join the expedition of Léry, 1100; bring to the French rumors of the attack upon Ticonderoga, 1101; their ways described by Duchat, 1103; trouble the English in their transportation of stores, 1108; sent to harass Oswego, 1112; join the French at Montreal, 1121; capture of Oswego, 1122–27; the attack upon Kittanning, 1132–34; assist the English at Fort William Henry, 1135; join the war-party of Perière, 1136–37; sent to Ticonderoga, 1141, 1145; fight with Rogers' rangers, 1145–46, 1280–82; join Vaudreuil's war-parties, 1148–49; exaggerated accounts of Vaudreuil in relation to, 1158–59, 1160; ceremony of the war-song, 1167; fortified camps of, 1168; described by Bougainville, 1169; their Manitou, 1169; their ornaments and dress, 1169, 1172; their rations, 1169; their religion, 1169; their war-feast described, 1172–73; capture of Colonel Parker's company, 1174; scalping-party at Fort Edward, 1175; a council called by Montcalm, 1175–78; French officers having command of, 1176; speeches made by the chiefs, 1176–78; their interpreters, 1177; the attack and massacre at Fort William Henry, 1179–94, 1194 note, 1489–92; encounter on Lake George, 1179–80; death and burial of a chief, 1181; interview with Montcalm, 1185; prisoners bought from, 1200; the fight at German Flats, 1200–01; brutal murder of Lieutenant Phillips, 1206; sent to guard Louisbourg, 1233; serve under Marin, 1280; carry off Major Putnam, 1280–81; Bradstreet forbids cruelty, 1284; effect of the French victory at Ticonderoga, 1284; serve under Forbes, 1291–92, 1293; convention of, 1293–94, 1297–98, 1306; influence and visit of Post the Moravian, 1294–99; effect of the victory at Fort Duquesne, 1306; sent to Montcalm, 1308–09; Vaudreuil's admiration for, 1312; number ready to defend Canada, 1317; resolutions of Vaudreuil, 1318; assist in the defence of Quebec, 1336, 1345, 1347, 1398, 1411; complaints of British soldiers, 1349; encounter with Carleton, 1351; the siege of Niagara, 1364–68; expedition of Rogers against the village of St. Francis, 1371–74; expedition of Lévis against Quebec, 1430–42; the attack on Montreal, 1448, 1450.

Ingoldsby, Colonel, acting governor of Connecticut, 427.

Innes, Colonel James, 955, 1001, 1163; commander at Fort Cumberland, 1000; plans of Dinwiddie, 1072.

Inverawe, 1261, 1271; castle of, 1494; legend of, 1494–96.

Inverness, 1322.

Iowas, Indians, in council with Bourgmont, 576; their language, 1169; called to a council by Montcalm, 1176–78.

Ipswich, 420, 1275.

Ireland, 1469; the regiments arrive at Hampton, 974.

Irish, the, in Pennsylvania, 866, 881, 1077, 1147.

Irondequoit Bay, muster of Indians there, 113.

Iroquois (Five Nations), 59, 62, 343; their strength, 62, 65; policy, 63; craft, 68; pride, 74; offences against the French, 83, 127–28; Denonville

seeks to chastise them, 95; approached by Dongan, 98; they distrust Denonville, 105; seizure at Fort Frontenac, 107; converts as allies, 114, 118; claimed as subjects by Andros, 124; invasion of Canada, 127, 133–35; seize the ruins of Fort Frontenac, 144; their inroads, 209; relations with Bellomont, 304–05; their suspicions of the French, 316; treat with Callières, 316–17; conference at Montreal, 317–24; their ill-faith 319; their numbers, 324 *note;* join in war-parties from Montreal, 719.

Iroquois Indians, the. See *Five Nations.*

Iroquois mission, the, 889.

Irwin, Lieutenant, serves with Rogers, 1280.

Island Battery, the, 1233, 1238, 1239.

Isle-au-Cochon, near Fort Detroit, 531.

Isle-aux-Œufs, the disaster to Admiral Walker's fleet at, 451.

Isle of Wight, 406.

Isles of Shoals, the, 626.

Italy, the Family Compact, 1466.

Jack, Captain, story of, 985.

Jacobites, the, 847, 976.

Jacobs, Captain, Indian chief, 1132; reduction of Kittanning, 1132–34.

Jacques-Cartier, 1386, 1405, 1406, 1408, 1410, 1414, 1430, 1443, 1445.

James II., 93, 104, 340, 435; assumes protectorate over the Iroquois, 122; puts the colonies under command of Andros, 124; is deposed, 136; plan for uniting the northern colonies in America, 868.

James III., acknowledged king by Louis XIV., 340.

James River, 1131 *note.*

Jaques, Benjamin, shot the missionary Sebastien Rale, 499.

Jefferson, 956.

Jersey, Island of, 1018.

"Jersey Blues," the, 1064, 1105.

Jervis, Jean, with Wolfe in the "Sutherland," 1391.

Jesuits, the, 889, 1341; in Canada, 24; Frontenac's charges, 27, 29, 38, 214;

English suspicions, 73; protected by Denonville, 96; excluded by Dongan, 120; hostile to Frontenac, 143; during the attack on Quebec, 205; their intrigues, 239–40; the amount of their possessions in Canada, 353; attempt to convert Rev. John Williams to certain rites of their church, 388; their attempts to convert the Deerfield captives, 390; the zeal displayed by both early and later missionaries in New France, 478–79; they converted but did not civilize the Indians, 479; settlements of, 1295.

Joannès, his efforts to save Quebec, 1412–13.

Jogues, a Jesuit missionary, 348, 429, 479.

Johnson, Fort, 1043, 1065, 1111, 1127.

Johnson, Sergeant John, loyalty of the British soldiers, 1389, 1429, 1437, 1438; fight of Murray with, 1435, 1502; the assault on Quebec made by Lévis, 1437–42 note; his writings on Quebec, 1500.

Johnson, Sir William, 715 note, 739 note, 887 note, 1063, 1068, 1268; made a war-chief of the Mohawks, 716; complains of certain persons selling liquor to the Indians, 717; sends war-parties of Indians to check French invasion, 717; his influence over the Indians, 888, 962, 963, 977, 1042, 1043, 1110–11, 1293, 1294, 1365; Indian treachery, 899; appointed leader of the expedition against Crown Point, 977, 1041; made Indian commissioner, 977, 1042, 1110; his birth and characteristics, 1042, 1047; encamps near Albany, 1044; his troops, 1044–46, 1047–48, 1051 and note, 1057, 1106; the expedition marches on to Lake George, 1046–47; gives the name to Lake George, 1047; ambush prepared for, by Dieskau, 1048, 1051; sends a letter of warning to Colonel Blanchard, 1048; movements of Dieskau, 1048–51; forces sent in advance repelled by Dieskau, 1051–54; the battle of Lake George, 1053–62, 1257; wounded, 1054, 1056; Dieskau

brought into camp, and kindly treated, 1056; his camp at Lake George, 1059–60; fails to capture Crown Point, 1059–61, 1104; the English and French losses, 1059 note; a council of war held, 1060; urged to attack Ticonderoga, 1060; raised to the rank of baron, 1061, 1110; eulogies of, 1061; cause of the quarrel with Shirley, 1069; his letter to the Lords of Trade, 1069; the loss of Fort Bull, 1100; difficulties thrown in his path, 1111; joins Webb at Fort Edward, 1198; money expended by Massachusetts on his expedition, 1255; Indian convention at Easton, 1297; takes command in Prideaux's place, 1365; Pouchot's allies cut to pieces, 1367; his fight at Niagara, 1367; restrains the Indians from cruelty, 1368, 1450, 1452; superseded by Gage, 1368; the army embarks for Montreal, 1449.

Johnstone, 1252 note, 1267 note; aide-decamp to Lévis, 1346; description of the attack on the French camp, 1356; despatched to assemble the troops, 1396; fired upon by the British, 1403–04; the general disorder of the troops at Quebec, 1404–05; the death of Montcalm, 1405, 1408, 1500–01; his opinion of the French retreat, 1407–08; his opportunities for observation, 1499; his "Dialogue in Hades," 1499–1500.

Joncaire-Chabert, 1111, 1365; able to converse in the Indian dialects, 875; discovers an intended Indian attack, 877; sent as a messenger by Céloron, 878; meets with hostile treatment, 878–79; his influence over the Indians, 885, 888, 961, 1294; anti-English speeches made to the Ohio Indians, 885 note; leaden plate stolen from, 887 note; at Niagara, 893; assists Father Piquet, 893, 896; report concerning the Ohio Indians, 901; in command at Venango, 935; invites Washington to supper, 935.

Joncaire-Clauzonne, 1365.

Joncaire, an agent among the Five Nations, 344, 345, 428, 611; his adventures among the Indians, 317, 318; a French emissary among the Seneca Indians, 716.

Jones, Esther, a heroine of Oyster River, 399.

Jones, Josiah, in the fight at Lovewell's Pond, 512; arrived at Biddeford, 512.

Jones, Lieutenant, killed by the French in their attack on Grand Pré, 704.

Jonquière, Marquis de la, governor of Canada, 602, 898, 924; charged St. Pierre with the search for the Pacific, 602; remains with the fleet at Chibucto, 684; succeeds to the command of D'Anville's fleet, 684; sails for Annapolis, but abandons his design of attack, 685; reaches Port Louis in Brittany, 685; the breaking up of his fleet, 685; sent with a fleet for the conquest of Acadia, etc., 687; meets with an English fleet, and is totally defeated, 687; illegal trade of Tournois stopped, 889 note; his character and description of, 898, 900; his instructions with regard to injuring the English, 898–900; his unhappiness, sickness, and death, 900 note, 900–01; orders given to Céleron, 902; report of, concerning the Acadians, 910, 916; a despatch sent to the colonial minister, 912–14; assists the Indians to harass the English, 913–14, 915–16; his efforts to regain the Acadians for French subjects, 915–16; issues a proclamation, 927.

Jordan River in Carolina, 608.

Joseph, 1091; his voyage, 1092–93.

Journal of Governor, etc., cited, 446 note.

Journal of the Siege of Louisbourg, cited, 647 note.

Juchereau de Saint-Denis, explored in Louisiana, 570; seized by Spaniards, 571.

Juchereau de Saint-Denis, Mother, quoted concerning the effect upon the ladies of Montreal, etc., of the news of Walker's expected attack, 454–55.

Jumonville, Charlotte, 947 note.

Jumonville, Coulon de, 944; matters pertaining to his alleged assassination, 945–47, 952, 1484–85; his summons and instructions, 945 note; 945–46; his widow receives a pension, 947 note.

Juniata River, the, 985, 1132.

Justinien, Père, 465, 473.

Kalm, Swedish naturalist, 454, 744 note; his prediction concerning the British colonies in America, 1471.

Kaministiguia River, a post established at, 580, 586.

Kanaouagon, the, 875.

Kannan, H., cited, 683 note.

Kanon, 1333, 1420 note; his fleet, 1336.

Karl, Prince, 1223.

Kaskaskia, town of, settled by Canadians, etc., 553, 873.

Kaskaskias, Indians, form a settlement on the Mississippi, 553.

Kaskékouké, eastern tributary of the Hudson, 732.

Kaunitz, 1086.

Keene (Upper Ashuelot), the settlement of, 718 note; attacked by Indians, 718; its defences, 718.

Kellogg, ——, escape from Indian captivity, 393–94.

Kellogg, Joanna, married Indian chief, 396.

Kenawha River, the, 878, 885.

Kennebec lands, parted with by the Indians, 483–84.

Kennebec River, the, 340, 360, 864, 969, 975, 1014, 1369; a dividing line between French possessions and New England, 477; forts to be built upon, by the English, 960.

Kennedy, Captain, sent to the Abenakis of St. Francis, 1369.

Kennedy, Lieutenant, consults with Captain Murray, 1030; his exploits against the French, 1135; adventures of a scouting-party of Rogers, 1144–46; killed by the French, 1145.

Kennetcook River, 701.

Kennington Cove, 1235 note.

Kent, ——, killed by Indians at Casco, Me., 366.

Keppel, Commodore, his arrival at Hampton, 972; accompanies Braddock to Alexandria, 974–75; sailors furnished by, for Braddock, 983.

Keyes, Solomon, in the fight at Lovewell's Pond, wounded, 511; arrived at Fort Ossipee, 512.

Kidder, Benjamin, a member of Lovewell's expedition, 509.

Kidder, Frederic, cited, 483 *note,* 507 *note,* 515 *note.*

Kikensick, chief of the Nipissings, speech of, 1176–77.

Kilgore, Ralph, 899 *note.*

Killick, master of an English transport, 1338; passage of the Traverse, 1338–39.

King, Colonel, letter on the manners, etc., of the colonists at Boston, 446–47; in Walker's expedition, escape of his ship from wreck, 451.

King's Bastion, the, 1231, 1233; the Governor's dwelling, 1242.

Kingston, 891; annoyed by Indians, 402.

Kinshon (the Fish), Indian name of New England, 148.

Kirkland, Dr., a surgeon, 1113.

Kittanning, attack upon, 1132–34.

Kittery, a town in Maine, 362; annoyed by Indians, 402.

Kittery Point, the view of the Piscataqua from, 625; the house of William Pepperrell at, 625.

Kloster-Zeven, convention of, 1227.

Kneeland, S., printer, Boston, 730 *note.*

Knowles, Commodore Charles, advises the removal of the Acadians, 693; presents a sword to Captain Phineas Stevens, 727.

Knowlton, Thomas, killed in the defence of Fort Massachusetts, 739, 744 *note.*

Knox, Captain John, 1234 *note;* character of Le Loutre described, 1018 *note;* at Annapolis, 1249; rejoicing at the fall of Louisbourg, 1249; his regiment ordered to Louisbourg, 1320;

his impressions of Wolfe, 1322; account of the Canadian coasts, 1339; description of the scenery on the St. Lawrence River, 1340–41; visits the Church of Saint-Laurent, 1340; description of the fireships, 1343, 1353; his view of Quebec from Point Levi, 1344; visits the falls, 1348; reports obtained from a Canadian, 1350; his account of Canadian prisoners, 1352–53; losses reported, 1357; the illness of Wolfe, 1379–80; the defence of Cap-Rouge, 1388; the dying words of Wolfe, 1400 *note;* describes Quebec after the siege, 1422–23; his stay in the General Hospital, 1423; the troops described by, 1425–26; skirmish at Lorette, 1427–28; action between Lévis and Murray, 1434–36; arrival of aid, 1439–40; the troops of Murray sail for Montreal, 1444–47; death of Montcalm, 1501.

Kolin, 1223.

Kondiaronk (the Rat), a Huron chief, 64; his craft, which brings on the Iroquois invasion, 130–32, 152; at Montreal, 317, 319; death and burial, 319–21; a Christian convert, 320.

Kunersdorf, the allies attacked, 1461.

Kushkushkee, 1295.

La Barolon, 1156.

La Barre, governor of Canada, 1682–1684, finds Lower Quebec in ruins, 61; his boasting, 65–66; proposes to attack the Senecas, 68; expedition to the Illinois, seizes Fort St. Louis, 70; campaign against the Senecas, 79; charges of Meules, 80; council at Fort La Famine, 82–86; La Barre's speech, 83; embassy to the Upper Lakes, 87; wrath of the Ottawas, 88; is recalled, 90.

Labat, M., at Port Royal, 414.

La Baye, fort, on Green Bay, 614.

Lac des Cristineaux (Lake of the Woods), a post established at, 580.

La Chasse, Père, quoted, 482 *note;* aids Rale in inciting the Indians to insurrection, 490; account of destruction of Norridgewock, cited, 500 *note;* acts as interpreter at an interview between Indians and the embassy from Governor Dummer, 504.

La Chesnaye, partner of Duchesneau, 52; in favor with La Barre, 67; seizes Fort Frontenac, 67; his forest trade, 69 (see *Chesnaye*).

La Chine, 355, 871, 1156, 1200, 1202, 1450, 1451; massacre of, 133–34.

La Clue, Admiral, 1229; imprisoned by Osborn, 1229–30.

La Corne, Saint-Luc de, 1176, 1187, 1279, 1492; suggested to the French the fortifying of Crown Point, 614; Récollet missionary at Miramichi, 698; in Ramesay's expedition, 698; assists in attack on Grand Pré, 702; blockades the principal guard-house at Grand Pré, 705; allows a suspension of arms while a surgeon attends Captain Howe, 705; makes terms of capitulation to the English, 706; his attentions to the English after capitulation at Grand Pré, 707; returns to Beaubassin, 708; his account of the French victory cited, 708 *note;* sent to Acadia to watch the frontier, 915, 924; circumstances attending the massacre at Fort William Henry, 1183, 1188, 1190; ordered to Quebec, 1331, 1333, 1364; to defend the rapids, 1444, 1450; shipwrecked, 1458–59.

Lacroix, a French prisoner of war, 706–07.

La Demoiselle (Old Britain), an Indian chief, 879–80, 902; his course of action with Céloron, 880; his village, 883; councils held with Gist, 883–84; the English invited to a feather dance, 884; devoured by the Indians, 903.

La Force, joins Rigaud's war-party, 734.

La Forest, in the fur-trade at Fort St. Louis, 519.

La Forêt, commander of Fort Frontenac, 67; returns to France, 67.

Lafresnière, Sieur de, 543; sent to fortify Crown Point, 614.

La Galette, 1449.

Lagny, assists in attack on Grand Pré, 702.

La Grange, father-in-law of Frontenac, 16.

La Harpe, Bénard de, 537 *note;* explorations along Red River, 571; reaches the land of the Nassonites, 571; arrives at an Indian village, 572; pushes on to Arkansas River, 572; explores it, 573; returned to Natchitoches, 573.

La Hontan, romances of, mentioned, 570.

Lainé, 1215.

La Jemeraye, joins La Vérendrye's enterprise, 585; death of, 586.

Lake tribes, English alliance, 74; great gathering at Montreal, 185–86; conciliated by Frontenac, 228–29; their threatening attitude, 290; treaty with Callières, 321–24.

Lalande, a prisoner among the Indians, 392.

Lalemant (Lallemant), a Jesuit mission priest, 429, 479.

Lalerne, fight at Beaubassin, 925.

La Loire des Ursins, in council at "the Illinois," 554 *note.*

Lamberville, Jacques, a Jesuit missionary at Onondaga, 65, 76, 82, 428; correspondence with La Barre, 77, 88–89; protected by Dongan, 97; in danger among the Iroquois, 105; escapes to Denonville, 109; an agent among the Five Nations, 344.

La Mothe-Cadillac, Antoine de, in command at Michillimackinac, 348; portrayed, 349 and *note;* plan to attack Boston, etc., 349 *note;* his antipathy against Carheil, 350; his plans for the occupation of Detroit, 351; his memorial to Comte de Maurepas, 352; some of the features of his plan, 352; opposition to his scheme, 352; his plan opposed by Callières, Champigny, and others, 353; sails for France, 354; presents his plan to M. de Ponchartrain, 354; returns to Canada, 355; proceeds to found the city of Detroit, 355; lures the Michillimackinac Indians to Detroit, 356; letters to Ponchartrain, 357; desires to be appointed governor of Detroit, 357; given the control of the fur-trade, 358; governor of colony of Louisiana, 521; succeeds Bienville at Louisiana, 541; denounces the country, products, etc., 541; his spite towards Bienville, 543; supplanted by L'Epinay, 547; quoted, 557 *note;* cited, 569 *note.*

La Motte, Captain, 1404.

La Motte, Dubois de, French admiral, 1164; commands the French fleet for America, 968–69; effort of Boscawen to intercept his fleet, 970; the English fleet wrecked, 1165.

La Motte-Cadillac (see *Cadillac*).

"La Mutine," frigate, 914.

Lanaudière in Ramesay's expedition, 698.

Lancaster, town of, joins in Lovewell's expedition, 508; infested by Indians, 402.

Langlade, Charles, a French trader, 902, 1347, 1451 *note,* 1487; to receive a pension, 903; the Ojibwas led to attack the Miamis, 988; his Indian wife, 1176; matters in relation to Braddock's defeat, 1487–88.

Languedoc, 1154; battalion of, 968, 971, 1050, 1103, 1168; stationed at Ticonderoga, 1101, 1268; the advance upon Fort William Henry, 1179; the fall of Quebec, 1396.

Langy, rangers captured by, 1256; reports the approach of the English, 1256, 1257; meeting with the English in the woods, 1261–63; detachment of, 1272.

La Noue, Lieutenant, engaged in the exploration for the Pacific Ocean, 581.

La Paille Coupée, village of, 875.

"La Palme," the suffering and starvation of her crew, 686.

La Pause, M. de, 1452.

La Perade, Chevalier de, 989.

La Perelle, sent with flag of truce from Duchambon to Pepperrell, 663.

La Plaine, reports an attack on Quebec, 431.

La Plante, 1176.

La Plaque, a Christian Indian, 186–87.

La Prairie, 1155; attacked by John Schuyler, 188; by Peter Schuyler, 211; his retreat, 212–14.

La Présentation, 893, 949, 1098, 1175, 1449; description of, 889–91; effort of Piquet to gain converts, 893, 895–96; Jesuit influence, 1295.

La Reine, battalion, of, 968, 971, 1050, 1168, 1268; to defend Ticonderoga, 1100–01; the advance upon Fort William Henry, 1179.

La Reine, Fort, built by La Vérendrye, 587.

La Ronde Denys. (See *Denys, La Ronde.*)

La Salle, Nicolas de, mentioned, 355, 561; his relations with Frontenac, 30–31, 48; at Fort St. Louis, 63; which is seized by La Barre, 70; gave Louisiana her name, 534; accuses Iberville, 539; accuses Artaguette, 540; his settlement at St. Louis mentioned, 553; proposed expedition, 570.

La Sarre, battalion of, 1092, 1122, 1168; encamped at Fort Frontenac, 1100; advances upon Fort William Henry, 1179; serves under Montcalm, 1268; the fall of Quebec, 1396.

Lascelles' regiment, 1357 *note.*

La Suède, 1431.

"La Superbe," ship, 1155.

La Touche, clerk in Department of Marine, etc., 354.

La Tour, mentioned, 617.

Lauder, Sir Thomas Dick, 1494.

"Launceston," a war-ship of Commodore Warren, 632, 638.

Laurain, an explorer on the Missouri, 570.

Laurel Hill, 943, 944, 947, 950, 1293.

Lauverjat, Father, a missionary, 497; a missionary of the Penobscots, 498.

Laval, bishop of Canada, 27, 38, 42, 205.

La Vente, *curé* of Mobile, accuses Bienville, 539.

La Vérendrye, Chevalier and Pierre de (sons of Pierre Gaultier), join in the search for the Pacific, 590–91; journey towards the West, 592–93; arrive at the camp of Les Beaux Hommes, 594; reach the camp of the Horse Indians, 595; join in a march of Indians against the Snake Indians, 595–96; visit the lodge of the Choke-Cherry Indians, 600; return to Fort La Reine, 600; discovered the Saskatchawan River, 601; their fur-trade, 601; badly treated by M. de Saint-Pierre, 602; receive bad treatment from La Jonquière, 602.

La Vérendrye, Chevalier de, death of, 605.

La Vérendrye, Pierre Gaultier de Varennes de, his search for the Pacific, 584; given a monopoly of the fur-trade, 585; raises a company of associates, 585; winters at Fort Pierre, 586; massacre of some of his party, 586; develops the fur-trade, builds forts, etc., 587; continued his explorations westward, 588; certain Indian tribes join his party, 588; arrived at a village of the Mandan Indians, 588; returns to Fort La Reine, 590; his sons join in the search for the Pacific, 590–91; promotion and honor bestowed upon him, 601; death of, 601.

Law, John, his undertaking to save the credit of France, 545; failure of his scheme, 547.

Lawrence, Brigadier, Governor of Nova Scotia, 1009, 1228, 1329 *note;* succeeds Hopson in office, 922; his treatment of the Acadians, 922; the occupation of Beaubassin, 924–27; the attack on Beauséjour, 975, 1009–13; his characteristics, 1021; quoted concerning the Acadians, 1021, 1025, 1029–30; exacts the oath of allegiance from the Acadians, 1023; a memorial sent to, from the Acadians, 1023–1025; matters pertaining to the expulsion of the Acadians, 1025–28, 1032–33, 1038; serves in the expedition against Louisbourg, 1228, 1234.

Lawrence, Fort, erected, 925, 1009,

1010, 1012; demands of Le Loutre, 927–28; encampment of the English, 1015.

Lawson, an illicit trader, 408.

Le Bâtard, Étienne, the murder of Captain Howe, 926.

Le Ber, Mademoiselle, a patriotic nun at Montreal, 455.

Le Blanc, a notary to the Acadians, 691.

Le Boëuf, Fort, 933, 991, 1305, 1365; erection of, 932; garrison at, 934; arrival of Washington, 936, 1049; burned, 1367.

Le Borgne, 1215, 1487.

Le Brun, 853.

Le Calvaire, 1427.

Le Canada Français, cited, 708 *note.*

Lechmere, Lieutenant, killed by the French in their attack on Grand Pré, 704.

Lee, Colonel, quoted, 456 *note.*

Legge, chancellor of the exchequer, 1464.

Le Guerne, a priest, his description of the embarkation of the Acadians, 1037–38.

Leisler, Jacob, at Fort William, 157, 211; mentioned, 342.

Le Loutre, Joseph Louis, missionary to the Micmac Indians, 690; vicar-general of Acadia, 695, 916, 922; accused of instigating the murder of Captain Howe, 695; instigates the Indians to murder the English, 913, 915–17, 1006; injures the Acadians by his machinations, 913–14, 922–23, 928, 1008, 1012; letter of, concerning Halifax, 914; pension received by, 917; his dealings discovered by Cornwallis, 918; encourages the Acadians to leave their farms, 919–20, 927, 1012–13, 1016, 1023; his double-dealing and cruelty, 922–23, 1011–12, 1018 *note,* 1483; arrival of, at Beaubassin, 924; treacherous murder of Captain Howe, 926; his letter in answer to Lawrence's proclamation, 927–28; letters from officials, urging dishonest conduct, 1009, 1011; relations with Vergor, 1012–13; siege and capitulation of Beauséjour, 1013–19;

imprisoned by the English, 1018; departs for France, 1018.

Le Marchant, Sir Denis, 1398 *note.*

Le Mercier, Chevalier, 951, 1158, 1210, 1257; plans of, to attack the English, 949–50; serves as messenger between the French and English, 1149; his fraudulent contracts, 1220, 1459.

Le Moyne, mission to the Onondagas, 68, 82, 210.

Lenisse, Madame de, 1156.

"Léopard," the, ship, 1092.

Le Page du Pratz, cited, 550 *note.*

Lepaon, 853.

L'Epinay, supplanted La Mothe-Cadillac at Louisiana, 547; his removal, 547.

"Le Prudent," 1232 *note.*

Le Rocher, station on the Illinois, 561.

Léry, a French officer, 1100; assists in attack on Grand Pré, 702; his plan of Detroit, 897 *note.*

Les Beaux Hommes, Indians of the Little Missouri, 594.

Les Mines, 919.

Leslie, Lieutenant, 995 *note.*

Lestock, Admiral, in command of British troops, 678.

Le Sueur, expedition to the Sioux country of Minnesota, 566; given command and monopoly of trade, 567; his commission revoked, 567; makes a voyage up the Mississippi, 567; encounters war-parties, 568; builds a fort on the river St. Peter, 568; opens trade with the Sioux Indians, 568–69; sailed for France, 569; death of, 570.

Lettres Edifiantes, cited, 491 *note.*

Leuthen, 1223.

Leverett, John, sent to counsel with Colonel March at Port Royal, 423.

Le Verrier, in command at Michillimackinac, 1217.

Levi, Point, 1344–46, 1348, 1349, 1351, 1354, 1384, 1387, 1389; position of Wolfe's army, 1348, 1354, 1355–57; held by the English at, 1377, 1382; embarkation of the artillery, 1385, 1389.

Lévis, Chevalier de, 946, 1090, 1173, 1443; opinion of, in regard to the killing of Jumonville, 946–47; beloved by Montcalm, 1092, 1102, 1154, 1408; embarks for America, 1092; joins Montcalm, 1099; at Montreal, 1101; his command at Ticonderoga, 1102–03, 1121; his description of Montcalm, 1102–03; his manner of life at Montreal, 1154–55, 1216, 1488–89; treatment received from Vaudreuil, 1159, 1203, 1410, 1453; his characteristics and popularity, 1161, 1168, 1410–11, 1444; encampment of, 1168; matters pertaining to the attack at Fort William Henry, 1175, 1179–94, 1194 *note;* his account of the slaughter at German Flats, 1201 *note;* quiets the mutiny at Montreal, 1203; statements concerning the fight at Rogers Rock, 1207 *note;* the victory at Ticonderoga, 1256–57, 1267–74, 1492–96; his promotion, 1315; the siege and fall of Quebec, 1346–57, 1375–1419; attacked by Wolfe, 1355–57; sent to protect Montreal, 1369, 1370, 1379; assumes the command after Montcalm's death, 1408, 1410–11, 1414, 1426; letter to Bourlamaque, 1412; his scaling-ladders, 1428, 1440, 1441; his expedition to attack Quebec, 1430–42; the encounter at Ste.-Foy, 1431–34, 1502–03; the courtesies of war, 1439; the fall of Canada, 1443–57; the terms of capitulation for Montreal, 1451–52; tries to preserve the honor of France, 1452–53; escapes from shipwreck, 1458; his letters, 1498.

Lévis, Fort, 1449, 1452; attacked by Amherst, 1449.

Lewis and Clark, Captains, visit to the Mandans, 589 *note;* discover the Rocky Mountains, 600; explore their way to the Pacific, 600.

Lewis, C. W., cited, 515 *note.*

Lewis, Major, 1291; the expedition of Major Grant, 1299–1302.

L'Huillier, Fort, built by Le Sueur, 568.

"Licorne," the, ship, 1092.

Liegnitz, successes of Frederic, 1461.

Lighthouse Point, 1231, 1238.

Lighthouse Point, Louisbourg, a battery planted at, 657; Beaubassin ordered to recapture it from the English, 658; Gridley's effective firing at, 662.

Ligneris, Captain, 1365, 1366; at Fort Duquesne, 988; encounter with the English under Braddock, 993; orders concerning prisoners, 1072 *note;* attack expected from Forbes, 1293; danger of starvation at the fort, 1302; Fort Duquesne abandoned, 1304; at Venango, 1306; letter of Montcalm concerning, 1311; departs from Presqu'isle, 1366; taken prisoner, 1367; matters pertaining to a pension for, 1485; receives the cross of the Order of St. Louis, 1488.

Lignery, Sieur de, called a council of Outagamies, 558; led an expedition against the Outagamies, 560; he does not succeed in it, 560.

Ligonier, General, 965.

Ligonier Bay, 1370.

Limoges, Jesuit missionary at the Illinois, 567.

"Lis," the, fate of, 970.

L'Isle-Dieu, Abbé de, 917, 918 *note;* assertion concerning Jumonville, 947 *note.*

Lismahago, 952.

Little Butte des Morts, 563.

Little Harbor, the house of Benning Wentworth at, 625.

Little Meadows, arrival of Braddock's army at, 986.

Little Missouri River, 593.

Little Niagara, Fort, 1364–65.

Littlefield, Edmond, his house at Wells, Me., 364.

Littlefield, Francis, inventory of his personal property, 364.

Livingston, ——, New York, 342.

Livingston, Captain, of Albany, an envoy to ransom the Deerfield captives, 393.

Livingston, Philip, concerning a fort at Niagara, 611.

Livingston, Robert, 351 *note,* 426.

Livingston, William, 1129; manor of, 867.

Logstown, 876, 877, 881, 886 *note,* 935.

"London Chronicle," the article upon provincial soldiery, 1278.

Long Saut, the, 1450.

Longueuil, ——, an agent among the Five Nations, 344.

Longueuil, Baron de, Governor of Canada, 901, 915, 1176, 1256, 1374 *note;* desired peace with the Indians, 558; complaints of English traders, 901, 902; correspondence with Girard, 918; paper drawn up by, 949–50; seeks to secure Indian allies, 1167.

Loppinot, sent from Louisbourg for terms of capitulation, 1244–47.

Loramie Creek, the, 879.

Lords of Trade, the, instructions to the colonial Assemblies, 962; leadership of Lord Halifax, 966; quoted concerning the Acadians and their want of loyalty, 1021–22; complaints of Johnson, 1069.

Lorette, 480, 988, 1098, 1175, 1391, 1397, 1408, 1431, 1441; mission of, 1295 *note;* English outpost at, 1426; skirmish at, 1427–28.

Lorimier, 1176.

Loring, Captain, the navy built by order of Amherst, 1363, 1369–70.

Lotbinière, ——, a French officer who assisted in the attack on Grand Pré, 704.

Lotbinière, a Canadian engineer, 1099, 1257; his work at Ticonderoga, 1102.

Lothrop, Lieut.-Colonel, mentioned, 671 *note.*

Loudon, Earl, to be the commander-in-chief of the American troops, 1105; difficulties in providing for the soldiers, 1108, 1143; arrives at Albany, 1116; royal orders concerning military rank, 1116; the provincial forces examined, 1117; orders Winslow to abandon Ticonderoga expedition, 1120; sends reinforcements to Oswego, 1120; his charges against Shirley, 1125 *note,* 1130; English losses, 1130; his campaign, 1131; his orders to Winslow, 1142; exaggeration of Vaudreuil, 1158; his plans for reducing Louisbourg, 1162–64, 1165 *note,* 1286;

soldiers drawn from New York, 1166; frontier exposed to attack, 1183; letters sent from Webb, 1183 *note,* 1186; despatches sent to Webb, 1197; his plan of action, 1197; plans an attack upon Ticonderoga, 1204; his failures, 1226; recalled from his command, 1228, 1253; money expended by Massachusetts on this expedition, 1255; consulted by Bradstreet, 1284; his influence on the army, 1456; letters concerning the massacre at Fort William Henry, 1489–90.

Louis XIII., 855; infancy of, 326.

Louis XIV., 1040 *note,* 1476; admonishes Frontenac, 45–46, 49–50, 51–52; recalls La Barre, 89–90; supports Denonville, 93, 104; his reign, 138; designs respecting the English colonies, 141–42; announces the treaty of Ryswick, 303–04; caused the War of the Spanish Succession, 339; places his grandson on the throne of Spain, 339; mentioned, 357; his throne threatened, 416; concerning republics, 442; his concessions in the Treaty of Utrecht, 458, 460; his old age, 458; commands the evacuation of Placentia, etc., 461; the foundations of Louisiana laid in his name, 536; refuses to allow some Huguenots to settle in Louisiana, 537; contests with Spain the Louisiana country, 538; his instructions to D'Iberville at Louisiana, 538; orders the destruction of the Outagamies, 558.

Louis XV., 695, 874, 890, 893, 896, 932, 1091; demanded restitution of Louisbourg by Peace of Aix-la-Chapelle, 745; possibility of the conquest of Canada, 843–44; condition of France during his reign, 852–56; scenes at Versailles, 853; adornments given to Paris, 854; feeling towards, 855; position of Madame de Pompadour, 855, 966; subjects of, in Acadia, 907, 910–11, 915, 917, 1006, 1008, 1023, 1040; the English denounced by, 923; political alliances with, 1086; his detestation of Frederic the Great,

1087; the promotion of Montcalm, 1090; troops sent against Austria, 1092; troops sent to reinforce New France, 1092; instructions sent to Vaudreuil, 1095; expenses in Canada, 1097, 1098, 1208–21, 1311–13, 1416–17; sends the *cordon rouge* to Montcalm, 1153; his portrait on Indian medals, 1172; promises of the Indians, 1177; corruption at court, 1226; Vaudreuil's efforts to slander Montcalm, 1308–10, 1416–17; the refusal of forces from France to Canada, 1315–17; the loss of New France, 1453.

Louisbourg, Cape Breton, 864, 917, 918, 920, 970, 1009, 1011, 1044, 1045; founded, 460–61; called the Dunquerque of America, 461; received news of the breaking out of the War of Austrian Succession, 616; an attack upon proposed by the English, 619 and *note;* called the American Dunkirk, 619; its powerful defences, 619; Governor Shirley furthers the design of taking, 620–23; the appointment of William Pepperrell to command a siege of, 624–25; a plan for sounding the fort at, 628; gathering the troops, 630; the naval force gathered intended for the siege of, 631; the directions of Governor Shirley for the attack upon, 633, 634 and *note;* the naval force arrive at Canseau, 637; a delay in the attack upon, 637; arrival of Commander Warren with his fleet, 638; her situation and defences, 638–39; the naval force arrive at, 638; the garrison at, 639; alarmed at the arrival of the naval fleet, 640; the Grand Battery attacked, 641; the French abandon the Grand Battery at, 643; English occupation of the battery, 644; Pepperrell's army encamped at, 644; their difficulties in landing cannon, 644; the planting of the batteries at, 645–46; Titcomb's battery the most destructive at, 647; a battery attacked by the French, 648; the destruction accomplished by the advanced battery under Captain Sherburn, 648–

49; good conduct of the troops, 650; the attack upon the Island Battery, 654–55; it proves unsuccessful, 656–57; the English loss in the attack, 657; capture of the ship-of-war "Vigilant," 658; skirmishes by Duchambon, etc., 658–59; the effective firing of the English at Lighthouse Point, 662; the surrender, 663–64; the French and English loss at, 664; the terms of capitulation consented to by Pepperrell and Warren, 664; the disgust of the New England soldiers at the capitulation, 666; the jealousies between the sea and land force concerning the taking of, 667–68; news of its surrender, 669–70; papers relating to the siege of, 671 *note;* after the conquest, dissatisfaction and mutiny of the troups, 672–73; arrival of Governor Shirley, 673; arrival of supply troops from Gibralter, 675; "Siege of Louisbourg as described by French witnesses," 761; fortress of, 907, 909, 1096, 1231–33; restored to the French, 907; commanders at, 914, 915, 916; aid refused to Beauséjour, 1017; plan of Loudon for the reduction of, 1162–63, 1164, 1166; the English fleet wrecked, 1165; policy of Pitt regarding, 1228; the siege and reduction of, by the English, 1228, 1229, 1231–52, 1273, 1285, 1307, 1317, 1327; inhabitants of the town, 1232; the batteries silenced by the enemy, 1238; Drucour's efforts to protect the harbor, 1239; the shipping burned, 1241–42, 1243; the Governor's lodgings in flames, 1242; position of the besieged, 1243–44; the terms of capitulation finally accepted, 1244–47; 1248 *note;* statistics of prisoners, cannon, etc., 1247–48; Governor Drucour succeeded by Governor Whitmore, 1248; rejoicing at the fall of, 1248–49; Wolfe ordered to scatter the neighboring settlers, 1251; arrival of 43d Regiment, 1321; departure of the fleet with Gen. Wolfe, 1329; dismantled and abandoned, 1445.

Louisbourg Grenadiers, the, at Quebec, 1401 *note.*

Louisiana, 894, 1094, 1197, 1302; named by La Salle, 534; the seizure of, urged by Henri de Tonty, 534; the probable result of an English settlement at, 534; the English prevented from settling at, 534; Iberville's colonists at, 539; wives, priests, nuns, etc., sent to the colony of, 539; discord and disorder, 539; official disputes, 540; an attempt to import slaves from the West Indies, 540–41; discontent of the colonists, 541; farmed out to Antoine Crozat, 542; disaffection of the colonists, 543; wives sent to the colonists, 544 and *note;* abandoned to the Crown by Crozat, 545; leased to the Mississippi Company, 545; its condition under the Mississippi Company, 545–46; concerning the wives sent to, 546; Bienville re-appointed governor of, 547; at war with the Natchez Indians, 548; a royal edict concerning live-stock in, 548; the cost of its settlement, 548; Sieur Perier succeeds Bienville as governor, 548; transferred from the Mississippi Company to the Crown, 549; fights the Chickasaws under Bienville as governor, 550; shows signs of growth, 550; compared with the Canadian colony, 551; desired trade communication with New Mexico, 578; ceded to the United States, 600; French possessions in, 859, 861, 872; communication with Canada, 870, 872, 900–01; arrival of the exiles from Acadia, 1039; proposal of Montcalm concerning, 1318; given to Spain, 1473.

Louisville, 885.

Louvigny, 1156.

Louvigny, expedition against the Outagamies, 555, 558; makes a treaty with them, 557–558.

Lovelace, Lord, 427 *note;* death of, 427.

Lovewell, John, of Dunstable, Massachusetts, 506; his father served in King Philip's War, 506–07; his expedition against the Indians, 507; the triumph of his first attack, 508; his second expedition, 509; his fight at Lovewell's Pond, 509; death of, 510, 513.

Lovewell, Mrs. John (Hannah), 507.

Lovewell's fight, 509–12; return of the survivors, 512–13; aid sent to the wounded, the dead buried, etc., 513; verses in commemoration of, 515 *note*.

Lovewell's Pond, 506.

Lowendal, 852.

"Lowestoffe," an English war-ship, 437, 1439, 1440.

Lowry, 899.

Lowther, Miss Katherine, 1327; Wolfe's last message to, 1391.

Loyal, Fort, at Casco Bay, 168–69; surrenders to Portneuf, 170.

Loyalhannon, 1298, 1299, 1301–02.

Loyalhannon Creek, 1293.

Loyola, mentioned, 478.

Lund, Thomas, killed by Indians, 507 *note*.

Lusignan, commandant at Ticonderoga, 1147.

Lusignan, *fils* and *père*, cited, 708 *note*.

Lusignan, in Ramesay's expedition, 698; assists in attack on Grand Pré, 702; wounded, 703.

Lutherans, the, 866, 867.

Lutterberg, battle of, 1228.

Lycurgus, 1259.

Lydius, a trader, 1139.

Lydius, Fort, 429.

Lyman, Caleb, kills some Indians at Coos Meadows, 369.

Lyman, Fort, 1047–49, 1051, 1056–57; building of, 1046; afterwards called Fort Edward, 1046–47, 1061.

Lyman, Phineas, in the expedition against Crown Point, 1044, 1059; origin of Fort Lyman, 1046; takes command of Johnson's troops, 1054; conflicting reports concerning, 1061; at Fort Edward, 1117, 1118; his chaplain, 1118; report concerning the camp, 1118; regiment of, 1262; meeting with Langy in the woods, 1263.

Lynn, 420.

Lyon's Cove, 1028.

Macartney, Captain, his humanity, 1431, 1432.

McBryer, Andrew, 903.

Macdonald, Captain, serves in the expedition of Major Grant, 1300; his death, 1300.

McDonald, Captain, a messenger to Duchambon from Commodore Warren, 659.

MacDonald, Captain Donald, sent to attack the French at Le Calvaire, 1427; his death, 1436.

McDonough, Thomas, 1500.

McGinnis, Captain, 1056.

McGregory, expedition to Lake Huron, 99, 112.

Machault d'Arnouville, minister of marine and colonies (1754–1757), 854, 855, 966, 1095, 1226.

Machault, Fort, 1305.

Mackay, Captain, 948; at Great Meadows, 948, 952, 1484–85.

Mackellar, Patrick, serves as engineer under Braddock and Wolfe, 996 *note*, 1340; to strengthen Fort Ontario, 1130 *note*.

McKenney, killed by Indians at Keene, 719.

Mackenzie, Captain, 1300–02.

Macleane, Allan, 1365 *note*.

McMullen, Lieutenant, sent to Crown Point, 1372.

Macnamara, Admiral, accompanies La Motte's expedition, 968.

Macquas (Mohawks), name given to Caughnawagas, 386 *note*.

MacVicar, Anne, recollections of Albany, 1063–64.

Madawaska, 1039.

Madeleine de Verchères, her heroism, 220–24.

Madocawando, Penobscot chief, 250, 260, 262.

Magazine of American History, cited, 434 *note*, 737 *note*.

Mahon, Lord, 966.

Maillard, a missionary at Shubenacadie, furnishes aid to Ramesay's troops, 698; missionary at Cape Breton, 917, 926.

Maillebois, 852, 1090.

Maine, the forest of, 359; the various tribes of Indians dwelling in, 360; a continuation of warfare in her borders, 483; English possessions in, 859.

Maine Historical Society, 481, *note.*

Maisonfort, Marquis de la, commander of the French ship-of-war "Vigilant," 658; informs Duchambon of cruel treatment to English captives, 659; held a prisoner by Warren, 659.

Maître, Abraham, 1394.

Makisabie, chief of the Pottawattamies, at Huron fort, 523; harangued the Outagamies in the midst of the fight, 526.

Malecite Indians, encamped with De Ramesay near Acadia, 688.

Mallet brothers explore their way from Louisiana to Mexico, 578.

Manach, Father, 1018; letter of Boishébert to, quoted, 1027.

Mandans, Indians, visit of La Vérendrye to the, 588; their descriptions of the Spaniards, 588–89, 590; their population, 589; visit of Prince Maximillian to, 589; (*Blancs Barbus*), 591 *note;* description of the village, 591–92.

Manila, 1470.

Manitoba, 584.

Manitou, the, 1169, 1176, 1177.

Mann, Fort, on Arkansas River, 572.

Mann, Sir Horace, letters from Horace Walpole quoted, 973; ambassador at Florence, 1418.

Mansfield, 849.

Mante, Major Thomas, 1252 *note,* 1263; statistics of the force sent against Louisbourg, 1234 *note.*

Maps of the Illinois colony, 873 *note;* map of Bonnecamp, 887 *note;* of French and British dominion in North America, 930–31 *note.*

March, Colonel John, attacked by Indians at Casco, Me., 366; captures Indians at Casco, 369, 373 *note;* commander of the expedition to Port Royal, 420; his unfitness for commander, 420, 421; the skirmish at Port Royal, 421; his miserable failure at Port Royal, 422; the disorder among his soldiers, 422; counsellors sent to him, 423; returns to Boston, 424.

Marest, ——, Jesuit missionary at Michillimackinac, 349; discontent at the conduct of the Michillimackinacs, 356; missionary to the Kaskaskias, 553; warns Le Sueur of war-parties, 568.

Mareuil, ——, Jesuit priest at Onondaga, 428.

Mareuil interdicted for play-acting, 235–37.

Margry, Pierre, cited, 350 *note,* 355 *note,* 605 *note.*

Marguerite, baptismal name of Abigail Stebbins, 395.

Marguerite, baptismal name of Martha French, 395.

Maria Theresa, her inheritance from Charles VI., 858; her heritage taken from her, 858, 1086; flatters Pompadour, 1086; the enemy of Frederic the Great, 1086; the war in Europe, 1222–23, 1475; condition of France, 1464.

Maricourt, ——, an agent among the Five Nations, 344.

"Marie-Joseph," vessel, 465.

Marietta, 878.

Marigalante Island, restored by England, 1472.

Marin, 1176, 1210, 1216, 1280, 1365; promotion of, 904; commander of Duquesne's expedition to the Ohio, 932–34, 938; his sickness and death, 932–34.

Marin, ——, a French trader, attacks the Outagamies, 563; makes an attack upon Annapolis, 660; ordered by Duchambon to assist in the resistance of Louisbourg to the New England soldiers, 660; in Ramesay's expedition, 698; assists in the attack on Grand Pré, 704.

"Marin," frigate, 535.

Marin, Madame, 1210.

Marin joins the war-party of Perière, 1136–37; the slaughter at Fort Edward, 1175; official knavery, 1214; victory over, 1280–83; taken prisoner, 1367–68.

Marlborough, Duke of, 416, 444, 445, 1061.

Marlborough, Mass., annoyed by Indians, 402.

Marlborough, Sara, Duchess of, 445.

Marolles, correspondence of, 1251 *note.*

Marquette, Jesuit missionary at St. Louis, 348, 553.

Marshall, N., of York, Me., 628 *note.*

Martel, the King's storekeeper, 1210, 1216.

Martin, Abraham. See *Abraham.*

Martin, Father, evidence in relation to the massacre at Fort William Henry, 1194 *note.*

Martin, Judge M. L., 563 *note.*

Martin, Sergeant Joshua, one of Rogers' rangers, 1146.

Martinique, 1470, 1472.

Martissan, an *habitant* of Louisbourg, 646.

Maryland, 342, 1072, 1287; contributes men, to capture Canada, 677; government and characteristics of, 862, 867; aid asked from by Dinwiddie, 939; aids Virginia, 959; commissioners sent to Albany for an Indian congress, 962–64; council of governors held with Braddock, 975–77; sufferings caused by Indian warfare, 1071–72, 1131.

Mascarene, Paul, *Narrative,* cited, 463 *note;* quoted, 467 *note;* in charge of the fort at Annapolis, 617; a threatened attack on the fort, 618; refuses Duvivier's terms of capitulation, 618; receives a reinforcement from Boston, 618; commandant, quoted concerning Acadia, 690; expels an Acadian priest, 694 *note;* reports the French and English losses at Grand Pré, 707.

Mascoutins, join with the Outagamies in a settlement at Detroit, 522.

Masham, Mrs., 445, 456.

Massachusetts, 342, 959, 1023, 1060, 1261; condition of the colony, 179, 208; desires aid from England for an attack upon Port Royal, 433; preparations in, for the attack upon Port Royal, 435; prediction concerning the possible independence of, 443; her financial exhaustion from war contingencies, 457 *note;* determined to destroy the village of the Penobscots, 498; sends a force to destroy Norridgewock, 498–500; her contribution towards the siege of Louisbourg, 631; the cost to her of the taking of Louisbourg, 670; reimbursed by England, 670; sends troops to protect Acadia, 696; builds Fort Dummer on the Connecticut River, 720; disputes with New Hampshire concerning Fort Dummer, 720; religion, finance, and politics of, 862–64, 1255 (see *Assembly of Massachusetts*); commissioners sent to meet the Indians at Albany, 887; council of governors held with Braddock, 975–77; characteristics of the officers from, 1032; distribution of the exiled Acadians, 1038; the Crown Point expedition fitted out, 1041–42, 1045, 1059–60; money received from Parliament, 1104 *note,* 1255; method of raising and paying troops, 1106–08, 1253, 1255; tablet erected to Lord Howe, in Westminster Abbey, 1259–60; utterances from the pulpits after the fall of Canada, 1454–56.

"Massachusetts," a gun-ship commanded by Captain Tyng, 631.

Massachusetts, Fort, built near the present town of Adams, Mass., 728; description of, 735; attack made upon, by Rigaud's war-party, 737; a "parley" desired, 739; capitulation, 740; the French flag raised, 740; rebuilt, 744.

Massachusetts Archives, cited, 424 *note,* 488 *note.*

Massachusetts Historical Society, the, 1061 *note;* portrait of Captain Winslow in, 1032 *note.*

Mass. Hist. Coll., cited, 424 *note,* 671 *note.*

Mass. Hist. Coll., 2d Series, cited, 402 *note.*

Mass. Hist. Coll., 5th Series, cited, 407 *note.*

Massey, Colonel, 1367.

Matchedash Bay, 348.

Mather, Cotton, mentioned, 178, 181 *note,* 369; his dislike for Governor Dudley, 406–07.

Mather, Increase, 178, 406.

Mathevet, missionary for the Nipissings, 1176.

Matinicus, the rendezvous of Colonel Church's troops, 418.

Maumee River, the, 873, 880, 901, 902; a fort built at, by the French, 614.

Maurault, Abbé, missionary at St. Francis, 1372 *note;* quoted concerning the Gill family, 397.

Maurepas, Comte de, memorial of La Mothe-Cadillac to, 352 and *note;* cited, 708 *note,* 732 *note,* 1022 *note.*

Maurepas, Fort, built by La Vérendrye, 587.

Maurepas, Lake, Le Moyne d'Iberville at, 536.

Maurin, François, 1210; official knavery, 1211–13, 1216; thrown into the Bastille, 1459.

Mauritius, Island of, 852.

Maxen, 1461.

Maximillian, Prince, visit to the Mandan Indians, 589, 591 *note.*

Maxwell, Thomas, 1374 *note.*

Mayhew, Jonathan, his prediction for the American colonies, 1419.

Maynard, Captain, 1281 *note.*

Mazade, Madame, 1091.

Mediterranean Sea, the, 1229.

Meech, Lieutenant, his encounter with the enemy, 1340.

Meeting-house Hill, a palisaded enclosure at Deerfield, 374.

Mellen, Reverend John, pastor of the Second Church in Lancaster, 1454; his sermon on the fall of Canada, 1455.

Memeramcook, 927, 928.

Memorial of Deplorable State of New England, etc., cited, 407 *note.*

Memphremagog, Lake, 1372, 1373.

Ménard, Jean Louis, a Canadian, 395.

Ménard, Mrs. Jean Louis (Martha French), 395.

Meneval, governor of Port Royal, 174; a prisoner at Boston, 176.

Menomonies, Indians, of Michigan, 519, 1121; aid Dubuisson at Detroit, 524; called to council by Montcalm, 1175–78.

Mercer, Colonel, commandant at Oswego, 1114, 1123; his death, 1125.

Mercer, Lieutenant-Colonel, to hold the new Fort Duquesne, 1305.

Mercier, ——, assists in attack on Grand Pré, 702.

Meriel, Father, a priest of St. Sulpice, 391, 396 *note.*

"Mermaid," a war-ship of Commodore Warren, 632, 658, 1014.

Merrimac River, 360, 508.

Merry-meeting Bay, attack of Indians at, 494.

Meserve, ——, lieutenant-colonel of New Hampshire regiment at siege of Louisbourg, 645.

Messalina, 1086.

Meules, intendant of Canada, 61; letter to La Barre, 79; representations to the king, 89; recalled, 104.

Mexico, 534, 858.

Mexico, Gulf of, 872, 986.

Miami confederacy, the, 873, 880.

Miami Indians, the, 879, 899, 901, 988; their chief (see *La Demoiselle*), home of, 873, 879–80, 883, 902; visited by Céloron, 880; visited by Gist, 883–84; their feeling towards the English, 885, 933; attacked and killed at Pickawillany, 903; become allies of the French, 933, 1293; called to a council by Montcalm, 1176–78.

Miami River, the, 873, 879, 883, 902.

Michigan, Lake, 896, 1121, 1141, 1175; groups of Indians at, 519, 562.

Michigan, the country claimed by the English, 95.

Michillimackinac, 896, 902, 1176, 1368; trouble there, 64; French stores threatened, 68, 69, 71; expedition of Perrot, 87; threatened Indian hostilities, 94; Indian muster, 111; English traders seized, 112; craft of the Rat,

132; burning of an Iroquois prisoner, 152–53; in command of Cadillac, 239; a Jesuit mission station settled by Huron and Ottawa Indians, 348; the Indian defences at, 348; the French colony at, 348; mentioned, 560, 582.

Micmacs, the Indians, 861, 918, 1320, 1329; to emigrate to Isle Royale, 461; attack Canso, etc., 497; join in an attack upon Louisbourg, 617; encamped with De Ramesay near Acadia, 688; under control of their missionary, Le Loutre, 690; disposition and characteristics of, 922; their missionary, 922, 928 (see *Le Loutre*); at Beaubassin, 924; murder of Captain Howe, 926; chief of, killed, 1018; called to a council by Montcalm, 1175–78; under Boishébert, 1241.

Middle Ages, the, 856.

Milbank, Mr., 1441.

Mildmay, questions of boundary, 928.

Militia, recruited for the expedition against Louisbourg, 630–31, 631 *note*.

Miller, Captain, 1135, 1424.

Mines, basin of, 701, 909, 1008, 1010, 1023, 1028–29, 1034.

Mines, district of Acadia, 696, 1007; the French in possession, 710; population of, 1026; the people summoned to hear the mandate of the King, 1030–31. See *Acadians*.

Mingoes, the, 872, 876, 886, 988; attitude towards the English, 885, 1299; border warfare of, 1070.

Minneconjou Indians, a tribe of the Sioux, 600 *note*.

Minnesota, Le Sueur's expedition into, 566.

Minnetarees, a tribe of the Missouri Indians, 592 *note*.

Minorca, 870, 1223; garrisons of, 849; restored by France, 1473.

Minot, John, cited, 490 *note*.

Miquelon Island given to France, 1472.

Miramichi, 1213, 1251; a missionary station, 698.

Mirepoix, French ambassador at London, 967; correspondence of, 969.

Missaguash River, the, 924, 925, 927, 1006, 1011, 1015, 1320.

Mission Indians, the illegal traffic carried on by the French, by means of, 889; allies of the French, 1098, 1167, 1169, 1204; their ferocity, 1295.

Missionaries, French, among the Indians, 28–29, 58; to be protected (Denonville), 96, 123 *note;* (Dongan), 98, 100, 121; instigate Indians to torture and kill their prisoners, 152; incite to murderous attacks, 269; their work among the Indians, 862, 889, 896, 1012–13, 1477; intrigues with regard to the Indians, Acadians, and English, 913–15, 1012–13, 1482–83.

Missisqui, 1175.

Missisquoi Bay, 1371.

Mississagas, 892, 1175; called to aid Dubuisson at Detroit, 523.

Mississippi, the, 536, 859, 861, 873, 874, 930, 933, 960, 1074, 1098, 1317, 1472, 1473; French settlements made upon, 534.

Mississippi and Great Lakes, considered in the Treaty of Utrecht, 459.

Mississippi Company, given the monopoly of Louisiana, 545; its powers and privileges, 545; its despotic government over Louisiana, 545–46; its efforts to people Louisiana, 547–48; its stockholders, 547; failure of the, 547; resigns the charge of Louisiana, 549.

Missouri River, 568.

Missouries, Indians, aid Dubuisson at Detroit, 524; in council with Bourgmont, 576.

Mitchell, his map of the British and French Dominions, 931 *note*.

Mobile Bay, a fort established at, 538.

Mogg, Indian chief, killed, 500.

Mohawks, the, 864, 889, 895, 905, 1042, 1048, 1065, 1069, 1162, 1198, 1480; fear the French, 62; their settlements, 75; at Schenectady, 157–58; visit Albany, 161; mission village at Saut St. Louis, 225; expedition against the tribe, 225–28; settle at Caughnawaga, 345; chiefs, taken to England by Peter Schuyler, 434; their reception, 434;

complaints of the tribe, 961; join Johnson's expedition, 1044, 1048–58; their chief, 1051, 1052, 1057; their bravery and ferocity, 1053, 1057; council held with Johnson, 1111.

Mohawk River, the, 864, 866, 887 *note,* 888, 899, 1042, 1063, 1065, 1099, 1100, 1112, 1120, 1200, 1256, 1276, 1284, 1363.

Mohegans, the, 1111, 1372; council held with Johnson, 1111; ally themselves with the English, 1297.

Mollwitz, battle of, 858.

Monckton, Robert, 1014; appointed leader of the expedition against Acadia, 977, 980; the capture of Beauséjour, 980, 1009, 1015, 1019, 1023, 1329; the Acadians removed from their homes, 1019, 1027–40 (see *Acadians*); despatched to the Bay of Fundy, 1249; serves under Wolfe, at the siege of Quebec, 1328–29, 1344, 1352, 1355–57, 1380, 1385, 1395, 1398 and *note,* 1400 *note,* 1405, 1498; disabled by his wounds, 1405, 1413–14; joins Rodney, 1470.

"Monmouth," the, 1229–30.

Monongahela River, the, 937, 943, 950, 987, 988, 1290, 1300, 1304, 1305; the battle of, 989–91, 995 and *note,* 998 and *note,* 1070.

Monro, Lieutenant-Colonel, commandant at Fort William Henry, 1182; his danger, 1182–83; his correspondence with Webb concerning aid, 1183, 1187; his correspondence with Montcalm, 1184; his brave resistance, 1186–87, 1257; the garrison capitulates, 1188; the massacre, 1188–94, 1489–92.

Montagu, George, letter from Walpole, 1463.

Montcalm-Gozon de Saint-Véran, Louis Joseph, Marquis de, 946, 1088, 1177; his aides-de-camp, 1039, 1092; succeeds Dieskau in command, 1087–88; birth, education, and traits of character, 1088, 1094–95, 1160, 1310, 1414–17; his military service, 1089–90; his wife and family, 1089, 1414; his letters to his mother quoted, 1090–91, 1098–99, 1153, 1160, 1273 *note,* 1274 *note,* 1308, 1314, 1316,

1488–89; the letter from D'Argenson, 1090; his salary, 1091; letters to his wife quoted, 1091, 1092–94, 1153–55, 1166, 1272–73, 1318; embarks for America, 1092–93; his opinion of Lévis, 1092, 1102, 1154, 1408; his relations with Bougainville, 1092; his arrival in Canada, 1093–94; his relations with Vaudreuil, 1094–95, 1101, 1158–62, 1198, 1199, 1201–03, 1308–18, 1332, 1337, 1397, 1403, 1414–18; his relations with his troops, 1096, 1131, 1159–60, 1279, 1341, 1353, 1375, 1389; his relations with the Indians, 1098, 1103, 1154, 1159–60, 1166–67, 1176, 1177, 1185; letters to the minister of war, 1101, 1159–60; life at Montreal and Quebec, 1101, 1121, 1153–57, 1201, 1203; hastens to the defence of Ticonderoga, 1102; his victory at Oswego, 1120–27, 1158, 1167, 1283, 1396, 1416; his situation at Ticonderoga, 1131; his descriptions of men and things, 1153–55; letters to Bourlamaque quoted, 1153, 1155–57, 1201–03, 1310–11, 1343, 1385; receives the *cordon rouge,* 1153; plans a new attack, 1165; the French troops at Ticonderoga, 1168; calls a council of Indians, 1175–78; joined by Lévis, 1179; prisoners taken on the lake, 1180; his letter to Monro, 1184; the attack and conquest of Fort William Henry, 1184–94, 1194 *note,* 1310, 1488–89; his position in relation to Fort Edward, 1198, 1310; retires to Quebec, 1201; meeting at Montreal, 1201; reveals the frauds in trade, 1220, 1416–17; expedition against Ticonderoga, 1256–74, 1274 *note,* 1361–62, 1492–96; joined by Lévis, 1268; the fight with Abercromby, 1268–74; letter to Doreil, 1273; the cross planted on the battlefield, 1273; parties sent to harass Abercromby, 1279; questions Major Putnam, 1283; his camp broken up, 1285, 1311; his condition after the battle of Ticonderoga, 1308–11; resolves to stand by Canada, 1313; his promotion, 1315; the refusal of forces from France, 1315–17; marriage of his children, 1316; letter from Belleisle, 1316–17; his plans for a final effort for Canada, 1317–18; death of a child of, 1318; his arrival at Quebec, 1333; the siege and reduction of Quebec by Wolfe, 1333–58, 1375–1419; his headquarters and camp, 1335–36, 1341; his plan of battle and course of action, 1341–42, 1347–48, 1350–51, 1353, 1376–82; condition of Canadians, 1352; Montmorenci evacuated, 1384; deceived as to Wolfe's movements, 1390–92; the English army ascends the Heights, 1393–94; the night before the battle, 1395–96; his last words to the army, and the final attack, 1396–1403, 1433–34; his remarks to the people, 1400 and *note;* his wounds, 1400, 1405; his death and burial, 1406–09, 1414, 1420 *note,* 1501; his last letter to Townshend, 1408; his protecting care for the Canadians and French, 1408; papers given to Roubaud, 1416–17, 1419 *note.*

Montcalm, brother of Louis, his prodigious knowledge and early death, 1088–89.

Montcalm, Chevalier de, son of the Marquis, appointed to command a regiment in France, 1089–90; his marriage, 1316.

Montcalm, father of Louis, the Marquis, 1088; death of, 1089.

Montcalm, Madame de, mother of the Marquis. See *Saint-Véran.*

Montcalm, Madame de, wife of the Marquis, 1091, 1310; her family, 1089; letters from her husband quoted, 1091, 1153, 1166, 1488, 1489.

Montcalm, Mademoiselle de, daughter of the Marquis, her marriage, 1316.

Montcalm, Marquis de (1884), 1094 *note.*

Montcalm, Miréte de, 1318.

Montespan, Mme., 20.

Montesquieu, 856.

Montgomery, Captain Alexander, 1376.

Montgomery, Colonel, his regiment, 1287; advance of Forbes's army, 1304.

Montgomery, General Richard, 1376.

Montguet, 1404.

Montguy, 1264.

Montigny, ——, a member of Rigaud's war-party, 739.

Montigny, taken prisoner, 1367.

Montmorenci, the heights of, 1335, 1341; the cataract, 1340, 1348, 1497; position occupied by Wolfe, 1346–49; the disaster and evacuation of, 1354–57, 1375, 1381, 1384, 1457.

Montmorency, M. de, 756.

Montour, Andrew, the expedition with Gist, 882–86.

Montour, Catharine, 882.

Montpellier, 1094, 1155.

Montpensier, Princess, 13; at Orleans, 13; her exile, 14; relations with Mme. Frontenac, 19 (see 20 *note*).

Montreal, 387, 880, 889, 890, 905, 932, 934, 1094, 1121, 1126, 1129, 1135, 1153, 1161, 1166, 1174, 1193, 1199, 1200, 1201, 1257, 1283, 1369, 1414, 1428; condition under Perrot, 31, 56; arrests made by Perrot, 56; terror at the Iroquois invasion, 134, 143; threatened attack from New York, 173; condition of the country during the Indian invasions, 219; great gathering of traders and Indians, 229; great council of Indians, 318–24; an Indian war-party mustered at, 400; a proposed attack upon, 426; consternation at, expecting an attack of the English, 431; to be attacked by the English expedition, 446; preparations for defence against Walker's attack, 454; the number of war-parties sent from, in 1746, 719; social life among the officials, 1153, 1155–56, 1209–11; scarcity of flour, 1203; La Friponne, 1212; census of, 1317; call to arms, 1331, 1333; approach of Amherst, 1359, 1379, 1444–50; Lévis sent to protect, 1369; supplies sent to Quebec, 1378; Lévis departs for Quebec, 1410; preparations to attack Quebec, 1430; the fall of Canada, 1443–57; the city described, 1450; capitulation of, 1452, 1458, 1471; the French soldiers return to France, 1452, 1458.

Montreuil, Adjutant-General, 1101; aids Dieskau, 1055; his letter concerning Montcalm, quoted, 1101; delay in sending aid to Montcalm, 1403; his letters, 1498.

Moody, Captain, a British naval captain at Boston, 433 *note;* attacks Fort William, Newfoundland, 424; dismissed from office, 496.

Moody, Rev. Samuel, chaplain of the expedition against Louisbourg, 628; his despotic rule over his parishioners, 628; his long prayers and sermons, 629; preached to the soldiers at Canseau, 637; says grace at Pepperrell's dinner given at Louisbourg, 666.

Moore, Colonel William, his soldiers camped at Louisbourg, 644; mentioned, 671 *note;* letter to Governor Morris, 1082.

Moravian brotherhood, the, 1294.

Moravians, the, 866, 882, 1082; mission of Frederic Post, 1294–99.

Moro Castle, 1470.

Morpain, Captain, opposes the landing of the enemy at Louisbourg, 640.

Morris, ——, of Cambridge, mentioned, 652.

Morris, Captain Roger, aide-de-camp to General Braddock, 984; wounded in the battle of the Monongahela, 995, 1002.

Morris, Robert Hunter, Governor of Pennsylvania, 958, 1001, 1004 *note,* 1143, 1286, 1294; correspondence with the younger Shirley quoted, 972, 983–84, 1066–67, 1077–78, 1079; council of governors held with Braddock, 975–77; relations of the Penns with, 1076; questions of taxing proprietary lands, 1076–78, 1080–83; his relations with the Assembly, 1077–84; letter to, from William Moore, 1082; declares war against the Indians, 1111; sends Colonel Armstrong to attack Kittanning, 1132; Indian convention held at Easton, 1297.

Moulton, Captain, sent to attack Norridgewock, 498; his soldiers camped at Louisbourg, 644.

Mount Desert, Colonel Church's troops sent to, 418.

Mouse River, 591.

Moyne, Le, 83.

Muis de Poubomcoup, Marie, married at Port Royal, 415.

Murdering Town, hamlet of, 937.

Murray, Captain Alexander, 1029; a memorial sent to, from the Acadians, 1023–25; his relations and correspondence with Colonel Winslow, 1029–31, 1036; the removal of the Acadians, from their homes, 1029–31, 1033, 1036–38. See *Acadians.*

Murray, James, 1437; serves under Wolfe at the reduction at Quebec, 1328, 1346, 1377, 1380, 1385, 1395 (see *Quebec*); his character, 1329, 1424, 1433; remains in command at Quebec, 1414, 1424; an attack expected from the French, 1426–28; expedition of Lévis against Quebec, 1430–42, 1502–03; his relations with his soldiers, 1437, 1446; the courtesies of war, 1439; the fall of Canada, 1443–57; ascends the St. Lawrence to Montreal, 1444–47, 1451.

Muskingum River, the, 877, 882.

Musquawkies, a name by which the Outagamie Indians called themselves, 564 *note.*

Mussey, widow, murdered by Indians, 368.

Nantasket Roads, 635; arrival of English fleet in, 446.

Naples, 852.

Napoleon I., 843.

Narrows of Lake George, the, 1136, 1139, 1144, 1179, 1260.

Nassonites, Indians, on the Red River, 571, 572.

Natchez, the tribe of sun-worshippers, 538; attack the colonists in Louisiana, 548.

Natchitoches, a settlement on the Red River, 570.

Nathaniel, Captain, Indian chief, 371.

Naval force, the equipment of, for the

expedition against Louisbourg, 631; its arrival at Canseau, 637; encounters the French frigate "Renommée," 637; takes some French prizes, 637; sails from Canseau, 638; arrives at Louisbourg, 638.

Neal, Andrew, the house of, attacked by Indians, 368.

Necessity, Fort, 561, 947, 950, 1387; retreat of Washington's forces, 953–54; matters pertaining to the capitulation of, 1484–85.

Negroes, 865, 976, 1001, 1002.

Nelson, Fort, on Hudson's Bay, 282–83.

Nelson, John, a prisoner at Quebec, warns the Massachusetts colony, 258–59.

"Neptune," the, 1328.

Nesmond (Marquis), to command in attack on Boston, 275, 277.

Netherlands, the, 1472.

Neutrality, treaty of, proposed between Canada and the New England colonies, 405.

Neuvillette, Lieutenant, killed in fight with a privateer, 410.

New Brunswick, 906, 929 note.

New Brunswick, originally Acadia, 410, 477.

New England, 883, 929, 1045; French schemes for conquest in, 340; colonies, their attitude as regarded war, 342; encroaches on Acadian fisheries, 410; determines to attack Port Royal, 433; desires aid from England, 434; prediction concerning the possible independence of, 443; barred out from the fur-trade, 517; the Peace of Aix-la-Chapelle proclaimed in, 744; characteristics of her colonies, 862–64, 866–68, 1014, 1032, 1039–40, 1042, 1258, 1276, 1454; confederation of the colonies, 868; the provincial troops, 1106–08, 1116–18, 1428; rejoicing at the fall of Louisbourg, 1248–49; her joy over the victories in Canada, 1419, 1454–56.

New England colonies unfit for war, 179, 208, 284; relations with Canada, 269; frontier hostilities, 277.

New England troops raised for an attack on Port Royal, 436; their camping at Louisbourg, 644; at Louisbourg, their cheerfulness under hardship, 646; their orderly conduct, 650; sickness, etc., 651; their disatisfaction and mutiny after the conquest of Louisbourg, 672; sickness and death of, 674.

New Eng. Hist. Gen. Register, cited, 708 *note.*

New France, the zeal displayed by Jesuit missionaries in, 478–79; the influence upon, by the occupation of Louisiana, 534; her two colonies, Canada and Louisiana, 551; character of the country with regard to attack and defence, 861; extent of, in America, 861, 872–74, 881, 894, 896, 899, 1285, 1413; the downfall of, 1455–57. See *Canada.*

New Hampshire, 1279; sends soldiers to Port Royal, 420; called upon for troops, 427; assists in an attack upon Louisbourg, 623; her contribution towards the siege of Louisbourg, 631; reimbursed for expenses of taking Louisbourg, 670; contributes men to capture Canada, 677; sends troops to protect Acadia, 696; disputes with Massachusetts concerning Fort Dummer, 720; invaded by parties from Canada, 964; the expedition sent against Crown Point, 1042, 1044, 1045; money granted to, by Parliament, 1105 *note;* Rogers' rangers, 1138; her sacrifices in time of war, 1256.

N. H. Historical Collections, cited, 487 *note.*

New Haven, 427, 1045.

New Jersey, 342, 939, 1069, 1129, 1261; called upon for troops, 426; her contributions towards the reduction of Canada, 428; contributes men to capture Canada, 677; characteristics of, 867; aids Virginia, 959; Crown Point to be seized, 976; the "Jersey Blues," 1064; money granted to, by Parliament, 1105 *note;* Indian warfare, 1131.

New London, a conference of governors at, concerning England's attack on Canada, 446.

New Mexico, desire of the French explorers to open trade with, 565; a route discovered from Louisiana to, 578.

New Netherland, colony of, 72.

New Orleans, 1472; the foundations laid by Bienville, 547; chain of forts connecting the city with Quebec, 870, 872–73; in the possession of France, 1472; given to Spain, 1473.

New Oswego, 1115, 1124.

New York, 872, 930, 940, 1045, 1057, 1060, 1197, 1198, 1250, 1261, 1306, 1368, 1471; plan of a French officer to destroy, 340; the bulwark of the Southern colonies, 342; destitution of her soldiers, and unfitness for war, 342; the pacific relations with Canada, 405; joins in the reduction of Canada, 427; her interest in the fur-trade, 517; a rival of Canada for the control of the West, 517; her attitude toward the Five Nations, 518; their friendship necessary to her for her fur-trade, 519; her communication with the West carried on through the Five Nations, 520; contributes men to capture Canada, 677; her condition respecting military efficiency, 712; questions of boundary, 864, 899, 977; matters of interest concerning the people and the place, 866–69, 885–87, 1069, 1084; expeditions of war fitted out by, 941, 955, 1042, 1045, 1105, 1166, 1328; Indian complaints, 961, 964; council of governors held with Braddock, 974–77; plans of Shirley to repel French invasion, 976 (see *Shirley*); orders for the removal of the Protestant population of, 1040 *note;* attitude of the Five Nations in time of war, 1098; council of war held, 1104; money granted to, by Parliament, 1105 *note;* expeditions of war planned, 1106, 1163; Indian warfare, 1131; difficulty in quartering the troops in winter, 1143; exposed condition of the forts, 1166;

rejoicing at the fall of Louisbourg, 1248.

New York, English colonies of, relations with the Iroquois, 63; claims to the western country, 92; intrigues with the Hurons, 92; trade with the north-west, 99; checked by La Durantaye, 112 (see *Dongan*); relations with Canada, 269.

New York Colonial Documents, cited, 715 *note.*

Newbury, an intended Indian attack upon, 400.

Newcastle, Duke of, 849, 977, 1223, 1224, 1467; orders the protection of Acadia by Commodore Warren, 632; sends aid to the expedition against Louisbourg, 633; letter to Governor Shirley quoted, 670 *note;* approves Governor Shirley's proposal to capture Canada, 676; promises British troops, 677; fails to send them, 678; his apathy of interest in the protection of Acadia, 688, 695; at the head of the English government, 965; error in Braddock's campaign, 980; his influence over England, 1224–25; blight of his administration, 1227; his idea of promotion in the army, 1327; influence upon the army, 1456–57; disliked by George III., 1464, 1469.

Newell, Chaplain, preached to the army before Lake George, 1048.

Newfoundland, 970, 1164, 1470; its conflicting powers, 424; the fisheries of, considered in the Treaty of Utrecht, 459; the fisheries, 1472, 1476.

Niagara, Fort, 893, 896, 899, 1104, 1203, 1283, 1293, 1305, 1363, 1449; planned by Denonville, 97; Indians muster at, 110; the fort built, 118; destroyed, 126; an important post for the French to secure, 610; situation and importance of the post, 896, 899, 1063, 1067, 1364, 1365, 1368; expedition against, 974–77, 1004, 1063–70, 1099, 1100, 1116, 1350; capture of, by Prideaux, 1363–68, 1371.

Niagara River, the, 1364.

Niaouré Bay, 1122.

Nicholson, Colonel Francis (Lieut.-Governor of New York), takes part in the scheme for reduction of Canada, 427; in command of New York troops, 429 and *note*; his advance towards Canada, 430; builds several forts, 430; stations his army at Wood Creek, 431; his troops disbanded, 433; sails for England, 434; given command of a new enterprise against Port Royal, 434; his plans, etc., 435; a dinner at the Green Dragon Tavern, 436; lands at Port Royal, 437; receives a messenger from Governor Subercase, 437; demands the surrender of the fort, 438; changes the name to Annapolis Royal, 439; sent to Boston from England to make preparations for England's attack on Canada, 445; encamped at Wood Creek, 454; receives news of Admiral Walker's retreat, 454; disbands his army, 454; governor at Annapolis, 465; his behavior towards the Acadians, 466; conquest of Acadia, 906.

Nicholson, Fort, on the Hudson, 429.

Niles, *Indian and French Wars,* cited, 366 *note.*

Nîmes, 1088.

Nims, ——, escapes from Indian captivity, 393.

Nipegon Lake, a French post, 584.

Nipissing Lake, 1175.

Nipissings, the, 873, 895, 949, 1175–78; their missionary, 1176; death of a chief, 1181.

Nivernois, Duc de, sent to London to negotiate for peace, 1471.

Niverville, 1176.

Niverville, Boucher de, ensign under St. Pierre in the search for the Pacific, 603, 604; commanded the Canadian troops in an attack against Number Four, 723; demands the surrender of the fort, 725; disappointed of success, he retires with his troops from the place, 726.

Noble, Colonel Arthur, commands troops sent to protect Acadia, 696; occupies the village of Grand Pré, 697; his quarters at Grand Pré attacked by Coulon de Villiers' troops, 702–04; killed by the French, 704.

Noble, Ensign, a brother of Colonel Noble, at Grand Pré, 702; killed in the attack by the French, 704.

Noddles Island (East Boston), English troops quartered at, 446.

Noix, Isle aux, 1317, 1331, 1408, 1448; the French entrenched at, 1361, 1363, 1368, 1379; the French retreat from 1370–71.

Normanville, brothers, 989.

Norridgewock, the village of, in 1716, 480–81; the government of Massachusetts determines to destroy, 498–500.

Norridgewocks, Indians of Maine, pretend a peace with Governor Dudley, 360; join a war-party, 400; a guard to the French colony on the Kennebec, 478; in charge of Father Sebastien Rale, 478; how they parted with their lands, 484; alarmed by the intrusion of settlers, 484; join in council to meet Governor Shute, 485; they annoy the English settlers, 489; invited to another council at Georgetown, 490; their interview with Captain Penhallow, 491; attack the fort at Georgetown, 492; interview with the embassy from Governor Dummer, 504; the scattering of the tribe, 506.

North America, 852. See *America.*

North Carolina, 867, 972, 1105, 1287; answers the appeal of Dinwiddie, 941; condition of forces from, 955; council of governors held with Braddock, 974–77; effect of the victory at Fort Duquesne, 1306.

North Pole, the, 858.

Northampton, 1044.

Northampton, Mass., 369, 379, 399, 729.

Northern Department, the, 1464.

Northfield, Mass., abandoned, 374; mentioned, 720; particularly liable to Indian attack, 729; the labors of the Rev. Benjamin Doolittle at, 729; the Sunday drum-beat at, 729.

"Northumberland," the war-ship of the Duc d'Anville, 682 and *note*.

Northwest Bay, 1178.

Norton, ——, chaplain at Fort Massachusetts, 736; quoted, 738; his account of their march from the fort as prisoners, 741; invited by De Muy to visit the fort at Crown Point, 744.

Nova Scotia, 410, 1009, 1016, 1197, 1320, 1321, 1328, 1457; *Archives* cited, 476 *note;* originally Acadia, 477; matters pertaining to Acadia, 906 (see *Acadia* and *Acadians*); rejoicing at the fall of Louisbourg, 1248–49; solitude of the forts, 1248–49.

Noyes, Dr., built a stone fort at Cushnoc (Augusta), 483.

Noyon, Jacques de, sergeant in colony troops, 395.

Noyon, Mrs. Jacques de (Abigail Stebbins), 395.

Number Four, a settlement formed by the brothers Farnsworth, of Groton, 720; the fort built at, 722; a small garrison sent from Massachusetts, 722; attacked by Indians, 722; abandoned by its settlers, 723; Captain Phineas Stevens sent to garrison it, 723; again attacked by Indians, 724; defended by Captain Stevens, 724; Niverville demands its surrender, 725; which being refused, he retires from the scene, 725–26; the inhabitants return to, 727.

Nuns, the, at Quebec, 1423. See *Ursulines*.

Nutfield, 509.

Oath of allegiance. See *Acadians*.

Obadiah, name used in New England, 1014.

O'Callaghan, 1194 *note*.

Ochterlony, Captain, escapes from Indians' cruelty, 1356.

Ogden, Captain, 1372; sufferings of the rangers, 1373.

Ogdensburg, 871.

Ohio Company, the, 881, 941, 950, 980; their trading-houses, 885, 935, 943, 982.

Ohio Indians, the, 885 *note,* 946, 949.

Ohio River, the, 859, 861, 871, 872, 874, 875, 879, 886, 888, 889, 903, 931, 932, 964, 987, 988, 1210, 1293–94; the French propose to build forts at, 610; valley of, controlled by the French, 896 (see *French*); conflict of French and English for the surrounding territory, 932–37, 941–54, 1063, 1071–84, 1294–99, 1365, 1367; forts on, 938, 941, 942.

Ojibwas, 933, 988, 1175; called to aid Dubuisson at Detroit, 523.

"Old Indian House," the house of John Sheldon at Deerfield, 381.

Oncpapa Indians, a tribe of the Sioux, 600 *note*.

Oneida Lake, 1065, 1363.

Oneidas, the, 75, 1043, 1111, 1200, 1284; settle at Caughnawaga, 345; in the Iroquois mission, 889.

Onondaga, 75, 961, 962, 1113; council at, 146–49, 289; the Iroquois capital, 344, 890; council held by Johnson, 1110.

Onondaga River, the, 895, 1066, 1284, 1363.

Onondagas, the, 1111, 1367; efforts of the French to convert, 889, 961.

Onontio, Indian name for governor of Canada, 59, 65, 74 (La Barre); addressed by Big Mouth, 84–86.

Onontio, the, 890, 949.

Ontario, Fort, 1115, 1123, 1124, 1130; burned to the ground, 1126.

Ontario, Lake, 871, 889, 894, 896, 977, 1043, 1065, 1066, 1099, 1100, 1104, 1105, 1106, 1115, 1122, 1126, 1129, 1283–85, 1307, 1331, 1364, 1368, 1444; journey of Father Piquet, 892.

Ord, Captain, mentioned in Campbell's letter, 1001.

Orléans, Duke of, 545; approves the plan for the discovery of the Pacific Ocean, 580.

Orléans, Fort, built by Bourgmont on Missouri River, 574.

Orleans, holds for the Fronde, 13.

Orléans, Isle d', 1335, 1338, 1340, 1354, 1432, 1444; position of Wolfe, 1344.

Orléans, Point of, 1337, 1342, 1346, 1348, 1349, 1382, 1384, 1389.

Orme, Captain Robert, aide-de-camp of Braddock, 975, 984, 998; wounded in the battle of the Monongahela, 995, 999; his account of Braddock's death, 999; correspondence with Dinwiddie, 1002–04.

Orry, 855.

Osages, Indians, 571, 874, 901.

Osborn, Admiral, expedition under, 1229, 1230.

Osborne, ——, chairman of the Committee of War, 652.

Osgood, Captain, 1030, 1031.

Ossipee Lake, 506, 510.

Oswegatchie, 880, 1449; La Présentation, 889–91.

Oswegatchie River, the, 871.

Oswego, 871, 880, 893, 895, 899, 905, 977, 1065, 1099, 1161, 1284, 1363, 1449, 1480; a trading-house built at, 612; its demolition ordered by Beauharnois, 612; life of the garrison at, 887, 891–92, 895, 1084, 1114–15; French enmity towards, 898 and note, 1043, 1067, 1099, 1112, 1120–27; arrival of Shirley's expedition, 1066; importance of, 1115; account of the capture by the French, 1120–27, 1158–59, 1238, 1396, 1416; murders committed by the French, 1197; return of Bradstreet, 1284; to be re-established, 1359; plans of Amherst, 1368.

Otoes, Indians, on the Missouri River, 576.

Otréouati (Big Mouth), 76.

Ottawa River, the, 930, 1098; its importance to the French, 217–18.

Ottawas, the, 873, 884, 902, 988, 1176 note; their hostility, 88; a generic name, 111 and note; join Denonville, 113; their barbarities, 117; claimed as British subjects, 120; greet Perrot, 152; jealous of the Hurons, 152; their neutrality overcome, 185–86; a tribe of the "Far Indians," 345; settled about Detroit, 519; their houses, crops, etc., 522; village of, 897; their cannibalism, 1174; called to a council by Montcalm, 1175–78; French allies, 1293.

Otter Creek, 731, 1363.

Otway, his regiment at Albany, 1116.

Ouacos, Indians on Arkansas River, 572 note.

Oudenarde, battle of, 1463.

Oueskak, inhabitants removed from, 1019–20.

Ourehaoué, a Cayuga chief, 145, 149.

Oushala, a chief of the Outagamies, 558.

Outagamies, Indians of Michigan, 519; the terror of the West, 521; settle themselves at Detroit, 522; their hostile intentions, 523; their camp attacked, 525; a fight ensues, 526; they ask an interview of Dubuisson, 527; more fighting, 528; they leave Detroit, 531; surrender to the French, 532; attack the Illinois, 554; expedition of Louvigny against the, 555; Vaudreuil determined to destroy, 555; their defences, 556–57, 557 note; make treaty of peace, 557–58; they attack the Illinois, 558; their war-chief burned by the Illinois, 558; order of King Louis for their destruction, 558; conflicting opinions concerning their extermination, 558–59; in council with Sieur de Lignery, 558; an expedition against them by Lignery, 560; again attacked Sieur de Villiers, 561; again attacked by Hurons, etc., 562; and defeated, 562–63; attacked by a French trader, Marin, 563; derivation of the name, 564 note; the survivors incorporate themselves with the Sacs, etc., 564.

Oxford, 941.

Oxford, the village of, attacked by Indians, 497.

Oyster River, attack and massacre, 263–65; attacked by Indians, 399.

Pacific Ocean, 1473; search for the, begun, 580; Charlevoix's search for the, 581–82; a company sent from Canada under La Perrière, 582; the enterprise and explorations of Varennes de la Vérendrye in search of, 584–91; the search of the brothers de la Vérendrye for, 591–601; Captains Lewis and Clark explore their way to, 600; the search for, undertaken by M. de St. Pierre, 602, 603 *note*.

Paddon, Captain, of the "Edgar," 450.

Padoucas, Indians, 574; name given to the Comanche Indians, 577 *note*.

Pain, Father, at Acadia, 462.

Paine, Timothy, 1119.

Palfrey, *New England*, cited, 516 *note*, 671 *note*.

Panama, 1470.

Panawamské, an Indian village, 498.

Panet, Jean Claude, 1499.

Paradis, ——, acted as pilot in Walker's expedition, 449.

"Parfait," a French war-ship, 685.

Parfouru, Madame de, 1489.

Paris Documents, 406 *note*.

Paris, 854, 856, 970, 975, 1058, 1090, 1155, 1228, 1417; questions of American boundary, 903 (see *France*); trial of the dishonest officials, 1459–60.

Paris, the peace of, 1458–74.

Parker, Colonel, his party captured by Indians, 1174, 1178.

Parkman, George Francis, 1500.

Parkman, Rev. Ebenezer, 1258 *note*.

Parkman, William, opinion of Abercromby, 1258.

Parliament, the, 847, 848, 958, 960, 967, 1224, 1253, 1255; taxation by, 961, 965, 976, 1478; raises money for campaigns in America, 977, 1061, 1104; money paid to Massachusetts, 1256; elections in 1761, 1464; the peace between England and France, 1473; resistance of the British colonies, 1478.

Parliament of Paris, the, 1092.

Parsons, Widow, carried off by Indians, 368.

Parsons's *Life of Pepperrell*, cited, 626 *note*, 639 *note*, 669 *note*.

Parthena, a negro woman, 377.

Partridge, Colonel Samuel, letters of, cited, 383 *note*.

Passamaquoddy Bay, 1321; Colonel Church's attack on Canadians at, 418.

Patten, Captain, assists Bradstreet, 1113.

Patterson's Creek, 1079.

Patterson's memoir, cited, 426 *note*.

Patton, John, 899.

Paugus, war-chief of the Pequawkets, 506; killed, 513 and *note*.

Pawnees, Indians, on the Missouri, visited by Du Tisné, 573.

Paxton, town of, 1080.

Payne, John, letter to Colonel Robert Hale, 635 *note*.

Peabody, his bravery, 1135.

Peace of Ryswick, 303; celebrated in Quebec, 306; mentioned, 340, 375.

Péan, 1156, 1202, 1210; his wife, 904, 1202, 1209, 1215, 1216; promotion of, 904; his official knavery, 932, 1211–13, 1215, 1217–18, 1221 *note;* letter to Duquesne, 933; effort to descend the Ohio thwarted, 934; at La Chine, 1202; thrown into the Bastille, 1459.

Péan, Madame, 904, 1202, 1209, 1215–16.

Pelham, Fort, built on the site of the present town of Rowe, Mass., 728.

Pemaquid, capture by French and Indians, 165, 250; scheme of Frontenac, 258; its defences, 259; attack and capture, 272–75.

Pemoussa, an Outagamie chief at the fight of Detroit, appeals to Dubuisson for peace, 527; makes a second appeal to Dubuisson, 530; surrenders and escapes, 532.

Penacooks, Indians, pretended peace with Governor Dudley, 360.

Penecaut, accompanies Le Sueur on his voyage, 567; *Relation of,* cited, 570 *note*.

Penhallow, Captain, his interview with hostile Indians at the Georgetown council, 491.

Penhallow's *History of Wars of New England,* etc., 361 *note,* 366 *note,* 383 *note,* 424 *note,* 483 *note,* 491 *note,* 510 *note,* 515 *note*.

Penisseault, Antoine, 1210; official knavery, 1211; thrown into the Bastille, 1459.

Penisseault, Madame, 1216.

Penn, Richard, proprietary of Pennsylvania, 1076.

Penn, Thomas, proprietary of Pennsylvania, 1076.

Penn, William, his plan of union for the colonies, 868; first proprietary of Pennsylvania, 1076.

Pennahouel, chief of the Ottawas, his speech, 1176–77.

Pennoyer, Jesse, 1374 *note*.

Pennsylvania, 1000, 1285; called upon for troops, 426; refused aid in the reduction of Canada, 428; men raised in, to capture Canada, 677; matters of interest concerning the people and the place, 862, 866–68, 871, 874, 876, 882, 885, 886, 903, 980–82, 1077; efforts of Dinwiddie to obtain help from, 939; relations of the Assembly with the people, 941, 957–59, 1075, 1077–84, 1131, 1286; commissioners sent to Albany, 962–64; German population, 976; sufferings of the settlers, 1071–72, 1075, 1084, 1131, 1286, 1287; question of taxing proprietary lands, 1076–78, 1080–82, 1084; a militia law passed, 1083; roads to be made by the army, 1287–88; Indian allies sought for, 1293–97; expedition of Major Grant, 1300.

Penobscot River, the, 1175.

Penobscot, Me., 340.

Penobscots, Indians, 1194 *note;* pretended peace with Governor Dudley, 360; join a war-party, 400; join in a council to meet Governor Shute, 485; the mission village of the, destroyed, 498–500; their new village burned by Captain Heath, 504–05; conclude a treaty of peace, 505; encamped with De Ramesay near Acadia, 688.

Pensacola, 426; Le Moyne d'Iberville at, 535; also Spanish ships, 535.

Pensens, ——, induced the Acadians to migrate, 465.

Pentegoet (Castine), 244; attacked by Andros, 250; held by Saint-Castin, 250.

Pepin, Lake, a fort built at, 566, 568.

Pepperell, Fort, condition of, 1123.

Pepperrell Papers, the, cited, 671 *note.*

Pepperrell, William, cited, 619 *note;*

given the chief command of an attack upon Louisbourg, 624–25; his mansion-house at Kittery Point, 625; his portrait, 625; his early life, education, etc., 626; held many offices, 626; consults Rev. George Whitefield when appointed to command the siege of Louisbourg, 627; a plan suggested to him for reconnoitering Louisbourg, 628; receives commissions from three Provinces, 630; manages the landing of the fleet at Louisbourg, 640; his soldiers camped at Louisbourg, 644; the cheerfulness of his men under difficulties, 646; orderly conduct of his men, 650; his popularity with his army, 651; his cares and annoyances, 652; receives Warren's plan for taking Louisbourg, 661; agrees with Warren upon a mode of attack, 662; makes terms of capitulation to Duchambon, 664; quoted concerning the surrender, 664; gives a dinner to celebrate the surrender, 665; jealousies between his soldiers and the sea force of Warren, 667–68; as compared with Warren, 669 and *note;* receives the keys of the fortress, 669; delivers them to Governor Shirley, 669; knighted and given a commission in British army, 670; in charge with Warren at Louisbourg, 672; his regiment, 976, 1064, 1105, 1115, 1123.

Pequawket Indians, 369; join in a council to meet Governor Shute, 485; a tribe of the Abenakis living on the Saco, 506; Lovewell's expedition against the, 507; the fight at Lovewell's Pond, 509–10; cowed by the English, 514.

Perelle, Ensign, carries a flag of truce from Governor Subercase to the English camp, 437.

Perier, Sieur, succeeds Bienville in Louisiana, 548; recalled from Louisiana, 549.

Perière, war-party sent out under, 1136.

Peronney, Captain, killed in battle, 1002.

Perrière, Boucher de la, military chief of the mission to the Sioux Indians, 582.

Perrot, Fort, built by Nicolas Perrot, 568 and *note.*

Perrot, governor of Montreal, 31; his anger at Bizard, 33; arrested at Quebec by Frontenac, 35; the king's opinion, 39–40; is restored, 56; his greed, 56–57; his enmity to Saint-Castin, 249; at the Montreal council, 322.

Perrot, Isle, 1450.

Perrot, Nicolas, the *voyageur,* 80 *note,* 566; at Michillimackinac, 87; his skill in dealing with the Indians, 87–88, 111, 151, 153; built a fort at Lake Pepin, 568 and *note,* 582.

Perry, John, Mrs., a war prisoner on the march from Fort Massachusetts, 742.

Perry, Professor A. L., 734 *note.*

Perth, 1322.

Peter III., 1468.

Peter the Great, 857.

Peter, Captain, the mission of Frederic Post, 1298.

Peticodiac, disaster to the English, 1034.

Petit Lorembec, several Englishmen captured and killed at, 659.

Petition, to General Court for compensation of losses from the Indian attack on Deerfield, 381 *note.*

Petrie, Johan Jost, taken prisoner, 1201.

Petty, ——, escapes from Indian captivity, 393.

Petty's Plain, near Deerfield, 374.

Peyroney, Ensign, 952. See *Peronney.*

Peyton, Lieutenant, his escape from Indians, 1356.

Philadelphia, 980, 995 *note,* 1001, 1003, 1004, 1287, 1306; relative size of, 866; influence of the Quakers, 1075, 1077; its prosperity, 1075; council of, 1134; difficulty in quartering the troops, 1143; rejoicing at the fall of Louisbourg, 1248.

Philippines, the, 1470.

Philipps, Governor Richard, concerning the government of Annapolis, 467; advises recall of French priests from Acadia, 471; orders the Acadians to swear allegiance to George I., 473; succeeded by Lieutenant-Governor Armstrong, 474.

Philip's (King) war, 162.

Philipsbourg, siege of, 1089.

Phillips, an illicit trader, 408.

Phillips, governor of Acadia, 911, 914 *note.*

Phillips, Lieutenant, surrender of, 1205–06.

Phippeny, ——, killed by Indians at Casco, Me., 366.

Phipps, Governor, letter from John Ashley to, 1108.

Phipps, Hon. Spencer, mentioned, 736 *note.*

Phips, Sir William, 403, 452; commands the expedition to Port Royal, 174; early life and character, 177–78; as governor of Massachusetts, 178; his expedition to Quebec, 192–208; the summons to surrender, 195; mistakes and delays, 197; cannonade, 199; retreat, 203; French supply-ships, 206; arrival at Boston, 207; captured Port Royal, 439.

Piacenza, 1090.

Piankishaws, the, 901.

Pichon, Thomas, commissary at Fort Beauséjour, 1252 *note;* his treachery, 1012; his writings, 1012 *note,* 1017 *note,* 1252 *note.*

Pickawillany, 880, 883–84, 900, 988; the Indians cajoled by the English, 901, 902; the town attacked, and the English traders slaughtered, 903.

Pickering, Lieutenant, killed by the French in their attack on Grand Pré, 704.

Pierce, Captain, killed at siege of Louisbourg, 648.

Pigiquid, now Windsor, 475.

Pine Hill, on the banks of the Saco, 506.

Pinet, Jesuit missionary, established the village of Cahokia, 553.

Pique Town (Pickawillany), importance of, 880.

Piquet, Abbé, 889 *note,* 1111; his mission

and plans, 871, 880, 898–99, 961, 1126, 1364, 1449, 1480; his banners, 1480.

Piscataqua River, a view of from Kittery Point, 625.

Pisiquid (now Windsor), an Acadian village, 475, 701, 909, 1012.

Pisiquid River, the, 1029.

Pitt, Fort, built by Stanwix, 1305.

Pitt, William, 444, 458, 848, 1223, 1327, 1493; his characteristics and his politics, 849, 1224–29, 1463, 1464, 1468, 1469, 1473; his relations with Newcastle, 966; his decline in power, 1163, 1164 note, 1224, 1226, 1227, 1468, 1469; his views and plans for war, 1228, 1253–55, 1258, 1277, 1286, 1327, 1359, 1362, 1463, 1464, 1469, 1475; report made by Pownall, 1255; naming of Pittsburg, 1305; the expeditions against Louisbourg and Quebec, 1327–29, 1330 note, 1381–83, 1418, 1433; disliked by George III., 1463, 1464, 1467; negotiations with Choiseul, 1465–67; an explanation demanded of Spain, 1467; the peace of Paris, 1469–74; carried into the House of Commons, 1473.

Pittsburg, 1359, 1365; site of, 876, 886, 941, 987; naming of the place, 1305.

Placentia, a French station in Newfoundland, 424; the people of, ordered to evacuate, 461.

Plaisted, Elisha, married to Hannah Wheelwright, 370; captured by Indians on his wedding-day, 370; ransomed, 371.

Plassey, the victory of, 1227, 1475.

Plates, leaden, bearing inscriptions, 874–75. See Céloron.

Platte River, 578.

Plessis, Joseph, Bishop of Quebec, 395.

Plymouth Colony, the, 1013.

Plymouth, Mass., 417.

Pococke, Admiral, Sir George, 1470.

Pointe-aux-Trembles, 1209, 1351, 1378, 1387, 1430, 1443.

Poisson, Jeanne. See Pompadour.

Poland, 852.

Polson, Captain, 1001, 1002.

Pomeroy, Abigail, 1360.

Pomeroy, Daniel, in the expedition against Crown Point, 1045, 1058.

Pomeroy, Lieutenant-Colonel Seth, in the expedition against Crown Point, 1044–45; quotations from his letters, 1046–47, 1058, 1061 note; the battle of Lake George, 1053, 1054, 1059 note.

Pomeroy, Rachel, 1058.

Pomeroy, Rev. Benjamin, 1360.

Pomeroy, Seth, gunsmith of Northampton, 636; at battle of Bunker Hill, 636; saluted by General Putnam, 636; major in expedition against Louisbourg, 636; extract from his diary at the siege of Louisbourg, 636–37; at the Grand Battery, 643; his journal cited, 671 note.

Pomeroy, Seth, Jr., 1045.

Pomeroy, Theodore, 1061 note.

Pomeroy, Theodore, Esq., 636 note.

Pompadour, Madame de (Jeanne Poisson), 843, 1086, 1226, 1465; her political influence, 843, 855, 966, 1086, 1092, 1222–26, 1314, 1464, 1475.

Ponchartrain, Fort, built at Detroit, 355, 521.

Ponchartrain, M. de, approves Cadillac's plan for occupation of Detroit, 355; concerning the Indian warfare, 404; gossiping letters sent to him from Port Royal, 415; concerning the designs of England against Massachusetts, 441.

Pondicherry, 1462, 1469.

Pont-à-Buot, 1015.

Pontbriand, Bishop, 1379, 1408.

Pontiac, 988, 1082 note, 1280.

Pontleroy, 1265.

Pontoosuc (Pittsfield), settlement, 728.

Popple, Mr., 428 note.

"Porcupine," the, 1391.

Porpoise, Cape, Me., attacked by Indians, 365.

Port à l'Anglois (Louisbourg), a fortress to be built at, 460.

Port Royal (Annapolis), 919; the seat of government at Acadia, 411; the internal dissensions at, 412; official gossip at, 414; the claim of "The Church" for authority, 415; Colonel

Church at, 419; an expedition sent to, by Governor Dudley, 420; the attack upon, 421; proves a failure, 423; the New England colonies determine to attack, 433; an attack to be made upon, 436; arrival of the squadron at, 436; Nicholson and Vetch land at, 437; capitulates to the English, 438; name changed to Annapolis Royal, 439.

Port Royal captured, 174–77.

Portland, former name of, 960.

Portland, town on Lake Erie, 871.

Portneuf, to build a trading-house at Toronto, 892.

Portsmouth, England, 427.

Portsmouth, N.H., place of assault of the French, 340; troops sent for defence against the Indians at, 369; an attack upon intended by the Indians, 400.

Portugal, 1470, 1477.

Poskoiac, River, 587.

Post, Christian Frederic, 1294; his mission, 1294–99; sent as envoy to the hostile tribes, 1294–99; his journal, 1297 note, 1307 note.

Potomac River, the, 885, 974, 982.

Pottawattamie Indians, a tribe of the Far Indians, 345, 897, 933, 988, 1141–42, 1175–78, 1293; settled about Detroit, 519.

Pottawattamie, the village of, 521.

Pouchot, Captain, 1099, 1203; the attack on Oswego, 1123; arrives at the camp of Montcalm, 1267; attacked, and surrenders at Niagara, 1364–68; the surrender of Fort Lévis, 1449.

Poulariez, Colonel, the capitulation of Quebec, 1396, 1405.

Poutrincourt, Baron de, 412.

Powder River Range, 593–94.

Pownall, Thomas, Governor of Massachusetts, 1194 note, 1255, 1491, 1492; despatch sent to Loudon, 1197; statement concerning the war-debt of Massachusetts, 1255–56.

Prague, the battle of, 1223.

Prairie à la Roche, 873.

Preble, Captain, an English officer at Grand Pré, 706.

Preble, Major Jedediah, 1034.

Prentice, Rev. ――, mentioned, 652.

Presburg, the Diet at, 858.

Presbyterians, the, 867, 1277; in Pennsylvania, 866, 1075, 1082.

Presquisle, 905, 932, 934, 938, 942, 1304, 1305, 1365; the fort burned, 1367.

Prévost, the intendant at Louisbourg, 916–17, 1245, 1251 note; memorial brought to Drucour, 1245–47.

Price, ――, militia officer at Haverhill, 401.

Prideaux, Brigadier, 1359; the capture of Fort Niagara, 1363–68, 1371; his death, 1365, 1368.

"Prince d'Orange," French war-ship, 681.

Prince Edward's Island, 912, 1247.

Prince, Rev. Thomas, quoted concerning the backsliding of his flock, 627.

Princess's Bastion, the, 1233, 1240.

Pringle, Captain, joins a scouting-party, 1204; his bravery, 1205–07.

Prisoners (English), their treatment in Canada, 272; French, among the Indians, 302, 304; restored, 304.

Privateers, encroach on Acadian fisheries, 410.

Proceedings of Mass. Hist. Soc., 382 note.

Protestant Reformation, the, 478.

Protestantism, 866, 1087.

Province Arms, the, 1248.

"Province Galley," a Massachusetts armed vessel, 366.

Provincial Papers of New Hampshire, cited, 491 note.

Provincial troops, the, 1276, 1278. See Army.

"Prudent," the, 1242–43.

Prussia, political condition of, 843, 857, 858, 1085–86, 1473, 1475; the Seven Years War, 1222, 1223, 1475; successes of, 1227; campaigns under Frederic, 1460, 1461; policy of George III., 1464; number of lives lost in the war, 1475.

Public Documents of Nova Scotia, 476 note.

Puritans, the settlers in Massachusetts,

863; the class holding Roundhead traditions, 864; dislike of the ways of the Virginians, 865.

Purpooduck Point, Me., attacked by Indians, 366.

Putnam, General Israel, salute to Seth Pomeroy at the battle of Bunker Hill, 636; in the expedition against Crown Point, 1045; his bravery, 1135; meeting with Langy's men, 1263; his adventures, 1281–83; his biography, 1281; taken prisoner, 1281, 1282; tortures inflicted upon, 1282–83; exchanged, 1283.

Puysieux, Marquis de, 855.

Pygmalion, 1160.

Pynchon, Doctor, 1055.

Pyrrhic dance, the, 1121.

Pythoness, the, 1142.

Quakers, the, their attitude toward the Indians, and their influence in Pennsylvania, 866, 941, 957, 976, 980, 1075–78, 1080–83, 1131, 1293; their trades, 1077.

Quary, Colonel ——, quoted, 342.

Quebec, 341, 931 note, 969 note, 1013, 1038, 1162, 1209, 1343, 1351, 1369, 1376, 1407; capital of Canada, 22; municipal government established by Frontenac, 25; the Lower Town burned, 61; greeting to Frontenac, 143; design of attack by Massachusetts, 179–81 (see Phips, Sir W.); the defences, 184; arrival of Frontenac with troops, 189; defence against Phips's attack, 192–203; its imminent danger, 204; construction of fortifications, 216; in possession of the Jesuits, 353; expects an attack from the English, 431; to be attacked by the English expedition, 446; prepares for defence against Walker's attack, 454; arrival of Sieur de la Valterie with news of the retreat of Walker, 455; rule of the military governor, 860; chain of French forts connecting the city with New Orleans, 870, 872–73; priests of Acadia controlled by the diocese of, 909–10, 1020; questions of French conquest, 1008; relations with the Acadians, 1011, 1038–39 (see Acadians); described by Montcalm, 1154; the Lenten season, 1155–56; Montcalm retires to, 1201–02; social life among the officials, 1209–16; La Friponne, 1212; war-policy of Pitt, 1228; preparations for an English attack, 1250, 1316; census of, 1317; natural defences of, 1317, 1341, 1394–95; the expedition fitted out against, 1327–29; the siege and reduction of, 1331–57, 1402–19, 1419–20 note, 1497–98, 1502–03; preparations for the defence of, 1333–37, 1341–42, 1344–45 (see Montcalm); the fire-ships, 1336, 1342–43, 1353; the Palace Gate, 1336; scarcity of food, 1337; the Cathedral, 1341; the Jesuits, 1341; the Recollets, 1341; the Seminary garden, 1341; the Ursulines, 1341; the proclamations issued by Wolfe, 1344, 1350, 1352, 1376; the town bombarded, and dwellings burned, 1345, 1376–77, 1379; the disaster of Montmorenci, 1354–57, 1375, 1381; the siege continued, 1375–83; the Upper and Lower Towns, 1380; despatches sent from Wolfe to England, 1382–83; the Heights of Abraham ascended, 1384–94; action of Holmes's squadron, 1387–88; the last battle between Wolfe and Montcalm, 1394–1400, 1400–01 note, 1406; the Plains of Abraham, 1394; the death of Wolfe, 1400; the French routed, 1402–06; the town abandoned by the army, 1407–09; the death of Montcalm, 1408; the grief and poverty of the people, 1409, 1410; Lévis attempts to save the city, 1410–12; the capitulation, of, 1412–14; the city left in command of Murray, 1414; the rejoicing over the victory, 1418–19; authorities for information concerning, 1419 note; confusion after the siege, 1421–23; drawings made of the ruins, 1421 note; kindness of the nuns, 1423–24, 1426; the rule of Murray, 1424; rumors of an attack from the French, 1426–28; the expedition of Lévis against, and the battle of Ste.-Foy, 1430–42, 1502–03; arrival of the British squadron, 1440; the siege raised, 1441; the fall of Canada, 1443–57; self-devotion of the missionaries, 1477; maps referring to, 1500.

Quebec, basin of, 1344, 1390.

Quebec, Bishop of, 918, 1020, 1023.

Queen Anne's War, the part of the American colonies in, 339; called also War of the Spanish Succession, 339; the beginnings of, 367.

Queen's Bastion, the, 1233, 1242.

Queen's Battery, the, at Quebec, 1341.

Querdisien-Tremais, to investigate the frauds in Canada, 1220.

Quesnel, a Frenchman in Bourgmont's party, 576.

Race, Cape, 970.

"Racehorse," the, 1431, 1441.

Rainy Lake, a fort built at, 586.

Rale, Sebastien, Jesuit missionary at Norridgewock, 361 note, 478; as missionary to the Abenakis, 480–81; opposed to the ministrations of the Rev. Joseph Baxter, 488; his correspondence with Baxter, 488; his correspondence with other ministers, 488; his power over the Indians, 489; quoted, 489 note; fears to lose his influence over the Indians, 490; stirs up an insurrection at the council at Georgetown, 490; his account of the attack on Georgetown, 492 note; he escapes arrest, 494; the government of Massachusetts demand him from the Indians, 494 and note; his death, 499; his character portrayed, 500–01; Jesuit missionary at St. Louis, 553.

Rameau, his estimate concerning Canadian population, 859 note; Acadian emigrants, 1007 note.

Ramesay, Chevalier de, 1336; his battery refused to Montcalm, 1397, 1433; his field-pieces in action, 1398; his last interview with Montcalm, 1408; at Montcalm's funeral, 1409; left in charge at Quebec, without supplies, 1409–12; calls a council of war, 1410; the capitulation of Quebec, 1413–14; his sister, 1423.

Ramesay, M. de, Governor of Montreal, quoted, 383 note, 555; sent with troops to surprise Nicholson advancing on Canada, 430; lands his troops at Crown Point, 430; retreats to Chambly, 430; sent to cooperate with D'Anville in retaking Acadia, 688; encamps at Chignecto with a force of Penobscot Indians, 688; builds a fort at Baye Verte, 692; endeavors to excite the Acadians to insurrection, 696; retreats before the coming of Colonel Arthur Noble, 697–98; plan for attacking Colonel Noble at Grand Pré, 698; the winter march of his troops, 699–701; his troops divided into ten parties for attack, 701; the plan of attack upon Grand Pré, 701–02; the attack upon Grand Pré and its results, 701–07; threatens the Acadians against intercourse with the English, 708; orders the Acadians to take arms against the English, 709.

Ramillies, 445.

Ramsay, R. A., 398 note.

Ranelagh Gardens, the, 848.

Rapide Plat, the, 1450.

Rascal, Fort, 1115, 1124, 1126.

Rat (the), a Huron chief, see Kondiaronk.

Raudot, Intendant at Canada, mentioned, 416; urged the settlement of Cape Breton, 460.

Raymond, Comte de, commandant at the post on the Maumee, 880, 901; command taken at Louisbourg, 915; royal instructions given to, with regard to the Indians and Acadians, 915, 1483.

Raynal, Abbé, his ideal picture of the Acadians, 1022.

Raystown, 1287, 1289, 1290, 1293, 1301, 1302.

Rea, Dr. Caleb, his religious views, 1276–77.

Reade, General J. Meredith, mentioned, 567 note.

Reading, 1080.

Rébald, Père, cited, 579 *note*.

Récollets, the, 1341, 1421; friars befriended by Frontenac, 39, 60, 233–34, 313; their eulogy of him, 309; friars at Port Royal, 415.

Red River, 571.

Rednap, an engineer, in the expedition to Port Royal, 420; quoted, 422.

Redstone Creek, 950; English storehouse on, 943; the storehouse burned, 954.

Reed, Josiah, on the march as a prisoner of war from Fort Massachusetts, 742; death of, 744 *note*.

Rehoboam, 1276.

Rémonville, Sieur de, proposed the settlement of Louisiana, 534.

Renaissance, the, produced also a revival in religious life, 478.

Renaudière, an engineer in Bourgmont's party, 575, 576.

Rennes, 1091.

"Renommée," a French frigate, 637.

Repentigny, 1215, 1347; in Ramesay's expedition, 698.

Restoration, the, 847.

Revolution, the French, 855.

Revolution, the, in America, 844, 868, 956 *note*, 995, 1063, 1278, 1437.

Reynolds, Sir Joshua, 984.

Rhine, the, 856, 1469.

Rhode Island, 342, 1105 *note*, 1261; sends soldiers to Port Royal, 420; called upon for troops, 427; promises assistance in an attack upon Louisbourg, 623, 624; failed to join in the siege of Louisbourg, 631; reimbursed for expenses incurred, 670; contributes men to capture Canada, 677; sends troops to protect Acadia, 696; the colony compared with others, 862; men voted for the expedition against Crown Point, 1042; character of the troops from, 1045.

Rhodes, Captain, hurt by the bursting of a gun at Louisbourg, 650 *note*.

Ribaut, mentioned, 608.

Richelieu River, the, 1043, 1102, 1135, 1152, 1369, 1424.

Richelieu, Cardinal de, 138, 756, 852, 1228; power given to, by Louis XIII., 855.

Richmond, Colonel, an officer in Pepperrell's army, 663.

Richmond, Fort, built on the Kennebec, 483, 498.

Richmond, Me., 483.

"Richmond," the, frigate, 1339.

Rickson, Lieutenant-Colonel, 1327.

Rigaud de Vaudreuil, brother of Governor Vaudreuil, 1122, 1159, 1175, 1256; capture of Oswego, 1121–27; his party attacks Fort William Henry, 1148–51, 1154; festivities given to his officers, 1155; his command, 1156, 1168; seeks to gain Indian allies, 1167; frauds in trade, 1214.

Rigaud de Vaudreuil, ordered to defend Fort Frederic against English attack, 731; intended to attack Schenectady, 732; the march of his war-party to attack Fort Massachusetts, 732–35; forms his war-party into two brigades, 733; the numbers of his war-party, 733; the plan of attack, 734–35; the attack made, 737; wounded, 738; offers terms of capitulation, 739; delivers some of the English prisoners to the Indians, 740; his party kill some people at Deerfield, 741; induces the Indians to treat the prisoners humanely, 742; allows his war-party to devastate the towns of the Hoosac Valley, 743; return to Crown Point, 743.

Rigaud, Madame de, 1210.

Rigauville, assists in attack on Grand Pré, 702.

Rimouski, country of, 930.

Rivière-aux-Canards, 706.

Roanoke, return of Gist, 885.

Robbins, Jonathan, signs petition to fight Indians, 507; wounded by Indians, 510; killed in the fight at Lovewell's Pond, 511.

Roberts, Colonel, burned the fort at Saratoga by advice of Governor Clinton, 715.

Robinson, John, re-captures some fishing vessels, 497.

Robinson, Sir Thomas, 983; in the House of Commons, 966; correspondence of, 969, 1009, 1010.

Robison, Professor John, 1392.

Rochbeaucourt, stationed at Pointe-aux-Trembles, 1443.

Roche, Lieutenant, 1204, 1205; his adventures, and escape from death, 1206–07.

Rochefort, 968, 969, 970, 1229–30; the expedition against, 1326.

Rochelle, France, 680; colonists from, in Louisiana, 540.

Rochester, 893.

Rock River, 562.

Rocky Mountains, 569, 574 *note*, 858, 933; discovered by La Vérendrye brothers, 597; discovered by Captains Lewis and Clark, 600.

Rodney, Admiral, sails for Martinique, 1470.

Rogers, John, minister of Boxford, 514.

Rogers, Richard, 1138; his corpse outraged, 1200 *note*.

Rogers, Robert, 1109, 1200 *note;* exploits of his rangers, 1137–38, 1144–47, 1204–07, 1258–61, 1263, 1279–82, 1309, 1349, 1369–74 *note*, 1376, 1448; his character and bravery, 1137–39, 1371, 1373; his portrait, 1137–38; sent to destroy the Abenakis town, 1369–74; suffers from hunger, 1372–74.

Rogers, Susanna, her engagement to Jonathan Frye, 514; her verses on the fate of Jonathan Frye, 515 *note*.

Rogers Rock, 1136, 1144, 1168, 1178, 1204, 1206, 1261, 1262.

Rolfe, Rev. ——, killed by Indians at Haverhill, 401.

Rollo, Lord, 1249; follows Murray, 1445.

Roma, quotation from, 911.

Roman Empire, the, 856.

Roman politique, disquisition entitled, 931.

Romans, 1418.

Rome, 1065.

Ronde, M. de la, an officer at Port Royal, 414.

Rooseboom, a Dutch trader, 99, 111, 112.

Roosevelt, Theodore, mentioned, 643 *note*.

Roquemaure, 1049; joined by Bougainville, 1448; at Montreal, 1451.

Rosalie, Fort, uprising of the Natchez Indians at, 548.

Rose, Captain, 1001.

Rossbach, 1223, 1227, 1475.

Rostaing killed, 971.

Roubaud, Jesuit missionary, 1172, 1176; his description of an Indian warfeast, 1172–73; Indian cruelty described, 1173–74, 1180, 1188; statements in relation to the massacre at Fort William Henry, 1193, 1194 *note;* the dishonesty in Canada, 1416–17; papers given to, by Montcalm, 1416, 1417, 1419 *note*, 1420 *note*.

Rouge, Fort, built by La Vérendrye, 587.

Rouillé, De, colonial minister at Versailles, 917 *note;* instructions given to La Jonquière injurious to the English, 898, 900, 902, 917 *note;* instructions to Duquesne, 904; official documents relating to the Acadians, 910–11; aids the French to destroy the English, 914, 915, 1480; treachery and double-dealing of, 917 *note*.

Rouillé, Monseigneur, cited, 603 *note*.

Rous, ——, an illicit trader, 408.

Rous, Captain, commands the warship "Shirley," 631; commended for gallant conduct at siege of Louisbourg, 670 *note;* fires on the "St. François," 923; in the expedition sent against Nova Scotia, 1014–16, 1018.

Rousseau, 856; mentioned, 339; philosophy of, 931.

Roussillon, Royal, battalion of, 1092, 1268, 1270, 1355; sent to defend Ticonderoga, 1102; advance of the French upon Fort William Henry, 1179; the fall of Quebec, 1396.

Rouville, Hertel de, commands a war-party to attack Deerfield, 373–79; wounded, 381; commands an Indian war-party to attack New England towns, 400.

Rowe, Mass., 728.

Roy, Jacques, a Canadian, married Martha French, 395.

Roy, Mrs. Jacques (Martha French), 395.

Royal Americans, the, 1260, 1287, 1356; serve in the expedition of Forbes, 1287–1307; in Grant's expedition, 1299; at the siege of Quebec, 1355–57, 1395.

Royal Battery, the, 1341; at Louisbourg, 633.

"Royal William," the, 1414.

Royale, l'Isle, 919.

Ruggles, the battle at Lake George, 1055; his regiment, 1455.

Runaways from Canada, sheltered by Dongan, 98.

Rupert, Fort (Hudson's Bay), seized by Canadians, 102.

Russell, 1501.

Russia, influence of Peter the Great, 857; political outlook of, 1086, 1222–23, 1460, 1464; peace with Prussia and Sweden, 1469.

Rutland, 498.

Ryswick, peace of, 303, 324; the treaty of, 875.

S——, Miss Sylvia, 973.

Sabbath, the, observance of, 1014, 1048.

Sabrevois, Sieur de, a member of Rigaud's war-party, 733; mentioned, 1176.

Sackett's Harbor, former name of, 1121.

Saco, town of, rebuilt, 483.

Saco River, 360, 506.

Sacs and Foxes settle on the Mississippi, 564; in war against American frontiersmen, 564; a party of their chiefs at Boston, 564.

Sacs, the, a tribe of the "Far Indians," 345, 933, 1175–78; at Michigan, 519; aid Dubuisson at Detroit, 524.

Sadler, ——, of Deerfield, 741.

Sagean, Matthieu, romances mentioned, 570.

Saginaws, the, attacked the Outagamies, 555.

Saguina, an Ottawa chief, 523.

St. André River, named by Fabry de la Bruyère, 579.

Saint-Andrew, 1283.

Saint-Ange, 901.

Saint-Ange, Sieurs de (father and son), attack the Outagamies, 561; sent by Bourgmont to the village of the Kansas Indians, 574.

St. Antoine, Fort, built by Nicolas Perrot, 568 note.

St. Augustin, 1408, 1412, 1427, 1431.

Saint-Blin, 1221 note.

Saint-Castin, Baron Vincent de, on the Penobscot, 163, 277; attacks Fort Loyal, 168; at Castine, 244; his career, 248–50; plan to kidnap him, 259; at the attack on Pemaquid, 274; plan to attack Boston, 341 note; mentioned, 493.

Saint-Castin, (son of Baron de Saint-Castin), Abenaki chief, 362; brought to Boston, charged with rebellion, 493.

St. Castin's Fort, now Castine, 418.

St. Charles, Fort, built by La Vérendrye, 587.

St. Charles River, the, 1211, 1335, 1336, 1392, 1395, 1402, 1405, 1407, 1412, 1435, 1497; the French camp, 1341.

St. Christopher, Island, a contribution for, 403 note.

Saint Clair, Lieutenant-General, given command of British troops to capture Canada, 677.

St. Croix River, 478.

St.-Denis, Ruisseau, 1393.

Saint Florentine, Marquis de, 856.

St. Francis, a Jesuit mission settlement, 388, 480, 988, 1098, 1172, 1175, 1369, 1416; Jesuit influence, 1295; the Abenakis attacked by Rogers, 1369, 1371–74 note.

St. Francis River, the, 1372.

"St. François," brig, 923.

St. George, 1163, 1247, 1439.

St. George River, a dividing line, 477 note; the fort at, attacked, 497.

St. Germain, 854.

St. Helen, Island of, 1156, 1453.

Saint-Ignace, Mère Aimable Dubé de, 1501.

St. James, 865.

St. Jean, Isle, 912, 918, 919, 920, 1007, 1038, 1247, 1249.

St. Jean River, the, 923, 1010, 1018, 1038, 1039, 1249, 1459.

St. Joachim burned by order of Wolfe, 1376.

St. John, an English station in Newfoundland, 424; attacked by Subercase, 424.

St. John, city, 1135, 1403, 1448.

St. John, Fort, 861, 1152; abandoned by the French, 1448.

St. John Isle, 699.

St. John (Lord Bolingbroke), 444; scheme for attacking Canada, 445.

St. John River, 478.

Saint John's taken by the French, and retaken by the English, 1470–71.

St. Joseph, a fort built on the, by the French, 614.

St. Joseph River, 523, 562, 873.

Saint-Julien, Lieutenant-Colonel de, the defence of Louisbourg, 1235.

St.-Laurent, visit of Knox to the church of, 1340.

St. Lawrence, Gulf of, 872, 923, 929, 1250, 1251, 1459; islands in, ceded to Great Britain, 1472.

St. Lawrence River, the, 460, 844, 859, 860, 871, 889, 891, 930, 1093, 1152, 1201, 1250, 1313, 1315, 1316, 1317, 1320, 1328–31, 1368–71, 1448; rapids of, 1317, 1364, 1450; measures of defence taken during the siege of Quebec, 1335, 1336, 1338, 1341–44, 1348, 1395, 1406; danger in passing through the Traverse, 1338–40; steepness of the banks, 1354; action of the fleet of Holmes, 1387–92; expedition of Lévis, 1430; humanity rewarded, 1431–32; arrival of the "Lowestoffe," 1439; the river blockaded, 1443; islands ceded to Great Britain, 1472.

St. Louis, 345, 871, 1215.

Saint Louis (Saut de), mission village, 214, 225.

Saint Louis, Fort, on the Illinois, 70, 111.

St. Louis, Lake, 1450.

St. Louis, site of, 873.

St. Louis, the cross of the Order of, 1315, 1488.

St. Lucia, 1470, 1473.

St. Malo, 1218, 1228.

St. Michael, 1380.

St. Michael, name of the Canadian mission to the Sioux Indians, 582.

St. Nicolas, 1388.

Saint-Ours des Chaillons, 1179; commanded an Indian war-party, 400; in Ramesay's expedition, 698.

Saint-Ours, Madame de, 1156.

Saint-Ovide, Sieur de, attacks Fort William, Newfoundland, 424; quoted, 467; keeps his agents at work among the Acadians, 469.

St. Patrick's Day, 1147; at Fort Cumberland, 1320.

St. Paul, village sacked and burned, 1376.

St. Paul's Bay, 353.

St. Paul's Church, 1248, 1468.

St. Peter River, settlement of Le Sueur on the, 568.

St. Philippe, a French hamlet, 873.

Saint-Pierre, Legardeur de, 933, 942; abandons the Sioux mission, 583; undertakes the search for the Pacific, 603 and note; spends the winter at Fort La Reine, 604; visited by hostile Assinniboins, 604; returns to Quebec, 605; in Ramesay's expedition, 698; journey of exploration made by, 933–38; letter from Governor Dinwiddie introducing Washington, 934–36; his dealings with Washington, 936–37; leads the Indians in the expedition of Dieskau, 1049; his death, 1053.

St. Pierre, Fort, built at Rainy Lake, 586.

St. Pierre Island, given to France, 1472.

Saint-Poncy, an Acadian missionary, 469.

St. Roch, 1350, 1403, 1410, 1432.

St. Sacrement, Lac, name of, changed to Lake George, 1061.

St.-Servan, capture of, 1228.

Saint-Simon, quoted, 546.

Saint Sulpice, priests of, 32, 34, 35, 40, 391.

Saint-Vallier, bishop of Canada, 91; applauds Denonville, 128, 137; at Quebec, 181; during Phips's attack, 205; relations with Frontenac, 233, 236; excess of zeal, 237–38; returns to France, 240.

Saint-Vallier, M. de, 431 *note*.

Saint-Véran, Madame de, the mother of Montcalm, 1089; letters from her son quoted, 1090–91, 1098–99, 1153, 1155, 1273 *note*, 1308, 1314, 1316.

Saint-Vincent, Madame de, at Port Royal, 414.

St. Vincent, 1470, 1473.

St. Yotoc, 878.

Sainte Anna-de-la-Pérade, 1209.

Sainte-Claude, Mère de, 1423.

Sainte-Foy, 1407, 1421–42, 1457; Quebec after the siege, 1421–23; occupied by the English, 1426, 1431; expedition of Lévis against Quebec, 1431–42, 1502–03.

Sainte-Hélène, son of Le Moyne, 102, 155; in the attack on Schenectady, 156–57; in the defence of Quebec, 198–200; is killed, 202.

Sainte Marie, Fort, garrison at, 896.

Sainte-Thérèse, 1447.

Salem, Mass., 420.

Salmon Falls, attack on, 162, 167.

Saltonstall, ——, governor of Connecticut, 427.

Samos, post of, 1386, 1394, 1396.

Samuel, Captain, a chief of the Eastern Indians, 361.

Sander. See *Lauder*.

Santa Fé, a route explored from Louisiana to, 579 and *note*.

"Sapphire," one of Admiral Walker's war-ships, 453.

Saratoga, 429, 1108, 1117, 1152; the garrison withdrawn from the fort by Governor Clinton, 715; the fort at, burned by order of Governor Clinton, 715; attacked by Marin, 715 *note;* the fort burned, 963.

Sardanapalus, 1226.

Sardinia, 858.

Saul, George, commissary of supplies, 1036.

Saunders, Admiral, 1328; aids Wolfe in the reduction of Quebec, 1328, 1330 *note,* 1381, 1383–85, 1390, 1395; his fleet sails for England, 1414.

Saunderson, *History of Charlestown, N.H.,* cited, 720 *note.*

"Sauvage," the, ship, 1092.

Sauvolle, Sieur de, in charge of fort at Biloxi, near the Mississippi, 536.

Saxe, Marshal, 854, 968, 1057; his death, 852, 967.

Saxony, 852, 1222; joins the league against Prussia, 1087.

Saxony, Elector of, the, 852.

Scalp Point (Crown Point), the intention of the English to seize, 613.

Scarborough, Me., attacked by Indians, 365–66; rebuilt, 483.

Scarroyaddy, Indian chief, 985.

Schaticook, name given to eastern tributary of the Hudson, 732.

Schenectady, destruction of, 156–59; its effect in Canada, 171; on the Indians, 185; an intended attack upon, by Rigaud's war party, 732.

Schenectady, village of, 1065, 1066, 1201, 1256.

Schuyler, Abraham, induces the Five Nations to aid in the reduction of Canada, 428.

Schuyler, General Peter, 342, 345, 375, 1063, 1264, 1283; endeavors to keep alliance with the Five Nations, 343; sets the people of Newbury, &c., on guard against an Indian attack, 400; gets promise of peace from Indians, 403; enters into the scheme for the reduction of Canada, 428; goes to England with some Mohawk chiefs, 434; concerning a fort at Niagara, 611; stationed at Saratoga, 715; action between Bradstreet and Villiers, 1112–13.

Schuyler, John, attacks La Prairie, 188.

Schuyler, Peter, mayor of Albany, 148; leads an attack, his successful retreat, 211–14; in the Mohawk expedition, 227–28; convokes an Indian council,

287; carries the treaty of Ryswick to Quebec, 303.

Schuyler, Mrs., 1063; her affection for Lord Howe, 1259, 1264.

Schuyler, Pedrom, 1264.

Schuyler family, the, 867.

Schuyler's *Colonial New York,* cited, 715 *note.*

Scioto River, the, 883.

Scioto, town of, 878.

Scotch, the, in Pennsylvania, 866, 1077.

Scotland, 1229, 1322.

Scott, Lieutenant-Colonel George, 1014; the siege of Beauséjour, 1016–19; his gallant action, 1237.

Scott, Moses, a prisoner of war from Fort Massachusetts, 742.

Scurvy, 934, 1429, 1437.

Sedgwick, Major, captured Port Royal, 439.

Ségur, Count, quotation from, 856.

Seignelay, son of Colbert, colonial minister, 53, 80; advices to Denonville, 128.

Seminary, the, at Quebec, burned, 391 *note.*

Seneca, Lake, 882.

Senecas, 875; the most powerful of the Iroquois, 62, 63; prepare for hostilities, 77; pass for cowards, 79; their fortifications, 89; attack the Illinois, 92; intrigue with the Hurons, 92; Denonville plans to attack them, 95, 104; his campaign, 114–19; they threaten Fort Niagara, 125; visited by Bienville, 875; efforts of the French to convert, 889, 893, 961; their alliances, 1294.

Senegal, 1228, 1469, 1473.

Senezergues, mortally wounded, 1405.

Serier, Captain, mentioned, 682 *note.*

Seven Years War, the, 477, 844, 1222, 1472–74, 1475; deportment of British officers, 1278.

Seventy-eighth Regiment, the, at Quebec, 1401 *note.*

Sewall, Judge Samuel, diary quoted, 361 *note,* 402 *note,* 484 and *note;* his feeling toward Governor Dudley, 406; oath administered by, at coun-

cil of Indians, 485; his speech before the Councillors, 495.

Sewell, Colonel Matthew, 1057; letter to Holdernesse quoted, 1057–58.

Seymour, 450.

Shannon, Richard Viscount, commissioned to attack Quebec, 435 and *note.*

Sharpe, Governor of Maryland, 975, 983; council of governors held with Braddock, 974–77.

Shawanoes, the, 872, 876, 878, 884, 933, 988, 1111; their attitude towards the English, 885, 984, 1070, 1080, 1299; present at a convention of Indians, 1293–94.

Shebbeare, Dr., 980 *note.*

Sheldon, Ensign John, the house of, at Deerfield, defensible against Indians, 375; the attack upon his house by Indians, 378; the door of his house preserved, 381 and *note;* sent by Governor Dudley to ransom the Deerfield captives, 393; makes a second journey to Canada for release of prisoners, 394; a third visit, 395; a paper on, by Alice C. Baker, 395 *note.*

Sheldon, George, of Deerfield, 376 *note,* 381 *note,* 383 *note,* 395 *note.*

Sheldon, Hannah, wife of John, Jr., 379; a prisoner in Canada, 393; ransomed, 393.

Sheldon, John, Jr., 379.

Sheldon, Mary, captured by Indians, 379.

Sheldon, Mercy, killed by Indians, 379.

Sheldon, Mrs. John, killed by Indians, 378.

Sheldon's *Early History of Michigan,* cited, 354 *note.*

Shepherd, Captain, his capture and escape, 1139.

Sheppard, Jack, 848.

Sherbrooke, 1374 *note.*

Sherburn, Captain Joseph, placed in charge of a battery at siege of Louisbourg, 648; extracts from his diary concerning the siege, 649; receives a flag of truce from Duchambon, 663.

Sherburn, Henry, commissary of New Hampshire regiment, 627.

Shingas, Indian chief, 1295.

Ship-building, 894.

Ship, sign of the, a tavern, 1001.

Shippensburg, 1289–90, 1293.

"Shirley," a war-ship in Pepperrell's squadron, 631, 658; Massachusetts frigate sent to reinforce Annapolis, 685.

Shirley, Captain John, son of Governor Shirley, 1068; extracts from his letter to Governor Morris, 1066–67; a victim of the war, 1067 *note;* his popularity, 1067 *note.*

Shirley, Fort, 1132; built to protect settlements in the Berkshire valley, 728.

Shirley, Mrs., arrived at Louisbourg, 673.

Shirley, William, Governor of Massachusetts, mentioned, 617, 928, 959; advised to attack Louisbourg, 619 and *note;* made governor of Massachusetts, 620; proposes to the General Court an attack upon Louisbourg, 621; his disappointment at their vote, 621; at last prevails with the court, 622; induces Governor Wentworth to assist in the attack upon Louisbourg, 623; writes to the Duke of Newcastle concerning the siege of Louisbourg, 633; has directions for the attack upon Louisbourg, 633–34 and *note;* used his influence to obtain compensation to Massachusetts for the siege of Louisbourg, 671 *note;* arrived at Louisbourg and quieted the discontented soldiers, 673; urges upon the Duke of Newcastle the conquest of Canada, 675–76; does not receive the promised troops from England, 678; designs an attack against Crown Point, 679; urges upon the Duke of Newcastle the protection of Acadia, 688; sends militia, &c., to protect it, 689; proposes the removal of the Acadians, 692; his plan concerning them, 693 and *note,* 694; proposed to exclude French priests from Acadia, 694 and *note;* correspondence with the Duke of Newcastle concerning the Acadians, quoted, 694 *note,* 695–

96; sends troops to the defence of Acadia, 696–97; sends Massachusetts troops to occupy Grand Pré, 709; quoted concerning the condition of the Acadians, 711; tries to repel the French invasions, 940, 960–61, 975, 1006; his dealings with the Assembly of Massachusetts, 959, 1010–11, 1041 *note;* council held with Braddock, 975–77; his French wife, 975; defends taxation by Parliament, 976; his troops, 976, 1014, 1064, 1068, 1456; the decisions of the council at Alexandria, 976–77; leads the expedition against Niagara and Fort Frontenac, 976–77, 1063–70, 1099, 1283; desires Mackellar to draw plans for Braddock's expedition, 996 *note;* becomes commander-in-chief of the troops in America, 1004, 1013, 1069; his view of Dunbar's conduct, 1004 *note;* his plans with regard to expelling the French from Nova Scotia, 1006, 1009–11, 1013–14, 1021; his correspondence with Governor Lawrence quoted, 1009; the expedition sent against Crown Point, 1041–62; his campaigns boldly planned, 1063; border warfare, 1063–84; at Fort Oswego, 1066–68; loss of his sons, 1066–67 and *note;* councils of war called, 1067–68; the Niagara expedition abandoned, 1068; his quarrels with Johnson and with Delancey, 1069–70; letters from Governor Morris quoted, 1077, 1079; plans for a new campaign, 1104–05, 1112; renews his expedition against Niagara, and Frontenac, 1104–05, 1111–12; recalled from command, 1105, 1116, 1117; a cabal formed against, 1105; his zeal and courage, 1106, 1117; his boatmen placed under Bradstreet, 1112; sends men to defend Oswego, 1112–15, 1125 *note;* interview with Loudon, 1116; Oswego seized by the French, 1121–27; vindicates himself, 1125 *note,* 1130 and *note;* causes leading to his failure, 1128–29; Loudon prejudiced against, 1130, 1162; sails for England, 1130; the opinion of Franklin concerning, 1130; made governor of the Bahamas, 1131; succeeded by Governor Pownall, 1255.

Shirley, William, son of the governor, secretary of Braddock, 972, 975; letter quoted concerning Braddock's expedition, 983–84; shot through the head, 995, 1002, 1066; letter to Governor Morris quoted, 1066.

Shirreff, William, proposal to remove the Acadians, 692.

Short, Richard, drawings of Quebec after the siege, 1421 note.

Shrewsbury, Duke of, presents Mohawks to Queen Anne, 434.

Shubenacadie, a missionary station, 698.

Shubenacadie River, 700, 922.

Shute, Governor Samuel, succeeds Dudley as governor, 485; called a council of Eastern Indians at Georgetown, 485; his speech at council of Indians, 485; the Indians renew their treaty with him, 487; declares war against the Abenakis, 494; hampered by the Government in making conciliation with the Indians, 494; returns to England, 495.

Shute, John, 1146.

Sibley, John Langdon, cited, 642 note.

Silesia, 858, 1086, 1223, 1461; seized by Frederic of Prussia, 616.

Silhouette, 929.

Sillery, 1345, 1385, 1386, 1394, 1424, 1432, 1434, 1503.

Simons, Benjamin, a wounded prisoner from Fort Massachusetts, 742.

Sinclair, Sir John, quartermaster-general, 981, 1287, 1291; in Braddock's expedition, 992; wounded in the battle of the Monongahela, 995, 1000; despatch sent from General Forbes, 1289–91; his peculiarities, 1291; his dealings with Lieutenant-Colonel Stephen, 1291.

Sioux Indians, a tribe of the "Far Indians," 345; La Sueur opens trade with, 568–69; a company formed in Canada to establish a mission among, 581–82.

Sioux mission, the, sent from Canada, 582; the company establish themselves at Lake Pepin, 582; name their mission St. Michael, 582; name their fort Fort Beauharnois, 582; the mission a failure, 583.

"Siren," the, 1014.

"Sirène," the, ship, 1092.

Six Nations, the, 884; desire to remain neutral, 1110. See *Five Nations*.

Skene Mountain, near Whitehall, 733.

Slade, Dr. D. D., mentioned, 737 *note*.

Small-pox, the, 901.

Smead, Captivity, child of John Smead, 742.

Smead, John, a prisoner of war on the march from Fort Massachusetts, 742; killed by Indians, 744.

Smead, Mrs. John, has a child born while on the march from Fort Massachusetts, 742; death of, 744.

Smibert, ——, his portrait of William Pepperrell, 625.

Smith, Colonel James, 990; cruelties practised by the Indians upon, 989; his statement concerning the defeat of Braddock's army, 997–98.

Smith, *History of New York*, cited, 434 *note*, 715 *note*.

Smith, John, 1001.

Smith, William, a Rhode Island soldier, his bravery, 1270.

Smith, William, his remark concerning the provincial army, 1045.

Smollett, 848, 952, 965.

Smollett, cited, 619 *note*, 745.

Smyth, an English traveller, 956 *note*.

Snake Indians of the West, 591; attack the tribe of Horse Indians, 595; a march of Horse Indians against them, 595–97; they flee before the enemy, 598.

Snelling, *Tales of the Northwest*, 563 *note*.

Snow, E. A., 605 *note*.

Sodus Bay, 894.

Soissons, Le Comte de, 756.

Sokokis Indians, living on the Saco River, 506.

Sorel, town of, 388, 1446.

Soubise, 852.

South Bay, 1048, 1050, 1051, 1059, 1108, 1140, 1182, 1279, 1363.

South Carolina, 867, 947, 964; commissioners sent to meet the Indians at Albany, 887; extent of British frontier, 1457.

Southack, Captain, defends Major March against the Indians at Casco, 366.

Spafford, John, Jr., one of the settlers of Number Four, on the Connecticut, 721; on committee for the protection of the settlement, 721.

Spain, 852, 858, 1229, 1466; the power gained by Great Britain over, 339; bent on claiming the Mississippi, etc., 535; succession of Carlos III., 1466; the Family Compact, 1466; change of rulers, 1466, 1468; influence of Pitt, 1469; expedition of Pococke, 1470; receives Havana from England, 1472; the peace of Paris, 1472–74; acquisitions in America, 1473, 1478; sinking into decay, 1477.

Spaniards, the, of Mexico, jealous of French designs, 571; attempt to attack the French at the Illinois, 574; the Mandans' description of, 588–89, 590.

Spanish Succession, War of, caused by Louis XIV., 339.

Sparhawk, Nathaniel, son-in-law of Pepperrell, 652; desires some plunder from Louisbourg, 666.

Sparks's American Biography cited, 488 *note.*

Speakman, Captain, despatches sent to Winslow, 1034.

Spikeman, Captain, one of Rogers' scouting-party, 1144; adventures of the expedition, 1144–46.

Spithead, embarkation of Wolfe, 1328.

Split, Cape, 1028.

Spruce-beer, 1022, 1360, 1439.

Spurwink, Me., Indian attack upon, 365.

"Squirrel," frigate, 485.

Stanhope, Earl, 1330 *note.*

Stanley, Dean, 1494.

Stanley, his sketch of the Duc de Choiseul, 1465; at Versailles, 1465.

Stanwix, Brigadier, new fort to be erected at the Great Carrying Place, 1285; builds Fort Pitt, 1305; to relieve Pittsburg, 1359; Pittsburg endangered, 1365.

Stanwix, Fort, 1363.

Stark, John, 1138, 1147; his celebrity, 1045; in the expedition against Crown Point, 1045; adventures in a scouting-party of Rogers, 1144–46; wounded, 1151 *note;* serves under Abercromby, 1261.

Stebbins, Abigail, mentioned, 395 *note;* married Jacques de Noyon, 395.

Stebbins, Benoni, sergeant in militia at Deerfield, 374; the Indians attack his house, 378; killed, 378.

Steele, 434.

Stella, 456.

Stephen, Lieutenant Adam, matters pertaining to Washington and Jumonville, 947 *note,* 1484; trouble with Sir J. Sinclair, 1291; sent to succor Rogers, 1373; expelled from the service, 1373.

Sterne, 848.

Stevens, B. F., mentioned, 727 *note.*

Stevens, Phineas, a settler of Number Four on the Connecticut, 721; his ingenious defences of Number Four from the Indian attack, 724; refuses to surrender to Niverville, and compels his departure, 724–25; his gallant conduct recognized by Commodore Charles Knowles, 727.

Stevens, the Indian interpreter, 1043; escapes from Quebec, 1387.

Stewart, Captain, 996.

Still, Isaac, 1299,

Stillwater, 1108, 1152.

Stirling, 1322.

Stobo, Major Robert, 952; detained at Quebec as a hostage, 1387; his escape, 1387; gives Wolfe the result of his knowledge of Quebec, 1387; his memoirs, 1387 *note.*

Stockbridge, 1372–73.

Stoddard, ——, escaped from Deerfield, 378.

Stoddard, John, superintendent of defence, etc., of Western Massachusetts, 721; charged with construction of forts in Berkshire valley, 729.

Stone, *Life and Times of Sir William Johnson,* 715 *note,* 739 *note.*

Stone, William L., 1061 *note,* 1360 *note.*

Storer, John, major in the Maine militia, 630.

Storer, Joseph, his house at Wells a garrison against Indians, 362.

Storer, Mary, carried off prisoner by Indians, 365.

Strait of Canso, 460.

Stuarts, the, 847, 1229, 1464.

Stuckley, Captain, of British frigate "Deptford," 423.

Subercase, a French officer, proposes to attack the Iroquois, but is overruled, 133–34; in the Onondaga expedition, 296.

Subercase, Governor, quoted concerning the attack on Haverhill, 404 *note,* 411; quoted concerning affairs at Port Royal, 413; offers the capitulation of Port Royal to General Nicholson, 438; quoted, 439 *note.*

"Success," the, 1014.

Suffield, 1118.

Sugar-trade, the, 1471.

Sulpitian priests, the, 871, 880, 890, 1156, 1295.

Sulte, M. Benjamin, cited, 584 *note.*

Sunderland, Earl of, cited, 427 *note.*

"Superbe," a war-ship of Commodore Warren, 632.

Superior, Lake, 580, 584, 585, 896, 1098, 1175.

Susquehanna River, the, 1079, 1111, 1294.

"Sutherland," the, 1351, 1388, 1391.

Swanzey (Lower Ashuelot) a settlement in New Hampshire, 718 *note.*

Sweden joins the league against Prussia, 1087; the Seven Years War, 1222; peace with Prussia, 1469.

Swedes in Pennsylvania, 866.

Swift, ——, quoted concerning the failure of Walker's expedition, 456.

Sydney, 1249.

Sydney, the fleet of Admiral Walker at, 453.

Symmes, Rev. Thomas, preached a sermon on the fate of Lovewell and his men, 514 *note.*

Taconic Falls, Maine, 498.

Tadoussac, 931 *note.*

Taensas, a tribe of sun-worshippers, 538.

Tailor, Colonel, sent with summons for the surrender of Port Royal, 438.

Talon du Boulay, Angélique Louise, 1089.

Talon, the intendant, 23; declines to attend meeting of the estates, 26; returns to France, 27; hostile to Frontenac at the court, 39.

Tantemar, 927, 1011, 1019, 1320.

Tarbell, John, captured, and becomes Indian chief, 398 *note.*

Tarbell, Zechariah, captured, and becomes Indian chief, 398 *note.*

"Tartar," a war-sloop fitted out by Rhode Island, 624, 631.

Tassé, citation from, 890 *note.*

Tatmagouche, village of, 699.

Tatten, Captain, 1001.

Taunton, Mass., 420.

Taxation, 961, 976, 1075–76, 1080–82, 1464, 1471, 1478.

Teedyuscung, Indian chief, 1294.

Temple and Sheldon, *History of Northfield* cited, 729 *note.*

Temple, Lord, 1330 *note,* 1467.

Tennessee River, the French propose to build forts at, 610.

Thames River, the, 1339.

Thaxter, Colonel Samuel, sent as ambassador to Vaudreuil, 503; has an interview with the Indians, 503–04.

The Boston Post Boy cited, 708 *note.*

"The Illinois," a settlement on the Mississippi, 552; settled by Canadians, etc., 553; the mixed marriages at, 553; annexed to Louisiana, 553.

The Importance and Advantage of Cape Breton quoted, 645 *note.*

Theatricals at Quebec, 234–36, 241.

Thierry, Captain of the Royal Battery at Louisbourg, 643.

Thirty-fifth Regiment, the, 1401 *note.*

Thomas, Surgeon John, his diary quoted, 1017.

Thomassy, *Géologie,* etc., cited, 571 *note.*

Thompson, James, 1437; diary of, 1499.

Thousand Islands, the, 891, 1449.

Three Rivers, 583, 731, 1175, 1210, 1378, 1410, 1430, 1443, 1445; census of, 1317.

Thury, the priest, 166, 260; persuades Taxous, 262, 265; instigates hostilities, 271.

Ticonderoga, 1084, 1152, 1197, 1207 *note,* 1253, 1266–67, 1278, 1307, 1309, 1343, 1396; advance of Dieskau, 1049–50; occupied by the French, 1059–60; attempt against, 1099; camp at, 1099; held by the French, 1099, 1101, 1109–10, 1126, 1145; its importance and position, 1102, 1135, 1168, 1265; plans of the English to capture, 1104–5, 1008–11, 1116, 1120, 1149; war-parties sent out from, 1136–37; exploits of Rogers' rangers, 1139–41, 1144–47, 1203–07; a small party left in charge, 1142; preparations to attack Fort William Henry, 1168; held by Montcalm's forces, 1178; expedition against, led by General Abercromby, 1256–74 *note;* the battle and Montcalm's victory, 1268–74 *note,* 1284, 1308, 1492–96; war-parties sent from, by the French, 1279–82; Putnam carried to, 1283; question of renewing the attack upon, by the English, 1285, 1332; Bourlamaque established at, 1331; approach of Amherst, 1342, 1350; captured by the English, 1359–62; blown up by the French, 1362, 1378; the legend of Inverawe, 1494–96.

Ticonderoga, Fort, 732–33.

Titcomb, Colonel Moses, his service at Louisbourg, 1044; the battle at Lake George, 1055.

Titcomb's battery at Louisbourg, 647.

Tiverton, R.I., 417.

Tobacco, 865, 867.

Tobago Island, to belong to England, 1473.

Tomahawk Camp, 1306.

Tongue Mountain, 1179.

Tonty at Fort St. Louis, 111; at Fort Niagara, 112; in the fight with the Senecas, 114.

Tonty, Alphonse de, accompanies Cadillac to Detroit, 355.

Tonty, Henri de, brother of Alphonse, 355; in the fur-trade at Fort St. Louis, 519; a letter written by him found among the Indians, 536 and *note.*

Topsfield, Mass., 420.

Tories, the, 847, 1463, 1468; eager for peace with France, 458.

Toronto, 99, 901; a trading-post established at, 613; trading-house at, 892–93, 894.

Toronto, Fort, 892; plan of capture by the English, 1104.

Torture practised by Indians, 135, 219, 297; instigated by the French, 152–53, 291.

Toulon, 1229, 1230.

Toulouse, Comte de, interested in the discovery of the Pacific, 581.

Touraine, 897.

Tourmente, Cape, 1338, 1339, 1376.

Tournois, Father, his illegal trade, 889 and *note.*

Townshend, Captain, his efforts to assist the German settlement, 1201; his death, 1361.

Townshend, Charles, secretary of war, 849, 1464.

Townshend, George, his character, 1329; serves under Wolfe at the siege of Quebec, 1328, 1346, 1380, 1385, 1395, 1398, 1400–01 *note,* 1412; succeeds Monckton in command, 1405; note sent from the dying Montcalm, 1408; the terms of capitulation for Quebec, 1413; returns to England, 1414.

Tracy, Lieutenant, 1281.

Trading-posts, 862, 893, 904, 975; a chain of, established by the French from Canada to Louisiana, 615; at Will's Creek, 885, 935, 941, 982.

Treaty of Casco, between the Abenaki Indians and Governor Dudley, 360–61.

Treaty of Utrecht, 608; the conditions of, 458–60.

Trent, William, 874; at Pickawillany, 903 *note;* in Washington's expedition to the West, 939; his band of backwoodsmen, 941, 943; sufferings of the people, 1079.

Trepezec, 1261, 1262.

"Trident," French war-ship, 682.

Trinity Bay, Newfoundland, 424.

Troupes de terre, 1095–96.

Trout Brook, 1204, 1261–62.

Troyes, Chevalier de, 102; at Fort Niagara, 118.

Truro, 909.

Tucker, Sergeant, wounded by Indians after a wedding-feast, 370.

Tufts, William, his exploit at Louisbourg, 642, 656 *note.*

Tulpehocken, settlement destroyed by the Indians, 1082.

Turenne, 852.

Turkey Creek, 1304.

Turner, ——, a militia officer at Haverhill, 401.

Turner, Lieutenant, 1372; attacked by the French, 1373.

Turner, *Reports upon Indian Tribes* cited, 577 *note.*

Turpin, Dick, 848.

Turtle Creek, 987.

Turtle, the, clan of, 1167.

Tuscaroras Indians joined to the Five Nations, 518, 888.

Twenty-eighth Regiment, the, 1401 *note.*

Two Mountains, Lake of the, 949, 1166, 1167, 1175,

Two Mountains, the, 1098; mission at, 562, 889 *note;* ceremony in the Mission Church of, 1167 *note.*

Tyburn, 848.

Tyng, Captain, captures and scalps several Indians, 369, 373 *note.*

Tyng, Captain Edward, chosen naval commander by Shirley, 631.

Tyng, Colonel, sent to aid the wounded in Lovewell's fight, 513.

Tyrrell, name applied to Thomas Pichon, 1012 *note.*

Ulster, 866.

United States, the, 877, 976; her growth and opportunities, 845, 1475, 1477, 1478–79.

Upton, Mrs., 973.

Ursuline Convent at Quebec, 29, 1409; during the attack, 204–05.

Ursulines, the, 1038, 1341, 1350, 1409;

1501; at the General Hospital, 1379; matters pertaining to the burial of Montcalm, 1414, 1501.

Usher, Robert, killed in the fight at Lovewell's Pond, 511.

Utrecht, the treaty of, 875, 899, 906–07, 910, 928–31, 1007–08.

Vaillant, ——, Jesuit, an agent among the Five Nations, 344.

Vaillant, the Jesuit, negotiates with Dongan, 123.

Vallière, Sieur de la, attempts to burn Pepperrell's storehouses near Louisbourg, 659.

Valrenne destroys Fort Frontenac, 144; sent to defend La Prairie, 212–14.

Valterie, Sieur de la, arrives at Quebec with accounts of the wreck of Walker's fleet, 455; a member of Rigaud's war-party, 733.

Valtry, M. de, 895.

Van Renselaer, 867.

Vanbraam, 937; interpreter for Washington, 935, 952; matters pertaining to the alleged assassination of Jumonville, 952, 1484–85.

"Vanguard," the, 1440.

Vannes, the siege at Beauséjour, 1016, 1017.

Vantadour, Le Duc de, 756.

Varennes, de la Vérendrye, Pierre Gaultier, his action at battle of Malplaquet, 583–84.

Varennes, René Gaultier de, governor of Three Rivers, 583; marriage of, 583.

Varin, Madame, 1155, 1489.

Varin, naval commissary, 1210; number of French in the fight at Great Meadows, 953 *note;* official knavery, 1216, 1459.

Vaudreuil, Cavagnal Pierre Rigaud de, French governor in Quebec, 361; instigated some Indian attacks, 367; sends a war-party to attack Deerfield, Mass., 373 and *note;* quoted, 381, 383, 403 *note;* ransoms Rev. John Williams from the Indians, 389; terms for the ransom of prisoners, 393;

bought Stephen Williams from Indians, 394; organizes a war-party of French and Indians, 400; quoted on losses at Haverhill, 402; quoted, 403 *note;* his terms of a neutrality with the colonies, 405; sends troops to surprise Colonel Nicholson advancing on Canada, 430; notified of English expedition against Canada, 454; lends aid to Rale in rousing the Indians to insurrection, 490; allows a pension to Rale, 492; pleased with the attack on Georgetown, 492; correspondence with Governor Dummer on the death of Rale, 502; receives an embassy from Governor Dummer, 503; determined to destroy the Outagamies, 555; gains the consent of the Five Nations to build a fort at Niagara, 611.

Vaudreuil, Chevalier de, in the Seneca campaign, 115; in the defence against the Iroquois, 127, 134; in the attack of the Onondagas, 295, 297.

Vaudreuil, Madame de, joins in the quarrel of her husband with Montcalm, 1310.

Vaudreuil, Philippe de, early governor of Canada, 1094.

Vaudreuil, Pierre François Rigaud, Marquis de, governor of New France, 968, 1043; his estimate concerning the population of Canada, 859 *note;* his friendship for Vergor, 1019, 1387; his relations with Montcalm, 1094–95, 1101, 1154, 1158–62, 1198, 1201–03, 1220, 1308–11, 1314, 1315, 1318, 1319 *note,* 1337, 1397, 1403, 1413–17; his traits of character, and his double-dealing, 1094–95, 1101, 1109 *note,* 1155, 1158–63, 1201, 1210–17, 1301 *note,* 1310, 1312–14, 1332–35, 1374 *note,* 1407, 1415, 1417, 1454; life at Montreal, 1094, 1154, 1201–03, 1208–11, 1429; his plans for defence, 1099, 1100; induces the Indians to fight against the English, 1112, 1141, 1161, 1199, 1200, 1377; party sent to cut off the supplies from Oswego, 1112; at Fort Frontenac, 1121; the French victorious at Oswego, 1125; despatches sent to Versailles, 1134–35; war-party sent to reduce Fort William Henry, 1148–51; his choice of Rigaud for commander, 1156; detractions made in regard to the French regulars, 1159–60; calls for troops, 1162; the attack on Fort William Henry planned, 1165, 1194 *note* (see *William Henry, Fort*); animus of Loudon towards, 1197; the affair at German Flats, 1200–01; his relations with Bigot, 1208, 1417; his official corruption, 1210–17, 1312, 1415; receives ministerial rebukes, 1217–20; his plans in regard to Ticonderoga, 1256–57, 1308–09; extracts from his letters to the colonial minister, 1293, 1313–15; provides for the defence of Fort Duquesne, 1293; letters blaming Montcalm, 1308–09, 1314; the loyalty of the Canadians, 1311; appeal made at court, for aid for Canada, 1312–14; receives the grand cross of the Order of St. Louis, 1315; a census of Canada made, 1317; ordered to defer to Montcalm, 1318; circular letter issued by, 1331; the siege and reduction of Quebec, 1331–57, 1375–1419, 1419–20 *note,* 1497–98; measures taken by, in the defence of Quebec, 1333–37, 1339, 1341, 1347, 1350, 1378–79, 1385–86, 1393, 1396–97, 1403, 1404; his friendship for Cadet, 1333, 1417; tries to burn the English fleet, 1342–43, 1353; proclamations of Wolfe, 1344, 1350, 1352, 1376, 1377; councils of war held, 1347, 1406; his delight over the English disaster at Montmorenci, 1357; the siege of Niagara by the English, 1359, 1364–68; his orders to Bourlamaque, 1361; the final battle and the death of Montcalm, 1397–1400, 1408–09; the question of capitulation discussed at Quebec, 1404–07; orders a retreat, 1407; his flight, 1408–09; summons Lévis to his assistance, 1410; steps taken to repair his errors, 1410–12; Quebec surrenders, 1412–13; defames Ramesay, 1414; his correspondence, 1417, 1419 *note,* 1498; his hope of retaking Quebec through the expedition of Lévis, 1430–42; his spirit, and chances of success, 1443–44, 1447–48, 1454; his proclamation to the Canadians, 1447; orders given to Bougainville, 1448; the English encamp near Montreal, 1451; the articles of capitulation for Montreal drawn up and signed, 1451–52; repairs to France, 1453, 1459; reproved for his action at Montreal, 1453; imprisoned and tried, 1459; acquitted, 1460; matters relating to Dumas and Ligneris, 1485–86.

Vaudreuil, Rigaud de. (See *Rigaud de Vandreuil*.)

Vaughan, William, his character portrayed, 619–20; of Damariscotta, advised the siege of Louisbourg, 619–20; attacks the Grand Battery at Louisbourg, 641; reinforced by Lieutenant-Colonel Bradstreet, 642; announces the taking of the Grand Battery to Pepperrell, 642; proposes to attack the Island Battery, 654–55.

Vauquelin, his bravery at Louisbourg, 1239, 1430; attacked by the English, 1440.

Vauvert, 1094.

Venango, 935, 937, 1132, 1305–06, 1365; the fort burned, 1367.

Vendôme, 852.

Vera Cruz, 536.

Verazan, Jean, 748.

Verchères, M. de, 895.

Verchères, the heroine of, 220–24.

Verelst, Dutch artist, paints the portraits of Mohawk chiefs, 434.

Vergor, Duchambon de, commandant at Beauséjour, 1009–11; letter from Bigot advising official corruption, 1011; sustains Le Loutre, 1011–13; the siege of Beauséjour, 1013–19; capitulation of the fort, 1017; tried and acquitted, 1019, 1387; his command on the Heights of Abraham, 1386–87; chances of success for Wolfe in his last venture, 1387, 1391–92; shot in the heel, 1393.

Vermont, 1044; new road made across, 1363.

Vernet, 853.

Verrazzano, mentioned, 608.

Verreau, Abbé H., 1221 *note*, 1420 *note*.

Versailles, 13, 138, 853, 899, 900, 904, 910, 914, 921, 967, 968, 1019, 1091, 1166, 1217, 1439, 1465; corruption at court, 1226; arrival of the envoys from Canada, 1314.

Verte, Baye, 1018–20.

Vetch, Captain Samuel, goes to Canada to negotiate for release of prisoners, 394, 405; suspected of illicit trade, 405, 408; mentioned, 421; his antecedents, 425; his marriage, 426; his scheme for the reduction of Canada, etc., 426; sails to England for aid, 426; perfects his plans in Boston and New York, 427; awaits at Boston the arrival of the English squadron, 432; his disappointment at the non-arrival, 432; made adjutant-general of a new enterprise, 434; a dinner at the Green Dragon Tavern, 436; lands at Port Royal, 437; takes command as governor of Annapolis Royal, 439; commands in Walker's expedition against Canada, 449; his escape from shipwreck, 451; offers to pilot the fleet, 453; expresses his mind at the retreat of Walker, 453; his neglected condition at Annapolis, 463 and *note*.

Vetch, William, death of, 426.

Vicars, Captain John, 1100 *note*, 1115 *note*; at Albany, 1114.

Viele, his mission to Onondaga, 74, 78.

Viger, Hon. D. B., 1498.

Viger, Jacques, 1480.

"Vigilant," a French ship-of-war taken by the English in Louisbourg harbor, 658.

Villars, 852.

Villebon, governor of Acadia, 251, 272.

Villejoin, 1156.

Villemont, assists in attack on Grand Pré, 702.

Villeray, a tool of the Jesuits, 44; at Quebec, 181; his negotiations with Frontenac, 183.

Villeray, commandant at Fort Gaspereau, 1018; surrenders to the English, 1018; brought to trial, 1019.

Villiers, Coulon de, mentioned, 561; attacked the Outagamies, 561; at Fort Necessity, 698; commands the Ramesay expedition, 699; receives aid from the priests Maillard and Girard, 700; receives information concerning his attack on Grand Pré, 702; makes the attack on Grand Pré and is wounded, 703; the number of his troops in the attack upon Grand Pré, 707; sent to Fort Duquesne, 948–49; the fight at Great Meadows, 948–54, 1484–85; the fight with Bradstreet's boatmen, 1112–13; condition of his camp, 1118; encamped at Niaouré Bay, 1121; taken prisoner, 1367.

Villieu, commands the Indian allies, 261; nearly perishes in the Penobscot, 262; attacks Oyster River, 263; returns to Quebec, 265; takes Pemaquid, 274; is captured, 277.

Villieu, M. de, accuses the ecclesiastics of illicit trade, 415.

Vincennes, 901.

Vincennes, on the Wabash River, 614.

Vincennes, Sieur de, arrived at Detroit to aid Dubuisson, 523; follows up an attack upon the Outagamies, 531.

Vincent, Earl St., 1391.

Virginia, 342, 891, 892, 941, 955, 968, 1104, 1132; contributes men to capture Canada, 677; manners, customs, and other matters of interest, pertaining to, 864–68, 874, 886, 903, 956 note, 957, 980, 1211; questions of boundary, 871, 881, 886, 963; unpopularity of Lord Albemarle, 937–38; the settlers need protection from the Indians, 939–40, 1071–75, 1079, 1094, 1103, 1131, 1286; meeting of the Assembly with Dinwiddie, 956–57; enlistments in and preparations for Braddock's campaign, 980, 983; disposal of the Acadians, 1039; fears of a slave insurrection, 1071; condition of its forts, 1131–32, 1131 note; roads to Ohio, 1287. See Assembly of Virginia.

Virginia regiment, the, commanded by George Washington, 935, 941, 947; distress of their marches, and difficulties of the service, 948, 950–53, 955, 993–94; the troops praised by Braddock and by Washington, 999, 1002.

Virginians, the, their service in the army, and merited commendation, 948, 952, 983, 999, 1002, 1287, 1291, 1300, 1305.

Vitré, Denis de, pilots the English fleet, 1338.

Voltaire, 843, 856, 860; letter from Frederic II., 1461.

Voyageurs, 859 note.

Wabash River, the, 873, 883, 901.

Waggoner, Captain, 994, 1071.

Wainwright, Colonel Francis, a commander in the expedition to Port Royal, 420.

Waldo, Brigadier, sent to occupy the Grand Battery at siege of Louisbourg, 643; to Shirley, cited, 643 note; quoted, 655; mentioned, 671 note.

Waldron at Cocheco, 165.

Waldron, Mrs. Adelaide Cilley, 626 note.

Walker, Sir Hovenden, admiral of the Canada expedition from England, 445; his reception in Boston, 446; preparations in Boston to join his expedition, 447; quoted concerning deserters, 448; he sails from Boston, 448; quotations from his journal, 449; his fleet barely escapes shipwreck, 450; the loss of his fleet by wreck, 451, 1337; anxious for retreat, 452; holds a council of war, 452; sails for Spanish River, 453; wild reports at Quebec concerning the wreck of his fleet, 455; sails for England, 456; holds council of war concerning Placentia, 456; emigrated to South Carolina, thence to Barbadoes, where he died, 457; his journal, 457 note.

Wallace, town of, Acadia, 699.

Walley, John, in command under Phips at Quebec, 180; commands the land attack, 198; in camp, 201–02; retreat, 203.

Walpole, Horace, 848; his opinion of Edward Cornwallis, 909, 920; remark and anecdote concerning the Duke of Newcastle, 965; observation concerning Mirepoix, 967; sketch of General Braddock, 973, 974, 981; remark concerning George Townshend, 1329; letters concerning Wolfe and Quebec, 1418, 1441; recounts the death of George II., 1463; his writing concerning Pitt, 1473.

Walton, Colonel, called to account by the Massachusetts Assembly, 495.

Wanton, governor of Rhode Island, 624 note, 627 note, 630 note.

War-parties sent from Montreal in 1746, 719.

War-songs, 1166, 1167, 1172.

Ward, Ensign, attacked by the French, and surrenders, 942.

Warde, George, 1327.

Warren, Mrs., arrived at Louisbourg, 673.

Warren, Sir Peter, Admiral, 1042; at Antigua, invited to aid in the siege of Louisbourg, 632; ordered to the protection of Acadia by the Duke of Newcastle, 632; joins the expedition against Louisbourg, 632, 638; quoted, 647; impatient for attack, 655; his desire to secure humane treatment to captives, 659; his plan for the immediate taking of Louisbourg, 661; agrees with Pepperrell upon a mode of attack, 662; together with Pepperrell agrees upon terms of capitulation from Louisbourg, 664; his proposed "ball" at Louisbourg, 665; the French prizes taken by his squadron, 667; jealousies of his squadron and the army of Pepperrell, 667–68; his speech to the New England soldiers, 668 note; compared with Pepperrell, 669; made an admiral, 670; remains with Pepperrell in charge of Louisbourg, 672; received commission as governor of the fortress, 675; defeats La Jonquière in command of a French fleet, 687; mentioned, 716.

Washington, George, 561, 881; sequence of events dating from the time of his youth, 843; enters upon his career, 935; adjutant-general of the Virginia militia, 935, 941, 947, 1071; his embassy to Fort Le Boeuf, with letter of introduction to Saint-Pierre, 935–37, 1049; his adventure at Murdering Town, 937; the site of Pittsburg examined by, 941; the battle at Great Meadows, and the alleged assassination of Jumonville, 943–54, 1484–85; his traits of character, 944, 946, 991, 995, 1072–73; at Fort Necessity, 950; the capitulation drawn up by Villiers, 951, 952; retreat from Fort Necessity, 953, 954; opinion of, expressed by Half-King, 953 note; the Fourth of July, 954; quoted concerning Braddock, 983; serves as aide-de-camp to Braddock in his expedition against Fort Duquesne, 984; consultation with Braddock, 986; letter to his brother quoted, 987; crosses the Monongahela, 990, 991; battle of the Monongahela, and retreat of the English troops, 991–1005; letter quoted concerning the defeat, 996, 1002; quoted concerning the sufferings of the people, 1071–73; his relations with Dinwiddie, 1072, 1073, 1286; report of the affair at Kittanning, by Dumas, 1134; his relations with General Forbes, in his expedition against Fort Duquesne, 1288, 1290, 1304.

Waterbury, 1135.

Webb, Colonel Daniel, 1143; resigns his position as commander-in-chief, 1105; arrives at Albany, 1116; sent to reinforce Oswego, 1120, 1126; at Fort Edward, 1182–83, 1182 note, 1198–99; his lack of support for Monro, at Fort William Henry, 1182–83, 1186, 1194 note, 1197–98, 1489, 1490; his correspondence with Monro, 1183; his regiment at the siege of Quebec, 1400.

Webster, Mount, 506.

Wedding, a notable, in Wells, 370.

Wedell, General, 1460.

Weems at Pemaquid, 165, 166.

Weiser, Conrad, 890, 895, 953; letter to Governor Morris, 1082.

Weld, Chaplain, 1119 and *note*.

Wells, attacked by French and Abenakis, 255–57.

Wells, John, an envoy to ransom the Deerfield captives, 393.

Wells, Jonathan, his house at Deerfield fortified against Indians, 375; assists in driving the enemy out of Deerfield, 380; petition for compensation of losses from the attack, 381 *note*.

Wells, Me., its garrisons, 362; its "turbulent women," 363; its judicial officers, 363; its people, 363; the church at, 363; Indian attack upon, 365; troops sent for defence against the Indians at, 369; annoyed by Indians, 402.

Wells, Thomas, murder of his wife by Indians at Wells, Me., 365.

Wendell, Jacob, cited, 683 *note*.

Wentworth, Governor Benning, of New Hampshire, 515 *note;* induced to aid in the attack upon Louisbourg, 623; his desire to command the troops, 625; his old mansion at Little Harbor, 625.

Wentworth, Governor, 1191 *note*.

Wesley, John, 848.

West India Company, built a fort on river Kansas, 574.

West Indies, the, 411, 852, 937, 1003 *note*, 1087, 1240, 1328, 1470; power of England over, 1469, 1472.

West Mountain, 1051.

West, Benjamin, 1305.

West, Captain, leads a party to bury the dead, 1305.

West, the, conflict for, of the French and English, 844, 888–905, 935, 936, 938–40, 960, 975, 1003, 1004, 1063, 1071, 1126; the forests, 986; French and English settlements compared, 1296.

Westbrook, Colonel, 481 *note;* sent to demand Rale from the Indians, 494; burns the mission village of the Penobscots, 498.

Western Posts, the, Canada's endeavor to control, 552.

Westminster Abbey, tablet erected to Lord Howe, 1259–60.

Weymouth, Mass., 420.

Wheeling Creek, 877.

Wheelwright, Hannah, married to Elisha Plaisted, 370; her husband captured by Indians, 370.

Wheelwright, John, the notable wedding of his daughter, 370.

Whigs, the, 847, 966, 1223, 1464, 1469; fallen from power, 458.

Whipple, *Reports upon Indian Tribes,* cited, 577 *note*.

White Mountains, 506, 1152.

White Point, 1234.

White River, 386, 588.

White Woman's Creek, 882.

White's Chocolate-House, 848.

Whitefield, George, 848; his advice to William Pepperrell, 627; his motto for a flag, 627.

Whitehall, 1049, 1280, 1370; on Lake Champlain, 733.

Whiting, ——, a member of Lovewell's expedition, 509.

Whiting, Lieutenant-Colonel, 1052; his men fall into Dieskau's ambush, 1052, 1053.

Whitmore, brigadier, serves in the expedition against Louisbourg, 1228, 1234–48; becomes the governor of Louisbourg, 1248.

Whitworth, Dr. Miles, 1190; summons to the Acadians drawn up, 1030–31; present at the massacre at Fort William Henry, 1190, 1194 *note*, 1491–92.

Wichitas, Indians, on Arkansas River, 572 *note*.

Wiggins, George, 1252 *note*.

Wilhelmina, death of, 1462.

Willard, ——, his soldiers camped at Louisbourg, 644.

Willard, Rev. Joseph, killed by Indians, 498.

William III., 138; deed of Northwestern country given to, by the Five Nations, 358; his accession to the throne of England, 847.

William, Duke of Cumberland, son of George II., 849.

William, Fort, Newfoundland, attacked by the French, 424; again attacked by Sieur de Saint-Ovide, 425.

William and Mary College, 956.

William Henry Hotel, 1117.

William Henry, Fort, 1108, 1152, 1155, 1257, 1275; its situation, 1061, 1180; winter life of the garrison, 1084; its condition, 1117, 1180, 1182; exploits of Lieutenant Kennedy and Captain Hodges, 1135–36; exploits of Rogers' rangers, 1139–41, 1144–46; attacked by Vaudreuil's war-party, 1148–51, 1154–55; a new attack planned, and the expedition prepared by the French, 1166–81; besieged and conquered by the French, 1181–94, 1197–1200, 1360, 1396, 1416, 1457, 1489–92; some of the garrison massacred by the Indians, 1188–94, 1489–92.

Williams, Captain Ephraim, in command at Fort Shirley, 729; the founder of Williams College, 735; killed in battle at Lake George, 736 note.

Williams, Colonel Ephraim, 1044; origin of Williams College, 1044; serves in the expedition against Crown Point, 1044–58; his wounds and death, 1052, 1058.

Williams, Colonel Israel, 1279 note; letters to quoted, 1045, 1046, 1275.

Williams, Colonel W., cited, 724 note.

Williams, Colonel William, account of the loss of Oswego, 1121; letters quoted concerning the army and the battle at Ticonderoga, 1275, 1279.

Williams, Eleazer, grandson of Eunice Williams, 396, 397 note.

Williams, Esther, ransomed, 393.

Williams, Eunice, child of Rev. John, 386; kept at the Mission of St. Louis, 389; remains in captivity, 395; married an Indian, 396; visits to Deerfield, 396.

Williams, Fort, 1099, 1100.

Williams, Josiah, 1058.

Williams, Major Israel, commissary at Fort Shirley, 729.

Williams, Mrs. (Rev.) John, death of, 384.

Williams, Rev. John, minister at Deerfield, 374; mentioned, 375 note, 674; his house attacked by Indians, 377; taken captive, 377; estimates the losses of the enemy, 382 note; account of their march, 383; preached to his flock during their march into captivity, 385; separated from his family, 386; his sufferings while on the march, 387; at the village of St. Francis, 388; entertained kindly by a Frenchwoman, 388; refuses to be converted to certain rites of the Jesuit church, 388; ransomed by Governor Vaudreuil and sent to Montreal, 389; sent to Quebec, 390; his experience with the Jesuit priests, 390, 391; sent to Château Richer, 390; released from captivity, 394; returns to Deerfield, 396; quoted, 399.

Williams, Roger, mentioned, 624.

Williams, Samuel, child of Rev. John, 386; conversion to Roman faith, 391; return to Deerfield and death, 392.

Williams, Stephen W., 374 note.

Williams, Stephen, son of Rev. John, 1044; captured by Indians, 382 note; released from captivity, 394; becomes a minister, 396; minister of Long Meadow, Mass., and chaplain in the army at Louisbourg, 674; preaches to the army at Lake George, 1048.

Williams, Thomas, surgeon at Fort Massachusetts, 736; serves in the expedition sent against Crown Point, 1044–45; letters from, quoted, 1047, 1058, 1061 note, 1120–21; his account of the battle of Lake George, 1054–55, 1059 note; his anxiety for Oswego, 1120–21.

Williams, William, justice of peace, 736 note.

Williams College, 734, 1044.

Williams River, named for Rev. John Williams, 385 note.

Williamsburg, 937, 941, 1001, 1072; society at, 956.

Williamson, ——, History of Maine, cited, 367 note, 483 note, 487 note, 492 note, 510 note.

Williamstown, Mass., 734.

Will's Creek, 885, 939, 941–43, 947, 954; the trading-station established on, 935, 982.

Wilson, General James Grant, cited, 426 *note*.

Winchester, 940, 1071.

Wind River Range of the Rocky Mountains, 598.

Windsor, 909, 1029.

Winnebagoes, Indians of Michigan, 519.

Winnebagoes, the, 1175.

Winnepesaukee, Lake, the rendezvous of an Indian war-party, 400, 508.

Winnipeg, Lake, a post established at, 580, 585.

Winslow, John, 960, 1181; his education and circumstances, 1013–14; the siege at Fort Beauséjour, 1014–19; his letters and journal quoted concerning the Acadians, 1016, 1018 and *note*, 1019–20, 1027 *note*, 1028–31, 1033, 1035 and *note*, 1036; circumstances with regard to the removal of the Acadians, 1016–19, 1027–40; relations with Captain Murray, 1029, 1033, 1036; delivers the orders of George II. to the Acadians, 1030–33; his portrait, 1032; his quarters at Half-Moon, 1108; letter to Colonel Fitch, 1109; letters hastening the preparations for an attack on Ticonderoga, 1109, 1120, 1142; difficulty concerning the rank of provincials and regulars, 1116–17; his camp at Lake George, 1117, 1131, 1142; his opinion of Israel Putnam, 1135; his *Letter Book* cited, 1136; prisoners brought into camp, 1137; his sentinels killed, 1141; ordered to remain in a defensive attitude, 1142; his letter to Shirley concerning the failure of the campaign, 1142; his troops garrisoned in winter-quarters, 1142–43; money expended on his expedition, 1255.

Winsor, Justin, *Nar. and Crit. Hist.*, cited, 434 *note*, 483 *note*.

Winter Harbor, Me., attack upon by Indians, 365, 367; annoyed by Indians, 402.

Winthrop, commander at Albany, 188.

Winthrop, Fitz-John, sends relief to Deerfield, 382 *note*.

Wisconsin, 1175.

Wisconsin Historical Collections, cited, 561 *note*.

Wisconsin Historical Society, the, 1487.

Wisconsin River, 582.

Wiwurna, Indian chief, in dialogue with Governor Shute, 485–86.

Wolcott, General Roger, commands Connecticut troops in an attack upon Louisbourg, 624; commander of Connecticut forces in siege of Louisbourg, 630; quoted concerning the Grand Battery at Louisbourg, 644; quoted, 656, 669; mentioned, 671 *note*.

Wolf Island, 1122.

Wolfe, James, 444, 1228, 1433; his opinion of Cornwallis, 909; serves in the expedition against Louisbourg, 1228–29, 1234–51; his characteristics and his ill health, 1229, 1235, 1250–51, 1321–28, 1348, 1349–52, 1379–83, 1386, 1389, 1394, 1398; plans of attack at Louisbourg, 1234–35; holds Lighthouse Point, 1238–39; the Island Battery silenced, 1238, 1239; the French ships burned, 1241–42, 1243; the capitulation of Louisbourg, 1244–47; ordered to disperse the French settlers, 1251; sails for England, 1251; his opinion of Abercromby and of Lord Howe, 1258; an expedition fitted out to serve under, 1320–22; his age, 1322; his rank and campaigns, 1322, 1327; confidential relation existing with his mother, 1323–27, 1381–82; the Rochefort expedition, 1326; letters to Major Wolfe and Lieutenant-Colonel Rickson, 1327–28; his betrothed, 1327, 1391; to command the expedition against Quebec, 1327–29; embarks for America, 1328; authorities on his life, 1329 *note;* siege and reduction of Quebec, 1331–57, 1375–1402, 1497–1500; arrival of the fleet in the St. Lawrence, and passage of the Traverse, 1337–40; at the Island of

Orléans, 1340; his view of the French camp, 1340–41; the descent of the fire-ships, 1342–43, 1353; seizes Point Levi, 1344; his proclamations to the Canadians, 1344, 1350, 1352, 1376; Quebec bombarded, 1345–46, 1353; his position at Montmorenci, 1346–50; his determination to persevere in the siege, 1353–54; the disaster at Montmorenci, 1354–57, 1375, 1381; ballads written concerning, 1357 *note;* the expected aid from Amherst, 1362–63, 1369, 1383; plans of attack considered by, 1375–76, 1380–84; proposes to fortify Isle-aux-Coudres, 1376; despatches sent to Pitt, 1381–83, 1418; the discovery of the path ascending the heights, 1384, 1387; his determination to climb the heights, and attack the French, 1384–89; movements of the squadron under Holmes, 1387–93; his last orders from the "Sutherland," 1388–89; statistics of his troops, 1389, 1395, 1400–01 *note,* 1497–98, 1503; assisted by Saunders, 1390; the pretended attack at Beauport, 1390; makes use of the French provision-boats, 1391–92; his presentiment, 1391; his chances of success, 1391–92; the ascent of the heights, 1391–94; remark concerning Gray's Elegy, 1392; the challenge to the boats, 1392–93; his troops drawn up ready for action, 1394–97; the charge and victory of the English, 1398–1400; his wounds, 1399; his last words, 1400 and *note;* his death, 1400, 1414, 1418, 1419; his remains carried to England, 1414; his death written upon by Walpole, 1418–19; the fruits of the victory, 1419, 1437, 1469; remarks of the Rev. E. Forbes, 1455; his *Instructions to Young Officers,* 1499.

Wolfe, Major-General Edward, 1322.

Wolfe, Mrs., the filial devotion of her son, 1323–27; last letter from General Wolfe, 1381–82; mourns his loss, 1419.

Wolfe, Walter, the uncle of James Wolfe, 1326, 1328; letters from his nephew quoted, 1327–28.

Wolfe's Cove, 1387.

Wood Creek, 426, 429, 728, 733, 1048, 1049, 1065, 1099, 1108, 1120, 1279.

Wooden Horse, the, 1107.

Woods, Lake of the, 586.

Woods, Sergeant, a member of Lovewell's expedition, 509.

Woolsey, Colonel, 1492, 1493.

Wooster, Colonel David, 1109.

Worcester, 1119.

Wraxall, 1051 *note;* eulogies of Johnson, 1061.

Wright, Daniel, Northfield, Mass., 729.

Wright, Dr., sickness in the army, 1279.

Wright, Ebenezer, petition for compensation of losses from Indian attack on Deerfield, 381 *note.*

Wright, his Life of Wolfe, 1252 *note,* 1329.

Wroth, Ensign, gains the submission of the Acadians, 474.

Wyandot, 882, 897.

Wyandots, the, 872, 873, 884.

Wyatt, Lieutenant, attacked by Indians at Black Point, Me., 368.

Wyman, Ensign Seth, in the fight with Indians at Lovewell's Pond, 511; arrived at Dunstable, 513; joined in Lovewell's expedition, 508.

Wyoming, 1294.

Xavier, mentioned, 478.

Yadkin, the, 885.

Yale College, 1044.

Yankton Indians, a tribe of the Sioux, 600 *note.*

Yellowstone Park, 597.

Yellowstone River, 578.

York, 848.

York, massacre at, 252–54.

York, Me., attack upon the people at, by Indians, 368; annoyed by Indians, 402.

Youghiogany River, the, 943, 1290.

Young, Lieutenant-Colonel, 1182; sent to Montcalm for terms of capitulation, 1188.

Zeisberger, David, 882 *note.*

Zinzendorf, Count, 882.

This book is set in 10 point Linotron Galliard, a face designed for photocomposition by Matthew Carter and based on the sixteenth-century face Granjon. The paper is Olin Nyalite and conforms to guidelines adopted by the Committee on Book Longevity of the Council on Library Resources. The binding material is Brillianta, a 100% rayon cloth made by Van Heek-Scholco Textielfabrieken, Holland. Composition by Haddon Craftsmen, Inc. and The Clarinda Company. Printing and binding by R. R. Donnelley & Sons Company. Designed by Bruce Campbell.